DOING ETHICS

Moral Reasoning and Contemporary Issues

Second Edition

About W. W. Norton & Company

W. W. Norton & Company has been independent since its founding in 1923, when William Warder Norton and Mary D. Herter Norton first published lectures delivered at the People's Institute, the adult education division of New York City's Cooper Union. The firm soon expanded its program beyond the Institute, publishing books by celebrated academics from America and abroad. By midcentury, the two major pillars of Norton's publishing program—trade books and college texts—were firmly established. In the 1950s, the Norton family transferred control of the company to its employees, and today—with a staff of four hundred and a comparable number of trade, college, and professional titles published each year—W. W. Norton & Company stands as the largest and oldest publishing house owned wholly by its employees.

DOING ETHICS

Moral Reasoning and Contemporary Issues

Second Edition

Lewis Vaughn

W. W. NORTON & COMPANY Independent and Employee-Owned New York · London

Composition by Matrix Publishing Services
Manufacturing by R. R. Donnelley—Crawfordsville, IN
Book design by Gooddesign Resource/Joan Greenfield
Editor: Peter J. Simon
Manuscript/copy editor: Carol Flechner
Production manager: Benjamin Reynolds
Editorial assistant: J. Conor Sullivan
Cover design: Gearbox
Managing editor, college: Marian Johnson

Library of Congress Cataloging-in-Publication Data

Vaughn, Lewis.
Doing ethics : moral reasoning and contemporary issues / Lewis Vaughn. — 2nd ed.
p. cm.
Includes bibliographical references and index.

ISBN 978-0-393-93428-1 (pbk.)

1. Ethics.   I. Title.
BJ1012.V385 2010
170—dc22
2009033799
ISBN: 978-0-393-93428-1 (pbk.)

W. W. Norton & Company, Inc., 500 Fifth Avenue, New York, NY 10110
www.wwnorton.com

W. W. Norton & Company Ltd., Castle House, 75/76 Wells Street, London W1T 3QT

1 2 3 4 5 6 7 8 9 0

CONTENTS

PART 2: MORAL REASONING

CHAPTER 3 **Evaluating Moral Arguments** 43

PART 4: ETHICAL ISSUES

CHAPTER 11 **Pornography and Censorship**

CHAPTER 14   Environmental Ethics   498

CHAPTER 15   Animal Rights   555

PREFACE

This second edition of *Doing Ethics* is a greatly expanded revision dedicated to the same ambitious goals that guided the first: to help students (1) see why ethics matters to society and to themselves; (2) understand core concepts (theories, principles, values, virtues, and the like); (3) be familiar with the background (scientific, legal, and otherwise) of contemporary moral problems; and (4) know how to apply critical reasoning to those problems—to assess moral judgments and principles, construct and evaluate moral arguments, and apply and critique moral theories. In other words, this book aspires to be a loyal ally to teachers of applied ethics who want students, above all, to think for themselves and competently do what is often required of morally mature persons.

These aims are reflected in the book's extensive introductions to concepts, cases, and issues; its large collection of readings and exercises; and its chapter-by-chapter coverage of moral reasoning—perhaps the most thorough introduction to these skills available in an applied-ethics text. This latter theme gets systematic treatment in five chapters, threads prominently throughout all the others, and is reinforced everywhere by "Critical Thought" text boxes prompting students to apply critical thinking to real debates and cases. The point, as reflected in the book's title, is to show students how to do ethics, not just to study it.

NEW FEATURES

- The addition of 2 to 3 readings in each of the original chapters covering moral issues—24 new articles in all.

- Two new moral-issues chapters: Chapter 12: *Sexual Morality and Marriage* and Chapter 18: *Global Economic Justice*. Each chapter contains 7 readings. These changes add another 14 selections, bringing the total additions to 38.

- Coverage of torture, added to the chapter on terrorism.

ORGANIZATION

Part 1 ("Fundamentals") prepares students for the tasks enumerated above. Chapter 1 explains why ethics is important and why thinking critically about ethical issues is essential to the examined life. It introduces the field of moral philosophy, defines and illustrates basic terminology, clarifies the connection between religion and morality, and explains why moral reasoning is crucial to moral maturity and personal freedom. Chapter 2 investigates a favorite doctrine of undergraduates—ethical relativism—and examines its distant cousin, emotivism.

Part 2 ("Moral Reasoning") consists of Chapter 3, which starts by reassuring students that moral reasoning is neither alien nor difficult but is simply ordinary critical reasoning applied to ethics. They've seen this kind of reasoning before and done it before. Thus, the chapter focuses on identifying, devising, and evaluating moral arguments and encourages practice and competence in finding implied premises, testing moral premises, assessing nonmoral premises, and dealing with common argument fallacies.

Part 3 ("Theories of Morality") is about applying critical reasoning to moral theories. Chapter 4 explains how moral theories work and how they relate to other important elements in moral experience: considered judgments, moral arguments, moral principles and rules, and cases and issues. It reviews major theories and shows how students can evaluate them using plausible criteria. The rest of Part 3 (Chapters 5–7) covers key theories in depth—utilitarianism, ethical egoism, Kant's theory, natural law theory, and the ethics of virtue. Students see how each theory is applied to moral issues and how their strengths and weaknesses are revealed by applying the criteria of evaluation.

In Part 4 ("Ethical Issues"), each of eleven chapters explores a timely moral issue through discussion and relevant readings: abortion, euthanasia and physician-assisted suicide, capital punishment, pornography and censorship, sexual morality and marriage, equality and affirmative action, environmental ethics, animal rights, warfare, terrorism and torture, and global economic justice. Each chapter supplies legal, scientific, and other background information on the issue; discusses how major theories have been applied to the problem; examines arguments that have been used in the debate; and includes additional cases for analysis with questions. The readings are a mix of well-known essays and surprising new voices, both classic and contemporary.

PEDAGOGICAL FEATURES

In addition to the "Critical Thought" boxes and "Cases for Analysis," there are other pedagogical devices:

- "Quick Review" boxes that reiterate key points or terms mentioned in previous pages
- Text boxes that discuss additional topics or issues related to main chapter material

- End-of-chapter review and discussion questions
- Chapter summaries
- Suggestions for further reading for each issues chapter
- Glossary

SUPPLEMENTS

Two Web sites—one for student review and research, and the other offering instructor's resources—accompany this text. To learn more about these two supplements, visit www.wwnorton.com/college/philosophy.

ACKNOWLEDGMENTS

No text like this can come to much without the help and insight of many. Among these I think first of my editor at W. W. Norton, Pete Simon, who believed in the project from the outset and helped me shape and improve it. Others at Norton also gave their time and talent to this text: Marian Johnson, managing editor; Carol Flechner, manuscript editor; Benjamin Reynolds, production manager; Nancy Rodwan, permissions manager; Joan Greenfield, text designer; and Conor Sullivan, assistant editor.

The silent partners in this venture are the many reviewers who helped in countless ways to make the book better. They include Harry Adams (Prairie View A&M University), Edwin Aiman (University of Houston), Peter Amato (Drexel University), Robert Bass (Coastal Carolina University), Vanda Bozicevic (Bergen Community College), Mark Raymond Brown (University of Ottawa), Robert Colter (Centre College), Steve Dickerson (South Puget Sound Community College), David Drebushenko (University of Southern Indiana), Clint Dunagan (Northwest Vista College), Paul Eckstein (Bergen Community College), Andrew

Fiala (California State University, Fresno), Stephen Finlay (University of Southern California), Mark Greene (University of Delaware), Barbara M. Hands (University of North Carolina, Greensboro), Ed Harris (Texas A&M University), Marko Hilgersom (Lethbridge Community College), John Holder III (Pensacola Junior College), Mark Hollifield (Clayton College and State University), Margaret Houck (University of South Carolina), Frances Howard-Snyder (Western Washington University), Robert Hull (Western Virginia Wesleyan College), Clayton Littlejohn (Southern Methodist University), Ernâni Magalhães (West Virginia University), Jon S. Moran (Southwest Missouri State University), Dale Murray (Virginia Commonwealth University), Thomas Nadelhoffer (Dickinson College), Leonard Olson (California State University, Fresno), Trisha Philips (Mississippi State University), Thomas M. Powers (University of Delaware), Joseph J. Rogers (University of Texas, San Antonio), Robert M. Seltzer (Western Illinois University), Aeon J. Skoble (Bridgewater Community College), Eric Sotnak (University of Akron), John Stilwell (University of Texas at Dallas), Allen Thompson (Virginia Commonwealth University), Julie C. Van Camp (California State University, Long Beach), and Phillip Wiebe (Trinity Western University).

DOING ETHICS

Moral Reasoning and Contemporary Issues

Second Edition

P A R T

1

Fundamentals

Ethics and the Examined Life

Ethics, or moral philosophy, is the philosophical study of morality. **Morality** refers to beliefs concerning right and wrong, good and bad—beliefs that can include judgments, values, rules, principles, and theories. They help guide our actions, define our values, and give us reasons for being the persons we are. (*Ethical* and *moral,* the adjective forms, are often used to mean simply "having to do with morality," and *ethics* and *morality* are sometimes used to refer to the moral norms of a specific group or individual, as in "Greek ethics" or "Russell's morality.") Ethics, then, addresses the powerful question that Socrates formulated twenty-four hundred years ago: how ought we to live?

The scope and continued relevance of this query suggest something compelling about ethics: you cannot escape it. You cannot run away from all the choices, feelings, and actions that accompany ideas about right and wrong, good and bad—ideas that persist in your culture and in your mind. After all, for much of your life, you have been assimilating, modifying, or rejecting the ethical norms you inherited from your family, community, and society. Unless you are very unusual, from time to time you deliberate about the rightness or wrongness of actions, embrace or reject particular moral principles or codes, judge the goodness of your character or intentions (or someone else's), perhaps even question (and agonize over) the soundness of your own moral outlook when it conflicts with that of others. In other words, you are involved in ethics—you *do ethics.* Even if you try to remove yourself from the ethi-

cal realm by insisting that all ethical concepts are irrelevant or empty, you assume a particular view, a theory in the broadest sense, about morality and its place in your life. If at some point you are intellectually brave enough to wonder whether your moral beliefs rest on some coherent supporting considerations, you will see that you cannot even begin to sort out such considerations without—again—doing ethics. In any case, in your life you must deal with the rest of the world, which turns on moral conflict and resolution, moral decision and debate.

What is at stake when we do ethics? In an important sense, the answer is *everything we hold dear.* Ethics is concerned with values—specifically, *moral values.* Through the sifting and weighing of moral values we determine what the most important things are in our lives, what is worth living for and what is worth dying for. We decide what is the greatest good, what goals we should pursue in life, what virtues we should cultivate, what duties we should or should not fulfill, what value we should put on human life, and what pain and perils we should be willing to endure for notions such as the common good, justice, and rights.

Does it matter whether the state executes criminals who have the mental capacity of a ten year old? Does it matter whether scientists conduct dangerous experiments on people without their full knowledge and consent? Does it matter who actually writes the term paper you turn in and represent as your own? Does it matter whether we regard the terrorists who killed nearly three thousand innocent people on September 11, 2001, as heroes or as murderers? Does it matter whether U.S. soldiers tortured detainees at Iraq's infamous Abu Ghraib prison? Does it matter whether we can easily save a drowning child but casually decide not to? Does it matter whether young girls in Africa have their genitals painfully mutilated for reasons of custom or religion? Do these actions and a million others just as controversial matter at all? Most of us—regardless of our opinion on these issues—would say that they matter a great deal. If they matter, then ethics matters, because these are ethical concerns requiring careful reflection using concepts and reasoning peculiar to ethics.

But even though in life ethics is inescapable and important, you are still free to take the easy way out, and many people do. You are free *not* to think too deeply or too systematically about ethical concerns. You can simply embrace the moral beliefs and norms given to you by your family and your society. You can just accept them without question or serious examination. In other words, you can try *not* to do ethics. This approach can be simple and painless—at least for a while—but it has some drawbacks.

First, it undermines your personal freedom. If you accept and never question the moral beliefs handed to you by your culture, then those beliefs are not really yours—and they, not you, control the path you take in life. Only if you critically examine these beliefs *yourself* and decide for *yourself* whether they have merit will they be truly yours. Only then will you be in charge of your own choices and actions.

Second, the no-questions-asked approach increases the chances that your responses to moral dilemmas or contradictions will be incomplete, confused, or mistaken. Sometimes in real life, moral codes or rules do not fit the situations at hand, or moral principles conflict with one another, or entirely new circumstances are not covered by any moral policy at all. Solving these problems requires something that a hand-me-down morality does not include: the intellectual tools to critically evaluate (and reevaluate) existing moral beliefs.

Third, if there is such a thing as intellectual moral growth, you are unlikely to find it on the safe route. To not do ethics is to stay locked in a kind of intellectual limbo, where exploration in ethics and personal moral progress are barely possible.

The philosopher Paul Taylor suggests that there is yet another risk in taking the easy road. If someone blindly embraces the morality bequeathed to him by his society, he may very well be a fine embodiment of the rules of his culture and accept them with certainty. But he also will lack the ability to defend his beliefs by rational argument against criticism. What happens when he encounters others who also have very strong beliefs that contradict his? "He will feel lost and bewildered," Taylor says, and his confusion might leave him disillusioned about morality. "Unable to give an objective, reasoned justification for his own convictions, he may turn from dogmatic certainty to total skepticism. And from total skepticism it is but a short step to an 'amoral' life. . . . Thus the person who begins by accepting moral beliefs blindly can end up denying all morality."[1]

There are other easy roads—roads that also bypass critical and thoughtful scrutiny of morality. We can describe most of them as various forms of subjectivism, a topic that we closely examine in the next chapter. You may decide, for example, that you can establish all your moral beliefs by simply consulting your feelings. In situations calling for moral judgments, you let your emotions be your guide. If it feels right, it is right. Alternatively, you may come to believe that moral realities are relative to each person, a view known as subjective relativism (also covered in the next chapter). That is, you think that what a person

---

[1] Paul W. Taylor, *Principles of Ethics: An Introduction* (Encino, CA: Dickenson, 1975), 9–10.

believes or approves of determines the rightness or wrongness of actions. If you believe that abortion is wrong, then it *is* wrong. If you believe it is right, then it *is* right.

But these facile ways through ethical terrain are no better than blindly accepting existing norms. Even if you want to take the subjectivist route, you still need to critically examine it to see if there are good reasons for choosing it—otherwise your choice is arbitrary and therefore not really yours. And unless you thoughtfully consider the merits of moral beliefs (including subjectivist beliefs), your chances of being wrong about them are substantial.

Ethics does not give us a royal road to moral truth. Instead, it shows us how to ask critical questions about morality and systematically seek answers supported by good reasons. This is a tall order because, as we have seen, many of the questions in ethics are among the toughest we can ever ask—and among the most important in life: What makes an action right (or wrong)? Is this moral argument sound? Should an action be judged by its consequences, or by the kind of action it is? Can a war ever be just? Is the moral principle "Never lie" valid? Is morality based on religion? Do animals have rights? Is it permissible to break a promise in order to save a person's life? Were his intentions good? Is she a good person? Is capital punishment ever permissible? What is the greatest good in life?

THE ETHICAL LANDSCAPE

The domain of ethics is large, divided into several areas of investigation and cordoned off from related subjects. So let us map the territory carefully. As the term *moral philosophy* suggests, ethics is a branch of philosophy. A very rough characterization of philosophy is the systematic use of critical reasoning to answer the most fundamental questions in life. Moral philosophy, obviously, tries to answer the fundamental questions of morality. The other major philosophical divisions address other basic questions; these are *logic* (the study of correct reasoning), *metaphysics* (the study of the fundamental nature of reality), and *epistemology* (the study of knowledge). As a division of philosophy, ethics does its work primarily through critical reasoning. Critical reasoning is the careful, systematic evaluation of statements, or claims—a process used in all fields of study, not just in ethics. Mainly this process includes both the evaluation of logical arguments and the careful analysis of concepts.

Science also studies morality, but not in the way that moral philosophy does. Its approach is known as **descriptive ethics**—the *scientific* study of moral beliefs and practices. Its aim is to describe and explain how people actually behave and think when dealing with moral issues and concepts. This kind of empirical research is usually conducted by sociologists, anthropologists, and psychologists. In contrast, the focus of moral philosophy is not what people actually believe and do, but what they *should* believe and do. The point of inquiry is to determine what actions are right (or wrong) and what things are good (or bad). As we have seen, this kind of investigation is done by philosophers and nonphilosophers alike.

Philosophers distinguish three major divisions in ethics, each one representing a different way to approach the subject. The first is **normative ethics**—the study of the principles, rules, or theories that guide our actions and judgments. (The word *normative* refers to norms, or standards, of judgment—in this case, norms for judging rightness and goodness.) The ultimate purpose of doing normative ethics is to try to establish the soundness of moral norms, especially the norms embodied in a comprehensive moral system, or theory. We do normative ethics when we use critical reasoning to demonstrate that a moral principle is justified, or that a professional code of conduct is contradictory, or that one proposed moral theory is better than another, or that a person's motive is good. Should the rightness of actions be judged by their consequences? Is happiness the greatest good in life? Is utilitarianism a good moral theory? Such questions are the preoccupation of normative ethics.

Another major division is **metaethics**—the study of the meaning and logical structure of moral beliefs. It asks not whether an action is right or whether a person's character is good. It takes a step back from these concerns and asks more fundamental questions about them: What does it mean for an action to be *right*? Is *good* the same thing as *desirable*? How can a moral principle be justified? Is there such a thing as moral truth? To do normative ethics, we must assume certain things about the meaning of moral terms and the logical relations among them. But the job of metaethics is to question all these assumptions, to see if they really make sense.

Finally, there is **applied ethics**—the application of moral norms to specific moral issues or cases, particularly those in a profession such as medicine or law. Applied ethics in these fields goes under names such as medical ethics, journalistic ethics, and business ethics. In applied ethics we study the results derived from applying a moral principle or theory to specific circumstances. The purpose of the exercise is to learn something important about either the moral characteristics of the situation or the adequacy of the moral norms. Did the doctor do right in performing that abortion? Is it morally permissible for scientists to perform experiments on people without their consent? Was it right for the journalist to distort her reporting to aid a particular side in the war? Questions like these drive the search for answers in applied ethics.

In every division of ethics, we must be careful to distinguish between *values* and *obligations*. Sometimes we may be interested in concepts or judgments of *value*—that is, about what is morally *good*, *bad*, *blameworthy*, or *praiseworthy*. We properly use these kinds of terms to refer mostly to per-

sons, character traits, motives, and intentions. We may say "She is a good person" or "He is to blame for that tragedy." Other times, we may be interested in concepts or judgments of *obligation*—that is, about what is obligatory or a duty or what we should or ought to do. We use these terms to refer to *actions*. We may say "She has a duty to tell the truth" or "What he did was wrong."

When we talk about value in the sense just described, we mean *moral* value. If she is a good person, she is good in the moral sense. But we can also talk about *nonmoral* value. We can say that things such as televisions, rockets, experiences, and artwork (things other than persons, intentions, etc.) are good, but we mean "good" only in a nonmoral way. It makes no sense to assert that in themselves televisions or rockets are morally good or bad. Perhaps a rocket could be used to perform an action that is morally wrong. In that case, the action would be immoral, while the rocket itself would still have nonmoral value only.

Many things in life have value for us, but they are not necessarily valuable in the same way. Some things are valuable because they are a means to something else. We might say that gasoline is good because it is a means to make a gas-powered vehicle work, or that a pen is good because it can be used to write a letter. Such things are said to be **instrumentally**, or **extrinsically**, **valuable**—they are valuable as a means to something else. Some things, however, are valuable in themselves or for their own sakes. They are valuable simply because they are what they are, without being a means to something else. Things that have been regarded as valuable in themselves include happiness, pleasure, virtue, and beauty. These are said to be **intrinsically valuable**—they are valuable in themselves.

THE ELEMENTS OF ETHICS

We all do ethics, and we all have a general sense of what is involved. But we can still ask, What are

---

QUICK REVIEW

ethics (moral philosophy)—The philosophical study of morality.

morality—Beliefs concerning right and wrong, good and bad; they can include judgments, rules, principles, and theories.

descriptive ethics—The scientific study of moral beliefs and practices.

normative ethics—The study of the principles, rules, or theories that guide our actions and judgments.

metaethics—The study of the meaning and logical structure of moral beliefs.

applied ethics—The application of moral norms to specific moral issues or cases, particularly those in a profession such as medicine or law.

instrumentally (or extrinsically) valuable—Valuable as a means to something else.

intrinsically valuable—Valuable in itself, for its own sake.

---

the elements of ethics that make it the peculiar enterprise that it is? We can include at least the following factors:

The Preeminence of Reason

Doing ethics typically involves grappling with our feelings, taking into account the facts of the situation (including our own observations and relevant knowledge), and trying to understand the ideas that bear on the case. But above all, it involves, even requires, critical reasoning—the consideration of reasons for whatever statements (moral or otherwise) are in question. Whatever our view on moral issues and whatever moral outlook we subscribe to, our commonsense moral experience suggests that if a moral judgment is to be

worthy of acceptance, it must be supported by good reasons, and our deliberations on the issue must include a consideration of those reasons.

The backbone of critical reasoning generally and moral reasoning in particular is logical argument. This kind of argument—not the angry-exchange type—consists of a statement to be supported (the assertion to be proved, the conclusion) and the statements that do the supporting (the reasons for believing the statement, the premises). With such arguments, we try to show that a moral judgment is or is not justified, that a moral principle is or is not sound, that an action is or is not morally permissible, or that a moral theory is or is not plausible. (See Chapter 3 for an in-depth discussion of moral arguments.)

Our use of critical reasoning and argument helps us keep our feelings about moral issues in perspective. Feelings are an important part of our moral experience. They make empathy possible, which gives us a deeper understanding of the human impact of moral norms. They also can serve as internal alarm bells, warning us of the possibility of injustice, suffering, and wrongdoing. But they are unreliable guides to moral truth. They may simply reflect our own emotional needs, prejudices, upbringing, culture, and self-interests. Careful reasoning, however, can inform our feelings and help us decide moral questions on their merits.

The Universal Perspective

Logic requires that moral norms and judgments follow the *principle of universalizability*—the idea that a moral statement (a principle, rule, or judgment) that applies in one situation must apply in all other situations that are relevantly similar. If you say, for example, that lying is wrong in a particular situation, then you implicitly agree that lying is wrong for anyone in relevantly similar situations. If you say that killing in self-defense is morally permissible, then you say in effect that killing in self-defense is permissible for everyone in relevantly similar situations. It cannot be the case that an action performed by A is *wrong* while the same action performed by B in relevantly similar circumstances is *right*. It cannot be the case that the moral judgments formed in these two situations must differ just because two different people are involved.

This point about universalizability also applies to reasons used to support moral judgments. If reasons apply in a specific case, then those reasons also apply in all relevantly similar cases. It cannot be true that reasons that apply in a specific case do not apply to other cases that are similar in all relevant respects.

The Principle of Impartiality

From the moral point of view, all persons are considered equal and should be treated accordingly. This sense of impartiality is implied in all moral statements. It means that the welfare and interests of each individual should be given the same weight as all others. Unless there is a morally relevant difference between people, we should treat them the same: we must treat equals equally. We would think it outrageous for a moral rule to say something like "Everyone must refrain from stealing food in grocery stores—except for Mr. X, who may steal all he wants." Imagine that there is no morally relevant reason for making this exception to food stealing; Mr. X is exempted merely because, say, he is a celebrity known for outrageous behavior. We not only would object to this rule, we might even begin to wonder if it was a genuine moral rule at all since it lacks impartiality. Similarly, we would reject a moral rule that says something like "Everyone is entitled to basic human rights—except Native Americans." Such a rule would be a prime example of unfair discrimination based on race. We can see this blatant partiality best if we ask what morally relevant difference there is between Native Americans and everyone else. Differences in income, social status,

skin color, ancestry, and the like are not morally relevant. Apparently there are no morally relevant differences. Because there are none, we must conclude that the rule sanctions unfair discrimination.

We must keep in mind, however, that sometimes there are good reasons for treating someone differently. Imagine a hospital that generally gives equal care to patients, treating equals equally. But suppose a patient comes to the hospital in an ambulance because she has had a heart attack and will die without immediate care. The hospital staff responds quickly, giving her faster and more sophisticated care than other patients receive. The situation is a matter of life and death—a good reason for *not* treating everyone the same and for providing the heart attack patient with special consideration. This instance of discrimination is justified.

The Dominance of Moral Norms

Not all norms are moral norms. There are legal norms (laws, statutes), aesthetic norms (for judging artistic creations), prudential norms (practical considerations of self-interest), and others. Moral norms seem to stand out from all these in an interesting way: they dominate. Whenever moral principles or values conflict in some way with nonmoral principles or values, the moral considerations usually override the others. Moral considerations seem more important, more critical, or more weighty. A principle of prudence such as "Never help a stranger" may be well justified, but it must yield to any moral principle that contradicts it, such as "Help a stranger in an emergency if you can do so without endangering yourself." An aesthetic norm that somehow involved violating a moral principle would have to take a backseat to the moral considerations. A law that conflicted with a moral principle would be suspect, and the latter would have to prevail over the former. Ultimately the justification for civil disobedience is that specific laws conflict with moral norms and are therefore invalid. If we judge a law to be bad, we usually do so on moral grounds.

RELIGION AND MORALITY

Many people believe that morality and religion are inseparable—that religion is the source or basis of morality and that moral precepts are simply what God says should be done. This view is not at all surprising, since all religions imply or assert a perspective on morality. The three great religions in the Western tradition—Christianity, Judaism, and Islam—provide to their believers commandments or principles of conduct that are thought to constitute the moral law, the essence of morality. For millions of these adherents, the moral law is the will of God, and the will of God is the moral law. In the West at least, the powerful imprint of religion is evident in secular laws and in the private morality of believers and unbelievers alike. Secular systems of morality—for example, those of the ancient Greek philosophers, Immanuel Kant, the utilitarians, and others—have of course left their mark on Western ethics. But they have not moved the millions who think that morality is a product exclusively of religion.

So what is the relationship between religion and morality? For our purposes, we should break this question into two parts: (1) what is the relationship between religion and *ethics* (the philosophical study of morality), and (2) what is the relationship between religion and *morality* (beliefs about right and wrong)? Question 1 is a query about how religion relates to the kind of investigation we conduct in this book—the use of experience and critical reasoning to study morality. The key point about the relationship is that whatever your views on religion and morality, an open-minded expedition into ethics is more useful and empowering than you may realize, especially now at the beginning of your journey into moral philosophy. You may believe, for example, that God determines what is right and wrong, so there is no need to apply critical reasoning to morality—you just need to know what God says. But this judgment—and similar dismissals of ethics—would be premature. Consider the following:

Believers Need Moral Reasoning

It is difficult—perhaps impossible—for most people to avoid using moral reasoning. Religious people are no exception. One cause is that religious moral codes (such as the Ten Commandments) and other major religious rules of conduct are usually vague, laying out general principles that may be difficult to apply to specific cases. (Secular moral codes have the same disadvantage.) For example, we may be commanded to love our neighbor, but what neighbors are included—people of a different religion? people who denounce our religion? the gay or lesbian couple? those who steal from us? the convicted child molester next door? the drug dealers on the corner? the woman who got an abortion? Also, what does loving our neighbor demand of us? How does love require us to behave toward the drug dealers, the gay couple, or the person who denounces our religion? If our terminally ill neighbor asks us in the name of love to help him kill himself, what should we do? Does love require us to kill him—or to refrain from killing him? And, of course, commandments can conflict—as when, for example, the only way to avoid killing an innocent person is to tell a lie, or the only way to save the life of one person is to kill another. All these situations force the believer to interpret religious directives, to try to apply general rules to specific cases, to draw out the implications of particular views—in other words, to do ethics.

When Conflicts Arise, Ethics Steps In

Very often moral contradictions or inconsistencies confront the religious believer, and only moral reasoning can help resolve them. Believers some-

CRITICAL THOUGHT: Ethics, Religion, and Tough Moral Issues

How can we hope to grapple with complex moral issues that have emerged only in recent years? Can religion alone handle the job? Consider the following case:

> According to a report by CNN, Jack and Lisa Nash made history when they used genetic testing to save the life of their six-year-old daughter, Molly, by having another child. Molly had a rare genetic disorder known as Fanconi anemia, which prevents the generation of bone marrow and produces a fatal leukemia. Molly's best chance to live was to get a transplant of stem cells from the umbilical cord of a sibling, and Molly's parents were determined to give her that sibling, brother Adam. Through genetic testing (and in vitro fertilization), Jack and Lisa were able to select a child who would not only be born without a particular disease (Fanconi anemia, in this case) but also would help a sibling combat the disease by being the optimal tissue match

for a transplant—a historic combination. As Lisa Nash said, "I was going to save Molly no matter what, and I wanted Molly to have siblings."*

Is it right to produce a child to save the life or health of someone else? More to the point, Do the scriptures of the three major Western religions provide any guidance on this question? Do any of these traditions offer useful methods for productively discussing or debating such issues with people of different faiths? How might ethics help with these challenges? Is it possible to formulate a reasonable opinion on this case *without doing ethics*? Why or why not?

*"Genetic Selection Gives Girl a Brother and a Second Chance," *CNN.com*, 3 October 2000, http://archives.cnn.com/2000/HEALTH/10/03/testube.brother/index.html (8 December 2005).

times disagree with their religious leaders on moral issues. Adherents of one religious tradition may disagree with those from another tradition on whether an act is right or wrong. Sincere devotees in a religious tradition may wonder if its moral teachings make sense. In all such cases, intelligent resolution of the conflict of moral claims can be achieved only by applying a neutral standard that helps sort out the competing viewpoints. Moral philosophy supplies the neutral standard in the form of critical thinking, well-made arguments, and careful analysis. No wonder then that many great religious minds—Aquinas, Leibniz, Descartes, Kant, Maimonides, Averroës, and others—have relied on reason to examine the nature of morality. In fact, countless theists have regarded reason as a gift from God that enables human beings to grasp the truths of science, life, and morality.

Moral Philosophy Enables Productive Discourse

Any fruitful discussions about morality undertaken between people from different religious traditions or between believers and nonbelievers will require a common set of ethical concepts and a shared procedure for deciding issues and making judgments. Ethics provides these tools. Without them, conversations will resolve nothing, and participants will learn little. Without them, people will talk past each other, appealing only to their own religious views. Furthermore, in a pluralistic society, most of the public discussions about important moral issues take place in a context of shared values such as justice, fairness, equality, and tolerance. Just as important, they also occur according to an unwritten understanding that (1) moral positions should be explained, (2) claims should be supported by reasons, and (3) reasoning should be judged by common rational standards. These skills, of course, are at the heart of ethics.

Now consider Question 2: What is the relationship between religion and morality? For many people, the most interesting query about the relationship between religion and morality is this: is God the maker of morality? That is, is God the author of the moral law? Those who answer yes are endorsing a theory of morality known as the *divine command theory*. It says that right actions are those that are willed by God, that God literally defines right and wrong. Something is right or good only because God makes it so. In the simplest version of the theory, God can determine right and wrong because he is omnipotent. He is all-powerful—powerful enough even to create moral norms. On this view, God is a divine lawgiver, and his laws constitute morality.

In general, believers are divided on whether the divine command theory gives an accurate account of the source of morality. Notable among the theory's detractors are the great theistic philosophers Gottfried Leibniz (1646–1716) and Thomas Aquinas (1225–74). And conversely, as odd as it may sound, some nonbelievers have subscribed to it. In *The Brothers Karamazov* (1879–80), the character Ivan Karamazov declares, "If God doesn't exist, everything is permissible." This very sentiment was espoused by, among others, the famous atheist philosopher Jean-Paul Sartre.

Both religious and secular critics of the divine command theory believe that it poses a serious dilemma, one first articulated by Socrates two and one-half millennia ago. In the dialogue *Euthyphro*, Socrates asks, Is an action morally right because God wills it to be so, or does God will it to be so because it is morally right? Critics say that if an action is right only because God wills it (that is, if right and wrong are dependent on God), then many heinous crimes and evil actions would be right if God willed them. If God willed murder,

theft, or torture, these deeds would be morally right. If God has unlimited power, he could easily will such actions. If the rightness of an action depended on God's will alone, he could not have reasons for willing what he wills. No reasons would be available and none required. Therefore, if God commanded an action, the command would be without reason, completely arbitrary. Neither the believer nor the nonbeliever would think this state of affairs plausible. On the other hand, if God wills an action because it is morally right (if moral norms are independent of God), then the divine command theory must be false. God does not create rightness; he simply knows what is right and wrong and is subject to the moral law just as humans are.

For some theists, this charge of arbitrariness is especially worrisome. Leibniz, for example, rejects the divine command theory, declaring that it implies that God is unworthy of worship:

In saying, therefore, that things are not good according to any standard of goodness, but simply by the will of God, it seems to me that one destroys, without realizing it, all the love of God and all his glory; for why praise him for what he has done, if he would be equally praiseworthy in doing the contrary? Where will be his justice and his wisdom if he has only a certain despotic power, if arbitrary will takes the place of reasonableness, and if in accord with the definition of tyrants, justice consists in that which is pleasing to the most powerful?[2]

Defenders of the divine command theory may reply to the arbitrariness argument by contending that God would never command us to commit heinous acts, because God is all-good. Because of his supreme goodness, he would will only what is good. Some thinkers, however, believe that such

[2]G. W. von Leibniz, "Discourse on Metaphysics," in *Selections*, ed. Philip P. Wiener (New York: Scribner, 1951), 292.

reasoning renders the very idea of God's goodness meaningless. As one philosopher says,

[O]n this view, the doctrine of the goodness of God is reduced to nonsense. It is important to religious believers that God is not only all-powerful and all-knowing, but that he is also good; yet if we accept the idea that good and bad are defined by reference to God's will, this notion is deprived of any meaning. What could it mean to say that God's commands are good? If "X is good" means "X is commanded by God," then "God's commands are good" would mean only "God's commands are commanded by God," an empty truism.[3]

In any case, it seems that through critical reasoning we can indeed learn much about morality and the moral life. After all, there are complete moral systems (some of which are examined in this book) that are not based on religion, that contain genuine moral norms indistinguishable from those embraced by religion, and that are justified not by reference to religious precepts but by careful thinking and moral arguments. As the philosopher Jonathan Berg says, "Those who would refuse to recognize as adequately justified any moral beliefs not derived from knowledge of or about God, would have to refute the whole vast range of arguments put by Kant and all others who ever proposed a rational basis for ethics!"[4] Moreover, if we can do ethics—if we can use critical reasoning to discern moral norms certified by the best reasons and evidence—then critical reasoning is sufficient to guide us to moral standards and values. Since we obviously can do ethics (as the following chapters demonstrate), morality is both accessible and meaningful to us whether we are religious or not.

[3]James Rachels, *The Elements of Moral Philosophy,* 4th ed. (Boston: McGraw-Hill, 2003), 51.
[4]Jonathan Berg, "How Could Ethics Depend on Religion?" in *A Companion to Ethics,* ed. Peter Singer, corr. ed. (Oxford: Blackwell, 1993), 525–33.

SUMMARY

Ethics is the philosophical study of morality, and morality consists of beliefs concerning right and wrong, good and bad. These beliefs can include judgments, principles, and theories. Participating in the exploration of morality—that is, doing ethics—is inescapable. We all must make moral judgments, assess moral norms, judge people's character, and question the soundness of our moral outlooks. A great deal is at stake when we do ethics, including countless decisions that determine the quality of our lives.

You can decide to forgo any ethical deliberations and simply embrace the moral beliefs and norms you inherited from your family and culture. But this approach undermines your freedom, for if you accept without question whatever moral beliefs come your way, they are not really yours. Only if you critically examine them for yourself are they truly yours.

The three main divisions of ethics proper are normative ethics (the study of the moral norms that guide our actions and judgments), metaethics (the study of the meaning and logical structure of moral beliefs), and applied ethics (the application of moral norms to specific moral issues or cases).

Ethics involves a distinctive set of elements. These include the preeminence of reason, the universal perspective, the principle of impartiality, and the dominance of moral norms.

Some people claim that morality depends on God, a view known as the divine command theory. Both theists and nontheists have raised doubts about this doctrine. The larger point is that doing ethics—using critical reasoning to examine the moral life—can be a useful and productive enterprise for believer and nonbeliever alike.

EXERCISES

Review Questions

1. What is ethics? What is morality? (p. 3)
2. In what ways are we forced to do ethics? What is at stake in these deliberations? (pp. 3–4)
3. What is the unfortunate result of accepting moral beliefs without questioning them? (pp. 4–5)

4. Can our feelings be our sole guide to morality? Why or why not? (p. 4)
5. What is descriptive ethics? In this field, what do researchers study? (p. 5)
6. What is normative ethics? applied ethics? (pp. 5–6)
7. What is metaethics? What is the difference between normative ethics and metaethics? (pp. 5–6)
8. What is the difference between judgments of value and judgments of obligation? (p. 6)
9. What is the difference between moral and nonmoral value? (p. 6)
10. What is the difference between instrumental value and intrinsic value? (p. 6)
11. To what does the "preeminence of reason" refer? (p. 7)
12. What is the principle of universalizability? (pp. 7–8)
13. What is the relationship between morality and religion? (pp. 9–12)

Discussion Questions

1. Do you think that morality ultimately depends on God (that God is the author of the moral law)? Why or why not?

2. Do you believe that you have absorbed or adopted without question most of your moral beliefs? Why or why not?
3. Formulate an argument against the divine command theory, then formulate one for it.
4. Give an example of how you or someone you know has used reasons to support a moral judgment.
5. Identify at least two normative ethical questions that you have wondered about in the past year.
6. Name two things (persons, objects, experiences, etc.) in your life that you consider intrinsically valuable. Name three that are instrumentally valuable.
7. How do your feelings affect the moral judgments you make? Do they *determine* your judgments? Do they inform them? If so, how?
8. What is the logic behind the principle of universalizability? Cite an example of how the principle has entered into your moral deliberations.
9. How does racial discrimination violate the principle of impartiality?
10. What is the "dominance of moral norms"? Does it strike you as reasonable—or do you believe that sometimes nonmoral norms can outweigh moral ones? If the latter, provide an example.

READINGS

From *What Is the Socratic Method?*

CHRISTOPHER PHILLIPS

The Socratic method is a way to seek truths by your own lights.

It is a system, a spirit, a method, a type of philosophical inquiry, an intellectual technique, all rolled into one.

Socrates himself never spelled out a "method." However, the Socratic method is named after him because Socrates, more than any other before or since, models for us *philosophy practiced*—philosophy as deed, as way of living, as something that any of us can do. It is an *open system* of philosophical inquiry that allows one to interrogate from many vantage points.

Gregory Vlastos, a Socrates scholar and professor of philosophy at Princeton, described Socrates' method of inquiry as "among the greatest achievements of humanity." Why? Because, he says, it makes philosophical inquiry "a common human enterprise, open to every man." Instead of requiring allegiance to a specific philosophical viewpoint or analytic technique or specialized vocabulary, the Socratic method "calls for common sense and common speech." And this, he says, "is as it should be, for how many should live is every man's business."

I think, however, that the Socratic method goes beyond Vlastos' description. It does not merely call for common sense but examines what common sense *is*. The Socratic method asks: Does the common sense of our day offer us the greatest potential for self-understanding and human excellence? Or is the prevailing common sense in fact a roadblock to realizing this potential?

Vlastos goes on to say that Socratic inquiry is by no means simple, and "calls not only for the highest degree of mental alertness of which anyone is capable" but also for "moral qualities of a high order: sincerity, humility, courage." Such qualities "protect against the possibility" that Socratic dialogue, no matter how rigorous, "would merely grind out . . . wild conclusions with irresponsible premises." I agree, though I would replace the quality of sincerity with honesty, since one can hold a conviction sincerely without examining it, while honesty would require that one subject one's convictions to frequent scrutiny.

A Socratic dialogue reveals how different our outlooks can be on concepts we use every day. It reveals how different our philosophies are, and often how tenable—or untenable, as the case may be—a range of philosophies can be. Moreover, even the most universally recognized and used concept, when subjected to Socratic scrutiny, might reveal not only that there is *not* universal agreement, after all, on the meaning of any given concept, but that every single person has a somewhat different take on each and every concept under the sun.

What's more, there seems to be no such thing as a concept so abstract, or question so off base, that it can't be fruitfully explored [using the Socratic method]. In the course of Socratizing, it often turns out to be the case that some of the most so-called abstract concepts are intimately related to the most profoundly relevant human experiences. In fact, it's been my experience that virtually any question can be plumbed Socratically. Sometimes you don't know what question will have the most lasting and signif-

---

Although not specifically concerned with ethics, this short piece by Christopher Phillips makes a persuasive case for using the "Socratic method" to think through difficult philosophical issues. To see the Socratic method applied to ethics, read the excerpt from Plato's *Euthyphro* that follows on p. 16.

Christopher Phillips, "What Is the Socratic Method?" in *Socrates Café: A Fresh Taste of Philosophy* (New York: W. W. Norton, 2001), 18–23 (edited). Copyright © 2001 by Christopher Phillips. Used by permission of W. W. Norton & Company, Inc. Reprinted by permission of Christopher Phillips.

icant impact until you take a risk and delve into it for a while.

What distinguishes the Socratic method from mere nonsystematic inquiry is the sustained attempt to explore the ramifications of certain opinions and then offer compelling objections and alternatives. This scrupulous and exhaustive form of inquiry in many ways resembles the scientific method. But unlike Socratic inquiry, scientific inquiry would often lead us to believe that whatever is not measurable cannot be investigated. This "belief" fails to address such paramount human concerns as sorrow and joy and suffering and love.

Instead of focusing on the outer cosmos, Socrates focused primarily on human beings and their cosmos within, utilizing his method to open up new realms of self-knowledge while at the same time exposing a great deal of error, superstition, and dogmatic nonsense. The Spanish-born American philosopher and poet George Santayana said that Socrates knew that "the foreground of human life is necessarily moral and practical" and that "it is so even so for artists"— and even for scientists, try as some might to divorce their work from these dimensions of human existence.

Scholars call Socrates' method the *elenchus,* which is Hellenistic Greek for *inquiry* or *cross-examination.* But it is not just any type of inquiry or examination. It is a type that reveals people to themselves, that makes them see what their opinions really amount to. C. D. C. Reeve, professor of philosophy at Reed College, gives the standard explanation of an elenchus in saying that its aim "is not simply to reach adequate definitions" of such things as virtues; rather, it also has a "moral reformatory purpose, for Socrates believes that regular elenctic philosophizing makes people happier and more virtuous than anything else. . . . Indeed philosophizing is so important for human welfare, on his view, that he is willing to accept execution rather than give it up."

Socrates' method of examination can indeed be a vital part of existence, but I would not go so far as to say that it *should* be. And I do not think that Socrates felt that habitual use of this method "makes people happier." The fulfillment that comes from Socratizing comes only at a price—it could well make us *unhappier,* more uncertain, more troubled, as well as more fulfilled. It can leave us with a sense that we *don't* know the answers after all, that we are much further from knowing the answers than we'd ever realized before engaging in Socratic discourse. And this is fulfilling—and exhilarating and humbling and perplexing.

* * *

There is no neat divide between one's views of philosophy and of life. They are overlapping and kindred views. It is virtually impossible in many instances to *know* what we believe in daily life until we engage others in dialogue. Likewise, to discover our philosophical views, we must engage with ourselves, with the lives we already lead. Our views form, change, evolve, as we participate in this dialogue. It is the only way truly to discover what philosophical colors we sail under. Everyone at some point preaches to himself and others what he does not yet practice; everyone acts in or on the world in ways that are in some way contradictory or inconsistent with the views he or she confesses or professes to hold. For instance, the Danish philosopher Søren Kierkegaard, the influential founder of existentialism, put Socratic principles to use in writing his dissertation on the concept of irony in Socrates, often using pseudonyms so he could argue his own positions with himself. In addition, the sixteenth-century essayist Michel de Montaigne, who was called "the French Socrates" and was known as the father of skepticism in modern Europe, would write and add conflicting and even contradictory passages in the same work. And like Socrates, he believed the search for truth was worth dying for.

The Socratic method forces people "to confront their own dogmatism," according to Leonard Nelson, a German philosopher who wrote on such subjects as ethics and theory of knowledge until he was forced by the rise of Nazism to quit. By doing so, participants in Socratic dialogue are, in effect, "*forcing* themselves to be free," Nelson maintains. But they're not just confronted with their own dogmatism. In the course of a [Socratic dialogue], they may be confronted with an array of hypotheses, convictions, conjectures and theories offered by the other participants, and themselves—all of which subscribe to some sort of dogma. The Socratic method requires that—honestly and openly, rationally and imaginatively—they confront the dogma by asking such questions as: What does this mean? What speaks for and against it? Are there alternative ways of considering it that are even more plausible and tenable?

At certain junctures of a Socratic dialogue, the "forcing" that this confrontation entails—the insistence that each participant carefully articulate her singular philosophical perspective—can be upsetting. But that is all to the good. If it never touches any nerves, if it doesn't upset, if it doesn't mentally and spiritually challenge and perplex, in a wonderful and exhilarating way, it is not Socratic dialogue. This "forcing" opens us up to the varieties of experiences of others—whether through direct dialogue, or through other means, like drama or books, or through a work of art or a dance. It compels us to explore alternative perspectives, asking what might be said for or against each.

* * *

From *The Euthyphro*

PLATO

* * *

Euthyphro. Piety . . . is that which is dear to the gods, and impiety is that which is not dear to them.

Socrates. Very good, Euthyphro; you have now given me the sort of answer which I wanted. But whether what you say is true or not I cannot as yet tell, although I make no doubt that you will prove the truth of your words.

Euthyphro. Of course.

Socrates. Come, then, and let us examine what we are saying. That thing or person which is dear to the gods is pious, and that thing or person which is hateful to the gods is impious, these two being the extreme opposites of one another. Was not that said?

Euthyphro. It was.

Socrates. And well said?

Euthyphro. Yes, Socrates, I thought so; it was certainly said.

Socrates. And further, Euthyphro, the gods were admitted to have enmities and hatreds and differences?

Euthyphro. Yes, that was also said.

Socrates. And what sort of difference creates enmity and anger? Suppose for example that you and I, my good friend, differ about a number; do differences of this sort make us enemies and set us at variance with one another? Do we not go at once to arithmetic, and put an end to them by a sum?

Euthyphro. True.

Socrates. Or suppose that we differ about magnitudes, do we not quickly end the differences by measuring?

Euthyphro. Very true.

Socrates. And we end a controversy about heavy and light by resorting to a weighing machine?

Euthyphro. To be sure.

Socrates. But what differences are there which cannot be thus decided, and which therefore make us angry and set us at enmity with one another? I dare say the answer does not occur to you at the moment, and therefore I will suggest that these enmities arise when the matters of difference are the just and unjust, good and evil, honourable and dishonourable. Are not these the points about which men differ, and about which when we are unable satisfactorily to decide our differences, you and I and all of us quarrel, when we do quarrel?

Plato, *The Euthyphro*, translated by Benjamin Jowett.

Euthyphro. Yes, Socrates, the nature of the differences about which we quarrel is such as you describe.

Socrates. And the quarrels of the gods, noble Euthyphro, when they occur, are of a like nature?

Euthyphro. Certainly they are.

Socrates. They have differences of opinion, as you say, about good and evil, just and unjust, honourable and dishonourable: there would have been no quarrels among them, if there had been no such differences—would there now?

Euthyphro. You are quite right.

Socrates. Does not every man love that which he deems noble and good, and hate the opposite of them?

Euthyphro. Very true.

Socrates. But, as you say, people regard the same things, some as just and others as unjust,—about these they dispute; and so there arise wars and fightings among them.

Euthyphro. Very true.

Socrates. Then the same things are hated by the gods and loved by the gods, and are both hateful and dear to them?

Euthyphro. True.

Socrates. And upon this view the same things, Euthyphro, will be pious and also impious?

Euthyphro. So I should suppose.

Socrates. Then, my friend, I remark with surprise that you have not answered the question which I asked. For I certainly did not ask you to tell me what action is both pious and impious: but now it would seem that what is loved by the gods is also hated by them. And therefore, Euthyphro, in thus chastising your father you may very likely be doing what is agreeable to Zeus but disagreeable to Cronos or Uranus, and what is acceptable to Hephaestus but unacceptable to Here, and there may be other gods who have similar differences of opinion.

Euthyphro. But I believe, Socrates, that all the gods would be agreed as to the propriety of punishing a murderer: there would be no difference of opinion about that.

Socrates. Well, but speaking of men, Euthyphro, did you ever hear any one arguing that a murderer or any sort of evil-doer ought to be let off?

Euthyphro. I should rather say that these are the questions which they are always arguing, especially in courts of law: they commit all sorts of crimes, and there is nothing which they will not do or say in their own defence.

Socrates. But do they admit their guilt, Euthyphro, and yet say that they ought not to be punished?

Euthyphro. No; they do not.

Socrates. Then there are some things which they do not venture to say and do: for they do not venture to argue that the guilty are to be unpunished, but they deny their guilt, do they not?

Euthyphro. Yes.

Socrates. Then they do not argue that the evil-doer should not be punished, but they argue about the fact of who the evil-doer is, and what he did and when?

Euthyphro. True.

Socrates. And the gods are in the same case, if as you assert they quarrel about just and unjust, and some of them say while others deny that injustice is done among them. For surely neither God nor man will ever venture to say that the doer of injustice is not to be punished?

Euthyphro. That is true, Socrates, in the main.

Socrates. But they join issue about the particulars—gods and men alike; and, if they dispute at all, they dispute about some act which is called in question, and which by some is affirmed to be just, by others to be unjust. Is not that true?

Euthyphro. Quite true.

Socrates. Well then, my dear friend Euthyphro, do tell me, for my better instruction and information, what proof have you that in the opinion of all the gods a servant who is guilty of murder, and is put in chains by the master of the dead man, and dies because he is put in chains before he who bound him can learn from the interpreters of the gods what he ought to do with him, dies unjustly; and that on behalf of such an one a son ought to proceed against his father and accuse him of murder. How would you show that all the gods absolutely agree in approving of his act? Prove to me that they do, and I will applaud your wisdom as long as I live.

Euthyphro. It will be a difficult task; but I could make the matter very dear indeed to you.

Socrates. I understand; you mean to say that I am not so quick of apprehension as the judges: for to them you will be sure to prove that the act is unjust, and hateful to the gods.

Euthyphro. Yes indeed, Socrates; at least if they will listen to me.

Socrates. But they will be sure to listen if they find that you are a good speaker. There was a notion that came into my mind while you were speaking; I said to myself: "Well, and what if Euthyphro does prove to me that all the gods regarded the death of the serf as unjust, how do I know anything more of the nature of piety and impiety? for granting that this action may be hateful to the gods, still piety and impiety are not adequately defined by these distinctions, for that which is hateful to the gods has been shown to be also pleasing and dear to them." And therefore, Euthyphro, I do not ask you to prove this; I will suppose, if you like, that all the gods condemn and abominate such an action. But I will amend the definition so far as to say that what all the gods hate is impious, and what they love pious or holy; and what some of them love and others hate is both or neither. Shall this be our definition of piety and impiety?

Euthyphro. Why not, Socrates?

Socrates. Why not! certainly, as far as I am concerned, Euthyphro, there is no reason why not. But whether this admission will greatly assist you in the task of instructing me as you promised, is a matter for you to consider.

Euthyphro. Yes, I should say that what all the gods love is pious and holy, and the opposite which they all hate, impious.

Socrates. Ought we to enquire into the truth of this, Euthyphro, or simply to accept the mere statement on our own authority and that of others? What do you say?

Euthyphro. We should enquire; and I believe that the statement will stand the test of enquiry.

Socrates. We shall know better, my good friend, in a little while. The point which I should first wish to understand is whether the pious or holy is beloved by the gods because it is holy, or holy because it is beloved of the gods.

Euthyphro. I do not understand your meaning, Socrates.

Socrates. I will endeavour to explain: we speak of carrying and we speak of being carried, of leading and being led, seeing and being see. You know that in all such cases there is a difference, and you know also in what the difference lies?

Euthyphro. I think that I understand.

Socrates. And is not that which is beloved distinct from that which loves?

Euthyphro. Certainly.

Socrates. Well; and now tell me, is that which is carried in this state of carrying because it is carried, or for some other reason?

Euthyphro. No; that is the reason.

Socrates. And the same is true of what is led and of what is seen?

Euthyphro. True.

Socrates. And a thing is not seen because it is visible, but conversely, visible because it is seen; nor is a thing led because it is in the state of being led, or carried because it is in the state of being carried, but the converse of this. And now I think, Euthyphro, that my meaning will be intelligible; and my meaning is, that any state of action or passion implies previous action or passion. It does not become because it is becoming, but it is in a state of becoming because it becomes; neither does it suffer because it is in a state of suffering, but it is in a state of suffering because it suffers. Do you not agree?

Euthyphro. Yes.

Socrates. Is not that which is loved in some state either of becoming or suffering?

Euthyphro. Yes.

Socrates. And the same holds as in the previous instances; the state of being loved follows the act of being loved, and not the act the state.

Euthyphro. Certainly.

Socrates. And what do you say of piety, Euthyphro; is not piety, according to your definition, loved by all the gods?

Euthyphro. Yes.

Socrates. Because it is pious or holy, or for some other reason?

Euthyphro. No, that is the reason.

Socrates. It is loved because it is holy, not holy because it is loved?

Euthyphro. Yes.

Socrates. And that which is dear to the gods is loved by them, and is in a state to be loved of them because it is loved of them?

Euthyphro. Certainly.

Socrates. Then that which is dear to the gods, Euthyphro, is not holy, nor is that which is holy loved of God, as you affirm; but they are two different things.

Euthyphro. How do you mean, Socrates?

Socrates. I mean to say that the holy has been acknowledged by us to be loved of God because it is holy, not to be holy because it is loved.

Euthyphro. Yes.

Socrates. But that which is dear to the gods is dear to them because it is loved by them, not loved by them because it is dear to them.

Euthyphro. True.

Socrates. But, friend Euthyphro, if that which is holy is the same with that which is dear to God, and is loved because it is holy, then that which is dear to God would have been loved as being dear to God; but if that which dear to God is dear to him because loved by him, then that which is holy would have been holy because loved by him. But now you see that the reverse is the case, and that they are quite different from one another. For one (Θεοφιλὲς) is of a kind to be loved because it is loved, and the other (ο´σιον) is loved because it is of a kind to be loved. Thus you appear to me, Euthyphro, when I ask you what is the essence of holiness, to offer an attribute only, and not the essence—the attribute of being loved by all the gods. But you still refuse to explain to me the nature of holiness. And therefore, if you please, I will ask you not to hide your treasure, but to tell me once more what holiness or piety really is, whether dear to the gods or not (for that is a matter about which we will not quarrel) and what is impiety?

Euthyphro. I really do not know, Socrates, how to express what I mean. For somehow or other our arguments, on whatever ground we rest them, seem to turn around and walk away from us.

* * *

From *Common-Sense Religion*

DANIEL C. DENNETT

* * *

It isn't easy being moral, and it seems to be getting harder and harder these days. It used to be that most of the world's ills—disease, famine, war—were quite

Daniel C. Dennett, "Common-Sense Religion," *The Chronicle Review* 52, no. 20 (20 January 2006), pp. B6. Reprinted by permission of Daniel Dennett.

beyond the capacities of everyday people to ameliorate. There was nothing they could do about it, so people could ignore the catastrophes on the other side of the globe—if they even knew about them—with a clear conscience. Living by a few simple, locally applicable maxims could more or less guarantee that one lived about as good a life as was possible at the time. No longer.

Thanks to technology, what almost anybody can do has been multiplied a thousandfold, but our moral understanding about what we ought to do hasn't kept pace. You can have a test-tube baby or take a morning-after pill to keep from having a baby; you can satisfy your sexual urges in the privacy of your room by downloading Internet pornography, or you can copy your favorite music free instead of buying it; you can keep your money in secret offshore bank accounts or purchase stock in cigarette companies that are exploiting impoverished third-world countries; and you can lay minefields, smuggle nuclear weapons in suitcases, make nerve gas, and drop "smart bombs" with pinpoint accuracy. Also, you can arrange to have $100 a month automatically sent from your bank account to provide education for 10 girls in an Islamic country who otherwise would not learn to read and write, or to benefit 100 malnourished people, or provide medical care for AIDS sufferers in Africa. You can use the Internet to organize citizen monitoring of environmental hazards or to check the honesty and performance of government officials—or to spy on your neighbors. Now, what ought we to do?

In the face of such truly imponderable questions, it is entirely reasonable to look for a short set of simple answers. H. L. Mencken cynically said, "For every complex problem, there is a simple answer . . . and it is wrong." But maybe he was wrong! Maybe one Golden Rule or the Ten Commandments or some other short list of absolutely nonnegotiable Dos and Don'ts resolves all the predicaments just fine, once you figure out how to apply them. Nobody would deny, however, that it is far from obvious how any of the favored rules or principles can be interpreted to fit all our quandaries. "Thou shalt not kill" is cited by religious opponents of the death penalty, and by proponents as well. The principle of the Sanctity of Human Life sounds bracingly clear and absolute: Every human life is equally sacred, equally inviolable; as with the king in chess, no price can be placed on it, since to lose it is to lose everything. But in fact we all know that life isn't, and can't be, like chess. There are multitudes of interfering "games" going on at once. What are we to do when more than one human life is at stake? If each life is infinitely valuable and none more valuable than another, how are we to dole out the few transplantable kidneys that are available, for instance? Modern technology only exacerbates the issues, which are ancient. Solomon faced tough choices with notable wisdom, and every mother who has ever had less than enough food for her own children (let alone her neighbor's children) has had to confront the impracticality of applying the principle of the Sanctity of Human Life.

Surely just about everybody has faced a moral dilemma and secretly wished, "If only somebody—somebody I trusted—could tell me what to do!" Wouldn't that be morally inauthentic? Aren't we responsible for making our own moral decisions? Yes, but the virtues of "do it yourself" moral reasoning have their limits, and if you decide, after conscientious consideration, that your moral decision is to delegate further moral decisions in your life to a trusted expert, then you have made your own moral decision. You have decided to take advantage of the division of labor that civilization makes possible and get the help of expert specialists.

We applaud the wisdom of that course in all other important areas of decision making (don't try to be your own doctor, the lawyer who represents himself has a fool for a client, and so forth). Even in the case of political decisions, like which way to vote, the policy of delegation can be defended. When my wife and I go to a town meeting, I know that she has studied the issues so much more assiduously than I that I routinely follow her lead, voting the way she tells me. Even if I'm not sure why, I have plenty of evidence for my conviction that, if we did take the time and energy to thrash it all out, she'd persuade me that, all things considered, her opinion was correct. Is that a dereliction of my duties as a citizen? I don't think so, but it does depend on my having good grounds for trusting her judgment. Love is not enough. That's why those who have an unquestioning faith in the correctness of the moral teachings of their religion are a problem: If they haven't conscientiously considered, on their own, whether their pastors or priests or rabbis or imams are worthy of such delegated authority over their lives, then they are taking a personally immoral stand.

That is perhaps the most shocking implication of my inquiry into the role religion plays in our lives, and I do not shrink from it, even though it may offend many who think of themselves as deeply moral. It is commonly supposed that it is entirely exemplary to adopt the moral teachings of one's own religion without question because—to put it simply—it is the word of God (as interpreted, always, by the specialists to whom one has delegated authority). I am urging, on the contrary, that anybody who professes that a particular point of moral conviction is not discussable, not debatable, not negotiable, simply because it is the word of God, or because the Bible says so, or because "that is what all Muslims (Hindus, Sikhs . . .) believe, and I am a Muslim (Hindu, Sikh . . .)" should be seen to be making it impossible for the rest of us to take their views seriously, excusing themselves from the moral conversation, inadvertently acknowledging that their own views are not conscientiously maintained and deserve no further hearing.

The argument is straightforward. Suppose I have a friend, Fred, who is (in my carefully considered opinion) always right. If I tell you I'm against stem-cell research because "my friend Fred says it's wrong, and that's all there is to it," you will just look at me as if I were missing the point of the discussion. I have not given you a reason that, in good faith, I could expect you to appreciate. Suppose you believe that stem-cell research is wrong because God has told you so. Even if you are right—that is, even if God does exist and has, personally, told you that stem-cell research is wrong—you cannot reasonably expect others who do not share your faith or experience to accept that as a reason. The fact that your faith is so strong that you cannot do otherwise just shows (if you really can't) that you are disabled for moral persuasion, a sort of robotic slave to a meme that you are unable to evaluate. And if you reply that you can, but you won't consider reasons for and against your conviction (because it is God's word, and it would be sacrilegious even to consider whether it might be in error), you avow your willful refusal to abide by the minimal conditions of rational discussion. Either way, your declarations of your deeply held views are posturings that are out of place, part of the problem, not part of the solution, and we others will just have to work around you as best we can.

Notice that my stand involves no disrespect and no prejudging of the possibility that God has told you. If God has told you, then part of your problem is convincing others, to whom God has not (yet) spoken. If you refuse or are unable to attempt that, you are actually letting your God down, in the guise of demonstrating your helpless love. You can withdraw from the discussion if you must—that is your right—but then don't blame us if we don't "get it."

Many deeply religious people have all along been eager to defend their convictions in the court of reasonable inquiry and persuasion. They will have no difficulty at all with my observations—aside from confronting the diplomatic decision of whether they will join me in trying to convince their less reasonable co-religionists that they are making matters worse for their religion by the intransigence.

* * *

Subjectivism, Relativism, and Emotivism

Consider the following: Abdulla Yones killed his sixteen-year-old daughter Heshu in their apartment in west London. The murder was yet another example of an "honor killing," an ancient tradition still practiced in many parts of the world. Using a kitchen knife, Yones stabbed Heshu eleven times and slit her throat. He later declared that he *had* to kill her to expunge a stain from his family, a stain that Heshu had caused by her outrageous behavior. What was outrageous behavior to Yones, however, would seem to many Westerners to be typical teenage antics, annoying but benign. Heshu's precise offense against her family's honor is unclear, but the possibilities include wearing makeup, having a boyfriend, and showing an independent streak that would be thought perfectly normal throughout the West. In some countries, honor killings are sometimes endorsed by the local community or even given the tacit blessing of the state.

What do you think of this time-honored way of dealing with family conflicts? Specifically, what is your opinion regarding the *morality* of honor killing? Your response to this question is likely to reveal not only your view of honor killing but your overall approach to morality as well. Suppose your response is something like this: "Honor killing is morally *wrong*—wrong no matter where it's done or who does it." With this statement, you implicitly embrace moral **objectivism,** the doctrine that some moral norms or principles are valid for everyone—*universal,* in other words—regardless of how cultures may differ in their moral outlooks. However, you need not hold that the objective

principles are rigid rules that have no exceptions (a view known as *absolutism*) or that they must be applied in exactly the same way in every situation and culture.

On the other hand, let us say that you assess the case like this: "In societies that approve of honor killing, the practice is morally right; in those that do not approve, it is morally wrong. My society approves of honor killing, so it is morally right." If you believe what you say, then you are a cultural relativist. **Cultural relativism** is the view that an action is morally right if one's culture approves of it. Moral rightness and wrongness are therefore relative to cultures. So in one culture, an action may be morally right; in another culture, it may be morally wrong.

Perhaps you prefer an even narrower view of morality, and so you say, "Honor killing may be right for you, but it is most certainly not right for me." If you mean this literally, then you are committed to another kind of relativism called **subjective relativism**—the view that an action is morally right if one approves of it. Moral rightness and wrongness are relative not to cultures but to individuals. An action then can be right for you but wrong for someone else. Your approving of an action makes it right. There is therefore no objective morality, and cultural norms do not make right or wrong—individuals make right or wrong.

Finally, imagine that you wish to take a different tack regarding the subject of honor killing. You say, "I abhor the practice of honor killing"—but you believe that in uttering these words you are saying nothing that is true or false. You believe that despite what your statement seems to mean, you are simply expressing your emotions. You therefore hold to **emotivism**—the view that moral utterances are neither true nor false but are instead expressions of emotions or attitudes. So in your sentence about honor killing, you are not stating a fact—you are merely emoting and possibly trying to influence someone's behavior. Even when emotivists express a more specific preference regarding other people's behavior—by saying, for instance, "No one should commit an honor killing"—they are still not making a factual claim. They are simply expressing a preference, and perhaps hoping to persuade other people to see things their way.

These four replies represent four distinctive perspectives on morality (though certainly not the *only* perspectives), four divergent views of the meaning and import of moral judgments. Moreover, they are not purely theoretical but real and relevant. People actually live their lives (or try to) as moral objectivists, or relativists, or emotivists, or some strange and inconsistent mixture of these. (There is an excellent chance, for example, that you were raised as an objectivist but now accept some form of relativism—or even try to hold to objectivism in some instances and relativism in others.)

In any case, the question that you should ask (and that ethics can help you answer) is not whether you in fact accept any of these views, but whether you are justified in doing so. Let us see then where an examination of reasons for and against them will lead.

SUBJECTIVE RELATIVISM

What view of morality could be more tempting (and convenient) than the notion that an action is right if someone approves of it? Subjective relativism says that action X is right for Ann if she approves of it yet wrong for Greg if he disapproves of it. Thus action X can be both right and wrong—

QUICK REVIEW

objectivism—The view that some moral principles are valid for everyone.

cultural relativism—The view that an action is morally right if one's culture approves of it. *Implications*: that cultures are morally infallible, that social reformers can never be morally right, that moral disagreements between individuals in the same culture amount to arguments over whether someone disagrees with her culture, that other cultures cannot be legitimately criticized, and that moral progress is impossible.

subjective relativism—The view that an action is morally right if one approves of it. *Implications*: that individuals are morally infallible and that genuine moral disagreement between individuals is nearly impossible.

emotivism—The view that moral utterances are neither true nor false but are expressions of emotions or attitudes. *Implications*: that people cannot disagree over the moral facts because there are no moral facts, that presenting reasons in support of a moral utterance is a matter of offering nonmoral facts that can influence someone's attitude, and that nothing is actually good or bad.

right for Ann but wrong for Greg. A person's approval of an action *makes it right* for that person. Action X is not *objectively* right (or wrong). It is right (or wrong) relative to individuals. In this way, moral rightness becomes a matter of personal taste. If to Ann strawberry ice cream tastes good, then it is good (for her). If to Greg strawberry ice cream tastes bad, then it is bad (for him). There is no such thing as strawberry ice cream tasting good objectively or generally. Likewise, the morality of an action depends on Ann and Greg's moral tastes.

Judge Not?

Jesus said "Judge not that ye be not judged." Some have taken this to mean that we should not make moral judgments about others, and many who have never heard those words are convinced that to judge others is to be insensitive, intolerant, or absolutist. Professor Jean Bethke Elshtain examines this attitude and finds it both mistaken and harmful.

> I have also found helpful the discussion of the lively British philosopher, Mary Midgley. In her book *Can't We Make Moral Judgments?* Midgley notes our contemporary search for a nonjudgmental politics and quotes all those people who cry, in effect, "But surely it's always wrong to make moral judgments." We are not permitted to make anyone uncomfortable, to be "insensitive." Yet moral judgment of "some kind," says Midgley, "is a necessary element to our thinking." Judging involves our whole nature—it isn't just icing on the cake of self-identity. Judging makes it possible for us to "find our way through a whole forest of possibilities."

Midgley argues that Jesus was taking aim at sweeping condemnations and vindictiveness: he was not trashing the "whole faculty of judgment." Indeed, Jesus is making the "subtle point that while we cannot possibly avoid judging, we can see to it that we judge fairly, as we would expect others to do to us." This is part and parcel, then, of justice as fairness, as a discernment about a particular case and person and deed. Subjectivism in such matters—of the "I'm okay, you're okay," variety—is a cop-out, a way to stop forming and expressing moral judgments altogether. This strange suspension of specific moments of judgment goes hand-in-glove, of course, with an often violent rhetoric of condemnation of whole categories of persons, past and present—that all-purpose villain, the Dead White European Male, comes to mind.*

*Jean Bethke Elshtain, "Judge Not?" *First Things,* no. 46 (October 1994): 36–40.

Many people claim they are subjective relativists—until they realize the implications of the doctrine, implications that are at odds with our commonsense moral experience. First, subjective relativism implies that in the rendering of any moral opinion, each person is incapable of being in error. Each of us is *morally infallible.* If we approve of an action—and we are sincere in our approval—then that action is morally right. We literally cannot be mistaken about this, because our approval makes the action right. If we say that inflicting pain on an innocent child for no reason is right (that is, we approve of such an action), then the action is right. Our moral judgment is correct, and it cannot be otherwise. Yet if anything is obvious about our moral experience, it is that we are *not* infallible. We sometimes *are* mistaken in our moral judgments. We are, after all, not gods.

From all accounts, Adolf Hitler approved of (and ordered) the extermination of vast numbers of innocent people, including six million Jews. If so, by the lights of subjective relativism, his facilitating those deaths was morally right. It seems that the totalitarian leader Pol Pot approved of his murdering more than a million innocent people in Cambodia. If so, it was right for him to murder those people. But it seems obvious that what these men did was wrong, and their approving of their actions did not make the actions right. Because subjective relativism suggests otherwise, it is a dubious doctrine.

Another obvious feature of our commonsense moral experience is that from time to time we have moral disagreements. Maria says that capital punishment is right, but Carlos says that it is wrong. This seems like a perfectly clear case of two people disagreeing about the morality of capital punishment. Subjective relativism, however, implies that such disagreements cannot happen. Subjective relativism says that when Maria states that capital punishment is right, she is just saying that she approves of it. And when Carlos states that capital punishment is wrong, he is just saying that he disapproves of it. But they are not really disagreeing, because they are merely describing their attitudes toward capital punishment. In effect, Maria is saying "This is my attitude on the subject," and Carlos is saying "Here is my attitude on the subject." But these two claims are not opposed to one another. They are about different subjects, so both statements could be true. Maria and Carlos might as well be discussing how strawberry ice cream tastes to each of them, for nothing that Maria says could contradict what Carlos says. Because genuine disagreement is a fact of our moral life, and subjective relativism is inconsistent with this fact, the doctrine is implausible.

In practice, subjective relativism is a difficult view to hold consistently. At times, of course, you can insist that an action is right for you but wrong for someone else. But you may also find yourself saying something like "Pol Pot committed absolutely heinous acts; he was evil" or "What Hitler did was wrong"—and what you mean is that what Pol Pot and Hitler did was objectively wrong, not just wrong relative to you. Such slides from subjective relativism to objectivism suggest a conflict between these two perspectives and the need to resolve it through critical reasoning.

CULTURAL RELATIVISM

To many people, the idea that morality is relative to culture is obvious. It seems obvious primarily because modern sociology has left no doubt that people's moral judgments differ from culture to culture. We now know that the moral judgments of people in other cultures are often shockingly different from our own. In some societies, it is morally permissible to kill infants at birth, burn widows alive with the bodies of their husbands, steal and commit acts of treachery, surgically remove the clitorises of young girls for no medical reason, kill one's elderly parents, have multi-

ple husbands or wives, and make up for someone's death by murdering others. There is only a small step from acknowledging this moral diversity among cultures to the conclusion that cultures determine moral rightness and that objective morality is a myth.

The philosopher Walter T. Stace (1886–1967) illustrates how easily this conclusion has come to many in Western societies:

It was easy enough to believe in a single absolute morality in older times when there was no anthropology, when all humanity was divided clearly into two groups, Christian peoples and the "heathen." Christian peoples knew and possessed the one true morality. The rest were savages whose moral ideas could be ignored. But all this changed. Greater knowledge has brought greater tolerance. We can no longer exalt our own moralities as alone true, while dismissing all other moralities as false or inferior. The investigations of anthropologists have shown that there exist side by side in the world a bewildering variety of moral codes. On this topic endless volumes have been written, masses of evidence piled up. Anthropologists have ransacked the Melanesian Islands, the jungles of New Guinea, the steppes of Siberia, the deserts of Australia, the forests of central Africa, and have brought back with them countless examples of weird, extravagant, and fantastic "moral" customs with which to confound us. We learn that all kinds of horrible practices are, in this, that, or the other place, regarded as essential to virtue. We find that there is nothing, or next to nothing, which has always and everywhere been regarded as morally good by all men. Where then is our universal morality? Can we, in face of all this evidence, deny that it is nothing but an empty dream?[1]

Here, Stace spells out in rough form the most common argument for cultural relativism, an inference from differences in the moral beliefs of cultures to the conclusion that cultures make

---

[1]Walter Stace, *The Concept of Morals* (1937; reprint, New York: Macmillan, 1965), 8–58.

morality. Before we conclude that objectivism is in fact an empty dream, we should state the argument more precisely and examine it closely. We can lay out the argument like this:

1. People's judgments about right and wrong differ from culture to culture.

2. If people's judgments about right and wrong differ from culture to culture, then right and wrong are relative to culture, and there are no objective moral principles.

3. Therefore, right and wrong are relative to culture, and there are no objective moral principles.

A good argument gives us good reason to accept its conclusion, and an argument is good if its logic is solid (the conclusion follows logically from the premises) *and* the premises are true. So is the foregoing argument a good one? We can see right away that the logic is in fact solid. That is, the argument is valid: the conclusion does indeed follow from the premises. The question then becomes whether the premises are true. As we have seen, Premise 1 is most certainly true. People's judgments about right and wrong do vary from culture to culture. But what of Premise 2? Does the diversity of views about right and wrong among cultures show that right and wrong are determined by culture, that there are no universal moral truths? There are good reasons to think this premise false.

Premise 2 says that because there are disagreements among cultures about right and wrong, there must not be any universal standards of right and wrong. But even if the moral judgments of

---

CRITICAL THOUGHT: "Female Circumcision" and Cultural Relativism

In recent years many conflicts have flared between those who espouse universal human rights and those who embrace cultural relativism. One issue that has been a flashpoint in the contentious debates is a practice called *female genital cutting* (FGC). Other names include *female circumcision* and *female genital mutilation.*

In FGC, all or part of the female genitals are removed. The procedure, used mostly in Africa and the Middle East, is usually performed on girls between the ages of four and eight, but sometimes on young women. A report in the *Yale Journal of Public Health* states that in Sudan 89 percent of girls receive FGC and that the cutting tools "include knives, scissors, razors, and broken glass. The operation is typically performed by elderly women or traditional birth attendants, though increasing numbers of doctors are taking over these roles."* The practice occurs for various reasons, including religious and sociological, and is defended by some

who say that it prepares girls for their role in society and marriage and discourages illicit sex.

Public health officials regard FGC as a serious health problem. It can cause reproductive tract infections, pain during intercourse, painful menstruation, complications during childbirth, greater risk of HIV infection, bleeding, and even death. International health agencies denounce FGC, but many say that no one outside a culture using FGC has a right to criticize the practice.

Do you think that FGC is morally permissible? If you judge the practice wrong, are you appealing to some notion of objective morality? If you judge it permissible, are you doing so because you are a cultural relativist? In either case, explain your reasoning.

*Sarah Cannon and Daniel Berman, "Cut Off: The Female Genital-Cutting Controversy," *Yale Journal of Public Health* 1, no. 2 (2004), www.yaleph.com (31 December 2006).

people in various cultures do differ, such difference in itself does not show that morality is relative to culture. Just because people in different cultures have different views about morality, their disagreement does not prove that no view can be objectively correct—no more than people's disagreements about the size of a house show that no one's opinion about it can be objectively true. Suppose Culture A endorses infanticide, but Culture B does not. Such a disagreement does not demonstrate that both cultures are equally correct or that there is no objectively correct answer. After all, it is possible that infanticide is objectively right (or wrong) and that the relevant moral beliefs of either Culture A or Culture B are false.

Another reason to doubt the truth of Premise 2 comes from questioning how deep the disagreements among cultures really are. Judgments about the rightness of actions obviously do vary across cultures. But people can differ in their moral judgments not just because they accept different moral principles, but also because they have divergent *nonmoral* beliefs. They may actually embrace the *same* moral principles, but their moral judgments conflict because their nonmoral beliefs lead them to apply those principles in very different ways. If so, the diversity of moral judgments across cultures does not necessarily indicate deep disagreements over fundamental moral principles or standards. Here is a classic example:

[T]he story is told of a culture in which a son is regarded as obligated to kill his father when the latter reaches age sixty. Given just this much information about the culture and the practice in question it is tempting to conclude that the members of that culture differ radically from members of our culture in their moral beliefs and attitudes. We, after all, believe it is immoral to take a human life, and regard patricide as especially wrong. But suppose that in the culture we are considering, those who belong to it believe (a) that at the moment of death one enters heaven; (b) one's physical and mental condition in

the afterlife is exactly what it is at the moment of death; and (c) men are at the peak of their physical and mental powers when they are sixty. Then what appeared at first to be peculiarities in moral outlook on the part of the cultural group in question regarding the sanctity of life and respect for parents, turn out to be located rather in a nonmoral outlook of the group. A man in that culture who kills his father is doing so out of concern for the latter's well-being—to prevent him, for example, from spending eternity blind or senile. It is not at all clear that, if we shared the relevant nonmoral beliefs of this other culture, we would not believe with them that sons should kill their fathers at the appropriate time.[2]

To find similar examples, we need not search for the exotic. In Western cultures we have the familiar case of abortion, an issue hotly debated among those who at first glance appear to be disagreeing about moral principles. But in fact the disputants agree about the moral principle involved: that murder is morally wrong. What they do disagree about is a nonmoral factual matter—whether the fetus is an entity that can be murdered (that is, whether it is a person). Disagreement over the nonmoral facts masks substantial agreement on fundamental moral standards.

The work of several anthropologists provides some evidence for these kinds of disagreements as well as for the existence of cross-cultural moral agreement in general. The social psychologist Solomon Asch, for instance, maintains that differing moral judgments among societies often arise when the same moral principles are operating but the particulars of cultural situations vary.[3] Other observers claim that across numerous diverse

[2]Phillip Montague, "Are There Objective and Absolute Moral Standards?" in *Reason and Responsibility: Readings in Some Basic Problems in Philosophy,* ed. Joel Feinberg, 5th ed. (Belmont, CA: Wadsworth, 1978), 490–91.
[3]Solomon Asch, *Social Psychology* (Englewood Cliffs, NJ: Prentice-Hall, 1952), 378–79.

cultures we can find many common moral elements such as prohibitions against murder, lying, incest, and adultery and obligations of fairness, reciprocity, and consideration toward parents and children.[4] Some philosophers argue that a core set of moral values—including, for example, truth telling and prohibitions against murder—*must* be universal, otherwise cultures would not survive.

These points demonstrate that Premise 2 of the argument for cultural relativism is false. The argument therefore gives us no good reasons to believe that an action is right simply because one's culture approves of it.

For many people, however, the failure of the argument for cultural relativism may be beside the point. They find the doctrine appealing mainly because it seems to promote the humane and enlightened attitude of tolerance toward other cultures. Broad expanses of history are drenched with blood and marked by cruelty because of the evil of intolerance—religious, racial, political, and social. Tolerance therefore seems a supreme virtue, and cultural relativism appears to provide a justification and vehicle for it. After all, if all cultures are morally equal, does not cultural relativism both entail and promote tolerance?

We should hope that tolerance does reign in a pluralistic world, but there is no necessary connection between tolerance and cultural relativism. For one thing, cultural relativists cannot consistently advocate tolerance. To advocate tolerance is to advocate an objective moral value. But if tolerance is an objective moral value, then cultural relativism must be false, because it says that there are no objective moral values. So instead of justifying tolerance toward all, cultural relativism actually undercuts universal tolerance. Moreover,

according to cultural relativism, intolerance can be justified just as easily as tolerance can. If a culture approves of intolerance, then intolerance is right for that culture. If a culture approves of tolerance, then tolerance is right for that culture. Cultural relativists are thus committed to the view that intolerance can in fact be justified, and they cannot consistently claim that tolerance is morally right everywhere.

At this point we are left with no good reasons to believe that cultural relativism is true. But the problems for the doctrine are deeper than that. Like subjective relativism, it has several implications that render it highly implausible.

First, as is the case with subjective relativism, cultural relativism implies moral infallibility. A culture simply cannot be mistaken about a moral issue. If it approves of an action, then that action is morally right, and there is no possibility of error as long as the culture's approval is genuine. But, of course, cultural infallibility in moral matters is flagrantly implausible, just as individual infallibility is. At one time or another, cultures have sanctioned witch burning, slavery, genocide, racism, rape, human sacrifice, and religious persecution. Does it make any sense to say that they could not have been mistaken about the morality of these actions?

Cultural relativism also has the peculiar consequence that social reformers of every sort would *always be wrong*. Their culture would be the ultimate authority on moral matters, so if they disagree with their culture, they could not possibly be right. If their culture approves of genocide, genocide would be right, and antigenocide reformers would be wrong to oppose the practice. In this upside-down world, the antigenocide reformers would be immoral and the genocidal culture would be the real paragon of righteousness. Reformers such as Martin Luther King Jr., Mahatma Gandhi, Mary Wollstonecraft (champion of women's rights), and Frederick Douglass (American abolitionist) would be great crusaders—

---

[4]See, for example, Clyde Kluckhohn, "Ethical Relativity: Sic et Non," *Journal of Philosophy* 52 (1955): 663–77, and E. O. Wilson, *On Human Nature* (1978; reprint, New York: Bantam, 1979).

for immorality. Our moral experience, however, suggests that cultural relativism has matters exactly backward. Social reformers have often been right when they claimed their cultures were wrong, and this fact suggests that cultural relativism is wrong about morality.

Where cultural relativism holds, if you have a disagreement with your culture about the rightness of an action, you automatically lose. You are in error by definition. But what about a disagreement among members of the same society? What would such a disagreement amount to? It amounts to something very strange, according to cultural relativism. When two people in the same culture disagree on a moral issue, what they are really disagreeing about—the only thing they can rationally disagree about—is whether their society endorses a particular view. After all, society makes actions right by approving or disapproving of them. According to cultural relativism, if René and Michel (both members of society X) are disagreeing about capital punishment, their disagreement must actually be about whether society X approves of capital punishment. Since right and wrong are determined by one's culture, René and Michel are disagreeing about what society X says. But this view of moral disagreement is dubious, to say the least. When we have a moral disagreement, we do not think that the crux of it is whether our society approves of an action. We do not think that deciding a moral issue is simply a matter of polling the public to see which way opinion leans. We do not think that René and Michel will ever find out whether capital punishment is morally permissible by consulting public opinion. Determining whether an action is right is a very different thing from determining what most people think. This odd consequence of cultural relativism suggests that the doctrine is flawed.

One of the more disturbing implications of cultural relativism is that other cultures cannot be legitimately criticized. If a culture approves of the actions that it performs, then those actions are morally right regardless of what other cultures have to say about the matter. One society's practices are as morally justified as any other's, as long as the practices are socially sanctioned. This consequence of cultural relativism may not seem too worrisome when the societies in question are long dead. But it takes on a different tone when the societies are closer to us in time. Consider the 1994 genocide committed in Rwanda in which a million people died. Suppose the killers' society (their tribe) approved of the murders. Then the genocide was morally justified. And what of Hitler's "final solution"—the murder of millions of Jews in World War II? Say that German society approved of Hitler's actions (and those of the men who carried out his orders). Then Hitler's final solution was morally right; engineering the Holocaust was morally permissible. If you are a cultural relativist, you cannot legitimately condemn these monstrous deeds. Because they were approved by their respective societies, they were morally justified. They were just as morally justified as the socially sanctioned activities of Albert Schweitzer, Jonas Salk, or Florence Nightingale. But all this seems implausible. We do in fact sometimes criticize other cultures and believe that it is legitimate to do so.

Contrary to the popular view, rejecting cultural relativism (embracing moral objectivism) does not entail intolerance. In fact, it provides a plausible starting point for tolerance. A moral objectivist realizes that she can legitimately criticize other cultures—and that people of other cultures can legitimately criticize her culture. A recognition of this fact together with an objectivist's sense of fallibility can lead her to an openness to criticism of her own culture and to acceptance of everyone's right to disagree.

We not only criticize other cultures, but we also compare the past with the present. We compare the actions of the past with those of the present and judge whether moral progress has been made. We see that slavery has been abolished, that we no longer burn witches, that we recognize racism as evil—then we judge that these changes represent moral progress. For moral relativists, however, there is no objective standard by which to compare the ways of the past with the ways of the present. Societies of the past approved or disapproved of certain practices, and contemporary societies approve or disapprove of them, and no transcultural moral assessments can be made. But if there is such a thing as moral progress, then there must be some cross-cultural moral yardstick by which we can evaluate actions. There must be objective standards by which we can judge that actions of the present are better than those of the past. If there are no objective moral standards, our judging that we are in fact making moral progress is hard to explain.

Finally, there is a fundamental difficulty concerning the application of cultural relativism to moral questions: the doctrine is nearly impossible to use. The problem is that cultural relativism applies to societies (or social groups), but we all belong to several societies, and there is no way to choose which one is the proper one. What society do you belong to if you are an Italian American Buddhist living in Atlanta, Georgia, who is a member of the National Organization for Women and a breast cancer support group? The hope of cultural relativists is that they can use the doctrine to make better, more enlightened moral decisions. But this society-identification problem seems to preclude any moral decisions, let alone enlightened ones.

What, then, can we conclude from our examination of cultural relativism? We have found that the basic argument for the view fails; we therefore have no good reasons to believe that the doctrine is true. Beyond that, we have good grounds for thinking the doctrine false. Its surprising implications regarding moral infallibility, moral reformers, moral progress, the nature of moral disagreements within societies, and the possibility of cross-cultural criticism show it to be highly implausible. The crux of the matter is that cultural relativism does a poor job of explaining some important features of our moral experience. A far better explanation of these features is that some form of moral objectivism is true.

EMOTIVISM

The commonsense view of moral judgments is that they ascribe moral properties to such things as actions and people and that they are therefore statements that can be true or false. This view of moral judgments is known as *cognitivism*. The opposing view, called *noncognitivism,* denies that moral judgments are statements that can be true or false; they do not ascribe properties to anything. Probably the most famous noncognitivist view is emotivism, which says that moral judgments cannot be true or false because they do not make any claims—they merely express emotions or attitudes. For the emotivist, moral utterances are something akin to exclamations that simply express approving or disapproving feelings: "Violence against women—disgusting!" or "Shoplifting—love it!"

The English philosopher A. J. Ayer (1910–89), an early champion of emotivism, is clear and blunt about what a moral utterance such as "Stealing money is wrong" signifies. This sentence, he says,

expresses no proposition which can be either true or false. It is as if I had written "Stealing money!!"—where the shape and thickness of the exclamation marks show, by a suitable convention, that a special sort of moral disapproval is the feeling which is being expressed. It is clear that there is nothing said here which can be true or false. . . . For in saying that a certain type of action is right or wrong, I am not making any factual statement, not even a statement about my own state of mind.[5]

[5]A. J. Ayer, "Critique of Ethics and Theology," in *Language, Truth and Logic* (1936; reprint, New York: Dover, 1952), 107.

If moral judgments are about feelings and not the truth or falsity of moral assertions, then ethics is a very different sort of inquiry than most people imagine. As Ayer says,

[A]s ethical judgements are mere expressions of feeling, there can be no way of determining the validity of any ethical system, and, indeed, no sense in asking whether any such system is true. All that one may legitimately enquire in this connection is, What are the moral habits of a given person or group of people, and what causes them to have precisely those habits and feelings? And this enquiry falls wholly within the scope of the existing social sciences.[6]

The emotivist points out that while moral utterances express feelings and attitudes, they also function to influence people's attitudes and behavior. So the sentence "Stealing money is wrong" not only expresses feelings of disapproval, it also can influence others to have similar feelings and act accordingly.

Emotivists also take an unusual position on moral disagreements. They maintain that moral disagreements are not conflicts of beliefs, as is the case when one person asserts that something is the case and another person asserts that it is not the case. Instead, moral disagreements are *disagreements in attitude*. Jane has positive feelings or a favorable attitude toward abortion, but Ellen has negative feelings or an unfavorable attitude toward abortion. The disagreement is emotive, not cognitive. Jane may say "Abortion is right," and Ellen may say "Abortion is wrong," but they are not really disagreeing over the facts. They are expressing conflicting attitudes and trying to influence each other's attitude and behavior.

Philosophers have criticized emotivism on several grounds, and this emotivist analysis of disagreement has been a prime target. As you might suspect, their concern is that this notion of disagreement is radically different from our ordinary

view. Like subjective relativism, emotivism implies that disagreements in the usual sense are impossible. People cannot disagree over the moral facts, because there are no moral facts. But we tend to think that when we disagree with someone on a moral issue, there really is a conflict of statements about what is the case. Of course, when we are involved in a conflict of beliefs, we may also experience conflicting attitudes. But we do not think that we are *only* experiencing a disagreement in attitudes.

Emotivism also provides a curious account of how reasons function in moral discourse. Our commonsense view is that a moral judgment is the kind of thing that makes a claim about moral properties and that such a claim can be supported by reasons. If someone asserts "Euthanasia is wrong," we may sensibly ask her what reasons she has for believing that claim. If she replies that there are no reasons to back up her claim or that moral utterances are not the kind of things that can be supported by reasons, we would probably think that she misunderstood the question or the nature of morality. For the emotivist, "moral" reasons have a very different function. Here reasons are intended not to support statements (since there are no moral statements) but to influence the emotions or attitudes of others. Since moral utterances express emotions or attitudes, "presenting reasons" is a matter of offering nonmoral facts that can influence those emotions and attitudes. Suppose A has a favorable attitude toward abortion, and B has an unfavorable one (that is, A and B are having a disagreement in attitude). For A, to present reasons is to provide information that might cause B to have a more favorable attitude toward abortion.

This conception of the function of reasons, however, implies that good reasons encompass *any* nonmoral facts that can alter someone's attitude. On this view, the relevance of these facts to the judgment at hand is beside the point. The essential criterion is whether the adduced facts are suf-

6. Ayer, "Critique of Ethics," 112.

ficiently influential. They need not have any logical or cognitive connection to the moral judgment to be changed. They may, for example, appeal to someone's ignorance, arrogance, racism, or fear. But we ordinarily suppose that reasons *should* be relevant to the cognitive content of moral judgments. Moreover, we normally make a clear distinction between influencing someone's attitudes and showing (by providing reasons) that a claim is true—a distinction that emotivism cannot make.

The final implication of emotivism is also problematic: there is no such thing as goodness or badness. We cannot legitimately claim that anything is good or bad, because these properties do not exist. To declare that something is good is just to express positive emotions or a favorable attitude toward it. We may say that pain is bad, but badness (or goodness) is not a feature of pain. Our saying that pain is bad is just an expression of our unfavorable attitude toward pain.

Suppose a six-year-old girl is living in a small village in Iraq during the brutal reign of Saddam Hussein. Saddam's henchmen firebomb the village, destroying it and incinerating everyone except the girl, who is burned from head to toe and endures excruciating pain for three days before she dies. Suppose that we are deeply moved by this tragedy as we consider her unimaginable suffering and we remark, "How horrible. The little girl's suffering was a very bad thing."[7] When we say something like this, we ordinarily mean that the girl's suffering had a certain moral property: that the suffering was bad. But according to emotivism, her suffering had no moral properties at all. When we comment on the girl's suffering, we are simply expressing our feelings; the suffering itself was neither good nor bad. But this view of things seems implausible. Our moral experience

suggests that some things in fact are bad and some are good.

The philosopher Brand Blanshard (1892–1987) makes the point in the following way:

[T]he emotivist is cut off by his theory from admitting that there has been anything good or evil in the past, either animal or human. There have been Black Deaths, to be sure, and wars and rumours of war; there have been the burning of countless women as witches, and the massacre in the Katlyn forest, and Oswiecim, and Dachau, and an unbearable procession of horrors; but one cannot meaningfully say that anything evil has ever happened. The people who suffered from these things did indeed take up attitudes of revulsion toward them; we can now judge that they took them; but in such judgments we are not saying that anything evil occurred. . . . [Emotivism], when first presented, has some plausibility. But when this is balanced against the implied unplausibility of setting down as meaningless every suggestion that good or evil events have ever occurred, it is outweighed enormously.[8]

Obviously, emotivism does not fare well when examined in light of our commonsense moral experience. We must keep in mind, though, that common sense is fallible. On the other hand, we should not jettison common sense in favor of another view unless we have good reasons to do so. In the case of emotivism, we have no good reasons to prefer it over common sense—and we have good grounds for rejecting it.

SUMMARY

Subjective relativism is the view that an action is morally right if one approves of it. A person's approval makes the action right. This doctrine (as well as cultural relativism) is in stark contrast to *moral objectivism*, the view that some moral principles are valid for everyone. Subjective relativism, though, has some troubling implications. It implies that each per-

[7]This scenario is inspired by some of Brand Blanshard's examples from "Emotivism," in *Reason and Goodness* (1961; reprint, New York: G. Allen and Unwin, 1978).

[8]Blanshard, "Emotivism," 204–5.

son is morally infallible and that individuals can never have a genuine moral disagreement.

Cultural relativism is the view that an action is morally right if one's culture approves of it. The argument for this doctrine is based on the diversity of moral judgments among cultures: because people's judgments about right and wrong differ from culture to culture, right and wrong must be relative to culture, and there are no objective moral principles. This argument is defective, however, because the diversity of moral views does not imply that morality is relative to cultures. In addition, the alleged diversity of basic moral standards among cultures may be only apparent, not real. Societies whose moral judgments conflict may be differing not over moral principles but over nonmoral facts.

Some think that tolerance is entailed by cultural relativism. But there is no necessary connection between tolerance and the doctrine. Indeed, the cultural relativist cannot consistently advocate tolerance while maintaining his relativist standpoint. To advocate tolerance is to advocate an objective moral value. But if tolerance is an objective moral value, then cultural relativism must be false, because it says that there are no objective moral values.

Like subjective relativism, cultural relativism has some disturbing consequences. It implies that cultures are morally infallible, that social reformers can never be morally right, that moral disagreements between individuals in the same culture amount to arguments over whether they disagree with their culture, that other cultures cannot be legitimately criticized, and that moral progress is impossible.

Emotivism is the view that moral utterances are neither true nor false but are expressions of emotions or attitudes. It leads to the conclusion that people can disagree only in attitude, not in beliefs. People cannot disagree over the moral facts, because there are no moral facts. Emotivism also implies that presenting reasons in support of a moral utterance is a matter of offering nonmoral facts that can influence someone's attitude. It seems that any nonmoral facts will do, as long as they affect attitudes. Perhaps the most far-reaching implication of emotivism is that nothing is actually good or bad. There simply are no

properties of goodness and badness. There is only the expression of favorable or unfavorable emotions or attitudes toward something.

EXERCISES

Review Questions

1. What is moral objectivism? (p. 22)
2. What is moral absolutism? Does objectivism require absolutism? (p. 22)
3. What is subjective relativism? What is cultural relativism? (p. 22)
4. What is emotivism? How does emotivism differ from objectivism? (p. 23)
5. How does subjective relativism imply moral infallibility? (p. 24)
6. According to moral subjectivism, are moral disagreements possible? Why or why not? (pp. 24–25)
7. What is the argument for cultural relativism? Is the argument sound? Why or why not? (pp. 25–28)
8. Does the diversity of moral outlooks in cultures show that right and wrong are determined by culture? Why or why not? (pp. 26–28)
9. According to the text, how is it possible for people in different cultures to disagree about moral judgments and still embrace the same fundamental moral principles? (pp. 27–28)
10. Is there a necessary connection between cultural relativism and tolerance? Why or why not? (p. 28)
11. What does cultural relativism imply about the moral status of social reformers? (pp. 28–29)
12. What is the emotivist view of moral disagreements? (p. 30)
13. According to emotivism, how do reasons function in moral discourse? (pp. 31–32)

Discussion Questions

1. Are you a subjective relativist? If so, how did you come to adopt this view? If not, what is your explanation for not accepting it?

2. Suppose a serial killer approves of his murderous actions. According to subjective relativism, are the killer's actions therefore justified? Do you believe a serial killer's murders are justified? If not, is your judgment based on a subjective relativist's perspective or an objectivist perspective?

3. Are you a cultural relativist? Why or why not?

4. Suppose a majority of the German people approved of Hitler's murdering six million Jews in World War II. Would this approval make Hitler's actions morally justified? If so, why? If not, why not—and what moral outlook are you using to make such a determination?

5. When cultural relativists say that every culture should embrace a policy of tolerance, are they contradicting themselves? If so, how? If cultural relativism were true, would this fact make wars between societies less or more likely? Explain your answer.

6. If you traveled the world and saw that cultures differ dramatically in their moral judgments,

would you conclude from this evidence that cultural relativism was true? Why or why not?

7. According to a cultural relativist, would the civil rights reforms that Martin Luther King Jr. sought be morally right or wrong? Do *you* think that his efforts at reform were morally wrong? What are your reasons for your decision?

8. Do you believe that there has been moral progress in the past thousand years of human history? Why or why not?

9. Suppose a deer that had been shot by a hunter writhed in agony for days before dying. You exclaim, "How she must have suffered! Her horrendous pain was a bad thing." In this situation, does the word *bad* refer to any moral properties? Is there really something *bad* about the deer's suffering—or is your use of the word just a way to express your horror without making any moral statement at all? Explain your answers.

READINGS

From *Anthropology and the Abnormal*

RUTH BENEDICT

Modern social anthropology has become more and more a study of the varieties and common elements of cultural environment and the consequences of these in human behavior. For such a study of diverse social orders primitive peoples fortunately provide a laboratory not yet entirely vitiated by the spread of a standardized worldwide civilization. Dyaks and Hopis, Fijians and Yakuts are significant for psychological and sociological study because only among these simpler peoples has there been sufficient iso-

Ruth Benedict, "The Case for Moral Relativism from Anthropology and the Abnormal," *Journal of General Psychology* 10 (1934): 59–75 (edited). Reprinted with permission of the Helen Dwight Reid Educational Foundation. Published by Heldref Publications, 1319 Eighteenth Street, NW, Washington D.C. 20036-1802. Copyright © 1934.

lation to give opportunity for the development of localized social forms. In the higher cultures the standardization of custom and belief over a couple of continents has given a false sense of the inevitability of the particular forms that have gained currency, and we need to turn to a wider survey in order to check the conclusions we hastily base upon this near-universality of familiar customs. Most of the simpler cultures did not gain the wide currency of the one which, out of our experience, we identify with human nature, but this was for various historical reasons, and certainly not for any that gives us as its carriers a monopoly of social good or of social sanity. Modern civilization, from this point of view, becomes not a necessary pinnacle of human achievement but one entry in a long series of possible adjustments.

These adjustments, whether they are in mannerisms like the ways of showing anger, or joy, or grief in any society, or in major human drives like those of sex, prove to be far more variable than experience in any one culture would suggest. In certain fields, such as that of religion or of formal marriage arrangements, these wide limits of variability are well known and can be fairly described. In others it is not yet possible to give a generalized account, but that does not absolve us of the task of indicating the significance of the work that has been done and of the problems that have arisen.

One of these problems relates to the customary modern normal-abnormal categories and our conclusions regarding them. In how far are such categories culturally determined, or in how far can we with assurance regard them as absolute? In how far can we regard inability to function socially as diagnostic of abnormality, or in how far is it necessary to regard this as a function of the culture?

As a matter of fact, one of the most striking facts that emerge from a study of widely varying cultures is the ease with which our abnormals function in other cultures. It does not matter what kind of "abnormality" we choose for illustration, those which indicate extreme instability, or those which are more in the nature of character traits like sadism or delusions of grandeur or of persecution, there are well-described cultures in which these abnormals function at ease and with honor, and apparently without danger or difficulty to the society.

The most notorious of these is trance and catalepsy. Even a very mild mystic is aberrant in our culture. But most peoples have regarded even extreme psychic manifestations not only as normal and desirable, but even as characteristic of highly valued and gifted individuals. This was true even in our own cultural background in that period when Catholicism made the ecstatic experience the mark of sainthood. It is hard for us, born and brought up in a culture that makes no use of the experience, to realize how important a rôle it may play and how many individuals are capable of it, once it has been given an honorable place in any society.

* * *

Cataleptic and trance phenomena are, of course, only one illustration of the fact that those whom we regard as abnormals may function adequately in other cultures. Many of our culturally discarded traits are selected for elaboration in different societies. Homosexuality is an excellent example, for in this case our attention is not constantly diverted, as in the consideration of trance, to the interruption of routine activity which it implies. Homosexuality poses the problem very simply. A tendency toward this trait in our culture exposes an individual to all the conflicts to which all aberrants are always exposed, and we tend to identify the consequences of this conflict with homosexuality. But these consequences are obviously local and cultural. Homosexuals in many societies are not incompetent, but they may be such if the culture asks adjustments of them that would strain any man's vitality. Wherever homosexuality has been given an honorable place in any society, those to whom it is congenial have filled adequately the honorable rôles society assigns to them. Plato's *Republic* is, of course, the most convincing statement of such a reading of homosexuality. It is presented as one of the major means to the good life, and it was generally so regarded in Greece at that time.

The cultural attitude toward homosexuals has not always been on such a high ethical plane, but it has been varied. Among many American Indian tribes there exists the institution of the berdache, as the French called them. These men-women were men who at puberty or thereafter took the dress and the occupations of women. Sometimes they married other men and lived with them. Sometimes they were men with no inversion, persons of weak sexual endowment who chose this rôle to avoid the jeers of the women. The berdaches were never regarded as of first-rate supernatural power, as similar men-women were in Siberia, but rather as leaders in women's occupations, good healers in certain diseases, or, among certain tribes, as the genial organizers of social affairs. In any case, they were socially placed. They were not left exposed to the conflicts that visit the deviant who is excluded from participation in the recognized patterns of his society.

* * *

No one civilization can possibly utilize in its mores the whole potential range of human behavior. Just as there are great numbers of possible phonetic articulations, and the possibility of language depends on a selection and standardization of a few of these in order that speech communication may be possible at all, so the possibility of organized behavior of every sort, from the fashions of local dress and houses to the dicta of a people's ethics and religion, depends upon a similar selection among the possible behavior traits. In the field of recognized economic obligations or sex tabus this selection is as nonrational and subconscious a process as it is in the field of phonetics. It is a process which goes on in the group for long periods of time and is historically conditioned by innumerable accidents of isolation or of contact of peoples. In any comprehensive study of psychology, the selection that different cultures have made in the course of history within the great circumference of potential behavior is of great significance.

Every society, beginning with some slight inclination in one direction or another, carries its preference farther and farther, integrating itself more and more completely upon its chosen basis, and discarding those types of behavior that are uncongenial. Most of these organizations of personality that seem to us most incontrovertibly abnormal have been used by different civilizations in the very foundations of their institutional life. Conversely the most valued traits of our normal individuals have been looked on in differently organized cultures as aberrant. Normality, in short, within a very wide range, is culturally defined. It is primarily a term for the socially elaborated segment of human behavior in any culture; and abnormality, a term for the segment that that particular civilization does not use. The very eyes with which we see the problem are conditioned by the long traditional habits of our own society.

It is a point that has been made more often in relation to ethics than in relation to psychiatry. We do not any longer make the mistake of deriving the morality of our own locality and decade directly from the inevitable constitution of human nature. We do not elevate it to the dignity of a first principle. We recognize that morality differs in every society, and is a convenient term for socially approved habits. Mankind has always preferred to say, "It is a morally good," rather than "It is habitual," and the fact of this preference is matter enough for a critical science of ethics. But historically the two phrases are synonymous.

The concept of the normal is properly a variant of the concept of the good. It is that which society has approved. A normal action is one which falls well within the limits of expected behavior for a particular society. Its variability among different peoples is essentially a function of the variability of the behavior patterns that different societies have created for themselves, and can never be wholly divorced from a consideration of culturally institutionalized types of behavior.

Each culture is a more or less elaborate working-out of the potentialities of the segment it has chosen. In so far as a civilization is well integrated and consistent within itself, it will tend to carry farther and farther, according to its nature, its initial impulse toward a particular type of action, and from the point of view of any other culture those elaborations will include more and more extreme and aberrant traits.

Each of these traits, in proportion as it reinforces the chosen behavior patterns of that culture, is for that culture normal. Those individuals to whom it is congenial either congenitally, or as the result of childhood sets, are accorded to prestige in that culture, and are not visited with the social contempt or disapproval which their traits would call down upon them in a society that was differently organized. On the other hand, those individuals whose characteristics are not congenial to the selected type of human behavior in that community are the deviants, no matter how valued their personality traits may be in a contrasted civilization.

* * *

I have spoken of individuals as having sets toward certain types of behavior, and of these sets as running sometimes counter to the types of behavior which are institutionalized in the culture to which they belong. From all that we know of contrasting cultures it seems clear that differences of temperament occur in every society. The matter has never been made the subject of investigation, but from the available material it would appear that these temperament types are very likely of universal recurrence. That is, there is an ascertainable range of human behavior that is found wherever a sufficiently large series of individuals is observed. But the proportion in which behavior types stand to one another in different societies is not universal. The vast majority of the individuals in any group are shaped to the fashion of that culture. In other words, most individuals are plastic to the moulding force of the society into which they are born. In a society that values trance, as in India, they will have supernormal experience. In a society that institutionalized homosexuality, they will be homosexual. In a society that sets the

gathering of possessions as the chief human objective, they will amass property. The deviants, whatever the type of behavior the culture has institutionalized, will remain few in number, and there seems no more difficulty in moulding the vast malleable majority to the "normality" of what we consider an aberrant trait, such as delusions of reference, than to the normality of such accepted behavior patterns as acquisitiveness. The small proportion of the number of the deviants in any culture is not a function of the sure instinct with which that society has built itself upon the fundamental sanities, but of the universal fact that, happily, the majority of mankind quite readily take any shape that is presented to them.

* * *

Trying Out One's New Sword

MARY MIDGLEY

All of us are, more or less, in trouble today about trying to understand cultures strange to us. We hear constantly of alien customs. We see changes in our lifetime which would have astonished our parents. I want to discuss here one very short way of dealing with this difficulty, a drastic way which many people now theoretically favour. It consists in simply denying that we can ever understand any culture except our own well enough to make judgements about it. Those who recommend this hold that the world is sharply divided into separate societies, sealed units, each with its own system of thought. They feel that the respect and tolerance due from one system to another forbids us ever to take up a critical position to any other culture. Moral judgment, they suggest, is a kind of coinage valid only in its country of origin.

I shall call this position 'moral isolationism'. I shall suggest that it is certainly not forced upon us,

Mary Midgley, "Trying Out One's New Sword," in *Heart and Mind: The Varieties of Moral Experience* (Brighton, Sussex: Harvester Press, 1981), 69–75. Reprinted by permission of David Higham Associates.

and indeed that it makes no sense at all. People usually take it up because they think it is a respectful attitude to other cultures. In fact, however, it is not respectful. Nobody can respect what is entirely unintelligible to them. To respect someone, we have to know enough about him to make a *favourable* judgement, however general and tentative. And we do understand people in other cultures to this extent. Otherwise a great mass of our most valuable thinking would be paralysed.

To show this, I shall take a remote example, because we shall probably find it easier to think calmly about it than we should with a contemporary one, such as female circumcision in Africa or the Chinese Cultural Revolution. The principles involved will still be the same. My example is this. There is, it seems, a verb in classical Japanese which means 'to try out one's new sword on a chance wayfarer'. (The word is *tsujigiri*, literally 'crossroads-cut'.) A samurai sword had to be tried out because, if it was to work properly, it had to slice through someone at a single blow, from the shoulder to the opposite flank. Otherwise, the warrior bungled his stroke. This could injure his honour, offend his ancestors, and even let down his emperor. So tests were needed, and wayfarers had to be expended. Any wayfarer would do—provided, of course, that he was not another Samurai. Scientists will recognize a familiar problem about the rights of experimental subjects.

Now when we hear of a custom like this, we may well reflect that we simply do not understand it; and therefore are not qualified to criticize it at all, because we are not members of that culture. But we are not members of any other culture either, except our own. So we extend the principle to cover all extraneous cultures, and we seem therefore to be moral isolationists. But this is, as we shall see, an impossible position. Let us ask what it would involve.

We must ask first. Does the isolating barrier work both ways? Are people in other cultures equally unable to criticize *us*? This question struck me sharply when I read a remark in *The Guardian* by an anthropologist about a South American Indian who had been taken into a Brazilian town for an operation, which saved his life. When he came back to his village, he made several highly critical remarks about the white Brazilians' way of life. They may very well have been justified. But the interesting point was that the anthropologist called these remarks 'a damning indictment of Western civilization'. Now the Indian had been in that town about two weeks. Was he in a position to deliver a damning indictment? Would we ourselves be qualified to deliver such an indictment on the Samurai, provided we could spend two weeks in ancient Japan? What do we really think about this?

My own impression is that we believe that outsiders can, in principle, deliver perfectly good indictments—only, it usually takes more than two weeks to make them damning. Understanding has degrees. It is not a slapdash yes-or-no matter. Intelligent outsiders can progress in it, and in some ways will be at an advantage over the locals. But if this is so, it must clearly apply to ourselves as much as anybody else.

Our next question is this: Does the isolating barrier between cultures block praise as well as blame? If I want to say that the Samurai culture has many virtues, or to praise the South American Indians, am I prevented from doing *that* by my outside status? Now, we certainly do need to praise other societies in this way. But it is hardly possible that we could praise them effectively if we could not, in principle, criticize them. Our praise would be worthless if it rested on no definite grounds, if it did not flow from some understanding. Certainly we may need to praise things which we do not *fully* understand. We say 'there's something very good here, but I can't quite make out what it is yet'. This happens when we want to learn from strangers. And we can learn from strangers. But to do this we have to distinguish between those strangers who are worth learning from and those who are not. Can we then judge which is which?

This brings us to our third question: What is involved in judging? Now plainly there is no question here of sitting on a bench in a red robe and sentencing people. Judging simply means forming an opinion, and expressing it if it is called for. Is there anything wrong about this? Naturally, we ought to avoid forming—and expressing—*crude* opinions, like that of a simple-minded missionary, who might dismiss the whole Samurai culture as entirely bad, because non-Christian. But this is a different objection. The trouble with crude opinions is that they are crude, whoever forms them, not that they are formed by the wrong people. Anthropologists, after all, are outsiders quite as much as missionaries. Moral isolationism forbids us to form *any* opinions on these matters. Its ground for doing so is that we don't understand them. But there is much that we don't understand in our own culture too. This brings us to our last question: If we can't judge other cultures, can we really judge our own? Our efforts to do so will be much damaged if we are really deprived of our opinions about other societies, because these provide the range of comparison, the spectrum of alternatives against which we set what we want to understand. We would have to stop using the mirror which anthropology so helpfully holds up to us.

In short, moral isolationism would lay down a general ban on moral reasoning. Essentially, this is the programme of immoralism, and it carries a distressing logical difficulty. Immoralists like Nietzsche are actually just a rather specialized sect of moralists. They can no more afford to put moralizing out of business than smugglers can afford to abolish customs regulations. The power of moral judgement is, in fact, not a luxury, not a perverse indulgence of the self-righteous. It is a necessity. When we judge something to be bad or good, better or worse than something else, we are taking it as an example to aim at or avoid. Without opinions of this sort, we would have no framework of comparison for our own policy, no chance of profiting by other people's insights or mistakes. In this vacuum, we could form no judgements on our own actions.

Now it would be odd if Homo sapiens had really got himself into a position as bad as this—a position where his main evolutionary asset, his brain, was so little use to him. None of us is going to accept this sceptical diagnosis. We cannot do so, because our involvement in moral isolationism does not flow from apathy, but from a rather acute concern about human hypocrisy and other forms of wickedness. But we polarize that concern around a few selected moral truths. We are rightly angry with those who despise, oppress or steamroll other cultures. We think that doing these things is actually *wrong*. But this is itself a moral judgement. We could not condemn oppression and insolence if we thought that all our condemnations were just a trivial local quirk of our own culture. We could still less do it if we tried to stop judging altogether.

Real moral scepticism, in fact, could lead only to inaction, to our losing all interest in moral questions, most of all in those which concern other societies. When we discuss these things, it becomes instantly clear how far we are from doing this. Suppose, for instance, that I criticize the bisecting Samurai, that I say his behaviour is brutal. What will usually happen next is that someone will protest, will say that I have no right to make criticisms like that of another culture. But it is most unlikely that he will use this move to end the discussion of the subject. Instead, he will justify the Samurai. He will try to fill in the background, to make me understand the custom, by explaining the exalted ideals of discipline and devo-

tion which produced it. He will probably talk of the lower value which the ancient Japanese placed on individual life generally. He may well suggest that this is a healthier attitude than our own obsession with security. He may add, too, that the wayfarers did not seriously mind being bisected, that in principle they accepted the whole arrangement.

Now an objector who talks like this is implying that it *is* possible to understand alien customs. That is just what he is trying to make me do. And he implies, too, that if I do succeed in understanding them, I shall do something better than giving up judging them. He expects me to change my present judgement to a truer one—namely, one that is favourable. And the standards I must use to do this cannot just be Samurai standards. They have to be ones current in my own culture. Ideals like discipline and devotion will not move anybody unless he himself accepts them. As it happens, neither discipline nor devotion is very popular in the West at present. Anyone who appeals to them may well have to do some more arguing to make *them* acceptable, before he can use them to explain the Samurai. But if he does succeed here, he will have persuaded us, not just that there was something to be said for them in ancient Japan, but that there would be here as well.

Isolating barriers simply cannot arise here. If we accept something as a serious moral truth about one culture, we can't refuse to apply it—in however different an outward form—to other cultures as well, wherever circumstance admit it. If we refuse to do this, we just are not taking the other culture seriously. This becomes clear if we look at the last argument used by my objector—that of justification by consent of the victim. It is suggested that sudden bisection is quite in order, *provided* that it takes place between consenting adults. I cannot now discuss how conclusive this justification is. What I am pointing out is simply that it can only work if we believe that *consent* can make such a transaction respectable—and this is a thoroughly modern and Western idea. It would probably never occur to a Samurai; if it did, it would surprise him very much. It is *our* standard. In applying it, too, we are likely to make another typically Western demand. We shall ask for good factual evidence that the wayfarers actually do have this rather surprising taste—that they are really willing to be bisected. In applying Western standards in this way, we are not being confused or irrelevant. We are asking the questions which arise *from where we stand*, questions which we can see the sense of. We do this because asking questions which you can't see the sense of is humbug. Certainly we can extend our questioning by imaginative effort. We can come to understand other societies better. By doing so, we may make their questions our own, or we may see that they are really forms of the questions which we are asking already. This is not impossible. It is just very hard work. The obstacles which often prevent it are simply those of ordinary ignorance, laziness and prejudice.

If there were really an isolating barrier, of course, our own culture could never have been formed. It is no scaled box, but a fertile jungle of different influences—Greek, Jewish, Roman, Norse, Celtic and so forth, into which further influences are still pouring—American, Indian, Japanese, Jamaican, you name it. The moral isolationist's picture of separate, unmixable cultures is quite unreal. People who talk about British history usually stress the value of this fertilizing mix, no doubt rightly. But this is not just an odd fact about Britain. Except for the very smallest and most remote, all cultures are formed out of many streams. All have the problem of digesting and assimilating things which, at the start, they do not understand. All have the choice of learning something from this challenge, or, alternatively, of refusing to learn, and fighting it mindlessly instead.

This universal predicament has been obscured by the fact that anthropologists used to concentrate largely on very small and remote cultures, which did not seem to have this problem. These tiny societies, which had often forgotten their own history, made neat, self-contained subjects for study. No doubt it was valuable to emphasize their remoteness, their extreme strangeness, their independence of our cultural tradition. This emphasis was, I think, the root of moral isolationism. But, as the tribal studies themselves showed, even there the anthropologists were able to interpret what they saw and make judgements—often favourable—about the tribesmen. And the tribesmen, too, were quite equal to making judgements about the anthropologists—and about the tourists and Coca-Cola salesmen who followed them. Both sets of judgements, no doubt, were somewhat hasty, both have been refined in the light of further experience. A similar transaction between us and the Samurai might take even longer. But that is no reason at all for deeming it impossible. Morally as well as physically, there is only one world, and we all have to live in it.

PART

2

Moral Reasoning

CHAPTER 3

Evaluating Moral Arguments

As we have seen, we cannot escape the ethical facts of life. We often must make moral judgments, assess moral principles or rules, contend with moral theories, and argue the pros and cons of moral issues. Typically we do all these things believing that in one way or another they *really matter*. And because we think they matter, moral reasoning matters, for we could make little headway in these difficult waters without the use of reasons and arguments. Along the way we may take into account our feelings, desires, beliefs, and other factors, but getting to our destination depends mostly on the quality of our moral reasoning. Through moral reasoning we assess what is right and wrong, good and bad, virtuous and vicious. We make and dismantle arguments for this view and for that. In our finest moments, we follow the lead of reason in the search for answers, trying to rise above subjectivism, prejudice, delusion, and confusion.

In this chapter you will discover (if you haven't already) that you are no stranger to moral reasoning. Moral reasoning is ordinary critical reasoning applied to ethics. Critical reasoning (or critical thinking) is the careful, systematic evaluation of statements or claims. We use critical reasoning every day to determine whether a statement is worthy of acceptance—that is, whether it is true. We harness critical reasoning to assess the truth of all sorts of claims in all kinds of contexts—personal, professional, academic, philosophical, scientific, political, and ethical. Moral reasoning, then, is not a type of reasoning that you have never seen before.

We therefore begin this chapter with the basics of critical reasoning. The focus is on the skills that are at the heart of this kind of thinking—the formulation and evaluation of logical arguments. The rest of the chapter is about applying critical reasoning to the claims and arguments of ethics.

CLAIMS AND ARGUMENTS

When you use critical reasoning, your ultimate aim is usually to figure out whether to accept, or believe, a statement—either someone else's statement or one of your own. A **statement,** or claim, is an assertion that something is or is not the case; it is either true or false. These are statements:

- The ship sailed on the wind-tossed sea.
- I feel tired and listless.
- Murder is wrong.
- 5 + 5 = 10.
- A circle is not a square.

These statements assert that something is or is not the case. Whether you accept them, reject them, or neither, they are still statements because they are assertions that can be either true or false.

The following, however, are not statements; they do not assert that something is or is not the case:

- Why is Anna laughing?
- Is abortion immoral?
- Hand me the screwdriver.
- Don't speak to me.

- Hello, Webster.
- For heaven's sake!

A fundamental principle of critical reasoning is that we should not accept a statement as true without good reasons. If a statement is supported by good reasons, we are entitled to believe it. The better the reasons supporting a statement, the more likely it is to be true. Our acceptance of a statement, then, can vary in strength. If a statement is supported by strong reasons, we are entitled to believe it strongly. If it is supported by weaker reasons, our belief should likewise be weaker. If the reasons are equivocal—if they do not help us decide one way or another—we should suspend judgment until the evidence is more definitive.

Reasons supporting a statement are themselves statements. To lend credence to another claim, these supporting statements may assert something about scientific evidence, expert opinion, relevant examples, or other considerations. In this way they provide reasons for believing that a statement is true, that what is asserted is actual. When this state of affairs exists—when at least one statement attempts to provide reasons for believing another statement—we have an **argument.** An argument is a group of statements, one of which is supposed to be supported by the rest. An argument in this sense, of course, has nothing to do with the common notion of arguments as shouting matches or vehement quarrels.

In an argument, the supporting statements are known as **premises;** the statement being supported is known as a **conclusion.** Consider these arguments:

Argument 1. Capital punishment is morally permissible because it helps to deter crime.

Argument 2. If John killed Bill in self-defense, he did not commit murder. He did act in self-defense. Therefore, he did not commit murder.

Argument 3. Telling a white lie is morally permissible. We should judge the rightness of an act by its impact on human well-being. If an act increases human well-being, then it is right. Without question, telling a white lie increases human well-being because it spares people's feelings; that's what white lies are for.

These arguments are fairly simple. In Argument 1, a single premise ("because it helps to deter crime") supports a straightforward conclusion—"Capital punishment is morally permissible." Argument 2 has two premises: "If John killed Bill in self-defense, he did not commit murder" and "He did act in self-defense." And the conclusion is "Therefore, he did not commit murder." Argument 3 has three premises: "We should judge the rightness of an act by its impact on human well-being," "If an act increases human well-being, then it is right," and "Without question, telling a white lie increases human well-being because it spares people's feelings." Its conclusion is "Telling a white lie is morally permissible."

As you can see, these three arguments have different structures. Argument 1, for example, has just one premise, but Arguments 2 and 3 have two and three premises. In Arguments 1 and 3, the conclusion is stated first; in Argument 2, last. Obviously, arguments can vary dramatically in their number of premises, in the placement of premises and conclusion, and in the wording of each of these parts. But all arguments share a common pattern: at least one premise is intended to support a conclusion. This pattern is what makes an argument an argument.

Despite the simplicity of this premise-conclusion arrangement, though, arguments are not always easy to identify. They can be embedded in long passages of nonargumentative prose, and nonargumentative prose can often look like arguments. Consider:

The number of abortions performed in this state is increasing. More and more women say that they favor greater access to abortion. This is an outrage.

Do you see an argument in this passage? You shouldn't, because there is none. The first two sentences are meant to be assertions of fact, and the last one is an expression of indignation. There is no premise providing reasons to accept a conclusion. But what if we altered the passage to make it an argument? Look:

The number of abortions performed in this state is increasing, and more and more women say that they favor greater access to abortion. Therefore, in this state the trend among women is toward greater acceptance of abortion.

This is now an argument. There is a conclusion ("Therefore, in this state the trend among women is toward greater acceptance of abortion") supported by two premises ("The number of abortions performed in this state is increasing, and more and more women say that they favor greater access to abortion"). We are given reasons for accepting a claim.

Notice how easy it would be to elaborate on the nonargumentative version, adding other unsupported claims and more expressions of the writer's attitude toward the subject matter. We would end up with a much longer passage piled high with more assertions—but with no argument in sight. Often those who write such passages believe that because they have stated their opinion, they have presented an argument. But a bundle of unsupported claims—however clearly stated—does not an argument make. Only when reasons are given for believing one of these claims is an argument made.

Learning to distinguish arguments from nonargumentative material takes practice. The job gets easier, however, if you pay attention to **indicator words.** Indicator words are terms that often appear in arguments and signal that a premise or conclusion may be nearby. Notice that in the argument about abortion, the word *therefore* indicates that the conclusion follows, and in Argument 1 the word *because* signals the beginning of a prem-

ise. In addition to *therefore,* common conclusion indicators include *consequently, hence, it follows that, thus, so, it must be that,* and *as a result.* Besides *because,* some common premise indicators are *since, for, given that, due to the fact that, for the reason that, the reason being, assuming that,* and *as indicated by.*

Understand that indicator words are not foolproof evidence that a premise or conclusion is near. Sometimes words that often function as indicators appear when no argument at all is present. Indicator words are simply hints that an argument may be close by.

Probably the most reliable way to identify arguments is to *always look for the conclusion first.* When you know what claim is being supported, you can more easily see what statements are doing the supporting. A true argument always has something to prove. If there is no statement that the writer is trying to convince you to accept, no argument is present and you need not look further.

Finally, understand that an argument (as we have used the term here) is not the same thing as *persuasion.* To offer a good argument is to present reasons why a particular assertion is true. To persuade someone of something is to influence her opinion by any number of means, including emotional appeals, linguistic or rhetorical tricks, deception, threats, propaganda, and more. Reasoned argument does not necessarily play any part at all. You may be able to use some of these ploys to persuade people to believe a claim. But if you do, you will not have established that the claim is worth believing. On the other hand, if you articulate a good argument, then you prove something—and others just might be persuaded by your reasoning.

ARGUMENTS GOOD AND BAD

A good argument shows that its conclusion is worthy of belief or acceptance; a bad argument fails to show this. A good argument gives you good reasons to accept a claim; a bad argument proves

CRITICAL THOUGHT: The Morality of Critical Thinking

You might be surprised to learn that some philosophers consider reasoning itself a moral issue. That is, they think that believing a claim without good reasons (an unsupported statement) is immoral. Probably the most famous exposition of this point comes from the philosopher and mathematician W. K. Clifford (1845–79). He has this to say on the subject:

It is wrong always, everywhere, and for anyone, to believe anything upon insufficient evidence. If a man, holding a belief which he was taught in childhood or persuaded of afterwards, keeps down and pushes away any doubts which arise about it in his mind . . . and regards as impious those questions which cannot easily be asked without disturbing it—the life of that man is one long sin against mankind.*

Do you agree with Clifford? Can you think of a counterexample to his argument—that is, instances in which believing without evidence would be morally permissible? Suppose the power of reason is a gift from God to be used to help you live a good life. If so, would believing without evidence (failing to use critical thinking) be immoral?

*W. K. Clifford, "The Ethics of Belief," in *The Rationality of Belief in God,* ed. George I. Mavrodes (Englewood Cliffs, NJ: Prentice-Hall, 1970), 159–60.

---

nothing. So the crucial question is, How can you tell which is which? To start, you can learn more about different kinds of arguments and how they get to be good or bad.

There are two basic types of arguments: **deductive** and **inductive.** Deductive arguments are supposed to give logically conclusive support to their conclusions. Inductive arguments, on the other hand, are supposed to offer only probable support for their conclusions.

Consider this classic deductive argument:

All men are mortal.

Socrates is a man.

Therefore, Socrates is mortal.

It is deductive because the support offered for the conclusion is meant to be absolutely unshakable. When a deductive argument actually achieves this kind of conclusive support, it is said to be **valid.** In a valid argument, if the premises are true, then the conclusion absolutely has to be true. In the Socrates argument, if the premises are true, the conclusion *must be true.* The conclusion follows inexorably from the premises. The argument is therefore valid. When a deductive argument does not offer conclusive support for the conclusion, it is said to be **invalid.** In an invalid argument, it is not the case that if the premises are true, the conclusion must be true. Suppose the first premise of the Socrates argument was changed to "All ducks are mortal." Then the argument would be invalid because even if the premises were true, the conclusion would not necessarily be true. The conclusion would not follow inexorably from the premises.

Notice that the validity or invalidity of an argument is a matter of its *form,* not its content. The structure of a deductive argument renders it either valid or invalid, and validity is a separate matter from the truth of the argument's statements. Its statements (premises and conclusion) may be either true or false, but that has nothing to do with validity. Saying that an argument is valid means that it has a particular form that ensures that if the premises are true, the conclusion can be nothing but true. There is no way that the premises can be true and the conclusion false.

Recall that there are indicator words that point to the presence of premises and conclusions. There are also indicator words that suggest (but do not prove) that an argument is deductive. Some of the more common terms are *it necessarily follows that, it must be the case that, it logically follows that, conclusively,* and *necessarily.*

Now let us turn to inductive arguments. Examine this one:

Almost all the men at this college have high SAT scores.

Therefore, Julio (a student at the college) probably has high SAT scores.

This argument is inductive because it is intended to provide probable, not decisive, support to the conclusion. That is, the argument is intended to show only that, at best, the conclusion is probably true. With any inductive argument, it is possible for the premises to be true and the conclusion false. An inductive argument that manages to actually give probable support to the conclusion is said to be **strong.** In a strong argument, if the premises are true, the conclusion is probably true (more likely to be true than not). The SAT argument is strong. An inductive argument that does not give probable support to the conclusion is said to be **weak.** In a weak argument, if the premises are true, the conclusion is not probable (not more likely to be true than not true). If we change the first premise in the SAT argument to "Twenty percent of the men at this college have high SAT scores," the argument would be weak.

Like deductive arguments, inductive ones are often accompanied by indicator words. These terms include *probably, likely, in all probability, it is reasonable to suppose that, odds are,* and *chances are.*

Good arguments provide you with good reasons for believing their conclusions. You now know that good arguments must be valid or strong. But they must also have true premises. Good arguments must both have the right form (be valid or strong) and have reliable content (have true premises). Any argument that fails in either of these respects is a bad argument. A valid argument with true premises is said to be **sound;** a strong argument with true premises is said to be **cogent.**

To evaluate an argument is to determine whether it is good or not, and establishing that requires you to check the argument's form and the truth of its premises. You can check the truth of premises in many different ways. Sometimes you can see immediately that a premise is true (or false). At other times you may need to examine a premise more closely or even do some research. Assessing an argument's form is also usually a very straightforward process. With inductive arguments, sometimes common sense is all that's required to see whether they are strong or weak (whether the conclusions follow from the premises). With deductive arguments, just thinking about how the premises are related to the conclusion is often sufficient. In all cases the key to correctly and efficiently determining the validity or strength of arguments is practice.

Fortunately, there are some techniques that can improve your ability to check the validity of deductive arguments. Some deductive forms are so common that just being familiar with them can give you a big advantage. Let's look at some of them.

To begin, understand that you can easily indicate an argument's form by using a kind of standard shorthand, with letters standing for statements. Consider, for example, this argument:

If Maria walks to work, then she will be late.

She is walking to work.

Therefore, she will be late.

Here's how we symbolize this argument's form:

If p, then q.

p.

Therefore, q.

We represent each statement with a letter, thereby laying bare the argument's skeletal form. The first premise is a compound statement, consisting of two constituent statements, *p* and *q*. This particular argument form is known as a *conditional*. A conditional argument has at least one conditional premise—a premise in an if-then pattern (If *p*, then *q*). The two parts of a conditional premise are known as the *antecedent* (which begins with *if*) and the *consequent* (which follows *then*).

This argument form happens to be very common—so common that it has a name, *modus ponens*, or affirming the antecedent. The first premise is conditional ("If Maria walks to work, then she will be late"), and the second premise affirms the antecedent of that conditional ("She is walking to work"). This form is *always valid:* if the premises are true, the conclusion *has to be true.* Any argument that has this form will be valid regardless of the subject matter.

Another frequently occurring form is known as *modus tollens,* or denying the consequent:

If Maria walks to work, then she will be late.

She will not be late.

Therefore, she will not walk to work.

Symbolized, *modus tollens* looks like this:

If *p*, then *q*.

Not *q*.

Therefore, not *p*.

Modus tollens is always valid, no matter what statements you plug into the formula.

Here are two more common argument forms. These, however, are *always invalid.*

Denying the antecedent:

If Maria walks to work, then she will be late.

She will not walk to work.

Therefore, she will not be late.

If *p*, then *q*.

Not *p*.

Therefore, not *q*.

Affirming the consequent:

If Maria walks to work, then she will be late.

She will be late.

Therefore, she will walk to work.

If *p*, then *q*.

q.

Therefore, *p*.

Do you see the problem with these two? In the first one (denying the antecedent), even a false antecedent (if Maria will not walk to work) doesn't mean that she will not be late. Maybe she will sit at home and be late, or be late for some other reason. When the antecedent is denied, the premises can be true and the conclusion false—clearly an invalid argument. In the second argument (affirming the consequent), even a true consequent (if Maria will be late) doesn't mean that she will walk to work. Some other factor besides her walking could cause Maria to be late. Again, the premises can be true while the conclusion is false—definitely invalid.

Consider one last form, the hypothetical syllogism (*hypothetical* means *conditional;* a *syllogism* is a three-statement deductive argument):

If Maria walks to work, then she will be late.

If she is late, she will be fired.

Therefore, if Maria walks to work, she will be fired.

If *p*, then *q*.

If *q*, then *r*.

Therefore, if *p*, then *r*.

The hypothetical syllogism is a valid argument form. If the premises are true, the conclusion must be true.

Obviously, if *modus ponens, modus tollens,* and the hypothetical syllogism are always valid, then any arguments you encounter that have the same form will also be valid. And if denying the antecedent and affirming the consequent are always invalid, any arguments you come across that have the same form will also be invalid. The best way to make use of these facts is to memorize each argument form so you can tell right away when an argument matches one of them—and thereby see immediately that it is valid (or invalid).

But what if you bump into a deductive argument that does not match one of these common forms? You can try the *counterexample method.* This approach is based on a fundamental fact that you already know: *it is impossible for a valid argument to have true premises and a false conclusion.* So to test the validity of an argument, you first invent a twin argument that has exactly the same form as the argument you are examining—but you try to give this new argument true premises and a false conclusion. If you can construct such an argument, you have proven that your original argument is invalid.

Suppose you want to test this argument for validity:

If capital punishment deters crime, then the number of death row inmates will decrease over time.

But capital punishment does not deter crime.

Therefore, the number of death row inmates will not decrease over time.

You can probably see right away that this argument is an example of denying the antecedent, an invalid form. But for the sake of example, let's use the counterexample method in this case. Suppose we come up with this twin argument:

If lizards are mammals, then they have legs.

But they are not mammals.

Therefore, they do not have legs.

QUICK REVIEW

statement—An assertion that something is or is not the case.

argument—A group of statements, one of which is supposed to be supported by the rest.

premise—A supporting statement in an argument.

conclusion—The statement supported in an argument.

indicator words—Terms that often appear in arguments to signal the presence of a premise or conclusion, or to indicate that an argument is deductive or inductive.

deductive argument—An argument that is supposed to give logically conclusive support to its conclusion.

inductive argument—An argument that is supposed to offer probable support to its conclusion.

valid argument—A deductive argument that does in fact provide logically conclusive support for its conclusion.

invalid argument—A deductive argument that does not offer logically conclusive support for the conclusion.

strong argument—An inductive argument that does in fact provide probable support for its conclusion.

weak argument—An inductive argument that does not give probable support to the conclusion.

sound argument—A valid argument with true premises.

cogent argument—A strong argument with true premises.

We have invented a twin argument that has true premises and a false conclusion, so we know that the original argument is invalid.

IMPLIED PREMISES

Most of the arguments that we encounter in everyday life are embedded in larger tracts of nonargumentative prose—in essays, reports, letters to the editor, editorials, and the like. The challenge is to pick out the premises and conclusions and evaluate the assembled arguments. In many cases, though, there is an additional obstacle: some premises may be implied instead of stated. Sometimes the premises are implicit because they are too obvious to mention; readers mentally fill in the blanks. But in most cases, implicit premises should not be left unstated. It is often unclear what premises have been assumed; and unless these are spelled out, argument evaluation becomes difficult or impossible. More to the point, unstated premises are often the most dubious parts of an argument. This problem is especially common in moral arguments, where the implicit premises are frequently the most controversial and the most in need of close scrutiny.

Here is a typical argument with an unstated premise:

The use of condoms is completely unnatural. They have been manufactured for the explicit purpose of interfering in the natural process of procreation. Therefore, the use of condoms should be banned.

In this argument, the first two sentences constitute a single premise, the gist of which is that using condoms is unnatural. The conclusion is that the use of condoms should be banned. This conclusion, however, does not follow from the stated premise. There is a logical gap between premise and conclusion. The argument will work only if the missing premise is supplied. Here's a good possibility: "Anything that interferes in a

natural process should not be allowed." The argument then becomes:

The use of condoms is completely unnatural. They have been manufactured for the explicit purpose of interfering in the natural process of procreation. Anything that interferes in a natural process should not be allowed. Therefore, the use of condoms should be banned.

By adding the implicit premise, we have filled out the argument, making it valid and a little less mysterious. But now that the missing premise has been brought out into the open, we can see that it is dubious or, at least, controversial. Should everything that interferes in a natural process be banned? If so, we would have to ban antibiotics, cancer drugs, deodorants, and automobiles. (Later in this chapter, ways to judge the truth of moral premises are discussed.)

When you evaluate an argument, you should try to explicitly state any implied premise (or premises) when (1) there seems to be a logical gap between premises or between premises and the conclusion and (2) the missing material is not a commonsense assumption. In general, the supplied premise should make the argument valid (when the argument is supposed to be deductive) or strong (when the argument is supposed to be inductive). It should also be *plausible* (as close to the truth as possible) and *fitting* (coinciding with what you think is the author's intent). The point of these stipulations is that when you supply a missing premise, you should be fair and honest, expressing it in such a way that the argument is as solid as possible and in keeping with the author's purpose. Adding a premise that renders an argument ridiculous is easy, and so is distorting the author's intent—and with neither tack are you likely to learn anything or uncover the truth.

Be aware, though, that some arguments are irredeemably bad, and no supplied premise that is properly made can save them. They cannot be turned into good arguments without altering them beyond recognition or original intent. You need not take these arguments seriously, and the responsibility of recasting them lies with those who offer them.

MORAL STATEMENTS AND ARGUMENTS

When we deliberate about the rightness of our actions, make careful moral judgments about the character or behavior of others, or strive to resolve complex ethical issues, we are usually making or critiquing moral arguments—or trying to. And rightly so. To a remarkable degree, moral arguments are the vehicles that move ethical thinking and discourse along. The rest of this chapter should give you a demonstration of how far skill in devising and evaluating moral arguments can take you.

Recall that arguments are made up of statements (premises and conclusions), and thus moral arguments are too. What makes an argument a moral argument is that its conclusion is always a moral statement. A **moral statement** is a statement affirming that an action is right or wrong or that a person (or one's motive or character) is good or bad. These are moral statements:

- Capital punishment is wrong.
- Jena should not have lied.
- You ought to treat him as he treated you.
- Tania is a good person.
- Cruelty to animals is immoral.

Notice the use of the terms *wrong, should, ought, good,* and *immoral.* Such words are the mainstays of moral discourse, though some of them (for example, *good* and *wrong*) are also used in nonmoral senses.

Nonmoral statements are very different. They do not affirm that an action is right or wrong or that a person is good or bad. They assert that a state of affairs is actual (true or false) but do not

assign a moral value to it. Most of the statements that we encounter every day are nonmoral. Of course, nonmoral statements may assert nonmoral normative judgments, such as "This is a good library" or "Jack ought to invest in stocks," but these are clearly not moral statements. They may also describe a state of affairs that touches on moral concerns—without *being* moral statements. For example:

- Many people think that capital punishment is wrong.
- Jena did not lie.
- You treated him as he treated you.
- Tania tries to be a good person.
- Animals are treated cruelly.

Now we can be more specific about the structure of moral arguments. A typical moral argument consists of premises and a conclusion, just as any other kind of argument does, with the conclusion being a moral statement, or judgment. The premises, however, are a combination of the moral and nonmoral. At least one premise must be a moral statement affirming a moral principle or rule (a general moral standard), and at least one premise must be a nonmoral statement about a state of affairs, usually a specific type of action. Beyond these simple requirements, the structure of moral arguments can vary in standard ways: there may be many premises or few; premises may be implicit not overt; and extraneous material may be present or absent. Take a look at this moral argument:

1. Committing a violent act to defend yourself against physical attack is morally permissible.
2. Assaulting a mugger who is attacking you is a violent act of self-defense.
3. Therefore, assaulting a mugger who is attacking you is morally permissible.

Premise 1 is a moral statement asserting a general moral principle about the rightness of a category of actions (violent acts in self-defense). Premise 2 is a nonmoral statement about the characteristics of a specific kind of action (violent acts against a mugger). It asserts that a specific kind of action falls under the general moral principle expressed in Premise 1. Premise 3, the conclusion, is a moral judgment about the rightness of the specific kind of action in light of the general moral principle.

Why must we have at least one premise that is a moral statement? Without a moral premise, the argument would not get off the ground. We cannot infer a moral statement (conclusion) from a nonmoral statement (premise). That is, we cannot reason that a moral statement must be true because a nonmoral state of affairs is actual. Or as philosophers say, we cannot establish what *ought to be* or *should be* based solely on what *is*. What if our self-defense argument contained no moral premise? Look:

2. Assaulting a mugger who is attacking you is a violent act of self-defense.

3. Therefore, assaulting a mugger who is attacking you is morally permissible.

The conclusion no longer follows. It says something about the rightness of an action, but the premise asserts nothing about rightness—it just characterizes the nonmoral aspects of an action. Perhaps the action described is morally permissible or perhaps it is not—Premise 2 does not say.

Another example:

1. Not using every medical means available to keep a seriously ill newborn infant alive is allowing the infant to die.

3. Therefore, not using every medical means available to keep a seriously ill newborn infant alive is wrong.

As it stands, this argument is seriously flawed. The conclusion (a moral statement) does not follow from the nonmoral premise. Even if we know that "not using every medical means" is equivalent to allowing a seriously ill newborn to die, we cannot then conclude that the action is wrong. We need a premise making that assertion:

2. Allowing terminally ill newborn infants to die is wrong.

Here's the complete argument:

1. Not using every medical means available to keep a seriously ill newborn infant alive is allowing the infant to die.

2. Allowing terminally ill newborn infants to die is wrong.

3. Therefore, not using every medical means available to keep a seriously ill newborn infant alive is wrong.

A nonmoral premise is also necessary in a moral argument. Why exactly? Recall that the conclusion of a typical moral argument is a moral judgment, or claim, about a particular kind of action. The moral premise is a general moral principle, or standard, concerning a wider category of actions. But we cannot infer a statement (conclusion) about a *particular kind of action* from a moral statement (premise) about a *broad category of actions*—unless we have a nonmoral premise to link the two. We saw, for example, that we cannot infer from the general principle that "committing a violent act to defend yourself . . . is morally permissible" the conclusion that "assaulting a mugger who is attacking you is morally permissible" unless a nonmoral premise tells us that assaulting a mugger is an instance of self-defense. (The nonmoral premise may seem obvious here, but not everyone would agree that violence against a mugger is an example of self-defense. Some might claim that such violence is an unnecessary act of retaliation or revenge.) The role of the nonmoral premise, then, is to affirm that the general moral principle does indeed apply to the particular case.

Unfortunately, both moral and nonmoral premises are often left unstated in moral arguments. As we noted in the previous section, making implicit premises explicit is always a good idea, but in moral arguments it is critical. The unseen premises (an argument may have several) are the ones most likely to be dubious or unfounded, a problem that can arise whether an argument is yours or someone else's. Too many times, unstated premises are assumptions that you may be barely aware of; they might be the true, unacknowledged source of disagreement between you and others. No premise should be left unexamined. (More about assessing the truth of premises in the next section.)

The general guidelines discussed earlier about uncovering unstated premises apply to moral arguments—but we need to add a proviso. Remember, in a moral argument, as in any other kind of argument, you have good reason to look for implicit premises if there is a logical gap between premises, and the missing premise is not simply common sense. And any premise you supply should be both plausible and fitting. But note: The easiest way to identify implied premises in a moral argument is to treat it as *deductive*. Approaching moral arguments this way helps you not only find implied premises but also assess the worth of *all* the premises.

For example:

1. The use of capital punishment does not deter crime.

2. Therefore, the use of capital punishment is immoral.

This is an invalid argument. Even if the premise is true, the conclusion does not follow from it. The argument needs a premise that can bridge the gap between the current premise and the conclusion. So we should ask, "What premise can we add that will be plausible and fitting *and* make the argument valid?" This premise will do: "Administering a punishment to criminals that does not deter crime is immoral." The argument then becomes:

1. Administering a punishment to criminals that does not deter crime is immoral.

2. The use of capital punishment does not deter crime.

3. Therefore, the use of capital punishment is immoral.

Now the argument is valid, and trying to make it valid has helped us find at least one premise that might work. Moreover, if we know that the argument is valid, we can focus our inquiry on the truth of the premises. After all, if there is something wrong with a valid argument (that is, if the argument is not sound), we know that the trouble is in the premises—specifically, that at least one premise must be false. To put it another way, whether or not such an argument is a good argument depends entirely on the truth of the premises.

As it turns out, our added premise is a general moral principle. And like many implied premises, it is questionable. Deterrence is not necessarily the only reason for administering punishment. Some would say that justice is a better reason; others, that rehabilitation is. (The second premise is also dubious, but we won't worry about that now.)

In any case, if the supplied premise renders the argument valid, and the premise is plausible and fitting, we can then conclude that we have filled out the argument properly. We can then examine the resulting argument and either accept or reject it. And if we wish to explore the issue at greater depth, we can overhaul the argument altogether to see what we can learn. We can radically change or add premises until we have a sound argument or at least a valid one with plausible premises.

TESTING MORAL PREMISES

But how can we evaluate moral premises? After all, we cannot check them by consulting a scientific study or opinion poll as we might when examining nonmoral premises. Usually the best approach is to use counterexamples.

If we want to test a universal generalization such as "All dogs have tails," we can look for counterexamples—instances that prove the generalization false. All we have to do to show that the statement "All dogs have tails" is false is to find one tailless dog. And a thorough search for tailless dogs is a way to check the generalization. Likewise, if we want to test a moral premise (a variety of universal generalization), we can look for counterexamples.

Examine this valid moral argument:

1. Causing a person's death is wrong.

2. Individuals in a deep, irreversible coma are incapacitated persons.

3. "Pulling the plug" on someone in a deep, irreversible coma is causing a person to die.

4. Therefore, "pulling the plug" on someone in a deep, irreversible coma is wrong.

Premise 1 is the moral premise, a general moral principle about killing. Premises 2 and 3 are nonmoral premises. (Premise 2 is entailed by Premise 3, but we separate the two to emphasize the importance to this argument of the concept of personhood.) Statement 4, of course, is the conclusion, the verdict that causing someone in a deep coma to die is immoral.

Is Premise 1 true? It is at least dubious, because counterexamples abound in which the principle seems false. Is it wrong to kill one person to save a hundred? Is it wrong to kill a person in self-defense? Is it wrong to kill a person in wartime? As it stands, Premise 1 seems implausible.

To salvage the argument, we can revise Premise 1 (as well as Premise 3) to try to make it impervious to counterexamples. We can change it like this:

1. Causing the death of a person who is incapacitated is wrong.

2. Individuals in a deep, irreversible coma are persons.

3. "Pulling the plug" on someone in a deep, irreversible coma is causing an incapacitated person to die.

4. Therefore, "pulling the plug" on someone in a deep, irreversible coma is wrong.

Premise 1 now seems a bit more reasonable. In its current form, it rules out the counterexamples involving self-defense and war. But it does not escape the killing-to-save-lives counterexample. In some circumstances it may be morally permissible to kill someone to save many others, even if the person is incapacitated. To get around this problem, we can amend Premise 1 so the counterexample is no longer a threat (and make a corresponding change in the conclusion). For example:

1. Causing the death of a person who is incapacitated is wrong, except to save lives.

2. Individuals in a deep, irreversible coma are persons.

3. "Pulling the plug" on someone in a deep, irreversible coma is causing an incapacitated person to die.

4. Therefore, "pulling the plug" on someone in a deep, irreversible coma is wrong, except to save lives.

Premise 1 now seems much closer to being correct than before. It may not be flawless, but it is much improved. By considering counterexamples, we have made the whole argument better.

Checking a moral premise against possible counterexamples is a way to consult our considered moral judgments, a topic we broached in Chapter 1 and take up again in Part 3 (Theories of Morality). If our considered moral judgments are at odds with a moral premise that is based on a cherished moral principle or moral theory, we may have a prima facie reason to doubt not only the premise but also the principle or theory from which it is derived. We may then need to reexamine the claims involved and how they are related. If we do, we may find that our judgments are on solid ground and the premise, principle, or theory needs to be adjusted—or vice versa. If our purpose is solely to evaluate a moral premise in an argument, we need not carry our investigation this far. But we should understand that widening our investigation may sometimes be appropriate and that our moral beliefs are often more interconnected than we might realize. Our ultimate goal should be to ensure that all our moral beliefs are as logically consistent as we can make them.

ASSESSING NONMORAL PREMISES

Sometimes the sticking point in a moral argument is not a moral premise but a nonmoral one—a claim about a nonmoral state of affairs. Often people on both sides of a dispute may agree on a moral principle but differ dramatically on the nonmoral facts. Usually these facts concern the consequences of an action or the characteristics of the parties involved. Does pornography cause people to commit sex crimes? Does capital punishment deter crime? Is a depressed person competent to decide whether to commit suicide? When does the fetus become viable? Are African Americans underrepresented among executives in corporate America? Does gay marriage undermine the institution of heterosexual marriage? These and countless other questions arise—and must be answered—as we try to develop and analyze moral arguments.

The most important principle to remember is that nonmoral premises, like all premises, *must be supported by good reasons.* As we have already seen, simply believing or asserting a claim does not make it so. We should insist that our own nonmoral premises and those of others be backed by reliable scientific research, the opinions of trustworthy experts, pertinent examples and analogies, historical records, or our own background knowledge (claims that we have excellent reasons to believe).

QUICK REVIEW

- Look for an implicit premise when (1) there seems to be a logical gap between premises or between premises and the conclusion and (2) the missing material is not a commonplace assumption.

- Any supplied unstated premise should be valid or strong, plausible, and fitting.

- A typical moral argument has at least one moral premise and at least one nonmoral premise.

- The easiest way to identify implied premises in a moral argument is to treat it as deductive.

- Test moral premises with counterexamples.

moral statement—A statement affirming that an action is right or wrong or that a person (or one's motive or character) is good or bad.

nonmoral statement—A statement that does not affirm that an action is right or wrong or that a person (or one's motive or character) is good or bad.

Ensuring that nonmoral premises are supported by good reasons is sometimes difficult but always worth the effort. The process begins by simply asking, "Is this statement true?" and "What reasons do I have for believing this?"

In your search for answers, keep the following in mind:

1. *Use reliable sources.* If you have reason to doubt the accuracy of a source, do not use it. Doubt it if it produces statements you know to be false, ignores reliable data (such as the latest scientific research), or has a track record of presenting inaccurate information or dubious arguments. Make sure that any experts you rely on are in fact experts in their chosen field. In general, true

experts have the requisite education and training, the relevant experience in making reliable judgments, and a good reputation among peers.

Probably every major moral issue discussed in this book is associated with numerous advocacy groups, each one devoted to promoting its particular view of things. Too often the information coming from many of these groups is unreliable. Do not automatically assume otherwise. Double-check any information you get from them with sources you know are reliable and see if it is supported by scientific studies, expert opinion, or other evidence.

2. *Beware when evidence conflicts.* You have good reason to doubt a statement if it conflicts with other statements you think are well supported. If your nonmoral premise is inconsistent with another claim you believe is true, you cannot simply choose the one you like best. To resolve the conflict, you must evaluate them both by weighing the evidence for each one.

3. *Let reason rule.* Deliberating on moral issues is serious business, often involving the questioning of cherished views and the stirring of strong feelings. Many times the temptation to dispense with reason and blindly embrace a favorite outlook is enormous. This common—and very human—predicament can lead us to veer far from the relevant evidence and true nonmoral premises. Specifically, we may reject or disregard evidence that conflicts with what we most want to believe. We may even try to pretend that the conflicting evidence actually supports our preconceptions. Yet resisting the relevant evidence is just one side of the coin. We may also look for and find only evidence that supports what we want to believe, going around the world to confirm our prejudices.

Our best chance to avert these tendencies is to try hard to be both critical and fair—to make a deliberate effort to examine *all* the relevant evidence, the information both for and against our preferred beliefs. After all, the point of assessing a moral argument is to discover the truth. We must be brave enough to let the evidence point where it will.

AVOIDING BAD ARGUMENTS

Recall that a good argument has true premises plus a conclusion that follows from those premises. A bad argument fails at least one of these conditions—it has a false premise or a conclusion that does not follow. This failure, however, can appear in many different argument forms, some of which are extremely common. These commonly bad arguments are known as *fallacies*. They are so distinctive and are used so often that they have been given names and are usually covered in courses on critical reasoning. Though flawed, fallacies are often persuasive and frequently employed to mislead the unwary—even in (or *especially* in) moral reasoning. The best way to avoid using fallacies—or being taken in by them—is to study them so you know how they work and can easily identify them. The following is a brief review of some fallacies that are most prevalent in moral argumentation.

Begging the Question
Begging the question is the fallacy of arguing in a circle—that is, trying to use a statement as both a premise in an argument and the conclusion of that argument. Such an argument says, in effect, *p* is true because *p* is true. That kind of reasoning, of course, proves nothing.

For example:

1. Women in Muslim countries, regardless of their social status and economic limitations, are entitled to certain rights, including but not necessarily limited to suffrage.

2. Therefore, all women in Muslim countries have the right to vote in political elections.

This argument is equivalent to saying "Women in Muslim countries have a right to vote because women in Muslim countries have a right to vote." The conclusion merely repeats the premise but in different words. The best protection against circular reasoning is a close reading of the argument.

Equivocation

The fallacy of **equivocation** assigns two different meanings to the same term in an argument. Here's an example that, in one form or another, is a commonplace in the abortion debate:

1. A fetus is an individual that is indisputably human.

2. A human is endowed with rights that cannot be invalidated, including a right to life.

3. Therefore, a fetus has a right to life.

This argument equivocates on the word *human*. In Premise 1, the term means physiologically human, as in having human DNA. This claim, of course, is indeed indisputable. But in Premise 2, *human* is used in the sense of *person*— that is, an individual having full moral rights. Since the premises refer to two different things, the conclusion does not follow. If you are not paying close attention, though, you might not detect the equivocation and accept the argument as it is.

Appeal to Authority

This fallacy is relying on the opinion of someone thought to be an expert who is not. An expert, of course, can be a source of reliable information— but only if he really is an authority in the designated subject area. A true expert is someone who is both knowledgeable about the facts and able to make reliable judgments about them. Ultimately, experts are experts because they carefully base their opinions on the available evidence.

We make a fallacious **appeal to authority** when we (1) cite experts who are not experts in the field under discussion (though they may be experts in some other field) or (2) cite nonexperts as experts. Expertise in one field does not automatically carry over to another, and even nonexperts who are prestigious and famous are still just nonexperts. In general, on subjects outside an expert's area of expertise, her opinions are no more reliable than those of nonexperts.

Two rules of thumb should guide your use of expert opinion. First, if a claim conflicts with the consensus of opinion among experts, you have good reason to doubt the claim. Second, if experts disagree about a claim, you again have good reason to doubt it.

Appeal to Emotion

Emotions have a role to play in the moral life. In moral arguments, however, the use of emotions alone as substitutes for premises is a fallacy. We commit this fallacy when we try to convince someone to accept a conclusion not by providing them with relevant reasons but by appealing only to fear, guilt, anger, hate, compassion, and the like. For example:

> The defendant is obviously guilty of murder in this case. Look at him in the courtroom—he's terrifying and menacing. And no one can ignore the way he stabbed that girl and mutilated her body. And her poor parents. . . .

The question here is whether the defendant committed the crime, and the feelings of fear and pity that he evokes are not relevant to it. But if the question were about the anguish or torment inflicted on the victim or her parents, then our feelings of empathy would indeed be relevant— and so would any pertinent moral principles or theories.

Slippery Slope

Slippery slope is the fallacy of using dubious premises to argue that doing a particular action will inevitably lead to other actions that will result in disaster, so you should not do that first action. This way of arguing is perfectly legitimate if the premises are solid—that is, if there are good reasons to believe that the first step really will lead to ruin. Consider:

1. Rampant proliferation of pornography on the Internet leads to obsession with pornographic materials.

2. Obsession with pornographic materials disrupts relationships, and that disruption leads to divorce.

3. Therefore, we should ban pornography on the Internet.

Perhaps the chain of events laid out here could actually occur, but we have been given no reason to believe that it would. (You can see that this argument is also missing a moral premise.) Scientific evidence showing that this sequence of cause and effect does occur as described would constitute good reason to accept Premises 1 and 2.

Faulty Analogy

The use of an analogy to argue for a conclusion is known, not surprisingly, as argument by analogy. It is a type of inductive argument that says because two things are alike in some ways, they must be alike in some additional way. For example:

1. Humans feel pain, care for their young, live in social groups, and understand nuclear physics.

2. Apes also feel pain, care for their young, and live in social groups.

3. Therefore, apes can understand nuclear physics.

In argument by analogy, the probability that the conclusion is true depends on the relevant similarities between the two things being compared. The greater the relevant similarities, the more likely the conclusion is true. Humans and apes are relevantly similar in several ways, but the question is, Are they relevantly similar enough to render the conclusion probable? In this case, though humans and apes are similar in some ways, they are not relevantly similar enough to adequately support the conclusion. Humans and apes have many differences—the most relevant of which for this argument is probably in the physiology of their brains and in their capacity for advanced learning.

Arguments by analogy are common in moral reasoning. For example:

1. When a neighbor needs your help (as when he needs to borrow your garden hose to put out a fire in his house), it is morally permissible to lend the neighbor what he needs.

2. Britain is a neighbor of the United States, and it is in dire need of help to win the war against Germany.

3. Therefore, it is morally permissible for the United States to lend Britain the material and equipment it needs to defeat Germany.

This is roughly the moral argument that President Franklin Roosevelt made during World War II to convince Americans to aid Britain in its struggle. The strength of the argument depends on the degree of similarity between the two situations described. At the time, many Americans thought the argument strong.

The fallacy of **faulty analogy** is arguing by an analogy that is weak. In strong arguments by analogy, not only must the degree of similarity be great but also the similarities must be relevant. This means that the similarities must relate specifically to the conclusion. Irrelevant similarities cannot strengthen an argument.

Appeal to Ignorance

This fallacy consists of arguing that the *absence of evidence* entitles us to believe a claim. Consider these two arguments:

- No one has proven that the fetus is not a person, so it is in fact a person.
- It is obviously false that a fetus is a person, because science has not proven that it is a person.

Both these arguments are **appeals to ignorance.** The first one says that because a statement has not been proven false, it must be true. The second one has things the other way around: because a statement has not been proven true, it must be false. The problem in both these is that a *lack* of evidence cannot be evidence for anything. A dearth of evidence simply indicates that we are ignorant of the facts. If having no evidence could prove something, we could prove all sorts of outrageous claims. We could argue that because no one has proven that there are no space aliens controlling all our moral decisions, there are in fact space aliens controlling all our moral decisions.

Straw Man

Unfortunately, this fallacy is rampant in debates about moral issues. It amounts to misrepresenting someone's claim or argument so it can be more easily refuted. For example, suppose you are trying to argue that a code of ethics for your professional group should be secular so that it can be appreciated and used by as many people as possible, regardless of their religious views. Suppose further that your opponent argues against your claim in this fashion:

X obviously wants to strip religious faith away from every member of our profession and to banish religion from the realm of ethics. We should not let this happen. We should not let X have his way. Vote against the secular code of ethics.

This argument misrepresents your view, distorting it so that it seems outrageous and unacceptable. Your opponent argues against the distorted version and then concludes that your (original) position should be rejected.

The **straw man** fallacy is not just a bad argument—it flies in the face of the spirit of moral reasoning, which is about seeking understanding through critical thinking and honest and fair exploration of issues. If you agree with this approach, then you should not use the straw man fallacy—and you should beware of its use by others.

Appeal to the Person

Appeal to the person (also known as *ad hominem*) is arguing that a claim should be rejected solely because of the characteristics of the person who makes it. Look at these:

- We should reject Alice's assertion that cheating on your taxes is wrong. She's a political libertarian.
- Jerome argues that we should all give a portion of our income to feed the hungry people of the world. But that's just what you'd expect a rich guy like him to say. Ignore him.
- Maria says that animals have rights and that we shouldn't use animal products on moral grounds. Don't believe a word of it. She owns a fur coat—she's a big hypocrite.

In each of these arguments, a claim is rejected on the grounds that the person making it has a particular character, political affiliation, or motive. Such personal characteristics, however, are irrelevant to the truth of a claim. A claim must stand or fall on its own merits. Whether a statement is true or false, it must be judged according to the quality of the reasoning and evidence behind it. Bad people can construct good arguments; good people can construct bad arguments.

QUICK REVIEW

begging the question—The fallacy of arguing in a circle—that is, trying to use a statement as both a premise in an argument and the conclusion of that argument. Such an argument says, in effect, *p* is true because *p* is true.

equivocation—The fallacy of assigning two different meanings to the same term in an argument.

appeal to authority—The fallacy of relying on the opinion of someone thought to be an expert who is not.

slippery slope—The fallacy of using dubious premises to argue that doing a particular action will inevitably lead to other actions that will result in disaster, so you should not do that first action.

faulty analogy—The use of a flawed analogy to argue for a conclusion.

appeal to ignorance—The fallacy of arguing that the absence of evidence entitles us to believe a claim.

straw man—The fallacy of misrepresenting someone's claim or argument so it can be more easily refuted.

appeal to the person—The fallacy (also known as *ad hominem*) of arguing that a claim should be rejected solely because of the characteristics of the person who makes it.

hasty generalization—The fallacy of drawing a conclusion about an entire group of people or things based on an undersized sample of the group.

Hasty Generalization

Hasty generalization is a fallacy of inductive reasoning. It is the mistake of drawing a conclusion about an entire group of people or things based on an undersized sample of the group.

- In this town three pro-life demonstrators have been arrested for trespassing or assault. I'm telling you, pro-lifers are lawbreakers.

- In the past thirty years, at least two people on death row in this state have been executed and later found to be innocent by DNA evidence. Why is the state constantly executing innocent people?

In the first argument, a conclusion is drawn about all people with pro-life views from a sample of just three people. When it is spelled out plainly, the leap in logic is clearly preposterous. Yet such preposterous leaps are extremely common. In the second argument, the conclusion is that wrongful executions in the state happen frequently. This conclusion, though, is not justified by the tiny sample of cases.

SUMMARY

An argument is a group of statements, one of which is supposed to be supported by the rest. To be more precise, an argument consists of one or more premises and a conclusion. In a good argument, the conclusion must follow from the premises, and the premises must be true.

Arguments come in two basic types: deductive and inductive. Deductive arguments are meant to give logically conclusive support for their conclusions. A deductive argument that actually provides this kind of support is said to be valid. If it also has true premises, it is said to be sound. An inductive argument is meant to provide probable support for its conclusion. An inductive argument that actually provides this kind of support is said to be strong. If it also has true premises, it is said to be cogent.

Deductive arguments come in different forms. Some of these forms are known to be valid; some, invalid. Knowing these patterns helps you determine the validity of deductive arguments. Using the counterexample method can also aid your analysis.

The typical moral argument consists of at least one moral premise and at least one nonmoral premise. The best approach to evaluating moral arguments is to treat them as deductive. This tack enables you to uncover implicit premises. Implicit premises are often moral premises, which may be controversial or dubious. They can be tested through the use of counterexamples.

In moral reasoning, you frequently encounter fallacies—bad arguments that arise repeatedly. Some of those you are most likely to come across are begging the question, equivocation, appeal to authority, slippery slope, faulty analogy, appeal to ignorance, straw man, appeal to the person, and hasty generalization.

EXERCISES

Review Questions

1. What is the difference between persuasion and argument? (p. 45)
2. What is a deductive argument? an inductive argument? (p. 46)
3. What is a valid argument? a strong argument? (pp. 46–47)
4. What is the term designating a valid argument with true premises? a strong argument with true premises? (p. 47)
5. Is the following argument form valid or invalid? (p. 48)

   If *p*, then *q*.
   p.
   Therefore, *q*.
6. Is the following argument form valid or invalid? (p. 48)

   If *p*, then *q*.
   If *q*, then *r*.
   Therefore, if *p*, then *r*.

7. What is the counterexample method? (p. 49)
8. What is a moral argument? What kind of premises must it have? (p. 51)
9. What is the best method for evaluating moral premises? (p. 54)
10. What is the fallacy of the slippery slope? appeal to ignorance? straw man? (pp. 58–59)

Discussion Questions

1. Is it immoral to believe a claim without evidence? Why or why not?
2. If moral reasoning is largely about providing good reasons for moral claims, where do feelings enter the picture? Is it possible to present a good argument that you feel strongly about? If so, provide an example of such an argument.
3. Which of the following passages are arguments (in the sense of displaying critical reasoning)? Explain your answers.
   - If you harm someone, they will harm you.
   - Racial profiling is wrong. It discriminates against racial groups, and discrimination is wrong.
   - If you say something that offends me, I have the right to prevent you from saying it again. After all, words are weapons, and I have a right to prevent the use of weapons against me.
4. What is the difference between persuading someone to believe a claim and giving them reasons to accept it? Can a good argument be persuasive? Why or why not?
5. Why do you think people are tempted to use the straw man fallacy in disagreements on moral issues? How do you feel when someone uses this fallacy against you?

Theories of Morality

The Power of Moral Theories

Recall that Part 1 (Fundamentals) gave you a broad view of our subject, outlining the major concerns of moral philosophy, the function of moral judgments and principles, the nature of moral problems, the elements of our common moral experience, and the challenges of moral relativism and emotivism. Part 2 (Moral Reasoning) covered ethics at the ground level—the fundamentals of critical reasoning as applied to everyday moral claims, arguments, and conflicts. Here in Part 3 (Chapters 4–7) we touch again on a great deal of this previous material as we explore a central concern of contemporary ethics: moral theory.

THEORIES OF RIGHT AND WRONG

Whatever else the moral life entails, it surely has moral reasoning at its core. We act, we feel, we choose—guided in our best moments by the sifting of reasons and the weighing of arguments. Much of the time, we expect—and want—this process to yield plausible moral judgments. We confront the cases that unsettle us and hope to respond to them with credible assessments of the right and the good. In making these judgments, we may appeal to moral standards—principles or rules that help us sort out right and wrong, good and bad. Our deliberations may even work the other way around: moral judgments may help us mold moral principles. If we think carefully about our own deliberations, however, we will likely come to understand that this interplay between moral judgments and principles cannot be the whole story of moral reasoning. From time to time

we step back from such considerations and ask ourselves if a trusted moral principle is truly sound, whether a conflict of principles can be resolved, or if a new principle can handle cases that we have never had to address before. When we puzzle over such things, we enter the realm of moral theory. We theorize—trying to use, make, or revise a moral theory or a piece of one.

A **moral theory** is an explanation of what makes an action right or what makes a person or thing good. Its focus is not the rightness or goodness of specific actions or persons but the very nature of rightness or goodness itself. Moral theories concerned with the goodness of persons or things are known as *theories of value*. Moral theories concerned with the rightness or wrongness of actions are called *theories of obligation*. In this text, we focus mostly on theories of obligation and, unless otherwise indicated, will use the more general term *moral theories* to refer to them. A moral theory in this sense, then, is an explanation of what makes an action right or wrong. It says, in effect, that a particular action is right (or wrong) because it has *this* property, or characteristic.

Moral theories and theorizing are hard to avoid. To wonder what makes an action right is to theorize. To try *not* to think much about morality but to rely on your default moral theory—the one you inherited from your family or culture—is of course to live by the lights of a moral theory. To reject all moral theories, to deny the possibility of objective morality, or to embrace a subjectivist view of right and wrong is to have a particular overarching view of morality, a view

Moral Theories versus Moral Codes

A moral theory explains what makes an action right; a moral code is simply a set of rules. We value a moral theory because it identifies for us the essence of rightness and thereby helps us make moral judgments, derive moral principles, and resolve conflicts between moral statements. A moral code, however, is much less useful than a moral theory. The rules in a moral code inevitably conflict but provide no means for resolving their inconsistencies. Rules saying both "Do not kill" and "Protect human life," for example, will clash when the only way to protect human life is to kill. Also, rules are always general—usually too general to cover many specific situations that call for a moral decision—yet not general enough (in the way that theories are) to help us deal with such an array of specifics. How does a rule insisting "Children must obey their parents" apply when the parents are criminally insane or under the influence of drugs, or when there are no parents, just legal guardians? To make the rule apply, we would have to interpret it—and that gets us back into the realm of moral theory.

The point is that moral codes may have their place in the moral life, but they are no substitute for a plausible moral theory. Rules are rules, but a moral theory can help us see beyond the rules.

that in the broadest sense constitutes a moral theory or part of one.

A moral theory provides us with very general norms, or standards, that can help us make sense of our moral experiences, judgments, and principles. (Some moral theories feature only *one* overarching standard.) The standards are meant to be general enough and substantial enough to inform our moral reasoning—to help us assess the worth of less general principles, to shed light on our moral judgments, to corroborate or challenge aspects of our moral experience, and even to generate new lower-level principles if need be.

Moral theories and moral arguments often work together. A statement expressing a moral theory may itself act as the moral premise in an argument. More often, an argument's moral premise is ultimately backed by a moral theory from which the moral premise (principle or rule) is derived. Testing the premise may require examining one or more supporting principles or perhaps the most general norm (the theory) itself.

Classic utilitarianism (covered in the next chapter) is an example of a simple moral theory, one based on a single, all-encompassing standard: right actions are those that directly produce the greatest overall happiness, everyone considered. What matters most are the consequences of actions. Thus in a particular situation, if there are only two possible actions, and action X produces, say, 100 units of overall happiness for everyone involved (early utilitarians were the first to use this strange-sounding notion of *units* of happiness) while action Y produces only 50 units, action X is the morally right action to perform. The theory therefore identifies what is thought to be the most important factor in the moral life (happiness) and provides a procedure for making judgments about right and wrong actions.

Should we therefore conclude that a moral theory is the final authority in moral reasoning? Not at all. A moral theory is not like a mathematical axiom. From a moral theory we cannot derive in strict logical fashion principles or judgments that will solve all the problems of our real-world cases. Because moral theories are by definition general and theoretical, they cannot by themselves give us precisely tailored right answers. But neither can we dispense with moral theories and rely solely on judgments about particular cases and issues. In the field of ethics, most philosophers agree that carefully made moral judgments about cases and issues are generally reliable data that we should take very seriously. Such opinions are called *considered moral judgments* because they are formed after careful deliberation that is as free of bias as possible. Our considered judgments (including the principles or rules sanctioned by those judgments) by themselves, however, are sometimes of limited use. They may conflict. They may lack sufficient justification. A moral theory provides standards that can help overcome these limitations.

So where does theory fit in our moral deliberations? Theory plays a role along with judgments and principles or rules. In trying to determine the morally right thing to do in a specific case, we may find ourselves reflecting on just one of these elements or on all of them at once. We may, for example, begin by considering the insights embodied in our moral theory, which give some justification to several relevant principles. In light of these principles, we may decide to perform a particular action. But we may also discover that our considered judgment in the case conflicts with the deliverances of the relevant principles or even with the overarching theory. Depending on the weight we give to the particular judgment, we may decide to adjust the principles or the theory so that it is compatible with the judgment. A moral theory can crystallize important insights in morality and thereby give us general guidance as we make judgments about cases and issues. But the judgments—if they are indeed trustworthy—can compel us to reconsider the theory.

The ultimate goal in this give-and-take of theory and judgment (or principle) is a kind of close coherence between the two—what has come to be known as *reflective equilibrium*.[1] They should fit together as closely as possible, with maximum agreement between them. This process is similar to the one used in science to reconcile theory and experimental data, a topic we address in more detail later in this chapter.

MAJOR THEORIES

Moral philosophers have traditionally grouped theories of morality into two major categories:

[1]John Rawls, *A Theory of Justice,* rev. ed. (Cambridge, MA: Harvard University Press, Belknap Press, 1999).

consequentialist (or teleological) and nonconsequentialist (or deontological). In general, **consequentialist** moral theories say that what makes an action right is its *consequences*. Specifically, the rightness of an action depends on the amount of good it produces. A consequentialist theory may define the good in different ways—as, for example, pleasure, happiness, well-being, flourishing, or knowledge. But however good is defined, the morally right action is the one that results in the most favorable balance of good over bad.

Nonconsequentialist moral theories say that the rightness of an action does *not* depend entirely on its consequences. It depends primarily, or completely, on the nature of the action itself. To a nonconsequentialist, the balance of good over bad that results from an action may matter little or not at all. What is of primary concern is the *kind* of action in question. To a consequentialist, telling a lie may be considered wrong because it leads to more unhappiness than other actions do. To a nonconsequentialist, telling a lie may be considered wrong simply because it violates an exceptionless rule. Thus by nonconsequentialist lights, an action could be morally right—even though it produces less good than any alternative action.

Consequentialist Theories

There are several consequentialist theories, each differing on who is to benefit from the goods or what kinds of goods are to be pursued. But two theories have received the most attention from moral philosophers: utilitarianism and ethical egoism.

Utilitarianism says that the morally right action is the one that produces the most favorable balance of good over evil, everyone considered. That is, the right action maximizes the good (however *good* is defined) better than any alternative action, everyone considered. Utilitarianism insists that *everyone* affected by an action must be included in any proper calculation of overall consequences. The crucial factor is how much net good is produced when everyone involved is counted.

Moral philosophers distinguish two major types of utilitarianism, according to whether judgments of rightness focus on individual acts (without reference to rules) or on rules that cover various categories of acts. **Act-utilitarianism** says that right actions are those that *directly* produce the greatest overall good, everyone considered. The consequences that flow directly from a particular act are all that matter; rules are irrelevant to this calculation. In act-utilitarianism, each situation calling for a moral judgment is unique and demands a new calculation of the balance of good over evil. Thus, breaking a promise may be right in one situation and wrong in another, depending on the consequences. **Rule-utilitarianism**, on the other hand, says that the morally right action is the one *covered by a rule* that if generally followed would produce the most favorable balance of good over evil, everyone considered. The consequences of generally following a rule are of supreme importance—not the direct consequences of performing a particular action. Specific rules are justified because if people follow them all the time (or most of the time), the result will be a general maximization of good over evil. We are to follow such rules consistently even if doing so in a particular circumstance results in bad consequences.

Ethical egoism says that the morally right action is the one that produces the most favorable balance of good over evil *for oneself*. That is, in every situation the right action is the one that advances one's own best interests. In each circumstance, the ethical egoist must ask, Which action, among all possible actions, will result in the most good *for me*? Ironically, it may be possible for an ethical egoist to consistently practice this creed without appearing to be selfish or committing many selfishly unkind acts. The egoist may think that *completely* disregarding the welfare of others is not in his or her best interests. After all, people tend to resent such behavior and may

respond accordingly. Nevertheless, the bottom line in all moral deliberations is whether an action maximizes the good for the egoist. This approach to morality seems to radically conflict with commonsense moral experience as well as with the basic principles of most other moral theories.

Nonconsequentialist Theories

Nonconsequentialist (deontological) theories also take various forms. They differ on, among other things, the number of foundational principles or basic rules used and the ultimate basis of those principles.

By far the most influential nonconsequentialist theory is that of Immanuel Kant (1724–1804). Kant wants to establish as the foundation of his theory a single principle from which all additional maxims can be derived, a principle he calls the **categorical imperative.** One way that he states his principle is "Act only on that maxim through which you can at the same time will that it should become a universal law."[2] (Kant insists that he formulates just one principle but expresses it in several different forms; the forms, however, seem to be separate principles.) The categorical imperative, Kant says, is self-evident—and therefore founded on reason. The principle and the maxims derived from it are also universal (applying to all persons) and absolutist, meaning that they are moral laws that have no exceptions. **Kant's theory**, then, is the view that the morally right action is the one done in accordance with the categorical imperative.

For Kant, every action implies a rule or maxim saying, in effect, always do this in these circumstances. An action is right, he says, if and only if you could rationally will the rule to be universal—to have everyone in a similar situation always act according to the same rule. Breaking promises is wrong because if the implied rule (something like "Break promises whenever you want") were

[2]Immanuel Kant, *Groundwork of the Metaphysic of Morals,* trans. H. J. Paton (1948; reprint, New York: Harper & Row, 1964), 88.

universalized (if everyone followed the rule), then no promise anywhere could be trusted and the whole convention of promise making would be obliterated—and no one would be willing to live in such a world. In other words, universalizing the breaking of promises would result in a logically contradictory state of affairs, a situation that makes no moral sense.

Notice again the stark contrast between utilitarianism and Kant's theory. For the former, the rightness of an action depends solely on its consequences, on what results the action produces for the individuals involved. For the latter, the consequences of actions for particular individuals never enter into the equation. An action is right if and only if it possesses a particular property—the property of according with the categorical imperative, of not involving a logical contradiction.

Another notable nonconsequentialist view is the theory of natural law. **Natural law theory** says that the morally right action is the one that follows the dictates of nature. What does nature have to do with ethics? According to the most influential form of this theory (traditional natural law theory), the natural world, including humankind, exhibits a rational order in which everything has its proper place and purpose, with each thing given a specific role to play by God. In this grand order, natural laws reflect how the world is as well as how it should be. People are supposed to live according to natural law—that is, they are to fulfill their rightful, *natural* purpose. To act morally, they must act naturally; they must do what they were designed to do by God. They must obey the absolutist moral rules that anyone can read in the natural order.

A natural law theorist might reason like this: Lying is immoral because it goes against human nature. Truth telling is natural for humans because they are social creatures with an inborn tendency to care about the welfare of others. Truth telling helps humans get along, maintain viable societies, and show respect for others. Lying is therefore

QUICK REVIEW

moral theory—An explanation of what makes an action right or what makes a person or thing good.

consequentialist theory—A theory asserting that what makes an action right is its consequences.

nonconsequentialist theory—A theory asserting that the rightness of an action does not depend on its consequences.

utilitarianism—A theory asserting that the morally right action is the one that produces the most favorable balance of good over evil, everyone considered.

act-utilitarianism—A utilitarian theory asserting that the morally right action is the one that directly produces the most favorable balance of good over evil, everyone considered.

rule-utilitarianism—A utilitarian theory asserting that the morally right action is the one covered by a rule that if generally followed would produce the most favorable balance of good over evil, everyone considered.

ethical egoism—A theory asserting that the morally right action is the one that produces the most favorable balance of good over evil for oneself.

categorical imperative—An imperative that we should follow regardless of our particular wants and needs; also, the principle that defines Kant's ethical system.

Kant's theory—A theory asserting that the morally right action is the one done in accordance with the categorical imperative.

natural law theory—A theory asserting that the morally right action is the one that follows the dictates of nature.

divine command theory—A theory asserting that the morally right action is the one that God commands.

unnatural and wrong. Another example: Some natural law theorists claim that "unnatural" sexual activity is immoral. They argue that because the natural purpose of sex is procreation, and such practices as homosexual behavior or anal sex have nothing to do with procreation, these practices are immoral.

Another critical aspect of the traditional theory is that it insists that humans can discover what is natural, and thus moral, through reason. God has created a natural order and given humans the gift of rationality to correctly apprehend this order. This means that any rational person—whether religious or not—can discern the moral rules and live a moral life.

One of the simplest nonconsequentialist theories is the **divine command theory,** a view discussed in Chapter 1. It says that the morally right action is the one that God commands. An action is right if and only if God says it is. The rightness of an action does not depend in any way on its consequences. According to the divine command theory, an action may be deemed right even though it does *not* maximize the good, or deemed wrong even if it does maximize the good. It may incorporate one principle only (the core principle that God makes rightness) or the core principle plus several subordinate rules, as is the case with divine command views that designate the Ten Commandments as a God-made moral code.

EVALUATING THEORIES

We come now to the question that moral philosophers have been asking in one way or another for centuries: Is this moral theory a *good* theory? That is, Is it true? Does it reliably explain what makes an action right? As we have seen, not all moral theories are created equal. Some are better than others; some are seriously flawed; and some, though imperfect, have taught the world important lessons about the moral life.

The next question, of course, is, How do we go about answering the first question? At first glance, it seems that impartially judging the worth of a moral theory is impossible, since we all look at the world through our own tainted lens, our own moral theory or theory fragments. However, our review of subjectivism and relativism (Chapter 2) suggests that this worry is overblown. More to the point, there are plausible criteria that we can use to evaluate the adequacy of moral theories (our own and those of others), standards that moral philosophers and others have used to appraise even the most complex theories of morality. These are what we may call the *moral criteria of adequacy.*

The first step in any theory assessment (before using these criteria) is to ensure that the theory meets the minimum requirement of *coherence.* A moral theory that is coherent is *eligible* to be evaluated using the criteria of adequacy. A coherent theory is internally consistent, which means that its central claims are consistent with each other—they are not contradictory. An internally consistent theory would not assert, for example, both that (1) actions are right if and only if they are natural and (2) it is morally right to use unnatural means to save a life. Contradictory claims assert both that something *is* and *is not* the case; one statement says X and another says not-X. When claims conflict in this way, we know that at least one of them is false. So if two substantial claims in a theory are contradictory, one of the claims must be false—and the theory is refuted. This kind of inconsistency is such a serious shortcoming in a moral theory that further evaluation of it would be unnecessary. It is, in fact, not eligible for evaluation. Ineligible theories would get low marks on each criterion of adequacy.

Eligible moral theories are a different matter. Unlike ineligible theories, they are not guaranteed to fare poorly when evaluated, and testing their mettle with the moral criteria of adequacy is almost always revealing. But how do we use these criteria? The answer is that we apply them in much the same way and for a few of the same reasons that scientists apply their criteria to scientific theories.

Scientific theories are introduced to explain data concerning the causes of events—why something happens as it does or why it is the way it is. Usually scientists devise several theories (explanations) of a phenomenon, ensuring that each one is minimally adequate for evaluation. Then they try to determine which of these is best, which offers the best explanation for the data in question, for they know that the best theory is the one most likely to be true. To discover which is the best, they must judge each theory according to some generally accepted standards—the scientific criteria of adequacy. One criterion, for example, is *conservatism:* how well a theory fits with what scientists already know. A scientific theory that conflicts with existing knowledge (well-established facts, scientific laws, or extensively confirmed theories) is not likely to be true. On the other hand, the more conservative a theory is (that is, the less it conflicts with existing knowledge), the more likely it is to be true. All things being equal, a con-

servative theory is better than one that is not conservative. Another criterion is *fruitfulness:* how many successful novel predictions the theory makes. The more such predictions, the more plausible the theory is.

Now consider the following criteria of adequacy for moral theories:

Criterion 1: Consistency with Considered Judgments

To be worth evaluating, a plausible scientific theory must be consistent with the data it was introduced to explain. A theory meant to explain an epidemic, for example, must account for the nature of the disease and the method of transmission. Otherwise it is a very poor theory. A moral theory must also be consistent with the data it was introduced to explain. A moral theory is supposed to explain what makes an action right, and the data relevant to that issue are our *considered moral judgments*.

Recall that considered moral judgments are views that we form after careful deliberation under

---

Considered Moral Judgments

The philosopher John Rawls devised the notion of reflective equilibrium and put heavy emphasis on the quality of moral judgments in his own moral theory. This is what he has to say about the nature of considered moral judgments:

> Now, as already suggested, [considered judgments] enter as those judgments in which our moral capacities are most likely to be displayed without distortion. Thus in deciding which of our judgments to take into account we may reasonably select some and exclude others. For example, we may discard those judgments made with hesitation, or in which we have little confidence. Similarly, those given when we are upset or frightened, or when we stand to gain one way or the other can be left aside. All

these judgments are likely to be erroneous or to be influenced by an excessive attention to our own interests. Considered judgments are simply those rendered under conditions favorable to the exercise of the sense of justice, and therefore in circumstances where the more common excuses and explanations for making a mistake do not obtain. The person making the judgment is presumed, then, to have the ability, the opportunity, and the desire to reach a correct decision (or at least, not the desire not to). Moreover, the criteria that identify these judgments are not arbitrary. They are, in fact, similar to those that single out considered judgments of any kind.*

*John Rawls, *A Theory of Justice,* rev. ed. (Cambridge, MA: Harvard University Press, Belknap Press, 1999), 42.

conditions that minimize bias and error. They are therefore thought to have considerable weight as reasons or evidence in moral matters, even though they can be mistaken and other considerations (such as an established moral principle or a well-supported theory) can sometimes overrule them.

A moral theory that is inconsistent with trustworthy judgments is at least dubious and likely to be false, in need of drastic overhaul or rejection. There is something seriously wrong, for example, with a theory that approves of the murder of innocent people, the wanton torture of children, or the enslavement of millions of men and women. As we will see in the next chapter, inconsistency with considered judgments can be the undoing of even the most influential and attractive moral theories.

Consider Theory X. It says that right actions are those that enhance the harmonious functioning of a community. On the face of it, this theory appears to be a wise policy. But it seems to imply that certain heinous acts are right. It suggests, for example, that if killing an innocent person would enhance a community's harmonious functioning, killing that person would be right. This view conflicts dramatically with our considered judgment that murdering an innocent person just to make a community happy is wrong. Theory X should be rejected.

Criterion 2: Consistency with Our Moral Experiences

As we saw earlier, a good scientific theory should be conservative. It should, in other words, be consistent with scientific background knowledge—with the many beliefs that science has already firmly established. Likewise, a plausible moral theory should be consistent with moral background knowledge—with what we take to be the fundamental facts of our moral experience. Whatever

---

CRITICAL THOUGHT: A 100 Percent All-Natural Theory

Imagine that you come across a theory based on this moral standard: Only actions that are "natural" are morally right; "unnatural" actions are wrong. We can call it the all-natural theory. It defines natural actions as (1) those done in accordance with the normal biological urges and needs of human beings, (2) those that reflect typically human psychological tendencies and patterns, and (3) those that help ensure the survival of the human species. (This approach should not be confused with the more sophisticated and historically important natural law theory.) An all-natural theorist might view these actions as morally permissible: walking, talking, eating, having sex, cooperating with others, caring for loved ones, teaching children, creating art, growing food, building shelters, going to war, solving problems, and protecting the environ-ment. Impermissible actions might include building spaceships, using birth control, using performance-enhancing drugs, being a loner or a hermit, and intervening in reproductive processes (as in cloning, abortion, fertility treatments, in vitro fertilization, and stem cell research).

Is this a good theory? Is it internally inconsistent? (For example, do the three definitions of natural actions conflict? Would applying Definition 3 contradict the results of applying Definitions 1 and 2?) Is the all-natural theory consistent with our considered moral judgments? (Hint: Would it condone murder? Would it conflict with our usual concepts of justice?) If it is not consistent, supply an example (a counterexample). Is the theory consistent with our moral experience? Give reasons for your answer. Is the theory useful? If not, why not?

our views on morality, few of us would deny that we do in fact have these experiences:

- We sometimes make moral judgments.
- We often give reasons for particular moral beliefs.
- We are sometimes mistaken in our moral beliefs.
- We occasionally have moral disagreements.
- We occasionally commit wrongful acts.

As is the case with theories that conflict with considered judgments, a theory in conflict with these experiences is at least dubious and probably false. A moral theory is inconsistent with the moral life if it implies that we do not have one or more of these basic moral experiences.

Suppose Theory Y says that our feelings alone determine whether actions are right. If our feelings lead us to believe that an action is right, then it is right. But this theory suggests that we are *never* mistaken in our moral beliefs, for if our feelings determine what is right, we cannot be wrong. Whatever we happen to feel tells us what actions are right. Our moral experience, however, is good evidence that we are *not* morally infallible. Theory Y therefore is problematic, to say the least.

Could we possibly be mistaken about our moral experience? Yes. It is possible that our experience of the moral life is illusory. Perhaps we are morally infallible after all, or maybe we do not actually make moral judgments. But like our considered moral judgments, our commonsense moral experience carries weight as evidence—good evidence that the moral life is, for the most part, as we think it is. We therefore are entitled to accept this evidence as trustworthy unless we have good reason to think otherwise.

Criterion 3: Usefulness in Moral Problem Solving

Good scientific theories increase our understanding of the world, and greater understanding leads to greater usefulness—the capacity to solve problems and answer questions. The more useful a scientific theory is, the more credibility it acquires. A good moral theory is also useful—it helps us solve moral problems in real-life situations. It helps us make reliable judgments about moral principles and actions and resolve conflicts among conflicting judgments, principles, and the theory itself. A major reason for devising a moral theory is to obtain this kind of practical guidance.

Usefulness is a necessary, though not sufficient, characteristic of a good moral theory. This means that all good theories are useful, but usefulness alone does not make a moral theory good. It is possible for a bad theory to be useful as well (to be useful but fail some other criterion of adequacy). But any moral theory that lacks usefulness is a dubious theory.

Now we can be more specific about the similarities between science and ethics in handling theory and data. In science, the interaction between a theory and the relevant data is dynamic. The theory is designed to explain the data, so the data help shape the theory. But a plausible theory can give scientists good reasons to accept or reject specific data or to reinterpret them. Both the theory and the data contribute to the process of searching for the truth. Scientists work to get the balance between these two just right. They try to ensure a very close fit between them—so close that

QUICK REVIEW

The Moral Criteria of Adequacy

Criterion 1: Consistency with considered judgments.

Criterion 2: Consistency with our moral experience.

Criterion 3: Usefulness in moral problem solving.

there is no need for major alterations in either the theory or the data. In ethics, the link between theory and data (considered judgments) is similar. Considered judgments help shape theory (and its principles or rules), and a good theory sheds light on judgments and helps adjudicate conflicts beween judgments and other moral statements. As in science, we should strive for a strong logical harmony between theory, data, and subordinate principles.

Remember, though, theory evaluation is not a mechanical process, and neither is the application of theories to moral problems. There is no formula or set of instructions for applying our three criteria to a theory. Neither is there a calculating machine for determining how much weight to give each criterion in particular situations. We must make an informed judgment about the importance of particular criteria in each new instance. Nevertheless, applying the criteria is not a subjective, arbitrary affair. It is rational and objective—like, for example, the diagnosis of an illness, based on the educated judgment of a physician using appropriate guidelines.

Now suppose you apply the moral criteria of adequacy and reach a verdict on the worth of a theory: you reject it. Should this verdict be the end of your inquiry? In general, no. There is often much to be learned from even seriously defective theories. Many philosophers who reject utilitarianism, for example, also believe that it makes a valuable point that any theory should take into account: the consequences of actions do matter. Judiciously applying the criteria of adequacy to a theory can help us see a theory's strengths as well as its weakness. Such insights can inspire us to improve any moral theory—or perhaps create a new one.

You will get a chance to see firsthand how theory evaluation is done. In Chapters 5 and 6 we will apply the moral criteria of adequacy to several major moral theories.

SUMMARY

A moral theory is an explanation of what makes an action right or what makes a person or thing good. Theories concerned with the rightness or wrongness of actions are known as theories of obligation (or, in this text, simply moral theories). A moral theory is interconnected with considered judgments and principles. Considered judgments can shape a theory, and a theory can shed light on judgments and principles.

The two major types of theories are consequentialist and nonconsequentialist. Consequentialist theories say that what makes an action right is its consequences. Nonconsequentialist moral theories say that the rightness of an action does not depend entirely on its consequences. Consequentialist theories include utilitarianism (both act- and rule-utilitarianism) and ethical egoism; nonconsequentialist theories include Kant's theory, natural law theory, and divine command theory.

Since not all theories are of equal worth, we must try to discover which one is best—a task that we can perform by applying the moral criteria of adequacy to theories. The three criteria are (1) consistency with considered judgments, (2) consistency with our moral experience, and (3) usefulness in moral problem solving.

EXERCISES

Review Questions

1. What is a moral theory? (p. 65)
2. What is the difference between a moral theory and a moral code? (p. 66)
3. How can a moral theory be used in a moral argument? (p. 66)
4. What is a considered moral judgment? (p. 66)
5. What are the two main categories of moral theory? (p. 67)
6. What is utilitarianism? ethical egoism? (pp. 67–68)
7. According to Kant's moral theory, what makes an action right? (p. 68)

8. What are the three moral criteria of adequacy? (pp. 71–73)

Discussion Questions

1. Do you try to guide your moral choices with a moral code or a moral theory or both? If so, how?

2. Suppose you try to use the Ten Commandments as a moral code to help you make moral decisions. How would you resolve conflicts between commandments? Does your approach to resolving the conflicts imply a moral theory? If so, can you explain the main idea behind the theory?

3. What considered moral judgments have you made or appealed to in the past month? Do you think that these judgments are reflective of a moral principle or moral theory you implicitly appeal to? If so, what is it?

4. Would you describe your approach to morality as consequentialist, nonconsequentialist, or some combination of both? What reasons do you have for adopting this particular approach?

5. Give an example of a possible conflict between a consequentialist theory and a considered moral judgment. (Show how these two may be inconsistent.)

6. Provide an example of a conflict between a nonconsequentialist theory and a moral judgment based on the consequences of an action.

7. Using the moral criteria of adequacy, evaluate act-utilitarianism.

8. Using the moral criteria of adequacy, evaluate natural law theory.

CHAPTER 5

Consequentialist Theories: Maximize the Good

There is something in consequentialist moral theories that we find appealing, something simple and commonsensical that jibes with everyday moral experience. This attractive core is the notion that right actions must produce the best balance of good over evil. Never mind (for now) how *good* and *evil* are defined. The essential concern is how much good can result from actions performed. In this chapter, we examine the plausibility of this consequentialist maxim and explore how it is worked out in its two most influential theories: ethical egoism and utilitarianism.

ETHICAL EGOISM

Ethical egoism is the theory that the right action is the one that advances one's own best interests. It is a provocative doctrine, in part because it forces us to consider two opposing attitudes in ourselves. On the one hand, we tend to view selfish or flagrantly self-interested behavior as wicked, or at least troubling. Self-love is bad love. We frown on people who trample others in life to get to the head of the line. On the other hand, sometimes we want to look out for number one, to give priority to our own needs and desires. We think, If we do not help ourselves, who will? Self-love is good love.

Ethical egoism says that one's only moral duty is to promote the most favorable balance of good over evil for oneself. Each person must put his or her own welfare first. Advancing the interests of others is part of this moral equation only if it helps promote one's own good. Yet this extreme self-interest is not necessarily selfishness. Selfish acts advance one's own interests regardless of how others are affected. Self-interested acts promote one's own interests but not necessarily to the detriment of others. To further your own interests you may actually find yourself helping others. To gain some advantage, you may perform actions that are decidedly unselfish.

Just as we cannot equate ethical egoism with selfishness, neither can we assume it is synonymous with self-indulgence or recklessness. An ethical egoist does not necessarily do whatever she desires to do or whatever gives her the most immediate pleasure. She does what is in her best interests, and instant gratification may not be in her best interests. She may want to spend all her money at the casino or work eighteen hours a day, but over the long haul doing so may be disastrous for her. Even ethical egoists have to consider the long-term effects of their actions. They also have to take into account their interactions with others. At least most of the time, egoists are probably better off if they cooperate with others, develop reciprocal relationships, and avoid actions that antagonize people in their community or society.

Ethical egoism comes in two forms—one applying the doctrine to individual *acts* and one to relevant *rules*. **Act-egoism** says that to determine right action, you must apply the egoistic principle to individual acts. Act A is preferable to Act B because it promotes your self-interest better. **Rule-egoism** says that to determine right action, you must see if an act falls under a rule that if consistently followed would maximize your self-interest. Act A is preferable to Act B because it falls under a rule that maximizes your self-interest better than any other relevant rule applying to Act B. An ethical egoist can define self-interest in various ways. The Greek philosopher Epicurus (341–270 B.C.E.), a famous ethical egoist from whose name we derive the words *epicure* and *epicurean,* gave a hedonist answer: The greatest good is pleasure, and the greatest evil, pain. The duty of a good ethical egoist is to maximize pleasure for oneself. (Contrary to legend, Epicurus thought that wanton overindulgence in the delights of the senses was not in one's best interests. He insisted that the best pleasures were those of the contemplative life and that extravagant pleasures such as drunkenness and gluttony eventually lead to misery.) Other egoistic notions of the greatest good include self-actualization (fulfilling one's potential), security and material success, satisfaction of desires, acquisition of power, and the experience of happiness.

To many people, ethical egoism may sound alien, especially if they have heard all their lives about the noble virtue of altruism and the evils of self-centeredness. But consider that self-interest is a pillar on which the economic system of capitalism is built. In a capitalist system, self-interest is supposed to drive people to seek advantages for themselves in the marketplace, compelling them to compete against each other to build a better mousetrap at a lower price. Economists argue that the result of this clash of self-interests is a better, more prosperous society.

Applying the Theory

Suppose Rosa is a successful executive at a large media corporation, and she has her eye on the vice president's position, which has just become vacant. Vincent, another successful executive in the company, also wants the VP job. Management wants to fill the vacancy as soon as possible, and they are trying to decide between the two most qualified candidates—Rosa and Vincent. One day Rosa discovers some documents left near a pho-

tocopy machine and quickly realizes that they belong to Vincent. One of them is an old memo from the president of a company where Vincent used to work. In it, the president lambastes Vincent for botching an important company project. Rosa knows that despite what she reads in the memo, Vincent has had an exemplary professional career in which he has managed most of his projects extremely well. In fact, she believes that the two of them are about equal in professional skills and accomplishments. She also knows that if management saw the memo, they would almost certainly choose her over Vincent for the VP position. She figures that Vincent probably left the documents there by mistake and would soon return to retrieve them. Impulsively, she makes a copy of the memo for herself.

Now she is confronted with a moral choice. Let us suppose that she has only three options. First, she can destroy her copy of the memo and forget about the whole incident. Second, she can discredit Vincent by showing it to management, thereby securing the VP slot for herself. Third, she can achieve the same result by discrediting Vincent surreptitiously: she can simply leave a copy where management is sure to discover it. Let us also assume that she is an act-egoist who defines her self-interest as self-actualization. Self-actualization for her means developing into the most powerful, most highly respected executive in her profession while maximizing the virtues of loyalty and honesty.

So by the lights of her act-egoism what should Rosa do? Which choice is in her best interests? Option one is neutral regarding her self-interest. If she destroys her copy of the memo, she will neither gain nor lose an advantage for herself. Option two is more complicated. If she overtly discredits Vincent, she will probably land the VP spot—a feat that fits nicely with her desire to become a powerful executive. But such a barefaced sabotaging of someone else's career would likely trouble management, and their loss of some respect for Rosa would impede future advancement in her career. They may also come to distrust her. Rosa's back-stabbing would also probably erode the trust and respect of her subordinates (those who report to her). If so, their performance may suffer, and any deficiencies in Rosa's subordinates would reflect on her leadership skills. Over time, she may be able to regain the respect of management through dazzling successes in her field, but the respect and trust of others may be much harder to regain. Option two involves the unauthorized, deceitful use of personal information against another person—not an action that encourages the virtue of honesty in Rosa. In fact, her dishonesty may weaken her moral resolve and make similar acts of deceit more probable. Like option two, option three would likely secure the VP job for Rosa. But because the deed is surreptitious, it would probably not diminish the respect and trust of others. There is a low probability, however, that Rosa's secret would eventually be uncovered—especially if Vincent suspects Rosa, which is likely. If she is found out, the damage done to her reputation (and possibly her career) might be greater than that caused by the more up-front tack of option two. Also like option two, option three might weaken the virtue of honesty in Rosa's character.

Given this situation and Rosa's brand of act-egoism, she should probably go with option three—but only if the risk of being found out is extremely low. Option three promotes her self-interest dramatically by securing the coveted job at a relatively low cost (a possible erosion of virtue). Option two would also land the job but at very high cost—a loss of other people's trust and respect, a possible decrease in her chances for career advancement, damage to her professional reputation, and a likely lessening of a virtue critical to Rosa's self-actualization (honesty).

If Rosa believes that the risks to her career and character involved in options two and three are too high, she should probably choose option one.

This choice would not promote her best interests, but it would not diminish them either.

Would Rosa's action be any different if judged from the perspective of rule-egoism? Suppose Rosa, like many other ethical egoists, thinks that her actions should be guided by this rule (or something like it): People should be honest in their dealings with others—that is, except in insignificant matters (white lies), they should not lie to others or mislead them. She believes that adhering to this prohibition against dishonesty is in her best interests. The rule, however, would disallow both options two and three, for they involve significant deception. Only option one would be left. But if obeying the rule would lead to a major setback for her interests, Rosa might decide to ignore it in this case (or reject it altogether as contrary to the spirit of ethical egoism). If so, she might have to fall back to act-egoism and decide in favor of option three.

Evaluating the Theory

Is ethical egoism a plausible moral theory? Let us find out by examining arguments in its favor and applying the moral criteria of adequacy.

The primary argument for ethical egoism depends heavily on a scientific theory known as **psychological egoism,** the view that the motive for all our actions is self-interest. Whatever we do, we do because we want to promote our own welfare. Psychological egoism, we are told, is simply a description of the true nature of our motivations. We are, in short, born to look out for number one.

Putting psychological egoism to good use, the ethical egoist reasons as follows: We can never be morally obligated to perform an action that we cannot possibly do. This is just an obvious fact about morality. Since we are *not able* to prevent a hurricane from blasting across a coastal city, we are *not morally obligated* to prevent it. Likewise, since we are not able to perform an action except out of self-interest (the claim of psychological egoism), we are not morally obligated to perform an action unless motivated by self-interest. That is, we are morally obligated to do only what our self-interest motivates us to do. Here is the argument stated more formally:

1. We are not able to perform an action except out of self-interest (psychological egoism).

2. We are not morally obligated to perform an action unless motivated by self-interest.

3. Therefore, we are morally obligated to do only what our self-interest motivates us to do.

Notice that even if psychological egoism is true, this argument does not establish that an action is right if and only if it promotes one's self-interest (the claim of ethical egoism). But it does demonstrate that an action cannot be right unless it at least promotes one's self-interest. To put it another way, an action that does not advance one's own welfare cannot be right.

Is psychological egoism true? Many people think it is and offer several arguments in its favor. One line of reasoning is that psychological egoism is true because experience shows that all our actions are in fact motivated by self-interest. All our actions—including seemingly altruistic ones—are performed to gain some benefit for ourselves. This argument, however, is far from conclusive. Sometimes people do perform altruistic acts because doing so is in their best interests. Smith may contribute to charity because such generosity furthers his political ambitions. Jones may do volunteer work for the Red Cross because it looks good on her résumé. But people also seem to do things that are *not* motivated by self-interest. They sometimes risk their lives by rushing into a burning building to rescue a complete stranger. They may impair their health by donating a kidney to prevent one of their children from dying. Explanations that appeal to self-interest in such cases seem implausible. Moreover, people often have self-destructive habits (for example, drinking excessively

and driving recklessly)—habits that are unlikely to be in anyone's best interests.

Some ethical egoists may argue in a slightly different vein: People get satisfaction (or happiness or pleasure) from what they do, including their so-called unselfish or altruistic acts. Therefore, they perform unselfish or altruistic actions because doing so gives them satisfaction. A man saves a child from a burning building because he wants the emotional satisfaction that comes from saving a life. Our actions, no matter how we characterize them, are all about self-interest.

This argument is based on a conceptual confusion. It says that we perform selfless acts to achieve satisfaction. Satisfaction is the object of the whole exercise. But if we experience satisfaction in performing an action, that does not show that our goal in performing the action is satisfaction. A much more plausible account is that we desire something other than satisfaction and then experience satisfaction as a result of getting what we desired. Consider, for example, our man who saves the child from a fire. He rescues the child and feels satisfaction—but he could not have experienced that satisfaction unless he already had a desire to save the child or cared what happened to her. If he did not have such a desire or care about her, how could he have derived any satisfaction from his actions? To experience satisfaction he had to have a desire for something other than his own satisfaction. The moral of the story is that satisfaction is the result of getting what we want—not the object of our desires.

This view fits well with our own experience. Most often when we act according to some purpose, we are not focused on, or aware of, our satisfaction. We concentrate on obtaining the real object of our efforts, and when we succeed, we then feel satisfaction.

The philosopher Joel Feinberg makes a similar point about the pursuit of happiness. He asks us to imagine a person, Jones, who has no desire for much of anything—except happiness. Jones has

Can Ethical Egoism Be Advocated?

Some critics of ethical egoism say that it is a very strange theory because its adherents cannot urge others to become ethical egoists! The philosopher Theodore Schick Jr. makes the point:

> Even if ethical egoism did provide necessary and sufficient conditions for an action's being right, it would be a peculiar sort of ethical theory, for its adherents couldn't consistently advocate it. Suppose that someone came to an ethical egoist for moral advice. If the ethical egoist wanted to do what is in his best interest, he would not tell his client to do what is in her best interest because her interests might conflict with his. Rather, he would tell her to do what is in his best interest.

Such advice has been satirized on national TV. Al Franken, a former writer for *Saturday Night Live* and author of *Rush Limbaugh Is a Big Fat Idiot and Other Observations,* proclaimed on a number of *Saturday Night Live* shows in the early 1980s that whereas the 1970s were known as the "me" decade, the 1980s were going to be known as the "Al Franken" decade. So whenever anyone was faced with a difficult decision, the individual should ask herself, "How can I most benefit Al Franken?"*

*Theodore Schick Jr., in *Doing Philosophy: An Introduction through Thought Experiments*, by Schick and Lewis Vaughn, 2nd ed. (Boston: McGraw-Hill, 2003), 327.

---

no interest in knowledge for its own sake, the beauty of nature, art and literature, sports, crafts, or business. But Jones does have "an overwhelming passion for, a complete preoccupation with, his own happiness. The one desire of his life is to be happy."[1] The irony is that using this approach, Jones will *not* find happiness. He cannot pursue happiness directly and expect to find it. To achieve happiness, he must pursue other aims whose pursuit yields happiness as a by-product. We must conclude that it is not the case that our only motivation for our actions is the desire for happiness (or satisfaction or pleasure).

These reflections show that psychological egoism is a dubious theory, and if we construe self-interest as satisfaction, pleasure, or happiness, the theory seems false. Still, some may not give up the argument from experience (mentioned earlier), insisting that when properly interpreted, all our

actions (including those that seem purely altruistic or unselfish) can be shown to be motivated by self-interest. All the counterexamples that seem to suggest that psychological egoism is false actually are evidence that it is true. Smith's contributing to charity may look altruistic, but he is really trying to impress a woman he would like to date. Jones's volunteer work at the Red Cross may seem unselfish, but she is just trying to cultivate some business contacts. Every counterexample can be reinterpreted to support the theory.

Critics have been quick to charge that this way of defending psychological egoism is a mistake. It renders the theory untestable and useless. It ensures that no evidence could possibly count against it, and therefore it does not tell us anything about self-interested actions. Anything we say about such actions would be consistent with the theory. Any theory that is so uninformative could not be used to support another theory—including ethical egoism.

So far we have found the arguments for ethical egoism ineffective. Now we can ask another question: are there any good arguments *against*

---

[1] Joel Feinberg, "Psychological Egoism," in *Moral Philosophy: Selected Readings,* ed. George Sher (San Diego: Harcourt Brace Jovanovich, 1987), 11–12.

ethical egoism? This is where the moral criteria of adequacy come in.

Recall that an important first step in evaluating a moral theory (or any other kind of theory) is to determine if it meets the minimum requirement of coherence, or internal consistency. As it turns out, some critics of ethical egoism have brought the charge of logical or practical inconsistency against the theory. But in general these criticisms seem to fall short of a knockout blow to ethical egoism. Devising counterarguments that can undercut the criticisms seems to be a straightforward business. Let us assume, then, that ethical egoism is in fact eligible for evaluation using the criteria of adequacy.

We begin with Criterion 1, consistency with considered judgments. A major criticism of ethical egoism is that it is *not* consistent with many of our considered moral judgments—judgments that seem highly plausible and commonsensical. Specifically, ethical egoism seems to sanction actions that we would surely regard as abominable. Suppose a young man visits his elderly, bedridden father. When he sees that no one else is around, he uses a pillow to smother the old man in order to collect on his life insurance. Suppose also that the action is in the son's best interests; it will cause not the least bit of unpleasant feelings in him; and the crime will remain his own terrible secret. According to ethical egoism, this heinous act is morally right. The son did his duty.

An ethical egoist might object to this line by saying that *refraining* from committing evil acts is actually endorsed by ethical egoism—one's best interests are served by refraining. You should not murder or steal, for example, because it might encourage others to do the same to you, or it might undermine trust, security, or cooperation in society, which would not be in your best interests. For these reasons, you should obey the law or the rules of conventional morality (as the rule-egoist might do).

But following the rules is clearly not always in one's best interests. Sometimes committing a wicked act really does promote one's own welfare. In the case of the murdering son, no one will seek revenge for the secret murder, cooperation and trust in society will not be affected, and the murderer will suffer no psychological torments. There seems to be no downside here—but the son's rewards for committing the deed will be great. Consistently looking out for one's own welfare sometimes requires rule violations and exceptions. In fact, some argue that the interests of ethical egoists may be best served when they urge everyone else to obey the rules while themselves secretly breaking them.

If ethical egoism does conflict with our considered judgments, it is questionable at best. But it has been accused of another defect as well: it fails Criterion 2, consistency with our moral experience.

One aspect of morality is so fundamental that we may plausibly view it as a basic fact of the moral life: moral impartiality, or treating equals equally. We know that in our dealings with the world, we are supposed to take into account the treatment of others as well as that of ourselves. The moral life is lived with the wider world in mind. We must give all persons their due and treat all equals equally, for in the moral sense we are all equals. Each person is presumed to have the same rights—and to have interests that are just as important—as everyone else, unless we have good reason for thinking otherwise. If one person is qualified for a job, and another person is equally qualified, we would be guilty of discrimination if we hired one and not the other based solely on race, sex, skin color, or ancestry. These factors are not morally relevant. People who do treat equals unequally in such ways are known as racists, sexists, bigots, and the like. Probably the most serious charge against ethical egoism is that it discriminates against people in the same fashion. It arbitrarily treats the interests of some people

QUICK REVIEW

act-egoism—The theory that to determine right action, you must apply the egoistic principle to individual acts.

rule-egoism—The theory that to determine right action, you must see if an act falls under a rule that if consistently followed would maximize your self-interest.

psychological egoism—The view that the motive for all our actions is self-interest.

(oneself) as more important than the interests of all others (the rest of the world)—even though there is no morally relevant difference between the two.

The failure of ethical egoism to treat equals equally seems a serious defect in the theory. It conflicts with a major component of our moral existence. For many critics, this single defect is enough reason to reject the theory.

Recall that Criterion 3 is usefulness in moral problem solving. Some philosophers argue that ethical egoism fails this standard because the theory seems to lead to contradictory advice or conflicting actions. If real, this problem would constitute a significant failing of the theory. But these criticisms depend on controversial assumptions about ethical egoism or morality in general, so we will not dwell on them here. Our analysis of ethical egoism's problems using the first two criteria should be sufficient to raise serious doubts about the theory.

UTILITARIANISM

Are you a utilitarian? To find out, consider the following scenario: After years of research, a medical scientist—Dr. X—realizes that she is just one step

away from developing a cure for all known forms of heart disease. Such a breakthrough would save hundreds of thousands of lives—perhaps millions. The world could finally be rid of heart attacks, strokes, heart failure, and the like, a feat as monumental as the eradication of deadly smallpox. That one last step in her research, however, is technologically feasible but morally problematic. It involves the killing of a single healthy human being to microscopically examine the person's heart tissue just seconds after the heart stops beating. The crucial piece of information needed to perfect the cure can be acquired only as just described; it cannot be extracted from the heart of a cadaver, an accident victim, someone suffering from a disease, or a person who has been dead for more than sixty seconds. Dr. X decides that the benefits to humanity from the cure are just too great to ignore. She locates a suitable candidate for the operation: a homeless man with no living relatives and no friends—someone who would not be missed. Through some elaborate subterfuge she manages to secretly do what needs to be done, killing the man and successfully performing the operation. She formulates the cure and saves countless lives. No one ever discovers how she obtained the last bit of information she needed to devise the cure, and she feels not the slightest guilt for her actions.

Did Dr. X do right? If you think so, then you may be a utilitarian. A utilitarian is more likely to believe that what Dr. X did was right, because it brought about consequences that were more good than bad. One man died, but countless others were saved. If you think that Dr. X did wrong, you may be a nonconsequentialist. A nonconsequentialist is likely to believe that Dr. X did wrong, because of the nature of her action: it was murder. The consequences are beside the point.

In this example, we get a hint of some of the elements that have made utilitarianism so attractive (and often controversial) to so many. First, whether or not we agree with the utilitarian view in this case, we can see that it has some plausibility. We tend to think it entirely natural to judge the morality of an action by the effects that it has on the people involved. To decide if we do right or wrong, we want to know whether the consequences of our actions are good or bad, whether they bring pleasure or pain, whether they enhance or diminish the welfare of ourselves and others. Second, the utilitarian formula for distinguishing right and wrong actions seems exceptionally straightforward. We simply calculate which action among several possible actions has the best balance of good over evil, everyone considered—and act accordingly. Moral choice is apparently reduced to a single moral principle and simple math. Third, at least sometimes, we all seem to be utilitarians. We may tell a white lie because the truth would hurt someone's feelings. We may break a promise because keeping it causes more harm than good. We may want a criminal punished not because he broke the law but because the punishment may deter him from future crimes. We justify such departures from conventional morality on the grounds that they produce better consequences. Finally, some of the moral choices sanctioned by utilitarianism may conflict dramatically with choices derived from commonsense morality—or so we think.

Utilitarianism is one of the most influential moral theories in history. The English philosopher Jeremy Bentham (1748–1832) was the first to fill out the theory in detail, and the English philosopher and economist John Stuart Mill (1806–73) developed it further. In their hands utilitarianism became a powerful instrument of social reform. It provided a rationale for promoting women's rights, improving the treatment of prisoners, advocating animal rights, and aiding the poor—all radical ideas in Bentham's and Mill's day. In the twenty-first century, the theory still has a strong effect on moral and policy decision making in many areas, including health care, criminal justice, and government.

Classic utilitarianism—the kind of act-utilitarianism formulated by Bentham—is the simplest form of the theory. It affirms the principle that the right action is the one that directly produces the best balance of happiness over unhappiness for all concerned. Happiness is an intrinsic good—the *only* intrinsic good. What matters most is how much net happiness comes directly from performing an action (as opposed to following a rule that applies to such actions). To determine the right action, we need only compute the amount of happiness that each possible action generates and choose the one that generates the most. There are no rules to take into account—just the single, simple utilitarian principle. Each set of circumstances calling for a moral choice is unique, requiring a new calculation of the varying consequences of possible actions.

Bentham called the utilitarian principle the **principle of utility** and asserted that all our actions can be judged by it. (Mill called it the **greatest happiness principle.**) As Bentham says,

By the principle of utility is meant that principle which approves or disapproves of every action whatsoever, according to the tendency which it appears to have to augment or diminish the happiness of the party whose interest is in question: or, what is the same thing in other words, to promote or to oppose that happiness. . . .

By utility is meant that property in any object, whereby it tends to produce benefit, advantage, pleasure, good, or happiness, (all this in the present case comes to the same thing) or (what comes again to the same thing) to prevent the happening of mischief, pain, evil, or unhappiness to the party whose interest is considered[.][2]

The principle of utility, of course, makes the theory consequentialist. The emphasis on happiness or pleasure makes it hedonistic, for happiness is the only intrinsic good.

[2]Jeremy Bentham, "Of the Principle of Utility," in *An Introduction to the Principles of Morals and Legislation* (1789; reprint, Oxford: Clarendon Press, 1879), 1–7.

As you can see, there is a world of difference between the moral focus of utilitarianism (in all its forms) and that of ethical egoism. The point of ethical egoism is to promote one's own good. An underlying tenet of utilitarianism is that you should promote the good of *everyone concerned* and that everyone *counts equally*. When deliberating about which action to perform, you must take into account your own happiness as well as that of everyone else who will be affected by your decision—and no one is to be given a privileged status. Such evenhandedness requires a large measure of impartiality, a quality that plays a role in every plausible moral theory. Mill says it best:

[T]he happiness which forms the utilitarian standard of what is right in conduct, is not the agent's own happiness, but that of all concerned. As between his own happiness and that of others, utilitarianism requires him to be as strictly impartial as a disinterested and benevolent spectator.[3]

In classic act-utilitarianism, knowing how to tote up the amount of utility, or happiness, generated by various actions is essential. Bentham's answer to this requirement is the *hedonic calculus,* which quantifies happiness and handles the necessary calculations. His approach is straightforward in conception but complicated in the details: For each possible action in a particular situation, determine the total amount of happiness or unhappiness produced by it for one individual (that is, the *net* happiness—happiness minus unhappiness). Gauge the level of happiness with seven basic characteristics such as intensity, duration, and fecundity (how likely the pleasure or pain is to be followed by more pleasure or pain). Repeat this process for all individuals involved and sum their happiness or unhappiness to arrive at an overall net happiness for that particular action.

Repeat for each possible action. The action with the best score (the most happiness or least unhappiness) is the morally right one.

Notice that in this arrangement, only the *total amount* of net happiness for each action matters. How the happiness is distributed among the persons involved does not figure into the calculations. This means that an action that affects ten people and produces one hundred units of happiness is to be preferred over an action that affects those same ten people but generates only fifty units of happiness—even if most of the one hundred units go to just one individual, and the fifty units divide equally among the ten. The aggregate of happiness is decisive; its distribution is not. Classic utilitarianism, though, does ask that any given amount of happiness be spread among as many people as possible—thus the utilitarian slogan "The greatest happiness for the greatest number."

Both Bentham and Mill define happiness as pleasure. In Mill's words,

The creed which accepts as the foundation of morals *utility,* or the *greatest happiness principle,* holds that actions are right in proportion as they tend to promote happiness, wrong as they tend to produce the reverse of happiness. By "happiness" is intended pleasure, and the absence of pain; by "unhappiness," pain, and the privation of pleasure.[4]

They differ, though, on the nature of happiness and how it should be measured. Bentham thinks that happiness varies only in quantity—different actions produce different amounts of happiness. To judge the intensity, duration, or fecundity of happiness is to calculate its quantity. Mill contends that happiness can vary in quantity *and* quality. There are lower pleasures, such as eating, drinking, and having sex, and there are higher pleasures, such as pursuing knowledge, appreciating beauty, and creating art. The higher pleasures

---

[3]John Stuart Mill, "What Utilitarianism Is," in *Utilitarianism,* 7th ed. (London: Longmans, Green, 1879), Chapter II.

[4]Mill, "What Utilitarianism Is," Chapter II.

are superior to the lower ones. The lower ones can be intense and enjoyable, but the higher ones are qualitatively better and more fulfilling. In this scheme, a person enjoying a mere taste of a higher pleasure may be closer to the moral ideal than a hedonistic glutton who gorges on lower pleasures. Thus Mill declared, "It is better to be a human being dissatisfied than a pig satisfied; better to be Socrates dissatisfied than a fool satisfied."[5] In Bentham's view, the glutton—who acquires a larger quantity of pleasure—would be closer to the ideal.

The problem for Mill is to justify his hierarchical ranking of the various pleasures. He tries to do so by appealing to what the majority prefers—that is, the majority of people who have experienced both the lower and higher pleasures. But this approach probably will not help, because people can differ drastically in how they rank pleasures. It is possible, for example, that a majority of people who have experienced a range of pleasures would actually disagree with Mill's rankings. In fact, any effort to devise such rankings using the principle of utility seems unlikely to succeed.

Many critics have argued that the idea of defining right action in terms of some intrinsic nonmoral good (whether pleasure, happiness, or anything else) is seriously problematic. Attempts to devise such a definition have been fraught with complications—a major one being that people have different ideas about what things are intrinsically valuable. Some utilitarians have tried to sidestep these difficulties by insisting that maximizing utility means maximizing people's *preferences,* whatever they are. This formulation seems to avoid some of the difficulties just mentioned but falls prey to another: some people's preferences may be clearly objectionable when judged by almost any moral standard, whether utilitarian or nonconsequentialist. Some people, after all, have ghastly

preferences—preferences, say, for torturing children or killing innocent people for fun. Some critics say that repairing this preference utilitarianism to avoid sanctioning objectionable actions seems unlikely without introducing some nonutilitarian moral principles such as justice, rights, and obligations.

Like act-utilitarianism, rule-utilitarianism aims at the greatest good for all affected individuals, but it maintains that we travel an indirect route to that goal. In rule-utilitarianism, the morally right action is not the one that directly brings about the greatest good but the one covered by a rule that, if followed consistently, produces the greatest good for all. In act-utilitarianism, we must examine each action to see how much good (or evil) it generates. Rule-utilitarianism would have us first determine what rule an action falls under, then see if that rule would likely maximize utility if everyone followed it. In effect, the rule-utilitarian asks, "What if everyone followed this rule?"

An act-utilitarian tries to judge the rightness of actions by the consequences they produce, occasionally relying on "rules of thumb" (such as "Usually we should not harm innocents") merely to save time. A rule-utilitarian, however, tries to follow every valid rule—even if doing so may not maximize utility in a specific situation.

In our example featuring Dr. X and the cure for heart disease, an act-utilitarian might compare the net happiness produced by performing the lethal operation and by not performing it, opting finally for the former because it maximizes happiness. A rule-utilitarian, on the other hand, would consider what moral rules seem to apply to the situation. One rule might be "It is permissible to conduct medical procedures or experiments on people without their full knowledge and consent in order to substantially advance medical science." Another one might say "Do not conduct medical procedures or experiments on people without their full knowledge and consent." If the first rule is generally followed, happiness is not likely to be

---

[5]Mill, "What Utilitarianism Is," Chapter II.

maximized in the long run. Widespread adherence to this rule would encourage medical scientists and physicians to murder patients for the good of science. Such practices would outrage people and cause them to fear and distrust science and the medical profession, leading to the breakdown of the entire health care system and most medical research. But if the second rule is consistently adhered to, happiness is likely to be maximized over the long haul. Trust in physicians and medical scientists would be maintained, and promising research could continue as long as it was conducted with the patient's consent. The right action, then, is for Dr. X *not* to perform the gruesome operation.

Applying the Theory

Let us apply utilitarianism to another type of case. Imagine that for more than a year a terrorist has been carrying out devastating attacks in a developing country, killing hundreds of innocent men, women, and children. He seems unstoppable. He always manages to elude capture. In fact, because of his stealth, the expert assistance of a few accomplices, and his support among the general population, he will most likely never be captured or killed. The authorities have no idea where he hides or where he will strike next. But they are sure that he will go on killing indefinitely. They have tried every tactic they know to put an end to the slaughter, but it goes on and on. Finally, as a last resort, the chief of the nation's antiterrorist police orders the arrest of the terrorist's family—a wife and seven children. The chief intends to kill the wife and three of the children right away (to show that he is serious), then threaten to kill the remaining four unless the terrorist turns himself in. There is no doubt that the chief will make good on his

---

Peter Singer, Utilitarian

The distinguished philosopher Peter Singer is arguably the most famous (and controversial) utilitarian of recent years. Many newspaper and magazine articles have been written about him, and many people have declared their agreement with, or vociferous opposition to, his views. This is how one magazine characterizes Singer and his ideas:

The New Yorker calls him "the most influential living philosopher." His critics call him "the most dangerous man in the world." Peter Singer, the De Camp Professor of Bioethics at Princeton University's Center for Human Values, is most widely and controversially known for his view that animals have the same moral status as humans. . . .

Singer is perhaps the most thoroughgoing philosophical utilitarian since Jeremy Bentham. As such, he believes animals have rights because the relevant moral consideration is not whether a being can reason or talk but whether it can suffer. Jettisoning the traditional distinction between humans and nonhumans, Singer distinguishes instead between persons and non-persons. Persons are beings that feel, reason, have self-awareness, and look forward to a future. Thus, fetuses and some very impaired human beings are not persons in his view and have a lesser moral status than, say, adult gorillas and chimpanzees.

Given such views, it was no surprise that anti-abortion activists and disability rights advocates loudly decried the Australian-born Singer's appointment at Princeton last year. Indeed, his language regarding the treatment of disabled human beings is at times appallingly similar to the eugenic arguments used by Nazi theorists concerning "life unworthy of life." Singer, however, believes that only parents, not the state, should have the power to make decisions about the fates of disabled infants.*

*Ronald Bailey, "The Pursuit of Happiness," *ReasonOnline*, December 2000, www.reason.com/news/show/27886. html (21 November 2006).

intentions, and there is excellent reason to believe that the terrorist will indeed turn himself in rather than allow his remaining children to be executed.

Suppose that the chief has only two options: (1) refrain from murdering the terrorist's family and continue with the usual antiterrorist tactics (which have only a tiny chance of being successful) or (2) kill the wife and three of the children and threaten to kill the rest (a strategy with a very high chance of success). According to utilitarianism, which action is right?

As an act-utilitarian, the chief might reason like this: Action 2 would probably result in a net gain of happiness, everyone considered. Forcing the terrorist to turn himself in would save hundreds of lives. His killing spree would be over. The general level of fear and apprehension in the country might subside, and even the economy—which has slowed because of terrorism—might improve. The prestige of the terrorism chief and his agents might increase. On the downside, performing Action 2 would guarantee that four innocent people (and perhaps eight) would lose their lives, and the terrorist (whose welfare must also be included in the calculations) would be imprisoned for life or executed. In addition, many citizens would be disturbed by the killing of innocent people and the flouting of the law by the police, believing that these actions are wrong and likely to set a dangerous precedent. Over time, though, these misgivings may diminish. All things considered, then, Action 2 would probably produce more happiness than unhappiness. Action 1, on the other hand, maintains the status quo. It would allow the terrorist to continue murdering innocent people and spreading fear throughout the land—a decidedly unhappy result. It clearly would produce more unhappiness than happiness. Action 2, therefore, would produce the most happiness and would therefore be the morally right option.

As a rule-utilitarian, the chief might make a different choice. He would have to decide what rules would apply to the situation then determine

QUICK REVIEW

principle of utility—Bentham's definition: "that principle which approves or disapproves of every action whatsoever, according to the tendency which it appears to have to augment or diminish the happiness of the party whose interest is in question."

greatest happiness principle—Mill's definition: the principle that "holds that actions are right in proportion as they tend to promote happiness, wrong as they tend to produce the reverse of happiness."

which one, if consistently followed, would yield the most utility. Suppose he must decide between Rule 1 and Rule 2. Rule 1 says, "Do not kill innocent people in order to prevent terrorists from killing other innocent people." Rule 2 says, "Killing innocent people is permissible if it helps to stop terrorist attacks." The chief might deliberate as follows: We can be confident that consistently following Rule 2 would have some dire consequences for society. Innocent people would be subject to arbitrary execution, civil rights would be regularly violated, the rule of law would be severely compromised, and trust in government would be degraded. In fact, adhering to Rule 2 might make people more fearful and less secure than terrorist attacks would; it would undermine the very foundations of a free society. In a particular case, killing innocent people to fight terror could possibly have more utility than not killing them. But whether such a strategy would be advantageous to society over the long haul is not at all certain. Consistently following Rule 1 would have none of these unfortunate consequences. If so, a society living according to Rule 1 would be better off than one adhering to Rule 2, and therefore the innocent should not be killed to stop a terrorist.

Evaluating the Theory

Bentham and Mill do not offer ironclad arguments demonstrating that utilitarianism is the best moral theory. Mill, however, does try to show that the principle of utility is at least a plausible basis for the theory. After all, he says, humans by nature desire happiness and nothing but happiness. If so, happiness is the standard by which we should judge human conduct, and therefore the principle of utility is the heart of morality. But this kind of moral argument is controversial, because it reasons from what *is* to what *should be*. In addition, as pointed out in the discussion of psychological egoism, the notion that happiness is our sole motivation is dubious.

What can we learn about utilitarianism by applying the moral criteria of adequacy? Let us begin with classic act-utilitarianism and deal with rule-utilitarianism later. We can also postpone discussion of the minimum requirement of coherence, because critics have been more inclined to charge rule-utilitarianism than act-utilitarianism with having significant internal inconsistencies.

If we begin with Criterion 1 (consistency with considered judgments), we run into what some have called act-utilitarianism's most serious problem: it conflicts with commonsense views about justice. Justice requires equal treatment of persons. It demands, for example, that goods such as happiness be distributed fairly, that we not harm one person to make several other persons happy. Utilitarianism says that everyone should be included in utility calculations, but it does not require that everyone get an equal share. Consider this famous scenario from the philosopher H. J. McCloskey:

Suppose a utilitarian were visiting an area in which there was racial strife, and that, during his visit, a Negro rapes a white woman, and that race riots occur as a result of the crime, white mobs, with the connivance of the police, bashing and killing Negroes, etc. Suppose too that our utilitarian is in the area of the crime when it is committed such that his testimony would bring about the conviction of a particular Negro. If he knows that a quick arrest will stop the riots and lynchings, surely, as a utilitarian, he must conclude that he has a duty to bear false witness in order to bring about the punishment of an innocent person.[6]

If right actions are those that maximize happiness, then it seems that the utilitarian would be doing right by framing the innocent person. The innocent person, of course, would experience unhappiness (he might be sent to prison or even executed), but framing him would halt the riots and prevent many other innocent people from being killed, resulting in a net gain in overall happiness. Framing the innocent is unjust, though, and our considered moral judgments would be at odds with such an action. Here the commonsense idea of justice and the principle of utility collide. The conflict raises doubts about act-utilitarianism as a moral theory.

Here is another famous example:

This time you are to imagine yourself to be a surgeon, a truly great surgeon. Among other things you do, you transplant organs, and you are such a great surgeon that the organs you transplant always take. At the moment you have five patients who need organs. Two need one lung each, two need a kidney each, and the fifth needs a heart. If they do not get those organs today, they will all die; if you find organs for them today, you can transplant the organs and they will all live. But where to find the lungs, the kidneys, and the heart? The time is almost up when a report is brought to you that a young man who has just come into your clinic for his yearly check-up has exactly the right blood type, and is in excellent

[6]H. J. McCloskey, "A Non-Utilitarian Approach to Punishment," *Inquiry* 8 (1965): 239–49.

health. Lo, you have a possible donor. All you need do is cut him up and distribute his parts among the five who need them. You ask, but he says, "Sorry. I deeply sympathize, but no." Would it be morally permissible for you to operate anyway?[7]

This scenario involves the possible killing of an innocent person for the good of others. There seems little doubt that carrying out the murder and transplanting the victim's organs into five other people (and thus saving their lives) would maximize utility (assuming, of course, that the surgeon's deed would not become public, he or she suffered no untoward psychological effects, etc.). Compared to the happiness produced by doing the transplants, the unhappiness of the one unlucky donor seems minor. Therefore, according to act-utilitarianism, you (the surgeon) should commit the murder and do the transplants. But this choice appears to conflict with our considered moral judgments. Killing the healthy young man to benefit the five unhealthy ones seems unjust.

Look at one final case. Suppose a tsunami devastates a coastal town in Singapore. Relief agencies arrive on the scene to distribute food, shelter, and medical care to 100 tsunami victims—disaster aid that amounts to, say, 1,000 units of happiness. There are only two options for the distribution of the 1,000 units. Option A is to divide the 1,000 units equally among all 100 victims, supplying 10 units to each person. Option B is to give 901 units to one victim (who happens to be the richest man in town) and 99 units to the remaining victims, providing 1 unit per person. Both options distribute the same amount of happiness to the victims—1,000 units. Following the dictates of act-utilitarianism, we would have to say that the two actions (options) have equal utility and so are equally right. But this seems wrong. It seems unjust to distribute the units

of happiness so unevenly when all recipients are equals in all morally relevant respects. Like the other examples, this one suggests that act-utilitarianism may be an inadequate theory.

Detractors also make parallel arguments against the theory in many cases besides those involving injustice. A familiar charge is that act-utilitarianism conflicts with our commonsense judgments both about people's rights and about their obligations to one another. Consider first this scenario about rights: Mr. Y is a nurse in a care facility for the elderly. He tends to many bedridden patients who are in pain most of the time, are financial and emotional burdens to their families, and are not expected to live more than a few weeks. Despite their misery, they do not wish for death; they want only to be free of pain. Mr. Y, an act-utilitarian, sees that there would be a lot more happiness in the world and less pain if these patients died sooner rather than later. He decides to take matters into his own hands, so he secretly gives them a drug that kills them quietly and painlessly. Their families and the facility staff feel enormous relief. No one will ever know what Mr. Y has done, and no one suspects foul play. He feels no guilt—only immense satisfaction knowing that he has helped make the world a better place.

If Mr. Y does indeed maximize happiness in this situation, then his action is right, according to act-utilitarianism. Yet most people would probably say that he violated the rights of his patients. The commonsense view is that people have certain rights that should not be violated merely to create a better balance of happiness over unhappiness.

Another typical criticism of act-utilitarianism is that it appears to fly in the face of our considered judgments about our obligations to other people. Suppose Ms. Z must decide between two actions: Action A will produce 1,001 units of happiness; Action B, 1,000 units. The only other significant difference between them is that Action A

[7]Judith Jarvis Thomson, "The Trolley Problem," in *Rights, Restitution, and Risk: Essays in Moral Theory*, ed. William Parent (Cambridge, MA: Harvard University Press, 1986), 95.

entails the breaking of a promise. By act-utilitarian lights, Ms. Z should choose Action A because it yields more happiness than Action B does. But we tend to think that keeping a promise is more important than a tiny gain in happiness. We often try to keep our promises even when we know that doing so will result in a decrease in utility. Some say that if our obligations to others sometimes outweigh considerations of overall happiness, then act-utilitarianism must be problematic.[8]

What can an act-utilitarian say to rebut these charges about justice, rights, and obligations? One frequent response goes like this: The scenarios put forth by critics (such as the cases just cited) are misleading and implausible. They are always set up so that actions regarded as immoral produce the greatest happiness, leading to the conclusion that utilitarianism conflicts with commonsense morality and therefore cannot be an adequate moral theory. But in real life these kinds of actions almost never maximize happiness. In the case of Dr. X, her crime would almost certainly be discovered by physicians or other scientists, and she would be exposed as a murderer. This revelation would surely destroy her career, undermine patient-physician trust, tarnish the reputation of the scientific community, dry up funding for legitimate research, and prompt countless lawsuits. Scientists might even refuse to use the data from Dr. X's research because she obtained them through a heinous act. As one philosopher put it, "Given a clearheaded view of the world as it is and a realistic understanding of man's nature, it becomes more and more evident that injustice will never have, in the long run, greater utility than justice. . . . Thus injustice becomes, in actual practice, a source of great social disutility."[9]

The usual response to this defense is that the act-utilitarian is probably correct that most violations of commonsense morality do not maximize happiness—but at least some violations do. At least sometimes actions that have the best consequences do conflict with our credible moral principles or considered moral judgments. The charge is that the act-utilitarian cannot plausibly dismiss all counterexamples, and only one counterexample is required to show that maximizing utility is not a necessary and sufficient condition for right action.[10]

Unlike ethical egoism, act-utilitarianism (as well as rule-utilitarianism) does not fail Criterion 2 (consistency with our moral experience), so we can move on to Criterion 3 (usefulness in moral problem solving). On this score, some scholars argue that act-utilitarianism deserves bad marks. Probably their most common complaint is what has been called the "no-rest problem." Utilitarianism (in all its forms) requires that in our actions we *always* try to maximize utility, everyone considered. Say you are watching television. Utilitarianism would have you ask yourself, "Is this the best way to maximize happiness for everyone?" Probably not. You could be giving to charity or working as a volunteer for the local hospital or giving your coat to a homeless person or selling everything you own to buy food for hungry children. Whatever you are doing, there usually is something else you could do that would better maximize net happiness for everyone. This is how the philosopher James Rachels describes the problem:

In fact, faithful adherence to the utilitarian standard would require you to give away your resources until you have lowered your own standard of living to the level of the neediest people you could help. We might

---

[8]This case is based on one devised by W. D. Ross in *The Right and the Good* (Oxford: Clarendon Press, 1930), 34–35.

[9]Paul W. Taylor, *Principles of Ethics: An Introduction* (Encino, CA: Dickenson, 1975), 77–78.

[10]The points in this and the preceding paragraph were inspired by James Rachels, *The Elements of Moral Philosophy*, 4th ed. (Boston: McGraw-Hill, 2003), 111–12.

admire people who do this, but we do not regard them as simply doing their duty. Instead, we regard them as saintly people whose generosity goes *beyond* what duty requires. We distinguish actions that are morally required from actions that are praiseworthy but not strictly required. (Philosophers call the latter *supererogatory* actions.) Utilitarianism seems to eliminate this distinction.[11]

If act-utilitarianism does demand too much of us, then its usefulness as a guide to the moral life is suspect. One possible reply to this criticism is that the utilitarian burden can be lightened by devising rules that place limits on supererogatory actions. (We will deal with utilitarian rules in the following pages.) Another reply is that our moral common sense is simply wrong on this issue—we *should* be willing to perform, as our duty, many actions that are usually considered supererogatory. If necessary, we should be willing to give up our personal ambitions for the good of everyone. We should be willing, for example, to sacrifice a very large portion of our resources to help the poor.

To some, this reply seems questionable precisely because it challenges our commonsense moral intuitions—the very intuitions that we use to measure the plausibility of our moral judgments and principles. Moral common sense, they say, can be mistaken, and our intuitions can be tenuous or distorted—but we should cast them aside only for good reasons.

But a few utilitarians directly reject this appeal to common sense, declaring that relying so heavily on such intuitions is a mistake:

Admittedly utilitarianism does have consequences which are incompatible with the common moral consciousness, but I tended to take the view "so much the worse for the common moral consciousness." That is, I was inclined to reject the common methodology of testing general ethical principles by seeing how they square with our feelings in particular instances.[12]

These utilitarians would ask, Isn't it possible that in dire circumstances, saving a hundred innocent lives by allowing one to die would be the best thing to do even though allowing that one death would be a tragedy? Aren't there times when the norms of justice and duty *should* be ignored for the greater good of society?

To avoid the problems that act-utilitarianism is alleged to have, some utilitarians have turned to rule-utilitarianism. By positing rules that should be consistently followed, rule-utilitarianism seems to align its moral judgments closer to those of common sense. And the theory itself is based on ideas about morality that seem perfectly sensible:

In general, rule utilitarianism seems to involve two rather plausible intuitions. In the first place, rule utilitarians want to emphasize that moral rules are important. Individual acts are justified by being shown to be in accordance with correct moral rules. In the second place, utility is important. Moral rules are shown to be correct by being shown to lead, somehow, to the maximization of utility. . . . Rule utilitarianism, in its various forms, tries to combine these intuitions into a single, coherent criterion of morality.[13]

But some philosophers have accused the theory of being internally inconsistent. They say, in other words, that it fails the minimum requirement of coherence. (If so, we can forgo discussion of our three criteria of adequacy.) They argue as follows: Rule-utilitarianism says that actions are right if they conform to rules devised to maximize utility. Rules with exceptions or qualifications, however, maximize utility better than rules with-

---

[11]Rachels, *The Elements of Moral Philosophy*, 109.

[12]J. J. C. Smart, *Utilitarianism: For and Against* (Cambridge: Cambridge University Press, 1973), 68.

[13]Fred Feldman, *Introductory Ethics* (Englewood Cliffs, NJ: Prentice-Hall, 1978), 77–78.

CRITICAL THOUGHT: Cross-Species Transplants: What Would a Utilitarian Do?

Like any adequate moral theory, utilitarianism should be able to help us resolve moral problems, including new moral issues arising from advances in science and medicine. A striking example of one such issue is cross-species transplantation, the transplanting of organs from one species to another, usually from nonhuman animals to humans. Scientists are already bioengineering pigs so their organs will not provoke tissue rejection in human recipients. Pigs are thought to be promising organ donors because of the similarities between pig and human organs. Many people are in favor of such research because it could open up new sources of transplantable organs, which are now in short supply and desperately needed by thousands of people whose organs are failing.

Would an act-utilitarian be likely to condone cross-species transplants of organs? If so, on what grounds? Would the unprecedented, "unnatural" character of these operations bother a utilitarian? Why or why not? Would you expect an act-utilitarian to approve of cross-species organ transplants if they involved the killing of one hundred pigs for every successful transplant? If only a very limited number of transplants could be done successfully each year, how do you think an act-utilitarian would decide who gets the operations? Would she choose randomly? Would she ever be justified (by utilitarian considerations) in, say, deciding to save a rich philanthropist while letting a poor person die for lack of a transplant?

---

out them. For example, a rule like "Do not steal except in these circumstances" maximizes utility better than the rule "Do not steal." It seems, then, that the best rules are those with amendments that make them as specific as possible to particular cases. But if the rules are changed in this way to maximize utility, they would end up mandating the same actions that act-utilitarianism does. They all would say, in effect, "do not do this except to maximize utility." Rule-utilitarianism would lapse into act-utilitarianism.

Some rule-utilitarians respond to this criticism by denying that rules with a lot of exceptions would maximize utility. They say that people might fear that their own well-being would be threatened when others make multiple exceptions to rules. You might be reassured by a rule such as "Do not harm others" but feel uneasy about the rule "Do not harm others except in this situation." What if you end up in that particular situation?

Those who criticize the theory admit that it is indeed possible for an exception-laden rule to pro-

duce more unhappiness than happiness because of the anxiety it causes. But, they say, it is also possible for such a rule to generate a very large measure of happiness—large enough to more than offset any ill effects spawned by rule exceptions. If so, then rule-utilitarianism could easily slip into act-utilitarianism, thus exhibiting all the conflicts with commonsense morality that act-utilitarianism is supposed to have.

LEARNING FROM UTILITARIANISM

Regardless of how much credence we give to the arguments for and against utilitarianism, we must admit that the theory seems to embody a large part of the truth about morality. First, utilitarianism begs us to consider that the consequences of our actions do indeed make a difference in our moral deliberations. Whatever factors work to make an action right (or wrong), surely the consequences of what we do must somehow be among them. Even if lying is morally wrong primarily because of the kind of act it is, we cannot plausibly think that a lie that saves a thousand lives is morally equivalent to one that changes nothing. Sometimes our considered moral judgments may tell us that an action is right regardless of the good (or evil) it does. And sometimes they may say that the good it does matters a great deal.

Second, utilitarianism—perhaps more than any other moral theory—incorporates the principle of impartiality, a fundamental pillar of morality itself. Everyone concerned counts equally in every moral decision. As Mill says, when we judge the rightness of our actions, utilitarianism requires us to be "as strictly impartial as a disinterested and benevolent spectator." Discrimination is forbidden, and equality reigns. We would expect no less from a plausible moral theory.

Third, utilitarianism is through and through a moral theory for promoting human welfare. At its core is the moral principle of beneficence—the obligation to act for the well-being of others. Beneficence is not the whole of morality, but to most people it is at least close to its heart.

SUMMARY

Ethical egoism is the theory that the right action is the one that advances one's own best interests. It promotes self-interested behavior but not necessarily selfish acts. The ethical egoist may define his self-interest in various ways—as pleasure, self-actualization, power, happiness, or other goods. The most important argument for ethical egoism relies on the theory known as psychological egoism, the view that the motive for all our actions is self-interest. Psychological egoism, however, seems to ignore the fact that people sometimes do things that are not in their best interests. It also seems to misconstrue the relationship between our actions and the satisfaction that often follows from them. We seem to desire something other than satisfaction and then experience satisfaction as a result of getting what we desire.

Utilitarianism is the view that the morally right action is the one that produces the most favorable balance of good over evil, everyone considered. Act-utilitarianism says that right actions are those that directly produce the greatest overall happiness, everyone considered. Rule-utilitarianism says that the morally right action is the one covered by a rule that if generally followed would produce the most favorable balance of good over evil, everyone considered.

Critics argue that act-utilitarianism is not consistent with our considered judgments about justice. In many possible scenarios, the action that maximizes utility in a situation also seems blatantly unjust. Likewise, the theory seems to collide with our notions of rights and obligations. Again, it seems relatively easy to imagine scenarios in which utility is maximized while rights or obligations are shortchanged. An act-utilitarian might respond to these points by saying that such examples are unrealistic—that in real life, actions thought to be immoral almost never maximize happiness.

Rule-utilitarianism has been accused of being internally inconsistent—of easily collapsing into act-utilitarianism. The charge is that the rules that maximize happiness best are specific to particular cases, but such rules would sanction the same actions that act-utilitarianism does.

Regardless of criticisms lodged against it, utilitarianism offers important insights about the nature of morality: The consequences of our actions surely do matter in our moral deliberations and in our lives. The principle of impartiality is an essential part of moral decision making. And any plausible moral theory must somehow take into account the principle of beneficence.

EXERCISES

Review Questions

1. What is ethical egoism? What is the difference between act- and rule-egoism? (p. 76)
2. What is psychological egoism? (p. 78)
3. What is the psychological egoist argument for ethical egoism? (p. 79)
4. Is psychological egoism true? Why or why not? (pp. 79–80)

5. In what way is ethical egoism not consistent with our considered moral judgments? (p. 81)
6. What is the principle of utility? (p. 83)
7. What is the main difference between the ways that Mill and Bentham conceive of happiness? Which view seems more plausible? (pp. 84–85)
8. What is the difference between act- and rule-utilitarianism? (p. 85)
9. How do act- and rule-utilitarians differ in their views on rules? (p. 85)
10. Is act-utilitarianism consistent with our considered moral judgments regarding justice? Why or why not? (pp. 88–89)

Discussion Questions

1. Is psychological egoism based on a conceptual confusion? Why or why not?
2. Why do critics regard ethical egoism as an inadequate moral theory? Are the critics right? Why or why not?
3. How would your life change if you became a consistent act-utilitarianism?
4. How would your life change if you became a consistent rule-utilitarianism?

5. To what was Mill referring when he said, "It is better to be a human being dissatisfied than a pig satisfied"? Do you agree with this statement? Why or why not?
6. If you were on trial for your life (because of an alleged murder), would you want the judge to be an act-utilitarian, a rule-utilitarian, or neither? Why?
7. If you were the surgeon in the example about the five transplants, what would you do? Why?
8. Does act-utilitarianism conflict with commonsense judgments about rights? Why or why not?
9. Is there such a thing as a supererogatory act— or are all right actions simply our duty? What would an act-utilitarian say about supererogatory acts?
10. Suppose you had to decide which one of a dozen dying patients should receive a lifesaving drug, knowing that there was only enough of the medicine for one person. Would you feel comfortable making the decision as an act-utilitarian would? Why or why not?

READING

From *Utilitarianism*

JOHN STUART MILL

CHAPTER II.
WHAT UTILITARIANISM IS

* * *

The creed which accepts, as the foundation of morals, Utility, or the Greatest Happiness Principle, holds that actions are right in proportion as they tend to promote happiness, wrong as they tend to produce the reverse of happiness. By happiness is intended pleasure, and the absence of pain; by unhappiness, pain, and the privation of pleasure. To give a clear view of the moral standard set up by the theory, much more requires to be said; in particular, what things it includes in the ideas of pain and pleasure; and to what extent this is left an open question. But these supplementary explanations do not affect the theory of life on which this theory of morality is grounded—namely, that pleasure, and freedom from pain, are the only things desirable as ends; and that

John Stuart Mill, *Utilitarianism*, Chapter II (edited).

all desirable things (which are as numerous in the utilitarian as in any other scheme) are desirable either for the pleasure inherent in themselves, or as means to the promotion of pleasure and the prevention of pain.

Now, such a theory of life excites in many minds, and among them in some of the most estimable in feeling and purpose, inveterate dislike. To suppose that life has (as they express it) no higher end than pleasure—no better and nobler object of desire and pursuit—they designate as utterly mean and grovelling; as a doctrine worthy only of swine, to whom the followers of Epicurus were, at a very early period, contemptuously likened; and modern holders of the doctrine are occasionally made the subject of equally polite comparisons by its German, French, and English assailants.

When thus attacked, the Epicureans have always answered, that it is not they, but their accusers, who represent human nature in a degrading light; since the accusation supposes human beings to be capable of no pleasures except those of which swine are capable. If this supposition were true, the charge could not be gainsaid, but would then be no longer an imputation; for if the sources of pleasure were precisely the same to human beings and to swine, the rule of life which is good enough for the one would be good enough for the other. The comparison of the Epicurean life to that of beasts is felt as degrading, precisely because a beast's pleasures do not satisfy a human being's conceptions of happiness. Human beings have faculties more elevated than the animal appetites, and when once made conscious of them, do not regard anything as happiness which does not include their gratification. I do not, indeed, consider the Epicureans to have been by any means faultless in drawing out their scheme of consequences from the utilitarian principle. To do this in any sufficient manner, many Stoic, as well as Christian elements require to be included. But there is no known Epicurean theory of life which does not assign to the pleasures of the intellect, of the feelings and imagination, and of the moral sentiments, a much higher value as pleasures than to those of mere sensation. It must be admitted, however, that utilitarian writers in

general have placed the superiority of mental over bodily pleasures chiefly in the greater permanency, safety, uncostliness, &c., of the former—that is, in their circumstantial advantages rather than in their intrinsic nature. And on all these points utilitarians have fully proved their case; but they might have taken the other, and, as it may be called, higher ground, with entire consistency. It is quite compatible with the principle of utility to recognise the fact, that some *kinds* of pleasure are more desirable and more valuable than others. It would be absurd that while, in estimating all other things, quality is considered as well as quantity, the estimation of pleasures should be supposed to depend on quantity alone.

If I am asked, what I mean by difference of quality in pleasures, or what makes one pleasure more valuable than another, merely as a pleasure, except its being greater in amount, there is but one possible answer. Of two pleasures, if there be one to which all or almost all who have experience of both give a decided preference, irrespective of any feeling of moral obligation to prefer it, that is the more desirable pleasure. If one of the two is, by those who are competently acquainted with both, placed so far above the other that they prefer it, even though knowing it to be attended with a greater amount of discontent, and would not resign it for any quantity of the other pleasure which their nature is capable of, we are justified in ascribing to the preferred enjoyment a superiority in quality, so far outweighing quantity as to render it, in comparison, of small account.

Now it is an unquestionable fact that those who are equally acquainted with, and equally capable of appreciating and enjoying, both, do give a most marked preference to the manner of existence which employs their higher faculties. Few human creatures would consent to be changed into any of the lower animals, for a promise of the fullest allowance of a beast's pleasures; no intelligent human being would consent to be a fool, no instructed person would be an ignoramus, no person of feeling and conscience would be selfish and base, even though they should be persuaded that the fool, the dunce, or the rascal is better satisfied with his lot than they are with theirs. They would not resign what they possess more than he, for the most complete satisfaction of all the desires which they have in common with him. If they ever fancy they would, it is only in cases of unhappiness so extreme, that to escape from it they would exchange their lot for almost any other, however, undesirable in their own eyes. A being of higher faculties requires more to make him happy, is capable probably of more acute suffering, and is certainly accessible to it at more points, than one of an inferior type; but in spite of these liabilities, he can never really wish to sink into what he feels to be a lower grade of existence. We may give what explanation we please of this unwillingness; we may attribute it to pride, a name which is given indiscriminately to some of the most and to some of the least estimable feelings of which mankind are capable; we may refer it to the love of liberty and personal independence, an appeal to which was with the Stoics one of the most effective means for the inculcation of it; to the love of power, or the love of excitement, both of which do really enter into and contribute to it: but its most appropriate appellation is a sense of dignity, which all human beings possess in one form or other, and in some, though by no means in exact, proportion to their higher faculties, and which is so essential a part of the happiness of those in whom it is strong, that nothing which conflicts with it could be, otherwise than momentarily, an object of desire to them. Whoever supposes that this preference takes place at a sacrifice of happiness—that the superior being, in anything like equal circumstances, is not happier than the inferior—confounds the two very different ideas, of happiness, and content. It is indisputable that the being whose capacities of enjoyment are low, has the greatest chance of having them fully satisfied; and a highly-endowed being will always feel that any happiness which he can look for, as the world is constitute, is imperfect. But he can learn to bear its imperfections, if they are at all bearable; and they will not make him envy the being who is indeed unconscious of the imperfections, but only because he feels not at all the good which those imperfections qualify. It is better to be a human being dissatisfied than a pig satisfied; better to be Socrates dissatisfied than a fool satisfied. And if the fool, or the pig, is of a different opinion, it is because they only know their own side of the question. The other party to the comparison knows both sides.

It may be objected, that many who are capable of the higher pleasures, occasionally, under the influence of temptation, postpone them to the lower. But this is quite compatible with a full appreciation of the intrinsic superiority of the higher. Men often, from infirmity of character, make their election for the nearer good, though they know it to be the less valuable; and this no less when the choice is between two bodily pleasures, than when it is between bodily and mental. They pursue sensual indulgences to the injury of health, though perfectly aware that health is the greater good. It may be further objected, that many who begin with youthful enthusiasm for everything noble, as they advance in years sink into indolence and selfishness. But I do not believe that those who undergo this very common change, voluntarily choose the lower description of pleasures in preference to the higher. I believe that before they devote themselves exclusively to the one, they have already become incapable of the other. Capacity for the nobler feelings is in most natures a very tender plant, easily killed, not only by hostile influences, but by mere want of sustenance; and in the majority of young persons it speedily dies away if the occupations to which their position in life has devoted them, and the society into which it has thrown them, are not favourable to keeping that higher capacity in exercise. Men lose their high aspirations as they lose their intellectual tastes, because they have not time or opportunity for indulging them; and they addict themselves to inferior pleasures, not because they deliberately prefer them, but because they are either the only ones to which they have access, or the only ones which they are any longer capable of enjoying. It may be questioned whether any one who has remained equally susceptible to both classes of pleasures, ever knowingly and calmly preferred the lower; though many, in all ages, have broken down in an ineffectual attempt to combine both.

From this verdict of the only competent judges, I apprehend there can be no appeal. On a question which is the best worth having of two pleasures, or which of two modes of existence is the most grateful to the feelings, apart from its moral attributes and from its consequences, the judgment of those who are qualified by knowledge of both, or, if they differ, that of the majority among them, must be admitted as final. And there needs be the less hesitation to accept this judgment respecting the quality of pleasures, since there is no other tribunal to be referred to even on the question of quantity. What means are there of determining which is the acutest of two pairs, or the intensest of two pleasurable sensations, except the general suffrage of those who are familiar with both? Neither pains nor pleasures are homogeneous, and pain is always heterogeneous with pleasure. What is there to decide whether a particular pleasure is worth purchasing at the cost of a particular pain, except the feelings and judgment of the experienced? When, therefore, those feelings and judgment declare the pleasures derived from the higher faculties to be preferable *in kind*, apart from the question of intensity, to those of which the animal nature, disjoined from the higher faculties, is susceptible, they are entitled on this subject to the same regard.

I have dwelt on this point, as being a necessary part of a perfectly just conception of Utility or Happiness, considered as the directive rule of human conduct. But it is by no means an indispensable condition to the acceptance of the utilitarian standard; for that standard is not the agent's own greatest happiness, but the greatest amount of happiness altogether; and if it may possible be doubted whether a noble character is always the happier for its nobleness, there can be no doubt that it makes other people happier, and that the world in general is immensely a gainer by it. Utilitarianism, therefore, could only attain its end by the general cultivation of nobleness of character, even if each individual were only benefited by the nobleness of others, and his own, so far as happiness is concerned, were a sheer deduction from the benefit. But the bare enunciation of such an absurdity as this last, renders refutation superfluous.

According to the Greatest Happiness Principle, as above explained, the ultimate end, with reference to and for the sake of which all other things are desirable (whether we are considering our own good or that of other people), is an existence exempt as far as possible from pain, and as rich as possible in enjoyments, both in point of quantity and quality; the test of quality, and the rule for measuring it against quantity, being the preference felt by those who, in their opportunities of experience, to which must be added their habits of self-consciousness and self-observation, are best furnished with the means of comparison. This being, according to the utilitarian opinion, the end of human action, is necessarily also the standard of morality; which may accordingly be defined, the rules and precepts for human conduct, by the observance of which an existence such as has been described might be, to the greatest extent possible, secured to all mankind; and not to them only, but, so far as the nature of things admits, to the whole sentient creation.

* * *

I must again repeat, what the assailants of utilitarianism seldom have the justice to acknowledge, that the happiness which forms the utilitarian standard of what is right in conduct, is not the agent's own happiness, but that of all concerned. As between his own happiness and that of others, utilitarianism requires him to be as strictly impartial as a disinterested and benevolent spectator. In the golden rule of Jesus of Nazareth, we read the complete spirit of the ethics of utility. To do as one would be done by, and to love one's neighbour as oneself, constitute the ideal perfection of utilitarian morality. As the means of making the nearest approach to this ideal, utility would enjoin, first, that laws and social arrangements should place the happiness, or (as speaking practically it may be called) the interest, of every individual, as nearly as possible in harmony with the interest of the whole; and secondly, that education and opinion, which have so vast a power over human character, should so use that power as to establish in the mind of every individual an indissoluble association between his own happiness and the good of the whole; especially between his own happiness and the practice of such modes of conduct, negative and positive, as regard for the universal happiness prescribes: so that not only he may be unable to conceive the possibility of happiness to himself, consistently with conduct opposed to the general good, but also that a direct impulse to promote the general good may be in every individual one of the habitual motives of action, and the sentiments connected therewith may fill a large and prominent place in every human being's sentient existence. If the impugners of the utilitarian morality represented it to their own minds in this its true character, I know not what recommendation possessed by any other morality they could possibly affirm to be wanting to it: what more beautiful or more exalted developments of human nature any other ethical system can be supposed to foster, or what springs of action, not accessible to the utilitarian, such systems rely on for giving effect to their mandates.

* * *

It may not be superfluous to notice a few more of the common misapprehensions of utilitarian ethics, even those which are so obvious and gross that it might appear impossible for any person of candour and intelligence to fall into them: since persons, even of considerable mental endowments, often give themselves so little trouble to understand the bearings of any opinion against which they entertain a prejudice, and men are in general so little conscious of this voluntary ignorance as a defect, that the vulgarest misunderstandings of ethical doctrines are continually met with in the deliberate writings of persons of the greatest pretensions both to high principle and to philosophy. We not uncommonly hear the doctrine of utility inveighed against as a *godless* doctrine. If it be necessary to say anything at all against so mere an assumption, we may say that the question depends upon what idea we have formed of the moral character of the Deity. If it be a true belief that God desires, above all things, the happiness of his creatures, and that this was his purpose in their creation, utility is not only not a godless doctrine, but more profoundly religious than any other. If it be meant that utilitarianism does not recognise the revealed will of God as the supreme law of morals, I answer,

that an utilitarian who believes in the perfect goodness and wisdom of God, necessarily believes that whatever God has thought fit to reveal on the subject of morals, must fulfil the requirements of utility in a supreme degree. But others besides utilitarians have been of opinion that the Christian revelation was intended, and is fitted, to inform the hearts and minds of mankind with a spirit which should enable them to find for themselves what is right, and incline them to do it when found, rather than to tell them, except in a very general way, what it is: and that we need a doctrine of ethics, carefully followed out, to *interpret* to us the will of God. Whether this opinion is correct or not, it is superfluous here to discuss; since whatever aid religion, either natural or revealed, can afford to ethical investigation, is as open to the utilitarian moralist as to any other. He can use it as the testimony of God to the usefulness or hurtfulness of any given course of action, by as good a right as others can use it for the indication of a transcendental law, having no connexion with usefulness or with happiness.

Again, Utility is often summarily stigmatized as an immoral doctrine by giving it the name of Expediency, and taking advantage of the popular use of that term to contrast it with Principle. But the Expedient, in the sense in which it is opposed to the Right, generally means that which is expedient for the particular interest of the agent himself: as when a minister sacrifices the interest of his country to keep himself in place. When it means anything better than this, it means that which is expedient for some immediate object, some temporary purpose, but which violates a rule whose observance is expedient in a much higher degree. The Expedient, in this sense, instead of being the same thing with the useful, is a branch of the hurtful. Thus, it would often be expedient, for the purpose of getting over some momentary embarrassment, or attaining some object immediately useful to ourselves or others, to tell a lie. But inasmuch as the cultivation in ourselves of a sensitive feeling on the subject of veracity, is one of the most useful, and the enfeeblement of that feeling one of the most hurtful, things to which our conduct can be instrumental; and inasmuch as any, even unintentional, deviation from truth, does that much towards weakening the trustworthiness of human assertion, which is not only the principal support of all present social well-being, but the insufficiency of which does more than any one thing that can be named to keep back civilisation, virtue, everything on which human happiness on the largest scale depends; we feel that the violation, for a present advantage, of a rule of such transcendent expediency, is not expedient, and that he who, for the sake of a convenience to himself or to some other individual, does what depends on him to deprive mankind of the good, and inflict upon them the evil, involved in the greater or less reliance which they can place in each other's word, acts the part of one of their worst enemies. Yet that even this rule, sacred as it is, admits of possible exceptions, is acknowl-

edged by all moralists; the chief of which is when the withholding of some fact (as of information from a malefactor, or of bad news from a person dangerously ill) would preserve some one (especially a person other than oneself) from great and unmerited evil, and when the withholding can only be effected by denial. But in order that the exception may not extend itself beyond the need, and may have the least possible effect in weakening reliance on veracity, it ought to be recognized, and, if possible, its limits defined; and if the principle of utility is good for anything, it must be good for weighing these conflicting utilities against one another, and marking out the region within which one or the other preponderates.

* * *

CHAPTER 6

Nonconsequentialist Theories: Do Your Duty

For the consequentialist, the rightness of an action depends entirely on the effects of that action (or of following the rule that governs it). Good effects make the deed right; bad effects make the deed wrong. But for the nonconsequentialist (otherwise known as a "deontologist"), the rightness of an action can never be measured by such a variable, contingent standard as the quantity of goodness brought into the world. Rightness derives not from the consequences of an action but from its nature, its right-making characteristics. An action is right (or wrong) not because of what it produces but because of what it *is*. Yet for all their differences, both consequentialist and deontological theories contain elements that seem to go to the heart of morality and our moral experience. So in this chapter, we look at ethics through a deontological lens and explore the two deontological theories that historically have offered the strongest challenges to consequentialist views: Kant's moral system and natural law theory.

KANT'S ETHICS

The German philosopher Immanuel Kant (1724–1804) is considered one of the greatest moral philosophers of the modern era. Many scholars would go further and say that he is *the* greatest moral philosopher of the modern era. As a distinguished thinker of the Enlightenment, he sought to make reason the foundation of morality. For him, reason alone leads us to the right and the good. Therefore, to discover the true path we need not appeal to utility, religion, tradition, authority,

happiness, desires, or intuition. We need only heed the dictates of reason, for reason informs us of the moral law just as surely as it reveals the truths of mathematics. Because of each person's capacity for reason, he or she is a sovereign in the moral realm, a supreme judge of what morality demands. What morality demands (in other words, our duty) is enshrined in the moral law—the changeless, necessary, universal body of moral rules.

In Kant's ethics, right actions have moral value only if they are done with a "good will"—that is, a will to do your duty for duty's sake. To act with a good will is to act with a desire to do your duty *simply because it is your duty,* to act out of pure reverence for the moral law. Without a good will, your actions have no moral worth—even if they accord with the moral law, even if they are done out of sympathy or love, even if they produce good results. Only a good will is unconditionally good, and only an accompanying good will can give your talents, virtues, and actions moral worth. As Kant explains,

Nothing can possibly be conceived in the world, or even out of it, which can be called good without qualification, except a *good will*. Intelligence, wit, judgement, and the other *talents* of the mind, however they may be named, or courage, resolution, perseverance, as qualities of temperament, are undoubtedly good and desirable in many respects; but these gifts of nature may also become extremely bad and mischievous if the will which is to make use of them, and which, therefore, constitutes what is called *char-*

acter, is not good. It is the same with the *gifts of fortune.* Power, riches, honour, even health, and the general well-being and contentment with one's condition which is called *happiness,* inspire pride, and often presumption, if there is not a good will to correct the influence of these on the mind. . . . A good will is good not because of what it performs or effects, not by its aptness for the attainment of some proposed end, but simply by virtue of the volition—that is, it is good in itself, and considered by itself is to be esteemed much higher than all that can be brought about by it in favour of any inclination, nay, even of the sum-total of all inclinations.[1]

So to do right, we must do it for duty's sake, motivated solely by respect for the moral law. But how do we know what the moral law is? Kant sees the moral law as a set of principles, or rules, stated in the form of imperatives, or commands. Imperatives can be *hypothetical* or *categorical.* A **hypothetical imperative** tells us what we should do if we have certain desires: for example, "If you need money, work for it" or "If you want orange juice, ask for it." We should obey such imperatives only if we desire the outcomes specified. A **categorical imperative,** however, is not so iffy. It tells us that we should do something in all situations *regardless of our wants and needs.* A moral categorical imperative expresses a command like "Do not steal" or "Do not commit suicide." Such imperatives are universal and unconditional, containing no stipulations contingent on human desires or preferences. Kant says that the moral law consists entirely of categorical imperatives. They are the authoritative expression of our moral duties. Because they are the products of rational insight and we are rational agents, we can straightforwardly access, understand, and know them as the great truths that they are.

[1]Immanuel Kant, *Fundamental Principles of the Metaphysic of Morals,* trans. Thomas K. Abbott, 2nd ed. (London: Longmans, Green, 1879), 1–2.

Kant says that all our duties, all the moral categorical imperatives, can be logically derived from a principle that he calls *the* categorical imperative. It tells us to "Act only on that maxim through which you can at the same time will that it should become a universal law."[2] (Kant actually devised three statements, or versions, of the principle, the one given here and two others; in the next few pages we will examine only the two most important ones.) Kant believes that every action implies a general rule, or maxim. If you steal a car, then your action implies a maxim such as "In this situation, steal a car if you want one." So the first version of the categorical imperative says that an action is right if you can will that the maxim of an action become a moral law applying to all persons. That is, an action is permissible if (1) its maxim can be universalized (if everyone can consistently act on the maxim in similar situations) and (2) you would be willing to let that happen. If you can so will the maxim, then the action is right (permissible). If you cannot, the action is wrong (prohibited). Right actions pass the test of the categorical imperative; wrong actions do not.

Some of the duties derived from the categorical imperative are, in Kant's words, perfect duties and some, imperfect duties. **Perfect duties** are those that absolutely must be followed without fail; they have no exceptions. Some perfect duties cited by Kant include duties not to break a promise, not to lie, and not to commit suicide. **Imperfect duties** are not always to be followed; they do have exceptions. As examples of imperfect duties, Kant mentions duties to develop your talents and to help others in need.

Kant demonstrates how to apply the first version of the categorical imperative to several cases, the most famous of which involves a lying promise. Imagine that you want to borrow money from someone, and you know you will not be able to

[2]Kant, *Fundamental Principles of the Metaphysic of Morals,* 52.

CRITICAL THOUGHT: Sizing Up the Golden Rule

The Golden Rule—"Do unto others as you would have them do unto you"—has some resemblance to Kant's ethics and has been, in one form or another, implicit in many religious traditions and moral systems. Moral philosophers generally think that it touches on a significant truth about morality. But some have argued that taken by itself, without the aid of any other moral principles or theory, the Golden Rule can lead to implausible conclusions and absurd results. Here is part of a famous critique by Richard Whately (1787–1863):

> Supposing any one should regard this golden rule as designed to answer the purpose of a complete system of morality, and to teach us the difference of right and wrong; then, if he had let his land to a farmer, he might consider that the farmer would be glad to be excused paying any rent for it, since he would himself, if he were the farmer, prefer having the land rent-free; and that, therefore, the rule of doing as he would be done by requires him to give up all his property. So also the shopkeeper

might, on the same principle, think that the rule required him to part with his goods under prime cost, or to give them away, and thus to ruin himself. Now such a procedure would be *absurd*. . . .

You have seen, then, that the golden rule was far from being designed to impart to men the first notions of justice. On the contrary, it *presupposes* that knowledge; and if we had *no* such notions, we could not properly apply the rule. But the real design of it is to put us on our guard against the danger of being blinded by self-interest.*

How does the Golden Rule resemble Kant's theory? How does it differ? Do you agree with Whately's criticism? Why or why not? How could the Golden Rule be qualified or supplemented to blunt Whately's critique? John Stuart Mill said that the Golden Rule was the essence of utilitarianism. What do you think he meant by this?

*Richard Whately, quoted in Louis P. Pojman and Lewis Vaughn, *The Moral Life* (New York: Oxford University Press, 2007), 353–54.

repay the debt. You also know that you will get the loan if you falsely promise to pay the money back. Is such deceptive borrowing morally permissible? To find out, you have to devise a maxim for the action and ask whether you could consistently will it to become a universal law. Could you consistently will everyone to act on the maxim "If you need money, make a lying promise to borrow some"? Kant's emphatic answer is no. If all persons adopted this rule, then they would make lying promises to obtain loans. But then everyone would know that such promises are false, and the practice of giving loans based on a promise would no longer exist, because no promises could be trusted. The maxim says that everyone should make a false promise in order to borrow money, but then no one would loan money based on a promise. If acted

on by everyone, the maxim would defeat itself. As Kant says, the "maxim would necessarily destroy itself as soon as it was made a universal law."[3] Therefore, you cannot consistently will the maxim to become a universal law. The action, then, is not morally permissible.

Kant believes that besides the rule forbidding the breaking of promises, the categorical imperative generates several other duties. Among these he includes prohibitions against committing suicide, lying, and killing innocent people.

Some universalized maxims may fail the test of the categorical imperative (first version) not by being self-defeating (as in the case of a lying prom-

[3] Kant, *Fundamental Principles of the Metaphysic of Morals*, 55.

ise) but by constituting rules that you would not want everyone else to act on. (Remember that an action is permissible if everyone can consistently act on it in similar situations *and* you would be willing to let that happen.) Kant asks us to consider a maxim that mandates *not* contributing anything to the welfare of others or aiding them when they are in distress. If you willed this maxim to become a universal moral law (if everyone followed it), no self-defeating state of affairs would obtain. Everyone could conceivably follow this rule. But you probably would not want people to act on this maxim because one day *you* may need *their* help and sympathy. Right now you may will the maxim to become universal law, but later, when the tables are turned, you may regret that policy. The inconsistency lies in wanting the rule to be universalized and not wanting it to be universalized. Kant says that this alternative kind of inconsistency shows that the action embodied in the maxim is not permissible.

Kant's second version of the categorical imperative is probably more famous and influential than the first. (Kant thought the two versions virtually synonymous, but they seem to be distinct principles.) He declares, "So act as to treat humanity, whether in thine own person or in that of any other, in every case as an end withal, never as means only."[4] This rule—the **means-end principle**—says that we must always treat people (including ourselves) as ends in themselves, as creatures of great intrinsic worth, never merely as things of instrumental value, never merely as tools to be used for someone else's purpose.

This statement of the categorical imperative reflects Kant's view of the status of rational beings, or persons. Persons have intrinsic value and dignity because they, unlike the rest of creation, are rational agents who are free to choose their own ends, legislate their own moral laws, and assign

value to things in the world. Persons are the givers of value, so they must have ultimate value. They therefore must always be treated as ultimate ends and never merely as means.

Kant's idea is that people not only have intrinsic worth—they also have *equal* intrinsic worth. Each rational being has the same inherent value as every other rational being. This equality of value cannot be altered by, and has no connection to, social and economic status, racial and ethnic considerations, or the possession of prestige or power. Any two persons are entitled to the same moral rights, even if one is rich, wise, powerful, and famous—and the other is not.

To treat people merely as a means rather than as an end is to fail to recognize the true nature and status of persons. Since people are by nature free, rational, autonomous, and equal, we treat them merely as a means if we do not respect these attributes—if we, for example, interfere with people's right to make informed choices by lying to them, inhibit their free and autonomous actions by enslaving or coercing them, or violate their equality by discriminating against them. For Kant, lying or breaking a promise is wrong because to do so is to use people merely as a means to an end, rather than as an end in themselves.

Sometimes we use people to achieve some end, yet our actions are not wrong. To see why, we must understand that there is a moral difference between treating persons as a means and treating them *merely*, or *only*, as a means. We may treat a mechanic as a means to repair our cars, but we do not treat him merely as a means if we also respect his status as a person. We do not treat him only as means if we neither restrict his freedom nor ignore his rights.

As noted earlier, Kant insists that the two versions of the categorical imperative are two ways of stating the same idea. But the two principles seem to be distinct, occasionally leading to different conclusions about the rightness of an action. The maxim of an action, for example, may pass the

[4]Kant, *Fundamental Principles of the Metaphysic of Morals*, 66–67.

first version (be permissible) by being universalizable but fail the second by not treating persons as ends. A more plausible approach is to view the two versions not as alternative tests but as a single two-part test that an action must pass to be judged morally permissible. So before we can declare a maxim a bona fide categorical imperative, we must be able to consistently will it to become a universal law *and* know that it would have us treat persons not only as a means but as ends.

Applying the Theory

How might a Kantian decide the case of the antiterrorist chief of police, discussed in Chapter 5, who considers killing a terrorist's wife and children? Recall that the terrorist is murdering hundreds of innocent people each year and that the chief has good reasons to believe that killing the wife and children (who are also innocent) will end the terrorist's attacks. Recall also the verdict on this case rendered from both the act- and rule-utilitarian perspectives. By act-utilitarian lights, the chief should kill some of the terrorist's innocent relatives (and threaten to kill others). The rule-utilitarian view, however, is that the chief should *not* kill them.

Suppose the maxim in question is "When the usual antiterrorist tactics fail to stop terrorists from killing many innocent people, the authorities should kill (and threaten to kill) the terrorists' relatives." Can we consistently will this maxim to become a universal law? Does this maxim involve treating persons merely as a means to an end rather than an end in themselves? To answer the first question, we should try to imagine what would happen if everyone in the position of the relevant authorities followed this maxim. Would any inconsistencies or self-defeating states of affairs arise? We can see that the consequences of universalizing the maxim would not be pleasant. The authorities would kill the innocent—actions that could be as gruesome and frightening as terrorist attacks. But our willing that everyone act on the

maxim would not be self-defeating or otherwise contradictory. Would we nevertheless be willing to live in a world where the maxim was universally followed? Again, there seems to be no good reason why we could not. The maxim therefore passes the first test of the categorical imperative.

To answer the second (ends-means) question, we must inquire whether following the maxim would involve treating someone merely as a means. The obvious answer is yes. This antiterrorism policy would use the innocent relatives of terrorists as a means to stop terrorist acts. Their freedom and their rights as persons would be violated. The maxim therefore fails the second test, and the acts sanctioned by the maxim would not be permissible. From the Kantian perspective, using the innocent relatives would be wrong no matter what—regardless of how many lives the policy would save or how much safer the world would be. So in this case, the Kantian verdict would coincide with that of rule-utilitarianism but not that of act-utilitarianism.

Evaluating the Theory

Kant's moral theory meets the minimum requirement of coherence and is generally consistent with our moral experience (Criterion 2). In some troubling ways, however, it seems to conflict with our commonsense moral judgments (Criterion 1) and appears to have some flaws that restrict its usefulness in moral problem solving (Criterion 3).

As we saw earlier, some duties generated by the categorical imperative are absolute—they are, as Kant says, perfect duties, allowing no exceptions whatsoever. We have, for example, a perfect (exceptionless) duty not to lie—ever. But what should we do if lying is the only way to prevent a terrible tragedy? Suppose a friend of yours comes to your house in a panic and begs you to hide her from an insane man intent on murdering her. No sooner do you hide her in the cellar than the insane man appears at your door with a bloody knife in his hand and asks where your friend is.

The Kantian View of Punishment

Kant's philosophical position on punishment is radically different from that of the utilitarians. Generally, they think that criminals should not be punished for purposes of justice or retribution. Criminals should be corrected or schooled so they do not commit more crimes, or they should be imprisoned only to protect the public. To them, the point of "punishment" is to promote the good of society. Kant thinks that criminals should be punished *only* because they perpetrated crimes; the public good is irrelevant. In addition, Kant thinks that the central principle of punishment is that the punishment should fit the crime. For Kant, this principle constitutes a solid justification for capital punishment: killers should be killed. As Kant explains,

Even if a civil society resolved to dissolve itself with the consent of all its members—as might be supposed in the case of a people inhabiting an island resolving to separate and scatter throughout the whole world—that last murderer lying in prison ought to be executed before the resolution was carried out. This ought to be done in order that every one may realize the desert of his deeds, and that blood-guiltiness may not remain on the people; for otherwise they will all be regarded as participants in the murder as a public violation of justice.*

*Immanuel Kant, *The Philosophy of Law,* trans. W. Hostie (Edinburgh: Clark, 1887), 198.

You have no doubt that the man is serious and that your friend will in fact be brutally murdered if the man finds her. Imagine that you have only two choices (and saying "I don't know" is not one of them): either you lie to the man and thereby save your friend's life, or you tell the man where she is hiding and guarantee her murder. Kant actually considers such a case and renders this verdict on it: you should tell the truth though the heavens fall. He says, as he must, that the consequences of your action here are irrelevant, and not lying is a perfect duty. There can be no exceptions. Yet Kant's answer seems contrary to our considered moral judgments. Moral common sense seems to suggest that in a case like this, saving a life would be much more important than telling the truth.

Another classic example involves promise keeping, which is also a perfect duty. Suppose you promise to meet a friend for lunch, and on your way to the restaurant you are called upon to help someone injured in car crash. No one else can help her, and she will die unless you render aid. But if you help her, you will break your promise to meet your

friend. What should you do? Kant would say that come what may, your duty is to keep your promise to meet your friend. Under these circumstances, however, keeping the promise just seems wrong.

These scenarios are significant because, contrary to Kant's view, we seem to have no absolute, or exceptionless, moral duties. We can easily imagine many cases like those just mentioned. Moreover, we can also envision situations in which we must choose between two allegedly perfect duties, each one prohibiting some action. We cannot fulfill both duties at once, and we must make a choice. Such conflicts provide plausible evidence against the notion that there are exceptionless moral rules.[5]

Conflicts of duties, of course, are not just deficiencies regarding Criterion 1. They also indicate difficulties with Criterion 3. Like many moral theories, Kant's system fails to provide an effective means for resolving major conflicts of duties.

[5]I owe this point to James Rachels, *The Elements of Moral Philosophy,* 4th ed. (Boston: McGraw-Hill, 2003), 126.

Some additional inconsistencies with our common moral judgments seem to arise from applications of the first version of the categorical imperative. Remember that the first version says that an action is permissible if everyone can consistently act on it and if you would be willing to have that happen. At first glance, it seems to guarantee that moral rules are universally fair. But it makes the acceptability of a moral rule depend largely on whether *you personally* are willing to live in a world that conforms to the rule. If you are not willing to live in such a world, then the rule fails the first version of the categorical imperative, and your conforming to the rule is wrong. But if you are the sort of person who would prefer such a world, then conforming to the rule would be morally permissible. This subjectivity in Kant's theory could lead to the sanctioning of heinous acts of all kinds. Suppose the rule is "Kill everyone with dark skin" or "Murder all Jews." Neither rule would be contradictory if universalized; everyone could consistently act on it. Moreover, if you were willing to have everyone act on it—even willing to be killed if *you* have dark skin or are a Jew—then acts endorsed by the rule would be permissible. Thus the first version seems to bless acts that are clearly immoral.

Critics say that another difficulty with Kant's theory concerns the phrasing of the maxims to be universalized. Oddly enough, Kant does not provide any guidance for how we should state a rule describing an action, an oversight that allows us to word a rule in many different ways. Consider, for example, our duty not to lie. We might state the relevant rule like this: "Lie only to avoid injury or death to others." But we could also say "Lie only to avoid injury, death, or embarrassment to anyone who has green eyes and red hair (a group that includes you and your relatives)." Neither rule would lead to an inconsistency if everyone acted on it, so they both describe permissible actions. The second rule, though, is obviously not morally acceptable. More to the point, it shows that we could use the first version of the categorical imperative to sanction all sorts of immoral acts if we state the rule *in enough detail*. This result suggests not only a problem with Criterion 1 but also a limitation on the usefulness of the theory, a fault measured by Criterion 3. Judging the rightness of an action is close to impossible if the language of the relevant rule can change with the wind.

It may be feasible to remedy some of the shortcomings of the first version of the categorical imperative by combining it with the second. Rules such as "Kill everyone with dark skin" or "Lie only to avoid injury, death, or embarrassment to anyone who has green eyes and red hair" would be unacceptable because they would allow people to be treated merely as a means. But the means-ends principle itself appears to be in need of modification. The main difficulty is that our duties not to use people merely as a means can conflict, and Kant provides no counsel on how to resolve such dilemmas. Say, for example, that hundreds of innocent people are enslaved inside a brutal Nazi concentration camp, and the only way we can free them is to kill the Nazis guarding the camp. We must therefore choose between allowing the prisoners to be used merely as a means by the Nazis or using the Nazis merely as a means by killing them to free the prisoners.

Here is another example, a classic case from the philosopher C. D. Broad:

Again, there seem to be cases in which you must either treat A or treat B, not as an end, but as a means. If we isolate a man who is a carrier of typhoid, we are treating him merely as a cause of infection to others. But, if we refuse to isolate him, we are treating other people merely as means to his comfort and culture.[6]

Kant's means-ends principle captures an important truth about the intrinsic value of persons. But we apparently cannot fully implement it, because

[6]C. D. Broad, *Five Types of Ethical Theory* (1930; reprint, London: Routledge & Kegan Paul, 1956), 132.

sometimes we are forced to treat people merely as a means and not as an end in themselves.

LEARNING FROM KANT'S THEORY

Despite these criticisms, Kant's theory has been influential because it embodies a large part of the whole truth about morality. At a minimum, it promotes many of the duties and rights that our considered judgments lead us to embrace. More importantly, it emphasizes three of morality's most important features: (1) universality, (2) impartiality, and (3) respect for persons. Kant's first version of the categorical imperative rests firmly on universality—the notion that the moral law applies to all persons in relevantly similar situations. Impartiality requires that the moral law apply to everyone in the same way, that no one can claim a privileged moral status. In Kantian ethics, double standards are inherently bad. Ethical egoism fails as a moral theory in large part because it lacks this kind of impartiality. The first version of the categorical imperative, in contrast, enshrines impartiality as essential to the moral life. Kant's principle of respect for persons (the means-ends imperative) entails a recognition that persons have ultimate and inherent value, that they should not be used merely as a means to utilitarian ends, that equals should be treated equally, and that there are limits to what can be done to persons for the sake of good consequences. To many scholars, the central flaw of utilitarianism is that it does not incorporate a fully developed respect for persons. But in Kant's theory, the rights and duties of persons override any consequentialist calculus.

NATURAL LAW THEORY

The natural law theory of morality comes to us from ancient Greek and Roman philosophers (most notably, Aristotle and the Stoics) through the theologian and philosopher Thomas Aquinas

(1225–74). Aquinas molded it into its most influential form and bequeathed it to the world and the Roman Catholic Church, which embraced it as its official system of ethics. To this day, the theory is the primary basis for the church's views on abortion, homosexuality, euthanasia, and other controversial issues.

Here we focus on the traditional version of the theory derived from Aquinas. This form is theistic, assuming a divine lawgiver that has given us the gift of reason to comprehend the order of nature. But there are other natural law theories of a more recent vintage that dispense with the religious elements, basing objective moral standards on human nature and the natural needs and interests of humans.

According to Aquinas, at the heart of the traditional theory is the notion that right actions are those that accord with the natural law—the moral principles that we can "read" clearly in the very structure of nature itself, including human nature. We can look into nature and somehow uncover moral standards because nature is a certain way: it is rationally ordered and teleological (goal-directed), with every part having its own purpose or end at which it naturally aims. From this notion about nature, traditional natural law theorists draw the following conclusion: how nature *is* reveals how it *should be*. The goals to which nature inclines reveal the values that we should embrace and the moral purposes to which we should aspire.

In conformity with an inherent, natural purpose or goal—that is, according to natural law—an acorn develops into a seedling, then into a sapling and finally into an oak. The end toward which the acorn strives is the good (for acorns)—that is, to be a well-formed and well-functioning oak. Natural law determines how an oak functions—*and* indicates how an oak should function. If the oak does not function according to its natural purpose (if, for example, it is deformed or weak), it fails to be as it should be, deviating from its proper path laid down in natural law. Likewise, humans have a nature—a natural function and purpose unique among all living things. In human nature, in the mandates of the natural law for humanity, are the aims toward which human life strives. In these teleological strivings, in these facts about what human nature *is,* we can perceive what it *should be.*

What is it, exactly, that human nature aims at? Aquinas says that humans naturally incline toward preservation of human life, avoidance of harm, basic functions that humans and animals have in common (sexual intercourse, raising offspring, and the like), the search for truth, the nurturing of social ties, and behavior that is benign and reasonable. For humans, these inclinations constitute the good—the good of human flourishing and well-being. Our duty then is to achieve the good, to fully realize the goals to which our nature is already inclined. As Aquinas says,

[T]his is the first precept of law, that *good is to be done and promoted, and evil is to be avoided.* All other precepts of the natural law are based upon this; so that all things which the practical reason naturally apprehends as man's good belong to the precepts of the natural law under the form of things to be done or avoided.

Since, however, good has the nature of an end, and evil, the nature of the contrary, hence it is that all those things to which man has a natural inclination are naturally apprehended by reason as good, and consequently as objects of pursuit, and their contraries as evil, and objects of avoidance. Therefore, the order of the precepts of the natural law is according to the order of natural inclinations.[7]

In this passage, Aquinas refers to the aspect of human nature that enables us to decipher and implement the precepts of natural law: reason.

---

[7]Thomas Aquinas, *Summa Theologica,* in *Basic Writings of Saint Thomas Aquinas,* ed. and annotated Anton C. Pegis (New York: Random House, 1945), First Part of the Second Part, Question 94, Article 2.

Humans, unlike the rest of nature, are rational creatures, capable of understanding, deliberation, and free choice. Since all of nature is ordered and rational, only rational beings such as humans can peer into it and discern the inclinations in their nature, derive from the natural tendencies the natural laws, and apply the laws to their actions and their lives. Humans have the gift of reason (a gift from God, Aquinas says), and reason gives us access to the laws. Reason therefore is the foundation of morality. Judging the rightness of actions, then, is a matter of consulting reason, of considering rational grounds for moral beliefs.

It follows from these points that the natural (moral) laws are both objective and universal. The general principles of right and wrong do not vary from person to person or culture to culture. The dynamics of each situation may alter how a principle is applied, and not every situation has a relevant principle, but principles do not change with the tide. The natural laws are the natural laws. Further, they are not only binding on all persons, but they can be known by all persons. Aquinas insists that belief in God or inspiration from above is not a prerequisite for knowledge of morality. A person's effective use of reason is the only requirement.

Like Kant's categorical imperative, traditional natural law theory is, in the main, strongly absolutist. Natural law theorists commonly insist on several exceptionless rules. Directly killing the innocent is always wrong (which means that direct abortion is always wrong). Use of contraceptives is always wrong (on the grounds that it interferes with the natural human inclination toward procreation). Homosexuality is always wrong (again because it thwarts procreation). For Aquinas, lying, adultery, and blasphemy are always wrong.

As we have seen, moral principles—especially absolutist rules—can give rise to conflicts of duties. Kant's view on conflicting perfect duties is that such inconsistencies cannot happen. The natural law tradition gives a different answer: conflicts between duties are possible, but they can be resolved by applying the **doctrine of double effect.** This principle pertains to situations in which an action has both good and bad effects. It says that performing a good action may be permissible even if it has bad effects, but performing a bad action for the purpose of achieving good effects is never permissible. More formally, on a traditional interpretation of the doctrine, an action is permissible if four requirements are met:

1. *The action is inherently (without reference to consequences) either morally good or morally neutral.* That is, the action itself must at least be morally permissible.

2. *The bad effect is not used to produce the good effect (though the bad may be a side effect of the good).* Killing a fetus to save the mother's life is never permissible. However, using a drug to cure the mother's life-threatening disease—even though the fetus dies as a side effect of the treatment—may be permissible.

3. *The intention must always be to bring about the good effect.* For any given action, the bad effect may occur, and it may even be foreseen, but it must not be intended.

4. *The good effect must be at least as important as the bad effect.* The good of an action must be proportional to the bad. If the bad heavily outweighs the good, the action is not permissible. The good of saving your own life in an act of self-defense, for example, must be at least as great as the bad of taking the life of your attacker.

The doctrine of double effect is surprisingly versatile. Natural law theorists have used it to navigate moral dilemmas in medical ethics, reproductive health, warfare, and other life-and-death issues. The next section provides a demonstration.

Applying the Theory

Traditional natural law theory and its double-effect doctrine figure prominently in obstetrics

QUICK REVIEW

hypothetical imperative—An imperative that tells us what we should do if we have certain desires.

categorical imperative—An imperative that we should follow regardless of our particular wants and needs; also, the principle that defines Kant's ethical system.

perfect duty—A duty that has no exceptions.

imperfect duty—A duty that has exceptions.

means-ends principle—The rule that we must always treat people (including ourselves) as ends in themselves, never merely as a means.

doctrine of double effect—The principle that performing a good action may be permissible even if it has bad effects, but performing a bad action for the purpose of achieving good effects is never permissible; any bad effects must be unintended.

cases in which a choice must be made between harming a pregnant woman or her fetus. A typical scenario goes something like this: A pregnant woman has cancer and will die unless she receives chemotherapy to destroy the tumors. If she does take the chemotherapy, the fetus will die. Is it morally permissible for her to do so?

In itself, the act of taking the chemotherapy is morally permissible. There is nothing inherently wrong with using a medical treatment to try to cure a life-threatening illness. So the action meets Condition 1. We can also see that the bad effect (killing the fetus) is not used to produce the good effect (saving the woman's life). Receiving the chemotherapy is the method used to achieve the good effect. The loss of the fetus is an indirect, unintended result of the attempt to destroy the cancer. The action therefore meets Condition 2.

CRITICAL THOUGHT: Double Effect and the "Trolley Problem"

Consider the following thought experiment, first proposed by the philosopher Philippa Foot and set forth here by the philosopher Judith Jarvis Thomson:

> Suppose you are the driver of a trolley. The trolley rounds a bend, and there come into view ahead five track workmen, who have been repairing the track. The track goes through a bit of a valley at that point, and the sides are steep, so you must stop the trolley if you are to avoid running the five men down. You step on the brakes, but alas they don't work. Now you suddenly see a spur of track leading off to the right. You can turn the trolley onto it, and thus save the five men on the straight track ahead. Unfortunately, Mrs. Foot has arranged that there is one track workman on that spur of track. He can no more get off the track in time than the

five can, so you will kill him if you turn the trolley onto him. Is it morally permissible for you to turn the trolley?*

If you were the driver of the trolley, which option would you choose? Would you consider it morally permissible to turn the trolley onto the one workman to save the other five? Why or why not? What would the doctrine of double effect have you do in this case? Does your moral intuition seem to conflict with what the doctrine would have you do? What reasons can you give for the choice you make?

*Judith Jarvis Thomson (May 1985). The Trolley Problem. Reprinted by permission of The Yale Law Journal Company and William S. Hein Company from *The Yale Law Journal, Volume 94*, pp. 1395–1415.

The intention behind the action is to kill the cancer and thereby save the woman's life—not to kill the fetus. The woman and her doctors know that the unfortunate consequence of treating the cancer will be the death of the fetus. They foresee the death, but their intention is not to kill the fetus. Thus, the action meets Condition 3. Is the good effect proportional to the bad effect? In this case, a life is balanced against a life, the life of the woman and the life of the fetus. From the natural law perspective, both sides of the scale seem about equal in importance. If the good effect to be achieved for the woman was, say, a nicer appearance through cosmetic surgery, and the bad effect was the death of the fetus, the two sides would not have the same level of importance. But in this case, the action does meet Condition 4. Because the action meets all four conditions, receiving the chemotherapy is morally permissible for the woman.

Now let us examine a different kind of scenario. Remember that earlier in this chapter, we

applied both utilitarianism and Kant's theory to the antiterrorism tactic of killing a terrorist's relatives. To stop the murder of many innocent people by a relentless terrorist, the authorities consider killing his wife and three of his children and threatening to kill the remaining four children. What verdict would the doctrine of double effect yield in this case?

Here the action is the antiterrorist tactic just described. The good effect is preventing the death of innocent citizens; the bad effect is the killing of other innocents. Right away we can see that the action, in itself, is not morally good. Directly killing the innocent is never permissible, so the action does not meet Condition 1. Failing to measure up to even one condition shows the action to be prohibited, but we will continue our analysis anyway. Is the bad effect used to produce the good effect? Yes. The point of the action is to prevent further terrorist killings, and the means to that end is killing the terrorist's wife and children. The bad is used to achieve the good. So the action does not meet Condition 2, either. It does, however, meet Condition 3 because the intention behind the action is to bring about the good effect, preventing further terrorist killings. Finally, if we view the good effect (preventing the deaths of citizens) as comparable to the bad effect (the killing of the terrorist's wife and children), we should infer that the action meets Condition 4. In any case, since the action fails Conditions 1 and 2, we have to say that the action of the authorities in killing members of the terrorist's family is not permissible.

As suggested earlier, a Kantian theorist would likely agree with this decision, and a rule-utilitarian would probably concur. However, judging that the good consequences outweigh the bad, an act-utilitarian might very well say that killing the wife and children to prevent many other deaths would not only be permissible but obligatory.

Evaluating the Theory

Traditional natural law theory appears to contain no crippling internal inconsistencies, so we will regard it as an eligible theory for evaluation. But it does encounter difficulties with Criteria 1 and 3.

The theory seems to fall short of Criterion 1 (conflicts with commonsense moral judgments) in part because of its absolutism, a feature that also encumbers Kant's theory. As we have seen, natural law theorists maintain that some actions are *always* wrong: for example, intentionally killing the innocent, impeding procreation (through contraception, sterilization, or sexual preferences), or lying. Such absolutes, though, can lead to moral judgments that seem to diverge from common sense. The absolute prohibition against directly killing the innocent, for example, could actually result in great loss of life in certain extreme circumstances. Imagine that a thousand innocent people are taken hostage by a homicidal madman, and the only way to save the lives of nine hundred and ninety-nine is to intentionally kill one of them. If the one is not killed, all one thousand will die. Most of us would probably regard the

killing of the one hostage as a tragic but necessary measure to prevent a massive loss of life. The alternative—letting them all die—would seem a much greater tragedy. But many natural law theorists would condemn the killing of the one innocent person even if it would save the lives of hundreds.

Similarly, suppose a pregnant woman will die unless her fetus is aborted. Would it be morally permissible for her to have the abortion? Given the natural law prohibition against killing the innocent, many natural law theorists would say no. Aborting the fetus would be wrong even to save the mother's life. But most people would probably say that this view contradicts our considered moral judgments.

The absolutism of natural law theory arises from the notion that nature is authoritatively teleological. Nature aims toward particular ends that are ordained by the divine, and the values inherent in this arrangement cannot and must not be ignored or altered. How nature *is* reveals how it *should be*. Period. But the teleological character of nature has never been established by logical argument or empirical science—at least not to the satisfaction of most philosophers and scientists. In fact, science (including evolutionary theory) suggests that nature is not teleological at all but instead random and purposeless, changing and adapting according to scientific laws, blind cause and effect, chance mutation, and competition among species. Moreover, the idea that values can somehow be extracted from the facts of nature is as problematic for natural law theory as it is for ethical egoism and utilitarianism. From the fact that humans have a natural inclination toward procreation it does not follow that discouraging procreation through contraception is morally wrong.

Natural law theory seems to falter on Criterion 3 (usefulness) because, as just mentioned, discovering what values are inscribed in nature is problematic. The kind of moral principles that we might extract from nature depends on our conception of nature, and such conceptions can vary. Taking their cue from Aquinas, many natural law theorists see the inclinations of human nature as benign; others, as fundamentally depraved. Historically, humans have shown a capacity for both great good and monstrous evil. Which inclination is the true one? And even if we could accurately identify human inclinations, there seems to be no reliable procedure for uncovering the corresponding moral values or telling whether moral principles should be absolutist.

LEARNING FROM NATURAL LAW

Like Kantian ethics, natural law theory is universalist, objective, and rational, applying to all persons and requiring that moral choices be backed by good reasons. The emphasis on reason makes morality independent of religion and belief in God, a distinction also found in Kant's ethics. At the heart of natural law theory is a strong respect for human life, an attitude that is close to, but not quite the same thing as, Kant's means-ends principle. Respect for life or persons is, of course, a primary concern of our moral experience and seems to preclude the kind of wholesale end-justifies-the-means calculations that are a defining characteristic of many forms of utilitarianism.

Natural law theory emphasizes a significant element in moral deliberation that some other theories play down: intention. In general, intention plays a larger role in natural law theory than it does in Kant's categorical imperative. To many natural law theorists, the rightness of an action often depends on the intentions of the moral agent performing it. In our previous example of the pregnant woman with cancer, for example, the intention behind the act of taking the chemotherapy is to kill the cancer, not the fetus, though the fetus dies because of the treatment. So the action is thought to be morally permissible. If the intention had been to directly kill the fetus, the action would have been deemed wrong. In our everyday

moral experience, we frequently take intentions into account in evaluating an action. We usually would think that there must be some morally relevant difference between a terrorist's intentionally killing ten people and a police officer's accidentally killing those same ten people while chasing the terrorist, though both scenarios result in the same tragic loss of life.

SUMMARY

Kant's moral theory is perhaps the most influential of all nonconsequentialist approaches. In his view, right actions have moral value only if they are done with a "good will"—for duty's sake alone. The meat of Kant's theory is the categorical imperative, a principle that he formulates in three versions. The first version says that an action is right if you can will that the maxim of an action become a moral law applying to all persons. An action is permissible if (1) its maxim can be universalized (if everyone can consistently act on it) and (2) you would be willing to have that happen. The second version of the categorical imperative says that we must always treat people as ends in themselves and never merely as a means to an end.

Kant's theory seems to conflict with our commonsense moral judgments (Criterion 1) and has flaws that limit its usefulness in moral problem solving (Criterion 3). The theory falters on Criterion 1 mainly because some duties generated by the categorical imperative are absolute. Absolute duties can conflict, and Kant provides no way to resolve the inconsistencies, a failure of Criterion 3. Furthermore, we seem to have no genuine absolute duties.

Natural law theory is based on the notion that right actions are those that accord with natural law—the moral principles embedded in nature itself. How nature *is* reveals how it *should be*. The inclinations of human nature reveal the values that humans should live by. Aquinas, who gave us the most influential form of natural law theory, says that humans naturally incline toward preservation of human life, procreation, the search for truth, community, and benign and reasonable behavior.

Like Kant's theory, traditional natural law theory is absolutist, maintaining that some actions are always wrong. These immoral actions include directly killing the innocent, interfering with procreation, and lying. The theory's absolutist rules do occasionally conflict, and the proposed remedy for any such inconsistencies is the doctrine of double effect. The principle applies to situations in which an action produces both good and bad effects. It says that performing a good action may be permissible even if it has bad effects, but performing a bad action for the purpose of achieving good effects is never permissible. Despite the double-effect doctrine, the theory's biggest weakness is still its absolutism, which seems to mandate actions that conflict with our considered moral judgments. In some cases, for example, the theory might require someone to allow hundreds of innocent people to die just to avoid the direct killing of a single person.

EXERCISES

Review Questions

1. What is the significance of a "good will" in Kant's ethics? (pp. 100–101)
2. What is the difference between a hypothetical and a categorical imperative? (p. 101)
3. What is the moral principle laid out in the first version of Kant's categorical imperative? (p. 101)
4. What is a perfect duty? (p. 101)
5. What is Kant's means-ends principle? (p. 103)
6. How can the absolutism of Kant's theory lead to judgments that conflict with moral common sense? (pp. 104–5)
7. How might the subjectivity of Kant's theory lead to the sanctioning of heinous acts? (p. 106)
8. What is natural law theory? (pp. 107–8)

9. According to natural law theorists, how can nature reveal anything about morality? (pp. 107–8)
10. According to Aquinas, what is the good that human nature aims at? (p. 108)
11. According to natural law theory, how are moral principles objective? How are they universal? (p. 108)
12. What is the doctrine of double effect? (p. 109)
13. How can the absolutism of natural law theory lead to moral judgments that conflict with moral common sense? (p. 111)

Discussion Questions

1. Which moral theory—Kant's or natural law— seems more plausible to you? Why?
2. What elements of Kant's theory do you think could or should be part of any viable moral theory?
3. In what way is Kant's ethics independent of (not based on) religious belief? Is natural law theory independent of religious belief? Why or why not?
4. According to Kant, why is breaking a promise or lying immoral? Do you agree with Kant's reasoning? Why or why not?
5. How might your life change if you completely embraced Kant's theory of morality?
6. How might your life change if you adopted the natural law theory of morality?
7. Would a Kantian and a natural law theorist agree on whether having an abortion is moral? Why or why not?
8. Do you believe, as Kant does, that there are perfect (absolute) duties? Why or why not?
9. According to the text, natural law theory generates judgments that conflict with commonsense morality. Do you agree with this assessment? Why or why not?
10. Is natural law theory more plausible than utilitarianism? Why or why not?

READINGS

From *Fundamental Principles of the Metaphysic of Morals*

IMMANUEL KANT

* * *

Nothing can possibly be conceived in the world, or even out of it, which can be called good, without qualification, except a *good will*. Intelligence, wit, judgement, and the other talents of the mind, however, they may be named, or courage, resolution, perseverance, as qualities of temperament, are undoubtedly good and desirable in many respects; but these gifts of nature may also become extremely bad and mischievous if the will which is to make use of them, and which, therefore, constitutes what is called *character,* is not good. It is the same with the *gifts of fortune.* Power, riches, honour, even health, and the general well-being and contentment with one's condition which is called *happiness,* inspire pride, and often presumption, if there is not a good will to correct the influence of these on the mind, and with this also to rectify the whole principle of acting and adapt it to its end. The sight of a being who is not adorned with a single feature of a pure and good will, enjoying unbroken prosperity, can never give pleasure to an impartial rational spectator. Thus a good will appears to constitute the indispensable condition even of being worthy of happiness.

There are even some qualities which are of service to this good will itself and may facilitate its action, yet which have no intrinsic unconditional value, but always presuppose a good will, and this qualifies the esteem that we justly have for them and does not permit us to regard them as absolutely good. Moderation in the affections and passions, self-control, and calm deliberation are not only good in many respects, but even seem to constitute part of the intrinsic worth of the person; but they are far from deserving to be called good without

Immanuel Kant, *Fundamental Principles of the Metaphysic of Morals,* trans. Thomas K. Abbott (edited).

qualification, although they have been so unconditionally praised by the ancients. For without the principles of a good will, they may become extremely bad, and the coolness of a villain not only makes him far more dangerous, but also directly makes him more abominable in our eyes than he would have been without it.

A good will is good not because of what it performs or effects, not by its aptness for the attainment of some proposed end, but simply by virtue of the volition—that is, it is good in itself, and considered by itself is to be esteemed much higher than all that can be brought about by it in favour of any inclination, nay, even of the sum-total of all inclinations. Even if it should happen that, owing to special disfavour of fortune, or the niggardly provision of a stepmotherly nature, this will should wholly lack power to accomplish its purpose, if with its greatest efforts it should yet achieve nothing, and there should remain only the good will (not, to be sure, a mere wish, but the summoning of all means in our power), then, like a jewel, it would still shine by its own light, as a thing which has its whole value in itself. Its usefulness or fruitfulness can neither add nor take away anything from this value. It would be, as it were, only the setting to enable us to handle it the more conveniently in common commerce, or to attract to it the attention of those who are not yet connoisseurs, but not to recommend it to true connoisseurs, or to determine its value.

There is, however, something so strange in this idea of the absolute value of the mere will, in which no account is taken of its utility, that notwithstanding the thorough assent of even common reason to the idea, yet a suspicion must arise that it may perhaps really be the product of mere highflown fancy, and that we may have misunderstood the purpose of nature in assigning reason as the governor of our will. Therefore we will examine this idea from this point of view.

* * *

To be beneficent when we can is a duty; and besides this, there are many minds so sympathetically constituted that, without any other motive of vanity or self-interest, they find a pleasure in spreading joy around them and can take delight in the satisfaction of others so far as it is their own work. But I maintain that in such a case an action of this kind, however proper, however amiable it may be, has nevertheless no true moral worth, but is on a level with other inclinations, e.g., the inclination to honour, which, if it is happily directed to that which is in fact of public utility and accordant with duty and consequently honourable, deserves praise and encouragement, but not esteem. For the maxim lacks the moral import, namely, that such actions be done from duty, not from inclination. Put the case that the mind of that philanthropist were clouded by sorrow of his own, extinguishing all sympathy with the lot of others, and that, while he still has the power to benefit others in distress, he is not touched by their trouble because he is absorbed with his own; and now suppose that he tears himself out of this dead insensibility, and performs the action without any inclination to it, but simply from duty, then first has his action its genuine moral worth. Further still, if nature has put little sympathy in the heart of this or that man; if he, supposed to be an upright man, is by temperament cold and indifferent to the sufferings of others, perhaps because in respect of his own he is provided with the special gift of patience and fortitude and supposes, or even requires, that others should have the same—and such a man would certainly not be the meanest product of nature—but if nature had not specially framed him for a philanthropist, would he not still find in himself a source from whence to give himself a far higher worth than that of a good-natured temperament could be? Unquestionably. It is just in this that the moral worth of the character is brought out which is incomparably the highest of all, namely, that he is beneficent, not from inclination, but from duty.

* * *

Thus the moral worth of an action does not lie in the effect expected from it, nor in any principle of action which requires to borrow its motive from this expected effect. For all these effects—agreeableness of one's condition and even the promotion of the happiness of others—could have been also brought about by other causes, so that for this there would have been no need of the will of a rational being; whereas it is in this alone that the supreme and unconditional good can be found. The pre-eminent good which we call moral can therefore consist in nothing else than the conception of law in itself, which certainly is only possible in a rational being, in so far as this conception, and not the expected effect, determines the will. This is a good which is already present in the person who acts accordingly, and we have not to wait for it to appear first in the result.

* * *

But what sort of law can that be, the conception of which must determine the will, even without paying any regard to the effect expected from it, in order that this will may be called good absolutely and without qualification? As I have deprived the will of every impulse which could arise to it from obedience to any law, there remains nothing but the universal conformity of its actions to law in general, which alone is to serve the will as a principle, i.e., I am never to act otherwise than so that I could also will that my maxim should become a universal law. Here, now, it is the simple conformity to law in general, without assuming any particular law applicable to certain actions, that serves the will as its principle and must so serve it, if duty is not to be a vain delusion and a chimerical notion. The common reason of men in its practical judgements perfectly coincides with this and always has in view the principle here suggested. Let the question be, for example: May I when in distress make a promise with the intention not to keep it? I readily distinguish here between the two significations which the question may have: Whether it is prudent, or whether it is right, to make a false promise? The former may undoubtedly often be the case. I see clearly indeed that it is not enough to extricate myself from a present difficulty by means of this subterfuge, but it must be well considered whether there may not hereafter spring from this lie much greater inconvenience than that from which I now free myself, and as, with all my supposed cunning, the consequences cannot be so easily foreseen but that credit once lost may be much more injurious to me than any mischief which I seek to avoid at present, it should be considered whether it would not be more prudent to act herein according to a universal maxim and to make it a habit to promise nothing except with the intention of keeping it. But it is soon clear to me that such a maxim will still only be based on the fear of consequences. Now it is a wholly different thing to be truthful from duty, and to be so from apprehension of injurious consequences. In the first case, the very notion of the action already implies a law for me; in the second case, I must first look about elsewhere to see what results may be combined with it which would affect myself. For to deviate from the principle of duty is beyond all doubt wicked; but to be unfaithful to my maxim of prudence may often be very advantageous to me, although to abide by it is certainly safer. The shortest way, however, and an unerring one, to discover the answer to this question whether a lying promise is consistent with duty, is to ask myself, "Should I be content that my maxim (to extricate myself from difficulty by a false promise) should hold good as a universal law, for myself as well as for others?" and should I be able to say to myself, "Every one may make a deceitful promise when he finds himself in a difficulty from which he cannot otherwise extricate himself?" Then I presently become aware that while I can will the lie, I can by no means will that lying should be a universal law. For with such a law there would be no promises at all, since it would be in vain to allege my intention in regard to my future actions to those who would not believe this allegation, or if they over hastily did so would pay me back in my own coin. Hence my maxim, as soon as it should be made a universal law, would necessarily destroy itself.

I do not, therefore, need any far-reaching penetration to discern what I have to do in order that my will may be morally good. Inexperienced in the course of the world, incapable of being prepared for all its contingencies, I only ask myself: Canst thou also will that thy maxim should be a universal law? If not, then it must be rejected, and that not because of a disadvantage accruing from it to myself or even to others, but because it cannot enter as a principle into a possible universal legislation, and reason extorts from me immediate respect for such legislation. I do not indeed as yet discern on what this respect is based (this the philosopher may inquire), but at least I understand this, that it is an estimation of the worth which far outweighs all worth of what is recommended by inclination, and that the necessity of acting from pure respect for the practical law is what constitutes duty, to which every other motive must give place, because it is the condition of a will being good in itself, and the worth of such a will is above everything.

* * *

Nor could anything be more fatal to morality than that we should wish to derive it from examples. For every example of it that is set before me must be first itself tested by principles of morality, whether it is worthy to serve as an original example, i.e., as a pattern; but by no means can it authoritatively furnish the conception of morality. Even the Holy One of the Gospels must first be compared with our ideal of moral perfection before we can recognise Him as such; and so He says of Himself, "Why call ye Me (whom you see) good; none is good (the model of good) but God only (whom ye do not see)?" But whence have we the conception of God as the supreme good? Simply from the idea of moral perfection, which reason frames a priori and connects inseparably with the notion of a free will. Imitation finds no place at all in morality, and examples serve only for encouragement, i.e., they put beyond doubt the feasibility of what the law commands, they make visible that which the practical rule expresses more generally, but they can never authorize us to set aside the true original which lies in reason and to guide ourselves by examples.

* * *

From what has been said, it is clear that all moral conceptions have their seat and origin completely a priori in the reason, and that, moreover, in the commonest reason just as truly as in that which is in the highest degree speculative; that they cannot be obtained by abstraction from any empirical, and therefore merely contingent, knowledge; that it is just this purity of their origin that makes them worthy to serve as our supreme practical principle, and that just in proportion as we add anything empirical, we detract from their genuine influence and from the absolute value of actions; that it is not only of the greatest necessity, in a purely speculative point of view, but is also of the greatest practical importance, to derive these notions and laws from pure reason, to present them pure and unmixed, and even to determine the compass of this practical or pure rational knowledge, i.e., to determine the whole faculty of pure practical reason; and, in doing so, we must not make its principles dependent on the particular nature of human reason, though in speculative philosophy this may be permitted, or may even at times be necessary; but since moral laws ought to hold good for every rational creature, we must derive them from the general concept of a rational being. In this way, although for its application to man morality has need of anthropology, yet, in the first instance, we must treat it independently as pure philosophy, i.e., as metaphysic, complete in itself (a thing which in such distinct branches of science is easily done); knowing well that unless we are in possession of this, it would not only be vain to determine the moral element of duty in right actions for purposes of speculative criticism, but it would be impossible to base morals on their genuine principles, even for common practical purposes, especially of moral instruction, so as to produce pure moral dispositions, and to engraft them on men's minds to the promotion of the greatest possible good in the world.

But in order that in this study we may not merely advance by the natural steps from the common moral judgement (in this case very worthy of respect) to the philosophical, as has been already done, but also from a popular philosophy, which goes no further than it can reach by groping with the help of examples, to metaphysic (which does not allow itself to be checked by anything empirical and, as it must measure the whole extent of this kind of rational knowl-edge, goes as far as ideal conceptions, where even examples fail us), we must follow and clearly describe the practical faculty of reason, from the general rules of its determination to the point where the notion of duty springs from it.

Everything in nature works according to laws. Rational beings alone have the faculty of acting according to the conception of laws—that is, according to principles, that is, have a will. Since the deduction of actions from principles requires reason, the will is nothing but practical reason. If reason infallibly determines the will, then the actions of such a being which are recognised as objectively necessary are subjectively necessary also, that is, the will is a faculty to choose that only which reason independent of inclination recognises as practically necessary, that is, as good. But if reason of itself does not sufficiently determine the will, if the latter is subject also to subjective conditions (particular impulses) which do not always coincide with the objective conditions; in a word, if the will does not in itself completely accord with reason (which is actually the case with men), then the actions which objectively are recognised as necessary are subjectively contingent, and the determination of such a will according to objective laws is obligation, that is to say, the relation of the objective laws to a will that is not thoroughly good is conceived as the determination of the will of a rational being by principles of reason, but which the will from its nature does not of necessity follow.

The conception of an objective principle, in so far as it is obligatory for a will, is called a command (of reason), and the formula of the command is called an imperative.

All imperatives are expressed by the word ought [or shall], and thereby indicate the relation of an objective law of reason to a will, which from its subjective constitution is not necessarily determined by it (an obligation). They say that something would be good to do or to forbear, but they say it to a will which does not always do a thing because it is conceived to be good to do it. That is practically good, however, which determines the will by means of the conceptions of reason, and consequently not from subjective causes, but objectively, that is, on principles which are valid for every rational being as such. It is distinguished from the pleasant, as that which influences the will only by means of sensation from merely subjective causes, valid only for the sense of this or that one, and not as a principle of reason, which holds for every one.

* * *

Now all imperatives command either hypothetically or categorically. The former represent the practical necessity of a possible action as means to something else that is willed (or at least which one might possibly will). The categorical imperative would be that which represented an action as necessary of itself without reference to another end, that is, as objectively necessary.

Since every practical law represents a possible action as good and, on this account, for a subject who is practically determinable by reason, necessary, all imperatives are formulae determining an action which is necessary according to the principle of a will good in some respects. If now the action is good only as a means to something else, then the imperative is hypothetical; if it is conceived as good in itself and consequently as being necessarily the principle of a will which of itself conforms to reason, then it is categorical.

Thus the imperative declares what action possible by me would be good and presents the practical rule in relation to a will which does not forthwith perform an action simply because it is good, whether because the subject does not always know that it is good, or because, even if it know this, yet its maxims might be opposed to the objective principles of practical reason.

Accordingly the hypothetical imperative only says that the action is good for some purpose, possible or actual. In the first case it is a problematical, in the second an assertorial practical principle. The categorical imperative which declares an action to be objectively necessary in itself without reference to any purpose, i.e., without any other end, is valid as an apodeictic (practical) principle.

* * *

Finally, there is an imperative which commands a certain conduct immediately, without having as its condition any other purpose to be attained by it. This imperative is categorical. It concerns not the matter of the action, or its intended result, but its form and the principle of which it is itself a result; and what is essentially good in it consists in the mental disposition, let the consequence be what it may. This imperative may be called that of morality.

* * *

[The] question how the imperative of morality is possible, is undoubtedly one, the only one, demanding a solution, as this is not at all hypothetical, and the objective necessity which it presents cannot rest on any hypothesis, as is the case with the hypothetical imperatives. Only here we must never leave out of consideration that we cannot make out by any example, in other words empirically, whether there is such an imperative at all, but it is rather to be feared that all those which seem to be categorical may yet be at bottom hypothetical. For instance, when the precept is: "Thou shalt not promise deceitfully"; and it is assumed that the necessity of this is not a mere counsel to avoid some other evil, so that it should mean: "Thou shalt not make a lying promise, lest if it become known thou shouldst destroy thy credit," but that an action of this kind must be regarded as evil in itself, so that the imperative of the prohibition is categorical; then we cannot show with certainty in any example that the will was determined merely by the law, without any other spring of action, although it may appear to be so. For it is always possible that fear of disgrace, perhaps also obscure dread of other dangers, may have a secret influence on the will. Who can prove by experience the non-existence of a cause when all that experience tells us is that we do not perceive it? But in such a case the so-called moral imperative, which as such appears to be categorical and unconditional, would in reality be only a pragmatic precept, drawing our attention to our own interests and merely teaching us to take these into consideration.

We shall therefore have to investigate a priori the possibility of a categorical imperative, as we have not in this case the advantage of its reality being given in experience, so that [the elucidation of] its possibility should be requisite only for its explanation, not for its establishment. In the meantime it may be discerned beforehand that the categorical imperative alone has the purport of a practical law; all the rest may indeed be called principles of the will but not laws, since whatever is only necessary for the attainment of some arbitrary purpose may be considered as in itself contingent, and we can at any time be free from the precept if we give up the purpose; on the contrary, the unconditional command leaves the will no liberty to choose the opposite; consequently it alone carries with it that necessity which we require in a law.

Secondly, in the case of this categorical imperative or law of morality, the difficulty (of discerning its possibility) is a very profound one. It is an a priori synthetical practical proposition; and as there is so much difficulty in discerning the possibility of speculative propositions of this kind, it may readily be supposed that the difficulty will be no less with the practical.

* * *

In this problem we will first inquire whether the mere conception of a categorical imperative may not perhaps supply us also with the formula of it, containing the proposition which alone can be a categorical imperative; for even if we know the tenor of such an absolute command, yet how it is possible will require further special and laborious study, which we postpone to the last section.

When I conceive a hypothetical imperative, in general I do not know beforehand what it will contain until I am given the condition. But when I conceive a categorical imperative, I know at once what it contains. For as the imperative contains besides the law only the necessity that the maxims shall conform to this law, while the law contains no conditions restricting it, there remains nothing but the general statement that the maxim of the action should conform to a universal law, and it is this conformity alone that the imperative properly represents as necessary.

* * *

There is therefore but one categorical imperative, namely, this: Act only on that maxim whereby thou canst at the same time will that it should become a universal law.

Now if all imperatives of duty can be deduced from this one imperative as from their principle, then, although it should remain undecided what is called duty is not merely a vain notion, yet at least we shall be able to show what we understand by it and what this notion means.

Since the universality of the law according to which effects are produced constitutes what is properly called nature in the most general sense (as to form), that is the existence of things so far as it is determined by general laws, the imperative of duty may be expressed thus: Act as if the maxim of thy action were to become by thy will a universal law of nature.

We will now enumerate a few duties, adopting the usual division of them into duties to ourselves and to others, and into perfect and imperfect duties.

* * *

1. A man reduced to despair by a series of misfortunes feels wearied of life, but is still so far in possession of his reason that he can ask himself whether it would not be contrary to his duty to himself to take his own life. Now he inquires whether the maxim of his action could become a universal law of nature. His maxim is: "From self-love I adopt it as a principle to shorten my life when its longer duration is likely to bring more evil than satisfaction." It is asked then simply whether this principle founded on self-love can become a universal law of nature. Now we see at once that a system of nature of which it should be a law to destroy life by means of the very feeling whose special nature it is to impel to the improvement of life would contradict itself and, therefore, could not exist as a system of nature; hence that maxim cannot possibly exist as a universal law of nature and, consequently, would be wholly inconsistent with the supreme principle of all duty.

2. Another finds himself forced by necessity to borrow money. He knows that he will not be able to repay it, but sees also that nothing will be lent to him unless he promises stoutly to repay it in a definite time. He desires to make this promise, but he has still so much conscience as to ask himself: "Is it not unlawful and inconsistent with duty to get out of a

difficulty in this way?" Suppose however that he resolves to do so: then the maxim of his action would be expressed thus: "When I think myself in want of money, I will borrow money and promise to repay it, although I know that I never can do so." Now this principle of self-love or of one's own advantage may perhaps be consistent with my whole future welfare; but the question now is, "Is it right?" I change then the suggestion of self-love into a universal law, and state the question thus: "How would it be if my maxim were a universal law?" Then I see at once that it could never hold as a universal law of nature, but would necessarily contradict itself. For supposing it to be a universal law that everyone when he thinks himself in a difficulty should be able to promise whatever he pleases, with the purpose of not keeping his promise, the promise itself would become impossible, as well as the end that one might have in view in it, since no one would consider that anything was promised to him, but would ridicule all such statements as vain pretences.

3. A third finds in himself a talent which with the help of some culture might make him a useful man in many respects. But he finds himself in comfortable circumstances and prefers to indulge in pleasure rather than to take pains in enlarging and improving his happy natural capacities. He asks, however, whether his maxim of neglect of his natural gifts, besides agreeing with his inclination to indulgence, agrees also with what is called duty. He sees then that a system of nature could indeed subsist with such a universal law although men (like the South Sea islanders) should let their talents rest and resolve to devote their lives merely to idleness, amusement, and propagation of their species—in a word, to enjoyment; but he cannot possibly will that this should be a universal law of nature, or be implanted in us as such by a natural instinct. For, as a rational being, he necessarily wills that his faculties be developed, since they serve him and have been given him, for all sorts of possible purposes.

4. A fourth, who is in prosperity, while he sees that others have to contend with great wretchedness and that he could help them, thinks: "What concern is it of mine? Let everyone be as happy as Heaven pleases, or as he can make himself; I will take nothing from him nor even envy him, only I do not wish to contribute anything to his welfare or to his assistance in distress!" Now no doubt if such a mode of thinking were a universal law, the human race might very well subsist and doubtless even better than in a state in which everyone talks of sympathy and goodwill, or even takes care occasionally to put it into practice, but, on the other side, also cheats when he can, betrays the rights of men, or otherwise violates them. But although it is possible that a universal law of nature might exist in accordance with that maxim, it is impossible to will that such a principle should have the universal validity of a law of nature. For a will which resolved this would contradict itself, inasmuch as many cases might occur in which one would have need of the love and sympathy of others, and in which, by such a law of nature, sprung from his own will, he would deprive himself of all hope of the aid he desires.

These are a few of the many actual duties, or at least what we regard as such, which obviously fall into two classes on the one principle that we have laid down. We must be able to will that a maxim of our action should be a universal law. This is the canon of the moral appreciation of the action generally. Some actions are of such a character that their maxim cannot without contradiction be even conceived as a universal law of nature, far from it being possible that we should will that it should be so. In others this intrinsic impossibility is not found, but still it is impossible to will that their maxim should be raised to the universality of a law of nature, since such a will would contradict itself. It is easily seen that the former violate strict or rigorous (inflexible) duty; the latter only laxer (meritorious) duty. Thus it has been completely shown how all duties depend as regards the nature of the obligation (not the object of the action) on the same principle.

* * *

Now I say: man and generally any rational being exists as an end in himself, not merely as a means to be arbitrarily used by this or that will, but in all his actions, whether they concern himself or other rational beings, must be always regarded at the same time as an end. All objects of the inclinations have only a conditional worth, for if the inclinations and the wants founded on them did not exist, then their object would be without value. But the inclinations, themselves being sources of want, are so far from having an absolute worth for which they should be desired that on the contrary it must be the universal wish of every rational being to be wholly free from them. Thus the worth of any object which is to be acquired by our action is always conditional. Beings whose existence depends not on our will but on nature's, have nevertheless, if they are irrational beings, only a relative value as means, and are therefore called things; rational beings, on the contrary, are called persons, because their very nature points them out as ends in themselves, that is as something which must not be used merely as means, and so far therefore restricts freedom of actions (and is an object of respect). These, therefore, are not merely subjective ends whose existence has a worth for us as an effect of our action, but objective ends, that is, things whose existence is an end in itself; an end moreover for which no other can be substituted, which they should subserve merely as means, for otherwise nothing whatever would possess absolute worth; but if all worth were conditioned and therefore contingent, then there would be no supreme practical principle of reason whatever.

If then there is a supreme practical principle or, in respect of the human will, a categorical imperative, it must be one which, being drawn from the conception of that which is necessarily an end for everyone because it is an end in itself, constitutes an objective principle of will, and can therefore serve as a universal practical law. The foundation of this principle is: rational nature exists as an end in itself. Man necessarily conceives his own existence as being so; so far then this is a subjective principle of human actions. But every other rational being regards its existence similarly, just on the same rational principle that holds for me: so that it is at the same time an objective principle, from which as a supreme practical law all laws of the will must be capable of being deduced. Accordingly the practical imperative will be as follows: So act as to treat humanity, whether in thine own person or in that of any other, in every case as an end withal, never as means only. We will now inquire whether this can be practically carried out.

* * *

To abide by the previous examples:

Firstly, under the head of necessary duty to oneself: He who contemplates suicide should ask himself whether his action can be consistent with the idea of humanity as an end in itself. If he destroys himself in order to escape from painful circumstances, he uses a person merely as a mean to maintain a tolerable condition up to the end of life. But a man is not a thing, that is to say, something which can be used merely as means, but must in all his actions be always considered as an end in himself. I cannot, therefore, dispose in any way of a man in my own person so as to mutilate him, to damage or kill him. (It belongs to ethics proper to define this principle more precisely, so as to avoid all misunderstanding, for example, as to the amputation of the limbs in order to preserve myself as to exposing my life to danger with a view to preserve it, etc. This question is therefore omitted here.)

Secondly, as regards necessary duties, or those of strict obligation, towards others: He who is thinking of making a lying promise to others will see at once that he would be using another man merely as a mean, without the latter containing at the same time the end in himself. For he whom I propose by such a promise to use for my own purposes cannot possibly assent to my mode of acting towards him and, therefore, cannot himself contain the end of this action. This violation of the principle of humanity in other men is more obvious if we take in examples of attacks on the freedom and property of others. For then it is clear that he who transgresses the rights of men intends to use the person of others merely as a means, without considering that as rational beings they ought always to be esteemed also as ends, that is, as beings who must be capable of containing in themselves the end of the very same action.

* * *

Thirdly, as regards contingent (meritorious) duties to oneself: It is not enough that the action does not violate humanity in our own person as an end in itself, it must also harmonize with it. Now there are in humanity capacities of greater perfection, which belong to the end that nature has in view in regard to humanity in ourselves as the subject: to neglect these might perhaps be consistent with the maintenance of humanity as an end in itself, but not with the advancement of this end.

* * *

Looking back now on all previous attempts to discover the principle of morality, we need not wonder why they all failed. It was seen that man was bound to laws by duty, but it was not observed that the laws to which he is subject are only those of his own giving, though at the same time they are universal, and that he is only bound to act in conformity with his own will; a will, however, which is designed by nature to give universal laws. For when one has conceived man only as subject to a law (no matter what), then this law required some interest, either by way of attraction or constraint, since it did not originate as a law from his own will, but this will was according to a law obliged by something else to act in a certain manner. Now by this necessary consequence all the labour spent in finding a supreme principle of duty was irrevocably lost. For men never elicited duty, but only a necessity of acting from a certain interest. Whether this interest was private or otherwise, in any case the imperative must be conditional and could not by any means be capable of being a moral command. I will therefore call this the principle of autonomy of the will, in contrast with every other which I accordingly reckon as heteronomy.

The conception of the will of every rational being as one which must consider itself as giving in all the maxims of its will universal laws, so as to judge itself and its actions from this point of view—this conception leads to another which depends on it and is very fruitful, namely that of a kingdom of ends.

By a kingdom I understand the union of different rational beings in a system by common laws. Now since it is by laws that ends are determined as regards their universal validity, hence, if we abstract from the personal differences of rational beings and likewise from all the content of their private ends, we shall

be able to conceive all ends combined in a systematic whole (including both rational beings as ends in themselves, and also the special ends which each may propose to himself), that is to say, we can conceive a kingdom of ends, which on the preceding principles is possible.

For all rational beings come under the law that each of them must treat itself and all others never merely as means, but in every case at the same time as ends in themselves. Hence results a systematic union of rational being by common objective laws, that is, a kingdom which may be called a kingdom of ends, since what these laws have in view is just the relation of these beings to one another as ends and means. It is certainly only an ideal.

A rational being belongs as a member to the kingdom of ends when, although giving universal laws in it, he is also himself subject to these laws. He belongs to it as sovereign when, while giving laws, he is not subject to the will of any other.

A rational being must always regard himself as giving laws either as member or as sovereign in a kingdom of ends which is rendered possible by the freedom of will. He cannot, however, maintain the latter position merely by the maxims of his will, but only in case he is a completely independent being without wants and with unrestricted power adequate to his will.

Morality consists then in the reference of all action to the legislation which alone can render a kingdom of ends possible. This legislation must be capable of existing in every rational being and of emanating from his will, so that the principle of this will is never to act on any maxim which could not without contradiction be also a universal law and, accordingly, always so to act that the will could at the same time regard itself as giving in its maxims universal laws. If now the maxims of rational beings are not by their own nature coincident with this objective principle, then the necessity of acting on it is called practical necessitation, that is, duty. Duty does not apply to the sovereign in the kingdom of ends, but it does to every member of it and to all in the same degree.

* * *

From *Summa Theologica*, First Part of the Second Part

St. Thomas Aquinas

QUESTION 91.
OF THE VARIOUS KINDS OF LAW.

* * *

First Article.
Whether There Is an Eternal Law?

We proceed thus to the First Article:—

Objection 1. It would seem that there is no eternal law. Because every law is imposed on someone. But there was not someone from eternity on whom a law could be imposed: since God alone was from eternity. Therefore no law is eternal.

Obj. 2. Further, promulgation is essential to law. But promulgation could not be from eternity: because there was no one to whom it could be promulgated from eternity. Therefore no law can be eternal.

Obj. 3. Further, a law implies order to an end. But nothing ordained to an end is eternal: for the last end alone is eternal. Therefore no law is eternal.

On the contrary, Augustine says: *That Law which is the Supreme Reason cannot be understood to be otherwise than unchangeable and eternal.*

I answer that, . . . a law is nothing else but a dictate of practical reason emanating from the ruler who governs a perfect community. Now it is evident, granted that the world is ruled by Divine Providence, . . . that the whole community of the universe is governed by Divine Reason. Wherefore the very Idea of the government of things in God the Ruler of the universe, has the nature of a law. And since the Divine Reason's conception of things is not subject to time but is eternal, according to Proverbs 8.23, therefore it is that this kind of law must be called eternal.

Reply Obj. 1. Those things that are not in themselves, exist with God, inasmuch as they are foreknown and preordained by Him, according to

Romans 4.17: *Who calls those things that are not, as those that are.* Accordingly the eternal concept of the Divine law bears the character of an eternal law, in so far as it is ordained by God to the government of things foreknown by Him.

Reply Obj. 2. Promulgation is made by word of mouth or in writing; and in both ways the eternal law is promulgated: because both the Divine Word and the writing of the Book of Life are eternal. But the promulgation cannot be from eternity on the part of the creature that hears or reads.

Reply Obj. 3. The law implies order to the end actively, in so far as it directs certain things to the end; but not passively,—that is to say, the law itself is not ordained to the end,—except accidentally, in a governor whose end is extrinsic to him, and to which end his law must needs be ordained. But the end of the Divine government is God Himself, and His law is not distinct from Himself. Wherefore the eternal law is not ordained to another end.

Second Article.
Whether There Is in Us a Natural Law?

We proceed thus to the Second Article:—

Objection 1. It would seem that there is no natural law in us. Because man is governed sufficiently by the eternal law: for Augustine says that *the eternal law is that by which it is right that all things should be most orderly.* But nature does not abound in superfluities as neither does she fail in necessaries. Therefore no law is natural to man.

Obj. 2. Further, by the law man is directed, in his acts, to the end. . . . But the directing of human acts to their end is not a function of nature, as is the case in irrational creatures, which act for an end solely by their natural appetite; whereas man acts for an end by his reason and will. Therefore no law is natural to man.

Obj. 3. Further, the more a man is free, the less is he under the law. But man is freer than all the animals, on account of his free-will, with which he is endowed above all other animals. Since therefore other animals are not subject to a natural law, neither is man subject to a natural law.

On the contrary, A gloss on Romans 2.14: *When the Gentiles, who have not the law, do by nature those things that are of the law,* comments as follows: *Although they have no written law, yet they have the natural law, whereby each one knows, and is conscious of, what is good and what is civil.*

I answer that . . . law, being a rule and measure, can be in a person in two ways: in one way, as in him that rules and measures; in another way, as in that which is ruled and measured, since a thing is ruled and measured, in so far as it partakes of the rule or measure. Wherefore, since all things subject to Divine providence are ruled and measured by the eternal law, as was stated above (A. I); it is evident that all things partake somewhat of the eternal law, in so far as, namely, from its being imprinted on them, they derive their respective inclinations to their proper acts and ends. Now among all others, the rational creature is subject to Divine providence in the most excellent way, in so far as it partakes of a share of providence, by being provident both for itself and for others. Wherefore it has a share of the Eternal Reason, whereby it has a natural inclination to its proper act and end: and this participation of the eternal law in the rational creature is called the natural law. Hence the Psalmist after saying (Psalms 4.6): *Offer up the sacrifice of justice,* as though someone asked what the works of justice are, adds: *Many say, Who showeth us good things?* in answer to which question he says: *The light of Thy countenance, O Lord, is signed upon us :* thus implying that the light of natural reason, whereby we discern what is good and what is evil, which is the function of the natural law, is nothing else than an imprint on us of the Divine light. It is therefore evident that the natural law is nothing else than the rational creature's participation of the eternal law.

Reply Obj. 1. This argument would hold, if the natural law were something different from the eternal law: whereas it is nothing but a participation thereof, as stated above.

Reply Obj. 2. Every act of reason and will in us is based on that which is according to nature . . . : for every act of reasoning is based on principles that are known naturally, and every act of appetite in respect of the means is derived from the natural appetite in respect of the last end. Accordingly the first direction of our acts to their end must needs be in virtue of the natural law.

Reply Obj. 3. Even irrational animals partake in their own way of the Eternal Reason, just as the rational creature does. But because the rational creature partakes thereof in an intellectual and rational manner, therefore the participation of the eternal law in the rational creature is properly called a law, since a law is something pertaining to reason . . . Irrational creatures, however, do not partake thereof in a rational manner, wherefore there is no participation of the eternal law in them, except by way of similitude.

Third Article.
Whether There Is a Human Law ?

We proceed thus to the Third Article:—

Objection 1. It would seem that there is not a human law. For the natural law is a participation of the eternal law, as stated above (A.2). Now through the eternal law *all things are most orderly,* as Augustine states. Therefore the natural law suffices for the ordering of all human affairs. Consequently there is no need for a human law.

Obj. 2. Further, a law bears the character of a measure. . . . But human reason is not a measure of things, but vice versa. . . . Therefore no law can emanate from human reason.

Obj. 3. Further, a measure should be most certain. . . . But the dictates of human reason in matters of conduct are uncertain, according to Book of Wisdom 9.14: *The thoughts of mortal men are fearful, and our counsels uncertain.* Therefore no law can emanate from human reason.

On the contrary, Augustine distinguishes two kinds of law, the one eternal, the other temporal, which he calls human.

I answer that . . . a law is a dictate of the practical reason. Now it is to be observed that the same procedure takes place in the practical and in the speculative reason: for each proceeds from principles to conclusions. . . . Accordingly we conclude that just as, in the speculative reason, from naturally known indemonstrable principles, we draw the conclusions of the various sciences, the knowledge of which is not imparted to us by nature, but acquired by the efforts of reason, so too it is from the precepts of the natural law, as from general and indemonstrable principles, that the human reason needs to proceed to the more particular determination of certain matters. These particular determinations, devised by human reason, are called human laws, provided the other essential conditions of law be observed. . . . Wherefore Tully says in his *Rhetoric* that *justice has its source in nature ; thence certain things came into custom by reason of their utility ; afterwards these things which emanated from nature and were approved by custom, were sanctioned by fear and reverence for the law.*

Reply Obj. 1. The human reason cannot have a full participation of the dictate of the Divine Reason, but according to its own mode, and imperfectly. Consequently, as on the part of the speculative reason, by a natural participation of Divine Wisdom, there is in us the knowledge of certain general principles, but not proper knowledge of each single truth, such as that contained in the Divine Wisdom; so too, on the part of the practical reason, man has a natural participation of the eternal law, according to certain general principles, but not as regards the particular determinations of individual cases, which are, however, contained in the eternal law. Hence the need for human reason to proceed further to sanction them by law.

Reply Obj. 2. Human reason is not, of itself, the rule of things: but the principles impressed on it by nature, are general rules and measured of all things relating to human conduct, whereof the natural reason is the rule and measure, although it is not the measure of things that are from nature.

Reply Obj. 3. The practical reason is concerned with practical matters, which are singular and contingent: but not with necessary things, with which the speculative reason is concerned. Wherefore human laws cannot have that inerrancy that belongs to the demonstrated conclusions of sciences. Nor is it necessary for every measure to be altogether unerring and certain, but according as it is possible in its own particular genus.

Fourth Article.
Whether There Was Any Need for a Divine Law ?
We proceed thus to the Fourth Article:—

Objection 1. It would seem that there was no need for a Divine law. Because, as stated above (A. 2), the natural law is a participation in us of the eternal law. But the eternal law is a Divine law, as stated above (A. I). Therefore there is no need for a Divine law in addition to the natural law, and human laws derived therefrom.

Obj. 2. Further, it is written (Ecclesiasticus 15.14) that *God left man in the hand of his own counsel.* Now counsel is an act of reason. . . . Therefore man was left to the direction of his reason. But a dictate of human reason is a human law, as stated above (A. 3). Therefore there is no need for man to be governed also by a Divine law.

Obj. 3. Further, human nature is more self-sufficing than irrational creatures. But irrational creatures have no Divine law besides the natural inclination impressed on them. Much less, therefore, should the rational creature have a Divine law in addition to the natural law.

On the contrary, David prayed God to set His law before him, saying (Psalms 118.33): *Set before me for a law the way of Thy justifications, O Lord.*

I answer that, Besides the natural and the human law it was necessary for the directing of human conduct to have a Divine law. And this for four reasons. First, because it is by law that man is directed how to perform his proper acts in view of his last end. And indeed if man were ordained to no other end than that which is proportionate to his natural faculty, there would be no need for man to have any further direction on the part of his reason, besides the natural law and human law which is derived from it. But since man is ordained to an end of eternal happiness which is improportionate to man's natural faculty, . . . therefore it was necessary that, besides the natural and the human law, man should be directed to his end by a law given by God.

Secondly, because, on account of the uncertainty of human judgment, especially on contingent and particular matters, different people form different judgments on human acts; whence also different and contrary laws result. In order, therefore, that man may know without any doubt what he ought to do and what he ought to avoid, it was necessary for man to be directed in his proper acts by a law given by God, for it is certain that such a law cannot err.

Thirdly, because man can make laws in those matters of which he is competent to judge. But man is not competent to judge of interior movements, that are hidden, but only of exterior acts which appear: and yet for the perfection of virtue it is necessary for man to conduct himself aright in both kinds of acts. Consequently human law could not sufficiently curb and direct interior acts; and it was necessary for this purpose that a Divine law should supervene.

Fourthly, because, as Augustine says, human law cannot punish or forbid all evil deeds: since while aiming at doing away with all evils, it would do away with many good things, and would hinder the advance of the common good, which is necessary for human intercourse. In order, therefore, that no evil might remain unforbidden and unpunished, it was necessary for the Divine law to supervene, whereby all sins are forbidden.

And these four causes are touched upon in Psalms 118.8, where it is said: *The law of the Lord is unspotted,* i.e., allowing no foulness of sin; *converting souls,* because it directs not only exterior, but also interior acts; *the testimony of the Lord is faithful,* because of the certainty of what is true and right; *giving wisdom to little ones,* by directing man to an end supernatural and Divine.

Reply Obj. 1. By the natural law the eternal law is participated proportionately to the capacity of human nature. But to his supernatural end man needs to be directed in a yet higher way. Hence the additional law given by God, whereby man shares more perfectly in the eternal law.

Reply Obj. 2. Counsel is a kind of inquiry: hence it must proceed from some principles. Nor is it

enough for it to proceed from principles imparted by nature, which are the precepts of the natural law, for the reasons given above: but there is need for certain additional principles, namely, the precepts of the Divine law.

Reply Obj. 3. Irrational creatures are not ordained to an end higher than that which is proportionate to their natural powers: consequently the comparison fails.

Fifth Article.
Whether There Is But One Divine Law?

We proceed thus to the Fifth Article:—

Objection 1. It would seem that there is but one Divine law. Because, where there is one king in one kingdom there is but one law. Now the whole of mankind is compared to God as to one king, according to Psalms 46.8: *God is the King of all the earth.* Therefore there is but one Divine law.

Obj. 2. Further, every law is directed to the end which the lawgiver intends for those for whom he makes the law. But God intends one and the same thing for all men; since according to 1 Timothy 2.4: *He will have all men to be saved, and to come to the knowledge of the truth.* Therefore there is but one Divine law.

Obj. 3. Further, the Divine law seems to be more akin to the eternal law, which is one, than the natural law, according as the revelation of grace is of a higher order than natural knowledge. Therefore much more is the Divine law but one.

On the contrary, The Apostle says (Hebrews 7.12): *The priesthood being translated, it is necessary that a translation also be made of the law.* But the priesthood is twofold, as stated in the same passage, viz., the levitical priesthood, and the priesthood of Christ. Therefore the Divine law is twofold, namely, the Old Law and the New Law.

I answer that . . . distinction is the cause of number. Now things may be distinguished in two ways. First, as those things that are altogether specifically different, *e.g.,* a horse and an ox. Secondly, as perfect and imperfect in the same species, *e.g.,* a boy and a man: and in this way the Divine law is divided into Old and New. Hence the Apostle (Galatians 3.24, 25) compares the state of man under the Old Law to that of a child *under a pedagogue ;* but the state under the New Law, to that of a full grown man, who is *no longer under a pedagogue.*

Now the perfection and imperfection of these two laws is to be taken in connection with the three conditions pertaining to law, as stated above. For, in the first place, it belongs to law to be directed to the common good as to its end. . . . This good may be twofold. It may be a sensible and earthly good; and to this, man was directly ordained by the Old Law: wherefore, at the very outset of the law, the people were invited to the earthly kingdom of the Chananæans (Exodus 3.8, 17). Again it may be an intelligible and heavenly good: and to this, man is ordained by the New Law. Wherefore, at the very beginning of His preaching, Christ invited men to the kingdom of heaven, saying (Matthew 4.17): *Do penance, for the kingdom of heaven is at hand.* Hence Augustine says that *promises of temporal goods are contained in the Old Testament, for which reason it is called old; but the promise of eternal life belongs to the New Testament.*

Secondly, it belongs to the law to direct human acts according to the order of righteousness (A. 4): wherein also the New Law surpasses the Old Law, since it directs our internal acts, according to Matthew 5.20: *Unless your justice abound more than that of the Scribes and Pharisees, you shall not enter into the kingdom of heaven.* Hence the saying that *the Old Law restrains the hand, but the New Law controls the mind.*

Thirdly, it belongs to the law to induce men to observe its commandments. This the Old Law did by the fear of punishment: but the New Law, by love, which is poured into our hearts by the grace of Christ, bestowed in the New Law, but foreshadowed in the Old. Hence Augustine says that *there is little difference between the Law and the Gospel—fear and love.*

Reply Obj. 1. As the father of a family issues different commands to the children and to the adults, so also the one King, God, in His one kingdom, gave one law to men, while they were yet imperfect, and another more perfect law, when, by the preceding law, they had been led to a greater capacity for Divine things.

Reply Obj. 2. The salvation of man could not be achieved otherwise than through Christ, according to Acts 4.12: *There is no other name . . . given to men, whereby we must be saved.* Consequently the law that brings all to salvation could not be given until after the coming of Christ. But before His coming it was necessary to give to the people, of whom Christ was to be born, a law containing certain rudiments of righteousness unto salvation, in order to prepare them to receive Him.

Reply Obj. 3. The natural law directs man by way of certain general precepts, common to both the perfect and the imperfect: wherefore it is one and the same for all. But the Divine law directs man also in certain particular matters, to which the perfect and imperfect do not stand in the same relation. Hence the necessity for the Divine law to be twofold, as already explained.

* * *

QUESTION 94
OF THE NATURAL LAW.

First Article.
Whether the Natural Law Is a Habit?

We proceed thus to the First Article:—

Objection 1. It would seem that the natural law is a habit. Because, as the Philosopher [Aristotle] says, *there are three things in the soul, power, habit, and passion.* But the natural law is not one of the soul's powers: nor is it one of the passions; as we may see by going through them one by one. Therefore the natural law is a habit.

Obj. 2. Further, Basil says that the conscience or *synderesis is the law of our mind ;* which can only apply to the natural law. But the *synderesis* is a habit. . . . Therefore the natural law is a habit.

Obj. 3. Further, the natural law abides in man always, as will be shown further on (A. 6). But man's reason, which the law regards, does not always think about the natural law. Therefore the natural law is not an act, but a habit.

On the contrary, Augustine says that *a habit is that whereby something is done when necessary.* But such is not the natural law: since it is in infants and in the damned who cannot act by it. Therefore the natural law is not a habit.

I answer that, A thing may be called a habit in two ways. First, properly and essentially: and thus the natural law is not a habit. For . . . the natural law is something appointed by reason, just as a proposition is a work of reason. Now that which a man does is not the same as that whereby he does it: for he makes a becoming speech by the habit of grammar. Since then a habit is that by which we act, a law cannot be a habit properly and essentially.

Secondly, the term habit may be applied to that which we hold by a habit: thus faith may mean that which we hold by faith. And accordingly, since the precepts of the natural law are sometimes considered by reason actually, while sometimes they are in the reason only habitually, in this way the natural law may be called a habit. Thus, in speculative matters, the indemonstrable principles are not the habit itself whereby we hold those principles, but are the principles the habit of which we possess.

Reply Obj. 1. The Philosopher proposes there to discover the genus of virtue; and since it is evident that virtue is a principle of action, he mentions only those things which are principles of human acts, viz., powers, habits and passions. But there are other things in the soul besides these three: there are acts; thus *to will* is in the one that wills; again, things known are in the knower; moreover its own natural properties are in the soul, such as immortality and the like.

Reply Obj. 2. *Synderesis* is said to be the law of our mind, because it is a habit containing the precepts of the natural law, which are the first principles of human actions.

Reply Obj. 3. This argument proves that the natural law is held habitually: and this is granted.

To the argument advanced in the contrary sense we reply that sometimes a man is unable to make use of that which is in him habitually, on account of some impediment: thus, on account of sleep, a man is unable to use the habit of science. In like manner, through the deficiency of his age, a child cannot use the habit of understanding of principles, or the natural law, which is in him habitually.

Second Article.
Whether the Natural Law Contains Several Precepts, or One Only?
We proceed thus to the Second Article:—

Objection 1. It would seem that the natural law contains, not several precepts, but one only. For law is a kind of precept. . . . If therefore there were many precepts of the natural law, it would follow that there are also many natural laws.

Obj. 2. Further, the natural law is consequent to human nature. But human nature, as a whole, is one; though, as to its parts, it is manifold. Therefore, either there is but one precept of the law of nature, on account of the unity of nature as a whole; or there are many, by reason of the number of parts of human nature. The result would be that even things relating to the inclination of the concupiscible faculty belong to the natural law.

Obj. 3. Further, law is something pertaining to reason. . . . Now reason is but one in man. Therefore there is only one precept of the natural law.

On the contrary, The precepts of the natural law in man stand in relation to practical matters, as the first principles to matters of demonstration. But there are several first indemonstrable principles. Therefore there are also several precepts of the natural law.

I answer that . . . the precepts of the natural law are to the practical reason, what the first principles of demonstrations are to the speculative reason; because both are self-evident principles. Now a thing is said to be self-evident in two ways: first, in itself; secondly, in relation to us. Any proposition is said to be self-evident in itself, if its predicate is contained in the notion of the subject: although, to one who knows not the definition of the subject, it happens that such a proposition is not self-evident. For instance, this proposition, *Man is a rational being,* is, in its very nature, self-evident, since who says *man,* says *a rational being :* and yet to one who knows not what a man is, this proposition is not self-evident. Hence it is that, as Boethius says, certain axioms or propositions are universally self-evident to all; and such are those propositions whose terms are known to all, as, *Every whole is greater than its part,* and, *Things equal to one and the same are equal to one another.* But some propositions are self-evident only to the wise, who understand the meaning of the terms of such propositions: thus to one who understands that an angel is not a body, it is self-evident that an angel is not circumscriptively in a place: but this is not evident to the unlearned, for they cannot grasp it.

Now a certain order is to be found in those things that are apprehended universally. For that which, before aught else, falls under apprehension, is *being,* the notion of which is included in all things whatsoever a man apprehends. Wherefore the first indemonstrable principle is that *the same thing cannot be affirmed and denied at the same time,* which is based on the notion of *being* and *not-being:* and on this principle all others are based. . . . Now as *being* is the first thing that falls under the apprehension simply, so *good* is the first thing that falls under the apprehension of the practical reason, which is directed to action: since every agent acts for an end under the aspect of good. Consequently the first principle in the practical reason is one founded on the notion of good, viz., that *good is that which all things seek after.* Hence this is the first precept of law, that *good is to be done and ensued, and evil is to be avoided.* All other precepts of the natural law are based upon this: so that whatever the practical reason naturally apprehends as man's good (or evil) belongs to the precepts of the natural law as something to be done or avoided.

Since, however, good has the nature of an end, and evil, the nature of a contrary, hence it is that all those things to which man has a natural inclination, are naturally apprehended by reason as being good, and consequently as objects of pursuit, and their contraries as evil, and objects of avoidance. Wherefore according to the order of natural inclinations, is the order of the precepts of the natural law. Because in man there is first of all an inclination to good in accordance with the nature which he has in common with all substances: inasmuch as every substance seeks the preservation of its own being, according to its nature: and by reason of this inclination, whatever is a means of preserving human life, and of warding off its obstacles, belongs to the natural law.

Secondly, there is in man an inclination to things that pertain to him more specially, according to that nature which he has in common with other animals: and in virtue of this inclination, those things are said to belong to the natural law, *which nature has taught to all animals,* such as sexual intercourse, education of offspring and so forth. Thirdly, there is in man an inclination to good, according to the nature of his reason, which nature is proper to him: thus man has a natural inclination to know the truth about God, and to live in society: and in this respect, whatever pertains to this inclination belongs to the natural law; for instance, to shun ignorance, to avoid offending those among whom one has to live, and other such things regarding the above inclination.

Reply Obj. 1. All these precepts of the law of nature have the character of one natural law, inasmuch as they flow from one first precept.

Reply Obj. 2. All the inclinations of any parts whatsoever of human nature, *e.g.,* of the concupiscible and irascible parts, in so far as they are ruled by reason, belong to the natural law, and are reduced to one first precept, as stated above: so that the precepts of the natural law are many in themselves, but are based on one common foundation.

Reply Obj. 3. Although reason is one in itself, yet it directs all things regarding man; so that whatever can be ruled by reason, is contained under the law of reason.

Third Article.

Whether All Acts of Virtue Are Prescribed by the Natural Law ?

We proceed thus to the Third Article:—

Objection 1. It would seem that not all acts of virtue are prescribed by the natural law. Because . . . it is essential to a law that it be ordained to the common good. But some acts of virtue are ordained to the private good of the individual, as is evident especially in regard to acts of temperance. Therefore not all acts of virtue are the subject of natural law.

Obj. 2. Further, every sin is opposed to some virtuous act. If therefore all acts of virtue are prescribed by the natural law, it seems to follow that all sins are against nature: whereas this applies to certain special sins.

Obj. 3. Further, those things which are according to nature are common to all. But acts of virtue are not common to all: since a thing is virtuous in one, and vicious in another. Therefore not all acts of virtue are prescribed by the natural law.

On the contrary, Damascene says that *virtues are natural.* Therefore virtuous acts also are a subject of the natural law.

I answer that, We may speak of virtuous acts in two ways: first, under the aspect of virtuous; secondly, as such and such acts considered in their proper species. If then we speak of acts of virtue, considered as virtuous, thus all virtuous acts belong to the natural law. For it has been stated (A. 2) that to the natural law belongs everything to which a man is inclined according to his nature. Now each thing is inclined naturally to an operation that is suitable to it according to its form: thus fire is inclined to give heat. Wherefore, since the rational soul is the proper form of man, there is in every man a natural inclination to act according to reason: and this is to act according to virtue. Consequently, considered thus, all acts of virtue are prescribed by the natural law: since each one's reason naturally dictates to him to act virtuously. But if we speak of virtuous acts, considered in themselves, i.e., in their proper species, thus not all virtuous acts are prescribed by the natural law: for many things are done virtuously, to which nature does not incline at first; but which, through the inquiry of reason, have been found by men to be conducive to well-living.

Reply Obj. 1. Temperance is about the natural concupiscences of food, drink and sexual matters, which are indeed ordained to the natural common good, just as other matters of law are ordained to the moral common good.

Reply Obj. 2. By human nature we may mean either that which is proper to man—and in this sense all sins, as being against reason, are also against nature, as Damascene states: or we may mean that nature which is common to man and other animals; and in this sense, certain special sins are said to be against nature; thus contrary to sexual intercourse, which is natural to all animals, is unisexual lust, which has received the special name of the unnatural crime.

Reply Obj. 3. This argument considers acts in themselves. For it is owing to the various conditions of men, that certain acts are virtuous for some, as being proportionate and becoming to them, while they are vicious for others, as being out of proportion to them.

Fourth Article.
Whether the Natural Law Is the Same in All Men?

We proceed thus to the Fourth Article:—

Objection 1. It would seem that the natural law is not the same in all. For it is stated in the Decretals that *the natural law is that which is contained in the Law and the Gospel.* But this is not common to all men; because, as it is written (Romans 10.16), *all do not obey the gospel.* Therefore the natural law is not the same in all men.

Obj. 2. Further, *Things which are according to the law are said to be just. . . .* But . . . nothing is so universally just as not to be subject to change in regard to some men. Therefore even the natural law is not the same in all men.

Obj. 3. Further . . . to the natural law belongs everything to which a man is inclined according to his nature. Now different men are naturally inclined to different things; some to the desire of pleasures, others to the desire of honours, and other men to other things. Therefore there is not one natural law for all.

On the contrary, Isidore says: *The natural law is common to all nations.*

I answer that . . . to the natural law belongs those things to which a man is inclined naturally: and among these it is proper to man to be inclined to act according to reason. Now the process of reason is from the common to the proper. . . . The speculative reason, however, is differently situated in this matter, from the practical reason. For, since the speculative reason is busied chiefly with necessary things, which cannot be otherwise than they are, its proper conclusions, like the universal principles, contain the truth without fail. The practical reason, on the other hand, is busied with contingent matters, about which human actions are concerned: and consequently, although there is necessity in the general principles, the more we descend to matters of detail, the more frequently we encounter defects. Accordingly then in speculative matters truth is the same in all men, both as to principles and as to conclusions: although the truth is not known to all as regards the conclusions, but only as regards the principles which are called common notions. But in matters of action, truth or practical rectitude is not the same for all, as to matters of detail, but only as to the general principles: and where there is the same rectitude in matters of detail, it is not equally known to all.

It is therefore evident that, as regards the general principles whether of speculative or of practical reason, truth or rectitude is the same for all, and is equally known by all. As to the proper conclusions of the speculative reason, the truth is the same for all, but is not equally known to all: thus it is true for all that the three angles of a triangle are together equal to two right angles, although it is not known to all. But as to the proper conclusions of the practical reason, neither is the truth or rectitude the same for all, nor, where it is the same, is it equally known by all. Thus it is right and true for all to act according to reason: and from this principle it follows as a proper conclusion, that goods entrusted to another should be restored to their owner. Now this is true for the majority of cases: but it may happen in a particular case that it would be injurious, and therefore unreasonable, to restore goods held in trust; for instance if they are claimed for the purpose of fighting against one's country. And this principle will be found to fail the more, according as we descend further into detail, *e.g.*, if one were to say that goods held in trust should be restored with such and such a guarantee, or in such and such a way; because the greater the number of conditions added, the greater the number of ways in which the principle may fail, so that it be not right to restore or not to restore.

Consequently we must say that the natural law, as to general principles, is the same for all, both as to rectitude and as to knowledge. But as to certain matters of detail, which are conclusions, as it were, of those general principles, it is the same for all in the majority of cases, both as to rectitude and as to knowledge; and yet in some few cases it may fail, both as to rectitude, by reason of certain obstacles (just as natures subject to generation and corruption fail in some few cases on account of some obstacle), and as to knowledge, since in some the reason is perverted by passion, or evil habit, or an evil disposition of nature; thus formerly, theft, although it is expressly contrary to the natural law, was not considered wrong among the Germans, as Julius Cæsar relates.

Reply Obj. 1. The meaning of the sentence quoted is not that whatever is contained in the Law and the Gospel belongs to the natural law, since they contain many things that are above nature; but that whatever belongs to the natural law is fully contained in them. Wherefore Gratian, after saying that *the natural law is what is contained in the Law and the Gospel,* adds at once, by way of example, *by which everyone is commanded to do to others as he would be done by.*

Reply Obj. 2. The saying of the Philosopher is to be understood of things that are naturally just, not as general principles, but as conclusions drawn from them, having rectitude in the majority of cases, but failing in a few.

Reply Obj. 3. As, in man, reason rules and commands the other powers, so all the natural inclinations belonging to the other powers must needs be directed according to reason. Wherefore it is universally right for all men, that all their inclinations should be directed according to reason.

Fifth Article.
Whether the Natural Law Can Be Changed?

We proceed thus to the Fifth Article:—

Objection 1. It would seem that the natural law can be changed. Because on Ecclesiasticus 17.9, *He gave them instructions, and the law of life,* the gloss says: *He wished the law of the letter to be written, in order to correct the law of nature.* But that which is corrected is changed. Therefore the natural law can be changed.

Obj. 2. Further, the slaying of the innocent, adultery, and theft are against the natural law. But we find these things changed by God: as when God commanded Abraham to slay his innocent son (Genesis 22.2); and when He ordered the Jews to borrow and purloin the vessels of the Egyptians (Exodus 12.35); and when He commanded Osce to take to himself *a wife of fornications* (Hosea 1.2). Therefore the natural law can be changed.

Obj. 3. Further, Isidore says that *the possession of all things in common, and universal freedom, are matters of natural law.* But these things are seen to be changed by human laws. Therefore it seems that the natural law is subject to change.

On the contrary, It is said in the Decretals: *The natural law dates from the creation of the rational creature. It does not vary according to time, but remains unchangeable.*

I answer that, A change in the natural law may be understood in two ways. First, by way of addition. In this sense nothing hinders the natural law from being changed: since many things for the benefit of human life have been added over and above the natural law, both by the Divine law and by human laws.

Secondly, a change in the natural law may be understood by way of subtraction, so that what previously was according to the natural law, ceases to be so. In this sense, the natural law is altogether unchangeable in its first principles: but in its secondary principles, which, as we have said (A. 4), are certain detailed proximate conclusions drawn from the first principles, the natural law is not changed so that what it prescribes be not right in most cases. But it may be changed in some particular cases of rare occurrence, through some special causes hindering the observance of such precepts, as stated above (A. 4).

Reply Obj. 1. The written law is said to be given for the correction of the natural law, either because it supplies what was wanting to the natural law; or because the natural law was perverted in the hearts of some men, as to certain matters, so that they esteemed those things good which are naturally evil; which perversion stood in need of correction.

Reply Obj. 2. All men alike, both guilty and innocent, die the death of nature: which death of nature is inflicted by the power of God on account of orig-

inal sin, according to 1 Kings 2.6: *The Lord killeth and maketh alive.* Consequently, by the command of God, death can be inflicted on any man, guilty or innocent, without any injustice whatever.—In like manner adultery is intercourse with another's wife; who is allotted to him by the law emanating from God. Consequently intercourse with any woman, by the command of God, is neither adultery nor fornication.—The same applies to theft, which is the taking of another's property. For whatever is taken by the command of God, to Whom all things belong, is not taken against the will of its owner, whereas it is in this that theft consists.—Nor is it only in human things, that whatever is commanded by God is right; but also in natural things, whatever is done by God, is, in some way, natural. . . .

Reply Obj. 3. A thing is said to belong to the natural law in two ways. First, because nature inclines thereto: *e.g.,* that one should not do harm to another. Secondly, because nature did not bring in the contrary: thus we might say that for man to be naked is of the natural law, because nature did not give him clothes, but art invented them. In this sense, *the possession of all things in common and universal freedom* are said to be of the natural law, because, to wit, the distinction of possessions and slavery were not brought in by nature, but devised by human reason for the benefit of human life. Accordingly the law of nature was not changed in this respect, except by addition.

Sixth Article.
Whether the Law of Nature Can Be Abolished from the Heart of Man?

We proceed thus to the Sixth Article:—

Objection 1. It would seem that the natural law can be abolished from the heart of man. Because on Romans 2.14, *When the Gentiles who have not the law,* etc., a gloss says that *the law of righteousness, which sin had blotted out, is graven on the heart of man when he is restored by grace.* But the law of righteousness is the law of nature. Therefore the law of nature can be blotted out.

Obj. 2. Further, the law of grace is more efficacious than the law of nature. But the law of grace is blotted out by sin. Much more therefore can the law of nature be blotted out.

Obj. 3. Further, that which is established by law is made just. But many things are enacted by men, which are contrary to the law of nature. Therefore the law of nature can be abolished from the heart of man.

On the contrary, Augustine says: *Thy law is written in the hearts of men, which iniquity itself effaces not.* But the law which is written in men's hearts is the natural law. Therefore the natural law cannot be blotted out.

I answer that . . . there belong to the natural law, first, certain most general precepts, that are known to all; and secondly, certain secondary and more detailed precepts, which are, as it were, conclusions following closely from first principles. As to those general principles, the natural law, in the abstract, can nowise be blotted out from men's hearts. But it is blotted out in the case of a particular action, in so far as reason is hindered from applying the general principle to a particular point of practice on account of concupiscence or some other passion. . . . —But as to the other, *i.e.,* the secondary precepts, the natural law can be blotted out from the human heart, either by evil persuasions, just as in speculative matters errors occur in respect of necessary conclusions; or by vicious customs and corrupt habits, as among some men, theft, and even unnatural vices, as the Apostle states, were not esteemed sinful.

Reply Obj. 1. Sin blots out the law of nature in particular cases, not universally, except perchance in regard to the secondary precepts of the natural law, in the way stated above.

Reply Obj. 2. Although grace is more efficacious than nature, yet nature is more essential to man, and therefore more enduring.

Reply Obj. 3. This argument is true of the secondary precepts of the natural law, against which some legislators have framed certain enactments which are unjust.

Virtue Ethics: Be a Good Person

Consequentialist moral theories are concerned with the consequences of actions, for the consequences determine the moral rightness of conduct. The production of good over evil is the essence of morality. Nonconsequentialist moral theories are concerned with the moral nature of actions, for the right-making characteristics of actions determine the rightness of conduct. Virtue ethics, however, takes a different turn. **Virtue ethics** is a theory of morality that makes virtue the central concern. When confronted with a moral problem, a utilitarian or a Kantian theorist asks, "What should I *do*?" But a virtue ethicist asks, in effect, "What should I *be*?" For the former, moral conduct is primarily a matter of following or applying a moral principle or rule to a particular situation, and morality is mainly duty-based. For the latter, moral conduct is something that emanates from a person's moral virtues, from his or her moral character, not from obedience to moral laws. In this chapter we try to understand both the main attractions and the major criticisms of this virtue-centered approach to ethics and the moral life.

THE ETHICS OF VIRTUE

Most modern virtue ethicists trace their theoretical roots back to the ancients, most notably to Aristotle (384–322 B.C.E.). His ethics is a coherent, virtue-based view that interlocks with his broader philosophical concerns—his theories about causation, society, self, education, mind, and metaphysics. He says the moral life consists not in following moral rules that stipulate right actions but in striving to be a particular kind of person— a virtuous person whose actions stem naturally from virtuous character.

For Aristotle, every living being has an end toward which it naturally aims. Life is teleological; it is meant not just to *be* something but to *aspire toward* something, to fulfill its proper function. What is the proper aim of human beings? Aristotle argues that the true goal of humans— their greatest good—is **eudaimonia,** which means "happiness" or "flourishing" and refers to the full realization of the good life. To achieve *eudaimonia,* human beings must fulfill the function that is natural and distinctive to them: living fully in accordance with reason. The life of reason entails a life of virtue because the virtues themselves are rational modes of behaving. Thus Aristotle says, "Happiness is an activity of the soul in accordance with complete or perfect virtue." The virtuous life both helps human beings *achieve* true happiness and *is the realization of* true happiness. Virtues make you good, *and* they help you have a good life.

A **virtue** is a stable disposition to act and feel according to some ideal or model of excellence. It is a deeply embedded character trait that can affect actions in countless situations. Aristotle distinguishes between intellectual and moral virtues. Intellectual virtues include wisdom, prudence, rationality, and the like. Moral virtues include fairness, benevolence, honesty, loyalty, conscientiousness, and courage. He believes that intellectual virtues can be taught, just as logic and

CRITICAL THOUGHT: Learning Virtues in the Classroom

A few years ago the *New York Times* reported that the teaching of traditional virtues such as honesty and civility was becoming more common in public schools. The article highlighted Paul Meck, an elementary school guidance counselor who spent much of his time teaching students about virtues and values. Meck's approach was to visit classrooms and lead discussions on such topics as honesty, friendship, and shoplifting. When he talked to younger students, he played his guitar and sang lyrics that underscored his points. "Whether through song, discussion or simply a straightforward lecture," the reporter noted, "there is an effort afoot to awaken the interest of youngsters in these subjects."*

Would Aristotle approve of the methods cited here (song, discussion, lecture)? Why or why not? What type of virtue education would he approve of? Which approach—Aristotle's or the one mentioned in this excerpt—do you think would be most effective? Give reasons for your answer.

* Gene I. Maeroff, "About Education; Values Regain Their Popularity," *New York Times*, Science Desk, 10 April 1984.

mathematics can be taught. But moral virtues can be learned only through practice:

[M]oral virtue comes about as a result of habit. . . . From this it is also plain that none of the moral virtues arises in us by nature. . . . [B]ut the virtues we get by first exercising them, as also happens in the case of the arts as well. For the things we have to learn before we can do them, we learn by doing them, e.g. men become builders by building and lyreplayers by playing the lyre; so too we become just by doing just acts, temperate by doing temperate acts, brave by doing brave acts.[1]

Aristotle's notion of a moral virtue is what he calls the "**Golden Mean,**" a balance between two behavioral extremes. A moral virtue (courage, for example) is the midpoint between excess (an excess of courage, or foolhardiness) and deficit (a deficit of courage, or cowardice). For Aristotle, then, the virtuous—and happy—life is a life of moderation in all things.

Modern virtue ethicists follow Aristotle's lead in many respects. Some thinkers take issue with his teleological theory of human nature and his concept of a virtue as a mean between opposing tendencies. And some have offered interesting alternatives to his virtue ethics. But almost all virtue theories owe a debt to Aristotle in one way or another.

Like Aristotle, contemporary thinkers put the emphasis on quality of character and virtues (character traits), rather than on adherence to particular principles or rules of right action. They are of course concerned with doing the right thing, but moral obligations are derived from virtues. Virtue ethicists are, for example, less likely to ask whether lying is wrong in a particular situation than whether the action or person is honest or dishonest, or whether honesty precludes lying in this case, or whether an exemplar of honesty (say, Gandhi or Jesus) would lie in these circumstances.

Contemporary virtue ethicists are also Aristotelian in believing that a pure duty-based morality of rule adherence represents a barren, one-dimensional conception of the moral life. First, they agree with Aristotle that the cultivation

[1]Aristotle, *Nicomachean Ethics*, trans. W. D. Ross, book II, chapter 1, eBooks@Adelaide, 2004.

of virtues is not merely a moral requirement—it is a way (some would say the *only* way) to ensure human flourishing and the good life. Second, they maintain that a full-blown ethics must take into account motives, feelings, intentions, and moral wisdom—factors that they think duty-based morality neglects. This view contrasts dramatically with Kant's duty-based ethics. He argues that to act morally is simply to act out of duty—that is, to do our duty *because* it is our duty. We need not act out of friendship, loyalty, kindness, love, or sympathy. But in virtue ethics, acting from such motivations is a crucial part of acting from a virtuous character, for virtues are stable dispositions that naturally include motivations and feelings. Contrast the action of someone who methodically aids his sick mother solely out of a sense of duty with the person who tends to her mother out of sympathy, love, and loyalty (perhaps in addition to a sense of duty). Most people would probably think that the latter is a better model of the moral life, while the former seems incomplete.

Virtue in Action

If moral rules are secondary in virtue ethics, how does a virtue ethicist make moral decisions or guide his or her conduct or judge the behavior of others? Suppose Helen, a conscientious practitioner of Aristotelian virtue ethics, hears William lie to a friend to avoid paying a debt. She does not have to appeal to a moral rule such as "Do not lie" to know that William's action is an instance of dishonesty (or untruthfulness) and that William himself is dishonest. She can see by his actions that he lacks the virtue of honesty.

But to Helen, honesty is more than just a character trait: it is also an essential part of human happiness and flourishing. In her case, honesty is a virtue that she has cultivated for years by behaving honestly and truthfully in a variety of situations (not just in cases of lying). She has taken such trouble in part because cultivating this virtue has helped her become the kind of person she

wants to be. She has developed the disposition to act honestly; acting honestly is part of who she is. She sometimes relies on moral rules (or moral rules of thumb) to make moral decisions, but she usually does not need them, because her actions naturally reflect her virtuous character.

In addition, Helen's trained virtues not only guide her actions, but they also inspire the motivations and feelings appropriate to the actions. Helen avoids dishonest dealings, and she does so because that is what a virtuous person would do, because she has compassion and sympathy for innocent people who are cheated, and because dishonesty is not conducive to human happiness and flourishing.

What guidance can Helen obtain in her strivings toward a moral ideal? Like most virtue ethicists, she looks to moral exemplars—people who embody the virtues and inspire others to follow in their steps. (For exemplars of honesty, Helen has several moral heroes to choose from—Socrates, Gandhi, Jesus, the Buddha, Thomas Aquinas, and many others.) As the philosopher Louis Pojman says of virtue systems,

The primary focus is not on abstract reason but on ideal types of persons or on actual ideal persons. Discovering the proper moral example and imitating that person or ideal type thus replace casuistic reason as the most significant aspects of the moral life. Eventually, the apprentice-like training in virtue gained by imitating the ideal model results in a virtuous person who spontaneously does what is good.[2]

Evaluating Virtue Ethics

A case can be made for virtue ethics based on how well it seems to explain important aspects of the moral life. Some philosophers, for example, claim that the virtue approach offers a more plausible explanation of the role of motivation in moral

---

[2]Louis P. Pojman, *Ethics: Discovering Right and Wrong*, 4th ed. (Belmont, CA: Wadsworth, 2002), 165.

actions than duty-based moral systems do. By Kantian lights your conduct may be morally acceptable even if you, say, save a friend's life out of a sense of duty alone (that is, without any sincere regard for your friend). But this motivation—your calculating sense of duty—seems a very cold and anemic motivation indeed. Virtue theorists would say that a more natural and morally appropriate response would be to save your friend primarily out of compassion, love, loyalty, or something similar—and these motives are just what we would expect from a virtuous person acting from fully developed virtues.

Some philosophers also remind us that virtue ethics puts primary emphasis on being a good person and living a good life, a life of happiness and flourishing. They say that these aims are obviously central to the moral life and should be part of any adequate theory of morality. Duty-based moral systems, however, pay much less attention to these essential elements.

Many duty-based theorists are willing to concede that there is some truth in both these claims. They believe that motivation for moral action cannot be derived entirely from considerations of duty, just as appropriate motivation cannot be based solely on virtuous character. And they recognize that the moral life involves more than merely honoring rules and principles. As Aristotle insists, there should be room for moral achievement in morality, for striving toward moral ideals. But even if these claims of the virtue ethicist are true, it does not follow that traditional virtue ethics is the best moral theory or that an ethics without duties or principles is plausible.

Virtue-based ethics seems to meet the minimum requirement of coherence, and it appears to be generally consistent with our commonsense moral judgments and moral experience. Nevertheless critics have taken it to task, with most of the strongest criticisms centering on alleged problems with applying the theory—in other words, with usefulness (Criterion 3).

The critics' main contention is that appeals to virtues or virtuous character without reference to principles of duty cannot give us any useful guidance in deciding what to do. Suppose we are trying to decide what to do when a desperately poor stranger steals money from us. Should we have him arrested? Give him even more money? Ignore the whole affair? According to virtue ethics, we should do what a virtuous person would do, or do what moral exemplars such as Jesus or Buddha would do, or do what is benevolent or conscientious. But what exactly *would* a virtuous person do? Or what precisely *is* the benevolent or conscientious action? As many philosophers see it, the problem is that virtue ethics says that the right action is the one performed by the virtuous person and that the virtuous person is the one who performs the right action. But this is to argue in a circle and to give us no help in figuring out what to do. To avoid this circularity, they say, we must appeal to some kind of moral standard or principle to evaluate the action itself. Before we can decide if a person is virtuous, we need to judge if her actions are right or wrong—and such judgments take us beyond virtue ethics.

Some argue in a similar vein by pointing out that a person may possess all the proper virtues and still be unable to tell right from wrong actions. Dr. Green may be benevolent and just and still not know if stem cell research should be continued or stopped, or if he should help a terminal patient commit suicide, or if he should perform a late-term abortion. Likewise, we know that it is possible for a virtuous person to act entirely from virtue—and still commit an immoral act. This shows, critics say, that the rightness of actions does not necessarily (or invariably) depend on the content of one's character. We seem to have independent moral standards—independent of character considerations—by which we judge the moral permissibility of actions.

The virtue theorist can respond to these criticisms by asserting that there actually is plenty of

CRITICAL THOUGHT: Warrior Virtues and Moral Disagreements

A recent report from *Voice of America* told of a dispute over the war in Iraq among highly regarded war veterans. Democratic Representative John Murtha, a decorated Marine Corps veteran who fought in Vietnam, is a strong supporter of the military—but thought the war in Iraq was a disaster and demanded that U.S. forces be withdrawn from Iraq within six months. Democratic Senator John Kerry, also a decorated veteran of the Vietnam War, disagreed with Murtha's timetable for troop withdrawal. He proposed that troops start to leave Iraq later, in early 2007. Republican Senator John McCain, a former Navy fighter pilot and POW in the Vietnam conflict, supported the president's view that the troops should stay in Iraq until the job was done.*

Assume that all these men are honorable and have all the appropriate warrior virtues such as courage and loyalty. If they are then comparably virtuous in the ways indicated, how could they disagree about the conduct of the war? Suppose they all possessed exactly the same virtues to exactly the same degree and had access to the same set of facts about the war. Would it still be possible for them to disagree? Why or why not? Do you think that any of these considerations suggest that virtue ethics may be a flawed moral theory? Why or why not?

* Jim Malone, "Waning US Iraq War Support Stirs New Comparisons to Vietnam Conflict," *VOANews.com* (22 November 2005), www.voanews.com/english/2005-11-22-voa65.cfm (7 December 2005).

moral guidance to be had in statements about virtues and vices. According to the virtue ethicist Rosalind Hursthouse,

[A] great deal of specific action guidance could be found in rules employing the virtue and vice terms ("v-rules") such as "Do what is honest/charitable; do not do what is dishonest/uncharitable." (It is a noteworthy feature of our virtue and vice vocabulary that, although our list of generally recognised virtue terms is comparatively short, our list of vice terms is remarkably, and usefully, long, far exceeding anything that anyone who thinks in terms of standard deontological rules has ever come up with. Much invaluable action guidance comes from avoiding courses of action that would be irresponsible, feckless, lazy, inconsiderate, uncooperative, harsh, intolerant, selfish, mercenary, indiscreet, tactless, arrogant . . . and on and on.)[3]

[3]Rosalind Hursthouse, "Virtue Ethics," *The Stanford Encyclopedia of Philosophy* (Fall 2003 ed.), ed. Edward N. Zalta, http://plato.Stanford.edu/archives/fall2003/entries/ethics-virtue/ (21 November 2006).

Another usefulness criticism crops up because of apparent conflicts between virtues. What should you do if you have to choose between performing or not performing a particular action, and each option involves the same two virtues but in contradictory ways? Suppose your best friend is on trial for murder, and under oath you must testify about what you know of the case—and what you know will incriminate her. The question is, Should you lie? If you lie to save your friend, you will be loyal but dishonest. If you tell the truth, you will be honest but disloyal. The virtues of loyalty and honesty conflict; you simply cannot be both loyal and honest. Virtue ethics says you should act as a virtuous person would. But such advice gives you no guidance on how to do that in this particular case. You need to know which virtue is more important in this situation, but virtue ethics does not seem to provide a useful answer.

The proponent of virtue ethics has a ready reply to this criticism: Some duty-based moral theories, such as Kantian ethics, are also troubled by conflicts

(conflicts of rules or principles, for example). Obviously the existence of such conflicts is not a fatal flaw in duty-based ethics, and so it must not be in virtue approaches either. When principles seem to conflict, the duty-based theorist must determine if the conflict is real and, if so, if it can be resolved (by, say, weighting one principle more than another). Virtue ethics, the argument goes, can exercise the same kind of options. Some might observe, however, that incorporating a weighting rule or similar standard into virtue ethics seems to make the theory a blend of duty-based and virtue-based features.

THE ETHICS OF CARE

Associated with virtue ethics is an approach known as the **ethics of care.** The ethics of care is a perspective on moral issues that emphasizes close personal relationships and moral virtues such as compassion, love, and sympathy. It contrasts dramatically with traditional moral theories that are preoccupied with principles, rules, and legalistic moral reasoning. The ethics of care is probably best characterized as an important component of virtue ethics (or of *any* approach to morality), though some prefer to think of it as a full-fledged moral theory in its own right.

Much of the interest in the ethics of care was sparked by research done by the psychologist Carol Gilligan on how men and women think about moral problems.[4] She maintains that men and women think in radically different ways when making moral decisions. According to Gilligan, in moral decision making, men deliberate about rights, justice, and rules; women, on the other hand, focus on personal relationships, caring for others, and being aware of people's feelings, needs, and viewpoints. She dubbed these two approaches the *ethic of justice* and the *ethic of care.* Some fem-

[4]Carol Gilligan, *In a Different Voice: Psychological Theory and Women's Development* (Cambridge, MA: Harvard University Press, 1982).

QUICK REVIEW

virtue ethics—A theory of morality that makes virtue the central concern.

eudaimonia—Happiness, or flourishing.

virtue—A stable disposition to act and feel according to some ideal or model of excellence.

Golden Mean—Aristotle's notion of a virtue as a balance between two behavioral extremes.

ethics of care—A perspective on moral issues that emphasizes close personal relationships and moral virtues such as compassion, love, and sympathy.

inist thinkers have used this gender distinction as a starting point to advance the new way of looking at ethics known as the ethics of care.

More recent research has raised doubts about whether there really is a gap between the moral thinking styles of men and women. But these findings do not dilute the relevance of caring to ethics. The ethics of care, regardless of any empirical underpinnings, is a reminder that caring is a vital and inescapable part of the moral life—a conclusion that few philosophers would deny. If virtues are a part of the moral life (as they surely are), and if caring (or compassion, sympathy, or love) is a virtue, then there must be a place for caring alongside principles of moral conduct and moral reasoning. The philosopher Annette C. Baier, an early proponent of the ethics of care, makes a case for both care and justice: "It is clear, I think, that the best moral theory has to be a cooperative product of women and men, has to harmonize justice and care. The morality it theorizes about is after all for all persons, for men and women, and will need their combined insights."[5]

[5]Annette C. Baier, "The Need for More Than Justice," *Canadian Journal of Philosophy,* suppl. vol. 13 (1988): 56.

LEARNING FROM VIRTUE ETHICS

Why does the ancient moral tradition of virtue ethics persist—and not just persist but thrive, even enjoying a revival in modern times? Many thinkers would say that virtue ethics is alive and well because it is sustained by an important ethical truth: virtue and character are large, unavoidable constituents of our moral experience. As moral creatures, we regularly judge the moral permissibility of actions—*and* assess the goodness of character. If someone commits an immoral act (kills an innocent human being, for example), it matters to us whether the act was committed out of compassion (as in euthanasia), benevolence, loyalty, revenge, rage, or ignorance. The undeniable significance of virtue in morality has obliged many philosophers to consider how best to accommodate virtues into their principle-based theories of morality or to recast those theories entirely to give virtues a larger role.

The rise of virtue ethics has also forced many thinkers to reexamine the place of principles in morality. If we have virtues, do we need principles? Most philosophers would probably say yes and agree with the philosopher William Frankena that "principles without traits [virtues] are impotent and traits without principles are blind":

To be or to do, that is the question. Should we construe morality as primarily a following of certain principles or as primarily a cultivation of certain dispositions and traits? Must we choose? It is hard to see how a morality of principles can get off the ground except through the development of dispositions to act in accordance with its principles, else all motivation to act on them must be of an *ad hoc* kind, either prudential or impulsively altruistic. Moreover, morality can hardly be content with a mere conformity to rules, however willing and self-conscious it may be, unless it has no interest in the spirit of its law but only in the letter. On the other hand, one cannot conceive of traits of character except as including dispositions and tendencies to act in cer-

tain ways in certain circumstances. Hating involves being disposed to kill or harm, being just involves tending to do just acts (acts that conform to the principle of justice) when the occasion calls. Again, it is hard to see how we could know what traits to encourage or inculcate if we did not subscribe to principles, for example, to the principle of utility, or to those of benevolence and justice.[6]

SUMMARY

Virtue ethics is a moral theory that makes virtue the central concern. In virtue ethics, moral conduct is supposed to radiate naturally from moral virtues. That is, moral actions are derived from virtues. A virtue is a stable disposition to act and feel according to an ideal or model of excellence.

Most modern virtue ethicists take their inspiration from Aristotle. He argues that humankind's greatest good is happiness, or *eudaimonia*. To achieve happiness, human beings must fulfill their natural function—to live fully in accordance with reason. To live this way is to cultivate the virtues, for they are rational ways of being and flourishing. Aristotle suggests that a moral virtue is a Golden Mean, a midpoint between two extreme ways of behaving. So he says that the good life is a life in the middle, a life of moderation.

Virtue theorists think that acting out of duty alone is a distortion of true morality. A full-blown morality, they insist, must include motives, emotions, intentions, and moral wisdom. Acting morally means acting from virtue—from the appropriate motives and feelings, taking all the factors of the situation into account.

Virtue-based ethics seems to meet the minimum requirement of coherence, and it fits with our commonsense moral judgments and experience. But it has been accused of not being useful. The main criticism is that appeals to virtue alone (sans principles) give us little or no guidance about how to act. Critics argue that virtue ethics defines virtue in terms of

---

[6]William K. Frankena, *Ethics*, 2nd ed. (Englewood Cliffs, NJ: Prentice-Hall, 1973), 65.

right actions and defines right actions in terms of virtue. But this is circular reasoning and provides no help for making moral decisions. Virtue theorists, however, can reply that guidance in moral decision making is in fact available—it is inherent in statements about virtues and vices.

The ethics of care is a perspective on moral issues that emphasizes personal relationships and the virtues of compassion, love, sympathy, and the like. It can be thought of as an essential element in virtue ethics. The ethics of care is a reminder that caring is a crucial part of the moral life. Many philosophers have acknowledged this fact by trying to incorporate care into moral theories containing principles.

EXERCISES

Review Questions

1. What is virtue ethics? How does it differ from duty-based ethics? (p. 134)
2. In what way is Aristotle's virtue ethics considered teleological? (p. 134)
3. What is *eudaimonia?* What must humans do to achieve *eudaimonia?* (p. 134)
4. What is a virtue? Give three examples of moral virtues. Give two examples of intellectual virtues. (p. 134)
5. What important elements do virtue ethicists think are missing from traditional duty-based ethics? (p. 136)
6. How do virtue ethicists use moral exemplars? (p. 136)

7. Does virtue ethics seem to offer a more plausible explanation of the role of motivation in moral actions than does Kantian ethics? If so, how? (p. 137)
8. What is the chief argument against virtue ethics? How can the virtue ethicist respond? (p. 137)
9. What is the ethics of care? (p. 139)
10. According to Annette Baier, are justice and care compatible? (p. 139)

Discussion Questions

1. Critique Aristotle's virtue ethics theory. What are its strengths and weaknesses?
2. According to Aristotle, the virtuous life helps us *achieve* happiness and *is* happiness. What does this mean?
3. Is Aristotle's notion of the Golden Mean helpful in identifying the virtues in any situation? Why or why not?
4. Kant says that to act morally is to act out of duty. How does this differ from the virtue ethics approach? Are you likely to admire someone who always acts out of duty alone? Why or why not?
5. Compare the advantages and disadvantages of act-utilitarianism and virtue ethics. Which do you think is the better theory? How would you combine the two approaches to fashion a better theory?
6. William Frankena says that morality requires both principles and virtues. Do you agree? Why or why not?

READINGS

From *Nicomachean Ethics*

ARISTOTLE

BOOK I

1

Every art and every inquiry, and similarly every action and pursuit, is thought to aim at some good; and for this reason the good has rightly been declared to be that at which all things aim. But a certain difference is found among ends; some are activities, others are products apart from the activities that produce them. Where there are ends apart from the actions, it is the nature of the products to be better than the activities. Now, as there are many actions, arts, and sciences, their ends also are many; the end of the medical art is health, that of shipbuilding a vessel, that of strategy victory, that of economics wealth. But where such arts fall under a single capacity—as bridle-making and the other arts concerned with the equipment of horses fall under the art of riding, and this and every military action under strategy, in the same way other arts fall under yet others—in all of these the ends of the master arts are to be preferred to all the subordinate ends; for it is for the sake of the former that the latter are pursued. It makes no difference whether the activities themselves are the ends of the actions, or something else apart from the activities, as in the case of the sciences just mentioned.

2

If, then, there is some end of the things we do, which we desire for its own sake (everything else being desired for the sake of this), and if we do not choose everything for the sake of something else (for at that rate the process would go on to infinity, so that our desire would be empty and vain), clearly this must

be the good and the chief good. Will not the knowledge of it, then, have a great influence on life? Shall we not, like archers who have a mark to aim at, be more likely to hit upon what is right? If so, we must try, in outline at least, to determine what it is, and of which of the sciences or capacities it is the object. It would seem to belong to the most authoritative art and that which is most truly the master art. And politics appears to be of this nature; for it is this that ordains which of the sciences should be studied in a state, and which each class of citizens should learn and up to what point they should learn them; and we see even the most highly esteemed of capacities to fall under this, e.g. strategy, economics, rhetoric; now, since politics uses the rest of the sciences, and since, again, it legislates as to what we are to do and what we are to abstain from, the end of this science must include those of the others, so that this end must be the good for man. For even if the end is the same for a single man and for a state, that of the state seems at all events something greater and more complete whether to attain or to preserve; though it is worth while to attain the end merely for one man, it is finer and more godlike to attain it for a nation or for city-states. These, then, are the ends at which our inquiry aims, since it is political science, in one sense of that term.

3

* * *

Now each man judges well the things he knows, and of these he is a good judge. And so the man who has been educated in a subject is a good judge of that subject, and the man who has received an all-round education is a good judge in general. Hence a young man is not a proper hearer of lectures on political science; for he is inexperienced in the actions that occur in life, but its discussions start from these and are

Aristotle, Books I and II of *Nichomachean Ethics*, trans. W. D. Ross (edited).

about these; and, further, since he tends to follow his passions, his study will be vain and unprofitable, because the end aimed at is not knowledge but action. And it makes no difference whether he is young in years or youthful in character; the defect does not depend on time, but on his living, and pursuing each successive object, as passion directs. For to such persons, as to the incontinent, knowledge brings no profit; but to those who desire and act in accordance with a rational principle knowledge about such matters will be of great benefit. These remarks about the student, the sort of treatment to be expected, and the purpose of the inquiry, may be taken as our preface.

4

Let us resume our inquiry and state, in view of the fact that all knowledge and every pursuit aims at some good, what it is that we say political science aims at and what is the highest of all goods achievable by action. Verbally there is very general agreement; for both the general run of men and people of superior refinement say that it is happiness, and identify living well and doing well with being happy; but with regard to what happiness is they differ, and the many do not give the same account as the wise. For the former think it is some plain and obvious thing, like pleasure, wealth, or honour; they differ, however, from one another—and often even the same man identifies it with different things, with health when he is ill, with wealth when he is poor; but, conscious of their ignorance, they admire those who proclaim some great ideal that is above their comprehension. Now some thought that apart from these many goods there is another which is self-subsistent and causes the goodness of all these as well. To examine all the opinions that have been held were perhaps somewhat fruitless; enough to examine those that are most prevalent or that seem to be arguable.

* * *

5

Let us, however, resume our discussion from the point at which we digressed. To judge from the lives

that men lead, most men, and men of the most vulgar type, seem (not without some ground) to identify the good, or happiness, with pleasure; which is the reason why they love the life of enjoyment. For there are, we may say, three prominent types of life—that just mentioned, the political, and thirdly the contemplative life. Now the mass of mankind are evidently quite slavish in their tastes, preferring a life suitable to beasts, but they get some ground for their view from the fact that many of those in high places share the tastes of Sardanapallus. A consideration of the prominent types of life shows that people of superior refinement and of active disposition identify happiness with honour, for this is, roughly speaking, the end of the political life. But it seems too superficial to be what we are looking for, since it is thought to depend on those who bestow honour rather than on him who receives it, but the good we divine to be something proper to a man and not easily taken from him. Further, men seem to pursue honour in order that they may be assured of their goodness; at least it is by men of practical wisdom that they seek to be honoured, and among those who know them, and on the ground of their virtue; clearly, then, according to them, at any rate, virtue is better. And perhaps one might even suppose this to be, rather than honour, the end of the political life. But even this appears somewhat incomplete; for possession of virtue seems actually compatible with being asleep, or with lifelong inactivity, and, further, with the greatest sufferings and misfortunes; but a man who was living so no one would call happy, unless he were maintaining a thesis at all costs. But enough of this; for the subject has been sufficiently treated even in the current discussions. Third comes the contemplative life, which we shall consider later.

The life of money-making is one undertaken under compulsion, and wealth is evidently not the good we are seeking; for it is merely useful and for the sake of something else. And so one might rather take the aforenamed objects to be ends; for they are loved for themselves. But it is evident that not even these are ends; yet many arguments have been thrown away in support of them. Let us leave this subject, then.

* * *

7

Let us again return to the good we are seeking, and ask what it can be. It seems different in different actions and arts; it is different in medicine, in strategy, and in the other arts likewise. What then is the good of each? Surely that for whose sake everything else is done. In medicine this is health, in strategy victory, in architecture a house, in any other sphere something else, and in every action and pursuit the end; for it is for the sake of this that all men do whatever else they do. Therefore, if there is an end for all that we do, this will be the good achievable by action, and if there are more than one, these will be the goods achievable by action.

So the argument has by a different course reached the same point; but we must try to state this even more clearly. Since there are evidently more than one end, and we choose some of these (e.g. wealth, flutes, and in general instruments) for the sake of something else, clearly not all ends are final ends; but the chief good is evidently something final. Therefore, if there is only one final end, this will be what we are seeking, and if there are more than one, the most final of these will be what we are seeking. Now we call that which is in itself worthy of pursuit more final than that which is worthy of pursuit for the sake of something else, and that which is never desirable for the sake of something else more final than the things that are desirable both in themselves and for the sake of that other thing, and therefore we call final without qualification that which is always desirable in itself and never for the sake of something else.

Now such a thing happiness, above all else, is held to be; for this we choose always for self and never for the sake of something else, but honour, pleasure, reason, and every virtue we choose indeed for themselves (for if nothing resulted from them we should still choose each of them), but we choose them also for the sake of happiness, judging that by means of them we shall be happy. Happiness, on the other hand, no one chooses for the sake of these, nor, in general, for anything other than itself.

From the point of view of self-sufficiency the same result seems to follow; for the final good is thought to be self-sufficient. Now by self-sufficient we do not mean that which is sufficient for a man by himself, for one who lives a solitary life, but also for parents, children, wife, and in general for his friends and fellow citizens, since man is born for citizenship. But some limit must be set to this; for if we extend our requirement to ancestors and descendants and friends' friends we are in for an infinite series. Let us examine this question, however, on another occasion; the self-sufficient we now define as that which when isolated makes life desirable and lacking in nothing; and such we think happiness to be; and further we think it most desirable of all things, without being counted as one good thing among others— if it were so counted it would clearly be made more desirable by the addition of even the least of goods; for that which is added becomes an excess of goods, and of goods the greater is always more desirable. Happiness, then, is something final and self-sufficient, and is the end of action.

Presumably, however, to say that happiness is the chief good seems a platitude, and a clearer account of what it is still desired. This might perhaps be given, if we could first ascertain the function of man. For just as for a flute-player, a sculptor, or an artist, and, in general, for all things that have a function or activity, the good and the 'well' is thought to reside in the function, so would it seem to be for man, if he has a function. Have the carpenter, then, and the tanner certain functions or activities, and has man none? Is he born without a function? Or as eye, hand, foot, and in general each of the parts evidently has a function, may one lay it down that man similarly has a function apart from all these? What then can this be? Life seems to be common even to plants, but we are seeking what is peculiar to man. Let us exclude, therefore, the life of nutrition and growth. Next there would be a life of perception, but it also seems to be common even to the horse, the ox, and every animal. There remains, then, an active life of the element that has a rational principle; of this, one part has such a principle in the sense of being obedient to one, the other in the sense of possessing one and exercising thought. And, as 'life of the rational element' also has two meanings, we must state that life in the sense of activity is what we mean; for this seems to be the more proper sense of the term. Now if the function of man is an activity of soul which follows or implies a rational principle, and if we say 'so-and-so-and 'a good so-and-so' have a function which is the same in kind, e.g. a lyre, and a good lyre-player, and so without qualification in all cases, eminence in respect of goodness being added to the name of the function (for the function of a lyre-player is to play the lyre, and that of a good lyre-player is to do so well): if this is the case, and we state the function of man to be a certain kind of life, and this to be an activity or actions of the soul implying a rational principle, and the function of a good man to be the good and noble performance of these, and if any action is well performed when it is performed in accordance with the appropriate excellence: if this is the case, human good turns out to be activity of soul in accordance with virtue, and if there are more than one virtue, in accordance with the best and most complete.

But we must add 'in a complete life.' For one swallow does not make a summer, nor does one day; and so too one day, or a short time, does not make a man blessed and happy.

* * *

BOOK II
1

Virtue, then, being of two kinds, intellectual and moral, intellectual virtue in the main owes both its birth and its growth to teaching (for which reason it requires experience and time), while moral virtue comes about as a result of habit, whence also its name (ēthikē) is one that is formed by a slight variation from the word ethos (habit). From this it is also plain that none of the moral virtues arises in us by nature; for nothing that exists by nature can form a habit contrary to its nature. For instance the stone which by nature moves downwards cannot be habituated to move upwards, not even if one tries to train it by throwing it up ten thousand times; nor can fire be habituated to move downwards, nor can anything else that by nature behaves in one way be trained to behave in another. Neither by nature, then, nor contrary to nature do the virtues arise in us; rather we are adapted by nature to receive them, and are made perfect by habit.

Again, of all the things that come to us by nature we first acquire the potentiality and later exhibit the activity (this is plain in the case of the senses; for it was not by often seeing or often hearing that we got these senses, but on the contrary we had them before we used them, and did not come to have them by using them); but the virtues we get by first exercising them, as also happens in the case of the arts as well. For the things we have to learn before we can do them, we learn by doing them, e.g. men become builders by building and lyre-players by playing the lyre; so too we become just by doing just acts, temperate by doing temperate acts, brave by doing brave acts.

This is confirmed by what happens in states; for legislators make the citizens good by forming habits in them, and this is the wish of every legislator, and those who do not effect it miss their mark, and it is in this that a good constitution differs from a bad one.

Again, it is from the same causes and by the same means that every virtue is both produced and destroyed, and similarly every art; for it is from playing the lyre that both good and bad lyre-players are produced. And the corresponding statement is true of builders and of all the rest; men will be good or bad builders as a result of building well or badly. For if this were not so, there would have been no need of a teacher, but all men would have been born good or bad at their craft. This, then, is the case with the virtues also; by doing the acts that we do in our transactions with other men we become just or unjust, and by doing the acts that we do in the presence of danger, and being habituated to feel fear or confidence, we become brave or cowardly. The same is true of appetites and feelings of anger; some men become temperate and good-tempered, others self-indulgent and irascible, by behaving in one way or the other in the appropriate circumstances. Thus, in one word, states of character arise out of like activities. This is why the activities we exhibit must be of a certain kind; it is because the states of character correspond to the differences between these. It makes no small difference, then, whether we form habits of one kind or of another from our very youth; it makes a very great difference, or rather all the difference.

2

Since, then, the present inquiry does not aim at theoretical knowledge like the others (for we are inquiring not in order to know what virtue is, but in order to become good, since otherwise our inquiry would have been of no use), we must examine the nature of actions, namely how we ought to do them; for these determine also the nature of the states of character that are produced, as we have said. Now, that we must act according to the right rule is a common principle and must be assumed—it will be discussed later, i.e. both what the right rule is, and how it is related to the other virtues. But this must be agreed upon beforehand, that the whole account of matters of conduct must be given in outline and not precisely, as we said at the very beginning that the accounts we demand must be in accordance with the subject-matter; matters concerned with conduct and questions of what is good for us have no fixity, any more than matters of health. The general account being of this nature, the account of particular cases is yet more lacking in exactness; for they do not fall under any art or precept but the agents themselves must in each case consider what is appropriate to the occasion, as happens also in the art of medicine or of navigation.

But though our present account is of this nature we must give what help we can. First, then, let us consider this, that it is the nature of such things to be destroyed by defect and excess, as we see in the case of strength and of health (for to gain light on things imperceptible we must use the evidence of sensible things); both excessive and defective exercise destroys the strength, and similarly drink or food which is above or below a certain amount destroys the health, while that which is proportionate both produces and increases and preserves it. So too is it, then, in the case of temperance and courage and the other virtues. For the man who flies from and fears everything and does not stand his ground against anything becomes a coward, and the man who fears nothing at all but goes to meet every danger becomes rash; and similarly the man who indulges in every pleasure and abstains from none becomes self-indulgent, while the man who shuns every pleasure, as boors do, becomes in a way insensible; temperance and courage, then, are destroyed by excess and defect, and preserved by the mean.

But not only are the sources and causes of their origination and growth the same as those of their destruction, but also the sphere of their actualization will be the same; for this is also true of the things which are more evident to sense, e.g. of strength; it is produced by taking much food and undergoing much exertion, and it is the strong man that will be most able to do these things. So too is it with the virtues; by abstaining from pleasures we become temperate, and it is when we have become so that we are most able to abstain from them; and similarly too in the case of courage; for by being habituated to despise things that are terrible and to stand our ground against them we become brave, and it is when we have become so that we shall be most able to stand our ground against them.

* * *

4

The question might be asked, what we mean by saying that we must become just by doing just acts, and temperate by doing temperate acts; for if men do just and temperate acts, they are already just and temperate, exactly as, if they do what is in accordance with the laws of grammar and of music, they are grammarians and musicians.

Or is this not true even of the arts? It is possible to do something that is in accordance with the laws of grammar, either by chance or at the suggestion of another. A man will be a grammarian, then, only when he has both done something grammatical and done it grammatically; and this means doing it in accordance with the grammatical knowledge in himself.

Again, the case of the arts and that of the virtues are not similar; for the products of the arts have their goodness in themselves, so that it is enough that they should have a certain character, but if the acts that are in accordance with the virtues have themselves a certain character it does not follow that they are done justly or temperately. The agent also must be in a certain condition when he does them; in the first place he must have knowledge, secondly he must choose the acts, and choose them for their own sakes, and thirdly his action must proceed from a firm and unchangeable character. These are not reckoned in as conditions of the possession of the arts, except the bare knowledge; but as a condition of the possession of the virtues knowledge has little or no weight, while the other conditions count not for a little but for everything, i.e. the very conditions which result from often doing just and temperate acts.

Actions, then, are called just and temperate when they are such as the just or the temperate man would do; but it is not the man who does these that is just and temperate, but the man who also does them as just and temperate men do them. It is well said, then, that it is by doing just acts that the just man is produced, and by doing temperate acts the temperate man; without doing these no one would have even a prospect of becoming good.

But most people do not do these, but take refuge in theory and think they are being philosophers and will become good in this way, behaving somewhat like patients who listen attentively to their doctors, but do none of the things they are ordered to do. As the latter will not be made well in body by such a course of treatment, the former will not be made well in soul by such a course of philosophy.

5

Next we must consider what virtue is. Since things that are found in the soul are of three kinds—passions, faculties, states of character, virtue must be one of these. By passions I mean appetite, anger, fear, confidence, envy, joy, friendly feeling, hatred, longing, emulation, pity, and in general the feelings that are accompanied by pleasure or pain; by faculties the things in virtue of which we are said to be capable of feeling these, e.g. of becoming angry or being pained or feeling pity; by states of character the things in virtue of which we stand well or badly with reference to the passions, e.g. with reference to anger we stand badly if we feel it violently or too weakly, and well if we feel it moderately; and similarly with reference to the other passions.

Now neither the virtues nor the vices are passions, because we are not called good or bad on the ground of our passions, but are so called on the ground of our virtues and our vices, and because we are neither praised nor blamed for our passions (for the man who feels fear or anger is not praised, nor is the man who simply feels anger blamed, but the man who feels it in a certain way), but for our virtues and our vices we are praised or blamed.

Again, we feel anger and fear without choice, but the virtues are modes of choice or involve choice. Further, in respect of the passions we are said to be moved, but in respect of the virtues and the vices we are said not to be moved but to be disposed in a particular way.

For these reasons also they are not faculties; for we are neither called good nor bad, nor praised nor blamed, for the simple capacity of feeling the passions; again, we have the faculties by nature, but we are not made good or bad by nature; we have spoken of this before. If, then, the virtues are neither passions nor faculties, all that remains is that they should be states of character.

Thus we have stated what virtue is in respect of its genus.

6

We must, however, not only describe virtue as a state of character, but also say what sort of state it is. We may remark, then, that every virtue or excellence both brings into good condition the thing of which it is the excellence and makes the work of that thing be done well; e.g. the excellence of the eye makes both the eye and its work good; for it is by the excellence of the eye that we see well. Similarly the excellence of the horse makes a horse both good in itself and good at running and at carrying its rider and at awaiting the attack of the enemy. Therefore, if this is true in every case, the virtue of man also will be the state of character which makes a man good and which makes him do his own work well.

How this is to happen we have stated already, but it will be made plain also by the following consideration of the specific nature of virtue. In everything that is continuous and divisible it is possible to take more, less, or an equal amount, and that either in terms of the thing itself or relatively to us; and the equal is an intermediate between excess and defect. By the intermediate in the object I mean that which is equidistant from each of the extremes, which is one and the same for all men; by the intermediate relatively to us that which is neither too much nor too little—and this is not one, nor the same for all. For instance, if ten is many and two is few, six is the intermediate, taken in terms of the object; for it exceeds and is exceeded by an equal amount; this is intermediate according to arithmetical proportion. But the intermediate relatively to us is not to be taken so; if ten pounds are too much for a particular person to eat and two too little, it does not follow that the trainer will order six pounds; for this also is perhaps too much for the person who is to take it, or too little—too little for Milo, too much for the beginner in athletic exercises. The same is true of running and wrestling. Thus a master of any art avoids excess and defect, but seeks the intermediate and chooses this—the intermediate not in the object but relatively to us.

If it is thus, then, that every art does its work well—by looking to the intermediate and judging its works by this standard (so that we often say of good works of art that it is not possible either to take away or to add anything, implying that excess and defect destroy the goodness of works of art, while the mean preserves it; and good artists, as we say, look to this in their work), and if, further, virtue is more exact and better than any art, as nature also is, then virtue must have the quality of aiming at the intermediate. I mean moral virtue; for it is this that is concerned with passions and actions, and in these there is excess, defect, and the intermediate. For instance,

both fear and confidence and appetite and anger and pity and in general pleasure and pain may be felt both too much and too little, and in both cases not well; but to feel them at the right times, with reference to the right objects, towards the right people, with the right motive, and in the right way, is what is both intermediate and best, and this is characteristic of virtue. Similarly with regard to actions also there is excess, defect, and the intermediate. Now virtue is concerned with passions and actions, in which excess is a form of failure, and so is defect, while the intermediate is praised and is a form of success; and being praised and being successful are both characteristics of virtue. Therefore virtue is a kind of mean, since, as we have seen, it aims at what is intermediate.

Again, it is possible to fail in many ways (for evil belongs to the class of the unlimited, as the Pythagoreans conjectured, and good to that of the limited), while to succeed is possible only in one way (for which reason also one is easy and the other difficult—to miss the mark easy, to hit it difficult); for these reasons also, then, excess and defect are characteristic of vice, and the mean of virtue;

For men are good in but one way, but bad in many.

Virtue, then, is a state of character concerned with choice, lying in a mean, i.e. the mean relative to us, this being determined by a rational principle, and by that principle by which the man of practical wisdom would determine it. Now it is a mean between two vices, that which depends on excess and that which depends on defect; and again it is a mean because the vices respectively fall short of or exceed what is right in both passions and actions, while virtue both finds and chooses that which is intermediate. Hence in respect of its substance and the definition which states its essence virtue is a mean, with regard to what is best and right an extreme.

But not every action nor every passion admits of a mean; for some have names that already imply badness, e.g. spite, shamelessness, envy, and in the case of actions adultery, theft, murder; for all of these and suchlike things imply by their names that they are themselves bad, and not the excesses or deficiencies of them. It is not possible, then, ever to be right with regard to them; one must always be wrong. Nor does goodness or badness with regard to such things depend on committing adultery with the right women, at the right time, and in the right way, but simply to do any of them is to go wrong. It would be equally absurd, then, to expect that in unjust, cowardly, and voluptuous action there should be a mean, an excess, and a deficiency; for at that rate there would be a mean of excess and of deficiency, an excess of excess, and a deficiency of deficiency. But as there is no excess and deficiency of temperance and courage because what is intermediate is in a sense an extreme, so too of the actions we have mentioned there is no mean nor any excess and deficiency, but however they are done they are wrong; for in general there is neither a mean of excess and deficiency, nor excess and deficiency of a mean.

7

We must, however, not only make this general statement, but also apply it to the individual facts. For among statements about conduct those which are general apply more widely, but those which are particular are more genuine, since conduct has to do with individual cases, and our statements must harmonize with the facts in these cases. We may take these cases from our table. With regard to feelings of fear and confidence courage is the mean; of the people who exceed, he who exceeds in fearlessness has no name (many of the states have no name), while the man who exceeds in confidence is rash, and he who exceeds in fear and falls short in confidence is a coward. With regard to pleasures and pains—not all of them, and not so much with regard to the pains—the mean is temperance, the excess self-indulgence. Persons deficient with regard to the pleasures are not often found; hence such persons also have received no name. But let us call them 'insensible'.

With regard to giving and taking of money the mean is liberality, the excess and the defect prodigality and meanness. In these actions people exceed and fall short in contrary ways; the prodigal exceeds in spending and falls short in taking, while the mean man exceeds in taking and falls short in spending. (At present we are giving a mere outline or summary, and are satisfied with this; later these states will be more exactly determined.) With regard to money there are also other dispositions—a mean, magnificence (for the magnificent man differs from the liberal man; the former deals with large sums, the latter with small ones), an excess, tastelessness and vulgarity, and a deficiency, niggardliness; these differ from the states opposed to liberality, and the mode of their difference will be stated later. With regard to honour and dishonour the mean is proper pride, the excess is known as a sort of 'empty vanity', and the deficiency is undue humility; and as we said liberality was related to magnificence, differing from it by dealing with small sums, so there is a state similarly related to proper pride, being concerned with small honours while that is concerned with great. For it is possible to desire honour as one ought, and more than one ought, and less, and the man who exceeds in his desires is called ambitious, the man who falls short unambitious, while the intermediate person has no name. The dispositions also are nameless, except that that of the ambitious man is called ambition. Hence the people who are at the extremes lay claim to the middle place; and we ourselves sometimes call the intermediate person ambitious and sometimes unambitious, and sometimes praise the ambitious man and sometimes the unambitious. The reason of our doing this will be stated in what follows; but now let us speak of the remaining states according to the method which has been indicated.

With regard to anger also there is an excess, a deficiency, and a mean. Although they can scarcely be said to have names, yet since we call the intermediate person good-tempered let us call the mean good temper; of the persons at the extremes let the one who exceeds be called irascible, and his vice irascibility, and the man who falls short an inirascible sort of person, and the deficiency inirascibility.

There are also three other means, which have a certain likeness to one another, but differ from one another: for they are all concerned with intercourse in words and actions, but differ in that one is concerned with truth in this sphere, the other two with pleasantness; and of this one kind is exhibited in giving amusement, the other in all the circumstances of life. We must therefore speak of these two, that we may the better see that in all things the mean is praiseworthy, and the extremes neither praiseworthy nor right, but worthy of blame. Now most of these states also have no names, but we must try, as in the other cases, to invent names ourselves so that we may be clear and easy to follow. With regard to truth, then, the intermediate is a truthful sort of person and the mean may be called truthfulness, while the pretence which exaggerates is boastfulness and the person characterized by it a boaster, and that which understates is mock modesty and the person characterized by it mock-modest. With regard to pleasantness in the giving of amusement the intermediate person is ready-witted and the disposition ready wit, the excess is buffoonery and the person characterized by it a buffoon, while the man who falls short is a sort of boor and his state is boorishness. With regard to the remaining kind of pleasantness, that which is exhibited in life in general, the man who is pleasant in the right way is friendly and the mean is friendli-

ness, while the man who exceeds is an obsequious person if he has no end in view, a flatterer if he is aiming at his own advantage, and the man who falls short and is unpleasant in all circumstances is a quarrelsome and surly sort of person.

* * *

9

That moral virtue is a mean, then, and in what sense it is so, and that it is a mean between two vices, the one involving excess, the other deficiency, and that it is such because its character is to aim at what is intermediate in passions and in actions, has been sufficiently stated. Hence also it is no easy task to be good. For in everything it is no easy task to find the middle, e.g. to find the middle of a circle is not for every one but for him who knows; so, too, any one can get angry—that is easy—or give or spend money; but to do this to the right person, to the right extent, at the right time, with the right motive, and in the right way, that is not for every one, nor is it easy; wherefore goodness is both rare and laudable and noble.

* * *

The Need for More Than Justice

ANNETTE C. BAIER

In recent decades in North American social and moral philosophy, alongside the development and discussion of widely influential theories of justice, taken as Rawls takes it as the 'first virtue of social institutions,'[1] there has been a counter-movement gathering strength, one coming from some interesting sources. For some of the most outspoken of the diverse group who have in a variety of ways been challenging the assumed supremacy of justice among the moral and social virtues are members of those

Annette C. Baier, "The Need for More Than Justice," *Canadian Journal of Philosophy*, suppl. vol. 13 (1988): 41–56 (edited). Published by University of Calgary Press. Reprinted with permission of University of Calgary Press.

sections of society whom one might have expected to be especially aware of the supreme importance of justice, namely blacks and women. Those who have only recently seen the correction or partial correction of long-standing racist and sexist injustices to their race and sex, are among the philosophers now suggesting that justice is only one virtue among many, and one that may need the presence of the others in order to deliver its own undenied value. Among these philosophers of the philosophical counterculture, as it were—but an increasingly large counterculture— I include Alasdair MacIntyre, Michael Stocker, Lawrence Blum, Michael Slote, Laurence Thomas, Claudia Card, Alison Jaggar, Susan Wolf and a whole group of men and women, myself included, who have been influenced by the writings of Harvard educational psychologist Carol Gilligan, whose book *In a Different Voice* (Harvard 1982; hereafter D.V.) caused a considerable stir both in the popular press and, more slowly, in the philosophical journals.

Let me say quite clearly at this early point that there is little disagreement that justice is *a* social value of very great importance, and injustice an evil. Nor would those who have worked on theories of justice want to deny that other things matter besides justice. Rawls, for example, incorporates the value of freedom into his account of justice, so that denial of basic freedoms counts as injustice. Rawls also leaves room for a wider theory of the right, of which the theory of justice is just a part. Still, he does claim that justice is the 'first' virtue of social institutions, and it is only that claim about priority that I think has been challenged. It is easy to exaggerate the differences of view that exist, and I want to avoid that. The differences are as much in emphasis as in substance, or we can say that they are differences in tone of voice. But these differences do tend to make a difference in approaches to a wide range of topics not just in moral theory but in areas like medical ethics, where the discussion used to be conducted in terms of patients' rights, of informed consent, and so on, but now tends to get conducted in an enlarged moral vocabulary, which draws on what Gilligan calls the ethics of *care* as well as that of *justice*.

For 'care' is the new buzz-word. It is not, as Shakespeare's Portia demanded, mercy that is to season justice, but a less authoritarian humanitarian supplement, a felt concern for the good of others and for community with them. The 'cold jealous virtue of justice' (Hume) is found to be too cold, and it is 'warmer' more communitarian virtues and social ideals that are being called in to supplement it. One might say that liberty and equality are being found inadequate without fraternity, except that 'fraternity' will be quite the wrong word, if as Gilligan initially suggested, it is *women* who perceive this value most easily. ('Sorority' will do no better, since it is too exclusive, and English has no gender-neuter word for the mutual concern of siblings.) She has since modified this claim, allowing that there are two perspectives on moral and social issues that we all tend to alternate between, and which are not always easy to combine, one of them what she called the justice perspective, the other the care perspective. It is increasingly obvious that there are many male philosophical spokespersons for the care perspective (Laurence Thomas, Lawrence Blum, Michael Stocker) so that it cannot be the prerogative of women. Nevertheless Gilligan still wants to claim that women are most unlikely to take *only* the justice perspective, as some men are claimed to, at least until some mid-life crisis jolts them into 'bifocal' moral vision (see D.V., ch. 6).

Gilligan in her book did not offer any explanatory theory of why there should be any difference between female and male moral outlook, but she did tend to link the naturalness to women of the care perspective with their role as primary care-takers of young children, that is with their parental and specifically maternal role. She avoided the question of whether it is their biological or their social parental role that is relevant, and some of those who dislike her book are worried precisely by this uncertainty. Some find it retrograde to hail as a special sort of moral wisdom an outlook that may be the product of the socially enforced restriction of women to domestic roles (and the reservation of such roles for them alone). For that might seem to play into the hands of those who still favor such restriction. (Marxists, presumably, will not find it so surprising that moral truths might depend for their initial clear voicing on the social oppression, and memory of it, of those who voice the truths.) Gilligan did in the first chapter of D.V. cite the theory of Nancy Chodorow (as presented in *The Reproduction of Mothering* [Berkeley 1978]) which traces what appears as gender differences in personality to early social development, in particular to the effects of the child's primary care-taker being or not being of the same gender as the child. Later, both in 'The Conquistador and the Dark Continent: Reflections on the Nature of Love' (*Daedalus* [Summer 1984]), and 'The Origins of Morality in Early Childhood' (in press), she develops this explanation. She postulates two evils that any infant may become aware of, the evil of detachment or isolation from others whose love one needs, and the evil of relative powerlessness and weakness. Two dimensions of moral development are thereby set—one aimed at achieving satisfying community with others, the other aiming at autonomy or equality of power. The relative predominance of one over the other development will depend both upon the relative salience of the two evils in early childhood, and on early and later reinforcement or discouragement in attempts made to guard against these two evils. This provides the germs of a theory about *why*, given current customs of childrearing, it should be mainly women who are not content with only the moral outlook that she calls the justice perspective, necessary though that was and is seen by them to have been to their hard won liberation from sexist oppression. They, like the blacks, used the language of rights and justice to change their own social position, but nevertheless see limitations in that language, according to Gilligan's findings as a moral psychologist. She reports their discontent with the individualist more or less Kantian moral framework that dominates Western moral theory and which influenced moral psychologists such as Lawrence Kohlberg, to whose conception of moral maturity she seeks an alternative. Since the target of Gilligan's criticism is the dominant Kantian tradition, and since that has been the target also of moral philosophers as diverse in their own views as Bernard Williams, Alasdair MacIntyre, Philippa Foot, Susan Wolf, Claudia Card, her book is of interest as much for its attempt to articulate an alternative to the Kantian justice perspective as for its implicit raising of the question of male bias in Western moral theory, especially liberal-democratic theory. For whether the supposed blind spots of that outlook are due to male bias, or to non-parental bias, or to early traumas of powerlessness or to early resignation to 'detachment' from others, we need first to be persuaded that they *are* blind spots before we will have any interest in their cause and cure. Is justice blind to important social values, or at least only one-eyed? What is it that comes into view from the 'care perspective' that is not seen from the 'justice perspective'?

Gilligan's position here is mostly easily described by contrasting it with that of Kohlberg, against which she developed it. Kohlberg, influenced by Piaget and the Kantian philosophical tradition as developed by John Rawls, developed a theory about typical moral development which saw it to progress from a pre-conventional level, where what is seen to matter is pleasing or not offending parental authority-figures, through a conventional level in which the child tries to fit in with a group, such as a school community, and conform to its standards and rules, to a post-conventional critical level, in which such conventional rules are subjected to tests, and where those tests are of a Utilitarian, or, eventually, a Kantian sort—namely ones that require respect for each person's individual rational will, or autonomy, and conformity to any implicit social contract such wills are deemed to have made, or to any hypothetical ones they would make if thinking clearly. What was found when Kohlberg's questionnaires (mostly by verbal response to verbally sketched moral dilemmas) were applied to female as well as male subjects, Gilligan reports, is that the girls and women not only scored generally lower than the boys and men, but tended to *revert* to the lower stage of the conventional level even after briefly (usually in adolescence) attaining the post conventional level. Piaget's finding that girls were deficient in 'the legal sense' was confirmed.

These results led Gilligan to wonder if there might not be a quite different pattern of development to be discerned, at least in female subjects. She therefore conducted interviews designed to elicit not just how far advanced the subjects were towards an appreciation of the nature and importance of Kantian autonomy, but also to find out what the subjects themselves saw as progress or lack of it, what conceptions of moral maturity they came to possess by the time they were adults. She found that although the Kohlberg version of moral maturity as respect for fellow persons, and for their rights as equals (rights including that of free association), did seem shared by many young men, the women tended to speak in a different voice about morality itself and about moral maturity. To quote Gilligan, 'Since the reality of interconnexion is experienced by women as given rather than freely contracted, they arrive at an understanding of life that reflects the limits of autonomy and control. As a result, women's development delineates the path not only to a less violent life but also to a maturity realized by interdependence and taking care' (D.V., 172). She writes that there is evidence that 'women perceive and construe social reality differently from men, and that these differences center around experiences of attachment and separation . . . because women's sense of integrity appears to be intertwined with an ethics of care, so that to see themselves as women is to see themselves in a relationship of connexion, the major changes in women's lives would seem to involve changes in the understanding and activities of care' (D.V., 171). She contrasts this progressive understanding of care, from merely pleasing others to helping and nurturing, with the sort of progression that is involved in Kohlberg's stages, a progression in the understanding, not of mutual care, but of mutual *respect,* where this has its Kantian overtones of distance, even of some fear for the respected, and where personal autonomy and *in*dependence, rather than more satisfactory interdependence, are the paramount values.

This contrast, one cannot but feel, is one which Gilligan might have used the Marxist language of alienation to make. For the main complaint about the Kantian version of a society with its first virtue justice, constructed as respect for equal rights to formal goods such as having contracts kept, due process, equal opportunity including opportunity to participate in political activities leading to policy and lawmaking, to basic liberties of speech, free association and assembly, religious worship, is that none of these goods do much to ensure that the people who have and mutually respect such rights will have any other relationships to one another than the minimal relationship needed to keep such a 'civil society' going. They may well be lonely, driven to suicide, apathetic about their work and about participation in political processes, find their lives meaningless and have no wish to leave offspring to face the same meaningless existence. Their rights, and respect for rights, are quite compatible with very great misery, and misery whose causes are not just individual misfortunes and psychic sickness, but social and moral impoverishment.

What Gilligan's older male subjects complain of is precisely this sort of alienation from some dimly glimpsed better possibility for human beings, some richer sort of network of relationships. As one of Gilligan's male subjects put it, 'People have real emotional needs to be attached to something, and equality does not give you attachment. Equality fractures society and places on every person the burden of standing on his own two feet' (D.V., 167). It is not just the difficulty of self reliance which is complained of, but its socially 'fracturing' effect. Whereas the younger men, in their college years, had seen morality as a matter of reciprocal non-interference, this old man begins to see it as reciprocal attachment. 'Morality is . . . essential . . . for creating the kind of environment, interaction between people, that is a prerequisite to the fulfillment of individual goals. If you want other people not to interfere with your pursuit of whatever you are into, you have to play the game,' says the spokesman for traditional liberalism (D.V. 98). But if what one is 'into' is interconnexion, interdependence rather than an individual autonomy that may involve 'detachment,' such a version of morality will come to seem inadequate. And Gilligan stresses that the interconnexion that her mature women subjects, and some men, wanted to sustain was not merely freely chosen interconnexion, nor interconnexion between equals, but also the sort of interconnexion that can obtain between a child and her unchosen mother and father, or between a child and her unchosen older and younger siblings, or indeed between most workers and their unchosen fellow workers, or most citizens and their unchosen fellow citizens.

A model of a decent community different from the liberal one is involved in the version of moral maturity that Gilligan voices. It has in many ways more in common with the older religion-linked versions of morality and a good society than with the modern Western liberal idea. That perhaps is why some find it so dangerous and retrograde. Yet it seems clear that it also has much in common with what we call Hegelian versions of moral maturity and of social health and malaise, both with Marxist versions and with so-called right-Hegelian views.

Let me try to summarize the main differences, as I see them, between on the one hand Gilligan's version of moral maturity and the sort of social structures that would encourage, express and protect it, and on the other the orthodoxy she sees herself to be challenging. I shall from now on be giving my own interpretation of the significance of her challenges, not merely reporting them. The most obvious point is the challenge to the individualism of the Western tradition, to the fairly entrenched belief in the possibility and desirability of each person pursuing his own good in his own way, constrained only by a minimal formal common good, namely a working legal apparatus that enforces contracts and protects individuals from undue interference by others. Gilligan reminds us that noninterference can, especially for the relatively powerless, such as the very young, amount to neglect, and even between equals can be isolating and alienating. On her less individualist version of individuality, it becomes defined by responses to dependence and to patterns of interconnexion, both chosen and unchosen. It is not something a person *has,* and which she then chooses relationships to suit, but something that develops out of a series of dependencies and interdepencies, and responses to them. This conception of individuality is not flatly at odds with, say, Rawls' Kantian one, but there is at least a difference of tone of voice between speaking as Rawls does of each of us having our own rational life plan, which a just society's moral traffic rules will allow us to follow, and which may or may not include close association with other persons, and speaking as Gilligan does of a satisfactory life as involving 'progress of affiliative relationship' (D.V., 170) where 'the concept of identity expands to include the experience of interconnexion' (D.V., 173). Rawls can allow that progress to Gilligan-style moral maturity may be *a* rational life plan, but not a moral constraint on every life-pattern. The trouble is that it will not do just to say 'let this version of morality be an optional extra. Let us agree on the essential minimum, that is on justice and rights, and let whoever wants to go further and cultivate this more demanding ideal of responsibility and care.' For, first, it cannot be satisfactorily cultivated without closer cooperation from others than respect for rights and justice will ensure, and second, the encouragement of some to cultivate it while others do not could easily lead to exploitation of those who do. It obviously *has* suited some in most societies well enough that others take on the responsibilities of care (for the sick, the helpless, the young) leaving them free to pursue their own less altruistic goods. Volunteer forces of those who accept an ethic of care, operating within a society where the power is exercised and the institutions designed, redesigned, or maintained by those who accept a less communal ethic of minimally constrained self-advancement, will not be the solution. The liberal individualists may be able to 'tolerate' the more communally minded, if they keep the liberals' rules, but it is not so clear that the more communally minded can be content with just those rules, nor be content to be tolerated and possibly exploited.

For the moral tradition which developed the concept of rights, autonomy and justice is the same tradition that provided 'justifications' of the oppression of those whom the primary right-holders depended on to do the sort of work they themselves preferred not to do. The domestic work was left to women and slaves, and the liberal morality for right-holders was surreptitiously supplemented by a different set of demands made on domestic workers. As long as women could be got to assume responsibility for the care of home and children, and to train their children to continue the sexist system, the liberal morality could continue to be the official morality, by turning its eyes away from the contribution made by those it excluded. The long unnoticed moral proletariat were the domestic workers, mostly female. Rights have usually been for the privileged. Talking about laws, and the rights those laws recognize and protect, does not in itself ensure that the group of legislators and rights-holders will not be restricted to some elite. Bills of rights have usually been proclamations of the rights of some in-group, barons, landowners, males, whites, non-foreigners. The 'justice perspective,' and the legal sense that goes with it, are shadowed by their patriarchal past. What did

Kant, the great prophet of autonomy, say in his moral theory about women? He said they were incapable of legislation, not fit to vote, that they needed the guidance of more 'rational' males.[2] Autonomy was not for them, only for first class, really rational, persons. It is ironic that Gilligan's original findings in a way confirm Kant's views—it seems that autonomy really may not be for women. Many of them reject that ideal (D.V., 48), and have been found not as good at making rules as are men. But where Kant concludes—'so much the worse for women,' we can conclude—'so much the worse for the male fixation on the special skill of drafting legislation, for the bureaucratic mentality of rule worship, and for the male exaggeration of the importance of independence over mutual interdependence.'

It is however also true that the moral theories that made the concept of a person's rights central were not just the instruments for excluding some persons, but also the instruments used by those who demanded that more and more persons be included in the favored group. Abolitionists, reformers, women, used the language of rights to assert their claims to inclusion in the group of full members of a community. The tradition of liberal moral theory has in fact developed so as to include the women it had for so long excluded, to include the poor as well as rich, blacks and whites, and so on. Women like Mary Wollstonecraft used the male moral theories to good purpose. So we should not be wholly ungrateful for those male moral theories, for all their objectionable earlier content. They were undoubtedly patriarchal, but they also contained the seeds of the challenge, or antidote, to this patriarchal poison.

But when we transcend the values of the Kantians, we should not forget the facts of history—that those values were the values of the oppressors of women. The Christian church, whose version of the moral law Aquinas codified, in his very legalistic moral theory, still insists on the maleness of the God it worships, and jealously reserves for males all the most powerful positions in its hierarchy. Its patriarchical prejudice is open and avowed. In the secular moral theories of men, the sexist patriarchal prejudice is today often less open, not as blatant as

it is in Aquinas, in the later natural law tradition, and in Kant and Hegel, but is often still there. No moral theorist today would say that women are unfit to vote, to make laws, or to rule a nation without powerful male advisors (as most queens had), but the old doctrines die hard. In one of the best male theories we have, John Rawls's theory, a key role is played by the idea of the 'head of a household.' It is heads of households who are to deliberate behind a 'veil of ignorance' of historical details, and of details of their own special situation, to arrive at the 'just' constitution for a society. Now of course Rawls does not think or say that these 'heads' are fathers rather than mothers. But if we have really given up the age-old myth of women needing, as Grotius put it, to be under the 'eye' of a more 'rational' male protector and master, then how do families come to have any one 'head,' except by the death or desertion of one parent? They will either be two-headed, or headless. Traces of the old patriarchal poison still remain in even the best contemporary moral theorizing. Few may actually say that women's place is in the home, but there is much muttering, when unemployment figures rise, about how the relatively recent flood of women into the work force complicates the problem, as if it would be a good thing if women just went back home whenever unemployment rises, to leave the available jobs for the men. We still do not really have a wide acceptance of the equal rights of women to employment outside the home. Nor do we have wide acceptance of the equal duty of men to perform those domestic tasks which in no way depend on special female anatomy, namely cooking, cleaning, and the care of weaned children. All sorts of stories (maybe true stories), about children's need for one 'primary' parent, who must be the mother if the mother breast feeds the child, shore up the unequal division of domestic responsibility between mothers and fathers, wives and husbands. If we are really to transvalue the values of our patriarchal past, we need to rethink all of those assumptions, really test those psychological theories. And how will men ever develop an understanding of the 'ethics of care' if they continue to be shielded or kept from that experience of caring for a dependent child, which complements the experience we all have had of being cared for as dependent children? These experiences form the natural background for the development of moral maturity as Gilligan's women saw it.

Exploitation aside, why would women, once liberated, not be content to have their version of morality merely tolerated? Why should they not see themselves as voluntarily, for their own reasons, taking on *more* than the liberal rules demand, while having no quarrel with the content of those rules themselves, nor with their remaining the only ones that are expected to be generally obeyed? To see why, we need to move on to three more differences between the Kantian liberals (usually contractarians) and their critics. These concern the relative weight put on relationships between equals, and the relative weight put on freedom of choice, and on the authority of intellect over emotions. It is a typical feature of the dominant moral theories and traditions, since Kant, or perhaps since Hobbes, that relationships between equals or those who are deemed equal in some important sense, have been the relations that morality is concerned primarily to regulate. Relationships between those who are clearly unequal in power, such as parents and children, earlier and later generations in relation to one another, states and citizens, doctors and patients, the well and the ill, large states and small states, have had to be shunted to the bottom of the agenda, and then dealt with by some sort of 'promotion' of the weaker so that an appearance of virtual equality is achieved. Citizens collectively become equal to states, children are treated as adults-to-be, the ill and dying are treated as continuers of their earlier more potent selves, so that their 'rights' could be seen as the rights of equals. This pretence of an equality that is in fact absent may often lead to desirable protection of the weaker, or more dependent. But it somewhat masks the question of what our moral relationships *are* to those who are our superiors or our inferiors in power. A more realistic acceptance of the fact that we begin as helpless children, that at almost every point of our lives we deal with both the more and the less helpless, that equality of power and interdependency, between two persons or groups, is rare and hard to recognize when it does occur, might lead us to a more direct approach to questions concerning the design of institutions structuring these relationships between unequals (families, schools, hospitals, armies) and of the morality of our dealings with the more and the less powerful. One reason why those who agree with the Gilligan version of what morality is about will not want to agree that the liberals' rules are a good minimal set, the only ones we need pressure *everyone* to obey, is that these rules do little to protect the young or the dying or the starving or any of the relatively powerless against neglect, or to ensure an education that will form persons to be *capable* of conforming to an ethics of care and responsibility. Put baldly, and in a way Gilligan certainly has not put it, the liberal morality, if unsupplemented, may *unfit* people to be anything other than what is justifying theories suppose them to be, ones who have no interest in each others' interests. Yet some must take an interest in the next generation's interests. Women's traditional work, of caring for the less powerful, especially for the young, is obviously socially vital. One cannot regard any version of morality that does not ensure that it gets well done as an adequate 'minimal morality,' any more than we could so regard one that left any concern for more distant future generations an optional extra. A moral theory, it can plausibly be claimed, cannot regard concern for new and future persons as an optional charity left for those with a taste for it. If the morality the theory endorses is to sustain itself, it must provide for its own continuers, not just take out a loan on a carefully encouraged maternal instinct or on the enthusiasm of a self-selected group of environmentalists, who make it their business or hobby to be concerned with what we are doing to mother earth.

The recognition of the importance for all parties of relations between those who are and cannot but be unequal, both of these relations in themselves and for their effect on personality formation and so on other relationships, goes along with a recognition of the plain fact that not all morally important relationships can or should be freely chosen. So far I have discussed three reasons women have not to be content to pursue their own values within the framework of the liberal morality. The first was its dubious record. The second was its inattention to relations of inequality or its pretence of equality. The third reason is its exaggeration of the scope of choice, or its inattention to unchosen relations. Showing up the partial myth of equality among actual members of a community, and of the undesirability of trying to pretend that we are treating all of them as equals, tends to go along with an exposure of the companion myth that moral obligations arise from freely *chosen* associations between such equals. Vulnerable future generations do not choose their dependence on earlier generations. The unequal infant does not choose its place in a family or nation, nor is it treated as free to do as it likes until some association is freely entered into. Nor do its parents always choose their parental role, or freely assume their parental responsibilities any more than we choose our power to affect the conditions in which later generations will live. Gilligan's attention to the version of morality and moral maturity found in women, many of whom had faced a choice of whether or not to have an abortion, and who had at some point become mothers, is attention to the perceived inadequacy of the language of rights to help in such choices or to guide them in their parental role. It would not be much of an exaggeration to call the Gilligan 'different voice' the voice of the potential parents. The emphasis on care goes with a recognition of the often unchosen nature of the responsibilities of those who give care, both of children who care for their aged or infirm parents, and of parents who care for the children they in fact have. Contract soon ceases to seem the paradigm source of moral obligation once we attend to parental responsibility, and justice as a virtue of social institutions will come to seem at best only first equal with the virtue, whatever its name, that ensures that each new generation is made appropriately welcome and prepared for their adult lives.

This all constitutes a belated reminder to Western moral theorists of a fact they have always known, that as Adam Ferguson, and David Hume before him emphasized, we are born into families, and the first society we belong to, one that fits or misfits us for later ones, is the small society of parents (or some sort of child-attendants) and children, exhibiting as it may both relationships of near equality and of inequality in power. This simple reminder, with the fairly considerable implications it can have for the plausibility of contractarian moral theory, is at the same time a reminder of the role of human emotions as much as human reason and will in moral development as it actually comes about. The fourth feature of the Gilligan challenge to liberal orthodoxy is a challenge to its typical *rationalism,* or intellectualism, to its assumption that we need not worry what passions persons have, as long as their rational wills can control them. This Kantian picture of a controlling reason dictating to possibly unruly passions also tends to seem less useful when we are led to consider what sort of person we need to fill the role of parent, or indeed want in any close relationship. It might be important for father figures to have rational control over their violent urges to beat to death the children whose screams enrage them, but more than control of such nasty passions seems needed in the mother or primary parent, or parent-substitute, by most psychological theories. They need to love their children, not just to control their irritation. So the emphasis in Kantian theories on rational control of emotions, rather than on cultivating desirable forms of emotion, is challenged by Gilligan, along with the challenge to the assumption of the centrality of autonomy, or relations between equals, and of freely chosen relations.

The same set of challenges to 'orthodox' liberal oral theory has come not just from Gilligan and other women, who are reminding other moral theorists of the role of the family as a social institution and as an influence on the other relationships people want to or are capable of sustaining, but also, as I noted at the start, from an otherwise fairly diverse group of men, ranging from those influenced by both Hegelian and Christian traditions (MacIntyre) to all varieties of other backgrounds. From this group I want to draw attention to the work of one philosopher in particular, namely Laurence Thomas, the author of a fairly remarkable article[3] in which he finds sexism to be a more intractable social evil than racism. . . . Thomas makes a strong case for the importance of supplementing a concern for justice and respect for rights with an emphasis on equally needed virtues, and on virtues seen as appropriate *emotional* as well as rational capacities. Like Gilligan (and unlike MacIntyre) Thomas gives a lot of attention to the childhood beginnings of moral and social capacities, to the role of parental love in making that possible, and to the emotional as well as the cognitive development we have reason to think both possible and desirable in human persons.

It is clear, I think, that the best moral theory has to be a cooperative product of women and men, has to harmonize justice and care. The morality it theorizes about is after all for all persons, for men and for women, and will need their combined insights. As Gilligan said (D.V., 174), what we need now is a 'marriage' of the old male and the newly articulated female insights. If she is right about the special moral aptitudes of women, it will most likely be the women who propose the marriage, since they are the ones with moral natural empathy, with the better diplomatic skills, the ones more likely to shoulder responsibility and take moral initiative, and the ones who find it easiest to empathize and care about how the other party feels. Then, once there is this union of male and female moral wisdom, we maybe can teach each other the moral skills each gender currently lacks, so that the gender difference in moral outlook that Gilligan found will slowly become less marked.

NOTES

1. John Rawls, *A Theory of Justice* (Harvard University Press)

2. Immanuel Kant, *Metaphysics of Morals,* sec. 46

3. Laurence Thomas, 'Sexism and Racism: Some Conceptual Differences,' *Ethics* 90 (1980), 239–50; republished in *Philosophy, Sex and Language,* Vetterling-Braggin, ed. (Totowa, NJ: Littlefield Adams 1980)

PART

4

Ethical Issues

Abortion

If somehow you had unobstructed access for a single day to all the public and private dramas provoked by the issue of abortion, you might see scenes like this: a forty-year-old mother of five agonizing over whether she should terminate her pregnancy (which is both unexpected and unwanted); antiabortion activists shouting "Thou shall not kill!" at a woman hurrying inside a clinic that performs abortions; a frightened sixteen-year-old rape victim having an abortion against her family's wishes; a Catholic bishop pointing out on the eleven o'clock news that abortion in any form is murder; the head of an abortion rights organization declaring in a CNN interview that antiabortion activists are violent and dangerous; a politician getting elected solely because he favors a constitutional amendment to ban virtually all abortions; two women who have been friends for years disagreeing bitterly about whether a fetus has a right to life; and state legislators angrily debating a bill requiring any woman seeking an abortion to watch a fifteen-minute video titled "The Tragedy of Abortion."

Such scenes are emblematic of the abortion issue in that they are intensely emotional and usually accompanied by uncritical or dogmatic thinking. Passions surge because abortion touches on some of our deepest values and most basic beliefs. When we grapple with the issue of abortion, we must consider whose rights (the mother's or the unborn's) carry the most moral weight, what the meaning of *human being* or *person* is, when—if ever—the unborn achieves personhood, how having an abortion affects the health and mind of the mother, how much importance to assign to our most fundamental moral principles, and much more. For many women, the abortion controversy is *personal,* involving judgments about their own body, their own health and happiness, and their own inner turmoil provoked by life-and-death decisions. Uncritical acceptance of particular moral perspectives on abortion seems to be the norm for people on all sides of the debate. Often discussion of the issue is reduced to shouting; informed reflection, to knee-jerk conclusions; and reasoned argument, to cases built on assumptions never questioned.

In this chapter, we try to do better, relying heavily on critical reasoning and striving for a more objective approach. We begin with a review of the (nonmoral) facts of abortion—biological, medical, psychological, semantic, and legal. Then we consider how the moral theories discussed in previous chapters can be applied to this issue. Finally, we examine a range of common arguments in the debate, from liberal to conservative as well as some intermediate positions.

ISSUE FILE: BACKGROUND

Abortion (also called *induced abortion*) is the deliberate termination of a pregnancy by surgical or medical (with drugs) means. The unintentional termination of a pregnancy (due to a medical disorder or injury) is known as a *spontaneous abortion,* or *miscarriage.* An abortion performed to protect the life or health of the mother is referred to as a **therapeutic abortion.** Therapeutic abortions are usually not thought to be morally problematic. (The Roman Catholic stance, however, is that direct abortion is always wrong, though the unintended death of the fetus during attempts to save the mother's life is morally permissible.) But induced abortions are intensely controversial and are the focus of the ongoing moral debate.

Throughout our discussion of abortion in this chapter, we will use the word *fetus* to refer to the unborn during its entire development from conception to birth. But technically the term indicates a particular phase of this development. Development begins at **conception,** or fertilization, when a sperm cell enters an ovum and the two merge into a single cell called a *zygote*. The zygote con-tains a complete set of forty-six chromosomes, half of them from the female, half from the male—all the genetic information needed to make a unique human individual. Over the next few days the zygote inches down the fallopian tube toward the uterus, expanding as cells divide. In three to five days it reaches the uterus, where it grows in a tiny orb of cells called a *blastocyst*. By day ten the blastocyst fully implants itself in the lining of the uterus, and from implantation until the eighth week after fertilization it is known technically as an *embryo*. In the embryonic phase, most major organs form (though the brain and spinal cord will keep developing during pregnancy), and the embryo will grow to just over an inch long. At

---

Abortion in the United States: Facts and Figures

- 49 percent of all pregnancies are unintended (about 3.1 million per year).

- 42 percent of all unintended pregnancies end in abortions.

- 1.29 million pregnancies were ended by abortion in 2002.

- In 2002, approximately 2 percent of women ages 15–44 had an abortion.

- The abortion rate (number of abortions per 1,000 women of reproductive age in a given year) was 21 per 1,000 in 2002 (women ages 15–44).

- The abortion rate has been declining since 1980.

- Most Western industrialized countries have lower abortion rates than the United States does.

- At least 10,000–15,000 abortions occur each year among women whose pregnancies were the result of rape or incest (roughly 1 percent of all abortions).

- The risk of death associated with abortion is about 0.6 per 100,000 abortions; the risk of death for pregnancies carried to term is 7.1 per100,000.

- 56 percent of women having abortions are in their 20s; 19 percent are 15–19; less than 1 percent are younger than 15.

- 67 percent of abortions occur in never-married women; 17 percent in married women; 16 percent in women who are separated, divorced, or widowed.

- 41 percent of women having abortions are non-Hispanic white; 52 percent are black and Hispanic (a percentage greater than the percentage of blacks and Hispanics in the population).

- 43 percent of women having abortions are Protestants; 27 percent are Catholic; and 13 percent are "born-again or evangelical Christians."*

*Derived from "An Overview of Abortion in the United States," compiled and developed by Physicians for Reproductive Choice and Health and the Alan Guttmacher Institute, May 2006, www.guttmacher.org (21 November 2006).

about the third week the embryo first acquires a human shape; by the eighth, doctors can detect brain activity. By the end of the eighth week until birth (approximately week forty), the embryo is known in medical terminology as a *fetus.*

In the abortion debate, certain other aspects of fetal development are thought by some to be of special significance. For example, usually at about sixteen to twenty weeks, the mother can feel the fetus moving, an event known as **quickening.** At about twenty-three or twenty-four weeks, the fetus may be able to live outside the uterus, a state referred to as **viability.**

Abortion methods vary depending largely on the length of a woman's pregnancy. Within the first seven weeks or so, drugs can be used to induce an abortion. A combination of mifepristone (RU-486) and prostaglandins (hormonelike agents that provoke uterine contractions) can force the embryo out of the uterus and through the vagina. This approach, sometimes called a medical abortion, has an extremely high success rate.

With a method known as *menstrual aspiration* (or *manual vacuum aspiration*), an abortion can be performed in the first three weeks. In this procedure, a physician expands the opening of the uterus (the cervix) and uses a syringe to draw out the embryo from the uterus wall. Up until twelve weeks of pregnancy (a period when most abortions are performed), a method called *suction curettage* (or *dilation and suction curettage*) is often used. A physician widens the cervix, then inserts a thin, flexible tube through it and into the uterus itself. A vacuum device attached to the other end of the tube then provides suction to empty the uterus. A method often used after twelve weeks is *dilation and evacuation.* After the cervix is opened up, forceps and suction are used to extract the fetus. A nonsurgical technique used in some late abortions involves inducing the contractions of labor so the fetus is expelled from the uterus. To force the contractions, physicians often use drugs as well as *saline injection,* the substitution of saltwater for amniotic fluid in the uterus.

Like any medical procedure, abortion poses some risk of complications. Its risks, however, are relatively low. Less than 1 percent of women who have an abortion suffer from a major complication. The risk of death for women who have an abortion at eight weeks or earlier is one death per one million abortions. The risk for all abortions is about 0.6 deaths per 100,000 abortions. By comparison, the risk of death related to childbirth is much higher than that—about twelve times higher.[1] The health risks linked to abortion are directly related to the timing of the procedure. The earlier in the pregnancy an abortion is performed, the lower the risk.

When we try to evaluate arguments in the abortion debate, we must distinguish between the moral question (Is abortion right?) and the legal one (What should the law allow?). Our main concern is the former, not the latter. But to be fully informed about the issue, we should understand, at least in general terms, what the law does allow. In 1973, in the landmark case of *Roe v. Wade,* the United States Supreme Court ruled that a woman has a constitutional, but not unlimited, right to obtain an abortion in a range of circumstances. According to the Court, in the first three months of pregnancy (the first trimester), the woman's right is unrestricted. The decision to have an abortion is up to the woman in consultation with her physician. After the first trimester, a state may regulate (but not ban) abortion to protect the health of the mother. After viability, however, a state may regulate and even forbid abortions in the interests of "the potentiality of human life," except when abortion is necessary to preserve the health or life of the woman.[2]

[1] "An Overview of Abortion in the United States," developed by Physicians for Reproductive Choice and Health and the Alan Guttmacher Institute, May 2006, www. guttmacher.org (21 November 2006).
[2] *Roe v. Wade,* 410 U.S. 113, 164–65 (1973).

Majority Opinion in *Roe v. Wade*

Seven justices concurred with the opinion in *Roe v. Wade*, including Justice Harry Blackmun, who wrote it. Here is an excerpt:

> This right of privacy, whether it be founded in the Fourteenth Amendment's concept of personal liberty and restrictions upon state action, as we feel it is, or, as the District Court determined, in the Ninth Amendment's reservation of rights to the people, is broad enough to encompass a woman's decision whether or not to terminate her pregnancy. . . .
>
> [A]ppellant and some *amici* argue that the woman's right is absolute and that she is entitled to terminate her pregnancy at whatever time, in whatever way, and for whatever reason she alone chooses. With this we do not agree. Appellant's arguments that Texas either has no valid interest at all in regulating the abortion decision, or no interest strong enough to support any limitation upon the woman's sole determination, are unpersuasive. The Court's decisions recognizing a right of privacy also acknowledge that some state regulation in areas protected by that right is appropriate. As noted above, a State may properly assert important interests in safeguarding health, in maintaining medical standards, and in protecting potential life. At some point in pregnancy, these respective inter-
> ests become sufficiently compelling to sustain regulation of the factors that govern the abortion decision. The privacy right involved, therefore, cannot be said to be absolute. . . .
>
> We, therefore, conclude that the right of personal privacy includes the abortion decision, but that this right is not unqualified and must be considered against important state interests in regulation. . . .
>
> [This] decision leaves the State free to place increasing restrictions on abortion as the period of pregnancy lengthens, so long as those restrictions are tailored to the recognized state interests. The decision vindicates the right of the physician to administer medical treatment according to his professional judgment up to the points where important state interests provide compelling justifications for intervention. Up to those points, the abortion decision in all its aspects is inherently, and primarily, a medical decision, and basic responsibility for it must rest with the physician. If an individual practitioner abuses the privilege of exercising proper medical judgment, the usual remedies, judicial and intra-professional, are available.*

* *Roe v. Wade*, 410 U.S. 113, 153–54, 165–66 (1973).

In *Roe* the Court maintained that a woman's right to an abortion is based on a fundamental right of personal privacy and that this right, derived from several constitutional amendments, applies to numerous situations involving reproduction, families, and children. The Court also pointed out that the word *person* as used in the Constitution "does not include the unborn" and that "the unborn have never been recognized in the law as persons in the whole sense."[3]

Over the next thirty years the Court handed down other abortion decisions that clarified or

supplemented *Roe*. Among other things, the justices prohibited or constrained the use of Medicaid (a government entitlement program) to subsidize abortions; forbade the use of public employees and facilities to perform abortions (except to save the life of the mother); declared that a woman seeking an abortion does not have to notify her husband of her intent; affirmed that states may not impose restrictions that present an "undue burden," or excessive impediment, to women seeking abortions; and held that states may require a girl under eighteen to obtain either the informed consent of a parent or a court order before getting an abortion.

[3]*Roe*, 410 U.S. at 158, 162.

MORAL THEORIES

How would a utilitarian judge the moral permissibility of abortion? How would a Kantian theorist or a natural law theorist evaluate it? Let us take utilitarianism first. An act-utilitarian would say that an abortion is morally right if it results in the greatest overall happiness, everyone considered. To argue for abortion, she might point to all the unhappiness that could be caused by the mother's remaining pregnant against her wishes: the mother's impaired mental and physical health (and possible death), her loss of personal freedom and future opportunities, financial strain on the mother as well as on her family, the anguish of being pregnant as a result of rape or incest, the agony of bringing a seriously impaired baby to term only to see it die later, and the stress that all these social and financial problems would have on a child after birth. The philosopher Mary Anne Warren cites a possible consequentialist argument that says when women do not have the option of abortion, unhappiness can be created on a *global* scale:

In the long run, access to abortion is essential for the health and survival not just of individual women and families, but also that of the larger social and biological systems on which all our lives depend. Given the inadequacy of present methods of contraception and the lack of universal access to contraception, the avoidance of rapid population growth generally requires some use of abortion. Unless population growth rates are reduced in those impoverished societies where they remain high, malnutrition and starvation will become even more widespread than at present.[4]

An act-utilitarian, of course, could also argue against abortion on exactly the same grounds—

the overall happiness (or unhappiness) brought about by particular actions. She could contend, for example, that *not* having an abortion would produce more net happiness than having one because having one would cause the mother tremendous psychological pain, because the happiness brought into the world with the birth of the child would be considerable, and because the social stigma of having an abortion would be extremely painful for both the mother and her family.

A rule-utilitarian could also view abortion as either morally right or wrong depending on the rule being followed and how much net happiness results from adhering to it. He could argue on various grounds that generally following a rule such as "Abortion is not morally permissible except to save the mother's life" would maximize happiness. Or he could claim that generally following this rule instead would maximize happiness: "Abortion is morally permissible for any reason during the first trimester and always in cases of rape, incest, fetal impairment, and serious threats to the mother's health or life."

A premise (often unstated) in many arguments about abortion is that the fetus is (or is not) a **person**—an entity with full moral rights. In general, utilitarian arguments about abortion do not depend heavily, if at all, on whether the fetus is regarded as a person. Whether the fetus is a person is not likely to dramatically affect the hedonic calculus. The main issue is not personhood but utility. For the Kantian theorist, however, the moral status of the fetus is likely to matter much more. (Whether Kant himself thought the fetus a person is an open question.) If the Kantian maintains that the fetus is a person—that is, an end in itself, a thing of intrinsic value and dignity—then he would insist that it has all the rights and is due all the respect that any other person has. This would mean that the unborn should not be regarded as just another quantity in a utilitarian calculation of consequences. Like any adult human, the fetus has rights, and these rights cannot

[4]Mary Anne Warren, "Abortion," in *A Companion to Ethics*, ed. Peter Singer, corr. ed. (Cambridge, MA: Blackwell, 1993), 304.

be overridden merely for utility's sake. Only for the most compelling moral reasons can these rights be set aside. A Kantian might say that one such reason is self-defense: killing a person in self-defense is permissible. He might therefore argue that if the mother's life is being threatened by the fetus she carries (if being pregnant is somehow life-threatening), therapeutic abortion is permissible, just as killing someone who is trying to kill you is permissible. On this view, abortion would seem to be only rarely justified.

On the other hand, if the Kantian does not regard the fetus as a person, he may believe that abortion is often justified to protect the rights and dignity of the mother, who *is* a person. In other words, the fetus—like any other nonperson—can be used as a means to an end, whereas the mother must be treated as an end in herself.

Traditional natural law theorists would view abortion very differently for two reasons. First, to them, there is no question about the moral status of the fetus: it is a person with full moral rights. Second, the theory is very clear about the treatment of innocent persons: it is always morally wrong to directly kill the innocent. So the direct, intentional killing of a fetus through abortion is

---

Abortion and the Scriptures

Do the Jewish or Christian scriptures forbid abortion? Many people believe that they do, but the philosopher James Rachels argues that they do not:

> It is difficult to derive a prohibition of abortion from either the Jewish or the Christian Scriptures. The Bible does not speak plainly on the matter. There are certain passages, however, that are often quoted by conservatives because they seem to suggest that fetuses have full human status. One of the most frequently cited passages is from the first chapter of Jeremiah, in which God is quoted as saying: "Before I formed you in the womb I knew you, and before you were born I consecrated you." These words are presented as though they were God's endorsement of the conservative position: They are taken to mean that the unborn, as well as the born, are "consecrated" to God.
>
> In context, however, these words obviously mean something quite different. Suppose we read the whole passage in which they occur:
>
> > Now the word of the Lord came to me saying, "Before I formed you in the womb I knew you, and before you were born I consecrated you; I appointed you a prophet to the nations." Then I said, "Ah, Lord God! Behold, I do not know how to speak, for I am only a youth." But the Lord said to me, "Do not say, 'I am only a youth'

> for to all to whom I send you you shall go, and whatever I command you you shall speak. Be not afraid of them, for I am with you to deliver you," says the Lord.
>
> Neither abortion, the sanctity of fetal life, nor anything else of the kind is being discussed in this passage. Instead, Jeremiah is asserting his authority as a prophet. He is saying, in effect, "God authorized me to speak for him; even though I resisted, he commanded me to speak." But Jeremiah puts the point more poetically; he has God saying that God had intended him to be a prophet even before Jeremiah was born. . . .
>
> The scriptural passage that comes closest to making a specific judgment about the moral status of fetuses occurs in the 21st chapter of Exodus. This chapter is part of a detailed description of the law of the ancient Israelites. Here the penalty for murder is said to be death; however, it is also said that if a pregnant woman is caused to have a miscarriage, the penalty is only a fine, to be paid to her husband. Murder was not a category that included fetuses. The Law of Israel apparently regarded fetuses as something less than full human beings.*

*James Rachels, *The Elements of Moral Philosophy,* 4th ed. (Boston: McGraw-Hill, 2003), 59–60. Copyright © 1989 McGraw-Hill. Reprinted with permission of McGraw-Hill Companies.

never permissible. According to the doctrine of double effect, killing an innocent person for the purpose of achieving some greater good is immoral. But indirectly, unintentionally killing an innocent person while trying to do good may be permissible. Therefore, intentionally killing a fetus through abortion, even to save the mother's life, is wrong. But trying to, say, cure a pregnant woman's cancer by performing a hysterectomy on her or giving her chemotherapy—treatment that has the unintended side effect of aborting the fetus—may be morally acceptable. On this view, very few abortions are morally acceptable.

MORAL ARGUMENTS

Arguments for and against abortion are plentiful and diverse, their quality ranging from good to bad, and their conclusions varying from conservative ("pro-life") to liberal ("pro-choice") with several moderate positions in between. We can sum up the central issue of the debate like this: *When, if ever, is abortion morally permissible?* Recall that in ethics the proper reply to such a question is to provide good reasons for a particular position. The usual fireworks that accompany the abortion debate—strident denunciations of the other side, appeals to emotion and pity, extremist rhetoric, exaggerated claims, political posturing, and the like—are not appropriate, not germane, and not helpful. So here we try to cut through all that and examine a few of the main arguments offered for a range of views.

The conservative position is that abortion is never, or almost never, morally permissible. Typically the "almost never" refers to situations in which abortion may be permissible to save the life of the mother. (Generally, both the liberal and conservative hold that abortion may be permissible to save the mother's life, usually on the grounds that the mother has a right of self-defense. But as mentioned earlier, the Roman Catholic position is that in any case the death of the fetus must be unintended.)

Like many arguments about abortion, the conservative case is built on a proposition about the moral status of the fetus. For most conservatives, the fetus is a person (a human being, as some would say) with full moral rights, the same rights that any adult human has, and these rights emerge at the moment of conception. Of course, the moral right at the heart of it all is the right to life. Taking the life of a fetal person is just as immoral as killing an innocent adult human.

Here is one version of the conservative argument:

1. The unborn is obviously a human life.

2. It is wrong to take a human life.

3. Abortion is the taking of a human life.

4. Therefore, abortion is wrong.

To evaluate this argument (or *any* argument), we must determine (1) whether the conclusion follows from the premises and (2) whether the premises are true. A cursory glance at this argument might suggest that the conclusion does follow from the premises and that the premises are true. But we must be careful. This argument commits the fallacy of equivocation. The term *human life* is assigned two different meanings in the premises, rendering the argument invalid. In Premise 1, "human life" means something like "biologically human"—an entity with human DNA, an entity that is from the human species. But in Premises 2 and 3, the term means "person"—a being entitled to full moral rights. If "human life" is used in different senses in the premises, then the argument is not valid (the conclusion does not follow from the premises)—even if the premises, using their respective meanings of the term, are true. As it stands, Premise 1 is unmistakably true: a fetus born of human parents with human DNA is certainly biologically human. And in its present form, Premise 2 is also true: the killing of a person is indeed wrong (except perhaps to save a life). Still, the argument fails and does not provide us with good reasons to accept the conclusion.

Yet there are conservative arguments that do not equivocate. Consider this one:

1. The unborn is an innocent person from conception.
2. It is wrong to kill an innocent person.
3. Abortion is the killing of an innocent person.
4. Therefore, abortion is wrong.

This argument is valid. The only significant difference between it and the previous one is Premise 1, which asserts that the unborn is a being with full moral rights from the very moment of fertilization. If Premise 1 is true, then the argument is sound—the premises are true and the conclusion follows from them.

But *is* the premise true? The conservative insists that it is and can argue for it in this fashion. Birth is generally thought to be the point at

CRITICAL THOUGHT: Late-Term Abortions

Late-term abortion (what some opponents of abortion call "partial-birth abortion") is a controversial procedure known technically as *intact dilation and extraction*. It is a rare operation usually performed after the first trimester because the pregnancy endangers the mother's life, the fetus is seriously deformed or defective, or the mother is mentally impaired, homeless, addicted to drugs, or otherwise unprepared or unwilling to care for an infant. Late-term abortion has been hotly debated in society and frequently adjudicated in the courts.

Some late-term abortions are performed after the fetus becomes viable. Do such procedures then involve, as some have alleged, the killing of babies? Should all late-term abortions be outlawed? Why or why not? Are they different from earlier abortions in morally relevant respects? Why or why not?

which the fetus is most clearly (and legally) a person. The development of the unborn from conception to birth, however, is one continuous process, with no obvious points along the way that might signal a transition into personhood. Moreover, whatever essential properties a born human has that make it a person seem to be present at the moment of conception. Therefore, since no unambiguous point of personhood can be located in this process, the most reasonable option is to identify personhood with conception.

Opponents of this argument contend that it is fallacious. We may not be able to pinpoint a precise moment when day becomes night, they say, but that does not mean that day *is* night. Likewise, we may not be able to determine the precise point in the continuous process of human development when a zygote becomes a full-fledged person. But that does not mean that a zygote is a person.

The conservative, however, can propose a more nuanced reason for supposing that conception marks the beginning of personhood:

One evidence of the nonarbitrary character of the line drawn [at conception] is the difference of probabilities on either side of it. If a spermatozoon is destroyed, one destroys a being which had a chance of far less than 1 in 200 million of developing into a reasoning being, possessed of the genetic code, a heart and other organs, and capable of pain. If a fetus is destroyed, one destroys a being already possessed of the genetic code, organs and sensitivity to pain, and one which had an 80 percent chance of developing further into a baby outside the womb who, in time, would reason.

The positive argument for conception as the decision moment of humanization is that at conception the new being receives the genetic code. It is this genetic information which determines his characteristics, which is the biological carrier of the possibility of human wisdom, which makes him a self-evolving being. A being with a human genetic code is man.[5]

Others who oppose abortion argue that although the fetus may not be a person, it has the *potential* to become a person and is therefore entitled to the same rights as full-fledged persons. But critics reject this view:

This argument is implausible, since in no other case do we treat the potential to achieve some status entailing certain rights as itself entailing those same rights. For instance, every child born in the United States is a potential voter, but no-one under the age of 18 has the right to vote in that country. If a fetus

is a potential person, then so is an unfertilized human ovum, together with enough viable spermatozoa to achieve fertilization; yet few would seriously suggest that *these* living human entities should have full and equal moral status.[6]

The liberal position is that abortion is always (or almost always) permissible. Like the conservative's argument, the liberal's is based on a particular view of the moral status of the fetus. But in opposition to the conservative view, the liberal asserts that the fetus is not a person, not a being with full moral rights. Abortion therefore is morally permissible because the fetus does not possess a right to life (unlike the mother, who has a full complement of rights). Generally, for the liberal, the event that makes the unborn a person is not conception but birth.

Here is a version of a common liberal argument:

1. The unborn is not a person until birth (and thus does not have a right to life).

2. It is wrong to kill an innocent person.

3. Abortion before birth would not be the killing of an innocent person.

4. If abortion before birth is not the killing of an innocent person, it is permissible.

5. Therefore, abortion before birth is permissible.

Notice that this argument and the conservative one have a common premise: it is wrong to kill an innocent person. Thus the liberal and the conservative agree on the immorality of murder. Their disagreement is not over this fundamental moral principle, but over the nature of persons and who does or does not qualify as such an entity. Premise 1, then, is the crux of the liberal's argument (just as Premise 1 is the heart of the conservative's argument). How might the liberal defend this premise?

[5]John T. Noonan Jr., "An Almost Absolute Value in History," in *The Morality of Abortion: Legal and Historical Perspectives,* ed. Noonan (Cambridge, MA: Harvard University Press, 1970), 56–57.

[6]Warren, "Abortion," 312.

The obvious approach is to plausibly explain what a person is and then show that the fetus does not qualify as one. The most influential argument along these lines is that of Mary Anne Warren. "What characteristics entitle an entity to be considered a person?" she asks. What criteria, for example, would we use to decide whether alien beings encountered on an unknown planet deserve to be treated morally or treated as, say, a source of food? How would we tell whether the creatures are persons? Warren says that the characteristics most important to our idea of personhood are (1) consciousness, (2) the ability to reason, (3) self-motivated activity, (4) the capacity to communicate, and (5) the presence of self-concepts and self-awareness. Any being that has all of these traits we would surely regard as a person. Even a being that has only some of these traits would probably qualify as a person. More to the point, Warren says, we must admit that any being that has none of these traits is unquestionably *not* a person. And since a fetus lacks all these, we have to conclude that it too is not a person.

These considerations suggest that being genetically human is not the same thing as being a person in the moral sense, the sense of having full moral rights. As Warren notes,

Now if [these five traits] are indeed the primary criteria of personhood, then it is clear that genetic humanity is neither necessary nor sufficient for establishing that an entity is a person. Some human beings are not people [persons], and there may well be people who are not human beings. A man or woman whose consciousness has been permanently obliterated but who remains alive is a human being which is no longer a person; defective human beings, with no appreciable mental capacity, are not and presumably never will be people; and a fetus is a human being which is not yet a person, and which therefore cannot coherently be said to have full moral rights.

Citizens of the next century should be prepared to recognize highly advanced, self-aware robots or computers, should such be developed, and intelligent inhabitants of other worlds, should such be found, as people in the fullest sense, and to respect their moral rights.[7]

Against the liberal's argument, the conservative can lodge the following objections. First, he can point out that if Warren's view of personhood is correct, then a fetus is not a person—but neither is a newborn. After all, it is doubtful that a newborn (or perhaps even an older baby) can meet Warren's criteria for personhood. If a newborn is not a person, then killing it—the crime of infanticide—would seem to be permissible. But we tend to think that infanticide is obviously wrong.

To this criticism the liberal may say that though a newborn is not a person, it still has value—either because it is a potential person or because it is valued by others. The liberal might even argue that though a baby is not a person, infanticide should never be permitted because it is a gruesome act that cheapens life or cultivates a callous attitude toward it.

The conservative can offer a related objection to the liberal's position. The liberal argument implies that the unborn is a person at birth but not a person a day or even an hour *before* birth, that abortion is immoral after birth but permissible an hour before. But since in such a case the physiological and psychological differences between the born and unborn are virtually nil, the liberal's distinction seems both arbitrary and ghastly.

The moderate rejects the claim that abortions are almost never permissible (as conservatives say) as well as the notion that they almost always are (as liberals maintain). In a variety of ways, mod-

---

[7]Mary Anne Warren, "On the Moral and Legal Status of Abortion," *The Monist* 57, no. 4 (1973): 56.

erates take intermediate positions between these two ends of the spectrum, asserting that abortion may be justified in more cases than conservatives would allow and fewer than liberals would like.

One moderate approach is to argue that the fetus becomes a person (and acquires full rights) some time after conception and before birth—at viability, quickening, sentience (sensory experience), or other notable milestone. Each of these points, however, is problematic in one way or another. The viability of the fetus (the point when it can survive outside the womb) is largely a function of modern medical know-how. Physicians are getting better at sustaining fetal life outside the womb, gradually pushing viability farther back toward conception. But this suggests, implausibly, that personhood depends on medical expertise. Quickening, the first detection of fetal movement by the mother, signifies nothing that can be plausibly linked to personhood. It does not indicate the start of fetal movement—the fetus begins moving in the very first week of life. Sentience refers to consciousness, specifically the capacity to have sense experiences. If being sentient (especially the capacity to feel pleasure and pain) is proof of personhood, then personhood must not arise in the fetus until the second trimester, when neurological pathways are developed enough to make sense experience possible. But why should we regard sentience as a marker for personhood in the first place? Kittens, birds, crabs, and spiders are sentient, but few of us would insist that they are persons with full moral rights.

Some moderate positions can be mapped out without reference to the issue of personhood. The most impressive argument for this sort of view is that of Judith Jarvis Thomson. She contends that even if we grant that the fetus is a person with full moral rights, abortion still may be permissible in certain cases—more cases than the conservative would permit and fewer than the liberal would.

The fetus has a right to life but not a right to sustain that life by using the mother's body against her will. To underscore her argument, Thomson asks us to consider this strange scenario:

You wake up in the morning and find yourself back to back in bed with an unconscious violinist. A famous unconscious violinist. He has been found to have a fatal kidney ailment, and the Society of Music Lovers has canvassed all the available medical records and found that you alone have the right blood type to help. They have therefore kidnapped you, and last night the violinist's circulatory system was plugged into yours, so that your kidneys can be used to extract poisons from his blood as well as your own. The director of the hospital now tells you, "Look, we're sorry the Society of Music Lovers did this to you—we would never have permitted it if we had known. But still, they did it, and the violinist now is plugged into you. To unplug you would be to kill him. But never mind, it's only for nine months. By then he will have recovered from his ailment, and can safely be unplugged from you."[8]

Would you agree to such an arrangement? Would you be morally obligated to do so? The violinist, like all persons, has a right to life. But does this right, in Thomson's phrase, "[outweigh] your right to decide what happens in and to your body"? Thomson concludes that the unborn's right to life does not entail the right to use the mother's body without her consent; the mother has a right to defend herself against unauthorized exploitation of her body. Abortion then is morally permissible when pregnancy is forced on the mother—that is, in cases of rape, incest, and defective contraception. (Like most people involved in the abortion debate, Thomson also thinks that abortion is morally acceptable to save the life of the mother.)

[8]Judith Jarvis Thomson, "A Defense of Abortion," *Philosophy & Public Affairs* 1, no. 1 (1971): 48–49.

While laying out her argument, Thomson makes a distinction that further moderates her views. She points out that though women have a right to terminate a pregnancy in some cases, they do not have a right to "secure the death of the unborn child":

It is easy to confuse these two things in that up to a certain point in the life of the fetus it is not able to survive outside the mother's body; hence removing it from her body guarantees its death. But they are importantly different. I have argued that you are not morally required to spend nine months in bed, sustaining the life of that violinist; but to say this is by no means to say that if, when you unplug yourself, there is a miracle and he survives, you then have a right to turn round and slit his throat. You may detach yourself even if this costs him his life; you have no right to be guaranteed his death, by some other means, if unplugging yourself does not kill him.[9]

Here is a greatly simplified version of Thomson's basic argument:

1. Whether or not the unborn has a right to life, it does not have a right to sustain its life by using the mother's body against her will.

2. The mother has a right to defend herself against the unborn's use of her body against her will (a right to have an abortion).

3. The unborn uses the mother's body against her when the pregnancy is the result of rape, incest, or defective contraception.

4. Therefore, abortion is permissible in cases of rape, incest, or defective contraception.

Probably the most common criticism of this argument is that the mother may in fact not have the right to disconnect herself from the fetus if she bears some responsibility for being connected. In the case of Thomson's violinist, the woman was not at all responsible for being connected to him. However, if the woman's own actions somehow precipitated her being attached to the violinist, then she would be responsible for her predicament and thus would have no right to disconnect herself. Likewise, this objection goes, if a woman consents to sexual intercourse and knows that her actions can lead to pregnancy, she bears some responsibility for getting pregnant and therefore has no right to abort the fetus, even though it is using her body to survive. If this view is right, an abortion would seem to be justified only in cases of rape, when the woman is clearly not responsible for her pregnancy.

SUMMARY

Abortion is the deliberate termination of a pregnancy by surgical or medical means. Therapeutic abortions are those performed to protect the life of the mother. An abortion can be performed at any point in the development of the unborn—from conception to birth.

Abortion methods vary depending on how long the woman has been pregnant. Very early abortions can be done with drugs. Other types of abortions are performed by widening the uterus and drawing out the embryo with a syringe (manual vacuum aspiration), by opening the cervix and using a thin suction tube to empty the uterus (suction curettage), by using forceps and suction to extract the fetus (dilation and evacuation), and by using drugs or saline solution to cause contractions to expel the fetus from the uterus.

In 1973, in the famous case of *Roe v. Wade*, the United States Supreme Court ruled that a woman has a constitutional, but limited, right to obtain an abortion. According to the Court, in the first trimester, the woman's right is unrestricted. The decision to have an abortion is up to the woman in consultation with her physician. After the first trimester, a state may regulate but not ban abortion to protect the health of the mother. After the fetus reaches viability, a state may regulate and even for-

[9]Thomson, "A Defense of Abortion," 66.

bid abortions in the interests of the fetus, except when an abortion is necessary to preserve the health or life of the woman.

Major moral theories offer different perspectives on the issue of abortion. An act-utilitarian would argue that an abortion is morally right (or wrong) depending on its consequences. A rule-utilitarian could also judge abortion to be either morally right or wrong depending on the rule being followed and how much net happiness results from adhering to it. A Kantian theorist is likely to judge the issue according to the moral status of the fetus. If the Kantian believes that the fetus is a person, then she would say that the fetus has full moral rights and that these rights cannot be overridden on utilitarian grounds. If she does not think the fetus a person, she may believe that abortion is sometimes justified to protect the rights and dignity of the mother.

Arguments for and against abortion can be roughly grouped into three major categories—conservative, liberal, and moderate. The conservative position is that abortion is never, or almost never, morally permissible. The conservative case is built on the supposition that the fetus is a person with full moral rights. The liberal position is that abortion is always, or almost always, permissible. The liberal asserts that the fetus is not a person and therefore does not have a right to life. The moderate can take a number of intermediate positions between these two extremes, asserting on various grounds that abortion may be permissible in more situations than would be allowed by the conservative and in fewer situations than would be accepted by the liberal. A moderate position can be formulated by arguing that the unborn is a person some time after conception and before birth—perhaps at viability, quickening, or sentience.

READINGS

A Defense of Abortion

JUDITH JARVIS THOMSON

Most opposition to abortion relies on the premise that the fetus is a human being, a person, from the moment of conception. The premise is argued for, but, as I think, not well. Take, for example, the most common argument. We are asked to notice that the development of a human being from conception through birth into childhood is continuous; then it is said that to draw a line, to choose a point in this development and say "before this point the thing is not a person, after this point it is a person" is to make an arbitrary choice, a choice for which in the nature of things no good reason can be given. It is concluded that the fetus is, or anyway that we had better say it

Judith Jarvis Thomson, "A Defense of Abortion," *Philosophy & Public Affairs* 1, no. 1 (1971): 47–66 (edited). Reprinted with permission of Blackwell Publishers.

is, a person from the moment of conception. But this conclusion does not follow. Similar things might be said about the development of an acorn into an oak tree, and it does not follow that acorns are oak trees, or that we had better say they are. Arguments of this form are sometimes called "slippery slope arguments"—the phrase is perhaps self-explanatory—and it is dismaying that opponents of abortion rely on them so heavily and uncritically.

I am inclined to agree, however, that the prospects for "drawing a line" in the development of the fetus look dim. I am inclined to think also that we shall probably have to agree that the fetus has already become a human person well before birth. Indeed, it comes as a surprise when one first learns how early in its life it begins to acquire human characteristics.

By the tenth week, for example, it already has a face, arms and legs, fingers and toes; it has internal organs, and brain activity is detectable. On the other hand, I think that the premise is false, that the fetus is not a person from the moment of conception. A newly fertilized ovum, a newly implanted clump of cells, is no more a person than an acorn is an oak tree. But I shall not discuss any of this. For it seems to me to be of great interest to ask what happens if, for the sake of argument, we allow the premise. How, precisely, are we supposed to get from there to the conclusion that abortion is morally impermissible? Opponents of abortion commonly spend most of their time establishing that the fetus is a person, and hardly any time explaining the step from there to the impermissibility of abortion. Perhaps they think the step too simple and obvious to require much comment. Or perhaps instead they are simply being economical in argument. Many of those who defend abortion rely on the premise that the fetus is not a person, but only a bit of tissue that will become a person at birth; and why pay out more arguments than you have to? Whatever the explanation, I suggest that the step they take is neither easy nor obvious, that it calls for closer examination than it is commonly given, and that when we do give it this closer examination we shall feel inclined to reject it.

I propose, then, that we grant that the fetus is a person from the moment of conception. How does the argument go from here? Something like this, I take it. Every person has a right to life. So the fetus has a right to life. No doubt the mother has a right to decide what shall happen in and to her body; everyone would grant that. But surely a person's right to life is stronger and more stringent than the mother's right to decide what happens in and to her body, and so outweighs it. So the fetus may not be killed; an abortion may not be performed.

It sounds plausible. But now let me ask you to imagine this. You wake up in the morning and find yourself back to back in bed with an unconscious violinist. A famous unconscious violinist. He has been found to have a fatal kidney ailment, and the Society of Music Lovers has canvassed all the available medical records and found that you alone have the right blood type to help. They have therefore kidnapped you, and last night the violinist's circulatory system was plugged into yours, so that your kidneys can be used to extract poisons from his blood as well as your own. The director of the hospital now tells you, "Look, we're sorry the Society of Music Lovers did this to you—we would never have permitted it if we had known. But still, they did it, and the violinist now is plugged into you. To unplug you would be to kill him. But never mind, it's only for nine months. By then he will have recovered from his ailment, and can safely be unplugged from you." Is it morally incumbent on you to accede to this situation? No doubt it would be very nice of you if you did, a great kindness. But do you *have* to accede to it? What if it were not nine months, but nine years? Or longer still? What if the director of the hospital says, "Tough luck, I agree, but you've now got to stay in bed, with the violinist plugged into you, for the rest of your life. Because remember this. All persons have a right to life, and violinists are persons. Granted you have a right to decide what happens in and to your body, but a person's right to life outweighs your right to decide what happens in and to your body. So you cannot ever be unplugged from him." I imagine you would regard this as outrageous, which suggests that something really is wrong with that plausible-sounding argument I mentioned a moment ago.

In this case, of course, you were kidnapped; you didn't volunteer for the operation that plugged the violinist into your kidneys. Can those who oppose abortion on the ground I mentioned make an exception for a pregnancy due to rape? Certainly. They can say that persons have a right to life only if they didn't come into existence because of rape; or they can say that all persons have a right to life, but that some have less of a right to life than others, in particular, that those who came into existence because of rape have less. But these statements have a rather unpleasant sound. Surely the question of whether you have a right to life at all, or how much of it you have, shouldn't turn on the question of whether or not you are the product of a rape. And in fact the people who oppose abortion on the ground I mentioned do not make this distinction, and hence do not make an exception in case of rape.

Nor do they make an exception for a case in which the mother has to spend the nine months of her pregnancy in bed. They would agree that would be a great pity, and hard on the mother; but all the same, all persons have a right to life, the fetus is a person, and so on. I suspect, in fact, that they would not make an exception for a case in which, miraculously enough, the pregnancy went on for nine years, or even the rest of the mother's life.

Some won't even make an exception for a case in which continuation of the pregnancy is likely to shorten the mother's life; they regard abortion as impermissible even to save the mother's life. Such cases are nowadays very rare, and many opponents of abortion do not accept this extreme view. All the same, it is a good place to begin: a number of points of interest come out in respect to it.

1. Let us call the view that abortion is impermissible even to save the mother's life "the extreme view." I want to suggest first that it does not issue from the argument I mentioned earlier without the addition of some fairly powerful premises. Suppose a woman has become pregnant, and now learns that she has a cardiac condition such that she will die if she carries the baby to term. What may be done for her? The fetus, being a person, has a right to life, but as the mother is a person too, so has she a right to life. Presumably they have an equal right to life. How is it supposed to come out that an abortion may not be performed? If mother and child have an equal right to life, shouldn't we perhaps flip a coin? Or should we add to the mother's right to life her right to decide what happens in and to her body, which everybody seems to be ready to grant—the sum of her rights now outweighing the fetus' right to life?

The most familiar argument here is the following. We are told that performing the abortion would be directly killing[1] the child, whereas doing nothing would not be killing the mother, but only letting her die. Moreover, in killing the child, one would be killing an innocent person, for the child has committed no crime, and is not aiming at his mother's death. And then there are a variety of ways in which

this might be continued. (1) But as directly killing an innocent person is always and absolutely impermissible, an abortion may not be performed. Or, (2) as directly killing an innocent person is murder, and murder is always and absolutely impermissible, an abortion may not be performed. Or, (3) as one's duty to refrain from directly killing an innocent person is more stringent than one's duty to keep a person from dying, an abortion may not be performed. Or, (4) if one's only options are directly killing an innocent person or letting a person die, one must prefer letting the person die, and thus an abortion may not be performed.

Some people seem to have thought that these are not further premises which must be added if the conclusion is to be reached, but that they follow from the very fact that an innocent person has a right to life. But this seems to me to be a mistake, and perhaps the simplest way to show this is to bring out that while we must certainly grant that innocent persons have a right to life, the theses in (1) through (4) are all false. Take (2), for example. If directly killing an innocent person is murder, and thus is impermissible, then the mother's directly killing the innocent person inside her is murder, and thus is impermissible. But it cannot seriously be thought to be murder if the mother performs an abortion on herself to save her life. It cannot seriously be said that she *must* refrain, that she *must* sit passively by and wait for her death. Let us look again at the case of you and the violinist. There you are, in bed with the violinist, and the director of the hospital says to you, "It's all most distressing, and I deeply sympathize, but you see this is putting an additional strain on your kidneys, and you'll be dead within the month. But you *have* to stay where you are all the same. Because unplugging you would be directly killing an innocent violinist, and that's murder, and that's impermissible." If anything in the world is true, it is that you do not commit murder, you do not do what is impermissible, if you reach around to your back and unplug yourself from that violinist to save your life.

The main focus of attention in writings on abortion has been on what a third party may or may not do in answer to a request from a woman for an abortion. This is in a way understandable. Things being as they are, there isn't much a woman can safely do to abort herself. So the question asked is what a third party may do, and what the mother may do, if it is mentioned at all, is deduced, almost as an afterthought, from what it is concluded that third parties may do. But it seems to me that to treat the matter in this way is to refuse to grant to the mother that very status of person which is so firmly insisted on for the fetus. For we cannot simply read off what a person may do from what a third party may do. Suppose you find yourself trapped in a tiny house with a growing child. I mean a very tiny house, and a rapidly growing child—you are already up against the wall of the house and in a few minutes you'll be crushed to death. The child on the other hand won't be crushed to death; if nothing is done to stop him from growing he'll be hurt, but in the end he'll simply burst open the house and walk out a free man. Now I could well understand it if a bystander were to say, "There's nothing we can do for you. We cannot choose between your life and his, we cannot be the ones to decide who is to live, we cannot intervene." But it cannot be concluded that you too can do nothing, that you cannot attack it to save your life. However innocent the child may be, you do not have to wait passively while it crushes you to death. Perhaps a pregnant woman is vaguely felt to have the status of house, to which we don't allow the right of self-defense. But if the woman houses the child, it should be remembered that she is a person who houses it.

I should perhaps stop to say explicitly that I am not claiming that people have a right to do anything whatever to save their lives. I think, rather, that there are drastic limits to the right of self-defense. If someone threatens you with death unless you torture someone else to death, I think you have not the right, even to save your life, to do so. But the case under consideration here is very different. In our case there are only two people involved, one whose life is threatened, and one who threatens it. Both are innocent: the one who is threatened is not threatened because of any fault, the one who threatens does not threaten

because of any fault. For this reason we may feel that we bystanders cannot intervene. But the person threatened can.

In sum, a woman surely can defend her life against the threat to it posed by the unborn child, even if doing so involves its death. And this shows not merely that the theses in (1) through (4) are false; it shows also that the extreme view of abortion is false, and so we need not canvass any other possible ways of arriving at it from the argument I mentioned at the outset.

2. The extreme view could of course be weakened to say that while abortion is permissible to save the mother's life, it may not be performed by a third party, but only by the mother herself. But this cannot be right either. For what we have to keep in mind is that the mother and the unborn child are not like two tenants in a small house which has, by an unfortunate mistake, been rented to both: the mother *owns* the house. The fact that she does adds to the offensiveness of deducing that the mother can do nothing from the supposition that third parties can do nothing. But it does more than this: it casts a bright light on the supposition that third parties can do nothing. Certainly it lets us see that a third party who says "I cannot choose between you" is fooling himself if he thinks this is impartiality. If Jones has found and fastened on a certain coat, which he needs to keep him from freezing, but which Smith also needs to keep him from freezing, then it is not impartiality that says "I cannot choose between you" when Smith owns the coat. Women have said again and again "This body is *my* body!" and they have reason to feel angry, reason to feel that it has been like shouting into the wind. Smith, after all, is hardly likely to bless us if we say to him, "Of course it's your coat, anybody would grant that it is. But no one may choose between you and Jones who is to have it."

We should really ask what it is that says "no one may choose" in the face of the fact that the body that houses the child is the mother's body. It may be simply a failure to appreciate this fact. But it may be something more interesting, namely the sense that one has a right to refuse to lay hands on people, even where it would be just and fair to do so, even where justice seems to require that somebody do so. Thus justice might call for somebody to get Smith's coat back from Jones, and yet you have a right to refuse to be the one to lay hands on Jones, a right to refuse to do physical violence to him. This, I think, must be granted. But then what should be said is not "no one may choose," but only "*I* cannot choose," and indeed not even this, but "*I* will not *act*," leaving it open that somebody else can or should, and in particular that anyone in a position of authority, with the job of securing people's rights, both can and should. So this is no difficulty. I have not been arguing that any given third party must accede to the mother's request that he perform an abortion to save her life, but only that he may.

I suppose that in some views of human life the mother's body is only on loan to her, the loan not being one which gives her any prior claim to it. One who held this view might well think it impartiality to say "I cannot choose." But I shall simply ignore this possibility. My own view is that if a human being has any just, prior claim to anything at all, he has a just, prior claim to his own body. And perhaps this needn't be argued for here anyway, since, as I mentioned, the arguments against abortion we are looking at do grant that the woman has a right to decide what happens in and to her body.

But although they do grant it, I have tried to show that they do not take seriously what is done in granting it. I suggest the same thing will reappear even more clearly when we turn away from cases in which the mother's life is at stake, and attend, as I propose we now do, to the vastly more common cases in which a woman wants an abortion for some less weighty reason than preserving her own life.

3. Where the mother's life is not at stake, the argument I mentioned at the outset seems to have a much stronger pull. "Everyone has a right to life, so the unborn person has a right to life." And isn't the child's right to life weightier than anything other than the mother's own right to life, which she might put forward as ground for an abortion?

This argument treats the right to life as if it were unproblematic. It is not, and this seems to me to be precisely the source of the mistake.

For we should now, at long last, ask what it comes to, to have a right to life. In some views having a right to life includes having a right to be given at least the bare minimum one needs for continued life. But suppose that what in fact *is* the bare minimum a man needs for continued life is something he has no right at all to be given? If I am sick unto death, and the only thing that will save my life is the touch of Henry Fonda's cool hand on my fevered brow, then all the same, I have no right to be given the touch of Henry Fonda's cool hand on my fevered brow. It would be frightfully nice of him to fly in from the West Coast to provide it. It would be less nice, though no doubt well meant, if my friends flew out to the West Coast and carried Henry Fonda back with them. But I have no right at all against anybody that he should do this for me. Or again, to return to the story I told earlier, the fact that for continued life that violinist needs the continued use of your kidneys does not establish that he has a right to be given the continued use of your kidneys. He certainly has no right against you that *you* should give him continued use of your kidneys. For nobody has any right to use your kidneys unless you give him such a right; and nobody has the right against you that you shall give him this right—if you do allow him to go on using your kidneys, this is a kindness on your part, and not something he can claim from you as his due. Nor has he any right against anybody else that *they* should give him continued use of your kidneys. Certainly he had no right against the Society of Music Lovers that they should plug him into you in the first place. And if you now start to unplug yourself, having learned that you will otherwise have to spend nine years in bed with him, there is nobody in the world who must try to prevent you, in order to see to it that he is given something he has a right to be given.

Some people are rather stricter about the right to life. In their view, it does not include the right to be given anything, but amounts to, and only to, the right not to be killed by anybody. But here a related difficulty arises. If everybody is to refrain from killing that violinist, then everybody must refrain from doing a great many different sorts of things. Everybody must refrain from slitting his throat, everybody must refrain from shooting him—and everybody must refrain from unplugging you from him. But does he have a right against everybody that they shall refrain from unplugging you from him? To refrain from doing this is to allow him to continue to use your kidneys. It could be argued that he has a right against us that *we* should allow him to continue to use your kidneys. That is, while he had no right against us that we should give him the use of your kidneys, it might be argued that he anyway has a right against us that we shall not now intervene and deprive him of the use of your kidneys. I shall come back to third-party interventions later. But certainly the violinist has no right against you that *you* shall allow him to continue to use your kidneys. As I said, if you do allow him to use them, it is a kindness on your part, and not something you owe him.

The difficulty I point to here is not peculiar to the right to life. It reappears in connection with all the other natural rights; and it is something which an adequate account of rights must deal with. For present purposes it is enough just to draw attention to it. But I would stress that I am not arguing that people do not have a right to life—quite to the contrary, it seems to me that the primary control we must place on the acceptability of an account of rights is that it should turn out in that account to be a truth that all persons have a right to life. I am arguing only that having a right to life does not guarantee having either a right to be given the use of or a right to be allowed continued use of another person's body—even if one needs it for life itself. So the right to life will not serve the opponents of abortion in the very simple and clear way in which they seem to have thought it would.

4. There is another way to bring out the difficulty. In the most ordinary sort of case, to deprive someone of what he has a right to is to treat him unjustly. Suppose a boy and his small brother are jointly given a box of chocolates for Christmas. If the older boy takes the box and refuses to give his brother any of the chocolates, he is unjust to him, for the brother has been given a right to half of them. But suppose that, having learned that otherwise it means nine years in bed with that violinist, you unplug

yourself from him. You surely are not being unjust to him, for you gave him no right to use your kidneys, and no one else can have given him any such right. But we have to notice that in unplugging yourself, you are killing him; and violinists, like everybody else, have a right to life, and thus in the view we were considering just now, the right not to be killed. So where you do what he supposedly has a right you shall not do, but you do not act unjustly to him in doing it.

The emendation which may be made at this point is this: the right to life consists not in the right not to be killed, but rather in the right not to be killed unjustly. This runs a risk of circularity, but never mind: it would enable us to square the fact that the violinist has a right to life with the fact that you do not act unjustly toward him in unplugging yourself, thereby killing him. For if you do not kill him unjustly, you do not violate his right to life, and so it is no wonder you do him no injustice.

But if this emendation is accepted, the gap in the argument against abortion stares us plainly in the face: it is by no means enough to show that the fetus is a person, and to remind us that all persons have a right to life—we need to be shown also that killing the fetus violates its right to life, i.e., that abortion is unjust killing. And is it?

I suppose we may take it as a datum that in a case of pregnancy due to rape the mother has not given the unborn person a right to the use of her body for food and shelter. Indeed, in what pregnancy could it be supposed that the mother has given the unborn person such a right? It is not as if there were unborn persons drifting about the world, to whom a woman who wants a child says "I invite you in."

But it might be argued that there are other ways one can have acquired a right to the use of another person's body than by having been invited to use it by that person. Suppose a woman voluntarily indulges in intercourse, knowing of the chance it will issue in pregnancy, and then she does become pregnant; is she not in part responsible for the presence, in fact the very existence, of the unborn person inside her? No doubt she did not invite it in. But doesn't her partial responsibility for its being there itself give it a right to the use of her body? If so, then her aborting it would be more like the boy's taking away the chocolates, and less like your unplugging yourself from the violinist—doing so would be depriving it of what it does have a right to, and thus would be doing it an injustice.

And then, too, it might be asked whether or not she can kill it even to save her own life: If she voluntarily called it into existence, how can she now kill it, even in self-defense?

The first thing to be said about this is that it is something new. Opponents of abortion have been so concerned to make out the independence of the fetus, in order to establish that it has a right to life, just as its mother does, that they have tended to overlook the possible support they might gain from making out that the fetus is *dependent* on the mother, in order to establish that she has a special kind of responsibility for it, a responsibility that gives it rights against her which are not possessed by any independent person—such as an ailing violinist who is a stranger to her.

On the other hand, this argument would give the unborn person a right to its mother's body only if her pregnancy resulted from a voluntary act, undertaken in full knowledge of the chance a pregnancy might result from it. It would leave out entirely the unborn person whose existence is due to rape. Pending the availability of some further argument, then, we would be left with the conclusion that unborn persons whose existence is due to rape have no right to the use of their mothers' bodies, and thus that aborting them is not depriving them of anything they have a right to and hence is not unjust killing.

And we should also notice that it is not at all plain that this argument really does go even as far as it purports to. For there are cases and cases, and the details make a difference. If the room is stuffy, and I therefore open a window to air it, and a burglar climbs in, it would be absurd to say, "Ah, now he can stay, she's given him a right to the use of her house—for she is partially responsible for his presence there, having voluntarily done what enabled him to get in, in full knowledge that there are such things as burglars, and that burglars burgle." It would be still more

absurd to say this if I had had bars installed outside my windows, precisely to prevent burglars from getting in, and a burglar got in only because of a defect in the bars. It remains equally absurd if we imagine it is not a burglar who climbs in, but an innocent person who blunders or falls in. Again, suppose it were like this: people-seeds drift about in the air like pollen, and if you open your windows, one may drift in and take root in your carpets or upholstery. You don't want children, so you fix up your windows with fine mesh screens, the very best you can buy. As can happen, however, and on very, very rare occasions does happen, one of the screens is defective; and a seed drifts in and takes root. Does the person-plant who now develops have a right to the use of your house? Surely not—despite the fact that you voluntarily opened your windows, you knowingly kept carpets and upholstered furniture, and you knew that screens were sometimes defective. Someone may argue that you are responsible for its rooting, that it does have a right to your house, because after all you *could* have lived out your life with bare floors and furniture, or with sealed windows and doors. But this won't do—for by the same token anyone can avoid a pregnancy due to rape by having a hysterectomy, or anyway by never leaving home without a (reliable!) army.

It seems to me that the argument we are looking at can establish at most that there are *some* cases in which the unborn person has a right to the use of its mother's body, and therefore *some* cases in which abortion is unjust killing. There is room for much discussion and argument as to precisely which, if any. But I think we should sidestep this issue and leave it open, for at any rate the argument certainly does not establish that all abortion is unjust killing.

5. There is room for yet another argument here, however. We surely must all grant that there may be cases in which it would be morally indecent to detach a person from your body at the cost of his life. Suppose you learn that what the violinist needs is not nine years of your life, but only one hour: all you need do to save his life is to spend one hour in that bed with him. Suppose also that letting him use your kidneys for that one hour would not affect your

health in the slightest. Admittedly you were kidnapped. Admittedly you did not give anyone permission to plug him into you. Nevertheless it seems to me plain you *ought* to allow him to use your kidneys for that hour—it would be indecent to refuse.

Again, suppose pregnancy lasted only an hour, and constituted no threat to life or health. And suppose that a woman becomes pregnant as a result of rape. Admittedly she did not voluntarily do anything to bring about the existence of a child. Admittedly she did nothing at all which would give the unborn person a right to the use of her body. All the same it might well be said, as in the newly emended violinist story, that she *ought* to allow it to remain for that hour—that it would be indecent in her to refuse.

Now some people are inclined to use the term "right" in such a way that it follows from the fact that you ought to allow a person to use your body for the hour he needs, that he has a right to use your body for the hour he needs, even though he has not been given that right by any person or act. They may say that it follows also that if you refuse, you act unjustly toward him. This use of the term is perhaps so common that it cannot be called wrong; nevertheless it seems to me to be an unfortunate loosening of what we would do better to keep a tight rein on. Suppose that box of chocolates I mentioned earlier had not been given to both boys jointly, but was given only to the older boy. There he sits, stolidly eating his way through the box, his small brother watching enviously. Here we are likely to say "You ought not to be so mean. You ought to give your brother some of those chocolates." My own view is that it just does not follow from the truth of this that the brother has any right to any of the chocolates. If the boy refuses to give his brother any, he is greedy, stingy, callous—but not unjust. I suppose that the people I have in mind will say it does follow that the brother has a right to some of the chocolates, and thus that the boy does act unjustly if he refuses to give his brother any. But the effect of saying this is to obscure what we should keep distinct, namely the difference between the boy's refusal in this case and the boy's refusal in the earlier case, in which the box was given to both boys jointly, and in which the

small brother thus had what was from any point of view clear title to half.

A further objection to so using the term "right" that from the fact that A ought to do a thing for B, it follows that B has a right against A that A do it for him, is that it is going to make the question of whether or not a man has a right to a thing turn on how easy it is to provide him with it; and this seems not merely unfortunate, but morally unacceptable. Take the case of Henry Fonda again. I said earlier that I had no right to the touch of his cool hand on my fevered brow, even though I needed it to save my life. I said it would be frightfully nice of him to fly in from the West Coast to provide me with it, but that I had no right against him that he should do so. But suppose he isn't on the West Coast. Suppose he has only to walk across the room, place a hand briefly on my brow—and lo, my life is saved. Then surely he ought to do it, it would be indecent to refuse. Is it to be said "Ah, well, it follows that in this case she has a right to the touch of his hand on her brow, and so it would be an injustice in him to refuse"? So that I have a right to it when it is easy for him to provide it, though no right when it's hard? It's rather a shocking idea that anyone's rights should fade away and disappear as it gets harder and harder to accord them to him.

So my own view is that even though you ought to let the violinist use your kidneys for the one hour he needs, we should not conclude that he has a right to do so—we should say that if you refuse, you are, like the boy who owns all the chocolates and will give none away, self-centered and callous, indecent in fact, but not unjust. And similarly, that even supposing a case in which a woman pregnant due to rape ought to allow the unborn person to use her body for the hour he needs, we should not conclude that he has a right to do so; we should conclude that she is self-centered, callous, indecent, but not unjust, if she refuses. The complaints are no less grave; they are just different. However, there is no need to insist on this point. If anyone does wish to deduce "he has a right" from "you ought," then all the same he must surely grant that there are cases in which it is not morally required of you that you allow that violinist to use your kidneys, and in which he does not have a right to use them, and in which you do not do him an injustice if you refuse. And so also for mother and unborn child. Except in such cases as the unborn person has a right to demand it—and we were leaving open the possibility that there may be such cases—nobody is morally *required* to make large sacrifices, of health, of all other interests and concerns, of all other duties and commitments, for nine years, or even for nine months, in order to keep another person alive.

6. We have in fact to distinguish between two kinds of Samaritan: the Good Samaritan and what we might call the Minimally Decent Samaritan. The story of the Good Samaritan, you will remember, goes like this:

A certain man went down from Jerusalem to Jericho, and fell among thieves, which stripped him of his raiment, and wounded him, and departed, leaving him half dead.

And by chance there came down a certain priest that way; and when he saw him, he passed by on the other side.

And likewise a Levite, when he was at the place, came and looked on him, and passed by on the other side.

But a certain Samaritan, as he journeyed, came where he was; and when he saw him he had compassion on him.

And went to him, and bound up his wounds, pouring in oil and wine, and set him on his own beast, and brought him to an inn, and took care of him.

And on the morrow, when he departed, he took out two pence, and gave them to the host, and said unto him, "Take care of him; and whatsoever thou spendest more, when I come again, I will repay thee."

(Luke 10:30–35)

The Good Samaritan went out of his way, at some cost to himself, to help one in need of it. We are not told what the options were, that is, whether or not the priest and the Levite could have helped by doing less than the Good Samaritan did, but assuming they could have, then the fact they did nothing at all shows they were not even Minimally Decent Samaritans, not because they were not Samaritans, but because they were not even minimally decent.

These things are a matter of degree, of course, but there is a difference, and it comes out perhaps most clearly in the story of Kitty Genovese, who, as you

will remember, was murdered while thirty-eight people watched or listened, and did nothing at all to help her. A Good Samaritan would have rushed out to give direct assistance against the murderer. Or perhaps we had better allow that it would have been a Splendid Samaritan who did this, on the ground that it would have involved a risk of death for himself. But the thirty-eight not only did not do this, they did not even trouble to pick up a phone to call the police. Minimally Decent Samaritanism would call for doing at least that, and their not having done it was monstrous.

After telling the story of the Good Samaritan, Jesus said "Go, and do thou likewise." Perhaps he meant that we are morally required to act as the Good Samaritan did. Perhaps he was urging people to do more than is morally required of them. At all events it seems plain that it was not morally required of any of the thirty-eight that he rush out to give direct assistance at the risk of his own life, and that it is not morally required of anyone that he give long stretches of his life—nine years or nine months—to sustaining the life of a person who has no special right (we were leaving open the possibility of this) to demand it.

Indeed, with one rather striking class of exceptions, no one in any country in the world is *legally* required to do anywhere near as much as this for anyone else. The class of exceptions is obvious. My main concern here is not the state of the law in respect to abortion, but it is worth drawing attention to the fact that in no state in this country is any man compelled by law to be even a Minimally Decent Samaritan to any person; there is no law under which charges could be brought against the thirty-eight who stood by while Kitty Genovese died. By contrast, in most states in this country women are compelled by law to be not merely Minimally Decent Samaritans, but Good Samaritans to unborn persons inside them. This doesn't by itself settle anything one way or the other, because it may well be argued that there should be laws in this country—as there are in many European countries—compelling at least Minimally Decent Samaritanism. But it does show that there is a gross injustice in the existing state of the law. And it shows also that the groups currently working against liberalization of abortion laws, in fact working toward having it declared unconstitutional for a state to permit abortion, had better start working for the adoption of Good Samaritan laws generally, or earn the charge that they are acting in bad faith.

I should think, myself, that Minimally Decent Samaritan laws would be one thing, Good Samaritan laws quite another, and in fact highly improper. But we are not here concerned with the law. What we should ask is not whether anybody should be compelled by law to be a Good Samaritan, but whether we must accede to a situation in which somebody is being compelled—by nature, perhaps—to be a Good Samaritan. We have, in other words, to look now at third-party interventions. I have been arguing that no person is morally required to make large sacrifices to sustain the life of another who has no right to demand them, and this even where the sacrifices do not include life itself; we are not morally required to be Good Samaritans or anyway Very Good Samaritans to one another. But what if a man cannot extricate himself from such a situation? What if he appeals to us to extricate him? It seems to me plain that there are cases in which we can, cases in which a Good Samaritan would extricate him. There you are, you were kidnapped, and nine years in bed with that violinist lie ahead of you. You have your own life to lead. You are sorry, but you simply cannot see giving up so much of your life to the sustaining of his. You cannot extricate yourself, and ask us to do so. I should have thought that—in light of his having no right to the use of your body—it was obvious that we do not have to accede to your being forced to give up so much. We can do what you ask. There is no injustice to the violinist in our doing so.

7. Following the lead of the opponents of abortion, I have throughout been speaking of the fetus merely as a person, and what I have been asking is whether or not the argument we began with, which proceeds only from the fetus' being a person, really does establish its conclusion. I have argued that it does not.

But of course there are arguments and arguments, and it may be said that I have simply fastened on the wrong one. It may be said that what is important is not merely the fact that the fetus is a person, but that it is a person for whom the woman has a special kind of responsibility issuing from the fact that she is its mother. And it might be argued that all my analogies are therefore irrelevant—for you do not have that special kind of responsibility for that violinist, Henry Fonda does not have that special kind of responsibility for me. And our attention might be drawn to the fact that men and women both *are* compelled by law to provide support for their children.

I have in effect dealt (briefly) with this argument in section 4 above; but a (still briefer) recapitulation now may be in order. Surely we do not have any such "special responsibility" for a person unless we have assumed it, explicitly or implicitly. If a set of parents do not try to prevent pregnancy, do not obtain an abortion, and then at the time of birth of the child do not put it out for adoption, but rather take it home with them, then they have assumed responsibility for it, they have given it rights, and they cannot *now* withdraw support from it at the cost of its life because they now find it difficult to go on providing for it. But if they have taken all reasonable precautions against having a child, they do not simply by virtue of their biological relationship to the child who comes into existence have a special responsibility for it. They may wish to assume responsibility for it, or they may not wish to. And I am suggesting that if assuming responsibility for it would require large sacrifices, then they may refuse. A Good Samaritan would not refuse—or anyway, a Splendid Samaritan, if the sacrifices that had to be made were enormous. But then so would a Good Samaritan assume responsibility for that violinist; so would Henry Fonda, if he is a Good Samaritan, fly in from the West Coast and assume responsibility for me.

8. My argument will be found unsatisfactory on two counts by many of those who want to regard abortion as morally permissible. First, while I do argue that abortion is not impermissible, I do not argue that it is always permissible. There may well be cases in which carrying the child to term requires only Minimally Decent Samaritanism of the mother, and this is a standard we must not fall below. I am

inclined to think it a merit of my account precisely that it does *not* give a general yes or a general no. It allows for and supports our sense that, for example, a sick and desperately frightened fourteen-year-old schoolgirl, pregnant due to rape, may *of course* choose abortion, and that any law which rules this out is an insane law. And it also allows for and supports our sense that in other cases resort to abortion is even positively indecent. It would be indecent in the woman to request an abortion, and indecent in a doctor to perform it, if she is in her seventh month, and wants the abortion just to avoid the nuisance of postponing a trip abroad. The very fact that the arguments I have been drawing attention to treat all cases of abortion, or even all cases of abortion in which the mother's life is not at stake, as morally on a par ought to have made them suspect at the outset.

Secondly, while I am arguing for the permissibility of abortion in some cases, I am not arguing for the right to secure the death of the unborn child. It is easy to confuse these two things in that up to a certain point in the life of the fetus it is not able to survive outside the mother's body; hence removing it from her body guarantees its death. But they are importantly different. I have argued that you are not morally required to spend nine months in bed, sustaining the life of that violinist; but to say this is by no means to say that if, when you unplug yourself, there is a miracle and he survives, you then have a right to turn round and slit his throat. You may detach yourself even if this costs him his life; you have no right to be guaranteed his death, by some other means, if unplugging yourself does not kill him. There are some people who will feel dissatisfied by this feature of my argument. A woman may be utterly devastated by the thought of a child, a bit of herself, put out for adoption and never seen or heard of again. She may therefore want not merely that the child be detached from her, but more, that it die. Some opponents of abortion are inclined to regard this as beneath contempt—thereby showing insensitivity to what is surely a powerful source of despair. All the same, I agree that the desire for the child's death is not one which anybody may gratify, should it turn out to be possible to detach the child alive.

At this place, however, it should be remembered that we have only been pretending throughout that the fetus is a human being from the moment of conception. A very early abortion is surely not the killing of a person, and so is not dealt with by anything I have said here.

NOTE

1. The term "direct" in the arguments I refer to is a technical one. Roughly, what is meant by "direct killing" is either killing as an end in itself, or killing as a means to some end, for example, the end of saving someone else's life.

On the Moral and Legal Status of Abortion

MARY ANNE WARREN

We will be concerned with both the moral status of abortion, which for our purposes we may define as the act which a woman performs in voluntarily terminating, or allowing another person to terminate, her pregnancy, and the legal status which is appropriate for this act. I will argue that, while it is not possible to produce a satisfactory defense of a woman's right to obtain an abortion without showing that a fetus is not a human being, in the morally relevant sense of that term, we ought not to conclude that the difficulties involved in determining whether or not a fetus is human make it impossible to produce any satisfactory solution to the problem of the moral status of abortion. For it is possible to show that, on the basis of intuitions which we may expect

Mary Anne Warren, "On the Moral and Legal Status of Abortion, *The Monist* 57, no. 4 (1973): 43–61 (edited). Copyright © 1973, The Monist: An International Quarterly Journal of General Philosophical Inquiry, Peru, Illinois, USA 61354. Published by permission.

even the opponents of abortion to share, a fetus is not a person, and hence not the sort of entity to which it is proper to ascribe full moral rights.

Of course, while some philosophers would deny the possibility of any such proof, others will deny that there is any need for it, since the moral permissibility of abortion appears to them to be too obvious to require proof. But the inadequacy of this attitude should be evident from the fact that both the friends and the foes of abortion consider their position to be morally self-evident. Because proabortionists have never adequately come to grips with the conceptual issues surrounding abortion, most if not all, of the arguments which they advance in opposition to laws restricting access to abortion fail to refute or even weaken the traditional antiabortion argument, i.e., that a fetus is a human being, and therefore abortion is murder.

These arguments are typically of one of two sorts. Either they point to the terrible side effects of the restrictive laws, e.g., the deaths due to illegal abortions, and the fact that it is poor women who suffer the most as a result of these laws, or else they state that to deny a woman access to abortion is to deprive her of her right to control her own body. Unfortunately, however, the fact that restricting access to abortion has tragic side effects does not, in itself, show that the restrictions are unjustified, since murder is wrong regardless of the consequences of prohibiting it; and the appeal to the right to control one's body, which is generally construed as a property right, is at best a rather feeble argument for the permissibility of abortion. Mere ownership does not give me the right to kill innocent people whom I find on my property, and indeed I am apt to be held responsible if such people injure themselves while on my property. It is equally unclear that I have any moral right to expel an innocent person from my property when I know that doing so will result in his death.

Furthermore, it is probably inappropriate to describe a woman's body as her property, since it seems natural to hold that a person is something distinct from her property, but not from her body. Even those who would object to the identification of a person with his body, or with the conjunction of his body and his mind, must admit that it would be very odd to describe, say, breaking a leg, as damaging one's property, and much more appropriate to describe it as injuring one*self*. Thus it is probably a mistake to argue that the right to obtain an abortion is in any way derived from the right to own and regulate property.

But however we wish to construe the right to abortion, we cannot hope to convince those who consider abortion a form of murder of the existence of any such right unless we are able to produce a clear and convincing refutation of the traditional antiabortion argument, and this has not, to my knowledge, been done. With respect to the two most vital issues which that argument involves, i.e., the humanity of the fetus and its implication for the moral status of abortion, confusion has prevailed on both sides of the dispute.

Thus, both proabortionists and antiabortionists have tended to abstract the question of whether abortion is wrong to that of whether it is wrong to destroy a fetus, just as though the rights of another person were not necessarily involved. This mistaken abstraction has led to the almost universal assumption that if a fetus is a human being, with a right to life, then it follows immediately that abortion is wrong (except perhaps when necessary to save the woman's life), and that it ought to be prohibited. It has also been generally assumed that unless the question about the status of the fetus is answered, the moral status of abortion cannot possibly be determined.

* * *

Judith Thomson is . . . the only writer I am aware of who has seriously questioned this assumption; she has argued that, even if we grant the antiabortionist his claim that a fetus is a human being, with the same right to life as any other human being, we can still demonstrate that, in at least some and perhaps most cases, a woman is under no moral obligation to complete an unwanted pregnancy.[1] Her argument is worth examining, since if it holds up it may enable us to establish the moral permissibility of abortion without becoming involved in problems about what entitles an entity to be considered human, and accorded full moral rights. To be able to do this would be a great gain in the power and simplicity of the proabortion position, since, although I will argue that these problems can be solved at least as decisively as can any other moral problem, we should certainly be pleased to be able to avoid having to solve them as part of the justification of abortion.

On the other hand, even if Thomson's argument does not hold up, her insight, i.e., that it requires *argument* to show that if fetuses are human then abortion is properly classified as murder, is an extremely valuable one. The assumption she attacks is particularly invidious, for it amounts to the decision that it is appropriate, in deciding the moral status of abortion, to leave the rights of the pregnant woman out of consideration entirely, except possibly when her life is threatened. Obviously, this will not do; determining what moral rights, if any, a fetus possesses is only the first step in determining the moral status of abortion. Step two, which is at least equally essential, is finding a just solution to the conflict between whatever rights the fetus may have, and the rights of the woman who is unwillingly pregnant. While the historical error has been to pay far too little attention to the second step, Ms. Thomson's suggestion is that if we look at the second step first we may find that a woman has a right to obtain an abortion *regardless* of what rights the fetus has.

Our own inquiry will also have two stages. In Section I, we will consider whether or not it is possible to establish that abortion is morally permissible even on the assumption that a fetus is an entity with a full-fledged right to life. I will argue that in fact this cannot be established, at least not with the conclusiveness which is essential to our hopes of convincing those who are skeptical about the morality of abortion, and that we therefore cannot avoid dealing with the question of whether or not a fetus really does have the same right to life as a (more fully developed) human being.

In Section II, I will propose an answer to this question, namely, that a fetus cannot be considered a member of the moral community, the set of beings with full and equal moral rights, for the simple reason that it is not a person, and that it is personhood, and not genetic humanity, . . . which is the basis for membership in this community. I will argue that a fetus, whatever its stage of development, satisfies none of the basic criteria of personhood, and is not even enough *like* a person to be accorded even some of the same rights on the basis of this resemblance. Nor, as we will see, is a fetus's *potential* personhood a threat to the morality of abortion, since, whatever the rights of potential people may be, they are invariably overridden in any conflict with the moral rights of actual people.

I

We turn now to Professor Thomson's case for the claim that even if a fetus has full moral rights, abortion is still morally permissible, at least sometimes, and for some reasons other than to save the woman's life. Her argument is based upon a clever, but I think faulty, analogy. She asks us to picture ourselves waking up one day, in bed with a famous violinist. Imagine that you have been kidnapped, and your bloodstream hooked up to that of the violinist, who happens to have an ailment which will certainly kill him unless he is permitted to share your kidneys for a period of nine months. No one else can save him, since you alone have the right type of blood. He will be unconscious all that time, and you will have to stay in bed with him, but after the nine months are over he may be unplugged, completely cured, that is provided that you have cooperated.

Now then, she continues, what are your obligations in this situation? The antiabortionist, if he is consistent, will have to say that you are obligated to stay in bed with the violinist: for all people have a right to life, and violinists are people, and therefore it would be murder for you to disconnect yourself from him and let him die [p. 174]. But this is outrageous, and so there must be something wrong with the same argument when it is applied to abortion. It would certainly be commendable of you to agree to save the violinist, but it is absurd to suggest that your refusal to do so would be murder. His right to life does not obligate you to do whatever is required to keep him alive; nor does it justify anyone else in forcing you to do so. A law which required you to stay in bed with the violinist would clearly be an unjust law, since it is no proper function of the law to force unwilling people to make huge sacrifices for the sake of other people toward whom they have no such prior obligation.

Thomson concludes that, if this analogy is an apt one, then we can grant the antiabortionist his claim that a fetus is a human being, and still hold that it is at least sometimes the case that a pregnant woman has the right to refuse to be a Good Samaritan towards the fetus, i.e., to obtain an abortion. For there is a great gap between the claim that *x* has a right to life, and the claim that *y* is obligated to do whatever is necessary to keep *x* alive, let alone that he ought to be forced to do so. It is *y*'s duty to keep *x* alive only if he has somehow contracted a *special* obligation to do so; and a woman who is unwillingly pregnant, e.g., who was raped, has done nothing which obligates her to make the enormous sacrifice which is necessary to preserve the conceptus.

This argument is initially quite plausible, and in the extreme case of pregnancy due to rape it is probably conclusive. Difficulties arise, however, when we try to specify more exactly the range of cases in which abortion is clearly justifiable even on the assumption that the fetus is human. Professor Thomson considers it a virtue of her argument that it does not enable us to conclude that abortion is *always* permissible. It would, she says, be "indecent" for a woman in her seventh month to obtain an abortion just to avoid having to postpone a trip to Europe. On the other hand, her argument enables us to see that "a sick and desperately frightened schoolgirl pregnant due to rape may *of course* choose abortion, and that any law which rules this out is an insane law" [p. 183]. So far, so good; but what are we to say about the woman who becomes pregnant not through rape but as a result of her own carelessness, or because of contraceptive failure, or who gets pregnant intentionally and then changes her mind about wanting a child? With respect to such cases, the violinist analogy is of much less use to the defender of the woman's right to obtain an abortion.

Indeed, the choice of a pregnancy due to rape, as an example of a case in which abortion is permissible

even if a fetus is considered a human being, is extremely significant; for it is only in the case of pregnancy due to rape that the woman's situation is adequately analogous to the violinist case for our intuitions about the latter to transfer convincingly. The crucial difference between a pregnancy due to rape and the *normal* case of an unwanted pregnancy is that in the normal case, we cannot claim that the woman is in no way responsible for her predicament; she could have remained chaste, or taken her pills more faithfully, or abstained on dangerous days, and so on. If, on the other hand, you are kidnapped by strangers, and hooked up to a strange violinist, then you are free of any shred of responsibility for the situation, on the basis of which it could be argued that you are obligated to keep the violinist alive. Only when her pregnancy is due to rape is a woman clearly just as nonresponsible.[2]

Consequently, there is room for the antiabortionist to argue that in the normal case of unwanted pregnancy a woman has, by her own actions, assumed responsibility for the fetus. For if *x* behaves in a way which he could have avoided, and which he knows involves, let us say, a 1 percent chance of bringing into existence a human being, with a right to life, and does so knowing that if this should happen then that human being will perish unless *x* does certain things to keep him alive, then it is by no means clear that when it does happen *x* is free of any obligation to what he knew in advance would be required to keep that human being alive.

The plausibility of such an argument is enough to show that the Thomson analogy can provide a clear and persuasive defense of a woman's right to obtain an abortion only with respect to those cases in which the woman is in no way responsible for her pregnancy, e.g., where it is due to rape. In all other cases, we would almost certainly conclude that it was necessary to look carefully at the particular circumstances in order to determine the extent of the woman's responsibility, and hence the extent of her obligation. This is an extremely unsatisfactory outcome, from the viewpoint of the opponents of restrictive abortion laws, most of whom are convinced that a woman has a right to obtain an abortion regardless of how and why she got pregnant.

Of course a supporter of the violinist analogy might point out that it is absurd to suggest that forgetting her pill one day might be sufficient to obligate a woman to complete an unwanted pregnancy. And indeed it *is* absurd to suggest this. As we will see, the moral right to obtain an abortion is not in the least dependent upon the extent to which the woman is responsible for her pregnancy. But unfortunately, once we allow the assumption that a fetus has full moral rights, we cannot avoid taking this absurd suggestion seriously. Perhaps we can make this point more clear by altering the violinist story just enough to make it more analogous to a normal unwanted pregnancy and less to a pregnancy due to rape, and then seeing whether it is still obvious that you are not obligated to stay in bed with the fellow.

Suppose, then, that violinists are peculiarly prone to the sort of illness the only cure for which is the use of someone else's bloodstream for nine months, and that because of this there has been formed a society of music lovers who agree that whenever a violinist is stricken they will draw lots and the loser will, by some means, be made the one and only person capable of saving him. Now then, would you be obligated to cooperate in curing the violinist if you had voluntarily joined this society, knowing the possible consequences, and then your name had been drawn and you had been kidnapped? Admittedly, you did not promise ahead of time that you would, but you did deliberately place yourself in a position in which it might happen that a human life would be lost if you did not. Surely this is at least a prima facie reason for supposing that you have an obligation to stay in bed with the violinist. Suppose that you had gotten your name drawn deliberately; surely *that* would be quite a strong reason for thinking that you had such an obligation.

It might be suggested that there is one important disanalogy between the modified violinist case and the case of an unwanted pregnancy, which makes the woman's responsibility significantly less, namely, the fact that the fetus *comes into existence* as the result of the woman's actions. This fact might give her a right to refuse to keep it alive, whereas she would not have had this right had it existed previously, independently, and then as a result of her actions become dependent upon her for its survival.

My own intuition, however, is that x has no more right to bring into existence, either deliberately or as a foreseeable result of actions he could have avoided, a being with full moral rights (*y*), and then refuse to do what he knew beforehand would be required to keep that being alive, then he has to enter into an agreement with an existing person, whereby he may be called upon to save that person's life, and then refuse to do so when so called upon. Thus, *x*'s responsibility for *y*'s existence does not seem to lessen his obligation to keep *y* alive, if he is also responsible for *y*'s being in a situation in which only he can save him.

Whether or not this intuition is entirely correct, it brings us back once again to the conclusion that once we allow the assumption that a fetus has full moral rights it becomes an extremely complex and difficult question whether and when abortion is justifiable. Thus the Thomson analogy cannot help us produce a clear and persuasive proof of the moral permissibility of abortion. Nor will the opponents of the restrictive laws thank us for anything less; for their conviction (for the most part) is that abortion is obviously *not* a morally serious and extremely unfortunate, even though sometimes justified act, comparable to killing in self-defense or to letting the violinist die, but rather is closer to being a morally neutral act, like cutting one's hair.

The basis of this conviction, I believe, is the realization that a fetus is not a person, and thus does not have a full-fledged right to life. Perhaps the reason why this claim has been so inadequately defended is that it seems self-evident to those who accept it. And so it is, insofar as it follows from what I take to be perfectly obvious claims about the nature of personhood, and about the proper grounds for ascribing moral rights, claims which ought, indeed, to be obvious to both the friends and foes of abortion. Nevertheless, it is worth examining these claims, and showing how they demonstrate the moral innocuousness of abortion, since this apparently has not been adequately done before.

II

The question which we must answer in order to produce a satisfactory solution to the problem of the moral status of abortion is this: How are we to define the moral community, the set of beings with full and equal moral rights, such that we can decide whether a human fetus is a member of this community or not? What sort of entity, exactly, has the inalienable rights to life, liberty, and the pursuit of happiness? . . . What reason is there for identifying the moral community with the set of all human beings, in whatever way we have chosen to define that term?

1. On the Definition of 'Human'

One reason why this vital . . . question is so frequently overlooked in the debate over the moral status of abortion is that the term 'human' has two distinct, but not often distinguished, senses. This fact results in a slide of meaning, which serves to conceal the fallaciousness of the traditional argument that since (1) it is wrong to kill innocent human beings, and (2) fetuses are innocent human beings, then (3) it is wrong to kill fetuses. For if 'human' is used in the same sense in both (1) and (2) then, whichever of the two senses is meant, one of these premises is question-begging. And if it is used in two different senses then of course the conclusion doesn't follow.

Thus, (1) is a self-evident moral truth,[3] and avoids begging the question about abortion, only if 'human being' is used to mean something like "a full-fledged member of the moral community." (It may or may not also be meant to refer exclusively to members of the species *Homo sapiens*.) We may call this the *moral* sense of 'human'. It is not to be confused with what we will call the *genetic* sense, i.e., the sense in which *any* member of the species is a human being, and no member of any other species could be. If (1) is acceptable only if the moral sense is intended, (2) is non-question-begging only if what is intended is the genetic sense.

In "Deciding Who is Human," [John] Noonan argues for the classification of fetuses with human beings by pointing to the presence of the full genetic code, and the potential capacity for rational thought.[4] It is clear that what he needs to show, for his version of the traditional argument to be valid, is that fetuses are human in the moral sense, the sense in which it is analytically true that all human beings have full moral rights. But, in the absence of any argument showing that whatever is genetically human is also morally human, and he gives none, nothing more than genetic humanity can be demonstrated by the presence of the human genetic code. And, as we will see, the *potential* capacity for rational thought can at most show that an entity has the potential for *becoming* human in the moral sense.

2. Defining the Moral Community

Can it be established that genetic humanity is sufficient for moral humanity? I think that there are very good reasons for not defining the moral community in this way. I would like to suggest an alternative way of defining the moral community, which I will argue for only to the extent of explaining why it is, or should be, self-evident. The suggestion is simply that the moral community consists of all and only *people,* rather than all and only human beings;[5] and probably the best way of demonstrating its self-evidence is by considering the concept of personhood, to see what sorts of entity are and are not persons, and what the decision that a being is or is not a person implies about its moral rights.

What characteristics entitle an entity to be considered a person? This is obviously not the place to attempt a complete analysis of the concept of personhood, but we do not need such a fully adequate analysis just to determine whether and why a fetus is or isn't a person. All we need is a rough and approximate list of the most basic criteria of personhood, and some idea of which, or how many, of these an entity must satisfy in order to properly be considered a person.

In searching for such criteria, it is useful to look beyond the set of people with whom we are acquainted, and ask how we would decide whether a totally alien being was a person or not. (For we have no right to assume that genetic humanity is necessary for personhood.) Imagine a space traveler who lands on an unknown planet and encounters a race of beings utterly unlike any he has ever seen or heard of. If he wants to be sure of behaving morally toward these beings, he has to somehow decide whether they are people, and hence have full moral rights, or whether they are the sort of thing which he need not feel guilty about treating as, for example, a source of food.

How should he go about making this decision? If he has some anthropological background, he might look for such things as religion, art, and the manufacturing of tools, weapons, or shelters, since these factors have been used to distinguish our human from our prehuman ancestors, in what seems to be closer to the moral than the genetic sense of 'human'. And no doubt he would be right to consider the presence of such factors as good evidence that the alien beings were people, and morally human. It would, however, be overly anthropocentric of him to take the absence of these things as adequate evidence that they were not, since we can imagine people who have progressed beyond, or evolved without ever developing, these cultural characteristics.

I suggest that the traits which are most central to the concept of personhood, or humanity in the moral sense, are, very roughly, the following:

(1) consciousness (of objects and events external and/or internal to the being), and in particular the capacity to feel pain;
(2) reasoning (the *developed* capacity to solve new and relatively complex problems);
(3) self-motivated activity (activity which is relatively independent of either genetic or direct external control);
(4) the capacity to communicate, by whatever means, messages of an indefinite variety of types, that is, not just with an indefinite number of possible contents, but on indefinitely many possible topics;
(5) the presence of self-concepts, and self-awareness, either individual or racial, or both.

Admittedly, there are apt to be a great many problems involved in formulating precise definitions of these criteria, let alone in developing universally valid behavioral criteria for deciding when they apply. But I will assume that both we and our explorer know approximately what (1)–(5) mean, and that he is also able to determine whether or not they apply. How, then should he use his findings to decide whether or not the alien beings are people? We needn't suppose that an entity must have *all* of these attributes to be properly considered a person; (1) and (2) alone may well be sufficient for personhood, and quite probably (1)–(3) are sufficient. Neither do we need to insist that any one of these criteria is *necessary* for personhood, although once again (1) and (2) look like fairly good candidates for necessary conditions, as does (3), if 'activity' is construed so as to include the activity of reasoning.

All we need to claim, to demonstrate that a fetus is not a person, is that any being which satisfies *none* of (1)–(5) is certainly not a person. I consider this claim to be so obvious that I think anyone who denied it, and claimed that a being which satisfied none of (1)–(5) was a person all the same, would thereby demonstrate that he had no notion at all of what a person is—perhaps because he had confused the concept of a person with that of genetic humanity. If the opponents of abortion were to deny the appropriateness of these five criteria, I do not know what further arguments would convince them. We would probably have to admit that our conceptual schemes were indeed irreconcilably different, and that our dispute could not be settled objectively.

I do not expect this to happen, however, since I think that the concept of a person is one which is very nearly universal (to people), and that it is common to both proabortionists and antiabortionists, even though neither group has fully realized the relevance of this concept to the resolution of their dispute. Furthermore, I think that on reflection even the antiabortionists ought to agree not only that (1)–(5) are central to the concept of personhood, but also that it is a part of this concept that all and only people have full moral rights. The concept of a person is in part a moral concept; once we have admitted that *x* is a person we have recognized, even if we have not agreed to respect, *x*'s right to be treated as a member of the moral community. It is true that the claim that *x* is a *human being* is more commonly voiced as part of an appeal to treat *x* decently than is the claim that *x* is a person, but this is either because 'human being' is here used in the sense which implies personhood, or because the genetic and moral senses of 'human' have been confused.

Now if (1)–(5) are indeed the primary criteria of personhood, then it is clear that genetic humanity is neither necessary nor sufficient for establishing that an entity is a person. Some human beings are not people, and there may well be people who are not human beings. A man or woman whose consciousness has been permanently obliterated but who remains alive is a human being which is no longer a person; defective human beings, with no appreciable mental capacity, are not and presumably never will be people; and a fetus is a human being which is not yet a person, and which therefore cannot coherently be said to have full moral rights. Citizens of the next century should be prepared to recognize highly advanced, self-aware robots or computers, should such be developed, and intelligent inhabitants of other worlds, should such be found, as people in the fullest sense, and to respect their moral rights. But to ascribe full moral rights to an entity which is not a person is as absurd as to ascribe moral obligations and responsibilities to such an entity.

3. Fetal Development and the Right to Life

Two problems arise in the application of these suggestions for the definition of the moral community to the determination of the precise moral status of a human fetus. Given that the paradigm example of a person is a normal adult human being, then (1) How like this paradigm, in particular how far advanced since conception, does a human being need to be before it begins to have a right to life by virtue, not of being fully a person as of yet, but of being *like* a person? and (2) To what extent, if any, does the fact that a fetus has the *potential* for becoming a person endow it with some of the same rights? Each of these questions requires some comment.

In answering the first question, we need not attempt a detailed consideration of the moral rights of organisms which are not developed enough, aware enough, intelligent enough, etc., to be considered people, but which resemble people in some respects. It does seem reasonable to suggest that the more like a person, in the relevant respects, a being is, the stronger is the case for regarding it as having a right to life, and indeed the stronger its right to life is. Thus we ought to take seriously the suggestion that, insofar as "the human individual develops biologically in a continuous fashion . . . the rights of a human person might develop in the same way."[6] But we must keep in mind that the attributes which are relevant in determining whether or not an entity is enough like a person to be regarded as having some of the same moral rights are no different from those which are relevant to determining whether or not it is fully a person—i.e., are no different from (1)–(5)—and that being genetically human, or having recognizably human facial and other physical features, or detectable brain activity, or the capacity to survive outside the uterus, are simply not among these relevant attributes.

Thus it is clear that even though a seven- or eight-month fetus has features which make it apt to arouse in us almost the same powerful protective instinct as is commonly aroused by a small infant, nevertheless it is not significantly more personlike than is a very small embryo. It is *somewhat* more personlike; it can apparently feel and respond to pain, and it may even have a rudimentary form of consciousness, insofar as its brain is quite active. Nevertheless, it seems safe to say that it is not fully conscious, in the way that an infant of a few months is, and that it cannot reason, or communicate messages of indefinitely many sorts, does not engage in self-motivated activity, and has no self-awareness. Thus, in the *relevant* respects, a fetus, even a fully developed one, is considerably less personlike than is the average mature mammal, indeed the average fish. And I think that a rational person must conclude that if the right to life of a fetus is to be based upon its resemblance to a person, then it cannot be said to have any more right to life than, let us say, a newborn guppy (which also seems to be capable of feeling pain), and that a right of that magnitude could never override a woman's right to obtain an abortion, at any stage of her pregnancy.

There may, of course, be other arguments in favor of placing legal limits upon the stage of pregnancy in which an abortion may be performed. Given the relative safety of the new techniques of artificially inducing labor during the third trimester, the danger to the woman's life or health is no longer such an argument. Neither is the fact that people tend to respond to the thought of abortion in the later stages of pregnancy with emotional repulsion, since mere emotional responses cannot take the place of moral reasoning in determining what ought to be permitted. Nor, finally, is the frequently heard argument that legalizing abortion, especially late in the pregnancy, may erode the level of respect for human life, leading, perhaps, to an increase in unjustified euthanasia and other crimes. For this threat, if it is a threat, can be better met by educating people to the kinds of moral distinctions which we are making here than by limiting access to abortion (which limitation may, in its disregard for the rights of women, be just as damaging to the level of respect for human rights).

Thus, since the fact that even a fully developed fetus is not personlike enough to have any significant right to life on the basis of its personlikeness shows that no legal restrictions upon the stage of pregnancy in which an abortion may be performed can be justified on the grounds that we should protect the rights of the older fetus; and since there is no other apparent justification for such restrictions, we may conclude that they are entirely unjustified. Whether or not it would be *indecent* (whatever that means) for a woman in her seventh month to obtain an abortion just to avoid having to postpone a trip to Europe, it would not, in itself, be *immoral*, and therefore it ought to be permitted.

4. Potential Personhood and the Right to Life

We have seen that a fetus does not resemble a person in any way which can support the claim that it has even some of the same rights. But what about its *potential*, the fact that if nurtured and allowed to develop naturally it will very probably become a person? Doesn't that alone give it at least some right to life? It is hard to deny that the fact that an entity is a potential person is a strong prima facie reason for not destroying it; but we need not conclude from this that a potential person has a right to life, by virtue of that potential. It may be that our feeling that it is better, other things being equal, not to destroy a potential person is better explained by the fact that potential people are still (felt to be) an invaluable resource, not to be lightly squandered. Surely, if every speck of dust were a potential person, we would be much less apt to conclude that every potential person has a right to become actual.

Still, we do not need to insist that a potential person has no right to life whatever. There may well be something immoral, and not just imprudent, about wantonly destroying potential people, when doing so isn't necessary to protect anyone's rights. But even if a potential person does have some prima facie right to life, such a right could not possibly outweigh the right of a woman to obtain an abortion, since the rights of any actual person invariably outweigh those of any potential person, whenever the two conflict. Since this may not be immediately obvious in the case of a human fetus, let us look at another case.

Suppose that our space explorer falls into the hands of an alien culture, whose scientists decide to create a few hundred thousand or more human beings, by breaking his body into its component cells, and using these to create fully developed human beings, with, of course, his genetic code. We may imagine that each of these newly created men will have all of the original man's abilities, skills, knowledge, and so on, and also have an individual self-concept, in short that each of them will be a bona fide (though hardly unique) person. Imagine that the whole project will take only seconds, and that its chances of success are extremely high, and that our explorer knows all of this, and also knows that these people will be treated fairly. I maintain that in such a situation he would have every right to escape if he could, and thus to deprive all of these potential people of their potential lives; for his right to life outweighs all of theirs together, in spite of the fact that they are all genetically human, all innocent, and all have a very high probability of becoming people very soon, if only he refrains from acting.

Indeed, I think he would have a right to escape even if it were not his life which the alien scientists planned to take, but only a year of his freedom, or, indeed, only a day. Nor would he be obligated to stay if he had gotten captured (thus bringing all these people-potentials into existence) because of his own carelessness, or even if he had done so deliberately, knowing the consequences. Regardless of how he got captured, he is not morally obligated to remain in captivity for *any* period of time for the sake of permitting any number of potential people to come into actuality, so great is the margin by which one actual person's right to liberty outweighs whatever right to life even a hundred thousand potential people have. And it seems reasonable to conclude that the rights of a woman will outweigh by a similar margin whatever right to life a fetus may have by virtue of its potential personhood.

Thus, neither a fetus's resemblance to a person, nor its potential for becoming a person provides any basis whatever for the claim that it has any significant right to life. Consequently, a woman's right to protect her health, happiness, freedom, and even her life,[7] by terminating an unwanted pregnancy, will always override whatever right to life it may be appropriate to ascribe to a fetus, even a fully developed one. And thus, in the absence of any overwhelming social need for every possible child, the laws which restrict the right to obtain an abortion, or limit the period of pregnancy during which an abortion may be performed, are a wholly unjustified violation of a woman's most basic moral and constitutional rights.

NOTES

1. Judith Thomson, "A Defense of Abortion," *Philosophy & Public Affairs* 1, no. 1 (Fall 1971): 47–66.

2. We may safely ignore the fact that she might have avoided getting raped, e.g., by carrying a gun, since by similar means you might likewise have avoided getting kidnapped, and in neither case does the victim's failure to take all possible precautions against a highly unlikely event (as opposed to reasonable precautions against a rather likely event) mean that he is morally responsible for what happens.

3. Of course, the principle that it is (always) wrong to kill innocent human beings is in need of many other modifications, e.g., that it may be permissible to do so to save a greater number of other innocent human beings, but we may safely ignore these complications here.

4. John Noonan, "Deciding Who Is Human," *Natural Law Forum* 13 (1968): 135.

5. From here on, we will use 'human' to mean genetically human, since the moral sense seems closely connected to, and perhaps derived from, the assumption that genetic humanity is sufficient for membership in the moral community.

6. Thomas L. Hayes, "A Biological View," *Commonweal* 85 (March 17, 1967): 677–78; quoted by Daniel Callahan, in *Abortion, Law, Choice, and Morality* (London: Macmillan & Co., 1970).

7. That is, insofar as the death rate, for the woman, is higher for childbirth than for early abortion.

Why Abortion Is Immoral

Don Marquis

The view that abortion is, with rare exceptions, seriously immoral has received little support in the recent philosophical literature. No doubt most philosophers affiliated with secular institutions of

Don Marquis, "Why Abortion Is Immoral," *The Journal of Philosophy* 86, no. 4 (April 1989): 183–202 (edited). Reprinted by permission of the Journal of Philosophy and Don Marquis.

higher education believe that the anti-abortion position is either a symptom of irrational religious dogma or a conclusion generated by seriously confused philosophical argument. The purpose of this essay is to undermine this general belief. This essay sets out an argument that purports to show, as well as any argument in ethics can show, that abortion is, except possibly in rare cases, seriously immoral, that it is in the same moral category as killing an innocent adult human being.

The argument is based on a major assumption. Many of the most insightful and careful writers on the ethics of abortion . . . believe that whether or not abortion is morally permissible stands or falls on whether or not a fetus is the sort of being whose life it is seriously wrong to end. The argument of this essay will assume, but not argue, that they are correct.

Also, this essay will neglect issues of great importance to a complete ethics of abortion. Some anti-abortionists will allow that certain abortions, such as abortion before implantation or abortion when the life of a woman is threatened by a pregnancy or abortion after rape, may be morally permissible. This essay will not explore the casuistry of these hard cases. The purpose of this essay is to develop a general argument for the claim that the overwhelming majority of deliberate abortions are seriously immoral.

I.

A sketch of standard anti-abortion and pro-choice arguments exhibits how these arguments possess certain symmetries that explain why partisans of those positions are so convinced of the correctness of their own positions, why they are not successful in convincing their opponents, and why, to others, this issue seems to be unresolvable. An analysis of the nature of this standoff suggests a strategy for surmounting it.

Consider the way a typical anti-abortionist argues. She will argue or assert that life is present from the moment of conception or that fetuses look like babies or that fetuses possess a characteristic such as a genetic code that is both necessary and sufficient for being human. Anti-abortionists seem to believe that (1) the truth of all of these claims is quite obvious, and (2) establishing any of these claims is sufficient to show that abortion is morally akin to murder.

A standard pro-choice strategy exhibits similarities. The prochoicer will argue or assert that fetuses are not persons or that fetuses are not rational agents or that fetuses are not social beings. Pro-choicers seem to believe that (1) the truth of any of these claims is quite obvious, and (2) establishing any of these claims is sufficient to show that an abortion is not a wrongful killing.

In fact, both the pro-choice and the anti-abortion claims do seem to be true, although the "it looks like a baby" claim is more difficult to establish the earlier the pregnancy. We seem to have a standoff. How can it be resolved?

As everyone who has taken a bit of logic knows, if any of these arguments concerning abortion is a good argument, it requires not only some claim characterizing fetuses, but also some general moral principle that ties a characteristic of fetuses to having or not having the right to life or to some other moral characteristic that will generate the obligation or the lack of obligation not to end the life of a fetus. Accordingly, the arguments of the anti-abortionist and the pro-choicer need a bit of filling in to be regarded as adequate.

Note what each partisan will say. The anti-abortionist will claim that her position is supported by such generally accepted moral principles as "It is always prima facie seriously wrong to take a human life" or "It is always prima facie seriously wrong to end the life of a baby." Since these are generally accepted moral principles, her position is certainly not obviously wrong. The pro-choicer will claim that her position is supported by such plausible moral principles as "Being a person is what gives an individual intrinsic moral worth" or "It is only seriously prima facie wrong to take the life of a member of the human community." Since these are generally accepted moral principles, the pro-choice position is certainly not obviously wrong. Unfortunately, we have again arrived at a standoff.

Now, how might one deal with this standoff? The standard approach is to try to show how the moral principles of one's opponent lose their plausibility under analysis. It is easy to see how this is possible. On the one hand, the anti-abortionist will defend a moral principle concerning the wrongness of killing which tends to be broad in scope in order that even fetuses at an early stage of pregnancy will fall under it. The problem with broad principles is that they often embrace too much. In this particular instance, the principle "It is always prima facie wrong to take a human life" seems to entail that it is wrong to end the existence of a living human cancer-cell culture, on the grounds that the culture is both living and human. Therefore, it seems that the anti-abortionist's favored principle is too broad.

On the other hand, the pro-choicer wants to find a moral principle concerning the wrongness of killing which tends to be narrow in scope in order that fetuses will *not* fall under it. The problem with narrow principles is that they often do not embrace enough. Hence, the needed principles such as "It is prima facie seriously wrong to kill only persons" or "It is prima facie wrong to kill only rational agents" do not explain why it is wrong to kill infants or young children or the severely retarded or even perhaps the severely mentally ill. Therefore, we seem again to have a standoff. The anti-abortionist charges, not unreasonably, that pro-choice principles concerning killing are too narrow to be acceptable; the pro-choicer charges, not unreasonably, that anti-abortionist principles concerning killing are too broad to be acceptable.

Attempts by both sides to patch up the difficulties in their positions run into further difficulties. The anti-abortionist will try to remove the problem in her position by reformulating her principle concerning killing in terms of human beings. Now we end up with: "It is always prima facie seriously wrong to end the life of a human being." This principle has the advantage of avoiding the problem of the human cancer-cell culture counterexample. But this advantage is purchased at a high price. For although it is clear that a fetus is both human and alive, it is not at all clear that a fetus is a human *being*. There is at least something to be said for the view that something becomes a human being only after a process of development, and that therefore first trimester fetuses and perhaps all fetuses are not yet human beings. Hence, the anti-abortionist by this move, has merely exchanged one problem for another.

The pro-choicer fares no better. She may attempt to find reasons why killing infants, young children,

and the severely retarded is wrong which are independent of her major principle that is supposed to explain the wrongness of taking human life, but which will not also make abortion immoral. This is no easy task. Appeals to social utility will seem satisfactory only to those who resolve not to think of the enormous difficulties with a utilitarian account of the wrongness of killing and the significant social costs of preserving the lives of the unproductive. A pro-choice strategy that extends the definition of 'person' to infants or even to young children seems just as arbitrary as an anti-abortion strategy that extends the definition of 'human being' to fetuses. Again, we find symmetries in the two positions and we arrive at a standoff.

There are even further problems that reflect symmetries in the two positions. In addition to counterexample problems, or the arbitrary application problems that can be exchanged for them, the standard anti-abortionist principle "It is prima facie seriously wrong to kill a human being," or one of its variants, can be objected to on the grounds of ambiguity. If 'human being' is taken to be a *biological* category, then the anti-abortionist is left with the problem of explaining why a merely biological category should make a moral difference. Why, it is asked, is it any more reasonable to base a moral conclusion on the number of chromosomes in one's cells than on the color of one's skin? If 'human being', on the other hand, is taken to be a *moral* category, then the claim that a fetus is a human being cannot be taken to be a premise in the anti-abortion argument, for it is precisely what needs to be established. Hence, either the anti-abortionist's main category is a morally irrelevant, merely biological category, or it is of no use to the anti-abortionist in establishing (noncircularly, of course) that abortion is wrong.

Although this problem with the anti-abortionist position is often noticed, it is less often noticed that the pro-choice position suffers from an analogous problem. The principle "Only persons have the right to life" also suffers from an ambiguity. The term 'person' is typically defined in terms of psychological characteristics, although there will certainly be disagreement concerning which characteristics are most important. Supposing that this matter can be settled, the pro-choicer is left with the problem of explaining why *psychological* characteristics should make a *moral* difference. If the pro-choicer should attempt to deal with this problem by claiming that an explanation is not necessary, that in fact we do treat such a cluster of psychological properties as having moral significance, the sharp-witted anti-abortionist should have a ready response. We do treat being both living and human as having moral significance. If it is legitimate for the pro-choicer to demand that the anti-abortionist provide an explanation of the connection between the biological character of being a human being and the wrongness of being killed (even though people accept this connection), then it is legitimate for the anti-abortionist to demand that the pro-choicer provide an explanation of the connection between psychological criteria for being a person and the wrongness of being killed (even though that connection is accepted).

[Joel] Feinberg has attempted to meet this objection (he calls psychological personhood "commonsense personhood"):

The characteristics that confer commonsense personhood are not arbitrary bases for rights and duties, such as race, sex or species membership; rather they are traits that make sense out of rights and duties and without which those moral attributes would have no point or function. It is because people are conscious; have a sense of their personal identities; have plans, goals, and projects; experience emotions; are liable to pains, anxieties, and frustrations; can reason and bargain, and so on—it is because of these attributes that people have values and interests, desires and expectations of their own, including a stake in their own futures, and a personal well-being of a sort we cannot ascribe to unconscious or nonrational beings. Because of their developed capacities they can assume duties and responsibilities and can have and make claims on one another. Only because of their sense of self, their life plans, their value hierarchies, and their stakes in their own futures can they be ascribed fundamental rights. There is nothing arbitrary about these linkages.[1]

The plausible aspects of this attempt should not be taken to obscure its implausible features. There is a

great deal to be said for the view that being a psychological person under some description is a necessary condition for having duties. One cannot have a duty unless one is capable of behaving morally, and a being's capability of behaving morally will require having a certain psychology. It is far from obvious, however, that having rights entails consciousness or rationality, as Feinberg suggests. We speak of the rights of the severely retarded or the severely mentally ill, yet some of these persons are not rational. We speak of the rights of the temporarily unconscious. The New Jersey Supreme Court based their decision in the Quinlan case on Karen Ann Quinlan's right to privacy, and she was known to be permanently unconscious at that time. Hence, Feinberg's claim that having rights entails being conscious is, on its face, obviously false.

Of course, it might not make sense to attribute rights to a being that would never in its natural history have certain psychological traits. This modest connection between psychological personhood and moral personhood will create a place for Karen Ann Quinlan and the temporarily unconscious. But then it makes a place for fetuses also. Hence, it does not serve Feinberg's pro-choice purposes. Accordingly, it seems that the pro-choicer will have as much difficulty bridging the gap between psychological personhood and personhood in the moral sense as the anti-abortionist has bridging the gap between being a biological human being and being a human being in the moral sense.

Furthermore, the pro-choicer cannot any more escape her problem by making person a purely moral category than the anti-abortionist could escape by the analogous move. For if person is a moral category, then the pro-choicer is left without the recourses for establishing (noncircularly, of course) the claim that a fetus is not a person, which is an essential premise in her argument. Again, we have both a symmetry and a standoff between pro-choice and antiabortion views.

Passions in the abortion debate run high. There are both plausibilities and difficulties with the standard positions. Accordingly, it is hardly surprising that partisans of either side embrace with fervor the moral generalizations that support the conclusions they pre-analytically favor, and reject with disdain the moral generalizations of their opponents as being subject to inescapable difficulties. It is easy to believe that the counterexamples to one's own moral principles are merely temporary difficulties that will dissolve in the wake of further philosophical research, and that the counterexamples to the principles of one's opponents are as straightforward as the contradiction between *A* and *O* propositions in traditional logic. This might suggest to an impartial observer (if there are any) that the abortion issue is unresolvable.

There is a way out of this apparent dialectical quandary. The moral generalizations of both sides are not quite correct. The generalizations hold for the most part, for the usual cases. This suggests that they are all *accidental* generalizations, that the moral claims made by those on both sides of the dispute do not touch on the *essence* of the matter.

This use of the distinction between essence and accident is not meant to invoke obscure metaphysical categories. Rather, it is intended to reflect the rather atheoretical nature of the abortion discussion. If the generalization a partisan in the abortion dispute adopts were derived from the reason why ending the life of a human being is wrong, then there could not be exceptions to that generalization unless some special case obtains in which there are even more powerful countervailing reasons. Such generalizations would not be merely accidental generalizations; they would point to, or be based upon, the essence of the wrongness of killing, what it is that makes killing wrong. All this suggests that a necessary condition of resolving the abortion controversy is a more theoretical account of the wrongness of killing. After all, if we merely believe, but do not understand, why killing adult human beings such as ourselves is wrong, how could we conceivably show that abortion is either immoral or permissible?

II.

In order to develop such an account, we can start from the following unproblematic assumption concerning our own case: it is wrong to kill *us*. Why is it wrong? Some answers can be easily eliminated. It might be said that what makes killing us wrong is that a killing brutalizes the one who kills. But the brutalization consists of being inured to the performance of an act that is hideously immoral; hence, the brutalization does not explain the immorality. It might be said that what makes killing us wrong is the great loss others would experience due to our absence. Although such hubris is understandable, such an explanation does not account for the wrongness of killing hermits, or those whose lives are relatively independent and whose friends find it easy to make new friends.

A more obvious answer is better. What primarily makes killing wrong is neither its effect on the murderer nor its effect on the victim's friends and relatives, but its effect on the victim. The loss of one's life is one of the greatest losses one can suffer. The loss of one's life deprives one of all the experiences, activities, projects, and enjoyments that would otherwise have constituted one's future. Therefore, killing someone is wrong, primarily because the killing inflicts (one of) the greatest possible losses on the victim. To describe this as the loss of life can be misleading, however. The change in my biological state does not by itself make killing me wrong. The effect of the loss of my biological life is the loss to me of all those activities, projects, experiences, and enjoyments which would otherwise have constituted my future personal life. These activities, projects, experiences, and enjoyments are either valuable for their own sakes or are means to something else that is valuable for its own sake. Some parts of my future are not valued by me now, but will come to be valued by me as I grow older and as my values and capacities change. When I am killed, I am deprived both of what I now value which would have been part of my future personal life, but also what I would come to value. Therefore, when I die, I am deprived of all of the value of my future. Inflicting this loss on me is ultimately what makes killing me wrong. This being the case, it would seem that what makes killing *any* adult human being prima facie seriously wrong is the loss of his or her future.

How should this rudimentary theory of the wrongness of killing be evaluated? It cannot be faulted for deriving an 'ought' from an 'is', for it does not. The analysis assumes that killing me (or you, reader) is prima facie seriously wrong. The point of the analysis is to establish which natural property ultimately explains the wrongness of the killing, given that it is wrong. A natural property will ultimately explain the wrongness of killing, only if (1) the explanation fits with our intuitions about the matter and (2) there is no other natural property that provides the basis for a better explanation of the wrongness of killing. This analysis rests on the intuition that what makes killing a particular human or animal wrong is what it does to that particular human or animal. What makes killing wrong is some natural effect or other of the killing. Some would deny this. For instance, a divine-command theorist in ethics would deny it. Surely this denial is, however, one of those features of divine-command theory which renders it so implausible.

The claim that what makes killing wrong is the loss of the victim's future is directly supported by two considerations. In the first place, this theory explains why we regard killing as one of the worst of crimes. Killing is especially wrong, because it deprives the victim of more than perhaps any other crime. In the second place, people with AIDS or cancer who know they are dying believe, of course, that dying is a very bad thing for them. They believe that the loss of a future to them that they would otherwise have experienced is what makes their premature death a very bad thing for them. A better theory of the wrongness of killing would require a different natural property associated with killing which better fits with the attitudes of the dying. What could it be?

The view that what makes killing wrong is the loss to the victim of the value of the victim's future gains additional support when some of its implications are examined. In the first place, it is incompatible with the view that it is wrong to kill only beings who are biologically human. It is possible that there exists a different species from another planet whose members have a future like ours. Since having a future like that is what makes killing someone wrong, this theory entails that it would be wrong to kill members of such a species. Hence, this theory is opposed to the claim that only life that is biologically human has great moral worth, a claim which many anti-abortionists have seemed to adopt. This opposition, which this theory has in common with personhood theories, seems to be a merit of the theory.

In the second place, the claim that the loss of one's future is the wrong-making feature of one's being killed entails the possibility that the futures of some actual nonhuman mammals on our own planet are sufficiently like ours that it is seriously wrong to kill them also. Whether some animals do have the same right to life as human beings depends on adding to the account of the wrongness of killing some additional account of just what it is about my future or the futures of other adult human beings which makes it wrong to kill us. No such additional account will be offered in this essay. Undoubtedly, the provision of such an account would be a very difficult matter. Undoubtedly, any such account would be quite controversial. Hence, it surely should not reflect badly on this sketch of an elementary theory of the wrongness of killing that it is indeterminate with respect to some very difficult issues regarding animal rights.

In the third place, the claim that the loss of one's future is the wrong-making feature of one's being killed does not entail, as sanctity of human life theories do, that active euthanasia is wrong. Persons who are severely and incurably ill, who face a future of pain and despair, and who wish to die will not have suffered a loss if they are killed. It is, strictly speaking, the value of a human's future which makes killing wrong in this theory. This being so, killing does not necessarily wrong some persons who are sick and dying. Of course, there may be other reasons for a prohibition of active euthanasia, but that is another matter. Sanctity-of-human-life theories seem to hold that active euthanasia is seriously wrong even in an individual case where there seems to be good reason for it independently of public policy considerations. This consequence is most implausible, and it is a plus for the claim that the loss of a future of value is what makes killing wrong that it does not share this consequence.

In the fourth place, the account of the wrongness of killing defended in this essay does straightforwardly entail that it is prima facie seriously wrong to kill children and infants, for we do presume that they have futures of value. Since we do believe that it is wrong to kill defenseless little babies, it is important that a theory of the wrongness of killing easily account for this. Personhood theories of the wrongness of killing, on the other hand, cannot straightforwardly account for the wrongness of killing infants and young children. Hence, such theories must add special ad hoc accounts of the wrongness of killing the young. The plausibility of such ad hoc theories seems to be a function of how desperately one wants such theories to work. The claim that the primary wrong-making feature of a killing is the loss to the victim of the value of its future accounts for the wrongness of killing young children and infants directly; it makes the wrongness of such acts as obvious as we actually think it is. This is a further merit of this theory. Accordingly, it seems that this value of a future-like-ours theory of the wrongness of killing shares strengths of both sanctity-of-life and personhood accounts while avoiding weaknesses of both. In addition, it meshes with a central intuition concerning what makes killing wrong.

The claim that the primary wrong-making feature of a killing is the loss to the victim of the value of its future has obvious consequences for the ethics of abortion. The future of a standard fetus includes a set of experiences, projects, activities, and such which are identical with the futures of adult human beings and are identical with the futures of young children. Since the reason that is sufficient to explain why it is wrong to kill human beings after the time of birth is a reason that also applies to fetuses, it follows that abortion is prima facie seriously morally wrong.

This argument does not rely on the invalid inference that, since it is wrong to kill persons, it is wrong to kill potential persons also. The category that is morally central to this analysis is the category of having a valuable future like ours; it is not the category of personhood. The argument to the conclusion that

abortion is prima facie seriously morally wrong proceeded independently of the notion of person or potential person or any equivalent. Someone may wish to start with this analysis in terms of the value of a human future, conclude that abortion is, except perhaps in rare circumstances, seriously morally wrong, infer that fetuses have the right to life, and then call fetuses "persons" as a result of their having the right to life. Clearly, in this case, the category of person is being used to state the *conclusion* of the analysis rather than to generate the *argument* of the analysis.

The structure of this anti-abortion argument can be both illuminated and defended by comparing it to what appears to be the best argument for the wrongness of the wanton infliction of pain on animals. This latter argument is based on the assumption that it is prima facie wrong to inflict pain on me (or you, reader). What is the natural property associated with the infliction of pain which makes such infliction wrong? The obvious answer seems to be that the infliction of pain causes suffering and that suffering is a misfortune. The suffering caused by the infliction of pain is what makes the wanton infliction of pain on me wrong. The wanton infliction of pain on other adult humans causes suffering. The wanton infliction of pain on animals causes suffering. Since causing suffering is what makes the wanton infliction of pain wrong and since the wanton infliction of pain on animals causes suffering, it follows that the wanton infliction of pain on animals is wrong.

This argument for the wrongness of the wanton infliction of pain on animals shares a number of structural features with the argument for the serious prima facie wrongness of abortion. Both arguments start with an obvious assumption concerning what it is wrong to do to me (or you, reader). Both then look for the characteristic or the consequence of the wrong action which makes the action wrong. Both recognize that the wrong–making feature of these immoral actions is a property of actions sometimes directed at individuals other than postnatal human beings. If the structure of the argument for the wrongness of the wanton infliction of pain on animals is sound, then the structure of the argument for the prima facie serious wrongness of abortion is also sound, for the structure of the two arguments is the same. The structure common to both is the key to the explanation of how the wrongness of abortion can be demonstrated without recourse to the category of person. In neither argument is that category crucial.

This defense of an argument for the wrongness of abortion in terms of a structurally similar argument for the wrongness of the wanton infliction of pain on animals succeeds only if the account regarding animals is the correct account. Is it? In the first place, it seems plausible. In the second place, its major competition is Kant's account. Kant believed that we do not have direct duties to animals at all, because they are not persons. Hence, Kant had to explain and justify the wrongness of inflicting pain on animals on the grounds that "he who is hard in his dealings with animals becomes hard also in his dealing with men."[2] The problem with Kant's account is that there seems to be no reason for accepting this latter claim unless Kant's account is rejected. If the alternative to Kant's account is accepted, then it is easy to understand why someone who is indifferent to inflicting pain on animals is also indifferent to inflicting pain on humans, for one is indifferent to what makes inflicting pain wrong in both cases. But, if Kant's account is accepted, there is no intelligible reason why one who is hard in his dealings with animals (or crabgrass or stones) should also be hard in his dealings with men. After all, men are persons: animals are no more persons than crabgrass or stones. Persons are Kant's crucial moral category. Why, in short, should a Kantian accept the basic claim in Kant's argument?

Hence, Kant's argument for the wrongness of inflicting pain on animals rests on a claim that, in a world of Kantian moral agents, is demonstrably false. Therefore, the alternative analysis, being more plausible anyway, should be accepted. Since this alternative analysis has the same structure as the anti-abortion argument being defended here, we have further support for the argument for the immorality of abortion being defended in this essay.

Of course, this value of a future-like-ours argument, if sound, shows only that abortion is prima facie wrong, not that it is wrong in any and all circumstances. Since the loss of the future to a standard fetus, if killed, is, however, at least as great a loss as the loss of the future to a standard adult human being who is killed, abortion, like ordinary killing, could be justified only by the most compelling reasons. The loss of one's life is almost the greatest misfortune that can happen to one. Presumably abortion could be justified in some circumstances, only if the loss consequent on failing to abort would be at least as great. Accordingly, morally permissible abortions will be rare indeed unless, perhaps, they occur so early in pregnancy that a fetus is not yet definitely an individual. Hence, this argument should be taken as showing that abortion is presumptively very seriously wrong, where the presumption is very strong—as strong as the presumption that killing another adult human being is wrong.

III.

How complete an account of the wrongness of killing does the value of a future-like-our account have to be in order that the wrongness of abortion is a consequence? This account does not have to be an account of the necessary conditions for the wrongness of killing. Some persons in nursing homes may lack valuable human futures, yet it may be wrong to kill them for other reasons. Furthermore, this account does not obviously have to be the sole reason killing is wrong where the victim did have a valuable future. This analysis claims only that, for any killing where the victim did have a valuable future like ours, having that future by itself is sufficient to create the strong presumption that the killing is seriously wrong.

One way to overturn the value of a future-like-ours argument would be to find some account of the wrongness of killing which is at least as intelligible and which has different implications for the ethics of abortion. Two rival accounts possess at least some degree of plausibility. One account is based on the obvious fact that people value the experience of living and wish for that valuable experience to continue. Therefore, it might be said, what makes killing wrong is the discontinuation of that experience for the victim. Let us call this the *discontinuation account.* Another rival account is based upon the obvious fact that people strongly desire to continue to live. This suggests that what makes killing us so wrong is that it interferes with the fulfillment of a strong and fundamental desire, the fulfillment of which is necessary for the fulfillment of any other desires we might have. Let us call this the *desire account.*

Consider first the desire account as a rival account of the ethics of killing which would provide the basis for rejecting the anti-abortion position. Such an account will have to be stronger than the value of a future-like-ours account of the wrongness of abortion if it is to do the job expected of it. To entail the wrongness of abortion, the value of a future-like-ours account has only to provide a sufficient, but not a necessary, condition for the wrongness of killing. The desire account, on the other hand, must provide us also with a necessary condition for the wrongness of killing in order to generate a pro-choice conclusion on abortion. The reason for this is that presumably the argument from the desire account moves from the claim that what makes killing wrong is interference with a very strong desire to the claim that abortion is not wrong because the fetus lacks a strong desire to live. Obviously, this inference fails if someone's having the desire to live is not a necessary condition of its being wrong to kill that individual.

One problem with the desire account is that we do regard it as seriously wrong to kill persons who have little desire to live or who have no desires to live or, indeed, have a desire not to live. We believe it is seriously wrong to kill the unconscious, the sleeping, those who are tired of life, and those who are suicidal. The value-of-a-human-future account renders standard morality intelligible in these cases; these cases appear to be incompatible with the desire account.

The desire account is subject to a deeper difficulty. We desire life, because we value the goods of this life. The goodness of life is not secondary to our desire for it. If this were not so, the pain of one's own premature death could be done away with merely by an appropriate alteration in the configuration of one's desires. This is absurd. Hence, it would seem that it is the loss of the goods of one's future, not the interference with the fulfillment of a strong desire to live, which accounts ultimately for the wrongness of killing.

It is worth noting that, if the desire account is modified so that it does not provide a necessary, but only a sufficient, condition for the wrongness of killing, the desire account is compatible with the value of a future-like-ours account. The combined accounts will yield an anti-abortion ethic. This suggests that one can retain what is intuitively plausible about the desire account without a challenge to the basic argument of this paper.

It is also worth nothing that, if future desires have moral force in a modified desire account of the wrongness of killing, one can find support for an anti-abortion ethic even in the absence of a value of a future-like-ours account. If one decides that a morally relevant property, the possession of which is sufficient to make it wrong to kill some individual, is the desire at some future time to live—one might decide to justify one's refusal to kill suicidal teenagers on these grounds, for example—then, since typical fetuses will have the desire in the future to live, it is wrong to kill typical fetuses. Accordingly, it does not seem that a desire account of the wrongness of killing can provide a justification of a pro-choice ethic of abortion which is nearly as adequate as the value of a human-future justification of an anti-abortion ethic.

The discontinuation account looks more promising as an account of the wrongness of killing. It seems just as intelligible as the value of a future-like-ours account, but it does not justify an anti-abortion position. Obviously, if it is the continuation of one's activities, experiences, and projects, the loss of which makes killing wrong, then it is not wrong to kill fetuses for that reason, for fetuses do not have experiences, activities, and projects to be continued or discontinued. Accordingly, the discontinuation account does not have the anti-abortion consequences that the value of a future-like-ours account has. Yet, it seems as intelligible as the value of a future-like-ours account, for when we think of what would be wrong with our being killed, it does seem as if it is the discontinuation of what makes our lives worthwhile which makes killing us wrong.

Is the discontinuation account just as good an account as the value of a future-like-ours account? The discontinuation account will not be adequate at all, if it does not refer to the *value* of the experience that may be discontinued. One does not want the discontinuation account to make it wrong to kill a patient who begs for death and who is in severe pain that cannot be relieved short of killing. (I leave open the question of whether it is wrong for other reasons.) Accordingly, the discontinuation account must be more than a bare discontinuation account. It must make some reference to the positive value of the patient's experiences. But, by the same token, the value of a future-like-ours account cannot be a bare future account either. Just having a future surely does not itself rule out killing the above patient. This account must make some reference to the value of the patient's future experiences and projects also. Hence, both accounts involve the value of experiences, projects, and activities. So far we still have symmetry between the accounts.

The symmetry fades, however, when we focus on the time period of the value of the experiences, etc., which has moral consequences. Although both accounts leave open the possibility that the patient in our example may be killed, this possibility is left open only in virtue of the utterly bleak future for the patient. It makes no difference whether the patient's immediate past contains intolerable pain, or consists in being in a coma (which we can imagine is a situation of indifference), or consists in a life of value. If the patient's future is a future of value, we want our account to make it wrong to kill the patient. If the patient's future is intolerable, whatever his or her immediate past, we want our account to allow killing the patient. Obviously, then, it is the value of that patient's future which is doing the work in rendering the morality of killing the patient intelligible.

This being the case, it seems clear that whether one has immediate past experiences or not does not work in the explanation of what makes killing wrong. The addition the discontinuation account makes to the value of a human future account is otiose. Its addition to the value-of-a-future account plays no role at all in rendering intelligible the wrongness of

killing. Therefore, it can be discarded with the discontinuation account of which it is a part.

IV.

The analysis of the previous section suggests that alternative general accounts of the wrongness of killing are either inadequate or unsuccessful in getting around the anti-abortion consequences of the value of a future-like-ours argument. A different strategy for avoiding these anti-abortion consequences involves limiting the scope of the value of a future argument. More precisely, the strategy involves arguing that fetuses lack a property that is essential for the value-of-a-future argument (or for any anti-abortion argument) to apply to them.

One move of this sort is based upon the claim that a necessary condition of one's future being valuable is that one values it. Value implies a valuer. Given this one might argue that, since fetuses cannot value their futures, their futures are not valuable to them. Hence, it does not seriously wrong them deliberately to end their lives.

This move fails, however, because of some ambiguities. Let us assume that something cannot be of value unless it is valued by someone. This does not entail that my life is of no value unless it is valued by me. I may think, in a period of despair, that my future is of no worth whatsoever, but I may be wrong because others rightly see value—even great value—in it. Furthermore, my future can be valuable to me even if I do not value it. This is the case when a young person attempts suicide, but is rescued and goes on to significant human achievements. Such young people's futures are ultimately valuable to them, even though such futures do not seem to be valuable to them at the moment of attempted suicide. A fetus's future can be valuable to it in the same way. Accordingly, this attempt to limit the anti-abortion argument fails.

Another similar attempt to reject the anti-abortion position is based on [Michael] Tooley's claim that an entity cannot possess the right to life unless it has the capacity to desire its continued existence. It follows that, since fetuses lack the conceptual capacity to desire to continue to live, they lack the right to life. Accordingly, Tooley concludes that abortion cannot be seriously prima facie wrong.[3]

What could be the evidence for Tooley's basic claim? Tooley once argued that individuals have a prima facie right to what they desire and that the lack of the capacity to desire something undercuts the basis of one's right to it.[4] This argument plainly will not succeed in the context of the analysis of this essay, however, since the point here is to establish the fetus's right to life on other grounds. Tooley's argument assumes that the right to life cannot be established in general on some basis other than the desire for life. This position was considered and rejected in the preceding section of this paper.

One might attempt to defend Tooley's basic claim on the grounds that, because a fetus cannot apprehend continued life as a benefit, its continued life cannot be a benefit or cannot be something it has a right to or cannot be something that is in its interest. This might be defended in terms of the general proposition that, if an individual is literally incapable of caring about or taking an interest in some X, then one does not have a right to X or X is not a benefit or X is not something that is in one's interest.

Each member of this family of claims seems to be open to objections. As John C. Stevens[5] has pointed out, one may have a right to be treated with a certain medical procedure (because of a health insurance policy one has purchased), even though one cannot conceive of the nature of the procedure. And, as Tooley himself has pointed out, persons who have been indoctrinated, or drugged, or rendered temporarily unconscious may be literally incapable of caring about or taking an interest in something that is in their interest or is something to which they have a right, or is something that benefits them. Hence, the Tooley claim that would restrict the scope of the value of a future-like-ours argument is undermined by counterexamples.

Finally, Paul Bassen[6] has argued that, even though the prospects of an embryo might seem to be a basis for the wrongness of abortion, an embryo cannot be a victim and therefore cannot be wronged. An embryo cannot be a victim, he says, because it lacks sentience. His central argument for this seems to be

that, even though plants and the permanently unconscious are alive, they clearly cannot be victims. What is the explanation of this? Bassen claims that the explanation is that their lives consist of mere metabolism and mere metabolism is not enough to ground victimizability. Mentation is required.

The problem with this attempt to establish the absence of victimizability is that both plants and the permanently unconscious clearly lack what Bassen calls "prospects" or what I have called "a future life like ours." Hence, it is surely open to one to argue that the real reason we believe plants and the permanently unconscious cannot be victims is that killing them cannot deprive them of a future life like ours; the real reason is not their absence of present mentation.

Bassen recognizes that his view is subject to this difficulty, and he recognizes that the case of children seems to support this difficulty, for "much of what we do for children is based on prospects." He argues, however, that, in the case of children and in other such cases, "potentially comes into play only where victimizability has been secured on other grounds" (p. 333).

Bassen's defense of his view is patently question-begging, since what is adequate to secure victimizability is exactly what is at issue. His examples do not support his own view against the thesis of this essay. Of course, embryos can be victims: when their lives are deliberately terminated, they are deprived of their futures of value, their prospects. This makes them victims, for it directly wrongs them.

The seeming plausibility of Bassen's view stems from the fact that paradigmatic cases of imagining someone as a victim involve empathy, and empathy requires mentation of the victim. The victims of flood, famine, rape, or child abuse are all persons with whom we can empathize. That empathy seems to be part of seeing them as victims.

In spite of the strength of these examples, the attractive intuition that a situation in which there is victimization requires the possibility of empathy is subject to counterexamples. Consider a case that Bassen himself offers: "Posthumous obliteration of an author's work constitutes a misfortune for him only if he had wished his work to endure" (p. 318). The conditions Bassen wishes to impose upon the possibility of being victimized here seem far too strong. Perhaps this author, due to his unrealistic standards of excellence and his low self-esteem, regarded his work as unworthy of survival, even though it possessed genuine literary merit. Destruction of such work would surely victimize its author. In such a case, empathy with the victim concerning the loss is clearly impossible.

Of course, Bassen does not make the possibility of empathy a necessary condition of victimizability; he requires only mentation. Hence, on Bassen's actual view, this author, as I have described him, can be a victim. The problem is that the basic intuition that renders Bassen's view plausible is missing in the author's case. In order to attempt to avoid counterexamples, Bassen has made his thesis too weak to be supported by the intuitions that suggested it.

Even so, the mentation requirement on victimizability is still subject to counterexamples. Suppose a severe accident renders me totally unconscious for a month, after which I recover. Surely killing me while I am unconscious victimizes me, even though I am incapable of mentation during that time. It follows that Bassen's thesis fails. Apparently, attempts to restrict the value of a future-like-ours argument so that fetuses do not fall within its scope do not succeed.

V.

In this essay, it has been argued that the correct ethic of the wrongness of killing can be extended to fetal life and used to show that there is a strong presumption that any abortion is morally impermissible. If the ethic of killing adopted here entails, however, that contraception is also seriously immoral, then there would appear to be a difficulty with the analysis of this assay.

But this analysis does not entail that contraception is wrong. Of course, contraception prevents the actualization of a possible future of value. Hence, it follows from the claim that futures of value should be maximized that contraception is prima facie immoral. This obligation to maximize does not exist, however; furthermore, nothing in the ethics of killing in this paper entails that it does. The ethics of killing in this essay would entail that contraception is wrong only if something were denied a human future of value by contraception. Nothing at all is denied such a future by contraception, however.

Candidates for a subject of harm by contraception fall into four categories: (1) some sperm or other, (2) some ovum or other, (3) a sperm and an ovum separately, and (4) a sperm and an ovum together. Assigning the harm to some sperm is utterly arbitrary, for no reason can be given for making a sperm the subject of harm rather than an ovum. Assigning the harm to some ovum is utterly arbitrary, for no reason can be given for making an ovum the subject of harm rather than a sperm. One might attempt to avoid these problems by insisting that contraception deprives both the sperm and the ovum separately of a valuable future like ours. On this alternative, too many futures are lost. Contraception was supposed to be wrong, because it deprived us of one future of value, not two. One might attempt to avoid this problem by holding that contraception deprives the combination of sperm and ovum of a valuable future like ours. But here the definite article misleads. At the time of contraception, there are hundreds of millions of sperm, one (released) ovum and millions of possible combinations of all of these. There is no actual combination at all. Is the subject of the loss to be a merely possible combination? Which one? This alternative does not yield an actual subject of harm either. Accordingly, the immorality of contraception is not entailed by the loss of a future-like-ours argument simply because there is no nonarbitrarily identifiable subject of the loss in the case of contraception.

VI.

The purpose of this essay has been to set out an argument for the serious presumptive wrongness of abortion subject to the assumption that the moral permissibility of abortion stands or falls on the moral status of the fetus. Since a fetus possesses a property, the possession of which in adult human beings is sufficient to make killing an adult human being wrong, abortion is wrong. This way of dealing with the problem of abortion seems superior to other approaches to the ethics of abortion, because it rests on an ethics of killing which is close to self-evident, because the crucial morally relevant property clearly applies to fetuses, and because the argument avoids the usual equivocations of 'human life', 'human being', or 'person'. The argument rests neither on religious claims nor on Papal dogma. It is not subject to the objection of "speciesism." Its soundness is compatible with the moral permissibility of euthanasia and contraception. It deals with our intuitions concerning young children.

Finally, this analysis can be viewed as resolving a standard problem—indeed, *the* standard problem—concerning the ethics of abortion. Clearly, it is wrong to kill adult human beings. Clearly, it is not wrong to end the life of some arbitrarily chosen single human cell. Fetuses seem to be like arbitrarily chosen human cells in some respects and like adult humans in other respects. The problem of the ethics of abortion is the problem of determining the fetal property that settles this moral controversy. The thesis of this essay is that the problem of the ethics of abortion, so understood, is solvable.

NOTES

1. Joel Feinberg, "Abortion," in *Matters of Life and Death: New Introductory Essays in Moral Philosophy*, ed. Tom Regan (New York: Random House, 1986), p. 270.

2. "Duties to Animals and Spirits," in *Lectures on Ethics*, trans. Loius Infeld (New York: Harper, 1963), p. 239.

3. Michael Tooley, *Abortion and Infanticide* (New York: Oxford, 1984), pp. 46–47.

4. Tooley, *Abortion and Infanticide*, pp. 44–45.

5. "Must the Bearer of a Right Have the Concept of That to Which He Has a Right?" *Ethics* 95, no. 1 (1984): 68–74.

6. "Present Sakes and Future Prospects: The Status of Early Abortion," *Philosophy and Public Affairs* 11, no. 4 (1982): 322–26.

The Abortion Debate That Wasn't

Wendy McElroy

Although the political dust has yet to settle, the pro-life movement has won the abortion debate by virtue of the fact that pro-choice advocates have refused to deal with the moral issues it raises. The preceding statement brings me no pleasure. I stand firmly by the principle of "a woman's body, a woman's right" but, like many pro-choice advocates, I have always had moral reservations about late term abortion. The reservations increase dramatically when confronted with partial birth abortions performed for any reason other than valid concern about the pregnant women's health. Even with partial birth abortion, however, I believe the law must protect a woman's right to control her own body—that is, it must acknowledge a woman's right to abort.

Wendy McElroy, "The Abortion Debate That Wasn't," ifeminists.com (24 April 2001), http://www.ifeminists.net/introduction/editorials/2001/0424.html. Reprinted by permission of Wendy McElroy.

(No similar moral or emotional problem arises with RU486 and other means of early abortion because all that exists at that point—to my mind—is a potential human being. But, given that I value human life, I also value its potential. As the fetus comes closer to viability, the value I place on it increases as well . . . though its value is never so high as that of the pregnant woman.)

Why has feminism been conspicuously silent about the morality of late term abortion? My experiences may be indicative. Years ago, when I began speaking out in favor of abortion rights, I routinely included my moral reservations and followed up with a question. I asked, "What is the purpose of law in society?" and I answered, "It is to protect person and property," to protect individual rights. In other words, in my worldview, the purpose of law is to preserve the peace. This contrasts sharply with the view that law should preserve virtue: for example, that there should be laws against pornography, blasphemy, and sexual deviance because such activities constitute a breach of public morality. In drawing the distinction between "the legal" and "the moral," I argued that individuals have the right to do anything with their own bodies and property whether or not those actions are "moral" by some standard. Women have a right to undergo any medical procedure they wished to have performed upon their own bodies whether or not the morality of the procedure was questionable. Morality is a matter of individual conscience, not of law.

A more seasoned feminist took me aside and urged me to stop mentioning 'moral reservations.' Such statements, I was told, gave ammunition to the enemy and harmed "the cause." Since then, I have heard manifold versions of this argument regarding every controversial issue I've addressed. "You should be less than candid, you should quote this study and ignore that one, you should never acknowledge a good argument from the other side" . . . My response has remained basically the same. The minute you start ignoring facts, refusing to address arguments, and being anything less than candid, you have lost the debate. And you deserve to. The pro-choice movement has lost the debate on abortion because it has refused to grapple with the moral issues that have come to define this matter.

When is a human life present? When does an individual with individual rights exist? Is it wrong to destroy the potential for life even though it may be lawful to do so? In answering these questions, I remain pro-choice and have a clear conscience besides. In refusing to deal with these questions, feminism has become an ally of the pro-life movement. The mainstream feminist movement has surrendered the moral high ground to pro-life forces: it has refused to enter into honest debate.

In the early days (the '70s), when abortion opponents still spoke to each other, I remember how vigorously pro-choice advocates objected to the pro-life tactic of propping blown-up photos of aborted fetuses against the dais of debate. (Ironically, the same women who strenuously objected often tried to prop up the worst S/M photos from pornography during debate on that subject.) The tactic was denounced as a raw appeal to emotions. Well . . . perhaps there is nothing wrong with that. Emotions are an integral part of every decision we make as human beings. By refusing to deal with the emotions surrounding abortion—just as it refused to deal with the moral questions—feminism has relegated itself to the sidelines of debate.

I want to look at the photographs of aborted fetuses. I want to see the pictures that result from partial birth abortions—the same photos that have convinced some non-political nurses in attendance to become anti-abortion zealots. If feminists are not willing to look at the practical consequences of their policies, then we should retire from the political arena.

In fairness, however, I ask the pro-life movement to honestly confront their own difficult questions. For example, like many women of my generation, I had a first-trimester abortion that was entirely discretionary. By pro-life standards, I am guilty of first-degree, premeditated murder and the doctor who performed the procedure is guilty of the same—a crime that has no time limit under law. I ask every pro-life advocate: are you willing to subject me to the maximum penalties being imposed for such a crime, up to and including a death sentence? If not, why not? Anything less constitutes an admission on your part that abortion is, in fact, less than the murder of an innocent human being.

According to pro-life doctrine, a substantial portion of an entire generation deserves a death sentence or its equivalent. By eschewing moral issues, feminism has allowed the hideous practical consequences of the pro-life position to stand without contradiction. I am not so generous. Let me repeat my question: are pro-life advocates willing to send police to my home, are they willing to throw me in prison and subject me to the maximum penalty for premeditated murder? If not, then feminists are not the only ones avoiding the difficult questions.

The Morality of Abortion

Margaret Olivia Little

It is often noted that public discussion of the moral status of abortion is disappointingly crude. The positions staked out and the reasoning proffered seem to reflect little of the subtlety and nuance—not to mention ambivalence—that mark more private reflections on the subject. Despite attempts by various parties to find middle ground, the debate remains largely polarized: at its most dramatic, with extreme conservatives claiming abortion to be the moral equivalent of murder, even as extreme liberals think it devoid of moral import.

To some extent, this polarization is due to the legal battle that continues to shadow moral discussions. Admissions of ethical nuance, it is feared, will play as concession on the deeply contested question of whether abortion should be a legally protected option for women. But, to some extent, blame for the continued crudeness can be laid at the doorstep of moral theory itself.

For one thing, the ethical literature on abortion has focused almost exclusively on the thinnest moral assessment—on whether and when abortion is "morally permissible." This question is, of course, a crucial one, its answer often desperately sought. But many of our deepest struggles with the morality of abortion concern much more textured questions about its placement on the scales of *decency, respectfulness,* and *responsibility*. It is one thing to decide that an abortion was permissible, quite another to decide that it was *honorable*; one thing to decide that an abortion was impermissible, quite another to decide that it was *monstrous*. It is these latter categories that determine what we might call the thick moral interpretation of the act—and, with it, the meaning the woman must live with, and the reactive attitudes such as disgust, forbearance, or admiration that she

and others think the act deserves. A moral theory that moves too quickly or focuses too exclusively on moral permissibility will not address these crucial issues.

Moreover, the tools that mainstream moral theory has used for analyzing abortion fit only awkwardly to this subject matter. Many treatments analyze abortion in the same terms used for assessing when war is justified, or the extent of our obligations to needy strangers, or the protection owed to the paintings of Leonardo da Vinci. While there is some overlap of issues, such treatments end up leaving aside many of the most important themes relevant to the ethics of gestation: what it means to play a role in *creating* a person; how to assess responsibilities that involve *sharing*, not just risking, one's body and life; what follows from the fact that the entity in question is or would be *one's child*. Nor are such lacunae incidental glitches. As theorists such as Catharine MacKinnon (1991) and Robin West (1993) have pointed out, our moral and political theories have been forged, by and large, to deal with interactions between independently situated and relatively equal strangers. However well this might work for soldierly heroism and barroom brawls (a question worth pressing in its own right), such a theory might not be expected to do well with moral questions dealing with the sort of intertwinement at issue in pregnancy.

If this is right, it means it is especially important not to focus all our energies, as many treatments are wont to do, arbitrating the question of fetal personhood. The question certainly matters: the moral contours of abortion, as we shall see, are importantly different depending on the answer we give it. The question is, moreover, a genuinely complex one, pressing, in essence, on the extent to which moral status is a function of the sort of being something already is, as judged by its occurrent properties, and the sort of creature it would become if it developed. (My own view, which I will not defend here, is that full moral status is in part anticipatory and in part something achieved; the fetus's status becomes pro-

Margaret Olivia Little, "Abortion," in *A Companion to Applied Ethics* (Malden, MA: Blackwell, 2005), 313–24 (edited). Reprinted with permission of Blackwell Publishing.

gressively more weighty as pregnancy continues. For the debate on moral status, see Brody, 1975; Marquis, 1989; Feinberg, 1992; Steinbock, 1992; Quinn, 1993.) Complex as the issue of personhood is, though, the temptation to think our work done if only we could settle it—as though the moral status of abortion follows lockstep from the moral status of the fetus—has led theorists to ignore the rich ethical issues that are raised by the, shall we say, rather distinctive situation in which the fetus is located.

To make progress on the moral status of abortion, it turns out, requires us not just to arbitrate already familiar controversies in metaphysics and ethics, but to attend to the distinctive aspects of pregnancy that often stand at their margins. In the following, I want to argue that if we acknowledge gestation as an *intimacy*, motherhood as a *relationship*, and creation as a *process*, we will be in a far better position to appreciate the moral textures of abortion. I explore these textures, in the first half on stipulation that the fetus is a person, in the second half under supposition that early human life has an important value worthy of respect.

FETAL PERSONHOOD: FROM WRONGFUL INTERFERENCE TO POSITIVE RESPONSIBILITIES

If fetuses are persons, then abortion is surely an enormously serious matter: what is at stake is nothing less than the life of a creature with full moral standing. To say that the stakes are high, though, is not to say that moral analysis is obvious (which is why, elsewhere in moral theory, conversation usually starts, not stops, once we realize people's lives are at issue). I think the most widely held objection to abortion is badly misguided; more importantly, it obscures the deeper ethical question at issue.

On the usual view, it is perfectly obvious what to say about abortion on supposition of fetal personhood: if fetuses are persons, then abortion is murder. Persons, after all, have a fundamental right to life, and abortion, it would seem, counts as its gross violation. On this view, we can assess the status of abortion quite cleanly. In particular, we need not delve

too deeply into the burdens that continued gestation might present for women—not because their lives do not matter or because we do not sympathize with their plight, but because we do not take hardship as justification for murder.

In fact, though, abortion's assimilation to murder will seem clear cut only if we have already ignored key features of gestation. While certain metaphors depict gestation as passive carriage—as though the fetus were simply occupying a room until it is born—the truth is of course far different. One who is gestating is providing the fetus with sustenance—donating nourishment, creating blood, delivering oxygen, providing hormonal triggers for development—without which it could not live. For a fetus, to live is inextricably tied to receiving aid (see Bolton, 1979). And whether the assistance is delivered by way of intentional activity (as when the woman eats or takes her prenatal vitamins) or by way of biological mechanism, assistance it plainly is. But this has crucial implications for abortion's alleged status as murder. To put it simply, the right to life, as Judith Thomson (1971) famously put it, does not include the right to have all assistance needed to maintain that life. Ending gestation will, at early stages at least, certainly lead to the fetus's demise, but that does not mean that doing so would constitute murder.

Now Thomson herself illustrated the point with an (in)famous thought experiment in which one person is kidnapped and used as life support for another: staying connected to the Famous Violinist, she points out, may be the kind thing to do, but disconnecting oneself does not violate the Violinist's rights. The details of this rather esoteric example have led to widespread charges that Thomson's point ignores the distinction between killing and letting die, and would apply at any rate only to cases in which the woman was not responsible for procreation occurring. In fact, though, I think the central insight here is broader than the example, or Thomson's own analysis, indicates.

As Frances Kamm's work points out (Kamm, 1992), in the usual case of a killing—if you stab a person on the street, for instance—you interfere with the trajectory the person had independently of you. She faced a happy enough future, we will say; your action changed that, taking away from her something she would have had but for your action. In ending gestation, though, what you are taking away from this person is something she would not have had to begin with without your aid. She comes to you with a "downward trajectory," as it were: but for you she would already be dead. In removing that assistance, you are not violating the person's right to life, judged in the traditional terms of a right against interference. While all killings are tragedies, then, not all are alike: some killings, as Kamm puts it, share the crucial "formal" feature of letting die, which is that they leave the person no worse off than before she encountered you.

The argument is not some crude utilitarian one, according to which you get to kill the person because you saved her life (as though, having given you a nice lamp for your birthday, I may therefore later steal it with impunity). The point, rather, is that where I am still in the process of saving—or sustaining or enabling—your life, and that life cannot be thus saved or sustained by anyone else, ending that assistance, even by active means, does not violate your right to life.

Now some, of course, will argue that matters change when the woman is causally responsible for procreation. In such cases, it will be said, she is responsible for introducing the person's need. She is not like someone happening by an accident on the highway who knows CPR; she is like the person who *caused* the accident. Her actions introduced a set of vulnerabilities or needs, and we have a special duty to lessen vulnerabilities and repair harms we have inflicted on others.

But there is a deep disanalogy between causing the accident and procreating. The fact of causing a crash itself introduces a harm to surrounding drivers: they are in a worse position for having encountered that driver. But the simple act of procreating does not worsen the fetus's position: without procreation, the fetus would not exist at all, and the mere fact of being brought into existence is not a bad thing. To be sure, creating a human is creating someone who comes with needs. But this, crucially, is not the same as

inflicting a need *onto* someone (see Silverstein, 1987). It is not as though the fetus already existed with one level of needs and the woman added a new one (as does happen, for instance, if a woman takes a drug after conception that increases the fetus's vulnerability to, say, certain cancers). The woman is (partially) responsible for creating a life, and it is a life that necessarily includes needs, but that is not the same as being responsible for the person being needy rather than not. The pregnant woman has not made the fetus more vulnerable than it would otherwise have been: without her procreative actions, it would not have existed at all.

Even if the fetus is a person, then, abortion would not be murder. More broadly put, abortion, whatever its rights and wrongs, is not a species of *wrongful interference*.

None of this, though, is to say that abortion under such supposition is therefore unproblematic. It is to argue, instead, that the crucial moral issue needs to be relocated. Wrongful interference is a central concern in morality, but it is not the only one. We are also concerned with notions of *neglect, abandonment,* and *disregard*. These are issues that involve abrogations of positive responsibilities to help others, not injunctions against interfering with them. If fetuses are persons, the question we really need to decide is: what positive responsibilities, if any, do pregnant women have to continue gestational assistance? This is a question that takes us into far richer, and far more interesting, territory than that occupied by discussions of murder.

One key question is what we should say pregnant women owe to the fetuses they carry as a matter of *general beneficence*. Philosophers, of course, familiarly divide over the ambitions of beneficence, generically construed, but abortion raises distinct difficulties of its own. On the one hand, the beneficence called for her is of a particularly urgent kind: the stakes are life and death, and the pregnant woman is the *only* one who can render the assistance needed. It is a rare (and, many of us will think, dreadful) moral theory that will think she faces no responsibilities to assist here: passing a drowning person for mere convenience when no one else is within shouting distance is a very good example of moral indecency. On the other hand, gestation is not just any activity. It involves sharing one's very body. It brings with it an emotional intertwinement that can reshape one's entire life. It adds another person to one's family. Being asked to gestate another person, that is, is not like being asked to write a check to support an impoverished child; it is more like being asked to adopt the child. Doing so is a caring, compassionate act; it is also an enormous undertaking that has reverberations for an entire lifetime. Deciding whether, and if so when, such action is obligatory rather than admirable is no light matter.

I do not think moral theory has begun to address the right questions at issue here. When are intimate actions owed to generic others? How do we weigh the sacrifice morality requires of us when it is measured, not in terms of risk, but of intertwinement? What should we think of such obligations if the required acts would be performed under conditions of profound self-alienation? The *type* of issue paradigmatically represented by gestation—an assistance that combines life and death stakes with deep intimacy—is virtually nowhere discussed in ethical theory. (We are not called upon in the usual course of events to save people's lives by, say, having sexual intercourse with them.) By ignoring these issues, mainstream moral theory has ended up deeply underselling the moral complexity of abortion.

Difficult as these questions are, though, it is actually a second issue, I suspect, that is responsible for much of the passion that surrounds abortion on supposition of fetal personhood. On reflection, many will say, the issues confronting the pregnant woman are not about generic beneficence at all. The considerations she faces are not just those that would face someone uniquely well placed to serve as Good Samaritan to some stranger, as when one passes the drowning person: for the pregnant woman and fetus, crucially, are not strangers. If the fetus is a person, many will say, it is *her child*; and for this reason she has special responsibilities to meet its needs. In the end, I believe, much of the animating concern with abortion is not about what we owe to generic others; it is about what parents owe their children.

But if it is parenthood that is carrying normative weight, then we need an ethics of parenthood—a theory of what makes someone a parent in this thickly normative sense and what the contours of its responsibilities really are. This should raise something of a warning flag. Philosophers, it must be said, have by and large done a rather poor job when it comes to parenthood, variously avoiding it, romanticizing it, or assimilating it to categories, like contractual relations, to which it stands in paradigmatic contrast. This general shortcoming is evident in discussions of abortion, where two remarkably unhelpful models dominate.

One position, advocated by Judith Thomson and some of the most recent treatments of abortion, is a classically liberal one. It agrees that special responsibilities attach to parenthood but argues that parenthood is thereby a status that is entered into only by consent. That consent is usually tacit, to be sure: taking the baby home from the hospital qualifies. None the less, special responsibilities to a child accrue only when one voluntarily assumes them.

Such a model is surely an odd one. The model yields the plausible view that the rape victim does not face the very same set of duties as many other pregnant women, but it does so by implying that a man who fathers a child during a one-night stand has no special responsibilities toward that child unless he decides he does. Perhaps most strikingly, such a view has no resources for acknowledging that there may be moral reasons why one *should* consent to the status. Those who sustain a biological connection may have a tendency to enter the role of parent, but on this scheme it is a mere psychological proclivity that rides atop nothing normative.

Another position is classically conservative. According to this view, the special responsibilities of parenthood are grounded in biological progenitorship. It is blood ties, to use the old-fashioned vernacular—"passing on one's genes," in more current translation—that makes one a parent and grounds heightened responsibilities. This view has its own blind spot. It has the resources for agreeing that a man who fathers a child from a one-night stand faces special responsibilities for the child whether he likes it or not, but none for distinguishing between the responsibilities of someone who has served as the special steward for a child—who has engaged for years in the *activity* of parenting—and the responsibilities to someone who bears literally no connection beyond a genetic or causal contribution to existence. On this view, a sperm donor faces all the responsibilities of a social father.

What both positions have in common is the supposition that parenthood is an all-or-nothing affair. Applied to pregnancy, the gestating woman either owes everything we imagine we owe to the children we love and rear or she owes nothing beyond general beneficence unless she decides she does. But parenthood—like all familial relations—is surely a more complicated moral notion than this. Parenthood, and its attendant responsibilities, admits of *layers*. It has a crucial existence as a social *role*: something with institutionally defined entrances, exits, and expectations that can attach us quite independently of what our self-conceptions might say. It also has a crucial existence as a *relationship*, an emotional connection, a shared history, an intertwinement of lives. it is because of that intertwinement that parents' motivation to sacrifice is so often immediate. But it is also because of that relationship that even especially ambitious sacrifices are legitimately expected, and why failure to undertake them would be so problematic: absent unusual circumstances, it becomes a betrayal of the relationship itself. In short, parenthood is not monolithic: some of the responsibilities we paradigmatically associate as parental attach, not to the role, but to the relationship that so often accompanies it.

These layers matter especially when we get to gestation, for the pregnant woman stands precisely at their intersection. If a fetus is a person, then there is surely an important sense in which she is its mother: to regard her as just a passing stranger uniquely able to help it would grossly distort the situation. But she is not yet a mother most thickly described—a mother in standing relationship with a child, with the responsibilities born of shared history and the enterprise of caretaking.

These demarcations are integral, I think, to understanding the distinctive sorts of conflicts that pregnancy can represent, including, most notably, the conflicts it can bring *within* the mantle of motherhood. Women sometimes decide to abort, even though they regard the fetus they carry as their child, because they realize, grimly, that bringing the child into the world will leave too little room to care adequately for the children they are already raising. This is a conflict we cannot even name, much less arbitrate, on standard views: if the fetus is her child, how could she possibly choose to sacrifice its life unless the stakes are literally equivalent for the others? But this is to ignore the layers of parenthood. She occupies the role of mother to the fetus, but with the other children, she is, by dint of time, interaction, and intertwinement, in a relationship of motherhood. The fetus is her baby, then, not just some passing stranger she alone can help, which is why this conflict brings the kind of agony it does. But if it is her child in the role sense only, she does not yet owe all that she owes to her other children. Depending on the circumstances, other family members with whom she is already in relationship may, tragically, come first.

None of this is to make light of the responsibilities pregnant women face on supposition of fetal personhood. If fetuses are persons, such responsibilities are surely profound. It is, rather, to insist that they admit of layer and degree, and that these distinctions, while delicate, are crucial to capturing the *types* of tragedy—and the types of moral compromise—abortion can here represent.

THE SANCTITY OF LIFE: RESPECT REVISITED

Just as we cannot assume that abortion is monstrous if fetuses are persons, so too we cannot assume that abortion is empty of moral import if they are not. Given all the ink that has been split on arbitrating the question of fetal personhood, one might be forgiven for having thought so: on some accounts, decisions about whether to continue or end a pregnancy really are, from a moral point of view, just like decisions about whether to cut one's hair.

But as Ronald Dworkin (1993) has urged, to think abortion morally weighty does not require supposition that the fetus is a person, or even a creature with interests in continued life. Destruction of a Da Vinci painting, he points out, is not bad *for the painting*—the painting has no interests. Instead, it is regrettable because of the deep value it has. So, too, one of the reasons we might regard abortion as morally weighty does not have to do with its being bad *for the fetus*—a setback to its interests—for it may not satisfy the criteria of having interests. Abortion may be weighty, instead, because there is something precious and significant about germinating human life that deserves our deep respect. This, as Dworkin puts it, locates issues of abortion in a different neighborhood of our moral commitments: namely, the accommodation we owe to things of value. That an organism is a potential person may not make it a claims-bearer, but it does mean it has a kind of stature that is worthy of respect.

This intuition, dismissed by some as mere sentimentality, is, I think, both important and broadly held. Very few people regard abortion as the moral equivalent of contraception. Most think a society better morally—not just by public health measures—if it regards abortion as a back-up to failed contraception rather than as routine birth control. Reasons adequate for contraception do not translate transparently as reasons adequate for abortion. Indeed, there is a telling shift in presumption: for most people, it takes no reason at all to justify contracepting; it takes *some* reason to justify ending a pregnancy. That a human life has now begun matters morally.

Burgeoning human life, we might put it, is *respect-worthy*. This is why we care not just whether, but how, abortion is done—while crass jokes are made or with solemnity—and why we care how the fetal remains are treated. It is why the thought of someone aborting for genuinely trivial reasons—to fit into a favorite party dress, say—makes us morally queasy. Perhaps, most basically, it is why the thought of someone aborting with casual indifference fills us with misgiving. Abortion involves loss. Not just loss of the hope that various parties might have invested, but loss of something valuable in its own right. To respect something is to appreciate fully the value it has and the claims it presents to us; someone who aborts but never gives it a second thought has not exhibited genuine appreciation of the value and moral status of that which is now gone.

But if many share the intuition that early human life has a value deserving of respect, there is considerable disagreement about what that respect looks like. There is considerable conflict, that is, over what accommodation we owe to burgeoning human life. In part, of course, this is due to disagreement over the *degree* of value such life should be accorded: those for whom it is thoroughly modest will have very different views on issues, from abortion to stem-cell research, from those for whom it is transcendent. But this is only part of the story. Obscured by analogies to Da Vinci paintings, some of the most important sources of conflict, especially for the vast middle rank of moderates, ride atop rough agreement on "degree" of fetal value. If we listen to women's own struggles about when it is morally decent to end pregnancy, what we hear are themes about *motherhood* and *respect for creation*. These themes are enormously complex, I want to argue, for they enter stories on both sides of the ledger: for some women, as reasons to continue pregnancy, and, for others, as reasons to end it. Let me start with motherhood.

For many women who contemplate abortion, the desire to end pregnancy is not, or not centrally, a desire to avoid the nine months of pregnancy; it is to avoid what lies on the far side of those months—namely, motherhood. If gestation were simply a matter of rendering, say, somewhat risky assistance to help a burgeoning human life they have come across—if they could somehow render that assistance without thereby adding a member to their family—the decision faced would be a far different one. But gestation does not just allow cells to become a person; it turns one into a mother.

One of the most common reasons women give for wanting to abort is that they do not want to become a mother—now, ever, again, with this partner, or no reliable partner, with these few resources, or these many that are now, after so many years of mothering, slated finally to another cause (Hursthouse, 1987: ch. 8.4). Nor does adoption represent a universal solution. To give up a child would be for some a lifelong trauma; others occupy fortunate circumstances that would, by their own lights, make it unjustified to give over a child for others to rear. Or again—and most frequently—she does not want to raise a child just now but knows that if she *does* carry the pregnancy to term, she will not *want* to give up the child for adoption. Gestation, she knows, is likely to reshape her heart and soul, transforming her into a mother emotionally, not just officially; and it is precisely that transformation she does not want to undergo. It is because continuing pregnancy brings with it this new identity and, likely, relationship, then, that many feel it legitimate to decline.

But pregnancy's connection to motherhood also enters the phenomenology of abortion in just the opposite direction. For some women, that it would be her child is precisely why she feels she must continue the pregnancy, even if motherhood is not what she desired. To be pregnant is to have one's potential child knocking at one's door; to abort is to turn one's back on it, a decision, many women say, that would haunt them forever. On this view, the desire to avoid motherhood, so compelling as a reason to use contraception, is uneasy grounds to abort: for once an embryo is on the scene, it is not about rejecting motherhood, it is about rejecting one's *child*. Not literally, of course, since there is no child yet extant to stand as the object of rejection. But the stance one should take to pregnancy, sought or not, is one of *acceptance*: when a potential family member is knocking at the door, one should move over, make room, and welcome her in.

These two intuitive stances represent just profoundly different ways of *gestalting* the situation of ending pregnancy. On the first view, abortion is closer to contraception: hardly equivalent, because it means the demise of something of value. But the desire to avoid the enterprise and identity of motherhood is an understandable and honorable basis for deciding to end a pregnancy. Given that there is no child yet on the scene, one does not owe special openness to the relationship that stands at the end of pregnancy's trajectory. On the second view, abortion is closer to exiting a parental relationship: hardly equivalent, for one of the key relata is not yet fully present. But one's decision about whether to continue the pregnancy already feels specially constrained; that one would be related to the resulting person exerts now some moral force. It would take especially grave reasons to refuse assistance here, for the norms of parenthood already have toehold. Assessing the moral status of abortion, it turns out, then, is not just about assessing the contours of generic respect owed to burgeoning human life, it is about assessing the salience of *impending relationship*. And this is an issue that functions in different ways for different women—and, sometimes, in one and the same woman.

In my own view, until the fetus is a person, we should recognize a moral prerogative to decline parenthood and end the pregnancy. Not because motherhood is necessarily a burden (though it can be), but because it so thoroughly changes what we might call one's fundamental *practical identity*. The enterprise of mothering restructures the self—changing the shape of one's heart, the primary commitments by which one lives one's life, the terms by which one judges one's life a success or a failure. If the enterprise is eschewed and one decides to give the child over to another, the identity of mother still changes the normative facts that are true of one, as there is now someone by whom one does well or poorly (see Ross, 1982). And either way—whether one rears the child or lets it go—to continue a pregnancy means that a piece of one's heart, as the saying goes, will forever walk outside one's body. As profound as the respect we should have for burgeoning human life, we should acknowledge moral prerogatives over identity-constituting commitments and enterprises as profound as motherhood.

Whether one agrees with this view or not, there is at any rate another layer of the moral story here. If women find themselves with different ways of *gestalting* the prospective relationship involved in pregnancy, it is in part because they have different identities, commitments, and ideals that such a prospect intersects with, commitments which, while permissibly idiosyncratic, re morally authoritative for *them*. If one woman feels already duty-bound by the norms of parenthood to nurture this creature, for example, it may be for the very good reason that, in an important personal sense, she already *is* its mother. She finds herself (perhaps to her surprise) with a maternal commitment to this creature. But taking on the identity of mother toward something just *is* to take on certain imperatives about its well-being as categorical. Her job is thus clear: it is to help this creature reach its fullest potential. For another woman, on the other hand, the identity of mother is yet to be taken on; it is tried on, perhaps accepted, but perhaps declined—in which case respect is owed, but love is saved, or confirmed, for others—other relationships, other projects, other passions.

And, again, if one woman feels she owes a stance of welcome to burgeoning human life that comes her way, it may be, not because she thinks such a stance authoritative for all, but because of the virtues around which her practical identity is now oriented: receptivity to life's agenda, for instance, or responsiveness to that which is most vulnerable. For another woman, the virtues to be exercised may tug in just the other direction: loyalty to treasured life plans, a commitment that it be she, not the chances of biology, that should determine her life's course, bolstering self-direction after a life too long ruled by serendipity and fate.

Deciding when it is morally decent to end a pregnancy, it turns out, is an admixture of setting impersonally or universally authoritative moral requirements, and of discovering and arbitrating—sometimes after agonizing deliberation, sometimes in a decision no less deep for its immediacy—one's own commitments, identity, and defining virtues.

A similarly complex story appears when we turn to the second theme. Another thread that appears in many women's stories in the face of unsought pregnancy is respect for the weighty responsibility involved in creating human life. Once again, it is a theme that pulls and tugs in different directions.

In its most familiar direction, it shows up in many stories of why an unsought pregnancy is continued. Many people believe that one's responsibility to nurture new life is importantly amplified if one is responsible for bringing about its existence in the first place. Just what it takes to count as responsible here is a

point on which individuals diverge (whether voluntary intercourse with contraception is different from intercourse without use of birth control, and again from intentionally deciding to become pregnant at the IVF clinic). But triggering the relevant standard of responsibility for creation, it is felt, brings with it a heightened responsibility to nurture: it is disrespectful to create human life only to allow it to wither. Put more rigorously, one who is responsible for bringing about a creature that has intrinsic value in virtue of its potential to become a person has a special responsibility to enable it to reach that end state.

But the idea of respect for creation is also, if less frequently acknowledged, sometimes the reason why women are moved to *end* pregnancies. As Barbara Katz Rothman (1989) puts it, decisions to abort often represent, not a decision to destroy, but a refusal to create. Many people have deeply felt convictions about the circumstances under which they feel it right for them to bring a child into the world. Can it be brought into a decent world, an intact family, a society that can minimally respect its agency? These considerations may persist even after conception has taken place; for while the *embryo* has already been created, a person has not. Some women decide to abort, that is, not because they do not *want* the resulting child—indeed, they may yearn for nothing more, and desperately wish that their circumstances were otherwise—but because they do not think bringing a child into the world the right thing for them to do.

These are abortions marked by moral language. A woman wants to abort because she knows she could not give up a child for adoption but feels she could not give the child the sort of life, or be the sort of parent, she thinks a child *deserves*; a woman who would have to give up the child thinks it would be *unfair* to bring a child into existence already burdened by rejection, however well grounded its reasons; a woman living in a country marked by poverty and gender apartheid wants to abort because she decides it would be *wrong* for her to bear a daughter whose life, like hers, would be filled with so much injustice and hardship.

Some have thought that such decisions betray a simple fallacy: unless the child's life were literally going to be worse than non-existence, how can one abort out of concern for the future child? But the worry here is not that one would be imposing a *harm* on the child by bringing it into existence (as though children who are in the situations mentioned have lives that are not worth living). The claim is that bringing about a person's life in these circumstances would do violence to her ideals of creating and parenthood. She does not want to bring into existence a daughter she cannot love and care for, she does not want to bring into existence a person whose life will be marked by disrespect or rejection.

Nor does the claim imply judgment on women who *do* continue pregnancies in similar circumstances—as though there were here an obligation to abort. For the norms in question, once again, need not be impersonally authoritative moral claims. Like ideals of good parenting, they mark out considerations all should be sensitive to, perhaps, but equally reasonable people may adhere to different variations and weightings. Still, they are normative for those who do have them; far from expressing mere matters of taste, the ideals one does accept carry an important kind of categoricity, issuing imperatives whose authority is not reducible to mere desire. These are, at root, issues about *integrity*, and the importance of maintaining integrity over one's participation in this enterprise precisely because it is so normatively weighty.

What is usually emphasized in the morality of abortion is the ethics of destruction, but there is a balancing ethics of creation. And for many people, conflict about abortion is a conflict *within* that ethics. On the one hand, we now have on hand an entity that has a measure of sanctity: that it has begun is reason to help it continue, perhaps especially if one has had a role in its procreation, which is why even early abortion is not normatively equivalent to contraception. On the other hand, not to end a pregnancy *is* to do something else, namely, to continue creating a person, and, for some women, pregnancy strikes in circumstances in which they cannot countenance that enterprise. For some, the sanctity of developing human life will be strong enough to tip the balance toward continuing the pregnancy; for others, their norms of respectful creation will hold sway. For those who believe that the norms governing creation of a person are mild relative to the normative telos of embryonic life, being a responsible creator means continuing to gestate, and doing the best one can to bring about the conditions under which that creation will be more respectful. For others, though, the normativity of fetal telos is mild and their standards of respectful creation high, and the lesson goes in just the other direction: it is a sign of respect not to continue creating when certain background conditions, such as a loving family or adequate resources, are not in place.

However one thinks these issues settle out, they will not be resolved by austere contemplation of the value of human life. They require wrestling with the rich meanings of creation, responsibility, and kinship. And these issues, I have suggested, are just as much issues about one's integrity as they are about what is impersonally obligatory. On many treatments of abortion, considerations about whether or not to continue a pregnancy are exhausted by preferences, on the one hand, and universally authoritative moral demands, on the other; but some of the most important terrain lies in between.

REFERENCES

Bolton, M. B. (1979) Responsible women and abortion decisions. In O. O'Neill and W. Ruddick (eds), *Having Children*. New York: Oxford University Press.

Brody, B. (1975) *Abortion and the Sanctity of Life*. Cambridge, MA: MIT Press.

Dworkin, R. (1993) *Life's Dominion: An Argument about Abortion, Euthanasia, and Individual Freedom*. New York: Alfred A. Knopf.

Feinberg, J. (1992) Abortion. In *Freedom and Fulfillment: Philosophical Essays*. Princeton, NJ: Princeton University Press.

Hursthouse, R. (1987) *Beginning Lives*. Oxford: Open University Press.

Kamm, F. M. (1992) *Creation and Abortion: A Study in Moral and Legal Philosophy*. New York: Oxford University Press.

MacKinnon, C. A. (1991) Reflections on sex equality under law. *The Yale Law Journal,* 100 (5): 1281–328.

Marquis, D. (1989) Why abortion is immoral. *The Journal of Philosophy,* 76: 183–202.

Quinn, W. (1993) Abortion: identity and loss. In *Morality and Action.* New York: Cambridge University Press.

Ross, S. L. (1982) Abortion and the death of the fetus. *Philosophy and Public Affairs,* 11: 232–45.

Rothman, B. K. (1989) *Recreating Motherhood: Ideology and Technology in a Patriarchal Society.* New York: Norton.

Silverstein, H. S. (1987) On a woman's "responsibility" for the fetus. *Social Theory and Practice,* 13: 103–19.

Steinbock, B. (1992) *Life before Birth: The Moral and Legal Status of Embryos and Fetuses.* New York: Oxford University Press.

Thomson, J. J. (1971) A defense of abortion. *Philosophy and Public Affairs,* 1: 47–66.

West, R. (1993) Jurisprudence and gender. In D. Kelly Weisberg (ed.), *Feminist Legal Theory: Foundations,* pp. 75–98. Philadelphia: Temple University Press.

An Almost Absolute Value in History

John T. Noonan Jr.

The most fundamental question involved in the long history of thought on abortion is: How do you determine the humanity of a being? To phrase the question that way is to put in comprehensive humanistic terms what the theologians either dealt with as an explicitly theological question under the heading of "ensoulment" or dealt with implicitly in their treatment of abortion. The Christian position as it originated did not depend on a narrow theological or philosophical concept. It had no relation to theories of infant baptism. It appealed to no special theory of instantaneous ensoulment. It took the world's view on ensoulment as that view changed from Aristotle to Zacchia. There was, indeed, theological influence affecting the theory of ensoulment finally adopted, and, of course, ensoulment itself was a theological concept, so that the position was always explained in theological terms. But the theological notion of ensoulment could easily be translated into humanistic language by substituting "human" for "rational soul"; the problem of knowing when a man is a man is common to theology and humanism.

John T. Noonan, "An Almost Absolute Value in History," in *The Morality of Abortion* (Cambridge, MA: Harvard University Press, 1970), 51–59 (edited). Reprinted with permission of Harvard University Press.

If one steps outside the specific categories used by the theologians, the answer they gave can be analyzed as a refusal to discriminate among human beings on the basis of their varying potentialities. Once conceived, the being was recognized as man because he had man's potential. The criterion for humanity, thus, was simple and all-embracing: if you are conceived by human parents, you are human.

The strength of this position may be tested by a review of some of the other distinctions offered in the contemporary controversy over legalizing abortion. Perhaps the most popular distinction is in terms of viability. Before an age of so many months, the fetus is not viable, that is, it cannot be removed from the mother's womb and live apart from her. To that extent, the life of the fetus is absolutely dependent on the life of the mother. This dependence is made the basis of denying recognition to its humanity.

There are difficulties with this distinction. One is that the perfection of artificial incubation may make the fetus viable at any time: it may be removed and artificially sustained. Experiments with animals already show that such a procedure is possible. This hypothetical extreme case relates to an actual difficulty: there is considerable elasticity to the idea of viability. Mere length of life is not an exact measure.

The viability of the fetus depends on the exent of its anatomical and functional development. The weight and length of the fetus are better guides to the state of its development than age, but weight and length vary. Moreover, different racial groups have different ages at which their fetuses are viable. Some evidence, for example, suggests that Negro fetuses mature more quickly than white fetuses. If viability is the norm, the standard would vary with race and with many individual circumstances.

The most important objection to this approach is that dependence is not ended by viability. The fetus is still absolutely dependent on someone's care in order to continue existence; indeed a child of one or three or even five years of age is absolutely dependent on another's care for existence; uncared for, the older fetus or the younger child will die as surely as the early fetus detached from the mother. The unsubstantial lessening in dependence at viability does not seem to signify any special acquisition of humanity.

A second distinction has been attempted in terms of experience. A being who has had experience, has lived and suffered, who possesses memories, is more human than one who has not. Humanity depends on formation by experience. The fetus is thus "unformed" in the most basic human sense.

This distinction is not serviceable for the embryo which is already experiencing and reacting. The embryo is responsive to touch after eight weeks and at least at that point is experiencing. At an earlier stage the zygote is certainly alive and responding to its environment. The distinction may also be challenged by the rare case where aphasia has erased adult memory: has it erased humanity? More fundamentally, this distinction leaves even the older fetus or the younger child to be treated as an unformed inhuman thing. Finally, it is not clear why experience as such confers humanity. It could be argued that certain central experiences such as loving or learning are necessary to make a man human. But then human beings who have failed to love or to learn might be excluded from the class called man.

A third distinction is made by appeal to the sentiments of adults. If a fetus dies, the grief of the parents is not the grief they would have for a living child. The fetus is an unnamed "it" till birth, and is not perceived as personality until at least the fourth month of existence when movements in the womb manifest a vigorous presence demanding joyful recognition by the parents.

Yet feeling is notoriously an unsure guide to the humanity of others. Many groups of humans have had difficulty in feeling that persons of another tongue, color, religion, sex, are as human as they. Apart from reactions to alien groups, we mourn the loss of a ten-year-old boy more than the loss of his one-day-old brother or his 90-year-old grandfather. The difference felt and the grief expressed vary with the potentialities extinguished, or the experience wiped out; they do not seem to point to any substantial difference in the humanity of baby, boy, or grandfather.

Distinctions are also made in terms of sensation by the parents. The embryo is felt within the womb only after about the fourth month. The embryo is seen only at birth. What can be neither seen nor felt is different from what is tangible. If the fetus cannot be seen or touched at all, it cannot be perceived as man.

Yet experience shows that sight is even more untrustworthy than feeling in determining humanity. By sight, color became an appropriate index for saying who was a man, and the evil of racial discrimination was given foundation. Nor can touch provide the test; a being confined by sickness, "out of touch" with others, does not thereby seem to lose his humanity. To the extent that touch still has appeal as a criterion, it appears to be a survival of the old English idea of "quickening"—a possible mistranslation of the Latin *animatus* used in the canon law. To that extent touch as a criterion seems to be dependent on the Aristotelian notion of ensoulment, and to fall when this notion is discarded.

Finally, a distinction is sought in social visibility. The fetus is not socially perceived as human. It cannot communicate with others. Thus, both subjectively and objectively, it is not a member of society. As moral rules are rules for the behavior of members of society to each other, they cannot be made for behavior toward what is not yet a member. Excluded from the society of men, the fetus is excluded from the humanity of men.

By force of the argument from the consequences, this distinction is to be rejected. It is more subtle than that founded on an appeal to physical sensation, but it is equally dangerous in its implications. If humanity depends on social recognition, individuals or whole groups may be dehumanized by being denied any status in their society. Such a fate is fictionally portrayed in *1984* and has actually been the lot of many men in many societies. In the Roman empire, for example, condemnation to slavery meant the practical denial of most human rights; in the Chinese Communist world, landlords have been classified as enemies of the people and so treated as nonpersons by the state. Humanity does not depend on social recognition, though often the failure of society to recognize the prisoner, the alien, the heterodox as human has led to the destruction of human beings. Anyone conceived by a man and a woman is human. Recognition of this condition by society follows a real event in the objective order, however imperfect and halting the recognition. Any attempt to limit humanity to exclude some group runs the risk of furnishing authority and precedent for excluding other groups in the name of the consciousness or perception of the controlling group in the society.

A philosopher may reject the appeal to the humanity of the fetus because he views "humanity" as a secular view of the soul and because he doubts the existence of anything real and objective which can be identified as humanity. One answer to such a philosopher is to ask how he reasons about moral questions without supposing that there is a sense in which he and the others of whom he speaks are human. Whatever group is taken as the society which determines who may be killed is thereby taken as human. A second answer is to ask if he does believe that there is a right and wrong way of deciding moral questions. If there is such a difference, experience may be appealed to: to decide who is human on the basis of the sentiment of a given society has led to consequences which rational men would characterize as monstrous.

The rejection of the attempted distinctions based on viability and visibility, experience and feeling, may be buttressed by the following considerations: Moral judgments often rest on distinctions, but if the distinctions are not to appear arbitrary fiat, they should relate to some real difference in probabilities. There is a kind of continuity in all life, but the earlier stages of the elements of human life possess tiny probabilities of development. Consider for example, the spermatozoa in any normal ejaculate: There are about 200,000,000 in any single ejaculate, of which one has a chance of developing into a zygote. Consider the oocytes which may become ova: there are 100,000 to 1,000,000 oocytes in a female infant, of which a maximum of 390 are ovulated. But once spermatozoon and ovum meet and the conceptus is formed, such studies as have been made show that roughly in only 20 percent of the cases will spontaneous abortion occur. In other words, the chances are about 4 out of 5 that this new being will develop. At this stage in the life of the being there is a sharp shift in probabilities, an immense jump in potentialities. To make a distinction between the rights of spermatozoa and the rights of the fertilized ovum is to respond to an enormous shift in possibilities. For about twenty days after conception the egg may split to form twins or combine with another egg to form a chimera, but the probability of either event happening is very small.

It may be asked, What does a change in biological probabilities have to do with establishing humanity? The argument from probabilities is not aimed at establishing humanity but at establishing an objective discontinuity which may be taken into account in moral discourse. As life itself is a matter of probabilities, as most moral reasoning is an estimate of probabilities, so it seems in accord with the structure of reality and the nature of moral thought to found a moral judgment on the change in probabilities at conception. The appeal to probabilities is the most commensensical of arguments, to a greater or small degree all of us base our actions on probabilities, and in morals, as in law, prudence and negligence are often measured by the account one has taken of the probabilities. If the chance is 200,000,000 to 1 that the movement in the bushes into which you shoot is a man's, I doubt if many persons would hold you careless in shooting; but if the chances are 4 out of 5 that the movement is a human being's, few would acquit you of blame. Would the argument be different if only one out of ten children conceived came to term? Of course this argument would be different. This argument is an appeal to probabilities that actually exist, not to any and all states of affairs which may be imagined.

The probabilities as they do exist do not show the humanity of the embryo in the sense of a demonstration in logic any more than the probabilities of the movement in the bush being a man demonstrate beyond all doubt that the being is a man. The appeal is a "buttressing" consideration, showing the plausibility of the standard adopted. The argument focuses on the decisional factor in any moral judgment and assumes that part of the business of a moralist is drawing lines. One evidence of the nonarbitrary character of the line drawn is the difference of probabilities on either side of it. If a spermatozoon is destroyed, one destroys a being which had a chance of far less than 1 in 200 million of developing into a reasoning being, possessed of the genetic code, a heart and other organs, and capable of pain. If a fetus is destroyed, one destroys a being already possessed of the genetic code, organs, and sensitivity to pain, and one which had an 80 percent chance of developing further into a baby outside the womb who, in time, would reason.

The positive argument for conception as the decisive moment of humanization is that at conception the new being receives the genetic code. It is this genetic information which determines his characteristics, which is the biological carrier of the possibility of human wisdom, which makes him a self-evolving being. A being with a human genetic code is man.

This review of current controversy over the humanity of the fetus emphasizes what a fundamental question the theologians resolved in asserting the inviolability of the fetus. To regard the fetus as possessed of equal rights with other humans was not, however, to decide every case where abortion might be employed. It did decide the case where the argument was that the fetus should be aborted for its own good. To say a being was human was to say it had a destiny to decide for itself which could not be taken from it by another man's decision. But human beings with equal rights often come in conflict with each other, and some decision must be made as whose claims are to prevail. Cases of conflict involving the fetus are different only in two respects: the total inability of the fetus to speak for itself and the fact that the right of the fetus regularly at stake is the right to life itself.

The approach taken by the theologians to these conflicts was articulated in terms of "direct" and "indirect." Again, to look at what they were doing from outside their categories, they may be said to have been drawing lines or "balancing values." "Direct" and "indirect" are spatial metaphors; "line-drawing" is another. "To weigh" or "to balance" values is a metaphor of a more complicated mathematical sort hinting at the process which goes on in moral judgments. All the metaphors suggest that, in the moral judgments made, comparisons were necessary, that no value completely controlled. The principle of double effect was no doctrine fallen from heaven, but a method of analysis appropriate where two relative values were being compared. In Catholic moral theology, as it developed, life even of the innocent was not taken as an absolute. Judgments on acts affecting life issued from a process of weighing. In the weighing, the fetus was always given a value greater than zero, always a value separate and independent from its parents. This valuation was crucial and fundamental in all Christian thought on the subject and marked it off from any approach which considered that only the parents' interests needed to be considered.

Even with the fetus weighed as human, one interest could be weighed as equal or superior: that of the mother in her own life. The casuists between 1450 and 1895 were wiling to weigh this interest as superior. Since 1895, that interest was given decisive weight only in the two special cases of the cancerous uterus and the ectopic pregnancy. In both of these cases the fetus itself had little chance of survival even if the abortion were not performed. As the balance was once struck in favor of the mother whenever her life was endangered, it could be so struck again. The balance reached between 1895 and 1930 attempted prudentially and pastorally to forestall a multitude of exceptions for interests less than life.

The perception of the humanity of the fetus and the weighing of fetal rights against other human rights constituted the work of the moral analysts. But what spirit animated their abstract judgments? For the Christian community it was the injunction of Scripture to love your neighbor as yourself. The fetus as human was a neighbor; his life had parity with one's own. The commandment gave life to what otherwise would have been only rational calculation.

The commandment could be put in humanistic as well as theological terms: Do not injure your fellow man without reason. In these terms, once the humanity of the fetus is perceived, abortion is never right except in self-defense. When life must be taken to save life, reason alone cannot say that a mother must prefer a child's life to her own. With this exception, now of great rarity, abortion violates the rational humanist tenet of the equality of human lives.

For Christians the commandment to love had received a special imprint in that the examplar proposed of love was the love of the Lord for this disciples. In the light given by this example, self-sacrifice carried to the point of death seemed in the extreme situations not without meaning. In the less extreme cases, preference for one's own interests to the life of another seemed to express cruelty or selfishness irreconcilable with the demands of love.

Virtue Theory and Abortion

ROSALIND HURSTHOUSE

* * *

As everyone knows, the morality of abortion is commonly discussed in relation to just two considerations: first, and predominantly, the status of the fetus and whether or not it is the sort of thing that may or may not be innocuously or justifiably killed; and second, and less predominantly (when, that is, the discussion concerns the *morality* of abortion rather than the question of permissible legislation in a just society), women's rights. If one thinks within this familiar framework, one may well be puzzled about what virtue theory, as such, could contribute. Some people assume the discussion will be conducted solely in terms of what the virtuous agent would or would not do * * * . Others assume that only justice, or at most justice and charity, will be applied to the issue, generating a discussion very similar to Judith Jarvis Thomson's.[1]

Rosalind Hursthouse, "Virtue Theory and Abortion," *Philosophy & Public Affairs* 20, no. 3 (Summer 1991): 223–46 (edited). Reprinted with permission of Blackwell Publishing.

Now if this is the way the virtue theorist's discussion of abortion is imagined to be, no wonder people think little of it. It seems obvious in advance that in any such discussion there must be either a great deal of extremely tendentious application of the virtue terms *just, charitable,* and so on or a lot of rhetorical appeal to "this is what only the virtuous agent knows." But these are caricatures; they fail to appreciate the way in which virtue theory quite transforms the discussion of abortion by dismissing the two familiar dominating considerations as, in a way, fundamentally irrelevant. In what way or ways, I hope to make both clear and plausible.

Let us first consider women's rights. Let me emphasize again that we are discussing the *morality* of abortion, not the rights and wrongs of laws prohibiting or permitting it. If we suppose that women do have a moral right to do as they choose with their own bodies, or, more particularly, to terminate their pregnancies, then it may well follow that a *law* forbidding abortion would be unjust. Indeed, even if they have no such right, such a law might be, as things stand at the moment, unjust, or impractical, or inhumane: on this issue I have nothing to say in this article. But, putting all questions about the justice or injustice of laws to one side, and supposing only that women have such a moral right, *nothing* follows from this supposition about the morality of abortion, according to virtue theory, once it is noted (quite generally, not with particular reference to abortion) that in exercising a moral right I can do something cruel, or callous, or selfish, light-minded, self-righteous, stupid, inconsiderate, disloyal, dishonest—that is, act viciously.[2] Love and friendship do not survive their parties' constantly insisting on their rights, nor do people live well when they think that getting what they have a right to is of preeminent importance; they harm others, and they harm themselves. So whether women have a moral right to terminate their pregnancies is irrelevant within virtue theory, for it is irrelevant to the question "In having an abortion in these circumstances, would the agent be acting virtuously or viciously or neither?"

What about the consideration of the status of the fetus—what can virtue theory say about that? One might say that this issue is not in the province of *any* moral theory; it is a metaphysical question, and an extremely difficult one at that. Must virtue theory then wait upon metaphysics to come up with the answer?

At first sight it might seem so. For virtue is said to involve knowledge, and part of this knowledge consists in having the *right* attitude to things. "Right" here does not just mean "morally right" or "proper" or "nice" in the modern sense; it means "accurate, true." One cannot have the right or correct attitude to something if the attitude is based on or involves false beliefs. And this suggests that if the status of the fetus is relevant to the rightness or wrongness of abortion, its status must be known, as a truth, to the fully wise and virtuous person.

But the sort of wisdom that the fully virtuous person has is not supposed to be recondite; it does not call for fancy philosophical sophistication, and it does not depend upon, let alone wait upon, the discoveries of academic philosophers.[3] And this entails

the following, rather startling, conclusion: that the status of the fetus—that issue over which so much ink has been spilt—is, according to virtue theory, simply not relevant to the rightness or wrongness of abortion (within, that is, a secular morality).

Or rather, since that is clearly too radical a conclusion, it is in a sense relevant, but only in the sense that the familiar biological facts are relevant. By "the familiar biological facts" I mean the facts that most human societies are and have been familiar with—that, standardly (but not invariably), pregnancy occurs as the result of sexual intercourse, that it lasts about nine months, during which time the fetus grows and develops, that standardly it terminates in the birth of a living baby, and that this is how we all come to be.

It might be thought that this distinction—between the familiar biological facts and the status of the fetus—is a distinction without a difference. But this is not so. To attach relevance to the status of the fetus, in the sense in which virtue theory claims it is not relevant, is to be gripped by the conviction that we must go beyond the familiar biological facts, deriving some sort of conclusion from them, such as that the fetus has rights, or is not a person, or something similar. It is also to believe that this exhausts the relevance of the familiar biological facts, that all they are relevant to is the status of the fetus and whether or not it is the sort of thing that may or may not be killed.

These convictions, I suspect, are rooted in the desire to solve the problem of abortion by getting it to fall under some general rule such as "You ought not to kill anything with the right to life but may kill anything else." But they have resulted in what should surely strike any nonphilosopher as a most bizarre aspect of nearly all the current philosophical literature on abortion, namely, that, far from treating abortion as a unique moral problem, markedly unlike any other, nearly everything written on the status of the fetus and its bearing on the abortion issue would be consistent with the human reproductive facts (to say nothing of family life) being totally different from what they are. Imagine that you are an alien extraterrestrial anthropologist who does not know that the human race is roughly 50 percent female and 50 percent male, or that our only (natural) form of reproduction involves heterosexual intercourse, viviparous birth, and the female's (and only the female's) being pregnant for nine months, or that females are capable of childbearing from late childhood to late middle age, or that childbearing is painful, dangerous, and emotionally charged—do you think you would pick up these facts from the hundreds of articles written on the status of the fetus? I am quite sure you would not. And that, I think, shows that the current philosophical literature on abortion has got badly out of touch with reality.

Now if we are using virtue theory, our first question is not "What do the familiar biological facts show—what can be derived from then about the status of the fetus?" but "How do these facts figure in the practical reasoning, actions and passions, thoughts and reactions, of the virtuous and the non-virtuous? What is the mark of having the right attitude to these facts and what manifests having the wrong attitude to them?" This immediately makes essentially relevant not only all the facts about human reproduction I mentioned above, but a whole range of facts about our emotions in relation to them as well. I mean such facts as that human parents, both male and female, tend to care passionately about their offspring, and that family relationships are among the deepest and strongest in our lives—and, significantly, among the longest-lasting.

These facts make it obvious that pregnancy is not just one among many other physical conditions; and hence that anyone who genuinely believes that an abortion is comparable to a haircut or an appendectomy is mistaken.[4] The fact that the premature termination of a pregnancy is, in some sense, the cutting off of a new human life, and thereby, like the procreation of a new human life, connects with all our thoughts about human life and death, parenthood, and family relationships, must make it a serious matter. To disregard this fact about it, to think of abortion as nothing but the killing of something that does not matter, or as nothing but the exercise of some right or rights one has, or as the incidental means to some desirable state of affairs, is to do something callous and light-minded, the sort of thing that no virtuous and wise person would do. It is to have the wrong attitude not only to fetuses, but more generally to human life and death, parenthood, and family relationships.

Although I say that the facts make this obvious, I know that this is one of my tendentious points. In partial support of it I note that even the most dedicated proponents of the view that deliberate abortion is just like an appendectomy or haircut rarely hold the same view of spontaneous abortion, that is, miscarriage. It is not so tendentious of me to claim that to react to people's grief over miscarriage by saying, or even thinking, "What a fuss about nothing!" would be callous and light-minded, whereas to try to laugh someone out of grief over an appendectomy scar or a botched haircut would not be. It is hard to give this point due prominence within act-centered theories, for the inconsistency is an inconsistency in attitude about the seriousness of loss of life, not in beliefs about which acts are right or wrong. Moreover, an act-centered theorist may say, "Well, there is nothing wrong with *thinking* 'What a fuss about nothing!' as long as you do not say it and hurt the person who is grieving. And besides, we cannot be held responsible for our thoughts, only for the intentional actions they give rise to." But the character traits that virtue theory emphasizes are not simply dispositions to intentional actions, but a seamless disposition to certain actions and passions, thoughts and reactions.

To say that the cutting off of a human life is always a matter of some seriousness, at any stage, is not to deny the relevance of gradual fetal development. Notwithstanding the well-worn point that clear boundary lines cannot be drawn, our emotions and attitudes regarding the fetus do change as it develops, and again when it is born, and indeed further as the baby grows. Abortion for shallow reasons in the later stages is much more shocking than abortion for the same reasons in the early stages in a way that matches the fact that deep grief over miscarriage in the later stages is more appropriate than it is over miscarriage in the earlier stages (when, that is, the grief is solely about the loss of *this* child, not about, as might be the case, the loss of one's only hope of having a child or of having one's husband's child). Imagine (or recall) a woman who already has children; she had not intended to have more, but finds herself unexpectedly pregnant. Though contrary to her plans, the pregnancy, once established as a fact, is welcomed—and then she loses the embryo almost immediately. If this were bemoaned as a tragedy, it would, I think, be a misapplication of the concept of what is tragic. But it may still properly be mourned as a loss. The grief is expressed in such terms as "I shall always wonder how she or he would have turned out" or "When I look at the others, I shall think, 'How different their lives would have been if this other one had been part of them.'" It would, I take it, be callous and light-minded to say, or think, "Well, she has already *got* four children; what's the problem?"; it would be neither, nor arrogantly intrusive in the case of a close friend, to try to correct prolonged mourning by saying, "I know it's sad, but it's not a tragedy; rejoice in the ones you have." The application of *tragic* becomes more appropriate as the fetus grows, for the mere fact that one has lived with it for longer, conscious of its existence, makes a difference. To shrug off an early abortion is understandable just because it is very hard to be fully conscious of the fetus's existence in the early stages and hence hard to appreciate that an early abortion is the destruction of life. It is particularly hard for the young and inexperienced to appreciate this, because appreciation of it usually comes only with experience.

I do not mean "with the experience of having an abortion" (though that may be part of it) but, quite generally, "with the experience of life." Many women who have borne children contrast their later pregnancies with their first successful one, saying that in the later ones they were conscious of a new life growing in them from very early on. And, more generally, as one reaches the age at which the next generation is coming up close behind one, the counterfactuals "If I, or she, had had an abortion, Alice, or Bob, would not have been born" acquire a significant application, which casts a new light on the conditionals "If I or Alice have an abortion then some Caroline or Bill will not be born."

The fact that pregnancy is not just one among many physical conditions does not mean that one can never regard it in that light without manifesting a vice. When women are in very poor physical health, or worn out from childbearing, or forced to do very physically demanding jobs, then they cannot be described as self-indulgent, callous, irresponsible, or light-minded if they seek abortions mainly with a view to avoiding pregnancy as the physical condition that it is. To go through with a pregnancy when one is utterly exhausted, or when one's job consists of crawling along tunnels hauling coal, as many women in the nineteenth century were obliged to do, is perhaps heroic, but people who do not achieve heroism are not necessarily vicious. That they can view the pregnancy only as eight months of misery, followed by hours if not days of agony and exhaustion, and abortion only as the blessed escape from this prospect, is entirely understandable and does not manifest any lack of serious respect for human life or a shallow attitude or motherhood. What it does show is that something is terribly amiss in the conditions of their lives, which make it so hard to recognize pregnancy and childbearing as the good that they can be.

* * *

The foregoing discussion, insofar as it emphasizes the right attitude to human life and death, parallels to a certain extent those standard discussions of abortion that concentrate on it solely as an issue of killing. But it does not, as those discussions do, gloss over the fact, emphasized by those who discuss the morality of abortion in terms of women's rights, that abortion, wildly unlike any other form of killing, is the termination of a pregnancy, which is a condition of a woman's body and results in *her* having a child if it is not aborted. This fact is given due recognition not by appeal to women's rights but by emphasizing the relevance of the familiar biological and psychological facts and their connection with having the right attitude to parenthood and family relationships. But it may well be thought that failing to bring in women's rights still leaves some important aspects of the problem of abortion untouched.

Speaking in terms of women's rights, people sometimes say things like, "Well, it's her life you're talking about too, you know; she's got a right to her own life, her own happiness." And the discussion stops there. But in the context of virtue theory, given that we are particularly concerned with what constitutes a good human life, with what true happiness or *eudaimonia* is, this is no place to stop. We go on to ask, "And is this life of hers a good one? Is she living well?"

If we are to go on to talk about good human lives, in the context of abortion, we have to bring in our thoughts about the value of love and family life, and our proper emotional development through a natural life cycle. The familiar facts support the view that parenthood in general, and motherhood and childbearing in particular, are intrinsically worthwhile, are among the things that can be correctly thought to be partially constitutive of a flourishing human life. If this is right, then a woman who opts for not being a mother (at all, or again, or now) by opting for abortion may thereby be manifesting a flawed grasp of what her life should be, and be about—a grasp that is childish, or grossly materialistic, or shortsighted, or shallow.

I said "*may* thereby": this *need* not be so. Consider, for instance, a woman who has already had several children and fears that to have another will seriously affect her capacity to be a good mother to the ones she has—she does not show a lack of appreciation of the intrinsic value of being a parent by opting for abortion. Nor does a woman who has been a good mother and is approaching the age at which she may be looking forward to bring a good grandmother. Nor does a woman who discovers that her pregnancy may well kill her, and opts for abortion and adoption. Nor, necessarily, does a woman who has decided to lead a life centered around some other worthwhile activity or activities with which motherhood would compete.

People who are childless by choice are sometimes described as "irresponsible," or "selfish," or "refusing to grow up," or "not knowing what life is about." But one can hold that having children is intrinsically worthwhile without endorsing this, for we are, after all, in the happy position of there being more worthwhile things to do than can be fitted into one life-time. Parenthood, and motherhood in particular, even if granted to be intrinsically worthwhile, undoubtedly take up a lot of one's adult life, leaving no room for some other worthwhile pursuits. But some women who choose abortion rather than have their first child, and some men who encourage their partners to choose abortion, are not avoiding parenthood for the sake of other worthwhile pursuits, but for the worthless one of "having a good time," or for the pursuit of some false vision of the ideals of freedom or self-realization. And some others who say "I am not ready for parenthood yet" are making some sort of mistake about the extent to which one can manipulate the circumstances of one's life so as to make it fulfill some dream that one has. Perhaps one's dream is to have two perfect children, a girl and a boy, within a perfect marriage, in financially secure circumstances, with an interesting job of one's own. But to care too much about that dream, to demand of life that it give it to one and act accordingly, may be both greedy and foolish, and is to run the risk of missing out on happiness entirely. Not only may fate make the dream impossible, or destroy it, but one's own attachment to it may make it impossible. Good marriages, and the most promising children, can be destroyed by just one adult's excessive demand for perfection.

Once again, this is not to deny that girls may quite properly say "I am not ready for motherhood yet," especially in our society, and, far from manifesting irresponsibility or light-mindedness, show an appropriate modesty or humility, or a fearfulness that does not amount to cowardice. However, even when the decision to have an abortion is the right decision—one that does not itself fall under a vice-related term and thereby one that the perfectly virtuous could recommend—it does not follow that there is no sense in which having the abortion is wrong, or guilt inappropriate. For, by virtue of the fact that a human life has been cut short, some evil has probably been brought about,[5] and that circumstances make the decision to bring about some evil the right decision will be a ground for guilt if getting into those circumstances in the first place itself manifested a flaw in character.

What "gets one into those circumstances" in the case of abortion is, except in the case of rape, one's sexual activity and one's choices, or the lack of them, about one's sexual partner and about contraception. The virtuous woman (which here of course does not mean simply "chaste woman" but "woman with the virtues") has such character traits as strength, independence, resoluteness, decisiveness, self-confidence, responsibility, serious-mindedness, and self-determination—and no one, I think, could deny that many women become pregnant in circumstances in which they cannot welcome or cannot face the thought of having *this* child precisely because they lack one or some of these character traits. So even in the cases where the decision to have an abortion is the right one, it can still be the reflection of a moral failing—not because the decision itself is weak or cowardly or irresolute or irresponsible or light-minded, but because lack of the requisite opposite of these failings landed one in the circumstances in the first place. Hence the common universalized claim that guilt and remorse are never appropriate emotions about an abortion is denied. They may be appropriate, and appropriately inculcated, even when the decision was the right one.

Another motivation for bringing women's rights into the discussion may be to attempt to correct the implication, carried by the killing-centered approach, that insofar as abortion is wrong, it is a wrong that only women do, or at least (given the preponderance of male doctors) that only women instigate. I do not myself believe that we can thus escape the fact that nature bears harder on women than it does on men, but virtue theory can certainly correct many of the injustices that the emphasis on women's rights is rightly concerned about. With very little amendment, everything that has been said above applies to boys and men too. Although the abortion decision is, in a natural sense, the woman's decision, proper to her, boys and men are often party to it, for well or ill, and even when they are not, they are bound to have been party to the circumstances that brought it up. No less than girls and women, boys and men can, in their actions, manifest self-centeredness, callousness, and light-mindedness about life and par-

enthood in relation to abortion. They can be self-centered or courageous about the possibility of disability in their offspring; they need to reflect on their sexual activity and their choices, or the lack of them, about their sexual partner and contraception; they need to grow up and take responsibility for their own actions and life in relation to fatherhood. If it is true, as I maintain, that insofar as motherhood is intrinsically worthwhile, being a mother is an important purpose in women's lives, being a father (rather than a mere generator) is an important purpose in men's lives as well, and it is adolescent of men to turn a blind eye to this and pretend that they have many more important things to do.

* * *

NOTES

1. Judith Jarvis Thomson, "A Defense of Abortion," *Philosophy & Public Affairs* 1, no. 1 (Fall 1971): 47–66. One could indeed regard this article as proto–virtue theory (no doubt to the surprise of the author) if the concepts of callousness and kindness were allowed more weight.

2. One possible qualification: if one ties the concept of justice very closely to rights, then if women do have a moral right to terminate their pregnancies it *may* follow that in doing so they do not act unjustly. (Cf. Thomson, "A Defense of Abortion.") But it is debatable whether even that much follows.

3. This is an assumption of virtue theory, and I do not attempt to defend it here. An adequate discussion of it would require a separate article, since, although most moral philosophers would be chary of claiming that intellectual sophistication is a necessary condition of moral wisdom or virtue, most of us, from Plato onward, tend to write as if this were so. Sorting out which claims about moral knowledge are committed to this kind of elitism and which can, albeit with difficulty, be reconciled with the idea that moral knowledge can be acquired by anyone who really wants it would be a major task.

4. Mary Anne Warren, in "On the Moral and Legal Status of Abortion," *Monist* 57 (1973), sec. 1, says of the opponents of restrictive laws governing abortion that "their conviction (for the most part) is that abortion is not a *morally* serious and extremely unfortunate, even though sometimes justified, act, comparable to killing in self-defense or to letting the violinist die, but rather is closer to being a *morally neu-*

tral act, like cutting one's hair" (italics mine). I would like to think that no one *genuinely* believes this. But certainly in discussion, particularly when arguing against restrictive laws or the suggestion that remorse over abortion might be appropriate, I have found that some people *say* they believe it (and often cite Warren's article, albeit inaccurately, despite its age). Those who allow that it is morally serious, and far from morally neutral, have to argue against restrictive laws, or the appropriateness of remorse, on a very different ground from that laid down by the premise "The fetus is just part of the woman's body (and she has a right to determine what hap-

pens to her body and should not feel guilty about anything she does to it)."

5. I say "some evil has probably been brought about" on the ground that (human) life is (usually) a good and hence (human) death usually an evil. The exceptions would be (*a*) where death is actually a good or a benefit, because the baby that would come to be if the life were not cut short would be better off dead than alive, and (*b*) where death, though not a good, is not an evil either, because the life that would be led (e.g., in a state of permanent coma) would not be a good.

CASES FOR ANALYSIS

1. Aborting Daughters

China plans to jail anyone who helps prospective parents to learn the sex of their unborn child, in an attempt to halt the abortion of female foetuses.

It is already illegal to scan a foetus to discover its gender. But an amendment submitted to the standing committee of the National People's Congress, or parliament, will mean up to three years in jail and heavy fines for anyone helping with gender selection. It is rare for the parliament not to pass a Bill.

Most couples are limited by law to just one child. Many, especially in the countryside, yearn for a son to work the land, provide for parents and carry on the family name. Many rural clinics provide unauthorised ultrasound scans to determine the sex of the foetus and parents generally abort daughters.

As a result, the ratio of boys to girls now stands at 119 to 100, significantly higher than the world average of 106 to 100. In southern provinces such as Hainan and Guangdong the imbalance is as high as 130 boys per 100 girls, despite numerous incentives offered to farmers to stop them aborting daughters.

As part of a drive to reduce the gender imbalance to 105 to 100 by 2010, slogans are daubed on village walls across the country, reading: "Daughters are as good as sons." A Care for Girls campaign ensures free schooling for females and provides tax breaks and other privileges to their families.

But parents still slip money to doctors or nurses to learn the sex of their unborn child. For a boy, parents may pay £7, or £4 if the foetus is female. The owner of one illegal clinic hidden in a huge vegetable market on the outskirts of Beijing told the *Beijing Times:* "Ninety-nine percent of the women who ask for an abortion are those who have found out they are carrying a girl."

An estimated 500,000 babies are abandoned in China each year, 95 per cent of them healthy females.*

Do you think sex-selection abortions are morally permissible? What reasons can you provide to back up your view? Some Chinese parents could argue that such abortions are acceptable on utilitarian grounds: Aborting female fetuses prevents economic harm to the family. Is this a good moral argument? Why or why not?

* Jane Macartney, "Chinese Facing Jail to Protect Unborn Girls," *Times Online,* 27 December 2005, www.timesonline.co.uk/article/0,,25689-1959596,00.html (accessed 13 February 2006). © The Times, London, December 27, 2005.

2. Parental Notification

USA Today—Sabrina Holmquist trained as a physician in low-income neighborhoods in the Bronx, N.Y. She says she often saw pregnant teenagers in desperate health and family crises, including some girls who had been abused at home. That, Holmquist says, led her to believe that doctors sometimes should be able to perform abortions on minors without informing a parent.

But in Texas, Linda W. Flower, who practiced obstetrics for two decades, disagrees. She says that in the vast majority of cases in which a teenage girl seeks an abortion, a parent's guidance is helpful and needed. Flower says she knows of young women who have regretted having abortions.

The doctors' views reflect the dueling arguments in the first abortion case to come before the Supreme Court in five years: a New Hampshire dispute that tests whether a state may bar physicians from performing an abortion on a girl younger than 18 unless one of her parents has been notified at least 48 hours in advance—even in instances in which the girl faces a health emergency.

The case, to be heard by the court Wednesday, is the first abortion dispute before the justices since 2000, when they voted 5–4 to strike down Nebraska's ban on a procedure that critics call "partial birth" abortion because the ban lacked an exception for cases in which the woman's health was at risk. The new dispute tests whether such a health exception should be required in parental-involvement mandates, which have been passed in various forms by 43 states.[†]

Which doctor do you think is right about parental notification? Under what circumstances, if any, do you think it morally permissible for an under-eighteen girl to have an abortion without notifying a parent or guardian? when the girl's life is at stake? when she is a victim of sexual abuse including incest? Would it be reasonable to require parental notification in *all* cases without exception?

†Joan Biskupic, "High Court Case May Signal Shift on Abortion," *USA Today,* 30 November 2005. Copyright © USA Today, 2005. Reprinted with permission.

3. No Abortion to Avert Health Risks

Medical News Today—The European Court of Human Rights on Tuesday began considering the appeal of a Polish woman who says that in 2000 she was denied an abortion despite warnings from physicians that she could become blind if she continued the pregnancy, the *Scotsman* reports (Neighbour, *Scotsman,* 2/8). Alicja Tysiac—who has three children—alleges that Poland's abortion law violated her rights under Article 8 and Article 14 of the European Convention for the Protection of Human Rights and Fundamental Freedoms, which guarantee "respect for privacy and family life" and "prohibition of discrimination," respectively. Polish law allows abortion only if a woman has been raped, if there is danger to the life of the woman or if the fetus will have birth defects, according to the *Jurist* (Onikepe, *Jurist,* 2/8). The European Court could rule that Tysiac's rights were violated but cannot mandate that Poland change its abortion laws (*Reuters,* 2/7).‡

Should Alicia Tysiac have been permitted an abortion even though her life was not at risk? Why or why not? How serious must pregnancy-related health problems be before a risk-lowering abortion is permissible (if ever)? When such health dangers are involved, why should—or should not—a woman be allowed to decide for herself about whether to have an abortion?

‡"In the Courts: European Court of Human Rights Considers Appeal of Polish Woman Allegedly Denied Abortion," 10 February 2006, www.medicalnewstoday.com/medicalnews.php?newsid=37619 (4 October 2006). Reprinted with permission from kaisernetwork.org. You can view the entire Kaiser Daily Women's Health Policy report, search the archives, and sign up for email delivery at http://www.kaisernetwork.org/daily_reports/rep_women.cmf. The Kaiser Daily Women's Health Policy report is published for kaisernetwork.org, a free service of The Henry J. Kaiser Family Foundation. © 2006 Advisory Board Company.

Euthanasia and Physician-Assisted Suicide

For fifteen years, Terri Schiavo existed between life and death in that shadow land called a persistent vegetative state, a place where she was wakeful but without awareness or any purposeful behavior. Severe brain damage had left her there, with virtually no chance of recovery. And all the while, a storm of caustic debate swirled around her, reaching its greatest strength in the last few days before her death on March 31, 2005. In 1990 her heart had stopped briefly because of a chemical imbalance, leaving her brain damaged and her in a twilight state, kept alive by a feeding tube. She had left no living will, no written record of her wishes should she become indefinitely incapacitated. Her husband, Michael Schiavo, insisted that Terri had told him once that she would prefer death to being kept alive with machines. Her parents rejected his claim and demanded that Terri be kept alive, holding out hope that with proper care she might recover.

The battle between Michael Schiavo and Terri's parents raged on in the courts for years. Again and again, state and federal courts sided with the husband, while the U.S. Supreme Court repeatedly refused to hear the case. In the final days before Terri died, President George W. Bush, the U.S. Congress, the governor of Florida (where she lived), and Florida legislators weighed in on the controversy, supporting Terri's parents.

Finally, a judge allowed the feeding tube to be removed, and Terri Schiavo, age forty-one, died thirteen days later. The parents called the removal "judicial homicide." A Vatican official called it "an attack against God."[1]

So it goes with all public debates on the moral permissibility of euthanasia. Passions rise, claims and counterclaims collide, and stakes are high. In the balance are issues of life and death, science and religion, murder and mercy. The tragic end of Terri Schiavo is only the most dramatic (and dramatized) case in a series of tragic ends that turned into widely publicized moral battlegrounds. (See the box "The Death of Karen Ann Quinlan.") The moral questions it incited are typical of such cases: Was removing Terri Schiavo's feeding tube really a case of murder? Or was it a morally permissible act allowing her to die with dignity and escape her bleak condition? What if instead of stopping the tube feeding, her doctors never started it because they deemed her situation hopeless? Would *that* have been murder—or a permissible act of mercy? Or suppose that soon after Schiavo collapsed, her doctors had decided to give her a lethal injection? Would such an act have been morally wrong? What if Schiavo had left a living will that clearly specified that she did *not* want to be kept alive by any means if she fell into a persistent vegetative state? Would withdrawing the feeding tube or giving her a lethal injection then have been morally acceptable?

[1]Larry Copeland and Laura Parker, "Terri Schiavo's Case Doesn't End with Her Passing," *USAToday*, 31 March 2005, www.usatoday.com/news/nation/2005-03-31-schiavo_x.htm (25 April 2005).

The Death of Karen Ann Quinlan

Like nothing else before it, the case of Karen Ann Quinlan focused the world's attention on the medical truths, the legal complexities, and the moral problems of euthanasia. She was just twenty-one years old when she sustained acute brain damage after imbibing alcohol along with a tranquilizer. She was left in a persistent vegetative state, kept alive by a feeding tube and a respirator, a machine that maintained her breathing mechanically. After several months, members of her family came to accept that her recovery was hopeless and sought permission from the courts to unplug the respirator to allow her to die. Finally in 1976 the New Jersey Supreme Court granted their request. But to everyone's surprise, she continued to breathe without the respirator until 1985, ten years after she slipped into the vegetative state. She died on June 11.*

* See "Famous Cases: Karen Ann Quinlan," *CBC News Online,* 22 March 2005, www.cbc.ca/news/background/schiavo/vegetative_state.html (23 November 2006); Barran H. Lerner, "Planning for the Long Goodbye," *New York Times,* 18 June 2004.

Of course, in every instance of euthanasia there are plenty of nonmoral questions too—primarily legal, judicial, medical, scientific, and political. (In the Schiavo case, for example, the moral questions arose side by side with what most informed observers saw as the *real* issue: who, if anyone, had the legal right to decide for Schiavo what was to become of her?) But these nonmoral concerns are intertwined with the moral concerns. Our task here is to apply moral reasoning to try to unravel the knot.

ISSUE FILE: BACKGROUND

Euthanasia is directly or indirectly bringing about the death of another person for that per-

son's sake.[2] It is thought to provide a benefit or a good for the person by ending a life deemed no longer worth living—a situation that typically arises when someone has an incurable or terminal disease that causes great suffering or when someone experiences an irreversible loss of consciousness (as in the Schiavo case). This notion of dying as a kind of blessing is preserved in the Greek roots of *euthanasia,* which literally means "easy death." Euthanasia makes sense to many people because they believe that a quick and painless death would be preferable to a slow and painful dying (such as the kind that some terminal cancer patients endure) or a long, vegetative sleep without a chance for a meaningful life.

As you might expect, the moral permissibility of euthanasia depends heavily on the consent of the patient (the person whose death is being considered). Moral philosophers therefore distinguish between euthanasia that is voluntary, nonvoluntary, and involuntary. In **voluntary euthanasia,** the patient requests or agrees to the act. She may make the request in person or leave instructions to be followed in case she becomes incapacitated. Such instructions are usually in the form of an **advance directive** (for example, a living will), a legal document allowing physicians to withhold or withdraw treatments if a patient becomes terminally ill and unable to express her wishes. For any voluntary euthanasia request to be valid, the patient at the time of the request must be competent—that is, capable of making an informed, rational choice. In **nonvoluntary euthanasia,** others besides the patient (family or physicians, for example) choose euthanasia for her because she is not competent (due to illness or

[2] I owe the notion of a good death "for the sake" of the person dying to Philippa Foot (in "Euthanasia," *Philosophy & Public Affairs* 6, no. 2, [1977]: 85–112): and to Helga Kuhse (in "Euthanasia," in *A Companion to Ethics,* ed. Peter Singer, corr. ed. [Oxford: Blackwell, 1993], 294–302).

injury) and has left no instructions regarding her end-of-life preferences. Euthanasia performed on infants and small children is, of course, nonvoluntary. In **involuntary euthanasia,** the act is carried out against the wishes of the patient and is therefore illegal and widely regarded as immoral.

People also draw a distinction between active and passive euthanasia. **Active euthanasia** is taking a direct action to kill someone, to carry out a "mercy killing." A doctor who gives a patient a lethal injection is performing active euthanasia, and so is a man who suffocates his dying brother to spare him from an unbearably painful passing. **Passive euthanasia** is allowing someone to die by *not* doing something—by withholding or withdrawing measures necessary for sustaining life. A doctor, then, would be performing passive euthanasia if she removed a patient's respirator, did not administer antibiotics to halt a life-threatening infection, or withdrew hydration and nutrition (fluids and nutrients).

Many believe that this active-passive distinction is essential to understanding the moral permissibility of euthanasia. It allows them to maintain that whereas active euthanasia is always wrong, in some cases passive euthanasia may be permissible. This view is widespread among physicians and fits with the popular notion that killing people is morally worse than letting them die. Others, however, argue that there is no moral difference between killing and letting die: in both active and passive euthanasia the patient's death is caused, and they are therefore morally equivalent.

Taking into account the categories of *voluntary, nonvoluntary, active,* and *passive* (and disregarding *involuntary*), we can identify four kinds of euthanasia: (1) *active voluntary* (mercy killing at the patient's request), (2) *active nonvoluntary* (mercy killing without the patient's consent or request), (3) *passive voluntary* (letting the patient die at her request), and (4) *passive nonvoluntary* (letting the

patient die without his consent or request). Generally, the law forbids active euthanasia (either voluntary or nonvoluntary), and the medical profession is officially opposed to it (though the views of individual physicians vary). Passive voluntary euthanasia is legal; by law, competent patients have the right to refuse any kind of medical treatment. Passive nonvoluntary euthanasia may be legal provided that someone (a family member, for example) can be designated to make decisions on behalf of the patient.

Related to, but distinct from, active voluntary euthanasia is **physician-assisted suicide**—the killing of a person by the person's own hand with the help of a physician. Like active voluntary euthanasia, physician-assisted suicide is requested by the patient, and the intended outcome is the patient's death for the relief of pain and suffering. But the agent who ultimately causes the death in active voluntary euthanasia is the physician, whereas the ultimate causal agent in physician-assisted suicide is the patient. In the former, the physician is primarily responsible for the killing; in the latter, the patient is. In most cases, the physician provides help by prescribing a lethal dose of drugs, which the patient then administers to himself.

In the United States, physician-assisted suicide is legal only in Oregon. Supreme Court rulings allow each state to decide for itself whether to legalize assisted suicide. The official position of the American Medical Association (AMA), the main professional group for physicians, is that "physician-assisted suicide is unethical and fundamentally inconsistent with the pledge physicians make to devote themselves to healing and life."[3]

---

[3]Lonnie R. Bristow (for the American Medical Association), testimony before the U.S. House of Representatives Committee on the Judiciary, Subcommittee on the Constitution, 104th Cong., 2nd sess., *Congressional Record* (29 April 1996).

Landmark Court Rulings

In the past three decades, U.S. courts have several times weighed in on the controversial issues of euthanasia and physician-assisted suicide. The following are some of the more far-reaching rulings:

- **1976** The New Jersey Supreme Court rules that a life-sustaining respirator could be legally disconnected from Karen Ann Quinlan, a young woman who had lapsed into a persistent vegetative state. After it was removed, she remained comatose and lived for another ten years, finally dying in June 1985.

- **1990** The U.S. Supreme Court (in *Cruzan v. Director, Missouri Department of Health*) rules that a feeding tube could be removed from Nancy Cruzan, a woman in a persistent vegetative state due to an automobile accident, if "clear and convincing evidence" shows that she would have approved of the withdrawal. The ruling recognized the legitimacy of living wills, surrogates to act for incapacitated individuals, and a qualified "right to die."

- **1997** The U.S. Supreme Court (in *Washington v. Glucksberg*) rules that a Washington State prohibition of physician-assisted suicide does not violate the due process clause of the Fourteenth Amendment.

- **1997** The U.S. Supreme Court (in *Vacco v. Quill*) rules that a New York State prohibition of physician-assisted suicide does not violate the equal protection clause of the Fourteenth Amendment. The Court acknowledges a crucial distinction between withdrawing life-sustaining treatment and assisted suicide. People may refuse life-sustaining treatment, but assisted suicide is prohibited.

A factor that can complicate all the foregoing issues is the concept of death itself. One problem is that thanks to modern medical technology, determining when a person is dead is not as straightforward as it once seemed. Death has become more difficult to define. Years ago the prevailing notion was that a person is dead when his breathing and blood flow stop (no respiration and no heartbeat). But nowadays machines can keep an individual's heart and lungs functioning long after the brain permanently and completely shuts down. Thus we can have an individual whose organs are mechanically operated while he is in a coma or persistent vegetative state—*for years*. By the traditional definition of death, such an individual would still be alive, but many people would insist that he is no longer there: he is dead. So the conventional notion of death seems to be inadequate.

Why does correctly defining death matter at all? Say an individual is in the kind of state just described. If we judge him to be dead and thus no longer a person, then perhaps it would be morally permissible to disconnect him from the machines, or administer a fatal drug overdose, or remove his feeding tube, or even harvest his organs for transplant into another person. Or would it? If we deem him alive and still a person, perhaps we are not justified in doing *any* of the above. Maybe taking any one of these actions is to commit murder. Depending on the concept of death accepted by the legal system, killing him or allowing him to die could have serious legal consequences.

To overcome the drawbacks of the traditional definition of death, alternative definitions have been suggested. According to the *whole-brain* definition of death, an individual is dead when all brain functions (including those performed in the brain stem) permanently stop. It has become the primary standard in both medicine and the law for determining death. Critics of the whole-brain standard, though, have pointed out that it is based

QUICK REVIEW

euthanasia—Directly or indirectly bringing about the death of another person for that person's sake.

voluntary euthanasia—Euthanasia performed on a person with his or her permission.

advance directive—A legal document allowing physicians to withhold or withdraw treatments if a patient becomes terminally ill and unable to express his or her wishes.

nonvoluntary euthanasia—Euthanasia performed on a person who is not competent to decide the issue and has left no instructions regarding end-of-life preferences. In such cases, family or physicians usually make the decision.

involuntary euthanasia—Euthanasia performed on a person against his or her wishes.

active euthanasia—Euthanasia performed by taking a direct action to cause someone's death; "mercy killing."

passive euthanasia—Euthanasia performed by withholding or withdrawing measures necessary for sustaining life.

physician-assisted suicide—The killing of a person by the person's own hand with the help of a physician.

on a faulty assumption: that the brain is the control center for all physiological functions. Yet some functions (such as respiration) are partially independent of brain activity. In addition, by the whole-brain standard, individuals in an irreversible persistent vegetative state (who have some detectable brain activity) are thought to be alive—a result that some regard as counterintuitive or puzzling.

The *higher brain* definition of death says that an individual is dead when higher brain func-

tions—those that give rise to consciousness—permanently stop. Some have maintained that because consciousness is necessary for personhood, an individual whose higher brain functions have disappeared is no longer a person and is therefore rightly considered dead. By the higher-brain standard, individuals in a persistent vegetative state (who continue to breathe and have a heartbeat) but whose higher brain functions have ceased are thought to be dead—also a result that some people find counterintuitive.

MORAL THEORIES

Utilitarianism, Kant's ethics, and natural law theory lead to divergent conclusions on the issue of euthanasia. An act-utilitarian would certainly try to take into account how much overall happiness various possible actions could bring about, everyone considered. But she could make this calculation in different ways. The basic approach would be to consider the patient's suffering (as well as that of others involved, such as family members) and the likely success of any treatments and try to determine how much overall happiness would be generated by different actions, including bringing about the patient's death. If the patient's situation is hopeless and his suffering great, an act-utilitarian could decide that the greatest net happiness would result from killing the patient or letting him die. The patient's consent to euthanasia may or may not be a primary concern, depending on how consent would affect overall happiness. On the other hand, the act-utilitarian might say that euthanasia is contrary to the goal of maximizing happiness because killing a person rules out any possibility of his experiencing happiness in the future. Happiness does not occur in a vacuum; it exists only when persons experience it. So eliminating a person eliminates potential happiness.

Some people—even those who are not thoroughgoing utilitarians—argue against euthanasia on what amounts to rule-utilitarian grounds or something close to it. They contend that regardless of the moral permissibility of euthanasia in specific cases, a general rule (that is, a social policy or law) permitting some types of euthanasia would cause more harm than good. They offer slippery-slope arguments such as the following: Passing a law (making a rule) permitting active voluntary euthanasia would inevitably lead to abuses such as more frequent use of nonvoluntary euthanasia and unnecessary killing; therefore, no such law should be passed. Similarly, some argue that a general rule allowing physician-assisted suicide would destroy the "moral center" of the medical profession; if physicians are allowed to kill patients, they will violate their pledge to protect life and to heal, causing patients to distrust them. Of course, it is also possible to argue *for* euthanasia on rule-utilitarian grounds. (Whether such arguments are sound is another matter.) A rule-utilitarian could devise a rule that he thinks would result in a maximization of happiness for everyone if the rule were consistently followed.

Like the utilitarian, the Kantian theorist could also take several different positions on euthanasia, consistent with Kantian principles. She could argue that euthanasia is never permissible because it would entail treating persons as mere disposable things. Kant underscores this view in his discussion of suicide. He maintains that "suicide is in no circumstances permissible" because it robs individuals of their personhood, which is the very foundation of all moral values. Furthermore, it treats persons as if they had no more value than that of a beast. As Kant puts it, "But the rule of morality does not admit of [suicide] under any condition because it degrades human nature below the level of animal nature and so destroys it."[4] This stern prohibition against suicide may or may not apply equally well to euthanasia—depending on whether those considered for euthanasia are to be regarded as persons. Certainly those who are competent (coherent and rational) are persons and therefore should not be killed or allowed to die. But what would Kant say about individuals who have slipped from waking life into a coma or a vegetative state? Are they still persons with full moral rights? If they are persons, then performing euthanasia on them would be immoral. If they are not persons, then euthanasia might be morally acceptable. In fact, a Kantian might argue that performing euthanasia on individuals in comas or vegetative states may be morally permissible precisely because persons have intrinsic worth and dignity. The bioethicist Ronald Munson explains this view well:

It may be more in keeping with our freedom and dignity for us to instruct others either to put us to death or to take no steps to keep us alive should we ever be in such a state. Voluntary euthanasia may be compatible with (if not required by) Kant's ethics.

By a similar line of reasoning, it may be that nonvoluntary euthanasia might be seen as a duty that we have to others. We might argue that by putting to death a comatose and hopeless person we are recognizing the dignity that person possessed in his or her previous state.[5]

According to the dominant reading of natural law theory, euthanasia is wrong in almost every instance. It is wrong because we have a moral duty to preserve life. So intentionally performing any kind of euthanasia, active or passive, is impermissible. The doctrine of double effect, however, allows one exception to this rule. Recall that this doctrine makes a distinction between (1) performing a good action that happens to have a bad effect and (2) performing a

[4]Immanuel Kant, "Suicide," in *Lectures on Ethics,* trans. Louis Infield (New York: Harper & Row, 1963), 147–54.

[5]Ronald Munson, *Intervention and Reflection: Basic Issues in Medical Ethics,* ed. Munson, 7th ed. (Belmont, CA: Wadsworth, 2004), 696–97.

CRITICAL THOUGHT:
Dr. Kevorkian and
Physician-Assisted Suicide

Dr. Jack Kevorkian is known as a champion of the right-to-die movement, having helped many incurably ill people commit suicide. He is also known as "Dr. Death," the physician who helps desperate people kill themselves. After many unsuccessful tries, prosecutors finally won a conviction against him for murder: in 1999, he was sentenced to ten to twenty-five years in prison. The *New York Times* reported that the sentence was handed down "despite emotional courtroom pleas on his behalf from the widow and brother of the terminally ill man he was convicted of killing."*

Do you agree with the verdict in this case? Why or why not? If you do not agree, would your opinion change if you knew that many of Dr. Kevorkian's suicide patients were not mentally competent at the time of their deaths (because of depression), as some people allege? If so, why? If you were terminally ill and in horrendous pain with no hope of relief, might you think it morally permissible to use the services of someone like Dr. Kevorkian? If not, why not?

* Dirk Johnson, "Kevorkian Sentenced to 10 to 25 Years in Prison," *New York Times,* 14 April 1999.

bad action to achieve a good effect. The former may be permissible, but the latter is not. In the case of euthanasia, the doctrine implies that giving a pain-racked patient a large dose of morphine to end her life (a practice known as *terminal sedation*) is never morally acceptable. But giving her a large dose of morphine with the intention of easing her pain—an act that has the side effect of expediting her death—is permissible. The hastening of the patient's death is permissible because even though it was foreseen, it

was not intended. In the doctrine of double effect, intention makes all the difference.

MORAL ARGUMENTS

Most plausible euthanasia arguments are about *active* euthanasia (mercy killing, as opposed to letting the patient die). As suggested earlier, passive euthanasia (both voluntary and nonvoluntary) is legal, provided certain conditions are met, and both forms of it are widely believed to be morally acceptable. So let us confine our evaluation here to moral arguments for and against *active voluntary euthanasia* (mercy killing at the patient's request). The question these arguments address then is straightforward: *Is active voluntary euthanasia morally permissible?*

As we proceed, we must keep an important distinction in mind: moral permissibility is not the same thing as legal permissibility. Whether euthanasia is morally acceptable is a separate issue from whether it should be legalized. It is possible that we could be justified in believing both that euthanasia is morally permissible *and* that it should not be legalized—or vice versa. We might plausibly argue that in some cases, performing active voluntary euthanasia is the right thing to do but that legalizing it would have terrible consequences. Legalization could, say, lead doctors to practice active *nonvoluntary* euthanasia or encourage them to care less about preserving life or cause patients to fear or mistrust doctors. To mix up these two kinds of issues—moral and legal—is to invite confusion.

We begin by examining arguments *for* active voluntary euthanasia. The strongest of these are built on two fundamental moral principles: persons have (1) a right of self-determination and (2) an obligation to help someone in serious distress or peril (if they are in a position to help without great risk to themselves). Principle (1) refers to the patient's right of self-determination, and principle (2) to other persons who might be able to benefit her. Principle (1) assumes that persons have autonomy—the capacity, as Kant would have it, to use reason to guide their own actions and make their own decisions. It asserts that persons have the right to exercise this power to direct their lives as they see fit (with the proviso that their actions not violate the rights of others). Many who appeal to this principle argue that if it applies to how persons live, then it surely applies to how they die, because their dying is part of their life. This is how the bioethicist Dan W. Brock explains the importance of this end-of-life self-determination:

Most people are very concerned about the nature of the last stage of their lives. This reflects not just a fear of experiencing substantial suffering when dying, but also a desire to retain dignity and control during this last period of life. Death is today increasingly preceded by a long period of significant physical and mental decline, due in part to the technological interventions of modern medicine. Many people adjust to these disabilities and find meaning and value in new activities and ways. Others find the impairments and burdens in the last stage of their lives at some point sufficiently great to make life no longer worth living. For many patients near death, maintaining the quality of one's life, avoiding great suffering, maintaining one's dignity, and insuring that others remember us as we wish them to become of paramount importance and outweigh merely extending one's life. But there is no single, objectively correct answer for everyone as to when, if at all, one's life becomes all things considered a burden and unwanted. If self-determination is a fundamental value, then the great variability among people on this question makes it especially important that individuals control the manner, circumstances, and timing of their dying and death.[6]

Principle (2) is a duty of beneficence (a duty to benefit others). Applied to euthanasia, it says

that if we are in a position to ease the agony of another, and we can do so without excessive cost to ourselves, we should try to render aid. This tenet applies to persons generally, but it carries extra weight for people with a special relationship with the suffering person, such as family members, close friends, and doctors. Physicians have an explicit obligation to try to relieve the misery of their patients—especially dying patients who often must endure horrific pain and suffering. Many advocates of euthanasia contend that if a competent dying patient is in agony and asks to be put out of her misery (active voluntary euthanasia), rejecting her plea for mercy would be both cruel and wicked. They also insist that merely withholding treatment from her to hasten her death (passive euthanasia) would only prolong her suffering.

Here is one way to incorporate both principles (1) and (2) into a single argument for active voluntary euthanasia:

1. Competent persons have a right of self-determination (as long as exercising this right does not violate others' rights).

2. The right of self-determination includes the right of competent persons to decide the manner of their dying and to choose active (voluntary) euthanasia.

3. We have an obligation to help others in serious distress or peril (if we are in a position to help without great risk to themselves).

4. This duty of beneficence includes the duty, under appropriate conditions, to ease the pain and suffering of competent dying persons by performing active (voluntary) euthanasia.

5. Therefore, active voluntary euthanasia for competent dying persons is permissible.

The central idea behind this argument is that if competent dying persons have a right to choose active euthanasia, and if the duty of beneficence includes performing active voluntary euthanasia,

[6]Dan W. Brock, "Voluntary Active Euthanasia," *Hastings Center Report* 22, no. 2 (March/April 1992): 11.

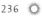

Public Opinion and Euthanasia

Many opinion polls have shown that most people favor some form of euthanasia or physician assistance in dying. A 2005 Harris poll of 1,010 adults ages eighteen and over echoed these findings:*

- 70 percent agree that "a law should allow doctors to comply with the wishes of a dying patient in severe distress who asks to have his or her life ended."

- 64 percent do not agree with the 1997 U.S. Supreme Court ruling that "individuals do not have a constitutional right to doctor-assisted suicide."

- 72 percent agree that the instructions they would want in a living will in case they became unconscious and, "to a reasonable degree of medical certainty would never regain consciousness," would say that they should be "allowed to die so nutrition and hydration should be withheld or withdrawn."

- 67 percent favor a law in their own state similar to the Oregon law that legalizes doctor-assisted suicide (and specifies that certain conditions must be met).

*The Harris Poll® #32. April 27, 2005, "Majorities of U.S. Adults Favor Euthanasia and Physician-Assisted Suicide." Harris Interactive Inc. All rights reserved. Reprinted with permission of Harris Interactive.

then active voluntary euthanasia is morally permissible. But does the conclusion follow from the premises, and are the premises true? The answer to the first part of this question is yes. The answer to the second part is more complicated. Look at Premises 1 and 3; they articulate the two basic moral principles we began with. These principles qualify as considered moral judgments and are accepted by virtually all parties to the euthanasia debate. We have good reason, then, to say that Premises 1 and 3 are true.

Premises 2 and 4, however, are controversial. Critics of Premise 2 would say that we do indeed have a right of self-determination but that this right *does not* include the right to opt for active voluntary euthanasia. The reason is that active euthanasia is killing, and killing is always wrong. We may have all sorts of rights, but killing is still killing.

This reply, though, is based on a superficial understanding of prohibitions against killing. Some kinds of killing are considered by most people to be morally permissible—for example, killing in self-defense and killing in war. These are regarded as justified killings; unjustified killings are known as *murder*. So even though all killing may be regrettable, not all killing is immoral. Active euthanasia may in fact be a form of acceptable killing.

The opponent of active euthanasia can make a stronger reply along the same lines. He can say that the problem with active euthanasia is not that it is a type of killing but that it is a type of *unwarranted* killing. A dying patient in the grip of unimaginable pain, for example, does not have to be killed to escape her agony. Modern medicine is better than ever at alleviating pain—even very intense pain. Spinal blocks, drug combinations, new ways to deliver powerful analgesics (drugs that ease pain)—these options and others can offer dying patients unprecedented levels of pain relief. So euthanasia is uncalled for. If this claim is correct, then opponents can argue that contrary to Premise 4, active euthanasia will actually harm patients by cutting their lives short unnecessarily and thus depriving them of the benefits that may accrue in their remaining days—benefits such as profoundly meaningful moments spent with their families, the chance to come to terms with their dying, and even the possibility of a newfound cure for their disease.[7] Proponents of active euthana-

---

[7]I owe this point to Thomas F. Wall, *Thinking Critically about Moral Problems* (Belmont, CA: Wadsworth, 2003), 176.

sia, however, charge that this upbeat view of pain management is not accurate. They point to several unpleasant facts: though it is *possible* to manage even severe pain well, too often pain is not well-managed (for a variety of reasons, including the reluctance of health care workers to administer large doses of pain-relieving drugs); the side effects of the best pain medications (especially when used long term) often add to the suffering of the patient; and many dying patients endure not physical pain but psychological suffering that is unbearable and untreatable by any medication.

Proponents can put forth another kind of argument for active voluntary euthanasia, this one based on the moral significance of killing (active euthanasia) and letting die (passive euthanasia). As we saw earlier, active euthanasia is taking a direct action to kill someone, while passive euthanasia is allowing someone to die by withholding or withdrawing measures necessary for sustaining life. Passive euthanasia is legal (competent patients have the right to refuse treatment) and widely believed to be morally permissible. Active euthanasia is generally illegal, and debate continues over its moral permissibility. Opponents of active euthanasia generally think that there is a profound *moral* difference between killing and letting die: killing is far worse than letting die; in fact, killing is morally wrong while letting die is permissible. But proponents of active voluntary euthanasia assert that the two are morally equivalent. Using this alleged moral equivalence, proponents can construct an argument like this:

1. Passive euthanasia is morally permissible.

2. If passive euthanasia is morally equivalent to active euthanasia, active euthanasia is also morally permissible.

3. Passive euthanasia is morally equivalent to active euthanasia.

4. Therefore, active (voluntary) euthanasia is morally permissible.

The conclusion follows from the premises, and Premises 1 and 2 are uncontroversial. The crux of the matter is Premise 3. What reasons are there for thinking that it is true? Here is an argument for Premise 3 in the form of a classic thought experiment. Suppose Smith will inherit a fortune if his six-year-old cousin dies. So he decides to take matters into his own hands. He slips into the bathroom while his little cousin is taking a bath and drowns him. He makes the whole thing look like an accident and leaves undetected. Now consider Jones, who also will inherit a fortune if his six-year-old cousin dies. He too decides to kill the child, and he too slips into the bathroom while the boy is bathing. But before Jones has a chance to commit the deed, the boy slips in the tub, gets knocked unconscious, and will surely drown unless Jones rescues him. Jones is happy to do nothing and lets the boy drown on his own—a simple "accident." Now which man behaves better morally? If there is a significant moral difference between killing and letting die, we would want to say that Jones's actions are less blameworthy than Smith's. But this distinction doesn't seem correct. The motives and aims of both men are the same.[8]

The line taken here is that if the difference between killing and letting die really is important morally, then we would judge one man's action (either Smith's or Jones's) to be more blameworthy than the other. But our judgment is the same for both, so there must be no moral difference.

Some reject this argument and insist that there is in fact a moral difference between killing and letting die but that the distinction is often obscured in thought experiments like the Smith-Jones story. One critic claims, for example, that in this scenario the two men are equally reprehensible and the two actions appear to be morally equivalent simply because both men *were prepared*

---

[8]James Rachels, "Active and Passive Euthanasia," *New England Journal of Medicine* 292, no. 2 (9 January 1975): 79.

to kill. Remove this common factor, and the moral difference between killing and letting die will be apparent.[9]

Some of the strongest arguments *against* active voluntary euthanasia take a slippery-slope approach. The gist of most of them is that lifting a moral or legal prohibition against this kind of mercy killing will dilute respect for life and encourage a slow slide from active voluntary euthanasia to active *nonvoluntary* euthanasia and then perhaps to *involuntary* euthanasia. This argument is therefore consequentialist: active voluntary euthanasia is wrong because it leads to bad consequences. (The argument is also sometimes lodged against legalizing this form of euthanasia.) Here is how one bioethicist describes the descent down the slope:

A person apparently hopelessly ill may be allowed to take his own life. Then he may be permitted to deputize others to do it for him should he no longer be able to act. The judgment of others then becomes the ruling factor. Already at this point euthanasia is not personal and voluntary, for others are acting "on behalf of" the patient as they see fit. This may well incline them to act on behalf of other patients who have not authorized them to exercise their judgment. It is only a short step, then, from voluntary euthanasia (self-inflicted or authorized), to directed euthanasia administered to a patient who has given no authorization, to involuntary euthanasia conducted as part of a social policy.[10]

We can formulate a version of the argument thus:

1. If the general acceptance or approval of active voluntary euthanasia leads to widespread abuses

(unjustified killing), then the practice is morally wrong.

2. The general acceptance or approval of active voluntary euthanasia will lead to widespread abuses (unjustified killing).

3. Therefore, active voluntary euthanasia is morally wrong.

This is a valid argument, an instance of *modus ponens,* so we need to focus only on the truth or falsity of the premises. Probably most people who have thought carefully about this kind of argument accept Premise 1 or a variation of it. Premise 2 is the sticking point. Because of a lack of solid evidence on the subject, the social consequences of a general acceptance of active euthanasia are difficult to ascertain. For example, to prove their case, some opponents of euthanasia cite reports on the Dutch experience with physician-assisted suicide. Proponents point to the same reports to undermine that case. The difficulty is that the research is not robust enough to lend unequivocal support to one side or the other. It therefore does not show that Premise 2 is true. Many of the arguments for Premise 2 are arguments by analogy or inferences based on observations concerning human behavior. Generally, these too are weak and conjectural.

Those who are skeptical of Premise 2 often simply point out that no good reasons have been provided to support it. At best, they say, arguments for Premise 2 show only that dreadful consequences from widespread use of active euthanasia are possible. As one skeptic puts it,

Now it cannot be denied that it is *possible* that permitting euthanasia could have these fateful consequences, but that cannot be enough to warrant prohibiting it if it is otherwise justified. A similar *possible* slippery slope worry could have been raised to securing competent patients' rights to decide about life support, but recent history shows such a worry would have been unfounded.[11]

---

[9]Winston Nesbitt, "Is Killing No Worse Than Letting Die?" *Journal of Applied Philosophy* 12, no. 1 (1995): 101–5.

[10]J. Gay-Williams, "The Wrongfulness of Euthanasia," in *Intervention and Reflection: Basic Issues in Medical Ethics,* [selected by] Ronald Munson, 7th ed. (Belmont, CA: Wadsworth, 2004), 710–11.

[11]Brock, "Voluntary Active Euthanasia," 20.

SUMMARY

Euthanasia is directly or indirectly bringing about the death of another person for that person's sake. Its moral status depends in large measure on the consent of the patient. In voluntary euthanasia, the patient agrees to the act. In nonvoluntary euthanasia, others besides the patient decide on euthanasia because he or she is incompetent and has left no statement about end-of-life preferences. In involuntary euthanasia, the act is performed against the patient's wishes. Active euthanasia is taking direct action to kill someone (administering a lethal injection, for example); passive euthanasia is allowing the patient to die by withholding or withdrawing life-sustaining measures.

The traditional notion of death as the cessation of breathing and heartbeat has been revised in light of new developments in medical technology. According to the whole-brain view of death, the individual is dead when all brain functions permanently stop. The higher-brain view of death says that an individual is dead when higher brain functions permanently stop.

An act-utilitarian might see euthanasia as morally permissible because it results in the greatest happiness for all concerned. She could also consistently say that euthanasia is contrary to the goal of maximizing happiness because killing an individual rules out any possibility of that person's future happiness. A rule-utilitarian might say that a general rule permitting some kinds of euthanasia would do more harm than good—or that such a rule would maximize happiness in the long run. A Kantian theorist could consistently reject euthanasia because it entails treating persons as disposable things. Or he could consistently maintain that individuals in comas or persistent vegetative states are no longer persons, and therefore euthanasia is morally acceptable.

Arguments in favor of active voluntary euthanasia are often based on a right of self-determination and a duty to help others in distress. Some arguments for euthanasia, however, depend on the alleged equivalence between active and passive euthanasia. Some of the strongest arguments against euthanasia are of the slippery-slope type: active voluntary euthanasia is wrong because it leads to bad consequences, such as an increased risk of unjustified killings.

R E A D I N G S

Active and Passive Euthanasia

JAMES RACHELS

The distinction between active and passive euthanasia is thought to be crucial for medical ethics. The idea is that it is permissible, at least in some cases, to withhold treatment and allow a patient to die, but it is never permissible to take any direct action designed to kill the patient. This doctrine seems to be accepted by most doctors, and it is endorsed in

James Rachels, "Active and Passive Euthanasia," *The New England Journal of Medicine* 292, no. 2 (9 January 1975): 78–80 (edited). Copyright © 1975 Massachusetts Medical Society. All rights reserved.

a statement adopted by the House of Delegates of the American Medical Association on December 4, 1973:

The intentional termination of the life of one human being by another—mercy killing—is contrary to that for which the medical profession stands and is contrary to the policy of the American Medical Association.

The cessation of the employment of extraordinary means to prolong the life of the body when there is irrefutable evidence that biological death is imminent is the decision of the patient and/or his immediate family. The advice and judgment of the physician should be freely available to the patient and/or his immediate family.

However, a strong case can be made against this doctrine. In what follows I will set out some of the relevant arguments, and urge doctors to reconsider their views on this matter.

To begin with a familiar type of situation, a patient who is dying of incurable cancer of the throat is in terrible pain, which can no longer be satisfactorily alleviated. He is certain to die within a few days, even if present treatment is continued, but he does not want to go on living for those days since the pain is unbearable. So he asks the doctor for an end to it, and his family joins in the request.

Suppose the doctor agrees to withhold treatment, as the conventional doctrine says he may. The justification for his doing so is that the patient is in terrible agony, and since he is going to die anyway, it would be wrong to prolong his suffering needlessly. But now notice this. If one simply withholds treatment, it may take the patient longer to die, and so he may suffer more than he would if more direct action were taken and a lethal injection given. This fact provides strong reason for thinking that, once the initial decision not to prolong his agony has been made, active euthanasia is actually preferable to passive euthanasia, rather than the reverse. To say otherwise is to endorse the option that leads to more suffering rather than less, and is contrary to the humanitarian impulse that prompts the decision not to prolong his life in the first place.

Part of my point is that the process of being "allowed to die" can be relatively slow and painful, whereas being given a lethal injection is relatively quick and painless. Let me give a different sort of example. In the United States about one in 600 babies is born with [Down] syndrome. Most of these babies are otherwise healthy—that is, with only the usual pediatric care, they will proceed to an otherwise normal infancy. Some, however, are born with congenital defects such as intestinal obstructions that require operations if they are to live. Sometimes, the parents and the doctor will decide not to operate, and let the infant die. Anthony Shaw describes what happens then:

. . . When surgery is denied [the doctor] must try to keep the infant from suffering while natural forces sap the baby's life away. As a surgeon whose natural inclination is to use the scalpel to fight off death, standing by and watching a salvageable baby die is the most emotionally exhausting experience I know. It is easy at a conference, in a theoretical discussion, to decide that such infants should be allowed to die. It is altogether different to stand by in the nursery and watch as dehydration and infection wither a tiny being over hours and days. This is a terrible ordeal for me and the hospital staff—much more so than for the parents who never set foot in the nursery.[1]

I can understand why some people are opposed to all euthanasia, and insist that such infants must be allowed to live. I think I can also understand why other people favor destroying these babies quickly and painlessly. But why should anyone favor letting "dehydration and infection wither a tiny being over hours and days?" The doctrine that says that a baby may be allowed to dehydrate and wither, but may not be given an injection that would end its life without suffering, seems so patently cruel as to require no further refutation. The strong language is not intended to offend, but only to put the point in the clearest possible way.

My second argument is that the conventional doctrine leads to decisions concerning life and death made on irrelevant grounds.

Consider again the case of the infants with [Down] syndrome who need operations for congenital defects unrelated to the syndrome to live. Sometimes, there is no operation, and the baby dies, but when there is no such defect, the baby lives on. Now, an operation such as that to remove an intestinal obstruction is not prohibitively difficult. The reason why such operations are not performed in these cases is, clearly, that the child has [Down] syndrome and the parents and doctor judge that because of that fact it is better for the child to die.

But notice that this situation is absurd, no matter what view one takes of the lives and potentials of such babies. If the life of such an infant is worth preserving, what does it matter if it needs a simple operation? Or, if one thinks it better that such a baby should not live on what difference does it make that it happens to have an unobstructed intestinal tract? In either case, the matter of life and death is being decided on irrelevant grounds. It is the [Down] syndrome, and not the intestines, that is the issue. The matter should be decided, if at all, on that basis, and not be allowed to depend on the essentially irrelevant question of whether the intestinal tract is blocked.

What makes this situation possible, of course, is the idea that when there is an intestinal blockage, one can "let the baby die," but when there is no such defect there is nothing that can be done, for one must not "kill" it. The fact that this idea leads to such results as deciding life or death on irrelevant grounds is another good reason why the doctrine should be rejected.

One reason why so many people think that there is an important moral difference between active and passive euthanasia is that they think killing someone is morally worse than letting someone die. But is it? Is killing, in itself, worse than letting die? To investigate this issue, two cases may be considered that are exactly alike except that one involves killing whereas the other involves letting someone die. Then, it can be asked whether this difference makes any difference to the moral assessments. It is important that the cases be exactly alike, except for this one difference, since otherwise one cannot be confident that it is this difference and not some other that accounts for any variation in the assessments of the two cases. So, let us consider this pair of cases:

In the first, Smith stands to gain a large inheritance if anything should happen to his six-year-old cousin. One evening while the child is taking his bath, Smith sneaks into the bathroom and drowns the child, and then arranges things so that it will look like an accident.

In the second, Jones also stands to gain if anything should happen to his six-year-old cousin. Like Smith, Jones sneaks in planning to drown the child in his bath. However, just as he enters the bathroom Jones sees the child slip and hit his head, and fall face down in the water. Jones is delighted; he stands by, ready to push the child's head back under if it is

necessary, but it is not necessary. With only a little thrashing about, the child drowns all by himself, "accidentally," as Jones watches and does nothing.

Now Smith killed the child, whereas Jones "merely" let the child die. That is the only difference between them. Did either man behave better, from a moral point of view? If the difference between killing and letting die were in itself a morally important matter, one should say that Jones's behavior was less reprehensible than Smith's. But does one really want to say that? I think not. In the first place, both men acted from the same motive, personal gain, and both had exactly the same end in view when they acted. It may be inferred from Smith's conduct that he is a bad man, although that judgment may be withdrawn or modified if certain further facts are learned about him—for example, that he is mentally deranged. But would not the very same thing be inferred about Jones from his conduct? And would not the same further considerations also be relevant to any modification of this judgment? Moreover, suppose Jones pleaded, in his own defense, "After all, I didn't do anything except just stand there and watch the child drown. I didn't kill him: I only let him die." Again, if letting die were in itself less bad than killing, this defense should have at least some weight. But it does not. Such a "defense" can only be regarded as a grotesque perversion of moral reasoning. Morally speaking, it is no defense at all.

Now, it may be pointed out, quite properly, that the case of euthanasia with which doctors are concerned are not like this at all. They do not involve personal gain or the destruction of normal healthy children. Doctors are concerned only with cases in which the patient's life is of no further use to him, or in which the patient's life has become or will soon become a terrible burden. However, the point is the same in these cases: the bare difference between killing and letting die does not, in itself, make a moral difference. If a doctor lets a patient die, for humane reasons, he is in the same moral position as if he had given the patient a lethal injection for humane reasons. If his decision was wrong—if, for example, the patient's illness was in fact curable—the decision would be equally regrettable no matter which method was used to carry it out. And if the doctor's decision was the right one, the method used is not in itself important.

The AMA policy statement isolates the crucial issue very well: the crucial issue is "the intentional termination of the life of one human being by another." But after identifying this issue, and forbidding "mercy killing," the statement goes on to deny that the cessation of treatment is the intentional termination of a life. This is where the mistake comes in, for what is the cessation of treatment, in these circumstances, if it is not "the intentional termination of the life of one human being by another"? Of course it is exactly that, and if it were not, there would be no point to it.

Many people will find this judgment hard to accept. One reason, I think, is that it is very easy to conflate the question of whether killing is, in itself, worse than letting die, with the very different question of whether most actual cases of killing are more reprehensible than most actual cases of letting die. Most actual cases of killing are clearly terrible (think, for example, of all the murders reported in the newspapers), and one hears of such cases every day. On the other hand, one hardly ever hears of a case of letting die, except for the actions of doctors who are motivated by humanitarian reasons. So one learns to think of killing in a much worse light than of letting die. But this does not mean that there is something about killing that makes it in itself worse than letting die, for it is not the bare difference between killing and letting die that makes the difference in these cases. Rather, the other factors—the murderer's motive of personal gain, for example, contrasted with the doctor's humanitarian motivation—account for different reactions to the different cases.

I have argued that killing is not in itself any worse than letting die: if my contention is right, it follows that active euthanasia is not any worse than passive euthanasia. What arguments can be given on the other side? The most common, I believe, is the following:

"The important difference between active and passive euthanasia is that, in passive euthanasia, the doctor does not do anything to bring about the patient's death. The doctor does nothing, and the patient dies of whatever ills already afflict him. In active euthanasia, however, the doctor does something to bring about the patient's death: he kills him. The doctor who gives the patient with cancer a lethal injection has himself caused his patient's death: whereas if he merely ceases treatment, the cancer is the cause of the death."

A number of points need to be made here. The first is that it is not exactly correct to say that in passive euthanasia the doctor does nothing, for he does do one thing that is very important: he lets the patient die. "Letting someone die" is certainly different, in some respects, from other types of action—mainly in that it is a kind of action that one may perform by way of not performing certain other actions. For example, one may let a patient die by way of not giving medication, just as one may insult someone by way of not shaking his hand. But for any purpose of moral assessment, it is a type of action nonetheless. The decision to let a patient die is subject to moral appraisal in the same way that a decision to kill him would be subject to moral appraisal: it may be assessed as wise or unwise, compassionate or sadistic, right or wrong. If a doctor deliberately let a patient die who was suffering from a routinely curable illness, the doctor would certainly be to blame for what he had done, just as he would be to blame if he had needlessly killed the patient. Charges against him would then be appropriate. If so, it would be no defense at all for him to insist that he didn't "do anything." He would have done something very serious indeed, for he let his patient die.

Fixing the cause of death may be very important from a legal point of view, for it may determine whether criminal charges are brought against the doctor. But I do not think that this notion can be used to show a moral difference between active and passive euthanasia. The reason why it is considered bad to be the cause of someone's death is that death is regarded as a great evil—and so it is. However, if it has been decided that euthanasia—even passive euthanasia—is desirable in a given case, it has also been decided that in this instance death is no greater an evil than the patient's continued existence. And if this is true, the usual reason for not wanting to be the cause of someone's death simply does not apply.

Finally, doctors may think that all of this is only of academic interest—the sort of thing that philosophers may worry about but that has no practical bearing on their own work. After all, doctors must be concerned about the legal consequences of what they do, and active euthanasia is clearly forbidden by the law. But even so, doctors should also be concerned with the fact that the law is forcing upon them a moral doctrine that may well be indefensible, and has a considerable effect on their practices. Of course, most doctors are not now in the position of being coerced in this matter, for they do not regard themselves as merely going along with what the law requires. Rather, in statements such as the AMA policy statement that I have quoted, they are endorsing this doctrine as a central point of medical ethics. In that statement, active euthanasia is condemned not merely as illegal but as "contrary to that for which the medical profession stands," whereas passive euthanasia is approved. However, the preceding considerations suggest that there is really no moral difference between the two, considered in themselves (there may be important moral differences in some cases in their *consequences,* but, as I pointed out, these differences may make active euthanasia, and not passive euthanasia, the morally preferable option). So, whereas doctors may have to discriminate between active and passive euthanasia to satisfy the law, they should not do any more than that. In particular, they should not give the distinction any added authority and weight by writing it into official statements of medical ethics.

NOTE

1. Anthony Shaw, "Doctor, Do We Have a Choice?" *New York Times Magazine,* 30 January 1972, 54.

The Wrongfulness of Euthanasia

J. GAY-WILLIAMS

My impression is that euthanasia—the idea, if not the practice—is slowly gaining acceptance within our society. Cynics might attribute this to an increasing tendency to devalue human life, but I do not believe this is the major factor. The acceptance is much more likely to be the result of unthinking sympathy and benevolence. Well-publicized, tragic stories like that of Karen Quinlan elicit from us deep feelings of compassion. We think to ourselves, "She and her family would be better off if she were dead." It is an easy step from this very human response to the view that if someone (and others) would be better off dead, then it might be all right to kill that person. Although I respect the compassion that leads to this conclu-

J. Gay-Williams, "The Wrongfulness of Euthanasia," 709–11 (edited). Copyright © 1979 by Ronald Munson. Published from Ronald Munson, *Intervention and Reflection: Basic Issues in Medical Ethics, 4th Edition.* Wadsworth Publishing Company: Belmont, California. Reprinted with permission.

sion, I believe the conclusion is wrong. I want to show that euthanasia is wrong. It is inherently wrong, but it is also wrong judged from the standpoints of self-interest and of practical effects.

Before presenting my arguments to support this claim, it would be well to define "euthanasia." An essential aspect of euthanasia is that it involves taking a human life, either one's own or that of another. Also, the person whose life is taken must be someone who is believed to be suffering from some disease or injury from which recovery cannot reasonably be expected. Finally, the action must be deliberate and intentional. Thus, euthanasia is intentionally taking the life of a presumably hopeless person. Whether the life is one's own or that of another, the taking of it is still euthanasia.

It is important to be clear about the deliberate and intentional aspect of the killing. If a hopeless person is given an injection of the wrong drug by mistake and this causes his death, this is wrongful killing but not euthanasia. The killing cannot be the result of accident. Furthermore, if the person is given an injection of a drug that is believed to be necessary to treat his disease or better his condition and the person dies as a result, then this is neither wrongful killing nor euthanasia. The intention was to make the patient well, not kill him. Similarly, when a patient's condition is such that it is not reasonable to hope that any medical procedures or treatments will save his life, a failure to implement the procedures or treatments is not euthanasia. If the person dies, this will be as a result of his injuries or disease and not because of his failure to receive treatment.

The failure to continue treatment after it has been realized that the patient has little chance of benefiting from it has been characterized by some as "passive euthanasia." This phrase is misleading and mistaken. In such cases, the person involved is not killed (the first essential aspect of euthanasia), nor is the death of the person intended by the withholding of additional treatment (the third essential aspect of euthanasia). The aim may be to spare the person additional and unjustifiable pain, to save him from the indignities of hopeless manipulations, and to avoid increasing the financial and emotional burden on his family. When I buy a pencil it is so that I can use it to write, not to contribute to an increase in the gross national product. This may be the unintended consequence of my action, but it is not the aim of my action. So it is with failing to continue the treatment of a dying person. I intend his death no more than I intend to reduce the GNP by not using medical supplies. His is an unintended dying, and so-called "passive euthanasia" is not euthanasia at all.

1. THE ARGUMENT FROM NATURE

Every human being has a natural inclination to continue living. Our reflexes and responses fit us to fight attackers, flee wild animals, and dodge out of the way of trucks. In our daily lives we exercise the caution and care necessary to protect ourselves. Our bodies are similarly structured for survival right down to the molecular level. When we are cut, our capillaries seal shut, our blood clots, and fibrogen is produced to start the process of healing the wound. When we are invaded by bacteria, antibodies are produced to fight against the alien organisms, and their remains are swept out of the body by special cells designed for clean-up work.

Euthanasia does violence to this natural goal of survival. It is literally acting against nature because all the processes of nature are bent towards the end of bodily survival. Euthanasia defeats these subtle mechanisms in a way that, in a particular case, disease and injury might not.

It is possible, but not necessary, to make an appeal to revealed religion in this connection. Man as trustee of his body acts against God, its rightful possessor, when he takes his own life. He also violates the commandment to hold life sacred and never to take it without just and compelling cause. But since this appeal will persuade only those who are prepared to accept that religion has access to revealed truths, I shall not employ this line of argument.

It is enough, I believe, to recognize that the organization of the human body and our patterns of behavioral responses make the continuation of life a natural goal. By reason alone, then, we can recognize that euthanasia sets us against our own nature. Furthermore, in doing so, euthanasia does violence to our dignity. Our dignity comes from seeking our ends. When one of our goals is survival, and actions are taken that eliminate that goal, then our natural dignity suffers. Unlike animals, we are conscious through reason of our nature and our ends. Euthanasia involves acting as if this dual nature—inclination towards survival and awareness of this as an end—did not exist. Thus, euthanasia denies our basic human character and requires that we regard ourselves or others as something less than fully human.

2. THE ARGUMENT FROM SELF-INTEREST

The above arguments are, I believe, sufficient to show that euthanasia is inherently wrong. But there are reasons for considering it wrong when judged by standards other than reason. Because death is final and irreversible, euthanasia contains within it the possibility that we will work against our own interest if we practice it or allow it to be practiced on us.

Contemporary medicine has high standards of excellence and a proven record of accomplishment, but it does not possess perfect and complete knowledge. A mistaken diagnosis is possible, and so is a mistaken prognosis. Consequently, we may believe that we are dying of a disease when, as a matter of fact, we may not be. We may think that we have no hope of recovery when, as a matter of fact, our chances are quite good. In such circumstances, if euthanasia were permitted, we would die needlessly. Death is final and the chance of error too great to approve the practice of euthanasia.

Also, there is always the possibility that an experimental procedure or a hitherto untried technique will pull us through. We should at least keep this option open, but euthanasia closes it off. Furthermore, spontaneous remission does occur in many cases. For no apparent reason, a patient simply recovers when those all around him, including his physicians, expected him to die. Euthanasia would just guarantee their expectations and leave no room for the "miraculous" recoveries that frequently occur.

Finally, knowing that we can take our life at any time (or ask another to take it) might well incline us to give up too easily. The will to live is strong in all of us, but it can be weakened by pain and suffering and feelings of hopelessness. If during a bad time we allow ourselves to be killed, we never have a chance to reconsider. Recovery from a serious illness requires that we fight for it, and anything that weakens our determination by suggesting that there is an easy way out is ultimately against our own interest. Also, we may be inclined towards euthanasia because of our concern for others. If we see our sickness and suffering as an emotional and financial burden on our family, we may feel that to leave our life is to make their lives easier. The very presence of the possibility of euthanasia may keep us from surviving when we might.

3. THE ARGUMENT FROM PRACTICAL EFFECTS

Doctors and nurses are, for the most part, totally committed to saving lives. A life lost is, for them, almost a personal failure, an insult to their skills and knowledge. Euthanasia as a practice might well alter this. It could have a corrupting influence so that in any case that is severe doctors and nurses might not try hard enough to save the patient. They might decide that the patient would simply be "better off dead" and take the steps necessary to make that come about. This attitude could then carry over to their dealings with patients less seriously ill. The result would be an overall decline in the quality of medical care.

Finally, euthanasia as a policy is a slippery slope. A person apparently hopelessly ill may be allowed to take his own life. Then he may be permitted to deputize others to do it for him should he no longer be able to act. The judgment of others then becomes the ruling factor. Already at this point euthanasia is not personal and voluntary, for others are acting "on behalf of" the patient as they see fit. This may well incline them to act on behalf of other patients who have not authorized them to exercise their judgment. It is only a short step, then, from voluntary euthanasia (self-inflicted or authorized), to directed euthanasia administered to a patient who has given no authorization, to involuntary euthanasia conducted as part of a social policy. Recently many psychiatrists and sociologists have argued that we define as "mental illness" those forms of behavior that we disapprove of. This gives us license then to lock up those who display the behavior. The category of the "hopelessly ill" provides the possibility of even worse abuse. Embedded in a social policy, it would give society or its representatives the authority to eliminate all those who might be considered too "ill" to function normally any longer. The dangers of euthanasia are too great to all to run the risk of approving it in any form. The first slippery step may well lead to a serious and harmful fall.

I hope that I have succeeded in showing why the benevolence that inclines us to give approval of euthanasia is misplaced. Euthanasia is inherently wrong because it violates the nature and dignity of human beings. But even those who are not convinced by this must be persuaded that the potential personal and social dangers inherent in euthanasia are sufficient to forbid our approving it either as a personal practice or as a public policy.

Suffering is surely a terrible thing, and we have a clear duty to comfort those in need and to ease their suffering when we can. But suffering is also a natural part of life with values for the individual and for others that we should not overlook. We may legitimately seek for others and for ourselves an easeful death, as Arthur Dyck has pointed out.[1] Euthanasia, however, is not just an easeful death. It is a wrongful death. Euthanasia is not just dying. It is killing.

NOTE

1. Arthur Dyck, "Beneficent Euthanasia and Benemortasia," in *Beneficent Euthanasia,* ed. Marvin Kohl (Buffalo, NY: Prometheus Books, 1975), 177–29.

From *Voluntary Active Euthanasia*

Dan W. Brock

* * *

THE CENTRAL ETHICAL ARGUMENT FOR VOLUNTARY ACTIVE EUTHANASIA

The central ethical argument for euthanasia is familiar. It is that the very same two fundamental ethical values supporting the consensus on patient's rights to decide about life-sustaining treatment also support the ethical permissibility of euthanasia. These values are individual self-determination or autonomy and individual well-being. By self-determination as it bears on euthanasia, I mean people's interest in making important decisions about their lives for themselves according to their own values or conceptions of a good life, and in being left free to act on those decisions. Self-determination is valuable because it permits people to form and live in accordance with their own conception of a good life, at least within the bounds of justice and consistent with others doing so as well. In exercising self-determination people take responsibility for their lives and for the kinds of persons they become. A central aspect of human dignity lies in people's capacity to direct their lives in this way. The value of exercising self-determination presupposes some minimum of deci-

Dan W. Brock, "Voluntary Active Euthanasia," *Hastings Center Report* 22, no. 2 (March/April 1992): 11–12, 14–17, 19–21 (edited). © The Hastings Center. Reprinted by permission. This article first appeared in The Hastings Center Report.

sion making capacities or competence, which thus limits the scope of euthanasia supported by self-determination; it cannot justifiably be administered, for example, in cases of serious dementia or treatable clinical depression.

Does the value of individual self-determination extend to the time and manner of one's death? Most people are very concerned about the nature of the last stage of their lives. This reflects not just a fear of experiencing substantial suffering when dying, but also a desire to retain dignity and control during this last period of life. Death is today increasingly preceded by a long period of significant physical and mental decline, due in part to the technological interventions of modern medicine. Many people adjust to these disabilities and find meaning and value in new activities and ways. Others find the impairments and burdens in the last stage of their lives at some point sufficiently great to make life no longer worth living. For many patients near death, maintaining the quality of one's life, avoiding great suffering, maintaining one's dignity, and insuring that others remember us as we wish them to become of paramount importance and outweigh merely extending one's life. But there is no single, objectively correct answer for everyone as to when, if at all, one's life becomes all things considered a burden and unwanted. If self-determination is a fundamental value, then the great variability among people on this question makes it especially important that individuals control the manner, circumstances, and timing of their dying and death.

The other main value that supports euthanasia is individual well-being. It might seem that individual well-being conflicts with a person's self-determination when the person requests euthanasia. Life itself is commonly taken to be a central good for persons, often valued for its own sake, as well as necessary for pursuit of all other goods within a life. But when a competent patient decides to forgo all further life-sustaining treatment then the patient, either explicitly or implicitly, commonly decides that the best life possible for him or her with treatment is of sufficiently poor quality that it is worse than no further life at all. Life is no longer considered a benefit by the patient, but has now become a burden. The same judgment underlies a request for euthanasia: continued life is seen by the patient as no longer a benefit, but now a burden. Especially in the often severely compromised and debilitated states of many critically ill or dying patients, there is no objective standard, but only the competent patient's judgment of whether continued life is no longer a benefit.

Of course, sometimes there are conditions, such as clinical depression, that call into question whether the patient has made a competent choice, either to forgo life-sustaining treatment or to seek euthanasia, and then the patient's choice need not be evidence that continued life is no longer a benefit for him or her. Just as with decisions about treatment, a determination of incompetence can warrant not honoring the patient's choice: in the case of treatment, we then transfer decisional authority to a surrogate, though in the case of voluntary active euthanasia a determination that the patient is incompetent means that choice is not possible.

The value or right of self-determination does not entitle patients to compel physicians to act contrary to their own moral or professional values. Physicians are moral and professional agents whose own self-determination or integrity should be respected as well. If performing euthanasia became legally permissible, but conflicted with a particular physician's reasonable understanding of his or her moral or professional responsibilities, the care of a patient who requested euthanasia should be transferred to another.

Most opponents do not deny that there are some cases in which the values of patient self-determination and well-being support euthanasia. Instead, they commonly offer two kinds of arguments against it that on their view outweigh or override this support. The first kind of argument is that in any individual case where considerations of the patient's self-determination and well-being do support euthanasia, it is nevertheless always ethically wrong or impermissible. The second kind of argument grants that in some individual cases euthanasia may not be ethically wrong, but maintains nonetheless that public and legal policy should never permit it. The first kind of argument focuses on features of any individual case of euthanasia, while the second kind focuses on social or legal policy. In the next section I consider the first kind of argument.

* * *

WOULD THE BAD CONSEQUENCES OF EUTHANASIA OUTWEIGH THE GOOD?

The argument against euthanasia at the policy level is stronger than at the level of individual cases, though even here I believe the case is ultimately unpersuasive, or at best indecisive. The policy level is the place where the main issues lie, however, and where moral considerations that might override arguments in favor of euthanasia will be found, if they are found anywhere. It is important to note two kinds of disagreement about the consequences for public policy of permitting euthanasia. First, there is empirical or factual disagreement about what the consequences would be. This disagreement is greatly exacerbated by the lack of firm data on the issue. Second, since on any reasonable assessment there would be both good and bad consequences, there are moral disagreements about the relative importance of different effects. In addition to these two sources of disagreement, there is also no single, well-specified policy proposal for legalizing euthanasia on which policy assessments can focus. But without such specification, and especially without explicit procedures for protecting against well-intentioned misuse and ill-intentioned abuse, the consequences for policy are largely speculative. Despite these difficulties, a preliminary account of the main likely good and bad consequences is possible. This should help clarify where better data or more moral analysis and argument are needed, as well as where policy safeguards must be developed.

Potential Good Consequences of Permitting Euthanasia

What are the likely good consequences? First, if euthanasia were permitted it would be possible to respect the self-determination of competent patients who want it, but now cannot get it because of its illegality. We simply do not know how many such patients and people there are. In the Netherlands, with a population of about 14.5 million (in 1987), estimates in a recent study were that about 1,900 cases of voluntary active euthanasia or physician-assisted suicide occur annually. No straightforward extrapolation to the United States is possible for many reasons, among them, that we do not know how many people here who want euthanasia now get it, despite its illegality. Even with better data on the number of persons who want euthanasia but cannot get it, significant moral disagreement would remain about how much weight should be given to any instance of failure to respect a person's self-determination in this way.

One important factor substantially affecting the number of persons who would seek euthanasia is the extent to which an alternative is available. The widespread acceptance in the law, social policy, and medical practice of the right of a competent patient to forgo life-sustaining treatment suggests that the number of competent persons in the United States who would want euthanasia if it were permitted is probably relatively small.

A second good consequence of making euthanasia legally permissible benefits a much larger group. Polls have shown that a majority of the American public believes that people should have a right to obtain euthanasia if they want.[1] No doubt the vast majority of those who support this right to euthanasia will never in fact come to want euthanasia for themselves. Nevertheless, making it legally permissible would reassure many people that if they ever do want euthanasia they would be able to obtain it. This reassurance would supplement the broader control over the process of dying given by the right to decide about life-sustaining treatment. Having fire insurance on one's house benefits all who have it, not just those whose houses actually burn down, by reassuring them that in the unlikely event of their house burning down, they will receive the money needed to rebuild it. Likewise, the legalization of euthanasia can be thought of as a kind of insurance policy against being forced to endure a protracted dying process that one has come to find burdensome and unwanted, especially when there is no life-sustaining treatment to forgo. The strong concern about losing control of their care expressed by many people who face serious illness likely to end in death suggests that they give substantial importance to the legalization of euthanasia as a means of maintaining this control.

A third good consequence of the legalization of euthanasia concerns patients whose dying is filled with severe and unrelievable pain or suffering. When there is a life-sustaining treatment that, if forgone, will lead relatively quickly to death, then doing so can bring an end to these patients' suffering without recourse to euthanasia. For patients receiving no such treatment, however, euthanasia may be the only release from their otherwise prolonged suffering and agony. This argument from mercy has always been the strongest argument for euthanasia in those cases to which it applies.

The importance of relieving pain and suffering is less controversial than is the frequency with which patients are forced to undergo untreatable agony that only euthanasia could relieve. If we focus first on suffering caused by physical pain, it is crucial to distinguish pain that could be adequately relieved with modern methods of pain control, though it in fact is not, from pain that is relievable only by death. For a variety of reasons, including some physicians' fear of hastening the patient's death, as well as the lack of a publicly accessible means for assessing the amount of the patient's pain, many patients suffer pain that could be, but is not, relieved.

Specialists in pain control, as for example the pain of terminally ill cancer patients, argue that there are very few patients whose pain could not be adequately controlled, though sometimes at the cost of so sedating them that they are effectively unable to interact with other people or their environment. Thus, the argument from mercy in cases of physical pain can probably be met in a large majority of cases by providing adequate measures of pain relief. This should be a high priority, whatever our legal policy on euthanasia—the relief of pain and suffering has long been, quite properly, one of the central goals of medicine. Those cases in which pain could be effectively relieved, but in fact is not, should only count significantly in favor of legalizing euthanasia if all reasonable efforts to change pain management techniques have been tried and have failed.

Dying patients often undergo substantial psychological suffering that is not fully or even principally the result of physical pain. The knowledge about how to relieve this suffering is much more limited than in the case of relieving pain, and efforts to do so are probably more often unsuccessful. If the argument from mercy is extended to patients experiencing great and unrelievable psychological suffering, the numbers of patients to which it applies are much greater.

One last good consequence of legalizing euthanasia is that once death has been accepted, it is often more humane to end life quickly and peacefully, when that is what the patient wants. Such a death will often be seen as better than a more prolonged one. People who suffer a sudden and unexpected death, for example by dying quickly or in their sleep from a heart attack or stroke, are often considered lucky to have died in this way. We care about how we die in part because we care about how others remember us, and we hope they will remember us as we were in "good times" with them and not as we might be when disease has robbed us of our dignity as human beings. As with much in the treatment and care of the dying, people's concerns differ in this respect, but for at least some people, euthanasia will be a more humane death than what they have often experienced with other loved ones and might otherwise expect for themselves.

Some opponents of euthanasia challenge how much importance should be given to any of these good consequences of permitting it, or even whether some would be good consequences at all. But more frequently, opponents cite a number of bad consequences that permitting euthanasia would or could produce, and it is to their assessment that I now turn.

Potential Bad Consequences of Permitting Euthanasia

Some of the arguments against permitting euthanasia are aimed specifically against physicians, while others are aimed against anyone being permitted to perform it. I shall first consider one argument of the former sort. Permitting physicians to perform euthanasia, it is said, would be incompatible with their fundamental moral and professional commitment as healers to care for patients and to protect life. Moreover, if euthanasia by physicians became common, patients would come to fear that a medication was intended not to treat or care, but instead to kill, and would thus lose trust in their physicians. This position was forcefully stated in a paper by Willard Gaylin and his colleagues:

The very soul of medicine is on trial. . . . This issue touches medicine at its moral center; if this moral center collapses, if physicians become killers or are even licensed to kill, the profession—and, therewith, each physician—will never again be worthy of trust and respect as healer and comforter and protector of life in all its frailty.

These authors go on to make clear that, while they oppose permitting anyone to perform euthanasia, their special concern is with physicians doing so:

We call on fellow physicians to say that they will not deliberately kill. We must also say to each of our fellow physicians that we will not tolerate killing of patients and that we shall take disciplinary action against doctors who kill. And we must say to the broader community that if it insists on tolerating or legalizing active euthanasia, it will have to find nonphysicians to do its killing.[2]

If permitting physicians to kill would undermine the very "moral center" of medicine, then almost certainly physicians should not be permitted to perform euthanasia. But how persuasive is this claim? Patients should not fear, as a consequence of permitting voluntary active euthanasia, that their physicians will substitute a lethal injection for what patients want and believe is part of their care. If active euthanasia is restricted to cases in which it is truly voluntary, then no patient should fear getting it unless she or he has voluntarily requested it. (The fear that we might in time also come to accept nonvoluntary, or even involuntary, active euthanasia is a slippery slope worry I address below.) Patients' trust of their physicians could be increased, not eroded, by knowledge that physicians will provide aid in dying when patients seek it.

. . . In spelling out above what I called the positive argument for voluntary active euthanasia, I suggested that two principal values—respective patients' self-determination and promoting their well-being—underlie the consensus that competent patients, or the surrogates of incompetent patients, are entitled to refuse any life-sustaining treatment and to choose from among available alternative treatments. It is the commitment to these two values in guiding physicians' actions as healers, comforters, and protectors of their patients' lives that should be at the "moral center" of medicine, and these two values support physicians' administering euthanasia when their patients make competent requests for it.

What should not be at that moral center is a commitment to preserving patients' lives as such, without regard to whether those patients want their lives preserved or judge their preservation a benefit to them. . . .

A second bad consequence that some foresee is that permitting euthanasia would weaken society's commitment to provide optimal care for dying patients. We live at a time in which the control of health care costs has become, and is likely to continue to be, the dominant focus of health care policy. If euthanasia is seen as a cheaper alternative to adequate care and treatment, then we might become less scrupulous about providing sometimes costly support and other services to dying patients. Particularly if our society comes to embrace deeper and more explicit rationing of health care, frail, elderly, and dying patients will need to be strong and effective advocates for their own health care and other needs, although they are hardly in a position to do this. We should do nothing to weaken their ability to obtain adequate care and services.

This second worry is difficult to assess because there is little firm evidence about the likelihood of the feared erosion in the care of dying patients. There are at least two reasons, however, for skepticism about this argument. The first is that the same worry could have been directed at recognizing patients' or surrogates' rights to forgo life-sustaining treatment, yet there is no persuasive evidence that recognizing the right to refuse treatment has caused a serious erosion in the quality of care of dying patients. The second reason for skepticism about this worry is that only a very small proportion of deaths would occur from euthanasia if it were permitted. In the Netherlands, where euthanasia under specified circumstances is permitted by the courts, though not authorized by statute, the best estimate of the proportion of overall deaths that result from it is about 2 percent.[3] Thus, the vast majority of critically ill and dying patients will not request it, and so will still have to be cared for by physicians, families, and others. Permitting euthanasia should not diminish people's commitment and concern to maintain and improve the care of these patients.

A third possible bad consequence of permitting euthanasia (or even a public discourse in which strong support for euthanasia is evident) is to threaten the progress made in securing the rights of patients or their surrogates to decide about and to refuse life-sustaining treatment. This progress has been made against the backdrop of a clear and firm legal prohibition of euthanasia, which has provided a relatively bright line limiting the dominion of others over patients' lives. It has therefore been an important reassurance to concerns about how the authority to take steps ending life might be misused, abused, or wrongly extended.

Many supporters of the right of patients or their surrogates to refuse treatment strongly oppose euthanasia, and if forced to choose might well withdraw their support of the right to refuse treatment rather than accept euthanasia. Public policy in the last fifteen years has generally let life-sustaining treatment decisions be made in health care settings between physicians and patients or their surrogates, and without the involvement of the courts. However, if euthanasia is made legally permissible greater involvement of the courts is likely, which could in turn extend to a greater court involvement in life-sustaining treatment decisions. Most agree, however, that increased involvement of the courts in these decisions would be undesirable, as it would make sound decisionmaking more cumbersome and difficult without sufficient compensating benefits.

As with the second potential bad consequence of permitting euthanasia, this third consideration too is speculative and difficult to assess. The feared erosion of patients' or surrogates' rights to decide about life-sustaining treatment, together with greater court involvement in those decisions, are both possible. However, I believe there is reason to discount this generally worry. The legal rights of competent patients and, to a lesser degree, surrogates of incompetent patients to decide about treatment are very firmly embedded in a long line of informed consent and life-sustaining treatment cases, and are not likely to be eroded by a debate over, or even acceptance of, euthanasia. It will not be accepted without safeguards that reassure the public about abuse, and if that debate shows the need for similar safeguards for some life-sustaining treatment decisions they should be adopted there as well. In neither case are the only possible safeguards greater court involvement, as the recent growth of institutional ethics committees shows.

The fourth potential bad consequence of permitting euthanasia . . . turns on the subtle point that making a new option or choice available to people can sometimes make them worse off, even if once they have the choice they go on to choose what is best for them. Ordinarily, people's continued existence is viewed by them as given, a fixed condition

with which they must cope. Making euthanasia available to people as an option denies them the alternative of staying alive by default. If people are offered the option of euthanasia, their continued existence is now a choice for which they can be held responsible and which they can be asked by others to justify. We care, and are right to care, about being able to justify ourselves to others. To the extent that our society is unsympathetic to justifying a severely dependent or impaired existence, a heavy psychological burden of proof may be placed on patients who think their terminal illness or chronic infirmity is not a sufficient reason for dying. Even if they otherwise view their life as worth living, the opinion of others around them that it is not can threaten their reason for living and make euthanasia a rational choice. Thus the existence of the option becomes a subtle pressure to request it.

This argument correctly identifies the reason why offering some patients the option of euthanasia would not benefit them. [David] Velleman takes it not as a reason for opposing all euthanasia, but for restricting it to circumstances where there are "unmistakable and overpowering reasons for persons to want the option of euthanasia,"[4] and for denying the option in all other cases. But there are at least three reasons why such restriction may not be warranted. First, polls and other evidence support that most Americans believe euthanasia should be permitted (though the recent defeat of the referendum to permit it in the state of Washington raises some doubt about this support). Thus, many more people seem to want the choice than would be made worse off by getting it. Second, if giving people the option of ending their life really makes them worse off, then we should not only prohibit euthanasia, but also take back from people the right they now have to decide about-life-sustaining treatment. The feared harmful effect should already have occurred from securing people's right to refuse life-sustaining treatment, yet there is no evidence of any such widespread harm or any broad public desire to rescind that right. Third, since there is a wide range of conditions in which reasonable people can and do disagree about whether they would want continued life, it is not possible to restrict the permissibility of euthanasia as narrowly as Velleman suggests without thereby denying it to most persons who would want it; to permit it only in cases in which virtually everyone would want it would be to deny it to most who would want it.

A fifth potential bad consequence of making euthanasia legally permissible is that it might weaken the general legal prohibition of homicide. This prohibition is so fundamental to civilized society, it is argued, that we should do nothing that erodes it. If most cases of stopping life support are killing, as I have already argued, then the court cases permitting such killing have already in effect weakened this prohibition. However, neither the courts nor most people have seen these cases as killing and so as challenging the prohibition of homicide. The courts have usually grounded patients' or their surrogates' rights to refuse life-sustaining treatment in rights to privacy, liberty, self-determination, or bodily integrity, not in exceptions to homicide laws.

Legal permission for physicians or others to perform euthanasia could not be grounded in patients' rights to decide about medical treatment. Permitting euthanasia would require qualifying, at least in effect, the legal prohibition against homicide, a prohibition that in general does not allow the consent of the victim to justify or excuse the act. Nevertheless, the very same fundamental basis of the right to decide about life-sustaining treatment—respecting a person's self-determination—does support euthanasia as well. Individual self-determination has long been a well-entrenched and fundamental value in the law, and so extending it to euthanasia would not require appeal to novel legal values or principles. That suicide or attempted suicide is no longer a criminal offense in virtually all states indicates an acceptance of individual self-determination in the taking of one's own life analogous to that required for voluntary active euthanasia. The legal prohibition (in most states) of assisting in suicide and the refusal in the law to accept the consent of the victim as a possible justification of homicide are both arguably a result of difficulties in the legal process of establishing the consent of the victim after the fact. If procedures can be designed that clearly establish the voluntariness

of the person's request for euthanasia it would under those procedures represent a carefully circumscribed qualification on the legal prohibition of homicide. Nevertheless, some remaining worries about this weakening can be captured in the final potential bad consequence, to which I will now turn.

This final potential bad consequence is the central concern of many opponents of euthanasia and, I believe, is the most serious objection to a legal policy permitting it. According to this "slippery slope" worry, although active euthanasia may be morally permissible in cases in which it is unequivocally voluntary and the patient finds his or her condition unbearable, a legal policy permitting euthanasia would inevitably lead to active euthanasia being performed in many other cases in which it would be morally wrong. To prevent those other wrongful cases of euthanasia we should not permit even morally justified performance of it.

Slippery slope arguments of this form are problematic and difficult to evaluate. From one perspective, they are the last refuge of conservative defenders of the status quo. When all the opponent's objections to the wrongness of euthanasia itself have been met, the opponent then shifts ground and acknowledges both that it is not in itself wrong and that a legal policy which resulted only in its being performed would not be bad. Nevertheless, the opponent maintains, it should still not be permitted because doing so would result in its being performed in other cases in which it is not voluntary and would be wrong. In this argument's most extreme form, permitting euthanasia is the first and fateful step down the slippery slope to Nazism. Once on the slope we will be unable to get off.

Now it cannot be denied that it is *possible* that permitting euthanasia could have these fateful consequences, but that cannot be enough to warrant prohibiting it if it is otherwise justified. A similar *possible* slippery slope worry could have been raised to securing competent patients' rights to decide about life support, but recent history shows such a worry would have been unfounded. It must be relevant how likely it is that we will end with horrendous consequences and an unjustified practice of euthanasia. How *like,* and *widespread* would the abuses and unwarranted extensions of permitting it be? By abuses, I mean the performance of euthanasia that fails to satisfy the conditions required for voluntary active euthanasia, for example, if the patient has been subtly pressured to accept it. By unwarranted extensions of policy, I mean later changes in legal policy to permit not just voluntary euthanasia, but also euthanasia in cases in which, for example, it need not be fully voluntary. Opponents of voluntary euthanasia on slippery slope grounds have not provided the data or evidence necessary to turn their speculative concerns into well-grounded likelihoods.

It is at least clear, however, that both the character and likelihood of abuses of a legal policy permitting euthanasia depend in significant part on the procedures put in place to protect against them. I will not try to detail fully what such procedures might be, but will just give some examples of what they might include:

1. The patient should be provided with all relevant information about his or her medical condition, current prognosis, available alternative treatments, and the prognosis of each.
2. Procedures should ensure that the patient's request for euthanasia is stable or enduring (a brief waiting period could be required) and fully voluntary (an advocate for the patient might be appointed to ensure this).
3. All reasonable alternatives must have been explored for improving the patient's quality of life and relieving any pain or suffering.
4. A psychiatric evaluation should ensure that the patient's request is not the result of a treatable psychological impairment such as depression.

These examples of procedural safeguards are all designed to ensure that the patient's choice is fully informed, voluntary, and competent, and so a true exercise of self-determination. Other proposals for euthanasia would restrict its permissibility further—for example, to the terminally ill—a restriction that cannot be supported by self-determination. Such additional restrictions might, however, be justified by concern for limiting potential harms from abuse. At the same time, it is important not to impose procedural or substantive safeguards so restrictive as to make euthanasia impermissible or practically infeasible in a wide range of Justified cases.

These examples of procedural safeguards make clear that it is possible to substantially reduce, though not to eliminate, the potential for abuse of a policy permitting voluntary active euthanasia. Any legalization of the practice should be accompanied by a well-considered set of procedural safeguards together with an ongoing evaluation of its use. Introducing euthanasia into only a few states could be a form of carefully limited and controlled social experiment that would give us evidence about the benefits and harms of the practice. Even then firm and uncontroversial data may remain elusive, as the continuing controversy over what has taken place in the Netherlands in recent years indicates.[5]

* * *

THE ROLE OF PHYSICIANS

If euthanasia is made legally permissible, should physicians take part in it? Should only physicians be permitted to perform it, as is the case in the Netherlands? In discussing whether euthanasia is incompatible with medicine's commitment to curing, caring for, and comforting patients, I argued that it is not at odds with a proper understanding of the aims of medicine, and so need not undermine patients' trust in their physicians. If that argument is correct, then physicians probably should not be prohibited, either by law or by professional norms, from taking part in a legally permissible practice of euthanasia (nor, of course, should they be compelled to do so if their personal or professional scruples forbid it). Most physicians in the Netherlands appear not to understand euthanasia to be incompatible with their professional commitments.

Sometimes patients who would be able to end their lives on their own nevertheless seek the assistance of physicians. Physician involvement in such cases may have important benefits to patients and others beyond simply assuring the use of effective means. Historically, in the United States suicide has carried a strong negative stigma that many today believe unwarranted. Seeking a physician's assistance, or what can almost seem a physician's blessing, may be a way of trying to remove that stigma and show others that the decision for suicide was made with due seriousness and was justified under the circumstances. The physician's involvement provides a kind of social approval, or more accurately helps counter what would otherwise be unwarranted social disapproval.

There are also at least two reasons for restricting the practice of euthanasia to physicians only. First, physicians would inevitably be involved in some of the important procedural safeguards necessary to a defensible practice, such as seeing to it that the patient is well-informed about his or her condition, prognosis, and possible treatments, and ensuring that all reasonable means have been taken to improve the quality of the patient's life. Second, and probably more important, one necessary protection against abuse of the practice is to limit the persons given authority to perform it, so that they can be held accountable for their exercise of that authority. Physi-

cians, whose training and professional norms give some assurance that they would perform euthanasia responsibly, are an appropriate group of persons to whom the practice may be restricted.

* * *

NOTES

1. P. Painton and E. Taylor, "Love or Let Die," *Time,* 19 March 1990, 62–71; Boston Globe/Harvard University Poll, *Boston Globe,* 3 November 1991.

2. Willard Gaylin, Leon R. Kass, Edmund D. Pellegrino, and Mark Siegler, "Doctors Must Not Kill," *Journal of the American Medical Association* 259 (1988): 2139–40.

3. Paul J. Van der Maas et al., "Euthanasia and Other Medical Decisions Concerning the End of Life," *Lancet* 338 (1991): 669–74.

4. David Velleman commented on an earlier version of the paper delivered at the American Philosophical Association Central Division meetings.

5. Richard Fenigsen, "A Case against Dutch Euthanasia," *Special Supplement, Hastings Center Report* 19, no. 1 (1989): 22–30.

From *Is There a Duty to Die?*

JOHN HARDWIG

* * *

When Richard Lamm made the statement that old people have a duty to die, it was generally shouted down or ridiculed. The whole idea is just too preposterous to entertain. Or too threatening. In fact, a fairly common argument against legalizing physician-assisted suicide is that if it were legal, some people might somehow get the idea that they have a duty to die. These people could only be the victims of twisted moral reasoning or vicious social pressure. It goes without saying that there is no duty to die.

John Hardwig, "Is There a Duty to Die?" *Hastings Center Report* 27, no. 2 (1997): 34–42 (edited). © The Hastings Center. Reprinted by permission. This article first appeared in The Hastings Center Report.

But for me the question is real and very important. I feel strongly that I may very well some day have a duty to die. I do not believe that I am idiosyncratic, morbid, mentally ill, or morally perverse in thinking this. I think many of us will eventually face precisely this duty. But I am first of all concerned with my own duty. I write partly to clarify my own convictions and to prepare myself. Ending my life might be a very difficult thing for me to do.

This notion of a duty to die raises all sorts of interesting theoretical and metaethical questions. I intend to try to avoid most of them because I hope my argument will be persuasive to those holding a wide variety of ethical views. Also, although the claim that there is a duty to die would ultimately require theoretical underpinning, the discussion needs to begin on the normative level. As is appropriate to my attempt to steer clear of theoretical commitments, I will use "duty," "obligation," and "responsibility" interchangeably, in a pretheoretical or pre-analytic sense.[1]

CIRCUMSTANCES AND A DUTY TO DIE

Do many of us really believe that no one ever has a duty to die? I suspect not. I think most of us probably believe that there is such a duty, but it is very uncommon. Consider Captain Oates, a member of Admiral Scott's expedition to the South Pole. Oates became too ill to continue. If the rest of the team stayed with him, they would all perish. After this had become clear, Oates left his tent one night, walked out into a raging blizzard, and was never seen again. That may have been a heroic thing to do, but we might be able to agree that it was also no more than his duty. It would have been wrong for him to urge—or even to allow—the rest to stay and care for him.

This is a very unusual circumstance—a "lifeboat case"—and lifeboat cases make for bad ethics. But I expect that most of us would also agree that there have been cultures in which what we would call a duty to die has been fairly common. These are relatively poor, technologically simple, and especially nomadic cultures. In such societies, everyone knows that if you manage to live long enough, you will eventually become old and debilitated. Then you will need to take steps to end your life. The old people in these societies regularly did precisely that. Their cultures prepared and supported them in doing so.

Those cultures could be dismissed as irrelevant to contemporary bioethics; their circumstances are so different from ours. But if that is our response, it is instructive. It suggests that we assume a duty to die is irrelevant to us because our wealth and technological sophistication have purchased exemption for us . . . except under very unusual circumstances like Captain Oates's.

But have wealth and technology really exempted us? Or are they, on the contrary, about to make a duty to die common again? We like to think of mod-

ern medicine as all triumph with no dark side. Our medicine saves many lives and enables most of us to live longer. That is wonderful, indeed. We are all glad to have access to this medicine. But our medicine also delivers most of us over to chronic illnesses and it enables many of us to survive longer than we can take care of ourselves, longer than we know what to do with ourselves, longer than we even are ourselves.

The costs—and these are not merely monetary—of prolonging our lives when we are no longer able to care for ourselves are often staggering. If further medical advances wipe out many of today's "killer diseases"—cancers, heart attacks, strokes, ALS, AIDS, and the rest—then one day most of us will survive long enough to become demented or debilitated. These developments could generate a fairly widespread duty to die. A fairly common duty to die might turn out to be only the dark side of our life-prolonging medicine and the uses we choose to make of it.

Let me be clear. I certainly believe that there is a duty to refuse life-prolonging medical treatment and also a duty to complete advance directives refusing life-prolonging treatment. But a duty to die can go well beyond that. There can be a duty to die before one's illnesses would cause death, even if treated only with palliative measures. In fact, there may be a fairly common responsibility to end one's life in the absence of any terminal illness at all. Finally, there can be a duty to die when one would prefer to live. Granted, many of the conditions that can generate a duty to die also seriously undermine the quality of life. Some prefer not to live under such conditions. But even those who want to live can face a duty to die. These will clearly be the most controversial and troubling cases; I will, accordingly, focus my reflections on them.

THE INDIVIDUALISTIC FANTASY

Because a duty to die seems such a real possibility to me, I wonder why contemporary bioethics has dismissed it without serious consideration. I believe that most bioethics still shares in one of our deeply embedded American dreams: the individualistic fantasy. This fantasy leads us to imagine that lives are separate and unconnected, or that they could be so if we chose. If lives were unconnected, things that happened in my life would not or need not affect others. And if others were not (much) affected by my life, I would have no duty to consider the impact of my decisions on others. I would then be free morally to live my life however I please, choosing whatever life and death I prefer for myself. The way I live would be nobody's business but my own. I certainly would have no duty to die if I preferred to live.

Within a health care context, the individualistic fantasy leads us to assume that the patient is the only one affected by decisions about her medical treatment. If only the patient were affected, the relevant questions when making treatment decisions would be precisely those we ask: What will benefit the patient? Who can best decide that? The pivotal issue would always be simply whether the patient wants to live like this and whether she would consider herself better off dead. "Whose life is it, anyway?" we ask rhetorically.

But this is morally obtuse. We are not a race of hermits. Illness and death do not come only to those who are all alone. Nor is it much better to think in terms of the bald dichotomy between "the interests of the patient" and "the interests of society" (or a third-party payer), as if we were isolated individuals connected only to "society" in the abstract or to the other, faceless members of our health maintenance organization.

Most of us are affiliated with particular others and most deeply, with family and loved ones. Families and loved ones are bound together by ties of care and affection, by legal relations and obligations, by inhabiting shared spaces and living units, by interlocking finances and economic prospects, by common projects and also commitments to support the different life projects of other family members, by shared histories, by ties of loyalty. This life together of family and loved ones is what defines and sustains us; it is what gives meaning to most of our lives. We would not have it any other way. We would not want to be all alone, especially when we are seriously ill, as we age, and when we are dying.

But the fact of deeply interwoven lives debars us from making exclusively self-regarding decisions, as the decisions of one member of a family may dramatically affect the lives of all the rest. The impact of my decisions upon my family and loved ones is the source of many of my strongest obligations and also the most plausible and likeliest basis of a duty to die. "Society," after all, is only very marginally affected by how I live, or by whether I live or die.

A BURDEN TO MY LOVED ONES

Many older people report that their one remaining goal in life is not to be a burden to their loved ones. Young people feel this, too: when I ask my undergraduate students to think about whether their death could come too late, one of their very first responses always is, "Yes, when I become a burden to my family or loved ones." Tragically, there are situations in which my loved ones would be much better off—all things considered, the loss of a loved one notwithstanding—if I were dead.

The lives of our loved ones can be seriously compromised by caring for us. The burdens of providing care or even just supervision twenty-four hours a day, seven days a week are often overwhelming. When this kind of caregiving goes on for years, it leaves the caregiver exhausted, with no time for herself or life of her own. Ultimately, even her health is often destroyed. But it can also be emotionally devastating simply to live with a spouse who is increasingly distant, uncommunicative, unresponsive, foreign, and unreachable. Other family members' needs often go unmet as the caring capacity of the family is exceeded. Social life and friendships evaporate, as there is no opportunity to go out to see friends and the home is no longer a place suitable for having friends in.

We must also acknowledge that the lives of our loved ones can be devastated just by having to pay for health care for us. One . . . study documented the financial aspects of caring for a dying member of a family. Only those who had illnesses severe enough to give them less than a 50 percent chance to live six more months were included in this study. When these patients survived their initial hospitalization and were discharged about one-third required considerable caregiving from their families; in 20 percent of cases a family member had to quit work or make some other major lifestyle change; almost one-third of these families lost all of their savings; and just under 30 percent lost a major source of income.[2]

If talking about money sounds venal or trivial, remember that much more than money is normally at stake here. When someone has to quit work, she may well lose her career. Savings decimated late in life cannot be recouped in the few remaining years of employability, so the loss compromises the quality of the rest of the caregiver's life. For a young person, the chance to go to college may be lost to the attempt to pay debts due to an illness in the family, and this decisively shapes an entire life.

A serious illness in a family is a misfortune. It is usually nobody's fault; no one is responsible for it. But we face choices about how we will respond to this misfortune. That's where the responsibility comes in and fault can arise. Those of us with families and loved ones always have a duty not to make selfish or self-centered decisions about our lives. We have a responsibility to try to protect the lives of loved ones from serious threats or greatly impoverished quality, certainly an obligation not to make choices that will jeopardize or seriously compromise their futures. Often, it would be wrong to do just what we want or just what is best for ourselves; we should choose in light of what is best for all concerned. That is our duty in sickness as well as in health. It is out of these responsibilities that a duty to die can develop.

I am not advocating a crass, quasi-economic conception of burdens and benefits, nor a shallow, hedonistic view of life. Given a suitably rich understanding of benefits, family members sometimes do benefit from suffering through the long illness of a loved one. Caring for the sick or aged can foster growth, even as it makes daily life immeasurably harder and the prospects for the future much bleaker. Chronic illness or a drawn-out death can also pull a family together, making the care for each other stronger and more evident. If my loved ones are truly benefiting from coping with my illness or debility, I have no duty to die based on burdens to them.

But it would be irresponsible to blithely assume that this always happens, that it will happen in my family, or that it will be the fault of my family if they cannot manage to turn my illness into a positive experience. Perhaps the opposite is more common: a hospital chaplain once told me that he could not think of a single case in which a family was strengthened or brought together by what happened at the hospital.

Our families and loved ones also have obligations, of course—they have the responsibility to stand by us and to support us through debilitating illness and death. They must be prepared to make significant sacrifices to respond to an illness in the family. I am far from denying that. Most of us are aware of this responsibility and most families meet it rather well. In fact, families deliver more than 80 percent of the long-term care in this country, almost always at great personal cost. Most of us who are a part of a family can expect to be sustained in our time of need by family members and those who love us.

But most discussions of an illness in the family sound as if responsibility were a one-way street. It is not, of course. When we become seriously ill or debilitated, we too may have to make sacrifices. To think that my loved ones must bear whatever burdens my illness, debility, or dying process might impose upon them is to reduce them to means to my well-being. And that would be immoral. Family solidarity, altruism, bearing the burden of a loved one's misfortune, and loyalty are all important virtues of families, as well. But they are all also two-way streets.

OBJECTIONS TO A DUTY TO DIE

To my mind, the most serious objections to the idea of a duty to die lie in the effects on my loved ones of ending my life. But to most others, the important objections have little or nothing to do with family and loved ones. Perhaps the most common objections are: (1) there is a higher duty that always takes precedence over a duty to die; (2) a duty to end one's own life would be incompatible with a recognition of human dignity or the intrinsic value of a person; and (3) seriously ill, debilitated, or dying people are already bearing the harshest burdens and so it would be wrong to ask them to bear the additional burden of ending their own lives.

These are all important objections; all deserve a thorough discussion. Here I will only be able to suggest some moral counterweights—ideas that might provide the basis for an argument that these objections do not always preclude a duty to die.

An example of the first line of argument would be the claim that a duty to God, the giver of life, forbids that anyone take her own life. It could be argued that this duty always supersedes whatever obligations we might have to our families. But what convinces us that we always have such a religious duty in the first place? And what guarantees that it always supersedes our obligations to try to protect our loved ones?

Certainly, the view that death is the ultimate evil cannot be squared with Christian theology. It does not reflect the actions of Jesus or those of his early followers. Nor is it clear that the belief that life is sacred requires that we never take it. . . . In any case, most of us—bioethicists, physicians, and patients alike—do not subscribe to the view that we have an obligation to preserve human life as long as possible. But if not, surely we ought to agree that I may legitimately end my life for other-regarding reasons, not just for self-regarding reasons.

Secondly, religious considerations aside, the claim could be made that an obligation to end one's own life would be incompatible with human dignity or would embody a failure to recognize the intrinsic value of a person. But I do not see that in thinking I had a duty to die I would necessarily be failing to respect myself or to appreciate my dignity or worth. Nor would I necessarily be failing to respect you in thinking that you had a similar duty. There is surely also a sense in which we fail to respect ourselves if in the face of illness or death, we stoop to choosing just what is best for ourselves. Indeed, Kant held that the very core of human dignity is the ability to act on a self-imposed moral law, regardless of whether it

is in our interest to do so.[3] We shall return to the notion of human dignity.

A third objection appeals to the relative weight of burdens and thus, ultimately, to considerations of fairness or justice. The burdens that an illness creates for the family could not possibly be great enough to justify an obligation to end one's life—the sacrifice of life itself would be a far greater burden than any involved in caring for a chronically ill family member.

But is this true? Consider the following case:

An 87-year-old woman was dying of congestive heart failure. Her APACHE [Acute Physiology and Chronic Health Evaluation] score predicted that she had less than a 50 percent chance to live for another six months. She was lucid, assertive, and terrified of death. She very much wanted to live and kept opting for rehospitalization and the most aggressive life-prolonging treatment possible. That treatment successfully prolonged her life (though with increasing debility) for nearly two years. Her 55-year-old daughter was her only remaining family, her caregiver, and the main source of her financial support. The daughter duly cared for her mother. But before her mother died, her illness had cost the daughter all of her savings, her home, her job, and her career.

This is by no means an uncommon sort of case. Thousands of similar cases occur each year. Now, ask yourself which is the greater burden:

a) To lose a 50 percent chance of six more months of life at age 87?
b) To lose all your savings, your home, and your career at age 55?

Which burden would you prefer to bear? Do we really believe the former is the greater burden? Would even the dying mother say that (a) is the greater burden? Or has she been encouraged to believe that the burdens of (b) are somehow morally irrelevant to her choices?

I think most of us would quickly agree that (b) is the greater burden. That is the evil we would more hope to avoid in our lives. If we are tempted to say that the mother's disease and impending death are the greater evil, I believe it is because we are taking a "slice of time" perspective rather than a "lifetime perspective."[4] But surely the lifetime perspective is the appropriate perspective when weighing burdens. If (b) is the greater burden, then we must admit that we have been promulgating an ethics that advocates imposing greater burdens on some people in order to provide smaller benefits for others just because they are ill and thus gain our professional attention and advocacy.

A whole range of cases like this one could easily be generated. In some, the answer about which burden is greater will not be clear. But in many it is. Death—or ending your own life—is simply not the greatest evil or the greatest burden.

This point does not depend on a utilitarian calculus. Even if death were the greatest burden (thus disposing of any simple utilitarian argument), serious questions would remain about the moral justifiability of choosing to impose crushing burdens on loved ones in order to avoid having to bear this burden oneself. The fact that I suffer greater burdens than others in may family does not license me simply to choose what I want for myself, nor does it necessarily release me from a responsibility to try to protect the quality of their lives.

I can readily imagine that, through cowardice, rationalization, or failure of resolve, I will fail in this obligation to protect my loved ones. If so, I think I would need to be excused or forgiven for what I did. But I cannot imagine it would be morally permissible for me to ruin the rest of my partner's life to sustain mine or to cut off my sons' careers, impoverish them, or compromise the quality of their children's lives simply because I wish to live a little longer. This is what leads me to believe in a duty to die.

WHO HAS A DUTY TO DIE?

Suppose, then, that there can be a duty to die. Who has a duty to die? And when? To my mind, these are the right questions, the questions we should be asking. Many of us may one day badly need answers to just these questions.

But I cannot supply answers here, for two reasons. In the first place, answers will have to be very particular and contextual. Our concrete duties are often situated, defined in part by the myriad details of our circumstances, histories, and relationships. Though there may be principles that apply to a wide range of cases and some cases that yield pretty straightforward answers, there will also be many situations in which it is very difficult to discern whether one has a duty to die. If nothing else, it will often be very difficult to predict how one's family will bear up under the weight of the burdens that a protracted illness would impose on them. Momentous decisions will often have to be made under conditions of great certainty.

Second and perhaps even more importantly, I believe that those of us with family and loved ones should not define our duties unilaterally, especially not a decision about a duty to die. It would be isolating and distancing for me to decide without consulting them what is too much of a burden for my loved ones to bear. That way of deciding about my moral duties is not only atomistic, it also treats my family and loved ones paternalistically. They must be allowed to speak for themselves about the burdens my life imposes on them and how they feel about bearing those burdens.

Some may object that it would be wrong to put a loved one in a position of having to say, in effect, "You should end your life because caring for you is too hard on me and the rest of my family." Not only will it be almost impossible to say something like that to someone you love, it will carry with it a heavy load of guilt. On this view, you should decide by yourself whether you have a duty to die and approach your loved ones only after you have made up your mind to say good-bye to them. Your family could then try to change your mind, but the tremendous weight of moral decision would be lifted from their shoulders.

Perhaps so. But I believe in family decisions. Important decisions for those whose lives are interwoven should be made together, in a family discussion. Granted, a conversation about whether I have a duty to die would be a tremendously difficult conversation. The temptations to be dishonest could be enormous. Nevertheless, if I am contemplating a duty to die, my family and I should, if possible, have just such an agonizing discussion. It will act as a check on the information, perceptions, and reasoning of all of us. But even more importantly, it affirms our connectedness at a critical juncture in our lives and our life together. Honest talk about difficult matters almost always strengthens relationships.

However, many families seem unable to talk about death at all, much less a duty to die. Certainly most families could not have this discussion all at once, in one sitting. It might well take a number of discussions to be able to approach this topic. But even if talking about death is impossible, there are always behavioral clues—about your caregiver's tiredness, physical condition, health, prevailing mood, anxiety, financial concerns, outlook, overall well-being, and so on. And families unable to talk about death can often talk about how the caregiver is feeling, about finances, about tensions within the family resulting from the illness, about concerns for the future. Deciding whether you have a duty to die based on these behavioral clues and conversation about them honors your relationships better than deciding on your own about how burdensome you and your care must be.

I cannot say when someone has a duty to die. Still, I can suggest a few features of one's illness, history, and circumstances that make it more likely that one has a duty to die. I present them here without much elaboration or explanation.

1. A duty to die is more likely when continuing to live will impose significant burdens—emotional burdens, extensive caregiving, destruction of life plans, and, yes, financial hardship—on your family and loved ones. This is the fundamental insight underlying a duty to die.

2. A duty to die becomes greater as you grow older. As we age, we will be giving up less by giving up our lives, if only because we will sacrifice fewer remaining years of life and a smaller portion of our life plans. After all, it's not as if we would be immortal and live forever if we could just manage to avoid a duty to die. To have reached the age of, say, seventy-five or eighty years without being ready to die is itself a moral failing, the sign of a life out of touch with life's basic realities.

3. A duty to die is more likely when you have already lived a full and rich life. You have already had a full share of the good things life offers.

4. There is greater duty to die if your loved ones' lives have already been difficult or impoverished, if they have had only a small share of the good things that life has to offer (especially if through no fault of their own).

5. A duty to die is more likely when your loved ones have already made great contributions—perhaps even sacrifices—to make your life a good one. Especially if you have not made similar sacrifices for their well-being or for the well-being of other members of your family.

6. To the extent that you can make a good adjustment to your illness or handicapping condition, there is less likely to be a duty to die. A good adjustment means that smaller sacrifices will be required of loved ones and there is more compensating interaction for them. Still, we must also recognize that some diseases—Alzheimer's or Huntington's chorea—will eventually take their toll on your loved ones no matter how courageously, resolutely, even cheerfully you manage to face that illness.

7. There is less likely to be a duty to die if you can still make significant contributions to the lives of others, especially your family. The burdens to family members are not only or even primarily financial, neither are the contributions to them. However, the old and those who have terminal illnesses must also bear in mind that the loss their family members will feel when they die cannot be avoided, only postponed.

8. A duty to die is more likely when the part of you that is loved will soon be gone or seriously compromised. Or when you soon will no longer be capable of giving love. Part of the horror of dementing disease is that it destroys the capacity to nurture and sustain relationships, taking away a person's agency and the emotions that bind her to others.

9. There is a greater duty to die to the extent that you have lived a relatively lavish lifestyle instead of saving for illness or old age. Like most upper

middle-class Americans, I could easily have saved more. It is a greater wrong to come to your family for assistance if your need is the result of having chosen leisure or a spendthrift lifestyle. I may eventually have to face the moral consequences of decisions I am now making.

These, then, are some of the considerations that give shape and definition to the duty to die. If we can agree that these considerations are all relevant, we can see that the correct course of action will often be difficult to discern. A decision about when I should end my life will sometimes prove to be every bit as difficult as the decision about whether I want treatment for myself.

CAN THE INCOMPETENT HAVE A DUTY TO DIE?

Severe mental deterioration springs readily to mind as one of the situations in which I believe I could have a duty to die. But can incompetent people have duties at all? We can have moral duties we do not recognize or acknowledge, including duties that we never recognized. But can we have duties we are unable to recognize? Duties when we are unable to understand the concept of morality at all? If so, do others have a moral obligation to help us carry out this duty? These are extremely difficult theoretical questions. The reach of moral agency is severely strained by mental incompetence.

I am tempted to simply bypass the entire question by saying that I am talking only about competent persons. But the idea of a duty to die clearly raises the specter of one person claiming that another—who cannot speak for herself—has such a duty. So I need to say that I can make no sense of the claim that someone has a duty to die if the person has never been able to understand moral obligation at all. To my mind, only those who were formerly capable of making moral decisions could have such a duty.

But the case of formerly competent persons is almost as troubling. Perhaps we should simply stipulate that no incompetent person can have a duty to die, not even if she affirmed belief in such a duty in an advance directive. If we take the view that formerly competent people may have such a duty, we should surely exericise extreme caution when claiming a formerly competent person would have acknowledged a duty to die or that any formerly competent person has an unacknowledged duty to die. Moral dangers loom regardless of which way we decide to resolve such issues.

But for me personally, very urgent practical matters turn on their resolution. If a formerly competent person can no longer have a duty to die (or if other people are not likely to help her carry out this duty), I believe that my obligation may be to die while I am still competent, before I become unable to make and carry out that decision for myself. Surely it would be irresponsible to evade my moral duties by temporizing until I escape into incompetence. And so I must die sooner than I otherwise would have to. On the other hand, if I could count on others to end my life after I become incompetent, I might be able to fulfill my responsibilities while also living out all my competent or semi-competent days. Given our society's reluctance to permit physicians, let alone family members, to perform aid-in-dying, I believe I may well have a duty to end my life when I can see mental incapacity on the horizon.

There is also the very real problem of sudden incompetence—due to a serious stroke or automobile accident, for example. For me, that is the real nightmare. If I suddenly become incompetent, I will fall into the hands of a medical-legal system that will conscientiously disregard my moral beliefs and do what is best for me, regardless of the consequences for my loved ones. And that is not at all what I would have wanted!

SOCIAL POLICIES AND A DUTY TO DIE

The claim that there is a duty to die will seem to some a misplaced response to social negligence. If our society were providing for the debilitated, the chronically ill, and the elderly as it should be, there would be only very rare cases of a duty to die. On this view, I am asking the sick and debilitated to step in and accept responsibility because society is derelict in its responsibility to provide for the incapacitated.

This much is surely true: there are a number of social policies we could pursue that would dramatically reduce the incidence of such a duty. Most obviously, we could decide to pay for facilities that provided excellent long-term care (not just health care!) for all chronically ill, debilitated, mentally ill, or demented people in this country. We probably could still afford to do this. If we did, sick, debilitated, and dying people might still be morally required to make sacrifices for their families. I might, for example, have a duty to forgo personal care by a family member who knows me and really does care for me. But these sacrifices would only rarely include the sacrifice of life itself. The duty to die would then be virtually eliminated.

I cannot claim to know whether in some abstract sense a society like ours should provide care for all who are chronically ill or debilitated. But the fact is that we Americans seem to be unwilling to pay for this kind of long-term care, except for ourselves and our own. In fact, we are moving in precisely the opposite direction—we are trying to shift the burdens of caring for the seriously and chronically ill onto families in order to save costs for our health care system. As we shift the burdens of care onto families, we also dramatically increase the number of Americans who will have a duty to die.

I must not, then, live my life and make my plans on the assumption that social institutions will protect my family from my infirmity and debility. To do so would be irresponsible. More likely, it will be up to me to protect my loved ones.

A DUTY TO DIE AND THE MEANING OF LIFE

A duty to die seems very harsh, and often it would be. It is one of the tragedies of our lives that someone who wants very much to live can nevertheless have a duty to die. It is both tragic and ironic that it is precisely the very real good of family and loved ones that gives rise to this duty. Indeed, the genuine love, closeness, and supportiveness of family members is a major source of this duty: we could not be

such a burden if they did not care for us. Finally, there is deep irony in the fact that the very successes of our life-prolonging medicine help to create a widespread duty to die. We do not live in such a happy world that we can avoid such tragedies and ironies. We ought not to close our eyes to this reality or pretend that it just doesn't exist. We ought not to minimize the tragedy in any way.

And yet, a duty to die will not always be as harsh as we might assume. If I love my family, I will want to protect them and their lives. I will want not to make choices that compromise their futures. Indeed, I can easily imagine that I might want to avoid compromising their lives more than I would want anything else. I must also admit that I am not necessarily giving up so much in giving up my life: the conditions that give rise to a duty to die would usually already have compromised the quality of the life I am required to end. In any case, I personally must confess that at age fifty-six, I have already lived a very good life, albeit not yet nearly as long a life as I would like to have.

We fear death too much. Our fear of death has led to a massive assault on it. We still crave after virtually any life-prolonging technology that we might conceivably be able to produce. We still too often feel morally impelled to prolong life virtually any form of life as long as possible. As if the best death is the one that can be put off longest.

We do not even ask about meaning in death, so busy are we with trying to postpone it. But we will not conquer death by one day developing a technology so magnificent that no one will have to die. Nor can we conquer death by postponing it ever longer. We can conquer death only by finding meaning in it.

Although the existence of a duty to die does not hinge on this, recognizing such a duty would go some way toward recovering meaning in death. Paradoxically, it would restore dignity to those who are seriously ill or dying. It would also reaffirm theconnections required to give life (and death) meaning. I close now with a few words about both of these points.

First, recognizing a duty to die affirms my agency and also my moral agency. I can still do things that make an important difference in the lives of my loved ones. Moreover, the fact that I still have responsibilities keeps me within the community of moral agents. My illness or debility has not reduced me to a mere moral patient (to use the language of the philosophers). Though it may not be the whole story, surely Kant was onto something important when he claimed that human dignity rests on the capacity for moral agency within a community of those who respect the demands of morality.

By contrast, surely there is something deeply insulting in a medicine and an ethic that would ask only what I want (or would have wanted) when I become ill. To treat me as if I had no moral responsibilities when I am ill or debilitated implies that my condition has rendered me morally incompetent. Only small children, the demented or insane, and those totally lacking in the capacity to act are free from moral duties. There is dignity, then, and a kind of meaning in moral agency, even as it forces extremely difficult decisions upon us.

Second, recovering meaning in death requires an affirmation of connections. If I end my life to spare the futures of my loved ones, I testify in my death that I am connected to them. It is because I love and care for precisely these people (and I know they care for me) that I wish not to be such a burden to them. By contrast, a life in which I am free to choose whatever I want for myself is a life unconnected to others. A bioethics that would treat me as if I had no serious moral responsibilities does what it can to marginalize, weaken, or even destroy my connections with others.

But life without connection is meaningless. The individualistic fantasy, though occasionally liberating, is deeply destructive. When life is good and vitality seems unending, life itself and life lived for yourself may seem quite sufficient. But if not life, certainly death without connection is meaningless. If you are only for yourself, all you have to care about as your life draws to a close is yourself and your life. Everything you care about will then perish in your death. And that—the end of everything you care about—is precisely the total collapse of meaning. We can, then, find meaning in death only through a

sense of connection with something that will survive our death.

This need not be connections with other people. Some people are deeply tied to land (for example, the family farm), to nature, or to a transcendent reality. But for most of us, the connections that sustain us are to other people. In the full bloom of life, we are connected to others in many ways—through work, profession, neighborhood, country, shared faith and worship, common leisure pursuits, friendship. Even the guru meditating in isolation on his mountain top is connected to a long tradition of people united by the same religious quest.

But as we age or when we become chronically ill, connections with other people usually become much more restricted. Often, only ties with family and close friends remain and remain important to us. Moreover, for many of us, other connections just don't go deep enough. . . .

If I am correct, death is so difficult for us partly because our sense of community is so weak. Death seems to wipe out everything when we can't fit it into the lives of those who live on. A death motivated by the desire to spare the futures of my loved ones might well be a better death for me than the one I would get as a result of opting to continue my life as long as there is any pleasure in it for me. Pleasure is nice, but it is meaning that matters.

I don't know about others, but these reflections have helped me. I am now more at peace about facing a duty to die. Ending my life if my duty required might still be difficult. But for me, a far greater horror would be dying all alone or stealing the futures of my loved ones in order to buy a little more time for myself. I hope that if the time comes when I have a duty to die, I will recognize it, encourage my loved ones to recognize it too, and carry it out bravely.

NOTES

1. Given the importance of relationships in my thinking, "responsibility"—rooted as it is in "respond"—would perhaps be the most appropriate word. Nevertheless, I often use "duty" despite its legalistic overtones, because Lamm's famous statement has given the expression "duty to die" a

certain familiarity. But I intend no implication that there is a law that grounds this duty, nor that someone has a right corresponding to it.

2. Kenneth E. Covinsky et al., "The Impact of Serious Illness on Patients' Families," *Journal of the American Medical Association* 272 (1994): 1839–44.

3. Kant, as is well known, was opposed to suicide. But he was arguing against taking your life out of self-interested motives. It is not clear that Kant would or we should consider taking your life out of a sense of duty to be wrong. See Hilde L. Nelson, "Death with Kantian Dignity," *Journal of Clinical Ethics* 7 (1996): 215–21.

4. I owe this distinction to Norman Daniels. Normal Daniels, *Am I My Parents' Keeper? An Essay on Justice between the Young and the Old* (New York: Oxford University Press, 1988). Daniels is not committed to my use of it here.

Euthanasia

Philippa Foot

The widely used *Shorter Oxford English Dictionary* gives three meanings for the word "euthanasia": the first, "a quiet and easy death"; the second, "the means of procuring this"; and the third, "the action of inducing a quiet and easy death." It is a curious fact that no one of the three gives an adequate definition of the word as it is usually understood. For "euthanasia" means much more than a quiet and easy death, or the means of procuring it, or the action of inducing it. The definition species only the manner of the death, and if this were all that was implied a murderer, careful to drug his victim, could claim that his act was an act of euthanasia. We find this ridiculous because we take it for granted that in euthanasia it is death itself, not just the manner of death, that must be kind to the one who dies.

To see how important it is that "euthanasia" should not be used as the dictionary definition allows it to be used, merely to signify that a death was quiet and easy, one has only to remember that Hitler's "euthanasia" program traded on this ambiguity. Under this program, planned before the War but brought into full operation by a decree of 1 September 1939, some 275,000 people were gassed in centers which were to be a model for those in which Jews were later exterminated. Anyone in a state institution could be sent to the gas chambers if it was considered that he could not be "rehabilitated" for useful work. As Dr. Leo Alexander reports, relying on the testimony of a neuropathologist who received 500 brains from one of the killing centers,

In Germany the exterminations included the mentally defective, psychotics (particularly schizophrenics), epileptics and patients suffering from infirmities of old age and from various organic neurological disorders such as infantile paralysis, Parkinsonism, multiple sclerosis and brain tumors. . . . In truth, all those unable to work and considered nonrehabilitable were killed.[1]

These people were killed because they were "useless" and "a burden on society"; only the manner of their deaths could be thought of as relatively easy and quiet.

Let us insist, then, that when we talk about euthanasia we are talking about a death understood as a good or happy event for the one who dies. This stipulation follows etymology, but is itself not exactly in line with current usage, which would be captured by the condition that the death should *not* be an evil rather than that it *should* be a good. That this is how people talk is shown by the fact that the case of Karen Ann Quinlan and others in a state of permanent coma is often discussed under the heading of "euthanasia." Perhaps it is not too late to object to the use of the word "euthanasia" in this sense. Apart from the break

Philippa Foot, "Euthanasia," *Philosophy & Public Affairs* 6, no. 2 (Winter, 1977): 85–112 (edited). Reprinted with permission of Blackwell Publishing.

with the Greek origins of the word there are other unfortunate aspects of this extension of the term. For if we say that the death must be supposed to be a good to the subject we can also specify that it shall be for his sake that an act of euthanasia is performed. If we say merely that death shall not be an evil to him, we cannot stipulate that benefiting him shall be the motive where euthanasia is in question. Given the importance of the question, For whose sake are we acting? it is good to have a definition of euthanasia which brings under this heading only cases of opting for death for the sake of the one who dies. Perhaps what is most important is to say either that euthanasia is to be for the good of the subject or at least that death is to be no evil to him, thus refusing to talk Hitler's language. However, in this paper it is the first condition that will be understood, with the additional proviso that by an act of euthanasia we mean one of inducing or otherwise opting for death for the sake of the one who is to die.

A few lesser points need to be cleared up. In the first place it must be said that the word "act" is not to be taken to exclude omission: we shall speak of an act of euthanasia when someone is deliberately allowed to die, for his own good, and not only when positive measures are taken to see that he does. The very general idea we want is that of a choice of action or inaction directed at another man's death and causally effective in the sense that, in conjunction with actual circumstances, it is a sufficient condition of death. Of complications such as overdetermination, it will not be necessary to speak.

A second, and definitely minor, point about the definition of an act of euthanasia concerns the question of fact versus belief. It has already been implied that one who performs an act of euthanasia thinks that death will be merciful for the subject since we have said that it is on account of this thought that the act is done. But is it enough that he acts with this thought, or must things actually be as he thinks them to be? If one man kills another, or allows him to die, thinking that he is in the last stages of a terrible disease, though in fact he could have been cured, is this an act of euthanasia or not? Nothing much seems to hang on our decision about this. The same condition

has got to enter into the definition whether as an element in reality or only as an element in the agent's belief. And however we define an act of euthanasia culpability or justifiability will be the same: if a man acts through ignorance his ignorance may be culpable or it may not.[2]

These are relatively easy problems to solve, but one that is dauntingly difficult has been passed over in this discussion of the definition, and must now be faced. It is easy to say, as if this raised no problems, that an act of euthanasia is by definition one aiming at the *good* of the one whose death is in question, and that it is *for his sake* that his death is desired. But how is this to be explained? Presumably we are thinking of some evil already with him or to come on him if he continues to live, and death is thought of as a release from this evil. But this cannot be enough. Most people's lives contain evils such as grief or pain, but we do not therefore think that death would be a blessing to them. On the contrary life is generally supposed to be a good even for someone who is unusually unhappy or frustrated. How is it that one can ever wish for death for the sake of the one who is to die? This difficult question is central to the discussion of euthanasia, and we shall literally not know what we are talking about if we ask whether acts of euthanasia defined as we have defined them are ever morally permissible without first understanding better the reason for saying that life is a good, and the possibility that it is not always so.

If a man should save my life he would be my benefactor. In normal circumstances this is plainly true; but does one always benefit another in saving his life? It seems certain that he does not. Suppose, for instance, that a man were being tortured to death and was given a drug that lengthened his sufferings; this would not be a benefit but the reverse. Or suppose that in a ghetto in Nazi Germany a doctor saved the life of someone threatened by disease, but that the man once cured was transported to an extermination camp; the doctor might wish for the sake of the patient that he had died of the disease. Nor would a longer stretch of life always be a benefit to the person who was given it. Comparing Hitler's camps with those of Stalin, Dmitri Panin observes that in the latter the method of extermination was made worse by agonies that could stretch out over months.

Death from a bullet would have been bliss compared with what many millions had to endure while dying of hunger. The kind of death to which they were condemned has nothing to equal it in treachery and sadism.[3]

These examples show that to save or prolong a man's life is not always to do him a service: it may be better for him if he dies earlier rather than later. It must therefore be agreed that while life is normally a benefit to the one who has it, this is not always so.

The judgment is often fairly easy to make—that life is or is not a good to someone—but the basis for it is very hard to find. When life is said to be a benefit or a good, on what grounds is the assertion made?

The difficulty is underestimated if it is supposed that the problem arises from the fact that one who is dead has nothing, so that the good someone gets from being alive cannot be compared with the amount he would otherwise have had. For why should this particular comparison be necessary? Surely it would be enough if one could say whether or not someone whose life was prolonged had more good than evil in the extra stretch of time. Such estimates are not always possible, but frequently the year; we say, for example, "He was very happy in those last years," or, "He had little but unhappiness then." If the balance of good and evil determined whether life was a good to someone we would expect to find a correlation in the judgments. In fact, of course, we find nothing of the kind. First, a man who has no doubt that existence is a good to him may have no idea about the balance of happiness and unhappiness in his life, or of any other positive and negative factors that may be suggested. So the supposed criteria are not always operating where the judgment is made. And secondly the application of the criteria gives an answer that is often wrong. Many people have more evil than good in their lives; we do not, however, conclude that we would do these people no service by rescuing them from death.

To get around this last difficulty Thomas Nagel has suggested that experience itself is a good which must be brought in to balance accounts.

. . . life is worth living even when the bad elements of experience are plentiful, and the good ones too meager to outweigh the bad ones on their own. The additional positive weight is supplied by experience itself, rather than by any of its contents.[4]

This seems implausible because if experience itself is a good it must be so even when what we experience is wholly bad, as in being tortured to death. How should one decide how much to count for this experiencing; and why count anything at all?

Others have tried to solve the problem by arguing that it is a man's desire for life that makes us call life a good: if he wants to live then anyone who prolongs his life does him a benefit. Yet someone may cling to life where we would say confidently that it would be better for him if he died, and he may admit it too. Speaking of those same conditions in which, as he said, a bullet would have been merciful, Panin writes,

I should like to pass on my observations concerning the absence of suicides under the extremely severe conditions of our concentration camps. The more that life became desperate, the more a prisoner seemed determined to hold onto it.[5]

One might try to explain this by saying that hope was the ground of this wish to survive for further days and months in the camp. But there is nothing unintelligible in the idea that a man might cling to life though he knew those facts about his future which would make any charitable man wish that he might die.

The problem remains, and it is hard to know where to look for a solution. Is there a conceptual connection between *life* and *good*? Because life is not always a good we are apt to reject this idea, and to think that it must be a contingent fact that life is usually a good, as it is a contingent matter that legacies are usually a benefit, if they are. Yet it seems not to be a contingent matter that to save someone's life is ordinarily to benefit him. The problem is to find where the conceptual connection lies.

It may be good tactics to forget for a time that it is euthanasia we are discussing and to see how *life* and *good* are connected in the case of living beings other than men. Even plants have things done to them that are harmful or beneficial, and what does them good must be related in some way to their living and dying. Let us therefore consider plants and animals, and then come back to human beings. At least we shall get away from the temptation to think that the connection between life and benefit must everywhere be a matter of happiness and unhappiness or of pleasure and pain; the idea being absurd in the case of animals and impossible even to formulate for plants.

In case anyone thinks that the concept of the beneficial applies only in a secondary or analogical way to plants, he should be reminded that we speak quite straightforwardly in saying, for instance, that a certain amount of sunlight is beneficial to most plants. What is in question here is the habitat in which plants of particular species flourish, but we can also talk, in a slightly different way, of what does them good, where there is some suggestion of improvement or remedy. What has the beneficial to do with sustaining life? It is tempting to answer, "everything," thinking that a healthy condition just is the one apt to secure survival. In fact, however, what is beneficial to a plant may have to do with reproduction rather than the survival of the individual member of the species. Nevertheless there is a plain connection between the beneficial and the life-sustaining even for the individual plant; if something makes it better able to survive in conditions normal for that species it is ipso facto good for it. We need go no further, and could go no further, in explaining why a certain environment or treatment is good for a plant than to show how it helps this plant to survive.[6]

This connection between the life-sustaining and the beneficial is reasonably unproblematic, and there is nothing fanciful or zoomorphic in speaking of benefiting or doing good to plants. A connection with its survival can make something beneficial to a plant. But this is not, of course, to say that we count life as a good to a plant. We may save its life by giving it what is beneficial; we do not benefit it by saving its life.

A more ramified concept of benefit is used in speaking of animal life. New things can be said, such as that an animal is better or worse off for something that happened, or that it was a good or bad thing for it that it did happen. And new things count as benefit. In the first place, there is comfort, which often is, but need not be, related to health. When loosening a collar which is too tight for a dog we can say, "That will be better for it." So we see that the words "better for it" have two different meanings which we mark when necessary by a difference of emphasis, saying "better *for* it" when health is involved. And secondly an animal can be benefited by having its life saved. "Could you do anything for it?" can be answered by, "Yes, I managed to save its life." Sometimes we may understand this, just as we would for a plant, to mean that we had checked some disease. But we can also do something for an animal by scaring away its predator. If we do this, it is a good thing for the animal that we did, unless of course it immediately meets a more unpleasant end by some other means. Similarly, on the bad side, an animal may be worse off for our intervention, and this not because it pines or suffers but simply because it gets killed.

The problem that vexes us when we think about euthanasia comes on the scene at this point. For if we can do something for an animal—can benefit it—by relieving its suffering but also by saving its life, where does the greater benefit come when only death will end pain? It seemed that life was a good in its own right; yet pain seemed to be an evil with equal status and could therefore make life not a good after all. Is it only life without pain that is a good when animals are concerned? This does not seem a crazy suggestion when we are thinking of animals, since unlike human beings they do not have suffering as part of their normal life. But it is perhaps the idea of ordinary life that matters here. We would not say that we had done anything for an animal if we had merely kept it alive, either in an unconscious state or in a condition where, though conscious, it was unable to operate in an ordinary way; and the fact is that animals in severe and continuous pain simply do not operate normally. So we do not, on the whole, have the option of doing the animal good by saving its life though the life would be a life of pain. No doubt there are borderline cases, but that is no problem. We are not trying to make new judgments possible, but rather to find the principle of the ones we do make.

When we reach human life the problems seem even more troublesome. For now we must take quite new things into account, such as the subject's own view of his life. It is arguable that this places extra constraints on the solution: might it not be counted as a necessary condition of life's being a good to a man that he should see it as such? Is there not some difficulty about the idea that a benefit might be done to him by the saving or prolonging of his life even though he himself wished for death? Of course he might have a quite mistaken view of his own prospects, but let us ignore this and think only of cases where it is life as he knows it that is in question. Can we think that the prolonging of his life would be a benefit to him even though he would rather have it end than continue? It seems that this cannot be ruled out. That there is no simple incompatibility between life as a good and the wish for death is shown by the possibility that a man should wish himself dead, not for his own sake, but for the sake of someone else. And if we try to amend the thesis to say that life cannot be a good to one who wishes *for his own sake* that he should die, we find the crucial concept slipping through our fingers. As Bishop Butler pointed out long ago not all ends are either benevolent or self-interested. Does a man wish for death for his own sake in the relevant sense if, for instance, he wishes to revenge himself on another by his death. Or what if he is proud and refuses to stomach dependence or incapacity even though there are many good things left in life for him? The truth seems to be that the wish for death is sometimes compatible with life's being a good and sometimes not, which is possible because the description "wishing for death" is one covering diverse states of mind from that of the determined suicide, pathologically depressed, to that of one who is surprised to find that the thought of a fatal accident is viewed with relief. On the one hand, a man may see his life as a burden but go about his business in a more or less ordinary way; on the other hand, the wish for death may take the form of a rejection of everything that is in life, as it does in severe depression. It seems reasonable to say that life is not a good to one permanently in the latter state, and we must return to this topic later on.

When are we to say that life is a good or a benefit to a man? The dilemma that faces us is this. If we say that life as such is a good we find ourselves refuted by the examples given at the beginning of this discussion. We therefore incline to think that it is as bringing good things that life is a good, where it is a good. But if life is a good only because it is the condition of good things why is it not equally an evil when it brings bad things? And how can it be a good even when it brings more evil than good?

It should be noted that the problem has here been formulated in terms of the balance of good and evil, not that of happiness and unhappiness, and that it is not to be solved by the denial (which may be reasonable enough) that unhappiness is the only evil or happiness the only good. In this paper no view has been expressed about the nature of goods other than life itself. The point is that on any view of the goods and evils that life can contain, it seems that a life with more evil than good could still itself be a good.

It may be useful to review the judgments with which our theory must square. Do we think that life can be a good to one who suffers a lot of pain? Clearly we do. What about severely handicapped people; can life be a good to them? Clearly it can be, for even if someone is almost completely paralyzed, perhaps living in an iron lung, perhaps able to move things only by means of a tube held between his lips, we do not rule him out of order if he says that some benefactor saved his life. Nor is it different with mental handicap. There are many fairly severely handicapped people—such as those with [Down] Syndrome (Mongolism)—for whom a simple affectionate life is possible. What about senility? Does this break the normal connection between life and good? Here we must surely distinguish between forms of senility. Some forms leave a life which we count someone as better off having than not having, so that a doctor who prolonged it would benefit the person concerned. With some kinds of senility this is however no longer true. There are some in geriatric wards who are barely conscious, though they can move a little and swallow food put into their mouths. To prolong such a state, whether in the old or in the very severely mentally handicapped is not to do them a service or confer a benefit. But of course it need not be the reverse: only if there is suffering would one wish for the sake of the patient that he should die.

It seems, therefore, that merely being alive even without suffering is not a good, and that we must make a distinction similar to that which we made when animals were our topic. But how is the line to be drawn in the case of men? What is to count as ordinary human life in the relevant sense? If it were only the very senile or very ill who were to be said not to have this life it might seem right to describe it in terms of *operation*. But it will be hard to find the sense in which the men described by Panin were not operating, given that they dragged themselves out to the forest to work. What is it about the life that the prisoners were living that makes us put it on the other side of the dividing line from that of some severely ill or suffering patients, and from most of the physically or mentally handicapped? It is not that they were in captivity, for life in captivity can certainly be a good. Nor is it merely the unusual nature of their life. In some ways the prisoners were living more as other men do than the patient in an iron lung.

The suggested solution to the problem is, then, that there is a certain conceptual connection between *life* and *good* in the case of human beings as in that of animals and even plants. Here, as there, however, it is not the mere state of being alive that can determine, or itself count as, a good, but rather life coming up to some standard of normality. It was argued that it is as part of ordinary life that the elements of good that a man may have are relevant to the question of whether saving his life counts as benefiting him. Ordinary human lives, even very hard lives, contain a minimum of basic goods, but when these are absent the idea of life is no longer linked to that of good. And since it is in this way that the elements of good contained in a man's life are relevant to the question of whether he is benefited if his life is preserved, there is no reason why it should be the balance of good and evil that counts.

It should be added that evils are relevant in one way when, as in the examples discussed above, they destroy the possibility of ordinary goods, but in a different way when they invade a life from which the goods are already absent for a different reason. So, for instance, the connection between *life* and *good* may be broken because consciousness has sunk to a very low level, as in extreme senility or severe brain damage. In itself this kind of life seems to be neither good nor evil, but if suffering sets in one would hope for a speedy end.

The idea we need seems to be that of life which is ordinary human life in the following respect—that it contains a minimum of basic human goods. What is ordinary in human life—even in very hard lives—is that a man is not driven to work far beyond his capacity; that he has the support of a family or community; that he can more or less satisfy his hunger; that he has hopes for the future; that he can lie down to rest at night. Such things were denied to the men in the Vyatlag camps described by Panin; not even rest at night was allowed them when they were tormented by bed-bugs, by noise and stench, and by routines such as body-searches and bath-parades—arranged for the night time so that work norms would not be reduced. Disease too can so take over a man's life that the normal human goods disappear. When a patient is so overwhelmed by pain or nausea that he cannot eat with pleasure, if he can eat at all, and is out of the reach of even the most loving voice, he no longer has ordinary human life in the sense in which the words are used here. And we may now pick up a thread from an earlier part of the discussion by remarking that crippling depression can destroy the enjoyment of ordinary goods as effectively as external circumstances can remove them.

This, admittedly inadequate, discussion of the sense in which life is normally a good, and of the reasons why it may not be so in some particular case, completes the account of what euthanasia is here taken to be. An act of euthanasia, whether literally act or rather omission, is attributed to an agent who opts for the death of another because in his case life seems to be an evil rather than a good. The question now to be asked is whether acts of euthanasia are ever justifiable. But there are two topics here rather than one. For it is one thing to say that some acts of euthanasia considered only in themselves and their results are morally unobjectionable, and another to say that it would be all right to legalize them. Perhaps the practice of euthanasia would allow too many abuses, and perhaps there would be too many mistakes. Moreover the practice might have very important and highly undesirable side effects, because it is unlikely that we could change our principles about the treatment of the old and the ill without changing fundamental emotional attitudes and social relations. The topics must, therefore, be treated separately. In the next part of the discussion, nothing will be said about the social consequences and possible abuses of the practice of euthanasia, but only about acts of euthanasia considered in themselves.

What we want to know is whether acts of euthanasia, defined as we have defined them, are ever morally permissible. To be more accurate, we want to know whether it is ever sufficient justification of the choice of death for another that death can be counted a benefit rather than harm, and that this is why the choice is made.

It will be impossible to get a clear view of the area to which this topic belongs without first marking the distinct grounds on which objection may lie when one man ops for the death of another. There are two different virtues whose requirements are, in general, contrary to such actions. An unjustified act of killing, or allowing to die, is contrary to justice or to charity, or to both virtues, and the moral failings are distinct. Justice has to do with what men *owe* each other in the way of noninterference and positive service. When used in this wide sense, which has its history in the doctrine of the cardinal virtues, justice is not especially connected with, for instance, law courts but with the whole area of rights, and duties corresponding to rights. Thus murder is one form of injustice, dishonesty another, and wrongful failure to keep contracts a third; chicanery in a law court or defrauding someone of his inheritance are simply other cases of injustice. Justice as such is not directly linked to the good of another, and may require that something

be rendered to him even where it will do him harm, as Hume pointed out when he remarked that a debt must be paid even to a profligate debauchee who "would rather receive harm than benefit from large possessions."[7] Charity, on the other hand, is the virtue which attaches us to the good of others. An act of charity is in question only where something is not demanded by justice, but a lack of charity and of justice can be shown where a man is denied something which he both needs and has a right to; both charity and justice demand that widows and orphans are not defrauded, and the man who cheats them is neither charitable nor just.

It is easy to see that the two grounds of objection to inducing death are distinct. A murder is an act of injustice. A culpable failure to come to the aid of someone whose life is threatened is normally contrary, not to justice, but to charity. But where one man is under contract, explicit or implicit, to come to the aid of another injustice too will be shown. Thus injustice may be involved either in an act or an omission, and the same is true of a lack of charity; charity may demand that someone be aided, but also that an unkind word not be spoken.

The distinction between charity and justice will turn out to be of the first importance when voluntary and nonvoluntary euthanasia are distinguished later on. This is because of the connection between justice and rights, and something should now be said about this. I believe it is true to say that wherever a man acts unjustly he has infringed a right, since justice has to do with whatever a man is owed, and whatever he is owed is his as a matter of right. Something should therefore be said about the different kinds of rights. The distinction commonly made is between having a right in the sense of having a liberty, and having a "claim-right" or "right of recipience." The best way to understand such a distinction seems to be as follows. To say that a man has a right in the sense of liberty is to say that no one can demand that he do not do the thing which he has a right to do. The fact that he has a right to do it consists in the fact that a certain kind of objection does not lie against his doing it. Thus a man has a right in this sense to walk down a public street or park his car in a public parking space. It does not follow that no one else may prevent him from doing so. If for some reason I want a certain man not to park in a certain place I may lawfully park there myself or get my friends to do so, thus preventing him from doing what he has a right (in the sense of a liberty) to do. It is different, however, with a claim-right. This is the kind of right which I have in addition to a liberty when, for example, I have a private parking space; now others have duties in the way of noninterference, as in this case, or of service, as in the case where my claim-right is to goods or services promised to me. Sometimes one of these rights gives other people the duty of securing to me that to which I have a right, but at other times their duty is merely to refrain from interference. If a fall of snow blocks my private parking space there is normally no obligation for anyone else to clear it away. Claim-rights generate duties; sometimes these duties are duties of noninterference; sometimes they are duties of service. If your right gives me the duty not to interfere with you I have "no right" to do it; similarly, if your right gives me the duty to provide something for you I have "no right" to refuse to do it. What *I* lack is the right which is a liberty; I am not "at liberty" to interfere with you or to refuse the service.

Where in this picture does the right to life belong? No doubt people have the right to live in the sense of a liberty, but what is important is the cluster of claim-rights brought together under the title of the right to life. The chief of these is, of course, the right to be free from interferences that threaten life. If other people aim their guns at us or try to pour poison into our drink we can, to put it mildly, demand that they desist. And then there are the services we can claim from doctors, health officers, bodyguards, and firemen; the rights that depend on contract or public arrangement. Perhaps there is no particular point in saying that the duties these people owe us belong to the right to life; we might as well say that all the services owed to anyone by tailors, dressmakers, and couturiers belong to a right called the right to be elegant. But contracts such as

those understood in the patient-doctor relationship come in an important way when we are discussing the rights and wrongs of euthanasia, and are therefore mentioned here.

Do people have the right to what they need in order to survive, apart from the right conferred by special contracts into which other people have entered for the supplying of these necessities? Do people in the underdeveloped countries in which starvation is rife have the right to the food they so evidently lack? Joel Feinberg, discussing this question, suggests that they should be said to have "a claim," distinguishing this from a "valid claim," which gives a claim-right.

The manifesto writers on the other side who seem to identify needs, or at least basic needs, with what they call "human rights," are more properly described, I think, as urging upon the world community the moral principle that *all* basic human needs ought to be recognized as *claims* (in the customary *prima facie* sense) worthy of sympathy and serious consideration right now, even though, in many cases, they cannot yet plausibly be treated as *valid* claims, that is, as grounds of any other people's duties. This way of talking avoids the anomaly of ascribing to all human beings now, even those in pre-industrial societies, such "economic and social rights" as "periodic holidays with pay."[8]

This seems reasonable, though we notice that there are some actual rights to service which are not based on anything like a contract, as for instance the right that children have to support from their parents and parents to support from their children in old age, though both sets of rights are to some extent dependent on existing social arrangements.

Let us now ask how the right to life affects the morality of acts of euthanasia. Are such acts sometimes or always ruled out by the right to life? This is certainly a possibility; for although an act of euthanasia is, by our definition, a matter of opting for death for the good of the one who is to die, there is, as we noted earlier, no direct connection between that to which a man has a right and that which is for his good. It is true that men have the right only to the kind of thing that is, in general, a good: we do not think that people have the right to garbage or polluted air. Nevertheless, a man may have the right to something which he himself would be better off without; where rights exist it is a man's will that counts not his or anyone else's estimate of benefit or harm. So the duties complementary to the right to life—the general duty of noninterference and the duty of service incurred by certain persons—are not affected by the quality of a man's life or by his prospects. Even if it is true that he would be, as we say, "better off dead," so long as he wants to live this does not justify us in killing him and may not justify us in deliberately allowing him to die. All of us have the duty of noninterference, and some of us may have the duty to sustain his life. Suppose, for example, that a retreating army has to leave behind wounded or exhausted soldiers in the wastes of an arid or snowbound land where the only prospect is death by starvation or at the hands of an enemy notoriously cruel. It has often been the practice to accord a merciful bullet to men in such desperate straits. But suppose that one of them demands that he should be left alive? It seems clear that his comrades have no right to kill him, though it is a quite different question as to whether they should give him a life-prolonging drug. The right to life can sometimes give a duty of positive service, but does not do so here. What it does give is the right to be left alone.

Interestingly enough we have arrived by way of a consideration of the right to life at the distinction normally labeled "active" versus "passive" euthanasia, and often thought to be irrelevant to the moral issue. Once it is seen that the right to life is a distinct ground of objection to certain acts of euthanasia, and that this right creates a duty of noninterference more widespread than the duties of care there can be no doubt about the relevance of the distinction between passive and active euthanasia. Where everyone may have the duty to leave someone alone, it may be that no one has the duty to maintain his life, or that only some people do.

Where then do the boundaries of the "active" and "passive" lie? In some ways the words are themselves misleading, because they suggest the difference between act and omission which is not quite what we want. Certainly the act of shooting someone is the kind of thing we were talking about under the heading of "interference," and omitting to give him a drug a case of refusing care. But the act of turning off a respirator should surely be thought of as no different from the decision not to start it; if doctors had decided that a patient should be allowed to die, either course of action might follow, and both should be counted as passive rather than active euthanasia if euthanasia were in question. The point seems to be that interference in a course of treatment is not the same as other interference in a man's life, and particularly if the same body of people are responsible for the treatment and for its discontinuance. In such a case we could speak of the disconnecting of the apparatus as killing the man, or of the hospital as allowing him to die. By and large, it is the act of killing that is ruled out under the heading of noninterference, but not in every case.

Doctors commonly recognize this distinction, and the grounds on which some philosophers have denied it seem untenable. James Rachels, for instance, believes that if the difference between active and passive is relevant anywhere, it should be relevant everywhere, and he has pointed to an example in which it seems to make no difference which is done. If someone saw a child drowning in a bath it would seem just as bad to let it drown as to push its head under water. If "it makes no difference" means that one act would be as iniquitous as the other this is true. It is not that killing is *worse* than allowing to die, but that the two are contrary to distinct virtues, which gives the possibility that in some circumstances one is impermissible and the other permissible. In the circumstances invented by Rachels, both are wicked: it is contrary to justice to push the child's head under the water—something one has no right to do. To leave it to drown is not contrary to justice, but it is a particularly glaring example of lack of charity. Here it makes no practical difference because the requirements of justice and charity coincide; but in the case of the retreating army they did not: charity would have required that the wounded soldier be killed had not justice required that he be left alive.[9] In such a case it makes all the difference whether a man opts for the death of another in a positive action, or whether he allows him to die. An analogy with the right to property will make the point clear. If a man owns something he has the right to it even when its possession does him harm, and we have no right to take it from him. But if one day it should blow away, maybe nothing requires us to get it back for him; we could not deprive him of it, but we may allow it to go. This is not to deny that it will often be an unfriendly act or one based on an arrogant judgment when we refuse to do what he wants. Nevertheless, we would be within our rights, and it might be that no moral objection of any kind would lie against our refusal.

It is important to emphasize that a man's rights may stand between us and the action we would dearly like to take for his sake. They may, of course, also prevent action which we would like to take for the sake of others, as when it might be tempting to kill one man to save several. But it is interesting that the limits of allowable interference, however uncertain, seem stricter in the first case than the second. Perhaps there are no cases in which it would be all right to kill a man against his will *for his own sake* unless they could equally well be described as cases of allowing him to die, as in the example of turning off the respirator. However, there are circumstances, even if these are very rare, in which one man's life would justifiably be sacrificed to save others, and "killing" would be the only description of what was being done. For instance, a vehicle which had gone out of control might be steered from a path on which it would kill more than one man to a path on which it would kill one. But it would not be permissible to steer a vehicle towards someone in order to kill him, against his will, for his own good. An analogy with property rights illustrates the point. One may not destroy a man's property against his will on the grounds that he would be better off without it; there are however circumstances in which it could be destroyed for the sake of others. If his house is liable to fall and kill him that is his affair; it might, how-ever, without injustice be destroyed to stop the spread of a fire.

We see then that the distinction between active and passive, important as it is elsewhere, has a special importance in the area of euthanasia. It should also be clear why James Rachels' other argument, that it is often "more humane" to kill than to allow to die, does not show that the distinction between active and passive euthanasia is morally irrelevant. It might be "more humane" in this sense to deprive a man of the property that brings evils on him, or to refuse to pay what is owed to Hume's profligate debauchee; but if we say this we must admit that an act which is "more humane" than its alternative may be morally objectionable because it infringes rights.

So far we have said very little about the right to service as opposed to the right to noninterference, though it was agreed that both might be brought under the heading of "the right to life." What about the duty to preserve life that may belong to special classes of persons such as bodyguards, firemen, or doctors? Unlike the general public they are not within their rights if they merely refrain from inter-fering and do not try to sustain life. The subject's claim-rights are two-fold as far as they are concerned and passive as well as active euthanasia may be ruled out here if it is against his will. This is not to say that he has the right to any and every service needed to save or prolong his life; the rights of other people set limits to what may be demanded, both because they have the right not to be interfered with and because they may have a competing right to services. Fur-thermore one must enquire just what the contract or implicit agreement amounts to in each case. Firemen and bodyguards presumably have a duty which is simply to preserve life, within the limits of justice to others and of reasonableness to themselves. With doctors it may however be different, since their duty relates not only to preserving life but also to the relief of suffering. It is not clear what a doctor's duties are to his patient if life can be prolonged only at the cost of suffering or suffering relieved only by measures that shorten life. George Fletcher has argued that what the doctor is under contract to do depends on what is generally done, because this is what a patient will reasonably expect.[10] This seems right. If procedures are part of normal medical practice then it seems that the patient can demand them however much it may be against his interest to do so. Once again it is not a matter of what is "most humane."

That the patient's right to life may set limits to permissible acts of euthanasia seems undeniable. If he does not want to die no one has the right to practice active euthanasia on him, and passive euthanasia may also be ruled out where he has a right to the services of doctors or others.

Perhaps few will deny what has so far been said about the impermissibility of acts of euthanasia simply because we have so far spoken about the case of one who positively wants to live, and about his rights, whereas those who advocate euthanasia are usually thinking either about those who wish to die or about those whose wishes cannot be ascertained either because they cannot properly be said to have wishes or because, for one reason or another, we are unable to form a reliable estimate of what they are. The question that must now be asked is whether the latter type of case, where euthanasia though not involuntary would again be nonvoluntary, is different from the one discussed so far. Would we have the right to kill someone for his own good so long as we had no idea that he positively wished to live? And what about the life-prolonging duties of doctors in the same circumstances? This is a very difficult problem. On the one hand, it seems ridiculous to suppose that a man's right to life is something which generates duties only where he has signaled that he wants to live; as a borrower does indeed have a duty to return something lent on indefinite loan only if the lender indicates that he wants it back. On the other hand, it might be argued that there is something illogical about the idea that a right has been infringed if someone incapable of saying whether he wants it or not is deprived of something that is doing him harm rather than good. Yet on the analogy of property we would say that a right has been infringed. Only if someone had earlier told us that in such circumstances he would not want to keep the thing could we think that his right had been waived. Perhaps if

we could make confident judgments about what anyone in such circumstances would wish, or what he would have wished beforehand had he considered the matter, we could agree to consider the right to life as "dormant," needing to be asserted if the normal duties were to remain. But as things are we cannot make any such assumption; we simply do not know what most people would want, or would have wanted, us to do unless they tell us. This is certainly the case so far as active measures to end life are concerned. Possibly it is different, or will become different, in the matter of being kept alive, so general is the feeling against using sophisticated procedures on moribund patients, and so much is this dreaded by people who are old or terminally ill. Once again the distinction between active and passive euthanasia has come on the scene, but this time because most people's attitudes to the two are so different. It is just possible that we might presume, in the absence of specific evidence, that someone would not wish, beyond a certain point, to be kept alive; it is certainly not possible to assume that he would wish to be killed.

In the last paragraph we have begun to broach the topic of voluntary euthanasia, and this we must now discuss. What is to be said about the case in which there is no doubt about someone's wish to die: either he has told us beforehand that he would wish it in circumstances such as he is now in, and has shown no sign of a change of mind, or else he tells us now, being in possession of his faculties and of a steady mind. We should surely say that the objections previously urged against acts of euthanasia, which it must be remembered were all on the ground of rights, had disappeared. It does not seem that one would infringe someone's right to life in killing him with his permission and in fact at his request. Why should someone not be able to waive his right to life, or rather, as would be more likely to happen, to cancel some of the duties of noninterference that this right entails? (He is more likely to say that he should be killed by this man at this time in this manner, than to say that anyone may kill him at any time and in any way.) Similarly someone may give permission for the destruction of his property, and request it. The important thing is that he gives a critical permission, and it seems that this is enough to cancel the duty normally associated with the right. If someone gives you permission to destroy his property it can no longer be said that you have no right to do so, and I do not see why it should not be the case with taking a man's life. An objection might be made on the ground that only God has the right to take life, but in this paper religious as opposed to moral arguments are being left aside. Religion apart, there seems to be no case to be made out for an infringement of rights if a man who wishes to die is allowed to die or even killed. But of course it does not follow that there is no moral objection to it. Even with property, which is after all a relatively small matter, one might be wrong to destroy what one had the right to destroy. For, apart from its value to other people, it might be valuable to the man who wanted it destroyed, and charity might require us to hold our hand where justice did not.

Let us review the conclusion of this part of the argument, which has been about euthanasia and the right to life. It has been argued that from this side come stringent restrictions on the acts of euthanasia that could be morally permissible. Active nonvoluntary euthanasia is ruled out by that part of the right to life which creates the duty of noninterference though passive nonvoluntary euthanasia is not ruled out, except where the right to life-preserving action has been created by some special condition such as a contract between a man and his doctor, and it is not always certain just what such a contract involves. Voluntary euthanasia is another matter: as the preceding paragraph suggested, no right is infringed if a man is allowed to die or even killed at his own request.

Turning now to the other objection that normally holds against inducing the death of another, that it is against charity, or benevolence, we must tell a very different story. Charity is the virtue that gives attachment to the good of others, and because life is normally a good, charity normally demands that it should be saved or prolonged. But as we so defined an act of euthanasia that it seeks a man's death for his own sake—for his good—charity will normally

speak in favor of it. This is not, of course, to say that charity can require an act of euthanasia which justice forbids, but if an act of euthanasia is not contrary to justice—that is, it does not infringe rights—charity will rather be in its favor than against.

Once more the distinction between nonvoluntary and voluntary euthanasia must be considered. Could it ever be compatible with charity to seek a man's death although he wanted to live, or at least had not let us know that he wanted to die? It has been argued that in such circumstances active euthanasia would infringe his right to life, but passive euthanasia would not do so, unless he had some special right to life-preserving service from the one who allowed him to die. What would charity dictate? Obviously when a man wants to live there is a presumption that he will be benefited if his life is prolonged, and if it is so the question of euthanasia does not arise. But it is, on the other hand, possible that he wants to live where it would be better for him to die: perhaps he does not realize the desperate situation he is in, or perhaps he is afraid of dying. So, in spite of a very proper resistance to refusing to go along with a man's own wishes in the matter of life and death, someone might justifiably refuse to prolong the life even of someone who asked him to prolong it, as in the case of refusing to give the wounded soldier a drug that would keep him alive to meet a terrible end. And it is even more obvious that charity does not always dictate that life should be prolonged where a man's own wishes, hypothetical or actual, are not known.

So much for the relation of charity to nonvoluntary passive euthanasia, which was not, like nonvoluntary active euthanasia, ruled out by the right to life. Let us now ask what charity has to say about voluntary euthanasia both active and passive. It was suggested in the discussion of justice that if of sound mind and steady desire a man might give others the *right* to allow him to die or even to kill him, where otherwise this would be ruled out. But it was pointed out that this would not settle the question of whether the act was morally permissible, and it is this that we must now consider. Could not charity speak against what justice allowed? Indeed it might do so. For while the fact that a man wants to die suggests that his life is wretched, and while his rejection of life may itself tend to take the good out of the things he might have enjoyed, nevertheless his wish to die might here be opposed for his own sake just as it might be if suicide were in question. Perhaps there is hope that his mental condition will improve. Perhaps he is mistaken in thinking his disease incurable. Perhaps he wants to die for the sake of someone else on whom he feels he is a burden, and we are not ready to accept this sacrifice whether for ourselves or others. In such cases, and there will surely be many of them, it could not be for his own sake that we kill him or allow him to die, and therefore euthanasia as defined in this paper would not be in question. But this is not to deny that there could be acts of voluntary euthanasia both passive and active against which neither justice nor charity would speak.

We have now considered the morality of euthanasia both voluntary and nonvoluntary, and active and passive. The conclusion has been that nonvoluntary active euthanasia (roughly, killing a man against his will or without his consent) is never justified; that is to say, that a man's being killed for his own good never justifies the act unless he himself has consented to it. A man's rights are infringed by such an action, and it is therefore contrary to justice. However, all the other combinations, nonvoluntary passive euthanasia, voluntary active euthanasia, and voluntary passive euthanasia are sometimes compatible with both justice and charity. But the strong condition carried in the definition of euthanasia adopted in this paper must not be forgotten; an act of euthanasia as here understood is one whose purpose is to benefit the one who dies.

In the light of this discussion let us look at our present practices. Are they good or are they bad? And what changes might be made, thinking now not only of the morality of particular acts of euthanasia but also of the indirect effects of instituting different practices, of the abuses to which they might be subject and of the changes that might come about if euthanasia became a recognized part of the social scene.

The first thing to notice is that it is wrong to ask whether we should introduce the practice of euthanasia as if it were not something we already had. In fact we do have it. For instance it is common, where the medical prognosis is very bad, for doctors to recommend against measures to prolong life, and particularly where a process of degeneration producing one medical emergency after another has already set in. If these doctors are not certainly within their legal rights this is something that is apt to come as a surprise to them as to the general public. It is also obvious that euthanasia is often practiced where old people are concerned. If someone very old and soon to die is attacked by a disease that makes his life wretched, doctors do not always come in with life-prolonging drugs. Perhaps poor patients are more fortunate in this respect than rich patients, being more often left to die in peace; but it is in any case a well recognized piece of medical practice, which is a form of euthanasia.

No doubt the case of infants with mental or physical defects will be suggested as another example of the practice of euthanasia as we already have it, since such infants are sometimes deliberately allowed to die. That they are deliberately allowed to die is certain; children with severe spina bifida malformations are not always operated on even where it is thought that without the operation they will die; and even in the case of children with [Down] Syndrome who have intestinal obstructions the relatively simple operation that would make it possible to feed them is sometimes not performed.[11] Whether this is euthanasia in our sense or only as the Nazis understood it is another matter. We must ask the crucial question, "Is it for the sake of the child himself that the doctors and parents choose his death?" In some cases the answer may really be yes, and what is more important it may really be true that the kind of life which is a good is not possible or likely for this child, and that there is little but suffering and frustration in store for him.[12] But this must presuppose that the medical prognosis is wretchedly bad, as it maybe for some spina bifida children. With children who are born with [Down] Syndrome it is, however, quite different. Most of these are able to live on for quite a time in a reasonably contented way, remaining like children all their lives but capable of affectionate relationships and able to play games and perform simple tasks. The fact is, of course, that the doctors who recommend against life-saving procedures for handicapped infants are usually thinking not of them but rather of their parents and of other children in the family or of the "burden on society" if the children survive. So it is not for their sake but to avoid trouble to others that they are allowed to die. When brought out into the open this seems unacceptable: at least we do not easily accept the principle that adults who need special care should be counted too burdensome to be kept alive. It must in any case be insisted that if children with [Down] Syndrome are deliberately allowed to die this is not a matter of euthanasia except in Hitler's sense. And for our children, since we scruple to gas them, not even the manner of their death is "quiet and easy"; when not treated for an intestinal obstruction a baby simply starves to death. Perhaps some will take this as an argument for allowing active euthanasia, in which case they will be in the company of an S.S. man stationed in the Warthgenau who sent Eichmann a memorandum telling him that "Jews in the coming winter could no longer be fed" and submitting for his consideration a proposal as to whether "it would not be the most humane solution to kill those Jews who were incapable of work through some quicker means."[13] If we say we are *unable* to look after children with handicaps we are no more telling the truth than was the S.S. man who said that the Jews could not be fed.

Nevertheless if it is ever right to allow deformed children to die because life will be a misery to them, or not to take measures to prolong for a little the life of a newborn baby whose life cannot extend beyond a few months of intense medical intervention, there is a genuine problem about active as opposed to passive euthanasia. There are well-known cases in which the medical staff has looked on wretchedly while an infant died slowly from starvation and dehydration because they did not feel able to give a lethal injection. According to the principles discussed in the earlier part of this paper they would indeed have had no right to give it, since an infant cannot ask that it should be done. The only possible solution—supposing that voluntary active euthanasia were to be legalized—would be to appoint guardians to act on the infant's behalf. In a different climate of opinion this might not be dangerous, but at present, when people so readily assume that the life of a handicapped baby is of no value, one would be loath to support it.

Finally, on the subject of handicapped children, another word should be said about those with severe mental defects. For them too it might sometimes be right to say that one would wish for death for their sake. But not even severe mental handicap automatically brings a child within the scope even of a possible act of euthanasia. If the level of consciousness is low enough it could not be said that life is a good to them, any more than in the case of those suffering from extreme senility. Nevertheless if they do not suffer it will not be an act of euthanasia by which someone opts for their death. Perhaps charity does not demand that strenuous measures are taken to keep people in this state alive, but euthanasia does not come into the matter, any more than it does when someone is, like Karen Ann Quinlan, in a state of permanent coma. Much could be said about this last case. It might even be suggested that in the case of unconsciousness this "life" is not the life to which "the right to life" refers. But that is not our topic here.

What we must consider, even if only briefly, is the possibility that euthanasia, genuine euthanasia, and not contrary to the requirements of justice or charity, should be legalized over a wider area. Here we are up against the really serious problem of abuse. Many people want, and want very badly, to be rid of their elderly relatives and even of their ailing husbands or wives. Would any safeguards ever be able to stop them describing as euthanasia what was really for their own benefit? And would it be possible to prevent the occurrence of acts which were genuinely acts of euthanasia but morally impermissible because infringing the rights of a patient who wished to live?

Perhaps the furthest we should go is to encourage patients to make their own contracts with a doctor by making it known whether they wish him to prolong their life in case of painful terminal illness or of incapacity. A document such as the Living Will seems eminently sensible, and should surely be allowed to give a doctor following the previously expressed wishes of the patient immunity from legal proceedings by relatives.[14] Legalizing active euthanasia is, however, another matter. Apart from the special repugnance doctors feel towards the idea of a lethal injection, it may be of the very greatest importance to keep a psychological barrier up against killing. Moreover it is active euthanasia which is the most liable to abuse. Hitler would not have been able to kill 275,000 people in his "euthanasia" program if he had had to wait for them to need life-saving treatment. But there are other objections to active euthanasia, even voluntary active euthanasia. In the first place it would be hard to devise procedures that would protect people from being persuaded into giving their consent. And secondly the possibility of active voluntary euthanasia might change the social scene in ways that would be very bad. As things are, people do, by and large, expect to be looked after if they are old or ill. This is one of the good things that we have, but we might lose it, and be much worse off without it. It might come to be expected that someone likely to need a lot of looking after should call for the doctor and demand his own death. Something comparable could be good in an extremely poverty-stricken community where the children genuinely suffered from lack of food; but in rich societies such as ours it would surely be a spiritual disaster. Such possibilities should make us very wary of supporting large measures of euthanasia, even where moral principle applied to the individual act does not rule it out.

NOTES

1. Leo Alexander, "Medical Science under Dictatorship," *New England Journal of Medicine,* 14 July 1949, p. 40.

2. For a discussion of culpable and nonculpable ignorance see Thomas Aquinas, *Summa Theologica,* First Part of the Sec-

ond Part, Question 6, article 8, and Question 19, articles 5 and 6.

3. Dmitri Panin, *The Notebooks of Sologdin* (London, 1976), pp. 66–67.

4. Thomas Nagel, "Death," in James Rachels, ed., *Moral Problems* (New York, 1971), p. 362.

5. Panin, *Sologdin,* p. 85.

6. Yet some detail needs to be filled in to explain why we should not say that a scarecrow is beneficial to the plants it protects. Perhaps what is beneficial must either be a feature of the plant itself, such as protective prickles, or else must work on the plant directly, such as a line of trees which give it shade.

7. David Hume, *Treatise,* Book III, Part II, Section 1.

8. Feinberg, "Human Rights," *Moral Problems in Medicine,* p. 465.

9. It is not, however, that justice and charity conflict. A man does not lack charity because he refrains from an act of injustice which would have been for someone's good.

10. George Fletcher, "Legal Aspects of the Decision not to Prolong Life," *Journal of the American Medical Association* 203, no. 1 (1 Jan. 1968): 119–122. Reprinted in Gorovitz.

11. I have been told this by a pediatrician in a well-known medical center in the United States. It is confirmed by Anthony M. Shaw and Iris A. Shaw, "Dilemma of Informed Consent in Children," *The New England Journal of Medicine* 289, no. 17 (25 Oct. 1973): 885–890. Reprinted in Gorovitz.

12. It must be remembered, however, that many of the social miseries of spina bifida children could be avoided. Professor R.B. Zachary is surely right to insist on this. See, for example, "Ethical and Social Aspects of Spina Bifida," *The Lancet,* 3 Aug. 1968, pp. 274–276. Reprinted in Gorovitz.

13. Quoted by Hannah Arendt, *Eichmann in Jerusalem* (London, 1963), p. 90.

14. Details of this document are to be found in J.A. Behnke and Sissela Bok, eds., *The Dilemmas of Euthanasia* (New York, 1975), and in A.B. Downing, ed., *Euthanasia and the Right to Life: The Case for Voluntary Euthanasia* (London, 1969).

Killing and Allowing to Die

Daniel Callahan

* * *

If a lessened worry about the consequences of legal euthanasia has been gaining ground, there has been an even more powerful threat to the traditional prohibition against it. No valid distinction, many now argue, can be made between killing and allowing to die, or between an act of commission and one of omission. The standard distinction being challenged rests on the commonplace observation that lives can come to an end as the result of: (a) the direct action of another who becomes the cause of death (as in shooting a person), and (b) the result of impersonal forces where no human agent has acted (death by lightning, or by disease). The purpose of the distinction has been to separate those deaths caused by human action, and those caused by nonhuman events. It is, as a distinction, meant to say something about human beings and their relationship to the world. It is a way of articulating the difference between those actions for which human beings can be held rightly responsible, or blamed, and those of which they are innocent. At issue is the difference between physical causality, the realm of impersonal events, and moral culpability, the realm of human responsibility.

The challenges encompass two points. The first is that people can become equally dead by our omissions as well as our commissions. We can refrain from saving them when it is possible to do so, and they will be just as dead as if we shot them. It is our decision itself that is the reason for their death, not necessarily how we effectuate that decision. That fact establishes the basis of the second point: if we *intend* their death, it can be brought about as well by omitted acts as by those we commit. The crucial moral point is not how they die, but our intention about

their death. We can, then, be responsible for the death of another by intending that they die and accomplish that end by standing aside and allowing them to die.

Despite these criticisms—resting upon ambiguities that can readily be acknowledged—the distinction between killing and allowing to die remains, I contend, perfectly valid. It not only has a logical validity but, no less importantly, a social validity whose place must be central in moral judgments. As a way of putting the distinction into perspective, I want to suggest that it is best understood as expressing three different, though overlapping, perspectives on nature and human action. I will call them the metaphysical, the moral, and the medical perspectives.

Metaphysical. The first and most fundamental premise of the distinction between killing and allowing to die is that there is a sharp difference between the self and the external world. Unlike the childish fantasy that the world is nothing more than a projection of the self, or the neurotic person's fear that he or she is responsible for everything that goes wrong, the distinction is meant to uphold a simple notion: there is a world external to the self that has its own, and independent, causal dynamism. The mistake behind a conflation of killing and allowing to die is to assume that the self has become master of everything within and outside of the self. It is as if the conceit that modern man might ultimately control nature has been internalized: that, if the self might be able to influence nature by its actions, then the self and nature must be one.

Of course that is a fantasy. The fact that we can intervene in nature, and cure or control many diseases, does not erase the difference between the self and the external world. It is as "out there" as ever, even if more under our sway. That sway, however great, is always limited. We can cure disease, but not always the chronic illness that comes with the cure.

Daniel Callahan, "Can We Return Death to Disease?" *Hastings Center Report* 19, no. 1 (January–February 1989: 5–6 (edited). Reprinted with permission of the *Hastings Center Report*.

We can forestall death with modern medicine, but death always wins in the long run because of the innate limitations of the body, inherently and stubbornly beyond final human control. And we can distinguish between a diseased body and an aging body, but in the end if we wait long enough they always become one and the same body. To attempt to deny the distinction between killing and allowing to die is, then, mistakenly to impute more power to human action than it actually has and to accept the conceit that nature has now fallen wholly within the realm of human control. Not so.

Moral. At the center of the distinction between killing and allowing to die is the difference between physical causality and moral culpability. To bring the life of another to an end by an injection kills the other directly; our action is the physical cause of the death. To allow someone to die from a disease we cannot cure (and that we did not cause) is to permit the disease to act as the cause of death. The notion of physical causality in both cases rests on the difference between human agency and the action of external nature. The ambiguity arises precisely because we can be morally culpable for killing someone (if we have no moral right to do so, as we would in self-defense) and no less culpable for allowing someone to die (if we have both the possibility and the obligation of keeping that person alive). Thus there are cases where, morally speaking, it makes no difference whether we killed or allowed to die; we are equally responsible. In those instances, the lines of physical causality and moral culpability happen to cross. Yet the fact that they can cross in some cases in no way shows that they are always, or even usually, one and the same. We can normally find the difference in all but the most obscure cases. We should not, then, use the ambiguity of such cases to do away altogether with the distinction between killing and allowing to die. The ambiguity may obscure, but does not erase, the line between the two.

There is one group of ambiguous cases that is especially troublesome. Even if we grant the ordinary validity between killing and allowing to die, what about those cases that combine (a) an illness that renders a patient unable to carry out an ordinary bio-logical function (to breathe or eat on his own, for example), and (b) our turning off a respirator or removing an artificial feeding tube? On the level of physical causality, have we killed the patient or allowed him to die? In one sense, it is our action that shortens his life, and yet in another sense his underlying disease brings his life to an end. I believe it reasonable to say that, since his life was being sustained by artificial means (respirator or feeding tube) made necessary because of the fact that he had an incapacitating disease, his disease is the ultimate reality behind his death. But for its reality, there would be no need for artificial sustenance in the first place and no moral issue at all. To lose sight of the paramount reality of the disease is to lose sight of the difference between our selves and the outer world.

I quickly add, and underscore, a moral point: the person who, without good moral reason, turns off a respirator or pulls a feeding tube, can be morally culpable; that the patient has been allowed to die of his underlying condition does not morally excuse him. The moral question is whether we are obliged to continue treating a life that is being artificially sustained. To cease treatment may or may not be morally acceptable; but it should be understood, in either case, that the physical cause of death was the underlying disease.

Medical. An important social purpose of the distinction between killing and allowing to die has been that of protecting the historical role of the physician as one who tries to cure or comfort patients rather than to kill patients. Physicians have been given special knowledge about the body, knowledge that can be used to kill or to cure. They are also given great privileges in making use of that knowledge. It is thus all the more important that physicians' social role and power be, and be seen to be, a limited power. It may be used only to cure or comfort, never to kill. They have not been given, nor should they be given, the power to use their knowledge and skills to bring life to an end. It would open the way for powerful misuse and, no less importantly, represent an intrinsic violation of what it has meant to be a physician.

Yet if it is possible for physicians to misuse their knowledge and power to kill people directly, are they thereby required to use that same knowledge always to keep people alive, always to resist a disease that can itself kill the patient? The traditional answer has been: not necessarily. For the physician's ultimate obligation is to the welfare of the patient, and excessive treatment can be as detrimental to that welfare as inadequate treatment. Put another way, the obligation to resist the lethal power of disease is limited— it ceases when the patient is unwilling to have it resisted, or where the resistance no longer serves the patient's welfare. Behind this moral premise is the recognition that disease (of some kind) ultimately triumphs and that death is both inevitable sooner or later and not, in any case, always the greatest human evil. To demand of the physician that he always struggle against disease, as if it was in his power always to conquer it, would be to fall into the same metaphysical trap mentioned above: that of assuming that no distinction can be drawn between natural and human agency.

A final word. I suggested earlier that the most potent motive for active euthanasia and assisted suicide stems from a dread of the power of medicine. That power then seems to take on a drive of its own regardless of the welfare or wishes of patients. No one can easily say no—not physicians, not patients, not families. My guess is that happens because too many have already come to believe that it is their choice, and their choice alone, which brings about death; and they do not want to exercise that kind of authority. The solution is not to erase the distinction between killing and allowing to die, but to underscore its validity and importance. We can bring disease as a cause of death back into the care of the dying.

The Intentional Termination of Life

BONNIE STEINBOCK

According to James Rachels and Michael Tooley, * * * a common mistake in medical ethics is the belief that there is a moral difference between active and passive euthanasia. This is a mistake, they argue, because the rationale underlying the distinction between active and passive euthanasia is the idea that there is a significant moral difference between intentionally killing and intentionally letting die. "This idea," Tooley says, "is admittedly very common. But I believe that it can be shown to reflect either confused thinking or a moral point of view unrelated to the interests of individuals." Whether or not the belief that there is a significant moral difference is mistaken is not my concern here. For it is far from clear that this distinction *is* the basis of the doctrine of the American Medical Association which Rachels attacks. And if the killing/letting die distinction is not the basis of

the AMA doctrine, then arguments showing that the distinction has no moral force do not, in themselves, reveal in the doctrine's adherents either "confused thinking" or "a moral point of view unrelated to the interests of individuals." Indeed, as we examine the AMA doctrine, I think it will become clear that it appeals to and makes use of a number of overlapping distinctions, which may have moral significance in particular cases, such as the distinction between intending and foreseeing, or between ordinary and extraordinary care. Let us then turn to the 1973 statement, from the House of Delegates of the American Medical Association, which Rachels cites:

The intentional termination of the life of one human being by another—mercy killing—is contrary to that for which the medical profession stands and is contrary to the policy of the American Medical Association.

The cessation of the employment of extraordinary means to prolong the life of the body when there is irrefutable evidence that biological death is imminent is the decision of the patient and/or his immediate family. The

Bonnie Steinbock, "The Intentional Termination of Life," in *Killing and Letting Die* (Englewood Cliffs, NJ: Prentice-Hall, 1980), 69–77 (edited). Reprinted with permission of Prentice-Hall, Inc.

advice and judgment of the physician should be freely available to the patient and/or his immediate family.

Rachels attacks this statement because he believes that it contains a moral distinction between active and passive euthanasia. Tooley also believes this to be the position of the AMA, saying:

> Many people hold that there is an important moral distinction between passive euthanasia and active euthanasia. Thus, while the AMA maintains that people have a right "to die with dignity," so that it is morally permissible for a doctor to allow someone to die if that person wants to and is suffering from an incurable illness causing pain that cannot be sufficiently alleviated, the AMA is unwilling to countenance active euthanasia for a person who is in similar straits, but who has the misfortune not to be suffering from an illness that will result in a speedy death.

Both men, then, take the AMA position to prohibit active euthanasia, while allowing, under certain conditions, passive euthanasia.

I intend to show that the AMA statement does not imply support of the active/passive euthanasia distinction. In forbidding the intentional termination of life, the statement rejects both active and passive euthanasia. It does allow for "the cessation of the employment of extraordinary means" to prolong life. The mistake Rachels and Tooley make is in identifying the cessation of life-prolonging treatment with passive euthanasia, or intentionally letting die. If it were right to equate the two, then the AMA statement would be self-contradictory, for it would begin by condemning, and end by allowing, the intentional termination of life. But if the cessation of life-prolonging treatment is not always or necessarily passive euthanasia, then there is no confusion and no contradiction.

Why does Rachels think that the cessation of life-prolonging treatment is the intentional termination of life? He says:

The AMA policy statement isolates the crucial issue very well: the crucial issue is "the intentional termination of the life of one human being by another." But after identifying this issue, and forbidding "mercy killing," the statement goes on to deny that the cessation of treatment is the intentional termination of a life. This is where the mistake comes in, for what is the cessation of treatment, in these circumstances, if it is not "the intentional termination of the life of one human being of another"? Of course it is exactly that, and if it were not, there would be no point to it.

However, there *can* be a point (to the cessation of life-prolonging treatment) other than an endeavor to bring about the patient's death, and so the blanket identification of cessation of treatment with the intentional termination of a life is inaccurate. There are at least two situations in which the termination of life-prolonging treatment cannot be identified with the intentional termination of the life of one human being by another.

The first situation concerns the patient's right to refuse treatment. Both Tooley and Rachels give the example of a patient dying of an incurable disease, accompanied by unrelievable pain, who wants to end the treatment which cannot cure him but can only prolong his miserable existence. Why, they ask, may a doctor accede to the patient's request to stop treatment, but not provide a patient in a similar situation with a lethal dose? The answer lies in the patient's right to refuse treatment. In general, a competent adult has the right to refuse treatment, even where such treatment is necessary to prolong life. Indeed, the right to refuse treatment has been upheld even when the patient's reason for refusing treatment is generally agreed to be inadequate.[1] This right can be overridden (if, for example, the patient has dependent children) but, in general, no one may legally compel you to undergo treatment to which you have not consented. "Historically, surgical intrusion has always been considered a technical battery upon the person and one to be excused or justified by consent of the patient or justified by necessity created by the circumstances of the moment. . . ."[2]

At this point, an objection might be raised that if one has the right to refuse life-prolonging treatment, then consistency demands that one have the right to decide to end his or her life, and to obtain help in doing so. The idea is that the right to refuse treatment somehow implies a right to voluntary euthanasia, and we need to see why someone might think this. The right to refuse treatment has been considered by legal writers as an example of the right to privacy or, better, the right to bodily self-determination. You have the right to decide what happens to your own body, and the right to refuse treatment is an instance of that right. But if you have the right to determine what happens to your own body, then should you not have the right to choose to end your life, and even a right to get help in doing so?

However, it is important to see that the right to refuse treatment is not the same as, nor does it entail, a right to voluntary euthanasia, even if both can be derived from the right to bodily self-determination. The right to refuse treatment is not itself a "right to die"; that one may choose to exercise this right even at the risk of death, or even *in order to die*, is irrelevant. The purpose of the right to refuse medical treatment is not to give persons a right to decide whether to live or die, but to protect them from the unwanted interferences of others. Perhaps we ought to interpret the right to bodily self-determination more broadly, so as to include a right to die; but this would be a substantial extension of our present understanding of the right to bodily self-determination, and not a consequence of it. If we were to recognize a right to voluntary euthanasia, we would have to agree that people have the right not merely to be left alone but also the right to be killed. I leave to one side that substantive moral issue. My claim is simply that there can be a reason for terminating life-prolonging treatment other than "to bring about the patient's death."

The second case in which termination of treatment cannot be identified with intentional termination of life is where continued treatment has little chance of improving the patient's condition and brings greater discomfort than relief.

The question here is what treatment is appropriate to the particular case. A cancer specialist describes it in this way:

My general rule is to administer therapy as long as a patient responds well and has the potential for a reasonably good quality of life. But when all feasible therapies have been administered and a patient shows signs of rapid deterioration, the continuation of therapy can cause more discomfort than the cancer. From that time I recommend surgery, radiotherapy, or chemotherapy only as a means of relieving pain. But if a patient's condition should once again stabilize after the withdrawal of active therapy and if it should appear that he could still gain some good time, I would immediately reinstitute active therapy. The decision to cease anticancer treatment is never irrevocable, and often the desire to live will push a patient to try for another remission, or even a few more days of life.[3]

The decision here to cease anticancer treatment cannot be construed as a decision that the patient die, or as the intentional termination of life. It is a decision to provide the most appropriate treatment for that patient at that time. Rachels suggests that the point of the cessation of treatment is the intentional termination of life. But here the point of discontinuing treatment is not to bring about the patient's death but to avoid treatment that will cause more discomfort than the cancer and has little hope of benefiting the patient. Treatment that meets this description is often called "extraordinary."[4] The concept is flexible, and what might be considered "extraordinary" in one situation might be ordinary in another. The use of a respirator to sustain a patient through a severe bout with a respiratory disease would be considered ordinary; its use to sustain the life of a severely brain-damaged person in an irreversible coma would be considered extraordinary.

Contrasted with extraordinary treatment is ordinary treatment, the care a doctor would normally be expected to provide. Failure to provide ordinary care constitutes neglect, and can even be construed as the intentional infliction of harm, where there is a legal obligation to provide care. The importance of the ordinary/extraordinary care distinction lies partly in its connection to the doctor's intention. The withholding of extraordinary care should be seen as a decision not to inflict painful treatment on a patient without reasonable hope of success. The withholding of ordinary care, by contrast, must be seen as neglect. Thus, one doctor says, "We have to draw a distinction between ordinary and extraordinary means. We never withdraw what's needed to make a baby comfortable, we would never withdraw the care a parent would provide. We never kill a baby. . . . But we may decide certain heroic intervention is not worthwhile."[5]

We should keep in mind the ordinary/extraordinary care distinction when considering an example given by both Tooley and Rachels to show the irrationality of the active/passive distinction with regard to infanticide. The example is this: a child is born with [Down] syndrome and also has an intestinal obstruction that requires corrective surgery. If the surgery is not performed, the infant will starve to death, since it cannot take food orally. This may take days or even weeks, as dehydration and infection set in. Commenting on this situation in his article in this book, Rachels says:

I can understand why some people are opposed to all euthanasia, and insist that such infants must be allowed to live. I think I can also understand why other people favor destroying these babies quickly and painlessly. But why should anyone favor letting "dehydration and infection wither a tiny being over hours and days"? The doctrine that says that a baby may be allowed to dehydrate and wither, but may not be given an injection that would end its life without suffering, seems so patently cruel as to require no further refutation.

Such a doctrine perhaps does not need further refutation; but this is not the AMA doctrine. The AMA statement criticized by Rachels allows only for the cessation of extraordinary means to prolong life when death is imminent. Neither of these conditions is satisfied in this example. Death is not imminent in this situation, any more than it would be if a normal child had an attack of appendicitis. Neither the corrective surgery to remove the intestinal obstruction nor the intravenous feeding required to keep the infant alive until such surgery is performed can be regarded as extraordinary means, for neither is particularly expensive, nor does either place an overwhelming burden on the patient or others. (The continued existence of the child might be thought to place an overwhelming burden on its parents, but that has nothing to do with the characterization of the means to prolong its life as extraordinary. If it had, then *feeding* a severely defective child who

required a great deal of care could be regarded as extraordinary.) The chances of success if the operation is undertaken are quite good, though there is always a risk in operating on infants. Though the [Down] syndrome will not be alleviated, the child will proceed to an otherwise normal infancy.

It cannot be argued that the treatment is withheld for the infant's sake, unless one is prepared to argue that all mentally retarded babies are better off dead. This is particularly implausible in the case of [Down] syndrome babies, who generally do not suffer and are capable of giving and receiving love, of learning and playing, to varying degrees.

In a film on this subject entitled, "Who Should Survive?", a doctor defended a decision not to operate, saying that since the parents did not consent to the operation, the doctors' hands were tied. As we have seen, surgical intrusion requires consent, and in the case of infants, consent would normally come from the parents. But, as legal guardians, parents are required to provide medical care for their children, and failure to do so can constitute criminal neglect or even homicide. In general, courts have been understandably reluctant to recognize a parental right to terminate life-prolonging treatment.[6] Although prosecution is unlikely, physicians who comply with invalid instructions from the parents and permit the infant's death could be liable for aiding and abetting, failure to report child neglect, or even homicide. So it is not true that, in this situation, doctors are legally bound to do as the parents wish.

To sum up, I think that Rachels is right to regard the decision not to operate in the [Down] syndrome example as the intentional termination of life. But there is no reason to believe that either the law or the AMA would regard it otherwise. Certainly the decision to withhold treatment is not justified by the AMA statement. That such infants have been allowed to die cannot be denied; but this, I think, is the result of doctors misunderstanding the law and the AMA position.

Withholding treatment in this case is the intentional termination of life because the infant is deliberately allowed to die; that is the point of not operating. But there are other cases in which that is not the point. If the point is to avoid inflicting painful treatment on a patient with little or no reasonable hope of success, this is not the intentional termination of life. The permissibility of such withholding of treatment, then, would have no implications for the permissibility of euthanasia, active or passive.

The decision whether or not to operate, or to institute vigorous treatment, is particularly agonizing in the case of children born with spina bifida, an opening in the base of the spine usually accompanied by hydrocephalus and mental retardation. If left unoperated, these children usually die of meningitis or kidney failure within the first few years of life. Even if they survive, all affected children face a lifetime of illness, operations, and varying degrees of disability. The policy used to be to save as many as possible, but the trend now is toward selective treatment, based on the physician's estimate of the chances of success. If operating is not likely to improve significantly the child's condition, parents and doctors may agree not to operate. This is not the intentional termination of life, for again the purpose is not the termination of the child's life but the avoidance of painful and pointless treatment. Thus, the fact that withholding treatment is justified does not imply that killing the child would be equally justified.

Throughout the discussion, I have claimed that intentionally ceasing life-prolonging treatment is not the intentional termination of life unless the doctor has, as his or her purpose in stopping treatment, the patient's death.

It may be objected that I have incorrectly characterized the conditions for the intentional termination of life. Perhaps it is enough that the doctor intentionally ceases treatment, foreseeing that the patient will die.

In many cases, if one acts intentionally, foreseeing that a particular result will occur, one can be said to have brought about that result intentionally. Indeed, this is the general legal rule. Why, then, am I not willing to call the cessation of life-prolonging treatment, in compliance with the patient's right to refuse treatment, the intentional termination of life?

It is not because such an *identification* is necessarily opprobrious; for we could go on to *discuss* whether such cessation of treatment is a *justifiable* intentional termination of life. Even in the law, some cases of homicide are justifiable; e.g., homicide in self-defense.

However, the cessation of life-prolonging treatment, in the cases which I have discussed, is not regarded in law as being justifiable homicide, because it is not homicide at all. Why is this? Is it because the doctor "doesn't do anything," and so cannot be guilty of homicide? Surely not, since, as I have indicated, the law sometimes treats an omission as the cause of death. A better explanation, I think, has to do with the fact that in the context of the patient's right to refuse treatment, a doctor is not at liberty to continue treatment. It seems a necessary ingredient of intentionally letting die that one could have done something to prevent the death. In this situation, of course the doctor can physically prevent the patient's death, but since we do not regard the doctor as *free* to continue treatment, we say that there is "nothing he can do." Therefore he does not intentionally let the patient die.

To discuss this suggestion fully, I would need to present a full-scale theory of intentional action. However, at least I have shown, through the discussion of the above examples, that such a theory will be very complex, and that one of the complexities concerns the agent's reason for acting. The reason why an agent acted (or failed to act) may affect the characterization of what he did intentionally. The mere fact that he did *something* intentionally, foreseeing a certain result, does not necessarily mean that he brought about that *result* intentionally.

In order to show that the cessation of life-prolonging treatment, in the cases I've discussed, is the intentional termination of life, one would either have to show that treatment was stopped in order to bring about the patient's death, or provide a theory of intentional action according to which the reason for ceasing treatment is irrelevant to its characterization as the intentional termination of life. I find this suggestion implausible, but am willing to consider arguments for it. Rachels has provided no such arguments: indeed, he apparently shares my view about the intentional termination of life. For when he claims that the cessation of life-prolonging treatment *is* the intentional termination of life, his reason for making the claim is that "if it were not, there would be no point to it." Rachels believes that the point of ceasing treatment, "in these cases," is to bring about the patient's death. If that were not the point, he suggests, why would the doctor cease treatment? I have shown, however, that there can be a point to ceasing treatment which is not the death of the patient. In showing this, I have refuted Rachels' reason for identifying the cessation of life-prolonging treatment with the intentional termination of life, and thus his argument against the AMA doctrine.

Here someone might say: Even if the withholding of treatment is not the intentional termination of life, does that make a difference, morally speaking? if life-prolonging treatment may be withheld, for the sake of the child, may not an easy death be provided, for the sake of the child, as well? The unoperated child with spina bifida may take months or even years to die. Distressed by the spectacle of children "lying around, waiting to die," one doctor has written, "It is time that society and medicine stopped perpetuating the fiction that withholding treatment is ethically different from terminating a life. It is time that society began to discuss mechanisms by which we can alleviate the pain and suffering for those individuals whom we cannot help."[7]

I do not deny that there may be cases in which death is in the best interests of the patient. In such cases, a quick and painless death may be the best thing. However, I do not think that, once active or vigorous treatment is stopped, a quick death is always preferable to a lingering one. We must be cautious about attributing to defective children *our* distress at seeing them linger. Waiting for them to die may be tough on parents, doctors, and nurses—it isn't necessarily tough on the child. The decision not to operate need not mean a decision to neglect, and it may be possible to make the remaining months of the child's life comfortable, pleasant, and filled with love. If this alternative is possible, surely it is more decent and humane than killing the child. In such a situa-

tion, withholding treatment, foreseeing the child's death, is not ethically equivalent to killing the child, and we cannot move from the permissibility of the former to that of the latter. I am worried that there will be a tendency to do precisely that if active euthanasia is regarded as morally equivalent to the withholding of life-prolonging treatment.

CONCLUSION

The AMA statement does not make the distinction Rachels and Tooley wish to attack, that between active and passive euthanasia. Instead, the statement draws a distinction between the intentional termination of life, on the one hand, and the cessation of the employment of extraordinary means to prolong life, on the other. Nothing said by Rachels and Tooley shows that this distinction is confused. It may be that doctors have misinterpreted the AMA statement, and that this has led, for example, to decisions to allow defective infants to starve slowly to death. I quite agree with Rachels and Tooley that the decisions to which they allude were cruel and made on irrelevant grounds. Certainly it is worth pointing out that allowing someone to die *can* be the intentional termination of life, and that it can be just as bad as, or worse than, killing someone. However, the withholding of life-prolonging treatment is not necessarily the intentional termination of life, so that if it is permissible to withhold life-prolonging treatment it does not follow that, other things being equal, it is permissible to kill. Furthermore, most of the time, other things are not equal. In many of the cases in which it would be right to cease treatment, I do not think that it would also be right to kill.

NOTES

1. For example, *In re Yetter*, 62 Pa. D & C. 2d 619 (C.P., Northampton County Ct. 1974).

2. David W. Meyers, "Legal Aspects of Voluntary Euthanasia," in *Dilemmas of Euthanasia*, ed. John Behnke and Sissela Bok (New York: Anchor Books, 1975), p. 56.

3. Ernest H. Rosenbaum, M.D., *Living With Cancer* (New York: Praeger, 1975), p. 27.

4. See Tristram Engelhardt, Jr.; "Ethical Issues in Aiding the Death of Young Children," in *Beneficent Euthanasia*, ed. Marvin Kohl (Buffalo, N.Y.: Prometheus Books, 1975). . . .

5. B. D. Colen, *Karen Ann Quinlan: Living and Dying in the Age of Eternal Life* (Los Angeles: Nash, 1976), p. 115.

6. See Norman L. Cantor, "Law and the Termination of an Incompetent Patient's Life-Preserving Care," in *Dilemmas of Euthanasia*, pp. 69–105.

7. John Freeman, "Is There a Right to Die—Quickly?", *Journal of Pediatrics*, 80, no. 5 (1972), 904–905.

CASES FOR ANALYSIS

1. Euthanasia and Hurricane Katrina

NEW ORLEANS, Louisiana (CNN)—More than one medical professional is under scrutiny as a possible person of interest as Louisiana's attorney general investigates whether hospital workers resorted to euthanasia in the chaotic days after Hurricane Katrina shattered New Orleans, a source familiar with the investigation has told CNN.

CNN first reported in October that staff members at Memorial Medical Center had discussions about euthanizing patients after the hurricane flooded the city on Monday, August 29, cutting off power and stranding hundreds of thousands of residents. Now, for the first time, Louisiana Attorney General Charles Foti has told CNN that allegations of possible euthanasia at Memorial Medical Center are "credible and worth investigating."

Foti would not provide any details of his investigation. However, a source familiar with it, who did not want to be identified publicly, told CNN that more than one person is being scrutinized as a possible person of interest for crimes related to euthanasia that may have been committed there.

CNN has learned the investigation is looking at the possibility that medical personnel at the hospital were afraid of anarchy in the city, feared they could be the next targets of violence as they grew increasingly tired of horrible conditions inside the hospital.

Memorial Hospital had been a storm refuge for up to 2,000 people. Patients, staff and their families rode out the storm inside. But by Thursday, four days after Katrina hit, despair was setting in. The hospital was surrounded by floodwater. There was no power, no water and stifling heat. Food was running low. Nurses were forced to fan patients by hand. And outside the hospital windows, nurses tell CNN they saw looters breaking into a credit union.

The hours, and then days, passed with only the occasional boat or helicopter stopping by to pick up patients. On Thursday, according to people who were there, there was a shift in tone at the hospital.

Angela McManus of New Orleans was at the side of her critically ill mother Wilda on the hospital's seventh floor and sensed the change: Nurses, she says, were now discussing who would be evacuated and, for the first time, who would not.

"These were grown men who were buckling down to their knees, because they were saying they couldn't believe FEMA was making them stay there and watch people dying. They had decided not to evacuate the DNR patients," McManus said, referring to the patients who had signed "do not resuscitate" forms.

At about the same time, some members of the hospital staff were discussing euthanizing patients, medical personnel who were at the scene tell CNN.*

Give reasons for your answers to the following questions. Suppose doctors at Memorial Hospital did perform active euthanasia on some patients (a supposition, of course, that may very well be false). Considering the horrid conditions in the hospital at the time and the suffering of the patients there, would doctors have been justified in using active nonvoluntary euthanasia on unconscious DNR patients? Or on conscious, suffering patients who were expected to die soon and had no advance directives? Would doctors have been justified in performing active involuntary euthanasia on a few dying patients to conserve medicines so that many more patients could be saved?

* Drew Griffin and Kathleen Johnson, "Katrina Investigation Focuses on More Than One Person," *CNN.com,* 21 December 2005, www.cnn.com/2005/US/12/21/katrina.hospital/index.html (accessed 19 February 2006). © 2005 Cable News Network. Reprinted courtesy of CNN.

---

2. Euthanasia for Newborns

Paris (CNSNews.com)—Four years after becoming the first nation formally to legalize euthanasia, the Netherlands is set to amend its legislation to provide for the euthanasia of newborn babies, under certain circumstances.

In 2001, the Dutch government passed a law allowing doctors to end the life of adult patients at their own request.

The new directive, which will be debated in parliament later this month and most likely approved without a vote, will extend the regulations to incorporate what is known as the Groningen Protocol.

Under these guidelines, parents can give consent for children to be killed, if they are suffering from severe pain and are terminally ill.

"This is dangerous because the question is, what will be the next extension?" said Bert Dorenbos, chairman of Cry for Life, a pro-life organization in the Netherlands.

"It can be very dangerous when our lives are in the hands of political parties or subjective groups," he said.

The Groningen Academic Hospital, where doctors drew up the guidelines, made headlines last year when it admitted publicly that it had carried out euthanasia on terminally ill newborn babies.

The hospital claimed the practice was common elsewhere in the world, including in the U.S.

Government officials said there were 10–15 cases of child euthanasia in the Netherlands every year and doctors were eager for the directive to be adopted so they will not be prosecuted. . . .

The Groningen Protocol lists several criteria for making a decision on ending a child's life. There should be severe pain and suffering and no hope for a cure or relief through medical treatment, and an independent doctor must provide a second opinion. Parents must also give consent.[†]

Provide reasons for your answers to the following questions. Under the circumstances described (severe pain, terminal illness), would child euthanasia ever be morally permissible? Would child euthanasia be permissible if the newborn was not terminal but in an unalterable vegetative state? Would it be permissible if the newborn suffered from a severe birth defect such as Down's syndrome, which causes severe disabilities but does not rule out a worthwhile life?

†Excerpt from Eva Cahen, "Next Up in the Netherlands: Euthanasia for Babies," *CNSNews.com*, 5 October 2005, www.cnsnews.com/ViewForeignBureaus.asp?Page=/ForeignBureaus/archive/200510.FOR20051005b.html (accessed 23 November 2006). © 2005 Cybercast News Service. Reprinted with permission from Cnsnews.com–Cybercast News Service.

3. The Suicide of Admiral Nimitz

The name of Chester W. Nimitz is legendary in the annals of naval warfare. In June 1942, Admiral Nimitz commanded the U.S. forces assigned to block a Japanese invasion of Midway.

In the Battle of Midway, Nimitz's fighter-bombers caught the Japanese fleet off guard, as its carrier aircraft were being refueled on deck. His pilots swooped in and sent to the bottom four of the Japanese carriers—Hiryu, Soryu, Akagi and Kaga—that had led the attack on Pearl Harbor. Midway broke the back of Japanese naval power and was among the most decisive battles in all of history.

Nimitz's son and namesake, Chester W. Nimitz Jr., would rise to the same rank of admiral and become a hero of the Pacific war—a submarine commander who would sink a Japanese destroyer bearing down on his boat by firing torpedoes directly into its bow.

But Chester W. Nimitz Jr., achieved another kind of fame on Jan. 2. In a suicide pact with his 89-year-old wife, the 86-year-old hero ended his life with an overdose of sleeping pills.

Having lost 30 pounds from a stomach disorder, suffering from congestive heart failure and in constant back pain, the admiral had been determined to dictate the hour of his death. His wife, who suffered from osteoporosis so severe her bones were breaking, had gone blind. She had no desire to live without her husband.

So, as the devoted couple had spent their lives together, they decided to end their lives together. The admiral's final order read: "Our decision was made over a considerable period of time and was not carried out in acute desperation. Nor is it the expression of a mental illness. We have consciously, rationally, deliberately and of our own free will taken measures to end our lives today because of the physical limitations on our quality of life placed upon us by age, failing vision, osteoporosis, back and painful orthopedic problems."

According to The New York Times obituary, "The Nimitzes did not believe in any afterlife or God, and embraced no religion. But one of Mr. Nimitz's three surviving sisters, Mary Aquinas, 70, is a Catholic nun. . . . Sister Mary said that she could not condone her brother's decision to end his life, but that she felt sympathetic. 'If you cannot see any value to suffering for yourself or others,' she said, 'Then maybe it does make sense to end your life.' "‡

Provide reasons for your answers: Was Admiral Nimitz justified in his decision to commit suicide? Is suicide morally wrong in all circumstances? Is suicide a matter of personal choice, morally permissible if a person freely opts to end her life for whatever reason?

‡ Patrick J. Buchanan, "The Sad Suicide of Admiral Nimitz," *WorldNetDaily*, 18 January 2002, www.wnd.com/news/article.asp?ARTICLE_ID=26106 (accessed 19 February 2006). Reprinted with permission of Patrick J. Buchanan and Creators Syndicate.

Capital Punishment

Few moral issues provoke the kind of fiery emotions and fervent debate that capital punishment does. In some circles, the very mention of the words *death penalty* is enough to set off a cross fire of opinions on the subject—as well as an onslaught of zealotry and moral confusion. At the center of all the commotion is a clash of fundamental moral values, a conflict heightened by the realization that weighing in the balance is, ultimately and tragically, the life or death of a human being.

In this controversy, the **abolitionists** (those who wish to abolish capital punishment) most often appeal to basic moral principles such as "Do not kill," "Honor the sanctity of life," or "Respect human dignity." The **retentionists** (those who wish to retain the death penalty) are likely to appeal to other principles: "Punish the guilty," "Give murderers the punishment they deserve," "A life for a life," or "Deter the ultimate crime (murder) with the ultimate punishment." On the most general and fundamental of these principles—not killing, respecting human dignity, and punishing the guilty—almost all parties to the dispute agree. But retentionists and abolitionists are usually at odds over how these principles should be interpreted.

Retentionists like to remind us of murderers whose crimes are so horrific that the death penalty may seem the only fitting punishment. Thus they bring up such moral monsters as Timothy McVeigh (used a bomb to kill 168 men, women, and children), Ted Bundy (murdered, by his own count, more than 100 women), John Wayne Gacy (raped and murdered 33 boys and men), and Adolf Eichmann (facilitated the murder of millions during the Holocaust). Abolitionists, on the other hand, tell of the horrors that often accompany the death penalty: innocent people who are wrongly convicted and executed, executions that go wrong and cause excruciating pain to those executed, and the suspiciously high percentage of poor and minority people who are executed in the United States. Commonplace in the capital punishment debate, such facts may move us to anger, pity, disgust, or sadness, and they may inform our thinking in important ways. But we should not allow our emotional reaction to them interfere with the vital task that we begin in this chapter—the careful evaluation of arguments for and against capital punishment.

ISSUE FILE: BACKGROUND

In the legal sense, **punishment** is the deliberate and authorized causing of pain or harm to someone thought to have broken a law. It is a legal sanction imposed by society on offenders for violating society's official norms. The justification for punishment—the reason why society uses it—generally takes one of two forms. As we will see later, many believe that the sole reason we should punish the wrongdoer is because he morally *deserves* punishment. His desert is the only justification required, and meting out punishment to those who deserve it is morally obligatory and a morally good thing. Others believe that the only proper justification is the good consequences for society that the punishment of offenders will bring—most notably, the prevention of future crimes and the maintenance of an orderly society.

Capital punishment is punishment by execution of someone officially judged to have committed a serious, or capital, crime. For thousands of years, this extreme sanction has been used countless times in the Western world for a variety of offenses—rape, murder, horse theft, kidnapping, treason, sodomy, spying, blasphemy, witchcraft, and many others. A wide assortment of execution methods have also been employed, ranging from the ancient and medieval (crucifixion, drawing and quartering, burning alive, impalement, etc.) to the handful of standard techniques of the past two centuries (hanging, firing squad, lethal gas, electrocution, and lethal injection). In twenty-first century America, most death-penalty states (thirty-eight in 2004) reserve capital punishment for the crime of murder, and lethal injection is the sole method of execution in about two dozen of those (with most of the rest offering a choice between lethal injection and either gas or electrocution).[1]

In December 2003, there were 3,374 prisoners on death row in the United States, and eleven states and the federal government executed 65 of them. Of those 65, 41 were white; 20 black; 3 Hispanic (all white); and 1 Native American. Only one of these executions was by electrocution; all others were by lethal injection. California held the largest number of death row inmates, 629; Texas held 453; and Pennsylvania, 230. Texas carried out 24 executions in 2003, more than any other state. Oklahoma executed 14 and North Carolina 7, with all other jurisdictions each executing 3 or fewer. However, no death penalty was in force in the District of Columbia and twelve states: Alaska,

Hawaii, Iowa, Maine, Massachusetts, Michigan, Minnesota, North Dakota, Rhode Island, Vermont, West Virginia, and Wisconsin.[2]

The trend in executions in the United States has varied over the past few decades. The number of executions carried out each year between the mid-1930s and the 1970s gradually declined, from a high of 200 down to 0 in 1976. But from 1977 to 1999, the annual toll ramped up again, from 1 in 1977 to 98 in 1999. Since this high point, another downward trend has set in, with the number of executions in 2004 dropping to 59.[3] Over the past decade or so, the gradual decrease in executions has coincided with significant public support for the death penalty for convicted murderers. Gallup polls show that between 1994 and 2004, the percentage of American adults in favor of capital punishment for murder has fluctuated annually but always stayed within the 64 to 80 percent range. These numbers decreased significantly when people were asked to consider life in prison without parole as an option.[4]

Most other countries have officially abolished the death penalty or simply stopped using it. One hundred twenty-one nations—including Canada, Mexico, and all Western European countries—are in this category. Seventy-five countries and territories, however, continue to employ capital punishment. In 2004, at least 90 percent of executions around the world were carried out by China, which is thought to have put to death at least 3,400 people. Though twenty-four other countries executed people that year, four of these nations accounted for most of the executions: Iran (159),

---

[1]Tracy L. Snell, "Capital Punishment 1996," U.S. Department of Justice, Bureau of Justice Statistics Bulletin, NJC-167031 (December 1997), table 2; updated by the Death Penalty Information Center.

[2]Thomas P. Bonczar and Tracy L. Snell, "Capital Punishment, 2003," U.S. Department of Justice, Bureau of Justice Statistics Bulletin, NJC 206627 (November 2004), 1, 9.

[3]*Bureau of Justice Statistics Bulletin,* Capital Punishment, 2003 (November 2004), 10.

[4]"Facts about the Death Penalty," *Death Penalty Information Center,* www.deathpenaltyinfo.org (2 November 2005).

Vietnam (64), United States (59), and Saudi Arabia (33).[5]

The use of capital punishment in the United States has been shaped by several landmark Supreme Court decisions. In 1972, in *Furman v. Georgia*, the Court ruled that capital punishment as it was then being applied in certain states was unconstitutional. The ruling put a halt to executions across the country. Yet the Court declared not that the death penalty itself was unconstitutional, only that its current method of administration was. The majority on the Court thought that the usual administration—which allowed juries to impose the death penalty arbitrarily without any legal guidance—constituted "cruel and unusual punishment," a violation of the Eighth Amendment of the Constitution.

Many states then promptly rewrote their death penalty statutes to try to minimize administrative arbitrariness. A few states passed laws decreeing that the death penalty would be mandatory for particular capital crimes. But in *Woodson v. North Carolina* (1976), the Supreme Court declared mandatory death sentences unconstitutional. Some states instituted sentencing guidelines to provide standards for the judge or jury deliberating about whether to impose the death penalty. In *Gregg v. Georgia* (1976), the Court ruled that such death penalty laws prescribing proper guidelines were constitutional, at least in cases of murder. This ruling in effect reinstated capital punishment in the country, and executions resumed in the following year. Since 1976, few state statutes have allowed the death penalty for anything but homicide cases.

More recently the Court has banned the use of the death penalty for particular kinds of offenders. In *Atkins v. Virginia* (2002), the Court held that the execution of mentally retarded persons is cruel

and unusual punishment and is therefore unconstitutional. In *Roper v. Simmons* (2005), the Court held that executing those who were under the age of eighteen when they committed their crimes is also a violation of Eighth Amendment protection against cruel and unusual punishment. Before *Roper,* seven states had no minimum age for execution, and fifteen states had set the minimum at between fourteen and seventeen years old.

An important tradition in law that bears on capital punishment is the distinction between types of punishable killing: namely, between first-degree murder, second-degree murder, and manslaughter. Statutes vary by jurisdiction, but generally first-degree murder is killing (1) with premeditation; (2) while performing a major crime (felony) such as armed robbery, kidnapping, or rape; or (3) involving particular egregious circumstances such as the deaths of several people or of a child or police officer. Second-degree murder is killing without premeditation but with some degree of intent ("malice aforethought"). Manslaughter is killing without premeditation or intent, as when one person kills another in "the heat of passion" or by driving drunk. Usually, only first-degree murder makes a defendant eligible for the death penalty.

MORAL THEORIES

Both retentionists and abolitionists appeal to consequentialist and nonconsequentialist moral theories. Retentionist arguments are often thoroughly utilitarian, contending that use of capital punishment can create a favorable balance of happiness over unhappiness for society. One common argument is that the death penalty achieves such utility through *prevention*—by preventing the criminal from striking again. Better than any other form of punishment, the retentionist says, the death penalty protects society from repeat criminals, those violent and dangerous offenders who cannot be reformed. The retentionist claims that life

[5]Amnesty International, "Death Sentences and Executions in 2004," *Death Penalty News: June 2005,* 1 June 2005, http://web.amnesty.org/library/index/engact 530022005 (27 November 2006).

CRITICAL THOUGHT: Medicated for the Death Penalty

Consider this excerpt from a 2004 news report on an infamous execution in the United States:

> (CNN)—The voices inside Charles Singleton's head varied, in volume and number, regardless of whether he had taken medication for his schizophrenia. Inside his Arkansas cell, he said he could often hear voices that speak of killing him.
>
> Singleton was executed by lethal injection Tuesday night at the Cummins prison unit in Varner, about 70 miles south of Little Rock.
>
> Singleton's attorney said his 44-year-old client welcomed his execution because he was tired of living with mental illness. Singleton understood that he would be put to death and why—the current legal standards to qualify for execution, said his attorney, Jeff Rosenzweig.
>
> Singleton, however, was rational only when he was on medication. It was that fact, as well as an 18-year-old Supreme Court ruling barring executing the insane, that his attorney, some members of the legal and medical communities and death penalty critics pointed to in opposing Singleton's execution.
>
> "If [Singleton] is artificially made to be competent, then the situation is an oxymoron," said

Ronald Tabak, a New York–based attorney who has represented clients in death penalty cases.

> But the prosecutor in the Singleton case claimed the defendant was sane at the time of the crime, and therefore unaffected by the Supreme Court ruling.
>
> "I do not feel he is being medicated in order to put him to death," said John Frank Gibson, who hasn't dealt with the Singleton case in recent years. "He's being medicated to . . . keep him healthy, to control him."*

Do you think it is morally permissible to execute a convicted murderer who was sane at the time of his crime but is now insane? Why or why not? Is it morally permissible to medicate such a person to ensure that he is sane enough for execution? To what moral theory, if any, are you appealing to help you decide?

*Excerpt from Kevin Drew, "Executed Mentally Ill Inmate Heard Voices Until End," *CNN.com,* 6 January 2004, www.cnn.com/2004/LAW/01/06/singleton.death.row/index.html (accessed 8 November 2005). © 2004 Cable News Network. Reprinted courtesy of CNN.

in prison without parole—the usual alternative to the death penalty—is an inadequate substitute. Violent lifers can kill other inmates and prison guards, or they can escape to terrorize society again. By also appealing to utility, the abolitionist may object to this line by insisting that the retentionist produce empirical evidence showing that executing violent criminals does indeed protect society better than the use of life sentences. After all, such premises about deterrence are empirical claims, and empirical claims require supporting evidence.

A related retentionist argument asserts that the death penalty, more than any other form of pun-

ishment (including life in prison), can achieve great overall utility through *deterrence*—the dissuading of possible offenders from committing capital crimes. This utilitarian argument is thought by many to be the retentionist's strongest. The utilitarian philosopher John Stuart Mill claims that for a particular kind of would-be criminal, capital punishment is the most effective deterrent of all:

But the influence of punishment is not to be estimated by its effect on hardened criminals. Those whose habitual way of life keeps them, so to speak, at all times within sight of the gallows, do grow to care less about it; as, to compare good things with bad, an old soldier is not much affected by the chance of dying in battle. I can afford to admit all that is often said about the indifference of the professional criminals to the gallows. Though of that indifference one-third is probably bravado and another third confidence that they shall have the luck to escape, it is quite probable that the remaining third is real. But the efficacy of a punishment which acts principally through the imagination, is chiefly to be measured by the impression it makes on those who are still innocent; by the horror with which it surrounds the first promptings of guilt; the restraining influence it exercises over the beginning of the thought which, if indulged, would become a temptation; the check which it exerts over the graded declension towards the state—never suddenly attained—in which crime no longer revolts, and punishment no longer terrifies.[6]

Like the prevention appeal, the deterrence argument requires supporting evidence—specifically, evidence showing that the execution of criminals really does deter serious criminal behavior better than lesser punishments such as imprisonment. Abolitionists, however, are quick to question any such evidence. In fact, even many retentionists agree that the relevant scientific studies on the deterrence question are conflicting or otherwise inconclusive.

The central difficulty in conducting these studies is the number of variables that must be controlled to get reliable results. A social scientist, for example, could select two very similar jurisdictions, one with the death penalty and one without, and compare the murder rates in each. Presumably, if capital punishment deters murderers, then the jurisdiction using the death penalty should have a lower murder rate than the no-death penalty jurisdiction. But it is virtually impossible to rule out the influence of extraneous factors on the study results. Besides being influenced by the penal system, murder rates may be affected by many variables—unemployment, cultural conventions, moral beliefs, political climate, media influence, availability of lethal weapons, incidence of illegal drug use, history of violence, income level, and on and on. No two jurisdictions are exactly alike, and many differences (both known and unknown) could contribute to the rise or fall of serious crime rates.

Despite these research problems, many retentionists still consider the case for deterrence strong. They argue that even if science does not yet offer unequivocal support for the death penalty's power to deter capital crimes, common sense does. The philosopher Louis Pojman takes this tack. He contends that it is obvious that most people want to avoid jail and that long sentences will deter most potential criminals better than short ones—and that there are good reasons to believe that the death penalty deters better still. One reason, he says, is that a large proportion of crimes are committed by criminals who weigh the risks and benefits of their criminal activity and become more attracted to particular crimes the milder the punishments are. And there are good indications that the death penalty would exert maximum deterrence in these cases: "The fact that those who are condemned to death do everything in their power to get their sentences postponed or reduced to long-term prison sentences, in the way *lifers* do not, shows that they fear death more than life in prison."[7]

The abolitionist can offer a couple of responses to this argument from common sense. First, even if the death penalty is a more severe punishment than life in prison, it does not follow that the

[6]John Stuart Mill, "Speech in Favor of Capital Punishment," to the English Parliament, 1868, http://ethics.sandiego.edu/Mill.html (13 April 2007).

[7]Louis P. Pojman, "Why the Death Penalty Is Morally Permissible," in *Debating the Death Penalty: Should America Have Capital Punishment? The Experts on Both Sides Make Their Best Case,* ed. Hugo Adam Bedau and Paul G. Cassell (Oxford: Oxford University Press, 2004), 60–61.

death penalty deters murderers better. The prospect of life in prison may very well deter future murderers just as effectively as the death penalty can. Second, it is possible that the threat of capital punishment motivates potential killers not to avoid killing but to try harder not to get caught.

Recognizing the uncertainties in trying to assess levels of deterrence, some retentionists argue that despite the unknowns, our wisest and most morally responsible move is to bet that capital punishment does deter murderers. The reasoning that leads to this conclusion is essentially a utilitarian calculation. The philosopher Ernest van den Haag was the first to articulate this argument. The choice we are faced with, he says, is either to use the death penalty or not to use it—and we must choose while not knowing for sure whether it is a superior deterrent. If we use the penalty, we risk killing convicted murderers (and saving innocent lives). If we abolish the penalty, we risk bringing about the deaths of innocent victims (and saving the lives of murderers). If we must risk something, he says, it is better to risk the lives of convicted murderers than those of innocent people. Thus, our best bet is to retain the death penalty. "I believe we have no right to risk additional future victims of murder for the sake of sparing convicted murderers," van den Haag asserts, "on the contrary, our moral obligation is to risk the possible ineffectiveness of executions."[8]

A common abolitionist reply to this argument is that the utilitarian calculation is incomplete. The assessment of net happiness, says the abolitionist, fails to take into account the possibility that the death penalty could *encourage* violent crime instead of just deterring it. How? Some argue that violent criminals who know they are likely to get the death penalty may commit murder to avoid being captured. In addition, some aboli-

tionists maintain that capital punishment has a brutalizing effect on society—it makes killing human beings seem more morally and psychologically acceptable. If so, executing people could cause more harm than good and be a very poor bet for society.

On utilitarian grounds, abolitionists can attack capital punishment directly (as opposed to simply countering retentionist arguments). In perhaps the most common of such approaches, the abolitionist argues that more net happiness is created in society by sentencing murderers to life in prison without parole than by executing them. Life sentences promote the welfare of society by preventing murderers from killing again—and they do so without generating the disadvantages and pain inherent in a system of capital punishment.

Another utilitarian argument against the death penalty is that this form of punishment is simply too costly:

The death penalty is much more expensive than its closest alternative—life imprisonment with no parole. Capital trials are longer and more expensive at every step than other murder trials. Pre-trial motions, expert witness investigations, jury selection, and the necessity for two trials—one on guilt and one on sentencing—make capital cases extremely costly, even before the appeals process begins. Guilty pleas are almost unheard of when the punishment is death. In addition, many of these trials result in a life sentence rather than the death penalty, so the state pays the cost of life imprisonment on top of the expensive trial.[9]

Retentionists often respond to this argument by questioning whether the costs have been calculated accurately and fairly. Perhaps more often, they offer a nonconsequentialist reply: if the death

[8]Ernest van den Haag, "On Deterrence and the Death Penalty," *Journal of Criminal Law, Criminology, and Police Science* 60, no. 2 (1969).

[9]Richard C. Dieter, "Millions Misspent: What Politicians Don't Say about the High Cost of the Death Penalty," Fall 1994, www.deathpenaltyinfo.org/article.php?scid=45&did=385 (27 November 2006).

QUICK REVIEW

abolitionists—Those who wish to abolish capital punishment.

retentionists—Those who wish to retain the death penalty.

punishment—The deliberate and authorized causing of pain or harm to someone thought to have broken a law.

capital punishment—Punishment by execution of someone officially judged to have committed a serious, or capital, crime.

retributivism—The view that offenders deserve to be punished, or "paid back," for their crimes and to be punished in proportion to the severity of their offenses.

penalty is a just punishment, then the costs involved are irrelevant.

In the death penalty debate, appeals to non-consequentialist theories are common on both sides of the issue. Abolitionists devise arguments against capital punishment using what they take to be fundamental moral principles regarding the value or dignity of human life. For them, regardless of its social utility, the death penalty is wrong because it violates these principles. For example, they may argue that everyone has a right to life (a basic moral principle), even hardened criminals, and that the death penalty is a violation of this right—therefore, executing criminals is wrong. To this argument, retentionists usually reply along these lines: people do indeed have a right to life, but this right is not absolute. That is, a person's right to life can sometimes be overridden for good reasons. For example, if your life is being threatened, it is morally permissible to kill an attacker in self-defense. So the right to life does not hold in every situation no matter what. It may be

morally permissible, then, to sometimes set this right aside.

To make their case, abolitionists often appeal to notions of fairness or justice. One prevalent argument is based on the assertion that our penal system is inherently unjust, sometimes executing innocent people (numerous cases have come to light in which people who had been executed or who were on death row were later found to be innocent). Because the death penalty is irrevocable—that is, there is no way to "undo" an execution or to compensate the executed—the execution of the innocent is an especially egregious miscarriage of justice. Therefore, we should get rid of the death penalty, since abolition is the only way to avoid such tragedies. Retentionists are generally unmoved by this argument, offering counterarguments like this one:

Miscarriages of justice result in innocent people being sentenced to death and executed, even in criminal-law systems in which greatest care is taken to ensure that it never comes to that. But this does not stem from the intrinsic nature of the institution of capital punishment; it results from deficiencies, limitations, and imperfections of the criminal law procedures in which this punishment is meted out. Errors of justice do not demonstrate the need to do away with capital punishment; they simply make it incumbent on us to do everything possible to improve even further procedures of meting it out.[10]

The main nonconsequentialist argument for the death penalty is based on the theory of punishment known as **retributivism**—the view that offenders deserve to be punished, or "paid back," for their crimes and to be punished in proportion to the severity of their offenses. Retributivism says that offenders should be punished because *they deserve to be punished.* Punishment is a matter of justice, not social utility. If offenders are not pun-

[10]Igor Primoratz, *Justifying Legal Punishment* (Atlantic Highlands, NJ: Humanities Press International, 1989), 165.

ished, justice is not done. Kant, probably the most influential retributivist, declares that there is only one reason to punish someone for his offenses:

Juridical punishment can never be administered merely as a means for promoting another good either with regard to the criminal himself or to civil society, but must in all cases be imposed only because the individual on whom it is inflicted has committed a crime.[11]

We can distinguish two kinds of retributivism according to the nature of the penal payback required. Kant accepts retributivism based on the doctrine of *lex talionis*—the idea that the punishment should match the crime in kind, that justice demands "an eye for an eye, a life for a life." He thinks that whatever harm the criminal does to the innocent, that same kind of harm should be done to the criminal. Thus, the only just punishment for a man who wrongfully and deliberately takes someone's life is the taking of *his* life. Other retributivists are uncomfortable with the notion of punishing in kind (should rapists be raped? should torturers be tortured?). They favor *proportional retributivism,* in which punishment reflects the seriousness of the crime but does not necessarily *resemble* the crime. For these retributivists, murder is the worst possible crime and deserves the worst possible punishment—the death of the offender.

Underpinning many retributive views of capital punishment is a Kantian emphasis on respect for persons. Persons have dignity and inherent worth and are ends in themselves. Deliberately killing an innocent person, says the retributivist, is so heinous a crime, such an intolerable evil, that it merits the ultimate punishment—the death of the murderer. So when the killer takes a life, she must forfeit her own. As Kant says,

Even if a civil society resolved to dissolve itself with the consent of all its members . . . the last murderer lying in prison ought to be executed before the resolution was carried out. This ought to be done in order that every one may realize the desert of his deeds, and that blood-guiltiness may not remain on the people; for otherwise they will all be regarded as participants in the murder as a public violation of justice.[12]

Perhaps surprisingly, often the retributivist also appeals to the dignity and worth of the murderer. As Kant notes, treating persons with respect means treating them as rational agents who make free choices and are responsible for their actions. To justly punish persons—to give them what they deserve—is to acknowledge their status as responsible agents deserving of respect. He asserts, then, that executing a murderer is not an affront to human dignity but a recognition of it.

A frequent reaction to the retributivist view is that penal retribution is not justice—but revenge. The retributivist replies that this charge is muddled: vengeance refers to making the offender suffer because of one's sense of outrage, grief, or frustration toward her and her crime; retribution involves moral deliberation about an offender's just deserts.

MORAL ARGUMENTS

Is the death penalty a morally permissible form of punishment? As you know by now, many arguments have been put forth on both sides of this issue—too many for any single book to tackle, let alone a single chapter. But we can dissect one of the more widely used (and interesting) examples. Let us begin with a popular argument *against* the death penalty:

1. If the death penalty discriminates against blacks, it is unjust.

[11]Immanuel Kant, *The Philosophy of Law,* trans. W. Hastie (Edinburgh: Clark, 1887), 195.

[12]Kant, *Philosophy of Law,* 198.

2. If the death penalty is unjust, it should be abolished.

3. The death penalty discriminates against blacks.

4. Therefore, the death penalty should be abolished.

This argument is valid, so our evaluation of it should focus on the truth of the premises. Premises 1 and 2 are moral statements; Premise 3 is an empirical statement about the use of the death penalty against African Americans. (Arguments like this are used with equal force when focusing on other minority groups as well as the poor and uneducated; for simplicity's sake we focus on blacks, who make up the largest segment of minority death row inmates.)

Let us examine the empirical claim first: is Premise 3 true? We can give it more precision by recasting it like this: The administration of the death penalty is biased against blacks. Many abolitionists insist that this claim is indeed accurate. They say, for example, that blacks convicted of murder are more likely to be sentenced to death than whites convicted of murder. How is this claim supported? Here is one way:

[T]he Reverend Jesse Jackson, in his book *Legal Lynching,* argues that "[n]umerous researchers have shown conclusively that African American defendants are far more likely to receive the death penalty than are white defendants charged with the same crime." The support for this claim is said to be the undisputed fact that when compared to their percentage in the overall population African Americans are overrepresented on death row. For example, while 12 percent of the population is African American, about 43 percent of death row inmates are African American, and 38 percent of prisoners executed since 1977 are African American.[13]

But such statistical comparisons can be misleading, say some retentionists:

The relevant population for comparison is not the general population, but rather the population of murderers. If the death penalty is administered without regard to race, the percentage of African American death row inmates found at the end of the process should not exceed the percentage of African American defendants charged with murder at the beginning. The available statistics indicate that is precisely what happens. The Department of Justice found that while African Americans constituted 48 percent of adults charged with homicide, they were only 41 percent of those admitted to prison under sentence of death. In other words, once arrested for murder, blacks are actually less likely to receive a capital sentence than are whites.[14]

Needless to say, Premise 3 (in the form examined here and in several other variations) is controversial. That does not mean, of course, that its truth or falsity is unknowable. New research or conscientious examination of existing research may provide the support that Premise 3 requires. In any event, the support must come in the form of solid statistical data carefully interpreted. Anecdotal evidence—for example, news stories of apparent unequal treatment of whites and blacks—cannot help us much.

As we did with Premise 3, we can restate Premise 1 to make it more specific: If the administration of the death penalty is biased against blacks, it is unjust. On a straightforward reading, this assertion would seem to be acceptable to both retentionists and abolitionists. Few would deny that applying the death penalty in a discriminatory fashion is unjust, for equals must be treated equally. On this reading, the premise is almost certainly true. But many abolitionists would interpret the statement differently. They would contend that if the administration of the death penalty is

---

[13]Paul G. Cassell, "In Defense of the Death Penalty," in Bedau and Cassell, eds., *Debating the Death Penalty,* 201.

[14]Cassell, "In Defense of the Death Penalty," 201.

biased against blacks, then the death penalty itself is unjust. Some abolitionists accept this view because they believe there is no way to apply the death penalty fairly; the administration of capital punishment is inherently unjust. Others would say that there is no way to separate the "death penalty itself" from the way it is administered. In the real world, there is only the death-penalty-as-actually-applied, which is inescapably unfair.

A common reply to the abolitionist understanding of Premise 1 is that it misses an important distinction: the unjust administration of a punishment does not entail the injustice of the punishment itself. As one retentionist says,

[This charge of unfairness] is not an argument, either against the death penalty or against any other form of punishment. It is an argument against unjust and inequitable distribution of penalties. If the trials of wealthy men are less likely to result in convictions than those of poor men, then something must be done to reform the procedure in criminal courts. . . . But the maldistribution of penalties is no argument against any particular form of penalty.[15]

It seems that we cannot decide the truth of Premise 1 without a much more thorough examination of the arguments for and against it, a task beyond the scope of this discussion. So let us move to our revised Premise 2: If the administration of the death penalty is unjust, it should be abolished. As you can see, this premise has the same kind of ambiguity that we see in Premise 1. Again the abolitionist reading is that an unjust application of the death penalty is an indictment against capital punishment itself, so capital punishment should be abolished. Thus the same arguments and counterarguments surrounding Premise 1 also apply here.

At this point, we have not determined whether this abolitionist argument is a good one. But we

have gained insight into this part of the capital punishment debate. Look again at the argument in its revised form:

1. If the administration of the death penalty is biased against blacks, it is unjust.

2. If the administration of the death penalty is unjust, it should be abolished.

3. The administration of the death penalty is biased against blacks.

4. Therefore, the death penalty should be abolished.

We have seen how difficult it can be to make this argument work. If any one of the premises is false, the conclusion is not supported and the argument fails. (Also, the argument is now valid only on the reading preferred by abolitionists.) But we have also found that the lynchpin of the argument is the abolitionist view that injustice in the system of capital punishment is the same as injustice in lethal punishment itself. If abolitionists can establish this equivalence, the argument is much more likely to succeed. The other links in the chain of reasoning—the injustice of discrimination and the need to abolish unjust punishments—are generally accepted by all parties to the dispute.

We have also learned something about the retentionist position. We have discovered how retentionists can readily agree that the application of the death penalty discriminates against blacks, that this biased treatment is unconscionable and unjust, and that such a discriminatory system should be reformed or abolished—and still consistently believe that it can be morally permissible for the state to put a convicted murderer to death.

SUMMARY

Capital punishment is a form of legal punishment—execution—reserved for someone convicted of committing a capital crime, usually some form of murder. Abolitionists wish to abolish capital punishment;

---

[15]B. M. Leiser, *Liberty, Justice and Morals: Contemporary Value Conflicts* (New York: Macmillan, 1973), 225.

retentionists want to retain it. In several decisions, the U.S. Supreme Court has sanctioned and circumscribed the use of the death penalty. In *Gregg v. Georgia*, the Court ruled that administration of the death penalty—if used according to proper guidelines—is constitutional in cases of murder. Other rulings banned the execution of retarded persons and of those who were under eighteen when they committed their crimes.

Both retentionists and abolitionists appeal to utilitarianism and nonconsequentialist moral theories to make their case. Retentionists often argue that the death penalty maximizes the welfare of society by preventing repeat crimes or deterring future crimes. Retributivists argue on nonconsequentialist grounds that capital punishment is morally permissible because it accords with the demands of justice. Abolitionists, on the other hand, often contend that the death penalty does more harm than good to society and that life in prison without parole results in more net happiness than executions do. Many abolitionists also take the nonconsequentialist route by insisting that the death penalty violates some fundamental moral principles—the right to life, the dignity of human beings, and the injustice of executing the innocent.

READINGS

The Ultimate Punishment: A Defense

ERNEST VAN DEN HAAG

In an average year about 20,000 homicides occur in the United States. Fewer than 300 convicted murderers are sentenced to death. But because no more than thirty murderers have been executed in any recent year, most convicts sentenced to death are likely to die of old age.[1] Nonetheless, the death penalty looms large in discussions: it raises important moral questions independent of the number of executions.[2]

The death penalty is our harshest punishment.[3] It is irrevocable: it ends the existence of those punished, instead of temporarily imprisoning them. Further, although not intended to cause physical pain, execution is the only corporal punishment still applied to adults. These singular characteristics contribute to the perennial, impassioned controversy about capital punishment.

Ernest van den Haag, "The Ultimate Punishment: A Defense," *Harvard Law Review* 99 (1986): 1662–69 (edited). Copyright © 1986 by Harvard Law Review Association. Reproduced by permission of Harvard Law Review via Copyright Clearance Center.

I. DISTRIBUTION

Consideration of the justice, morality, or usefulness, of capital punishment is often conflated with objections to its alleged discriminatory or capricious distribution among the guilty. Wrongly so. If capital punishment is immoral *in se*, no distribution among the guilty could make it moral. If capital punishment is moral, no distribution would make it immoral. Improper distribution cannot affect the quality of what is distributed, be it punishment or rewards. Discriminatory or capricious distribution thus could not justify abolition of the death penalty. Further, maldistribution inheres no more in capital punishment than in any other punishment.

Maldistribution between the guilty and the innocent is, by definition, unjust. But the injustice does not lie in the nature of the punishment. Because of the finality of the death penalty, the most grievous maldistribution occurs when it is imposed upon the innocent. However, the frequent allegations of discrimination and capriciousness refer to maldistribution among the guilty and not to the punishment of the innocent.

Maldistribution of any punishment among those who deserve it is irrelevant to its justice or morality. Even if poor or black convicts guilty of capital offenses suffer capital punishment, and other convicts equally guilty of the same crimes do not, a more equal distribution, however desirable, would merely be more equal. It would not be more just to the convicts under sentence of death.

Punishments are imposed on persons, not on racial or economic groups. Guilt is personal. The only relevant question is: does the person to be executed deserve the punishment? Whether or not others who deserved the same punishment, whatever their economic or racial group, have avoided execution is irrelevant. If they have, the guilt of the executed convicts would not be diminished, nor would their punishment be less deserved. To put the issue starkly, if the death penalty were imposed on guilty blacks, but not on guilty whites, or, if it were imposed by a lottery among the guilty, this irrationally discriminatory or capricious distribution would neither make the penalty unjust, nor cause anyone to be unjustly punished, despite the undue impunity bestowed on others.

Equality, in short, seems morally less important than justice. And justice is independent of distributional inequalities. The ideal of equal justice demands that justice be equally distributed, not that it be replaced by equality. Justice requires that as many of the guilty as possible be punished, regardless of whether others have avoided punishment. To let these others escape the deserved punishment does not do justice to them, or to society. But it is not unjust to those who could not escape.

These moral considerations are not meant to deny that irrational discrimination, or capriciousness, would be inconsistent with constitutional requirements. But I am satisfied that the Supreme Court has in fact provided for adherence to the constitutional requirement of equality as much as is possible. Some inequality is indeed unavoidable as a practical matter in any system.[4] But, *ultra posse nemo obligatur.* (Nobody is bound beyond ability.)

Recent data reveal little direct racial discrimination in the sentencing of those arrested and convicted of murder.[5] The abrogation of death penalty for rape has eliminated a major source of racial discrimination. Concededly, some discrimination based on the race of murder victims may exist; yet, this discrimination affects criminal victimizers in an unexpected way. Murderers of whites are thought more likely to be executed than murderers of blacks. Black victims, then, are less fully vindicated than white ones. However, because most black murderers kill blacks, black murderers are spared the death penalty more often than are white murderers. They fare better than most white murderers.[6] The motivation behind unequal distribution of the death penalty may well have been to discriminate against blacks, but the result has favored them. Maldistribution is thus a straw man for empirical as well as analytical reasons.

II. MISCARRIAGES OF JUSTICE

In a recent survey Professors Hugo Adam Bedau and Michael Radelet found that 7000 persons were executed in the United States between 1900 and 1985 and that 25 were innocent of capital crimes.[7] Among the innocents they list Sacco and Vanzetti as well as Ethel and Julius Rosenberg. Although their data may be questionable, I do not doubt that, over a long enough period, miscarriages of justice will occur even in capital cases.

Despite precautions, nearly all human activities, such as trucking, lighting, or construction, cost the lives of some innocent bystanders. We do not give up these activities, because the advantages, moral or material, outweigh the unintended losses.[8] Analogously, for those who think the death penalty just, miscarriages of justice are offset by the moral benefits and the usefulness of doing justice. For those who think the death penalty unjust even when it does not miscarry, miscarriages can hardly be decisive.

III. DETERRENCE

Despite much recent work, there has been no conclusive statistical demonstration that the death penalty is a better deterrent than are alternative punishments. However, deterrence is less than decisive for either side. Most abolitionists acknowledge that they would continue to favor abolition even if the death penalty were shown to deter more murders than alternatives could deter.[9] Abolitionists appear to value the life of a convicted murderer or, at least, his non-execution, more highly than they value the lives of the innocent victims who might be spared by deterring prospective murderers.

Deterrence is not altogether decisive for me either. I would favor retention of the death penalty as retribution even if it were shown that the threat of execution could not deter prospective murderers not already deterred by the threat of imprisonment.[10] Still, I believe the death penalty, because of its finality, is more feared than imprisonment, and deters some prospective murderers not deterred by the threat of imprisonment. Sparing the lives of even a few prospective victims by deterring their murderers is more important than preserving the lives of convicted murderers because of the possibility, or even the probability, that executing them would not deter others. Whereas the lives of the victims who might be saved are valuable, that of the murderer has only negative value, because of his crime. Surely the criminal law is meant to protect the lives of potential victims in preference to those of actual murderers.

Murder rates are determined by many factors; neither the severity nor the probability of the threatened sanction is always decisive. However, for the long run, I share the view of Sir James Fitzjames Stephen: "Some men, probably, abstain from murder because they fear that if they committed murder they would be hanged. Hundreds of thousands abstain from it because they regard it with horror. One great reason why they regard it with horror is that murderers are hanged."[11] Penal sanctions are useful in the long run for the formation of the internal restraints so necessary to control crime. The severity and finality of the death penalty is appropriate to the seriousness and the finality of murder.[12]

IV. INCIDENTAL ISSUES: COST, RELATIVE SUFFERING, BRUTALIZATION

Many nondecisive issues are associated with capital punishment. Some believe that the monetary cost of appealing a capital sentence is excessive. Yet most comparisons of the cost of life imprisonment with the cost of execution, apart from their dubious relevance, are flawed at least by the implied assumption that life prisoners will generate no judicial costs during their imprisonment. At any rate, the actual monetary costs are trumped by the importance of doing justice.

Others insist that a person sentenced to death suffers more than his victim suffered, and that this (excess) suffering is undue according to the *lex talionis* (rule of retaliation). We cannot know whether the murderer on death row suffers more than his victim suffered; however, unlike the murderer, the victim deserved none of the suffering inflicted. Further, the limitations of the *lex talionis* were meant to restrain private vengeance, not the social retribution that has taken its place. Punishment—regardless of the motivation—is not intended to revenge, offset, or compensate for the victim's suffering, or to be measured by it. Punishment is to vindicate the law and the social order undermined by the crime. This is why a kidnapper's penal confinement is not limited to the period for which he imprisoned his victim; nor is a burglar's confinement meant merely to offset the suffering or the harm he caused his victim; nor is it meant only to offset the advantage he gained.[13]

Another argument heard . . . is that, by killing a murderer, we encourage, endorse, or legitimize unlawful killing. Yet, although all punishments are meant to be unpleasant, it is seldom argued that they legitimize the unlawful imposition of identical unpleasantness. Imprisonment is not thought to legitimize kidnapping; neither are fines thought to legitimize robbery. The difference between murder and execution, or between kidnapping and imprisonment, is that the first is unlawful and undeserved, the second a lawful and deserved punishment for an unlawful act. The physical similarities of the punishment to the crime are irrelevant. The relevant difference is not physical, but social.[14]

V. JUSTICE, EXCESS, DEGRADATION

We threaten punishments in order to deter crime. We impose them not only to make the threats credible but also as retribution (justice) for the crimes that were not deterred. Threats and punishments are necessary to deter and deterrence is a sufficient practical justification for them. Retribution is an independent moral justification. Although penalties can be unwise, repulsive, or inappropriate, and those punished can be pitiable, in a sense the infliction of legal punishment on a guilty person cannot be unjust. By committing the crime, the criminal volunteered to assume the risk of receiving a legal punishment that he could have avoided by not committing the crime. The punishment he suffers is the punishment he voluntarily risked suffering and, therefore, it is no more unjust to him than any other event for which one knowingly volunteers to assume the risk. Thus, the death penalty cannot be unjust to the guilty criminal.[15]

There remain, however, two moral objections. The penalty may be regarded as always excessive as retribution and always morally degrading. To regard the death penalty as always excessive, one must believe that no crime—no matter how heinous—could possibly justify capital punishment. Such a belief can be neither corroborated nor refuted; it is an article of faith.

Alternatively, or concurrently, one may believe that everybody, the murderer no less than the victim, has an imprescriptible (natural?) right to life. The law therefore should not deprive anyone of life. I share Jeremy Bentham's view that any such "natural and imprescriptible rights" are "nonsense upon stilts."[16]

Justice Brennan has insisted that the death penalty is "uncivilized," "inhuman," inconsistent with "human dignity" and with "the sanctity of life," that it "treats members of the human race as nonhumans, as objects to be toyed with and discarded," that it is "uniquely degrading to human dignity" and "by its very nature, [involves] a denial of the executed person's humanity." Justice Brennan does not say why he thinks execution "uncivilized." Hitherto most civilizations have had the death penalty, although it has been discarded in Western Europe, where it is currently unfashionable probably because of its abuse by totalitarian regimes.

By "degrading," Justice Brennan seems to mean that execution degrades the executed convicts. Yet philosophers, such as Immanuel Kant and G. W. F. Hegel, have insisted that, when deserved, execution, far from degrading the executed convict, affirms his humanity by affirming his rationality and his responsibility for his actions. They thought that execution, when deserved, is required for the sake of the convict's dignity. (Does not life imprisonment violate human dignity more than execution, by keeping alive a prisoner deprived of all autonomy?)

Common sense indicates that it cannot be death—our common fate—that is inhuman. Therefore, Justice Brennan must mean that death degrades when it comes not as a natural or accidental event, but as a deliberate social imposition. The murderer learns through his punishment that his fellow men have found him unworthy of living; that because he has murdered, he is being expelled from the community of the living. This degradation is self-inflicted. By murdering, the murderer has so dehumanized himself that he cannot remain among the living. The social recognition of his self-degradation is the punitive essence of execution. To believe, as Justice Brennan appears to, that the degradation is inflicted by the execution reverses the direction of causality.

Execution of those who have committed heinous murders may deter only one murder per year. If it does, it seems quite warranted. It is also the only fitting retribution for murder I can think of.

NOTES

1. Death row as a semipermanent residence is cruel, because convicts are denied the normal amenities of prison life. Thus, unless death row residents are integrated into the prison population, the continuing accumulation of convicts on death row should lead us to accelerate either the rate of executions or the rate of communications. I find little objection to integration.

2. The debate about the insanity defense is important for analogous reasons.

3. Some writers, for example, Cesare Bonesana, Marchese di Beccaria, have thought that life imprisonment is more severe. However, the overwhelming majority of both aboli-

tionists and of convicts under death sentence prefer life imprisonment to execution.

4. The ideal of equality, unlike the ideal of retributive justice (which can be approximated separately in each instance), is clearly unattainable unless all guilty persons are apprehended, and therefore tried, convicted and sentenced by the same court, at the same time. Unequal justice is the best we can do; it is still better than the injustice, equal or unequal, which occurs if, for the sake of equality, we deliberately allow some who could be punished to escape.

5. *See* Bureau of Justice Statistics, U.S. Dep't of Justice, Bulletin No. NJC-98,399, Capital Punishment 1984, at 9 (1985); Johnson, *The Executioner's Bias,* Nat'l Rev., Nov. 15, 1985, at 44.

6. It barely need be said that any discrimination *against* (for example, black murderers of whites) must also be discrimination *for* (for example, black murderers of blacks).

7. Bedau & Radelet, *Miscarriages of Justice in Potentially Capital Cases* (1st draft, Oct. 1985) (on file at Harvard Law School Library).

8. An excessive number of trucking accidents or of miscarriages of justice could offset the benefits gained by trucking or the practice of doing justice. We are, however, far from this situation.

9. For most abolitionists, the discrimination argument, *see supra* pp. 1662–64, is similarly nondecisive: they would favor abolition even if there could be no racial discrimination.

10. If executions were shown to increase the murder rate in the long run, I would favor abolition. Sparing the innocent victims who would be spared by the nonexecution of murderers would be more important to me than the execution, however just, of murderers. But although there is a lively discussion of the subject, no serious evidence exists to support the hypothesis that executions produce a higher murder rate.

11. H. Gross, A Theory of Criminal Justice 489 (1979) (attributing this passage to Sir James Fitzjames Stephen).

12. Weems v. United States, 217 U.S. 349 (1910), suggests that penalties be proportionate to the seriousness of the crime—a common theme of the criminal law. Murder, therefore, demands more than life imprisonment, if, as I believe, it is a more serious crime than other crimes punished by life imprisonment. In modern times, our sensibility requires that the range of punishments be narrower than the range of crimes—but not so narrow as to exclude the death penalty.

13. Thus restitution (a civil liability) cannot satisfy the punitive purpose of penal sanctions, whether the purpose be retributive or deterrent.

14. Some abolitionists challenge: if the death penalty is just and serves as a deterrent, why not televise executions? The answer is simple. The death even of a murderer, however well-deserved, should not serve as public entertainment. It so served in earlier centuries. But in this respect our sensibility has changed for the better, I believe. Further, television unavoidably would trivialize executions, wedged in, as they would be, between game shows, situation comedies and the like. Finally, because televised executions would focus on the physical aspects of the punishment, rather than the nature of the crime and the suffering of the victim, a televised execution would present the murderer as the victim of the state. Far from communicating the moral significance of the execution, television would shift the focus to the pitiable fear of the murderer. We no longer place in cages those sentenced to imprisonment to expose them to public view. Why should we so expose those sentenced to execution?

15. An explicit threat of punitive action is necessary to the justification of any legal punishment: *nulla poena sine lege* (no punishment without [preexisting] law). To be sufficiently justified, the threat must in turn have a rational and legitimate purpose. "Your money or your life" does not qualify; nor does the threat of an unjust law; nor, finally, does a threat that is altogether disproportionate to the importance of its purpose. In short, preannouncement legitimizes the threatened punishment only if the threat is warranted. But this leaves a very wide range of justified threats. Furthermore, the punished person is aware of the penalty for his actions and thus volunteers to take the risk even of an unjust punishment. His victim, however, did not volunteer to risk anything. The question whether any self-inflicted injury—such as a legal punishment—ever can be unjust to a person who knowingly risked it is a matter that requires more analysis than is possible here.

16. The Works of Jeremy Bentham 105 (J. Bowring ed. 1972).

From *Justice, Civilization, and the Death Penalty: Answering van den Haag*

Jeffrey H. Reiman

On the issue of capital punishment, there is as clear a clash of moral intuitions as we are likely to see. Some (now a majority of Americans) feel deeply that justice requires payment in kind and thus that murderers should die; and others (once, but no longer, nearly a majority of Americans) feel deeply that the state ought not be in the business of putting people to death.[1] Arguments for either side that do not do justice to the intuitions of the other are unlikely to persuade anyone not already convinced. And, since, as I shall suggest, there is truth on both sides, such arguments are easily refutable, leaving us with nothing but conflicting intuitions and no guidance from reason in distinguishing the better from the worse. In this context, I shall try to make an argument for the abolition of the death penalty that does justice to the intuitions on both sides. I shall sketch out a conception of retributive justice that accounts for the justice of executing murderers, and then I shall argue that *though the death penalty is a just punishment for murder,* abolition of the death penalty is part of the civilizing mission of modern states.

* * *

[I.] JUST DESERTS AND JUST PUNISHMENTS

In my view, the death penalty is a just punishment for murder because the *lex talionis,* an eye for an eye, and so on, is just, although, as I shall suggest at the end of this section, it can only be rightly applied when its implied preconditions are satisfied. The *lex talionis* is a version of retributivism. Retributivism— as the word itself suggests—is the doctrine that the offender should be *paid back* with suffering he deserves because of the evil he has done, and the *lex*

talionis asserts that injury equivalent to that he imposed is what the offender deserves.[2] But the *lex talionis* is not the only version of retributivism. Another, which I shall call "proportional retributivism," holds that what retribution requires is not equality of injury between crimes and punishments, but "fit" or proportionality, such that the worst crime is punished with the society's worst penalty, and so on, though the society's worst punishment need not duplicate the injury of the worst crime.[3] Later, I shall try to show how a form of proportional retributivism is compatible with acknowledging the justice of the *lex talionis.* Indeed, since I shall defend the justice of the *lex talionis,* I take such compatibility as a necessary condition of the validity of any form of retributivism.

There is nothing self-evident about the justice of the *lex talionis* nor, for that matter, of retributivism. The standard problem confronting those who would justify retributivism is that of overcoming the suspicion that it does no more than sanctify the victim's desire to hurt the offender back. Since serving that desire amounts to hurting the offender simply for the satisfaction that the victim derives from seeing the offender suffer, and since deriving satisfaction from the suffering of others seems primitive, the policy of imposing suffering on the offender for no other purpose than giving satisfaction to his victim seems primitive as well. Consequently, defending retributivism requires showing that the suffering imposed on the wrongdoer has some worthy point beyond the satisfaction of victims. In what follows, I shall try to identify a proposition—which I call the *retributivist principle*—that I take to be the nerve of retributivism. I think this principle accounts for the justice of the *lex talionis* and indicates the point of the suffering demanded by retributivism. Not to do too much of the work of the death penalty advocate, I shall make no extended argument for the principle beyond sug-

Jeffrey H. Reiman, "Justice, Civilization, and the Death Penalty," *Philosophy & Public Affairs* 14, no. 2 (Spring 1985): 115–42 (edited). Reprinted with permission of Blackwell Publishing.

gesting the considerations that make it plausible. I shall identify these considerations by drawing, with considerable license, on Hegel and Kant.

I think that we can see the justice of the *lex talionis* by focusing on the striking affinity between it and the *golden rule*. The *golden rule* mandates "Do unto others as you would have others do unto you," while the *lex talionis* counsels "Do unto others as they have done unto you." It would not be too far-fetched to say that the *lex talionis* is the law enforcement arm of the golden rule, at least in the sense that if people were actually treated as they treated others, then everyone would necessarily follow the golden rule because then people could only willingly act toward others as they were willing to have others act toward them. This is not to suggest that the *lex talionis* follows from the golden rule, but rather that the two share a common moral inspiration: the equality of persons. Treating others as you *would* have them treat you means treating others as equal to you, because adopting the golden rule as one's guiding principle implies that one counts the suffering of others to be as great a calamity as one's own suffering, that one counts one's right to impose suffering on others as no greater than their right to impose suffering on one, and so on. This leads to the *lex talionis* by two approaches that start from different points and converge.

I call the first approach "Hegelian" because Hegel held (roughly) that crime upsets the equality between persons and retributive punishment restores that equality by "annulling" the crime.[4] As we have seen, acting according to the golden rule implies treating others as your equals. Conversely, violating the golden rule implies the reverse: Doing to another what you would *not* have that other do to you violates the equality of persons by asserting a right toward the other that the other does not possess toward you. Doing back to you what you did "annuls" your violation by reasserting that the other has the same right toward you that you assert toward him. Punishment according to the *lex talionis* cannot heal the injury that the other has suffered at your hands, rather it rectifies the indignity he has suffered, by restoring him to equality with you.

"Equality of persons" here does not mean equality of concern for their happiness, as it might for a utilitarian. On such a (roughly) utilitarian understanding of equality, imposing suffering on the wrongdoer equivalent to the suffering he has imposed would have little point. Rather, equality of concern for people's happiness would lead us to impose as little suffering on the wrongdoer as was compatible with maintaining the happiness of others. This is enough to show that retributivism (at least in this "Hegelian" form) reflects a conception of morality quite different from that envisioned by utilitarianism. Instead of seeing morality as administering doses of happiness to individual recipients, the retributivist envisions morality as maintaining the relations appropriate to equally sovereign individuals. A crime, rather than representing a unit of suffering added to the already considerable suffering in the world, is an assault on the sovereignty of an individual that temporarily places one person (the criminal) in a position of illegitimate sovereignty over another (the victim). The victim (or his representative, the state) then has the right to rectify this loss of standing relative to the criminal by meting out a punishment that reduces the criminal's sovereignty in the degree to which he vaunted it above his victim's. It might be thought that this is a duty, not just a right, but that is surely too much. The victim has the right to forgive the violator without punishment, which suggests that it is by virtue of having the right to punish the violator (rather than the duty), that the victim's equality with the violator is restored.

I call the second approach "Kantian" since Kant held (roughly) that, since reason (like justice) is no respecter of the sheer difference between individuals, when a rational being decides to act in a certain way toward his fellows, he implicitly authorizes similar action by his fellows toward him.[5] A version of the golden rule, then, is a requirement of reason: acting rationally, one always acts as he would have others act toward him. Consequently, to act toward a person as he has acted toward others is to treat him as a rational being, that is, as if his act were the product of a rational decision. From this, it may be concluded that we have a duty to do to offenders what they have done, since this amounts to according them the respect due rational beings.[6] Here too, however, the assertion of a duty to punish seems excessive, since, if this duty arises because doing to people what they have done to others is necessary to accord them the respect due rational beings, then we would have a duty to do to all rational persons *everything*—good, bad, or indifferent—that they do to others. The point rather is that, by his acts, a rational being *authorizes* others to do the same to him, he doesn't *compel* them to. Here too, then, the argument leads to a right, rather than a duty, to exact the *lex talionis*. And this is supported by the fact that we can conclude from Kant's argument that a rational being cannot validly complain of being treated in the way he has treated others, and where there is no valid complaint, there is no injustice, and where there is no injustice, others have acted within their rights.[7] It should be clear that the Kantian argument also rests on the equality of persons, because a rational agent only implicitly authorizes having done to him action similar to what he has done to another, if he and the other are similar in the relevant ways.

The "Hegelian" and "Kantian" approaches arrive at the same destination from opposite sides. The "Hegelian" approach starts from the victim's equality with the criminal, and infers from it the victim's right to do to the criminal what the criminal has done to the victim. The "Kantian" approach starts from the criminal's rationality, and infers from it the criminal's authorization of the victim's right to do to the criminal what the criminal has done to the victim. Taken together, these approaches support the following proposition: The equality and rationality of persons implies that an offender deserves and his victim has the right to impose suffering on the offender equal to that which he imposed on the victim. This is the proposition I call the *retributivist principle,* and I shall assume henceforth that it is true. This principle provides that the *lex talionis* is the criminal's just desert and the victim's (or as his representative, the state's) right. Moreover, the principle also indicates the point of retributive punishment, namely, it affirms the equality and rationality of persons, victims and offenders alike. And the point of this affir-

mation is, like any moral affirmation, to make a statement, to the criminal, to impress upon him his equality with his victim (which earns him a like fate) and his rationality (by which his actions are held to authorize his fate), and to the society, so that recognition of the equality and rationality of persons becomes a visible part of our shared moral environment that none can ignore in justifying their actions to one another.

* * *

The truth of the retributivist principle establishes the justice of the *lex talionis,* but, since it establishes this as a right of the victim rather than a duty, it does not settle the question of whether or to what extent the victim or the state should exercise this right and exact the *lex talionis.* This is a separate moral question because strict adherence to the *lex talionis* amounts to allowing criminals, even the most barbaric of them, to dictate our punishing behavior. It seems certain that there are at least some crimes, such as rape or torture, that we ought not try to match. And this is not merely a matter of imposing an alternative punishment that produces an equivalent amount of suffering, as, say, some number of years in prison that might "add up" to the harm caused by a rapist or a torturer. Even if no amount of time in prison would add up to the harm caused by a torturer, it still seems that we ought not torture him even if this were the only way of making him suffer as much as he has made his victim suffer. Or, consider someone who has committed several murders in cold blood. On the *lex talionis,* it would seem that such a criminal might justly be brought to within an inch of death and then revived (or to within a moment of execution and then reprieved) as many times as he has killed (minus one), and then finally executed. But surely this is a degree of cruelty that would be monstrous.

Since the retributivist principle establishes the *lex talionis* as the victim's right, it might seem that the question of how far this right should be exercised is "up to the victim." And indeed, this would be the case in the state of nature. But once, for all the good reasons familiar to readers of John Locke, the state comes into existence, public punishment replaces private, and the victim's right to punish reposes in the state. With this, the decision as to how far to exercise this right goes to the state as well. To be sure, since (at least with respect to retributive punishment) the victim's right is the source of the state's right to punish, the state must exercise its right in ways that are faithful to the victim's right. Later, when I try to spell out the upper and lower limits of just punishment, these may be taken as indicating the range within which the state can punish and remain faithful to the victim's right.

I suspect that it will be widely agreed that the state ought not administer punishments of the sort described above even if required by the letter of the *lex talionis,* and thus, even granting the justice of *lex talionis,* there are occasions on which it is morally appropriate to diverge from its requirements. We must, of course, distinguish such morally based divergence from that which is based on practicality. Like any moral principle, the *lex talionis* is subject to "ought implies can." It will usually be impossible to do to an offender exactly what he has done—for example, his offense will normally have had an element of surprise that is not possible for a judicially imposed punishment, but this fact can hardly free him from having to bear the suffering he has imposed on another. Thus, for reasons of practicality, the *lex talionis* must necessarily be qualified to call for doing to the offender *as nearly as possible* what he has done to his victim. When, however, we refrain from raping rapists or torturing torturers, we do so for reasons of morality, not of practicality. And, given the justice of the *lex talionis,* these moral reasons cannot amount to claiming that it would be *unjust* to rape rapists or torture torturers. Rather the claim must be that, even though it would be just to rape rapists and torture torturers, other moral considerations weigh against doing so.

* * *

This way of understanding just punishment enables us to formulate proportional retributivism so that it is compatible with acknowledging the justice of the *lex talionis:* If we take the *lex talionis* as spelling out the offender's just deserts, and if other moral considerations require us to refrain from matching the injury caused by the offender while still allowing us to punish justly, then surely we impose just punishment if we impose the closest morally acceptable approximation to the *lex talionis.* Proportional retributivism, then, in requiring that the worst crime be punished by the society's worst punishment and so on, could be understood as translating the offender's just desert into its nearest equivalent in the society's table of morally acceptable punishments. Then the two versions of retributivism (*lex talionis* and proportional) are related in that the first states what just punishment would be if nothing but the offender's just desert mattered, and the second locates just punishment at the meeting point of the offender's just deserts and the society's moral scruples. And since this second version only modifies the requirements of the *lex talionis* in light of other moral considerations, it is compatible with believing that the *lex talionis* spells out the offender's just deserts, much in the way that modifying the obligations of promisers in light of other moral considerations is compatible with believing in the binding nature of promises.

* * *

[II.] CIVILIZATION, PAIN, AND JUSTICE

As I have already suggested, from the fact that something is justly deserved, it does not automatically follow that it should be done, since there may be other moral reasons for not doing it such that, all told, the weight of moral reasons swings the balance against proceeding. The same argument that I have given for the justice of the death penalty for murderers proves the justice of beating assaulters, raping rapists, and torturing torturers. Nonetheless, I believe, and suspect that most would agree, that it would not be right for us to beat assaulters, rape rapists, or torture torturers, *even though it were their just deserts*—and even if this were the only way to make them suffer as much as they had made their victims suffer. Calling for the abolition of the death penalty, though it be just, then, amounts to urging that as a society we place execution in the same category of sanction as beating, raping, and torturing, and treat it as something it would also not be right for us to do to offenders, *even if it were their just deserts.*

To argue for placing execution in this category, I must show what would be gained therefrom; and to show that, I shall indicate what we gain from placing torture in this category and argue that a similar gain is to be had from doing the same with execution. I select torture because I think the reasons for placing it in this category are, due to the extremity of torture, most easily seen—but what I say here applies with appropriate modification to other severe physical punishments, such as beating and raping. First, and most evidently, placing torture in this category broadcasts the message that we as a society judge torturing so horrible a thing to do to a person that we refuse to do it even when it is deserved. Note that such a judgment does not commit us to an absolute prohibition on torturing. No matter how horrible we judge something to be, we may still be justified in doing it if it is necessary to prevent something even worse. Leaving this aside for the moment, what is gained by broadcasting the public judgment that torture is too horrible to inflict even if deserved?

I think the answer to this lies in what we understand as civilization. In *The Genealogy of Morals*, Nietzsche says that in early times "pain did not hurt as much as it does today."[8] The truth in this puzzling remark is that progress in civilization is characterized by a lower tolerance for one's own pain and that suffered by others. And this is appropriate, since, via growth in knowledge, civilization brings increased power to prevent or reduce pain and, via growth in the ability to communicate and interact with more and more people, civilization extends the circle of people with whom we empathize. If civilization is characterized by lower tolerance for our own pain and that of others, then publicly refusing to do horrible things to our fellows both signals the level of our civilization *and, by our example, continues the work of civilizing*. And this gesture is all the more powerful if we refuse to do horrible things to those who deserve them. I contend then that the more things we are able to include in this category, the more civilized we are and the more civil*izing*. Thus we gain from including torture in this category, and if execution is especially horrible, we gain still more by including it.

* * *

Thus far, by analogy with torture, I have argued that execution should be avoided because of how horrible it is to the one executed. But there are reasons of another sort that follow from the analogy with torture. Torture is to be avoided not only because of what it says about *what* we are willing to do to our fellows, but also because of what it says about *us* who are willing to do it. To torture someone is an awful spectacle not only because of the intensity of pain imposed, but because of what is required to be able to impose such pain on one's fellows. The tortured body cringes, using its full exertion to escape the pain imposed upon it—it literally begs for relief with its muscles as it does with its cries. To torture someone is to demonstrate a capacity to resist this begging, and that in turn demonstrates a kind of hardheartedness that a society ought not parade.

And this is true not only of torture, but of all severe corporal punishment. Indeed, I think this constitutes part of the answer to the puzzling question of why we refrain from punishments like whipping, even when the alternative (some months in jail versus some lashes) seems more costly to the offender. Imprisonment is painful to be sure, but it is a reflective pain, one that comes with comparing what is to what might have been, and that can be temporarily ignored by thinking about other things. But physical pain has an urgency that holds body and mind in a fierce grip. Of physical pain, as Orwell's Winston Smith recognized, "you could only wish one thing: that it should stop."[9] Refraining from torture in particular and corporal punishment in general, we both refuse to put a fellow human being in this grip *and* refuse to show our ability to resist this wish. The death penalty is the last corporal punishment used officially in the modern world. And it is corporal not only because administered via the body, but because the pain of foreseen, humanly administered death strikes us with the urgency that characterizes intense physical pain, causing grown men to cry, faint, and lose control of their bodily functions. There is something to be gained by refusing to endorse the hardness of heart necessary to impose such a fate.

By placing execution alongside torture in the category of things we will not do to our fellow human beings even when they deserve them, we broadcast the message that totally subjugating a person to the power of others *and* confronting him with the advent of his own humanly administered demise is too horrible to be done by civilized human beings to their fellows even when they have earned it: too horrible to do, and too horrible to be capable of doing. And I contend that broadcasting this message loud and clear would in the long run contribute to the general detestation of murder and be, to the extent to which it worked itself into the hearts and minds of the populace, a deterrent. In short, refusing to execute murderers though they deserve it both reflects and continues the taming of the human species that we call civilization. Thus, I take it that the abolition of the death penalty, though it is a just punishment for murder, is part of the civilizing mission of modern states.

* * *

NOTES

1. Asked, in a 1981 Gallup Poll, "Are you in favor of the death penalty for persons convicted of murder?" 66.25% were in favor, 25% were opposed, and 8.75% had no opinion. Asked the same question in 1966, 47.5% were opposed, 41.25% were in favor, and 11.25% had no opinion (Timothy J. Flanagan, David J. van Alstyne, and Michael R. Gottfredson, eds., *Sourcebook of Criminal Justice Statistics— 1981,* U.S. Department of Justice, Bureau of Justice Statistics [Washington, D.C.: U.S. Government Printing Office, 1982], p. 209).

2. I shall speak throughout of retribution as paying back for "harm caused," but this is shorthand for "harm intentionally attempted or caused"; likewise when I speak of the death penalty as punishment for murder, I have in mind premeditated, first-degree murder. Note also that the harm caused by an offender, for which he is to be paid back, is not necessarily limited to the harm done to his immediate victim. It may include as well the suffering of the victim's relatives or the fear produced in the general populace, and the like. For simplicity's sake, however, I shall continue to speak as if the harm for which retributivism would have us pay the offender back is the harm (intentionally attempted or done) to his immediate victim. Also, retribution is not to be confused with *restitution.* Restitution involves restoring the *status quo ante,* the condition prior to the offense. Since it was

in this condition that the criminal's offense was committed, it is this condition that constitutes the baseline against which retribution is exacted. Thus retribution involves imposing a loss on the offender measured from the status quo ante. For example, returning a thief's loot to his victim so that thief and victim now own what they did before the offense is *restitution.* Taking enough from the thief so that what he is left with is less than what he had before the offense is *retribution,* since this is just what he did to his victim.

3. "The most extreme form of retributivism is the law of retaliation: 'an eye for an eye'" (Stanley I. Benn, "Punishment," *The Encyclopedia of Philosophy* 7, ed. Paul Edwards [New York: Macmillan, 1967], p. 32). Hugo Bedau writes: "retributive justice need not be thought to consist of *lex talionis.* One may reject that principle as too crude and still embrace the retributive principle that the severity of punishments should be graded according to the gravity of the offense" (Hugo Bedau, "Capital Punishment," in *Matters of Life and Death,* ed. Tom Regan [New York: Random House, 1980], p. 177).

4. Hegel writes that "The sole positive existence which the injury [i.e., the crime] possesses is that it is the particular will of the criminal [i.e., it is the criminal's intention that distinguishes criminal injury from, say, injury due to an accident]. Hence to injure (or penalize) this particular will as a will determinately existent is to annul the crime, which otherwise would have been held valid, and to restore the right" (G. W. F. Hegel, *The Philosophy of Right,* trans. by T. M. Knox [Oxford: Clarendon Press, 1962; originally published in German in 1821], p. 69, see also p. 331n). I take this to mean that the right is a certain equality of sovereignty between the wills of individuals, crime disrupts that equality by placing one will above others, and punishment restores the equality by annulling the illegitimate ascendance. On these grounds, as I shall suggest below, the desire for revenge (strictly limited to the desire "to even the score") is more respectable than philosophers have generally allowed. And so Hegel writes that "The annulling of crime in this sphere where right is immediate [i.e., the condition prior to conscious morality] is principally revenge, which is just in its content in so far as it is retributive" (ibid., p. 73).

5. Kant writes that "any undeserved evil that you inflict on someone else among the people is one that you do to yourself. If you vilify him, you vilify yourself; if you steal from him, you steal from yourself; if you kill him, you kill yourself." Since Kant holds that "If what happens to someone is also willed by him, it cannot be a punishment," he takes

pains to distance himself from the view that the offender *wills* his punishment. "The chief error contained in this sophistry," Kant writes, "consists in the confusion of the criminal's [that is, the murderer's] own judgment (which one must necessarily attribute to his reason) that he must forfeit his life with a resolution of the will to take his own life" (Immanuel Kant, *The Metaphysical Elements of Justice, Part I of The Metaphysics of Morals,* trans. by J. Ladd [Indianapolis: Bobbs-Merrill, 1965; originally published in 1797], pp. 101, 105–106). I have tried to capture this notion of attributing a judgment to the offender rather than a resolution of his will with the term 'authorizes.'

6. "Even if a civil society were to dissolve itself by common agreement of all its members . . . , the last murderer remaining in prison must first be executed, so that everyone will duly receive what his actions are worth" (Kant, ibid., p. 102).

7. "It may also be pointed out that no one has ever heard of anyone condemned to death on account of murder who complained that he was getting too much [punishment] and therefore was being treated unjustly; everyone would laugh in his face if he were to make such a statement" (Kant, *Metaphysical Elements of Justice,* p. 104; see also p. 133).

8. Friedrich Nietzsche, *The Birth of Tragedy and The Genealogy of Morals,* trans. Francis Golffing (New York: Doubleday, 1956), pp. 199–200.

9. George Orwell, *1984* (New York: New American Library, 1983; originally published in 1949), p. 197.

A Life for a Life

Igor Primoratz

. . . According to the retributive theory, consequences of punishment, however important from the practical point of view, are irrelevant when it comes to its justification; *the* moral consideration is its justice. Punishment is morally justified insofar as it is meted out as retribution for the offense committed. When someone has committed an offense, he deserves to be punished: it is just, and consequently justified, that he be punished. The offense is the sole ground of the state's right and duty to punish. It is also the measure of legitimate punishment: the two ought to be proportionate. So the issue of capital punishment within the retributive approach comes down to the question, Is this punishment ever proportionate retribution for the offense committed, and thus deserved, just, and justified?

The classic representatives of retributivism believed that it was, and that it was the only proportionate and hence appropriate punishment, if the offense was *murder*—that is, criminal homicide perpetrated voluntarily and intentionally or in wanton disregard of human life. In other cases, the demand for proportionality between offense and punishment can be satisfied by fines or prison terms; the crime of murder, however, is an exception in this respect, and calls for the literal interpretation of the *lex talionis.* The uniqueness of this crime has to do with the uniqueness of the value which has been deliberately or recklessly destroyed. We come across this idea as early as the original formulation of the retributive view—the biblical teaching on punishment: "You shall accept no ransom for the life of a murderer who is guilty of death; but he shall be put to death."[1] The rationale of this command—one that clearly distinguishes the biblical conception of the criminal law from contemporaneous criminal law systems in the Middle East—is that man was not only created *by* God, like every other creature, but also, alone among all the creatures, *in the image of God:*

That man was made in the image of God . . . is expressive of the peculiar and supreme worth of man. Of all creatures, Genesis 1 relates, he alone possesses this attribute, bringing him into closer relation to God than all the rest and con-

Igor Primoratz, "A Life for a Life," in *Justifying Legal Punishment* (Amherst, NY: Humanity Books, 1990), 158–67 (edited). Reprinted with permission of publisher.

ferring upon him the highest value. . . . This view of the uniqueness and supremacy of human life . . . places life beyond the reach of other values. The idea that life may be measured in terms of money or other property . . . is excluded. Compensation of any kind is ruled out. The guilt of the murderer is infinite, because the murdered life is invaluable; the kinsmen of the slain man are not competent to say when he has been paid for. An absolute wrong has been committed, a sin against God which is not subject to human discussion. . . . Because human life is invaluable, to take it entails the death penalty.[2]

This view that the value of human life is not commensurable with other values, and that consequently there is only one truly equivalent punishment for murder, namely death, does not necessarily presuppose a theistic outlook. It can be claimed that, simply because we have to be alive if we are to experience and realize any other value at all, there is nothing equivalent to the murderous destruction of a human life except the destruction of the life of the murderer. Any other retribution, no matter how severe, would still be less than what is proportionate, deserved, and just. As long as the murderer is alive, no matter how bad the conditions of his life may be, there are always at least *some* values he can experience and realize. This provides a plausible interpretation of what the classical representatives of retributivism as a philosophical theory of punishment, such as Kant and Hegel, had to say on the subject.[3]

It seems to me that this is essentially correct. With respect to the larger question of the justification of punishment in general, it is the retributive theory that gives the right answer. Accordingly, capital punishment ought to be retained where it obtains, and reintroduced in those jurisdictions that have abolished it, although we have no reason to believe that, as a means of deterrence, it is any better than a very long prison term. It ought to be retained, or reintroduced, for one simple reason: that justice be done in cases of murder, that murderers be punished according to their deserts.

There are a number of arguments that have been advanced against this rationale of capital punishment.

Two of these arguments have to do, in different ways, with the idea of the right to life. The first is the famous argument of Beccaria that the state cannot have the right to take away the life of its citizen, because its rights in relation to him are based on the social contract, and it cannot be assumed that he has transferred his right to life to the state and consented to be executed.

What manner of right can men attribute to themselves to slaughter their fellow beings? Certainly not that from which sovereignty and the laws derive. These are nothing but the sum of the least portions of the private liberty of each person; they represent the general will, which is the aggregate of particular wills. Was there ever a man who can have wished to leave to other men the choice of killing him? Is it conceivable that the least sacrifice of each person's liberty should include sacrifice of the greatest of all goods, life? And if that were the case, how could such a principle be reconciled with the other, that man is not entitled to take his own life? He must be, if he can surrender that right to others or to society as a whole.[4]

The most obvious way of attacking Beccaria's argument would be to call into question its philosophical basis, the social contract theory of political obligation. This is what Hegel does, for instance, he conceives of the nature and grounds of political obligation in a completely different manner, so he can do away with Beccaria with a single sentence: "The state is not a contract at all."[5] I shall not argue along these lines, however. This is not the place to take up the problem of political obligation and to assess the social contract theory as a solution to it. What Beccaria is saying here can in any case be refuted even within the framework of that theory.

Both steps in his argument are wrong, and for the same reason. The act of consenting to be executed if one commits murder is presented as a kind of suicide. Against the background of this conflation, it seems convincing to claim that it would be utterly unreasonable to do that, and the case appears to be strengthened even further by the appeal to the moral prohibition of suicide. This latter prohibition is, of course, rather controversial, to say the least; it was controversial in Beccaria's time as well. But his argument fails even if we grant him this point. For by consenting to be executed if I murder someone, I do not commit a kind of suicide—I do not "sacrifice the greatest of all goods" I have, my own life. My consent could be described in these terms if it were unconditional, if it implied that others were entitled to do with my life whatever they chose, quite independently of my own choices and actions. In order to show that capital punishment is legitimate from the standpoint of the contract theory of political obligation, however, we need not assume that citizens have agreed to *that*. All that is needed is the assumption of a conditional consent—consent to be executed *if* one commits murder; and it is, of course, up to everyone to choose whether to commit such a crime or not. To agree to this, obviously, is not the same as to sacrifice one's life, to commit a suicide of sorts. And it is not so unreasonable to assume that citizens have agreed to this if, against the background of the social contract theory, we grant, first, that the laws, including criminal laws, ought to be just, and second, that the only proportionate and hence just punishment for murder is capital punishment.

The second abolitionist argument makes use of the idea of a right to life in a more straightforward manner: it simply says that capital punishment is illegitimate because it violates the right to life, which is a fundamental, absolute, sacred right belonging to each and every human being, and therefore ought to be respected even in a murderer.

If any rights are fundamental, the right to life is certainly one of them; but to claim that it is absolute, inviolable under any circumstances and for any reason, is a different matter. If an abolitionist wants to argue his case by asserting an absolute right to life, she will also have to deny moral legitimacy to taking human life in war, revolution, and self-defense. This kind of pacifism is a consistent but farfetched and hence implausible position.

I do not believe that the right to life (nor, for that matter, any other right) is absolute. I have no general theory of rights to fall back upon here; instead, let me pose a question. Would we take seriously the claim to an absolute, sacred, inviolable right to life—coming from the mouth of a *confessed murderer*? I submit that we would not, for the obvious reason that it is being put forward by the person who confessedly denied another human being this very right. But if the murderer cannot plausibly claim such a right for himself, neither can *anyone else* do that in his behalf. This suggests that there is an element of reciprocity in our general rights, such as the right to life or property. I can convincingly claim these rights only so long as I acknowledge and respect the same rights of others. If I violate the rights of others, I thereby lose the same rights. If I am a murderer, I have no *right* to live.

Some opponents of capital punishment claim that a criminal law system which includes this punishment is contradictory, in that it prohibits murder and at the same time provides for its perpetration: "It is one and the same legal regulation which prohibits the individual from murdering, while allowing the state to murder. . . . This is obviously a terrible irony, an abnormal and immoral logic, against which everything in us revolts."[6]

This seems to be one of the more popular arguments against the death penalty, but it is not a good one. If it were valid, it would prove too much. Exactly the same might be claimed of other kinds of punishment: of prison terms, that they are "contradictory" to the legal protection of liberty; of fines, that they are "contradictory" to the legal protection of property. Fortunately enough, it is not valid, for it begs the question at issue. In order to be able to talk of the state as "murdering" the person it executes, and to claim that there is "an abnormal and immoral logic" at work here, which thrives on a "contradiction," one has to use the word "murder" in the very same sense—that is, in the usual sense, which implies the idea of the *wrongful* taking the life of another—both when speaking of what the murderer has done to the victim and of what the state is doing to him by way of punishment. But this is precisely the question at issue: whether capital punishment *is* "murder," whether it is wrongful or morally justified and right.

The next two arguments attack the retributive rationale of capital punishment by questioning the claim that it is only this punishment that satisfies the demand for proportion between offense and punishment in the case of murder. The first points out that any two human lives are different in many important respects, such as age, health, physical and mental capability, so that it does not make much sense to consider them equally valuable. What if the murdered person was very old, practically at the very end of her natural life, while the murderer is young, with most of his life still ahead of him, for instance? Or if the victim was gravely and incurably ill, and thus doomed to live her life in suffering and hopelessness, without being able to experience almost anything that makes a human life worth living, while the murderer is in every respect capable of experiencing and enjoying things life has to offer? Or the other way round? Would not the death penalty in such cases amount either to taking a more valuable life as a punishment for destroying a less valuable one, or *vice versa*? Would it not be either too much, or too little, and in both cases disproportionate, and thus unjust and wrong, from the standpoint of the retributive theory itself?

Any plausibility this argument might appear to have is the result of a conflation of differences between, and value of, human lives. No doubt, any two human lives are *different* in innumerable ways, but this does not entail that they are not *equally valuable*. I have no worked-out general theory of equality to refer to here, but I do not think that one is necessary in order to do away with this argument. The modern humanistic and democratic tradition in ethical, social, and political thought is based on the idea that all human beings are equal. This finds its legal expression in the principle of equality of people under the law. If we are not willing to give up this principle, we have to stick to the assumption that, all differences notwithstanding, any two human lives, *qua* human lives, are equally valuable. If, on the other hand, we allow that, on the basis of such criteria as age, health, or mental or physical ability, it can be claimed that the life of one person is more or less valuable than the life of another, and we admit

such claims in the sphere of law, including criminal law, we shall thereby give up the principle of equality of people under the law. In all consistency, we shall not be able to demand that property, physical and personal integrity, and all other rights and interests of individuals be given equal consideration in courts of law either—that is, we shall have to accept systematic discrimination between individuals on the basis of the same criteria across the whole field. I do not think anyone would seriously contemplate an overhaul of the whole legal system along these lines.

The second argument having to do with the issue of proportionality between murder and capital punishment draws our attention to the fact that the law normally provides for a certain period of time to elapse between the passing of a death sentence and its execution. It is a period of several weeks or months; in some cases it extends to years. This period is bound to be one of constant mental anguish for the condemned. And thus, all things considered, what is inflicted on him is disproportionately hard and hence unjust. It would be proportionate and just only in the case of "a criminal who had warned his victim of the date at which he would inflict a horrible death on him and who, from that moment onward, had confined him at his mercy for months."[7]

The first thing to note about this argument is that it does not support a full-fledged abolitionist stand; if it were valid, it would not show that capital punishment is *never* proportionate and just, but only that it is *very rarely* so. Consequently, the conclusion would not be that it ought to be abolished outright, but only that it ought to be restricted to those cases that would satisfy the condition cited above. Such cases do happen, although, to be sure, not very often; the murder of Aldo Moro, for instance, was of this kind. But this is not the main point. The main point is that the argument actually does not hit at capital punishment itself, although it is presented with that aim in view. It hits at something else: a particular way of carrying out this punishment, which is widely adopted in our time. Some hundred years ago and more, in the Wild West, they frequently hanged the man convicted to die almost immediately after pronouncing the sentence. I am not arguing here that we should follow this example today; I mention this piece of historical fact only in order to show that the interval between sentencing someone to death and carrying out the sentence is not a *part* of capital punishment itself. However unpalatable we might find those Wild West hangings, whatever objections we might want to voice against the speed with which they followed the sentencing, surely we shall not deny them the *description* of "executions." So the implication of the argument is not that we ought to do away with capital punishment altogether, nor that we ought to restrict it to those cases of murder where the murderer had warned the victim weeks or months in advance of what he was going to do to her, but that we ought to reexamine the procedure of carrying out this kind of punishment. We ought to weigh the reasons for having this interval between the sentencing and executing, against the moral and human significance of the repercussions such an interval inevitably carries with it.

These reasons, in part, have to do with the possibility of miscarriages of justice and the need to rectify them. Thus we come to the argument against capital punishment which, historically, has been the most effective of all: many advances of the abolitionist movement have been connected with discoveries of cases of judicial errors. Judges and jurors are only human, and consequently some of their beliefs and decisions are bound to be mistaken. Some of their mistakes can be corrected upon discovery; but precisely those with most disastrous repercussions—those which result in innocent people being executed—can never be rectified. In all other cases of mistaken sentencing we can revoke the punishment, either completely or in part, or at least extend compensation. In addition, by exonerating the accused we give moral satisfaction. None of this is possible after an innocent person has been executed; capital punishment is essentially different from all other penalties by being completely irrevocable and irreparable. Therefore, it ought to be abolished.

A part of my reply to this argument goes along the same lines as what I had to say on the previous one. It is not so far-reaching as abolitionists assume; for it would be quite implausible, even fanciful, to claim that there have *never* been cases of murder which left no room whatever for reasonable doubt as to the guilt and full responsibility of the accused. Such cases may not be more frequent than those others, but they do happen. Why not retain the death penalty at least for them?

Actually, this argument, just as the preceding one, does not speak out against capital punishment itself, but against the existing procedures for trying capital cases. Miscarriages of justice result in innocent people being sentenced to death and executed, even in the criminal-law systems in which greatest care is taken to ensure that it never comes to that. But this does not stem from the intrinsic nature of the institution of capital punishment; it results from deficiencies, limitations, and imperfections of the criminal law procedures in which this punishment is meted out. Errors of justice do not demonstrate the need to do away with capital punishment; they simply make it incumbent on us to do everything possible to improve even further procedures of meting it out.

To be sure, this conclusion will not find favor with a diehard abolitionist. "I shall ask for the abolition of Capital Punishment until I have the infallibility of human judgement demonstrated to me," that is, as long as there is even the slightest possibility that innocent people may be executed because of judicial errors, Lafayette said in his day.[8] Many an opponent of this kind of punishment will say the same today. The demand to do away with capital punishment altogether, so as to eliminate even the smallest chance of that ever happening—the chance which, admittedly, would remain even after everything humanly possible has been done to perfect the procedure, although then it would be very slight indeed—is actually a demand to give a privileged position to murderers as against all other offenders, big and small. For if we acted on this demand, we would bring about a situation in which proportionate penalties would be meted out for all offenses, *except* for murder. Murderers would not be receiving the only punishment truly proportionate to their crimes, the punishment of death, but some other, lighter, and thus disproportionate penalty. All other offenders would be punished according to their deserts; only murderers would be receiving less than *they* deserve. In all other cases justice would be done in full; only in cases of the gravest of offenses, the crime of murder, justice would not be carried out in full measure. It is a great and tragic miscarriage of justice when an innocent person is mistakenly sentenced to death and executed, but systematically giving murderers advantage over all other offenders would also be a grave injustice. Is the fact that, as long as capital punishment is retained, there is a possibility that over a number of years, or even decades, an injustice of the first kind may be committed, unintentionally and unconsciously, reason enough to abolish it altogether, and thus end up with a system of punishments in which injustices of the second kind are perpetrated daily, consciously, and inevitably?

There is still another abolitionist argument that actually does not hit out against capital punishment itself, but against something else. Figures are sometimes quoted which show that this punishment is much more often meted out to the uneducated and poor than to the educated, rich, and influential people; in the United States, much more often to blacks than to whites. These figures are adduced as a proof of the inherent injustice of this kind of punishment. On account of them, it is claimed that capital punishment is not a way of doing justice by meting out deserved punishment to murderers, but rather a means of social discrimination and perpetuation of social injustice.

I shall not question these findings, which are quite convincing, and anyway, there is no need to do that in order to defend the institution of capital punishment. For there seems to be a certain amount of discrimination and injustice not only in sentencing people to death and executing them, but also in meting out other penalties. The social structure of the death rows in American prisons, for instance, does not seem to be basically different from the general social structure of American penitentiaries. If this

argument were valid, it would call not only for abolition of the penalty of death, but for doing away with other penalties as well.

But it is not valid; as Burton Leiser has pointed out,

this is not an argument, either against the death penalty or against any other form of punishment. It is an argument against the unjust and inequitable distribution of penalties. If the trials of wealthy men are less likely to result in convictions than those of poor men, then something must be done to reform the procedure in criminal courts. If those who have money and standing in the community are less likely to be charged with serious offenses than their less affluent fellow citizens, then there should be a major overhaul of the entire system of criminal justice. . . . But the maldistribution of penalties is no argument against any particular form of penalty.[9]

There is, finally, the argument that the moral illegitimacy of capital punishment is obvious from the widespread contempt for those who carry it out: "Logically, if the Death Penalty *were* morally justified, the executioner's calling would be considered an honourable one. The fact that even its keenest supporters shrink from such a man with loathing and exclude him from their circle, is in itself an indication that Capital Punishment stands morally condemned."[10]

This is also a poor argument, for several reasons. The contempt for the executioner and the accompanying social ostracism is by no means a universal phenomenon in history; on the contrary, it is a comparatively modern one. In earlier ages, the person who carried out capital punishment—whether the professional executioner or before this became an occupation in its own right, the judge, or some other high-ranking official, sometimes even the ruler himself, or a relative of the murdered person—was always regarded with respect. Quite apart from this, the so-called common moral consciousness, to which the argument appeals is not to be seen as some kind of supreme tribunal in moral matters. Among reasons of general nature for this is that it would be an unreliable, inconsistent, confused, and confusing tribunal. On the one hand, when viewed historically, it hardly seems a very good guide to the moral status of various occupations, for in earlier ages it used to condemn very resolutely and strongly the merchant, the banker, the actor, which no one would think of disparaging today, abolitionists included. On the other hand, it has proved itself quite inconsistent on the issue of the moral basis of punishment in general, voicing incompatible views, now retributive, now utilitarian. It is not at all surprising that both advocates and opponents of capital punishment have claimed its support for their views. But if it supports both sides in this more restricted dispute as well, then it actually supports neither.

There is still another facet of this illogical, irrational streak inherent to the common moral consciousness that comes to the fore in connection with this dispute. If the contempt for the executioner is really rooted in the belief that what he carries out is morally reprehensible, then it is surely heaped upon the wrong person. For he merely carries out decisions on which he has no say whatsoever. Those who are responsible are, in the first instance, the judge and members of the jury. They, on their part, act as they do against the background of criminal laws for which responsibility lies at a further remove still—with the legislators. These, again, legislate in the name of the people, if the political system is a representative one. But for some reason the common moral consciousness has never evinced contempt of any of these.

NOTES

1. Numbers 35.31

2. M. Greenberg, "Some Postulates of Biblical Criminal Law," in J. Goldin (ed.), *The Jewish Expression* (New York: Bantam, 1970), pp. 25–26.

3. "There is no *parallel* between death and even the most miserable life, so that there is no equality of crime and retribution [in the case of murder] unless the perpetrator is judicially put to death" (I. Kant, "The Metaphysics of Morals," *Kant's Political Writings,* ed. H. Reiss, trans. H. B. Nisbet [Cambridge: Cambridge University Press, 1970], p. 156). "Since life is the full compass of a man's existence, the punishment [for murder] cannot simply consist in a 'value', for none is great enough, but can consist only in taking away a second life" (G. W. F. Hegel, *Philosophy of Right,* trans. T. M. Knox [Oxford: Oxford University Press, 1965], p. 247).

4. C. Beccaria, *On Crimes and Punishments,* trans. H. Paolucci (Indianapolis: Bobbs-Merrill, 1977), p. 45.

5. G. W. F. Hegel, *Philosophy of Right,* p. 71.

6. S. V. Vulović, *Problem smrtne kazne* (Belgrade: Geca Kon, 1925), pp. 23–24.

7. A. Camus, "Reflections on the Guillotine," in *Resistance, Rebellion and Death,* trans. J. O'Brien (London: Hamish Hamilton, 1961), p. 143.

8. Quoted in E. R. Calvert, *Capital Punishment in the Twentieth Century* (London: G. P. Putnam's Sons, 1927), p. 132.

9. B. M. Leiser, *Liberty, Justice and Morals: Contemporary Value Conflicts* (New York: Macmillan, 1973), p. 225.

10. Calvert, *Capital Punishment,* p. 172.

Against the Death Penalty: The Minimal Invasion Argument

Hugo Adam Bedau

Abolitionists attacking the death penalty typically employ a wide variety of moral arguments. The value of human life, respect for human life—these norms play a decisive role for some. Others object on the

ground that the state has no right to kill any of its prisoners. Some oppose it because they regard it as an affront to human dignity. Many others object on the ground that the death penalty violates the offender's right to life. Some will insist that it is the unfair administration of the death penalty, and the impossibility of making it fair, that warrants abolishing it. Still others insist that the risk of executing the innocent outweighs whatever alleged benefits the death penalty provides, or that, all things considered, a policy of selective death sentences has less overall social utility—in particular, it squanders scarce resources—than does a policy of no death sentencing. Or (to borrow language from the Supreme Court) "evolving standards of decency" condemn the death penalty today, even if they did not a century ago. Some oppose the death penalty not so much for what it does to the offender as for what it reveals about *us* in tolerating, not to say advocating, such killings. These and perhaps other moral concerns can be connected in various ways; they show that there is much to think about from the moral point of view in evaluating and criticizing the death penalty.

This occasion does not present the opportunity to develop an adequate review and critique of all the arguments implied by these varied moral norms. For that reason I propose to present and discuss only one argument—the one I now think is the best argument against the death penalty. Its lineage can be traced back to the little book by Cesare Beccaria, *An Essay on Crimes and Punishments* (1764), the tract usually credited with inspiring the abolition movement during the period of the Enlightenment in Europe and a version of which reappears in the recent papal encyclical, *Evangelium Vitae*. The argument rests on a fundamental principle that neither Beccaria nor the Pope explicitly formulated: Given a compelling state interest in some goal or purpose, the government in a constitutional democracy built on the principle of equal freedom and human rights for all must use the least restrictive means sufficient to achieve that goal or purpose. More expansively, the principle (a near-neighbor to what students of constitutional law would recognize as the principle of "substantive due process") holds that if individual privacy, liberty, and autonomy (or other fundamental values) are to be invaded and deliberately violated, it must be because the end to be achieved is of undeniable importance to society, and no less severe interference will suffice. For convenience of reference, let us henceforth call this the Minimal Invasion argument against the death penalty and the principle that generates it the Minimal Invasion principle.

The Minimal Invasion argument is unlike most arguments against the death penalty in two important respects. First, it does not rely on such familiar values as the right to life, values that either are not widely shared or are widely shared but at the cost of excessive vagueness. Second, the argument (with the exception of the debate over deterrence) does not hinge on establishing the usual faults that plague this form of punishment as actually administered. Thus, this argument sidesteps worries about the risk of executing the innocent, the arbitrariness of death sentencing and executions, and demonstrable effects of racial bias (especially in the South), the evident vulnerability of the poor, the unavoidable economic costs that exceed those of imprisonment. Opponents of the death penalty are often challenged to declare where they would stand were these flaws to be corrected. Despite the current interest in reforming our several systems of capital punishment, it is doubtful whether all or even most of the reforms so far proposed will be adopted. In any case, the Minimal Invasion argument does not depend on such contingencies. While it is a far cry from a philosopher's a priori argument, it comes close to sharing with such arguments immunity to a wide variety of factual considerations.

If an argument against the death penalty is to be constructed around the Minimal Invasion principle, at least three further propositions must be accepted. First, punishment for crime must be judged to be a legitimate practice in society under a constitution such as ours. Second, the death penalty by its very nature must be judged to be more severe, invasive, and irremediable than the alternative of some form of long-term imprisonment. Third, the death penalty must be judged not to play a necessary role in securing public safety either by way of general deterrence or specific incapacitation. If these three propositions are true, as I think they are, then in conjunction with the principle with which we began they lead to the conclusion that we ought to abolish the death penalty for all crimes and all offenders. Restating this argument in semi-formal style, this is what we get:

The principle. Invasions by the government of an individual's privacy, liberty, and autonomy (or other fundamental value) are justified only if no less invasive practice is sufficient to achieve an important social goal.

1. Punishment is justified only if it is necessary as a means to some socially valid end.
2. The death penalty is more severe—more invasive—than long-term imprisonment.
3. Long-term imprisonment is sufficient as an invasion of individual liberty, privacy, and autonomy (and other fundamental values) to achieve valid social goals.
4. Society ought to abolish any lawful practice that imposes more violation of individual liberty, privacy, or autonomy (or other fundamental value) when it is known that a less invasive practice is available and is sufficient.

The conclusion. Society ought to abolish the death penalty.

There's the argument. What can be said on behalf of the truth of each of its premises? Consider first the Minimal Invasion principle (and its corollary, step [4]). How much defense does it require? Surely it is clear that only extreme socialists, fascists, theocrats, or other totalitarians who for various reasons want to extend state power and intervention into the lives of citizens as far as possible will quarrel with this principle. Liberals and conservatives alike, who accept the basic tenets of constitutional democracy and believe in human rights, should readily embrace it. The only issue calling for further discussion among these supporters is whether this principle might ever conflict with other principles worthier of respect in certain cases, so that it must yield to them. What might such an incompatible but superior principle be? What sort of case might arise where such a conflict occurs? A fuller account of the rationale behind this principle would require us to connect it with more fundamental principles of social justice, a topic that cannot be pursued here. As for the three other steps in the argument, each warrants a closer look.

The first premise. Affirming the legitimacy of a system of punishment poses no problem for supporters of the death penalty nor for any but a few of its opponents. No one disputes that public security—protec-

tion against criminal victimization—is a salient value and that intervention by government into the behavior of its citizens to achieve that goal is warranted. But pursuit of such a goal is subject to constraints. Not every imaginable weapon to fight crime is morally permissible. Principles of various sorts (e.g., due process of law) restrict the tactics of intervention. These constraints to the side, as things stand, society needs recourse to punitive methods as a necessary condition of public safety.

This is not, however, because punishment is an end in itself; it is because we know of no less invasive responses to individual behavior sufficient as a means to achieve the purpose. If we did, then it would be difficult and perhaps impossible to defend punishment as a morally permissible practice. After all, punishment by its very nature involves deliberately inflicting deprivations and hardships on persons that, if inflicted by private citizens, would be crimes. So punishment needs to be justified, and the only justification available is that it is a necessary means to a fundamental social goal. For present purposes, then, we can say that there is little dispute over the truth of the first proposition.

The second premise. Few will deny the greater brutality and violence of the death penalty when compared to imprisonment. From time to time one hears a friend of the death penalty—and even on occasion some of its enemies—claiming that life in prison is a much more severe punishment than death. Beccaria and his English admirer, Jeremy Bentham (1748–1832), both pioneering abolitionists, believed that life in prison involved more suffering than a few moments on the gallows. I think it is sufficient by way of a reply to point out that those in the best position to know behave in a manner that suggests otherwise.

Few death row prisoners try to commit suicide and fewer succeed. Few death row prisoners insist that all appeals on their behalf be dropped. Few convicted murderers sentenced to life in prison declare years later that they wish they had been sentenced instead to death and executed. Few if any death row prisoners refuse clemency if it is offered to them. No doubt prison life can be made unbearable and hideous; no doubt death row can be managed by the authorities in an inhumane fashion. But none of this is necessary. No doubt not all life-term prisoners find ways to make their imprisonment something more than an inhumane endurance test. So it should hardly come as a surprise that the vast majority of friends of the death penalty as well as its opponents believe that death is worse than imprisonment. This is why its opponents want to abolish it—and its supporters want to keep it. So we can accept the second proposition without further ado.

The third premise. The third proposition affirms that whatever the legitimate purposes of punishment are, imprisonment serves them as well as or better than the death penalty. This proposition rests on a variety of kinds of empirical evidence, ranging from statistical research on deterrence, the behavior in prison and on parole of convicted murderers not sentenced to death and executed, and above all on the experience of jurisdictions such as Michigan that have gone without the death penalty for decades.

Here is what the record shows: There is no evidence that prison officials, guards, or visitors in prisons where there is no death penalty are more at risk than are their counterparts in the death penalty states. There is no evidence that residents of abolition jurisdictions are at greater risk of murderous victimization than are residents in the death penalty jurisdictions. (The District of Columbia in recent years has had a very high homicide rate and is an abolition jurisdiction; but there is no research that connects the one fact with the other. Most other abolition jurisdictions have a noticeably lower homicide rate than do neighboring death penalty jurisdictions.) To be sure, some convicted murderers commit another murder while in prison or after release—the U.S. Bureau of Justice Statistics reports that 9 percent of those currently on death row had a previous homicide conviction.[1] But not all of these recidivist murderers were guilty in their first homicide of a death-eligible murder. For these murderers, their second homicide could not have been prevented by inflicting the death penalty on them for the first homicide, since their first homicide was not death-eligible. Furthermore, there is no way to predict in advance which convicted murderers are likely to

recidivate: the predictions of future dangerousness are plagued with false positives. If we could make accurate and reliable predictions of which prisoners would be dangerous in the future, these offenders could be kept under confinement, just as a typhoid carrier may be quarantined as a public health menace. The only way to prevent such recidivism would be to execute *every* convicted murderer—a policy that is politically unavailable and morally indefensible. Today's defenders of the death penalty must accept a pick-and-choose system of death sentences and executions, with all the adverse effects—as they see it—that such a system has on prevention and retribution.

It is also true that opponents of the death penalty who want to rest their case on the argument under discussion would be vulnerable to evidence—if there were any—showing that the death penalty is a better deterrent than imprisonment. Were there such evidence, opponents would have to rely on some other argument. (I have not claimed that the Minimal Invasion argument is the only argument for abolition, I claim only that I find it the most persuasive.[2]) But since there is so little reason to suppose that the death penalty is ever a marginally superior deterrent over imprisonment, or that such superiority (if any) can be detected by the currently available methods of social science, this "what-if" counterargument can be put to the side and disregarded. (Below, I return to the issue of deterrence.)

With worries about prevention, deterrence, and incapacitation behind us (for the moment), what might we reasonably expect to be the public response in quarters where the death penalty currently has wide support? Is there reason to believe that if the death penalty were abolished, the police would take to administering curbstone justice and the public would revolt? Would the clamor of surviving family members of murder victims force the authorities to restore the death penalty? Would outspoken abolitionists become targets for violent rage, as have some doctors in abortion clinics? Nothing of the sort has happened in any current abolition jurisdiction. However, given the utter lack of political leadership on all aspects of the death penalty in states in the Deep South, where the death penalty has been so conspicuously used, I must admit to some uneasiness over what might happen if Texas were told—say, by a Supreme Court ruling—that it could no longer use the death penalty. The heirs of those who plastered the South in the 1950s with billboards shouting "Impeach Earl Warren" would rise to the occasion and denounce whatever political leadership brought about abolition. Fundamentalist Christians, Mormons, and others who have persuaded themselves that the Bible decrees the death penalty for murder pose a somewhat different problem. How members of these religious groups—clergy and laity, concentrated in (but by no means confined to) the Bible Belt across the South—would behave is far from obvious.

The upshot is that the third premise in the argument under discussion is reasonably supported by the available facts; and that suffices to prove the conclusion.

* * *

Nevertheless, many friends of the death penalty will not be persuaded by my argument. They will advance at least two objections, one empirical and the other conceptual and normative. First, they will insist on the superiority of the death penalty as a deterrent. Second, they will object that my argument simply ignores a crucial conceptual element and normative principle that, when properly taken into account, leads to a different conclusion.

* * *

. . . The question that defenders of the death penalty need to answer is not "Does the death penalty deter?" Common sense assures us that punishments generally serve to deter some persons from some crimes on some occasions. There is no reason to think that the death penalty is an exception. As for measuring how much it deters, as econometricians try to do, that is a side issue. Answering the question above would be dispositive only if opponents of the death penalty favored *no* punishment for capital crimes. But of course they don't favor no punishment (with the exception, perhaps, of some pacificists). The question that death penalty advocates need to answer is this: "Does the death penalty deter *as well as or better than* imprisonment?" To date, no one has even tried to determine the extent to which imprisonment is a

deterrent to murder. For all we know, it is as good a deterrent as death, or even better. For all we know, the alleged deterrent effect detected by econometric methods is owing to increases in the use of long-term imprisonment concurrent with executions. Defenders of the death penalty who want to rest their case in whole or in part on the alleged deterrent effect of the death penalty at best refute those abolitionists who think (erroneously) that the death penalty never deters. They leave untouched those abolitionists who think there is no evidence that the death penalty is marginally a better deterrent than executions.

But for the sake of the argument, let us suppose that the death penalty as currently employed does have a marginally superior deterrent effect. Such an effect is of little use in defending the death penalty because the supposed benefit is obtained at an unacceptable cost. The cost comes in the many ways our death penalty system is dysfunctional. The latest study by James S. Liebman and his associates documents this conclusion in alarming detail. Perhaps their most disturbing finding was that the more a jurisdiction uses the death penalty, the greater the likelihood that it will make mistakes—notably, the mistake of convicting the innocent or the mistake of sentencing to death offenders whose crimes should not have made them death-eligible. Everyone agrees that the deterrent effect of a penalty is a function of the frequency with which it is employed; Liebman's research shows that the more courts strive for a deterrent effect by increasing the frequency of death sentences, the more likely they are to err in their judgments and sentences.[3] We have no right to secure a benefit for some (innocents protected by superior marginal deterrence), *knowing* that we do so by methods that impose injustice on others—defendants who may not be guilty (or not guilty of first-degree murder) and whose guilt is determined by violations of due process and equal protection of the law.

Today, would-be defenders of the death penalty no longer rely, as they once did, mainly on the claim of superior deterrence. And that is just as well. Quite apart from the difficulties just discussed in defending the death penalty on grounds of deterrence, those who rely on the principle that severe punishments

CHAPTER 10: CAPITAL PUNISHMENT ☼ 323

are justified by their superior deterrent and incapacitative effects are implicitly invited to go further. If death deters more than imprisonment, then death preceded by torture presumably deters more than death alone. If so, on what ground is the defender of the death penalty able to resist embracing torture as well as death? Surely, all sides agree that morality and politics require that there be some upper bound to the permissible severity of punishments no matter what their deterrent effect might be. The dispute is not over whether there is such a limit, but where to place that limit and why. The Minimal Invasion argument provides a reasonable solution to that problem. Preferring the death penalty because of its allegedly superior deterrent effects does not.

* * *

NOTES

1. U.S. Department of Justice, Bureau of Justice Statistics, "Capital Punishment 1998," Washington, D.C., 1999, p. 10.

2. A strong candidate for an argument equally as concise as but otherwise very different from mine is the "knockdown argument" offered by Stephen Nathanson, *An Eye for an Eye,* 2nd ed. (Lanham, Md.: Rowman and Littlefield, 2001), p. 175. Here it is, addressed to a death penalty supporter: "You accept justice and respect for human life as fundamental values; the death penalty is inconsistent with these values; therefore, based on your own values, you ought to reject the death penalty."

3. James S. Liebman et al., *Why There Is So Much Error in Capital Cases, and What Can Be Done about It* (New York: Columbia Law School, February 2002).

What Do Murderers Deserve?

David Gelernter

No civilized nation ever takes the death penalty for granted; two recent cases force us to consider it yet again. A Texas woman, Karla Faye Tucker, murdered two people with a pickaxe, was said to have repented in prison, and was put to death. A Montana man, Theodore Kaczynski, murdered three people with mail bombs, did not repent, and struck a bargain with the Justice Department; he pleaded guilty and will not be executed. (He also attempted to murder others and succeeded in wounding some, myself included.) Why did we execute the penitent and spare the impenitent? However we answer this question, we surely have a duty to ask it.

And we ask it—I do, anyway—with a sinking feeling, because in modern America, moral upside-downness is a specialty of the house. To eliminate

race prejudice we discriminate by race. We promote the cultural assimilation of immigrant children by denying them schooling in English. We throw honest citizens in jail for child abuse, relying on testimony so phony any child could see through it. Orgasm studies are okay in public high schools but the Ten Commandments are not. We make a point of admiring manly women and womanly men. None of which has anything to do with capital punishment directly, but it all obliges us to approach any question about morality in modern American in the larger context of this country's desperate confusion about elementary distinctions.

Why execute murderers? To deter? To avenge? Supporters of the death penalty often give the first answer, opponents the second. But neither can be the whole truth. If our main goal were deterring crime, we would insist on public executions—which are not on the political agenda, and not an item that many Americans are interested in promoting. If our main

David Gelernter, "What Do Murderers Deserve?" *Commentary* (April 1998): 21–24 (edited). Reprinted with permissions of *Commentary*.

goal were vengeance, we would allow the grieving parties to decide the murderer's fate; if the victim had no family or friends to feel vengeful on his behalf, we would call the whole thing off.

In fact, we execute murderers in order to make a communal proclamation: that murder is intolerable. A deliberate murderer embodies evil so terrible that it defiles the community. Thus the late social philosopher Robert Nisbet: "Until a catharsis has been effected through trial, through the finding of guilt and then punishment, the community is anxious, fearful, apprehensive, and above all, contaminated."

Individual citizens have a right and sometimes a duty to speak. A community has the right, too, and sometimes the duty. The community certifies births and deaths, creates marriages, educates children, fights invaders. In laws, deeds, and ceremonies it lays down the boundary lines of civilized life, lines that are constantly getting scuffed and needing renewal.

When a murder takes place, the community is obliged, whether it feels like it or not, to clear its throat and step up to the microphone. Every murder demands a communal response. Among possible responses, the death penalty is uniquely powerful because it is permanent and can never be retracted or overturned. An execution forces the community to assume forever the burden of moral certainty; it is a form of absolute speech that allows no waffling or equivocation. Deliberate murder, the community announces, is absolutely evil and absolutely intolerable, period.

Of course, we could make the same point less emphatically if we wanted to—for example, by locking up murderers for life (as we sometimes do). The question then becomes: is the death penalty overdoing it? Should we make a less forceful proclamation instead?

The answer might be yes if we were a community in which murder was a shocking anomaly and thus in effect a solved problem. But we are not. Our big cities are full of murderers at large. "One can guesstimate," writes the criminologist and political scientist John J. DiIulio, Jr., "that we are nearing or may already have passed the day when 500,000 murderers, convicted and undetected, are living in American society."

DiIulio's statistics show an approach to murder so casual as to be depraved. We are reverting to a pre-civilized state of nature. Our natural bent in the face of murder is not to avenge the crime but to shrug it off, except in those rare cases when our own near and dear are involved. (And even then, it depends.)

This is an old story. Cain murders Abel and is brought in for questioning: where is Abel, your brother? The suspect's response: how should I know? "What *am* I, my brother's keeper?" It is one of the very first statements attributed to mankind in the Bible; voiced here by an interested party, it nonetheless expressed a powerful and universal inclination. Why mess in other people's problems? And murder is always, in the most immediate sense, someone else's problem, because the injured party is dead.

Murder in primitive societies called for a private settling of scores. The community as a whole stayed out of it. For murder to count, as it does in the Bible, as a crime not merely against one man but against the whole community and against God—that was moral triumph that is still basic to our integrity, and that is never to be taken for granted. By executing murderers, the community reaffirms this moral understanding by restating the truth that absolute evil exists and must be punished.

Granted (some people say), the death penalty is a communal proclamation; it is nevertheless an incoherent one. If our goal is to affirm that human life is more precious than anything else, how can we make such a declaration by destroying life?

But declaring that human life is more precious than anything else is not our goal in imposing the death penalty. Nor is the proposition true. The founding fathers pledged their lives (and fortunes and sacred honor) to the cause of freedom; Americans have traditionally believed that some things are more precious than life. ("Living in a sanitary age, we are getting so we place too high a value on human life—which rightfully must always come second to human ideas." Thus E.B. White in 1938, pondering the Munich pact ensuring "peace in our time" between the Western powers and Hitler.) The point of capital punishment is not to pronounce on life in general but on the crime of murder.

Which is not to say that the sanctity of human life does not enter the picture. Taking a life, says the Talmud (in the course of discussing Cain and Abel), is equivalent to destroying a whole world. The rabbis used this statement to make a double point: to tell us why murder is the gravest of crimes, and to warn against false testimony in a murder trial. But to believe in the sanctity of human life does not mean, and the Talmud does not say it means, that capital punishment is ruled out.

A newer objection grows out of the seemingly random way in which we apply capital punishment. The death penalty might be a reasonable communal proclamation in principle, some critics say, but it has become so garbled in practice that it has lost all significance and ought to be dropped. DiIulio writes that "the ratio of persons murdered to persons executed for murder from 1977 to 1996 was in the ballpark of 1,000 to 1"; the death penalty has become in his view "arbitrary and capricious," a "state lottery" that is "unjust both as a matter of Judeo–Christian ethics and as a matter of American citizenship."

We can grant that, on the whole, we are doing a disgracefully bad job of administering the death penalty. After all, we are divided and confused on the issue. The community at large is strongly in favor of capital punishment; the cultural elite is strongly against it. Our attempts to speak with assurance as a community come out sounding in consequence like a man who is fighting off a choke-hold as he talks. But a community as cavalier about murder as we are has no right to back down. That we are botching things does not entitle us to give up.

Opponents of capital punishment tend to describe it as a surrender to our emotions—to grief, rage, fear, blood lust. For most supporters of the death penalty, this is exactly false. Even when we resolve in principle to go ahead, we have to steel ourselves. Many of us would find it hard to kill a dog, much less a man. Endorsing capital punishment means not that we yield to our emotions but that we overcome them. (Immanuel Kant, the great advocate of the

death penalty precisely on moral grounds, makes this point in his reply to the anti-capital-punishment reformer Cesare Beccaria—accusing Beccaria of being "moved by sympathetic sentimentality and an affectation of humanitarianism.") If we favor executing murderers it is not because we want to but because, however much we do *not* want to, we consider ourselves obliged to.

Many Americans, of course, no longer feel that obligation. The death penalty is hard for us as a community above all because of our moral evasiveness. For at least a generation, we have urged one another to switch off our moral faculties. "Don't be judgmental!" We have said it so many times, we are starting to believe it.

The death penalty is a proclamation about absolute evil, but many of us are no longer sure that evil even exists. We define evil out of existence by calling it "illness"—a tendency Aldous Huxley anticipated in his novel *Brave New World* (1932) and Robert Nisbet wrote about in 1982: "America has lost the villain, the evil one, who has now become one of the sick, the disturbed. . . . America has lost the moral value of guilt, lost it to the sickroom."

Our refusal to look evil in the face is no casual notion; it is a powerful drive. Thus we have (for example) the terrorist Theodore Kaczynski, who planned and carried out a hugely complex campaign of violence with a clear goal in mind. It was the goal most terrorists have: to get famous and not die. He wanted public attention for his ideas about technology; he figured he could get it by attacking people with bombs.

He was right. His plan succeeded. It is hard to imagine a more compelling proof of mental competence than this planning and carrying out over decades of a complex, rational strategy. (Evil, yes; irrational, no; they are different things.) The man himself has said repeatedly that he is perfectly sane, knew what he was doing, and is proud of it.

To call such a man insane seems to me like deliberate perversity. But many people do. Some of them insist that his thoughts about technology constitute "delusions," though every terrorist holds strong beliefs that are wrong, and many nonterrorists do, too. Some insist that sending bombs through the mail is *ipso facto* proof of insanity—as if the 20th century had not taught us that there is no limit to the bestiality of which sane men are capable.

Where dos this perversity come from? I said earlier that the community at large favors the death penalty, but intellectuals and the cultural elite tend to oppose it. This is not (I think) because they abhor killing more than other people do, but because the death penalty represents absolute speech from a position of moral certainty, and doubt is the black-lung disease of the intelligentsia—an occupational hazard now inflicted on the culture as a whole.

American intellectuals have long differed from the broader community—particularly on religion, crime and punishment, education, family, the sexes, race relations, American history, taxes and public spending, the size and scope of government, art, the environment, and the military. (Otherwise, I suppose, they and the public have been in perfect accord.) But not until the 60's and 70's were intellectuals finally in a position to act on their convictions. Whereupon they attacked the community's moral certainties with the enthusiasm of guard dogs leaping at throats. The result is an American community smitten with the disease of intellectual doubt—or, in this case, self-doubt.

The failure of our schools is a consequence of our self-doubt, of our inability to tell children that learning is not fun and they are required to master certain topics whether they want to or not. The tortured history of modern American race relations grows out of our self-doubt: we passed a civil-rights act in 1964, then lost confidence immediately in our ability to make a race-blind society work; racial preferences codify our refusal to believe in our own good faith. During the late stages of the cold war, many Americans laughed at the idea that the American way was morally superior or the Soviet Union was an "evil empire"; some are still laughing. Within their own community and the American community at large, doubting intellectuals have taken refuge (as doubters often do) in bullying, to the point where many of us are now so uncomfortable at the prospect of con-fronting evil that we turn away and change the subject.

Returning then to the penitent woman and the impenitent man: the Karla Faye Tucker case is the harder of the two. We are told that she repented of the vicious murders she committed. If that is true, we would still have had no business forgiving her, or forgiving any murderer. As Dennis Prager has written apropos this case, only the victim is entitled to forgive, and the victim is silent. But showing mercy to penitents is part of our religious tradition, and I cannot imagine renouncing it categorically.

Why was Cain not put to death, but condemned instead to wander the earth forever? Among the answers given by the rabbis in the Midrash is that he repented. The moral category of repentance is so important, they said, that it was created before the world itself. I would therefore consider myself morally obligated to think long and hard before executing a penitent. But a true penitent would have to have renounced (as Karla Faye Tucker did) all legal attempts to overturn the original conviction. If every legal avenue has been tried and has failed, the penitence window is closed. Of course, this still leaves the difficult problem of telling counterfeit penitence from the real thing, but everything associated with capital punishment is difficult.

As for Kaczynski, the prosecutors who accepted the murderer's plea-bargain say they got the best outcome they could, under the circumstances, and I believe them. But I also regard this failure to execute a cold-blooded impenitent terrorist murderer as a tragic abdication of moral responsibility. The tragedy lies in what, under our confused system, the prosecutors felt compelled to do. The community was called on to speak unambiguously. It flubbed its lines, shrugged its shoulders, and walked away.

Which brings me back to our moral condition as a community. I can describe our plight better in artistic than in philosophical terms. The most vivid illustrations I know of self-doubt and its consequences are the paintings and sculptures of Alberto Giacometti (who died in 1966). Giacometti was an artist of great integrity; he was consumed by intellectual and moral self-doubt, which he set down faithfully. His sculpted figures show elongated, shriveled human beings who seem corroded by acid, eaten-up to the bone, hurt and weakened past fragility nearly to death. They are painful to look at. And they are natural emblems of modern America. We ought to stick one on top of the Capitol and think it over.

In executing murderers, we declare that deliberate murder is absolutely evil and absolutely intolerable. This is a painfully difficult proclamation for a self-doubting community to make. But we dare not stop trying. Communities may exist in which capital punishment is no longer the necessary response to deliberate murder. America today is not one of them.

In Defense of the Death Penalty

Louis P. Pojman

THE RETRIBUTIVIST ARGUMENT FOR THE DEATH PENALTY

Let me say a word about the notion of *desert*. Part of justice, going back to Plato, Aristotle, Kant, the Biblical tradition, and virtually every major religion, holds that people ought to get what they deserve. Those who work hard for worthy goals deserve reward; those who do not make the effort deserve nothing; and those who purposefully do evil deserve punishment. The virtuous deserve to flourish to the degree of their virtue, and the vicious deserve to suffer to the degree of their vice. "Whatsoever a man soweth, that shall he reap," is an ancient adage perhaps as old as its metaphysical counterpart of eternal judgment (Jewish/Christian tradition) or karma (Hindu/Buddhist tradition)—that what one does in this life will be part of one's essential constitution in the next life. This notion presumes the notion of responsibility, that people are accountable for their actions and should be rewarded and punished accordingly. Even Karl Marx objected to applying the principle "From each according to his ability, to each according to his need," to people who did not work, who did not deserve to be helped.[1] Only in contemporary liberalism, such as Rawls's theory of justice as fairness, has the notion of natural desert been seriously undermined. But Rawls is wrong here. Although we may not deserve our initial endowments or capacities, we do deserve what we make with them. Our effort and contribution are worthy of moral assessment, and as agents we can be held accountable for our effort and contributions. That is, without the concept of desert, responsibility has no validity, and without the notion of responsibility, neither morality nor law has a footing.

Suppose, as most of us do, that each person has a right to life. That right, however, is not absolute, but conditional (otherwise we could not kill even in self-defense). Like our right to property and liberty, it can be overridden for weighty moral reasons. When an offender threatens or attempts to kill an innocent person, the offender deserves a punishment appropriate to the severity of the crime. When an offender with malice aforethought takes the life of an innocent person, he or she forfeits his or her own life. But the main idea in the retributivist theory is that not only is the death penalty permissible for the murderer, it is also deserved. The guilty deserve punishment, and that punishment should be proportional to the severity of their crime. A complete retributivist like Kant * * * holds that all and only those who are guilty should be so punished. The moderate retributivist holds that only the guilty should be so pun-

Louis P. Pojman, "The Death Penalty," in *Life and Death* (Belmont, CA: Wadsworth, 2000): 140–50 (edited). Reprinted with permission of Wadsworth.

ished—but not necessarily all of the guilty. Mitigating circumstances, the external costs of punishment, the possibility of reform, and so forth may prescribe lesser degrees of punishment than are deserved. Hell itself may be a just desert for Hitler, but morality doesn't require that we torture him. The moderate retributivist holds that giving people what they deserve (positive and negative) is a *prima facie* duty, not an absolute, nonoverridable one.

Some have objected that the death penalty is itself murder. To quote eighteenth-century abolitionist Cesare di Beccaria, "Putting the criminal to death only compounds evil. If killing is an evil, then the State actually doubles the evil by executing the murderer. The State violates the criminal's right to life. It carries out *legalized murder*. The death penalty cannot be useful because of the example of barbarity it gives to men. . . . it seems to me absurd that the laws which punish homicide should themselves commit it." But there is a difference. The murderer volunteered for his crime. The victim didn't volunteer for his fate. The murderer had reason to believe that he would be justly and severely punished for his crime, so he has no reason to complain when the state executes him. The murderer violated the victim's right to life, thereby forfeiting his own *prima facie* right to life. The Fifth and Fourteenth Amendments of our Bill of Rights state that no one should be deprived of life, liberty, or property without due process of the law, implying that so long as due process of the law has been observed, condemning a murderer to death is both legally and morally justified.

Society may rank punishments corresponding roughly to the gravity of the crime. That is, it draws up two lists. The first list consists of a list of crimes, from the most to the least serious. The second is a list of punishments that it considers acceptable, from the most severe to the least severe. So long as there is a rough correspondence between the two lists, a society is permitted to consult its own sense of justice in linking the various punishments with each crime in question. The death penalty, it seems, is at the head of the list of severe punishments, linked retributively with the worst crimes. Whether torture is also permitted for a torturer, mutilation for a rapist,

and so forth, may be debated. Strictly speaking I have no argument against the appropriate use of torture, though I think it is not necessary. It seems to me that death is a sufficient punishment for the most heinous crimes, but it's not part of my thesis to sort out these matters. Where to put the limit of harm to be imposed on the murderer is partly a cultural matter, as the history of legal punishment indicates.[2] Our notion of what is or is not "humane," connected with repulsion against torture and corporal punishment in general, is largely a cultural matter. It has to do with how we have been socialized. Torture shocks our sensibilities, but not those of our ancestors, and not necessarily our moral principles. Although I am a moral objectivist, holding that moral truth exists, part of morality is relative to culture, to the sensibilities of the majority of its members.

One objection to the retributivist argument is that although a criminal may deserve the death penalty, the justification of the State's execution of the criminal is another matter. It needs a separate justification. The correct response is that justice consists of giving people what they deserve. As Locke noted, in the state of nature we would each have the right and duty to punish the offender, but in organized society, we surrender that right and duty to the State. We may override justice because of mitigating circumstances, but insofar as the State has duty to dispense justice, it is justified in executing those who commit murder.

THE UTILITARIAN ARGUMENT

The utilitarian argument for capital punishment is that it deters would-be offenders from committing first-degree murder. If the death penalty deters, we have an auxiliary argument for its use. This argument may supplement (but not replace) the retributivist argument. Isaac Ehrlich's study, to my knowledge the most thorough study to date, takes into account complex sociological data and concludes that over the period 1933–1969, "an additional execution per year. . . . may have resulted on the average in seven or eight fewer murders."[3] Ehrlich's findings have been challenged by many opponents with the result that the issue is left in doubt. It seems an enormous undertaking to prove either that the death penalty deters or that it does not deter. The statistical evidence is inconclusive—which is different from saying that it is "zero," as abolitionists sometimes claim.

Commonsense reasons exist for believing that the death penalty deters some would-be murderers from murdering. Richard Herrnstein and James Q. Wilson have argued in *Crime and Human Nature* that a great deal of crime is committed in a cost-benefit scheme, wherein the criminal engages in some form of risk assessment as to his or her chances of getting caught and punished in some manner. If a would-be criminal estimates the punishment to be mild, the crime will become inversely attractive, and vice versa. If a potential murderer judges that he may be punished by imprisonment or death, he will be more deterred than if he judges that he will be punished only by imprisonment. Doesn't the fact that those condemned to death do everything in their power to postpone it, and to get their sentences reduced to long-term prison sentences, show that the death penalty is feared as an evil to be avoided? The potential criminal need not go through deliberate cost-benefit analysis. The association of murder with the death penalty may have embedded in the subconscious mind of potential criminals a powerful deterrence. Perhaps the abolition of the death penalty from the 1960s until the late 1970s, and the fact that it is only recently being carried out with any regularity, have eroded the association, accounting for the increased murder rate from 1980 until 1993. The fact that the death penalty is beginning to be carried out may partially account for the decrease of homicides in recent years.

Former Prosecuting Attorney for the State of Florida, Richard Gernstein, has set forth the commonsense case for deterrence. First of all, the death penalty certainly deters the murderer from committing any further murders, including those he or she might commit within the prison in which he is confined. Second, statistics cannot tell us how many potential criminals have refrained from taking another's life through fear of the death penalty. As Hyman Barshay puts it:

The death penalty is a warning, just like a lighthouse throwing its beams out to sea. We hear about shipwrecks, but we do not hear about the ships the lighthouse guides safely on their way. We do not have proof of the number of ships it saves, but we do not tear the lighthouse down.

Some of the commonsense evidence is anecdotal, as reported by British member of parliament Arthur Lewis, who was converted from being an abolitionist to a retentionist:

One reason that has stuck in my mind, and which has proved to me beyond question, is that there was once a professional burglar in my constituency who consistently boasted of the fact that the had spent about one-third of his life in prison. . . . he said to me, "I am a professional burglar. Before we go out on a job we plan it down to every detail. Before we go into the boozer to have a drink we say, 'Don't forget, no shooters'—shooters being guns." He adds, "We did our job and didn't have shooters because at that time there was capital punishment. Our wives, girlfriends and our mums said, 'Whatever you do, do not carry a shooter because if you are caught you might be topped.' If you do away with capital punishment they will all be carrying shooters."

It's difficult to know how widespread this kind of reasoning is. My own experience, growing up in a neighborhood where some of my acquaintances were criminals, corroborates this testimony. These criminals admitted being constrained in their behavior by the possibility of the death penalty. No doubt some crimes are committed in the heat of passion or by the temporarily insane, but not all crime fits that mold. Perhaps rational risk assessment, which involves the cost-benefit analysis of crime, is mainly confined to certain classes of potential and professional criminals, including burglars and kidnappers. It probably applies to people who are tempted to kill their enemies. We simply don't know how much capital punishment deters, but this sort of commonsense, anecdotal evidence cannot be dismissed as worthless. Common sense tells us that people will be deterred by greater punishments such as death than by lesser ones such as imprisonment.

I have been arguing that we do have some statistical and commonsense evidence that the death penalty deters would-be killers. Even if you are skeptical about that evidence, another argument, based on the *possibility* that it deters, is available to us. This is the argument set forth by Ernest van den Haag, which he calls the "Best Bet argument."[4] Van den Haag argues that even though we don't know for certain whether the death penalty deters or prevents other murders, we should bet that it does. Indeed, due to our ignorance, any social policy we take is a gamble. Not to choose capital punishment for first-degree murder is as much a bet that capital punishment doesn't deter as choosing the policy is a bet that it does. There is a significant difference in the betting, however: to bet *against* capital punishment is to bet against the innocent and for the murderer; while to bet *for* it is to bet against the murderer and for the innocent.[5]

The point is this: we are accountable for what we let happen as well as for what we actually do. If I fail to bring up my children properly and they are a menace to society, I am to some extent responsible for their bad behavior. I could have caused it to be somewhat better. If I have good evidence that a bomb will blow up the building in which you are working and I fail to notify you (assuming that I can), I am partly responsible for your death, if and when the bomb explodes. To refrain purposefully from a lesser evil that we know will allow a greater evil to occur, is to be at least partially responsible for the greater evil.

This responsibility for our omissions underlies van den Haag's argument, to which we now return. Suppose that we choose a policy of capital punishment for capital crimes. In this case we are betting that the death of some murderers will be more than compensated for by the lives of some innocents who will not be murdered (by either these murderers or others). If we're right, we have saved the lives of the innocent. If we're wrong, unfortunately, we've sacrificed the lives of some murderers. Suppose we choose not to have a social policy of capital punishment. If capital punishment doesn't work as a deterrent, we've come out ahead, but if it does, we've missed an opportunity to save innocent lives. If we value the saving of innocent lives more highly than the loss of the guilty, betting on a policy of capital punishment turns out to be rational. The reasoning goes like this: Let "CP" stand for Capital Punishment:

The Wager

	CP works	CP doesn't work
We bet on CP	a. We win: some murderers die and some innocents are saved.	b. We lose: some murderers die for no purpose.
We bet against CP	c. We lose: murderers live and some innocents die needlessly.	d. We win: murderers live and the lives of others are unaffected.

Suppose that we estimate the utility value of a murderer's life a 5 while the value of an innocent's life is 10. Although we cannot give lives exact numerical values, we can make rough comparative estimates: Mother Teresa's life is greater than Adolf Hitler's, and all things being equal, the life of an innocent person is at least twice the value of a murderer's. (My own sense is that the murderer has forfeited most, if not all, of his worth, but if I had to put a figure on it, that figure would be 1,000 to 1). Given van den Haag's figures, the sums work out this way:

A murderer saved	+5
A murderer executed	−5
An innocent saved	+10
An innocent murdered	−10

Suppose that for each execution only two innocent lives are spared. Then the outcomes read as follows:

1. $-5 + 20 = +15$
2. -5
3. $+5 - 20 = -15$
4. $+5$

If all of the possibilities are roughly equal, we can sum their outcomes as follows:

If we bet on capital punishment, (a) and (b) obtain = +10.

If we bet against capital punishment, (c) and (d) obtain = −10.

So to execute convicted murderers turns out to be a good bet. To abolish the death penalty for convicted murderers would be a bad bet. We unnecessarily put the innocent at risk.

Even if we value the utility of an innocent life only slightly more than that of a murderer, it is still rational to execute convicted murderers. As van den Haag writes, "Though we have no proof of the positive deterrence of the penalty, we also have no proof of zero or negative effectiveness. I believe we have no right to risk additional future victims of murder for the sake of sparing convicted murderers; on the contrary, our moral obligation is to risk the possible ineffectiveness of executions."[6]

THE GOLDEN RULE ARGUMENT

One more argument should be set forth, and that is the Golden Rule argument for the death penalty. The Golden Rule states that we should do unto others as we would have them do unto us if we were in their shoes. Reflect on the evil deeds perpetrated by Nazi war criminals, or by those who blew up the Murrah Federal Building in Oklahoma City on April 19, 1995, killing 168 people, or on any number of heinous murders well known to us. If you had yielded to temptation and blown up the Federal Building, or like Steven Judy had raped and murdered a helpless woman and then drowned her three small children, or if you had kidnapped a young girl, placed her in your trunk and then killed her, what punishment do you think would be fitting for *you*? What would you deserve? Would you want to live? Would not the moral guilt that you would doubtless feel demand the death penalty? And would you not judge that such moral guilt was appropriate and that anyone who did not feel it was morally defective? Would you not agree that you had forfeited your right to life, that you had brought upon yourself the hangman's noose? Would you not agree that you deserved noth-

ing les than death? Should we not apply these sentiments to murderers?

OBJECTIONS TO CAPITAL PUNISHMENT

Let us examine three major objections to capital punishment, as well as the retentionist's responses to those objections.

1. Objection: Capital punishment is a morally unacceptable thirst for revenge. As former British Prime Minister Edward Heath put it,

The real point which is emphasized to me by many constituents is that even if the death penalty is not a deterrent, murderers deserve to die. This is the question of revenge. Again, this will be a matter of moral judgment for each of us. I do not believe in revenge. If I were to become the victim of terrorists, I would not wish them to be hanged or killed in any other way for revenge. All that would do is deepen the bitterness which already tragically exists in the conflicts we experience in society, particularly in Northern Ireland.[7]

Response: Retributivism is not the same thing as revenge, although the two attitudes are often intermixed in practice. Revenge is a personal response to a perpetrator for an injury. Retribution is an impartial and impersonal response to an offender for an offense done against someone. You cannot desire revenge for the harm of someone to whom you are indifferent. Revenge always involves personal concern for the victim. Retribution is not personal but based on objective factors: the criminal has deliberately harmed an innocent party and so deserves to be punished, whether I wish it or not. I would agree that I, my son, or my daughter deserves to be punished for our crimes, but I don't wish any vengeance on myself, my son, or my daughter.

Furthermore, while revenge often leads us to exact more suffering from the offender than the offense warrant, retribution stipulates that the offender be punished in proportion to the gravity of the offense. In this sense, the *lex talionis* that we find in the Old Testament is actually a progressive rule, where retribution replaces revenge as the mode of punishment. It says that there are limits to what one may do to an offender. Revenge demands a life for an eye or a tooth, but Moses provides a rule that exacts a penalty equal to the harm done by the offender.

2. Objection: Miscarriages of justice occur. Capital punishment is to be rejected because of human fallibility in convicting innocent parties and sentencing them to death. In a survey done in 1985, Hugo Adam Bedau and Michael Radelet found that of the 7,000 persons executed in the United States between 1900 and 1985, 25 were innocent of capital crimes.[8] Although some compensation is available to those unjustly imprisoned, the death sentence is irrevocable. We can't compensate the dead. As John Maxton, a member of the British Parliament, puts it, "If we allow one innocent person to be executed, morally we are committing the same, or, in some ways, a worse crime than the person who committed the murder."[9]

Response: Mr. Maxton is incorrect in saying that mistaken judicial execution is morally the same as or worse than murder. A deliberate intention to kill the innocent occurs in a murder, whereas no such intention occurs in wrongful capital punishment.

Sometimes the objection is framed this way: It is better to let ten criminals go free than to execute one innocent person. If this dictum is a call for safeguards, it is well taken, but somewhere there seems to be a limit on the society's tolerance of capital offenses. Would these abolitionists argue that it is better that 50 or 100 or 1,000 murderers go free than that one innocent person be executed? Society has a right to protect itself from capital offenses even if this means taking a finite chance of executing an innocent person. If the basic activity or process is justified, it is regrettable but morally acceptable that some mistakes are made. Fire trucks occasionally kill innocent pedestrians while racing to fires, but we accept these losses as justified by the greater good of the activity of using fire trucks. We judge the use of automobiles to be acceptable even though such use causes an average

of 50,000 traffic fatalities each year. We accept the morality of a defensive war even though it will result in our troops accidentally or mistakenly killing innocent people.

The fact that we can err in applying the death penalty should give us pause and cause us to build an appeals process into the judicial system. Such a process is already in the American and British legal systems. Occasional errors may be made, but as regrettable as this is, it is not a sufficient reason for us to refuse to use the death penalty if, on balance, it serves a just and useful function.

Furthermore, abolitionists are simply misguided in thinking that prison sentences are a satisfactory alternative. It's not clear that we can always or typically compensate innocent parties who waste away in prison. Jacques Barzun has argued that a prison sentence can be worse than death and carries all the problems that the death penalty does regarding the impossibility of compensation:

In the preface of his useful volume of cases, *Hanged in Error*, Mr. Leslie Hale refers to the tardy recognition of a minor miscarriage of justice—one year in jail: "The prisoner emerged to find that his wife had died and that his children and his aged parents had been removed to the workhouse. By the time a small payment had been assessed as 'compensation' the victim was incurably insane." So far we are as indignant with the law as Mr. Hale. But what comes next? He cites the famous Evans case, in which it is very probable that the wrong man was hanged, and he exclaims: "While such mistakes are possible, should society impose an irrevocable sentence?" Does Mr. Hale really ask us to believe that the sentence passed on the first man, whose wife died and who went insane, was in any sense *revocable*? Would not any man rather be Evans dead than that other wretch "emerging" with his small compensation and his reason for living gone?[10]

The abolitionist is incorrect in arguing that death is different than long-term prison sentences because it is irrevocable. Imprisonment also takes good things away from us that may never be returned. We cannot restore to an inmate the freedom or opportunities he or she lost. Suppose an innocent twenty-five-year-old man is given a life sentence for murder. Thirty years later the mistake is discovered and he is set free. Suppose he equates three years of freedom to every one year of life. That is, he would rather live ten years as a free man than thirty as a prisoner. Given this man's values, the criminal justice system has taken the equivalent of ten years of life from him. If he lives until he is sixty-five, he has, by his estimate, lost ten years, so he may be said to have lived only fifty-five years.[11]

The numbers in this example are arbitrary, but the basic point is sound. Most of us would prefer a short life of high quality to a longer one of low quality. Death prevents all subsequent quality, but imprisonment also irrevocably harms one in diminishing the quality of life of the prisoner.

3. Objection: The death penalty is unjust because it discriminates against the poor and minorities, particularly African Americans. Former Supreme Court Justice William Douglas wrote that "a law which reaches that [discriminatory] result in practice has no more sanctity than a law which in terms provides the same."[12] Nathanson argues that "in many cases, whether one is treated justly or not depends not only on what one deserves but on how other people are treated."[13] He offers the example of unequal justice in a plagiarism case. "I tell the students in my class that anyone who plagiarizes will fail the course. Three students plagiarize papers, but I give only one a failing grade. The other two, in describing their motivation, win my sympathy, and I give them passing grades." Arguing that this is patently unjust, he likens this case to the imposition of the death penalty and concludes that it too is unjust.

Response: First of all, it is not true that a law applied in a discriminatory manner is unjust. Unequal justice is no less justice, however uneven its application. The discriminatory application, not the law itself, is unjust. A just law is still just, even if it is not applied consistently. For example, a friend of mine once got two speeding tickets during a 100-mile trip (having borrowed my car). He complained to the police officer who gave him his second ticket that many drivers were driving faster than he was at the time. They

had escaped detection, he argued, so it wasn't fair for him to get two tickets on one trip. The officer acknowledged the imperfections of the system but, justifiably, had no qualms about giving him the second ticket. Unequal justice is still justice, however regrettable. So Justice Douglas is wrong in asserting that discriminatory results invalidate the law itself. The discriminatory practice should be reformed, and in many cases it can be. But imperfect practices in themselves do not entail that the laws engendering these practices are themselves unjust.

With regard to Nathanson's analogy in the plagiarism case, two things should be said against it. First, if the teacher is convinced that the motivational factors are mitigating factors, then he or she may be justified in passing two of the plagiarizing students. Suppose that one student did no work whatsoever, showed no interest (Nathanson's motivation factor) in learning, and exhibited no remorse in cheating, whereas the other two spent long hours seriously studying the material and, upon apprehension, showed genuine remorse for their misdeeds. To be sure, they yielded to temptation at certain—though limited—sections of their long papers, but the vast majority of their papers represented their own diligent work. Suppose also that all three had C averages at this point. The teacher gives the unremorseful, gross plagiarizer an F but relents and gives the other two Ds. Her actions parallel the judge's use of mitigating circumstances and cannot be construed as arbitrary, let alone unjust.

The second problem with Nathanson's analogy is that it would have disastrous consequences for law and benevolent practices alike. If we concluded that we should abolish a rule or practice unless we always treated everyone by exactly the same rules, we would have to abolish, for example, traffic laws and laws against imprisonment for rape, theft, and even murder. Carried to its logical limits, we would also have to refrain from saving drowning victims if a number of people were drowning but only a few of them could be saved. Imperfect justice is the best that we humans can attain. We should reform our practices as much as possible to eradicate unjust discrimination wherever we can, but if we are not allowed to have a law without perfect application, we will be forced to have no laws at all.

Nathanson acknowledges this response but argues that the case of death is different. "Because of its finality and extreme severity of the death penalty, we need to be more scrupulous in applying it as punishment than is necessary with any other punishment."[14] The retentionist agrees that the death penalty is a severe punishment and that we need to be scrupulous in applying it. The difference between the abolitionist and the retentionist seems to lie in whether we are wise and committed enough as a nation to reform our institutions so that they approximate fairness. Apparently Nathanson is pessimistic here, whereas I have faith in our ability to learn from our mistakes and reform our systems. If we can't reform our legal system, what hope is there for us?

More specifically, the charge that a higher percentage of blacks than whites are executed was once true but is no longer so. Many states have made significant changes in sentencing procedures, with the result that currently whites convicted of first-degree murder are sentenced to death at a higher rate than blacks.[15]

One must be careful in reading too much into these statistics. Although great disparities in statistics should cause us to examine our judicial procedures, they do not in themselves prove injustice. For example, more males than females are convicted of violent crimes (almost 90 percent of those convicted of violent crimes are males—a virtually universal statistic), but this is not strong evidence that the law is unfair, for there are psychological explanations for the disparity in convictions. Males are on average and by nature more aggressive (usually tied to testosterone) than females. Likewise, there may be good explanations for why people of one ethnic group commit more crimes than do those of other groups, explanations that do not impugn the processes of the judicial system.[16]

4. *Objection:* The death penalty is a "cruel and unusual" punishment. It constitutes a denial of the wrongdoer's essential dignity as a human being. No matter

how bad a person becomes, no matter how terrible one's deed, we must never cease to regard a person as an end in himself or herself, as someone with inherent dignity. Capital punishment violates that dignity. As such, it violates the Constitution of the United States of America, which forbids "cruel and unusual" punishments. Here is how Justice Thurgood Marshall stated it in *Gregg v. Georgia:*

> To be sustained under the Eighth Amendment, the death penalty must [comport] with the basic concept of human dignity at the core of the Amendment; the objective in imposing it must be [consistent] with our respect for the dignity of [other] men. Under these standards, the taking of life "because the wrongdoer deserves it" surely must fail, for such a punishment has as its very basis the total denial of the wrongdoer's dignity and worth. The death penalty, unnecessary to promote the goal of deterrence or to further any legitimate notion of retribution, is an excessive penalty forbidden by the Eighth and Fourteenth Amendments.[17]

Similarly, in *Furman v. Georgia* (1972) Justice William Brennan condemned capital punishment because it treats "members of the human race as nonhumans, as objects to be toyed with and discarded," adding that it is "inconsistent with the fundamental premise of the Clause that even the vilest criminal remains a human being possessed of common human dignity."[18]

Response: First of all, Justice Marshall differs with the framers of the Constitution about the meaning of "cruel and unusual" in declaring that the death penalty violates the Eighth Amendment's prohibition against "cruel and unusual" punishments—unless one would accuse the framers of the Constitution of contradicting themselves. The Fifth and Fourteenth Amendments clearly authorize the death penalty.[19] The phrase "cruel and unusual" in the Eighth Amendment seems to mean cruel and *uncustomary or new* punishments, for, as van den Haag notes, "the framers did not want judges to invent *new* cruel punishments, but did not abolish customary ones."[20] However, even if the framers did intend to prohibit the death penalty, I would argue that it is morally justified. The law is not always identical to what is morally correct.

Rather than being a violation of a wrongdoer's dignity, capital punishment may constitute a recognition of human dignity. As noted in the discussion in Kant's view of retribution, the use of capital punishment respects the worth of victims in calling for an equal punishment to be extracted from offenders, and it respects the dignity of the offenders in treating them as free agents who must be respected for their decisions and who must bear the cost of their acts as responsible agents.

Let's look at these two points a bit more closely. The first—that capital punishment respects the worth of the victim—is bluntly articulated by newspaper columnist Mike Royko:

When I think of the thousands of inhabitants of Death Rows in the hundreds of prisons in this country, I don't react the way the kindly souls do—with revulsion that the state would take these lives. My reaction is: What's taking us so long? Let's get that electrical current flowing. Drop the pellets now!

Whenever I argue this with friends who have opposite views, they say that I don't have enough regard for that most marvelous of miracles—human life.

Just the opposite: It's because I have so much regard for human life that I favor capital punishment. Murder is the most terrible crime there is. Anything less than the death penalty is an insult to the victim and society. It says, in effect, that we don't value the victim's life enough to punish the killer fully.[21]

It is precisely because the victim's life is sacred that the death penalty is sometimes the only fitting punishment for first-degree murder. I am accepting here the idea that there is something "sacred" or "dignified" about human life, although earlier I gave reasons that should cause secularists to doubt this.

Second, it's precisely because murderers are autonomous, free agents that we regard their acts of murder as their own and hold them responsible. Not to hold a murderer responsible for his crime is to treat him as less than autonomous. Just as we praise and reward people in proportion to the merit of their good deeds, so we blame and punish them in proportion to the evil of their bad deeds. If there is evidence that the offender did not act freely, we would mitigate his sentence, but if he acted of his own free will, he bears the responsibility for those actions and deserves to be punished accordingly.

Of course, there are counterresponses to all of the retentionist's responses. Consider the utilitarian matter of cost. The appeals process, which is necessary to our system of justice, is so prolonged and expensive that it might not be worth the costs simply to satisfy our sense of retribution. Furthermore, most moderate retributivists do not argue that there is an absolute duty to execute first-degree murderers. Even the principle that the guilty should suffer in proportion to the harm they caused is not absolute; it can be overridden by mercy. But such mercy must be judicious, serving the public good.

In the same vein many argue that life imprisonment without parole will accomplish just as much as the death penalty. The retentionist would respond that death is a more fitting punishment for one who kills in cold blood, and utilitarians (deterrentists) would be concerned about the possibility of escape, murders committed by the murderer while incarcerated, and the enormous costs of keeping a prisoner incarcerated for life. Imprisonment without parole, advocated by many abolitionists as an alternative to the death penalty, should be given serious consideration in special cases, such as when there is evidence that the murderer has suitably repented. Even in these cases, however, the desert argument and the Best Bet argument lean toward the death penalty.

No doubt we should work toward the day when capital punishment is no longer necessary: when the murder rate becomes a tiny fraction of what it is today, when a civilized society can safely incarcerate the few violent criminals in its midst, and when moral reform of the criminal is a reality. Perhaps this is why several European nations have abolished capital punishment (e.g., the murder rate in one year in Detroit alone was 732 times that of the nation of Austria). I for one regret the use of the death penalty. I would vote for its abolition in an instant if only one condition were met: that those contemplating murder would set an example for me. Otherwise, it is better that the murderer perish than that innocent victims be cut down by the murderer's knife or bullet.

ENDNOTES

1. Karl Marx, "Critique of the Gotha Program," *Karl Marx: Selected Writings,* ed. B. McLellan (Oxford: Oxford University Press, 1977). For a fuller discussion of desert, see my article "Equality and Desert," *What Do We Deserve,* eds. L. Pojman and O. McLeod (Oxford: Oxford University Press, 1998).

2. Michael Davis has an excellent discussion of "humane punishment" in "Death, Deterrence, and the Method of Common Sense," *Social Theory and Practice* (summer 1981).

3. Isaac Ehrlich, "The Deterrent Effect of Capital Punishment: A Question of Life and Death," *American Economic Review* 65 (June 1975): 397–417.

4. Ernst van den Haag, "On Deterrence and the Death Penalty," *Ethics,* 78 (July 1968).

5. The Best Bet argument rejects the passive–active distinction involved in killing and letting die. Many people think that it is far worse to kill someone than to let him die, even with the same motivation. More generally, they hold that it is worse to *do* something bad than to *allow* something bad to happen. I think people feel this way because they are tacitly supposing different motivational stances. Judith Jarvis Thomson gives the following counterexample to this doctrine: John is a trolley driver who suddenly realizes that his brakes have failed. He is heading for a group of workers on the track before him and will certainly kill them if something isn't done immediately. Fortunately, there is a side track to the right onto which John can turn the trolley. Unfortunately, there is one worker on that track who will be killed if John steers the trolley onto the side track.

If the passive–active distinction holds, John should do nothing but simply allow the trolley to take its toll of the five men on the track before him, but that seems terrible. Surely by turning quickly and causing the trolley to move onto the side track, John will be saving a total of four lives. It seems morally preferable for John to turn the trolley onto the side track and actively cause the death of one man rather than passively allow the death of five. John is caught in a situation in which he cannot help doing or allowing harm, but he can act so that the lesser of the evils obtains.

6. van den Haag, op. cit.

7. British Parliamentary Debates, 1982, quoted in Sorrell, *Moral Theory,* 43.

8. Hugo Adam Bedau and Michael Radelet, *Miscarriages of Justice in Potential Capital Cases* (1st draft Oct. 1985, on file at Harvard Law School Library), quoted in E. van den Haag, "The Ultimate Punishment: A Defense," *Harvard Law Review,* 99, no. 7 (May 1896): 1664.

9. Ibid., 47.

10. Jacques Barzun, "In Favor of Capital Punishment," *The American Scholar,* 31, no. 2 (spring 1962).

11. I have been influenced by similar arguments by Michael Levin (unpublished manuscript) and Michael Davis, "Is the Death Penalty Irrevocable?" *Social Theory and Practice* 10:2 (summer 1984).

12. Justice William Douglas in *Furman v. Georgia* 408 U.S. 238 (1972).

13. Stephen Nathanson, *An Eye for an Eye?* (Totowa, NJ: Roman & Littlefield, 1987) 62.

14. Ibid., 67.

15. The Department of Justice's *Bureau of Justice Statistics Bulletin* for 1994 reports that between 1977 and 1994, 2,336 (51%) of those arrested for murder were white, 1838 (40%) were black, 316 (7%) were Hispanic. Of the 257 who were executed, 140 (54%) were white, 98 (38%) were black, 17 (7%) were Hispanic, and 2 (1%) were of other races. In 1994, 31 prisoners, 20 white men and 11 black men, were executed, although whites made up only 7,532 (41%) and blacks 9,906 (56%) of those arrested for murder. Of those sentenced to death in 1994, 158 were white men, 133 were black men, 25 were Hispanic men, 2 were Native American men, 2 were white women, and 3 were black women. Of those sentenced, relatively more blacks (72%) than whites (65%) or Hispanics (60%), had prior felony records. Overall, the criminal justice system does not seem to favor white criminals over black, though it does seem to favor rich defendants over poor ones.

16. For instance, according to FBI figures for 1992, the U.S. murder rate was 9.3, far higher than that of France (4.5), Germany (3.9) or Austria (3.9). Of the 23,760 murders committed in the United States that year, 55% of the offenders whose race was known were black and 43% white. Since blacks compose 12.1% of the U.S. population, the murder rate for blacks in 1992 was 45 per 100,000, while that for whites was 4.78—a figure much closer to that for European whites.

17. Justice Thurgood Marshall, *Gregg v. Georgia* (1976).

18. Justice William Brennan, *Furman v. Georgia* (1972).

19. The Fifth Amendment permits depriving people of "life, liberty or property" if the deprivation occurs with "due process of law," and the Fourteenth Amendment applies this provision to the states: "no State shall . . . deprive any person of life, liberty, or property, without due process of law."

20. Ernest van den Haag, "Why Capital Punishment?" *Albany Law Review* 54 (1990).

21. Mike Royko, *Chicago Sun-Times,* September 1983.

Capital Punishment

Anthony G. Amsterdam

My discussion of capital punishment will proceed in three stages. *First,* I would like to set forth certain basic factual realities about capital punishment, like the fact that capital punishment is a fancy word for legally killing people. Please forgive me for beginning with such obvious and ugly facts. Much of our political and philosophical debate about the death penalty is carried on in language calculated to conceal these realities and their implications. The implications, I will suggest, are that capital punishment is a great evil: surely the greatest evil except for war that our society can intentionally choose to commit.

This does not mean that we should do away with capital punishment. Some evils, like war, are occasionally necessary; and perhaps capital punishment is one of them. But the fact that it is a great evil means that we should not choose to do it without some very good and solid reason of which we are satisfactorily convinced upon sufficient evidence. The conclusion of my first point simply is that the burden of proof upon the question of capital punishment rightly rests on those who are asking us to use our laws to kill people with; and that this is a very heavy burden.

Second, I want to review the justifications that have been advanced to support capital punishment. I want to explore with you concepts such as retribution and deterrence, and some of the assumptions and evidence about them. The conclusion of my sec-

ond point will be that none of the reasons which we like to give ourselves for executing criminals can begin to sustain the burden of proof that rightfully rests upon them.

Third, I would like to say a word about history— about the slow but absolutely certain progress of maturing civilization that will bring an inevitable end to the punishment of death. That history does not give us the choice between perpetuating and abolishing capital punishment, because we could not perpetuate it if we wanted to. Our choice is narrower but not unimportant: whether we shall be numbered among the last generations of legal killers, or remembered as the first generation to put legal killing aside. I will end by asking you to cast your choice for life instead of death. But, first, let me begin with some basic facts about the death penalty.

The most basic fact, of course, is that capital punishment means taking living, breathing men and women, stuffing them into a chair, strapping them down, pulling a lever, and exterminating them. We have almost forgotten this fact because there have been no executions in this country for more than ten years, except for Gary Gilmore whose combined suicide and circus were so wildly extravagant as to seem unreal. For many people, capital punishment has become a sanitized and symbolic issue: Do you or do you not support your local police? Do you or do you not care enough about crime to get tough with criminals? These abstractions were never what capital punishment was about, although it was possible to think so during the ten-year moratorium on execu-

Anthony G. Amsterdam, "Capital Punishment," *Vital Speeches* (July 8, 1977): 677–82 (edited). Reprinted with permission of *Vital Speeches.*

tions caused by constitutional challenges to the death penalty in the courts. That is no longer possible. The courts have now said that we can start up executions again, if we want to. Today, a vote for capital punishment is a vote to kill real, live people.

What this means is, first, that we bring a man or woman into court and put them through a trial for their lives. They are expected to sit back quietly and observe decent courtroom decorum throughout a proceeding whose purpose is slowly and systematically to kill them. The jury hears evidence and votes; and you can always tell when a jury has voted for death because they come back into court and they will not look the defendant or defense counsel in the eyes. The judge pronounces sentence and the defendant is taken away to be held in a cell for two to six years, hoping that his appeals will succeed, not really knowing what they are all about, but knowing that if they fail, he will be taken out and cinched down and put to death. Most of the people in prison are reasonably nice to him, and even a little apologetic; but he realizes every day for that seven hundred or twenty-one hundred days that they are holding him there helpless for the approaching slaughter; and that, once the final order is given, they will truss him up and kill him, and that nobody in that vast surrounding machinery of public officials and servants of the law will raise a finger to save him. This is why Camus once wrote that an execution

" . . . is not simply death. It is just as different . . . from the privation of life as a concentration camp is from prison . . . It adds to death a rule, a public premeditation known to the future victim, an organization . . . which is itself a source of moral sufferings more terrible than death. . . . [Capital punishment] is . . . the most premeditated of murders, to which no criminal's deed, however calculated . . . , can be compared. . . . For there to be an equivalence, the death penalty would have to punish a criminal who had warned his victim of the date at which he would inflict a horrible death on him and who, from that moment onward, had confined him at his mercy for months. Such a monster is not encountered in private life."

I will spare you descriptions of the execution itself. Evelle Younger speaks to you next week, and he will probably describe some very gory, gruesome murders to you. All murders are horrible things, and executions are usually a lot cleaner physically— although, like Camus, I have never heard of a murderer who held his victim captive for two or more years waiting as the minutes and the hours ticked away toward his preannounced death. The clinical details of an execution are as unimaginable to me as they are to most of you. We have not permitted public executions in this country for over forty years. The law in every State forbids more than a few people to watch the deed done behind prison walls. Seven months ago, a federal judge in Texas ruled that executions could be photographed for television; but now the attorneys-general of twenty-five states have asked the federal Court of Appeals to set aside that ruling. I can only leave to your imagination what they are trying so very hard to hide from us. Oh, of course, executions are too hideous to put on television; we all know that. But let us not forget that it is the same hideous thing, done in secret, which we are discussing under abstract labels like "capital punishment" that permit us to talk about the subject over lunch instead of spitting up.

In any event, Mr. Younger will probably tell you about some very horrible murders, and I decline to insult your intelligence by playing "can you top this" with issues of life and death. I ask you only to remember two things, if and when you hear such descriptions.

First, the murders being described are not murders that are being done by us, or in our name, or with our approval; and our power to stop them is exceedingly limited even under the most exaggerated suppositions of deterrence, which I shall shortly return to question. Every execution, on the other hand, is done by our paid servants, in our collective name, and we can stop them all. Please do not be bamboozled into thinking that people who are against executions are in favor of murders. If we had the individual or the collective power to stop murders, we would stop them all—and for the same basic reason that we want to stop executions. Murders and executions are both ugly, vicious things, because they destroy the same sacred and mysterious gift of life which we do not understand and can never restore.

Second, please remember therefore that descriptions of murders are relevant to the subject of capital punishment only on the theory that two wrongs make a right, or that killing murderers can assuage their victims' sufferings or bring them back to life, or that capital punishment is the best deterrent to murder. The first two propositions are absurd, and the third is debatable—although, as I shall later show, the evidence is overwhelmingly against it. My present point is only that deterrence *is* debatable, whereas we *know* that persons whom we execute are dead beyond recall, no matter how the debate about deterrence comes out. That is a sufficient reason, I believe, why the burden of proof on the issue of deterrence should be places squarely upon the executioners.

There are other reasons too. Let me try to state them briefly.

Capital punishment not merely kills people; it also kills some of them in error; and these are errors which we can never correct. When I speak about legal error, I do not mean only the question whether "they got the right man" or killed somebody who "didn't do it." Errors of that sort do occur: Timothy Evans, for example—an innocent man whose execution was among the reasons for the abolition of the death penalty in Great Britain. If you read Anthony Scaduto's recent book, *Scapegoat,* you will come away with unanswerable doubts whether Bruno Richard Hauptmann was really guilt of kidnapping of the Lindbergh infant for which he was executed, or whether we killed Hauptmann, too, for a crime he did not commit. In 1975, the Florida Cabinet pardoned two black men, Freddie Lee Pitts and Wilbert Lee, who were twice tried and sentenced to death and spent twelve years apiece on death row for a murder committed by somebody else. This one, I am usually glibly told, "does not count," because Pitts and Lee were never actually put to death. Take comfort if you will but I cannot, for I know that only the general constitutional attack which we were then mounting upon the death penalty in Florida kept Pitts and Lee alive along enough to permit discovery of the evidence of their innocence. Our constitutional attack is now dead, and so would Pitts and Lee be if they were tried tomorrow. Sure, we catch some errors. But

we often catch them by extremely lucky breaks that could as easily not have happened. I represented a young man in North Carolina who came within a hair's breadth of being the Gary Gilmore of his day. Like Gilmore, he became so depressed under a death sentence that he tried to dismiss his appeal; he was barely talked out of it; his conviction was reversed; and on retrial jury acquitted him in eleven minutes.

We do not know how many "wrong men" have been executed. We think and pray that it is rare—although we can't be sure because, after a man is dead, people seldom continue to investigate the possibility that he was innocent. But that is not the biggest source of error anyway.

What about *legal* error? In 1968, the Supreme Court of the United States held that it was unconstitutional to exclude citizens from capital trial juries simply because they had general conscientious or religious objections to the death penalty. That decision was held retroactive; and I represented sixty or seventy men whose death sentences were subsequently set aside for constitutional errors in jury selection. While researching their cases, I found the cases of at least as many more men who had already been executed on the basis of trials infected with identical errors. Eight days ago, we finally won a decision from the Supreme Court of the United States that the death penalty is excessively harsh and therefore unconstitutional for the crime of rape. Fine, but it comes too late for the 455 men executed for rape in this country since 1930—405 of them black. In 1975, the Supreme Court held that the constitutional presumption of innocence forbids a trial judge to tell the jury that the burden of proof is on a homicide defendant to show provocation which reduces murder to manslaughter. Three weeks ago, the Court held that this decision was also retroactive. Jury charges of precisely that kind were standard forms for more than a century in many American states that punished murder with death. Can we even begin to guess how many people were unconstitutionally executed under this so-called retroactive decision?

Now what about errors of fact that go to the degree of culpability of a crime? In many States, the difference between first and second degree murder—

or between capital and non-capital murder—depends on whether the defendant acted with something called "premeditation" as distinguished from intent to kill. Premeditation means intent formed beforehand, but no particular amount of time is required. Courts tell juries that premeditation "may be as instantaneous as successive thoughts in the mind." Mr. Justice Cardozo wrote that *he* did not understand the concept of premeditation after several decades of studying and trying to apply it as a judge. Yet this is the kind of question to which a jury's answer spells out life or death in a capital trial—this, and the questions whether the defendant had "malice aforethought," or "provocation and passion," or "insanity," or the "reasonableness" necessary for killing in self-defense. I think of another black client, Johnny Coleman, whose conviction and death sentence for killing a white truck driver named "Screwdriver" Johnson we twice got reversed by the Supreme Court of the United States. On retrial a jury acquitted him on the grounds of self-defense upon exactly the same evidence that an earlier jury had had when it sentenced him to die. When ungraspable legal standards are thus applied to intangible mental states, there is not merely the possibility but the actuarial certainty that juries deciding substantial volumes of cases are going to be wrong in an absolutely large number of them. If you accept capital punishment, you must accept the reality—not the risk, but the reality—that we shall kill people whom the law says that it is not proper to kill. No other outcome is possible when we presume to administer an infallible punishment through a fallible system.

You will notice that I have taken examples of black defendants as some of my cases of legal error. There is every reason to believe that discrimination on grounds of race and poverty fatally infect the administration of capital justice in this country. Since 1930, an almost equal number of white and black defendants has been executed for the crime of murder, although blacks constituted only about a tenth of the nation's population during this period. No sufficiently careful studies have been done of these cases, controlling other variables than race, so as to determine exactly what part race played in the outcome.

But when that kind of systematic study *was* done in rape cases, it showed beyond the statistical possibility of a doubt that black men who raped white women were disproportionately sentenced to die on the basis of race alone. Are you prepared to believe that juries which succumbed to conscious or unconscious racial prejudices in rape cases were or are able to put those prejudices wholly aside where the crime charged is murder? Is it not much more plausible to believe that even the most conscientious juror—or judge, or prosecuting attorney—will be slower to want to inflict the death penalty on a defendant with whom he can identify as a human being; and that the process of identification in our society is going to be very seriously affected by racial identity? There have been two studies—one by the Stanford Law Review and the other by the Texas Judicial Council—which found no racial discrimination in capital sentencing in certain murder cases. But both of these studies had methodological problems and limitations; and both of them also found death-sentencing discrimination against the economically poor, who come disproportionately from minorities. The sum of the evidence stands where the National Crime Commission found it ten years ago, when it described the following "discriminatory patterns. The death sentence," said the Commission, "is disproportionately imposed and carried out on the poor, the Negro, and members of unpopular groups."

Apart from discrimination, there is a haphazard, crazy-quilt character about the administration of capital punishment that every knowledgeable lawyer or observer can describe but none can rationally explain. Some juries are hanging juries; some counties are hanging counties; some years are hanging years; and men live or die depending on these flukes.

However atrocious the crime may have been for which a particular defendant is sentenced to die, "[e]xperienced wardens know many prisoners serving life or less whose crimes were equally, or more atrocious." That is a quotation, by the way, from former Attorney General Ramsey Clark's statement to a congressional subcommittee; and Wardens Lewis Lawes, Clinton Duffy and others have said the same thing.

With it I come to the end of my first point. I submit that the deliberate judicial extinction of human life is intrinsically so final and so terrible an act as to cast the burden of proof for its justification upon those who want us to do it. But certainly when that act is executed through a fallible system which assures that we will kill some people wrongly, others because they are black or poor or personally ugly or socially unacceptable, and all of them quite freakishly in the sense that whether a man lives or dies for any particular crime is a matter of luck and happenstance, *then*, at the least, the burden of justifying capital punishment lies fully and heavily on its proponents.

Let us consider those justifications.

The first and the oldest is the concept of *retribution:* an eye for an eye, a life for a life. You may or may not believe in this kind of retribution, but I will not waste your time debating it because it cannot honestly be used to justify the only form of capital punishment that this country has accepted for the past half century. Even before the judicial moratorium, executions in the United States had dwindled to an average of about thirty a year. Only a rare, sparse handful of convicted murderers was being sentenced to die or executed for the self-same crimes for which many, many times as many murderers were sent away to prison. Obviously, as Herbert Wechsler said a generation ago, the issue of capital punishment is no longer "whether it is fair or just that one who takes another person's life should lose his own. . . . [W]e do not and cannot act upon . . . [that proposition] generally in the administration of the penal law. The problem rather is whether a small and highly random sample of people who commit murder . . . ought to be despatched, while most of those convicted of . . . [identical] crimes are dealt with by imprisonment."

Sometimes the concept of retribution is modernized a little with a notion called *moral reinforcement*—the idea that we should punish very serious crimes very severely in order to demonstrate how much we abhor them. The trouble with *this* justification for capital punishment, of course, is that it completely begs the question, which is *how severely* we ought to punish any particular crime to show appropriate

abhorrence for it. The answer can hardly be found in a literal application of the eye-for-an-eye formula. We do not burn down arsonists' houses or cheat back at bunco artists. But if we ought not punish all crimes exactly according to their kind, then what is the fit moral reinforcement for murder? You might as well say burning at the stake or boiling in oil as simple gassing or electrocution.

Or is it not more plausible—if what we really want to say is that the killing of a human being is wrong and ought to be condemned as clearly as we can—that we should choose the punishment of prison as the fitting means to make this point? So far as moral reinforcement goes, the difference between life imprisonment and capital punishment is precisely that imprisonment continues to respect the value of human life. The plain message of capital punishment, on the other hand, is that life ceases to be sacred whenever someone with the power to take it away decides that there is a sufficiently compelling pragmatic reason to do so.

But there is still another theory of a retributive sort which is often advanced to support the death penalty, particularly in recent years. This is the argument that *we*—(that is, the person making the argument)—*we* no longer believe in the outworn concept of retribution; but the *public*—the great and unwashed masses of the public—*they* believe in retribution; and so we must let them have their prey or they will lose respect for law. Watch for this argument because it is the surest sign of demagogic depravity. It is disgusting in its patronizing attribution to "the public" of a primitive, uneducable bloodthirstiness which the speaker is unprepared to defend but is prepared to exploit as a means of sidestepping the rational and moral limitations of a *just* theory of retribution. It out-judases Judas in its abnegation of governmental responsibility to respond to popular misinformation with enlightenment, instead of seizing on it as a pretext for atrocity. This argument asserts that the proper way to deal with a lynch mob is to string its victim up before they do. I will say no more about it.

Another supposed justification for capital punishment that deserves equally brief treatment is the notion of *isolation* or *specific deterrence*—the idea that we must kill a murderer to prevent him from murdering ever again. The usual forms that this argument takes are that a life sentence does not mean a life sentence—it means parole after seven, or twelve, or twenty-five years—; and that, within prisons themselves, guards and other prisoners are in constant jeopardy of death at the hands of convicted but unexecuted murderers. It amazes me that these argument can be made or taken seriously. Are we really going to kill a human being because we do not trust other people—the people whom we have chosen to serve on our own parole boards—to make a proper judgment in his case at some future time? We trust this same parole board to make far more numerous, difficult and dangerous decisions: hardly a week passes when they do not consider the cases of armed robbers, for example, although armed robbers are much, much more likely statistically to commit future murders than any murderer is to repeat his crime. But pass this point. If we refuse to trust the parole system, then let us provide by law that the murderers whose release we fear shall be given sentences of life imprisonment without parole which *do* mean life imprisonment without parole. I myself would be against that, but it is far more humane than capital punishment, and equally safe.

As for killings inside prisons, if you examine them you will find that they are very rarely done by convicted murderers, but are almost always done by people imprisoned for crimes that no one would think of making punishable by death. Warden Lawes of Sing Sing and Governor Wallace of Alabama, among others, regularly employed murder convicts as house servants because they were among the very safest of prisoners. There are exceptions of course; but these can be handled by adequate prison security. You cannot tell me or believe that a society which is capable of putting a man on the moon is incapable of putting a man in prison, keeping him there, and keeping him from killing while he is there. And if anyone says that this is costly, and that we should kill people in order to reduce government expenditures, I can only reply that the cost of housing a man for life in the most physically secure conditions imaginable is considerably less than the cost of putting the same man through all of the extraordinary legal proceedings necessary to kill him.

That brings me to the last supposed justification for the death penalty: *deterrence*. This is the subject that you most frequently hear debated, and many people who talk about capital punishment talk about nothing else. I have done otherwise today, partly for completeness, partly because it is vital to approach the subject of deterrence knowing precisely what question you want to ask and have answered. I have suggested that the proper question is *whether there is sufficiently convincing evidence that the death penalty deters murder better than does life imprisonment so that you are willing to accept responsibility for doing the known evil act of killing human beings—with all of the attending uglinesses that I have described—on the faith of your conviction in the superior deterrent efficacy of capital punishment.*

If this is the question, then I submit that there is only one fair and reasonable answer. When the Supreme Court of the United States reviewed the evidence last year, it described that evidence as "inconclusive." Do not let Evelle Younger or anybody else tell you that the Supreme Court held the death penalty justifiable as a deterrent. What the Court's plurality opinion said, exactly, was that "there is no convincing evidence *either supporting or refuting* . . . [the] view" that "the death penalty may not function as a significantly greater deterrent than lesser penalties." *Because* the evidence was inconclusive, the Court held that the Constitution did not forbid judgment either way. But if the evidence is inconclusive, is it *your* judgment that we should conclusively kill people on a factual theory that the evidence does not conclusively sustain?

I hope not. But let us examine the evidence more carefully because—even though it is not conclusive—it is very, very substantial; and the overwhelming weight of it refutes the claims of those who say that capital punishment is a better deterrent than life imprisonment for murder.

For more than forty years, criminologists have studied this question by a variety of means. They have compared homicide rates in countries and States that did and did not have capital punishment, or that actually executed people more and less frequently. Some of these studies compared large aggregates of abolitionist and retentionist States; others compared geographically adjacent pairs or triads of States, or States that were chosen because they were comparable in other socio-economic factors that might affect homicide. Other studies compared homicide rates in the same country or State before and after the abolition or reinstatement of capital punishment; or homicide rates for the same geographic area during periods preceding and following well-publicized executions. Special comparative studies were done relating to police killings and prison killings. All in all, there were dozens of studies. Without a single exception, *none* of them found that the death penalty had any statistically significant effect upon the rate of homicide or murder. Often I have heard advocates of capital punishment explain away its failures by likening it to a great lighthouse: "We count the ships that crash," they say, "but we never know how many saw the light and were saved." What these studies show, however, is that coastlines of the same shape and depth and tidal structure, with and without lighthouses, invariably have the same number of shipwrecks per year. On that evidence, would you invest your money in a lighthouse, or would you buy sonar if you really wanted to save lives?

In 1975, the first purportedly scientific study ever to find that capital punishment *did* deter homicides was published. This was done by Isaac Ehrlich of Chicago, who is not a criminologist but an economist. Using regression analysis involving an elaborate mathematical model, Ehrlich reported that every execution deterred something like eight murders. Naturally, supporters of capital punishment hurriedly clambered on the Ehrlich bandwagon.

Unhappily for them, the wagon was a factory reject. Several distinguished econometricians—including a team headed by Lawrence Klein, president of the American Economic Association—reviewed Ehrlich's work and found it fatally flawed with numerous methodological errors. Some of these were technical: it appeared, for example, that Ehrlich had produced his results by the unjustified and unex-plained use of a logarithmic form of regression equation instead of the more conventional linear form—which made his findings of deterrence vanish. Equally important, it was shown that Ehrlich's findings depended entirely on data from the post-1962 period, when executions declined and the homicide rate rose *as a part of a general rise in the over-all crime rate that Ehrlich incredibly failed to consider.* Incidentally, the non-scientific proponents of capital punishment are also fond of suggesting that the rise in homicide rates in the 1960's and the 1970's, when executions were halted, proves that executions used to deter homicides. This is ridiculous when you consider that crime as a whole has increased during this period; that homicide rates have increased about *half* as much as the rates for all other F.B.I. Index crimes; and that whatever factors are affecting the rise of most non-capital crimes (which *cannot* include cessation of executions) almost certainly affect the homicide-rate rise also.

In any event, Ehrlich's study was discredited; and a second, methodologically inferior study by a fellow named Yunker is not even worth criticizing here. These are the only two scientific studies in forty years, I repeat, which have ever purported to find deterrence. On the other hand, several recent studies have been completed by researchers who adopted Ehrlich's basic regression-analysis approach but corrected its defects. Peter Passell did such a study finding no deterrence. Kenneth Avio did such a study finding no deterrence. Brian Forst did such a study finding no deterrence. If you want to review all of these studies yourselves, you may find them discussed and cited in an excellent article that just appeared in the 1976 *Supreme Court Review* by Hans Zeisel, at page 317. The conclusion you will have to draw is that—during forty years and today—the scientific community has looked and looked and looked for any reliable evidence that capital punishment deters homicide better than life imprisonment; and it has found no such evidence at all.

Next week Evelle Younger will probably tell you about a different kind of study: one that was done by the Los Angeles Police Department. Police officers asked arrested robbers who did not carry guns, or did not use them, *why* they did not; and the answers, supposedly, were frequently that the robber "did not want to get the death penalty." It is noteworthy that the Los Angeles Police Department has consistently refused to furnish copies of this study and its underlying data to professional scholars, apparently for fear of criticism. I finally obtained a copy of the study from a legislative source, and I can tell you that it shows two things. First, an arrested person will tell a police officer anything that he thinks the officer wants to hear. Second, police officers—like all other human beings—hear what we want to hear. When a robber tries to say that he did not carry or use a gun because he did not wish to risk the penalties for homicide, he will describe those penalties in terms of whatever the law happens to be at that time and place. In Minnesota, which has no death penalty, he will say "I didn't want to get life imprisonment." In Los Angeles, he will say "I didn't want to get the death penalty." Both responses mean the same thing; neither tells you that death is a superior deterrent to life imprisonment.

The real mainstay of the deterrence thesis, however, is not evidence but intuition. You and I ask ourselves: are we not afraid to die? Of course! Would the threat of death, then, not intimidate us to forbear from a criminal act? Certainly! *Therefore,* capital punishment must be a deterrent. The trouble with this intuition is that the people who are doing the reasoning and the people who are doing the murdering are not the same people. You and I do not commit murder for a lot of reasons other than the death penalty. The death penalty might perhaps also deter us from murdering—but altogether needlessly, since we would not murder with it or without it. Those who are sufficiently dissocialized to murder are not responding to the world in the way that we are; and we simply cannot "intuit" their thinking processes from ours.

Consider, for example, the well-documented cases of persons who kill *because* there is a death penalty. One of these was Pamela Watkins, a baby sitter in San Jose who had made several unsuccessful suicide attempts and was frightened to try again. She finally strangled two children so that the State of Cal-

ifornia would execute her. In various bizarre forms, this "suicide-murder" syndrome is reported by psychiatrists again and again. (Parenthetically, Gary Gilmore was probably such a case.) If you intuit that somewhere, sometime, the death penalty *does* deter some potential murderers, are you also prepared to intuit that their numbers mathematically exceed the numbers of these wretched people who are actually induced to murder by the existence of capital punishment?

Here, I suggest, our intuition does—or should— fail, just as the evidence certainly does fail, to establish a deterrent justification for the death penalty. There is simply no credible evidence, and there is no rational way of reasoning about the real facts once you know them, which can sustain this or any other justification with the degree of confidence that should be demanded before a civilized society deliberately extinguishes human life.

I have only a little time for my final point, but it is sufficient because the point is perfectly plain. Capital punishment is a dying institution in this last quarter of the Twentieth Century. It has already been abandoned in law or in fact throughout most of the civilized world. England, Canada, the Scandinavian countries, virtually all of Western Europe except for France and Spain, have abolished the death penalty. The vast majority of countries in the Western Hemisphere have abolished it. Its last strongholds in the world—apart from the United States—are in Asia and Africa, particularly South Africa. Even the countries which maintain capital punishment on the books have almost totally ceased to use it in fact. In the United States, considering only the last half-century, executions have plummeted from 199 in 1935 to approximately 29 a year during the decade before 1967, when the ten-year judicial moratorium began.

Do you doubt that this development will continue? Do you doubt that it will continue because it is the path of civilization—the path up out of fear and terror and the barbarism that terror breeds, into self-confidence and decency in the administration of justice? The road, like any other built by men, has its detours; but over many generations it has run true, and will run true. And there will therefore come a time—perhaps in twenty years, perhaps in fifty or a hundred, but very surely and very shortly as the lifetime of nations is measured—when our children will look back at us in horror and unbelief because of what we did in their names and for their supposed safety, just as we look back in horror and unbelief at the thousands of crucifixions and beheadings and live disembowelments that our ancestors practiced for the supposed purpose of making our world safe from murderers and robbers, thieves, shoplifters, and pickpockets. All of these kinds of criminals are still with us, and will still be with our children—although we can certainly decrease their numbers and their damage, and protect ourselves from them a lot better, if we insist that our politicians stop pounding on the whipping boy of capital punishment and start coming up with some real solutions to the real problems of crime. Our children will cease to execute murderers for the same reason that we have ceased to string up pickpockets and shoplifters at the public crossroads, although there are still plenty of them around. Our children will cease to execute murderers because executions are a self-deluding, self-defeating, self-degrading, futile and entirely stupid means of dealing with the crime of murder, and because our children will prefer to be something better than murderers themselves. Should we not—can we not—make the same choice now?

CASES FOR ANALYSIS

1. Redemption and Capital Punishment

(CBS/AP)—Convicted killer Stanley Tookie Williams, the Crips gang co-founder whose case stirred a national debate about capital punishment versus the possibility of redemption, was executed Tuesday morning.

Williams, 51, died at 12:35 a.m. . . .

Five of his supporters witnessed his death.

"One witness pumped his fist in the air, a symbol of black power," said Crystal Carreon of the Sacramento Bee.

And three of Williams supporters shouted as they left the room after his death.

Barbara Becknell and the supporters said, "the State Of California just killed an innocent man," said Rita Cosby of MSNBC, another media witness. . . .

The case became the state's highest-profile execution in decades. Hollywood stars and capital punishment foes argued that Williams' sentence should be commuted to life in prison because he had made amends by writing children's books about the dangers of gangs and violence.

In the days leading up to the execution, state and federal courts refused to reopen his case. Monday, Gov. Arnold Schwarzenegger denied Williams' request for clemency, suggesting that his supposed change of heart was not genuine because he had not shown any real remorse for the killings committed by the Crips.

"Is Williams' redemption complete and sincere, or is it just a hollow promise?" Schwarzenegger wrote. "Without an apology and atonement for these senseless and brutal killings, there can be no redemption."

Williams was condemned in 1981 for gunning down convenience store clerk Albert Owens, 26, at a 7-Eleven in Whittier and killing Yen-I Yang, 76, Tsai-Shai Chen Yang, 63, and the couple's daughter Yu-Chin Yang Lin, 43, at the Los Angeles motel they owned. Williams claimed he was innocent.

Witnesses at the trial said he boasted about the killings, stating "You should have heard the way he sounded when I shot him." Williams then made a growling noise and laughed for five to six minutes, according to the transcript that the governor referenced in his denial of clemency. . . .

Among the celebrities who took up Williams' cause were Jamie Foxx, who played the gang leader in a cable movie about Williams; rapper Snoop Dogg, himself a former Crip; Sister Helen Prejean, the nun depicted in "Dead Man Walking"; and Bianca Jagger. During Williams' 24 years on death row, a Swiss legislator, college professors and others nominated him for the Nobel Prizes in peace and literature.

"There is no part of me that existed then that exists now," Williams said recently during an interview with The Associated Press.*

Suppose Williams was guilty of the murders for which he was convicted, and suppose he had a genuine change of heart and performed many commendable deeds while in prison. Should Williams' sentence then have been commuted to life in prison? Why or why not? Is redemption compatible with justice? If a murderer mends his ways, should this change have an effect on his punishment? Is mercy (giving someone a break) compatible with justice (giving someone what he deserves)?

*"Tookie Williams Is Executed," *CBSNews.com,* 13 December 2005, www.cbsnews.com/stories/2005/12/13/national/main1121576.shtml (accessed 25 February 2006). Reprinted with permission of The Associated Press. © 2005, CBS Broadcasting, Inc. Used by permission of CBS Broadcasting, Inc.

---

2. Cruel and Unusual Punishment

(Washington Post)—The Supreme Court agreed yesterday to decide when death row inmates may challenge lethal injection as a method of capital punishment, in a surprise decision issued after the justices dramatically stopped the execution of a Florida prisoner who was already strapped to a gurney preparing to die.

Clarence E. Hill, 48, convicted of murdering a Pensacola police officer in 1982, had refused a final meal and needles had punctured his arm when the Supreme Court stayed his execution. The court said it would hear his claim that he should have an opportunity to argue that his civil rights would be violated because the chemicals used to execute him would cause excessive pain.

It is a claim that has been pressed with growing frequency by capital defense lawyers around the country in recent years—but that has generally not yet succeeded, either in lower courts or at the Supreme Court.

Thirty-seven of the 38 death penalty states use lethal injection, as do the U.S. military and the federal government. Since the chemical mixtures in all jurisdictions are similar to those used in Florida, a victory for Hill at the Supreme Court could tie up the death penalty across the county in litigation, at least temporarily, legal analysts said. . . .

The Hill case does not ask the court to rule directly on the constitutionality of lethal injection—which states adopted as an alternative to hanging, gas, electrocution and shooting—even though Hill maintains that the particular mix of chemicals used in Florida would cause him an unconstitutional degree of suffering.

Rather, the case raises a procedural problem: what recourse there should be for a prisoner who finds out at or near the last minute that the method by which the state proposes to execute him might be "cruel and unusual" punishment. . . .

Hill tried to persuade the U.S. Court of Appeals for the 11th Circuit, based in Atlanta, to give him a day in court to argue against Florida's lethal-injection protocol, based in part on an article about lethal injection in the *Lancet,* a medical journal.

The article, published in 2005, said that 21 of 49 inmates executed by lethal injection in Arizona, Georgia, North Carolina and South Carolina may have been conscious and feeling pain.[†]

Suppose neither lethal injection nor any other form of execution can be made painless. Would this fact justify the abolition of the death penalty or provide any evidence against it? Why or why not? Does it really matter that executions not constitute cruel and unusual punishment? If so, why?

[†]Charles Lane, "High Court to Hear Lethal-Injection Case," *The Washington Post,* 26 January 2006, p. A03. © 2006 The Washington Post, reprinted with permission.

---

3. Poor Representation

Delma Banks, Jr. was charged in the 1980 murder of Richard Whitehead of Texas. The only evidence against Banks was the testimony of an informant who in exchange for his testimony received $200 and the dismissal of an arson charge that could have resulted in his life sentence as a habitual offender. Banks' lawyer did not vigorously cross-examine the informant, nor did he investigate the case. Had he done so, he would have learned of strong evidence that Banks was in another city at the time of the crime. Banks received such poor representation that former FBI director and United States District Court Judge William Sessions weighed in to urge the Supreme Court to temporarily stay his execution. On April 21, 2003 the U.S. Supreme Court accepted Banks' case for review.[‡]

Do you think Banks should get a new trial? Assuming capital punishment is morally permissible, would it ever be right to put someone to death who had not received adequate legal representation? Why or why not? What do you think would constitute adequate legal representation? Suppose someone who is duly sentenced to die got excellent legal representation except for one minor point—her lawyer dozed off for fifteen seconds during her trial. Should this small lapse be a good enough reason to throw out her conviction and demand a new trial?

[‡]ACLU, "Inadequate Representation," 8 October 2003, *ACLU,* www.aclu.org/captial/unequal/1039pub20031008. html (25 February 2006). Reprinted with permission of the American Civil Liberties Union.

CHAPTER 11

Pornography and Censorship

Pornography is nothing new. It graced (or disgraced) the walls of buildings in ancient Pompeii, adorning the houses of rich Romans and illustrating the sexual pleasures of local brothels. And even in those days, it was already ancient. Pornographic pictures predated Roman times by thousands of years. Now in the twenty-first century, after countless attempts by the powerful or concerned to eradicate pornography from the world for good, it is still with us—and spreading far and fast via technology and free enterprise.

Along with many other news organizations, the CBS News show *60 Minutes* has reported on how incredibly pervasive pornography of all kinds has become:

One of the biggest cultural changes in the United States over the past 25 years has been the widespread acceptance of sexually explicit material—pornography.

In the space of a generation, a product that once was available in the back alleys of big cities has gone corporate, delivered now directly into homes and hotel rooms by some of the biggest companies in the United States.

It is estimated that Americans now spend somewhere around $10 billion a year on adult entertainment, which is as much as they spend attending professional sporting events, buying music or going out to the movies.

Consumer demand is so strong that it has seduced some of America's biggest brand names, and companies like General Motors, Marriott and Time Warner are now making millions selling erotica to America.[1]

Not surprisingly, the moral questions that pornography raises have proliferated too. In the interests of clarity, we can separate them into two groups: (1) those concerning the morality of using, creating, or disseminating pornographic materials and (2) those relating to the legal prohibition or censorship of such materials. Some believe that answers to the former may help them decide what to do about the latter; others, that the two need not have anything much to do with one another. In any case, it is important to see that the morality of pornography and the moral permissibility of censoring it are logically distinct.

In this chapter we focus on the censorship question, which we can state as follows: *When, if ever, is it morally permissible for the government to limit or prohibit the exposure of consenting adults to pornographic materials?* Such limitations raise moral concerns because they involve the rights of persons, goods and evils, and social benefits and harms. The censorship question is, of course, extremely controversial—but only as it applies to consenting adults. There is little disagreement about laws prohibiting the display of pornography to minors and to adults who do not want to see it.

[1] "Porn in the U.S.A.," *60 Minutes*, 5 September 2004, www.cbsnews.com/stories/2003/11/21/60minutes/main 585049.shtml (16 February 2006).

ISSUE FILE: BACKGROUND

Though almost any proposed definition of pornography will be controversial, we can begin by positing one that is least troublesome and most useful in helping us understand the key issues. Therefore: **Pornography** is sexually explicit images or text meant to cause sexual excitement or arousal.

Defined this way, pornography includes an extensive array of materials that cater to many different tastes. It can be created in the media of photographs, drawings, paintings, sculpture, animation, videotape, film, fiction or nonfiction text, and live performances, and its modern modes of publication include books, magazines, DVDs, television, and the Internet. In all these modes, pornographic materials appeal to both heterosexuals and homosexuals and depict a remarkable variety of sexual behavior—intercourse, oral sex, anal sex, sexual bondage, fetishism, sadism, voyeurism, bestiality, and much more. In a large percentage of these depictions, the sexual activity is nonviolent, consented to by the adult participants, and regarded by many as neither degrading nor humiliating. In some pornography, however, people are shown being violently abused or degraded against their will. Sometimes women are depicted being raped or tortured, and sometimes both women and men are shown being beaten or forced to perform demeaning acts. Some pornographic materials display not consenting adults but actual children (though some materials may use computer-generated "children" or young adult actors who portray children).[2]

A concept entangled with the term *pornography* is obscenity. **Obscenity** is a characteristic or property believed to render sexually frank material morally or legally unacceptable. For some people, obscenity is the defining trait of pornography: any sexually explicit material that is obscene is pornography. They may judge such material obscene if, for example, it portrays what they consider immoral sexual behavior or if it is believed to corrupt the morals of individuals or society. Obscenity is also a legal term used to describe sexually graphic words or images that are not protected by the First Amendment's guarantee of free speech. Obscene materials can be legally banned. The criteria for judging whether a work is legally obscene were laid out in 1973 by the Supreme Court in *Miller v. California*. According to *Miller,* the criteria are

(a) whether "the average person, applying contemporary community standards" would find that the work, taken as a whole, appeals to the prurient interest [unwholesome sexual desire;] . . . (b) whether the work depicts or describes, in a patently offensive way, sexual conduct specifically defined by the applicable state law, and (c) whether the work, taken as a whole, lacks serious literary, artistic, political, or scientific value.[3]

A work is obscene if it meets all three requirements. Using the "**Miller test,**" the courts have rarely found pornographic materials to be obscene. Child pornography—visual images of real children under age eighteen engaged in sexually explicit conduct—is the notable exception. In many countries, including the United States, Canada, and the United Kingdom, the production, distribution, or possession of child pornography is a crime.

Another term often found alongside pornography is *erotica*. Some feminists define pornography as sexually explicit representations that degrade, demean, or subordinate women. For many of them, **erotica** is a contrasting term referring to sexually explicit material that does *not* portray women in

---

[2]See Caroline West, "Pornography and Censorship," *The Stanford Encyclopedia of Philosophy* (Fall 2005, ed.), ed. Edward N. Zalta, http://plato.stanford.edu/entries/pornography-censorship (15 February 2006).

[3]*Miller v. California,* 413 U.S. 15, 24 (1973).

this negative way but instead emphasizes mutually satisfying sexual relationships between equals.

The censorship question essentially centers on a conflict between personal freedom and the common good. Adding weight to the freedom side of the scales are such fundamental principles as personal autonomy, equality, self-determination, and individual rights—all blessed by the First Amendment and liberal democracy. Those who defend personal freedom against censorship usually understand the specific liberties involved to include freedom of speech or expression and the right to privacy. On the other side of the scales are claims to the effect that pornography is bad for individuals or society. Personal and institutional immorality, the lowering of moral standards, decay of religious values and traditions, the undermining of personal virtue, the debasement and subordination of women, increase in crime and social disorder, psychological damage—these and other ills are said to be the possible results of producing or using pornography.

Those who argue against censorship, then, usually do so in the name of individual liberty. On the anticensorship view, the government has no right to restrict an individual's freedom of expression, conscience, or personal choice without very powerful reasons. The most influential statement of this outlook comes from the utilitarian philosopher John Stuart Mill:

But there is a sphere of action in which society, as distinguished from the individual, has, if any, only an indirect interest. . . . This, then, is the appropriate region of human liberty. It comprises, first, the inward domain of consciousness; demanding liberty of conscience, in the most comprehensive sense; liberty of thought and feeling; absolute freedom of opinion and sentiment on all subjects, practical or speculative, scientific, moral, or theological. The liberty of expressing and publishing opinions may seem to fall under a different principle, since it belongs to that part of the conduct of an individual which concerns other people; but, being almost of as much importance as the liberty of thought itself, and resting in great part on the same reasons, is practically inseparable from it. Secondly, the principle requires liberty of tastes and pursuits; of framing the plan of our life to suit our own character; of doing as we like, subject to such consequences as may follow; without impediment from our fellow-creatures, so long as what we do does not harm them even though they should think our conduct foolish, perverse, or wrong. Thirdly, from this liberty of each individual, follows the liberty, within the same limits, of combination among individuals; freedom to unite, for any purpose not involving harm to others: the persons combining being supposed to be of full age, and not forced or deceived.

No society in which these liberties are not, on the whole, respected, is free, whatever may be its form of government; and none is completely free in which they do not exist absolute and unqualified. The only freedom which deserves the name, is that of pursuing our own good in our own way, so long as we do not attempt to deprive others of theirs, or impede their efforts to obtain it.[4]

According to Mill and his modern-day philosophical heirs, the only legitimate reason for limiting liberty is the prevention of harm to others. We are free to think, believe, say, desire, and choose as we see fit—as long as we do not harm our fellow citizens. (The meaning of *harm* is itself controversial, but the term usually refers to bodily injury or serious damage to important rights or interests.) The mere fact that most other people think our preferences distasteful, false, or immoral is not a good enough reason for the government to suppress or punish us. With some exceptions, the federal courts have generally taken this same stand—and so have most people opposed to the censorship of pornography.

---

[4]John Stuart Mill, from *On Liberty* (1859; reprint, Chicago: Henry Regnery, 1955), 17–18.

Where the possible harm of pornography has seemed substantial and obvious, the enemies of censorship (along with the courts) have recognized legitimate exceptions to the anticensorship principles. They have, for example, usually supported the banning of child pornography and have favored various restrictions on the public display of pornography to minors or nonconsenting adults.

On the procensorship side we find several arguments coming from both the political right and left. Many conservative and religious people argue that pornography should be prohibited for the best of reasons: it is immoral. Pornographic materials themselves are obscene and therefore morally abhorrent; they encourage immoral behavior such as promiscuity, premarital and extramarital intercourse, and deviant or unnatural sexuality; they weaken the moral underpinning of religious and family life; and they are offensive to people with strong moral values. According to this perspective, the important moral beliefs of the community should have the force of law, so the creation or use of pornography should be illegal.

The idea that a community's important moral beliefs should have the force of law is known as **legal moralism.** It is, of course, a far cry from Mill's doctrine. For him, legal moralism is nothing more than the many forcing their notion of morality on the few—"a tyranny of the majority." In contrast, many who advocate some form of legal moralism believe it justified because it is a way to prevent harm to society—*moral* harm.

Another procensorship approach is based on the idea that sometimes the government may legitimately restrict citizens' freedom for their own good, an outlook known as **legal paternalism** (which would sit no better than legal moralism with Mill). Some cite seat belt laws as prime examples of this doctrine: the state, like a kindly father, requires people to buckle up for their own safety— not because being unbuckled might harm others. Thus advocates of censorship argue that pornog-

raphy should be banned because it harms individuals who consume it. Looking at pornography, they contend, can cause psychological problems in viewers, engendering obsessive or deviant behavior and warped attitudes toward themselves, women, and sex. The state therefore should protect people from these self-inflicted harms.

Many argue for the censorship of pornography on grounds other than legal moralism or legal paternalism. They contend that men's consumption of pornography directly causes unmistakable harm to others: specifically, it provokes sexual violence against women and children. Presumably this is one procensorship argument that Mill would have to accept, assuming that pornography does indeed cause sexual violence.

The empirical evidence for this latter claim is conflicting and disputed, however. For example, in 1970 the U.S. government Commission on Obscenity and Pornography concluded that no scientific evidence shows that the consumption of pornographic materials causes sex crimes. But in 1986, the Attorney General's Commission on Pornography reported that there is an increased likelihood of some men committing sex crimes when they are exposed to materials that are either sexually violent or nonviolent and degrading. (No such link was found between sexual violence and erotica.) In contrast, long-term population studies of Denmark, Sweden, West Germany, and Japan showed that as the amount of available pornography increased, the incidence of rape or other sex crimes decreased.[5] Other studies have found links between exposure to violent or degrading pornography and aggressive or callous attitudes toward

[5]Milton Diamond and Ayako Uchiyama, "Pornography, Rape and Sex Crimes in Japan," *International Journal of Law and Psychiatry* 22, no. 1 (1999): 1–22; B. Kutchinsky, "Pornography and Rape: Theory and Practice? Evidence from Crime Data in Four Countries Where Pornography Is Easily Available," *International Journal of Law and Psychiatry* 14, nos. 1–2 (1991): 47–64.

women, but they fall short of demonstrating that pornography causes sexual violence.

More recently, another kind of argument for censorship has come from a number of feminists. These writers do not necessarily object to the sexually explicitness of sex-oriented material. Rather, they oppose sexually explicit material that portrays women as debased and dehumanized while commending this distorted perspective to the audience. The philosopher Helen E. Longino declares that

What makes a work a work of pornography, then, is not simply its representation of degrading and abusive sexual encounters, but its implicit, if not explicit, approval and recommendation of sexual behavior that is immoral, i.e., that physically or psychologically violates the personhood of one of its participants. Pornography, then, is verbal or pictorial material which represents or describes sexual behavior that is degrad-

ing or abusive to one or more of the participants *in such a way as to endorse the degradation.*[6]

Many feminists argue that such material causes serious harm to women that goes beyond merely provoking sexual violence against them. Pornography, they maintain, legitimizes discriminatory and hostile attitudes toward women, leading to such social and political injuries as defamation of character, general oppression and exploitation, violations of women's rights to equal treatment and consideration, and the devaluing of women's dignity and personhood.

But other feminists disagree. They are skeptical of the alleged causal link between consump-

[6]Helen E. Longino, "Pornography, Oppression, and Freedom," in *Take Back the Night: Women on Pornography,* ed. Laura Lederer (New York: William Morrow, 1980), 276.

CRITICAL THOUGHT: The Limits of Free Speech

The Supreme Court case of *Brandenburg v. Ohio* (1969) articulated a test for determining when *inflammatory* free speech can be lawfully punished or banned. It reaffirmed the notion that the right of free speech is not absolute but has limits. In the words of a famous phrase, we would not allow some types of free speech, such as someone "shouting 'fire!' in a crowded theater." But the Court also asserted that not just any kind of speech can be forbidden. Even inflammatory, offensive, or seditious speech cannot be banned unless it passes the "Brandenburg test." As the justices said,

the constitutional guarantees of free speech and free press do not permit a State to forbid or proscribe advocacy of the use of force or of law violation except where such advocacy is directed to inciting or producing imminent lawless action and is likely to incite or produce such action.*

To be prohibited, inflammatory speech must be intended to provoke "imminent lawless action" that is likely to occur. Suppose, as many people contend, that some kinds of pornography are inflammatory. Do you think that under the "Brandenburg test" some pornography would then be deemed eligible for prohibition? Can certain types of pornography provoke imminent lawless action? If pornography can be legitimately banned because it is inflammatory speech likely to provoke imminent lawless action, what other kinds of speech could be banned on the same basis? What about members of the KKK standing on a street corner shouting racial insults at blacks and Jews? What about a controversial speaker at a college advocating the killing of Muslims or gays?

* *Brandenburg v. Ohio,* 395 U.S. 444, 442 (1969).

tion of pornography and unfair treatment of women. They doubt that the relationship between the two is as clear and as toxic as antipornography feminists claim. Moreover, even if a great deal of pornography is unwholesome or misogynistic, they argue, the civil benefits of freedom of expression outweigh any possible goods produced by censorship. As the anticensorship feminist Wendy McElroy says:

Pornography is free speech applied to the sexual realm. Freedom of speech is the ally of those who seek change: it is the enemy of those who seek to maintain control. Pornography, along with all other forms of sexual heresy, such as homosexuality, should have the same legal protection as political heresy. This protection is especially important to women, whose sexuality has been controlled by censorship through the centuries.[7]

MORAL THEORIES

As you can see, many (if not most) of the disputes over the censorship of pornography are about the consequences of allowing (or disallowing) access to pornographic materials. So, naturally, underpinning many arguments on both sides of the issue are appeals to consequentialist moral theories.

Proponents of censorship, for example, can argue on utilitarian grounds that happiness can be maximized for society only by prohibiting the creation and consumption of pornography. The backbone of such arguments would consist of claims that pornography causes more harm than any kind of censorship would. The harms would include some or all of those mentioned earlier— increases in sexual violence against women and minors, the degradation of moral and social life, a higher incidence of mental and emotional prob-

lems, and more exploitation and unfair treatment of women. To be credible, these assertions would need to be backed by empirical evidence showing that, on balance, censorship does indeed lead to greater happiness than alternative proposals. The utilitarian case for censorship, however, would face a steep challenge because, as we have seen, much of the relevant empirical evidence is in doubt. And, of course, a consistent (and honest) utilitarian would have to switch to the anticensorship camp if the evidence suggested that censorship would do more harm than good.

In turn, anticensorship utilitarians would argue that permitting the production and use of pornography (except for some obviously pernicious types such as child pornography) would generate the greatest amount of overall happiness. They could contend both that censoring pornography can cause great harm and that consuming it can be beneficial. Many are opposed to censorship because they believe it injurious and dangerous to society. They argue that the free expression of divergent ideas about such important facets of life as art, politics, morality, and religion is vital to the welfare of a society. The freedom to express one's beliefs and desires is essential to social progress, the acquisition of knowledge, the examination of values and interests, and the pursuit of personal fulfillment.

On the positive side, some contend that reading or viewing pornography can provide important sexual information and be a useful form of emotional therapy:

- [Pornography] gives a panoramic view of the world's sexual possibilities. This is true even of basic sexual information such as masturbation. It is not uncommon for women to reach adulthood without knowing how to give themselves pleasure.

- It allows women to "safely" experience sexual alternatives and satisfy a healthy sexual curiosity. . . .

[7]Wendy McElroy, "A Feminist Defense of Pornography," *Free Inquiry* (Fall 1997): 17.

QUICK REVIEW

pornography—Sexually explicit images or text meant to cause sexual excitement or arousal.

obscenity—A characteristic or property believed to render sexually frank material morally or legally unacceptable; also, a legal term used to describe sexually graphic words or images that are not protected by the First Amendment's guarantee of free speech.

Miller test—Criteria for judging whether a work is legally obscene, as articulated in *Miller v. California* (1973).

erotica—Sexually explicit material that does not degrade or subordinate women; also, sexually explicit material that emphasizes mutually satisfying sexual relationships between equals.

legal moralism—The view that a community's important moral beliefs should have the force of law.

legal paternalism—The view that the government may legitimately restrict citizens' freedom for their own good.

• It offers the emotional information that comes only from experiencing something either directly or vicariously. It provides us with a sense [of] how it would "feel" to do something. . . .

Pornography can be good therapy. Pornography provides a sexual outlet for those who—for whatever reason—have no sexual partner. . . . Couples also use pornography to enhance their relationship.[8]

As we have seen, both those opposed to and in favor of censoring pornography may argue their cases by appealing to nonconsequentialist theories. People who want to ban pornography solely

[8]McElroy, "A Feminist Defense of Pornography," 16–17.

because they deem its creation and consumption immoral are taking a nonconsequentialist view: these actions are wrong in themselves, wrong because of their very nature, and their consequences are beside the point. Similarly, some people maintain that pornography devalues the personhood of women and encourages men to treat them as mere objects of pleasure—as mere means to an end rather than as an end in themselves. This tack is Kantian, condemning pornography as a violation of a fundamental moral principle.

Critics of censorship also frequently found their arguments on nonconsequentialist moral principles, the most common being respect for autonomy. Respecting people's autonomy means allowing them to freely make their own choices and to live their lives as they see fit (as long as others are not harmed). Recall Mill's declaration that personal freedom requires "liberty of tastes and pursuits; of framing the plan of our life to suit our own character; of doing as we like, subject to such consequences as may follow."

MORAL ARGUMENTS

Let us examine an artificial but instructive variation on a procensorship argument that has been extremely controversial, especially among feminists and others concerned about the treatment of women. The gist is that pornography, by its unsavory portrayal of women, degrades and dehumanizes them; this portrayal amounts to unlawful discrimination against women; therefore, pornography should be banned. Here is the argument laid out more precisely:

1. Pornography shows women being degraded, dehumanized, or subordinated and implies approval and encouragement of such illtreatment.

2. This way of portraying women is morally objectionable.

3. This way of portraying women *causes* sexual violence and discrimination against them.

4. This way of portraying women *is* a form of discrimination against them.

5. Censorship of pornography is necessary to prevent these harms.

6. Therefore, the censorship of pornography is justified.

Premise 1 seems to be true, although critics would want to qualify it: *some* pornography is clearly degrading and demeaning to women, and *some* of it does appear to recommend or endorse the degrading and demeaning treatment portrayed.

Most informed people involved in this debate (both pro- and anticensorship) would probably accept Premise 2. They would agree that much of pornography—especially the kind depicting and encouraging violence against women—is indeed morally repugnant. But notice that this premise, even if true, does not support the conclusion. The issue is whether pornography should be censored, not whether it is immoral. Someone can believe that producing and using pornography is morally wrong and that its view of women is demonstrably false and still consistently oppose censorship.

Premise 3 is problematic. As discussed earlier, the claim that pornography causes rape and other sexual violence is widely disputed. And the idea that pornography causes discrimination against women has even less support. To be acceptable, the premise needs to be substantiated by solid empirical evidence—meaning scientific studies, not merely anecdotes. The problem is that it is not at all obvious that this alleged causal connection is actual. As one critic puts it,

Most studies are limited to violent pornography. And even though some of these studies do suggest a *temporary* impact on *attitudes* (e.g., those who view violent pornography may be more likely to express the view that women seek and "enjoy" violence), this does not show that viewing violent pornography

causes violent *behavior*. Moreover, there is some evidence suggesting that the effect on attitudes is only temporary and that it can be effectively counteracted by additional information.[9]

We should note, however, that for the argument to work, Premise 3 does not need to be true. As long as *either* Premise 3 or Premise 4 is true (as well as Premises 1 and 5), we will have a good argument. For the argument to work, we need a premise establishing that pornography causes harm—and either Premise 3 or Premise 4 will do. But since the former is disputed, a proponent of this argument must rely on the latter.

Premise 4 says that pornography does not cause discrimination against women—it *is* discrimination against women. The feminist theorist Catharine MacKinnon has famously made this very point:

We define pornography as a practice of sex discrimination, a violation of women's civil rights, the opposite of sexual equality. . . . Pornography is a practice of discrimination on the basis of sex, on one level because of its role in creating and maintaining sex as a basis for discrimination. It harms many women one at a time and helps keep all women in an inferior status by defining our subordination as our sexuality and equating that with our gender. It is also sex discrimination because its victims, including men, are selected for victimization on the basis of their gender. But for their sex, they would not be so treated.[10]

MacKinnon asserts that pornography is not merely speech or expression (which is protected by the First Amendment) but a form of conduct. If pornography is a kind of harmful conduct (dis-

[9]Mark R. Wicclair, "Feminism, Pornography, and Censorship," in *Social Ethics: Morality and Social Policy,* ed. Thomas A. Mappes and Jane S. Zembaty, 6th ed. (Dubuque, IA: McGraw-Hill, 2002), 235.

[10]Catharine MacKinnon, "Pornography, Civil Rights, and Speech," *Harvard Civil Rights/Civil Liberties Law Review* 20 (1985): 22, 27.

crimination against women), then there is a good reason for outlawing it. After all, discrimination on the basis of race, creed, religion, or sex is illegal and widely recognized as immoral. But if pornography is a form of expression—even offensive and degrading expression—then we cannot automatically conclude that it should be censored. Free expression is considered a fundamental right that can be violated only for very strong reasons and in rare circumstances. In general, harm can be used as a justification for restricting expression only if the harm is in the form of an injury or an "immediate breach of the peace." Thus, the classic example of speech that can be lawfully curtailed is the word "fire!" shouted in a packed theater.

Many observers have rejected the equating of pornography with conduct. The courts, too, have made it clear that they regard pornography of whatever kind as a form of expression, not conduct.

If Premises 3 and 4 are in doubt, then the truth of Premise 5 does not matter. In any case, some would reject Premise 5, arguing that censorship is itself harmful and that there are better ways to counteract the harms of pornography than curtailing free expression. One suggested approach is to educate people about the dangers of sexism and sexual violence.

SUMMARY

In this chapter, *pornography* has been defined as sexually frank images or text meant to cause sexual excitement or arousal. *Obscenity* is used as a legal term defined by the courts: obscene materials are those that the "average person, applying contemporary community standards" would judge to be appealing to prurient interests, that are "patently offensive,"

and that lack "serious literary, artistic, political, or scientific value."

The censorship question (pertaining to state censorship of pornography) rests essentially on how to resolve a conflict between personal freedom and the common good. Those who argue against censorship usually appeal to individual liberty, affirming with John Stuart Mill that the only legitimate reason for limiting liberty is the prevention of harm to others. Those arguing for censorship often contend that pornography should be censored because it is immoral in itself and encourages immoral behavior. Also, many taking a procensorship stance maintain that the consumption of pornography provokes sexual violence against women and children. The existence of empirical evidence to support this claim is disputed. Some feminists argue that pornography causes serious harm to women by legitimizing discriminatory and hostile attitudes toward women—attitudes that lead to women's oppression and exploitation, violations of women's right to equal treatment, and the devaluing of women's dignity and personhood. Other feminists reject this view because they are skeptical of the alleged causal link between pornography and harm to women and because they think the benefits of freedom of expression outweigh any possible gains from censorship.

Consequentialist theories can be used to argue both for and against the censorship of pornography. Depending on the import of the empirical evidence, you could argue that the greatest benefits to society would result from censoring—or not censoring—pornography. Nonconsequentialist theories can also be used to support either position. You can argue, for example, that pornography should be censored because it treats women merely as a means to an end (a Kantian approach) or that it should not be censored because censorship is a violation of people's autonomy (another Kantian concern).

R E A D I N G S

From Attorney General's Commission on Pornography: Final Report

* * *

We present in the following sections our conclusions regarding the harms we have investigated with respect to the various subdividing categories we have found most useful. To the extent that these conclusions rest on findings from the social sciences, as they do to a significant extent, we do not in this Part of the Report describe and analyze the individual studies or deal in specifics with their methodologies. For that we rely on our analysis of the social science research which is included later in this Report. Each of us has relied on different evidence from among the different categories of evidence, and specific studies that some of us have found persuasive have been less persuasive to others of us. Similarly, some of us have found evidence of a certain type particularly valuable, while others of us have found other varieties of evidence more enlightening. And in many instances we have relied on certain evidence despite some flaws it may have contained, for it is the case that all of us have reached our conclusions about harms by assimilating and amalgamating a large amount of evidence. Many studies and statements of witnesses have both advantages and disadvantages, and often the disadvantages of one study or piece of testimony has been remedied by another. Thus, the conclusions we reach cannot be identified with complete acceptance or complete rejection by all of us of any particular item of evidence. As a result, we consider the social science analysis, which is much more specific than what we say in this section, to be an integral part of this Report, and we urge that it be read as such. We have not relied totally on that analysis, as all of us have gone beyond it in our reading.

United States Attorney General's Commission on Pornography, *Attorney General's Commission on Pornography: Final Report* (Washington: U.S. Department of Justice, 1986) (edited).

And we cannot say that each of us agrees with every sentence and word in it. Nevertheless, it seems to us a sensitive, balanced, comprehensive, accurate, and current report on the state of the research. We have relied on it extensively, and we are proud to include it here.

SEXUALLY VIOLENT MATERIAL

The category of material on which most of the evidence has focused is the category of material featuring actual or unmistakably simulated or unmistakably threatened violence presented in sexually explicit fashion with a predominant focus on the sexually explicit violence. Increasingly, the most prevalent forms of pornography, as well as an increasingly prevalent body of less sexually explicit material, fit this description. Some of this material involves sado-masochistic themes, with the standard accoutrements of the genre, including whips, chains, devices of torture, and so on. But another theme of some of this material is not sado-masochistic, but involves instead the recurrent theme of a man making some sort of sexual advance to a woman, being rebuffed, and then raping the woman or in some other way violently forcing himself on the woman. In almost all of this material, whether in magazine or motion picture form, the woman eventually becomes aroused and ecstatic about the initially forced sexual activity, and usually is portrayed as begging for more. There is also a large body of material, more "mainstream" in its availability, that portrays sexual activity or sexually suggestive nudity coupled with extreme violence, such as disfigurement or murder. The so-called "slasher" films fit this description, as does some material, both in films and in magazines, that is less or more sexually explicit than the prototypical "slasher" film.

It is with respect to material of this variety that the scientific findings and ultimate conclusions of the 1970 Commission are least reliable for today, precisely because material of this variety was largely absent from that Commission's inquiries. It is not, however, absent from the contemporary world, and it is hardly surprising that conclusions about this material differ from conclusions about material not including violent themes.

When clinical and experimental research has focused particularly on sexually violent material, the conclusions have been virtually unanimous. In both clinical and experimental settings, exposure to sexually violent materials has indicated an increase in the likelihood of aggression. More specifically, the research, which is described in much detail later in this Report, shows a causal relationship between exposure to material of this type and aggressive behavior towards women.

Finding a link between aggressive behavior towards women and sexual violence, whether lawful or unlawful, requires assumptions not found exclusively in the experimental evidence. We see no reason, however, not to make these assumptions. The assumption that increased aggressive behavior towards women is causally related, for an aggregate population, to increased sexual violence is significantly supported by the clinical evidence, as well as by much of the less scientific evidence. They are also to all of us assumptions that are plainly justified by our own common sense. This is not to say that all people with heightened levels of aggression will commit acts of sexual violence. But it is to say that over a sufficiently large number of cases we are confident in asserting that an increase in aggressive behavior directed at women will cause an increase in the level of sexual violence directed at women.

Thus we reach our conclusions by combining the results of the research with highly justifiable assumptions about the generalizability of more limited research results. Since the clinical and experimental evidence supports the conclusion that there is a causal relationship between exposure to sexually violent materials and an increase in aggressive behavior directed towards women, and since we believe that an increase in aggressive behavior towards women will in a population increase the incidence of sexual violence in that population, we have reached the conclusion, unanimously and confidently, that the available evidence strongly supports the hypothesis that substantial exposure to sexually violent materials as described here bears a causal relationship to antisocial acts of sexual violence and, for some subgroups, possibly to unlawful acts of sexual violence.

Although we rely for this conclusion on significant scientific empirical evidence, we feel it worthwhile to note the underlying logic of the conclusion. The evidence says simply that the images that people are exposed to bears a causal relationship to their behavior. This is hardly surprising. What would be surprising would be to find otherwise, and we have not so found. We have not, of course, found that the images people are exposed to are a greater cause of sexual violence than all or even many other possible causes the investigation of which has been beyond our mandate. Nevertheless, it would be strange indeed if graphic representations of a form of behavior, especially in a form that almost exclusively portrays such behavior as desirable, did not have at least some effect on patterns of behavior.

Sexual violence is not the only negative effect reported in the research to result from substantial exposure to sexually violent materials. The evidence is also strongly supportive of significant attitudinal changes on the part of those with substantial exposure to violent pornography. These attitudinal changes are numerous. Victims of rape and other forms of sexual violence are likely to be perceived by people so exposed as more responsible for the assault, as having suffered less injury, and as having been less degraded as a result of the experience. Similarly, people with a substantial exposure to violent pornography are likely to see the rapist or other sexual offender as less responsible for the act and as deserving of less stringent punishment.

These attitudinal changes have been shown experimentally to include a larger range of attitudes than those just discussed. The evidence also strongly supports the conclusion that substantial exposure to violent sexually explicit material leads to a greater acceptance of the "rape myth" in its broader sense—that women enjoy being coerced into sexual activity, that they enjoy being physically hurt in sexual context, and that as a result a man who forces himself on a woman sexually is in fact merely acceding to the "real" wishes of the woman, regardless of the extent to which she seems to be resisting. The myth is that a woman who says "no" really means "yes," and that men are justified in acting on the assumption that the "no" answer is indeed the "yes" answer. We have little trouble concluding that this attitude is both pervasive and profoundly harmful, and that any stimulus reinforcing or increasing the incidence of this attitude is for that reason alone properly designated as harmful.

Two vitally important features of the evidence supporting the above conclusions must be mentioned here. The first is that all of the harms discussed here, including acceptance of the legitimacy of sexual violence against women but not limited to it, are more pronounced when the sexually violent materials depict the woman as experiencing arousal, orgasm, or other form of enjoyment as the ultimate result of the sexual assault. This theme, unfortunately very common in the materials we have examined, is likely to be the major, albeit not the only, component of what it is in the materials in this category that causes the consequences that have been identified.

The second important clarification of all of the above is that the evidence lends some support to the conclusion that the consequences we have identified here do not vary with the extent of sexual explicitness so long as the violence is presented in an undeniably sexual context. Once a threshold is passed at which sex and violence are plainly linked, increasing the sexual explicitness of the material, or the bizarreness of the sexual activity, seems to bear little relationship to the extent of the consequences discussed here. Although it is unclear whether sexually violent material makes a substantially greater causal contribution to sexual violence itself than does material containing violence alone, it appears that increasing the amount of violence after the threshold of connecting sex with violence is more related to increase in the incidence or severity of harmful con-

sequences than is increasing the amount of sex. As a result, the so-called "slasher" films, which depict a great deal of violence connected with an undeniably sexual theme but less sexual explicitness than materials that are truly pornographic, are likely to produce the consequences discussed here to a greater extent than most of the materials available in "adults only" pornographic outlets.

Although we have based our findings about material in this category primarily on evidence presented by professionals in the behavioral sciences, we are confident that it is supported by the less scientific evidence we have consulted, and we are each personally confident on the basis of our own knowledge and experiences that the conclusions are justified. None of us has the least doubt that sexual violence is harmful, and that general acceptance of the view that "no" means "yes" is a consequence of the most serious proportions. We have found a causal relationship between sexually explicit materials featuring violence and these consequences, and thus conclude that the class of such materials, although not necessarily every individual member of that class, is on the whole harmful to society.

NONVIOLENT MATERIALS DEPICTING DEGRADATION, DOMINATION, SUBORDINATION, OR HUMILIATION

Current research has rather consistently separated out violent pornography, the class of materials we have just discussed, from other sexually explicit materials. With respect to further subdivision the process has been less consistent. A few researchers have made further distinctions, while most have merely classed everything else as "non-violent." We have concluded that more subdivision than that is necessary. Our examination of the variety of sexually explicit materials convinces us that once again the category of "non-violent" ignores significant distinctions within this category, and thus combines classes of material that are in fact substantially different.

The subdivision we adopt is one that has surfaced in some of the research. And it is also one that might explain a significant amount of what would otherwise seem to be conflicting research results. Some researchers have found negative effects from non-violent material, while others report no such negative effects. But when the stimulus material these researchers have used is considered, there is some suggestion that the presence or absence of negative effects from non-violent material might turn on the non-violent material being considered "degrading," a term we shall explain shortly. It appears that effects similar to although not as extensive as that involved with violent material can be identified with respect to such degrading material, but that these effects are likely absent when neither degradation nor violence is present.

An enormous amount of the most sexually explicit material available, as well as much of the material that is somewhat less sexually explicit, is material that we would characterize as "degrading," the term we use to encompass the undeniably linked characteristics of degradation, domination, subordination, and humiliation. The degradation we refer to is degradation of people, most often women, and here we are referring to material that, although not violent, depicts[1] people, usually women, as existing solely for the sexual satisfaction of others, usually men, or that depicts people, usually women, in decidedly subordinate roles in their sexual relations with others, or that depicts people engaged in sexual practices that would to most people be considered humiliating. Indeed, forms of degradation represent the largely predominant proportion of commercially available pornography.

With respect to material of this variety, our conclusions are substantially similar to those with respect to violent material, although we make them with somewhat less confidence and our making of them requires more in the way of assumption than was the case with respect to violent material. The evidence, scientific and otherwise, is more tentative, but supports the conclusion that the material we describe as degrading bears some causal relationship to the attitudinal changes we have previously identified. That is, substantial exposure to material of this variety is likely to increase the extent to which those exposed will view rape or other forms of sexual violence as

less serious than they otherwise would have, will view the victims of rape and other forms of sexual violence as significantly more responsible, and will view the offenders as significantly less responsible. We also conclude that the evidence supports the conclusion that substantial exposure to material of this type will increase acceptance of the proposition that women like to be forced into sexual practices, and, once again, that the woman who says "no" really means "yes."

With respect to material of this type, there is less evidence causally linking the material with sexual aggression, but this may be because this is a category that has been isolated in only a few studies, albeit an increasing number. The absence of evidence should by no means be taken to deny the existence of the causal link. But because the causal link is less the subject of experimental studies, we have been required to think more carefully here about the assumptions necessary to causally connect increased acceptance of rape myths and other attitudinal changes with increased sexual aggression and sexual violence. And on the basis of all the evidence we have considered, from all sources, and on the basis of our own insights and experiences, we believe we are justified in drawing the following conclusion: Over a large enough sample a population that believes that many women like to be raped, that believes that sexual violence or sexual coercion is often desired or appropriate, and that believes that sex offenders are less responsible for their acts, will commit more acts of sexual violence or sexual coercion than would a population holding these beliefs to a lesser extent.

We should make clear what we have concluded here. We are not saying that everyone exposed to material of this type has his attitude about sexual violence changed. We are saying only that the evidence supports the conclusion that substantial exposure to degrading material increases the likelihood for an individual and the incidence over a large population that these attitudinal changes will occur. And we are not saying that everyone with these attitudes will commit an act of sexual violence or sexual coercion. We are saying that such attitudes will increase the likelihood for an individual and the incidence for a population that acts of sexual violence, sexual coercion, or unwanted sexual aggression will occur. Thus, we conclude that substantial exposure to materials of this type bears some causal relationship to the level of sexual violence, sexual coercion, or unwanted sexual aggression in the population so exposed.

* * *

NON-VIOLENT AND NON-DEGRADING MATERIALS

Our most controversial category has been the category of sexually explicit materials that are not violent and are not degrading as we have used that term. They are materials in which the participants appear to be fully willing participants occupying substantially equal roles in a setting, devoid of actual or apparent violence or pain. This category is in fact quite small in terms of currently available materials. There is some, to be sure, and the amount may increase as the division between the degrading and the non-degrading becomes more accepted, but we are convinced that only a small amount of currently available highly sexually explicit material is neither violent nor degrading. We thus talk about a small category, but one that should not be ignored.

We have disagreed substantially about the effects of such materials, and that should come as no surprise. We are dealing in this category with "pure" sex, as to which there are widely divergent views in this society. That we have disagreed among ourselves does little more than reflect the extent to which we are representative of the population as a whole. In light of that disagreement, it is perhaps more appropriate to explain the various views rather than indicate a unanimity that does not exist, within this Commission or within society, or attempt the preposterous task of saying that some fundamental view about the role of sexuality and portrayals of sexuality was accepted or defeated by such-and-such vote. We do not wish to give easy answers to hard questions, and thus feel better with describing the diversity of opinion rather than suppressing part of it.

In examining the material in this category, we have not had the benefit of extensive evidence.

Research has only recently begun to distinguish the non-violent but degrading from material that is neither violent nor degrading, and we have all relied on a combination of interpretation of existing studies that may not have drawn the same divisions, studies that did draw these distinctions, clinical evidence, interpretation of victim testimony, and our own perceptions of the effect of images on human behavior. Although the social science evidence is far from conclusive, we are on the current state of the evidence persuaded that material of this type does not bear a causal relationship to rape and other acts of sexual violence. We rely once again not only on scientific studies outlined later in the Report, and examined by each of us, but on the fact that the conclusions of these studies seem to most of us fully consistent with common sense. Just as materials depicting sexual violence seem intuitively likely to bear a causal relationship to sexual violence, materials containing no depictions or suggestions of sexual violence or sexual dominance seem to most of us intuitively unlikely to bear a causal relationship to sexual violence. The studies and clinical evidence to date are less persuasive on this lack of negative effect than they are persuasive for the presence of negative effect for the sexually violent material, but they seem to us of equal persuasive power as the studies and clinical evidence showing negative effects for the degrading materials. The fairest conclusion from the social science evidence is that there is no persuasive evidence to date supporting the connection between non-violent and non-degrading materials and acts of sexual violence, and that there is some but very limited evidence, indicating that the connection does not exist. The totality of the social science evidence therefore, is slightly against the hypothesis that non-violence and non-degrading materials bear a causal relationship to acts of sexual violence.

* * *

NOTE

1. We restrict our analysis in large part to degradation that is in fact depicted in the material. It may very well be that degradation led to a woman being willing to pose for a pic-

ture of a certain variety, or to engage in what appears to be a non-degrading sexual act. It may be that coercion caused the picture to exist. And it may very well be that the existing disparity in the economic status of men and women is such that any sexually explicit depiction of a woman is at least suspect on account of the possibility that the economic disparity is what caused the woman to pose for a picture that most people in this society would find embarrassing.

We do not deny any of these possibilities, and we do not deny the importance of considering as pervasively as possible the status of women in contemporary America, including the effects of their current status and what might be done to change some of the detrimental consequences of that status. But without engaging in an inquiry of that breadth, we must generally, absent more specific evidence to the contrary, assume that a picture represents what it depicts.

From Pornography, Civil Rights, and Speech
CATHARINE A. MACKINNON

* * *

There is a belief that this is a society in which women and men are basically equals. Room for marginal corrections is conceded, flaws are known to exist, attempts are made to correct what are conceived as occasional lapses from the basic condition of sex equality. Sex discrimination law has centered most of its focus on these occasional lapses. It is difficult to overestimate the extent to which this belief in equality is an article of faith to most people, including most women, who wish to live in self-respect in an internal universe, even (perhaps especially) if not in the world. It is also partly an expression of natural law thinking: If we are inalienably equal, we can't "really" be degraded.

This is a world in which it is worth trying. In this world of presumptive equality, people make money based on their training or abilities or diligence or qualifications. They are employed and advanced on the basis of merit. In this world of just deserts, if someone is abused, it is thought to violate the basic rules of the community. If it doesn't, that person is seen to have done something she could have chosen to do differently, by exercise of will or better judgment. Maybe such people have placed themselves in a situation of vulnerability to physical abuse. Maybe

they have done something provocative. Or maybe they were just unusually unlucky. In such a world, if such a person has an experience, there are words for it. When they speak and say it, they are listened to. If they write about it, they will be published. If there are certain experiences that are never spoken, or certain people or issues seldom heard from, it is supposed that silence has been chosen. The law, including much of the law of sex discrimination and the first amendment, operates largely within the realm of these beliefs.

Feminism is the discovery that women do not live in this world, that the person occupying this realm is a man, so much more a man if he is white and wealthy. This world of potential credibility, authority, security, and just rewards, recognition of one's identity and capacity, is a world that some people do inhabit as a condition of birth, with variations *among them*. It is not a basic condition accorded humanity in this society, but a prerogative of status, a privilege, among other things, of gender.

I call this a discovery because it has not been an assumption. Feminism is the first theory, the first practice, the first movement, to take seriously the situation of all women from the point of view of all women, both on our situation and on social life as a whole. The discovery has therefore been made that the implicit social content of humanism, as well as the standpoint from which legal method has been designed and injuries have been defined, has not

Catharine MacKinnon, "Pornography, Civil Rights, and Speech," *Harvard Civil Rights/Civil Liberties Law Review* 20, no. 1 (1985): 10–68 (edited). Copyright © 1985 by the President and Fellows of Harvard College. Reprinted with permission.

been women's standpoint. Defining feminism in a way that connects epistemology with power as the politics of women's point of view, this discovery can be summed up by saying that women live in an other world: specifically, a world of *not* equality, a world of inequality.

Looking at the world from this point of view, a whole shadow world of previously invisible silent abuse has been discerned. Rape, battery, sexual harassment, forced prostitution, and the sexual abuse of children emerge as common and systematic. We find rape happens to women in all contexts, from the family, including rape of girls and babies, to students and women in the workplace, on the streets, at home, in their own bedrooms by men that they do not know, and by men that they do know, by men they are married to, men they have had a social conversation with, or, least often, men they have never seen before. Overwhelmingly, rape is something that men do or attempt to do to women (forty-four percent according to a recent study) at some point in our lives. Sexual harassment of women by men is common in workplaces and educational institutions. Up to eighty-five percent of women in one study report it, many in physical forms. Between a quarter and a third of women are battered in their homes by men. Thirty-eight percent of little girls are sexually molested inside or outside the family. Until women listened to women, this world of sexual abuse was *not spoken* of. It was the unspeakable. What I am saying is, if you *are* the tree falling in the epistemological forest, your demise doesn't make a sound if no one is listening. Women did not "report" these events, and overwhelmingly do not today, because no one is listening, because no one believes us. This silence does not mean nothing happened, and it does not mean consent. It is the silence of women of which Adrienne Rich has written, "Do not confuse it with any kind of absence."[1]

Believing women who say we are sexually violated has been a radical departure, both methodologically and legally. The extent and nature of rape, marital rape, and sexual harassment itself, were discovered in this way. Domestic battery as a syndrome, almost a habit, was discovered through refusing to believe that when a woman is assaulted by a man to whom she is connected, that is not an assault. The sexual abuse of children was uncovered, Freud notwithstanding, by believing that children were not making up all this sexual abuse. Now what is striking is that when each discovery is made, and somehow made real in the world, the response has been: It happens to men too. If women are hurt, men are hurt. If women are raped, men ar raped. If women are sexually harassed, men are sexually harassed. If women are battered, men are battered. Symmetry must be reasserted. Neutrality must be reclaimed. Equality must be reestablished.

The only places where the available evidence supports this, where anything like what happens to women also happens to men, are with children—little boys are sexually abused—and in prison. The liberty of prisoners is restricted, their freedom restrained, their humanity systematically diminished, their bodies and emotions confined, defined, and regulated. If paid at all, they are paid starvation wages. They can be tortured at will, and it is passed off as discipline or as means to an end. They become compliant. They can be raped at will, at any moment, and nothing will be done about it. When they scream, nobody hears. To be a prisoner means to be defined as a member of a group for whom the rules of what can be done to you, of what is seen as abuse of you, are reduced as part of the definition of your status. To be a woman is also that kind of definition and has that kind of meaning.

Men *are* damaged by sexism. (By men, I am referring to the status of masculinity which is accorded to males on the basis of their biology, but is not itself biological.) But whatever the damage of sexism is to men, the condition of being a man is not defined as subordinate to women by force. Looking at the facts of the abuses of women all at once, you see that a woman is socially defined as a person who, whether or not she is or has been, *can at any time* be treated in these ways by men, and little, if anything, will be done about it. This is what it means when feminists say that maleness is a form of power and femaleness is a form of powerlessness.

In this context, what all of this "men too" stuff is about, is that people don't really seem to believe that the things I have just said are true, though there really is little question about their empirical accuracy. The data are extremely simple, like women's fifty-nine cent on the dollar pay figure. People don't really seem to believe that either. Yet there is no question of its empirical validity. This is the workplace story: What women do is seen as not worth much or what is not worth much is seen as something for women to do. *Women* are not seen as worth much, is the thing. Now why are these basic realities of the sub-ordination of women to men, such that for example only 7.8 percent of women have never been sexually assaulted,[2] not effectively believed, not perceived as real in the face of all this evidence? Why don't *women* believe our own experiences? In the face of all this evidence, especially of systematic sexual abuse—sub-jection to violence with impunity is one extreme expression, although not the only expression, of a degraded status—the view that basically the sexes are equal in this society remains unchallenged and unchanged. The day I got this was the day I under-stood its real message, its real coherence: *This is equal-ity for us.*

I could describe this but I couldn't explain it until I started studying a lot of pornography. In pornog-raphy, there it is, in one place, all of the abuses that women had to struggle so long even to begin to artic-ulate, all the *unspeakable* abuse: the rape, the battery, the sexual harassment, the prostitution, and the sex-ual abuse of children. Only in the pornography it is called something else: sex, sex, sex, sex, and sex, respectively. Pornography sexualizes rape, battery, sexual harassment, prostitution, and child sexual abuse; it thereby celebrates, promotes, authorizes, and legitimizes them. More generally, it criticizes the dominance and submission that is the dynamic com-mon to them all. It makes hierarchy sexy and calls that "the truth about sex" or just a mirror of reality. Through this process, pornography constructs what a woman is as what men want from sex. This is what the pornography means. (I will talk about the way it works behaviorally, with the evidence on it, when I talk about the ordinance itself.)

Pornography constructs what a woman is in terms of its view of what men want sexually, such that acts of rape, battery, sexual harassment, prosti-tution, and sexual abuse of children become acts of sexual equality. Pornography's world of equality is a harmonious and balanced place. Men and women are perfectly complementary and perfectly bipolar. Women's desire to be fucked by men is equal to men's desire to fuck women. All the ways men love to take and violate women, women love to be taken and vio-lated. The women who most love this are most men's equals, the most liberated; the most participatory child is the most grown-up, the most equal to an adult. Their consent merely expresses or ratifies these preexisting facts.

The content of pornography is one thing. There, women substantively desire dispossession and cru-elty. We desperately want to be bound, battered, tortured, humiliated, and killed. Or, to be fair to the soft core, merely taken and used. This is erotic to the male point of view. Subjection itself with self-determination ecstatically relinquished is the content of women's sexual desire and desirability. Women are there to be violated and possessed, men to violate and possess us either on screen or by camera or pen on behalf of the consumer. On a simple descriptive level, the inequality of hierarchy, of which gender is the primary one, seems necessary for the sexual arousal to work. Other added inequalities identify various pornographic genres or sub-themes, although they are always added through gender: age, disabil-ity, homosexuality, animals, objects, race (including anti-semitism), and so on. Gender is never irrelevant.

What pornography *does* goes beyond its content: It eroticizes hierarchy, it sexualizes inequality. It makes dominance and submission sex. Inequality is its central dynamic; the illusion of freedom coming together with the reality of force is central to its work-ing. Perhaps because this is a bourgeois culture, the victim must look free, appear to be freely acting. Choice is how she got there. Willing is what she is when she is being equal. It seems equally important that then and there she actually be forced and that forcing be communicated on some level, even if only through still photos of her in postures of receptivity and access, available for penetration. Pornography in this view is a form of forced sex, a practice of sexual politics, an institution of gender inequality.

From this perspective, pornography is neither harmless fantasy nor a corrupt and confused misrepresentation of an otherwise natural and healthy sexual situation. It institutionalizes the sexuality of male supremacy, fusing the erotization of dominance and submission with the social construction of male and female. To the extent that gender is sexual, pornography is part of constituting the meaning of that sexuality. Men treat women as who they see women as being. Pornography constructs who that is. Men's power over women means that the way men see women defines who women can be. Pornography is that way. Pornography is not imagery in some relation to a reality elsewhere constructed. It is not a distortion, reflection, projection, expression, fantasy, representation, or symbol either. It is a sexual reality.

In Andrea Dworkin's definitive work on pornography, sexuality itself is a social construct gendered to the ground. Male dominance here is not an artificial overlay upon an underlying inalterable substratum of uncorrupted essential sexual being. Dworkin's *Pornography: Men Possessing Women* presents a sexual theory of gender inequality of which pornography is a constitutive practice. The way in which pornography produces its meaning constructs and defines men and women as such. Gender has no basis in anything other than the social reality its hegemony constructs. Gender is what gender means. The process that gives sexuality its male supremacist meaning is the same process through which gender inequality becomes socially real.

In this approach, the experience of the (overwhelmingly) male audiences who consume pornography is therefore not fantasy or simulation or catharsis but sexual reality, the level of reality on which sex itself largely operates. Understanding this dimension of the problem does not require noticing that pornography models are real women to whom, in most cases, something real is being done; nor does it even require inquiring into the systematic infliction of pornography and its sexuality upon women, although it helps. The way in which the pornography itself provides what those who consume it want matters. Pornography *participates* in its audience's eroticism through creating an accessible sexual object, the possession and consumption of which *is* male sexuality, as socially constructed; to be consumed and possessed as which, *is* female sexuality, as socially constructed; and pornography is a process that constructs it that way.

The object world is constructed according to how it looks with respect to its possible uses. Pornography defines women by how we look according to how we can be sexually used. Pornography codes how to look at women, so you know what you can do with one when you see one. Gender is an assignment made visually, both originally and in everyday life. A sex object is defined on the basis of its looks, in terms of its usability for sexual pleasure, such that both the looking—the quality of the gaze, including its point of view—and the definition according to use become eroticized as part of the sex itself. This is what the feminist concept "sex object" means. In this sense, sex in life is no less mediated than it is in art. One could say men have sex with *their image* of a woman. It is not that life and art imitate each other; in this sexuality, they *are* each other.

To give a set of rough epistemological translations, to defend pornography as consistent with the equality of the sexes is to defend the subordination of women to men as sexual equality. What in the pornographic view is love and romance looks a great deal like hatred and torture to the feminist. Pleasure and eroticism become violation. Desire appears as lust for dominance and submission. The vulnerability of women's projected sexual availability, that acting we are allowed (i.e. asking to be acted upon), is victimization. Play conforms to scripted roles. Fantasy expresses ideology, is not exempt from it. Admiration of natural physical beauty becomes objectification. Harmlessness becomes harm. Pornography is a harm of male supremacy made difficult to see because of its pervasiveness, potency, and, principally, because of its success in making the world a pornographic place. Specifically, its harm cannot be discerned, and will not be addressed, if viewed and approached neutrally, because it *is* so much of "what is." In other words, to the extent pornography succeeds in constructing social reality, it becomes invisible as harm. If we live in a world that pornography creates through the power of men in a male dominated situation the issue is not what the harm of pornography is, but how that harm is to become visible.

Obscenity law provides a very different analysis and conception of the problem. In 1973, the legal definition of obscenity became that which

the average person, applying contemporary community standards, would find that, taken as a whole, appeals to the prurient interest; that which depicts and describes in a patently offensive way [You feel like you're a cop reading someone's *Miranda* rights] sexual conduct as defined by the applicable state law; and that which, taken as a whole, lacks serious literary, artistic, political or scientific value.[3]

Feminism doubts whether the average gender-neutral person exists; has more questions about the content and process of defining what community standards are than it does about deviations from them; wonders why prurience counts but powerlessness does not, and why sensibilities are better protected from offense than women are from exploitation; defines sexuality, and thus its violation and expropriation, more broadly than does state law; and questions why a body of law which has not in practice been able to tell rape from intercourse should, without further guidance, be entrusted with telling pornography from anything less. Taking the work "as a whole" ignores that which the victims of pornography have long known: Legitimate settings diminish the injury perceived to be done to those whose trivialization and objectification it contextualizes. Besides, and this is a heavy one, if a woman is subjected, why should it matter that the work has other value? Maybe what redeems the work's value is what enhances its injury to women, not to mention that existing standards of literature, art, science, and politics, examined in a feminist light, are remarkably consonant with pornography's mode, meaning, and message. And finally—first and foremost, actually—although the subject of these materials is overwhelmingly women, their contents almost entirely comprised of women's

bodies, our invisibility has been such, our equation as a sex *with* sex has been such, that the law of obscenity has never even considered pornography a woman's issue.

Obscenity, in this light, is a moral idea; an idea about judgments of good and bad. Pornography, by contrast, is a political practice, a practice of power and powerlessness. Obscenity is ideational and abstract; pornography is concrete and substantive. The two concepts represent two entirely different things. Nudity, excess of candor, arousal or excitement, prurient appeal, illegality of the acts depicted, and unnaturalness or perversion are all qualities that bother obscenity law when sex is depicted or portrayed. Sex forced on real women so that it can be sold at a profit to be forced on other real women; women's bodies trussed and maimed and raped and made into things to be hurt and obtained and accessed and this presented as the nature of women in a way that is acted on and acted out over and over; the coercion that is visible and the coercion that has become invisible—this and more bothers feminists about pornography. Obscenity as such probably does little harm. Pornography is integral to attitudes and behaviors of violence and discrimination which define the treatment and status of half the population.

At the request of the city of Minneapolis, Andrea Dworkin and I conceived and designed a local human rights ordinance in accordance with our approach to the pornography issue. We define pornography as a practice of sex discrimination, a violation of women's civil rights, the opposite of sexual equality. Its point is to hold accountable, to those who are injured, those who profit from and benefit from that injury. It means that women's injury—our damage, our pain, our enforced inferiority—should outweigh their pleasure and their profits, or sex equality is meaningless.

We define pornography as the graphic sexually explicit subordination of women through pictures or words that also includes women dehumanized as sexual objects, things, or commodities, enjoying pain or humiliation or rape, being tied up, cut up, mutilated, bruised, or physically hurt, in postures of sexual submission or servility or display, reduced to body parts, penetrated by objects or animals, or presented in scenarios of degradation, injury, torture, shown as filthy or inferior, bleeding, bruised, or hurt in a context that makes these conditions sexual. Erotica, defined by distinction as not this, might be sexually explicit materials premised on equality. We also provide that the use of men, children or transsexuals in the place of women is pornography. The definition is substantive in that it is sex-specific, but it covers everyone in a sex-specific way, so is gender neutral in overall design.

* * *

This law aspires to guarantee women's rights consistent with the first amendment by making visible a conflict of rights between the equality guaranteed to all women and what, in some legal sense, is now the freedom of the pornographers to make and sell, and their consumers to have access to, the materials this ordinance defines. Judicial resolution of this conflict, if they do for women what they have done for others, is likely to entail a balancing of the rights of women arguing that our lives and opportunities, including our freedom of speech and action, are constrained by—and in many cases flatly precluded by, in, and through—pornography, against those who argue that the pornography is harmless, or harmful only in part but not in the whole of the definition; or that it is more important to preserve the pornography than it is to prevent or remedy whatever harm it does.

In predicting how a court would balance these interests, it is important to understand that this ordinance cannot now be said to be either conclusively legal or illegal under existing law or precedent, although I think the weight of authority is on our side. This ordinance enunciates a new form of the previously recognized governmental interest in sex equality. Many laws make sex equality a governmental interest. Our law is designed to further the equality of the sexes, to help make sex equality real. Pornography is a practice of discrimination on the basis of sex, on one level because of its role in creating and maintaining sex as a basis for discrimination. It harms many women one at a time and helps keep

all women in an inferior status by defining our subordination as our sexuality and equating that with our gender. It is also sex discrimination because its victims, including men, are selected for victimization on the basis of their gender. But for their sex, they would not be so treated.

The harm of pornography, broadly speaking, is the harm of the civil inequality of the sexes made invisible as harm because it has become accepted as the sex difference. Consider this analogy with race: If you see Black people as different, there is no harm to segregation; it is merely a recognition of that difference. To neutral principles, separate but equal was equal. The injury of racial separation to Blacks arises "solely because [they] choose to put that construction upon it."[4] Epistemologically translated: How you see it is not the way it is. Similarly, if you see women as just different, even or especially if you don't know that you do, subordination will not look like subordination at all, much less like harm. It will merely look like an appropriate recognition of the sex difference.

Pornography does not treat the sexes differently, so the case for sex differentiation can be made here. Men as a group do not tend to be (although some individuals may be) treated like women are treated in pornography. But as a social group, men are not hurt by pornography the way women as a social group are. Their social status is not defined as *less* by it. So the major argument does not turn on mistaken differentiation, particularly since women's treatment according to pornography's dictates makes it all too often accurate. The salient quality of a distinction between the top and the bottom in a hierarchy is not difference, although top is certainly different from bottom; it is power. So the major argument is: Subordinate but equal is not equal.

Particularly since this is a new legal theory, a new law, and "new" facts, perhaps the situation of women it newly exposes deserves to be considered on its own terms. Not to mention, why the problems of fifty-three percent of the population have to look like somebody else's problems before they can be recognized as existing, but then can't be addressed if they do look like other people's problems, about which something might have to be done if something is done about these, is a construction of things that truly deserves inquiry. Limiting the justification for this law to the situation of women would serve to limit the precedential value of a favorable ruling. Its particularity to one side, the *approach* to the injury is supported by a whole array of prior decisions that have justified exceptions to first amendment guarantees, when something that matters is seen to be directly at stake. What unites many cases where speech interests are raised and implicated but not, on balance, protected, is harm, harm that counts. In some existing exceptions, the definitions are much more open-ended than ours. In some, the sanctions are more severe, or potentially more so. For instance, ours is a civil law; most others are criminal, although not all. Almost none show as many people directly affected. Evidence of harm in other cases tends to be vastly less concrete and more conjectural, which is not to say that there is necessarily less of it. None of the previous cases addresses a problem of this scope or magnitude—for instance, an $8 billion a year industry. Nor do other cases address an abuse, the practice of which has such widespread legitimacy. Courts have seen harm in other cases. The question is, will they see it here, especially given that the pornographers got there first. I will confine myself here to arguing from cases on harm to people, on the supposition that, the pornographers notwithstanding, women are not flags.

* * *

To reach the magnitude of this problem on the scale it exists, our law makes trafficking in pornography— production, sale, exhibition, or distribution—actionable. Under the obscenity rubric, much legal and psychological scholarship has centered on a search for the elusive link between pornography defined as obscenity and harm. They have looked high and low—in the mind of the male consumer, in society or in its "moral fabric," in correlations between variations in levels of anti-social acts and liberalization of obscenity laws. The only harm they have found has been one they have attributed to "the social interest in order and morality."[5] Until recently, no one looked very persistently for harm to women, partic-

ularly harm to women through men. The rather obvious fact that the sexes *relate* has been overlooked in the inquiry into the male consumer and his mind. The pornography doesn't just drop out of the sky, go into his head and stop there. Specifically, men rape, batter, prostitute, molest, and sexually harass women. Under conditions of inequality, they also hire, fire, promote, and grade women, decide how much or whether or not we are worth paying and for what, define and approve and disapprove of women in ways that count, that determine our lives.

If women are not just born to be sexually used, the fact that we are seen and treated as though that is what we are born for becomes something in need of explanation. If we see that men relate to women in a pattern of who they see women as being, and that forms a pattern of inequality, it becomes important to ask where that view came from or, minimally, how it is perpetuated or escalated. Asking this requires asking different questions about pornography than the ones obscenity law made salient.

Now I'm going to talk about causality in its narrowest sense. Recent experimental research on pornography shows that the materials covered by our definition cause measurable harm to women through increasing men's attitudes and behaviors of discrimination in both violent and nonviolent forms. Exposure to some of the pornography in our definition increases normal men's immediately subsequent willingness to aggress against women under laboratory conditions. It makes normal men more closely resemble convicted rapists attitudinally, although as a group they don't look all that different from them to start with. It also significantly increases attitudinal measures known to correlate with rape and self-reports of aggressive acts, measures such as hostility toward women, propensity to rape, condoning rape, and predicting that one would rape or force sex on a woman if one knew one would not get caught. This latter measure, by the way, begins with rape at about a third of all men and moves to half with "forced sex."[6]

As to that pornography covered by our definition in which normal research subjects seldom perceive violence, long-term exposures still makes them see women as more worthless, trivial, non-human, and object-like, i.e., the way those who are discriminated against are seen by those who discriminate against them. Crucially, all pornography by our definition acts dynamically over time to diminish one's ability to distinguish sex from violence. The materials work behaviorally to diminish the capacity of both men and women to perceive that an account of a rape is an account of a rape. X-only materials, in which subjects perceive no force, also increase perceptions that a rape victim is worthless and decrease the perception she was harmed. The overall direction of current research suggests that the more expressly violent materials accomplish on less exposure what the less overtly violent—that is, the so-called "sex only materials"—accomplish over the longer term. Women are rendered fit for use and targeted for abuse. The only thing that the research cannot document is which individual women will be next on the list. (This cannot be documented experimentally because of ethics constraints on the researchers—constraints which do not operate in life.) Although the targeting is systematic on the basis of sex, it targets individuals at random. They are selected on the basis of roulette. Pornography can no longer be said to be just a mirror. It does not just reflect the world or some people's perceptions. It *moves* them. It increases attitudes that are lived out, circumscribing the status of half the population.

What the experimental data predict would happen, actually does happen in women's real lives. You know, it's fairly frustrating that women have known that these things do happen for some time. As Ed Donnerstein, an experimental researcher in this area, often puts it, "we just quantify the obvious." It is women, primarily, to whom the research results have been the obvious, because we live them. But not until a laboratory study predicts that these things *would* happen, do people begin to believe you when you say they *did* happen to you. There is no—*not any*—inconsistency between the patterns the laboratory studies predict and the data on what actually happens to real women. Show me an abuse of women in society, I'll show it to you made sex in the pornography. If you want to know who is being hurt in this

society, go see what is being done and to whom in pornography and then go look for them other places in the world. You will find them being hurt in just that way. We did in our hearings.

In our hearings, women spoke, to my knowledge for the first time in history in public, about the damage pornography does to them. We learned that pornography is used to break women, to train women to sexual submission, to season women, to terrorize women, and to silence their dissent. It is this that has previously been termed "having no effect." Men inflict on women the sex that they experience through the pornography in a way that gives women no choice about seeing the pornography or doing the sex. Asked if anyone ever tried to inflict sex acts on them they did not want that they knew came from pornography, ten percent of women in a recent random study said yes. Twenty-four percent of married women said yes. That is a lot of women. A lot more don't know. Some of those who do testified in Minneapolis. One wife said of her ex-husband: "He would read from the pornography like a text book, like a journal. In fact when he asked me to be bound, when he finally convinced me to do it, he read in the magazine how to tie the knots. . . ." Another woman said of her boyfriend: "[H]e went to this party, saw pornography, got an erection, got me . . . to inflict his erection on. . . . There is a direct causal relationship there." One woman who said her husband had rape and bondage magazines all over the house, discovered two suitcases full of Barbie dolls with rope tied on their arms and legs and with tape across their mouths. Now think about the silence of women. She said, "He used to tie me up and he tried those things on me." A therapist in private practice reported:

Presently or recently I have worked with clients who have been sodomized by broom handles, forced to have sex with over 20 dogs in the backseat of their car, tied up and then electrocuted on their genitals. These are children, [all] in the ages of 14 to 18, all of whom [have been directly affected by pornography,] [e]ither where the perpetrator has read the manuals and manuscripts at night and used these as recipe books by day or had the pornography present at the time of the sexual violence.

One woman, testifying that all the women in a group of ex-prostitutes were brought into prostitution as children through pornography, characterized their collective experience: "[I]n my experience there was not one situation where a client was not using pornography while he was using me or that he had not just watched pornography or that it was verbally referred to and directed me to pornography." "Men," she continued, "witness the abuse of women in pornography constantly and if they can't engage in that behavior with their wives, girl friends or children, they force a whore to do it."

Men also testified about how pornography hurts them. One young gay man who had seen *Playboy* and *Penthouse* as a child said of hetersexual pornography:

It was one of the places I learned about sex and it showed me that sex was violence. What I saw there was a specific relationship between men and women. . . . [T]he woman was to be used, objectified, humiliated and hurt; the man was in a superior position, a position to be violent. In pornography I learned that what it meant to be sexual with a man or to be loved by a man was to accept his violence.

For this reason, when he was battered by his first lover, which he described as "one of the most profoundly destructive experiences of my life," he accepted it.

Pornography also hurts men's capacity to relate to women. One young man spoke about this in a way that connects pornography—not the prohibition on pornography—with fascism. He spoke of his struggle to repudiate the thrill of dominance, of his difficulty finding connection with a woman to whom he is close. He said:

My point is that if women in a society filled by pornography must be wary for their physical selves, a man, even a man of good intentions, must be wary for his mind. . . . I do not want to be a mechanical, goose stepping follower of the Playboy bunny, because that is what I think it is. . . . [T]hese are the experiments a master race perpetuates on those slated for extinction.

The woman he lives with is Jewish. There was a very brutal rape near their house. She was afraid; she tried to joke. It didn't work. "She was still afraid. And just as a well-meaning German was afraid in 1933, I am also very much afraid."

Pornography stimulates and reinforces, it does not cathect or mirror, the connection between one-sided freely available sexual access to women and masculine sexual excitement and sexual satisfaction. The catharsis hypothesis is fantasy. The fantasy theory is fantasy. Reality is: Pornography conditions male orgasm to female subordination. It tells men what sex means, what a real woman is, and codes them together in a way that is behaviorally reinforcing. This is a real five-dollar sentence but I'm going to say it anyway: Pornography is a set of hermeneutical equivalences that work on the epistemological level. Substantively, pornography defines the meaning of what a woman is by connecting access to her sexuality with masculinity through orgasm. The behavioral data show that what pornography means *is* what it does.

So far, opposition to our ordinance centers on the trafficking provision. This means not only that it is difficult to comprehend a group injury in a liberal culture—that what it *means* to be a woman is defined by this and that it is an injury for all women, even if not for all women equally. It is not only that the pornography has got to be accessible, which is the bottom line of virtually every objection to this law. It is also that power, as I said, is when you say something, it is taken for reality. If you talk about rape, it will be agreed that rape is awful. But rape is a conclusion. If a victim describes the facts of a rape, maybe she was asking for it, or enjoyed it, or at least consented to it, or the man might have thought she did, or maybe she had had sex before. It is now agreed that there is something wrong with sexual harassment. But describe what happened to you, and it may be trivial or personal or paranoid, or maybe you should have worn a bra that day. People are against discrimination. But describe the situation of a real woman, and they are not so sure she wasn't just unqualified. In law, all these disjunctions between women's perspective on our injuries and the standards we have to meet go under dignified legal rubrics like burdens of proof, credibility, defenses, elements of the crime, and so on. These standards all contain a definition of what a woman is in terms of what sex is and the low value placed on us through it. They reduce injuries done to us to authentic expressions of who we are. Our silence is written all over them. So is the pornography.

By contrast, we have as yet encountered comparatively little objection to the coercion, force, or assault provisions of our ordinance. I think that's partly because the people who make and approve laws may not yet see what they do as that. They *know* they use the pornography as we have described it in this law, and our law defines that, the reality of pornography, as a harm to women. If they suspect that they might on occasion engage in or benefit from coercion or force or assault, they may think that the victims won't be able to prove it—and they're right. Women who charge men with sexual abuse are not believed. The pornographic view of them is: They want it; they all want it. When women bring charges of sexual assault, motives such as venality or sexual repression must be invented, because we cannot really have been hurt. Under the trafficking provision, women's lack of credibility cannot be relied upon to negate the harm. There's no woman's story to destroy, no credibility-based decision on what happened. The hearings establish the harm. The definition sets the standard. The grounds of reality definition are authoritatively shifted. Pornography is bigotry, *period*. We are now—*in the world pornography has decisively defined*—having to meet the burden of proving, once and for all, for all of the rape and torture and battery, all of the sexual harassment, all of the child sexual abuse, all of the forced prostitution, *all* of it that the pornography is part of and that is part of the pornography, that the harm *does happen* and that when it happens it looks like this. Which may be why all this evidence never seems to be enough.

It is worth considering what evidence has been enough when other harms involving other purported speech interests have been allowed to be legislated against. By comparison to our trafficking section, analytically similar restrictions have been allowed under the first amendment, with a legislative basis far less massive, detailed, concrete, and conclusive. Our statutory language is more ordinary, objective, and precise, and covers a harm far narrower than its legislative record substantiates. Under *Miller*, obscenity was allowed to be made criminal in the name of the "danger of offending the sensibilities of unwilling recipients, or exposure to juveniles."[7] Under our law, we have direct evidence of harm, not just a conjectural danger, that unwilling women in considerable numbers are not simply offended in their sensibilities, but are violated in their persons and restricted in their options. Obscenity law also suggests that the applicable standard for legal adequacy in measuring such connections may not be statistical certainty. The Supreme Court has said that it is not their job to resolve empirical uncertainties that underlie state obscenity legislation. Rather, it is for them to determine whether a legislature could reasonably have determined that a connection might exist between the prohibited material and harm of a kind in which the state has legitimate interest. Equality should be such an area. The Supreme Court recently recognized that prevention of sexual exploitation and abuse of children is, in their words, "a governmental objective of surpassing importance."[8] This might also be the case for sexual exploitation and abuse of women, although I think a civil remedy is initially more appropriate to the goal of empowering adult women than a criminal prohibition would be.

Other rubrics provide further support for the argument that this law is narrowly tailored to further a legitimate governmental interest consistent with the interests underlying the first amendment. Exceptions to the first amendment—you may have gathered from this—exist. The reason they exist is that the harm done by some speech outweighs its expressive value, if any. In our law, a legislature recognizes that pornography, as defined and made actionable, undermines sex equality. One can say—and I have—that pornography is a causal factor in violations of women; one can also say that women will be violated so long as pornography exists; but one can also say simply that pornography violates women. Perhaps this is what the woman had in mind who testified at our hearings that whether or not pornography causes violent acts to be perpetrated against some women is not her only issue. "Porn is already a violent act against women. It is our mothers, our daughters, our sisters, and our wives that are for sale for pocket change at the newsstands in this country." *Chaplinsky v. New Hampshire* recognizes the ability to restrict as "fighting words" speech which, "by [its] very utterance inflicts injury. . . ." Perhaps the only reason that pornography has not been "fighting words"—in the sense of words which by their utterance tend to incite immediate breach of the peace—is that women have seldom fought back, yet.

Some concerns close to those of this ordinance underlie group libel laws, although the differences are equally important. In group libel law, as Justice Frankfurter's opinion in *Beauharnais* illustrates, it has been understood that individuals' treatment and alternatives in life may depend as much on the reputation of the group to which such a person belongs as on their own merit. Not even a partial analogy can be made to group libel doctrine without examining the point made by Justice Brandeis, and recently underlined by Larry Tribe: Would more speech, rather than less, remedy the harm? In the end, the answer may be yes, but not under the abstract system of free speech, which only enhances the power of the pornographers while doing nothing substantively to guarantee the free speech of women, for which we need civil equality. The situation in which women presently find ourselves with respect to the pornography is one in which more *pornography* is inconsistent with rectifying or even counterbalancing its damage through speech, because so long as the pornography exists in the way it does there *will not be more speech by women*. Pornography strips and devastates women of credibility, from our accounts of sexual assault to our everyday reality of sexual subordination. We are deauthoritized and reduced and devalidated and silenced. Silenced here means that the purposes of the first amendment, premised upon conditions presumed and promoted by protecting free speech, do not pertain to women because they are not our conditions. Consider them: individual self-fulfillment—how does pornography promote our

individual self-fulfillment? How does sexual inequality even permit it? Even if she can form words, who listens to a woman with a penis in her mouth? Facilitating consensus—to the extent pornography does so, it does so one-sidedly by silencing protest over the injustice of sexual subordination. Participation in civic life . . . how does pornography enhance women's participation in civic life? Anyone who cannot walk down the street or even lie down in her own bed without keeping her eyes cast down and her body clenched against assault is unlikely to have much to say about the issues of the day, still less will she become Tolstoy. Facilitating change—*this law* facilitates the change the existing first amendment theory has been used to throttle. Any system of freedom of expression that does not address a problem where the free speech of men silences the free speech of women, a real conflict between speech interests as well as between people, is not serious about securing freedom of expression in this country.

For those of you who still think pornography is only an idea, consider the possibility that obscenity law got one thing right. Pornography is more act-like than thought-like. The fact that pornography, in a feminist view, furthers the idea of the sexual inferiority of women, which is a political idea, doesn't make the pornography itself into a political idea. One can express the idea a practice embodies. That does not make that practice into an idea. Segregation expresses the idea of the inferiority of one group to another on the basis of race. That does not make segregation an idea. A sign that says "Whites Only" is only words. Is it therefore protected by the first amendment? Is it not an act, a practice, of segregation because of the inseparability of what it means from what it does? *Law* is only words.

The issue here is whether the fact that the central link in the cycle of abuse that I have connected is words and pictures will immunize that entire cycle, about which we cannot do anything without doing something about the pornography. As Justice Stewart said in *Ginsburg*, "When expression occurs in a setting where the capacity to make a choice is absent, government regulation of that expression may coexist with and *even implement* First Amendment guarantees."[9] I would even go so far as to say that the pattern of evidence we have closely approaches Justice Douglas' requirement that "freedom of expression can be suppressed if, and to the extent that, it is so closely brigaded with illegal action as to be an inseparable part of it."[10] Those of you who have been trying to separate the acts from the speech—that's an act, that's an act, there's a law against that act, regulate that act, don't touch the speech—*notice here* that the fact that the acts involved are illegal doesn't mean that the speech that is "brigaded with" it, *cannot* be regulated. It is when it *can* be.

I take one of two penultimate points from Andrea Dworkin, who has often said that pornography is not speech for women, it is the silence of women. Remember the mouth taped, the woman gagged, "Smile I can get a lot of money for that." The smile is not her expression. It is her silence, and it is not her expression not because it didn't happen, but because it *did* happen. The screams of the women in pornography are silence, like Kitty Genovese's screams, whose plight was misinterpreted by some onlookers as a lovers' quarrel. The flat expressionless voice of the woman in the New Bedford gang rape, testifying, is the silence of women. She was raped as men cheered and watched like they do in and with the pornography. When women resist and men say, "Like this you stupid bitch, here is how to do it" and shove their faces into the pornography, this "truth of sex" is the silence of women. When they say, "If you love me, you'll try," the enjoyment we fake, the enjoyment we learn, is silence. Women who submit because there is more dignity in it than in losing the fight over and over live in silence. Having to sleep with your publisher or director to get access to what men call speech is silence. Being humiliated on the basis of your appearance, whether by approval or disapproval, because you have to look a certain way for a certain job, whether you get the job or not, is silence. The absence of a woman's voice, everywhere that it cannot be heard, is silence. And anyone who thinks that what women say in pornography is women's speech—the "Fuck me, do it to me, harder," all of that—has never heard the sound of a woman's voice.

The most basic assumption underlying first amendment adjudication is that, socially, speech is free. The first amendment says Congress shall not abridge the freedom of speech. Free speech, get it, *exists*. Those who wrote the first amendment *had* speech—they wrote the Constitution. *Their* problem was to keep it free from the only power that realistically threatened it: the federal government. They designed the first amendment to prevent government from constraining that which if unconstrained by government was free, meaning *accessible to them*. At the same time, we can't tell much about the intent of the Framers with regard to the question of women's speech, because I don't think we crossed their minds. It is consistent with this analysis that their posture to freedom of speech tends to presuppose that whole segments of the population are not systematically silenced, socially, prior to government action. If everyone's power were equal to theirs, if this were a non-hierarchical society, that might make sense. But the place of pornography in the inequality of the sexes makes the assumption of equal power untrue.

This is a hard question. It involves risks. Classically, opposition to censorship has involved keeping government off the backs of people. Our law is about getting some people off the backs of other people. The risks that it will be misused have to be measured against the risks of the status quo. Women will never have that dignity, security, compensation that is the promise of equality so long as the pornography exists as it does now. The situation of women suggests that the urgent issue of our freedom of speech is not primarily the avoidance of state intervention as such, but getting affirmative access to speech for those to whom it has been denied.

* * *

NOTES

1. A. Rich, "Cartographies of Silence," in *The Dream of a Common Language* [(New York: Norton, 1978), 16, 17].

2. This figure was calculated at my request by D. Russell on the random sample data base discussed in D. Russell, Rape in Marriage (1982). The figure includes all the forms of rape

or other sexual abuse or harassment surveyed, non-contact as well as contact, from gang-rape by strangers to obscene phone calls, unwanted sexual advances on the street, unwelcome requests to pose for pornography, and subjection to "Peeping Toms" and sexual exhibitionists.

3. Miller v. California, 413 U.S. 15, 24 (1973).

4. *See* Plessy v. Ferguson, 163 U.S. 537, 551 (1896).

5. Roth v. United States, 354 U.S. 476, 485 (1957) (quoting Chaplinsky v. New Hampshire, 315 U.S. 568, 572 (1942)).

6. *See* Briere & Malamuth, *Self-Reported Likelihood of Sexually Aggressive Behavior: Attitudinal Versus Sexual Explanations,* 37

J. Res. Personality 315, 318 (1983) (58% of college males in survey report some likelihood of forcing sex on woman if they knew they would not get caught).

7. *See* Miller v. California, 413 U.S. 15, 19 (1973).

8. New York v. Ferber, 458 U.S. 742, 757 (1982).

9. Ginsberg v. New York, 390 U.S. 629, 649 (1968) (Stewart, J., concurring in result) (emphasis added).

10. Roth v. United States, 354 U.S. 476, 514 (Douglas, J., dissenting) (citing Giboney v. Empire Storage & Ice Co., 336 U.S. 490, 498 (1949)).

Feminists against the First Amendment

Wendy Kaminer

Despite efforts to redevelop it, New York's Forty-second Street retains its underground appeal, especially for consumers of pornography. What city officials call "sex-related uses"—triple-X video (formerly book) stores, peep shows, and topless bars—have declined in number since their heyday in the 1970s, and much of the block between Seventh and Eighth avenues is boarded up, a hostage to development. New sex businesses—yuppie topless bars and downscale lap-dancing joints (don't ask)—are prospering elsewhere in Manhattan. But Peepland (MULTI-VIDEO BOOTHS! NUDE DANCING GIRLS!) still reigns, and Show World, a glitzy sex emporium, still anchors the west end of the block, right around the corner from *The New York Times*.

In the late 1970s I led groups of suburban women on tours through Show World and other Forty-second Street hot spots, exposing them, in the interests of consciousness-raising, to pornography's various genres: Nazi porn, nurse porn, lesbian porn, bondage porn—none of it terribly imaginative. The women didn't exactly hold hands as they ventured down the street with me, but they did stick close together; trav-

eling en masse, they were not so conspicuous as individuals. With only a little less discomfort than resolve, they dutifully viewed the pornography.

This was in the early days of the feminist anti-porn movement, when legislative strategies against pornography were mere gleams in the eye of the feminist writer Andrea Dworkin, when it seemed possible to raise consciousness about pornography without arousing demands for censorship. That period of innocence did not last long. By 1981 the New Right had mounted a nationwide censorship campaign to purge schools and public libraries of sex education and other secular-humanist forms of "pornography." Sex education was "filth and perversion," Jerry Falwell announced in a fund-raising letter that included, under the label "Adults Only, Sexually Explicit Material," excerpts from a college health text. By the mid-1980s right-wing advocates of traditional family values had co-opted feminist anti-porn protests—or, at least, they'd co-opted feminist rhetoric. The feminist attorney and law professor Catharine MacKinnon characterized pornography as the active subordination of women, and Phyllis Schlafly wrote, "Pornography really should be defined as the degradation of women. Nearly all porn involves the use of women in subordinate, degrading poses for the sexual, exploitative, and even sadistic and violent pleasures of men." Just like a feminist, Schlafly worried about how pornography might "affect a man who is already prone to violence against women." President Ronald Reagan deplored the link between pornography and violence against women.

PORNOGRAPHY AS SEX DISCRIMINATION

Of course, while feminists blamed patriarchy for pornography, moral majoritarians blamed feminism and other humanist rebellions. The alliance between feminists and the far right was not ideological but political. In 1984 anti-porn legislation devised by Andrea Dworkin and Catharine MacKinnon, defining pornography as a violation of women's civil rights, was introduced in the Indianapolis city council by an anti-ERA activist, passed with the support of the right, and signed into law by the Republican mayor, William Hudnut.

With the introduction of this bill, a new legislative front opened in the war against pornography, alienating civil-libertarian feminists from their more censorious sisters, while appealing to populist concerns about declining moral values. By calling for the censorship of pornography, some radical feminists found their way into the cultural mainstream—and onto the margins of First Amendment law.

The legislation adopted in Indianapolis offered a novel approach to prohibiting pornography which had all the force of a semantic distinction: pornography was not simply speech, Catharine MacKinnon suggested, but active sex discrimination, and was therefore not protected by the First Amendment. (In her 1989 book *Toward a Feminist Theory of the State,* MacKinnon characterized pornography as "a form of forced sex.") Regarding pornography as action, defining it broadly as any verbal or visual sexually explicit material (violent or not) that subordinates women, presuming that the mere existence of pornography oppresses women, the Indianapolis ordinance gave any woman offended by any arguably pornographic material the right to seek an order prohibiting it, along with damages for the harm it presumably caused. In other words, any woman customer brows-

ing in a bookstore or patrolling one, glancing at a newsstand or a triple-X video store, was a potential plaintiff in a sex-discrimination suit. Given all the literature, films, and videos on the mass market that could be said to subordinate women, this ordinance would have created lots of new business for lawyers—but it did not stand. Within a year of its enactment the Dworkin-MacKinnon law was declared unconstitutional by a federal appeals court, in a decision affirmed by the U.S. Supreme Court.

The feminist anti-porn movement retreated from the legislative arena and passed out of public view in the late 1980s, only to re-emerge with renewed strength on college campuses. College professors following fashions in poststructuralism asserted that legal principles, like those protecting speech, were mere rhetorical power plays: without any objective, universal merit, prevailing legal ideals were simply those privileged by the mostly white male ruling class. The dominant poststructural dogma of the late 1980s denied the First Amendment the transcendent value that the liberal belief in a marketplace of ideas has always awarded it.

MASSACHUSETTS MISCHIEF

This unlikely convergence of First Amendment critiques from multiculturalists, poststructuralists, and advocates of traditional family values, recently combined with high-profile rape and harassment cases and women's abiding concern with sexual violence, buoyed the feminist anti-porn movement. This year it re-emerged on the national and local scene with renewed legislative clout. The presumption that pornography oppresses women and is a direct cause of sexual violence is the basis for bills introduced in the U.S. Senate and the Massachusetts legislature. Last June the Senate Judiciary Committee passed the Pornography Victims' Compensation Act, which would make producers, distributors, exhibitors, and retailers convicted of disseminating material adjudged obscene liable for damages to victims of crimes who could claim that the material caused their victimization. The Massachusetts legislature held hearings on a much broader anti-porn bill, closely modeled on the Indianapolis ordinance. Disarmingly titled "An Act to Protect the Civil Rights of Women and Children," the Massachusetts bill would not only make purveyors of pornography liable for crimes committed by their customers; it would also allow any woman, whether or not she has been the victim of a crime, to sue the producers, distributors, exhibitors, or retailers of any sexually explicit visual material that subordinates women. (The exclusion of verbal "pornography" from the anti-trafficking provision would protect the likes of Norman Mailer, whom many feminists consider a pornographer, so long as his works are not adapted for the screen.) What this bill envisions is that the First Amendment would protect only that speech considered sexually correct.

The feminist case against pornography is based on the presumption that the link between pornography and sexual violence is clear, simple, and inexorable. The argument is familiar; censorship campaigns always blame unwanted speech for unwanted behavior: Jerry Falwell once claimed that sex education causes teenage pregnancy, just as feminists claim that pornography causes rape. One objection to this assertion is that it gives rapists and batterers an excuse for their crimes, and perhaps even a "pornography made me do it" defense.

The claim that pornography causes rape greatly oversimplifies the problem of sexual violence. We can hardly say that were it not for pornography, there would be no rape or battering. As feminists opposed to anti-porn legislation have pointed out, countries in which commercial pornography is illegal—Saudi Arabia, for example—are hardly safe havens for women.

This is not to deny that there probably is some link between violence in the media and violence in real life, but it is complicated, variable, and difficult to measure. Not all hate speech is an incantation; not all men are held spellbound by pornography. Poststructural feminists who celebrate subjectivism should be among the first to admit that different people respond to the same images differently. All we can confidently claim is that the way women are imagined is likely to have a cumulative effect on the way they're treated, but that does not mean any single image is the clear and simple cause of any single act.

The Dworkin-MacKinnon bill, however, did more than assume that pornography causes sex discrimination and other crimes against women. It said that pornography *is* violence and discrimination: the active subordination of women (and it assumed that we can all agree on what constitutes subordination). MacKinnon and her followers deny that prohibiting pornography is censorship, because they effectively deny that pornography is speech—and that is simply Orwellian. The line between speech and behavior is sometimes blurred: dancing nude down a public street is one way of expressing yourself which may also be a form of disorderly conduct. But if pornography is sex discrimination, then an editorial criticizing the President is treason.

Most feminists concerned about pornography are probably not intent on suppressing political speech, but the legislation they support, like the Massachusetts anti-porn bill, is so broad, and its definition of pornography so subjective, that it would be likely to jeopardize sex educators and artists more than it would hard-core pornographers, who are used to operating outside the law. Feminist legislation makes no exception for "pornography" in which some might find redeeming social value; it could, for example, apply in the case of a woman disfigured by a man who had seen too many paintings by Willem de Kooning. "If a woman is subjected," Catharine MacKinnon writes, "why should it matter that the work has other value?"

With this exclusive focus on prohibiting material that reflects incorrect attitudes toward women, anti-porn feminists don't deny the chilling effect of censorship; they embrace it. Any speech that subordinates women—any pornography—is yelling "Fire!" in a crowded theater, they say, falling back on a legal canard. But that's true only if, just as all crowds are deemed potential mobs, all men are deemed potential abusers whose violent impulses are bound to be sparked by pornography. It needs to be said, by feminists, that efforts to censor pornography reflect a profound disdain for men. Catharine MacKinnon has written that "pornography works as a behavioral conditioner, reinforcer and stimulus, not as idea or advocacy. It is more like saying 'kill' to a trained guard dog—and also the training process itself." That's more a theory of sexuality than of speech: pornography is action because all men are dogs on short leashes.

This bleak view of male sexuality condemns heterosexuality for women as an exercise in wish fulfillment (if only men weren't all dogs) or false consciousness (such as male-identified thinking). True feminism, according to MacKinnon, unlike liberal feminism, "sees sexuality as a social sphere of male power, of which forced sex is paradigmatic." With varying degrees of clarity, MacKinnon and Dworkin suggest that in a context of pervasive, institutionalized inequality, there can be no consensual sex between men and women: we can never honestly distinguish rape from intercourse.

AN ESOTERIC DEBATE

A modified version of this message may well have particular appeal to some college women today, who make up an important constituency for the anti-porn movement. In their late teens and early twenties, these women are still learning to cope with sexuality, in a violent and unquestionably misogynistic world. Feminism on campus tends to focus on issues of sexuality, not of economic equity. Anxiety about date rape is intense, along with anxiety about harassment and hate speech. Understanding and appreciation of the First Amendment is a lot less evident, and concern about employment discrimination seems somewhat remote. It's not hard to understand why: college women, in general, haven't experienced overt repression of opinions and ideas, or many problems in the workplace, but from childhood they've known what it is to fear rape. In the age of AIDS, the fear can be crippling.

Off campus the anti-porn feminist critique of male sexuality and heterosexuality for women has little appeal, but it is not widely known. MacKinnon's theoretical writings are impenetrable to readers who lack familiarity with poststructural jargon and the patience to decode sentences like this: "If objectivity is the epistemological stance of which women's sexual objectification is the social process, its imposition the paradigm of power in the male form, then the state will appear most relentless in imposing the male point of view when it comes closest to achieving its highest formal criterion of distanced aperspectivity." Dworkin is a much more accessible polemicist, but she is also much less visible outside feminist circles. Tailored, with an air of middle-class respectability and the authority of a law professor, MacKinnon looks far less scary to mainstream Americans than her theories about sexuality, which drive the anti-porn movement, might sound.

If anti-pornography crusades on the right reflect grassroots concern about changing sexual mores and the decline of the traditional family, anti-pornography crusades on the feminist left reflect the concerns and perceptions of an educated elite. In the battle for the moral high ground, anti-porn feminists claim to represent the interests of a racially diverse mixture of poor and working-class women who work in the pornography industry—and they probably do represent a few. But many sex-industry workers actively oppose anti-porn legislation (some feminists would say they've been brainwashed by patriarchy or actually coerced), and it's not at all clear that women who are abused in the making of pornography would be helped by forcing it deeper underground; working conditions in an illegal business are virtually impossible to police. It's hard to know how many other alleged victims of pornography feel represented by the anti-porn movement, and I know of no demographic study of the movement's active members.

Leaders of the feminist anti-porn movement, however, do seem more likely to emerge from academia and the professions than from the streets or battered-women's shelters. Debra Robbin, a former director of the New Bedford Women's Center, one of the first shelters in Massachusetts, doesn't believe that "women on the front lines," working with victims of sexual violence, will "put much energy into a fight against pornography." Activists don't have time: "They can barely leave their communities to go to the statehouses to fight for more funding." The poor and working-class women they serve would say, "Yeah, pornography is terrible, but I don't have food on my table." Carolin Ramsey, the executive director of the Massachusetts Coalition of Battered Women Service Groups, says that the pornography debate "doesn't have a lot to do with everyday life for me and the women I'm serving." She explains, "Violence in the home and the streets that directly threatens our lives and our families is more pressing than a movie. Keeping my kids away from drugs is more important than keeping them away from literature."

Ramsey is sympathetic to anti-porn feminists ("there's room in the movement for all of us"), and she believes that "violence in the media contributes to violence in real life." Still, she considers the pornography debate "esoteric" and "intellectual" and feels under no particular pressure from her constituents to take a stand against pornography.

If censoring pornography is the central feminist issue for Catharine MacKinnon, it is a peripheral issue for activists like Robbin and Ramsey. Robbin in particular does not believe that eliminating pornography would appreciably lessen the incidence of sexual abuse. David Adams, a co-founder and the executive director of Emerge, a Boston counseling center for male batterers, believes that only a minority of his clients (perhaps 10 to 20 percent) use hard-core pornography. He estimates that half may have substance-abuse problems, and adds that alcohol seems more directly involved in abuse than pornography. Adams agrees with feminists that pornography is degrading to women but does not support legislation regulating it, because "the legislation couldn't work and would only open the door to censorship."

What might work instead? Emerge conducts programs in Boston and Cambridge public schools on violence, aimed at both victims and perpetrators. "There's a lot of violence in teen relationships," Adams observes. Debra Robbin wishes that women in the anti-porn movement would "channel their energies into funding battered-women's shelters and rape-crisis centers."

Reforming the criminal-justice system is also a priority for many women concerned about sexual violence. Anti-stalking laws could protect many more women than raids on pornographic video stores are ever likely to; so could the efficient processing of cases against men who abuse women.

SENSATIONALISM AS AN ORGANIZING TOOL

Why do some women channel their energies into a fight against pornography? Antiporn legislation has the appeal of a quick fix, as Robbin notes. And, she adds, "there's notoriety to be gained from protesting pornography." The "harder work"—promoting awareness and understanding of sexual violence, changing the way children are socialized, and helping women victims of violence—is less sensationalist and less visible.

Sensationalism, however, is an organizing tool for anti-porn feminists. If questions about the effects of pornography seem intellectual to some women involved in social-service work, the popular campaign against pornography is aggressively anti-intellectual. Although advocates of First Amendment freedoms are stuck with intellectual defenses of the marketplace of ideas, anti-porn feminists whip up support for their cause with pornographic slide shows comprising hard-core pictures of women being tortured, raped, and generally degraded. Many feminists are equally critical of the soft-core porn movies available at local video stores and on cable TV, arguing that the violence in pornography is often covert (and they include mainstream advertising images in their slide shows). But hard-core violence is what works on the crowd. Feminist rhetoric often plays on women's worst fears about men: "Pornography tells us that there but for the grace of God go us." Gail Dines, a sociology professor at Wheelcock College, exclaimed during her recent slide show at Harvard, as she presented photographs of women being brutalized.

Dines's porn show was SRO, its audience some three hundred undergraduates who winced and gasped at the awful slides and cheered when Dines pointed to a pornographic picture of a woman and said, "When I walk down the street, what they know about me is what they know about her!" She warned her mostly female audience that pornographers have "aggressively targeted college men." She seemed pre-occupied with masturbation. Part of the problem of pornography, she suggested, is that men use it to masturbate, and "women weren't put on this world to facilitate masturbation." She advised a student concerned about the presence of *Playboy* in the college library that library collections of pornography aren't particularly worrisome, because men are not likely to masturbate in libraries.

In addition to condemnations of male sexuality, Dines offered questionable horror stories about pornography's atrocities, like this: Rape vans are roaming the streets of New York. Women are dragged into the vans and raped on camera; when their attackers sell the rape videos in commercial outlets, the women have no legal recourse.

A story like this is impossible to disprove (how do you prove a negative?), but it should probably not be taken at face value, as many students in Dines's audience seemed to take it. William Daly, the director of New York City's Office of Midtown Enforcement, which is responsible for monitoring the sex industry in New York, has never heard of rape vans; almost anything is possible on Forty-second Street, but he is skeptical that rape vans are a problem. Part of Dines's story, however, is simply untrue: under New York State privacy law, says Nan Hunter, a professor of law at Brooklyn Law School, women could seek damages for the sale of the rape videos, and also an injunction against their distribution.

It would be difficult even to raise questions about the accuracy of the rape-van story, however, in the highly emotional atmosphere of a slide show; you'd be accused of "not believing the women." Just as slides of bloody fetuses pre-empt rational debate about abortion, pornographic slide shows pre-empt argumentative questions and rational consideration of First Amendment freedoms, the probable effect of efforts to censor pornography, and the actual relationship between pornography and violence.

A PORNOGRAPHIC CULTURE?

Does pornography cause violence against women, as some feminists claim? Maybe, in some cases, under some circumstances involving explicitly violent material. Readers interested in the social-science debate should see both the report of the Attorney General's Commission on Pornography, which found a link between pornography and violence against women, and the feminist writer Marcia Pally's "Sense and Censorship," published by Americans for Constitutional Freedom and the Freedom to Read Foundation. In addition to the equivocal social-science data, however, we have the testimony of women who claim to have been brutalized by male consumers of pornography. Anti-porn feminists generally characterize pornography as a "how to" literature on abusing women, which men are apparently helpless to resist. But evidence of this is mainly anecdotal: At a hearing last March on the anti-porn bill in the Massachusetts legislature, several women told awful, lurid tales of sexual abuse, said to have been inspired by pornography. Like a TV talk show, the Attorney General's commission presented testimony from pornography's alleged victims, which may or may not have been true. It's difficult to cross-examine a sobbing self-proclaimed victim; you either take her testimony at face value or you don't.

Still, many people don't need reliable, empirical evidence about a link between pornography and behavior to believe that one exists. When feminists talk about pornography, after all, they mean a wide range of mainstream media images—Calvin Klein ads, Brian De Palma films, and the endless stream of TV shows about serial rapist stranglers and housewives who moonlight as hookers. How could we not be affected by the routine barrage of images linking sex and violence and lingerie? The more broadly pornography is defined, the more compelling are assertions about its inevitable effect on behavior, but the harder it is to control. How do we isolate the effect of any particular piece of pornography if we live in a pornographic culture?

Narrowly drawn anti-porn legislation, which legislators are most likely to pass and judges most likely to uphold, would not begin to address the larger cultural problem of pornography. Feminists themselves usually claim publicly that they're intent on prohibiting only hard-core pornography, although on its face their legislation applies to a much broader range of material. But if you accept the feminist critique of sexism in the media, hard-core porn plays a relatively minor role in shaping attitudes and behavior. If feminists are right about pornography, it is a broad social problem, not a discrete legal one—that is, pornography is not a problem the law can readily solve, unless perhaps we suspend the First Amendment entirely and give feminists the power to police the mainstream media, the workplace, and the schools.

The likelihood that feminists would not be the ones to police Forty-second Street should anti-porn legislation pass is one reason that many feminists oppose the anti-porn campaign. If society is as sexist as Andrea Dworkin and Catharine MacKinnon claim, it is not about to adopt a feminist agenda when it sets out to censor pornography. The history of anti-porn campaigns in this country is partly a history of campaigns against reproductive choice and changing roles for men and women. The first federal obscenity legislation, known as the Comstock Law, passed in 1873, prohibited the mailing of not only dirty pictures but also contraceptives and information about abortion. Early in this century Margaret Sanger and the sex educator Mary Ware Dennett were prosecuted for obscenity violations. Recently the New Right campaign against socially undesirable literature has focused on sex education in public schools. Anti-porn activists on the right consider feminism and homosexuality (which they link) to be threats to traditional family life (which, in fact, they are). In Canada a landmark Supreme Court ruling this year which adopted a feminist argument against pornography was first used to prohibit distribution of a small lesbian magazine, which a politically correct feminist would be careful to label erotica.

Gay and lesbian groups, as well as advocates of sex education and the usual array of feminist and nonfeminist civil libertarians, actively oppose anti-pornography legislation. Some state chapters of the National Organization for Women—New York, California, and Vermont—have taken strong anti-censorship stands, but at the national level NOW has not taken a position in the pornography debate. Its president, Patricia Ireland, would like to see pornography become socially unacceptable, "like smoking," but is wary of taking legal action against it, partly because she's wary of "giving people like Jesse Helms the power to decide what we read and see." But for major, national feminist organizations, like NOW and the NOW Legal Defense and Education Fund, the pornography debate is a minefield to be carefully avoided. Pornography is probably the most divisive issue feminists have faced since the first advocates of the ERA, in the 1920s, squared off against advocates of protective labor legislation for women. Feminists for and against anti-porn legislation are almost as bitterly divided as pro-choice activists and members of Operation Rescue.

Renewed concern about abortion rights may drain energy from the anti-porn movement. Feminists may awaken to the danger that anti-pornography laws will be used against sex educators and advocates of choice. (The imposition of a gag rule on family-planning clinics may have made some feminists more protective of the First Amendment.) Politicians courting women voters may find that anti-porn legislation alienates more feminists than it pleases. Still, censorship campaigns will always have considerable appeal. Like campaigns to reinstate the death penalty, they promise panaceas for profound social pathologies. They make their case by exploiting the wrenching anecdotal testimony of victims: politicians pushing the death penalty hold press conferences flanked by mothers of murdered children, just as feminists against pornography spotlight raped and battered women.

Rational argument is no match for highly emotional testimony. But it may be wishful thinking to believe that penalizing the production and distribution of hard-core pornography would have much effect on sexual violence. It would probably have little effect even on pornography given the black market. It would, however, complicate campaigns to distribute information about AIDS, let alone condoms, in the public schools. It would distract us from the harder, less popular work of reforming sexual stereotypes and roles, and addressing actual instead of metaphorical instruments of violence. The promise of the anti-porn movement is the promise of a world in which almost no one can buy pornography and almost anyone can buy a gun.

A Feminist Defense of Pornography

WENDY MCELROY

"Pornography benefits women, both personally and politically." This sentence opens my book *XXX: A Woman's Right to Pornography,* and it constitutes a more extreme defense of pornography than most feminists are comfortable with. I arrived at this position after years of interviewing hundreds of sex workers.

FEMINIST POSITIONS

Feminist positions on pornography currently break down into three rough categories. The most common one—at least, in academia—is that pornography is an expression of male culture through which women are commodified and exploited. A second view, the liberal position, combines a respect for free speech with the principle "a woman's body, a woman's right" and thus produces a defense of pornography along the lines of, "I don't approve of it, but everyone has the right to consume or produce words and images." A third view—a true defense of pornography—arises from feminists who have been labeled "pro-sex" and who argue that porn has benefits for women.

Little dialogue occurs between the three positions. Anti-pornography feminists treat women who disagree as either brainwashed dupes of patriarchy or as apologists for pornographers. In the anthology *Sexual Liberals and the Attack on Feminism* (1990), editor Dorchen Leidholdt claims that feminists who believe women make their own choices about pornography are spreading "a felicitous lie" (p. 131). In the same work, Sheila Jeffreys argues that "pro-sex" feminists are "eroticizing dominance and subordination." Wendy Stock accuses free speech feminists of identifying with their oppressors "much like . . . concentration camp prisoners with their jailors" (p. 150). Andrea Dworkin accuses them of running a "sex pro-

Wendy McElroy, "Sexual Freedom: A Feminist Defense of Pornography," *Free Inquiry* (Fall 1997): 14–17. Reprinted by permission of Wendy McElroy.

tection racket" (p. 136) and maintains that no one who defends pornography can be a feminist.

The liberal feminists who are personally uncomfortable with pornography tend to be intimidated into silence. Those who continue to speak out, like American Civil Liberties Union President Nadine Strossen (*Defending Pornography*) are ignored. For example, Catharine MacKinnon has repeatedly refused to share a stage with Strossen or any woman who defends porn. "Pro-sex" feminists—many of whom are current or former sex-workers—often respond with anger, rather than arguments.

Peeling back the emotions, what are the substantive questions raised by each feminist perspective?

Anti-porn Feminism

Page Mellish of Feminists Fighting Pornography has declared, "There's no feminist issue that isn't rooted in the porn problem." In her book *Only Words,* MacKinnon denies that pornography consists of words and images, both of which would be protected by the First Amendment. She considers pornography—in and of itself—to be an act of sexual violence. Why is pornography viewed as both the core issue of modern feminism and an inherent act of violence? The answer lies in radical feminist ideology, which Christina Hoff Sommers calls "gender feminism."

Gender feminism looks at history and sees an uninterrupted oppression of women by men that spans cultural barriers. To them, the only feasible explanation is that men and women are separate and antagonistic classes whose interests necessarily conflict. Male interests are expressed through and maintained by a capitalistic structure known as "patriarchy."

The root of the antagonism is so deep that it lies in male biology itself. For example, in the watershed book *Against Our Will,* Susan Brownmiller traces the inevitability of rape back to Neanderthal times when men began to use their penises as weapons. Brownmiller writes: "From prehistoric times to the present,

I believe, rape has played a critical function. It is nothing more or less than a conscious process of intimidation by which all men keep all women in a state of fear." How Brownmiller acquired this knowledge of prehistoric sex is not known.

Another tenet of gender oppression is that sex is a social construct. Radical feminists reject what they call "sexual essentialism"—the notion that sex is a natural force based on biology that inclines women toward natural tendencies, such as motherhood. Even deeply felt sexual preferences, such as heterosexuality, are not biological. They spring from ideology.

Men construct women's sexuality through the words and images of society, which the French philosopher Foucault called the "texts" of society. After such construction, men commercialize women's sexuality and market it back in the form of pornography. In other words, through porn man defines woman sexually—a definition that determines every aspect of her role in society. To end the oppression, patriarchy and its texts must be destroyed.

Liberal Feminism

Liberal feminism is a continuation of 1960s feminism that called for equality with men, who were not inherent oppressors so much as recalcitrant partners to be enlightened. Equality did not mean destroying the current system, but reforming it through such measures as affirmative action. The liberal principle "a woman's body, a woman's right" underlay arguments ranging from abortion rights to lifestyle freedoms like lesbianism. The stress was upon the act of choosing, rather than upon the content of any choice.

Liberal feminists share the general liberal bias toward free speech, but they are in flux on pornography. Some liberal organizations like Feminists for Free Expression (FFE) have consistently opposed censorship in any form. Some liberal feminists like Sallie Tisdale (*Talk Dirty to Me*) have staunchly defended sexual freedom. But many liberal feminists commonly reason as follows: "As a woman I am appalled by *Playboy* . . . but as a writer I understand the need for free expression."

Such arguments are not pro-pornography. They are anti-censorship ones based on several grounds, including: great works of art and literature would be banned; the First Amendment would be breached; political expression would be suppressed; and a creative culture requires freedom of speech.

Other liberal feminists, who have accepted many of the ideological assumptions of the anti-porn position, seem willing to sacrifice free speech for the greater good of protecting women. For example, they also condemn the free market for commercializing women as "body parts," which demeans women. In "A Capital Idea," an easy defending pornography, which sometimes seems to be an attack, Lisa Steel comments:

Sexist representation of women . . . is all part of the same system that, in the service of profits, reduces society to "consumer groups." And marketing is every bit as conservative as the military . . . we pay dearly for the "rights" of a few to make profits from the rest of us.

Such muddled and ambivalent "defenses" often offend the sex workers they are intended to protect.

Pro-sex Feminism

Over the past decade, a growing number of feminists—labeled "pro sex"—have defended a woman's choice to participate in and to consume pornography. Some of these women, such as Nina Hartley, are current or ex-sex-workers who know firsthand that posing for pornography is an uncoerced choice that can be enriching. Pro-sex feminists retain a consistent interpretation of the principle "a woman's body, a woman's right" and insist that every peaceful choice a woman makes with her own body must be accorded full legal protection, if not respect.

Pro-sex arguments sometimes seem to overlap with liberal feminist ones. For example, both express concern over who will act as censor because subjective words, such as "degrading," will be interpreted to mean whatever the censor wishes.

The statute that banned Margaret Sanger because she used the words *syphilis* and *gonorrhea* is no different, in principle, than the one that interprets obscenity today. There will be no protection even for the classics of feminism, such as *Our Bodies, Ourselves*, which provided a generation of women with the first explicit view of their own biology. Inevitably, censorship will be used again the least popular views, against the weakest members of society . . . including feminists and lesbians. When the Canadian Supreme Court decided in 1992 to protect women by restricting the importation of pornography, one of the first victims was the lesbian/gay Glad Day Bookstore, which had been on a police hit list. Among the books seized by Canadian customs were two books by Andrea Dworkin, *Pornography: Men Possessing Women* and *Women Hating*. Such an event should not have surprised Dworkin who declared in *Take Back the Night,* "There is not a feminist alive who could possibly look to the male legal system for real protection from the systematized sadism of men" (p. 257).

On the dangers of censoring pornography, pro-sex and liberal feminists often agree. On the possible benefits of pornography to women, they part company.

DISSECTING ANTI-PORN

Do the specific accusations hurled at pornography stand up under examination?

Pornography Is Degrading to Women

Degrading is a subjective term. I find commercials in which women become orgasmic over soapsuds to be tremendously degrading. The bottom line is that every woman has the right to define what is degrading and liberating for herself.

The assumed degradation is often linked to the "objectification" of women: that is, porn converts them into sexual objects. What does this mean? If taken literally, it means nothing because objects don't have sexuality; only beings do. But to say that porn portrays women as "sexual beings" makes for poor rhetoric. Usually, the term *sex objects* means showing women as body parts, reducing them to physical objects. What is wrong with this? Women are as much their bodies as they are their minds or souls. No one gets upset if you present women as "brains" or as spiritual beings. If I concentrated on a

woman's sense of humor to the exclusion of her other characteristics, is this degrading? Why is it degrading to focus on her sexuality?

Pornography Leads to Violence against Women

A cause-and-effect relationship is drawn between men viewing pornography and men attacking women, especially in the form of rape. But studies and experts disagree as to whether any relationship exists between pornography and violence, between images and behavior. Even the pro-censorship Meese Commission Report admitted that the data connecting pornography to violence was unreliable.

Other studies, such as the one prepared by feminist Thelma McCormick in 1983 for the Metropolitan Toronto Task Force on Violence Against Women, find no pattern to connect porn and sex crimes. Incredibly, the Task Force suppressed the study and reassigned the project to a pro-censorship male, who returned the "correct" results. His study was published.

What of real-world feedback? In Japan, where pornography depicting graphic and brutal violence is widely available, rape is much lower per capita than in the United States, where violence in porn is severely restricted.

Pornography Is Violence Because Women Are Coerced into Pornography

Not one of the dozens of women depicted in pornographic materials with whom I spoke reported being coerced. Not one knew of a woman who had been. Nevertheless, I do not dismiss reports of violence: every industry has its abuses. And anyone who uses force or threats to make a woman perform should be charged with kidnapping, assault, and/or rape. Any such pictures or films should be confiscated and burned because no one has the right to benefit from the proceeds of a crime.

Pornography Is Violence Because Women Who Pose for Porn Are So Traumatized by Patriarchy They Cannot Give Real Consent

Although women in pornography appear to be willing, anti-porn feminists know that no psychologically healthy woman would agree to the degradation of pornography. Therefore, if agreement seems to be present, it is because the women have "fallen in love with their own oppression" and must be rescued from themselves. A common characteristic of the porn actresses I have interviewed is a love of exhibitionism. Yet if such a woman declares her enjoyment in flaunting her body, anti-porn feminists claim she is not merely a unique human being who reacts from a different background or personality. She is psychologically damaged and no longer responsible for her actions. In essence, this is a denial of a woman's right to choose anything outside the narrow corridor of choices offered by political/sexual correctness. The right to choose hinges on the right to make a "wrong" choice, just as freedom of religion entails the right to be an atheist. After all, no one will prevent a woman from doing what she thinks she should do.

A PRO-SEX DEFENSE

As a "pro-sex" feminist, I contend: Pornography benefits women, both personally and politically. It provides sexual information on at least three levels:

- It gives a panoramic view of the world's sexual possibilities. This is true even of basic sexual information such as masturbation. It is not uncommon for women to reach adulthood without knowing how to give themselves pleasure.
- It allows women to "safely" experience sexual alternatives and satisfy a healthy sexual curiosity. The world is a dangerous place. By contrast, pornography can be a source of solitary enlightenment.
- It offers the emotional information that comes only from experiencing something either directly or vicariously. It provides us with a sense how it would "feel" to do something.

Pornography allows women to enjoy scenes and situations that would be anathema to them in real life. Take, for example, one of the most common fantasies reported by women—the fantasy of "being taken." The first thing to understand is that a rape fantasy does not represent a desire for the real thing. Why would a healthy woman daydream about being raped? Perhaps by losing control, she also sheds all

sense of responsibility for and guilt over sex. Perhaps it is the exact opposite of the polite, gentle sex she has now. Perhaps it is flattering to imagine a particular man being so overwhelmed by her that he must have her. Perhaps she is curious. Perhaps she has some masochistic feelings that are vented through the fantasy. Is it better to bottle them up?

Pornography breaks cultural and political stereotypes, so that each woman can interpret sex for herself. Anti-feminists tell women to be ashamed of their appetites and urges. Pornography tells them to accept and enjoy them.

Pornography can be good therapy. Pornography provides a sexual outlet for those who—for whatever reason—have no sexual partner. Perhaps they are away from home, recently widowed, isolated because of infirmity. Perhaps they simply choose to be alone. Couples also use pornography to enhance their relationship. Sometimes they do so on their own, watching videos and exploring their reactions together. Sometimes, the couples go to a sex therapist who advises them to use pornography as a way of opening up communication on sex. By sharing pornography, the couples are able to experience variety in their sex lives without having to commit adultery.

Pornography benefits women politically in many ways. Historically, pornography and feminism have been fellow travelers and natural allies. Although it is not possible to draw a cause-and-effect relationship between the rise of pornography and that of feminism, they both demand the same social conditions—namely, sexual freedom.

Pornography is free speech applied to the sexual realm. Freedom of speech is the ally of those who seek change: it is the enemy of those who seek to maintain control. Pornography, along with all other forms of sexual heresy, such as homosexuality, should have the same legal protection as political heresy. This protection is especially important to women, whose sexuality has been controlled by censorship through the centuries.

Viewing pornography may well have a cathartic effect on men who have violent urges toward women. If this is true, restricting pornography removes a protective barrier between women and abuse.

Legitimizing pornography would protect female sex-workers, who are stigmatized by our society. Anti-pornography feminists are actually undermining the safety of sex workers when they treat them as "indoctrinated women." Dr. Leonore Tiefer, a professor of psychology, observed in her essay "On Censorship and Women": "These women have appealed to feminists for support, not rejection. . . . Sex industry workers, like all women, are striving for economic survival and a decent life, and if feminism means anything it means sisterhood and solidarity with these women."

THE PURPOSE OF LAW

The porn debate is underscored by two fundamentally antagonistic views of the purpose of law in society.

The first view, to which pro-sex feminists subscribe, is that law should protect choice. "A woman's body, a woman's right" applies to every peaceful activity a woman chooses to engage in. The law should come into play only when a woman initiates force or has force initiated against her. The second view, to which both conservatives and anti-porn feminists subscribe, is that law should protect virtue. It should come into play whenever there has been a breach of public morality, or a breach of "women's class interests."

This is old whine in new battles. The issue at stake in the pornography debate is nothing less than the age-old conflict between individual freedom and social control.

Of Liberty

John Stuart Mill

The time, it is to be hoped, is gone by, when any defence would be necessary of the 'liberty of the press' as one of the securities against corrupt or tyrannical government. No argument, we may suppose, can now be needed, against permitting a legislature or an executive, not identified in interest with the people, to prescribe opinions to them, and determine what doctrines or what arguments they shall be allowed to hear. This aspect of the question, besides, has been so often and so triumphantly enforced by preceding writers, that it needs not be specially insisted on in this place. Though the law of England, on the subject of the press, is as servile to this day as it was in the time of the Tudors, there is little danger of its being actually put in force against political discussion, except during some temporary panic, when fear of insurrection drives ministers and judges from their

John Stuart Mill, "Of the Liberty of Thought and Discussion," in *On Liberty and Other Essays* (New York: Oxford University Press, 1991), 20–29 (edited). Reprinted with permission of Oxford University Press.

propriety;[1] and, speaking generally, it is not, in constitutional countries, to be apprehended, that the government, whether completely responsible to the people or not, will often attempt to control the expression of opinion, except when in doing so it makes itself the organ of the general intolerance of the public. Let us suppose, therefore, that the government is entirely at one with the people, and never thinks of exerting any power of coercion unless in agreement with what it conceives to be their voice. But I deny the right of the people to exercise such coercion, either by themselves or by their government. The power itself is illegitimate. The best government has no more title to it than the worst. It is as noxious, or more noxious, when exerted in accordance with public opinion, than when in opposition to it. If all mankind minus one, were of one opinion, and only one person were of the contrary opinion, mankind would be no more justified in silencing that one person, than he, if he had the power, would be justified in silencing mankind. Were an opinion a personal possession of no value except to the owner;

if to be obstructed in the enjoyment of it were simply a private injury, it would make some difference whether the injury was inflicted only on a few persons or on many. But the peculiar evil of silencing the expression of an opinion is, that it is robbing the human race; posterity as well as the existing generation; those who dissent from the opinion, still more than those who hold it. If the opinion is right, they are deprived of the opportunity of exchanging error for truth: if wrong, they lose, what is almost as great a benefit, the clearer perception and livelier impression of truth, produced by its collision with error.

It is necessary to consider separately these two hypotheses, each of which has a distinct branch of the argument corresponding to it. We can never be sure that the opinion we are endeavouring to stifle is a false opinion; and if we were sure, stifling it would be an evil still.

First: the opinion which it is attempted to suppress by authority may possibly be true. Those who desire to suppress it, of course deny its truth; but they are not infallible. They have no authority to decide the question for all mankind, and exclude every other person from the means of judging. To refuse a hearing to an opinion, because they are sure that it is false, is to assume that *their* certainty is the same thing as *absolute* certainty. All silencing of discussion is an assumption of infallibility. Its condemnation may be allowed to rest on this common argument, not the worse for being common.

Unfortunately for the good sense of mankind, the fact of their fallibility is far from carrying the weight in their practical judgement, which is always allowed to it in theory; for while every one well knows himself to be fallible, few think it necessary to take any precautions against their own fallibility, or admit the supposition that any opinion, of which they feel very certain, may be one of the examples of the error to which they acknowledge themselves to be liable. Absolute princes, or others who are accustomed to unlimited deference, usually feel this complete confidence in their own opinions on nearly all subjects. People more happily situated, who sometimes hear their opinions disputed, and are not wholly unused

to be set right when they are wrong, place the same unbounded reliance only on such of their opinions as are shared by all who surround them, or to whom they habitually defer: for in proportion to a man's want of confidence in his own solitary judgement, does he usually repose, with implicit trust, on the infallibility of 'the world' in general. And the world, to each individual, means the part of it with which he comes in contact; his party, his sect, his church, his class of society: the man may be called, by comparison, almost liberal and large-minded to whom it means anything so comprehensive as his own country or his own age. Nor is his faith in this collective authority at all shaken by his being aware that other ages, countries, sects, churches, classes, and parties have thought, and even now think, the exact reverse. He devolves upon his own world the responsibility of being in the right against the dissentient worlds of other people; and it never troubles him that mere accident has decided which of these numerous worlds is the object of his reliance, and that the same causes which make him a Churchman in London, would have made him a Buddhist or a Confucian in Pekin. Yet it is as evident in itself, as any amount of argument can make it, that ages are no more infallible than individuals; every age having held many opinions which subsequent ages have deemed not only false but absurd; and it is as certain that many opinions, now general, will be rejected by future ages, as it is that many, once general, are rejected by the present.

The objection likely to be made to this argument would probably take some such form as the following. There is no greater assumption of infallibility in forbidding the propagation of error, than in any other thing which is done by public authority on its own judgement and responsibility. Judgement is given to men that they may use it. Because it maybe used erroneously, are men to be told that they ought not to use it at all? To prohibit what they think pernicious, is not claiming exemption from error, but fulfilling the duty incumbent on them, although fallible, of acting on their conscientious conviction. If we were never to act on our opinions, because those opinions may be wrong, we should leave all our interests uncared for, and all our duties unperformed. An objection which applies to all conduct, can be no valid objection to any conduct in particular. It is the duty of governments, and of individuals, to form the truest opinions they can; to form them carefully, and never impose them upon others unless they are quite sure of being right. But when they are sure (such reasoners may say), it is not conscientiousness but cowardice to shrink from acting on their opinions, and allow doctrines which they honestly think dangerous to the welfare of mankind, either in this life or in another, to be scattered abroad without restraint, because other people, in less enlightened times, have persecuted opinions now believed to be true. Let us take care, if may be said, not to make the same mistake: but governments and nations have made mistakes in other things, which are not denied to be fit subjects for the exercise of authority: they have laid on bad taxes, made unjust wars. Ought we have therefore to lay on no taxes, and, under whatever provocation, make no wars? Men, and governments, must act to the best of their ability. There is no such thing as absolute certainty, but there is assurance sufficient for the purposes of human life. We may, and must, assume our opinion to be true for the guidance of our own conduct: and it is assuming no more when we forbid bad men to pervert society by the propagation of opinions which we regard as false and pernicious.

I answer, that it is assuming very much more. There is the greatest difference between presuming an opinion to be true, because, with every opportunity for contesting it, it has not been refuted, and assuming its truth for the purpose of not permitting its refutation. Complete liberty of contradicting and disproving our opinion, is the very condition which justifies us in assuming its truth for purposes of action; and on no other terms can a being with human faculties have any rational assurance of being right.

When we consider either the history of opinion, or the ordinary conduct of human life, to what is it to be ascribed that the one and the other are no worse than they are? Not certainly to the inherent force of the human understanding; for, on any matter not self-evident, there are ninety-nine persons totally incapable of judging of it, for one who is capable; and the capacity of the hundreth person is only comparative; for the majority of the eminent men of every past generation held many opinions now known to be erroneous, and did or approved numerous things which no one will now justify. Why is it, then, that there is on the whole a preponderance among mankind of rational opinions and rational conduct? If there really is this preponderance—which there must unless human affairs are, and have always been, in an almost desperate state—it is owing to a quality of the human mind, the source of everything respectable in men either as an intellectual or as a moral being, namely, that his errors are corrigible. He is capable of rectifying his mistakes, by discussion and experience. Not by experience alone. There must be discussion, to show how experience is to be interpreted. Wrong opinions and practices gradually yield to fact and argument: but facts and arguments, to produce any effect on the mind, must be brought before it. Very few facts are able to tell their own story, without comments to bring out their meaning. The whole strength and value, then, of human judgement, depending on the one property, that it can be set right when it is wrong, reliance can be placed on it only when the means of setting it right are kept constantly at hand. In the case of any person whose judgement is really deserving of confidence, how has it become so? Because he has kept his mind open to criticism of his opinions and conduct. Because it has been his practice to listen to all that could be said against him; to profit by as much of it as was just, and expound to himself, and upon occasion to others, the fallacy of what was fallacious. Because he has felt, that the only way in which a human being can make some approach to knowing the whole of a subject, is by hearing what can be said about it by persons of every variety of opinion, and studying all modes in which it can be looked at by every character of mind. No wise man ever acquired his wisdom in any mode but this; nor is it in the nature of human intellect to become wise in any other manner. The steady habit of correcting and completing his own opinion by collating it with those of others, so far from causing doubt and hesitation in carrying it in to practice, is the only stable foundation for a just reliance on it: for, being cognisant of all that can, at least obviously, be said against him, and having taken up his position against all gainsayers—knowing that he has sought for objections and difficulties, instead of avoiding them, and has shut out no light which can be thrown upon the subject from any quarter—he has a right to think his judgement better than that of any person, or any multitude, who have not gone through a similar process.

It is not too much to require that what the wisest of mankind, those who are best entitled to trust their own judgement, find necessary to warrant their relying on it, should be submitted to by that miscellaneous collection of a few wise and many foolish individuals, called the public. The most intolerant of churches, the Roman Catholic Church, even at the canonization of a saint, admits, and listens patiently to, a 'devil's advocate'. The holiest of men, it appears, cannot be admitted to posthumous honours, until all that the devil could say against him is known and weighed. If even the Newtonian philosophy were not permitted to be questioned, mankind could not feel as complete assurance of its truth as they now do. The beliefs which we have most warrant for, have no safeguard to rest on, but a standing invitation to the whole world to prove them unfounded. If the challenge is not accepted, or is accepted and the attempt fails, we are far enough from certainty still; but we have done the best that the existing state of human reason admits of; we have neglected nothing that could give the truth a chance of reaching us: if the lists are kept open, we may hope that if there be a better truth, it will be found when the human mind is capable of receiving it; and in the meantime we may rely on having attained such approach to truth, as is possible in our own day. This is the amount of certainty attainable by a fallible being, and this the sole way of attaining it.

Strange it is, that men should admit the validity of the arguments for free discussion, but object to their being 'pushed to an extreme'; not seeing that unless the reasons are good for an extreme case, they are not good for any case. Strange that they should

imagine that they are not assuming infallibility, when they acknowledge that there should be free discussion on all subjects which can possibly be *doubtful*, but think that some particular principle or doctrine should be forbidden to be questioned because it is so *certain*, that is, because *they are certain* that it is certain. To call any proposition certain, while there is any one who would deny its certainty if permitted, but who is not permitted, is to assume that we ourselves, and those who agree with us, are the judges of certainty, and judges without hearing the other side.

In the present age—which has been described as 'destitute of faith, but terrified at scepticism'—in which people feel sure, not so much that their opinions are true, as that they should not know what to do without them—the claims of an opinion to be protected from public attack are rested not so much on its truth, as on its importance to society. There are, it is alleged, certain beliefs, so useful, not to say indispensable to well-being, that it is as much the duty of governments to uphold those beliefs, as to protect any other of the interests of society. In a case of such necessity, and so directly in the line of their duty, something less than infallibility may, it is maintained, warrant, and even bind, governments, to act on their own opinion, confirmed by the general opinion of mankind. It is also often argued, and still oftener thought, that none but bad men would desire to weaken these salutary beliefs; and there can be nothing wrong, it is thought, in restraining bad men, and prohibiting what only such men would wish to practise. This mode of thinking makes the justification of restraints on discussion not a question of the truth of doctrines, but of their usefulness; and flatters itself by that means to escape the responsibility of claiming to be an infallible judge of opinions. But those who thus satisfy themselves, do not perceive that the assumption of infallibility is merely shifted from one point to another. The usefulness of an opinion is itself matter of opinion: as disputable, as open to discussion, and requiring discussion as much, as the opinion itself. There is the same need of an infallible judge of opinions to decide an opinion to be noxious, a to decide it to be false, unless the opinion condemned has full opportunity of defending itself. And it will not do to say that the heretic may be allowed to maintain the utility or harmlessness of his opinion, though forbidden to maintain its truth. The truth of an opinion is part of its utility. If we would know whether or not it is desirable that a proposition should be believed, is it possible to exclude the consideration of whether or not it is true? In the opinion, not of bad men, but of the best men, no belief which is contrary to truth can be really useful: and can you prevent such men from urging that pleas, when they are charged with culpability for denying some doctrine which they are told is useful, but which they believe to be false? Those who are on the side of received opinions, never fail to take all possible advantage of this plea; you do not find *them* handling the question of utility as if it could be completely abstracted from that of truth: on the contrary, it is, above all, because their doctrine is the 'truth', that the knowledge or the belief of it is held to be so indispensable. There can be no fair discussion of the question of usefulness, when an argument so vital may be employed on one side, but not on the other. And in point of fact, when law or public feeling do not permit the truth of an opinion to be disputed, they are just as little tolerant of a denial of its usefulness. The utmost they allow is an extenuation of its absolute necessity, or of the positive guilt of rejecting it.

In order more fully to illustrate the mischief of denying a hearing to opinions because we, in our own judgement, have condemned them, it will be desirable to fix down the discussion to a concrete case; and I choose, by preference, the cases which are least favourable to me—in which the argument against freedom of opinion, both on the score of truth and on that of utility, is considered the strongest. Let the opinions impugned be the belief in a God and in a future state, or any of the commonly received doctrines of morality. To fight the battle on such ground, gives a great advantage to an unfair antagonist; since he will be sure to say (and many who have no desire to be unfair will say it internally), are these the doctrines which you do not deem sufficiently certain to be taken under the protection of law? Is the belief in

a God one of the opinions, to feel sure of which, you hold to be assuming infallibility? But I must be permitted to observe, that it is not the feeling sure of a doctrine (be it what it may) which I call an assumption of infallibility. It is the undertaking to decide that question *for others*, without allowing them to hear what can be said on the contrary side. And I denounce and reprobate this pretension not the less, if put forth on the side of my most solemn convictions. However positive any one's persuasion may be, not only of the falsity but of the pernicious consequences—not only of the pernicious consequences, but (to adopt expressions which I altogether condemn) the immorality and impiety of an opinion; yet if, in pursuance of that private judgement, though backed by the public judgement of his country or his contemporaries, he prevents the opinion from being heard in its defence, he assumes infallibility. And so far from the assumption being less objectionable or less dangerous because the opinion is called immoral or impious, this is the case of all others in which it is most fatal. These are exactly the occasions on which the men of one generation commit those dreadful mistakes, which excite the astonishment and horror of posterity. It is among such that we find the instances memorable in history, when the arm of the law has been employed to root out the best men and the noblest doctrines; with deplorable success as to the man, though some of the doctrines have survived to be (as if in mockery) invoked, in defence of similar conduct towards those who dissent from *them*, or from their received interpretation.

Mankind can hardly be too often reminded, that there was once a man named Socrates, between whom and the legal authorities and public opinion of his time, there took place a memorable collision. Born in an age and country abounding in individual greatness, this man has been handed down to us by those who best knew both him and the age, as the most virtuous man in it; while *we* know him as the head and prototype of all subsequent teachers of virtue, the source equally of the lofty inspiration of Plato and the judicious utilitarianism of Aristotle, '*i maëstri di color che sanno,*' the two headsprings of ethical as of all other philosophy. This acknowledged master of all the eminent thinkers who have since lived—whose fame, still growing after more than two thousand years, all but outweighs the whole remainder of the names which make his native city illustrious—was put to death by his countrymen, after a judicial conviction, for impiety and immorality. Impiety, in denying the gods recognized by the State; indeed his accuser asserted (see the *Apologia*) that he believed in no gods at all. Immortality, in being, by his doctrines and instructions, a 'corruptor of youth'. Of these charges the tribunal, there is every ground for believing, honestly found him guilty, and condemned the man who probably of all then born had deserved best of mankind, to be put to death as a criminal.

* * *

NOTE

1. These words had scarcely been written, when, as if to give them an emphatic contradiction, occurred the Government Press Prosecutions of 1858. That ill-judged interference with the liberty of public discussion has not, however, induced me to alter a single word in the text, nor has it at all weakened my conviction that, moments of panic excepted, the era of pains and penalties for political discussion has, in our

own country, passed away. For, in the first place, the prosecutions were not persisted in; and, in the second, they were never, properly speaking, political prosecutions. The offence charged was not that of criticizing institutions, or the acts or persons of rulers, but of circulating what was deemed an immoral doctrine, the lawfulness of Tyrannicide.

If the arguments of the present chapter are of any validity, there ought to exist the fullest liberty of professing and discussing, as a matter of ethical conviction, any doctrine, however immoral it may be considered. It would, therefore, be irrelevant and out of place to examine here, whether the doctrine of Tyrannicide deserves that title. I shall content myself with saying that the subject has been at all times one of the open questions of morals; that the act of a private citizen in striking down a criminal, who, by raising himself above the law, has placed himself beyond the reach of legal punishment or control, has been accounted by whole nations, and by some of the best and wisest of men, not a crime, but an act of exalted virtue; and that, right or wrong, it is not of the nature of assassination, but of civil war. As such, I hold that the instigation to it, in a specific case, may be a proper subject of punishment, but only if an overt act has followed, and at least a probable connexion can be established between the act and the instigation. Even then, it is not a foreign government, but the very government assailed, which alone, in the exercise of self-defence, can legitimately punish attacks directed against its own existence.

"The Price We Pay"?: Pornography and Harm

Susan J. Brison

Defenders of civil liberties have typically held, with J. S. Mill, that governments may justifiably exercise power over individuals, against their will, only to prevent harm to others (Mill, 1978: ch. 1).[1] Until the 1970s, liberals and libertarians assumed that since producers and consumers of pornography clearly

Susan J. Brison, "'The Price We Pay'?: Pornography and Harm," in *Contemporary Debates in Applied Ethics*, ed. Andrew I. Cohen and Christopher Heath Wellman (Malden, MA: Blackwell Publishing, 2005), 236–50 (edited). Reprinted with permission by Blackwell Publishing.

didn't harm anyone else, the only reasons their opponents had for regulating pornography were that they considered it harmful to the producers or consumers, that they thought it an offensive nuisance, and that they objected, on moral or religious grounds, to certain private sexual pleasures of others. None of these reasons was taken to provide grounds for regulating pornography, however, since individuals are considered to be the best judges of what is in their own interest (and, in any case, they cannot be harmed by something to which they consent), what is merely offensive may be avoided (with the help of plain brown wrappers and zoning restrictions), and the private sexual activities, of consenting adults anyway, are no one else's, certainly not the state's, business.

In the 1970s, however, the nature of the pornography debate changed as an emerging group of feminists argued that what is wrong with pornography is not that it morally defiles its producers and consumers, nor that it is offensive or sinful, but, rather, that it is a species of hate literature as well as a particularly insidious method of sexist socialization. Susan Brownmiller was one of the first to take this stance in proclaiming that "[p]ornography is the undiluted essence of anti-female propaganda" (1975: 443). On this view, pornography (of the violent degrading variety) harms women by sexualizing misogynistic violence. According to Catharine MacKinnon, "[p]ornography sexualizes rape, battery, sexual harassment, prostitution, and child sexual abuse; it thereby celebrates, promotes, authorizes, and legitimizes them" (1987: 171).

The claim that women are harmed by pornography has changed the nature of the pornography debate, which is, for the most part, no longer a debate between liberals who subscribe to Mill's harm principle and legal moralists who hold that the state can legitimately legislate against so-called "morals offenses" that do not harm any non-consenting adults. Rather, the main academic debates now take place among those who subscribe to Mill's harm principle, but disagree about what its implications are for the legal regulation of pornography. Some theorists hold that violent degrading pornography does not harm anyone and, thus, cannot justifiably be legally regulated, socially stigmatized, or morally condemned. Others maintain that, although it is harmful to women, it cannot justifiably be regulated by either the civil or the criminal law, since that would cause even greater harms and/or violate the legal rights of pornography producers and consumers, but that, nevertheless, private individuals should do what they can (through social pressure, educational campaigns, boycotts, etc.) to put an end to it. Still others claim that such pornography harms women by violating their civil right to be free from sex discrimination and should, for that reason, be addressed by the law (as well as by other means), just as other forms of sex discrimination are. But others argue that restricting such pornography violates the moral right of pornography producers and consumers and, thus, restrictions are morally impermissible. Later in this chapter I will argue that there is no moral right to such pornography.

WHAT IS PORNOGRAPHY?

First, however, I need to articulate what is at issue, but this is hard to do, given various obstacles to describing the material in question accurately. (I have encountered the same problem in writing about sexual violence.) There is too much at stake to be put off writing about issues of urgent import to women because of squeamishness or fear of academic impropriety—but how can one write about this particular issue without reproducing the violent degrading pornography itself? (Recall the labeling of Anita Hill as "a little nutty and a little slutty" because she repeated, in public, the sexually demeaning language that Clarence Thomas had uttered to her in private.) However, if one doesn't write graphically about the content of violent degrading pornography, one risks being viewed as either crazy ("she must be imagining things!") or too prudish to talk frankly about sex. And what tone should one adopt—one of scholarly detachment or of outrage? There is a double bind here, similar to that faced by rape victims on the witness stand. If they appear calm and rational enough for their testimony to be credible, that may be taken as evidence that they cannot have been raped. But if they are emotional and out of control enough to appear traumatized, then their testimony is not considered reliable.

Any critic of violent degrading pornography risks being viewed not only as prudish (especially if the critic is a woman), but also as meddling in others' "private" business, since we tend not to see the harm in pornography—harm which is often made invisible and considered unspeakable. But "we" used not to see the harm in depriving women and minorities of their civil rights. And "we" used not to see the harm in distributing postcards depicting and celebrating lynchings. More recently, "we" didn't see the harm in marital or "date" rape, spousal battering, or sexual harassment. Even now, as Richard Delgado and Jean Stefancic point out:

[M]embers of the empowered group may simply announce to the disaffected that they do not see their problem, that they have looked for evidence of harm but cannot find it. Later generations may well marvel, "how could they have been so blind?" But paradigms change slowly. In the meantime, one may describe oneself as a cautious and principled social scientist interested only in the truth. And one's opponent, by a neat reversal, becomes an intolerant zealot willing to trample on the liberties of others without good cause. (1997: 37)

A further problem arises in critically analyzing violent degrading pornography, deriving from precisely those harmful aspects of it being critiqued, which is that descriptions of it and quotations from it can themselves be degrading, or even retraumatizing, especially for women who have been victimized by sexual violence. But one thing that is clear is that feminist critics of such pornography are *not* criticizing it on the grounds that it is erotic, or sexually arousing, or that it constitutes "obscenity," defined by the Court as "works which, taken as a whole, appeal to the prurient interest in sex, which portray sexual conduct in a patently offensive way, and which, taken as a whole, do not have serious literary, artistic, political or scientific value" (*Miller v. California*, 1973: 24). Those who work on this issue—and have familiarized themselves with the real world of the pornography industry—know all too well that pornography is not merely offensive. In contrast, here is how some of them define "pornography":

[T]he graphic sexually explicit subordination of women through pictures or words that also includes women dehumanized as sexual objects, things, or commodities; enjoying pain or humiliation or rape; being tied up, cut up, mutilated, bruised, or physically hurt; in postures of sexual submission, servility or display; reduced to body parts, penetrated by objects or animals, or presented in scenarios of degradation, injury, torture; shown as filthy or inferior;

bleeding, bruised, or hurt in a context that makes these conditions sexual. (MacKinnon, 1987: 176)[2]

I define "pornography," for the purposes of this chapter, as violent degrading misogynistic hate speech (where "speech" includes words, pictures, films, etc.). I will argue that, if pornography unjustly harms women (as there is reason to suppose it does), then there is no moral right to produce, sell, or consume it. (I will not here be arguing for or against its legal restriction and no position on that issue is dictated by my argument against the alleged moral right.)

PORNOGRAPHY AND HARM

I cannot hope to portray adequately the harms inflicted on girls and women in the production of pornography (for the reasons given above), but there is plenty of research documenting them. One of the most powerful forms of evidence for such harms is the first-person testimony of "participants" in pornography. * * * A not uncommon scenario in which a girl becomes trapped in the pornography industry is described by Evelina Giobbe in her testimony to the US Attorney-General's Commission on Pornography. After running away from home at age 13 and being raped her first night on the streets, Giobbe was befriended by a man who seemed initially kind and concerned, but who, after taking nude photographs of her, sold her to a pimp who raped and battered her, threatening her life and those of her family until she "agreed" to work as a prostitute for him. Her "customers" knew she was an adolescent and sexually inexperienced. "So," she testified, "they showed me pornography to teach me and ignored my tears and they positioned my body like the women in the pictures, and used me." She tried on many occasions to escape, but, as a teenager with no resources, cut off from friends and family, who believed she was a criminal, she was an easy mark for her pimp: "He would drag me down streets, out of restaurants, even into taxis, all the while beating me while I protested, crying and begging passers-by for help. No one wanted to get involved" (quoted in Russell, 1993: 38).

She was later sold to another pimp who "was a pornographer and the most brutal of all." According to her testimony, he recruited other girls and women into pornography by advertising for models:

When a woman answered his ad, he'd offer to put her portfolio together for free, be her agent, and make her a "star." He'd then use magazines like *Playboy* to convince her to pose for "soft-core" porn. He'd then engage her in a love affair and smooth talk her into prostitution. "Just long enough," he would say, "to get enough money to finance your career as a model." If sweet talk didn't work, violence and blackmail did. She became one of us. (Quoted in Russell, 1993: 39)

Giobbe escaped the pornography industry by chance, after "destroy[ing] herself with heroin" and becoming "no longer usable." She considers herself one of the lucky ones—"a rare survivor" (quoted in Russell, 1993: 39–40). And this was *before* the AIDS epidemic.

More recently, according to an article in the *Sunday New York Times Magazine,* pornography—of an increasingly violent sort—has played an important role in the global sex trafficking of girls and women who, lured by promises of employment (for example, as nannies or waitresses), end up trapped in foreign countries, with no money, no (legal) papers, no family or friends, and no ability to speak the local language. Immigrations and Customs Enforcement (ICE) agents at the Cyber Crimes Center in Fairfax, Virginia are "tracking a clear spike in the demand for harder-core pornography on the Internet. 'We've become desensitized by the soft stuff; now we need a harder and harder hit', says ICE Special Agent Perry Woo." With ICE agents, the author of the article looked up a website purporting to offer sex slaves for sale: "There were streams of Web pages of thumbnail images of young girls of every ethnicity in obvious distress, bound, gagged, contorted. The agents in the room pointed out probable injuries from torture" (Landesman, 2004: 72). "'With new Internet technology', Woo said, 'pornography is becoming more pervasive. With Web cams we're seeing more live molestation of children'" (Landesman, 2004: 74).

It is not enough to say that the participants in pornography consent, *even* in the case of adult women who apparently do, given the road many have been led (or dragged) down, since childhood in some cases, to get to that point. Genuine autonomous consent requires the ability to evaluate critically and to choose from a range of significant and worthwhile options. Even if all the participants genuinely consented to their use in the pornography industry, however, we would need to consider how pornography influences how *other* non-consenting women are viewed and treated. Compare the (thankfully imaginary) scenario in which some blacks consented to act servile or even to play the part of slaves—who are humiliated, beaten, and whipped for the pleasure of their masters. Suppose a *lot* of whites got off on this and some people got a lot of money from tapping into (and pumping up) the desire for such films. And suppose the widespread consumption of such entertainment—a multibillion-dollar industry, in fact—influenced how whites generally viewed and treated blacks, making it harder than it would otherwise be for blacks to overcome a brutal and ongoing legacy of hate and oppression. It is unimaginable that we would tolerate such "entertainment" simply because some people got off on it.

To give another analogy, the fact that scabs will work for less money (in worse conditions) than strikers harms the strikers. It makes it harder for the strikers to work under fair conditions. Sure, the scabs benefit; however, that's not the point. The point is that the strikers suffer. Suppose there were "slave auction" clubs where some blacks allowed themselves to be brutalized and degraded for the pleasure of their white customers. Suppose the black "performers" determined that, given the options, it was in their best interest to make money in this way. Their financial gain—imagine that they are highly paid—more than compensates for the social harm to them as individuals of being subjected to a slightly increased risk (resulting from the prevalence of such clubs) of being degraded and brutalized outside their workplace. Some of them even enjoy the work, having a level of ironic detachment that enables them to view their customers as pathetic or contemptible. Some, who don't actually enjoy their work, don't suffer distress, since they manage to dissociate during it. Others are distressed by it, but they have determined that the financial benefit outweighs the psychic and physical pain. For those blacks who did not work in the clubs, however, there would be nothing that compensated for their slightly increased risk of being degraded and brutalized as a result of it. They would be better off if the clubs did not exist. The work done by the blacks in the clubs would make it harder for other blacks to live their lives free of fear.

The harms caused by pornography to non-participants in its production—often called "indirect" or "diffuse" harms, which makes them sound less real and less serious than they actually are—include (1) harms to those who have pornography forced on them, (2) increased or reinforced discrimination against—and sexual abuse of—girls and women, (3) harms to boys and men whose attitudes toward women and whose sexual desires are influenced by pornography, and (4) harms to those who have already been victimized by sexual violence. The first three categories of harm have been amply documented. * * * That the proliferation of pornography leads to attitudinal changes in men, which, in turn, led to harmful behavior, should not be surprising, especially given the high rates of exposure to pornography of pre-teen and teenage boys. On the contrary, as Frederick Schauer, Frank Stanton Professor of the First Amendment at the John F. Kennedy School of Government at Harvard University, testified at the Pornography Civil Rights hearing in Boston, Massachusetts on March 16, 1992:

I find it a constant source of astonishment that a society that so easily and correctly accepts the possibility that a cute drawing of a camel can have such an effect on the number of people who take up smoking, has such difficulty accepting the proposition that endorsing images of rape or other forms of sexual violence can have an effect on the number of people who take up rape. (cited in MacKinnon and Dworkin, 1997: 396)

One might object, though, that pornography is merely a symptom (of a misogynistic, patriarchal society), not a cause. Even if this were the case, however, that would not mean that we should not be concerned about it. The fact that there are so few female legislators in the US at the federal level (and that it's still inconceivable that a woman could be elected president) is a symptom, not a cause, of patriarchy. But this does not mean that we should not do anything about the political status quo. In any case, pornography is more than a mere symptom: it fosters and perpetuates the sexist attitudes that are essential for its enjoyment, even if it does not create them.

It should be noted here that the fact that the *point* of pornography (from the standpoint of the producers) is to make money by giving pleasure does not mean that it cannot also be harmfully degrading. On the contrary, it is pleasurable (and profitable) *precisely because* it is degrading to others. And it is reasonable to expect a spill-over effect in the public domain, since its enjoyment requires the adoption of certain attitudes. Compare the case of pornography with that of sexist humor. Until quite recently, it used to be maintained that women who were offended by sexist jokes were simply humorless. After all, it was held, one can laugh at a sexist joke (because it's funny) and not *be* a sexist. Now it is widely acknowledged that such jokes are funny only if one holds certain sexist beliefs: in other words, the humor is contingent upon the beliefs.[3] With regard to pornographic depictions, it would be difficult to argue that the degradation and subordination of women they involve are merely incidental to their ability to arouse. The arousal is dependent on the depiction of degradation, just as, in sexist humor, the humor is dependent on the sexism. I stress this in order to deflect the objection that the *point* of pornography is to give pleasure, not to defame or degrade women.

It might be argued that one could laugh at sexist jokes and enjoy sexist pornography *in private* without this having any effect on one's ability to view women as equals *in public* and to treat them accordingly. But are we really so good at keeping our private and public attitudes distinct? Suppose it became known that a white public official—say, a judge—privately relished racist humor, collected racist paraphernalia, and showed old racist films at home for the entertainment of his close friends and family. Although one might not want there to be laws against such reprehensible behavior (for their enforcement would require gross invasions of privacy), one would presumably consider such *private* behavior to compromise the integrity of the judge's public position. (Were this judge's pastime to be made public during his confirmation hearings for a set on the Supreme Court, for example, it would presumably defeat his nomination.)

It is easier for us, now, to see the harm in the dehumanization of blacks and Jews in racist and anti-Semitic propaganda. We are well aware that the Nazis' campaign to exterminate the Jews utilized anti-Semitic propaganda which portrayed Jews as disgusting, disease-ridden vermin. In addition, "Nazis made Jews do things that would further associate them with the disgusting," making them scrub latrines to which they were then denied access (Nussbaum, 2001, p. 348). This in turn made them appear less than human. As Primo Levi observed in *The Drowned and the Saved*:

The SS escorts did not hide their amusement at the sight of men and women squatting wherever they could, on the platforms and in the middle of the tracks, and the German passengers openly expressed their disgust: people like this deserve their fate, just look how they behave. These are not *Menschen,* human beings, but animals, it's as clear as day. (Quoted in Nussbaum, 2001: 348)

It is harder for us to see the same process of dehumanization at work when girls and women are routinely portrayed as being worthy of degradation, torture, and even death. But empirical studies have shown that exposure to such portrayals increases the likelihood that people will take actual sexual violence less seriously—and even consider it to be justified in some cases (see Lederer and Delgado, 1995: 61–112; MacKinnon and Dworkin, 1993: 46–60; Russell, 1993: 113–213).

There is another connection between the dehumanization of girls and women in pornography and their brutalization in rape, battering, forced prostitu-

tion, and sexual murder, which is that, in a society where women are victimized in these ways at an alarming rate, it shows a callous disregard for the actual victims to have depictions of sexual violence bought and sold as entertainment. For a short while, after 9/11, we empathized so much with the victims of the terrorist attacks that films of similarly horrifying attacks were withdrawn because they were no longer considered entertaining. But victims of sexual violence are given so little respect that many of us see nothing wrong with being entertained by depictions of what they have had to endure.

If we take seriously the harm of pornography, then we want to know what to do about it. Should the government intervene by regulating it? The standard debate over pornography has framed it as a free speech issue. The drafters of an anti-pornography ordinance adopted by the city of Indianapolis argued that pornography constitutes a violation of the civil rights of women. In response to those who asserted that the First Amendment protected pornography, they argued that pornography violated the First Amendment rights of women (by "silencing" them—depriving them of credibility and making "no" appear to mean "yes" in rape scenarios) as well as their Fourteenth Amendment rights to equal protection. In his opinion in *American Booksellers Association v. Hudnut*, which ruled unconstitutional the Indianapolis anti-pornography ordinance, Judge Frank Easterbrook acknowledged that pornography harms women in very significant and concrete ways:

Depictions of subordination tend to perpetuate subordination. The subordinate status of women in turn leads to affront and lower pay at work, insult and injury at home, battery and rape on the streets. In the language of the legislature, "[p]ornography is central in creating and maintaining sex as a basis of discrimination. Pornography is a systematic practice of exploitation and subordination based on sex which differentially harms women. The bigotry and contempt it produce, with the acts of aggression it fosters, harm women's opportunities for equality and rights [of all kinds]." Indianapolis Code §16-1(a) (2). "Yet this simply demonstrates the power of pornography as speech" (*American Booksellers Association, Inc.* v. *Hudnut*, 1985: 329).[4]

Easterbrook seems to take the harms of pornography seriously, but he then goes on to talk about its "unhappy effects" which he considers to be the result of "mental intermediation." He assumes that speech has no (or merely negligible) effects that are not under the conscious control of the audience, although this assumption is undermined not only by the widely acknowledged power of advertising, but also by recent work in cognitive neuroscience on the prevalence of unconscious imitation in human beings.[5] It might be argued, though, that, if we consider the producers of pornography to be even partially responsible for the violence perpetrated by some of its consumers, then we must consider the perpetrators *not* to be responsible or to be less than fully responsible for their crimes. But this does not follow. Even if the perpetrators are considered to be 100 percent responsible, some responsibility can still be attributed to the pornographers. (In fact, two or more people can each be 100 percent responsible for the same crime, as in the case of multiple snipers who simultaneously fire many shots, fatally wounding their victim.)

The courts have, for now, decided that even if serious harm to women results from it, pornography is, qua speech, protected (except for that material which also meets the legal definition of obscenity). That is, there is, currently, a *legal* right to it, falling under the right to free speech. But *should* there be?

A MORAL RIGHT TO PORNOGRAPHY?

Of course we value freedom of speech. But how should we value it? What should we do when speech is genuinely harmful? Traditionally, in the US, the right to free speech is held to be of such high importance that it trumps just about everything else. For example, in the *Hudnut* case, discussed above, it was acknowledged that the pornography producers' and consumers' right to free speech was in conflict with women's right to equal protection, but it was asserted (without argumentation) that the free speech right had priority. Acceptance of this claim without requiring a defense of it, however, amounts to adopting a kind of free speech fundamentalism. To see how

untenable such a view is, suppose that uttering the words "you're dead" caused everyone within earshot (but the speaker) to fall down dead. Would anyone seriously say that such speech deserved protection? Granted, the harms of pornography are less obvious and less severe, but there is sufficient evidence for them for it to be reasonable to require an argument for why the legal right to it should take priority over others' legal rights not to be subjected to such harms.

If we reject free speech fundamentalism, the question of whether pornography should be legally restricted becomes much more complicated. My aim here is not to articulate or defend a position on this question, but I do want to stress that whatever view we take on it should be informed by an understanding of the harms of pornography—the price some people pay so that other people may get off on it.

In . . . "The Right to Get Turned On: Pornography, Autonomy, Equality," Andrew Altman shifts the debate over pornography in a promising way by arguing that there is a *moral* right to (even violent misogynistic) pornography, falling not under a right to free speech, but, rather, under a right to sexual autonomy (which also covers the right to use contraceptives and the right to homosexual sex).[6] On this view, which Altman dubs "liberal sexual morality," whatever harm results from pornography is just the price we pay for the right to sexual autonomy. Sexuality is an important, arguably central, aspect of a flourishing human life. Sexual expression is one of the primary ways we define ourselves and our relations to others, and a healthy society should value and celebrate it. But what does it add to these claims to say that we have a moral *right* to sexual autonomy? And, if we do have such a right, does it include a right to produce, distribute, and consume pornography (defined, as above, as violent degrading misogynistic hate speech)?

Although philosophers disagree about the nature of rights (and, indeed, even about whether such things exist at all), most hold that to say that someone, X, has a moral right to do something, y, means that others are under a duty not to interfere with X's doing y. (Of course, X's right is limited by others' rights, as expressed by the saying "your right to swing your arm ends at my face.") But beyond this, there is little agreement. Some hold that rights are natural, inalienable, and God-given. Others hold that rights-talk is just short-hand for talk about those interests that are especially important to us (for example, because protecting them tends to increase our welfare). Some hold that we have positive rights, just by virtue of being human, such that other people are under an obligation to provide us with whatever we need to exercise those rights. (If there is a positive right to education, for example, then society has an obligation to provide free public education for all.) Others hold that we have only negative rights (unless individuals *grant* us positive rights by, for example, making promises to assist us), which require only that other people do not interfere with our exercising those rights. (The right to privacy, if taken to be simply a right to be left alone, is an example of a negative right.)

On any account, the concept of a right is diffuse. To say that X has a moral right to do y does not, by itself, say very much, unless we specify what others are required to do (or to refrain from doing) in order not to violate that right. There is a wide range of different responses to X's doing y, given that X has a right to do y—from complete acceptance (or perhaps even positive support) to something just short of physical restraint or intervention. Where is the alleged right to pornography located on this spectrum of moral assessment?

Altman considers the right to pornography and the right to sexual orientation to have the same foundation in a right to sexual autonomy. What should our (society's) attitude be toward the exercising of that right? Should we tolerate it, that is, have no laws against it, while allowing private individuals to lobby against it or to try to dissuade people from it? Or should we actively embrace it? Assimilating the right to pornography to the right to sexual orientation muddies the waters here. Presumably, according to liberal sexual morality, the right to sexual orientation requires more than mere tolerance. It requires society's complete acceptance (and, I would argue, positive support, given that prejudice and violence against gays and lesbians persist in our society). It is

wrong to hold that gays and lesbians have "bad characters" or to try to get them to "reform."

The right to pornography, however, does not lie on the same end of the spectrum, since Altman claims that getting off on pornography is a sign of a bad character. Some feminists and liberals who defend a legal right to pornography hold at the same time that all sorts of private pressure—protests, boycotts, educational campaigns—should be brought to bear on the pornographers. Altman's position is that there is not just a legal right, but also a *moral* right to pornography, even if there is something bad about exercising it. There are persuasive reasons for holding that we have legal rights to do some things that are morally wrong, in cases in which enforcement would be impossible or would involve gross violations of privacy. But Altman seems to hold that we have a *moral* right to do some things that are morally wrong. What does this mean? It cannot mean that people have a right to do things that are wrong in that they harm others. It might mean that people have the right to do things that other people consider wrong (but that are not harmful to others)—that is, people have the right to do harmless things that other people morally disapprove of. However, if the behavior, e.g. engaging in homosexual sex, is not unjustly harming others, then liberals who subscribe to Mill's harm principle have no grounds for considering it to be wrong.

So where should the right to pornography be located on the spectrum of moral assessment? There is no one answer to this question. We need to look at particular cases. Suppose I have a 21-year-old son—leaving aside the question of whether minors have a right to pornography—who is a heavy consumer of pornography (of the kind I've been talking about). What does his (alleged) right to pornography entail? Given my opposition to pornography, presumably I would not be under an obligation positively to support his pornography habit by buying it for him. But would I have to pretend that I'm not aware of it? Would I be under a duty not to try to dissuade him from viewing pornography? Would his sister be under a duty not to throw the magazines out when she saw them in common areas of the house? Would it be wrong for his buddies to try to talk him out of it? Would his teachers have a duty to refrain from arguing against it? Would it be wrong for his neighbors to boycott the local convenience store that sold it? Would his girlfriend (or boyfriend) who became convinced it was ruining their relationship be under a moral duty not to rip it out of his hands? If the answer to each of the above questions is "no," which I think it is, then it's not clear what, if anything, his right entitles him to.[7] What is clear is that, if a right to pornography exists, it is quite unlike a right to engage in homosexual sex or to use contraceptives, and is located at the opposite end of the spectrum of moral assessment.

Perhaps there is, nevertheless, something special about sexual arousal ("getting turned on") that gives it special moral status. But Altman has not said what makes sexual arousal different (in a morally significant way) from other forms of arousal—for example, that of racial animus. It makes sense to say that there is a right to be turned on—not a special right, but, rather, one falling under a general right to liberty, but this general right to liberty is delimited by the harm principle. There is no general right to have pleasurable feelings (of any sort, sexual or otherwise) that override others' rights not to be harmed. There is no moral right to achieve a feeling of comfort by unjustly discriminating against homosexuals on the grounds that associating with them makes you uncomfortable. Likewise, there is no moral right to achieve a feeling of superiority (no matter how pleasurable such a feeling might be) by discriminating against those of a different race. And it doesn't matter how central to one's self-definition the feeling in question might be. For parents, the satisfaction of ensuring the good upbringing and education of their children is of paramount importance, and yet this degree of importance does not give racist parents the right to racially segregated housing or schools.

It might be argued that sexual arousal is special in that it is a bodily pleasure and, thus, more natural, possibly even immutable. Even if this were so, it would not follow that one has a right to achieve it by any means necessary. To take an example of another kind of "bodily" pleasure, support that there

are gustatory pleasures that can be achieved only in immoral ways—for example, by eating live monkey brains (which some people used to do), or organs or flesh "donated" by (or purchased from) living human beings, or food that has been stolen from the people on the verge of starvation. That there is a (general) right to enjoy eating what one chooses to eat—it would be (in general) wrong, for example, for me to force you to eat, or not to eat, something—does not mean that one has a right to eat whatever gives one pleasure.

But it is not the case that what people find sexually arousing is a simple biological fact about them, a given, something immutable. People can be conditioned to be aroused by any number of things. In one study, for example, men were conditioned to be aroused by a picture of a woman's boot (Russell, 1993: 129). Emotions, especially ones with strong physiological components, such as sexual arousal, *feel* natural. They don't seem to be socially constructed, because we don't (at the time) consciously choose them: they just *are*. But emotions are, at least to some extent, learned reactions to things. There are gender differences in emotional reactions; for example, men tend to get angry in some situations in which women tend to feel not angry, but hurt. But this does not mean that such differences are *natural*.

Given the wide variety of sexual fantasies and fetishes we know about, it's conceivable that just about *anything* could be a turn on for someone—looking at photos of dead, naked bodies piled in mass graves in Nazi death camps, for example, or looking at photos of lynched black men. According to liberal sexual morality, the only reason for supposing that there might not be a moral right to make a profit from and get off on such "pornography" would be that the photographed people are posthumously harmed by it (given that they did not consent to their images being used in this way). But suppose they had consented. Or suppose, more plausibly, that the images were computer-generated—completely realistic-looking, but not images *of* actual individuals. Liberal sexual morality would have to allow (some) people to make money by others' getting turned on by these images. Not only that, but, given that sexual desires are malleable, the pornographer also has a right to make money by acculturating others to be turned on by such images. (In other words, the pornographer has a right to turn the world into a place where people get turned on by such images.) And, if our attitude toward this is grounded in the right to sexual autonomy, it should be similar to our attitude toward homosexuality: we shouldn't merely tolerate it, we should come to accept and support it.

While conceding that there are limits to the right to sexual autonomy—it is constrained by the harm principle—Altman assumes (as most liberals do) that one cannot be harmed by something to which one consents. I argued earlier that the way many models get lured into the pornography industry should make us at least question the extent to which they are consenting to what is being done to them. But suppose they do consent. Does that mean that we must tolerate the production and use of whatever pornography results? Unfortunately, one doesn't have to construct a thought experiment to test our intuitions about this. According to *The New York Times*, Armin Meiwes, "[a] German computer technician who killed and ate a willing victim he found through the Internet" was recently convicted of manslaughter. His "victim," Bernd-Jürgen Brandes, had "responded to an Internet posting by Mr Meiwes seeking someone willing to be 'slaughtered'." "'Both were looking for the ultimate kick'," the judge said. It was "an evening of sexual role-playing and violence, much of it videotaped by Mr Meiwes," enough to convince the court that the "victim" had consented (Landler, 2004: A3). Does the right to sexual autonomy include the rights to produce, sell, and get turned on by the videotape of this "slaughter"—a real-life instance of a snuff film? If we cannot *prove* that there is a causal connection between the film and harm to others, the answer, according to liberal sexual morality, is "yes."

Altman claims that "even if a causal connection between violent pornography and sexual violence were clearly established, it would still be insufficient to conclude that, in contemporary society, the production, distribution and viewing of violent pornography lay beyond the limits of an adult's right to sexual autonomy" because *other* media—he cites "slasher films"—arguably "cause at least some amount of violence against women, sexual and otherwise. However, it is unreasonable to deny that adults have a right to produce, distribute, and view such movies" (2005: 229). Why, if one has established that, say, "slasher films" are harmful, we must hold that adults have a right to them is not explained. But even if we agree that adults have the right to produce/consume non-pornographic media even if it is as harmful as pornography, it does not follow that adults have the right to produce/consume pornography. To assume that it does would be like arguing against prohibiting driving while talking on cell phones on the grounds that this is not the *only* thing (or even the main thing) contributing to automobile accidents.

Altman accepts that "it is reasonable to hold that the existence of . . . pornography makes it more difficult for women to live their lives as the sexual equals of men—i.e., more difficult relative to a society which was ruled by a liberal sexual morality and had fewer women, or none at all, who were willing to engage in humiliating conduct as part of the production of pornographic materials" (Altman, 2005: 233), but he notes that women are better off in a society with liberal sexual morality than in a society with traditional sexual morality (for example, Saudi Arabia). I agree, but surely these are not the only two possibilities. I would advocate the alternative of a progressive sexual morality. What might that look like? We don't even know. Even our most deep-seated assumptions about sexuality may turn out to be mistaken. We used to view rape as being motivated purely by lust and battering as a way of showing spousal love. Some of us still do. Gradually, however, we are breaking the link between sexuality and violence. Perhaps some day we'll have reached the point where sexual violence is no longer arousing, where it makes no sense to talk of killing and being killed as the "ultimate" sexual "kick."

According to liberal sexual morality, the harms of pornography are the price we pay for having the right to sexual autonomy in other areas—e.g. the right to have sex (including homosexual sex) outside of marriage and the right to use contraceptives. But this view (of the right to sexual autonomy as an all-or-nothing package) is formed in response to legal moralism, and makes sense only if one considers all these rights to be rights to do harmless things that some people nevertheless morally condemn. In such cases, proponents of liberal sexual morality say: "If you don't like it, don't look at it (or hear about it or think about it)." This is a satisfactory response only if the behavior in question isn't harming anyone. But as our views about what constitutes harm have changed, our views of what is our business have also changed. Just as we no longer look the other way in response to marital or "date" rape, domestic violence, and sexual harassment, we should no longer accept pornography's harms as the price we pay for sexual autonomy.

NOTES

* * *

1. Mill considered his harm principle to apply equally to governmental regulation and to "the moral coercion of public opinion." The harm principle states that " . . . the only purpose for which power can be rightfully exercised over any member of a civilized community, against his will, is to prevent harm to others" (1978: 9). Mill does not specify what counts as harm. Following Joel Feinberg (1984), I consider it to be a wrongful setback to one's significant interests.

2. This is the definition used in the anti-pornography ordinance drafted by Andrea Dworkin and Catharine MacKinnon, passed by the city of Indianapolis, but ruled unconstitutional by the courts.

3. For a persuasive argument to that effect, see de Sousa (1987). In comparing sexist fantasies with sexist and racist humor, one might reply, however, that we have less control over, and thus are less responsible for, our fantasies than our jokes. This seems right, to the extent that we can refrain from laughing at or telling certain jokes (even though we might not be able to resist finding them funny). But the same distinction applies to fantasies. We do not always choose the fantasies that occur to us, but we can choose whether or not to cultivate them (voluntarily return to them repeatedly, make or view films about them, etc.). Even in the case of dreams, over which we, at the time, anyway, have no control, a white male liberal would be alarmed if he often had pleasurable dreams of watching blacks getting lynched.

This would presumably prompt some probing of his unconscious attitudes about blacks.

4. This view can't consistently be held, however, by liberals and feminists who support laws against sex or race discrimination and segregation in schools, workplace, and even private clubs. One doesn't hear the argument that if segregation harms minorities' opportunities for equal rights this simply demonstrates the power of freedom of association, which is also protected by the First Amendment.

5. The recent research discussed in Hurley (2004) suggests that the imitation of others' behavior, including others' violent acts, is not a consciously mediated process, under the autonomous control of the viewers/imitators.

6. Since some theorists ground the right to free speech in a right to autonomy, however, there may not be such a sharp distinction between these two approaches. See Brison (1998).

7. I also mean for the above thought experiment to illustrate the fact that the nature of the duty one has with respect to the holder of the alleged moral right to pornography depends on one's relationship to the right-holder. Presumably a neighbor would be under a duty not to snatch pornography out of the right-holder's hands. But if someone *else*, the right-holder's lover, say, is under no such duty, then it's not clear what the right amounts to.

REFERENCES

Altman, Andrew (2005). "The right to get turned on: pornography, autonomy, equality." In Andrew I. Cohen and Christopher Heath Wellman (eds.), *Contemporary Debates in Applied Ethics* (pp. 223–35). Oxford: Blackwell, 2005.

American Booksellers Association, Inc. v. *Hudnut* (1985). 771 F.2d 323.

Attorney General's Commission on Pornography (1986). *Final Report.* Washington, DC: US Department of Justice.

Brison, Susan J. (1998). "The autonomy defense of free speech." *Ethics*, 108: 312–39.

Brownmiller, Susan (1975). *Against Our Will: Men, Women and Rape.* New York: Bantam Books.

Delgado, Richard and Jean Stefancic (1997). *Must We Defend Nazis? Hate Speech, Pornography, and the New First Amendment.* New York: New York University Press.

de Sousa, Ronald (1987). "When is it wrong to laugh?" In *The Rationality of Emotion* (pp. 275–99). Cambridge, MA: MIT Press.

Feinberg, Joel (1984). *The Moral Limits of the Criminal Law,* vol. 1: *Harm to Others.* New York: Oxford University Press.

Hurley, Susan L. (2004). "Imitation, media violence, and freedom of speech." *Philosophical Studies,* 17/1–2 (January): 165–218.

Itzen, Catherine (ed.) (1992). *Pornography: Women, Violence and Civil Liberties.* New York: Oxford University Press.

Landesman, Peter (2004). "The girls next door." *Sunday New York Times Magazine* (January 25): 30–9, 66–74.

Landler, Mark (2004). "German court convicts Internet cannibal of manslaughter." *New York Times* (January 31): A3.

Lederer, Laura (ed.) (1980). *Take Back the Night: Women on Pornography.* New York: William Morrow and Co., Inc.

Lederer, Laura J. and Richard Delgado (eds.) (1995). *The Price We Pay: The Case Against Racist Speech, Hate Propaganda, and Pornography.* New York: Hill and Wang.

MacKinnon, Catharine A. (1987). *Feminism Unmodified: Discourses on Life and Law.* Cambridge, MA: Harvard University Press.

MacKinnon, Catharine A. (1993). *Only Words.* Cambridge, MA: Harvard University Press.

MacKinnon, Catharine A. and Andrea Dworkin (eds.) (1997). *In Harms' Way: The Pornography Civil Rights Hearings.* Cambridge, MA: Harvard University Press.

Mill, John Stuart (1978). *On Liberty.* Indianapolis, IN: Hackett Publishing Co. (Originally published 1859).

Miller v. California (1973). 413 US 15.

Nussbaum, Martha (2001). *Upheavals of Thought.* Cambridge: Cambridge University Press.

Russell, Diana E. H. (ed.) (1993). *Making Violence Sexy: Feminist Views on Pornography.* Buckingham: Open University Press.

CASES FOR ANALYSIS

1. Porn in the Courts

WASHINGTON, Feb. 16—In a case representing a major test of the Bush administration's campaign against pornography, the Justice Department said Wednesday that it would appeal a recent decision by a federal judge that declared federal obscenity laws unconstitutional.

The Justice Department said that if the judge's interpretation of federal law was upheld, it would undermine not only anti-obscenity prohibitions, but also laws against prostitution, bigamy, bestiality and others "based on shared views of public morality."

In a ruling last month in Pittsburgh, Judge Gary L. Lancaster of Federal District Court threw out a 10-count criminal indictment that charged a California video distributor, Extreme Associates, and the husband-and-wife team that owns it with violating federal obscenity laws. The company boasts of the particularly graphic content of its movies, with scenes of simulated gang rapes and other attacks on women, and its Web site declares, "See why the U.S. government is after us!"

While all sides agreed that the movies could be considered legally obscene, Judge Lancaster found that federal laws banning obscenity were unconstitutional as applied broadly to pornography distributors like Extreme Associates. The anti-obscenity laws "burden an individual's fundamental right to possess, read, observe and think about what he chooses in the privacy of his own home by completely banning the distribution of obscene materials," the judge wrote in a 45-page opinion. . . .

Louis Sirkin, a Cincinnati lawyer representing the pornography distributor, said he believed the judge's opinion would be upheld.

"You can't legislate morality," Mr. Sirkin said. "You have to let people make their own personal decisions, and that's the important principle at stake in this case." . . .

Judge Lancaster . . . relied on a 2003 Supreme Court decision, *Lawrence v. Texas,* that struck down a Texas homosexual sodomy law. In that case, the Supreme Court held that "liberty protects the person from unwarranted government intrusions into a dwelling or other private places."

Judge Lancaster interpreted that ruling to mean that "public morality is not a legitimate state interest sufficient to justify infringing on adult, private, consensual, sexual conduct even if that conduct is deemed offensive to the general public's sense of morality."*

Do you agree with the judge's ruling in this case? If you disagree, why? If you agree, what are your reasons? Are your reasons different from those given by the judge? The Justice Department declares that the ruling will cripple its campaign against many forms of obscenity. Do you think the privacy rights cited by the judge outweigh the department's obscenity concerns? Why or why not? Should the government "legislate morality"? If so, what moral values should be enforced?

*Eric Lichtblau, "Justice Dept. Fights Ruling on Obscenity," *New York Times,* 17 February 2005. Reprinted with permission.

---

2. Pornography on the Dean's Computer

CAMBRIDGE, Mass., May 19—In a case that has raised questions of privacy and propriety on the Harvard University campus, university officials said today that the dean of the Divinity School was forced to resign last fall because pornographic images had been discovered on his university-owned computer.

The dean, Ronald F. Thiemann, a nationally prominent theologian who had established a Center for the Study of Values in Public Life at the school, was asked to resign by Harvard's president, Neil L. Rudenstine, after several people saw the pornographic images on his computer, said the officials, who spoke on the condition that they not be named.

Harvard announced his sudden departure at the time, but there had been no explanation until a report about the pornographic material in today's issue of *The Boston Globe.*

Harvard officials familiar with the case said Mr. Thiemann made little effort to hide the material, sometimes leaving it on his computer screen in his official residence. At one point, they said, he even asked the computer department for more disk space for his computer and requested a university technician to transfer the pornographic files to the new drive.

Divinity School rules bar personal use of university computers outside the school's educational mission and specifically ban the "introduction" of material that is "inappropriate, obscene, bigoted or abusive." Mr. Thiemann is currently on leave, and Harvard has taken no action to revoke his tenured professorship. . . .

Richard J. Wood, the dean of the Yale University Divinity School, said the case was complex because many people keep personal items on their business computers. Dean Wood also said the pornography did not involve children and was not illegal.†

Supposing this account is true, do you agree that the dean should have been forced to resign? If so, on what grounds? If not, why not? Was the dean's right to privacy violated? Did Harvard inappropriately intrude on the dean's personal life? Is it likely that his viewing pornography harmed him in some way? If so, what would have been the nature of that harm? Is it likely that some kind of harm was done to others? If so, who could have been harmed and how?

†Fox Butterfield, "Pornography Cited in Ouster at Harvard," *New York Times,* 20 May 1999. Reprinted with permission.

---

3. Pornography and Rape

Here is part of the abstract of a scientific study published in the *International Journal of Law and Psychiatry* in 1991:

We have looked at the empirical evidence of the well-known feminist dictum: "pornography is the theory—rape is the practice" (Morgan, 1980). While earlier research, notably that generated by the U.S. Commission on Obscenity and Pornography (1970), had found no evidence of a causal link between pornography and rape, a new generation of behavioral scientists have, for more than a decade, made considerable effort to prove such a connection, especially as far as "aggressive pornography" is concerned. The first part of the article examines and discusses the findings of this new research. A number of laboratory experiments have been conducted, much akin to the types of experiments developed by researchers of the effects of nonsexual media violence. As in the latter, a certain degree of increased "aggressiveness" has been found under certain circumstances, but to extrapolate from such laboratory effects to the commission of rape in real life is dubious. Studies of rapists' and nonrapists' immediate sexual reactions to presentations of pornography showed generally greater arousal to non-violent scenes, and no difference can be found in this regard between convicted rapists, nonsexual criminals and noncriminal males. In the second part of the paper an attempt was made to study the necessary precondition for a substantial causal relationship between the availability of pornography, including aggressive pornography, and rape—namely, that obviously increased availability of such material was followed by an increase in cases of reported rape. The development of rape and attempted rape during the period 1964–1984 was studied in four countries: the U.S.A., Denmark, Sweden and West Germany. In all four countries there is clear and undisputed evidence that during this period the availability of various forms of pictorial pornography including violent/dominant varieties (in the form of picture magazines, and films/videos used at home or shown in arcades or cinemas) has developed from extreme scarcity to relative abundance. If (violent) pornography causes rape, this exceptional development in the availability of (violent) pornography should definitely somehow influence the rape statistics. Since, however, the rape figures could not simply be expected to remain steady during the period in question (when it is well known that most other crimes increased considerably), the development of rape rates was compared with that of non-sexual violent offences and nonviolent sexual offences (in so far as available statistics permitted). The results showed that in none of the countries did rape increase more than nonsexual violent crimes. This finding in itself would seem sufficient to discard the hypothesis that pornography causes rape.[‡]

Does this study prove conclusively that access to pornography does not cause rape? Why or why not? Suppose exposure to pornography does indeed lead to rape (increases its incidence). Would this fact justify the banning of all pornographic materials? How would you balance this harm (increased risk of rape) with freedom of expression? Which one would you give more weight to? But say pornography is harmless. Would you still want to see it banned? If so, on what grounds? Suppose pornography was actually helpful to people (enhancing sexuality, improving relationships, decreasing divorce rates, etc.). Would you still want it censored? Why or why not?

[‡]B. Kutchinsky, "Pornography and Rape: Theory and Practice? Evidence from Crime Data in Four Countries Where Pornography Is Easily Available," *International Journal of Law and Psychiatry* 14, nos. 1–2 (1991): 47–64. Reprinted from International Journal of Law and Psychiatry with permission from Elsevier.

Sexual Morality and Marriage

Sometimes it seems that almost anything having to do with sex or marriage is controversial. Frequently, topics that may be unremarkable in themselves trigger intense moral debates when sexuality or matrimony is inserted into the discussions. The moral issues most often focus on specific sexual acts, the context of the acts, the nature of marriage, and people's attitude toward that institution. Thus many may commend or condemn oral sex, anal sex, masturbation, homosexuality, group sex, premarital sex, promiscuous sex, contraception, infidelity, adultery, divorce, gay marriage, monogamy, and polygamy.

Unfortunately, people's positions on these questions usually have more to do with their upbringing, religious tradition, or cultural background than with plausible moral arguments. So let's see what critical thinking can tell us about the ethics of sex and marriage.

ISSUE FILE: BACKGROUND

The central question in the morality of sex is, What kind of sexual behavior is morally permissible, and under what circumstances? People generally give one of three answers: (1) sex is permissible only in a marriage between a man and a woman; (2) sex is permissible between informed, consenting adults; and (3) sex is permissible between informed, consenting adults who are bound by love or commitment.

The first answer is the **conventional view**: sex is morally acceptable only between one man and one woman who are married to each other by legal authority. Sex involving the unmarried or sex in adulterous relationships is impermissible—that is, premarital and extramarital sex are wrong. In a religious strain of the conventional view, some sex acts performed by married partners—acts that are incompatible with procreation—are also prohibited. These include masturbation, oral sex, anal sex, and sex using contraceptives.

The conventional attitude has been championed by Christianity, Judaism, and Islam, and has been vigorously defended in the natural law teachings of the Roman Catholic Church (see the next section). For a long time it was the dominant view of sexual ethics in the West, but since the 1960s its influence has faded. In a recent public opinion poll, 60 percent of respondents said they didn't believe it wrong for a man and woman to have sex before marriage.[1] And whatever people say they believe about the subject, their actual behavior is a far cry from the conventional standard. Research shows that sex before marriage is almost universal among Americans. By age forty-four, 95 percent have had premarital sexual relations.[2]

The second answer is the **liberal view** (not to be confused with the political outlook with the same name). Directly counter to the conventional stance, it says that as long as basic moral standards

<hr />

[1]CBS/New York Times Poll, 11–15 January 2009. N = 1,112 adults nationwide; MoE ± 3.

[2]Lawrence B. Finer, "Trends in Premarital Sex in the United States, 1954–2003," *Public Health Reports* 122 (January–February 2007), www.publichealthreports.org/userfiles/122_1/12_PHR122-1_73-78.pdf.

are respected (for example, no one is harmed or coerced), any sexual activity engaged in by informed, consenting adults is permissible. Provided that people adhere to the relevant moral principles, all kinds of sexual behavior condemned by the conventionalist would be morally acceptable, including premarital sex, extramarital sex, group sex, masturbation, and homosexuality.

The third answer is the **moderate view**, which says that sex is permissible, whether in marriage or not, if the consenting partners have a serious emotional connection. Moral sex does not require marriage, but it does entail more than just the informed, freely given consent of the people involved. For some, this needed connection is love, affection, or mutual caring; for others it's a commitment to sustaining the relationship. Provided that the necessary element is present, both premarital and extramarital sex could be permitted, but promiscuous sex would likely be disallowed.

As you would expect, the conventionalist and the liberal take opposing views on the rightness of **homosexuality** (sexual relations between people of the same sex). The conventionalist denounces it as abnormal, unnatural, harmful, or dangerous. It is always and everywhere wrong. The liberal sees no morally relevant difference between heterosexual and homosexual sex. The behavior is morally permissible if it conforms to legitimate moral standards and involves consenting adults.

Disputes over the moral rightness of homosexuality often seem tame compared to debates about the morality of same-sex marriage. Conventionalists think same-sex marriage is not only wrong but detrimental to social order, ethical standards, and the institution of marriage itself. It's wrong, they say, because marriage is for procreation and childrearing, and same-sex couples cannot procreate. It's detrimental because it perverts the true meaning of marriage, undercuts heterosexual marriage, and fractures family structure on which the welfare of children depends.

Liberals reject all these charges, insisting that marriage has other purposes besides procreation (such as promoting stable relationships and helping to nurture communities) and that same-sex marriages can fulfill these purposes as well as heterosexual marriages can. Besides, the liberal says, allowing same-sex couples to marry is the right thing to do.

MORAL THEORIES

Major moral theories have important implications for the morality of sexual behavior. As we have seen (in Chapter 6), natural law theory holds that right actions are those directed towards the aims revealed in nature. According to the Roman Catholic account of the theory, since procreation is foremost among these aims, actions consistent with it are permissible and actions incompatible with it are forbidden. Sexual intercourse between a man and a woman is the supreme act of procreation, and marriage provides the necessary stable context to nurture the fruits of procreation—children. Thus, only sex between a man and a woman joined by marriage can be morally legitimate. The Vatican declares:

Experience teaches us that love must find its safeguard in the stability of marriage, if sexual intercourse is truly to respond to the requirements of its own finality and to those of human dignity. These requirements call for a conjugal contract sanctioned and guaranteed by society—a contract which establishes a state of life of capital importance both for the exclusive union of the man and the woman and for the good of their family and of the human community.[3]

Premarital sex is, therefore, proscribed, as well as contraception and sexual activity not directed at procreation such as oral sex, masturbation, and homosexuality.

[3]Sacred Congregation for the Doctrine of the Faith, "*Persona Humana*: Declaration on Certain Questions Concerning Sexual Ethics" (29 December 1975).

VITAL STATS: Sex and Marriage

- On average, men first experience intercourse at 16.9 years, women at 17.4 years.

- By their late teens, up to 75 percent of all men and women have had intercourse.

- Over one-fourth of all women are married by their early twenties; fewer than one-fifth of men are.

- 60 percent of adults believe that sex before marriage is morally permissible.

- 95 percent of adult Americans have sex before marrying.

- 91 percent of adults believe it's wrong for married men and women to have an affair.

- 90 percent of adults think polygamy is wrong.

Statistic from CBS/New York Times Poll, 11–15 January 2009, N = 1,112 adults nationwide, MoE ± 3; The Alan Guttmacher Institute, published and unpublished data (2002), www.guttmacher.org/; Lawrence B. Finer, "Trends in Premarital Sex in the United States, 1954–2003," *Public Health Reports* 122 (January–February 2007), www.publichealthreports.org/userfiles/122_1/12_PHR122-1_73-78.pdf

---

Although Immanuel Kant favored a conventional approach to sex and marriage, some thinkers have derived from his theory a liberal view of sexual ethics. Recall Kant's dictum that we must always treat people as ends in themselves, never merely as a means to an end. Thomas Mappes says that to treat someone merely, or solely, as a means is to *use* that person, to treat that person without the respect that she deserves. He defines *using another person* as violating the requirement that interactions with that person be based on her voluntary informed consent. This implies that "using another person (in the morally significant sense) can arise in at least two ways: via *coercion*, which is antithetical to voluntary consent, and via *deception*, which undermines the informed character of voluntary consent."[4]

According to these guidelines, any sexual activity in which one person deceives or coerces another is wrong. But when the principle of voluntary informed consent is respected, a broad range of sexual practices is permissible.

[4]Thomas A. Mappes, "Sexual Morality and the Concept of Using Another Person," in *Social Ethics: Morality and Social Policy*, ed. Thomas A. Mappes and Jane S. Zembaty, 7th ed. (New York: McGraw-Hill, 2007), 171.

A utilitarian is likely to sanction many kinds of sexual activity on the grounds that they produce the greatest overall happiness or good for all concerned. Sexual behavior that results in the greatest net good (the greatest utility) is morally right regardless of whether it is unconventional, "unnatural," deviant, marital, nonmarital, procreative, or recreational.

Maximizing utility in sexual matters, however, requires weighing many possible harms and benefits. Those involved in a sexual relationship may risk sexually transmitted disease, pregnancy, emotional distress (humiliation, disappointment, guilt, etc.), disruptions in family life (as a result of adultery, for example), and social or legal censure. But they may also experience a great deal of sexual pleasure, attain a sense of well-being and psychological satisfaction, and forge strong bonds of affection and mutual caring.

MORAL ARGUMENTS

Probably the fiercest battles in sexual ethics are fought over homosexuality and same-sex marriage. A flash point in the former is the claim that homosexual behavior is immoral—precisely because it is unnatural or abnormal.

Some people take *unnatural* to mean something like "not commonly done by animals." If homosexual behavior is not found among animals in nature, then it is unnatural and, therefore, morally unacceptable. But biologists and others dispute this contention. For example:

We know that in species after species, right through the animal kingdom, students of animal behavior report unambiguous evidence of homosexual attachments and behavior—in insects, fish, birds, and lower and higher mammals. . . . Whatever the moral implications of homosexuality and naturalness may be, it is false that homosexuality is immoral because it does not exist amongst animals.[5]

For many who denounce homosexuality, *unnatural* means "out of the norm," "a deviation from the usual pattern," and this unnaturalness is reason enough to call homosexual behavior immoral. A common counterargument is that it does not follow from an action's statistical abnormality that it is immoral. Many acts are statistically out of the norm—skydiving, composing operas, eating snails—but we do not necessarily think them morally wrong.

While acknowledging the weaknesses of the foregoing definitions, some conventionalists offer more sophisticated abnormality arguments. Consider this line of reasoning:

This paper defends the view that homosexuality is abnormal and hence undesirable—not because it is immoral or sinful, or because it weakens society or hampers evolutionary development, but for a purely mechanical reason. It is a misuse of bodily parts. Clear empirical sense attaches to the idea of *the use* of such bodily parts as genitals, the idea that they are *for* something, and consequently to the idea of their misuse. I argue on grounds involving natural selection

that misuse of bodily parts can with high probability be connected to unhappiness. . . . I . . . draw a seemingly evident corollary from my view that homosexuality is abnormal and likely to lead to unhappiness.[6]

Homosexuality is a misuse of a bodily part—specifically, the penis, which is for injecting sperm into the vagina, not for the abnormal functions that gay men prefer. This misuse leads to unhappiness because it frustrates "an innately rewarding desire." Society has an interest in promoting happiness; and since homosexuality makes for unhappiness, society ought to discourage it by not legalizing it.

A typical rejoinder to this argument is that evolutionary adaptations, whatever their form, tell us nothing about how people *ought* to behave. Just because blind accidents of nature have shaped humans in a particular way, that doesn't mean people are obligated to stay as they are. As one philosopher puts it, "Human beings are completely at liberty to dispose of their work, their behavior, and even such things as their anatomy and physiology as they see fit."[7] Contrary to natural law theory, knowing how nature *is* tells us nothing about how we *ought to be*.

Debates about the morality of homosexuality may seem tranquil compared to the stormy controversies over same-sex marriage. To many, homosexuality challenges ideas about gender and biology, but gay marriage threatens one of the fundamental pillars of society itself—the institution of marriage. The moral question is, Should same-sex marriages be permitted—should they be recognized by law just as heterosexual marriages are?

The conventional answer is, of course, no. One argument for this position appeals to the benefits

---

[5]Michael Ruse, "Is Homosexuality Bad Sexuality?" in *Homosexuality: A Philosophical Inquiry* (Oxford: Blackwell, 1988), 179–192.

[6]Michael Levin, "Why Homosexuality Is Abnormal," *The Monist* (April 1984).

[7]Timothy F. Murphy, "Homosexuality and Nature: Happiness and the Law at Stake," *Journal of Applied Philosophy* 4, no. 2 (1987).

OPINION POLL: Same-Sex Marriage

- 42 percent of Americans claim that same-sex couples should be permitted to marry legally.

- 28 percent think same-sex couples should not receive any legal recognition.

- 25 percent advocate civil unions for same-sex couples but not marriage.

- 69 percent of liberals support gay marriage; 44 percent of conservatives insist on no legal recognition; 28 percent favor civil unions.

CBS/New York Times Poll (22–26 April 2009). N = 973 adults nationwide; MoE ± 3.

---

to society of preserving long-standing customs and traditions. The idea is that because these structures have evolved and endured in human societies, they embody a collective wisdom that must be preserved. However arbitrary or unjust they may seem, they work, and we are stuck with them. If we tamper with them, we risk wrecking their complex internal workings and destroying whole systems. The tradition of marriage is one such intricate structure, now solidly established as an institution joining male and female only.

Jonathan Rauch calls this the Hayekian view, which "argues strongly against gay marriage." It asserts that

once you say that marriage need not be male-female, soon marriage will stop being anything at all. You can't mess with the formula without causing unforeseen consequences, possibly including the implosion of marriage itself.[8]

But this position has serious problems, Rauch says:

In its extreme form, it implies that no social reforms should ever be undertaken. Indeed, no laws should be passed, because they interfere with the natural evolution of social mores. How could Hayekians abolish slavery?[9]

Other arguments against gay marriage appeal to the essence or real meaning of marriage. The

idea is that the true purpose and meaning of marriage is procreation and childrearing. Heterosexual couples can procreate and fulfill marriage's purpose; homosexual couples cannot. Same-sex marriage, therefore, amounts to a degradation of true marriage, a desertion from its essential meaning. Maggie Gallagher takes this view:

Marriage is the fundamental, cross-cultural institution for bridging the male-female divide so that children have loving, committed mothers and fathers. . . . Privately, religiously, emotionally, individually, marriage may have many meanings. But this is the core of its public, shared meaning: Marriage is the place where having children is not only tolerated but welcomed and encouraged, because it gives children mothers and fathers. . . . The problem with endorsing gay marriage is not that it would allow a handful of people to choose alternative family forms, but that it would require society at large to gut marriage of its central presumptions about family in order to accommodate a few adults' desires.[10]

Critics of this line reply that the traditional notion of marriage preferred by Gallagher and others is too narrow. Procreation is just one of several aims of marriage. This is how Rauch makes the point:

For the record, I would be the last to deny that children are one central reason for the privileged status

---

[8]Jonathan Rauch, "For Better or Worse? The Case for Gay (and Straight) Marriage," *The New Republic* (6 May 1996): 18–23.
[9]Rauch.

[10]Maggie Gallagher, "What Marriage Is For: Child Need Mothers and Fathers," *The Weekly Standard* 8, no. 45 (4–11 August 2003).

QUICK REVIEW

conventional view (of sexuality)—The idea that sex is morally acceptable only between a man and a woman who are legally married to each other.
liberal view (of sexuality)—The idea that as long as basic moral standards are respected, any sexual activity engaged in by informed, consenting adults is permissible.
moderate view (of sexuality)—The idea that sex is permissible, whether in marriage or not, if the consenting partners have a serious emotional connection.
homosexuality—Sexual relations between people of the same sex.

of marriage. When men and women get together, children are a likely outcome; and, as we are learning in ever more unpleasant ways, when children grow up without two parents, trouble ensues. Children are not a trivial reason for marriage; they just cannot be the only reason.

What are the others? It seems to me that the two strongest candidates are these: domesticating men and providing reliable caregivers. Both purposes are critical to the functioning of a humane and stable society, and both are much better served by marriage—that is, by one-to-one lifelong commitment—than by any other institution.[11]

These other purposes, Rauch says, can be realized through both same-sex and heterosexual marriage, so there is no reason to bar homosexual couples from this important social practice.

Some argue for the same conclusion another way. They doubt that procreation is the essential function of marriage because our civil marriage

[11]Rauch.

laws do not require procreation or fertility to be a necessary part of marriage. People who are infertile or who cannot or will not consummate their marriage may legally marry as easily as anyone else.

SUMMARY

The main question in the morality of sex is, What kind of sexual behavior is morally permissible, and under what circumstances? The most common answers are: (1) sex is permissible only in a marriage between a man and a woman (the conventional view); (2) sex is permissible between informed, consenting adults (the liberal view); and (3) sex is permissible between informed, consenting adults who are bound by love or commitment (the moderate view).

Natural law theory offers a conventional account of sexual morality, exemplified by Roman Catholic teachings on the subject. Premarital and extramarital sex are forbidden, as well as contraception, oral and anal sex, masturbation, and homosexuality. A liberal view of sexual ethics can be derived from Kantian theory. It says that any sexual activity in which one person deceives or coerces another is wrong, but when the principle of voluntary informed consent is respected, a broad range of sexual practices is permissible. Utilitarianism is likely to endorse many kinds of sexual activity on the grounds that they maximize utility.

A common charge against homosexuality is that it is unnatural or abnormal. People rebut these claims by trying to show that they are unfounded or confused, or by arguing that abnormality does not imply immorality.

A prevalent argument against same-sex marriage is that it is an abandonment of the true meaning of marriage. Marriage is for procreation and child-rearing, but same-sex couples cannot procreate. The main counterargument is that marriage has several purposes beyond procreation, and same-sex couples can participate in these as well as heterosexual couples can.

READINGS

On Marriage

JONATHAN RAUCH

Whatever else marriage may or may not be, it is certainly falling apart. Half of today's marriages end in divorce, and, far more costly, many never begin—leaving mothers poor, children fatherless and neighborhoods chaotic. With timing worthy of Neville Chamberlain, homosexuals have chosen this moment to press for the right to marry. What's more, Hawaii's courts are moving toward letting them do so. I'll believe in gay marriage in America when I see it, but if Hawaii legalizes it, even temporarily, the uproar over this final insult to a besieged institution will be deafening.

Whether gay marriage makes sense—and whether straight marriage makes sense—depends on what marriage is actually for. Current secular thinking on this question is shockingly sketchy. Gay activists say: marriage is for love, and we love each other, therefore we should be able to marry. Traditionalists say: marriage is for children, and homosexuals do not (or should not) have children, therefore you should not be able to marry. That, unfortunately, pretty well covers the spectrum. I say "unfortunately" because both views are wrong. They misunderstand and impoverish the social meaning of marriage.

So what is marriage for? Modern marriage is, of course, based upon traditions that religion helped to codify and enforce. But religious doctrine has no special standing in the world of secular law and policy (the "Christian nation" crowd notwithstanding). If we want to know what and whom marriage is for in modern America, we need a sensible secular doctrine.

At one point, marriage in secular society was largely a matter of business: cementing family ties, providing social status for men and economic sup-

port for women, conferring dowries, and so on. Marriages were typically arranged, and "love" in the modern sense was no prerequisite. In Japan, remnants of this system remain, and it works surprisingly well. Couples stay together because they view their marriage as a partnership: an investment in social stability for themselves and their children. Because Japanese couples don't expect as much emotional fulfillment as we do, they are less inclined to break up. They also take a somewhat more relaxed attitude toward adultery. What's a little extracurricular love provided that each partner is fulfilling his or her many other marital duties?

In the West, of course, love is a defining element. The notion of lifelong love is charming, if ambitious, and certainly love is a desirable element of marriage. In society's eyes, however, it cannot be the defining element. You may or may not love your husband, but the two of you are just as married either way. You may love your mistress, but that certainly doesn't make her your spouse. Love helps make sense of marriage emotionally, but it is not terribly important in making sense of marriage from the point of view of social policy.

If love does not define the purpose of secular marriage, what does? Neither the law nor secular thinking provides a clear answer. Today marriage is almost entirely a voluntary arrangement whose contents are up to the people making the deal. There are few if any behaviors that automatically end a marriage. If a man beats his wife, which is about the worst thing he can do to her, he may be convicted of assault, but his marriage is not automatically dissolved. Couples can be adulterous ("open") yet remain married. They can be celibate, too; consummation is not required. All in all, it is an impressive and also rather astonishing victory for modern individualism that so important an institution should be so bereft of for-

Jonathan Rauch, "For Better or Worse? The Case for Gay (and Straight) Marriage," *The New Republic* (6 May 1996): 18–19, 21–23 (edited). Reprinted with permission by *The New Republic*.

mal social instruction as to what should go on inside of it.

Secular society tells us only a few things about marriage. First, marriage depends on the consent of the parties. Second, the parties are not children. Third, the number of parties is two. Fourth, one is a man and the other a woman. Within those rules a marriage is whatever anyone says it is.

Perhaps it is enough simply to say that marriage is as it is and should not be tampered with. This sounds like a crudely reactionary position. In fact, however, of all the arguments against reforming marriage, it is probably the most powerful.

Call it a Hayekian argument, after the great libertarian economist F.A. Hayek, who developed this line of thinking in his book *The Fatal Conceit*. In a market system, the prices generated by impersonal forces may not make sense from any one person's point of view, but they encode far more information than even the cleverest person could ever gather. In a similar fashion, human societies evolve rich and complicated webs of nonlegal rules in the form of customs, traditions and institutions. Like prices, they may seem irrational or arbitrary. But the very fact that they are the customs that have evolved implies that they embody a practical logic that may not be apparent to even a sophisticated analyst. And the web of custom cannot be torn apart and reordered at will because once its internal logic is violated it falls apart. Intellectuals, such as Marxists or feminists, who seek to deconstruct and rationally rebuild social traditions, will produce not better order but chaos.

So the Hayekian view argues strongly against gay marriage. It says that the current rules may not be best and may even be unfair. But they are all we have, and, once you say that marriage need not be male-female, soon marriage will stop being anything at all. You can't mess with the formula without causing unforeseen consequences, possibly including the implosion of the institution of marriage itself.

However, there are problems with the Hayekian position. It is untenable in its extreme form and unhelpful in its milder version. In its extreme form, it implies that no social reforms should ever be undertaken. Indeed, no laws should be passed, because they interfere with the natural evolution of social mores. How could Hayekians abolish slavery? They would probably note that slavery violates fundamental moral principles. But in so doing they would establish a moral platform from which to judge social rules, and thus acknowledge that abstracting social debate from moral concerns is not possible.

If the ban on gay marriage were only mildly unfair, and if the costs of changing it were certain to be enormous, then the ban could stand on Hayekian grounds. But, if there is any social policy today that has a fair claim to be scaldingly inhumane, it is the ban on gay marriage. As conservatives tirelessly and rightly point out, marriage is society's most fundamental institution. To bar any class of people from marrying as they choose is an extraordinary deprivation. When not so long ago it was illegal in parts of America for blacks to marry whites, no one could claim that this was a trivial disenfranchisement. Granted, gay marriage raises issues that interracial marriage does not; but no one can argue that the deprivation is a minor one.

To outweigh such a serious claim it is not enough to say that gay marriage might lead to bad things. Bad things happened as a result of legalizing contraception, but that did not make it the wrong thing to do. Besides, it seems doubtful that extending marriage to, say, another 3 or 5 percent of the population would have anything like the effects that no-fault divorce has had, to say nothing of contraception. By now, the "traditional" understanding of marriage has been sullied in all kinds of ways. It is hard to think of a bigger affront to tradition, for instance, than allowing married women to own property independently of their husbands or allowing them to charge their husbands with rape. Surely it is unfair to say that marriage may be reformed for the sake of anyone and everyone except homosexuals, who must respect the dictates of tradition.

Faced with these problems, the milder version of the Hayekian argument says not that social traditions shouldn't be tampered with at all, but that they shouldn't be tampered with lightly. Fine. In this case, no one is talking about casual messing around; both sides have marshaled their arguments with deadly seriousness. Hayekians surely have to recognize that appeals to blind tradition and to the risks inherent in social change do not, a priori, settle anything in this instance. They merely warn against frivolous change.

So we turn to what has become the standard view of marriage's purpose. Its proponents would probably like to call it a child-centered view, but it is actually an anti-gay view, as will become clear. Whatever you call it, it is the view of marriage that is heard most often, and in the context of the debate over gay marriage it is heard almost exclusively. In its most straightforward form it goes as follows (I quote from James Q. Wilson's fine book *The Moral Sense*):

A family is not an association of independent people; it is a human commitment designed to make possible the rearing of moral and healthy children. Governments care—or ought to care—about families for this reason, and scarcely for any other.

Wilson speaks about "family" rather than "marriage" as such, but one may, I think, read him as speaking of marriage without doing any injustice to his meaning. The resulting proposition—government ought to care about marriage almost entirely because of children—seems reasonable. But there are problems. The first, obviously, is that gay couples may have children, whether through adoption, prior marriage or (for lesbians) artificial insemination. Leaving aside the thorny issue of gay adoption, the point is that if the mere presence of children is the test, then homosexual relationships can certainly pass it.

You might note, correctly, that heterosexual marriages are more likely to produce children than homosexual ones. When granting marriage licenses to heterosexuals, however, we do not ask how likely the couple is to have children. We assume that they are entitled to get married whether or not they end up with children. Understanding this, conservatives often make an interesting move. In seeking to justify the state's interest in marriage, they shift from the actual presence of children to the anatomical possibility of making them. Hadley Arkes, a political science professor and prominent opponent of homosexual marriage, makes the case this way:

The traditional understanding of marriage is grounded in the "natural teleology of the body"—in the inescapable fact that only a man and a woman, and only two people, not three, can generate a child. Once marriage is detached from that natural teleology of the body, what ground of principle would thereafter confine marriage to two people rather than some larger grouping? That is, on what ground of principle would the law reject the claim of a gay couple that their love is not confined to a coupling of two, but that they are woven into a larger ensemble with yet another person or two?

What he seems to be saying is that, where the possibility of natural children is nil, the meaning of marriage is nil. If marriage is allowed between members of the same sex, then the concept of marriage has been emptied of content except to ask whether the parties love each other. Then anything goes, including polygamy. This reasoning presumably is what those opposed to gay marriage have in mind when they claim that, once gay marriage is legal, marriage to pets will follow close behind.

But Arkes and his sympathizers make two mistakes. To see them, break down the claim into two components: (1) Two-person marriage derives its special status from the anatomical possibility that the partners can create natural children; and (2) Apart from (1), two-person marriage has no purpose sufficiently strong to justify its special status. That is, absent justification (1), anything goes.

The first proposition is wholly at odds with the way society actually views marriage. Leave aside the insistence that natural, as opposed to adopted, children define the importance of marriage. The deeper problem, apparent right away, is the issue of sterile heterosexual couples. Here the "anatomical possibility" crowd has a problem, for a homosexual union is, anatomically speaking, nothing but one variety of sterile union and no different even in principle: a woman without a uterus has no more potential for giving birth than a man without a vagina.

It may sound like carping to stress the case of barren heterosexual marriage: the vast majority of newlywed heterosexual couples, after all, can have children and probably will. But the point here is fundamental. There are far more sterile heterosexual unions in America than homosexual ones. The "anatomical possibility" crowd cannot have it both ways. If the possibility of children is what gives meaning to marriage, then a postmenopausal woman who applies for a marriage license should be turned away at the courthouse door. What's more, she should be hooted at and condemned for stretching the meaning of marriage beyond its natural basis and so reducing the institution to frivolity. People at the Family Research Council or Concerned Women for American should point at her an say, "If she can marry, why not polygamy?"

Obviously, the "anatomical" conservatives do not say this, because they are sane. They instead flail around, saying that sterile men and women were at least born with the right-shaped parts for making children, and so on. Their position is really a nonposition. It says that the "natural children" rationale defines marriage when homosexuals are involved but not when heterosexuals are involved. When the parties to union are sterile heterosexuals, the justification for marriage must be something else. But what?

Now arises the oddest part of the "anatomical" argument. Look at proposition (2) above. It says that, absent the anatomical justification for marriage, anything goes. In other words, it dismisses the idea that there might be other good reasons for society to sanctify marriage above other kinds of relationships. Why would anybody make this move? I'll hazard a guess: to exclude homosexuals. Any rationale that justifies sterile heterosexual marriages can also apply to homosexual ones. For instance, marriage makes women more financially secure. Very nice, say the conservatives. But that rationale could be applied to lesbians, so it's definitely out.

The end result of this stratagem is perverse to the point of being funny. The attempt to ground marriage in children (or the anatomical possibility thereof) falls flat. But, having lost that reason for marriage, the antigay people can offer no other. In their fixation on excluding homosexuals, they leave themselves no consistent justification for the privileged status of *heterosexual* marriage. They thus tear away any coherent foundation that secular marriage might have, which is precisely the opposite of what they claim they want to do. If they have to undercut marriage to save it from homosexuals, so be it!

For the record, I would be the last to deny that children are one central reason for the privileged status of marriage. When men and women get together, children are a likely outcome; and, as we are learning in ever more unpleasant ways, when children grow up without two parents, trouble ensues. Children are not a trivial reason for marriage; they just cannot be the only reason.

What are the others? It seems to me that the two strongest candidates are these: domesticating men and providing reliable caregivers. Both purposes are critical to the functioning of a humane and stable society, and both are much better served by marriage—that is, by one-to-one lifelong commitment—than by any other institution.

Civilizing young males is one of any society's biggest problems. Wherever unattached males gather in packs, you see no end of trouble: wildings in Central Park, gangs in Los Angeles, soccer hooligans in Britain, skinheads in Germany, fraternity hazings in universities, grope-lines in the military and, in a different but ultimately no less tragic way, the bathhouses and wanton sex of gay San Francisco or New York in the 1970s.

For taming men, marriage is unmatched. "Of all the institutions through which men may pass—schools, factories, the military—marriage has the largest effect," Wilson writes in *The Moral Sense*. (A token of the casualness of current thinking about marriage is that the man who wrote those words could, later in the very same book, say that government should care about fostering families for "scarcely any other" reason than children.) If marriage—that is, the binding of men into couples—did nothing else, its power to settle men, to keep them at home and out of trouble, would be ample justification for its special status.

Of course, women and older men don't generally travel in marauding or orgiastic packs. But in their case the second rationale comes into play. A second enormous problem for society is what to do when someone is beset by some sort of burdensome contingency. It could be cancer, a broken back, unemployment or depression; it could be exhaustion from work or stress under pressure. If marriage has any meaning at all, it is that, when you collapse from a stroke, there will be at least one other person whose "job" is to drop everything and come to your aid; or that when you come home after being fired by the postal service there will be someone to persuade you not to kill the supervisor.

Obviously, both rationales—the need to settle males and the need to have people looked after—apply to sterile people as well as fertile ones, and apply to childless couples as well as to ones with children. The first explains why everybody feels relieved when the town delinquent gets married, and the second explains why everybody feels happy when an aging widow takes a second husband. From a social point of view, it seems to me both rationales are far more compelling as justifications of marriage's special status than, say, love. And both of them apply to homosexuals as well as to heterosexuals.

Take the matter of settling men. It is probably true that women and children, more than just the fact of marriage, help civilize men. But that hardly means that the settling effect of marriage on homosexual men is negligible. To the contrary, being tied to a committed relationship plainly helps stabilize gay men. Even without marriage, coupled gay men have steady sex partners and relationships that they value and therefore tend to be less wanton. Add marriage, and you bring a further array of stabilizing influences. One of the main benefits of publicly recognized marriage is that it binds couples together not only in their own eyes but also in the eyes of society at large. Around the partners is woven a web of expectations that they will spend nights together, go to parties together, take out mortgages together, buy furniture at Ikea together, and so on—all of which helps tie them together and keep them off the streets and at home. Surely that is a very good thing, especially as compared to the closet-gay culture of furtive sex with innumerable partners in parks and bathhouses.

The other benefit of marriage—caretaking—clearly applies to homosexuals. One of the first things many people worry about when coming to terms with their homosexuality is: Who will take care of me when I'm ailing or old? Society needs to care about this, too, as the AIDS crisis has made horribly clear. If that crisis has shown anything, it is that homosexuals can and will take care of each other, sometimes with breathtaking devotion—and that no institution can begin to match the care of a devoted partner. Legally speaking, marriage creates kin. Surely society's interest in kin-creation is strongest of all for people who are unlikely to be supported by children in old age and who may well be rejected by their own parents in youth.

Gay marriage, then, is far from being a mere exercise in political point-making or rights-mongering. On the contrary, it serves two of the three social purposes that make marriage so indispensable and irreplaceable for heterosexuals. Two out of three may not be the whole ball of wax, but it is more than enough to give society a compelling interest in marrying off homosexuals.

There is no substitute. Marriage is the *only* institution that adequately serves these purposes. The power of marriage is not just legal but social. It seals its promise with the smiles and tears of family, friends and neighbors. It shrewdly exploits ceremony (big, public weddings) and money (expensive gifts, dowries) to deter casual commitment and to make bailing out embarrassing. Stag parties and bridal showers signal that what is beginning is not just a legal arrangement but a whole new stage of life. "Domestic partner" laws do none of these things.

I'll go further: far from being a substitute for the real thing, marriage-lite may undermine it. Marriage is a deal between a couple and society, not just between two people: society recognizes the sanctity and autonomy of the pair-bond, and in exchange each spouse commits to being the other's nurse, social worker and policeman of first resort. Each marriage is its own little society within society. Any step that weakens the deal by granting the legal benefits of marriage without also requiring the public commitment is begging for trouble.

So gay marriage makes sense for several of the same reasons that straight marriage makes sense. That would seem a natural place to stop. But the logic of the argument compels one to go a twist further. If it is good for society to have people attached, then it is not enough just to make marriage available. Marriage should also be *expected*. This, too, is just as true for homosexuals as for heterosexuals. So, if homosexuals are justified in expecting access to marriage, society is equally justified in expecting them to use it. I'm not saying that out-of-wedlock sex should be scandalous or that people should be coerced into marrying. The mechanisms of expectation are more subtle. When grandma cluck-clucks over a still-unmarried young man, or when mom says she wishes her little girl would settle down, she is expressing a strong and well-justified preference: one that is quietly echoed in a thousand ways throughout society and that produces subtle but important pressure to form and sustain unions. This is a good and necessary thing, and it will be as necessary for homosexuals as heterosexuals. If gay marriage is recognized, single gay people over a certain age should not be surprised when they are disapproved of or pitied. That is a vital part of what makes marriage work. It's stigma as social policy.

If marriage is to work it cannot be merely a "lifestyle option." It must be privileged. That is, it must be understood to be better, on average, than other ways of living. Not mandatory, not good where everything else is bad, but better: a general norm, rather than a personal taste. The biggest worry about gay marriage, I think, is that homosexuals might get it but then mostly not use it. Gay neglect of marriage wouldn't greatly erode the bonding power of heterosexual marriage (remember, homosexuals are only a tiny fraction of the population)—but it would certainly not help. And heterosexual society would rightly feel betrayed if, after legalization, homosexuals treated marriage as a minority taste rather than as a core institution of life. It is not enough, I think, for gay people to say we want the right to marry. If we do not use it, shame on us.

On Gay Rights

RICHARD D. MOHR

I. WHO ARE GAYS ANYWAY?

A recent Gallup poll found that only one in five Americans reports having a gay acquaintance. This finding is extraordinary given the number of practicing homosexuals in America. Alfred Kinsey's 1948 study of the sex lives of 5000 white males shocked the nation: 37 percent had at least one homosexual experience to orgasm in their adult lives; an additional 13 percent had homosexual fantasies to orgasm; 4 percent were exclusively homosexual in

Richard D. Mohr, "Gay Basics: Some Questions, Facts, and Values," in *Gays/Justice: A Study of Ethics, Society, and Law* (New York: Columbia University Press, 1988), 21–38 (edited). Reprinted with permission by Columbia University Press.

their practices; another 5 percent had virtually no heterosexual experience, and nearly 20 percent had at least as many homosexual as heterosexual experiences. With only slight variations, these figures held across all social categories: region, religion, political belief, class, income, occupation, and education.

Two out of five men one passes on the street have had orgasmic sex with men. Every second family in the country has a member who is essentially homosexual, and many more people regularly have homosexual experiences. Who are homosexuals? They are your friends, your minister, your teacher, your bankteller, your doctor, your mailcarrier, your secretary, your congressional representative, your sibling, parent, and spouse. They are everywhere, virtually all ordinary, virtually all unknown.

What follows? First, the country is profoundly ignorant of the actual experience of gay people. Second, social attitudes and practices that are harmful to gays have a much greater overall negative impact on society than is usually realized. Third, most gay people live in hiding—in the closet—making the "coming out" experience the central fixture of gay consciousness and invisibility the chief social characteristic of gays.

II. IGNORANCE, STEREOTYPE, AND MORALITY

Society's ignorance of gay people is, however, not limited to individuals' lack of personal acquaintance with gays. Stigma against gay people is so strong that even discussions of homosexuality are taboo. This taboo is particularly strong in academe, where it is reinforced by the added fear of the teacher as molester. So even within the hearth of reason irrational forces have held virtually unchallenged and largely unchallengeable sway. The usual sort of clarifying research that might be done on a stigmatized minority has with gays only just begun—haltingly—in history, literature, sociology, and the sciences.

Yet ignorance about gays has not stopped people from having strong opinions about them. The void which ignorance leaves has been filled with stereotypes. Society holds chiefly two groups of antigay stereotypes; the two are an oddly contradictory lot. One set of stereotypes revolves around alleged mistakes in an individual's gender identity: lesbians are women that want to be, or at least look and act like, men—bulldykes, diesel dykes; while gay men are those who want to be, or at least look and act like, women—queens, fairies, limp-wrists, nellies. Gays are "queer," which, remember, means at root not merely weird but chiefly counterfeit—"he's as queer as a three dollar bill." These stereotypes of mismatched or fraudulent genders provide the materials through which gays and lesbians become the butts of ethniclike jokes. These stereotypes and jokes, though derisive, basically view gays and lesbians as ridiculous.

Another set of stereotypes revolves around gays as a pervasive, sinister, conspiratorial, and corruptive threat. The core stereotype here is the gay person as child molester and, more generally, as sex-crazed maniac. These stereotypes carry with them fears of the very destruction of family and civilization itself. Now, that which is essentially ridiculous can hardly have such a staggering effect. Something must be afoot in this incoherent amalgam.

Sense can be made of this incoherence if the nature of stereotypes is clarified. Stereotypes are not *simply* false generalizations from a skewed sample of cases examined. Admittedly, false generalizing plays a part in most stereotypes a society holds. If, for instance, one takes as one's sample homosexuals who are in psychiatric hospitals or prisons, as was done in nearly all early investigations, not surprisingly one will probably find homosexuals to be of a crazed and criminal cast. Such false generalizations, though, simply confirm beliefs already held on independent grounds, ones that likely led the investigator to the prison and psychiatric ward to begin with. Evelyn Hooker, who in the mid-fifties carried out the first rigorous studies to use nonclinical gays, found that psychiatrists, when presented with results of standard psychological diagnostic tests—but with indications of sexual orientation omitted—were able to do no better than if they had guessed randomly in their attempts to distinguish gay files from nongay ones, even though the psychiatrists believed gays to be crazy and supposed themselves to be experts in detecting craziness. These studies provided a foundation embarrassment to the psychiatric establishment, the financial well-being of which was substantially enhanced by 'curing' allegedly insane gays. Eventually the studies contributed to the American Psychiatric Association's dropping homosexuality from its registry of mental illnesses in 1973. Nevertheless, the stereotype of gays as sick continues apace in the mind of America.

False generalizations *help maintain* stereotypes; they do not *form* them. As the history of Hooker's discoveries shows, stereotypes have a life beyond facts. Their origin lies in a culture's ideology—the general system of beliefs by which it lives—and they are sustained across generations by diverse cultural transmissions, hardly any of which, including slang and jokes, even purport to have a scientific basis. Stereotypes, then, are not the products of bad science, but are social constructions that perform central functions in maintaining society's conception of itself.

On this understanding, it is easy to see that the antigay stereotypes surrounding gender identification are chiefly means of reinforcing still powerful gender roles in society. If, as this stereotype presumes (and condemns), one is free to choose one's social roles independently of gender, many guiding social divisions, both domestic and commercial, might be threatened. The socially gender-linked distinctions would blur between breadwinner and homemaker, protector and protected, boss and secretary, doctor and nurse, priest and nun, hero and whore, saint and siren, lord and helpmate, and God and his world. The accusations "fag" and "dyke" (which recent philology has indeed shown to be rooted in slang referring to gender-bending, especially cross-dressing) exist in significant part to keep women in their place and to prevent men from breaking ranks and ceding away theirs.

The stereotypes of gays as child molesters, sex-crazed maniacs, and civilization destroyers function to displace (socially irresolvable) problems from their actual source to a foreign (and so, it is thought, manageable) one. Thus, the stereotype of child molester functions to give the family unit a false sheen of absolute innocence. It keeps the unit from being examined too closely for incest, child abuse, wife-battering, and the terrorism of constant threats. The stereotype teaches that the problems of the family are not internal to it, but external.

Because this stereotype has this central social function, it could not be dislodged even by empirical studies, paralleling Hooker's efforts, that showed heterosexuals to be child molesters to a far greater extent than the actual occurrence of heterosexuals in the general population. But one need not even be aware of such debunking empirical studies in order to see the same cultural forces at work in the social belief that gays are molesters as in its belief that they are crazy. For one can see them now in society's and the media's treatment of current reports of violence,

especially domestic violence. When a mother kills her child or a father rapes his daughter—regular Section B fare even in major urbane papers—this is never taken by reporters, columnists, or pundits as evidence that there is something wrong with heterosexuality or with traditional families. These issues are not even raised.

But when a homosexual child molestation is reported it is taken as confirming evidence of the way homosexuals are. One never hears of heterosexual murders, but one regularly reads of "homosexual" ones. Compare the social treatment of Richard Speck's sexually motivated mass murder in 1966 of Chicago nurses with that of John Wayne Gacy's serial murders of Chicago youths. Gacy was in the culture's mind taken as symbolic of gay men in general. To prevent the possibility that The Family was viewed as anything but an innocent victim in this affair, the mainstream press knowingly failed to mention that most of Gacy's adolescent victims were homeless hustlers, even though this was made obvious at his trial. That knowledge would be too much for the six o'clock news and for cherished beliefs.

The stereotype of gays as sex-crazed maniacs functions socially to keep individuals' sexuality contained. For this stereotype makes it look as though the problem of how to address one's considerable sexual drives can and should be answered with repression, for it gives the impression that the cyclone of dangerous psychic forces is *out there* where the fags are, not within one's own breast. With the decline of the stereotype of the black man as raping pillaging marauder (found in such works as *Birth of a Nation*, *Gone with the Wind*, and *Soul on Ice*), the stereotype of gay men as sex-crazed maniacs has become more aggravated. The stereotype of the sex-crazed threat seems one that society desperately needs to have somewhere in its sexual cosmology.

For the repressed homosexual, this stereotype has an especially powerful allure—by hating it consciously, he subconsciously appears to save himself from himself, at least as long as the ruse does not exhaust the considerable psychic energies required to maintain it, or until, like ultraconservative Congressman Robert E. Bauman (R-Md.) and Jon C. Hinson (R-Miss.), he is caught importuning hustlers or gentlemen in washrooms. If, as Freud and some of his followers thought, everyone feels an urge for sex partners of both genders, then the fear of gays works to show us that we have not "met the enemy and he is us."

By directly invoking sex acts, this second set of stereotypes is the more severe and serious of the two—one never hears child-molester jokes. These stereotypes are aimed chiefly against men, as in turn stereotypically the more sexed of the genders. They are particularly divisive for they create a very strong division between those conceived as "us" and those conceived as "them." This divide is not so strong in the case of the stereotype of gay men as effeminate. For women (and so the woman-like) after all do have their place. Nonstrident, nonuppity useful ones can even be part of "us," indeed, belong, like "our children," to "us." Thus, in many cultures with overweening gender-identified social roles (like prisons, truckstops, the armed forces, Latin America, and the Islamic world) only passive partners in male couplings are derided as homosexual.

Because "the facts" largely do not matter when it comes to the generation and maintenance of stereotypes, the effects of scientific and academic research and of enlightenment generally will be, at best, slight and gradual in the changing fortunes of gays. If this account of stereotypes holds, society has been profoundly immoral. For its treatment of gays is a grand scale rationalization and moral sleight-of-hand. The problem is not that society's usual standards of evidence and procedure in coming to judgments of social policy have been misapplied to gays, rather when it comes to gays, the standards themselves have simply been ruled out of court and disregarded in favor of mechanisms that encourage unexamined fear and hatred.

III. ARE GAYS DISCRIMINATED AGAINST? DOES IT MATTER?

Partly because lots of people suppose they do not know a gay person and partly through their willful ignorance of society's workings, people are largely unaware of the many ways in which gays are subject to discrimination in consequence of widespread fear and hatred. Contributing to this social ignorance of discrimination is the difficulty for gay people, as an invisible minority, even to complain of discrimination. For if one is gay, to register a complaint would suddenly target one as a stigmatized person, and so, in the absence of any protections against discrimination, would in turn invite additional discrimination.

Further, many people, especially those who are persistently downtrodden and so lack a firm sense of self to begin with, tend either to blame themselves for their troubles or to view their troubles as a matter of bad luck or as the result of an innocent mistake by others—as anything but an injustice indicating something wrong with society. Alfred Dreyfus went to his grave believing his imprisonment for treason and his degradation from the French military, in which he was the highest ranking Jewish officer, had all just been a sort of clerical error, merely requiring recomputation, rather than what it was— lightning striking a promontory from out of a storm of national bigotry. The recognition of injustice requires doing something to rectify wrong; the recognition of systematic injustices requires doing something about the system, and most people, especially the already beleaguered, simply are not up to the former, let alone the latter.

For a number of reasons, then, discrimination against gays, like rape, goes seriously underreported. What do they experience? First, gays are subject to violence and harassment based simply on their perceived status rather than because of any actions they have performed. A recent extensive study by the National Gay and Lesbian Task Force found that over 90 percent of gays and lesbians had been victimized in some form on the basis of their sexual orientation. Greater than one in five gay men and nearly one in ten lesbians had been punched, hit, or kicked; a quarter of all gays had had objects thrown at them; a third had been chased; a third had been sexually harassed and 14 percent had been spit on—all just for being perceived to be gay.

The most extreme form of antigay violence is queerbashing—where groups of young men target another man who they suppose is gay and beat and kick him unconscious and sometimes to death amid a torrent of taunts and slurs. Such seemingly random but in reality socially encouraged violence has the same social origin and function as lynchings of blacks—to keep a whole stigmatized group in line. As with lynchings of the recent past, the police and courts have routinely averted their eyes, giving their implicit approval to the practice.

Few such cases with gay victims reach the courts. Those that do are marked by inequitable procedures and results. Frequently judges will describe queerbashers as "just All-American Boys." In 1984, a District of Columbia judge handed suspended sentences to queerbashers whose victim had been stalked, beaten, stripped at knife point, slashed, kicked, threatened with castration, and pissed on, because the judge thought the bashers were good boys at heart—after all they went to a religious prep school.

In the summer of 1984, three teenagers hurled a gay man to his death from a bridge in Bangor, Maine. Though the youths could have been tried as adults and normally would have been, given the extreme violence of their crime, they were tried rather as children and will be back on the streets again automatically when they turn twenty-one.

Further, police and juries simply discount testimony from gays. They typically construe assaults on and murders of gays as "justified" self-defense—the killer need only claim his act was a panicked response to a sexual overture. Alternatively, when guilt seems patent, juries will accept highly implausible insanity or other "diminished capacity" defenses. In 1981 a former New York City Transit Authority policeman, later claiming he was just doing the work of God, machine-gunned down nine people, killing two, in two Greenwich Village gay bars. His jury found him innocent due to mental illness. The best known example of a successful "diminished capacity" defense is Dan White's voluntary manslaughter conviction for the 1978 assassination of openly gay San Francisco city councilman Harvey Milk—Hostess Twinkies, his lawyer successfully argued, made him do it.

These inequitable procedures and results collectively show that the life and liberty of gays, like those of blacks, simply count for less than the life and liberty of members of the dominant culture.

The equitable role of law is the heart of an orderly society. The collapse of the rule of law for gays shows that society is willing to perpetrate the worst possible injustices against them. Conceptually there is a difference only in degree between the collapse of the rule of law and systematic extermination of members of a population simply for having some group status independent of any act an individual has performed. In the Nazi concentration camps, gays were forced to wear pink triangles as identifying badges, just as Jews were forced to wear yellow stars. In remembrance of that collapse of the rule of law, the pink triangle has become the chief symbol of the gay rights movement.

Gays have been widely subject to discrimination in employment—the very means by which one puts bread on one's table and one of the chief means by which a person identifies himself to himself and achieves individual dignity. Governments are leading offenders here. They do a lot of discriminating themselves. They require that others, like government contractors, do it, and they set precedents and establish models favoring discrimination in the private sector. The federal government explicitly discriminates against gays in the armed forces, the CIA, the FBI, the National Security Agency, and the state department. The federal government refuses to give security clearances to gays and so forces the country's considerable private-sector military and aerospace contractors to fire known gay employees. State and local governments regularly fire gay teachers, police and fire personnel, social workers, and anyone who has contact with the public. Further, states through licensing laws officially bar gays from a vast array of occupations and professions—everything from doctors, lawyers, accountants, and nurses to hairdressers, morticians, and used car dealers. The American Civil Liberties Union's handbook *The Rights of Gay People* (1975) lists 307 such prohibited occupations.

Gays are subject to discrimination in a wide variety of other ways, including private-sector employment, public accommodations, housing, immigration and naturalization, insurance of all types, custody and adoption, and zoning regulations that bar "singles" or "non-related" couples. All of these discriminations affect central components of a meaningful life; some even reach to the means by which life itself is sustained. In half the states, where gay sex is illegal, the central role of sex to meaningful life is officially denied to gays.

All these sorts of discriminations also affect the ability of people to have significant intimate relations. It is difficult for people to live together as couples without having their sexual orientation perceived in the public realm and so becoming targets for discrimination. Illegality, discrimination, and the absorption by gays of society's hatred of them—all interact to impede or block altogether the ability of gays and lesbians to create and maintain significant personal relations with loved ones. So every facet of life is affected by discrimination. Only the most compelling reasons could justify it.

IV. BUT AREN'T THEY IMMORAL?

Many people think society's treatment of gays is justified because gays are extremely immoral. To evaluate this claim, different senses of "moral" must be distinguished. Sometimes by "morality" is meant the overall beliefs affecting behavior in a society—its current mores, norms, and customs. On this understanding, gays certainly are not moral: lots of people hate them and social customs are designed to register widespread disapproval of gays. The problem here is that this sense of morality is merely a *descriptive* one. On this understanding of what morality is, *every* society has a morality—even Nazi society, which had racism and mob rule as central features of its popular "morality." What is needed in order to use the notion of morality to praise or condemn behavior is a sense of morality that is *prescriptive* or *normative*—what is needed is a sense of morality whereby, for

instance, the descriptive morality of the Nazis is found wanting.

Moral thinking that carries a prescriptive or normative force has certain basic ground rules to which all people consent when attention is drawn to them. First, normative moral beliefs are not merely expressions of feelings. Rather we—normatively moral agents—both expect and are expected to be able to give reasons or justifications for them. We suspect that beliefs, especially strongly held ones, for which no reasons or justifications can be tendered, are mere expressions of phobias and neuroses. Second, moral thinking must be consistent and fair—we must recognize that our specific moral beliefs commit us to general moral principles in light of which we must be willing to treat relevantly similar cases similarly. Third, we must avoid prejudice and rationalization: we must be willing to apply to ourselves the same rules and standards of evidence and argument that we apply to others. And we must avoid being so peculiar and particular in the scope of our principles that we stand accused of being whimsical and arbitrary in picking them.

Even from this sketch of minimum requirements of a critical or normative morality, it should be clear that something's being descriptively moral or immoral is nowhere near enough to make it normatively moral or immoral. For one of our principles itself is that simply a lot of people's saying something is good, even over eons, does not make it so. Our rejection of the long history of socially approved and state-enforced slavery is a good example of this principle at work. Slavery would be wrong even if nearly everyone liked it. So consistency and fairness requires that the culture abandon the belief that gays are immoral simply because most people dislike or disapprove of gays or gay acts, or even because gay sex acts are illegal.

Further, recent historical and anthropological research has shown that opinion about gays has been by no means universally negative. Historically, it has varied widely even within the larger part of the Christian era and even within the Church itself. There are even societies—current ones—where homosexuality is not only tolerated but even a universal and compulsory part of social maturation. Society holds its current descriptive morality of gays not because it has to, but because it chooses to. Within the last thirty years, American society has undergone a grand turnabout from deeply ingrained, near total condemnation to near total acceptance on two emotionally charged "moral" or "family" issues: adult contraception and divorce. America could do the same with homosexuality if it thought to.

If popular opinion and custom are not enough to ground moral condemnation of homosexuality, perhaps religion can. Such argument proceeds along two lines. One claims that the condemnation is a direct revelation of God, usually through the Bible; the other claims to be able to detect condemnation in God's plan as manifested in nature.

One of the more remarkable discoveries of recent gay research is that the Bible may not be as univocal in its condemnation of homosexuality as has been usually believed. Christ never mentions homosexuality. Recent interpreters of the Old Testament have pointed out that the story of Lot at Sodom is probably intended to condemn inhospitality rather than homosexuality. Further, some of the Old Testament condemnations of homosexuality seem simply to be ways of tarring those of the Israelites' opponents who happen to accept homosexual practices when the Israelites themselves did not. If so, the condemnation is merely a quirk of history and rhetoric rather than a moral precept. All of this is hotly contested, and the debate continues.

What does seem clear, though, is that those who regularly cite the Bible to condemn an activity like homosexuality do so by reading it selectively. Do ministers who cite what they take to be condemnations of homosexuality in Leviticus maintain in their lives all the hygienic and dietary laws of Leviticus? If they cite the story of Lot at Sodom to condemn homosexuality, do they also cite the story of Lot in the Cave to praise incestuous rape? If not, they may be hypocrites (against whom Christ frequently riles), but more importantly they violate the normatively moral notions of consistency and fairness—unless of course they can cite some higher principle which gen-

erates exceptions to the (now) lower level principle: obey the Bible. But what could that be? It seems then not that the Bible is being used to ground condemnations of homosexuality as much as society's dislike of homosexuality is being used to interpret the Bible.

Even if a consistent portrait of condemnation could be gleaned from the bible, what social significance should it be given? One of the guiding principles of society, enshrined in the Constitution as a check against the government, is that decisions affecting social policy are not made on religious grounds. If the real ground of the alleged immorality invoked by governments to discriminate against gays is religious, then one of the major commitments of our nation is violated. But this principle is widely accepted as holding even beyond government. Usually one does not pick one's friends and acquaintances according to their religious beliefs or their accidental conformity to one's own religious tenets. And this is so because in America people deeply believe that one's religious life is a private matter. Indeed, one has to have built up a relationship of friendly trust with another for the question of religious beliefs even to be broached. No one (other than someone who is despicable on other grounds) points out with pride one's membership in a club that excludes Jews or Catholics—even where the exclusion is legal. People recognize that holding others accountable for religious beliefs is properly a source of shame, even if they go ahead and do it anyway. In respecting religious privacy, then, one does not hold others accountable to the beliefs one holds *solely* on religious grounds. Those who invoke religious sentiments for their attitudes toward gays, then, need to examine whether their religious beliefs are here not really a disguise for some animus for which they have no reasons.

V. BUT AREN'T THEY UNNATURAL?

The most noteworthy feature of the accusation of something being unnatural (where a moral rather than an advertising point is being made) is that the plaint is being made so infrequently. One used to hear the charge leveled against abortion, but it has dropped from public discourse as anti-abortionists have come to lay their chips on the hope that people in general will come to view abortion as murder. Incest used to be considered unnatural but discourse now usually assimilates it to the moral machinery of rape and violated trust. The charge comes up now in ordinary discourse only against homosexuality. This social pattern suggests that the charge is highly idiosyncratic and has little, if any, explanatory force. It fails to put homosexuality in a class with anything else so that one can learn by comparison with clear cases of the class just what exactly it is that is allegedly wrong with it. Nor is homosexuality even a paradigm case for a class of unnatural acts. In popular morality, the charge that homosexuality is immoral because unnatural appeals to a principle so narrow as to be arbitrary.

What the charge of unnaturalness lacks in moral content is compensated for by the emotional thrust with which it is delivered. In ordinary discourse, when the accusation of unnaturalness is applied to homosexuality, it is usually delivered with venom of forethought. It carries a high emotional charge, usually expressing disgust and evincing queasiness. Probably it has no content other than its expression of emotional aversion. For people get equally disgusted and queasy at all sorts of things that are perfectly natural—to be expected in nature apart from artifice—and that could hardly be fit subjects for moral condemnation. Two examples from current American culture are some people's responses to mothers suckling in public and to women who do not shave body hair. When people have strong emotional reactions, as they do in these cases, without being able to give good reasons for the reactions, one thinks of them not as operating morally and certainly not as grounding a morality for others, but rather as being obsessed and manic. So the feelings of disgust that some people have to gays will hardly ground a charge of immorality. People fling the term "unnatural" against gays in the same breath and with the same force as calling gays "sick" and "gross," and when they do this, they give every appearance of being neurotically fearful, while at the same time violating the

moral principle that one needs justifying reasons for moral beliefs.

When "nature" is taken in *technical* rather than ordinary usages, it looks like the notion also will not ground a charge of homosexual immorality. When unnatural means "by artifice" or "made by man," one need only point out that virtually everything that is good about life is unnatural in this sense, that one feature that distinguished people from most other animals is people's ability to make over the world to meet their needs and desires, and that people's well-being depends upon these departures from nature. On this understanding of the natural and people's nature, homosexuality is perfectly unobjectionable.

Another technical sense of natural is that something is natural, and so good, if it fulfills some function in nature. Homosexuality in this view is unnatural because it allegedly violates the function of genitals, which is to produce babies. One problem with this view is that lots of bodily parts have lots of functions and just because some one activity can be fulfilled by only one organ (say, the mouth for eating) this activity does not condemn other functions of the organ to immorality (say, the mouth for talking, licking stamps, blowing bubbles, or having sex). So the possible use of the genitals to produce children does not, without more, condemn the use of the genitals for other purposes, say, achieving ecstasy and intimacy.

The functional view of nature will provide a morally condemnatory sense to the unnatural only if a thing which might have many uses has but one proper function to the exclusion of all other possible functions. But whether this is so cannot be established simply by looking at the thing. For what is seen is all its possible functions: "it's a stamp-licker," "no, its a talker," "no, it's a bubble-blower," "no, it's a sex organ." It was thought that the notion of function might ground moral authority, but instead it turns out that moral authority is needed to define proper function.

Some people try to fill in this moral authority by appeal to the "design" or "order" of an organ, saying, for instance, that the genitals are designed for the purpose of procreation. But these people intellectually cheat if they fail to make explicit *who* the designer and orderer is. If it is God, the discussion is back to square one—they are holding others accountable for religious beliefs.

Further, ordinary moral attitudes about child-rearing will not provide the needed supplement which in conjunction with the natural-function view of bodily parts would produce a positive obligation to use the genitals for procreation. Society's attitude toward a childless couple is that of pity, not censure—even if the couple could have children. The pity may be an unsympathetic one—that is, not registering a course one would choose *for oneself*—but this does not make it a course one would *require* of others. The couple who discovers they cannot have children are viewed not as having thereby had a debt canceled, but rather as having to forgo some of the richness of life, just as a quadriplegic is not viewed as absolved from some moral obligation to hop, skip, and jump, but is viewed as missing some of the richness of life. Consistency requires, then, that, at most, gays who do not or cannot have children are to be pitied rather than condemned. What *is* immoral is the willful preventing of people from achieving the richness of life. Immorality in this regard lies with those social customs, regulations, and statutes that prevent lesbians and gay men from establishing blood or adoptive families, not with gays themselves.

Sometimes people attempt to establish authority for a moral obligation to use certain bodily parts in only one way simply by claiming that moral laws are natural laws and vice versa. On this account, inanimate objects and plants are good in that they follow natural laws by necessity, animals by instinct, and persons by a rational will. People are special in that they must first discover the laws that govern the species. Now, even if one believes the view—dubious in the post-Newtonian, post-Darwinian world—that natural laws in the usual sense ($e = mc^2$, for instance) have some moral content, it is not at all clear how

one is to discover the laws in nature that apply to people.

If, on the one hand, one looks to people themselves for a model—and looks hard enough—one finds amazing variety, including homosexual behavior as a social ideal (upper-class fifty-century B.C. Athenians) and even as socially mandatory (Melanesia today). When one looks to people, one is simply unable to strip away the layers of social custom, history, and taboo in order to see what's really there to any degree more specific than that people are the creatures which make over their world and are capable of abstract thought.

Most people, though, do not even try to see *what's there* but instead simply and by default end up projecting the peculiarities of their culture into the universe as cosmic principles. Anthropology has shown that each and every society—however much it may differ from the next—thinks that its own central norms are dictated by and conform with nature writ large. That this is so should raise doubts that neutral principles are to be found in man's nature that will condemn homosexuality. Man may very well be, as Hannah Arendt claimed, the creature whose nature it is to have no nature. It is by virtue of this human condition that people can be creative and make moral progress.

On the other hand, if for models one looks to nature apart from people, the possibilities are staggering. There are fish that change gender over their lifetimes: should people "follow nature" and be operative transsexuals? Orangutans, genetically our next of kin, live completely solitary lives without social organization of any kind: ought people to "follow nature" and be hermits? There are many species where only two members per generation reproduce: shall we be bees? The search in nature for people's purpose, far from finding sure models for action, is likely to leave people morally rudderless.

Plain Sex

ALAN H. GOLDMAN

I

* * *

I shall suggest here that sex continues to be misrepresented in recent writings, at least in philosophical writings, and I shall criticize the predominant form of analysis which I term "means-end analysis." Such conceptions attribute a necessary external goal or purpose to sexual activity, whether it be reproduction, the expression of love, simple communication, or interpersonal awareness. They analyze sexual activity as a means to one of these ends, implying that sexual desire is a desire to reproduce, to love or be loved, or to communicate with others. All definitions of this type suggest false views of the relation of sex to perversion and morality by implying that sex which does not fit one of these models or fulfill one of these functions is in some way deviant or incomplete.

The alternative, simpler analysis with which I will begin is that sexual desire is desire for contact with another person's body and for the pleasure which such contact produces; sexual activity is activity which tends to fulfill such desire of the agent. Whereas Aristotle and Butler were correct in holding that pleasure is normally a byproduct rather than a goal of purposeful action, in the case of sex this is not so clear. The desire for another's body is, principally among other things, the desire for the pleasure that physical contact brings. On the other hand, it is not a desire for a particular sensation detachable from its causal context, a sensation which can be derived in other ways. This definition in terms of the general goal of sexual desire appears preferable to an attempt to more explicitly list or define specific sexual activities, for many activities such as kissing, embracing, massaging, or holding hands may or may not be sex-

Alan H. Goldman, "Plain Sex," *Philosophy & Public Affairs* 6, no. 3 (Spring 1977): 268–75, 278–87 (edited). Reprinted with permission by Wiley-Blackwell Publishing.

ual, depending upon the context and more specifically upon the purposes, needs, or desires into which such activities fit. The generality of the definition also represents a refusal (common in recent psychological texts) to overemphasize orgasm as the goal of sexual desire or genital sex as the only norm of sexual activity (this will be hedged slightly in the discussion of perversion below).

Central to the definition is the fact that the goal of sexual desire and activity is the physical contact itself, rather than something else which this contact might express. By contrast, what I term "means-end analyses" posit ends which I take to be extraneous to plain sex, and they view sex as a means to these ends. Their fault lies not in defining sex in terms of its general goal, but in seeing plain sex as merely a means to other separable ends. I term these "means-end analyses" for convenience, although "means-separable-end analyses," while too cumbersome, might be more fully explanatory. The desire for physical contact with another person is a minimal criterion for (normal) sexual desire, but is both necessary and sufficient to qualify normal desire as sexual. Of course, we may want to express other feelings through sexual acts in various contexts; but without the desire for the physical contact in and for itself, or when it is sought for other reasons, activities in which contact is involved are not predominantly sexual. Furthermore, the desire for physical contact in itself, without the wish to express affection or other feelings through it, is sufficient to render sexual the activity of the agent which fulfills it. Various activities with this goal alone, such as kissing and caressing in certain contexts, qualify as sexual even without the presence of genital symptoms of sexual excitement. The latter are not therefore necessary criteria for sexual activity.

This initial analysis may seem to some either over- or underinclusive. It might seem too broad in leading us to interpret physical contact as sexual desire in activities such as football and other contact sports. In these cases, however, the desire is not for contact with another body per se, it is not directed toward a particular person for that purpose, and it is not the goal of the activity—the goal is winning or exercising or knocking someone down or displaying one's prowess. If the desire is purely for contact with another specific person's body, then to interpret it as sexual does not seem an exaggeration. A slightly more difficult case is that of a baby's desire to be cuddled and our natural response in wanting to cuddle it. In the case of the baby, the desire may be simply for the physical contact, for the pleasure of the caresses. If so, we may characterize this desire, especially in keeping with Freudian theory, as sexual or protosexual. It will differ nevertheless from full-fledged sexual desire in being more amorphous, not directed outward toward another specific person's body. It may also be that what the infant unconsciously desires is not physical contact per se but signs of affection, tenderness, or security, in which case we have further reason for hesitating to characterize its wants as clearly sexual. The intent of our response to the baby is often the showing of affection, not the pure physical contact, so that our definition in terms of action which fulfils sexual desire *on the part of the agent* does not capture such actions, whatever we say of the baby. (If it is intuitive to characterize our response as sexual as well, there is clearly no problem here for my analysis.) The same can be said of signs of affection (or in some cultures polite greeting) among men or women: these certainly need not be homosexual when the intent is only to show friendship, something extrinsic to plain sex although valuable when added to it.

Our definition of sex in terms of the desire for physical contact may appear too narrow in that a person's personality, not merely her or his body, may be sexually attractive to another, and in that looking or conversing in a certain way can be sexual in a given context without bodily contact. Nevertheless, it is not the contents of one's thoughts per se that are sexually appealing, but one's personality as embodied in certain manners of behavior. Furthermore, if a person is sexually attracted by another's personality, he

or she will desire not just further conversation, but actual sexual contact. While looking at or conversing with someone can be interpreted as sexual in given contexts it is so when intended as preliminary to, and hence parasitic upon, elemental sexual interest. Voyeurism or viewing a pornographic movie qualifies as a sexual activity, but only as an imaginative substitute for the real thing (otherwise a deviation from the norm as expressed in our definition). The same is true of masturbation as a sexual activity without a partner.

That the initial definition indicates at least an ingredient of sexual desire and activity is too obvious to argue. We all now what sex is, at least in obvious cases, and do not need philosophers to tell us. My preliminary analysis is meant to serve as a contrast to what sex is not, at least, not necessarily. I concentrate upon the physically manifested desire for another's body, and I take as central the immersion in the physical aspect of one's own existence and attention to the physical embodiment of the other. One may derive pleasure in a sex act from expressing certain feelings to one's partner or from awareness of the attitude of one's partner, but sexual desire is essentially desire for physical contact itself: it is a bodily desire for the body of another that dominates our mental life for more or less brief periods. Traditional writings were correct to emphasize the purely physical or animal aspect of sex; they were wrong only in condemning it. This characterization of sex as an intensely pleasurable physical activity and acute physical desire may seem to some to capture only its barest level. But it is worth distinguishing and focusing upon this least common denominator in order to avoid the false views of sexual morality and perversion which emerge from thinking that sex is essentially something else.

II

We may turn then to what sex is not, to the arguments regarding supposed conceptual connections between sex and other activities which it is necessary to conceptually distinguish. The more comprehensible attempt to build an extraneous purpose into the sex act identifies that purpose as reproduction, its primary biological function. While this may be "nature's" purpose, it certainly need not be ours (the analogy with eating, while sometimes overworked, is pertinent here). While this identification may once have had a rational basis which also grounded the identification of the value and morality of sex with that applicable to reproduction and childrearing, the development of contraception rendered the connection weak. Methods of contraception are by now so familiar and so widely used that it is not necessary to dwell upon the changes wrought by these developments in the concept of sex itself and in a rational sexual ethic dependent upon that concept. In the past, the ever present possibility of children rendered the concepts of sex and sexual morality different from those required at present. There may be good reasons, if the presence and care of both mother and father are beneficial to children, for restricting reproduction to marriage. Insofar as society has a legitimate role in protecting children's interests, it may be justified in giving marriage a legal status, although this question is complicated by the fact (among others) that children born to single mothers deserve no penalties. In any case, the point here is simply that these questions are irrelevant at the present time to those regarding the morality of sex and its potential social regulation. . . .

It is obvious that the desire for sex is not necessarily a desire to reproduce, that the psychological manifestation has become, if it were not always, distinct from its biological roots. There are many parallels, as previously mentioned, with other natural functions. The pleasures of eating and exercising are to a large extent independent of their roles in nourishment or health (as the junk-food industry discovered with a vengeance). Despite the obvious parallel with sex, there is still a tendency for many to think that sex acts which can be reproductive are, if not more moral or less immoral, at least more natural. These categories of morality and "naturalness," or normality, are not to be identified with each other, as will be argued below, and neither is applicable to sex by virtue of its connection to reproduction. The tendency to identify reproduction as the conceptu-

ally connected end of sex is most prevalent now in the pronouncements of the Catholic church. There the assumed analysis is clearly tied to a restrictive sexual morality according to which acts become immoral and unnatural when they are not oriented towards reproduction, a morality which has independent roots in the Christian sexual ethic as it derives from Paul. However, the means-end analysis fails to generate a consistent sexual ethic: homosexual and oral-genital sex is condemned while kissing or caressing, acts equally unlikely to lead in themselves to fertilization, even when properly characterized as sexual according to our definition, are not.

III

Before discussing further relations of means-end analyses to false or inconsistent sexual ethics and concepts of perversion, I turn to other examples of these analyses. One common position views sex as essentially an expression of love or affection between the partners. It is generally recognized that there are other types of love besides sexual, but sex itself is taken as an expression of one type, sometimes termed "romantic" love.[1] Various factors again ought to weaken this identification. First, there are other types of love besides that which it is appropriate to express sexually, and "romantic" love itself can be expressed in many other ways. I am not denying that sex can take on heightened value and meaning when it becomes a vehicle for the expression of feelings of love or tenderness, but so can many other usually mundane activities such as getting up early to make breakfast on Sunday, cleaning the house, and so on. Second, sex itself can be used to communicate many other emotions besides love, and, as I will argue below, can communicate nothing in particular and still be good sex.

On a deeper level, an internal tension is bound to result from an identification of sex, which I have described as a physical-psychological desire, with love as a long-term, deep emotional relationship between two individuals. As this type of relationship, love is permanent, at least in intent, and more or less exclusive. A normal person cannot deeply love more than a few individuals even in a lifetime. We may be suspicious that those who attempt or claim to love many love them weakly if at all. Yet, fleeting sexual desire can arise in relation to a variety of other individuals one finds sexually attractive. It may even be, as some have claimed, that sexual desire in humans naturally seeks variety, while this is obviously false of love. For this reason, monogamous sex, even if justified, almost always represents a sacrifice or the exercise of self-control on the part of the spouses, while monogamous love generally does not. There is no such thing as casual love in the sense in which I intend the term "love." It may occasionally happen that a spouse falls deeply in love with someone else (especially when sex is conceived in terms of love), but this is relatively rare in comparison to passing sexual desires for others; and while the former often indicates a weakness or fault in the marriage relation, the latter does not.

If love is indeed more exclusive in its objects than is sexual desire, this explains why those who view sex as essentially an expression of love would again tend to hold a repressive or restrictive sexual ethic. As in the case of reproduction, there may be good reasons for reserving the total commitment of deep love to the context of marriage and family—the normal personality may not withstand additional divisions of ultimate commitment and allegiance. There is no question that marriage itself is best sustained by a deep relation of love and affection; and even if love is not naturally monogamous, the benefits of family units to children provide additional reason to avoid serious commitments elsewhere which weaken family ties. It can be argued similarly that monogamous sex strengthens families by restricting and at the same time guaranteeing an outlet for sexual desire in marriage. But there is more force to the argument that recognition of a clear distinction between sex and love in society would help avoid disastrous marriages which result from adolescent confusion of the two when sexual desire is mistaken for permanent love, and would weaken damaging jealousies which arise in marriages in relation to passing sexual desires. The love and affection of a sound marriage certainly dif-

fers from the adolescent romantic variety, which is often a mere substitute for sex in the context of a repressive sexual ethic.

In fact, the restrictive sexual ethic tied to the means-end analysis in terms of love again has failed to be consistent. At least, it has not been applied consistently, but forms part of the double standard which has curtailed the freedom of women. It is predictable in light of this history that some women would now advocate using sex as another kind of means, as a political weapon or as a way to increase unjustly denied power and freedom. The inconsistency in the sexual ethic typically attached to the sex-love analysis, according to which it has generally been taken with a grain of salt when applied to men, is simply another example of the impossibility of tailoring a plausible moral theory in this area to a conception of sex which builds in conceptually extraneous factors.

I am not suggesting here that sex ought never to be connected with love or that it is not a more significant and valuable activity when it is. Nor am I denying that individuals need love as much as sex and perhaps emotionally need at least one complete relationship which encompasses both. Just as sex can express love and take on heightened significance when it does, so love is often naturally accompanied by an intermittent desire for sex. But again love is accompanied appropriately by desires for other shared activities as well. What makes the desire for sex seem more intimately connected with love is the intimacy which is seen to be a natural feature of mutual sex acts. Like love, sex is held to lay one bare psychologically as well as physically. Sex is unquestionably intimate, but beyond that the psychological toll often attached may be a function of the restrictive sexual ethic itself, rather than a legitimate apology for it. The intimacy involved in love is psychologically consuming in a generally healthy way, while the psychological tolls of sexual relations, often including embarrassment as a correlate of intimacy, are too often the result of artificial sexual ethics and taboos. The intimacy involved in both love and sex is insufficient in any case in light of previous points to render a means-end analysis in these terms appropriate.

* * *

V

I have now criticized various types of analysis sharing or suggesting a common means-end form. I have suggested that analyses of this form relate to attempts to limit moral or natural sex to that which fulfills some purpose or function extraneous to basic sexual desire. The attempts to brand forms of sex outside the idealized models as immoral or perverted fail to achieve consistency with intuitions that they themselves do not directly question. The reproductive model brands oral-genital sex a deviation, but cannot account for kissing or holding hands; the communication account holds voyeurism to be perverted but cannot accommodate sex acts without much conscious thought or seductive nonphysical foreplay; the sex-love model makes most sexual desire seem degrading or base. The first and last condemn extramarital sex on the sound but irrelevant grounds that reproduction and deep commitment are best confined to family contexts. The romanticization of sex and the confusion of sexual desire with love operate in both directions: sex outside the context of romantic love is repressed; once it is repressed, partners become more difficult to find and sex becomes romanticized further, out of proportion to its real value for the individual.

What all these analyses share in addition to a common form is accordance with and perhaps derivation from the Platonic-Christian moral tradition, according to which the animal or purely physical element of humans is the source of immorality, and plain sex in the sense I defined it is an expression of this element, hence in itself to be condemned. All the analyses examined seem to seek a distance from sexual desire itself in attempting to extend it conceptually beyond the physical. The love and communications analyses seek refinement or intellectualization of the desire; plain physical sex becomes vulgar, and too straightforward sexual encounters

without an aura of respectable cerebral communicative content are to be avoided. [Robert] Solomon explicitly argues that sex cannot be a "mere" appetite, his argument being that if it were, subway exhibitionism and other vulgar forms would be pleasing.[2] This fails to recognize that sexual desire can be focused or selective at the same time as being physical. Lower animals are not attracted by every other member of their species, either. Rancid food forced down one's throat is not pleasing, but that certainly fails to show that hunger is not a physical appetite. Sexual desire let us know that we are physical beings and, indeed, animals; this is why traditional Platonic morality is so thorough in its condemnation. Means-end analyses continue to reflect this tradition, sometimes unwittingly. They show that in conceptualizing sex it is still difficult, despite years of so-called revolution in this area, to free ourselves from the lingering suspicion that plain sex as physical desire is an expression of our "lower selves," that yielding to our animal natures is subhuman or vulgar.

VI

Having criticized these analyses for the sexual ethics and concepts of perversion they imply, it remains to contrast my account along these lines. To the question of what morality might be implied by my analysis, the answer is that there are no moral implications whatever. Any analysis of sex which imputes a moral character to sex acts in themselves is wrong for that reason. There is no morality intrinsic to sex, although general moral rules apply to the treatment of others in sex acts as they apply to all human relations. We can speak of a sexual ethic as we can speak of a business ethic, without implying that business in itself is either moral or immoral or that special rules are required to judge business practice which are not derived from rules that apply elsewhere as well. Sex is not in itself a moral category, although like business it invariably places us into relations with others in which moral rules apply. It gives us opportunity to do what is otherwise recognized as wrong, to harm others, deceive them or manipulate them against their wills. Just as the fact that an act is sexual in itself never renders it wrong or adds to its wrongness if it is wrong on other grounds (sexual acts towards minors are wrong on other grounds, as will be argued below), so no wrong act is to be excused because done from a sexual motive. If a "crime of passion" is to be excused, it would have to be on grounds of temporary insanity rather than sexual context (whether insanity does constitute a legitimate excuse for certain actions is too big a topic to argue here). Sexual motives are among others which may become deranged, and the fact that they are sexual has no bearing in itself on the moral character, whether negative or exculpatory, of the actions deriving from them. Whatever might be true of war, it is certainly not the case that all's fair in love or sex.

Our first conclusion regarding morality and sex is therefore that no conduct otherwise immoral should be excused because it is sexual conduct, and nothing in sex is immoral unless condemned by rules which apply elsewhere as well. The last clause requires further clarification. Sexual conduct can be governed by particular rules relating only to sex itself. But these precepts must be implied by general moral rules when these are applied to specific sexual relations or types of conduct. The same is true of rules of fair business, ethical medicine, or courtesy in driving a car. In the latter case, particular acts on the road may be reprehensible, such as tailgating or passing on the right, which seem to bear no resemblance as actions to any outside the context of highway safety. Nevertheless their immorality derives from the fact that they place others in danger, a circumstance which, when avoidable, is to be condemned in any context. This structures of general and specifically applicable rules describes a reasonable sexual ethic as well. To take an extreme case, rape is always a sexual act and it is always immoral. A rule against rape can therefore be considered an obvious part of sexual morality which has no bearing on nonsexual conduct. But the immorality of rape derives from its being an extreme violation of a person's body, of the right not to be humiliated, and of the general moral prohibition against using other persons against their wills, not from the fact that it is a sexual act.

The application elsewhere of general moral rules to sexual conduct is further complicated by the fact that it will be relative to the particular desires and preferences of one's partner (these may be influenced by and hence in some sense include misguided beliefs about sexual morality itself). This means that there will be fewer specific rules in the area of sexual ethics than in other areas of conduct, such as driving cars, where the relativity of preference is irrelevant to the prohibition of objectively dangerous conduct. More reliance will have to be placed upon the general moral rule, which in this area holds simply that the preferences, desires, and interests of one's partner or potential partner ought to be taken into account. This rule is certainly not specifically formulated to govern sexual relations; it is form of the central principle of morality itself. But when applied to sex, it prohibits certain actions, such as molestation of children, which cannot be categorized as violations of the rule without at the same time being classified as sexual. I believe this last case is the closest we can come to an action which is wrong *because* it is sexual, but even here its wrongness is better characterized as deriving from the detrimental effects such behavior can have on the future emotional and sexual life of the naive victims, and from the fact that such behavior therefore involves manipulation of innocent persons without regard for their interests. Hence, this case also involves violation of a general moral rule which applies elsewhere as well.

Aside from faulty conceptual analyses of sex and the influence of the Platonic moral tradition, there are two more plausible reasons for thinking that there are moral dimensions intrinsic to sex acts per se. The first is that such acts are normally intensely pleasurable. According to a hedonistic, utilitarian moral theory they therefore should be at least prima facie morally right, rather than morally neutral in themselves. To me this seems incorrect and reflects unfavorably on the ethical theory in question. The pleasure intrinsic to sex acts is a good, but not, it seems to me, a good with much positive moral significance. Certainly I can have no duty to pursue such pleasure myself, and while it maybe nice to give pleasure of any form to others, there is no ethical requirement to do so, given my right over my own body. The exception relates to the context of sex acts themselves, when one partner derives pleasure from the other and ought to return the favor. This duty to reciprocate takes us out of the domain of hedonistic utilitarianism, however, and into a Kantian moral framework, the central principles of which call for just such reciprocity in human relations. Since independent moral judgments regarding sexual activities constitute one area in which ethical theories are to be tested, these observations indicate here, as I believe others indicate elsewhere, the fertility of the Kantian, as opposed to the utilitarian, principles in reconstructing reasoned moral consciousness.

It may appear from this alternative Kantian viewpoint that sexual acts must be at least prima facie wrong in themselves. This is because they invariably involve at different stages the manipulation of one's partner for one's own pleasure, which might appear to be prohibited on the formulation of Kant's principle which holds that one ought not to treat another as a means to such private ends. A more realistic rendering of this formulation, however, one which recognizes its intended equivalence to the first universalizability principle, admits no such absolute prohibition. Many human relations, most economic transactions for example, involve using other individuals for personal benefit. These relations are immoral only when they are one-sided, when the benefits are not mutual, or when the transactions are not freely and rationally endorsed by all parties. The same holds true of sexual acts. The central principle governing them is the Kantian demand for reciprocity in sexual relations. In order to comply with the second formulation of the categorical imperative, one must recognize the subjectivity of one's partner (not merely by being aroused by her or his desire, as [Thomas] Nagel describes). Even in an act which by its nature "objectifies" the other, one recognizes a partner as a subject with demands and desires by yielding to those desires, by allowing oneself to be a sexual object as well, by giving pleasure or ensuring that the pleasures of the acts are mutual. It is this kind of reciprocity which forms the basis for morality in sex, which distinguished right acts from wrong

in this area as in others. (Of course, prior to sex acts one must gauge their effects upon potential partners and take these longer range interests into account.)

VII

I suggested earlier that in addition to generating confusion regarding the rightness or wrongness of sex acts, false conceptual analyses of the means-end form cause confusion about the value of sex to the individual. My account recognizes the satisfaction of desire and the pleasure this brings as the central psychological function of the sex act for the individual. Sex affords us a paradigm of pleasure, but not a cornerstone of value. For most of us it is not only a needed outlet for desire but also the most enjoyable form of recreation we know. Its value is nevertheless easily mistaken by being confused with that of love, when it is taken as essentially an expression of that emotion. Although intense, the pleasures of sex are brief and repetitive rather than cumulative. They give value to the specific acts which generate them, but not the lasting kind of value which enhances one's whole life. The briefness of these pleasures contributes to their intensity (or perhaps their intensity makes them necessarily brief), but it also relegates them to the periphery of most rational plans for the good life.

By contrast, love typically develops over a long term relation; while its pleasures may be less intense and physical, they are of more cumulative value. The importance of love to the individual may well be central in a rational system of value. And it has perhaps an even deeper moral significance relating to the identification with the interests of another person, which broadens one's possible relationships with others as well. Marriage is again important in preserving this relation between adults and children, which seems as important to the adults as it is to the children in broadening concerns which have a tendency to become selfish. Sexual desire, by contrast, is desire for another which is nevertheless essentially self-regarding. Sexual pleasure is certainly a good for the individual, and for many it may be necessary in order for them to function in a reasonably cheerful way. But it bears little relation to those other values just discussed, to which some analyses falsely suggest a conceptual connection.

VIII

While my initial analysis lacks moral implications in itself, as it should, it does suggest by contrast a concept of sexual perversion. Since the concept of perversion is itself a sexual concept, it will always be defined relative to some definition of normal sex; and any conception of the norm will imply a contrary notion of perverse forms. The concept suggested by my account again differs sharply from those implied by the means-end analyses examined above. Perversion does not represent a deviation from the reproductive function (or kissing would be perverted), from a loving relationship (or most sexual desire and many heterosexual acts would be perverted), or from efficiency in communicating (or unsuccessful seduction attempts would be perverted). It is a deviation from a norm, but the norm in question is merely statistical. Of course, not all sexual acts that are statistically unusual are perverted—a three-hour continuous sexual act would be unusual but not necessarily abnormal in the requisite sense. The abnormality in question must relate to the *form of the desire* itself in order to constitute sexual perversion; for example, desire, not for contact with another, but for merely looking, for harming or being harmed, for contact with items of clothing. This concept of sexual abnormality is that suggested by my definition of normal sex in terms of its typical desire. However not all unusual desires qualify either, only those with the typical physical sexual effects upon the individual who satisfies them. These effects, such as erection in males, were not built into the original definition of sex in terms of sexual desire, for they do not always occur in activities that are properly characterized as sexual, say, kissing for the pleasure of it. But they do seem to bear a closer relation to the definition of activities as perverted. (For those who consider only genital sex sexual, we could build such symptoms into a narrower definition, then speaking of sex in a broad sense as well as "proper" sex.)

Solomon and Nagel disagree with this statistical notion of perversion. For them the concept is evaluative rather than statistical. I do not deny that the term "perverted" is often used evaluatively (and purely emotively for that matter), or that it has a negative connotation for the average speaker. I do deny that we can find a norm, other than that of statistically usual desire, against which all and only activities that properly count as sexual perversions can be contrasted. Perverted sex is simply abnormal sex, and if the norm is not to be an idealized or romanticized extraneous end or purpose, it must express the way human sexual desires usually manifest themselves. Of course not all norms in other areas of discourse need be statistical in this way. Physical health is an example of a relatively clear norm which does not seem to depend upon the numbers of healthy people. But the concept in this case achieves its clarity through the connection of physical health with other clearly desirable physical functions and characteristics, for example, living longer. In the case of sex, that which is statistically abnormal is not necessarily incapacitating in other ways, and yet these abnormal desires with sexual effects upon their subject do count as perverted to the degree to which their objects deviate from usual ones. The connotations of the concept of perversion beyond those connected with abnormality or statistical deviation derive more from the attitudes of those likely to call certain acts perverted than from specifiable features of the acts themselves. These connotations add to the concept of abnormality that of *sub*normality, but there is no norm against which the latter can be measured intelligibly in accord with all and only acts intuitively called perverted.

The only proper evaluative norms relating to sex involve degrees of pleasure in the acts and moral norms, but neither of these scales coincides with statistical degrees of abnormality, according to which perversion is to be measured. The three parameters operate independently (this was implied for the first two when it was held above that the pleasure of sex is a good, but not necessarily moral good). Perverted sex may be more or less enjoyable to particular individuals than normal sex, and more or less moral, depending upon the particular relations involved. Raping a sheep may be more perverted than raping a woman, but certainly not more condemnable morally.[3] It is nevertheless true that the evaluative connotations attaching to the term "perverted" derive partly from the fact that most people consider perverted sex highly immoral. Many such acts are forbidden by long standing taboos, and it is sometimes difficult to distinguish what is forbidden from what is immoral. Others, such as sadistic acts, are genuinely immoral, but again not at all because of their connection with sex or abnormality. The principles which condemn these acts would condemn them equally if they were common and nonsexual. It is not true that we properly could continue to consider acts perverted which were found to be very common practice across societies. Such acts, if harmful, might continue to be condemned properly as immoral, but it was just shown that the immorality of an act does not vary with its degree of perversion. If not harmful, common acts previously considered abnormal might continue to be called perverted for a time by the moralistic minority; but the term when applied to such cases would retain only its emotive negative connotation without consistent logical criteria for application. It would represent merely prejudiced moral judgments.

To adequately explain why there is a tendency to so deeply condemn perverted acts would require a treatise in psychology beyond the scope of this paper. Part of the reason undoubtedly relates to the tradition of repressive sexual ethics and false conceptions of sex; another part to the fact that all abnormality seems to disturb and fascinate us at the same time. The former explains why sexual perversion is more abhorrent to many than other forms of abnormality; the latter indicates why we tend to have an emotive and evaluative reaction to perversion in the first place. It may be, as has been suggested according to a Freudian line,[4] that our uneasiness derives from latent desires we are loathe to admit, but this thesis takes us into psychological issues I am not competent to judge. Whatever the psychological explanation, it suffices to point out here that the conceptual connection between perversion and genuine or consistent moral evaluation is spurious and again suggested by misleading means-end idealizations of the concept of sex.

The position I have taken in this paper against those concepts is not totally new. Something similar to it is found in Freud's view of sex, which of course was genuinely revolutionary, and in the body of writings deriving from Freud to the present time. But in his revolt against romanticized and repressive conceptions, Freud went too far—from a refusal to view sex as merely a means to a view of it as the end of all human behavior, although sometimes an elaborately disguised end. This pansexualism led to the thesis (among others) that repression was indeed an inevitable and necessary part of social regulation of any form, a strange consequence of a position that began by opposing the repressive aspects of the means-end view. Perhaps the time finally has arrived when we can achieve a reasonable middle ground in this area, at least in philosophy if not in society.

NOTES

1. Even Bertrand Russell, whose writing in this area was a model of rationality, at least for its period, tends to make this identification and to condemn plain sex in the absence of love: "sex intercourse apart from love has little value, and is to be regarded primarily as experimentation with a view to love." *Marriage and Morals* (New York: Bantam, 1959), p. 87.

2. [Robert] Solomon, "Sex and Perversion," *Philosophy and Sex,* ed. R. Baker and F. Elliston (Buffalo: Prometheus, 1975), p. 285.

3. The example is like one from Sara Ruddick, "Better Sex," *Philosophy and Sex,* p. 96.

4. See Michael Slote, "Inapplicable Concepts and Sexual Perversion," *Philosophy and Sex.*

What Marriage Is For: Children Need Mothers and Fathers

MAGGIE GALLAGHER

Gay marriage is no longer a theoretical issue. Canada has it. Massachusetts is expected to get it any day. The Goodridge decision there could set off a legal, political, and cultural battle in the courts of 50 states and in the U.S. Congress. Every politician, every judge, every citizen has to decide: Does same-sex marriage matter? If so, how and why?

The timing could not be worse. Marriage is in crisis, as everyone knows: High rates of divorce and illegitimacy have eroded marriage norms and created millions of fatherless children, whole neighborhoods where lifelong marriage is no longer customary, driving up poverty, crime, teen pregnancy, welfare dependency, drug abuse, and mental and physical health problems. And yet, amid the broader negative trends, recent signs point to a modest but significant recovery.

Divorce rates appear to have declined a little from historic highs; illegitimacy rates, after doubling every decade from 1960 to 1990, appear to have leveled off, albeit at a high level (33 percent of American births are to unmarried women); teen pregnancy and sexual activity are down; the proportion of homemaking mothers is up; marital fertility appears to be on the rise. Research suggests that married adults are more committed to marital permanence than they were twenty years ago. A new generation of children of divorce appears on the brink of making a commitment to lifelong marriage. In 1977, 55 percent of American teenagers thought a divorce should be harder to get; in 2001, 75 percent did.

A new marriage movement—a distinctively American phenomenon—has been born. The scholarly consensus on the importance of marriage has broadened and deepened; it is now the conventional wisdom among child welfare organizations. As a Child Trends research brief summed up: "Research clearly

demonstrates that family structure matters for children, and the family structure that helps children the most is a family headed by two biological parents in a low-conflict marriage. Children in single-parent families, children born to unmarried mothers, and children in stepfamilies or cohabiting relationships face higher risks of poor outcomes. . . . There is thus value for children in promoting strong, stable marriages between biological parents."

What will court-imposed gay marriage do to this incipient recovery of marriage? For, even as support for marriage in general has been rising, the gay marriage debate has proceeded on a separate track. Now the time has come to decide: Will unisex marriage help or hurt marriage as a social institution?

Why should it do either, some may ask? How can Bill and Bob's marriage hurt Mary and Joe? In an exchange with me in the just-released book "Marriage and Same Sex Unions: A Debate," Evan Wolfson, chief legal strategist for same-sex marriage in the Hawaii case, Baer v. Lewin, argues that there is "enough marriage to share." What counts, he says, "is not family structure, but the quality of dedication, commitment, self-sacrifice, and love in the household."

Family structure does not count. Then what is marriage for? Why have laws about it? Why care whether people get married or stay married? Do children need mothers and fathers, or will any sort of family do? When the sexual desires of adults clash with the interests of children, which carries more weight, socially and legally?

These are the questions that same-sex marriage raises. Our answers will affect not only gay and lesbian families, but marriage as a whole.

In ordering gay marriage on June 10, 2003, the highest court in Ontario, Canada, explicitly endorsed a brand new vision of marriage along the lines Wolfson suggests: "Marriage is, without dispute, one of the most significant forms of personal relationships. . . . Through the institution of marriage, individuals

Maggie Gallagher, "What Marriage Is For: Children Need Mothers and Fathers," *Weekly Standard* 8, no. 45 (4–11 August 2003): 22–25 (edited). Reprinted with permission by *Weekly Standard*.

can publicly express their love and commitment to each other. Through this institution, society publicly recognizes expressions of love and commitment between individuals, granting them respect and legitimacy as a couple."

The Ontario court views marriage as a kind of Good Housekeeping Seal of Approval that government stamps on certain registered intimacies because, well, for no particular reason the court can articulate except that society likes to recognize expressions of love and commitment. In this view, endorsement of gay marriage is a no-brainer, for nothing really important rides on whether anyone gets married or stays married. Marriage is merely individual expressive conduct, and there is no obvious reason why some individuals' expression of gay love should hurt other individuals' expressions of non-gay love.

There is, however, a different view—indeed, a view that is radically opposed to this: Marriage is the fundamental, cross-cultural institution for bridging the male-female divide so that children have loving, committed mothers and fathers. Marriage is inherently normative: It is about holding out a certain kind of relationship as a social ideal, especially when there are children involved. Marriage is not simply an artifact of law; neither is it a mere delivery mechanism for a set of legal benefits that might as well be shared more broadly. The laws of marriage do not create marriage, but in societies ruled by law they help trace the boundaries and sustain the public meanings of marriage.

In other words, while individuals freely choose to enter marriage, society upholds the marriage option, formalizes its definition, and surrounds it with norms and reinforcements, so we can raise boys and girls who aspire to become the kind of men and women who can make successful marriages. Without this shared, public aspect, perpetuated generation after generation, marriage becomes what its critics say it is: a mere contract, a vessel with no particular content, one of a menu of sexual lifestyles, of no fundamental importance to anyone outside a given relationship.

The marriage idea is that children need mothers and fathers, that societies need babies, and that adults have an obligation to shape their sexual behavior so as to give their children stable families in which to grow up.

Which view of marriage is true? We have seen what has happened in our communities where marriage norms have failed. What has happened is not a flowering of libertarian freedom, but a breakdown of social and civic order that can reach frightening proportions. When law and culture retreat from sustaining the marriage idea, individuals cannot create marriage on their own.

In a complex society governed by positive law, social institutions require both social and legal support. To use an analogy, the government does not create private property. But to make a market system a reality requires the assistance of law as well as culture. People have to be raised to respect the property of others, and to value the traits of entrepreneurship, and to be law-abiding generally. The law cannot allow individuals to define for themselves what private property (or law-abiding conduct) means. The boundaries of certain institutions (such as the corporation) also need to be defined legally, and the definitions become socially shared knowledge. We need a shared system of meaning, publicly enforced, if market-based economies are to do their magic and individuals are to maximize their opportunities.

Successful social institutions generally function without people's having to think very much about how they work. But when a social institution is contested—as marriage is today—it becomes critically important to think and speak clearly about its public meanings.

Again, what is marriage for? Marriage is a virtually universal human institution. In all the wildly rich and various cultures flung throughout the ecosphere, in society after society, whether tribal or complex, and however bizarre, human beings have created systems of publicly approved sexual union between men and women that entail well-defined responsibilities of mothers and fathers. Not all these marriage systems look like our own, which is rooted in a fusion of Greek, Roman, Jewish, and Christian culture. yet everywhere, in isolated mountain valleys, parched deserts, jungle thickets, and broad plains, people have come up with some version of this thing called marriage. Why?

Because sex between men and women makes babies, that's why. Even today, in our technologically advanced contraceptive culture, half of all pregnancies are unintended: Sex between men and women still makes babies. Most men and woman are powerfully drawn to perform a sexual act that can and does generate life. Marriage is our attempt to reconcile and harmonize the erotic, social, sexual, and financial needs of men and women with the needs of their partner and their children.

How to reconcile the needs of children with the sexual desires of adults? Every society has to face that question, and some resolve it in ways that inflict horrendous cruelty on children born outside marriage. Some cultures decide these children don't matter: Men can have all the sex they want, and any children they create outside of marriage will be throwaway kids; marriage is for citizens—slaves and peasants need not apply. You can see a version of this elitist vision of marriage emerging in America under cover of acceptance of family diversity. Marriage will continue to exist as the social advantage of elite communities. The poor and the working class? Who cares whether their kids have dads? We can always import people from abroad to fill our need for disciplined, educated workers.

Our better tradition, and the only one consistent with democratic principles, is to hold up a single ideal for all parents, which is ultimately based on our deep cultural commitment to the equal dignity and social worth of all children. All kids needs and deserve a married mom and dad. All parents are supposed to at least try to behave in ways that will give their own children this important protection. Privately, religiously, emotionally, individually, marriage may have many meanings. But this is the core of its public, shared meaning: Marriage is the place where having children is not only tolerated but welcomed and encouraged, because it gives children mothers and fathers.

Of course, many couples fail to live up to this ideal. Many of the things men and women have to do to sustain their own marriages, and a culture of marriage, are hard. Few people will do them consistently if the larger culture does not affirm the critical importance of marriage as a social institution. Why stick out a frustrating relationship, turn down a tempting new love, abstain from sex outside marriage, or even take pains not to conceive children out of wedlock if family structure does not matter? If marriage is not a shared norm, and if successful marriage is not socially valued, do not expect it to survive as the generally accepted context for raising children. If marriage is just a way of publicly celebrating private love, then there is no need to encourage couples to stick it out for the sake of the children. If family structure does not matter, why have marriage laws at all? Do adults, or do they not, have a basic obligation to control their desires so that children can have mothers and fathers?

The problem with endorsing gay marriage is not that it would allow a handful of people to choose alternative family forms, but that it would require society at large to gut marriage of its central presumptions about family in order to accommodate a few adults' desires.

The debate over same-sex marriage, then, is not some sideline discussion. It is the marriage debate. Either we win—or we lose the central meaning of marriage. The great threat unisex marriage poses to marriage as a social institution is not some distant or nearby slippery slope, it is an abyss at our feet. If we cannot explain why unisex marriage is, in itself, a disaster, we have already lost the marriage ideal.

Same-sex marriage would enshrine in law a public judgment that the desire of adults for families of choice outweighs the need of children for mothers and fathers. It would give sanction and approval to the creation of a motherless or fatherless family as a deliberately chosen "good." It would mean the law was neutral as to whether children had mothers and fathers. Motherless and fatherless families would be deemed just fine.

Same-sex marriage advocates are startlingly clear on this point. Marriage law, they repeatedly claim, has nothing to do with babies or procreation or getting mothers and fathers for children. In forcing the state legislature to create civil unions for gay couples, the high court of Vermont explicitly ruled that marriage in the state of Vermont has nothing to do with procreation. Evan Wolfson made the same point in "Marriage and Same Sex Unions": "[I]sn't having the law pretend that there is only one family model that works (let alone exists) a lie?" He goes on to say that in law, "marriage is not just about procreation—indeed is not necessarily about procreation at all."

Wolfson is right that in the course of the sexual revolution the Supreme Court struck down many legal features designed to reinforce the connection of marriage to babies. The animus of elites (including legal elites) against the marriage idea is not brand new. It stretches back at least thirty years. That is part of the problem we face, part of the reason 40 percent of our children are growing up without their fathers.

It is also true, as gay-marriage advocates note, that we impose no fertility tests for marriage: Infertile and older couples marry, and not every fertile couple chooses procreation. But every marriage between a man and a woman is capable of giving any child they create or adopt a mother and a father. Every marriage between a man and a woman discourages either from creating fatherless children outside the marriage vow. In this sense, either older married couples nor childless husbands and wives publicly challenge or dilute the core meaning of marriage. Even when a man marries an older woman and they do not adopt, this marriage helps protect children. How? His marriage means, if he keeps his vows, that he will not produce out-of-wedlock children.

Does marriage discriminate against gays and lesbians? Formally speaking, no. There are no sexual-orientation tests for marriage; many gays and lesbians do choose to marry members of the opposite sex, and some of these unions succeed. Our laws do not require a person to marry the individual to whom he or she is most erotically attracted, so long as he or she is willing to promise sexual fidelity, mutual care-taking, and shared parenting of any children of the marriage.

But marriage is unsuited to the wants and desires of many gays and lesbians, precisely because it is designed to bridge the male-female divide and sustain the idea that children need mothers and fathers. To make a marriage, what you need is a husband and a wife. Redefining marriage so that it suits gays and lesbians would require fundamentally changing our legal, public, and social conception of what marriage is in ways that threaten its core public purposes.

Some who criticize the refusal to embrace gay marriage liken it to the outlawing of interracial marriage, but the analogy is woefully false. The Supreme Court overturned anti-miscegenation laws because they frustrated the core purpose of marriage in order to sustain a racist legal order. Marriage laws, by contrast, were not invented to express animus toward homosexuals or anyone else. Their purpose is not negative, but positive: They uphold an institution that developed, over thousands of years, in thousands of cultures, to help direct the erotic desires of men and women into a relatively narrow but indispensably fruitful channel. We need men and women to marry and make babies for our society to survive. We have no similar public stake in any other family form—in the union of same-sex couples or the singleness of single moms.

Meanwhile, cui bono? To meet the desires of whom would we put our most basic social institution at risk? No good research on the marriage intentions of homosexual people exists. For what it's worth, the Census Bureau reports that 0.5 percent of households now consist of same-sex partners. To get a proxy for how many gay couples would avail themselves of the health insurance benefits marriage can provide, I asked the top 10 companies listed on the Human Rights Campaign's website as providing same-sex insurance benefits how many of their employees use this option. Only one company, General Motors, released its data. Out of 1.3 million employees, 166 claimed benefits for a same-sex partner, one one-hundredth of one percent.

People who argue for creating gay marriage do so in the name of high ideals: justice, compassion, fairness. Their sincerity is not in question. Nevertheless, to take the already troubled institution most responsible for the protection of children and throw out its most basic presumption in order to further adult interests in sexual freedom would not be high-minded. It would be morally callous and socially irresponsible.

If we cannot stand and defend this ground, then face it: The marriage debate is over. Dan Quayle was wrong. We lost.

Sexual Morality

ROGER SCRUTON

* * *

We must now attempt to apply the Aristotelian strategy to the subject-matter of this book, and ask whether there is such a thing as sexual virtue, and, if so, what is it, and how is it acquired? Clearly, sexual desire, which is an interpersonal attitude with the most far-reaching consequences for those who are joined by it, cannot be morally neutral. On the contrary, it is in the experience of sexual desire that we are most vividly conscious of the distinction between virtuous and vicious impulses, and most vividly aware that, in the choice between them, our happiness is at stake.

The Aristotelian strategy enjoins us to ignore the actual conditions of any particular person's life, and to look only at the permanent features of human nature. We know that people feel sexual desire; that they feel erotic love, which may grow from desire; that they may avoid both these feelings, by dissipation or self-restraint. Is there anything to be said about desire, other than that it falls within the general scope of the virtue of temperance, which enjoins us to desire only what reason approves?

The first, and most important, observation to be made is that the capacity for love in general, and for erotic love in particular, is a virtue. In Chapter 8 I tried to show that erotic love involves an element of mutual self-enhancement; it generates a sense of the irreplaceable value, both of the other and of the self, and of the activities which bind them. To receive and to give this love is to achieve something of incomparable value in the process of self-fulfilment. It is to gain the most powerful of all interpersonal *guarantees*; in erotic love the subject becomes conscious of the full reality of his personal existence, not only in his own eyes, but in the eyes of another. Everything that he is and values gains sustenance from his love, and every project receives a meaning beyond the moment. All that exists for us as mere hope and hypothesis—the attachment to life and to the body—achieves under the rule of *erōs* the aspect of a radiant certainty. Unlike the cold glances of approval, admiration and pride, the glance of love sees value precisely in that which is the course of anxiety and doubt: in the merely contingent, merely 'empirical', existence of the flesh, the existence which we did not choose, but to which we are condemned. It is the answer to man's fallen condition—to his *Geworfenheit*.

To receive erotic love, however, a person must be able to give it: or if he cannot, the love of others will be a torment to him, seeking from him that which he cannot provide, and directing against him the fury of a disappointed right. It is therefore unquestionable that we have reason to acquire the capacity for erotic love, and, if this means bending our sexual impulses in a certain direction, that will be the direction of sexual virtue. Indeed, the argument of the last two chapters has implied that the development of the sexual impulse towards love may be impeded: there are sexual habits which are vicious, precisely in neutralising the capacity for love. The first thing that can

Roger Scruton, "Sexual Morality," in *Sexual Desire: A Moral Philosophy of the Erotic* (New York: Free Press, 1986), 337–47 (edited). Reprinted with permission by Simon & Schuster.

be said, therefore, is that we all have reason to avoid those habits and to educate our children not to possess them.

Here it may be objected that not every love is happy, that there are many—Anna Karenina, for example, or Phaedra—whose capacity for love was the cause of their downfall. But we must remind ourselves of the Aristotelian strategy. In establishing that courage or wisdom is a virtue, the Aristotelian does not argue that the possession of these virtues is in every particular circumstance bound to be advantageous. A parable of Derek Parfit's, adapted from T. C. Schelling, adequately shows what is a stake: Suppose a man breaks into my house and commands me to open the safe for him, saying that, if I do not comply, he will begin to shoot my children. He has heard me telephone the police, and knows that, if he leaves any of us alive, we will be able to give information sufficient to arrest him if he takes what the safe contains. Clearly it is irrational in these circumstances to open the safe—since that will not protect any of us—and also not to open it, since that would cause the robber to kill my children one by one in order to persuade me of his sincerity. Suppose, however, I possess a drug that causes me to become completely irrational. I swallow the pill, and cry out: 'I love my children, therefore kill them'; the man tortures me and I beg him to continue; and so on. In these changed circumstances, my assailant is powerless to obtain what he wants and can only flee before the police arrive. In other words, in such a case, it is actually in the interests of the subject to be irrational: he has overwhelming circumstantial *reason* to be irrational, just as Anna Karenina had an overwhelming circumstantial *reason* to be without the capacity for love. Clearly, however, it would be absurd, on these grounds, to inculcate a habit of irrationality in our children; indeed no *reason* could be given, in the absence of detailed knowledge of a person's future, for acquiring such a habit. In so far as reasons can be given now, for the cultivation of this or that state of character, they must justify the cultivation of rationality before all else—for how can I flourish according to my nature as a rational agent if I am not at least rational?

In like manner, it is not the particular personal tragedy but the generality of the human condition that determines the basis of sexual morality. Tragedy and loss are the rare but necessary outcomes of a process which we all have reason to undergo. (Indeed, it is part of the point of tragedy that it divorces in our imagination the right and the good from the merely prudential: that it sets the value of life against the value of mere survival.) We wish to know, in advance of any particular experience, which dispositions a person must have if he is successfully to express himself in sexual desire and to be fulfilled in his sexual endeavours. Love is the fulfilment of desire, and therefore love is its *telos*. A life of celibacy may also be fulfilled; but, assuming the general truth that most of us have a powerful, and perhaps overwhelming, urge to make love, it is in our interests to ensure that love—and not some other thing—is made.

Love, I have argued, is prone to jealousy, and the object of jealousy is defined by the thought of the beloved's desire. Because jealousy is one of the greatest of psychical catastrophes, involving the possible ruin of both partners, a morality based in the need for erotic love must forestall and eliminate jealousy. It is in the deepest human interest, therefore, that we form the habit of fidelity. This habit is natural and normal; but it is also easily broken, and the temptation to break it is contained in desire itself—in the element of generality which tempts us always to experiment, to verify, to detach ourselves from that which is too familiar in the interest of excitement and risk. Virtuous desire is faithful; but virtuous desire is also an artefact, made possible by a process of moral education which we do not, in truth, understand in its complexity.

If that observation is correct, a whole section of traditional sexual morality must be upheld. The fulfilment of sexual desire defines the nature of desire: *to telos phuseis estin*. And the nature of desire gives us our standard of normality. There are enormous varieties of human sexual conduct, and of 'common-sense' morality: some societies permit or encourage polygamy, others look with indifference upon pre-marital intercourse, or regard marriage itself as no more than an episode in a relation that pre-exists and perhaps survives it. But no society, and no 'common-sense' morality—not even, it seems, the morality of Samoa—looks with favour upon promiscuity or infidelity, unless influenced by a doctrine of 'emancipation' or 'liberation' which is dependent for its sense upon the very conventions which it defies. Whatever the institutional forms of human sexual union, and whatever the range of permitted partners, sexual desire is itself inherently 'nuptial': it involves concentration upon the embodied existence of the other, leading through tenderness to the 'vow' of erotic love. It is a telling observation that the civilisation which has most tolerated the institution of polygamy—the Islamic—has also, in its erotic literature, produced what are perhaps the intensest and most poignant celebrations of monogamous love, precisely through the attempt to capture, not the institution of marriage, but the human datum of desire.

The nuptiality of desire suggests, in its turn, a natural history of desire: a principle of development which defines the 'normal course' of sexual education. 'Sexual maturity' involves incorporating the sexual impulse into the personality, and so making sexual desire into an expression of the subject himself, even though it is, in the heat of action, a force which also overcomes him. If the Aristotetlian approach to these things is as plausible as I think it is, the virtuous habit will also have the character of a 'mean': it will involve the disposition to desire what is desirable, despite the competing impulses of animal lust (in which the intentionality of desire may be demolished) and timorous frigidity (in which the sexual impulse is impeded altogether). Education is directed towards the special kind of temperance which shows itself, sometimes as chastity, sometimes as fidelity, sometimes as passionate desire, according to the 'right judgement' of the subject. In wanting what is judged to be desirable, the virtuous person wants what may also be loved, and what may therefore be obtained without hurt or humiliation.

Virtue is a matter of degree, rarely attained in its completion, but always admired. Because traditional sexual education has pursued sexual virtue, it is worthwhile summarising its most important features, in order to see the power of the idea that underlies and justifies it.

The most important feature of traditional sexual education is summarised in anthropological language as the 'ethic of pollution and taboo'. The child was taught to regard his body as sacred, and as subject to pollution by misperception or misuse. The sense of pollution is by no means a trivial side-effect of the 'bad sexual encounter': it may involve a penetrating disgust, at oneself, one's body and one's situation, such as is experienced by the victim of rape. Those sentiments—which arise from our 'fear of the obscene'—express the tension contained within the experience of embodiment. At any moment we can become 'mere body', the self driven from its incarnation, and its habitation ransacked. The most important root idea of personal morality is that I am *in* my body, not (to borrow Descartes' image) as a pilot in a ship, but as an incarnate self. My body is identical with me, and sexual purity is the precious guarantee of this.

Sexual purity does not forbid desire: it simply ensures the status of desire as an interpersonal feeling. The child who learns 'dirty habits' detaches his sex from himself, sets it outside himself as something curious and alien. His fascinated enslavement to the body is also a withering of desire, a scattering of erotic energy and a loss of union with the other. Sexual purity sustains the *subject* of desire, making him present as a self in the very act which overcomes him.

The extraordinary spiritual significance accorded to sexual 'purity' has, of course, its sociobiological and its psychoanalytical explanations. But what, exactly, is its *meaning*, and have people been right to value it? In Wagner's *Parsifal*, the 'pure fool' is uniquely credited with the power to heal the terrible wound which is the physical sign of Amfortas's sexual 'pollution'. He alone can redeem Kundry, the 'fallen' woman, whose sexual licence is so resistant to her penitent personality, that it must be confined to another world, of which she retains only a dim and horrified consciousness. That other world is a world of pleasure and opportunity, a world of the 'permitted'. It is governed, however, by the impure eunuch

Klingsor, whose rule is a kind of slavery. Wagner finds the meaning of Christian redemption in the fool's chastity, which leads him to renounce the rewards of an impure desire for the sake of another's salvation. Parsifal releases Amfortas from the hold of 'magic', from the 'charm' which tempts Szymanowski's King Roger towards a vain apotheosis. Parsifal is the harbinger of peace and freedom, in a world that has been enslaved by the magic of desire.

The haunting symbols of this opera owe their power to feelings that are too deep to be lightly dismissed as aesthetic artefacts. But what is their meaning for people who live unsheltered by religion? The answer is to be found, not in religious, but in sexual, feeling. The purely human redemption which is offered to us in love is dependent, in the last analysis, upon public recognition of the value of chastity, and of the sacrilege involved in a sexual impulse that wanders free from the controlling impulse of respect. The 'pollution' of the prostitute is not that she gives herself for money, but that she gives herself to those whom she hates or despises. This is the 'wound' of unchastity, which cannot be healed in solitude by the one who suffers it, but only by his acceptance into a social order which confines the sexual impulse to the realm of intimate relations. The chaste person sustains the ideal of sexual innocence, by giving honourable form to chastity as a way of life. Through his example, it becomes not foolish but admirable to ignore the promptings of a desire that brings no intimacy or fulfilment. Chastity is not a private policy, followed by one individual alone for the sake of his peace of mind. It has a wider and more generous significance: it attempts to draw others into complicity, and to sustain a social order that confines the sexual impulse to the personal sphere.

Chastity exists in two forms: as a publicly declared and publicly recognised role or policy (the chastity of the monk, priest or nun); or as a private resolution, a recognition of the morality that lies dormant in desire. Thus Hans Sachs, in *Die Meistersinger*, who has the opportunity to fulfil his desire, chooses rather to renounce it, knowing that it will not be reciprocated. Sachs is loved and admired for the irreproachable aloneness which makes him the property

of all. He is the buttress of Nuremberg, whose satisfactions are public satisfactions, precisely because his own seed has not been sown. His melancholy and bookish contemplation of the trivialities of progenerative man are in one sense a sigh from the genetic depth: the species is alive in this sigh, just as the individual dies in it. In another sense, however, his melancholy is the supreme affirmation of the reality of others' joys: the recognition that desire must be silenced, in order that others may thrive in their desire.

The child was traditionally brought up to achieve sexual fulfilment only *through* chastity, which is the condition which surrounds him on his first entering the adult world—the world of commitments and obligations. At the same time, he was encouraged to ponder certain 'ideal objects' of desire. These, presented to him under the aspect of an idealised physical beauty, were never *merely* beautiful, but also endowed with the moral attributes that fitted them for love. This dual inculcation of 'pure' habits and 'ideal' love might seem, on the face of it, to be unworthy of the name of education. Is it not, rather, like the mere *training* of a horse or a dog, which arbitrarily forbids some things and fosters others, without offering the first hint of a reason why? And is it not the distinguishing mark of education that it engages with the rational nature of its recipient, and does not merely mould him indifferently to his own understanding of the process? Why, in short, is this moral education, rather than a transference into the sexual sphere—as Freud would have it—of those same processes of interdiction that train us to defecate, not in our nappies, but in a porcelain pot?

The answer is clear. The cult of innocence is an attempt to generate rational conduct, by incorporating the sexual impulse into the self-activity of the subject. It is an attempt to impede the impulse, until such a time as it may attach itself to the interpersonal project that leads to its fulfilment: the project of union with another person, who is wanted not merely for his body, but for the person who *is* this body. Innocence is the disposition to avoid sexual encounter, except with the person whom one may fully desire. Children who have lost their innocence have acquired the habit of gratification through the body alone, in a state of partial or truncated desire. Their gratification is detached from the conditions of personal fulfilment and wanders from object to object with no settled tendency to attach itself to any, pursued all the while by a sense of the body's obscene dominion. 'Debauching of the innocent' was traditionally regarded as a most serious offence, and one that offered genuine *harm* to the victim. The harm in question was not physical, but moral: the undermining of the process which prepares the child to enter the world of *erōs*. (Thus Nabokov's Lolita, who passes with such rapidity from childish provocativeness to a knowing interest in the sexual act, finds, in the end, a marriage devoid of passion, and dies without knowledge of desire.)

The personal and the sexual can become divorced in many ways. The task of sexual morality is to unite them, to sustain thereby the intentionality of desire, and to prepare the individual for erotic love. Sexual morality is the morality of embodiment: the posture which strives to unite us with our bodies, precisely in those situations when our bodies are foremost in our thoughts. Without such a morality the human world is subject to a dangerous divide, a gulf between self and body, at the verge of which all our attempts at personal union falter and withdraw. Hence the prime focus of sexual morality is not the attitude to others, but the attitude to one's own body and its uses. Its aim is to safeguard the integrity of our embodiment. Only on that condition, it is thought, can we inculcate either innocence in the young or fidelity in the adult. Such habits are, however, only one part of sexual virtue. Traditional morality has combined its praise of them with a condemnation of other things—in particular of the habits of lust and perversion. And it is not hard to find the reason for these condemnations.

Perversion consists precisely in a diverting of the sexual impulse from its interpersonal goal, or towards some act that is intrinsically destructive of personal relations and of the values that we find in them. The 'dissolution' of the flesh, which the Marquis de Sade regarded as so important an element in the sexual aim, is in fact that dissolution of the soul; the perversions described by de Sade are not so much attempts to destroy the flesh of the victim as to rid his flesh of its personal meaning, to wring out, with the blood, the rival perspective. That is true in one way or another of all perversion, which can be simply described as the habit of finding a sexual release that avoids or abolishes the *other*, obliterating his embodiment with the obscene perception of his body. Perversion is narcissistic, often solipsistic, involving strategies of replacement which are intrinsically destructive of personal feeling. Perversion therefore prepares us for a life without personal fulfilment, in which no human relation achieves foundation in the acceptance of the other, as this acceptance is provided by desire.

Lust may be defined as a genuine sexual desire, from which the goal of erotic love has been excluded, and in which whatever tends towards their goal—tenderness, intimacy, fidelity, dependence—is curtailed or obstructed. There need be nothing perverted in this. Indeed the special case of lust which I have discussed under the title of Don Juanism, in which the project of intimacy is constantly abbreviated by the flight towards another sexual object, provides one of our paradigms of desire. Nevertheless, the traditional condemnation of lust is far from arbitrary, and the associated contrast between lust and love far from a matter of convention. Lust is also a habit, involving the disposition to give way to desire, without regard to any personal relation with the object. (Thus perversions are all forms of lust even though lust is not in itself a perversion.) Naturally, we all feel the promptings of lust, but the rapidity with which sexual acts become sexual habits, and the catastrophic effect of a sexual act which cannot be remembered without shame or humiliation, give us strong reasons to resist them, reasons that Shakespeare captured in these words:

> Th'expence of Spirit in a waste of shame
> Is lust in action, and till action, lust
> Is perjur'd, murdrous, blouddy, full of blame,
> Savage, extreame, rude, cruell, not to trust,
> Injoyd no sooner but dispised straight,
> Past reason hunted, and no sooner had,
> Past reason hated as a swollowed bayt,

On purpose layd to make the taker mad:
Mad in pursuit and in possession so,
Had, having, and in quest to have, extreame,
A blisse in proofe, and prov'd, a very woe,
Before a joy proposd, behind, a dreame,
  All this the world well knowes, yet none knowes well
  To shun the heaven that leads men to this hell.

In addition to the condemnation of lust and perversion, however, some part of traditional sexual education can be seen as a kind of sustained war against fantasy. It is undeniable that fantasy can play an important part in all our sexual doings, and even the most passionate and faithful lover may, in the act of love, rehearse to himself other scenes of sexual abandon than the one in which he is engaged. Nevertheless, there is truth in the contrast (familiar, in one version, from the writings of Freud) between fantasy and reality, and in the sense that the first is in some way destructive of the second. Fantasy replaces the real, resistant, objective world with a pliant substitute—and that, indeed, is its purpose. Life in the actual world is difficult and embarrassing. Most of all it is difficult and embarrassing in our confrontation with other people, who, by their very existence, make demands that we may be unable or unwilling to meet. It requires a great force, such as the force of sexual desire, to overcome the embarrassment and self-protection that shield us from the most intimate encounters. It is tempting to take refuge in substitutes, which neither embarrass us nor resist the impulse of our spontaneous cravings. The habit grows, in masturbation, of creating a compliant world of desire, in which unreal objects become the focus of real emotions, and the emotions themselves are rendered incompetent to participate in the building of personal relations. The fantasy blocks the passage to reality, which becomes inaccessible to the will.

Even if the fantasy can be overcome so far as to engage in the act of love with another, a peculiar danger remains. The other becomes veiled in substitutes; he is never fully himself in the act of love; it is never clearly *him* that I desire, or *him* that I possess, but always rather a composite object, a universal body, of which he is but one among a potential infinity of

instances. Fantasy fills our thoughts with a sense of the obscene, and the orgasm becomes, not the possession of another, but the expenditure of energy on his depersonalised body. Fantasies are private property, which I can dispose according to my will, with no answerability to the other whom I abuse through them. He, indeed, is of no intrinsic interest to me, and serves merely as my opportunity for self-regarding pleasure. For the fantasist, the ideal partner is indeed the prostitute, who, because she can be purchased, solves at once the moral problem presented by the presence of another at the scene of sexual release.

The connection between fantasy and prostitution is deep and important. The effect of fantasy is to 'commodify' the object of desire, and to replace the law of sexual relationship between people with the law of the market. Sex itself can then be seen as a commodity: something that we pursue and obtain in quantifiable form, and which comes in a variety of packages: in the form of a woman or a man; in the form of a film or a dream; in the form of a fetish or an animal. In so far as the sexual act is seen in this way, it seems morally neutral—or, at best, impersonal. Such criticism as may be offered will concern merely the dangers for the individual and his partner of this or that sexual package: for some bring diseases and discomforts of which others are free. The most harmless and hygienic act of all, on this view, is the act of masturbation, stimulated by whatever works of pornography are necessary to prompt the desire for it in the unimaginative. This justification for pornography has, indeed, recently been offered.

As I have already argued, however, fantasy does not exist comfortably with reality. It has a natural tendency to realise itself: to remake the world in its own image. The harmless wanker with the video-machine can at any moment turn into the desperate rapist with a gun. The 'reality principle' by which the normal sexual act is regulated is a principle of personal encounter, which enjoins us to respect the other person, and to respect, also, the sanctity of his body, as the tangible expression of another self. The world of fantasy obeys no such rule, and is governed by monstrous myths and illusions which are at war with the human world—the illusions, for example, that women wish to be raped, that children have only to be awakened in order to give and receive the intensest sexual pleasure, that violence is not an affront but an affirmation of a natural right. All such myths, nurtured in fantasy, threaten not merely the consciousness of the man who lives by them, but also the moral structure of his surrounding world. They render the world unsafe for self and other, and cause the subject to look on everyone, not as an end in himself, but as a possible means to his private pleasure. In his world, the sexual encounter has been 'fetishised', to use the apt Marxian term, and every other human reality has been poisoned by the sense of the expendability and replaceability of the other.

It is a small step from the preoccupation with sexual virtue, to a condemnation of obscenity and pornography (which is its published form). Obscenity is a direct assault on the sentiment of desire, and therefore on the social order that is based on desire and which has personal love as its goal and fulfilment. There is no doubt that the normal conscience cannot remain neutral towards obscenity, any more than it can remain neutral towards paedophilia and rape (which is not to say that obscenity must also be treated as a *crime*). It is therefore unsurprising that traditional moral education has involved censorship of obscene material, and a severe emphasis on 'purity in thought, word and deed'—an emphasis which is now greeted with irony or ridicule.

Traditional sexual education was, despite its exaggerations and imbecilities, truer to human nature than the libertarian culture which has succeeded it. Through considering its wisdom and its shortcomings, we may understand how to resuscitate an idea of sexual virtue, in accordance with the broad requirements of the Aristotelian argument that I have, in this chapter, been presenting. The ideal of virtue remains one of 'sexual integrity'; of a sexuality that is entirely integrated into the life of personal affection, and in which the self and its responsibility are centrally involved and indissolubly linked to the pleasures and passions of the body.

Traditional sexual morality has therefore been the morality of the body. Libertarian morality, by con-

trast, has relied almost entirely on a Kantian view of the human subject, as related to his body by no coherent moral tie. Focussing as he does on an idea of purely personal respect, and assigning no distinctive place to the body in our moral endeavour, the Kantian inevitably tends towards permissive morality. No sexual act can be wrong merely by virtue of its physical character, and the ideas of obscenity, pollution and perversion have no obvious application. His attitude to homosexuality is conveniently summarised in this passage from a Quaker pamphlet:

We see no reason why the physical nature of the sexual act should be the criterion by which the question whether it is moral should be decided. An act which (for example) expresses true affection between two individuals and gives pleasure to them both, does not seem to us to be sinful by reason *alone* of the fact that it is homosexual. The same criteria seem to apply whether a relationship is heterosexual or homosexual.

Such sentiments are the standard offering of the liberal and utilitarian moralities of our time. However much we may sympathise with their conclusions, it is not possible to accept the shallow reasoning that leads up to them, and which bypasses the great metaphysical conundrum to which all sexual morality is addressed: the conundrum of embodiment. Lawrence asserts that 'sex is *you*', and offers some bad but revealing lines on the subject:

> And don't, with the nasty, prying mind, drag it out
>   from its deeps
> And finger it and force it, and shatter the rhythm it
>   keeps
> When it is left alone, as it stirs and rouses and sleeps.

If anything justifies Lawrence's condemnation of the 'nasty, prying mind', it is the opposite of what he supposes. Sex 'sleeps' in the soul precisely because, and to the extent that, it is buried there by education. If sex is you, it is because you are the product of that education, and not just its victim. It has endowed you with what I have called 'sexual integrity': the ability to be *in* your body, in the very moment of desire.

The reader may be reluctant to follow me in believing that traditional morality is largely justified by the ideal of sexual integrity. But if he accepts the main tenor of my argument, he must surely realise that the ethic of 'liberation', far from promising the release of the self from hostile bondage, in fact heralds the dissipation of the self in loveless fantasy: th'expence of Spirit, in a waste of shame.

What's Wrong with Homosexuality

JOHN FINNIS

The underlying thought is on the following lines. In masturbating, as in being masturbated or sodomized, one's body is treated as instrumental for the securing of the experiential satisfaction of the conscious self. Thus one disintegrates oneself in two ways, (1) by treating one's body as a mere instrument of the consciously operating self, and (2) by making one's choosing self the quasi-slave of the experiencing self which is demanding gratification. The worthlessness of the gratification, and the disintegration of oneself, are both the result of the fact that, in these sorts of behavior, one's conduct is not the actualizing and experiencing of a real common good. Marriage, with its double blessing—procreation and friendship—is a real common good. Moreover, it is a common good that can be both actualized and experienced in the orgasmic union of the reproductive organs of a man and a woman united in commitment to that good. Conjugal sexual activity, and—as Plato and Aristotle and Plutarch and Kant all argue—*only* conjugal activity is free from the shamefulness of instrumentalization that is found in masturbating and in being masturbated or sodomized.

At the very heart of the reflections of Plato, Xenophon, Aristotle, Musonius Rufus and Plutarch on the homoerotic culture around them is the very deliberate and careful judgment that homosexual *conduct* (and indeed all extramarital sexual gratification) is radically incapable of participating in, or actualizing, the common good of friendship. Friends who engage in such conduct are following a natural impulse and doubtless often wish their genital conduct to be an intimate expression of their mutual affection. But they are deceiving themselves. But they are deceiving themselves. The attempt to express affection by orgasmic nonmarital sex is the pursuit of an illusion. The orgasmic union of the reproductive organs of husband and wife really unites them biologically (and their biological reality is part of, not merely an instrument of, their *personal* reality); that orgasmic union therefore can actualize and allow them to experience their real common good—their marriage with the two goods, children and friendship, which are the parts of its wholeness as an intelligible common good. But the common good of friends who are not and cannot be married (man and man, man and boy, woman and woman) has nothing to do with their having children by each other, and their reproductive organs cannot make them a biological (and therefore a personal) unit. So their genital acts together cannot do what they may hope and imagine.

In giving their considered judgment that homosexual conduct cannot actualize the good of friendship, Plato and the many philosophers who follow him intimate an answer to the questions why it should be considered shameful to use, or allow another to use, one's body to give pleasure, and why this use of one's body differs from one's bodily participation in countless other activities (e.g., games) in which one takes and/or gets pleasure. Their response is that pleasure is indeed a good, when it is the experienced aspect of one's participation in some intelligible good, such as a task going well, or a game or a dance or a meal or a reunion. Of course, the activation of sexual organs with a view to the pleasures of

John Finnis, "Is Homosexual Conduct Wrong?—a Philosophical Exchange: Disintegrity," *The New Republic* (15 November 1993): 12–13 (edited). Reprinted with permission of *The New Republic*.

orgasm is sometimes spoken of as if it were a game. But it differs from real games in that its point is not the exercise of skill; rather, this activation of reproductive organs is focused upon the body precisely as a source of pleasure for one's consciousness. So this is a "use of the body" in a strongly different sense of "use." The body now is functioning not in the way one, as a bodily person, acts to instantiate some other intelligible good, but precisely as providing a service to one's consciousness, to satisfy one's desire for satisfaction.

This disintegrity is much more obvious when masturbation is solitary. Friends are tempted to think that pleasuring each other by some forms of mutual masturbation could be an instantiation or actualization or promotion of their friendship. But that line of thought overlooks the fact that if their friendship is not marital . . . activation of their reproductive organs cannot be, in reality, an instantiation or actualization of their friendship's common good. In reality, whatever the generous hopes and dreams with which the loving partners surround their use of their genitals, *that use* cannot express more than is expressed if two strangers engage in genital activity to give each other orgasm, or a prostitute pleasures a client, or a man pleasures himself. Hence, Plato's judgment, at the decisive moment of the *Gorgias*, that there is no important distinction in essential moral worthlessness between solitary masturbation, being sodomized as a prostitute and being sodomized for the pleasure of it. . . .

Societies such as classical Athens and contemporary England (and virtually every other) draw a distinction between behavior found merely (perhaps extremely) offensive (such as eating excrement) and behavior to be repudiated as destructive of human character and relationships. Copulation of humans with animals is repudiated because it treats human sexual activity and satisfaction as something appropriately sought in a manner that, like the coupling of animals, is divorced from the expressing of an intelligible common good—and so treats human bodily life, in one of its most intense activities, as merely animal. The deliberate genital coupling of persons of the same sex is repudiated for a very similar reason.

It is not simply that it is sterile and disposes the participants to an abdication of responsibility for the future of humankind. Nor is it simply that it cannot *really* actualize the mutual devotion that some homosexual persons hope to manifest and experience by it; nor merely that it harms the personalities of its participants by its disintegrative manipulation of different parts of their one personal reality. It is also that it treats human sexual capacities in a way that is deeply hostile to the self-understanding of those members of the community who are willing to commit themselves to real marriage [even one that happens to be sterile] in the understanding that its sexual joys are not mere instruments or accompaniments to, or mere compensation for, the accomplishments of marriage's responsibilities but rather are *the actualizing and experiencing* of the intelligent commitment top share in those responsibilities . . .

This pattern of judgment, both widespread and sound, conclude as follows. Homosexual orientation—the deliberate willingness to promote and engage in homosexual acts—is a standing denial of the intrinsic aptness of sexual intercourse to actualize and give expression to the exclusiveness and open-ended commitment of marriage as something good in itself. All who accept that homosexual acts can be a humanly appropriate use of sexual capacities must, if consistent, regard sexual capacities, organs and acts as instruments to be put to whatever suits the purposes of the individual "self" who has them. Such an acceptance is commonly (and in my opinion rightly) judged to be an active threat to the stability of existing and future marriages; it makes nonsense, for example, of the view that adultery is per se (and not merely because it may involve deception), and in an important way, inconsistent with conjugal love. A political community that judges that the stability and educative generosity of family life is of fundamental importance to the community's present and future can rightly judge that it has a compelling interest in denying that homosexual conduct is a valid, humanly acceptable choice and form of life, and in doing whatever it properly can, as a community with uniquely wide but still subsidiary functions, to discourage such conduct.

Homosexuality and Love

Martha Nussbaum

Finnis's arguments against homosexuality set themselves in a tradition of "natural law" argumentation that derives from ancient Greek traditions. The term "law of nature" was first used by Plato in his *Gorgias*. The approach is further developed by Aristotle, and, above all, by the Greek and Roman Stoics, who are usually considered to be the founders of natural law argumentation in the modern legal tradition, through their influence on Roman law. This being so, it is worth looking to see whether those traditions did in fact use "natural law" arguments to rule homosexual conduct morally or legally substandard.

Plato's dialogues contain several extremely moving celebrations of male-male love, and judge this form of love to be, on the whole, superior to male-female love because of its potential for spirituality and friendship. The *Symposium* contains a series of speeches, each expressing conventional views about this subject that Plato depicts in an appealing light. The speech by Phaedrus points to the military advantages derived by including homosexual couples in a fighting force; because of their intense love, each will fight better, wishing to show himself in the best light before his lover. The speech of Pausanias criticizes males who seek physical pleasure alone in their homosexual relationships, and praises those who seek in sex deeper spiritual communication. Pausanias mentions that tyrants will sometimes promulgate the view that same-sex relations are shameful in order to discourage the kind of community of dedication to political liberty that such relations foster. The speech of Aristophanes holds that all human beings are divided halves of formerly whole beings, and that sexual desire is the pursuit of one's lost other half; he points out that the superior people in any society are those whose lost "other half" is of the same sex—especially the male-male pairs—since these are likely to be the strongest

and most warlike and civically minded people. Finally, Socrates's speech recounts a process of religious-mystical education in which male-male love plays a central guiding role and is a primary source of insight and inspiration into the nature of the good and beautiful.

Platos' *Phaedrus* contains a closely related praise of the intellectual, political and spiritual benefits of a life centered around male-male love. Plato says that the highest form of human life is one in which a male pursues "the love of a young man along with philosophy," and is transported by passionate desire. He describes the experience of falling in love with another male in moving terms, and defends relationships that are mutual and reciprocal over relationships that are one-sided. He depicts his pairs of lovers as spending their life together in the pursuit of intellectual and spiritual activities, combined with political participation. (Although no marriages for these lovers are mentioned, it was the view of the time that this form of life does not prevent its participants from having a wife at home, whom they saw only rarely and for procreative purposes.)

Aristotle speaks far less about sexual love than does Plato, but it is evident that he too finds in male-male relationships the potential for the highest form of friendship, a friendship based on mutual well-wishing and mutual awareness of good character and good aims. He does not find this potential in male-female relationships, since he holds that females are incapable of good character. Like Pausanias in Plato's *Symposium*, Aristotle is critical of relationships that are superficial and concerned only with bodily pleasure; but he finds in male-male relationships—including many that begin in this way—the potential for much richer developments.

The ideal city of the Greek Stoics was built around the idea of pairs of male lovers whose bonds gave the city rich sources of motivation for virtue. Although the Stoics wished their "wise man" to eliminate most passions from his life, they encouraged him to foster

Martha Nussbaum, "Is Homosexual Conduct Wrong?—a Philosophical Exchange: Integrity," *The New Republic* (15 November 1993): 12–13 (edited). Reprinted with permission of *The New Republic*.

a type of erotic love that they defined as "the attempt to form a friendship inspired by the perceived beauty of young men in their prime." They held that this love, unlike other passions, was supportive of virtue and philosophical activity.

Furthermore, Finnis's argument, in his article against homosexuality, is a bad moral argument by any standard, secular or theological. First of all, it assumes that the purpose of a homosexual act is always or usually casual bodily pleasure and the instrumental use of another person for one's own gratification. But this is a false premise, easily disproved by the long historical tradition I have described and by the contemporary lives of real men and women. Finnis offers no evidence for this premise, or for the equally false idea that procreative relations cannot be selfish and manipulative. Second, having argued that a relationship is better if it seeks

no casual pleasure but the creation of a community, he then assumes without argument that the only sort of community a sexual relationship can create is a "procreative community." This is, of course, plainly false. A sexual relationship may create, quite apart from the possibility of procreation, a community of love and friendship, which no religious tradition would deny to be important human goods. Indeed, in many moral traditions, including those of Plato and Aristotle, the procreative community is ranked beneath other communities created by sex, since it is thought that the procreative community will probably not be based on the best sort of friendship and the deepest spiritual concerns. That may not be true in a culture that values women more highly than ancient Greek culture did; but the possibility of love and friendship between individuals of the same sex has not been removed by these historical changes.

CASES FOR ANALYSIS

1. Gay Marriage and Economics

Associated Press—Republicans can reach a broader base by recasting gay marriage as an issue that could dent pocketbooks as small businesses spend more on health care and other benefits, GOP Chairman Michael Steele said Saturday.

Steele said that was just an example of how the party can retool its message to appeal to young voters and minorities without sacrificing core conservative principles. Steele said he used the argument weeks ago while chatting on a flight with a college student who described herself as fiscally conservative but socially liberal on issues like gay marriage.

"Now all of a sudden I've got someone who wasn't a spouse before, that I had no responsibility for, who is now getting claimed as a spouse that I now have financial responsibility for," Steele told Republicans at the state convention in traditionally conservative Georgia. "So how do I pay for that? Who pays for that? You just cost me money." . . .

Vermont and Iowa have legalized gay marriage in recent weeks, and a Quinnipiac University poll released in April found that 57 percent of people questioned support civil unions that provide marriage-like rights. Although 55 percent said they opposed gay marriage, the poll indicated a shift toward more acceptance.*

Provide reasons for your answers. Is same-sex marriage an economic issue? If, as Chairman Steele suggests, gay marriage will cost small businesses money, is that a good reason to oppose legal recognition of gay couples? If gay marriage is an issue of fairness as many proponents argue, does the economic costs of allowing gay marriages matter?

*Russ Bynum, Associated Press, "RNC Chief: Gay Marriage Will Burden Small Business," 16 May 2009.

---

2. Executing Homosexuals

London (The Times)—Homosexuals deserve to be executed or tortured and possibly both, an Iranian leader told British MPs during a private meeting at a peace conference, *The Times* has learnt.

Mohsen Yahyavi is the highest-ranked politician to admit that Iran believes in the death penalty for homosexuality after a spate of reports that gay youths were being hanged.

President Ahmadinejad, questioned by students in New York two months ago about the executions, dodged the issue by suggesting that there were no gays in his country.

Britain regularly challenges Iran about its gay hangings, stonings and executions of adulterers and perceived moral criminals, Foreign and Commonwealth Office (FCO) papers show. . . .

Under the Freedom of Information Act, the FCO released papers to The Times about the death penalty being used in Iran for homosexuality, adultery and sex outside marriage. . . .

Iran, Mauritania, Saudi Arabia, Sudan, the United Arab Emirates, Yemen and Nigeria apply the death penalty for homosexuality, according to the International Lesbian and Gay Association.†

Explain your answers. Is it ever morally permissible to use legal punishment against persons considered sexually deviant? Suppose Iran's punishment of homosexuals is based on religious tradition. Would the execution of gays then be justified? What moral argument could you make against the legal punishment of homosexuality? Until recently, several states had antisodomy laws mandating imprisonment for homosexuality. Were those laws just?

†Dominic Kennedy, "Gays Should Be Hanged, Says Iranian Minister," *TimesOnline*, 13 November 2007, http://www.timesonline.co.uk/tol/news/world/middle_east/article2859606.ece (17 May 2009).

---

3. Premarital Abstinence Pledges

(Washington Post)—Teenagers who pledge to remain virgins until marriage are just as likely to have premarital sex as those who do not promise abstinence and are significantly less likely to use condoms and other forms of birth control when they do, according to a study released today.

The new analysis of data from a large federal survey found that more than half of youths became sexually active before marriage regardless of whether they had taken a "virginity pledge," but that the percentage who took precautions against pregnancy or sexually transmitted diseases was 10 points lower for pledgers than for non-pledgers.

"Taking a pledge doesn't seem to make any difference at all in any sexual behavior," said Janet E. Rosenbaum of the Johns Hopkins Bloomberg School of Public Health, whose report appears in the January issue of the journal *Pediatrics*. "But it does seem to make a difference in condom use and other forms of birth control that is quite striking."

The study is the latest in a series that have raised questions about programs that focus on encouraging abstinence until marriage, including those that specifically ask students to publicly declare their intention to remain virgins. The new analysis, however, goes beyond earlier analyses by focusing on teens who had similar values about sex and other issues before they took a virginity pledge.‡

Give reasons for your answers. Suppose, as this report suggests, abstinence pledges are ineffective and can reduce condom use and increase the risk of teen pregnancy. Would it be immoral to promote the pledges among teens? Should the effectiveness of the pledges in reducing teen pregnancy or STDs have any bearing on the morality of promoting the pledges? Is premarital sex among teens morally wrong regardless of its physical and social risks?

‡Rob Stein, "Premarital Abstinence Pledges Ineffective, Study Finds," *Washington Post,* 29 December 2008, p. A02.

Equality and Affirmative Action

A white man named Alan Bakke applies for admission to the Medical School of the University of California at Davis. Only one hundred slots are available, and there are many other applicants. His grades and admissions test scores, however, are good. The medical school denies him admission anyway—and grants admission to several others whose grades and scores are lower than his. As it turns out, the school has reserved sixteen of the available slots for minority students, many of whom had lower grades and test scores than Bakke. He sues, claiming that he has been denied admission solely because of his race. His case goes all the way to the Supreme Court, which is strongly divided but eventually decides in his favor. The majority opinion says that preferring members of a group solely on account of their race or ethnic origin is a clear-cut instance of discrimination. The Court finds that quota systems like the one used at the Davis Medical School are unconstitutional but that in some situations the use of race or minority status in admissions decisions may be permissible.

This famous Supreme Court case—*Regents of the University of California v. Bakke* (1978)—is one of many to grapple with the divisive and volatile issue of affirmative action, a social policy that is still being ferociously debated almost thirty years after the *Bakke* decision was handed down. It illustrates why this issue is so explosive, so complicated, and so important: disputes over affirmative action invariably involve complex collisions of beliefs and values about racism, sexism, discrimination, civil rights, justice, equality, desert, opportunity, and

social utility. Little wonder then that disagreements flare where agreement would be expected, and people often presumed to have different perspectives on the issue—liberals and conservatives, blacks and whites, men and women—may be just as likely to take the same side.

Affirmative action is notorious for touching off strong feelings that evoke simplistic, knee-jerk answers—precisely the kind of answers we want to avoid here. Only reflective, well-reasoned responses will do for moral questions like these: Are quota systems such as the one cited in the Bakke case morally permissible? Should people be given preference in college admissions or employment because they are members of a particular minority group? Should members of a minority group that was discriminated against in the past be given preferential treatment as compensation for that earlier discrimination? Is preferential treatment for minorities and women permissible even though it deprives white males of equal opportunities? Can affirmative action help create a more just and diverse society—or does it lead to a less just one, divided by race and culture?

ISSUE FILE: BACKGROUND

Affirmative action is a way of making amends for, or eradicating, discrimination based on race, ethnicity, and gender. It takes the form of policies and programs (usually mandated by government) designed to bring about the necessary changes in businesses, colleges, and other organizations. **Discrimination** in the sense used here is unfavorable treatment of people on irrelevant grounds. It refers to actions against people based on factors that cannot and should not be used to justify those actions. It includes, for example, failing to hire a qualified person just because she is a woman; refusing to give a good worker a raise in pay just because he is black or Hispanic; and denying an applicant admission to law school just because he is Asian.

The ideal that spawned affirmative action is this: all persons deserve equal respect and equal opportunity in employment and education. It is essentially an expression of the fundamental moral principle that *equals should be treated equally.* Two people should not be treated differently unless there are relevant differences between them—differences that would justify the dissimilar treatment.

Affirmative action in the United States evolved over the past half century from several groundbreaking laws, executive orders, and court cases. Most notable among these is the Civil Rights Act of 1964, enacted at a time when racial discrimination in the United States was a deeply implanted infection—painful, injurious, and widespread. Discrimination against minorities and women was rampant in the workplace, in college admissions offices, in government contracting, and in countless places of business, from barbershops to factories. Amounting to a direct assault on unequal treatment, the act outlawed discrimination in public accommodations (such as restaurants and hotels), public schools and universities, and business organizations of all kinds. Regarding the latter, the act declares

It shall be an unlawful employment practice for an employer—

(1) to fail or refuse to hire or discharge any individual or otherwise to discriminate against any individual with respect to his compensation, terms, conditions, or privileges of employment, because of such individuals' race, color, religion, sex, or national origin; or

(2) to limit, segregate, or classify his employees or applicants for employment in any way which would deprive or tend to deprive any individual of employment opportunities or otherwise adversely affect his status as an employee, because of such individual's race, color, religion, sex, or national origin.[1]

Later as the executive branch and the courts tried to interpret or implement antidiscrimination policies, affirmative action took on a broader meaning. Many companies and universities have gone beyond simply banning discriminatory practices. With prompting from the federal government, they have tried to institute equal opportunity ("to level the playing field") by ensuring that minority groups and women are represented in fair numbers (that is, numbers reflecting the proportion of such individuals in the whole community or the total workforce). But achieving fair or proportional representation has often required preferential treatment for the designated groups. Thus through the use of quotas or other means, members of the preferred groups have been favored over nonmembers, who typically are white males.

Thus we can say that there are actually two kinds of affirmative action—weak and strong.[2] **Weak affirmative action** is the use of policies and procedures to end discriminatory practices and ensure equal opportunity. It hews close to the spirit and the letter of the Civil Rights Act of 1964, which decrees in Title VI that "[No] person in the United States shall, on the ground of race, color or national origin, be excluded from participation in, denied the benefits of, or be subjected to discrimination under any program or activity receiv-

---

[1] Civil Rights Act of 1964, Section 601 of Title VI.
[2] Terms used by Louis P. Pojman in "The Case against Affirmative Action," *International Journal of Applied Philosophy* 12 (1998): 97–115 (reprinted in *Philosophy: The Quest for Truth*, ed. Louis P. Pojman [New York: Oxford University Press, 2006], 632–45). I attach very roughly the same meanings to them that Pojman does.

CRITICAL THOUGHT: Are Legacies Racist?

Take a look at this excerpt from a report on college "legacies" published in the *Christian Science Monitor*:

> WASHINGTON, D.C.—At Penn, they "take it very seriously." At Michigan it "gets you extra points." At Harvard, it "is not ignored," and at Notre Dame, they are "very open" to it. "It" is "legacy": an admissions designation used by most private and some public universities for applicants whose relatives attended the school, and who, as such, get some degree of preferential treatment. It's a practice as old as colleges themselves, and is intended to boost alumni support and donations and foster a sense of community.
>
> It's also racist, argue its critics.
>
> Following fast on the footsteps of last year's Supreme Court entry into the delicate area of affirmative-action admissions, lawmakers are taking a hard look at this so-called reverse affirmative action, which gives an edge to those whose parents and grandparents went to selective colleges at a time when most minorities there were few and far between[.]*

Are legacies indeed racist? If you think so, what are your reasons? If you think not, what argument would you put forth to support your belief? If you were the president of a state college, what policy toward legacies would you try to establish? Do legacies violate the Civil Rights Act of 1964? Why or why not?

* Danna Harman, "Family Ties: An Unfair Advantage?" *Christian Science Monitor,* 6 February 2004.

---

ing Federal financial assistance." Weak affirmative action can involve many strategies for expanding equal opportunity, but it stops short of preferential treatment. As the philosopher Louis P. Pojman explains it,

[Weak affirmative action] includes such things as dismantling of segregated institutions, widespread advertisement to groups not previously represented in certain privileged positions, special scholarships for the disadvantaged classes (e.g., the poor, regardless of race or gender), and even using diversity or under-representation of groups with a history of past discrimination as a tie breaker when candidates for these goods and offices are relatively equal. The goal of *Weak Affirmative Action* is equal opportunity to compete, not equal results. We seek to provide each citizen regardless of race or gender a fair chance to the most favored positions in society. There is no more moral requirement to guarantee that 12% of professors are Black than to guarantee that 85% of

the players in the National Basketball Association are White.[3]

Weak affirmative action, then, is hardly controversial. Probably few people nowadays would object to efforts to end discrimination against minorities and women and to give people an equal chance to get ahead. But strong affirmative action is a different matter.

Strong affirmative action is the use of policies and procedures to favor particular individuals because of their race, gender, or ethnic background. It is a kind of preferential treatment that is usually implemented through favoring plans, quota systems, or other approaches. The point of a quota system is to ensure that an organization has a predetermined number or percentage of minority members or women. Typically, a proportion of available positions or slots are

[3]Pojman, "The Case against Affirmative Action," 98.

reserved for the preferred people, as was the arrangement at the Medical School of UC Davis in the Bakke case. Sometimes the result of using a quota system is that less qualified people are hired or accepted while equally or more qualified people are not—with the difference being only that the preferred ones are women or members of a minority.

Defenders of strong affirmative action have offered several justifications for it. A leading argument is that because in generations past minorities were treated cruelly and unjustly, they now deserve compensation for those terrible wrongs. Giving minorities preferential treatment in employment and education is the best way to make amends. As one philosopher puts it, "Racism was directed against Blacks whether they were talented, average, or mediocre, and attenuating the effects of racism requires distributing remedies similarly. Affirmative action policies compensate for the harms of racism (overt and institutional) through antidiscrimination laws and preferential policies."[4]

Another argument is that strong affirmative action is necessary to foster *diversity* in a population—diversity of race, ethnicity, gender, culture, and outlook. Diversity is rightly thought to be an extremely valuable commodity for any free society. It promotes understanding of cultures and viewpoints different from one's own, which in turn encourages tolerance and cooperation in an increasingly heterogeneous world. Some think it valuable enough to use strong affirmative action to achieve it.

As you would expect, diversity is thought to be critical to education—especially in universities, where the issue of promoting diversity through preferences has been vigorously debated. Many universities have tested the use of preferences for diversity's sake, encouraged by the majority opinion in the Bakke case, which states that "The atmosphere of 'speculation, experiment and creation'—so essential to the quality of higher education—is widely believed to be promoted by a diverse student body."[5]

But strong affirmative action is strongly opposed by many who see it as *reverse discrimination*—unequal, preferential treatment against some people (mostly white males) to advance the interests of others (minorities and women). The main charge is that preferential treatment on the basis of race, gender, or minority status is *always* wrong. It is just as immoral when used against white males as it is when used against blacks or women. Speaking specifically of racial preferences, the philosopher Carl Cohen provides a succinct statement of this claim:

It uses categories that *must not* be used to distinguish among persons with respect to their entitlements in the community. Blacks and whites are equals, as blondes and brunettes are equals, as Catholics and Jews are equals, as Americans of every ancestry are equal. No matter who the beneficiaries may be or who the victims, preference on the basis of race is morally wrong. It was wrong in the distant past and in the recent past; it is wrong now; and it will always be wrong. Race preference violates the principle of human equality.[6]

MORAL THEORIES

In the debates over strong affirmative action, those who oppose it as well as those who endorse it appeal to conventional moral theories—both consequentialist and nonconsequentialist. Many who support strong affirmative action make the utili-

---

[4]Albert Mosley, "The Case for Affirmative Action," in *Philosophy: The Quest for Truth*, ed. Louis P. Pojman, 6th ed. (New York: Oxford University Press, 2006), 630.

[5]*Regents of the University of California v. Bakke*, 438 U.S. 265, 312 (1978).

[6]Carl Cohen, in *Affirmative Action and Racial Preference: A Debate*, by Carl Cohen and James P. Sterba (Oxford: Oxford University Press, 2003), 25.

CRITICAL THOUGHT: Are Whites-Only Scholarships Unjust?

After reading about weak and strong affirmative action in this chapter, consider the following news item:

(CNN)—A whites-only scholarship to be awarded Wednesday by a student Republican organization at Roger Williams University in Bristol, Rhode Island, has drawn both controversy and support.

"It all began two weeks ago as a way for the college Republican groups to express their opposition and tell people they are against race-based scholarships and affirmative action," June Speakman, faculty adviser for the College Republicans told CNN.

"We never expected such an overwhelming response of e-mails and media attention."

The scholarship is for $250, but College Republicans president Jason Mattera said he has received donations and pledges totaling $4,000 for future whites-only scholarships.

Mattera is of Puerto Rican descent and was awarded a $5,000 scholarship from the Hispanic College Fund. He said he believes being eligible for such scholarships gives him "an inherent advantage over my white peers." He wants the university to award scholarships based on merit and not ethnicity.

Applicants for the College Republicans' scholarship must be of Caucasian descent, have high hon-

ors, write an essay, and show an impressive list of accomplishments, Mattera said. Sixteen people applied.

Roger Williams University does not sponsor or endorse the scholarship, university spokesman Rick Goff told CNN.

"The scholarship is entirely initiated by the College Republicans at the university," he said. . . .

The state Republican Party has criticized the scholarship as having racist overtones.*

Is this whites-only scholarship an example of *weak* or *strong* affirmative action—or neither? Is it racist or discriminatory? If so, are blacks-only scholarships in the same category? If not, what distinguishes the one type of scholarship from the other? That is, what are your reasons for thinking that one is unjust while the other is not? Is there an implicit argument in the student organization's offering a white's only scholarship? If so, what is it?

*Jennifer Styles, "Whites-Only Scholarship Generates Controversy," *CNN.com,* 20 February 2004, www.cnn.com/2004/EDUCATION/02/18/whites.only.scholars/index.html (accessed 19 September 2005). © 2004 Cable News Network. Reprinted courtesy of CNN.

tarian argument that these policies can have enormous benefits for minorities and women as well as for society as a whole. They contend, as suggested earlier, that preferential programs can increase racial and cultural diversity, which helps promote tolerance, mutual understanding, better use of people's talents, and—in higher education—enhanced learning. They also argue that preferential policies can have great social utility by creating role models for minorities and women whose self-esteem and hopes for success have been dimmed by generations of discrimination. They assert that role models are essential for demonstrating to young people that significant achievement is pos-

sible. Finally, some think the best argument is that strong affirmative action may be able to eradicate racism and transform our race-conscious society. A proponent of this view outlines the argument as follows:

[Affirmative action programs] rest on two judgments. The first is a judgment of social theory: that the United States will continue to be pervaded by racial divisions as long as the most lucrative, satisfying, and important careers remain mainly the prerogative of members of the white race, while others feel themselves systematically excluded from a professional and social elite. The second is a calculation of strategy: that increasing the number of blacks who are at work in the professions will, in the long run, reduce the sense of frustration and injustice and racial self-consciousness in the black community to the point at which blacks may begin to think of themselves as individuals who can succeed like others through talent and initiative. At that future point the consequences of nonracial admissions programs, whatever these consequences might be, could be accepted with no sense of racial barriers or injustice.[7]

Many opponents of strong affirmative action also make utilitarian appeals. Their most straightforward counterargument is that those who favor race or gender preferences are simply wrong about the consequences of the policies: the consequences are either not as beneficial as supposed or are actually injurious. Opponents try to undermine the diversity argument by insisting that racial and ethnic diversity does not necessarily result in diversity of ideas or outlooks, that no scientific evidence supports the notion that diversity policies yield benefits in education or learning, and that giving priority to racial or gender diversity in the workplace would severely undermine competence and efficiency, which are highly valued by society. They reject the role model argument on the grounds that role models selected by race or gender are not necessarily the role models we need. The best role models in education, they say, are people who are the best—the most competent, knowledgeable, inspiring, and decent—*whatever the color of their skin, their background, or their gender.* Many opposed to racial preferences doubt that such treatment can help eliminate racism and promote a color-blind society. In fact, they argue that racial preferences can often have the opposite effect:

Preference puts distinguished minority achievement under a cloud. It imposes upon every member of the

---

QUICK REVIEW

affirmative action—A way of making amends for, or eradicating, discrimination based on race, ethnicity, and gender.

discrimination—Unfavorable treatment of people on irrelevant grounds.

weak affirmative action—The use of policies and procedures to end discriminatory practices and ensure equal opportunity.

strong affirmative action—The use of policies and procedures to favor particular individuals because of their race, gender, or ethnic background.

---

preferred minority the demeaning burden of presumed inferiority. Preference *creates* that burden; it *makes* a stigma of the race of those who are preferred by race. An ethnic group given special favor by the community is *marked* as needing special favor—and the mark is borne prominently by every one of its members. Nasty racial stereotypes are reinforced, and the malicious imputation of inferiority is inescapable because it is tied to the color of the skin.[8]

As noted earlier, a common nonconsequentialist argument for strong affirmative action is based on the notion of compensatory justice: historically, minorities (blacks, Native Americans, Hispanics, and others) were the victims of racism by the white majority; justice requires that members of those minorities now be compensated for that past mistreatment; racial preferences in employment and education are appropriate compensation; therefore, racial preferences are morally permissible. As you might guess, many who wish to counter this argument also appeal to justice. They argue that compensation is just only (1) if it is given in proper

---

[7]Ronald Dworkin, "Bakke's Case: Are Quotas Unfair?" in *A Matter of Principle* (Cambridge, MA: Harvard University Press, 1985), 294.

[8]Cohen, *Affirmative Action,* 110.

measure to specific persons who have been harmed, and (2) if the specific persons who caused the harm do the compensating. But with racial preferences, this direct connection that morality seems to require is missing. The result, they contend, is that often the nonminority person who suffers because of compensatory justice (because he is well-qualified but denied admission, for example) has had nothing to do with past racism, and the person who benefits from compensatory justice has suffered very little from racism (because he or she is well-educated with above-average income, say). They conclude that racial preferences are unjust.

MORAL ARGUMENTS

Let us look a little closer at the argument from compensatory justice, giving particular attention to how a supporter of strong affirmative action might articulate and defend it. Consider this version of the argument, narrowly focused on compensatory claims that blacks might have against whites for historical discrimination:

1. In the past, blacks have been cruelly and systematically discriminated against by whites.
2. Blacks thus are owed just compensation for this ill treatment.
3. Strong affirmative action in the form of racial preferences is the most morally appropriate form of such compensation.
4. Therefore, racial preferences (in employment and education) should be used to compensate blacks for past discrimination.

First note that this argument is valid and that Premise 1 is true. Both those for and those against racial preferences would be likely to accept this premise, a statement of historical fact that few thoughtful people would dispute. Premises 2 and 3, on the other hand, are very contentious claims.

The most common way to support Premise 2 is to appeal to our moral intuitions about the jus-tice of compensating people who have been wronged. We tend to think that people who have been wronged do in fact deserve reparations, that valid grievances warrant redress. Many argue that blacks have been mistreated and discriminated against for so many generations that today they still suffer the lingering effects—they are disadvantaged before they even begin to compete for jobs, school admissions, and grades. Racial preferences help give them the edge that they need—and that they justly deserve as repayment for cruelties suffered in the past.

Those who reject Premise 2 counter that the principle of just compensation is certainly legitimate, but compensation in the form of racial preferences is not just. Compensation, they argue, should go to the particular persons who have been wronged, and the compensation should be paid by the specific persons who wronged them. But with racial preferences, they contend, the blacks who benefit are not all equally deserving of redress. The ancestors of contemporary blacks were almost certainly not equally wronged, not all wronged in the same fashion, and not all wronged more than some poor white males were wronged. As Carl Cohen says,

[M]any of Hispanic ancestry now enjoy here, and have long enjoyed, circumstances as decent and as well protected as those enjoyed by Americans of all other ethnicities. The same is true of African Americans, some of whom are impoverished and some of whom are rich and powerful. Rewards distributed on the basis of ethnic membership assume that the damage suffered by some were suffered by all—an assumption that we know to be false.[9]

Advocates of race preferences can counter this criticism with an analogy. In the United States, veterans receive preferential treatment when they apply for civil service jobs. Their applications are automatically given extra weight, which means

[9]Cohen, *Affirmative Action,* 27–28.

that sometimes veterans may land jobs even when nonveteran applicants are equally qualified. The notion behind this policy is that a grateful nation owes veterans something for their service. The policy assumes that all veterans are owed preferential treatment even though some of them have served longer and more courageously than other of their comrades. So, the advocate of preferences asks, why should not blacks be treated according to a similar policy? Why should not all blacks be owed preferential treatment because of past discrimination—and owed it in equal measure even though some blacks have been wronged more than others?

Another kind of attack on Premise 2 focuses not on the people compensated but on those penalized so the debt can be paid. The claim is that racial preferences are unjust because they punish people who have done nothing to merit punishment. When blacks get preferential treatment in employment, the argument goes, some white males end up losing out—even though these whites had no part in past racism and may have never discriminated against anyone. Clearly, penalizing people for wrongdoing that they did not—and could not—commit is unjust; therefore, racial preferences are unjust.

A frequent reply to this argument is that the white males thought to be innocent victims of reverse discrimination are not as innocent as we might think. According to this response, white males are the recipients of advantages and privileges that have been unjustly extracted from blacks for generations—therefore, strong affirmative action does not take from white males anything that is rightfully theirs. The philosopher Judith Jarvis Thomson, an advocate of preferential hiring, makes the point in the following way:

No doubt few, if any, [young white male applicants] have themselves, individually, done any wrongs to blacks and women. But they have profited from the wrongs the community did. Many may actually have been direct beneficiaries of policies which excluded or down-graded blacks and women—perhaps in school admissions, perhaps in access to financial aid, perhaps elsewhere; and even those who did not directly benefit in this way had, at any rate, the advantage in the competition which comes of confidence in one's full membership, and of one's rights being recognized as a matter of course.[10]

Critics have tried to rebut this argument by questioning its underlying assumption—the notion that, as one philosopher puts it, "if someone gains from an unjust practice for which he is not responsible and even opposes, the gain is not really his and can be taken from him without injustice."[11] This rebuttal relies on the common-sense moral principle that a person who wrongs others is morally obligated to compensate them for that wrong but the wrongdoer's descendants are not. The sins of the parents cannot be transferred to the children.

Premise 3—that racial preferences are just and appropriate moral compensation for past discrimination—is defended by many, but probably most ably by Thomson:

[In] fact the nature of the wrongs done is such as to make jobs the best and most suitable form of compensation. What blacks and women were denied was full membership in the community; and nothing can more appropriately make amends for that wrong than precisely what will make them feel they now finally have it. And that means jobs. Financial compensation (the cost of which could be shared equally) slips through the fingers; having a job, and discovering you do it well, yield—perhaps better than anything else—that very self-respect which blacks and women have had to do without.[12]

[10]Judith Jarvis Thomson, "Preferential Hiring," *Philosophy & Public Affairs* 2, no. 4 (Summer 1973): 383–84.
[11]Robert Simon, "Preferential Hiring: A Reply to Judith Jarvis Thomson," *Philosophy & Public Affairs* 3, no. 3 (Spring 1974): 318.
[12]Thomson, "Preferential Hiring," 382–83.

Though several arguments can be tried against Premise 3, one in particular goes to the heart of the debate on racial preferences. It says that preferential treatment is not fitting compensation, because it ignores the true standard by which jobs and positions should be awarded—competence:

[T]he normal criterion of competence is a strong prima facie consideration when the most important positions are at stake. There are three reasons for this: (1) treating people according to their merits respects them as persons, as ends in themselves, rather than as means to social ends (if we believe that individuals possess a dignity that deserves to be respected, then we ought to treat that individual on the basis of his or her merits, not as a mere instrument for social policy); (2) society has given people expectations that if they attain certain levels of excellence they will be awarded appropriately; and (3) filling the most important positions with the best qualified is the best way to ensure efficiency in job-related areas and in society in general.[13]

SUMMARY

Affirmative action is meant to make up for or eliminate minority and gender discrimination, which is a form of unwarranted mistreatment. Affirmative action seeks to realize the ideal of equal respect and opportunity for all in employment and education.

[13]Pojman, "The Case against Affirmative Action," 101.

Weak affirmative action is generally not controversial, because it uses policies and procedures to ensure equal opportunity without demanding that one group be preferred over another. Strong affirmative action, on the other hand, is controversial, because it makes use of minority and gender preferences.

Those who defend strong affirmative action argue that it is needed to compensate certain groups for mistreatment and discrimination of the past. It is also thought to level the playing field—to give minorities and women an edge in the competition for jobs and educational admissions. Some also contend that such preferences are justified because they help promote cultural, ethnic, and intellectual diversity, a beneficial force for free societies. Strong affirmative action is opposed by many who think it is reverse discrimination, unequal treatment that penalizes white males to give advantages to blacks and women. These critics generally reject all forms of preferential treatment whether they favor white males or not.

Arguments for and against strong affirmative action can appeal to both consequentialist and nonconsequentialist theories. Some argue that preferential treatment is justified because it has positive consequences for minorities and for society as a whole. Others argue that such policies do not work as advertised and actually harm the people they are meant to help. Nonconsequentialist arguments appeal to justice, asserting either that affirmative action programs are just (doing compensatory justice, for example) or unjust (distorting compensatory justice).

READINGS

Reverse Discrimination as Unjustified

LISA H. NEWTON

I have heard it argued that "simple justice" requires that we favor women and blacks in employment and educational opportunities, since women and blacks were "unjustly" excluded from such opportunities for so many years in the not so distant past. It is a strange argument, an example of a possible implication of a true proposition advanced to dispute the proposition itself, like an octopus absent-mindedly slicing off his head with a stray tentacle. A fatal confusion underlies this argument, a confusion fundamentally relevant to our understanding of the notion of the rule of law.

Two senses of justice and equality are involved in this confusion. The root notion of justice, progenitor of the other, is the one that Aristotle (*Nichomachean Ethics* 5. 6; *Politics* 1. 2; 3. 1) assumes to be the foundation and proper virtue of the political association. It is the condition which free men establish among themselves when they "share a common life in order that their association bring them self-sufficiency"— the regulation of their relationship by law, and the establishment, by law, of equality before the law. Rule of law is the name and pattern of this justice; its equality stands against the inequalities—of wealth, talent, etc.—otherwise obtaining among its participants, who by virtue of that equality are called "citizens." It is an achievement—complete, or, more frequently, partial—of certain people in certain concrete situations. It is fragile and easily disrupted by powerful individuals who discover that the blind equality of rule of law is inconvenient for their interests. Despite its obvious instability, Aristotle assumed that the establishment of justice in this sense, the creation of citizenship, was a permanent possibility for men and that the resultant association of citizens was

Lisa H. Newton, "Reverse Discrimination as Unjustified," *Ethics*, 83, no. 4 (July 1973), 308–12 (edited). Copyright © 1973, University of Chicago Press. Reprinted with permission.

the natural home of the species. At levels below the political association, this rule-governed equality is easily found; it is exemplified by any group of children agreeing together to play a game. At the level of the political association, the attainment of this justice is more difficult, simply because the stakes are so much higher for each participant. The equality of citizenship is not something that happens of its own accord, and without the expenditure of a fair amount of effort it will collapse into the rule of a powerful few over an apathetic many. But at least it has been achieved, at some times in some places; it is always worth trying to achieve, and eminently worth trying to maintain, wherever and to whatever degree it has been brought into being.

Aristotle's parochialism is notorious; he really did not imagine that persons other than Greeks could associate freely in justice, and the only form of association he had in mind was the Greek *polis*. With the decline of the *polis* and the shift in the center of political thought, his notion of justice underwent a sea change. To be exact, it ceased to represent a political type and became a moral ideal: the ideal of equality as we know it. This ideal demands that all men be included in citizenship—that one Law govern all equally, that all men regard all other men as fellow citizens, with the same guarantees, rights, and protections. Briefly, it demands that the circle of citizenship achieved by any group be extended to include the entire human race. Properly understood, its effect on our associations can be excellent: it congratulates us on our achievement of rule of law as a process of government but refuses to let us remain complacent until we have expanded the associations to include others within the ambit of the rules, as often and as far as possible. While one man is a slave, none of us may feel truly free. We are constantly prodded by this ideal to look for possible justifiable discrimination, for inequalities not absolutely required for the functioning of the society and advantageous to all. And after twenty centuries of pressure, not at all constant, from this ideal, it might be said that some progress has been made. To take the cases in point for this problem, we are now prepared to assert, as Aristotle would never have been, the equality of sexes and of persons of different colors. The ambit of American citizenship, once restricted to white males of property, has been extended to include all adult free men, then all adult males including ex-slaves, then all women. The process of acquisition of full citizenship was for these groups a sporadic trail of half-measures, even now not complete; the steps on the road to full equality are marked by legislation and judicial decisions which are only recently concluded and still often not enforced. But the fact that we can now discuss the possibility of favoring such groups in hiring shows that over the area that concerns us, at least, full equality is presupposed as a basis for discussion. To that extent, they are full citizens, fully protected by the law of the land.

It is important for my argument that the moral idea of equality be recognized as logically distinct from the condition (or virtue) of justice in the political sense. Justice in this sense exists *among* a citizenry, irrespective of the number of the populace included in that citizenry. Further, the moral idea is parasitic upon the political virtue, for "equality" is unspecified—it means nothing until we are told in what respect that equality is to be realized. In a political context, "equality" is specified as "equal rights"—equal access to the public realm, public goods and offices, equal treatment under the law—in brief, the equality of citizenship. If citizenship is not a possibility, political equality is unintelligible. The ideal emerges as a generalization of the real condition and refers back to that condition for its content.

Now, if justice (Aristotle's justice in the political sense) is equal treatment under law for all citizens, what is injustice? Clearly, injustice is the violation of that equality, discriminating for or against a group of citizens, favoring them with special immunities and privileges or depriving them of those guaranteed to the others. When the southern employer refuses to hire blacks in white-collar jobs, when Wall Street will only hire women as secretaries with new titles, when Mississippi high schools routinely flunk all black boys above ninth grade, we have examples of injustice, and we work to restore the equality of the public realm by ensuring that equal opportunity will be provided in such cases in the future. But of course, when the employers and the schools *favor* women and blacks, the same injustice is done. Just as the previous discrimination did, this reverse discrimination violates the public equality which defines citizenship and destroys the rule of law for the areas in which these favors are granted. To the extent that we adopt a program of discrimination, reverse or otherwise, justice in the political sense is destroyed, and none of us, specifically affected or not, is a citizen, a bearer of rights—we are all petitioners for favors. And to the same extent, the ideal of equality is undermined, for it has content only where justice obtains, and by destroying justice we render the ideal meaningless. It is, then, an ironic paradox, if not a contradiction in terms, to assert that the ideal of equality justifies the violation of justice; it is as if one should argue, with William Buckley, that an ideal of humanity can justify the destruction of the human race.

Logically, the conclusion is simple enough: all discrimination is wrong prima facie because it violates justice, and that goes for reverse discrimination too. No violation of justice among the citizens may be justified (may overcome the prima facie objection) by appeal to the ideal of equality, for that ideal is logically dependent upon the notion of justice. Reverse discrimination, then, which attempts no other justification than an appeal to equality, is wrong. But let us try to make the conclusion more plausible by suggesting some of the implications of the suggested practice of reverse discrimination in employment and education. My argument will be that the problems raised there are insoluble, not only in practice, but in principle.

We may argue, if we like, about what "discrimination" consists of. Do I discriminate against blacks if I admit none to my school when none of the black applicants are qualified by the tests I always give?

How far must I go to root out cultural bias from my application forms and tests before I can say that I have not discriminated against those of different cultures? Can I assume that women are not strong enough to be roughnecks on my oil rigs, or must I test them individually? But this controversy, the most popular and well-argued aspect of the issue, is not as fatal as two others which cannot be avoided: if we are regarding the blacks as a "minority" victimized by discrimination, what is a "minority"? And for any group—blacks, women, whatever—that has been discriminated against, what amount of reverse discrimination wipes out the initial discrimination? Let us grant as true that women and blacks were discriminated against, even where laws forbade such discrimination, and grant for the sake of argument that a history of discrimination must be wiped out by reverse discrimination. What follows?

First, are there other groups which have been discriminated against? For they should have the same right of restitution. What about American Indians, Chicanos, Appalachian Mountain whites, Puerto Ricans, Jews, Cajuns, and Orientals? And if these are to be included, the principle according to which we specify a "minority" is simply the criterion of "ethnic (sub) group," and we're stuck with every hyphenated American in the lower-middle class clamoring for special privileges for *his* group—and with equal justification. For be it noted, when we run down the Harvard roster, we find not only a scarcity of blacks (in comparison with the proportion in the population) but an even more striking scarcity of those second-, third-, and fourth-generation ethnics who make up the loudest voice of Middle America. Shouldn't they demand *their* share? And eventually, the WASPs will have to form their own lobby, for they too are a minority. The point is simply this: there is no "majority" in America who will not mind giving up just a bit of their rights to make room for a favored minority. There are only other minorities, each of which is discriminated against by the favoring. The initial injustice is then repeated dozens of times, and if each minority is granted the same right of restitution as the others, an entire area of rule governance is dissolved into a pushing and shoving match

between self-interested groups. Each works to catch the public eye and political popularity by whatever means of advertising and power politics lend themselves to the effort, to capitalize as much as possible on temporary popularity until the restless mob picks another group to feel sorry for. Hardly an edifying spectacle, and in the long run no one can benefit: the pie is no larger—it's just that instead of setting up and enforcing rules for getting a piece, we've turned the contest into a free-for-all, requiring much more effort for no larger a reward. It would be in the interests of all the participants to reestablish an objective rule to govern the process, carefully enforced and the same for all.

Second, supposing that we do manage to agree in general that women and blacks (and all the others) have some right of restitution, some right to a privileged place in the structure of opportunities for a while, how will we know when that while is up? How much privilege is enough? When will the guilt be gone, the price paid, the balance restored? What recompense is right for centuries of exclusion? What criterion tells us when we are done? Our experience with the Civil Rights movement shows us that agreement on these terms cannot be presupposed: a process that appears to some to be going at a mad gallop into a black takeover appears to the rest of us to be at a standstill. Should a practice of reverse discrimination be adopted, we may safely predict that just as some of us begin to see "a satisfactory start toward righting the balance," others of us will see that we "have already gone too far in the other direction" and will suggest that the discrimination ought to be reversed again. And such disagreement is inevitable, for the point is that we could not *possibly* have any criteria for evaluating the kind of recompense we have in mind. The context presumed by any discussion of restitution is the context of rule of law: law sets the rights of men and simultaneously sets the method for remedying the violation of those rights. You may exact suffering from others and/or damage payments for yourself if and only if the others have violated your rights; the suffering you have endured is not sufficient reason for them to suffer. And remedial rights exist only where there is law: primary human rights are useful guides to legislation but cannot stand as reasons for awarding remedies for injuries sustained. But then, the context presupposed by any discussion of restitution is the context of preexistent full citizenship. No remedial rights could exist for the excluded; neither in law nor in logic does there exist a right to *sue* for a standing to sue.

From these two considerations, then, the difficulties with reverse discrimination become evident. Restitution for a disadvantaged group whose rights under the law have been violated is possible by legal means, but restitution for a disadvantaged group whose grievance is that there was no law to protect them simply is not. First, outside of the area of justice defined by the law, no sense can be made of "the group's rights," for no law recognizes that group or the individuals in it, qua members, as bearers of rights (hence *any* group can constitute itself as a disadvantaged minority in some sense and demand similar restitution). Second, outside of the area of protection of law, no sense can be made of the violation of rights (hence the amount of the recompense cannot be decided by any objective criterion). For both reasons, the practice of reverse discrimination undermines the foundation of the very ideal in whose name it is advocated; it destroys justice, law, equality, and citizenship itself, and replaces them with power struggles and popularity contests.

Affirmative Action and Fairness

Robert K. Fullinwider

I began by talking about four white men: David Duke, Brian Weber, William Bradford Reynolds, and George Bush.

David Duke has been much in the news of late. A former Klansman, a former leader of a white supremacist party, a purveyor of neo-Nazi literature, and now a representative in the state legislature. Duke took 40 percent of the vote in the 1990 senatorial primary in Louisiana—40 percent of the vote, 60 percent of the white vote. The main theme of his campaign: the injustice of affirmative action, the need for civil rights for whites. He tapped into something deep. He touched a nerve.

Brian Weber is also from Louisiana. In the 1970s he worked at a Kaiser Company chemical plant. That plant, like industry in general in the South, had a segregated work force. All of its black employees were relegated to a handful of unskilled jobs. There were none in the high-paying craft occupations. Moreover, given the company's rules and practices, little was likely to change. Kaiser hired craft workers by going outside the plant, using a regional labor market in which almost all workers trained in the crafts were white. The chemical workers' union and the company agreed to a plan to change things: the company would henceforth train its own craft workers instead of hiring from the outside, and it set up an on-the-job training program, admitting plant workers into the program from two lists—a white list and a black list. For every white worker admitted, one black worker would be admitted—until 30 percent of the craft workers at the plant were black. An explicit racial criterion. A quota.

In Brian Weber's eyes, this was unjustified reverse discrimination. He brought suit in federal court, and in 1979 the Supreme Court found in favor of the company.

There is a real irony in Weber's lawsuit. Weber himself was an unskilled worker at the plant. Had the company maintained its practice of going to outside markets for craft workers, Brian Weber would never

Robert K. Fullinwider, "Affirmative Action and Fairness," *Report from the Institute for Philosophy & Public Policy* 11, no. 1 (Winter 1991): 10–13. Reprinted by permission of the Philosophy & Public Policy Quarterly, Maryland School of Public Affairs.

have risen very far within the plant. The new program meant that he now had a chance to advance himself; he only had to wait his turn. No matter. The racial preferences in the program touched a nerve. They weren't tolerable. They had to go.

Nor, for George Bush, is the mere threat of preferences in favor of blacks or women acceptable. In October 1990 he vetoed the new Civil Rights Act, which would have clarified certain standards of proof in civil rights lawsuits. His objection was that these standards of proof made it hard for firms to defend themselves against charges of discrimination. Consequently, some firms might be tempted to avoid discrimination charges by using quotas—giving racial or gender preferences to make sure their work fores had the right racial or gender profile. This possibility was enough to cause the president to reject the bill.

WHY QUOTES ARE ANATHEMA

What is it, though, that makes a program like Kaiser's intolerable? What makes the mere risk of preferences unacceptable? Why is the Q-word anathema? That question brings me to the last man I'll talk about, William Bradford Reynolds. Reynolds headed the Office of Civil Rights in the Department of Justice during the Reagan Administration, and was that administration's leading spokesman on affirmative action and against quotas.

The debate about preferential treatment, he said, is between those (like himself) who believe in *equality of opportunity* and those who believe in *equality of results*. Those who *oppose* preferential treatment believe in individual rights and a colorblind, genderblind society. Those who *support* quotas believe in group rights and dividing up social benefits by race and gender. That's the way Reynolds put it.

Putting the matter this way is politically effective for opponents of affirmative action. Individual rights, equality of opportunity, success through effort and merit, reward because of what you do, not who you are—these values are as American as apple pie. Opposing preferential treatment isn't opposing racial and gender justice; it's just opposing an alien philosophy, an un-American ideology.

There may well be people who support preferential treatment because they believe in equality of results for its own sake, because they believe in group rights, or because they want a society shaped around color and gender. But the federal judges of this country are certainly not among those people, and it is federal courts who for twenty years have created or sustained the various parts of affirmative action, including the occasional use of quotas and preferences. Why have they done this? By their own account, to *prevent* discrimination and *secure* equality of opportunity.

Reynolds says that using racial and sexual preferences to end discrimination is nonsense; the way to end discrimination is not to discriminate in reverse but simply *to stop discriminating*. Exactly—if we can. If we can stop discriminating. That's the rub. And that's the problem courts ran into.

CAN'T WE JUST STOP DISCRIMINATING?

It takes more than good will and good intentions not to discriminate. It takes capability as well, and that may be hard to come by. To see what I'm talking about, let's look back at a company like Kaiser after the Civil Rights Act of 1964 outlawed discrimination in employment. The company may have employed no blacks at all. The sign in the window said: "No blacks apply." Now, how does the company comply with the law and stop discriminating? It takes the sign out of the window and says, "If blacks apply and meet all requirements, we will hire them." And suppose it is sincere. Is that enough?

Look at how other aspects of company policy may work. Suppose the company only advertises its jobs by word of mouth. It posts job openings on the bulletin board and lets the grapevine do the rest. Then few blacks will ever hear of openings since all the workers are white—a fact reflecting, of course, the company's past discrimination. A company policy not itself designed to keep blacks out nevertheless does exactly that. Or suppose that the company requires each applicant to provide a letter of recommendation from some current or former employee. All the current and former employees are white, so this policy, too, is going to exclude blacks. Taking the sign out of the window changes nothing at all.

This is what courts encountered when they began adjudicating civil rights cases in the 1960s. Because the system of discrimination had been so thorough and in place for so long, it was like the child's spinning top, which keeps on spinning even after you take your hand away. Ordinary business practices let a firm's prior discrimination keep reproducing itself—and that reproduction, whether intended or not, is *itself* discrimination. So concluded a unanimous Supreme Court in the landmark 1971 case *Griggs v. Duke Power Company*. In order to comply with the law, businesses must look at all parts of their operations—job classifications, work rules, seniority systems, physical organization, recruitment and retention policies, everything—and revise, where possible, those elements that reproduce past discrimination. That's the core idea of affirmative action, as it was born in the early 1970s from the experience of courts trying to assure nondiscrimination and equal opportunity, and as extended through federal rules to all recipients of government contracts and funds.

Make a plan (these rules say) that establishes a system for monitoring your workplace and operations; that changes procedures and operations where you see they may have discriminatory impact, and that predicts what your work force would look like were you successfully nondiscriminating, so you will have some measure of the success or failure of your efforts.

Those are the basic elements of affirmative action. They are surely reasonable. Even William Bradford Reynolds accepted most of this. Why is there ever a need for more? Why is there ever a need actually to impose racial or gender quotas? Or to risk their being adopted by firms?

Because sometimes it takes strong measures for us to see how to do what it is needed to secure the reality of equal opportunity, not just its form. If we've built a whole world around discrimination, then many of the ways the world discriminates may not be visible to us even when we go blocking. We may not be able to see all the ways our business practices

exclude women and blacks from the workplace or detract from their performance there until the workplace is actually changed by having women and blacks in it. And one quick way of changing the composition of the workplace is through quotas.

Courts have sometimes—not often—resorted to quotas when they were convinced that an institution was simply not capable of identifying and changing all the features of its practices that discriminate. Often the quotas have been imposed on companies or municipal agencies whose own histories showed them completely unwilling to make anything but token changes. But sometimes they've been imposed where the sheer inertial weight of company culture and organization convinced the court that the company would never be able to find "qualified" minorities or women, no matter how hard it tried. The culture itself had to be changed by putting minorities and women in the roles from which they had been excluded.

Here is where the real issue lies. It is about the nature and sweep of discrimination. Do we think discrimination is a relatively *shallow* or a very *deep* phenomenon? Do we think discrimination is *transparent* or *opaque?* The answer need not be a flat yes or no. Perhaps in some places discrimination is shallow, in some places deep; in some circumstances transparent, in others opaque. If discrimination is shallow and transparent, then modest affirmative action should be enough to cure it: we look for, find, and eliminate practices that are reproducing the effects of past discrimination. But if discrimination is deep and opaque, then we may not be able to find it even when we look, and more robust forms of affirmative action may be necessary. We may need rather sharp assistance to *see* the way our practices work to exclude and oppress. We may need to be shocked or shaken out of our old habits, to have our consciousness raised.

This, I think, is the heart of the controversy about affirmative action. The difference is not that some people want equal opportunity and some want equality of results, that some believe in individual rights and some believe in group entitlements. The difference is that some think discrimination is always transparent and shallow while others think it is—sometimes, at least, in some sectors or institutions—deep, enduring, and opaque.

THE LAND OF THE GIANTS

To drive home this point about the opacity of discrimination and how it can subvert good will and good intentions, I ask you to go through some experiments with me. Start with a simple fantasy. Imagine we were suddenly all transported to the land of the Giants. They would be puzzled and wonder what in the world to make of us; and in short order they would probably conclude that, though we were like them in many ways, still we were quite incapable, incompetent, *inferior* creatures—for although we have our charming side, we really can't manage to do well even the simplest tasks in Giant Land. We just don't measure up. Perhaps it's just our nature to be helpless, the Giants conclude. We must have been some unfortunate quirk in God's creation.

But we would know that the problem does not lie in us, it lies in the fact that everything in Giant Land is built to the scale of Giants. That world is built for Giants and of course we don't do well in that world—but give us back the world built for us and see what we can do! We can even outperform Giants!

What's my point? It's that the Giants see *their* world as *the* world. They just naturally measure us against it, so they see the problem to be in *us*.

This is just fantasy, you say, and besides, the Giants wouldn't have been so dense. If you think not, then turn to a second example—a real one.

Twenty-five years ago, we tended to think that people in wheelchairs couldn't do much. It was a shame they were in wheelchairs—it wasn't their fault—but it meant that they were incapable of doing what most of the rest of us did. They were very limited in their mobility, thus not qualified for most jobs. And so they were excluded. Left out. Omitted.

Why did we think that? Not because we disliked people in wheelchairs. It was because, when they had trouble performing operations we do easily, we naturally attributed the trouble to *them*—to *their* condi-tion—because we just took the world as it was for granted. And how was that world? It was a world of *curbs*. Curbs everywhere.

Now, curbs are not supplied by nature. The world of curbs was made—made by and for us, the walking, running, jumping types. It took federal law that mandated tearing up the sidewalks at nearly every intersection in this country to jar us into realizing that many of the problems people in wheelchairs faced lay not in them but in the fact that *we* had *made* a world that excluded them, and then, like the Giants, had assumed *that* world was *the* world.

UNAVOIDABLE UNFAIRNESS

The world of Giants—the world of curbs—the world of whites and men: imagine, if you will, a world built over a long time by and for men, by and for whites. In that world there would be a thousand and one impediments to women and blacks working effectively and successfully. That world and its institutions would be suffused through and through with inhospitality to blacks and women—just as Giant Land was inhospitable to us little people, and Curb World was inhospitable to wheelchair people. Imagine that world—or do we have to imagine it? That's the world we still live in, isn't it?

Isn't it plausible that strong measures may be needed to change it? Are those strong measures, if they involve racial or gender preferences, unfair to white men? Of course they are. Well, doesn't that settle the matter? It would if we could always be fair without sometimes being unfair. Does that sound puzzling?

Think a moment. What are our options? Consider the civil rights bill George Bush vetoed, and threatens to veto again. If we set high burdens of proof on businesses, some of them may resort to quotas—and that's unfair discrimination. But if we don't set high standards, some businesses won't make the necessary effort to change practices that still hinder blacks and women—and *that's* unfair discrimination. Sometimes we may be faced *only* with the choice of risking unfairness in one direction or risking it in another. Sometimes we may have no choice except to impose one unfairness or allow another to persist. Then what do we do?

President Bush vetoed the civil rights bill because it created the risk of quotas. Does he believe, then, that vetoing it creates no risks that some blacks and women will continue to be discriminated against, or is the unspoken premise this: that the risk of victimization is tolerable if the victims are not white men?

The Case against Affirmative Action

LOUIS P. POJMAN

Hardly a week goes by but that the subject of Affirmative Action does not come up. Whether in the form of preferential hiring, nontraditional casting, quotas, "goals and time tables," minority scholarships, race-norming, reverse discrimination, or employment of members of underutilized groups, the issue confronts us as a terribly perplexing problem. Affirmative action was one of the issues that divided the Democratic and Republican parties during the 1996 election, the Democrats supporting it ("Mend it don't end it") and the Republicans opposing it ("affirmative action is reverse racism"). During the last general election (November 7, 1996) California voters by a 55% to 45% vote approved Proposition 209 (called the "California Civil Rights Initiative") which made it illegal to discriminate on the basis of race or gender, hence ending Affirmative Action in public institutions in California. The Supreme Court recently refused to rule on the appeal, thus leaving it to the individual states to decide how they will deal with this issue. Both sides have reorganized for a renewed battle. Meanwhile, on Nov. 11, 1977, the European Union's High Court of Justice in Luxembourg approved Affirmative Action programs giving women preferential treatment in the 15 European Union countries.

Let us agree that despite the evidences of a booming economy, the poor are suffering grievously, with children being born into desperate material and psychological poverty; for them the ideal of "equal opportunity for all" is a cruel joke. Many feel that the federal government has abandoned its guarantee to provide the minimum necessities for each American, so that the pace of this tragedy seems to be worsening daily. In addition to this, African-Americans have a legacy of slavery and unjust discrimination to contend with, and other minorities have also suffered from injustice. Women have their own peculiar history of being treated unequally in relevant ways. What is the answer to this national problem? Is it increased welfare? More job training? More support for education? Required licensing of parents to have children? Negative income tax? More support for families or for mothers with small children? All of these have merit and should be part of the national debate. But, my thesis is, however tragic the situation may be (and we may disagree on just how tragic it is), one policy is *not* a legitimate part of the solution and that is *reverse, unjust discrimination* against young white males. Strong Affirmative Action, which implicitly advocates reverse discrimination, while no doubt well intentioned, is morally heinous, asserting, by implication, that *two wrongs make a right.*

The *Two Wrongs Make a Right* Thesis goes like this: Because *some* Whites once enslaved some Blacks, the descendants of those slaves (some of whom may now enjoy high incomes and social status) have a right to opportunities and offices over better qualified Whites and who had nothing to do with either slavery or the oppression of Blacks (and who may even have suffered hardship comparable to that of poor Blacks). In addition, Strong Affirmative Action creates a new Hierarchy of the Oppressed: Blacks get primary preferential treatment, women second, Native Americans

Louis P. Pojman, "The Case against Affirmative Action," *International Journal of Applied Philosophy* 12, no. 1 (1998): 97–115 (edited). Reprinted with permission of the Philosophy Document Center.

third, Hispanics fourth, Handicapped fifth, and Asians sixth and so on until White males, no matter how needy or well qualified, must accept the leftovers. Naturally, combinations of oppressed classes (e.g., a one-eyed, Black Hispanic female) trump all single classifications. The equal protection clause of the Fourteenth Amendment becomes reinterpreted as "Equal protection for all equals, but some equals are more equal than others."

Before analyzing arguments concerning Affirmative Action, I must define my terms.

By *Weak Affirmative Action* I mean policies that will increase the opportunities of disadvantaged people to attain social goods and offices. It includes such things as dismantling of segregated institutions, widespread advertisement to groups not previously represented in certain privileged positions, special scholarships for the disadvantaged classes (e.g., the poor, regardless of race or gender), and even using diversity or under-representation of groups with a history of past discrimination as a tie breaker when candidates for these goods and offices are relatively equal. The goal of *Weak Affirmative Action* is equal opportunity to compete, not equal results. We seek to provide each citizen regardless of race or gender a fair chance to the most favored positions in society. There is no more moral requirement to guarantee that 12% of professors are Black than to guarantee that 85% of the players in the National Basketball Association are White.

By *Strong Affirmative Action* I mean preferential treatment on the basis of race, ethnicity or gender (or some other morally irrelevant criterion), discriminating in favor of underrepresented groups against overrepresented groups, aiming at roughly equal results. *Strong Affirmative Action* is *reverse discrimination*. It says it is right to do wrong to correct a wrong. This is the policy currently being promoted under the name of *Affirmative Action,* so I will use that term or "AA" for short throughout this essay to stand for this version of affirmative action. I will not argue for or against the principle of *Weak Affirmative Action*. Indeed, I think it has some moral weight. *Strong affirmative Action* has none, or so I will argue.

This essay concentrates on AA policies with regard to race, but the arguments can be extended to cover ethnicity and gender. I think that if a case for Affirmative Action can be made it will be as a corrective to racial oppression. I will examine [nine] arguments regarding AA. The first six will be *negative,* attempting to show that the best arguments for Affirmative Action fail. The last three will be *positive* arguments for policies opposing Affirmative Action.

I. A CRITIQUE OF ARGUMENTS FOR AFFIRMATIVE ACTION

A. The Need for Role Models

This argument is straightforward. We all have need of role models, and it helps to know that others like us can be successful. We learn and are encouraged to strive for excellence by emulating our heroes and "our kind of people" who have succeeded.

In the first place it's not clear that role models of one's own racial or sexual type are necessary (let alone sufficient) for success. One of my heroes was Gandhi, an Indian Hindu, another was my grade school science teacher, Miss DeVoe, and another Martin Luther King, behind whom I marched in Civil Rights demonstrations. More important than having role models of one's "own type" is having genuinely good people, of whatever race or gender, to emulate. Our common humanity should be a sufficient basis for us to see the possibility of success in people of virtue and merit. To yield to the demand, however tempting it may be, for "role-models-just-like-us" is to treat people like means not ends. It is to elevate morally irrelevant particularity over relevant traits, such as ability and integrity. We don't need people exactly like us to find inspiration. As Steve Allen once quipped, "If I had to follow a role model exactly, I would have become a nun."

Furthermore, even if it is of some help to people with low self-esteem to gain encouragement from seeing others of their particular kind in successful positions, it is doubtful whether this is a sufficient reason to justify preferential hiring or reverse discrimination. What good is a role model who is inferior to other professors or physicians or business personnel? The best way to create role models is to promote people because they are the best qualified for the job. It is the violation of this fact that is largely responsible for the widespread whisper in the medical field (at least in New York), "Never go to a Black physician under 40" (referring to the fact that AA has affected the medical system during the past twenty years). Fight the feeling how I will, I cannot help wondering on seeing a Black or woman in a position of honor, "Is she in this position because she merits it or because of Affirmative Action?" Where Affirmative Action is the policy, the "figment of pigment" creates a stigma of undeservedness, whether or not it is deserved.[1]

Finally, entertain this thought experiment. Suppose we discovered that tall handsome white males somehow made the best role models for the most people, especially poor people. Suppose even large numbers of minority people somehow found inspiration in their sight. Would we be justified in hiring tall handsome white males over better qualified short Hispanic women, who were deemed less role-model worthy?

B. The Compensation Argument

The argument goes like this: blacks have been wronged and severely harmed by whites. Therefore white society should compensate blacks for the injury caused them. Reverse discrimination in terms of preferential hiring, contracts, and scholarships is a fitting way to compensate for the past wrongs.

This argument actually involves a distorted notion of compensation. Normally, we think of compensation as owed by a specific person A to another person B whom A has wronged in a specific way C. For example, if I have stolen your car and used it for a period of time to make business profits that would have gone to you, it is not enough that I return your car. I must pay you an amount reflecting your loss and my ability to pay. If I have made $5,000 and only have $10,000 in assets, it would not be possible for you to collect $20,000 in damages—even though that is the amount of loss you have incurred.

Sometimes compensation is extended to groups of people who have been unjustly harmed by the greater society. For example, the United States government has compensated the Japanese-Americans who were interred during the Second World War, and the West German government has paid reparations to the survivors of Nazi concentration camps. But here a specific people have been identified who were wronged in an identifiable way by the government of the nation in question.

On the face of it, demands by blacks for compensation do not fit the usual pattern. Southern States with Jim Crow laws could be accused of unjustly harming blacks, but it is hard to see that the United States government was involved in doing so. Much of the harm done to blacks was the result of private discrimination, not state action. So the Germany/US analogy doesn't hold. Furthermore, it is not clear that all blacks were harmed in the same way or whether some were *unjustly* harmed or harmed more than poor whites and others (e.g., short people). Finally, even if identifiable blacks were harmed by identifiable social practices, it is not clear that most forms of Affirmative Action are appropriate to restore the situation. The usual practice of a financial payment seems more appropriate than giving a high level job to someone unqualified or only minimally qualified, who, speculatively, might have been better qualified had he not been subject to racial discrimination. If John is the star tailback of our college team with a promising professional future, and I accidentally (but culpably) drive my pickup truck over his legs, and so cripple him, John may be due compensation, but he is not due the tailback spot on the football team.

Still, there may be something intuitively compelling about compensating members of an oppressed group who are minimally qualified. Suppose that the Hatfields and the McCoys are enemy clans and some youths from the Hatfields go over and steal diamonds and gold from the McCoys, distributing it within the Hatfield economy. Even though we do not know which Hatfield youths did the stealing, we would want to restore the wealth, as far as possible, to the

McCoys. One way might be to tax the Hatfields, but another might be to give preferential treatment in terms of scholarships and training programs and hiring to the McCoys.

This is perhaps the strongest argument for Affirmative Action, and it may well justify some weaker versions of AA, but it is doubtful whether it is sufficient to justify strong versions with quotas and goals and time tables in skilled positions. There are at least two reasons for this. First, we have no way of knowing how many people of any given group would have achieved some given level of competence had the world been different. This is especially relevant if my objections to the Equal Results Argument (below) are correct. Secondly, the normal criterion of competence is a strong prima facie consideration when the most important positions are at stake. There are three reasons for this: (1) treating people according to their merits respects them as persons, as ends in themselves, rather than as means to social ends (if we believe that individuals possess a dignity which deserves to be respected, then we ought to treat that individual on the basis of his or her merits, not as a mere instrument for social policy); (2) society has given people expectations that if they attain certain levels of excellence they will be awarded appropriately; and (3) filling the most important positions with the best qualified is the best way to ensure efficiency in job-related areas and in society in general. These reasons are not absolutes. They can be overridden.[2] But there is a strong presumption in their favor, so that a burden of proof rests with those who would override them.

At this point we get into the problem of whether innocent non-blacks should have to pay a penalty in terms of preferential hiring of blacks. We turn to that argument.

C. The Argument for Compensation from Those Who Innocently Benefitted from Past Injustice

Young White males as innocent beneficiaries of unjust discrimination against blacks and women have no grounds for complaint when society seeks to level the tilted field. They may be innocent of oppressing blacks, other minorities, and women, but they have unjustly benefitted from that oppression or discrimination. So it is perfectly proper that less qualified women and blacks be hired before them.

The operative principle is: He who knowingly and willingly benefits from a wrong must help pay for the wrong. Judith Jarvis Thomson puts it this way. "Many [white males] have been direct beneficiaries of policies which have downgraded blacks and women . . . and even those who did not directly benefit . . . had, at any rate, the advantage in the competition which comes of the confidence in one's full membership [in the community], and of one's right being recognized as a matter of course."[3] That is, white males obtain advantages in self respect and self-confidence deriving from a racist/sexist system which denies these to blacks and women.

Here is my response to this argument: As I noted in the previous section, compensation is normally individual and specific. If A harms B regarding x, B has a right to compensation from A in regards to x. If A steals B's car and wrecks it, A has an obligation to compensate B for the stolen car, but A's son has no obligation to compensate B. Furthermore, if A dies or disappears, B has no moral right to claim that society compensate him for the stolen car—though if he has insurance, he can make such a claim to the insurance company. Sometimes a wrong cannot be compensated, and we just have to make the best of an imperfect world.

Suppose my parents, divining that I would grow up to have an unsurpassable desire to be a basketball player, bought an expensive growth hormone for me. Unfortunately, a neighbor stole it and gave it to little Michael, who gained the extra 13 inches—my 13 inches—and shot up to an enviable 6 feet 6 inches. Michael, better known as Michael Jordan, would have been a runt like me but for his luck. As it is he profited from the injustice, and excelled in basketball, as I would have done had I had my proper dose.

Do I have a right to the millions of dollars that Jordan made as a professional basketball player—the unjustly innocent beneficiary of my growth hormone? I have a right to something from the neighbor who stole the hormone and it might be kind of Jordan to give me free tickets to the Bull's basketball games, and remember me in his will. As far as I can see, however, he does not *owe* me anything, either legally or morally.

Suppose further that Michael Jordan and I are in high school together and we are both qualified to play basketball, only he is far better than I. Do I deserve to start in his position because I would have been as good as he is had someone not cheated me as a child? Again, I think not. But if being the lucky beneficiary of wrongdoing does not entail that Jordan (or the coach) owes me anything in regards to basketball, why should it be a reason to engage in preferential hiring in academic positions or highly coveted jobs? If minimal qualifications are not adequate to override excellence in basketball, even when the minimality is a consequence of wrongdoing, why should they be adequate in other areas?

D. The Diversity Argument

It is important that we learn to live in a pluralistic world, learning to get along with those of other races, conditions, and cultures, so we should have schools and employment situations as fully integrated as possible. In a shrinking world we need to appreciate each other's culture and specific way of looking at life. Diversity is an important symbol and educative device. Thus, proponents of AA argue, preferential treatment is warranted to perform this role in society.

Once again, there is some truth in these concerns. Diversity of ideas challenges us to scrutinize our own values and beliefs, and diverse customs have aesthetic and moral value, helping us to appreciate the novelty and beauty in life. Diversity may expand our moral horizons. But, again, while we can admit the value of diversity, it hardly seems adequate to override the moral requirement to treat each person with equal respect. *Diversity for diversity's sake is moral promiscuity,* since it obfuscates rational distinctions, undermines treating individuals as ends, treating them, instead as mere means (to the goals of social engineering), and, furthermore, unless those hired are

highly qualified, the diversity factor threatens to become a fetish. At least at the higher levels of business and the professions, *competence* far outweighs considerations of diversity. I do not care whether the group of surgeons operating on me reflect racial or gender balance, but I do care that they are highly qualified. Neither do most football or basketball fans care whether their team reflects ethnic and gender diversity, but demand the best combination of players available. And likewise with airplane pilots, military leaders, business executives, and, may I say it, teachers and university professors. One need not be a white male to teach, let alone, appreciate Shakespeare, nor need one be Black to teach, let alone appreciate, Alice Walker's *Color Purple.*

There may be times when diversity may seem to be "crucial" to the well-being of a diverse community, such as for a police force. Suppose that White policemen tend to overreact to young Black males and the latter group distrust White policemen. Hiring more less qualified Black policemen, who would relate better to these youth, may have overall utilitarian value. But such a move, while we might take it as a lesser evil, could have serious consequences in allowing the demographic prejudices to dictate social policy. A better strategy would be to hire the best police, that is, those who can perform in disciplined, intelligent manner, regardless of their race. A White policeman must be able to arrest a Black burglar, even as a Black policeman must be able to arrest a White rapist. The quality of the police man or woman, not their race or gender is what counts.

On the other hand, if a Black policeman, though lacking some of the formal skills of the White policeman, really is able to do a better job in the Black community, this might constitute a case of merit, not Affirmative Action. As Stephen Kershnar points out, this is similar to the legitimacy of hiring Chinese men to act as undercover agents in Chinatown.[4]

E. The Equal Results Argument

Some philosophers and social scientists hold that human nature is roughly identical, so that on a fair playing field the same proportion from every race and ethnic group and both genders would attain to the highest positions in every area of endeavor. It would follow that any inequality of results itself is evidence for inequality of opportunity.

History is important when considering governmental rules like Test 21 because low scores by blacks can be traced in large measure to the legacy of slavery and racism: segregation, poor schooling, exclusion from trade unions, malnutrition, and poverty have all played their roles. Unless one assumes that blacks are naturally less able to pass the test, the conclusion must be that the results are themselves socially and legally constructed, not a mere given for which law and society can claim no responsibility.

The conclusion seems to be that genuine equality eventually requires equal results. Obviously blacks have been treated unequally throughout US history, and just as obviously the economic and psychological effects of that inequality linger to this day, showing up in lower income and poorer performance in school and on tests than whites achieve. Since we have no reason to believe that differences in performance can be explained by factors other than history, equal results are a good benchmark by which to measure progress made toward genuine equality. (John Arthur, *The Unfinished Constitution* [Belmont, CA: Wadsworth Publishing Co, 1990], p. 238)

Sterling Harwood seems to support a similar theory when he writes, "When will [AA] end? When will affirmative action stop compensating blacks? As soon as the unfair advantage is gone, affirmative action will stop. The elimination of the unfair advantage can be determined by showing that the percentage of blacks hired and admitted at least roughly equaled the percentage of blacks in the population."[5]

Albert G. Mosley develops a similar argument. "Establishing Blacks' presence at a level commensurate with their proportion in the relevant labor market need not be seen as an attempt to actualize some valid prediction. Rather, given the impossibility of determining what level of representation Blacks would have achieved were it not for racial discrimination, the assumption of proportional representation is the only *fair* assumption to make. This is not

to argue that Blacks should be maintained in such positions, but their contrived exclusion merits equally contrived rectification."[6] The result of a just society should be equal numbers in proportion to each group in the work force.

However, Arthur, Mosley, and Harwood fail even to consider studies that suggest that there are innate differences between races, sexes, and groups. If there are genetic differences in intelligence, temperament, and other qualities within families, why should we not expect such differences between racial groups and the two genders? Why should the evidence for this be completely discounted?

Mosley's reasoning is as follows: Since we don't know for certain whether groups proportionately differ in talent, we should presume that they are equal in every respect. So we should presume that if we were living in a just society, there would be roughly proportionate representation in every field (e.g., equal representation of dotors, lawyers, professors, carpenters, airplane pilots, basketball players, and criminals). Hence, it is only fair—productive of justice—to aim at proportionate representation in these fields.

But the logic is flawed. Under a situation of ignorance we should not presume equality or inequality of representation—but conclude that we *don't know* what the results would be in a just society. Ignorance doesn't favor equal group representation any more than it favors unequal group representation. It is neutral between them.

Consider this analogy. Suppose that you were the owner of a National Basketball Association team. Suppose that I and other frustrated White basketball players bring a class-action suit against you and all the other team owners, claiming that you have subtly and systematically discriminated against White and Asian basketball players who make up less than 20% of the NBA players. You reply that you and the other owners are just responding to individual merit, we respond that the discrimination is a function of deep prejudice against White athletes, especially basketball players, who are discouraged in every way from competing on fair terms with Blacks who dominate the

NBA. You would probably wish that the matter of unequal results was not brought up in the first place, but once it has been, would you not be in your rights to defend yourself by producing evidence, showing that *average* physiological differences exist between Blacks and Whites and Asians, so that we should not presume unjust discrimination?

Similarly, the proponents of the Doctrine of Equal Results open the door to a debate over average ability in ethnic, racial and gender groups. The proponent of equal or fair opportunity would just as soon downplay this feature in favor of judging people as individuals by their merit (hard though that may be). But if the proponent of AA insists on the Equal Results Thesis, we are obliged to examine the Equal Abilities Thesis, on which it is based—the thesis that various ethnic and gender groups all have the same distribution of talent on the relevant characteristic. With regard to cognitive skills we must consult the best evidence we have on average group differences. We need to compare average IQ scores, SAT scores, standard personality testing, success in academic and professional areas and the like. If the evidence shows that group differences are nonexistent, the AA proponent may win, but if the evidence turns out to be against the Equal Abilities Thesis, the AA proponent loses. Consider for a start that the average white and Asian scores 195 points higher on the SAT tests and that on virtually all IQ tests for the past seven or eight decades the average Black IQ is 85 as opposed to the average White and Asian IQ at over 100, or that males and females differ significantly on cognitive ability tests. Females outperform males in reading comprehension, perceptual speed, and associative memory (ratios of 1.4 to 2.2), but males typically outnumber females among high scoring individuals in mathematics, science and social science (by a ratio of 7.0 in the top 1% of overall mathematics distribution).[7] The results of average GRE, LSAT, MCAT scores show similar patterns or significant average racial difference. The Black scholar Glenn Loury notes, "In 1990 black high school seniors from families with annual incomes of $70,000 or more scored an average of 855 on the SAT, compared with average scores of 855 and 879 respectively for Asian-American and white seniors whose families had incomes between $10,000 and 20,000 per year."[8] Note, we are speaking about statistical averages. There are brilliant and retarded people in each group.

When such statistics are discussed many people feel uncomfortable and want to drop the subject. Perhaps these statistics are misleading, but then we need to look carefully at the total evidence. The proponent of equal opportunity urges us to get beyond racial and gender criteria in assignment of offices and opportunities and treat each person, not as an *average* white or Black or female or male, but as a *person* judged on his or her own merits.

Furthermore, on the logic of Mosley and company, we should take aggressive AA against Asians and Jews since they are overrepresented in science, technology, and medicine, and we should presume that Asians and Jews are no more talented than average. So that each group receives its fair share, we should ensure that 12% of the philosophers in the United States are Black, reduce the percentage of Jews from an estimated 15% to 2%—thus firing about 1,300 Jewish philosophers. The fact that Asians are producing 50% of Ph.D.s in science and math in this country and blacks less than 1% clearly shows, on this reasoning, that we are providing special secret advantages to Asians. By this logic, we should reduce the quota of Blacks in the NBA to 12%.

But why does society have to enter into this results game in the first place? Why do we have to decide whether all difference is environmental or genetic? Perhaps we should simply admit that we lack sufficient evidence to pronounce on these issues with any certainty—but if so, should we not be more modest in insisting on equal results? Here's a thought experiment. Take two families of different racial groups, Green and Blue. The Greens decide to have only two children, to spend all their resources on them, and to give them the best possible education. The two Green kids respond well and end up with achievement test scores in the 99th percentile. The Blues fail to practice family planning and have 15 children. They can only afford 2 children, but lack of ability or whatever prevents them from keeping their family size down. Now they need help for their large family. Why does society have to step in and help them? Society did not force them to have 15 children. Suppose that the achievement test scores of the 15 children fall below the 25th percentile. They cannot compete with the Greens. But now enters AA. It says that it is society's fault that the Blue children are not as able as the Greens and that the Greens must pay extra taxes to enable the Blues to compete. No restraints are put on the Blues regarding family size. This seems unfair to the Greens. Should the Green children be made to bear responsibility for the consequences of the Blues' voluntary behavior?

My point is simply that philosophers like Arthur, Harwood, and Mosley need to cast their net wider and recognize that demographics and childbearing and -rearing practices are crucial factors in achievement. People have to take some responsibility for their actions. The equal results argument (or axiom) misses a greater part of the picture.

F. The "No One Deserves His Talents" Argument Against Meritocracy

According to this argument, the competent do not deserve their intelligence, their superior character, their industriousness, or their discipline; therefore they have no right to the best positions in society; therefore it is not unjust to give these positions to less (but still minimally) qualified blacks and women. In one form this argument holds that since no one deserves anything, society may use any criteria it pleases to distribute goods. The criterion most often designated is social utility. Versions of this argument are found in the writings of John Arthur, John Rawls, Bernard Boxill, Michael Kinsley, Ronald Dworkin, and Richard Wasserstrom. Rawls writes, "No one deserves his place in the distribution of native endowments, any more than one deserves one's initial starting place in society. The assertion that a man deserves the superior character that enables him to make the effort to cultivate his abilities is equally problematic; for his character depends in large part upon fortunate family and social circumstances for which he can claim no credit. The notion of desert seems not

to apply to these cases."[9] Michael Kinsley is even more adamant.

Opponents of affirmative action are hung up on a distinction that seems more profoundly irrelevant: treating individuals versus treating groups. What is the moral difference between dispensing favors to people on their "merits" as individuals and passing out society's benefits on the basis of group identification?

Group identifications like race and sex are, of course, immutable. They have nothing to do with a person's moral worth. But the same is true of most of what comes under the label "merit." The tools you need for getting ahead in a meritocratic society—not all of them but most: talent, education, instilled cultural values such as ambition—are distributed just as arbitrarily as skin color. They are fate. The notion that people somehow "deserve" the advantages of these characteristics in a way they don't "deserve" the advantage of their race is powerful, but illogical.[10]

It will help to put the argument in outline form.

1. Society may award jobs and positions as it sees fit as long as individuals have no claim to these positions.
2. To have a claim to something means that one has earned it or deserves it.
3. But no one has earned or deserves his intelligence, talent, education or cultural values which produce superior qualifications.
4. If a person does not deserve what produces something, he does not deserve its products.
5. Therefore better qualified people do not deserve their qualifications.
6. Therefore, society may override their qualifications in awarding jobs and positions as it sees fit (for social utility or to compensate for previous wrongs).

So it is permissible if a minimally qualified black or woman is admitted to law or medical school ahead of a white male with excellent credentials or if a less qualified person from an "underutilized" group gets a professorship ahead of an eminently better qualified white male. Sufficiency and underutilization together outweigh excellence.

My response: Premise 4 is false. To see this, reflect that just because I do not deserve the money that I have been given as a gift (for instance) does not mean that I am not entitled to what I get with that money. If you and I both get a gift of $100 and I bury mine in the sand for 5 years while you invest yours wisely and double its value at the end of five years, I cannot complain that you should split the increase 50/50 since neither of us deserved the original gift. If we accept the notion of responsibility at all, we must hold that persons deserve the fruits of their labor and conscious choices. Of course, we might want to distinguish moral from legal desert and argue that, morally speaking, effort is more important than outcome, whereas, legally speaking, outcome may be more important. Nevertheless, there are good reasons in terms of efficiency, motivation, and rough justice for holding a strong prima facie principle of giving scarce high positions to those most competent.

The attack on moral desert is perhaps the most radical move that egalitarians like Rawls and company have made against meritocracy, and the ramifications of their attack are far reaching. Here are some implications: Since I do not deserve my two good eyes or two good kidneys, the social engineers may take one of each from me to give to those needing an eye or a kidney—even if they have damaged their organs by their own voluntary actions. Since no one deserves anything, we do not deserve pay for our labors or praise for a job well done or first prize in the race we win. The notion of moral responsibility vanishes in a system of levelling.

But there is no good reason to accept the argument against desert. We do act freely and, as such, we are responsible for our actions. We deserve the fruits of our labor, reward for our noble feats and punishment for our misbehavior.

We have considered six arguments for Affirmative Action and have found no compelling case for Strong AA and only one plausible argument (a version of the compensation argument) for Weak AA. We must now turn to the arguments against Affirmative Action to see whether they fare any better.

II. ARGUMENTS AGAINST AFFIRMATIVE ACTION

A. Affirmative Action Requires Discrimination Against a Different Group

Weak AA weakly discriminates against new minorities, mostly innocent young white males, and Strong Affirmative Action strongly discriminates against these new minorities. As I argued in I. C, this discrimination is unwarranted, since, even if some compensation to blacks were indicated, it would be unfair to make innocent white males bear the whole brunt of the payments. Recently I had this experience. I knew a brilliant philosopher, with outstanding publications in first level journals, who was having difficulty getting a tenure-track position. For the first time in my life I offered to make a phone call on his behalf to a university to which he had applied. When I got the Chair of the Search Committee, he offered that the committee was under instructions from the Administration to hire a woman or a Black. They had one of each on their short-list, so they weren't even considering the applications of White males. At my urging he retrieved my friend's file, and said, "This fellow looks far superior to the two candidates we're interviewing, but there's nothing I can do about it." Cases like this come to my attention regularly. In fact, it is poor white youth who become the new pariahs on the job market. The children of the wealthy have little trouble getting into the best private grammar schools and, on the basis of superior early education, into the best universities, graduate schools, managerial and professional positions. Affirmative Action simply shifts injustice, setting Blacks, Hispanics, Native Americans, Asians and women against young white males, especially ethnic and poor white males. It makes no more sense to discriminate in favor of a rich Black or female who had the opportunity of the best family and education available against a poor White, than it does to discriminate in favor of White males against Blacks or women. It does little to rectify the goal of providing equal opportunity to all.

At the end of his essay supporting Affirmative Action, Albert Mosley points out that other groups besides Blacks have been benefitted by AA, "women, the disabled, the elderly."[11] He's correct in including the elderly, for through powerful lobbies, such as the AARP, they do get special benefits, including medicare, and may sue on the grounds of being discriminated against due to *Agism*, prejudice against older people. Might this not be a reason to reconsider Affirmative Action? Consider the sheer rough percentages of those who qualify for AA programs.

GROUP	PERCENTAGE in Population
1. Women	52%
2. Blacks	12%
3. Hispanics	9%
4. Native Americans	2%
5. Asians	4%
6. Physically & Mentally Disabled	10%
7. Welfare recipients	6%
8. The Elderly	25% (est. Adults over 60)
9. Italians (in New York City)	3%
Totals	123%

The elderly can sue on the grounds of Agism, receive entitlements in terms of Social Security and Medicare, and have the AARP lobbying on their behalf. Recently, it has been proposed that homosexuals be included in oppressed groups deserving Affirmative Action. At Northeastern University in 1996 the faculty governing body voted to grant homosexuals Affirmative Action status at this university. How many more percentage points would this add? Several authors have advocated putting all poor people on the list. And if we took handicaps seriously would we not add ugly people, obese people, and, especially, short people, for which there is ample evidence of discrimination? How about left-handed people (about 9% of the population)—they can't play shortstop or third base and have to put up with a right-handedly biased world. The only group not the list is that of White males. Are they, especially healthy, middle class young White males, becoming the new "oppressed class"? Should we add them to our list?

Respect for persons entails that we treat each person as an end in him or herself, not simply as a means to be used for social purposes. What is wrong about discrimination against Blacks is that it fails to treat Black people as individuals, judging them instead by their skin color not their merit. What is wrong about discrimination against women is that it fails to treat them as individuals, judging them by their gender, not their merit. What is equally wrong about *Affirmative Action* is that it fails to treat White males with dignity as individuals, judging them by *both their race and gender,* instead of their merit. *Current Strong Affirmative Action is both racist and sexist.*

B. Affirmative Action Encourages Mediocrity and Incompetence

A few years ago Rev. Jesse Jackson joined protesters at Harvard Law School in demanding that the Law School faculty hire black women. Jackson dismissed Dean of the Law School, Robert C. Clark's standard of choosing the best qualified person for the job as "Cultural anemia." "We cannot just define who is qualified in the most narrow vertical academic terms," he said. "Most people in the world are yellow, brown, black, poor, non-Christian and don't speak English, and they can't wait for some white males with archaic rules to appraise them."[12] It might be noted that if Jackson is correct about the depth of cultural decadence at Harvard, blacks might be well advised to form and support their own more vital law schools and leave places like Harvard to their archaism.

At several universities, the administration has forced departments to hire members of minorities even when far superior candidates were available. Shortly after obtaining my PhD in the late 70s I was mistakenly identified as a black philosopher (I had a civil rights record and was once a black studies major) and was flown to a major university, only to be rejected for a more qualified candidate when it discovered that I was white.

Stories of the bad effects of Affirmative Action abound. The philosopher Sidney Hook writes that "At one Ivy League university, representatives of the Regional HEW[13] demanded an explanation of why there were no women or minority students in the Graduate Department of Religious Studies. They were told that a reading of knowledge of Hebrew and Greek was presupposed. Whereupon the representatives of HEW advised orally: 'Then end those old fashioned programs that require irrelevant languages. And start up programs on relevant things which minority group students can study without learning languages.' "[14]

Nicholas Capaldi notes that the staff of HEW itself was one-half women, three-fifths members of minorities, and one-half black—a clear case of racial over representation.

In 1972 officials at Stanford University discovered a proposal for the government to monitor curriculum in higher education: the "Summary Statement . . . Sex Discrimination Proposed HEW Regulation to Effectuate Title IX of the Education Amendment of 1972" to "establish and use internal procedure for reviewing curricula, designed both to ensure that they do not reflect discrimination on the basis of sex and to resolve complaints concerning allegations of such discrimination, pursuant to procedural standards to be prescribed by the Director of the office of Civil Rights." Fortunately, Secretary of HEW Caspar Weinberger discovered the intrusion and assured Stanford University that he would never approve of it.

Government programs of enforced preferential treatment tend to appeal to the lowest possible common denominator. Witness the 1974 HEW Revised Order No. 14 on Affirmative Action expectations for preferential hiring: "Neither minorities nor female employees should be required to possess higher qualifications than those of the lowest qualified incumbents."

Furthermore, no test may be given to candidates unless it is *proved* to be relevant to the job.

No standard or criteria which have, by intent or effect, worked to exclude women or minorities as a class can be utilized, unless the institution can demonstrate the necessity of such standard to the performance of the job in question.

Whenever a validity study is called for . . . the user should include . . . an investigation of suitable alternative selection procedures and suitable alternative methods of using the selection procedure which have as little adverse impact as possible. . . . Whenever the user is shown an alternative selection procedure with evidence of less adverse impact and substantial evidence of validity for the same job in similar circumstances, the user should investigate it to determine the appropriateness of using or validating it in accord with these guidelines.[15]

At the same time Americans are wondering why standards in our country are falling and the Japanese and Koreans are getting ahead. Affirmative Action with its twin idols, Sufficiency of Qualification and Diversity, is the enemy of excellence. I will develop this thought in the next section.

C. An Argument from the Principle of Merit

Traditionally, we have believed that the highest positions in society should be awarded to those who are best qualified. The Koran states that "A ruler who appoints any man to an office, when there is in his dominion another man better qualified for it, sins against God and against the State." Rewarding excellence both seems just to the individuals in the competition and makes for efficiency. Note that one of the most successful acts of racial integration, the Brooklyn Dodger's recruitment of Jackie Robinson in the late 40s, was done in just this way, according to merit. If Robinson had been brought into the major league as a mediocre player or had batted .200 he would have been scorned and sent back to the minors where he belonged.

As mentioned earlier, merit is not an absolute value, but there are strong *prima facie* reasons for awarding positions on that basis, and it should enjoy a weighty presumption in our social practices.

In a celebrated article Ronald Dworkin says that "Bakke had no case" because society did not owe Bakke anything. That may be, but then why does it owe anyone anything? Dworkin puts the matter in Utility terms, but if that is the case, society may owe Bakke a place at the University of California/Davis, for it seems a reasonable rule-utilitarian principle that achievement should be awarded in society. We generally want the best to have the best positions, the best qualified candidate to win the political office, the most brilliant and competent scientist to be chosen for the most challenging research project, the best qualified pilots to become commercial pilots, only the best soldiers to become generals. Only when little is at stake do we weaken the standards and content ourselves with sufficiency (rather than excellence)—there are plenty of jobs where "sufficiency" rather than excellence is required. Perhaps we have even come to feel that medicine or law or university professorships are so routine that they can be performed by minimally qualified people—in which case AA has a place.

Note! no one is calling for quotas or proportional representation of *underutilized* groups in the National Basketball Association where blacks make up 80% of the players. But, surely, if merit and merit alone reigns in sports, should it not be valued at least as much in education and industry?

The case for meritocracy has two pillars. One pillar is a deontological argument which holds that we ought to treat people as ends and not merely means. By giving people what they deserve as *individuals,* rather than as members of *groups* we show respect for their inherent worth. If you and I take a test, and you get 95% of the answers correct, and I only get 50% correct, it would be unfair to you for both of us to receive the same grade, say an A, and even more unfair to give me a higher grade A+ than your B+. Although I have heard cases where teachers have been instructed to "race norm" in grading (giving Blacks and Hispanics higher grades for the same numerical scores), most proponents of AA stop short of advocating such a practice. But, I would ask them, what's really the difference between taking the overall average of a White and a Black and "race norming" it? If teachers shouldn't do it, why should administrators?

The second pillar for meritocracy is utilitarian. In the end, we will be better off by honoring excellence. We want the best leaders, teachers, policemen, physicians, generals, lawyers, and airplane pilots that we can possibly produce in society. So our program should be to promote equal opportunity, as much as is feasible in a free market economy, and reward people according to their individual merit.

CONCLUSION

Let me sum up my discussion. The goal of the Civil Rights movement and of moral people everywhere has been justice for all, including equal opportunity. The question is: how best to get there. Civil Rights legislation removed the unjust legal barriers, opening the way towards equal opportunity, but it did not tackle the deeper causes that produce differential results. Weak Affirmative Action aims at encouraging minorities to strive for excellence in all areas of life, without unduly jeopardizing the rights of majorities. The problem of Weak Affirmative Action is that it easily slides into Strong Affirmative Action where quotas, goals and timetables," "equal results"—in a word—*reverse discrimination*—prevail and are forced onto groups, thus promoting mediocrity, inefficiency, and resentment. Furthermore, AA aims at the higher levels of society-universities and skilled jobs, but if we want to improve our society, the best way to do it is to concentrate on families, children, early education, and the like, so all are prepared to avail themselves of opportunity. Affirmative Action, on the one hand, is too much, too soon and on the other hand, too little, too late.

In addition to the arguments I have offered, Affirmative Action, rather than unite people of good will in the common cause of justice, tends to balkanize us into segregation-thinking. Professor Derrick Bell of Harvard Law School recently said that the African American Supreme Court Judge Clarence Thomas, in his opposition to Affirmative Action "doesn't think black." Does Bell really claim that there is a standard and proper "Black" (and presumably a White) way of thinking? Ideologues like Bell, whether radical Blacks like himself, or Nazis who advocate "think Aryan," both represent the same thing: cynicism about rational debate, the very antithesis of the quest for impartial truth and justice. People who believe in reason to resolve our differences will oppose this kind of balkanization of the races.

Martin Luther said that humanity is like a man mounting a horse who always tends to fall off on the other side of the horse. This seems to be the case with Affirmative Action. Attempting to redress the discriminatory iniquities of our history, our well-intentioned social engineers now engage in new forms of discriminatory iniquity and thereby think that they have successfully mounted the horse of racial harmony. They have only fallen off on the other side of the issue.

NOTES

1. This argument is related to *The Need of Breaking Stereotypes Argument.* Society may simply need to know that there are talented Blacks and women, so that it does not automatically assign them lesser respect or status. The right response is that hiring less qualified people is neither fair to those better qualified who are passed over nor an effective way to remove inaccurate stereotypes. If high competence is accepted as the criterion for hiring, then it is unjust to override it for purposes of social engineering. Furthermore, if Blacks and women are known to hold high positions simply because of reverse discrimination, they will still lack the respect due to those of their rank.

2. Merit sometimes may be justifiably overridden by need, as when parents choose to spend extra earnings on special education for their disabled child rather than for their gifted child. Sometimes we may override merit for utilitarian purposes. E.g., suppose you are the best short stop on a baseball team but are also the best catcher. You'd rather play short stop, but the manager decides to put you at catcher because, while your friend can do an adequate job at short, no one else is adequate at catcher. It's permissible for you to be assigned the job of catcher. Probably, some expression of appreciation would be due you.

3. Judith Jarvis Thomson, "Preferential Hiring," in Marshall Cohen, Thomas Nagel and Thomas Scanlon, eds., *Equality and Preferential Treatment* (Princeton: Princeton University Press, 1977).

4. Stephen Kershnar pointed this out in written comments (December 22, 1997).

5. Sterling Harwood, "The Justice of affirmative Action," in Yearger Hudson and C. Peden, eds., *The Bill of Rights: Bicentennial Reflections* (Lewiston, NY: Edwin Mellen).

6. Albert G. Mosley in his and Nicholas Capaldi's *Affirmative Action: Social Justice or Unfair Preference?* (Rowman and Littlefield, 1996), p. 28.

7. Larry Hedges and Amy Nowell, "Sex Differences in Mental Test Scores, Variability, and Numbers of High-Scoring Individuals," *Science* 269 (July 1995), pp. 41–45.

8. Glen Loury, " 'Getting Involved': An Appeal for Greater Community Participation in the Public Schools," *Washington Post Education Review* (August 6, 1995).

9. John Rawls, *A Theory of Justice* (Harvard University Press, 1971), p. 104.

10. Michael Kinsley, "Equal Lack of Opportunity," *Harper's* (June 1983).

11. Albert Mosley, op. cit., p. 53.

12. *New York Times,* May 10, 1990.

13. HEW stands for the Federal Department of "Health, Education & Welfare."

14. Quoted by Nicholas Capaldi, *Out of Order: Affirmative Action and the Crisis of Doctrinaire Liberalism* (Buffalo, NY: Prometheus, 1985).

15. Capaldi, op. cit., p. 95

Ten Myths about Affirmative Action

Scott Plous

In recent years, affirmative action has been debated more intensely than at any other time in its 35-year history. Many supporters view affirmative action as a milestone, many opponents see it as a

Scott Plous, "Ten Myths about Affirmative Action," *Understanding Prejudice and Discrimination,* ed. S. Plous (New York: McGraw-Hill, 2003), 206–11 (edited). Reprinted with permission of Scott Plous (understandingprejudice.org).

millstone, and many others regard it as both or neither—as a necessary, but imperfect, remedy for an intractable social disease. My own view is that the case against affirmative action is weak, resting, as it does so heavily, on myth and misunderstanding. Here are some of the most popular myths about affirmative action, along with a brief commentary on each one.

Myth 1: The only way to create a color-blind society is to adopt color-blind policies. Although this statement sounds intuitively plausible, the reality is that color-blind policies often put racial minorities at a disadvantage. For instance, all else being equal, color-blind seniority systems tend to protect White workers against job layoffs, because senior employees are usually White. Likewise, color-blind college admissions favor White students because of their earlier educational advantages. Unless preexisting inequities are corrected or otherwise taken into account, color-blind policies do not correct racial injustice—they reinforce it.

Myth 2: Affirmative action has not succeeded in increasing female and minority representation. Several studies have documented important gains in racial and gender equality as a direct result of affirmative action. For example, according to a report from the U.S. Labor Department, affirmative action has helped 5 million minority members and 6 million White and minority women move up in the workforce. Likewise, a study sponsored by the Office of Federal Contract Compliance Programs showed that between 1974 and 1980 federal contractors (who were required to adopt affirmative action goals) added Black and female officials and managers at twice the rate of noncontractors. There have also been a number of well-publicized cases in which large companies (e.g., AT&T, IBM, Sears Roebuck) increased minority employment as a result of adopting affirmative action policies.

Myth 3: Affirmative action may have been necessary 30 years ago, but the playing field is fairly level today. Despite the progress that has been made, the playing field is far from level. Women continue to earn 76 cents for every male dollar. Black people continue to have twice the unemployment rate of White people, twice the rate of infant mortality, and just over half the proportion of people who attend four years or more of college. In fact, without affirmative action the percentage of Black students at many selective schools would drop to only 2% of the student body. This would effectively choke off Black access to top universities and severely restrict progress toward racial equality.

Myth 4: The public doesn't support affirmative action anymore. Public opinion polls suggest that the majority of Americans support affirmative action, especially when the polls avoid an all-or-none choice between affirmative action as it currently exists and no affirmative action whatsoever. For example, a *Time*/CNN poll found that 80% of the public felt "affirmative action programs for minorities and women should be continued at some level." What the public opposes are quotas, set-asides, and "reverse discrimination." For instance, when the same poll asked people whether they favored programs "requiring businesses to hire a specific number or quota of minorities and women," 63% opposed such a plan. As these results indicate, most members of the public oppose racial preferences that violate notions of procedural justice—they do *not* oppose affirmative action.

Myth 5: A large percentage of White workers will lose out it affirmative action is continued. Government statistics do not support this myth. According to the U.S. Commerce Department, there are 1.3 million unemployed Black civilians and 112 million employed White civilians. Thus, even if every unemployed Black worker in the United States were to displace a White worker, only 1% of Whites would be affected. Furthermore, affirmative action pertains only to job-qualified applicants, so the actual percentage of affected Whites would be a fraction of 1%. The main sources of job loss among White workers have to do with factory relocations and labor contracting outside the United States, computerization and automation, and corporate downsizing.

Myth 6: If Jewish people and Asian Americans can rapidly advance economically, African Americans should be able to do the same. This comparison ignores the unique history of discrimination against Black people in America. As historian Roger Wilkins has pointed out, Blacks have a 375-year history on this continent: 245 involving slavery, 100 involving legalized discrimination, and only 30 involving anything else. Jews and Asians, on the other hand, are populations that *immigrated* to North America and included doctors, lawyers, professors, and entrepreneurs among their ranks. Moreover, European Jews are able to function as part of the White majority. To expect

Blacks to show the same upward mobility as Jews and Asians is to deny the historical and social reality that Black people face.

Myth 7: You can't cure discrimination with discrimination. The problem with this myth is that it uses the same word—*discrimination*—to describe two very different things. Job discrimination is grounded in prejudice and exclusion, whereas affirmative action is an effort to overcome prejudicial treatment through inclusion. The most effective way to cure society of exclusionary practices is to make special efforts at inclusion, which is exactly what affirmative action does. The logic of affirmative action is no different than the logic of treating a nutritional deficiency with vitamin supplements. For a healthy person, high doses of vitamin supplements may be unnecessary or even harmful, but for a person whose system is out of balance, supplements are an efficient way to restore the body's balance.

Myth 8: Affirmative action tends to undermine the self-esteem of women and racial minorities. Although affirmative action may have this effect in some cases, interview studies and public opinion surveys suggest that such reactions are rare. For instance, a 1995 Gallup poll asked employed Blacks and employed White women whether they had ever felt others questioned their abilities because of affirmative action. Nearly 90% of respondents said no (which is understandable—after all, White men, who have traditionally benefited from preferential hiring, do not feel hampered by self-doubt or a loss in self-esteem). Indeed, in many cases affirmative action may actually *raise* the self-esteem of women and minorities by providing them with employment and opportunities for advancement. There is also evidence that affirmative action policies increase job satisfaction and organizational commitment among beneficiaries.

Myth 9: Affirmative action is nothing more than an attempt at social engineering by liberal Democrats. In truth, affirmative action programs have spanned nine different presidential administrations—six Republican and three Democratic. Although the originating document of affirmative action was President Lyndon Johnson's Executive Order 11246, the policy was significantly expanded in 1969 by President Richard

Nixon and then Secretary of Labor George Schultz. President George Bush also enthusiastically signed the Civil Rights Act of 1991, which formally endorsed the principle of affirmative action. Thus, affirmative action has traditionally enjoyed the support of Republicans as well as Democrats.

Myth 10: Support for affirmative action means support for preferential selection procedures that favor unqualified candidates over qualified candidates. Actually, most supporters of affirmative action oppose this type of preferential selection. Preferential selection procedures can be ordered along the following continuum:

1. *Selection among equally qualified candidates.* The mildest form of affirmative action selection occurs when a female or minority candidate is chosen from a pool of equally qualified applicants (e.g., students with identical college entrance scores). Survey research suggests that three-quarters of the public does not see this type of affirmative action as discriminatory.

2. *Selection among comparable candidates.* A somewhat stronger form occurs when female or minority candidates are roughly comparable to other candidates (e.g., their college entrance scores are lower, but not by a significant amount). The logic here is similar to the logic of selecting among equally qualified candidates; all that is needed is an understanding that, for example, predictions based on an SAT score of 620 are virtually indistinguishable from predictions based on an SAT score of 630.

3. *Selection among unequal candidates.* A still stronger form of affirmative action occurs when qualified female or minority candidates are chosen over candidates whose records are better by a substantial amount.

4. *Selection among qualified and unqualified candidates.* The strongest form of preferential selection occurs when unqualified female or minority members are chosen over other candidates who are qualified. Although affirmative action is sometimes mistakenly equated with this form of preferential treatment, federal regulations explic-

itly prohibit affirmative action programs in which unqualified or unneeded employees are hired.

Even though these selection procedures occasionally blend into one another (due in part to the difficulty of comparing incommensurable records), a few general observations can be made. First, of the four different procedures, the selection of women and minority members among equal or roughly comparable candidates has the greatest public support, adheres most closely to popular conceptions of fairness, and reduces the chances that affirmative action beneficiaries will be perceived as unqualified or undeserving. Second, the selection of women and minority members among unequal candidates—used routinely in college admissions—has deeply divided the nation (with the strongest opposition coming from White males and conservative voters.) And finally, the selection of unqualified candidates is not permitted under federal affirma-

tive action guidelines and should not be equated with legal forms of affirmative action. By distinguishing among these four different selection procedures, it becomes clear that opposition to stronger selection procedures need not imply opposition to milder ones.

Some writers have criticized affirmative action as a superficial solution that does not address deeper societal problems by redistributing wealth and developing true educational equality. Yet affirmative action was never proposed as a cure-all solution to inequality. Rather, it was intended only to redress discrimination in hiring and academic admissions. In assessing the value of affirmative action, the central question is merely this: In the absence of sweeping societal reforms—unlikely to take place any time soon—does affirmative action help counteract the continuing injustice caused by discrimination? The research record suggests, unequivocally, that it does.

Affirmative Action and Quotas

Richard A. Wasserstrom

* * *

Someone might say something like this [about affirmative action]: it is just wrong in principle ever to take an individual's race or sex into account. Persons just have a right never to have race or sex considered. No reasons need be given; we just know they have that right. This is a common way of talking today in moral philosophy, but I find nothing persuasive or attractive about it. I do not know that persons have such a right. I do not "see" it. Instead, I think I can give and have given reasons in my discussion of the social realities as well as my discussion of ideals for why they might be said to have rights not to be

treated in certain ways. That is to say, I have tried to show something of what was wrong about the way blacks and women were and are treated in our culture. I have not simply proclaimed the existence of a right.

Another form of this objection is more convincing. The opponent of quotas and affirmative action programs might argue that any proponent of them is guilty of intellectual inconsistency, if not racism or sexism. At times past, employers, universities, and many social institutions did have racial or sexual quotas, when they did not practice overt racial or sexual exclusion, and it was clear that these quotas were pernicious. What is more, many of those who were most concerned to bring about the eradication of those racial quotes are now untroubled by the new programs which reinstitute them. And this is just a ter-

Richard A. Wasserstrom, "Affirmative Action and Quotas," *UCLA Law Review* 24, no. 581 (1977): 617–22 (edited). Reprinted with permission by *UCLA Law Review*.

rible sort of intellectual inconsistency which at worst panders to the fashion of the present moment and at best replaces intellectual honesty and integrity with understandable but misguided sympathy. The assimilationist ideal requires ignoring race and sex as distinguishing features of people.

Such an argument is a useful means by which to bring out the way in which the analysis I am proposing can respond. The racial quotas and practices of racial exclusion that were an integral part of the fabric of our culture, and which are still to some degree a part of it, were pernicious. They were a grievous wrong and it was and is important that all morally concerned individuals work for their eradication from our social universe. The racial quotas that are a part of contemporary affirmative action programs are, I think, commendable and right. But even if I am mistaken about the latter, the point is that there is no inconsistency involved in holding both views. For even if contemporary schemes of racial quotas are wrong, they are wrong for reasons very different from those that made quotas against blacks wrong.

As I have argued, the fundamental evil of programs that discriminated against blacks or women was that these programs were a part of a larger social universe which systematically maintained an unwarranted and unjust scheme which concentrated power, authority, and goods in the hands of white males. Programs which excluded or limited the access of blacks and women into these institutions were wrong both because of the direct consequences of these programs on the individuals most affected and because the system of racial and sexual superiority of which they were constituents was an immoral one in that it severely and without any adequate justification restricted the capacities, autonomy, and happiness of those who were members of the less favored categories.

Whatever may be wrong with today's affirmative action programs and quota systems, it should be clear that the evil, if any, is not the same. Racial and sexual minorities do not constitute the dominant social group. Nor is the conception of who is a fully developed member of the moral and social community one

of an individual who is either female or black. Quotas which prefer women or blacks do not add to the already relatively overabundant supply of resources and opportunities at the disposal of white males. If racial quotas are to be condemned or if affirmative action programs are to be abandoned, it should be because they will not work well to achieve the desired result. It is not because they seek either to perpetuate an unjust society or to realize a corrupt ideal.

Still a third version of this objection might be that when used in affirmative action programs, race and sex are categories that are too broad in scope. They include some persons who do not have the appropriate characteristics and exclude some persons who do. If affirmative action programs made race and sex the sole criteria of selection, this would certainly be a plausible objection, although even here it is very important to see that the objection is no different in kind from that which applies to all legislation and rules. For example, in restricting the franchise to those who are eighteen and older, we exclude some who have all the relevant qualifications for voting and we include some who lack them. The fit can never be precise. Affirmative action programs almost always make race or sex a *relevant* condition, not a conclusive one. As such, they function the way all other classificatory schemes do. The defect, if there is one, is generic, and not peculiar to programs such as these.

There is finally the third objection: that affirmative action programs are wrong because they take race and sex into account rather than the only thing that matters—an individual's qualifications. Someone might argue that what is wrong with these programs is that they deprive persons who are more qualified by bestowing benefits on those who are less qualified in virtue of their being either black or female.

There are many things wrong with the objection based on qualifications. Not the least of them is that we do not live in a society in which there is even the serious pretense of a qualification requirement for many jobs of substantial power and authority. Would anyone claim that the persons who comprise the judiciary are there because they are the most qualified lawyers or the most qualified persons to be judges?

Would anyone claim that Henry Ford II is the head of the Ford Motor Company because he is the most qualified person for the job? Or that the one hundred men who are Senators are the most qualified persons to be Senators? Part of what is wrong with even talking about qualifications and merit is that the argument derives some of its force from the erroneous notion that we would have a meritocracy were it not for affirmative action.

But there is a theoretical difficulty as well, which cuts much more deeply into the argument about qualifications. The argument cannot be that the most qualified ought to be selected because the most qualified will perform most efficiently, for this instrumental approach was what the opponent of affirmative action thought was wrong with taking the instrumental perspective in the first place. To be at all persuasive, the argument must be that those who are the most qualified *deserve* to receive the benefits (the job, the place in law school, etc.) because they are the most qualified. And there is just no reason to think that this is a correct premise. There is a logical gap in the inference that the person who is most qualified to perform a task, *e.g.*, be a good student, deserves to be admitted as a student. Of course, those who deserve to be admitted should be admitted. But why do the most qualified deserve anything? There is just no necessary connection between academic merit (in the sense of qualification) and deserving to be a member of a student body. Suppose, for instance, that there is only one tennis court in the community. Is it clear that the two best tennis players ought to be the ones permitted to use it? Why not those who were there first? Or those who will enjoy playing the most? Or those who are the worst and therefore need the greatest opportunity to practice? Or those who have the chance to play least frequently?

We might, of course, have a rule that says that the best tennis players get to use the court before the others. Under such a rule, the best players would deserve the court more than the poorer ones. But that is just to push the inquiry back one stage. Is there any reason to think that good tennis players are entitled to such a rule? Indeed, the arguments that might be given for or against such a rule are many and varied. And few if any of the arguments that might support the rule would depend upon a connection between ability and desert.

Someone might reply that the most able students deserve to be admitted to the university because all of their earlier schooling was a kind of competition, with university admission being the prize awarded to the winners. They deserve to be admitted because that is what the rule of the competition provides. In addition, it would be unfair now to exclude them in favor of others, given the reasonable expectations they developed about the way in which their industry and performance would be rewarded. Minority admission programs, which inevitably prefer some who are less qualified over some who are more qualified, all possess this flaw.

There are several problems with this argument. The most substantial of them is that it is an empirically implausible picture of our social world. Most of what are regarded as the decisive characteristics for higher education have a great deal to do with things over which the individual has neither control nor responsibility: such things as home environment, socioeconomic class of parents, and, of course, the quality of the primary and secondary schools attended. Since individuals do not deserve having had any of these things vis-à-vis other individuals, they do not, for the most part, deserve their qualifications. And since they do not deserve their abilities they do not in any strong sense deserve to be admitted because of their abilities.

To be sure, if there is a rule which connects, say, performance at high school with admission to college, then there is a weak sense in which those who do well at high school deserve, for that reason alone, to be admitted to college. But then, as I have said, the merits of this rule need to be explored and defended. In addition, if persons have built up or relied upon their reasonable expectations concerning performance and admission, they have a claim to be admitted on this ground as well. But it is certainly not obvious that these claims of desert are any stronger or more compelling than competing claims based upon the needs of or advantages to women or blacks.

Qualifications are also potentially relevant in at least three other respects. In the first place, there is some minimal set of qualifications without which the benefits of participation in higher education cannot be obtained by the individuals involved. In the second place, the qualifications of the students within the university will affect to some degree or other the benefits obtainable to anyone within it. And finally, the qualifications of students within the university may also affect the way the university functions vis-à-vis the rest of the world. The university will do some things better and some things worse depending upon the qualifications of those who make it up. If the students are "less qualified," teachers may have to spend more time with them and less time on research. Some teachers may find teaching now more interesting. Others may find it less so. But all these considerations only establish that qualifications, in this sense, are relevant, not that they are decisive. This is wholly consistent with the claim that minority group membership is also a relevant but not a decisive consideration when it comes to matters of admission. And that is all that virtually any preferential treatment program—even one with quotas—has ever tried to claim.

I do not think I have shown programs of preferential treatment to be right and desirable, because I have not sought to answer all of the empirical questions that may be relevant. But I have, I hope, shown that it is wrong to think that contemporary affirmative action programs are racist or sexist in the centrally important sense in which many past and present features of our society have been and are racist and sexist. The social realities do make a fundamental difference. It is also wrong to think that these programs are in any strong sense either unjust or unprincipled. The case for programs of preferential treatment can plausibly rest on the view that the programs are not unfair (except in the weak sense described above) to white males, and on the view that it is unfair to continue the present set of unjust— often racist and sexist—institutions that comprise the social reality. The case for these programs also rests on the thesis that it is fair, given the distribution of power and influence in the United States, to redistribute in this way, and that such programs may reasonably be viewed as useful means by which to achieve very significant social ideals.

In Defense of Affirmative Action

TOM L. BEAUCHAMP

Affirmative action policies have had their strongest appeal when discrimination that barred groups from desirable institutions persisted although forbidden by law. Policies that establish target goals, timetables, and quotas were initiated to ensure more equitable opportunities by counterbalancing apparently intractable prejudice and systemic favoritism. The policies that were initiated with such lofty ambitions

Tom L. Beauchamp, "In Defense of Affirmative Action," *Journal of Ethics* 2, no. 2 (June 1998): 143–58 (edited). Reprinted with permission by Springer Publishing.

are now commonly criticized on grounds that they establish quotas that unjustifiably elevate the opportunities of members of targeted groups, discriminate against equally qualified or even more qualified members of majorities, and perpetuate racial and sexual paternalism.

Affirmative action policies favoring *groups* have been controversial since former United States President Lyndon Johnson's 1965 executive order that required federal contractors to develop affirmative action policies.[1] Everyone now agrees that *individuals* who have been injured by past discrimination should be made whole for the inquiry, but it remains controversial whether and how past discrimination against groups justifies preferential treatment for the group's *current* members. Critics of group preferential policies hold that compensating individuals for unfair discrimination can alone be justified, but it is controversial whether individuals can be harmed merely by virtue of a group membership.[2]

Most who support affirmative action and those who oppose it both seek the best means to the same end: a color-blind, sex-blind society. Their goals do not differ. Nor do they entirely disagree over the means. If a color-blind, sex-blind society can be achieved and maintained by legal guarantees of equal opportunities to all, both parties agree that social policies should be restricted to this means. Here agreement ends. Those who support affirmative action do not believe such guarantees can be fairly and efficiently achieved other than by affirmative action policies. Those who seek an end to affirmative action believe that the goals can be achieved in other ways and that affirmative action policies themselves unjustifiably discriminate. I will be supporting affirmative action policies against this counterposition.

TWO PIVOTAL CONCEPTS

Like virtually all problems in practical ethics, the meaning of a few central terms can powerfully affect one's moral viewpoint. The terms "affirmative action" and "quotas" have proved particularly troublesome, because they have been defined in both minimal and maximal ways. The original meaning of "affirmative action" was minimalist. It referred to plans to safeguard equal opportunity, to protect against discrimination, to advertise positions openly, and to create scholarship programs to ensure recruitment from specific groups.[3] Few now oppose open advertisement and the like, and if this were all that were meant by "affirmative action," few would oppose it. However, "affirmative action" has assumed new and expanded meanings. Today it is typically associated with quotas and preferential policies that target specific groups, especially women or minority members.

I will not favor either the minimalist or the maximalist sense of "affirmative action." I will use the term to refer to positive steps taken to hire persons from groups previously and presently discriminated against, leaving open what will count as a "positive step" to remove discrimination. I thus adopt a broad meaning.

A number of controversies have also centered on the language of *quotas*.[4] A "quota," as I use the term, does not mean that fixed numbers of a group must be admitted, hired, or promoted—even to the point of including less qualified persons if they are the only available members of a targeted groups. Quotas are target numbers or percentages that an employer, admissions office, recruitment committee, and the like sincerely attempt to meet. Less qualified persons are occasionally hired or promoted under a policy that incorporates quotas; but it is no part of affirmative action or the meaning of "quotas" to hire persons who lack basic qualifications. Quotas are numerically expressible goals pursued in good faith and with due diligence.

The language of "quotas" can be toned down by speaking of hopes, objectives, and guidelines; but cosmetic changes of wording only thinly obscure a policy established to recruit from groups in which the goals are made explicitly by numbers. Thus, when John Sununu—presumably a strong opponent of quotas—told Secretary of Defense Richard Cheney that he "wanted 30 percent of the remaining 42 top jobs in the Defense Department to be filled by women and minorities,"[5] he was using a quota. Likewise, universities sometimes use quotas when the subtleties of faculty and staff hiring and promotion and student admission make no mention of them. For example, if the chair of a department says the department should hire 2 to 3 women in the next 5 available positions, the formula constitutes a quota, or at least a numerical target.

Reasons typically offered in defense of targeted affirmative action, with or without quotas, are the following: "We have many women students who need and do not have an ample number of role models and mentors." "The provost has offered a group of special fellowships to bring more minorities to the university." "More diversity is much needed in this department." "The goals and mission of this university strongly suggest a need for increased representation of women and minorities." In pursuing these objectives, members of departments and committees commonly act in ways that suggest they willingly endorse what either is or has a strong family resemblance to a specific target.

THE PREVALENCE OF DISCRIMINATION AS THE RATIONALE FOR AFFIRMATIVE ACTION

The moral problem of affirmative action is primarily whether specific targets, including quotas in the broad sense, can legitimately be used. To support affirmative action as a weapon against discrimination is not necessarily to endorse it in all institutions. Racial, sexual, and religious forms of discrimination affecting admission, hiring, and promotion have been substantially reduced in various sectors of US society, and perhaps even completely eliminated in some. The problem is that in other social sectors it is common to encounter discrimination in favor of a favored group or discrimination against disliked, distrusted, unattractive, or neglected groups. The pervasive attitudes underlying these phenomena are the most important background conditions of the debate over affirmative action, and we need to understand these pockets of discrimination in order to appreciate the attractions of affirmative action.

Statistics. Statistics constituting at least *prima facie* evidence of discrimination in society are readily available. These data indicate that in sizable parts of US society white males continue to receive the highest entry-level salaries when compared to all other social groups; that women with similar credentials and experience to those of men are commonly hired at lower positions or earn lower starting salaries than men and are promoted at one-half the rate of their male counterparts, with the consequence that the gap between salaries and promotion rates is still growing at an increasing rate; that 70% or more of white-collar positions are held by women, although they hold only about 10% of management positions;

that three out of seven US employees occupy white-collar positions, whereas the ratio is but one of seven of African-Americans; and, finally, that a significant racial gap in unemployment statistics is a consistent pattern in the US, with the gap now greatest for college-educated, African-American males.[6] Whether these statistics demonstrate invidious discrimination is controversial, but additional data drawn from empirical studies reinforce the judgment that racial and sexual discrimination are reasons for and perhaps the best explanation of these statistics.

Housing. For example, studies of real estate rentals, housing sales, and home mortgage lending show a disparity in rejection rates—for example, loan rejection rates between white applicants and minority applicants. Wide disparities exist even after statistics are adjusted for economic differences; minority applicants are over 50% more likely to be denied a loan than white applicants of equivalent economic status. Other studies indicate that discrimination in sales of houses is prevalent in the US. Race appears to be as important as socioeconomic status in failing to secure both houses and loans, and studies also show that the approval rate for African-Americans increases in lending institutions with an increase in the proportion of minority employees in that institution.[7]

Jobs. A similar pattern is found in employment. In 1985 the Grier Partnership and the Urban League produced independent studies that reveal striking disparities in the employment levels of college-trained African-Americans and whites in Washington, DC, one of the best markets for African-Americans. Both studies found that college-trained African-Americans have much more difficulty than their white counterparts in securing employment. Both cite discrimination as the major underlying factor.[8]

In a 1991 study by the Urban Institute, employment practices in Washington, DC and Chicago were examined. Equally qualified, identically dressed white and African-American applicants for jobs were used to test for bias in the job market, as presented by newspaper-advertised positions. Whites and African-Americans were matched identically for speech patterns, age, work experience, personal characteristics, and physical build. Investigators found repeated discrimination against African-American male applicants. The higher the position, the higher the level of discrimination. The white men received job offers three times more often than the equally qualified African-Americans who interviewed for the same position. The authors of the study concluded that discrimination against African-American men is "widespread and entrenched."[9]

These statistics and empirical studies help frame racial discrimination in the US. Anyone who believes that only a narrow slice of surface discrimination exists will be unlikely to agree with what I have been and will be arguing, at least if my proposals entail strong affirmative action measures. By contrast, one who believes that discrimination is securely and almost invisibly entrenched in many sectors of society will be more likely to endorse or at least tolerate resolute affirmative action policies.

Although racism and sexism are commonly envisioned as intentional forms of favoritism and exclusion, intent to discriminate is not a necessary condition of discrimination. Institutional networks can unintentionally hold back or exclude persons. Hiring by personal friendships and word of mouth are common instances, as are seniority systems. Numerical targets are important remedies for these camouflaged areas, where it is particularly difficult to shatter patterns of discrimination and reconfigure the environment.[10]

The US Supreme Court has rightly upheld affirmative action programs with numerically expressed hiring formulas when intended to quash the effects of both intentional and unintentional discrimination.[11] The Court has also maintained that such formulas have sometimes been structured so that they unjustifiably exceed proper limits.[12] The particulars of the cases will determine how we are to balance different interests and considerations.

THE JUSTIFICATION OF AFFIRMATIVE ACTION

This balancing strategy is warranted. Numerical goals or quotas are justified if and only if they are neces-

sary to overcome the discriminatory effects that could not otherwise be eliminated with reasonable efficiency. It is the intractable and often deeply hurtful character of racism and sexism that justified aggressive policies to remove their damaging effects. The history of affirmative action in the US, though short, is an impressive history of fulfilling once-failed promises, displacing disillusion, and protecting the most vulnerable members of US society against demeaning abuse. It has delivered the US from what was little more than a caste system and a companion of apartheid.

We have learned in the process that numerical formulas are sometimes essential tools, sometimes excessive tools, and sometimes permissible but optional tools—depending on the subtleties of the case. We can expect each case to be different, and for this reason we should be cautious about general pronouncements regarding the justifiability of numerical formulas—as well as the merit of merit-based systems and blinded systems. The better perspective is that until the facts of particular cases have been carefully assessed, we are not positioned to support or oppose any particular affirmative action policy or its abandonment.

The US Supreme Court has allowed these numerical formulas in plans that are intended to combat a manifest imbalance in traditionally segregated job categories (even if the particular workers drawn from minorities were not victims of past discrimination). In *Local 28 v. Equal Employment Opportunity Commission*, a minority hiring goal of 29.23 percent had been established. The Court held that such specific numbers are justified when dealing with persistent or egregious discrimination. The Court found that the history of Local 28 was one of complete "foot-dragging resistance" to the idea of hiring without discrimination in their apprenticeship training programs from minority groups. The Court argued that "affirmative race-conscious relief" may be the only reasonable means to the end of assuring equality of employment opportunities and to eliminate deeply ingrained discriminatory practices.[13]

In a 1989 opinion, by contrast, the US Supreme Court held in *City of Richmond v. J. A. Croson* that

Richmond, Virginia, officials could not require contractors to set aside 30 percent of their budget for subcontractors who owned "minority business enterprises." This particular plan was not written to remedy the effects of prior or present discrimination. The Court found that *this way* of fixing a percentage based on race, in the absence of evidence of identified discrimination, denied citizens an equal opportunity to compete for subcontracts. Parts of the reasoning in this case were reaffirmed in the 1995 case of *Adarand Constructors Inc. v. Pena.*

Some writers have interpreted *Croson, Adarand,* and the 1997 decision of a three-judge panel of the 9th US Circuit Court of Appeals to the effect that California's voter-approved ban on affirmative action (Proposition 209) is constitutional as the dismantling of affirmative action plans that use numerical goals. Perhaps this prediction will turn out to be correct, but the US Supreme Court has consistently adhered to a balancing strategy that I believe captures the fitting way to frame issues of affirmative action.[14] It allows us to use race and sex as relevant bases of policies if and only if it is essential to do so in order to achieve a larger and justified social purpose.

These reasons for using race and sex in policies are far distant from the role of these properties in invidious discrimination. Racial discrimination and sexual discrimination typically spring from feelings of superiority and a sense that other groups deserve lower social status. Affirmative action entails no such attitude or intent. Its purpose is to restore to persons a status they have been unjustifiably denied, to help them escape stigmatization, and to foster relationships of interconnectedness in society.[15]

Affirmative action in pockets of the most vicious and visceral racism will likely be needed for another generation in the US, after which the US should have reached its goals of fair opportunity and equal consideration. Once these goals are achieved, affirmative action will no longer be justified and should be abandoned in the US. The goal to be reached at that point is not proportional representation, which has occasionally been used as a basis for fixing target numbers in affirmative action policies, but as such is merely a means to the end of discrimination, not an end to be pursued for its own sake. The goal is simply fair opportunity and equal consideration.

* * *

TOLERATING REVERSE DISCRIMINATION

It has often been said that reverse discrimination is caused by affirmative action policies and that this discrimination is no better than the racial or sexual discrimination that affirmative actions allegedly frustrates.[16] Some instances of such discriminatory exclusion do occur, of course, and compensation or rectification for an injured party is sometimes the appropriate response. However, some of these setbacks to the interests of those excluded by a policy may be no more objectionable than various burdens produced by social policies that advantage some members of society and disadvantage others. Inheritance laws, for example, favor certain members of society over others, whereas policies of eminent domain disadvantage persons who wish to retain what is legitimately their property in order to advance the public good. Such laws and outcomes are warranted by a larger public benefit and by justice-based considerations that conflict with the interests of the disadvantaged parties. The point is that disadvantages to majorities produced by affirmative action may be warranted by the promotion of social ideals of equal treatment for groups that were severely mistreated in the past.

In assessing the disadvantages that might be caused to members of majorities (primarily white males), we should remember that there are disadvantages to other parties that operate in the current system, many of which will not be affected by affirmative action or by its absence. For example, just as young white males may now be paying a penalty for wrongs committed by older white males (who will likely never be penalized), so the older members of minority groups and older women who have been most disadvantaged in the past are the lest likely to gain an advantage from affirmative action policies. Paradoxically, the younger minority members and women who have suffered least from discrimination now stand to gain the most from affirmative action.

Despite these unfairnesses, there is no clear way to remedy them.

Policies of affirmative action may have many other shortcomings as well. For example, they confer economic advantages upon some who do not deserve them and generate court battles, jockeying for favored position by a multiple array of minorities, a lowering of admission and work standards in some institutions, heightened racial hostility, and continued suspicion that well-placed women and minority group members received their positions purely on the basis of quotas, thereby damaging their self-respect and the respect of their colleagues. Affirmative action is not a perfect social tool, but it is the best tool yet created as a way of preventing a recurrence of the far worse imperfections of our past policies of segregation and exclusion.

JUDGING THE PAST AND THE PRESENT

Looking back at this deplorable history and at the unprecedented development of affirmative action policies over the past thirty years in the US, what moral judgments can we reach about persons who either initiated these policies or those who failed to initiate such programs? Can we say that anyone has engaged in moral wrongdoing in implementing these policies, or exhibited moral failure in not implementing them? Addressing these questions should help us better judge the present in light of the past.

I will examine these questions through the classic AT&T affirmative action agreement in the 1970s. The salient facts of this case are as follows: The US Equal Employment Opportunity Commission (EEOC) had investigated AT&T in the 1960s on grounds of alleged discriminatory practices in hiring and promotion. In 1970 the EEOC stated that the firm engaged in "pervasive, system-wide, and blatantly unlawful discrimination in employment against women, African-Americans, Spanish-surnamed Americans, and other minorities."[17] The EEOC argued that the employment practices of AT&T violated several civil rights laws and had excluded women from all job classifications except low paying clerical and operator positions.

AT&T denied all charges and produced a massive array of statistics about women and minorities in the workforce. However, these statistics tended to undermine the corporation's own case. They showed that half the company's 700,000 employees were female, but that the women were all either secretaries or operators. It became apparent that the company categorized virtually all of its jobs in terms of men's work and women's work. The federal government was determined to obliterate this aspect of corporate culture in the belief that no other strategy would break the grip of this form of sexism. Eventually AT&T threw in the towel and entered a Consent Decree, which was accepted by a Philadelphia court in 1973. This agreement resulted in payments of $15 million in back wages to 13,000 women and 2,000 minority-group men and $23 million in raises to 36,000 employees who had been harmed by previous policies.

Out of this settlement came a companywide "model affirmative action plan" that radically changed the character of AT&T hiring and its promotion practices. The company agreed to create an "employee profile" in its job classifications to be achieved faster than would normally occur. It established racial and gender goals and intermediate targets in 15 job categories to be met in quarterly increments. The goals were determined by statistics regarding representative numbers of workers in the relevant labor market. The decree required that under conditions of a target failure, a less qualified (but qualified) person could take precedence over a more qualified person with greater seniority. This condition applied only to promotions, not to layoffs and rehiring, where seniority continued to prevail.

As was inevitable under this arrangement, reverse discrimination cases emerged. The well known McAleer case came before Judge Gerhard A. Gesell, who held in 1976 that McAleer was a faultless employee who became an innocent victim through an unfortunate but justifiable use of the affirmative action process.[18] Judge Gesell ruled that McAleer was entitled to monetary compensation (as damages), but not entitled to the promotion to which he thought he was entitled because the discrimination the Consent Decree had been designed to eliminate might be perpetuated if a qualified woman were not given the promotion.[19]

This AT&T case history, like many affirmative action cases, is a story of changed expectations and changing moral viewpoints. At the core of any framework for the evaluation of such cases is a distinction between *wrongdoing* and *culpability*, which derives from the need to evaluate the moral qualify of actions by contrast to agents. For example, we might want to say that AT&T's hiring practices were wrong and that many employees were wronged by them, without judging anyone culpable for the wrongs done.

Virtually everyone is now agreed, including AT&T officials, that AT&T's hiring and promotion practices did involve unjustified discrimination and serious wrongdoing. Even basic moral principles were violated—for example, that one ought to treat persons with equal consideration and respect, that racial and sexual discrimination are impermissible, and the like. Less clear is whether the agents involved should be blamed. Several factors place limits on our ability to make judgments about the blameworthiness of agents—or at least the fairness of doing so. These factors include culturally induced moral ignorance, a changing circumstance in the specification of moral principles, and indeterminacy in an organization's division of labor and designation of responsibility. All were present to some degree in the AT&T case.

Judgments of exculpation depend, at least to some extent, on whether proper moral standards were acknowledged in the culture in which the events transpired—for example, in the professional ethics of the period. If we had possessed clear standards regarding the justice of hiring and promotion in the 1950s and 1960s, it would be easier to find AT&T officials culpable. The absence of such standards is a factor in our reflections about culpability and exculpation, but need not be part of our reflection on the wronging that occurred.

The fact of culturally induced moral ignorance does not by itself entail exculpation or a lack of accountability for states of ignorance. The issue is the degree to which persons are accountable for holding and even perpetuating or disseminating the beliefs that they hold when an opportunity to remedy or modify the beliefs exists. If such opportunities are unavailable, a person may have a valid excuse; but the greater the opportunity to eliminate ignorance the less is exculpation appropriate. Persons who permit their culturally induced moral ignorance to persist through a series of opportunities to correct the beliefs thereby increase their culpability.

The more persons are obstinate in not facing issues, and the more they fail to perceive the plight of other persons who may be negatively affected by their failure to act, the more likely are we to find their actions or inactions inexcusable. No doubt culturally induced moral ignorance was a mitigating factor in the 1960s and early 1970s, but I believe US history also shows that it was mixed with a resolute failure to face moral problems when it was widely appreciated that they were serious problems and were being faced by other institutions.

The central issue for my purposes is not whether discriminatory attitudes should be judged harshly in the pre-affirmative action situation at AT&T, but whether the affirmative action policy that was adopted itself involved wrongdoing or constituted, then or now, an activity for which we would blame persons who establish such policies. I do not see how agents could be blamed for maintaining and enforcing this program, despite its toughness. Given AT&T's history as well as the desperate situation of discrimination in US society, under what conditions could agents be culpable even if McAleer-type cases of reverse discrimination occasionally resulted? Even if we assume that McAleer and others were wronged in the implementation of the policy, it does not follow that the agents were culpable for their support of the policy.

Today, many corporate programs similar to the AT&T policy are in place. We can and should ask both whether persons are wronged by these policies and whether those who use the policies are culpable. The answer seems to me the same in the 1990s as it was in the 1970s: As long as there is persistent, intractable discrimination in society, the policies will be justified and the agents nonculpable, even if some persons are harmed and even wronged by the policies. To say that we should right wrongs done by the policies is not to say that we should abandon the policies themselves.

Indeed, I defend a stronger view: Affirmative action was a noble struggle against a crippling social ill in the 1960s and 1970s, and those who took part in the struggle deserve acknowledgement for their courage and foresight. Those who failed to seize the opportunity to enact affirmative action policies or some functional equivalent such as company-wide enforcement of equal opportunity are culpable for what, in many cases, were truly serious moral failures.

There is no reason to believe that, in this respect, the situation is changed today from the 1970s. Today persons in corporations, universities, and government agencies who are aware or should be aware that a high level of racism or sexism exists are culpable if they fail to move to counteract its invidious effects by affirmative policies or similarly serious interventions such as meaningful enforcement of fair opportunity. To say that we should judge the officers of these institutions culpable for their moral failures is not to say that there are no mitigating conditions for their failures, such as the mixed messages they have received over the past fifteen years from federal officials and the general cultural climate of moral indifference to the problem. At the same time, the mitigating conditions are weaker today than in the 1970s because the excuse of culturally induced moral ignorance is weaker. In general, there are now fewer excuses available for not taking an aggressive posture to combat discrimination than ever before.

All of this is not to say that we are never culpable for the way we formulate or implement affirmative action policies. One aspect of these policies for which we likely will be harshly judged in the future is a failure of truthfulness in publicly disclosing and advertising the commitments of the policies—for example, in advertising for new positions.[20] Once it has been determined that a woman or a minority group member will most likely be hired, institutions now typically place advertisements that include lines such as the following:

Women and minority-group candidates are especially encouraged to apply. The University of X is an equal opportunity, affirmative action employer.

Advertisements and public statements rarely contain more information about an institution's affirmative action objectives, although often more information might be disclosed that would be of material relevance to applicants. The following are examples of facts or objectives that might be disclosed: A department may have reserved its position for a woman or minority; the chances may be overwhelming that only a minority group member will be hired; the interview team may have decided in advance that only women will be interviewed; the advertised position may be the result of a university policy that offers an explicit incentive (perhaps a new position) to a department if a minority representative is appointed, etc. Incompleteness in disclosure and advertising sometimes stems from fear of legal liability, but more often from fear of departmental embarrassment and harm either to reputation or to future recruiting efforts.

The greater moral embarrassment, however, is our ambivalence and weak conceptions of what we are doing. Many, including academics, fear making public what they believe to be morally commendable in their recruiting efforts. There is something deeply unsatisfactory about a reluctance to disclose one's real position. This situation is striking, because the justification for the position is presumably that it is a morally praiseworthy endeavor. Here we have a circumstance in which the actions taken may not be wrong, but the agents are culpable for a failure to clearly articulate the basis of their actions and to allow those bases to be openly debated so that their true merits can be assessed by all affected parties.

CONCLUSION

During the course of the last thirty years, the widespread acceptance of racial segregation and sexual dominance in the US has surrendered to a more polite culture that accepts racial integration and sexual equality. This discernible change of attitude and institutional policy has led to an imposing public opposition to preferential treatment on the basis of race and sex in general. In this climate what should happen to affirmative action?

As long as our choice are formulated in terms of the false dilemma of either special preference for groups or individual merit, affirmative action is virtually certain to be overthrown. US citizens are now wary and weary of all forms of group preference, other than the liberty to choose one's preferred groups. I would be pleased to witness the defeat of affirmative action were the choice the simple one of group preference or individual merit. But it is not. Despite the vast changes of attitudes in thirty years of US culture, the underlying realities are naggingly familiar. Perhaps in another thirty years we can rid ourselves of the perils of affirmative action. But at present the public good and our sense of ourselves as a nation will be well served by retaining what would in other circumstances be odious policies. They merit preservation as long as we can say that, on balance, they serve us better than they disserve us.

NOTES

1. Executive Order 11246. C.F.R. 339 (1964–65).

2. See J. Angelo Corlett, "Racism and Affirmative Action," *Journal of Social Philosophy* 24 (1993), pp. 163–175; and Cass R. Sunstein, "The Limits of Compensatory Justice," in John Chapman (ed.), *Nomos XXXIII: Compensatory Justice* (New York: New York University Press, 1991), pp. 281–310.

3. See Thomas Nagel, "A Defense of Affirmative Action," Testimony before the Subcommittee on the Constitution of the Senate Judiciary Committee, June 18, 1981; and Louis Pojman, "The Moral Status of Affirmative Action," *Public Affairs Quarterly* 6 (1992), pp. 181–206.

4. See the analyses in Gertrude Ezorsky, *Racism and Justice* (Ithaca, NY: Cornell University Press, 1991); and Robert Fullinwider, *The Reverse Discrimination Controversy* (Totowa, NJ: Rowman and Allanheld, 1980).

5. Bob Woodward, *The Commanders* (New York: Simon and Schuster, 1991), p. 72.

6. Bron Taylor, *Affirmative Action at Work: Law, Politics, and Ethics* (Pittsburgh: University of Pittsburgh Press, 1991); Morley Gunderson, "Male–Female Wage Differentials and Policy Responses," *Journal of Economic Literature* 27 (1989), and Morley Gunderson, "Pay and Employment Equity in the United States and Canada," *International Journal of Manpower* 15 (1994), pp. 26–43; Patricia Gaynor and Garey Durden, "Measuring the Extent of Earnings Discrimination: An Update," *Applied Economics* 27 (1995), pp. 669–767; Marjorie L. Baldwin and William G. Johnson, "The Employment Effects of Wage Discrimination Against Black Men," *Industrial & Labor Relations Review* 49 (1996), pp. 302–316; Franklin D. Wilson, Marta Tienda, and Lawrence Wu, "Race and Unemployment: Labor Market Experiences of Black and White Men, 1968–1988," *Work & Occupations* 22 (1995), pp. 245–270; National Center for Education Statistics, *Faculty in Higher Education Institutions, 1988, Contractor Survey Report*, compiled Susan H. Russell et al. (Washington: US Dept. of Education, 1990), pp. 5–13; Betty M. Vetter, ed., *Professional Women and Minorities: A Manpower Data Resource Service*, 8th edn. (Washington: Commission on Science and Technology, 1989); (anonymous) "Less Discrimination for Women but Poorer Prospect at Work than Men," *Management Services* 40 (1996), p. 6; Cynthia D. Anderson and Donald Tomaskovic-Devey, "Patriarchal Pressures: An Exploration of Organizational Processes that Exacerbate and Erode Gender Earnings Inequality," *Work & Occupations* 22 (1995), pp. 328–356; Thomas J. Bergman and G. E. Martin, "Tests for Compliance with Phases Plans to Equalize Discriminate Wages," *Journal of Applied Business Research* 11 (1994/1995), pp. 136–143.

7. Brent W. Ambrose, William T. Hughes, Jr., and Patrick Simmons, "Policy Issues concerning Racial and Ethnic Differences in Home Loan Rejection Rates," *Journal of Housing Research* 6 (1995), pp. 115–135; *A Common Destiny: Blacks and American Society*, ed. Gerald D. Jaynes and Robin M. Williams, Jr., Committee on the Status of Black Americans, Commission on Behavioral and Social Sciences and Education, National Research Council (Washington: NAS Press, 1989), pp. 12–13, 138–148; Sunwoong Kim, Gregory D. Squire, "Lender Characteristics and Racial Disparities in Mortgage Lending," *Journal of Housing Research* 6 (1995), pp. 99–113; Glenn B. Canner and Wayne Passmore, "Home Purchase Lending in Low-Income Neighborhoods and to Low-Income Borrowers," *Federal Reserve Bulletin* 81 (1995), pp. 71–103; Constance L. Hays, "Study Says Prejudice in Suburbs Is Aimed Mostly at Blacks," *The New York Times* (November 23, 1988), p. A16; John R. Walter, "The Fair Lending Laws and their Enforcement," *Economic Quarterly* 81 (1995), pp. 61–77; Stanley D. Longhofer, "Discrimination in Mortgage Lending: What Have We Learned?" *Economic Commentary* [Federal Reserve Bank of Cleveland] (August 15, 1996), pp. 1–4.

8. As reported by Rudolf A. Pyatt, Jr., "Significant Job Studies," *The Washington Post* (April 30, 1985), pp. D1–D2. See also Paul Burstein, *Discrimination, Jobs, and Politics* (Chicago: University of Chicago Press, 1985); Bureau of Labor Statistics, *Employment and Earnings* (Washington: US Dept. of Labor, Jan. 1989); *A Common Destiny,* op. cit., pp. 16–18, 84–88.

9. See Margery Austin Turner, Michael Fix, and Raymond Struyk, *Opportunities Denied, Opportunities Diminished: Discrimination in Hiring* (Washington, DC: The Urban Institute, 1991).

10. See Laura Purdy, "Why Do We Need Affirmative Action?" *Journal of Social Philosophy* 25 (1994), pp. 133–143; Farrell Bloch, *Antidiscrimination Law and Minority Employment: Recruitment Practices and Regulatory Constraints* (Chicago: University of Chicago Press, 1994); Joseph Sartorelli, "Gay Rights and Affirmative Action" in *Gay Ethics,* ed. Timothy F. Murphy (New York: Haworth Press, 1994); Taylor, *Affirmative Action at Work.*

11. *Fullilove v. Klutznick,* 448 U.S. 448 (1980); *United Steelworkers v. Weber,* 443 U.S. 193 (1979); *United States v. Paradise,* 480 U.S. 149 (1987); *Johnson v. Transportation Agency,* 480 U.S. 616 (1987); *Alexander v. Choate,* 469 U.S. 287, at 295.

12. *Firefighters v. Stotts,* 467 U.S. 561 (1984); *City of Richmond v. J. A. Croson Co.,* 109 S.Ct. 706 (1989); *Adarand Constructors Inc. v. Federico Pena,* 63 LW 4523 (1995); *Wygant v. Jackson Bd. of Education,* 476 U.S. 267 (1986); *Wards Cove Packing v. Atonio,* 490 U.S. 642.

13. In 1964 the New York Commission for Human Rights investigated the union and concluded that it excluded nonwhites through an impenetrable barrier of hiring by discriminatory selection. The state Supreme Court concurred and issued a "cease and desist" order. The union ignored it. Eventually, in a 1975 trial, the US District Court found a record "replete with instances of bad faith" and ordered a "remedial racial goal of 29% nonwhite membership" (based on the percentage of nonwhites in the local labor pool). Another court then found that the union had "consistently and egregiously violated" the law of the land (Title 7, in particular). In 1982 and 1983 court fines and civil contempt proceedings were issued. In the early 1980s virtually nothing had been done to modify the discriminatory hiring practices after 22 years of struggle.

14. For a very different view, stressing inconsistency, see Yong S. Lee, "Affirmative Action and Judicial Standards of Review: A Search for the Elusive Consensus," *Review of Public Personnel Administration* 12 (1991), pp. 47–69.

15. See Robert Ladenson, "Ethics in the American Workplace," *Business and Professional Ethics Journal* 14 (1995), pp. 17–31; Ezorsky, *Racism and Justice: The Case for Affirmative Action,* op. cit.; Thomas E. Hill, Jr., "The Message of Affirmative Action," *Social Philosophy and Policy* 8 (1991), pp. 108–129; Jorge L. Garcia, "The Heart of Racism," *Journal of Social Philosophy* 27 (1996), pp. 5–46.

16. See Robert Fullinwider, *The Reverse Discrimination Controversy,* op. cit.; Nicholas Capaldi, *Out of Order* (Buffalo, NY, 1985); F. R. Lynch, *Invisible Victims: White Males and the Crisis of Affirmative Action* (Westport, CT: Greenwood Press, 1989); Barry R. Gross, eds., *Reverse Discrimination* (Buffalo: Prometheus Books, 1977).

17. US Equal Employment Opportunity Commission, "Petition to Intervene," Federal Communications Commission Hearings on AT&T Revised Tariff Schedule (December 10, 1970), p. 1.

18. *McAleer v. American Telephone and Telegraph Company,* 416 F. Supp. 435 (1976); "AT&T Denies Job Discrimination Charges, Claims Firm Is Equal Employment Leader," *The Wall Street Journal* (December 14, 1970), p.6; Richard M. Hodgetts, "AT&T versus the Equal Employment Opportunity Commission," in *The Business Enterprise: Social Challenge, Social Response* (Philadelphia, W. B. Saunders Company, 1977), pp. 176–182.

19. According to a representative of the legal staff in AT&T's Washington Office (phone conversation on March 10, 1982).

20. See Steven M. Cahn, "Colleges Should be Explicit about Who Will be Considered for Jobs," *The Chronicle of Higher Education* (April 5, 1989), p. B3.

CASES FOR ANALYSIS

1. Racial Preferences for Whites?

While many whites seem to think the notion [of racial preference] originated with affirmative action programs, intended to expand opportunities for historically marginalized people of color, racial preference has actually had a long and very white history.

Affirmative action for whites was embodied in the abolition of European indentured servitude, which left black (and occasionally indigenous) slaves as the only unfree labor in the colonies that would become the U.S.

Affirmative action for whites was the essence of the 1790 Naturalization Act, which allowed virtually any European immigrant to become a full citizen, even while blacks, Asians, and American Indians could not.

Affirmative action for whites was the guiding principle of segregation, Asian exclusion laws, and the theft of half of Mexico for the fulfillment of Manifest Destiny.

In recent history, affirmative action for whites motivated racially-restrictive housing policies that helped 15 million white families procure homes with FHA loans from the 1930's to the '60's, while people of color were mostly excluded from the same programs.

In other words, it is hardly an exaggeration to say that white America is the biggest collective recipient of racial preference in the history of the cosmos. It has skewed our laws, shaped our public policy and helped create the glaring inequalities with which we still live.*

Do you agree with this commentator that racial preferences for whites have always been a major part of U.S. history? If so, do you think that the U.S. government should make amends for such past inequalities? Why or why not? If racial preferences for whites have indeed always been widespread, were they always unjust as well? Suppose they were unjust. Would racial preferences in favor of *nonwhites* now be just? Why or why not?

*Tim Wise, "The Mother of All Racial Preferences," *ZNet,* 24 May 2003, www.zmag.org/sustainers/content/2003-05/24wise.cfm (accessed 26 February 2006). Originally appeared as a ZNet Commentary at www.zmag.org. Reprinted with permission of Tim Wise.

2. Are Racial Preferences Harmful?

Over the past few years, researchers have begun to produce large datasets that make it possible to compare the fortunes of minority students who attend universities that use varying levels of admissions preferences. In many contexts, scholars find that students perform better, both in the short-term and the long-term, when students' credentials are closer to those of their classmates. When students are surrounded by peers who have much higher credentials, they often have more trouble persisting in a difficult major, graduating from college or getting a good job.

This phenomenon is known as the "mismatch effect," and last month I published a study in the *Stanford Law Review,* trying to determine whether the mismatch effect operates in law schools. . . . My study focused on black law students and compared black and white outcomes.

I found that law schools almost universally use very large preferences for blacks to achieve something very close to racial proportionality. The credentials gap between white and black students is about 30 times larger than it would be in a race-blind regime.

Starting a highly competitive curriculum with a large academic disadvantage, blacks wind up clustered in the bottom tenth of the class at nearly all law schools. I estimate the mismatch effect increases the number of black dropouts from law school by 40%, and increases the number of blacks failing their first bar exam by 80%.

The mismatch effect appears to operate in the job market as well. Law firms—once thought to be single-minded in their determination to recruit lawyers from the most elite schools possible—turn out to weigh law school grades more heavily than school prestige. The typical black law graduate, I estimate, loses about $10,000 in annual earnings because large preferences induce her to make a bad trade-off between law school prestige and law school grades.[†]

This study is controversial, but suppose it shows what the researcher says it does. Would you then favor *dismantling* preferences for black law students? Would you favor *maintaining* law school preference systems if they helped black students rather than harmed them? Why or why not? Some people advocate using preferences in higher education to redress the wrongs of past discrimination. To be logically consistent, should they disregard evidence suggesting that preferences hurt blacks?

[†]Richard Sander, "Preferences Hurt Black Law Students," *UCLA Today 25,* no. 1 (23 February 2005), www.today.ucla.edu/2005/050223voices_preferences.html (accessed 26 February 2006). Reprinted with permission of Richard Sander.

---

3. Diversity in Undergraduate Admissions

In 1998, California's ban on affirmative action went into effect in undergraduate admissions, and the effect at Berkeley was considerable. In its first year without race-based preferences, the school accepted its least diverse freshman class in 17 years, admitting 56 percent fewer blacks and 49 percent fewer Latinos than in 1997. Six months later, in February, 1999, several civil rights groups filed a class-action suit against the university on behalf of 750 minority students denied admission in the fall. The suit focused on the school's policy of weighting grade point averages with credit for Advanced Placement (AP) classes, and pointed to the fact that many minority students attend high schools without AP classes. The school countered that it had no other way to differentiate between all of its applicants with 4.0 averages. In 1998, more than 14,000 students with 4.0 averages applied for just 8,400 spots in the freshman class.[‡]

Provide reasons for your answers to the following questions. Is diversity in student population an important value in higher education? Is achieving it important enough to justify race-based preferences in admissions? Was Berkeley's system of weighting grade point averages with credit for AP classes fair to minority students who did not have access to such classes? Should admissions schemes take into account students' disadvantaged backgrounds?

‡*Frontline*, "Secrets of the SAT: Challenging Race Sensitive Admissions Policies—A Summary of Important Rulings," *PBS Online*, first aired 5 October 1999, www.pbs.org/wgbh/pages/frontline/shows/sats/race/summary. html (accessed 26 February 2006). From WGBH Educational Foundation Copyright © 2007 WGBH/Boston.

Environmental Ethics

For most of its history, Western ethics has focused on the moral values, rights, and obligations of *humans*. The relevant questions have been, What is the good for *humans*? What value should we place on a *human* life or person? What obligations or duties do we have to our fellow *humans*? What moral rights, if any, do *humans* have? In large part, the rest of the planet seems to have been left out of our moral equations. The nonhuman animals, the plants, the waters, the land—these have mattered, if at all, largely because they affect the well-being of humankind.

But the planet is not what it used to be. The world's natural resources are being depleted. Human technology, culture, and avarice are devouring forests and meadows, poisoning water and air, wiping out ecosystems and species—and threatening the interests of the very beings who have wielded so much technological and cultural power. Some predict doom. They say that humans have gone too far and that the world as we know it will end not with a bang or a whimper, but a gasp: a gasp for uncontaminated air, water, or food. But whether the situation is or is not this dire, the profound environmental changes that humans have produced on earth have inspired many to see the proper purview of ethics as encompassing not just humans but the whole natural world. Consequently a new set of ethical questions is demanding our attention: Is the environment valuable in its own right, regardless of its usefulness for people? Do animals or plants have moral rights? Are they somehow intrinsically valuable? If they are intrinsically valuable or worthy

of moral consideration, what makes them so? Does a dolphin have more moral value than a rat? or a rat more than redwood? or an individual mongoose more than its species? What obligations, if any, do humans have to the natural world? Should the interests of people take precedence over the interests or needs of the environment? Is it morally permissible, for example, to halt the construction of a dam that will bring prosperity to thousands of poor people but will also destroy a species of crayfish?

Trying to answer such questions through critical reasoning is the main business of *environmental ethics,* a branch of applied ethics. Let us explore how these questions arise, determine whether traditional moral theories can shed any light on them, and evaluate arguments that are frequently used to address important environmental issues.

ISSUE FILE: BACKGROUND

Environmental issues can emerge from a variety of real-world challenges: endangered species, pollution, wilderness preservation, treatment of animals, ecosystem protection, climate change, waste disposal, global population, resource allocation, energy use, economics, food production, world hunger, social justice, and the welfare of future generations. The problems are often intractable and maddeningly entangled.

As you would expect, serious disputes about environmental issues involve both the nonmoral and the moral—nonmoral facts (often scientific or technical) and moral principles or judgments.

More often than not, there is substantial agreement on the former but serious divergence on the latter. All parties may agree, for instance, that building a road through a forest would help a struggling town prosper and that the project would wipe out a rare species of butterfly, but the debate rages over whether prosperity is more valuable than the butterfly.

Moral arguments in environmental ethics depend heavily on notions of *value* and *moral status*. The distinction between *instrumental* and *intrinsic* value is especially important. Recall that something with instrumental (or extrinsic) value is valuable as a means to something else; something with intrinsic value is valuable in itself, for its own sake. For many people, nature possesses instrumental value (some think it has instrumental value *only*). They may therefore believe that a forest has value because of its economic worth, because it provides the raw materials for making houses, furniture, and paper. Or because it helps make the environment livable for humans by cleaning the air as it absorbs carbon dioxide and releases oxygen. Or because it adds to the quality of human life simply by being beautiful, inspiring, or impressive. Or because it provides a home to many animal and plant species that are themselves instrumentally valuable to humans. In all these cases, the value of the forest is measured by its positive effects on human well-being. The forest is good because it is good for human beings. On the other hand, for many other people, nature has intrinsic value—it is valuable regardless of its usefulness to humanity. (Keep in mind that nature or objects in nature can have both instrumental and intrinsic value.) So they might say that the forest should be cherished for what it is, for its own sake, regardless of whether it can contribute to the welfare or happiness of humankind. The forest has intrinsic value because of its aesthetic qualities, its organizational complexity, its status as a living thing, or some other value-granting property. Even without utility, it can have great intrinsic worth.

Many debates in environmental ethics revolve around the concept of **moral status, or moral considerability.** Something has moral status if it is a suitable candidate for moral concern or respect in its own right. A being with moral status is of moral importance regardless of whether it is a means to something else, and in our dealings with it we must somehow take this fact into account. Everyone agrees that humans have moral status; many believe that nonhuman animals also have moral status; some insist that *all* living things have moral status (including plants and even one-celled creatures); and a few think that the natural environment generally—mountains, oceans, rivers, and all—has moral status. A fundamental issue in environmental ethics is precisely what sorts of entities have moral status—and why.

Many things can have instrumental or intrinsic value yet have no moral status—that is, they may not deserve our direct moral concern. A bicycle can have instrumental value as a mode of transportation, but it is not the kind of thing that can have moral status. Michelangelo's magnificent sculpture *David* is generally thought to have intrinsic aesthetic value, but few philosophers would think that it has moral status. Some theorists draw such a distinction as follows: "We can have obligations *regarding* a painting, but not *to* a painting. We ought to treat beautiful paintings with respect, but not because we have obligations to the paintings. We ought to respect them because they are beautiful (or because their owners have rights), not because they have rights."[1]

Often the question at issue in environmental debates is not whether something has moral status, but whether it has greater or lesser moral status than something else. Does an ape have the same moral status as a domestic cow? Do animals (human and nonhuman) deserve the same level

[1]David Schmidtz and Elizabeth Willott, *Environmental Ethics: What Really Matters, What Really Works,* Introduction (New York: Oxford University Press, 2002), xvii.

Some Major Environmental Issues

GLOBAL WARMING

The Problem: *Global warming* refers to the increase in the average temperature of the earth, a rise that has occurred most dramatically over the twentieth century and has accelerated in the past thirty years. It worries scientists because even a tiny increase in the average temperature could affect climate worldwide. According to a growing scientific consensus, this warming is due largely to the "greenhouse effect" in which radiation from the sun is trapped in the earth's atmosphere by greenhouse gases such as carbon dioxide (CO_2) and CFCs (chlorofluorocarbons), heating up the lower atmosphere and the earth's surface. Scientists also generally agree that human activity in the past fifty years—notably the combustion of fossil fuels (which produces carbon dioxide)—is responsible for most of the buildup of these gases. Potentially, climate change due to global warming will have both positive and negative effects. The possible negative effects include melting glaciers and an accompanying rise in sea level (which could mean a loss of habitable land, extensive flooding, and displacement of populations), drought in some regions, the expansion of deserts, increased world hunger, changes in regional climates (for example, from dry to wet or cool to warm), and more hurricanes or even superhurricanes.

The Numbers: The earth's surface temperature has increased about 1 degree F in the past century. Scientists predict a warming of 5.4 degrees F by the end of this century. Annually, more than 60 percent of global CO_2 comes from industrialized nations. As of 1996, per capita emissions of carbon in the United States (5.37 thousand tons) are twenty times higher than emissions in India (0.29), and seven times higher than emissions in China (0.76). The United States has 4 percent of the world's population, but emits 23 percent of global greenhouse gases. The European Union nations constitute 3 percent of the world's population but account for 10 percent of global emissions.

The Questions: Should governments take steps to prevent global warming even if such measures would result in some human suffering—such as the loss of jobs and economic harm to businesses or whole industries? How should we weigh the benefits to a future generation against current economic harm to industries?

OZONE DEPLETION

The Problem: In the upper reaches of the earth's atmosphere, there is an airy layer of material known as ozone. The ozone layer absorbs a particularly harmful form of the sun's radiation, a segment of ultraviolet light known as UVB. Scientists have linked UVB to skin cancer and cataracts in humans and have shown that it can damage crops and marine life. A hole in the ozone layer or even its slight thinning in a particular area will allow more UVB to reach the earth's surface, increasing the risk of harm. The amount of ozone in the atmosphere waxes and wanes naturally over time, but scientists have discovered that some commercial products contain chemicals that can deplete the ozone layer faster than it can be replenished. Chlorofluorocarbons (CFCs)—found in refrigerants, aerosol sprays, solvents, and other products—were determined to be the main culprits. CFCs are stable compounds that drift into the ozone layer, undergo a chemical reaction, and destroy ozone. Ozone depletion happens over most of the planet, including North America, Europe, and Asia. Beginning in the 1970s, nations started to ban the use of CFCs, and eventually international agreements made the prohibition against CFCs almost universal. Consequently, the emissions of CFCs and other ozone-depleting substances have been dropping. Scientists say that if all goes well, the ozone layer may restore itself—in fifty years or so. At the same time, NASA reports that in a few years, climate change may do more to deplete the ozone layer than CFCs had done.

The Numbers: For every 1 percent decrease in the ozone layer, rates of skin cancer increase 5 percent.

Ninety percent of ozone exists in the stratosphere, 6 to 30 miles above the earth. It is estimated that without international agreements banning ozone-depleting products, 50 percent of the ozone over the Northern Hemisphere's mid-latitudes would be depleted by the year 2050, resulting in a doubling of the amount of UVB reaching the earth's surface.

The Questions: How should we weigh the saving of lives (by eliminating the risk of skin cancer) against the harm done to people's livelihoods? How much is one life worth? or a thousand lives? What if a single nation was responsible for most of the damage to the ozone layer and refused to be restrained by any international agreements? Should that nation be forced to comply?

FOREST CONSERVATION

The Problem: To a surprising degree, the planet and its inhabitants depend on its forests. From forests, people derive a long list of valuable products—aesthetic wood (for example, mahogany and teak), lumber, firewood, paper, rubber, fruit, nuts, and medicines. For many people, the commercial value of forests is mostly beside the point—forests are valuable for their beauty, their inspirational power, and their educational potential. For tribal hunter-gatherers, forests provide livelihoods, fuel, fiber, and homes. Tropical forests are an especially powerful force for biodiversity, offering habitats for tens of thousands of plant and animal species and enriching the world with potential sources of scientific, genetic, and evolutionary knowledge. At the most basic level, forests nourish life: they use up carbon dioxide and give off oxygen, helping to neutralize the global greenhouse effect in the process. But the world's forests are vanishing, along with many of the species they supported. As a consequence of the timber trade in valuable woods (both illegal and legal), the clearing of forests for agriculture and industry, the felling of trees for firewood, and the building of roads through wooded areas, millions of acres of forests are disappearing each year.

The Numbers: Forests now cover about 30 percent of the earth's land area. Each year more than 56,000 square miles of natural forests are lost. By the year 2050, global wood consumption is expected to increase 50 percent. Americans use 27 percent of the world's commercially harvested wood. Of the world's 1.2 billion people living in dire poverty, 80 to 90 percent depend on forests to make their living.

The Questions: How far should we go in preserving forests? Various industries, millions of impoverished people, and many tribal cultures depend economically on the clearing of forests. Are we justified in causing economic harm to save the world's forests? Are we justified in destroying someone's way of life to achieve that end?

Sources: National Academy of Sciences, "Understanding and Responding to Climate Change: Highlights of National Academies Reports," March 2006, http://dels.nas.edu/basc/Climate-HIGH.pdf (3 December 2006); Committee on the Science of Climate Change, National Research Council, *Climate Change Science: An Analysis of Some Key Questions* (Washington, DC: National Academy Press, 2001), available at http://darwin.nap.edu/html/climatechange/ (3 December 2006); U.S. EPA, *Global Warming: Climate,* 2000, http://yosemite.epa.gov/OAR/globalwarming.nsf/content/Climate.html (6 July 2006).

"Climate Change: Frequently Asked Questions," *New Scientist.com,* January 2006, www.newscientist.com/popuparticle.ns?id=in23 (7 July 2006); U.S. EPA, *Ozone Depletion,* 2006, www.epa.gov/ozone/science/effects.html (7 July 2006).

United Nations Environment Programme, "Backgrounder: Basic Facts and Data on the Science and Politics of Ozone Protection," 2 July 2003, www.unep.org/OZONE/pdf/Press-Backgrounder.pdf (3 December 2006); J. Louise Mastrantonio and John K. Francis, "A Student Guide to Tropical Forest Conservation," October 1997, www.fs.fed.us/global/lzone/student/tropical.htm (3 December 2006); World Wildlife Fund, "Forestry: Basic Information," 2006, www.worldwildlife.org/forests/basic.cfm (7 July 2006); Natural Resources Defense Council, "Forest Facts," 27 August 2004 www.nrdc.org/land/forests/fforestf.asp (7 July 2006).

of moral concern as plants? Do humans and non-human animals have the same moral status? Is a cat as morally important as a cabbage? Does a species have a stronger claim on our moral concern than any individual of a species? As we will soon see, on various grounds many people give priority to one or more species over others, some think all living things equal, and some rank species over individuals.

In light of these considerations, we should not be surprised that a central question in environmental ethics is, What entities have moral status and to what degree do they have it? The answer that has been assumed in the Western world for much of its history is known as **anthropocentrism,** the notion that only humans have moral standing. By anthropocentric (human-centered) lights, the rest of nature has only instrumental value—that is, nonhuman animals, plants, mountains, and streams have value only because they are valuable in some way to humans. An anthropocentrist sees animals, plants, and ecosystems as means to enhance the well-being of humankind, to serve the ends of human beings. This stance, however, does not imply a disregard for the environment. He may be genuinely concerned about the destruction of rain forests, the extinction of species, river and lake pollution, the destruction of wetlands, animal cruelty, and global warming—but only because these calamities might lead to a less livable environment for humans, or their loss of enjoyable aesthetic or spiritual experiences of nature, or their feelings of distress at the thought of animal suffering, or dramatic climate changes that could endanger human lives.

On what grounds should humans be granted this exclusive moral status? The traditional justification has been along Kantian lines: that humans are moral agents or persons—they are capable of making free, rational moral choices.

Another influential answer to our question is what could be called **zoocentrism,** the notion that animals—both human and nonhuman—have

moral status. Advocates for animal rights, notably the philosophers Peter Singer and Tom Regan, take this view, insisting that human and nonhuman animals are equally deserving of moral considerability or respect. Singer contends that moral status is justified for nonhuman animals when they, like humans, possess the psychological property of sentience. Sentient nonhuman animals can experience pain and pleasure, just as humans can; therefore, he says, they are entitled to the same level of moral respect. Some critics, however, object to this kind of animal egalitarianism, affirming that all sentient animals do have moral status but that humans have greater moral considerability than nonhuman animals.

Some theorists want to expand the sphere of moral status to include more than just animals. They hold to **biocentrism,** or life-centered ethics, the view that all living entities have moral status, whether sentient or not. People, cats, trees, weeds, algae, amoebas, germs—all these are worthy of some sort of moral concern simply because they are alive. This moral concern, many biocentrists say, is justified by the teleological nature of living things (*telos* is Greek for "goal"). Living things are goal-directed, striving consciously or unconsciously toward some good. They therefore have moral status. But biocentrists differ on how much respect to grant living things. Some assert that all living things have *equal* moral status: exactly the same moral considerability is accorded to human beings, dogs, redwood trees, and amoebas. These biocentrists are therefore **species egalitarians**. Other biocentrists, **species nonegalitarians,** think that not all living beings are created equal—some have more moral worth than others. A nonegalitarian might argue that a human deserves more respect than an elk, an elk more than a rat, and a rat more than a cactus.

In either form, biocentrism implies that in our moral deliberations we cannot ignore how our actions might affect both sentient and nonsentient living beings, as some forms of anthropocentrism might have us do. If we want to build a shopping mall on wetlands, we must consider all the plants and animals that the project would destroy—and judge whether their deaths would outweigh any benefits that the mall would provide to humans and other living things.

In both zoocentrism and biocentrism, the fundamental unit of moral consideration is the *individual*—the individual animal or plant. Only individuals have moral status. This perspective then is *individualistic,* its advocates being called **ecological individualists.** In contrast, some theorists say that the proper focus of moral concern is not the individual but the entire biosphere and its ecosystems, what has been called the "biotic community." This view then is *holistic*; its proponents, **ecological holists.** It implies that in considering our moral obligations to the environment, the good of the whole will always outweigh the good of an individual. An elk, for example, may be killed to preserve a species of plant or to ensure the health of its ecosystem. As one theorist expressed it, "A thing is right when it tends to preserve the integrity, stability, and beauty of the biotic community. It is wrong when it tends otherwise."[2] What properties might confer moral considerability on the biotic community or an ecosystem? A holist might say that such an environmental whole deserves our respect because it is a unity of beautifully integrated parts, or it is a self-regulating system, or its destruction would diminish the world's genetic possibilities.

MORAL THEORIES

On environmental issues, some traditional moral theories have been strongly anthropocentric. Kant's theory is a good example, mandating duties to people because they are ends in themselves but

---

> ### QUICK REVIEW
>
> ***moral status (or moral considerability)***—The property of being a suitable candidate for direct moral concern or respect.
>
> ***anthropocentrism***—The notion that only humans have moral status.
>
> ***zoocentrism***—The notion that both human and nonhuman animals have moral status.
>
> ***biocentrism***—The view that all living entities have moral status, whether sentient or not.
>
> ***species egalitarian***—One who believes that all living things have equal moral status.
>
> ***species nonegalitarian***—One who believes that some living things have greater moral status than others.
>
> ***ecological individualist***—One who believes that the fundamental unit of moral consideration in environmental ethics is the individual.
>
> ***ecological holist***—One who believes that the fundamental unit of moral consideration in environmental ethics is the biosphere and its ecosystems.

---

establishing no direct duties to animals. For Kant, animals have instrumental value only. As he puts it, "Animals . . . are there merely as means to an end. That end is man."[3] Thomas Aquinas, author of the most famous version of natural law theory, also thinks animals are tools to be employed at the discretion of humans. In addition, the Bible has seemed to many to suggest an anthropocentric attitude toward nature, commanding that humans "subdue" the earth and "have dominion over the fish of the sea and over the birds of the air and over every living thing that moves upon

---

[2]Aldo Leopold, "The Land Ethic," in *A Sand County Almanac* (Oxford: Oxford University Press, 1981), 237–65.

[3]Immanuel Kant, *Lectures on Ethics,* trans. Louis Infield (New York: Harper and Row, 1963), 239–40.

CRITICAL THOUGHT: Should Pandas Pay the Price?

Some of the most controversial disputes in environmental ethics involve conflicts between concern for endangered species and the economic needs and demands of humans. Here is just one of many recent examples:

(*China Daily*)—The more than 100 wild giant pandas in Northwest China's Gansu Province are now stepping onto the verge of extinction because of a decline in their ability to reproduce, according to Xinhua reports.

Researchers from the Gansu Baishuijiang Giant Panda Nature Reserve said the giant pandas in the province now live in five separate habitats, making mating among the groups almost impossible.

According to basic principles of genetics and the pandas' reproduction habits, a group of less than 50 giant pandas are predicted to become extinct at some point as a result of a weakening reproductive ability caused by inbreeding.

Wang Hao, a giant panda expert of Peking University, said the fragmentation of wild pandas' habitats had become the biggest threat to the survival of the species.

Wang said that the construction of highways is cutting large panda habitats into smaller and smaller ones, increasing the risk of degeneration of the species. . . .

Wang estimated that the annual cost to protect one wild panda exceeds 5 million yuan (US$617,000).*

Which should be given more moral weight—the people or the pandas? What are your reasons for preferring one over the other? If you agree that we should try to save endangered species like the panda, how much should we be willing to pay to do so? Is $617,000 per panda an acceptable price? How about $1 million? Suppose saving one panda would put one thousand people out of a job, forcing scores of families into poverty. Would saving the pandas be worth that cost? Why or why not? What moral principle would you devise to help you answer these questions (and similar questions regarding any endangered species)?

* Guo Nei, "Road Construction Segregates Giant Pandas' Habitats in Gansu," *China Daily*, 5 December 2005. Reprinted from China Daily.

the earth" (Genesis 1.28). But traditional theories can also be—and have been—construed in various ways to support nonanthropocentric approaches to environmental ethics.

As we have seen, some theorists adopt a nonconsequentialist or Kantian-like perspective on nature. They reject instrumentalist views in favor of the notion that the environment or its constituents have intrinsic value, just as persons are thought to be intrinsically valuable. Probably the most overtly Kantian theorist is the philosopher Paul Taylor, a biocentrist who argues that "it is the good (well-being, welfare) of individual organisms, considered as entities having inherent worth, that determines our moral relations with the Earth's wild communities of life" and that

"[their] well-being, as well as human well-being, is something to be realized *as an end in itself*."[4] Some zoocentrists also have a Kantian bent. For example, Tom Regan argues that sentient animals, human and nonhuman, possess equal intrinsic worth and therefore have an equal moral right not to be treated as mere things.[5] In this account, just as there are certain things that we should not do to humans regardless of the resulting utilitarian benefits, so there are ways of treating nonhuman animals that are wrong regardless

[4]Paul W. Taylor, "The Ethics of Respect for Nature," *Environmental Ethics* 3 (1981): 198.
[5]Tom Regan, "Animal Rights, Human Wrongs," *Environmental Ethics* 2, no. 2 (Summer 1980): 99–120.

of the advantages to humans. According to Regan, the result of applying this outlook to the treatment of animals would be the eradication of factory farming, animal experimentation, and hunting.

Utilitarianism has also been put to use in defense of nonhuman animals. Following the lead of the philosopher Jeremy Bentham, utilitarianism's founder, Peter Singer maintains that in calculating which action will produce the greatest overall satisfaction of interests (for example, an interest in avoiding pain), we must include the interests of all sentient creatures and give their interests equal weight. The pain suffered by a human is no more important than that experienced by a nonhuman animal. This view seems to imply that any factory farming in which animals suffer greatly before being slaughtered is wrong. But it also seems to suggest that if the animals could be raised without such suffering, factory farming may be morally permissible, even if they are killed in the end.

MORAL ARGUMENTS

Serious environmental issues and the arguments that surround them are numerous, varied, and complex, so for the purposes of evaluation let us focus on arguments pertaining to the one question that has concerned us most throughout this chapter: *When, if ever, do environmental entities or beings have moral status?* As we have seen, environmental philosophers and other thinkers have argued for and against different kinds of entities having moral considerability and for and against various justifications for that status. The entities thought to be worthy of such moral concern include human beings exclusively (anthropocentrism), human and nonhuman animals (zoocentrism), living things (biocentrism), and collections or systems of living things such as species or ecosystems (ecological holism). The properties that are supposed to validate their claim to moral

worth range across a broad spectrum of possibilities—from moral agency or sentience to complexity to self-regulation to beauty.

To begin, let us examine a simple argument containing a premise that offers a common answer to our question—the answer that entities in the environment have moral status because they are *natural* (lacking human interference or contrivance).

1. All natural entities have moral status (intrinsic value or rights, for example).

2. Old-growth forests are natural entities.

3. Therefore, old-growth forests have moral status.

We can see right away that this is a valid argument, but—as is so often the case in moral arguments—the moral premise (Premise 1) is not obviously true (though the other premise definitely is). What reasons might someone give to support the statement that objects in nature deserve our respect just because their properties are due solely to natural processes?

One reason that could be put forth is that Premise 1 is supported by our moral intuitions (our considered moral judgments, for example). To test this idea, mull over this thought experiment:

Imagine that a certain mine requires the destruction of a group of trees on a rocky outcrop and of the outcrop itself. Environmentalists protest that such destruction involves an uncompensated loss of value. The mining company promises to reconstruct the outcrop from synthetic parts and to replace the trees with plastic models. This bit of artificial environment will be indistinguishable, except by laboratory analysis, from what was originally there. It will be exactly as appealing to look at, no animals will be harmed as a consequence, and no ecosystem will be disrupted.[6]

---

[6]Robert Elliot, "Environmental Ethics," in *A Companion to Ethics*, ed. Peter Singer, corr. ed. (Oxford: Blackwell, 1993), 291.

What if anything, would be wrong with replacing these natural entities with synthetic ones? A few trees would be destroyed, and thus there is a loss of living things, but let us mentally discount the loss. Would this substitution of nonnatural for natural make a moral difference? Would the mining company be guilty of wrongdoing? If this scenario suggests to us that the property of naturalness does confer some kind of moral standing on objects, then perhaps our moral intuitions do support Premise 1.

The obvious move for a critic is to assert that it is not at all clear whether moral intuitions offer such support. Perhaps we are merely confused, actually worrying not about unnaturalness but about harm to ecosystems or extermination of wildlife.[7]

A defender of Premise 1 could try another tack. She could attempt to take our moral intuitions in a different direction, declaring that just as fake works of art seem to have less value for us than the originals, so synthetic objects in the environment have less intrinsic value than their natural counterparts or originals. We simply do not appreciate replicas of fine sculptures as much as we do the originals, and we do not respect artificial trees as much we do natural ones. The property of being natural, then, appears to confer some value on objects—and thus some level of moral standing.[8]

A detractor could cast doubt on this line by pointing out that there seem to be instances in which we do in fact value the artificial more than the natural. For example, Niagara Falls on the American side of the border with Canada is undeniably beautiful and majestic, exemplifying the ideal waterfall in its natural state. But oddly enough, the majestic, "natural" state of the falls is largely a product of human ingenuity. Because of natural erosion, the falls deteriorate over time and—without human intervention—would suffer so much damage that it would no longer look much like the falls people have come to expect. Through reconstruction and control of water flow, engineers have saved Niagara Falls, a now largely artificial phenomenon that people would almost certainly prefer over the natural but less impressive version.[9]

Let us now consider a "higher level" sort of argument, one that tries to establish the truth of a particular environmental theory, in this case biocentric egalitarianism. Recall that this doctrine asserts that all living things possess equal moral status—no being is superior to any other in moral considerability. Humans, then, are not entitled to more respect than apes or redwoods or elk. Here is how the philosopher Paul Taylor argues for this position:[10]

1. Humans are members of earth's community of life in exactly the same way that all other living things are members.

2. Human beings and all other living things constitute a dynamic system of interlinked and interdependent parts.

3. Each living thing is a "teleological center of life, pursuing its own good in its own way."

4. Human beings are not superior to other species.

5. Therefore, all living things have equal moral status.

This argument is complex and deserves far more close analysis than we can provide here. But we can home in on a few interesting elements.

Consider Premise 4. At the outset, note that the argument is not valid: the conclusion does not

---

[7]Elliot, "Environmental Ethics," 292.

[8]This argument is a vastly oversimplified rendering of Robert Elliot's argument in "Faking Nature," *Inquiry* 25, no. 1 (1982): 81–93.

[9]This example is adapted from Martin H. Krieger, "What's Wrong with Plastic Trees?" *Science* 179 (1973): 446–55.

[10]Taylor, "The Ethics of Respect for Nature," 197–218; quotation, 207.

follow from the first four premises. Taylor acknowledges this fact but suggests that if we accept Premises 1–4, then it would at least be more reasonable than not to accept the conclusion. He says the same thing about Premise 4: if we accept Premises 1–3, it would not be unreasonable to accept the fourth premise. But some argue that Premise 4 does not follow from Premises 1–3. More to the point, it could be argued that even if we accept that humans are part of an interdependent community of life in which all members are teleological centers pursuing their own good, we are not necessarily being unreasonable if we then reject the idea that humans are on a par with all other species. Even if Premises 1–3 are true, we are not obliged to accept Premise 4.

Some philosophers have argued directly against Taylor's conclusion (Statement 5) by drawing out its implications. If all species are morally equal, what would that imply about how we treat various species? One critic gives this answer:

What seems far more problematic for species egalitarianism is that it seems to suggest that it makes no difference *what* we kill. Vegetarians typically think it worse to kill a cow than to kill a carrot. Are they wrong? Yes they are, according to species egalitarianism. In this respect, species egalitarianism cannot be right. I believe we have reason to respect nature. But we fail to give nature due respect if we say we should have no more respect for a cow than for a potato.[11]

This counterargument is, of course, another appeal to our moral intuitions. We are asked to reflect on whether it would be morally permissible to treat a cow as if it had the same moral status as a potato. If they do deserve the same level of respect, then if we must kill one of them, we should not care which. They are moral equals. But if we think that it does matter which one we kill, we have reason to reject the notion that they are moral equals—and thus deny biocentric egalitarianism.

SUMMARY

Environmental ethics, a branch of applied ethics, explores questions about the value of nature and its constituents, the relationship between the environment and humans, and the moral obligations that humans have toward the environment. Logical arguments in the field rely on several key concepts, including instrumental value, intrinsic value, and moral status or considerability. Something with instrumental value is valuable as a means to something else; something with intrinsic value is valuable in itself. An entity has *moral status* if it is a suitable candidate for moral concern or respect in its own right.

Several positions have been staked out regarding the proper attitude of humans toward nature. Anthropocentrism is the view that only humans have moral standing; zoocentrism, that animals do; and biocentrism, that all living things do. Species egalitarians believe that all living things have equal moral status; species nonegalitarians, that they do not. Ecological individualists think that only individuals have moral status; ecological holists, that only the biosphere and its ecosystems do.

Some theorists have adopted a Kantian-like perspective on the environment. Paul Taylor insists that organisms have inherent worth and should not be treated merely as means to ends. Tom Regan asserts that sentient beings possess equal intrinsic worth and should not be considered mere things. A utilitarian stance is also possible, as Peter Singer has demonstrated in his position on animal rights.

[11]David Schmidtz, "Are All Species Equal?" *Journal of Applied Philosophy* 15 (1998): 59.

READINGS

People or Penguins

William F. Baxter

I start with the modest proposition that, in dealing with pollution, or indeed with any problem, it is helpful to know what one is attempting to accomplish. Agreement on how and whether to pursue a particular objective, such as pollution control, is not possible unless some more general objective has been identified and stated with reasonable precision. We talk loosely of having clean air and clean water, of preserving our wilderness areas, and so forth. But none of these is a sufficiently general objective: each is more accurately viewed as a means rather than as an end.

With regard to clean air, for example, one may ask, "how clean?" and "what does clean mean?" It is even reasonable to ask, "why have clean air?" Each of these questions is an implicit demand that a more general community goal be stated—a goal sufficiently general in its scope and enjoying sufficiently general assent among the community of actors that such "why" questions no longer seem admissible with respect to that goal.

If, for example, one states as a goal the proposition that "every person should be free to do whatever he wishes in contexts where his actions do not interfere with the interests of other human beings," the speaker is unlikely to be met with a response of "why." The goal may be criticized as uncertain in its implications or difficult to implement, but it is so basic a tenet of our civilization—it reflects a cultural value so broadly shared, at least in the abstract—that the question "why" is seen as impertinent or imponderable or both.

I do not mean to suggest that everyone would agree with the "spheres of freedom" objective just

stated. Still less do I mean to suggest that a society could subscribe to four or five such general objectives that would be adequate in their coverage to serve as testing criteria by which all other disagreements might be measured. One difficulty in the attempt to construct such a list is that each new goal added will conflict, in certain applications, with each prior goal listed; and thus each goal serves as a limited qualification on prior goals.

Without any expectation of obtaining unanimous consent to them, let me set forth four goals that I generally use as ultimate testing criteria in attempting to frame solutions to problems of human organization. My position regarding pollution stems from these four criteria. If the criteria appeal to you and any part of what appears hereafter does not, our disagreement will have a helpful focus: which of us is correct, analytically, in supposing that his position on pollution would better serve these general goals. If the criteria do not seem acceptable to you, then it is to be expected that our more particular judgments will differ, and the task will then be yours to identify the basic set of criteria upon which your particular judgments rest.

My criteria are as follows:

1. The spheres of freedom criterion stated above.
2. Waste is a bad thing. The dominant feature of human existence is scarcity—our available resources, our aggregate labors, and our skill in employing both have always been, and will continue for some time to be, inadequate to yield to every man all the tangible and intangible satisfactions he would like to have. Hence, none of those resources, or labors, or skills, should be wasted—that is, employed so as to yield less than they might yield in human satisfactions.
3. Every human being should be regarded as an end rather than as a means to be used for the better-

ment of another. Each should be afforded dignity and regarded as having an absolute claim to an evenhanded application of such rules as the community may adopt for its governance.

4. Both the incentive and the opportunity to improve his share of satisfactions should be preserved to every individual. Preservation of incentive is dictated by the "no-waste" criterion and enjoins against the continuous, totally egalitarian redistribution of satisfactions, or wealth; but subject to that constraint, everyone should receive, by continuous redistribution if necessary, some minimal share of aggregate wealth so as to avoid a level of privation from which the opportunity to improve his situation becomes illusory.

The relationship of these highly general goals to the more specific environmental issues at hand may not be readily apparent, and I am not yet ready to demonstrate their pervasive implications. But let me give one indication of their implications. Recently scientists have informed us that use of DDT in food production is causing damage to the penguin population. For the present purposes let us accept that assertion as an indisputable scientific fact. The scientific fact is often asserted as if the correct implication—that we must stop agricultural use of DDT—followed from the mere statement of the fact of penguin damage. But plainly it does not follow if my criteria are employed.

My criteria are oriented to people, not penguins. Damage to penguins, or sugar pines, or geological marvels is, without more, simply irrelevant. One must go further, by my criteria, and say: Penguins are important because people enjoy seeing them walk about rocks; and furthermore, the well-being of people would be less impaired by halting use of DDT than by giving up penguins. In short, my observations about environmental problems will be people-oriented, as are my criteria. I have no interest in preserving penguins for their own sake.

It may be said by way of objection to this position, that it is very selfish of people to act as if each person represented one unit of importance and nothing else was of any importance. It is undeniably self-

ish. Nevertheless I think it is the only tenable starting place for analysis for several reasons. First, no other position corresponds to the way most people really think and act—i.e., corresponds to reality.

Second, this attitude does not portend any massive destruction of nonhuman flora and fauna, for people depend on them in many obvious ways, and they will be preserved because and to the degree that humans do depend on them.

Third, what is good for humans is, in many respects, good for penguins and pine trees—clean air for example. So that humans are, in these respects, surrogates for plant and animal life.

Fourth, I do not know how we could administer any other system. Our decisions are either private or collective. Insofar as Mr. Jones is free to act privately, he may give such preferences as he wishes to other forms of life: he may feed birds in winter and do with less himself, and he may even decline to resist an advancing polar bear on the ground that the bear's appetite is more important than those portions of himself that the bear may choose to eat. In short my basic premise does not rule out private altruism to competing life-forms. It does rule out, however, Mr. Jones inclination to feed Mr. Smith to the bear, however hungry the bear, however despicable Mr. Smith.

Insofar as we act collectively on the other hand, only humans can be afforded an opportunity to participate in the collective decisions. Penguins cannot vote now and are unlikely subjects for the franchise—pine trees more unlikely still. Again each individual is free to cast his vote so as to benefit sugar pines if that is his inclination. But many of the more extreme assertions that one hears from some conservationists amount to tacit assertions that they are specially appointed representatives of sugar pines, and hence that their preferences should be weighted more heavily than the preferences of other humans who do not enjoy equal rapport with "nature." The simplistic assertion that agricultural use of DDT must stop at once because it is harmful to penguins is of that type.

Fifth, if polar bears or pine trees or penguins, like men, are to be regarded as ends rather than means, if they are to count in our calculus of social organization, someone must tell me how much each one counts, and someone must tell me how these life-forms are to be permitted to express their preferences, for I do not know either answer. If the answer is that certain people are to hold their proxies, then I want to know how those proxy-holders are to be selected: self-appointment does not seem workable to me.

Sixth, and by way of summary of all the foregoing, let me point out that the set of environmental issues under discussion—although they raise very complex technical questions of how to achieve any objective—ultimately raise a normative question: what *ought* we to do. Questions of *ought* are unique to the human mind and world—they are meaningless as applied to a nonhuman situation.

I reject the proposition that we *ought* to respect the "balance of nature" or to "preserve the environment" unless the reason for doing so, express or implied, is the benefit of man.

I reject the idea that there is a "right" or "morally correct" state of nature to which we should return. The word "nature" has no normative connotation. Was it "right" or "wrong" for the earth's crust to heave in contortion and create mountains and seas? Was it "right" for the first amphibian to crawl up out of the primordial ooze. Was it "wrong" for plants to reproduce themselves and alter the atmospheric composition in favor of oxygen? For animals to alter the atmosphere in favor of carbon dioxide both by breathing oxygen and eating plants? No answers can be given to these questions because they are meaningless questions.

All this may seem obvious to the point of being tedious, but much of the present controversy over environment and pollution rests on tacit normative assumptions about just such nonnormative phenomena that it is "wrong" to impair penguins with DDT, but not to slaughter cattle for prime rib roasts. That it is wrong to kill stands of sugar pines with industrial fumes, but not to cut sugar pines and build housing for the poor. Every man is entitled to his own preferred definition of Walden Pond, but there is no definition that has any moral superiority over another, except by reference to the selfish needs of the human race.

From the fact that there is no normative definition of the natural state, it follows that there is no normative definition of clean air or pure water—hence no definition of polluted air—or of pollution—except by reference to the needs of man. The "right" composition of the atmosphere is one which has some dust in it and some lead in it and some hydrogen sulfide in it—just those amounts that attend a sensibly organized society thoughtfully and knowledgeably pursuing the greatest possible satisfaction for its human members.

The first and most fundamental step toward solution of our environmental problems is a clear recognition that our objective is not pure air or water but rather some optimal state of pollution. That step immediately suggests the question: How do we define and attain the level of pollution that will yield the maximum possible amount of human satisfaction?

Low levels of pollution contribute to human satisfaction but so do food and shelter and education and music. To attain ever lower levels of pollution, we must pay the cost of having less of these other things. I contrast that view of the cost of pollution control with the more popular statement that pollution control will "cost" very large numbers of dollars. The popular statement is true in some senses, false in others; sorting out the true and false senses is of some importance. The first step in that sorting process is to achieve a clear understanding of the difference between dollars and resources. Resources are the wealth of our nation; dollars are merely claim checks upon those resources. Resources are of vital importance; dollars are comparatively trivial.

Four categories of resources are sufficient for our purposes: At any given time a nation, or a planet if you prefer, has a stock of labor, of technological skill, of capital goods, and of natural resources (such as mineral deposits, timber, water, land, etc.). These resources can be used in various combinations to yield goods and services of all kinds—in some limited quantity. The quantity will be larger if they are combined efficiently, smaller if combined inefficiently. But in either event the resource stock is limited, the goods and services that they can be made to yield are limited; even the most efficient use of them will yield less than our population, in the aggregate, would like to have.

If one considers building a new dam, it is appropriate to say that it will be costly in the sense that it will require x hours of labor, y tons of steel and concrete, and z amount of capital goods. If these resources are devoted to the dam, then they cannot be used to build hospitals, fishing rods, schools, or electric can openers. That is the meaningful sense in which the dam is costly.

Quite apart from the very important question of how wisely we can combine our resources to produce goods and services, is the very different question of how they get distributed—who gets how many goods? Dollars constitute the claim checks which are distributed among people and which control their share of national output. Dollars are nearly valueless pieces of paper except to the extent that they do represent claim checks to some fraction of the output of goods and services. Viewed as claim checks, all the dollars outstanding during any period of time are worth, in the aggregate, the goods and services that are available to be claimed with them during that period—neither more nor less.

It is far easier to increase the supply of dollars than to increase the production of goods and services—printing dollars is easy. But printing more dollars doesn't help because each dollar then simply becomes a claim to fewer goods, i.e., becomes worth less.

The point is this: many people fall into error upon hearing the statement that the decision to build a dam, or to clean up a river, will cost $X million. It is regrettably easy to say: "It's only money. This is a wealthy country, and we have lots of money." But you cannot build a dam or clean a river with $X million—unless you also have a match, you can't even make a fire. One builds a dam or cleans a river by diverting labor and steel and trucks and factories from making one kind of goods to making another. The cost in dollars is merely a shorthand way of describing the extent of the diversion necessary. If we build a dam for $X million, then we must recognize that we will have $X million less housing and food and medical care and electric can openers as a result.

Similarly, the costs of controlling pollution are best expressed in terms of the other goods we will have to give up to do the job. This is not to say the job should not be done. Badly as we need more housing, more medical care, and more can openers, and more symphony orchestras, we could do with somewhat less of them, in my judgment at least, in exchange for somewhat cleaner air and rivers. But that is the nature of the trade-off, and analysis of the problem is advanced if that unpleasant reality is kept in mind. Once the trade-off relationship is clearly perceived, it is possible to state in a very general way what the optimal level of pollution is. I would state it as follows:

People enjoy watching penguins. They enjoy relatively clean air and smog-free vistas. Their health is improved by relatively clean water and air. Each of these benefits is a type of good or service. As a society we would be well advised to give up one washing machine if the resources that would have gone into that washing machine can yield greater human satisfaction when diverted into pollution control. We should give up one hospital if the resources thereby freed would yield more human satisfaction when devoted to elimination of noise in our cities. And so on, trade-off by trade-off, we should divert our productive capacities from the production of existing goods and services to the production of a cleaner, quieter, more pastoral nation up to—and no further than—the point at which we value more highly the next washing machine or hospital that we would have to do without than we value the next unit of environmental improvement that the diverted resources would create.

Now this proposition seems to me unassailable but so general and abstract as to be unhelpful—at least unadministerable in the form stated. It assumes we can measure in some way the incremental units of human satisfaction yielded by very different types of goods. The proposition must remain a pious abstraction until I can explain how this measurement process can occur. In subsequent chapters I will attempt to show that we can do this—in some contexts with great precision and in other contexts only by rough approximation. But I insist that the proposition stated describes the result for which we should be striving—and again, that it is always useful to know what your target is even if your weapons are too crude to score a bull's eye.

The Ethics of Respect for Nature

PAUL W. TAYLOR

I. HUMAN-CENTERED AND LIFE-CENTERED SYSTEMS OF ENVIRONMENTAL ETHICS

In this paper I show how the taking of a certain ultimate moral attitude toward nature, which I call "respect for nature," has a central place in the foundations of a life-centered system of environmental ethics. I hold that a set of moral norms (both standards of character and rules of conduct) governing human treatment of the natural world is a rationally grounded set if and only if, first, commitment to those norms is a practical entailment of adopting the attitude of respect for nature as an ultimate moral attitude, and second, the adopting of that attitude on the part of all rational agents can itself be justified. When the basic characteristics of the attitude of respect for nature are made clear, it will be seen that a life-centered system of environmental ethics need not be holistic or organicist in its conception of the kinds of entities that are deemed the appropriate objects of moral concern and consideration. Nor does such a system require that the concepts of ecological homeostasis, equilibrium, and integrity provide us with normative principles from which could be derived (with the addition of factual knowledge) our obligations with regard to natural ecosystems. The "balance of nature" is not itself a moral norm, however important may be the role it plays in our general outlook on the natural world that underlies the attitude of respect of nature. I argue that finally it is the good (well-being, welfare) of individual organisms, considered as entities having inherent worth, that determines our moral relations with the Earth's wild communities of life.

In designating the theory to be set forth as life-centered, I intend to contrast it with all anthropocentric views. According to the latter, human actions affecting the natural environment and its

Paul W. Taylor, "The Ethics of Respect for Nature," *Environmental Ethics* 3, no. 3 (1981): 197–218 (edited). Reprinted with permission of Paul Taylor.

nonhuman inhabitants are right (or wrong) by either of two criteria: they have consequences which are favorable (or unfavorable) to human well-being, or they are consistent (or inconsistent) with the system of norms that protect and implement human rights. From this human-centered standpoint it is to humans and only to humans that all duties are ultimately owed. We may have responsibilities *with regard to* the natural ecosystems and biotic communities of our planet, but these responsibilities are in every case based on the contingent fact that our treatment of those ecosystems and communities of life can further the realization of human values and/or human rights. We have no obligation to promote or protect the good of nonhuman living things, independently of this contingent fact.

A life-centered system of environmental ethics is opposed to human-centered ones precisely on this point. From the perspective of a life-centered theory, we have prima facie moral obligations that are owed to wild plants and animals themselves as members of the Earth's biotic community. We are morally bound (other things being equal) to protect or promote their good for *their* sake. Our duties to respect the integrity of natural ecosystems, to preserve endangered species, and to avoid environmental pollution stem from the fact that these are ways in which we can help make it possible for wild species populations to achieve and maintain a healthy existence in a natural state. Such obligations are due those living things out of recognition of their inherent worth. They are entirely additional to and independent of the obligations we owe to our fellow humans. Although many of the actions that fulfill one set of obligations will also fulfill the other, two different grounds of obligation are involved. Their well-being, as well as human well-being, is something to be realized *as an end in itself*.

If we were to accept a life-centered theory of environmental ethics, a profound reordering of our moral universe would take place. We would begin to look at the whole of the Earth's biosphere in a new light. Our duties with respect to the "world" of nature would be seen as making prima facie claims upon us to be balanced against our duties with respect to the "world" of human civilization. We could no longer simply take the human point of view and consider the effects of our actions exclusively from the perspective of our own good.

II. THE GOOD OF A BEING AND THE CONCEPT OF INHERENT WORTH

What would justify acceptance of a life-centered system of ethical principles? In order to answer this it is first necessary to make clear the fundamental moral attitude that underlies and makes intelligible the commitment to live by such a system. It is then necessary to examine the considerations that would justify any rational agent's adopting that moral attitude.

Two concepts are essential to the taking of a moral attitude of the sort in question. A being which does not "have" these concepts, that is, which is unable to grasp their meaning and conditions of applicability, cannot be said to have the attitude as part of its moral outlook. These concepts are, first, that of the good (well-being, welfare) of a living thing, and second, the idea of an entity possessing inherent worth. I examine each concept in turn.

(1) Every organism, species population, and community of life has a good of its own which moral agents can intentionally further or damage by their actions. To say that an entity has a good of its own is simply to say that, without reference to any *other* entity, it can be benefited or harmed. One can act in its overall interest or contrary to its overall interest, and environmental conditions can be good for it (advantageous to it) or bad for it (disadvantageous to it). What is good for an entity is what "does it good" in the sense of enhancing or preserving its life and well-being. What is bad for an entity is something that is detrimental to its life and well-being.

We can think of the good of an individual non-human organism as consisting in the full development of its biological powers. Its good is realized to the extent that it is strong and healthy. It possesses whatever capacities it needs for successfully coping with its environment and so preserving its existence throughout the various stages of the normal life cycle of its species. The good of a population or community of such individuals consists in the population or community maintaining itself from generation to generation as a coherent system of genetically and ecologically related organisms whose average good is at an optimum level for the given environment. (Here *average good* means that the degree of realization of the good of *individual organisms* in the population or community is, on average, greater than would be the case under any other ecologically functioning order of interrelations among those species populations in the given ecosystem.)

The idea of a being having a good of its own, as I understand it, does not entail that the being must have interests or take an interest in what affects its life for better or for worse. We can act in a being's interest or contrary to its interest without its being interested in what we are doing to it in the sense of wanting or not wanting us to do it. It may, indeed, be wholly unaware that favorable and unfavorable events are taking place in its life. I take it that trees, for example, have no knowledge or desires or feelings. Yet it is undoubtedly the case that trees can be harmed or benefited by our actions. We can crush their roots by running a bulldozer too close to them. We can see to it that they get adequate nourishment and moisture by fertilizing and watering the soil around them. Thus we can help or hinder them in the realization of their good. It is the good of trees themselves that is thereby affected. We can similarly act so as to further the good of an entire tree population of a certain species (say, all the redwood trees in a California valley) or the good of a whole community of plant life in a given wilderness area, just as we can do harm to such a population or community.

When constructed in this way, the concept of a being's good is not coextensive with sentience or the capacity for feeling pain. William Frankena has argued for a general theory of environmental ethics in which the ground of a creature's being worthy of moral consideration is its sentience. I have offered some criticisms of this view elsewhere, but the full refutation of such a position, it seems to me, finally depends on the positive reasons for accepting a life-centered theory of a kind I am defending in this essay.

It should be noted further that I am leaving open the question of whether machines—in particular, those which are not only goal-directed, but also self-regulating—can properly be said to have a good of their own. Since I am concerned only with human treatment of wild organisms, species populations, and communities of life as they occur in our planet's natural ecosystems, it is to those entities alone that the concept "having a good of its own" will here be applied. I am not denying that other living things, whose genetic origin and environmental conditions have been produced, controlled, and manipulated by humans for human ends, do have a good of their own in the same sense as do wild plants and animals. It is not my purpose in this essay, however, to set out or defend the principles that should guide our conduct with regard to their good. It is only insofar as their production and use by humans have good or ill effects upon natural ecosystems and their wild inhabitants that the ethics of respect for nature comes into play.

(2) The second concept essential to the moral attitude of respect for nature is the idea of inherent worth. We take that attitude toward wild living things (individuals, species populations, or whole biotic communities) when and only when we regard them as entities possessing inherent worth. Indeed, it is only because they are conceived in this way that moral agents can think of themselves as having validly blinding duties, obligations, and responsibilities that are *owed* to them as their *due*. I am not at this juncture arguing why they *should* be so regarded; I consider it at length below. But so regarding them is a presupposition of our taking the attitude of respect toward them and accordingly understanding ourselves as bearing certain moral relations to them. This can be shown as follows:

What does it mean to regard an entity that has a good of its own as possessing inherent worth? Two general principles are involved: the principle of moral consideration and the principle of intrinsic value.

According to the principle of moral consideration, wild living things are deserving of the concern and consideration of all moral agents simply in virtue of their being members of the Earth's community of life. From the moral point of view their good must be taken into account whenever it is affected for better or worse by the conduct of rational agents. This holds no matter what species the creature belongs to. The good of each is to be accorded some value and so acknowledged as having some weight in the deliberation of all rational agents. Of course, it may be necessary for such agents to act in ways contrary to the good of this or that particular organism or group of organisms in order to further the good of others, including the good of humans. But the principle of moral consideration prescribes that, with respect to each being an entity having its own good, every individual is deserving of consideration.

The principle of intrinsic value states that, regardless of what kind of entity it is in other respects, if it is a member of the Earth's community of life, the realization of its good is something *intrinsically* valuable. This means that its good is prima facie worthy of being preserved or promoted as an end in itself and for the sake of the entity whose good it is. Insofar as we regard any organism, species population, or life community as an entity having inherent worth, we believe that it must never be treated as if it were a mere object or thing whose entire value lies in being instrumental to the good of some other entity. The well-being of each is judged to have value in and of itself.

Combining these two principles, we can now define what it means for a living thing or group of living things to possess inherent worth. To say that it possesses inherent worth is to say that its good is deserving of the concern and consideration of all moral agents, and that the realization of its good has intrinsic value, to be pursued as an end in itself and for the sake of the entity whose good it is.

The duties owed to wild organisms, species populations, and communities of life in the Earth's natural ecosystems are grounded on their inherent worth. When rational, autonomous agents regard such entities as possessing inherent worth, they place intrinsic value on the realization of their good and so hold themselves responsible for performing actions that will have this effect and for refraining from actions having the contrary effect.

III. THE ATTITUDE OF RESPECT FOR NATURE

Why should moral agents regard wild living things in the natural world as possessing inherent worth? To answer this question we must first take into account the fact that, when rational, autonomous agents subscribe to the principles of moral consideration and intrinsic value and so conceive of wild living things as having that kind of worth, such agents are *adopting a certain ultimate moral attitude toward the natural world*. This is the attitude I call "respect for nature." It parallels the attitude of respect for persons in human ethics. When we adopt the attitude of respect for persons as the proper (fitting, appropriate) attitude to take toward all persons as persons, we consider the fulfillment of the basic interests of each individual to have intrinsic value. We thereby make a moral commitment to live a certain kind of life in relation to other persons. We place ourselves under the direction of a system of standards and rules that we consider validly binding on all moral agents as such.

Similarly, when we adopt the attitude of respect for nature as an ultimate moral attitude we make a commitment to live by certain normative principles. These principles constitute the rules of conduct and standards of character that are to govern our treatment of the natural world. This is, first, an *ultimate* commitment because it is not derived from any higher norm. The attitude of respect for nature is not grounded on some other, more general, or more fundamental attitude. It sets the total framework for our responsibilities toward the natural world. It can be justified, as I show below, but its justification cannot consist in referring to a more general attitude or a more basic normative principle.

Second, the commitment is a *moral* one because it is understood to be a disinterested matter of principle. It is this feature that distinguishes the attitude of respect for nature from the set of feelings and dis-

positions that comprise the love of nature. The latter stems from one's personal interest in an response to the natural world. Like the affectionate feelings we have toward certain individual human beings, one's love of nature is nothing more than the particular way one feels about the natural environment and its wild inhabitants. And just as our love for an individual person differs from our respect for all persons as such (whether we happen to love them or not), so love of nature differs from respect for nature. Respect for nature is an attitude we believe all moral agents ought to have simply as moral agents, regardless of whether or not they also love nature. Indeed, we have not truly taken the attitude of respect for nature ourselves unless we believe this. To put it in a Kantian way, to adopt the attitude of respect for nature is to take a stance that one wills it to be a universal law for all rational beings. It is to hold that stance categorically, as being validly applicable to every moral agent without exception, irrespective of whatever personal feelings toward nature such an agent might have or might lack.

Although the attitude of respect for nature is in this sense a disinterested and universalizable attitude, anyone who does adopt it has certain steady, more or less permanent dispositions. These dispositions, which are themselves to be considered disinterested and universalizable, comprise three interlocking sets: dispositions to seek certain ends, dispositions to carry on one's practical reasoning and deliberation in a certain way, and dispositions to have certain feelings. We may accordingly analyze the attitude of respect for nature into the following components. (a) The disposition to aim at, and to take steps to bring about, as final and disinterested ends, the promoting and protecting of the good of organisms, species populations, and life communities in natural ecosystems. (These ends are "final" in not being pursued as means to further ends. They are "disinterested" in being independent of the self-interest of the agent.) (b) The disposition to consider actions that tend to realize those ends to be prima facie obligatory *because* they have that tendency. (c) The disposition to experience positive and negative feelings toward states of affairs in the world *because* they are favorable or unfavorable to the good of organisms, species populations, and life communities in natural ecosystems.

The logical connection between the attitude of respect for nature and the duties of a life-centered system of environmental ethics can now be made clear. Insofar as one sincerely takes that attitude and so has the three sets of dispositions, one will at the same time be disposed to comply with certain rules of duty (such as nonmaleficence and noninterference) and with standards of character (such as fairness and benevolence) that determine the obligations and virtues of moral agents with regard to the Earth's wild living things. We can say that the actions one performs and the character traits one develops in fulfilling these moral requirements are the way one *expresses* or *embodies* the attitude in one's conduct and character. In his famous essay, "Justice as Fairness," John Rawls describes the rules of the duties of human morality (such as fidelity, gratitude, honesty, and justice) as "forms of conduct in which recognition of others as persons is manifested."[1] I hold that the rules of duty governing our treatment of the natural world and its inhabitants are forms of conduct in which the attitude of respect for nature is manifested.

IV. THE JUSTIFIABILITY OF THE ATTITUDE OF RESPECT FOR NATURE

I return to the question posed earlier, which has not yet been answered: why *should* moral agents regard wild living things as possessing inherent worth? I now argue that the only way we can answer this question is by showing how adopting the attitude of respect for nature is justified for all moral agents. Let us suppose that we were able to establish that there are good reasons for adopting the attitude, reasons which are intersubjectively valid for every rational agent. If there are such reasons, they would justify anyone's having the three sets of dispositions mentioned above as constituting what it means to have the attitude. Since these include the disposition to promote or protect the good of wild living things as a disinterested and ultimate end, as well as the disposition to perform actions for the reason that they tend to realize that end, we see that such dispositions commit a person to the princi-

ples of moral consideration and intrinsic value. To be disposed to further, as an end in itself, the good of any entity in nature just because it is that kind of entity, is to be disposed to give consideration to *every* such entity and to place intrinsic value on the realization of its good. Insofar as we subscribe to these two principles we regard living things as possessing inherent worth. Subscribing to the principles is what it *means* to so regard them. To justify the attitude of respect for nature, then, is to justify commitment to these principles and thereby to justify regarding wild creatures as possessing inherent worth.

We must keep in mind that inherent worth is not some mysterious sort of objective property belonging to living things that can be discovered by empirical observation or scientific investigation. To ascribe inherent worth to an entity is not to describe it by citing some feature discernible by sense perception or inferable by inductive reasoning. Nor is there a logically necessary connection between the concept of a being having a good of its own and the concept of inherent worth. We do not contradict ourselves by asserting that an entity that has a good of its own lacks inherent worth. In order to show that such an entity "has" inherent worth we must give good reasons for ascribing that kind of value to it (placing that kind of value upon it, conceiving of it to be valuable in that way). Although it is humans (persons, valuers) who must do the valuing, for the ethics of respect for nature, the value so ascribed is not a human value. That is to say, it is not a value derived from considerations regarding human well-being or human rights. It is a value that is ascribed to non-human animals and plants themselves, independently of their relationship to what humans judge to be conducive to their own good.

Whatever reasons, then, justify our taking the attitude of respect for nature as defined above are also reasons that show why we *should* regard the living things of the natural world as possessing inherent worth. We saw earlier that, since the attitude is an ultimate one, it cannot be derived from a more fundamental attitude nor shown to be a special case of a more general one. On what sort of grounds, then, can it be established?

The attitude we take toward living things in the natural world depends on the way we look at them, on what kind of beings we conceive them to be, and on how we understand the relations we bear to them. Underlying and supporting your attitude is a certain *belief system* that constitutes a particular world view or outlook on nature and the place of human life in it. To give good reasons for adopting the attitude of respect for nature, then, we must first articulate the belief system which underlies and supports that attitude. If it appears that the belief system is internally coherent and well-ordered, and if, as far as we can now tell, it is consistent with all known scientific truths relevant to our knowledge of the object of the attitude (which in this case includes the whole set of the Earth's natural ecosystems and their communities of life), then there remains the task of indicating why scientifically informed and rational thinkers with a developed capacity of reality awareness can find it acceptable as a way of conceiving of the natural world and our place in it. To the extent we can do this we provide at least a reasonable argument for accepting the belief system and the ultimate moral attitude it supports.

I do not hold that such a belief system can be *proven* to be true, either inductively or deductively. As we shall see, not all of its components can be stated in the form of empirically verifiable propositions. Nor is its internal order governed by purely logical relationships. But the system as a whole, I contend, constitutes a coherent, unified, and rationally acceptable "picture" or "map" of a total world. By examining each of its main components and seeing how they fit together, we obtain a scientifically informed and well-ordered conception of nature and the place of humans in it.

This belief system underlying the attitude of respect for nature I call (for want of a better name) "the biocentric outlook on nature." Since it is not wholly analyzable into empirically confirmable assertions, it should not be thought of as simply a compendium of the biological sciences concerning our planet's ecosystems. It might best be described as a philosophical world view, to distinguish it from a scientific theory or explanatory system. However, one of its major tenets is the great lesson we have learned from the science of ecology: the interdependence of all living things in an organically unified order whose balance and stability are necessary conditions for the realization of the good of its constituent biotic communities.

Before turning to an account of the main components of the biocentric outlook, it is convenient here to set forth the overall structure of my theory of environmental ethics as it has now emerged. The ethics of respect for nature is made up of three basic elements: a belief system, an ultimate moral attitude, and a set of rules of duty and standards of character. These elements are connected with each other in the following manner. The belief system provides a certain outlook on nature which supports and makes intelligible an autonomous agent's adopting, as an ultimate moral attitude, the attitude of respect for nature. It supports and makes intelligible the attitude in the sense that, when an autonomous agent understands its moral relations to the natural world in terms of this outlook, it recognizes the attitude of respect to be the only *suitable* or *fitting* attitude to take toward all wild forms of life in the Earth's biosphere. Living things are now viewed as *the appropriate objects of the attitude of respect* and are accordingly regarded as entities possessing inherent worth. One then places intrinsic value on the promotion and protection of their good. As a consequence of this, one makes a moral commitment to abide by a set of rules of duty and to fulfill (as far as one can by one's own efforts) certain standards of good character. Given one's adoption of the attitude of respect, one makes that moral commitment because one considers those rules and standards to be validly binding on all moral agents. They are seen as embodying forms of conduct and character structures in which the attitude of respect for nature is manifested.

This three-part complex which internally orders the ethics of respect for nature is symmetrical with a theory of human ethics grounded on respect for persons. Such a theory includes, first, a conception of oneself and others as persons, that is, as centers of autonomous choice. Second, there is the attitude of respect for persons as persons. When this is adopted as an ultimate moral attitude it involves the disposition to treat every person as having inherent worth or "human dignity." Every human being, just in virtue of her or his humanity, is understood to be worthy of moral consideration, and intrinsic value is placed on the autonomy and well-being of each. This is what Kant meant by conceiving of persons as ends in themselves. Third, there is an ethical system of duties which are acknowledged to be owed by everyone to everyone. These duties are forms of conduct in which public recognition is given to each individual's inherent worth as a person.

This structural framework for a theory of human ethics is meant to leave open the issue of consequentialism (utilitarianism) versus nonconsequentialism (deontology). That issue concerns the particular kind of system of rules defining the duties of moral agents toward persons. Similarly, I am leaving open in this paper the question of what particular kind of system of rules defines our duties with respect to the natural world.

V. THE BIOCENTRIC OUTLOOK ON NATURE

The biocentric outlook on nature has four main components. (1) Humans are thought of as members of the Earth's community of life, holding that membership on the same terms as apply to all the nonhuman members. (2) The Earth's natural ecosystems as a totality are seen as a complex web of interconnected elements, with the sound biological functioning of each being dependent on the sound biological function of the others. (This is the component referred to above as the great lesson that the science of ecology has taught us). (3) Each individual organism is conceived of as a teleological center of life, pursuing its own good in its own way. (4) Whether we are concerned with standards of merit or with the concept of inherent worth, the claim that humans by their very nature are superior to other species is a groundless claim and, in the light of elements (1), (2), and (3) above, must be rejected as nothing more than an irrational bias in our own favor.

The conjunction of these four ideas constitutes the biocentric outlook on nature. In the remainder of this paper I give a brief account of the first three

components, followed by a more detailed analysis of the fourth. I then conclude by indicating how this outlook provides a way of justifying the attitude of respect for nature.

VI. HUMANS AS MEMBERS OF THE EARTH'S COMMUNITY OF LIFE

We share with other species a common relationship to the Earth. In accepting the biocentric outlook we take the fact of our being an animal species to be a fundamental feature of our existence. We consider it an essential aspect of "the human condition." We do not deny the differences between ourselves and other species, but we keep in the forefront of our consciousness the fact that in relation to our planet's natural ecosystems we are but one species population among many. Thus we acknowledge our origin in the very same evolutionary process that gave rise to all other species and we recognize ourselves to be confronted with similar environmental challenges to those that confront them. The laws of genetics, of natural selection, and of adaptation apply equally to all of us as biological creatures. In this light we consider ourselves as one with them, not set apart from them. We, as well as they, must face certain basic conditions of existence that impose requirements on us for our survival and well-being. Each animal and plant is like us in having a good of its own. Although our human good (what is of true value in human life, including the exercise of individual autonomy in choosing our own particular value systems) is not like the good of a nonhuman animal or plant, it can no more be realized than their good can without the biological necessities for survival and physical health.

When we look at ourselves from the evolutionary point of view, we see that not only are we very recent arrivals on Earth, but that our emergence as a new species on the planet was originally an event of no particular importance to the entire scheme of things. The Earth was teeming with life long before we appeared. Putting the point metaphorically, we are relative newcomers, entering a home that has been the residence of others for hundreds of millions of years, a home that must now be shared by all of us together.

The comparative brevity of human life on Earth may be vividly depicted by imagining the geological time scale in spatial terms. Suppose we start with algae, which have been around for at least 600 million years. (The earliest protozoa actually predated this by several *billion* years.) If the time that algae have been here were represented by the length of a football field (300 feet), then the period during which sharks have been swimming in the world's oceans and spiders have been spinning their webs would occupy three quarters of the length of the field; reptiles would show up at about the center of the field; mammals would cover the last third of the field; hominids (mammals of the family *Hominidae*) the last two feet; and the species *Homo sapiens* the last six inches.

Whether this newcomer is able to survive as long as other species remains to be seen. But there is surely something presumptuous about the way humans look down on the "lower" animals, especially those that have become extinct. We consider the dinosaurs, for example, to be biological failures, though they existed on our planet for 65 million years. One writer has made the point with beautiful simplicity:

> We sometimes speak of the dinosaurs as failures; there will be time enough for that judgment when we have lasted even for one tenth as long. . . . [2]

The possibility of the extinction of the human species, a possibility which starkly confronts us in the contemporary world, makes us aware of another respect in which we should not consider ourselves privileged beings in relation to other species. This is the fact that the well-being of humans is dependent upon the ecological soundness and health of many plant and animal communities, while their soundness and health does not in the least depend upon human well-being. Indeed, from their standpoint the very existence of humans is quite unnecessary. Every last man, woman, and child could disappear from the fact of the Earth without any significant detrimental consequence for the good of wild animals and plants. On the contrary, many of them would be greatly ben-

efited. The destruction of their habitats by human "developments" would cease. The poisoning and polluting of their environment would come to an end. The Earth's land, air, and water would no longer be subject to the degradation they are now undergoing as the result of large-scale technology and uncontrolled population growth. Life communities in natural ecosystems would gradually return to their former healthy state. Tropical forests, for example, would again be able to make their full contribution to a life-sustaining atmosphere for the whole planet. The rivers, lakes, and oceans of the world would (perhaps) eventually become clean again. Spilled oil, plastic trash, and even radioactive waste might finally, after many centuries, cease doing their terrible work. Ecosystems would return to their proper balance, suffering only the disruptions of natural events such as volcanic eruptions and glaciation. From these the community of life could recover, as it has so often done in the past. But the ecological disasters now perpetrated on it by humans—disasters from which it might never recover—these it would no longer have to endure.

If, then, the total, final, absolute extermination of our species (by our own hands?) should take place and if we should not carry all the others with us into oblivion, not only would the Earth's community of life continue to exist, but in all probability its well-being would be enhanced. Our presence, in short, is not needed. If we were to take the standpoint of the community and give voice to its true interest, the ending of our six-inch epoch would most likely be greeted with a hearty "Good riddance!"

VII. THE NATURAL WORLD AS AN ORGANIC SYSTEM

To accept the biocentric outlook and regard ourselves and our place in the world from its perspective is to see the whole natural order of the Earth's biosphere as a complex but unified web of interconnected organisms, objects, and events. The ecological relationships between any community of living things and their environment form an organic whole of functionally interdependent parts. Each ecosystem is a small universe itself in which the interactions of its various species populations comprise an intricately woven network of cause-effect relations. Such dynamic but at the same time relatively stable structures as food chains, predator-prey relations, and plant succession in a forest are self-regulating, energy-recycling mechanisms that preserve the equilibrium of the whole.

As far as the well-being of wild animals and plants is concerned, this ecological equilibrium must not be destroyed. The same holds true of the well-being of humans. When one views the realm of nature from the perspective of the biocentric outlook, one never forgets that in the long run the integrity of the entire biosphere of our planet is essential to the realization of the good of its constituent communities of life, both human and nonhuman.

Although the importance of this idea cannot be overemphasized, it is by now so familiar and so widely acknowledged that I shall not further elaborate on it here. However, I do wish to point out that this "holistic" view of the Earth's ecological systems does not itself constitute a moral norm. It is a factual aspect of biological reality, to be understood as a set of causal connections in ordinary empirical terms. Its significance for humans is the same as its significance for nonhumans, namely, in setting basic conditions for the realization of the good of living things. Its ethical implications for our treatment of the natural environment lie entirely in the fact that our *knowledge* of these causal connections is an essential *means* to fulfilling the aims we set for ourselves in adopting the attitude of respect for nature. In addition, its theoretical implications for the ethics of respect for nature lie in the fact that it (along with the other elements of the biocentric outlook) makes the adopting of that attitude a rational and intelligible thing to do.

VIII. INDIVIDUAL ORGANISMS AS TELEOLOGICAL CENTERS OF LIFE

As our knowledge of living things increases, as we come to a deeper understanding of their life cycles, their interactions with other organisms, and the manifold ways in which they adjust to the environment, we become more fully aware of how each of them is carrying out its biological functions according to the laws of its species-specific nature. But besides this, our increasing knowledge and understanding also develop in us a sharpened awareness of the uniqueness of each individual organism. Scientists who have made careful studies of particular plants and animals, whether in the field or in laboratories, have often acquired a knowledge of their subjects as identifiable individuals. Close observation over extended periods of time has led them to an appreciation of the unique "personalities" of their subjects. Sometimes a scientist may come to take a special interest in a particular animal or plant, all the while remaining strictly objective in the gathering and recording of data. Nonscientists may likewise experience this development of interest when, as amateur naturalists, they make accurate observations over sustained periods of close acquaintance with an individual organism. As one becomes more and more familiar with the organism and its behavior, one becomes fully sensitive to the particular way it is living out its life cycle. One may become fascinated by it and even experience some involvement with its good and bad fortunes (that is, with the occurrence of environmental conditions favorable or unfavorable to the realization of its good). The organism comes to mean something to one as a unique, irreplaceable individual. The final culmination of this process is the achievement of a genuine understanding of its point of view and, with that understanding, an ability to "take" that point of view. *Conceiving of it as a center of life, one is able to look at the world from its perspective.*

This development from objective knowledge to the recognition of individuality to full awareness of an organism's standpoint, is a process of heightening our consciousness of what it means to be an individual living thing. We grasp the particularity of the organism as a teleological center of life, striving to preserve itself and to realize its own good in its own unique way.

It is to be noted that we need not be falsely anthropomorphizing when we conceive of individual plants and animals in this manner. Understanding them as teleological centers of life does not necessitate "reading into" them human characteristics. We need not, for example, consider them to have consciousness. Some of them may be aware of the world around them and others may not. Nor need we deny that different kinds and levels of awareness are exemplified when consciousness in some form is present. But conscious or not, all are equally teleological centers of life in the sense that each is a unified system of goal-oriented activities directed toward their preservation and well-being.

When considered from an ethical point of view, a teleological center of life is an entity whose "world" can be viewed from the perspective of *its* life. In looking at the world from that perspective we recognize objects and events occurring in its life as being beneficent, maleficent, or indifferent. The first are occurrences which increase its powers to preserve its existence and realize its good. The second decrease or destroy those powers. The third have neither of these effects on the entity. With regard to our human role as moral agents, we can conceive of a teleological center of life as a being whose standpoint we can take in making judgments about what events in the world are good or evil, desirable or undesirable. In making these judgments it is what promotes or protects the being's own good, not what benefits moral agents themselves, that sets the standard of evaluation. Such judgments can be made about anything that happens to the entity which is favorable or unfavorable in relation to its good. As was pointed out earlier, the entity itself need not have any (conscious) *interest* in what is happening to it for such judgments to be meaningful and true.

It is precisely judgments of this sort that we are disposed to make when we take the attitude of respect for nature. In adopting that attitude those judgments are given weight as reasons for action in our practical deliberation. They become morally relevant facts in the guidance of our conduct.

IX. THE DENIAL OF HUMAN SUPERIORITY

This fourth component of the biocentric outlook on nature is the single most important idea in estab-

lishing the justifiability of the attitude of respect for nature. Its central role is due to the special relationship it bears to the first three components of the outlook. This relationship will be brought out after the concept of human superiority is examined and analyzed.

In what sense are humans alleged to be superior to other animals? We are different from them in having certain capacities that they lack. But why should these capacities be a mark of superiority? From what point of view are they judged to be signs of superiority and what sense of superiority is meant? After all, various nonhuman species have capacities that humans lack. There is the speed of a cheetah, the vision of an eagle, the agility of a monkey. Why should not these be taken as signs of *their* superiority over humans.

One answer that comes immediately to mind is that these capacities are not as *valuable* as the human capacities that are claimed to make us superior. Such uniquely human characteristics as rational thought, aesthetic creativity, autonomy and self-determination, and moral freedom, it might be held, have a higher value than the capacities found in other species. Yet we must ask: valuable to whom, and on what grounds?

The human characteristics mentioned are all valuable to humans. They are essential to the preservation and enrichment of our civilization and culture. Clearly it is from the human standpoint that they are being judged to be desirable and good. It is not difficult here to recognize a begging of the question. Humans are claiming human superiority from a strictly human point of view, that is, from a point of view in which the good of humans is taken as the standard of judgment. All we need to do is to look at the capacities of nonhuman animals (or plants, for that matter) from the standpoint of *their* good to find a contrary judgment of superiority. The speed of the cheetah, for example, is a sign of its superiority to humans when considered from the standpoint of the good of its species. If it were as slow a runner as a human, it would not be able to survive. And so for all the other abilities of nonhumans which further their good but which are lacking in humans. In each case the claim to human superiority would be rejected from a nonhuman standpoint.

When superiority assertions are interpreted in this way, they are based on judgments of *merit*. To judge the merits of a person or an organism one must apply grading or ranking standards to it. (As I show below, this distinguishes judgments of merit from judgments of inherent worth.) Empirical investigation then determines whether it has the "good-making properties" (merits) in virtue of which it fulfills the standards being applied. In the case of humans, merits may be either moral or nonmoral. We can judge one person to be better than (superior to) another from the moral point of view by applying certain standards to their character and conduct. Similarly, we can appeal to nonmoral criteria in judging someone to be an excellent piano player, a fair cook, a poor tennis player, and so on. Different social purposes and roles are implicit in the making of such judgments, providing the frame of reference for the choice of standards by which the nonmoral merits of people are determined. Ultimately such purposes and roles stem from a society's way of life as a whole. Now a society's way of life may be thought of as the cultural form given to the realization of human values. Whether moral or nonmoral standards are being applied, then, all judgments of people's merits finally depend on human values. All are made from an exclusively human standpoint.

The question that naturally arises at this juncture is: why should standards that are based on human values be assumed to be the only valid criteria of merit and hence the only true signs of superiority? This question is especially pressing when humans are being judged superior in merit to nonhumans. It is true that a human being may be a better mathematician than a monkey, but the monkey may be a better tree climber than a human being. If we humans value mathematics more than tree climbing, that is because our conception of civilized life makes the development of mathematical ability more desirable than the ability to climb trees. But is it not unreasonable to judge nonhumans by the values of human civilization, rather than by values connected with what it is for a member of *that* species to live a good

life? If all living things have a good of their own, it at least makes sense to judge the merits of nonhumans by standards derived from *their* good. To use only standards based on human values is already to commit oneself to holding that humans are superior to nonhumans, which is the point in question.

A further logical flaw arises in connection with the widely held conviction that humans are *morally* superior beings because they possess, while others lack, the capacities of a moral agent (free will, accountability, deliberation, judgment, practical reason). This view rests on a conceptual confusion. As far as moral standards are concerned, only beings that have the capacities of a moral agent can properly be judged to be *either* moral (morally good) *or* immoral (morally deficient). Moral standards are simply not applicable to beings that lack such capacities. Animals and plants cannot therefore be said to be morally inferior in merit to humans. Since the only beings that can have moral merits *or be deficient in such merits* are moral agents, it is conceptually incoherent to judge humans as superior to nonhumans on the ground that humans have moral capacities while nonhumans don't.

Up to this point I have been interpreting the claim that humans are superior to other living things as a grading or ranking judgment regarding their comparative merits. There is, however, another way of understanding the idea of human superiority. According to this interpretation, humans are superior to nonhumans not as regards their merits but as regards their inherent worth. Thus the claim of human superiority is to be understood as asserting that all humans, simply in virtue of their humanity, have *a greater inherent worth* than other living things.

The inherent worth of an entity does not depend on its merits. To consider something as possessing inherent worth, we have seen, is to place intrinsic value on the realization of its good. This is done regardless of whatever particular merits it might have or might lack, as judged by a set of grading or ranking standards. In human affairs, we are all familiar with the principle that one's worth as a person does not vary with one's merits or lack of merits. The same can hold true of animals and plants. To regard such entities as possessing inherent worth entails disregarding their merits and deficiencies, whether they are being judged from a human standpoint or from the standpoint of their own species.

The idea of one entity having more merit than another, and so being superior to it in merit, makes perfectly good sense. Merit is a grading or ranking concept, and judgments of comparative merit are based on the different degrees to which things satisfy a given standard. But what can it mean to talk about one thing being superior to another in inherent worth? In order to get at what is being asserted in such a claim it is helpful first to look at the social origin of the concept of degrees of inherent worth.

The idea that humans can possess different degrees of inherent worth originated in societies having rigid class structures. Before the rise of modern democracies with their egalitarian outlook, one's membership in a hereditary class determined one's social status. People in the upper classes were looked up to, while those in the lower classes were looked down upon. In such a society one's social superiors and social inferiors were clearly defined and easily recognized.

Two aspects of these class-structured societies are especially relevant to the idea of degrees of inherent worth. First, those born into the upper classes were deemed more worthy of respect than those born into the lower orders. Second, the superior worth of upper class people had nothing to do with their merits nor did the inferior worth of those in the lower classes rest on their lack of merits. One's superiority or inferiority entirely derived from a social position one was born into. The modern concept of a meritocracy simply did not apply. One could not advance into a higher class by any sort of moral or nonmoral achievement. Similarly, an aristocrat held his title and all the privileges that went with it just because he was the eldest son of a titled nobleman. Unlike the bestowing of knighthood in contemporary Great Britain, one did not earn membership in the nobility by meritorious conduct.

We who live in modern democracies no longer believe in such hereditary social distinctions. Indeed, we would wholeheartedly condemn them on moral grounds as being fundamentally unjust. We have come to think of class systems as a paradigm of social injustice, it being a central principle of the democratic way of life that among humans there are no superiors and no inferiors. Thus we have rejected the whole conceptual framework in which people are judged to have different degrees of inherent worth. That idea is incompatible with our notion of human equality based on the doctrine that all humans, simply in virtue of their humanity, have the same inherent worth. (The belief in universal human rights is one form that this egalitarianism takes.)

The vast majority of people in modern democracies, however, do not maintain an egalitarian outlook when it comes to comparing human beings with other living things. Most people consider our own species to be superior to all other species and this superiority is understood to be a matter of inherent worth, not merit. There may exist thoroughly vicious and depraved humans who lack all merit. Yet because they are human they are thought to belong to a higher class of entities than any plant or animal. That one is born into the species *Homo sapiens* entitles one to have lordship over those who are one's inferiors, namely, those born into other species. The parallel with hereditary social classes is very close. Implicit in this view is a hierarchical conception of nature according to which an organism has a position of superiority or inferiority in the Earth's community of life simply on the basis of its genetic background. The "lower" orders of life are looked down upon and it is considered perfectly proper that they serve the interests of those belonging to the highest order, namely humans. The intrinsic value we place on the well-being of our fellow humans reflects our recognition of their rightful positions as our equals. No such intrinsic value is to be placed on the good of other animals, unless we choose to do so out of fondness or affection for them. But their well-being imposes no moral requirement on us. In this respect there is an absolute difference in moral status between ourselves and them.

This is the structure of concepts and beliefs that people are committed to insofar as they regard humans to be superior in inherent worth to all other species. I now wish to argue that this structure of concepts and beliefs is completely groundless. If we accept the first three components of the biocentric outlook and from that perspective look at the major philosophical traditions which have supported that structure, we find it to be at bottom nothing more than the expression of an irrational bias in our own favor. The philosophical traditions themselves rest on very questionable assumptions or else simply beg the question. I briefly consider three of the main traditions to substantiate the point. These are classical Greek humanism, Cartesian dualism, and the Judeo-Christian concept of the Great Chain of Being.

The inherent superiority of humans over other species was implicit in the Greek definition of man as a rational animal. Our animal nature was identified with "brute" desires that need the order and restraint of reason to rule them (just as reason is the special virtue of those who rule in the ideal state). Rationality was then seen to be the key to our superiority over animals. It enables us to live on a higher plane and endows us with a nobility and worth that other creatures lack. This familiar way of comparing humans with other species is deeply ingrained in our Western philosophical outlook. The point to consider here is that this view does not actually provide an argument *for* human superiority but rather makes explicit the framework of thought that is implicitly used by those who think of humans as inherently superior to nonhumans. The Greeks who held that humans, in virtue of their rational capacities, have a kind of worth greater than that of any nonrational being, never looked at rationality as but one capacity of living things among many others. But when we consider rationality from the standpoint of the first three elements of the ecological outlook, we see that its value lies in its importance for *human* life. Other creatures achieve their species-specific good without the need of rationality, although they often make use of capacities that humans lack. So the humanistic outlook of classical Greek thought does not give us a neutral (non-question-begging) ground on which to construct a scale of degrees of inherent worth possessed by different species of living things.

The second tradition, centering on the Cartesian dualism of soul and body, also fails to justify the claim to human superiority. That superiority is supposed to derive from the fact that we have souls while animals do not. Animals are mere automata and lack the divine element that makes us spiritual beings. I wont' go into the now familiar criticisms of this two-substance view. I only add the point that, even if humans are composed of an immaterial, unextended soul and a material, extended body, this in itself is not a reason to deem them of greater worth than entities that are only bodies. Why is a soul substance a thing that adds value to its possessor? Unless some theological reasoning is offered here (which many, including myself, would find unacceptable on epistemological grounds), no logical connection is evident. An immaterial something which thinks is better than a material something which does not think only if thinking itself has value, either intrinsically or instrumentally. Now it is intrinsically valuable to humans alone, who value it as an end in itself, and it is instrumentally valuable to those who benefit from it, namely humans.

For animals that neither enjoy thinking for its own sake nor need it for living the kind of life for which they are best adapted, it has no value. Even if "thinking" is broadened to include all forms of consciousness, there are still many living things that can do without it and yet live what is for their species a good life. The anthropocentricity underlying the claim to human superiority runs throughout Cartesian dualism.

A third major source of the idea of human superiority is the Judeo-Christian concept of the Great Chain of Being. Humans are superior to animals and plants because their Creator has given them a higher place on the chain. It begins with God at the top, and then moves to the angels, who are lower than God but higher than humans, then to humans, positioned between the angels and the beasts (partaking of the nature of both), and then on down to the lower levels occupied by nonhuman animals, plants, and finally inanimate objects. Humans, being "made in God's image," are inherently superior to animals and plants by virtue of their being closer (in their essential nature) to God.

The metaphysical and epistemological difficulties with this conception of a hierarchy of entities are, in my mind, insuperable. Without entering into this matter here, I only point out that if we are unwilling to accept the metaphysics of traditional Judaism and Christianity, we are again left without good reasons for holding to the claim of inherent human superiority.

The foregoing considerations (and others like them) leave us with but one ground for the assertion that a human being, regardless of merit, is a higher kind of entity than any other living thing. This is the mere fact of the genetic makeup of the species *Homo sapiens*. But this is surely irrational and arbitrary. Why should the arrangement of genes of a certain type be a mark of superior value, especially when this fact about an organism is taken by itself, unrelated to any other aspect of its life? We might just as well refer to any other genetic makeup as a ground of superior value. Clearly we are confronted here with a wholly arbitrary claim that can only be explained as an irrational bias in our own favor.

That the claims is nothing more than a deep-seated prejudice is brought home to us when we look at our relation to other species in the light of the first three elements of the biocentric outlook. Those elements taken conjointly give us a certain overall view of the natural world and of the place of humans in it. When we take this view we come to understand other living things, their environmental conditions, and their ecological relationships in such a way as to awake in us a deep sense of our kinship with them as fellow members of the Earth's community of life. Humans and nonhumans alike are viewed together as integral parts of one unified whole in which all living things are functionally interrelated. Finally, when our awareness focuses on the individual lives of plants and animals, each is seen to share with us the characteristic of being a teleological center of life striving to realize its own good in its own unique way.

As this entire belief system becomes part of the conceptual framework through which we understand and perceive the world, we come to see ourselves as bearing a certain moral relation to nonhuman forms of life. Our ethical role in nature takes on a new significance. We begin to look at other species as we look at ourselves, seeing them as beings which have a good they are striving to realize just as we have a good we are striving to realize. We accordingly develop the disposition to view the world from the standpoint of their good as well as from the standpoint of our own good. Now if the groundlessness of the claim that humans are inherently superior to other species were brought clearly before our minds, we would not remain intellectually neutral toward that claim but would reject it as being fundamentally at variance with our total world outlook. In the absence of any good reasons for holding it, the assertion of human superiority would then appear simply as the expression of an irrational and self-serving prejudice that favors one particular species over several million others.

Rejecting the notion of human superiority entails its positive counterpart: the doctrine of species impartiality. One who accepts that doctrine regards all living things as possessing inherent worth—the *same* inherent worth, since no one species has been shown to be either "higher" or "lower" than any other. Now we saw earlier that, insofar as one thinks of a living thing as possessing inherent worth, one considers it to be the appropriate object of the attitude of respect and believes that attitude to be the only fitting or suitable one for all moral agents to take toward it.

Here, then, is the key to understanding how the attitude of respect is rooted in the biocentric outlook on nature. The basic connection is made through the denial of human superiority. Once we reject the claim that humans are superior either in merit or in worth to other living things, we are ready to adopt the attitude of respect. The denial of human superiority is itself the result of taking the perspective on nature built into the first three elements of the biocentric outlook.

Now the first three elements of the biocentric outlook, it seems clear, would be found acceptable to any rational and scientifically informed thinker who is fully "open" to the reality of the lives of nonhuman organisms. Without denying our distinctively human characteristics, such a thinker can acknowledge the fundamental respects in which we are members of the Earth's community of life and in which the biological conditions necessary for the realization of our human values are inextricably linked with the whole system of nature. In addition, the conception of individual living things as teleological centers of life simply articulates how a scientifically informed thinker comes to understand them as the result of increasingly careful and detailed observations. Thus, the biocentric outlook recommends itself as an acceptable system of concepts and beliefs to anyone who is clear-minded, unbiased, and factually enlightened, and who has a developed capacity of reality awareness with regard to the lives of individual organisms. This, I submit, is as good a reason for making the moral commitment involved in adopting the attitude of respect for nature as any theory of environmental ethics could possibly have.

X. MORAL RIGHTS AND THE MATTER OF COMPETING CLAIMS

I have not asserted anywhere in the foregoing account that animals or plants have moral rights. This omission was deliberate. I do not think that the reference class of the concept, bearer of moral rights, should be extended to include nonhuman living things. My reasons for taking this position, however, go beyond the scope of this paper. I believe I have been able to accomplish many of the same ends which those who ascribe rights to animals or plants wish to accomplish. There is no reason, moreover, why plants and animals, including whole species populations and life communities, cannot be accorded *legal* rights under my theory. To grant them legal protection could be interpreted as giving them legal entitlement to be protected, and this, in fact, would be a means by which a society that subscribed to the ethics of respect for nature could give public recognition to their inherent worth.

There remains the problem of competing claims, even when wild plants and animals are not thought of as bearers of moral rights. If we accept the biocentric outlook and accordingly adopt the attitude of respect for nature as our ultimate moral attitude, how do we resolve conflicts that arise from our respect for persons in the domain of human ethics and our respect for nature in the domain of environmental ethics? This is a question that cannot adequately be dealt with here. My main purpose in this paper has been to try to establish a base point from which we can start working toward a solution to the problem. I have shown why we cannot just begin with an initial presumption in favor of the interests of our own species. It is after all within our power as moral beings to place limits on human population and technology with the deliberate intention of sharing the Earth's bounty with other species. That such sharing is an ideal difficult to realize even in an approximate way does not take away its claim to our deepest moral commitment.

NOTES

1. John Rawls, "Justice As Fairness," *Philosophical Review* 67 (1958): 183.

2. Stephen R. L. Clark, *The Moral Status of Animals* (Oxford: Clarendon Press, 1977), p. 112.

Are All Species Equal?

DAVID SCHMIDTZ

I. RESPECT FOR NATURE

Species egalitarianism is the view that all species have equal moral standing.[1] To have moral standing is, at a minimum, to command respect, to be something more than a mere thing. Is there any reason to believe that all species have moral standing in even this most minimal sense? If so—that is, if all species command respect—is there any reason to believe they all command *equal* respect?

The following sections summarise critical responses to the most famous philosophical argument for species egalitarianism. I then try to explain why other species command our respect but also why they do not command equal respect. The intuition that we should have respect for nature is part of what motivates people to embrace species egalitarianism, but one need not be a species egalitarian to have respect for nature. I close by questioning whether species egalitarianism is even compatible with respect for nature.

II. THE GROUNDING OF SPECIES EGALITARIANISM

According to Paul Taylor, anthropocentrism 'gives either exclusive or primary consideration to human interests above the good of other species.'[2] The alternative to anthropocentrism is biocentrism, and it is biocentrism that, in Taylor's view, grounds species egalitarianism:

The beliefs that form the core of the biocentric outlook are four in number:

(a) The belief that humans are members of the Earth's Community of life in the same sense and on the same terms in which other living things are members of that community.

(b) The belief that the human species, along with all other species, are integral elements in a system of interdependence.

(c) The belief that all organisms are teleological centres of life in the sense that each is a unique individual pursuing its own good in its own way.

(d) The belief that humans are not inherently superior to other living beings.

Taylor concludes, 'Rejecting the notion of human superiority entails its positive counterpart: the doctrine of species impartiality. One who accepts that doctrine regards all living things as possessing inherent worth—the *same* inherent worth, since no one species has been shown to be either higher or lower than any other.'[3]

Taylor does not claim that this is a valid argument, but he thinks that if we concede (a), (b), and (c), it would be unreasonable not to move to (d), and then to his egalitarian conclusion. Is he right? For those who accept Taylor's three premises (and who thus interpret those premises in terms innocuous enough to render them acceptable), there are two responses. First, we may go on to accept (d), following Taylor, but then still deny that there is any warrant for moving from there to Taylor's egalitarian conclusion. Having accepted that our form of life is not superior, we might choose instead to regard it as inferior. More plausibly, we might view our form of life as noncomparable. We simply do not have the same kind of value as nonhumans. The question of how we compare to nonhumans has a simple answer: we do not compare to them.

Alternatively, we may reject (d) and say humans are indeed inherently superior but our superiority is a moot point. Whether we are inherently superior (that is, superior as a form of life) does not matter much. Even if we are superior, the fact remains that within the web of ecological interdependence mentioned in premises (a) and (b), it would be a mistake to ignore the needs and the telos of the other species

David Schmidtz, "Are All Species Equal?" *Journal of Applied Philosophy* 15, no. 1 (1998): 57–66 (edited). Reprinted with permission from Blackwell Publishing.

referred to in premise (c). Thus, there are two ways of rejecting Taylor's argument for species egalitarianism. Each, on its face, is compatible with the respect for nature that motivates Taylor's egalitarianism in the first place.

Taylor's critics, such as James Anderson and William French, have taken the second route. They reject (d). After discussing their arguments, and building on some while rejecting others, I explore some of our reasons to have respect for nature and ask whether they translate into reasons to be species egalitarians.

III. IS SPECIES EGALITARIANISM HYPOCRITICAL?

Paul Taylor and Arne Naess are among the most intransigent of species egalitarians, yet they allow that human needs override the needs of nonhumans.[4] William C. French argues that they cannot have it both ways.[5] French perceives a contradiction between the egalitarian principles that Taylor and Naess officially endorse and the unofficial principles they offer as the real principles by which we should live. Having proclaimed that we are all equal, French asks, what licenses Taylor and Naess to say that, in cases of conflict, nonhuman interests can legitimately be sacrificed to vital human interests?

French has a point. James C. Anderson makes a similar point.[6] Yet, somehow the inconsistency of Taylor and Naess is too obvious. Perhaps their position is not as blatantly inconsistent as it appears. Let me suggest how Taylor and Naess could respond to French. Suppose I find myself in a situation of mortal combat with an enemy soldier. If I kill my enemy to save my life, that does not entail that I regard my enemy as inherently inferior (i.e., as an inferior form of life). Likewise, if I kill a bear to save my life, that does not entail that I regard the bear as inherently inferior. Therefore, Taylor and Naess can, without hypocrisy, deny that species egalitarianism requires a radically self-effacing pacifism.

What, then, does species egalitarianism require? It requires us to avoid mortal combat whenever we can, not just with other humans but with living things in general. On this view, we ought to regret finding ourselves in kill-or-be-killed situations that we could have avoided. There is no point in regretting the fact that we must kill in order to eat, though, for there is no avoiding that. Species egalitarianism is compatible with our having a limited license to kill.

What seems far more problematic for species egalitarianism is that it seems to suggest that it makes no difference *what* we kill. Vegetarians typically think it is worse to kill a cow than to kill a potato. Are they wrong? Yes they are, according to species egalitarianism. In this respect, species egalitarianism cannot be right. I do believe we have reason to respect nature. But we fail to give nature due respect if we say we should have no more respect for a cow than for a potato.

IV. IS SPECIES EGALITARIANISM ARBITRARY?

Suppose interspecies comparisons are possible. Suppose the capacities of different species, and whatever else gives species moral standing, are commensurable. In that case, it could turn out that all species are equal, but that would be quite a fluke.

Taylor says a being has intrinsic worth if and only if it has a good of its own. Anderson does not disagree, but he points out that if we accept Taylor's idea of a thing having a good of its own, then that licenses us to notice differences among the various kinds of 'good of its own.' (We can notice differences without being committed to ranking them.) For example, we can distinguish, along Aristotelian lines, vegetative, animal, and cognitive goods of one's own. To have a vegetative nature is to be what Taylor, in premise (c), calls a teleological centre of life. A being with an animal nature is a teleological centre of life, and more. A being with a cognitive as well as animal nature is a teleological centre of life, and more still. Cognitive nature may be something we share with whales, dolphins, and higher primates. It is an empirical question. Anderson's view is that so long as we do not assume away this possibility, valuing cognitive capacity is not anthropocentric. The question is what would make *any* species superior to another (p. 348).

As mentioned earlier, Taylor defines anthropocentrism as giving exclusive or primary consideration to human interests above the good of other species. So, when we acknowledge that cognitive capacity is one valuable capacity among others, are we giving exclusive or primary considerations to human interests? Anderson thinks not, and surely he is right. Put it this way: if biocentrism involves resolving to ignore the fact that cognitive capacity is something we value—if biocentrism amounts to a resolution to value only those capacities that all living things share—then biocentrism is at least as arbitrary and question-begging as anthropocentrism.

It will not do to defend species egalitarianism by singling out a property that all species possess, arguing that this property is morally important, and then concluding that all species are therefore of equal moral importance. The problem with this sort of argument is that, where there is one property that provides a basis for moral standing, there might be others. Other properties might be possessed by some but not all species, and might provide bases for different kinds or degrees of moral standing.

V. THE MULTIPLE BASES OF MORAL STANDING

Taylor is aware of the Aristotelian classification scheme, but considers its hierarchy of capacities to be question-begging. Taylor himself assumes that human rationality is on a par with a cheetah's foot-speed. In this case, though, perhaps it is Taylor who begs the question. It hardly seems unreasonable to see the difference between the foot-speed of chimpanzees and cheetahs as a difference of degree, while seeing the difference between the sentience of a chimpanzee and the nonsentience of a tree as a difference in kind.

Anthropocentrists might argue that the good associated with cognitive capacity is superior to the good associated with vegetative capacity. Could they be wrong? Let us suppose they are wrong. For argument's sake, let us suppose *vegetative* capacity is the superior good. Even so, the exact nature of the good associated with an organism's vegetative capacity will depend upon the organism's other capacities. For example, Anderson (p. 358) points out that even if health in a human and health in a tree are instances of the same thing, they need not have the same moral standing. Why not? Because health in a human has an instrumental value that health in a tree lacks. John Stuart Mill's swine can take pleasure in its health but trees cannot. Animals have a plant's capacities plus more. In turn, humans (and possibly dolphins, apes, and so on) have an animal's capacities plus more. The comparison between Socrates and swine therefore is less a matter of comparing swine to non-swine and more a matter of comparing swine to 'swine-plus' (Anderson, p. 361). Crucially, Anderson's argument for the superiority of Socrates over swine does not presume that one capacity is higher than another. We do not need to make any assumptions about the respective merits of animal or vegetative versus cognitive capacities in order to conclude that the capacities of 'swine-plus' are superior to those of swine.

We may of course conclude that *one* of the grounds of our moral standing (i.e., our vegetative natures) is something we share with all living things. Beyond that, nothing about equality even suggests itself. In particular, it begs no questions to notice that there are grounds for moral standing that we do not share with all living things.

VI. IN PRAISE OF SPECIESISM

William French invites us to see species rankings not 'as an assessment of some inherent superiority, but rather as a considered moral recognition of the fact that greater ranges of vulnerability are generated by broader ranges of complexity and capacities' (p. 56). One species outranks another not because it is a superior form of life but rather because it is a more vulnerable form of life. French, if I understand correctly, interprets vulnerability as a matter of having *more* to lose. This interpretation is problematic. It implies that a millionaire, having more to lose than a pauper, is by that fact more vulnerable than the pauper. Perhaps this interpretation is forced upon French, though. If French had instead chosen a more natural interpretation—if he had chosen to interpret vulnerability as a matter of *probability* of loss—then a ranking by vulnerability would not be correlated to complex capacities in the way he wants. Ranking by probability of loss would change on a daily basis, and the top-ranked species often would be an amphibian.

If we set aside questions about how to interpret vulnerability, there remains a problem with French's proposal. If having complex capacities is not itself morally important, then being in danger of losing them is not morally important either. Vulnerability, on any interpretation, is essentially of derivative importance; any role it could play in ranking species must already be played by the capacities themselves.

Yet, although I reject French's argument, I do not reject his inegalitarian conclusion. The conclusion that mice are the moral equals of chimpanzees is about as insupportable as a conclusion can be. Suppose that, for some reason, we take an interest in how chimpanzees rank compared to mice. Perhaps we wonder what we would do in an emergency where we could save a drowning chimpanzee or a drowning mouse but not both. More realistically, we might wonder whether, other things equal, we have any reason to use mice in our medical experiments rather than chimpanzees. Species egalitarianism seems to say not.

Suppose we decide upon reflection that, from our human perspective, chimpanzees are superior to mice and humans are superior to chimpanzees. Would the perceived superiority of our form of life give us reason to think we have no obligations whatsoever to mice, or to chimpanzees? Those who believe we have fewer obligations to inferior species might be pressed to say whether they also would allow that we have fewer obligations to inferior human beings. Lawrence Johnson, for example, rhetorically asks whether it is worse to cause a person pain if the person is a Nobel Prize winner.[7] Well, why not? Echoing Peter Singer, Johnson argues that if medical researchers had to choose between harvesting the organs of a chimpanzee or a brain-damaged human baby, 'one thing we cannot justify is trying to have it both ways. If rationality is what makes the basic moral difference, then we cannot maintain that the brain-damaged infant ought to be exempt from utilisation just because it is human while at the same time allowing that the animal can be used if utility warrants' (p. 52).

Does this seem obvious? It should not. Johnson presumes that rationality is relevant to justification at the *token* level when speciesists (i.e., those who believe some species, the human species in particular, are superior to others) presumably would invoke rationality as a justification at the *type* level. One can say rationality makes a moral difference at the type level without thereby taking any position on whether rationality makes a moral difference at the token level. A speciesist could say humanity's characteristic rationality mandates respect for humanity, not merely for particular humans who exemplify human rationality. Similarly, once we note that chimpanzees have characteristic cognitive capacities that mice lack, we do not need to compare individual chimpanzees and mice on a case by case basis in order to have a moral justification for planning to use a mouse rather than a chimpanzee in an experiment.

Of course, some chimpanzees lack the characteristic features in virtue of which chimpanzees command respect as a species, just as some humans lack the characteristic features in virtue of which humans command respect as a species. It is equally obvious that some chimpanzees have cognitive capacities (for example) that are superior to the cognitive capacities of some humans. But whether every human being is superior to every chimpanzee is beside the point. The point is that we can, we do, and we should make decisions on the basis of our recognition that mice, chimpanzees, and humans are relevantly different types. We can have it both ways after all. Or so a speciesist could argue.

VII. EQUALITY AND TRANSCENDENCE

Even if speciesists are right to see a nonarbitrary distinction between humans and other species, though, the fact remains that, as Anderson (p. 362) points out, claims of superiority do not easily translate into justifications of domination. We can have reasons to treat nonhuman species with respect, regardless of whether we consider them to be on a moral par with *homo sapiens*.

What kind of reasons do we have for treating other species with respect? We might have respect for chimpanzees or even mice on the grounds that they are sentient. Even mice have a rudimentary point of view and rudimentary hopes and dreams, and we might well respect them for that. But what about plants? Plants, unlike mice and chimpanzees, do not care what happens to them. It is literally true that they could not care less. So, why should we care? Is it even possible for us to have any good reason, other than a purely instrumental reason, to care what happens to plants?

When we are alone in a forest wondering whether it would be fine to chop down a tree for fun, our perspective on what happens to the tree is, so far as we know, the only perspective there is. The tree does not have its own. Thus, explaining why we have reason to care about trees requires us to explain caring from our point of view, since that (we are supposing) is all there is. In that case, we do not have to satisfy *trees* that we are treating them properly; rather, we have to satisfy *ourselves*. So, again, can we have noninstrumental reasons for caring about trees—for treating them with respect?

One reason to care (not the only one) is that gratuitous destruction is a failure of self-respect. It is a repudiation of the kind of self-awareness and self-respect that we can achieve by repudiating wantonness. So far as I know, no one finds anything puzzling in the idea that we have reason to treat our lawns or living rooms with respect. Lawns and living rooms have instrumental value, but there is more to it than that. Most of us have the sense that taking reasonable care of our lawns and living rooms is somehow a matter of self-respect, not merely a matter of preserving their instrumental value. Do we have similar reasons to treat forests with respect? I think we do. There is an aesthetic involved, the repudiation of which would be a failure of self-respect. (Obviously, not everyone feels the same way about forests. Not everyone feels the same way about lawns and living rooms, either. But the point here is to make sense of respect for nature, not to argue that respect for nature

is in fact universal or that failing to respect nature is irrational.[8]) If and when we identify with a Redwood, in the sense of being inspired by it, having respect for its size and age and so on, then as a psychological fact, we really do face moral questions about how we ought to treat it. If and when we come to see a Redwood in that light, subsequently turning our backs on it becomes a kind of self-effacement. The values that we thereby fail to take seriously are *our* values, not the tree's.

A related way of grounding respect for nature is suggested by Jim Cheney's remark that 'moral regard is appropriate wherever we are *able* to manage it—in light of our sensibilities, knowledge, and cultural/personal histories. . . . The limits of moral regard are set only by the limitations of one's own (or one's species' or one's community's) ability to respond in a caring manner.'[9] Should we believe Cheney's rather startling proposal that moral regard is appropriate whenever we can manage it? One reason to take it very seriously is that exercising our capacity for moral regard is a way of expressing respect for that capacity. Developing that capacity is a form of self-realization.

Put it this way. I am arguing that the attitude we take toward gazelles (for example) raises issues of self-respect insofar as we see ourselves as relevantly like gazelles. My reading of Cheney suggests a different and complementary way of looking at the issue. Consider that lions owe nothing to gazelles. Therefore, if we owe it to gazelles not to hunt them, it must be because we are *unlike* lions, not (or not only) because we are *like* gazelles.

Unlike lions, we have a choice about whether to hunt gazelles, and we are capable of deliberating about that choice in a reflective way. We are capable of caring about the gazelle's pain, the gazelle's beauty, the gazelle's hopes and dreams (such as they are), and so forth. And if we do care, then in a more or less literal way, something is wrong with us—we are less than fully human—if we cannot adjust our behaviour in the light of what we care about. If we do not care, then we are missing something. For a human being, to lack a broad respect for living things and beautiful things and well-functioning things is to be stunted in a way.

Our coming to see other species as commanding respect is itself a way of transcending our animal natures. It is ennobling. It is part of our animal natures unthinkingly to see ourselves as superior, and to try to dominate accordingly; our capacity to see ourselves as equal is one of the things that makes us different. Thus, our capacity to see ourselves as equal may be one of the things that makes us superior. Coming to see all species as equal may not be the best way of transcending our animal natures—it does not work for me—but it is one way. Another way of transcending our animal natures and expressing due respect for nature is simply to not worry so much about ranking species. This latter way is, I think, better. It is more respectful of our own reflective natures. It does not dwell on rankings. It does not insist on seeing equality where a more reflective being simply would see what is there to be seen and would not shy away from respecting the differences as well as the commonalities. The whole idea of ranking species, even as equals, sometimes seems like a child's game. It seems beneath us.

VII. RESPECT FOR EVERYTHING

Thus, a broad respect for living or beautiful or well-functioning things need not translate into equal respect. It need not translate into universal respect, either. I can appreciate mosquitoes to a degree. My wife (a biochemist who studies mosquito immune systems) even finds them beautiful, or so she says. My own appreciation, by contrast, is thin and grudging and purely intellectual. In neither degree nor kind is it anything like the appreciation I have for my wife, or for human beings in general, or even for the rabbits I sometimes find eating my flowers in the morning. Part of our responsibility as moral agents is to be somewhat choosy about what we respect and how we respect it. I can see why people shy away from openly accepting that responsibility, but they still have it.

Johnson says speciesism is as arbitrary as racism unless we can show that the differences are morally relevant (p. 51). This is, to be sure, a popular sentiment among radical environmentalists and animal liberationists. But are we really like racists when we think it is worse to kill a dolphin than to kill a tuna? The person who says there is a relevant similarity between speciesism and racism has the burden of proof: go ahead and identify the similarity. Is seeing moral significance in biological differences between chimpanzees and potatoes anything like seeing moral significance in biological differences between races? I think not.

Is it true that we need good reason to *exclude* plants and animals from the realm of things we regard as commanding respect? Or do we need reason to *include* them? Should we be trying to identify properties in virtue of which a thing forfeits presumptive moral standing? Or does it make more sense to be trying to identify properties in virtue of which a thing commands respect? The latter seems more natural to me, which suggests the burden of proof lies with those who claim we should have respect for other species.

I would not say, though, that this burden is unbearable. One reason to have regard for other species has to do with self-respect. (As I said earlier, when we mistreat a tree that we admire, the values we fail to respect are our values, not the tree's.) A second reason has to do with self-realisation. (As I said, exercising our capacity for moral regard is a form of self-realisation.) Finally, at least some species seem to share with human beings precisely those cognitive and affective characteristics that lead us to see human life as especially worthy of esteem. Johnson describes experiments in which rhesus monkeys show extreme reluctance to obtain food by means that would subject monkeys in neighbouring cages to electric shock (p. 64n). He describes the case of Washoe, a chimpanzee who learned sign language. Anyone who has tried to learn a foreign language ought to be able to appreciate how astonishing an intellectual feat it is that an essentially nonlinguistic creature could learn a language—a language that is not merely foreign but the language of another species.

Johnson believes Washoe has moral standing (p. 27–31), but he does not believe that the moral standing of chimpanzees, and indeed of all living creatures, implies that we must resolve never to kill (p. 136). Thus, Johnson supports killing introduced animal species (feral dogs, rabbits, and so forth) to prevent the extermination of Australia's native species, including native plant species (p. 174).

Is Johnson guilty of advocating the speciesist equivalent of ethnic cleansing? Has he shown himself to be no better than a racist? I think not. Johnson is right to want to take drastic measures to protect Australia's native flora, and the idea of respecting trees is intelligible. Certainly one thing I feel in the presence of Redwoods is something like a feeling of respect. But I doubt that what underlies Johnson's willingness to kill feral dogs is mere respect for Australia's native plants. I suspect that his approval of such killings turns on the needs and aesthetic sensibilities of human beings, not just the interests of plants.[10] For example, if the endangered native species happened to be a malaria-carrying mosquito, I doubt that Johnson would advocate wiping out an exotic but minimally intrusive species of amphibian in order to save the mosquitoes.

Aldo Leopold urged us to see ourselves as plain citizens of, rather than conquerors of the biotic community, but there are some species with whom we can never be fellow citizens.[11] The rabbits eating my flowers in the back yard are neighbours, and I cherish their company, minor frictions notwithstanding. I feel no sense of community with mosquitoes, though, and not merely because they are not warm and furry. Some mosquito species are so adapted to making human beings miserable that moral combat is not accidental; rather, combat is a natural state. It is how such creatures live. Recall Cheney's remark that the limits of moral regard are set by the limits of our ability to respond in a caring manner. I think it is fair to say human beings are not able to respond to malaria-carrying mosquitoes in a caring manner. At very least, most of us would think less of a person who did respond to them in a caring manner. We would regard the person's caring as a parody of respect for nature.

The conclusion that *all* species have moral standing is unmotivated. For human beings, viewing apes as having moral standing is a form of self-respect. Viewing viruses as having moral standing is not. It is good to have a sense of how amazing living things are, but being able to marvel at living things is not the same as thinking all species have moral standing. Life as such commands respect only in the limited but nonetheless important sense that for self-aware and reflective creatures who want to act in ways that make sense, deliberately killing something is an act that does not make sense unless we have good reason to do it. Destroying something for no good reason is (at best) the moral equivalent of vandalism.

IX. THE HISTORY OF THE DEBATE

There is an odd project in the history of philosophy that equates what seem to be three distinct projects:

1. determining our essence;
2. specifying how we are different from all other species;
3. specifying what makes us morally important.

Equating these three projects has important ramifications. Suppose for the sake of argument that what makes us morally important is that we are capable of suffering. If what makes us morally important is necessarily the same property that constitutes our essence, then our essence is that we are capable of suffering. And if our essence necessarily is what makes us different from all other species, then we can deduce that dogs are not capable of suffering.

Likewise with rationality. If rationality is our essence, then rationality is what makes us morally important and also what makes us unique. Therefore, we can deduce that chimpanzees are not rational. Alternatively, if some other animal becomes rational, does that mean our essence will change? Is that why some people find Washoe, the talking chimpanzee, threatening?

The three projects, needless to say, should not be conflated in the way philosophy seems historically to have conflated them, but we can reject species equality without conflating them. If we like, we can select a property with respect to which all species are the same, then argue that that property confers moral standing, then say all species have moral standing. To infer that all species have the same standing, though, would be to ignore the possibility that there are other morally important properties with respect to which not all species are equal.

There is room to wonder whether species egalitarianism is even compatible with respect for nature. Is it true that we should have no more regard for dolphins than for tuna? Is it true that the moral standing of chimpanzees is no higher than that of mosquitoes? I worry that these things are not only untrue, but also disrespectful. Dolphins and chimpanzees command more respect than species egalitarianism allows.

There is no denying that it demeans us to destroy species we find beautiful or otherwise beneficial. What about species in which we find neither beauty nor benefit? It is, upon reflection, obviously in our interest to enrich our lives by finding them beautiful or beneficial, if we can. By and large, we must agree with Leopold that it is too late for conquering the biotic community. Our most pressing task now is to find ways of fitting in. Species egalitarianism is one way of trying to understand how we fit in. In the end, it is not an acceptable way. Having respect for nature and being a species egalitarian are two different things.

NOTES

1. A species egalitarian may or may not believe that individual living things all have equal moral standing. A species egalitarian may think a given whooping crane matters more than a given bald eagle because the cranes are endangered, despite believing that the differences between the two species qua species are not morally important.

2. Paul W. Taylor (1983) In defense of biocentrism, *Environmental Ethics*, 5: 237–43, here p. 240.

3. Taylor (1994), op. cit., p. 35.

4. Arne Naess (1973) The shallow and the deep, long-range ecology movement: a summary, *Inquiry*, 16: 95–100.

5. William C. French (1995) Against biospherical egalitarianism, *Environmental Ethics*, 17: 39–57, here pp. 44ff.

6. James C. Anderson (1993) Species equality and the foundations of moral theory, *Environmental Values*, 2: 347–65, here p. 350.

7. Lawrence Johnson (1991) *A Morally Deep World* (New York, Cambridge University Press), p. 52.

8. Thus, the objective is to explain how a rational agent could have respect for trees, not to argue that a rational agent could not fail to have respect. In utilitarian terms, a person whose utility function leaves no room to derive pleasure from respecting trees is not irrational for failing to respect trees, but people whose utility functions include a potential for deriving pleasure from respecting trees have reason (other things equal) to enrich their lives by realising that potential.

9. Jim Cheney (1987) Eco-feminism and deep ecology, *Environmental Ethics* 9: 115–45, here p. 144.

10. Johnson believes ecosystems as such have moral standing and that, consequently, 'we should always stop short of entirely destroying or irreparably degrading any ecosystem' (p. 276). 'Chopping some trees is one thing, then, but destroying a forest is something else' (p. 276). But this is impossible to square with his remark that there 'is an ecosystem in a tiny puddle of water in a rotting stump' (p. 265). Thus, when Johnson says ecosystems should never be destroyed, he does not mean ecosystems per se. Rather he means forests, deserts, marshes, and so on—ecosystems that are recognisable as habitat either for humans or for species that humans care about.

11. Aldo Leopold (1966, first published in 1949) *Sand County Almanac* (New York, Oxford University Press) p. 240.

Environmental Justice

JAMES P. STERBA

A central debate, if not the most central debate, in contemporary environmental ethics is between those who defend an anthropocentric ethics which holds that humans are superior overall to the members of other species, and those who defend a non-anthropocentric ethics which holds that the members of all species are equal. Here I propose to go some way toward resolving this debate by showing that when the most morally defensible versions of each of these perspectives are laid out, they do not lead to different practical requirements. In this way I hope to show how it is possible for defenders of anthropocentric and non-anthropocentric environmental ethics, despite their theoretical disagreement concerning whether humans are superior to members of other species, to agree on a common set of principles for achieving environmental justice.

NON-ANTHROPOCENTRIC ENVIRONMENTAL ETHICS

Consider first the non-anthropocentric perspective. In support of this, it can be argued that we have no non-question-begging grounds for regarding the members of any living species as superior to the members of any other. It allows that the members of species differ in a myriad of ways, but argues that these differences do not provide grounds for thinking that the members of any one species are superior to the members of any other. In particular, it denies that the differences between species provide grounds for thinking that humans are superior to the members of other species. Of course, the non-anthropocentric perspective recognizes that humans have distinctive traits which the members of other species lack, like rationality and moral agency. It just points out that the members of non-human species also

James P. Sterba, "Environmental Justice," in *Ethics: The Big Questions* (Malden, MA: Blackwell, 1998), 401–12 (edited). Reprinted with permission by Blackwell Publishing.

have distinctive traits that humans lack, like the homing ability of pigeons, the speed of the cheetah, and the ruminative ability of sheep and cattle.

Nor will it do to claim that the distinctive traits that humans have are more valuable than the distinctive traits that members of other species possess because there is no non-question-begging standpoint from which to justify that claim. From a human standpoint, rationality and moral agency are more valuable than any of the distinctive traits found in non-human species, since, as humans, we would not be better off if we were to trade in those traits for the distinctive traits found in non-human species. Yet the same holds true of non-human species. Generally, pigeons, cheetahs, sheep, and cattle would not be better off if they were to trade in their distinctive traits for the distinctive traits of other species.

Of course, the members of some species might be better off if they could retain the distinctive traits of their species while acquiring one or another of the distinctive traits possessed by some other species. For example, we humans might be better off if we could retain our distinctive traits while acquiring the ruminative ability of sheep and cattle. But many of the distinctive traits of species cannot be even imaginatively added to the members of other species without substantially altering the original species. For example, in order for the cheetah to acquire the distinctive traits possessed by humans, presumably it would have to be so transformed that its paws became something like hands to accommodate its humanlike mental capabilities, thereby losing its distinctive speed, and ceasing to be a cheetah. So possessing distinctively human traits would not be good for the cheetah. And with the possible exception of our nearest evolutionary relatives, the same holds true for the members of other species: they would not be better off having distinctively human traits. Only in fairy tales and in the world of Disney can the members of non-human species enjoy a full array of distinctively human traits. So there would appear to be no non-question-begging perspective from which to judge that distinctively human traits are more valuable than the distinctive traits possessed by other species. Judged from a non-question-begging perspective, we would seemingly have to regard the members of all species as equals.

It might be useful at this point to make my argument even more explicit. Here is one way this could be done.

(1) We should not aggress against any living being unless there are either self-evident or non-question-begging reasons for doing so. (It would be difficult to reject this principle given the various analogous principles we accept, such as the principle of formal equality: equals should be treated equally and unequals unequally.)

(2) To treat humans as superior overall to other living beings is to aggress against them by sacrificing their basic needs to meet the non-basic needs of humans. (Definition)

(3) Therefore, we should not treat humans as superior overall to other living beings unless we have either self-evident or non-question-begging reasons for doing so. (From 1 and 2)

(4) We do not have either self-evident or non-question-begging reasons for treating humans as superior overall to other living beings. (That we do not have any non-question-begging reasons for treating humans as superior overall to other living beings was established by the previous argument. That we do not have any self-evident reasons for doing so, I take it, is obvious.)

(5) Therefore, we should not treat humans as superior overall to other living beings. (From 3 and 4)

(6) Not to treat humans as superior overall to other living beings is to treat them as equal overall to other living beings. (Definition)

(7) Therefore, we should treat humans as equal overall to other living beings. (From 5 and 6)

Nevertheless, I want to go on to claim that regarding the members of all species as equals still allows for human preference in the same way that regarding all humans as equals still allows for self preference.

First of all, human preference can be justified on grounds of defense. Thus, we have

> A Principle of Human Defense: actions that defend oneself and other human beings against harmful aggression are permissible even when they necessitate killing or harming animals or plants.

This Principle of Human Defense allows us to defend ourselves and other human beings from harmful aggression first against our persons and the persons of other humans beings that we are committed to or happen to care about, and second against our justifiably held property and the justifiably held property of other humans beings that we are committed to or happen to care about.

This principle is analogous to the principle of self-defense that applies in human ethics and permits actions in defense of oneself or other human beings against harmful human aggression. In the case of human aggression, however, it will sometimes be possible to effectively defend oneself and other human beings by first suffering the aggression and then securing adequate compensation later. Since in the case of non-human aggression, this is unlikely to obtain, more harmful preventive actions such as killing a rabid dog or swatting a mosquito will be justified. There are simply more ways to effectively stop aggressive humans than there are to stop aggressive non-humans.

Second, human preference can also be justified on grounds of preservation. Accordingly, we have

> A Principle of Human Preservation: actions that are necessary for meeting one's basic needs or the basic needs of other human beings are permissible even when they require aggressing against the basic needs of animals and plants.

Now needs, in general, if not satisfied, lead to lacks or deficiencies with respect to various standards. The basic needs of humans, if not satisfied, lead to lacks or deficiencies with respect to a standard of a decent life. The basic needs of animals and plants, if not satisfied, lead to lacks or deficiencies with respect to a standard of a healthy life. The means necessary for meeting the basic needs of humans can vary widely from society to society. By contrast, the means necessary for meeting the basic needs of particular species of animals and plants are more invariant.

In human ethics, there is no principle that is strictly analogous to this Principle of Human Preservation. There is a principle of self-preservation in human ethics that permits actions that are necessary for meeting one's own basic needs or the basic needs of other people, even if this requires *failing to meet* (through an act of omission) the basic needs of still other people. For example, we can use our resources to feed ourselves and our family, even if this necessitates failing to meet the basic needs of people in Third World countries. But, in general, we don't have a principle that allows us to *aggress against* (through an act of commission) the basic needs of some people in order to meet our own basic needs or the basic needs of other people to whom we are committed or happen to care about. Actually, the closest we come to permitting aggressing against the basic needs of other people in order to meet our own basic needs or the basic needs of people to whom we are committed or happen to care about is our acceptance of the outcome of life and death struggles in lifeboat cases, where no one has an antecedent right to the available resources. For example, if you had to fight off others in order to secure the last place in a lifeboat for yourself or for a member of your family, we might say that you justifiably aggressed against the basic needs of those whom you fought to meet your own basic needs or the basic needs of the member of your family.

Nevertheless, our survival requires a principle of preservation that permits aggressing against the basic needs of at least some other living things whenever this is necessary to meet our own basic needs or the basic needs of other human beings. Here there are two possibilities. The first is a principle of preservation that allows us to aggress against the basic needs of both humans and non-humans whenever it would serve our own basic needs or the basic needs of other human beings. The second is the principle, given above, that allows us to aggress against the basic needs of only non-humans whenever it would serve our own basic needs or the basic needs of other

human beings. The first principle does not express any general preference for the members of the human species, and thus it permits even cannibalism provided that it serves to meet our own basic needs or the basic needs of other human beings. In contrast, the second principle does express a degree of preference for the members of the human species in cases where their basic needs are at stake. Happily, this degree of preference for our own species is still compatible with the equality of all species because favoring the members of one's own species to this extent is characteristic of the members of nearly all species with which we interact and is thereby legitimated. The reason it is legitimated is that we would be required to sacrifice the basic needs of members of the human species only if the members of other species were making similar sacrifices for the sake of members of the human species. In addition, if we were to prefer consistently the basic needs of the members of other species whenever those needs conflicted with our own (or even if we do so half the time), given the characteristic behavior of the members of other species, we would soon be facing extinction, and, fortunately, we have no reason to think that we are morally required to bring about our own extinction. For these reasons, the degree of preference for our own species found in the above Principle of Human Preservation is justified, even if we were to adopt a non-anthropocentric perspective.

Nevertheless, preference for humans can go beyond bounds, and the bounds that are compatible with a non-anthropocentric perspective are expressed by the following:

> *A Principle of Disproportionality*: actions that meet non-basic or luxury needs of humans are prohibited when they aggress against the basic needs of animals and plants.

This principle is strictly analogous to the principle in human ethics mentioned previously that prohibits meeting some people's non-basic or luxury needs by aggressing against the basic needs of other people.

Without a doubt, the adoption of such a principle with respect to non-human nature would significantly change the way we live our lives. Such a principle is required, however, if there is to be any substance to the claim that the members of all species are equal. We can no more consistently claim that the members of all species are equal and yet aggress against the basic needs of some animals or plants whenever this serves our own non-basic or luxury needs than we can consistently claim that all humans are equal and aggress against the basic needs of some other human beings whenever this serves our non-basic or luxury needs. Consequently, if species equality is to mean anything, it must be the case that the basic needs of the members of non-human species are protected against aggressive actions which only serve to meet the non-basic needs of humans, as required by the Principle of Disproportionality.

So while a non-anthropocentric perspective allows for a degree of preference for the members of the human species, it also significantly limits that preference.

To see why these limits on preference for the members of the human species are all that is required for recognizing the equality of species, we need to understand the equality of species by analogy with the equality of humans. We need to see that just as we claim that humans are equal but treat them differently, so too we can claim that all species are equal but treat them differently. In human ethics, there are various interpretations given to human equality that allow for different treatment of humans. In ethical egoism, everyone is *equally at liberty* to pursue his or her own interests, but this allows us to always prefer ourselves to others, who are understood to be like opponents in a competitive game. In libertarianism, everyone has an *equal right to liberty*, but although this imposes some limits on the pursuit of self-interest, it is said to allow us to refrain from helping others in severe need. In welfare liberalism, everyone has an *equal right to welfare and opportunity*, but this need not commit us to providing everyone with exactly the same resources. In socialism, everyone has an *equal right* to self-development, and although this may commit us to providing everyone with the same resources, it still sanctions some degree of self-preference. So just as there are these various ways to interpret human equality that still allow us to treat

humans differently, there are various ways that we can interpret species equality that allow us to treat species differently.

Now one might interpret species equality in a very strong sense, analogous to the interpretation of equality found in socialism. But the kind of species equality that I have defended is more akin to the equality found in welfare liberalism or in libertarianism than it is to the equality found in socialism. In brief, this form of equality requires that we not aggress against the basic needs of the members of other species for the sake of the non-basic needs of the members of our own species (the Principle of Disproportionality), but it permits us to aggress against the basic needs of the members of other species for the sake of the basic needs of the members of our own species (the Principle of Human Preservation), and also permits us to defend the basic and even the non-basic needs of the members of our own species against harmful aggression by members of other species (the Principle of Human Defense). In this way, I have argued that we can accept the claim of species equality, while avoiding imposing an unreasonable sacrifice on the members of our own species.

INDIVIDUALISM AND HOLISM

It might be objected here that I have not yet taken into account the conflict within a non-anthropocentric ethics between holists and individualists. According to holists, the good of a species or the good of an ecosystem or the good of the whole biotic community can trump the good of individual living things.[1] According to individualists, the good of each individual living thing must be respected.

Now one might think that holists would require that we abandon my Principle of Human Preservation. Yet consider. Assuming that people's basic needs are at stake, how could it be morally objectionable for them to try to meet those needs, even if this were to harm non-human individuals, or species, or whole ecosystems, or even, to some degree, the whole biotic community? Of course, we can ask people in such conflict cases not to meet their basic needs in order to prevent harm to non-human individuals or species, ecosystems or the whole biotic community. But if people's basic needs are at stake, we cannot reasonably demand that they make such a sacrifice. We could demand, of course, that people do all that they reasonably can to keep such conflicts from arising in the first place, for, just as in human ethics, many severe conflicts of interest can be avoided simply by doing what is morally required early on. Nevertheless, when people's basic needs are at stake, the individualist perspective seems incontrovertible. We cannot reasonably require people to be saints.

At the same time, when people's basic needs are not at stake, we would be justified in acting on holistic grounds to prevent serious harm to non-human individuals, or species, or ecosystems, or the whole biotic community. Obviously, it will be difficult to know when our interventions will have this effect, but when we can be reasonably sure that they will, such interventions (e.g. culling elk herds in wolf-free ranges or preserving the habitat of endangered species) would be morally permissible, and maybe even morally required.[2] This shows that it is possible to agree with individualists when the basic needs of human beings are at stake, and to agree with holists when they are not.

Yet this combination of individualism and holism appears to conflict with the equality of species by imposing greater sacrifices on the members of non-human species than it does on the members of the human species. Fortunately, appearances are deceiving here. Although the proposed resolution only justifies imposing holism when people's basic needs are not at stake, it does not justify imposing individuals at all. Rather it would simply permit individualism when people's basic needs *are* at stake. Of course, we could impose holism under all conditions. But given that this would, in effect, involve going to war against people who are simply striving to meet their own basic needs in the only way they can, as permitted by the Principle of Human Preservation, intervention in such cases would not be justified. It would involve taking away the means of survival from people, even when these means are not required for one's own survival.

Nevertheless, this combination of individualism and holism may leave animal liberationists wondering about the further implications of this resolution for the treatment of animals. Obviously, a good deal of work has already been done on this topic. Initially, philosophers taught that humanism could be extended to include animal liberation and eventually environmental concern. Then Baird Callicot argued that animal liberation and environmental concern were as opposed to each other as they were to humanism.[3] The resulting conflict Callicott called "a triangular affair." Agreeing with Callicott, Mark Sagoff contended that any attempt to link together animal liberation and environmental concern would lead to "a bad marriage and a quick divorce."[4] Yet more recently, such philosophers as Mary Ann Warren have tended to play down the opposition between animal liberation and environmental concern, and even Callicott now thinks he can bring the two back together again.[5] There are good reasons for thinking that such a reconciliation is possible.

Right off, it would be good for the environment if people generally, especially people in the First World, adopted a more vegetarian diet of the sort that animal liberationists are recommending. This is because a good portion of livestock production today consumes grains that could be more effectively used for direct human consumption. For example, 90 percent of the protein, 99 percent of the carbohydrate, and 100 percent of the fiber value of grain is wasted by cycling it through livestock, and currently 64 percent of the US grain crop is fed to livestock.[6] So by adopting a more vegetarian diet, people generally, and especially people in the First World, could significantly reduce the amount of farmland that has to be kept in production to feed the human population. This, in turn, could have beneficial effects on the whole biotic community by eliminating the amount of soil erosion and environmental pollutants that result from raising livestock. For example, it has been estimated that of 85 percent of US topsoil lost from cropland, pasture, range land, and forest land is directly associated with raising livestock.[7] So, in addition to preventing animal suffering, there are these additional reasons to favor a more vegetarian diet.

But even though a more vegetarian diet seems in order, it is not clear that the interests of farm animals would be well served if all of us became complete vegetarians. Sagott assumes that in a completely vegetarian human world people would continue to feed farm animals as before.[8] But it is not clear that we would have any obligation to do so. Moreover, in a completely vegetarian human world, we would probably need about half of the grain we now feed livestock to meet people's nutritional needs, particularly in Second and Third World countries. There simply would not be enough grain to go around. And then there would be the need to conserve cropland for future generations. So in a completely vegetarian human world, it seems likely that the population of farm animals would be decimated, relegating many of the animals that remain to zoos. On this account, it would seem to be more in the interest of farm animals generally that they be maintained under healthy conditions, and hence not in the numbers sustainable only with factory farms, but then killed relatively painlessly and eaten, rather than that they not be maintained at all. So a completely vegetarian human world would not seem to serve the interest of farm animals.

Nor, it seems, would it be in the interest of wild species who no longer have their natural predators not to be hunted by humans. Of course, where possible, it may be preferable to reintroduce natural predators. But this may not always be possible because of the proximity of farm animals and human populations, and then if action is not taken to control the populations of wild species, disaster could result for the species and their environment. For example, deer, rabbits, squirrels, quails, and ducks reproduce rapidly, and in the absence of predator can quickly exceed the carrying capacity of their environments. So it may be in the interest of certain wild species and their environments that humans intervene periodically to maintain a balance. Of course, there will be many natural environments where it is in the interest of the environment and the wild animals that inhabit it to be simply left alone. But here, too, animal liberation and environmental concern would not be in conflict. For these reasons, animal liberationists

would have little reason to object to the proposed combination of individualism and holism within a non-anthropocentric environmental ethics.

ANTHROPOCENTRIC ENVIRONMENTAL ETHICS

Suppose, however, we were to reject the central contention of the non-anthropocentric perspective and deny that the members of all species are equal. We might claim, for example, that humans are superior because they, through culture, "realize a greater range of values" than members of non-human species or we might claim that humans are superior in virtue of their "unprecedented capacity to create ethical systems that impart worth to other lifeforms."[9] Or we might offer some other grounds for human superiority. Suppose, then, we adopt this anthropocentric perspective. What follows?

First of all, we will still need a principle of human defense. However, there is no need to adopt a different principle of human defense from the principle favored by a non-anthropocentric perspective. Whether we judge humans to be equal or superior to the members of other species, we will still want a principle that allows us to defend ourselves and other human beings from harmful aggression, even when this necessitates killing or harming animals or plants.

Second, we will also need a principle of human preservation. But here too there is no need to adopt a different principle from the principle of human preservation favored by a non-anthropocentric perspective. Whether we judge humans to be equal or superior to the members of other species, we will still want a principle that permits actions that are necessary for meeting of other human beings, even when this requires aggressing against the basic needs of animals and plants.

The crucial question is whether we will need a different principle of disproportionality. If we judge humans to be superior to the members of other species, will we still have grounds for protecting the basic needs of animals and plants against aggressive action to meet the non-basic or luxury needs of humans?

Here it is important to distinguish between two degrees of preference that we noted earlier. First, we could prefer the basic needs of animals and plants over the non-basic or luxury needs of humans when to do otherwise would involve *aggressing against* (by an act of commission) the basic needs of animals and plants. Second, we could prefer the basic needs of animals and plants over the non-basic or luxury needs of humans when to do otherwise would involve simply *failing to meet* (by an act of omission) the basic needs of animals and plants.

Now in human ethics when the basic needs of some people are in conflict with the non-basic or luxury needs of others, the distinction between failing to meet and aggressing against basic needs seems to have little moral force. In such conflict cases, both ways of not meeting basic needs are objectionable.

But in environmental ethics, whether we adopt an anthropocentric or a non-anthropocentric perspective, we would seem to have grounds for morally distinguishing between the two cases, favoring the basic needs of animals and plants when to do otherwise would involve *aggressing against* those needs in order to meet our own non-basic or luxury needs, but not when it would involve simply *failing to meet* those needs in order to meet our own non-basic or luxury needs. This degree of preference for the members of the human species would be compatible with the equality of species in so far as members of non-human species similarly fail to meet the basic needs of members of the human species where there is a conflict of interest.

Even so, this theoretical distinction would have little practical force since most of the ways that we have of preferring our own non-basic needs over the basic needs of animals and plants actually involve aggressing against their basic needs to meet our own non-basic or luxury needs rather than simply failing to meet their basic needs.

Yet even if most of the ways that we have of preferring our own non-basic or luxury needs do involve aggressing against the basic needs of animals and plants, wouldn't human superiority provide grounds for preferring ourselves or other human beings in these ways? Or put another way, shouldn't human

superiority have more theoretical and practical significance than I am allowing? Not, I claim, if we are looking for the most morally defensible position to take.

For consider: the claim that humans are superior to the members of other species, if it can be justified at all, is something like the claim that a person came in first in a race where others came in second, third, fourth, and so on. It would not imply that the members of other species are without intrinsic value. In fact, it would imply just the opposite—that the members of other species are also intrinsically valuable as humans, just as the claim that a person came in first in a race implies that the persons who came in second, third, fourth, and so on are also meritorious, although not as meritorious as the person who came in first.

This line of argument draws further support once we consider the fact that many animals and plants are superior to humans in one respect or another, e.g. the sense of smell of the wolf, or the acuity of sight of the eagle, or the survivability of the cockroach, or the photosynthetic power of plants. So any claim of human superiority must allow for the recognition of excellences in non-human species, even for some excellences that are superior to their corresponding human excellences. In fact, it demands that recognition.

Moreover, if the claim of human superiority is to have any moral force, it must rest on non-question-begging grounds. Accordingly, we must be able to give a non-question-begging response to the non-anthropocentric argument for the equality of species. Yet for any such argument to be successful, it would have to recognize the intrinsic value of the members of non-human species. Even if it would be established that human beings have greater intrinsic value, we would still have to recognize that non-human nature has intrinsic value as well. So the relevant question is: how are we going to recognize the presumably lesser intrinsic value of non-human nature?

Now if human needs, even non-basic or luxury ones, are always preferred to even the basic needs of the members of non-human species, we would not be giving any recognition to the intrinsic value of non-human nature. But what if we allowed the non-basic or luxury needs of humans to trump the basic needs of non-human nature half the time, and half the time we allowed the basic needs of non-human nature to trump the non-basic or luxury needs of humans? Would that be enough? Certainly, it would be a significant advance over what we are presently doing. For what we are presently doing is meeting the basic needs of non-human nature, at best, only when it serves our own needs or the needs of those we are committed to or happen to care about, and that does not recognize the intrinsic value of non-human nature at all. A fifty-fifty arrangement would be an advanced indeed. But it would not be enough.

The reason why it would not be enough is that the claim that humans are superior to non-human nature no more supports the practice of aggressing against the basic needs of non-human nature to satisfy our own non-basic of luxury needs than the claim that a person who came in first in a race would support the practice of aggressing against the basic needs of those who came in second, third, fourth, and so on to satisfy the non-basic or luxury needs of the person who came in first. A higher degree of merit does not translate into a right of domination, and to claim a right to aggress against the basic needs of non-human nature in order to meet our own non-basic or luxury needs is clearly to claim a right of domination. All that our superiority as humans would justify is not meeting the basic needs of non-human nature when this conflicts with our non-basic or luxury needs. What it does not justify is aggressing against the basic needs of non-human nature when this conflicts with our non-basic or luxury needs.

OBJECTIVE AND SUBJECTIVE VALUE THEORY

Now it might be objected that my argument so far presupposes an objective theory of value which regards things as valuable because of the qualities they actually have rather than a subjective theory of value which regards things as valuable simply because humans happen to value them. However, I contend that when both these theories are defensi-bly formulated, they will lead to the same practical requirements.

For consider. Suppose we begin with a subjective theory of value that regards things as valuable simply because humans value them. Of course, some things would be valued by humans instrumentally, others intrinsically, but, according to this theory, all things would have the value they have, if they have any value at all, simply because they are valued by humans either instrumentally or intrinsically.

One problem facing such a theory is why should we think that humans alone determine the value that things have? For example, why not say that things are valuable because the members of other species value them? Why not say that grass is valuable because zebras value it, and that zebras are valuable because lions value them, and so on? Or why not say, assuming God exists, that things are valuable because God values them?

Nor would it do simply to claim that we authoritatively determine what is valuable for ourselves, that non-human species authoritatively determine what is valuable for themselves, and that God authoritatively determines what is valuable for the Godhead. For what others value should at least be relevant data when authoritatively determining what is valuable for ourselves.

Another problem for a subjective theory of value is that we probably would not want to say that just anything we happen to value determines what is valuable for ourselves. For surely we would want to say that at least some of the things that people value, especially people who are evil or deficient in certain ways, are not really valuable, even for them. Merely thinking that something is valuable doesn't make it so.

Suppose, then, we modified this subjective theory of value to deal with these problems. Let the theory claim that what is truly valuable for people is what they would value if they had all the relevant information (including, where it is relevant, knowledge of what others would value) and reasoned correctly. Of course, there will be many occasions where we are unsure that ideal conditions have been realized, unsure, that is, that we have all the relevant information and have reasoned correctly. And even when we are sure that ideal conditions have been realized, we may not always be willing to act upon what we come to value due to weakness of will.

Nevertheless, when a subjective theory of value is formulated in this way, it will have the same practical requirements as an objective theory of value that is also defensibly formulated. For an objective theory of value holds that what is valuable is determined by the qualities things actually have. But in order for the qualities things actually have to be valuable in the sense of being capable of being valued, they must be accessible to us, at least under ideal conditions, that is, they must be the sort of qualities that we would value if we had all the relevant information and reasoned correctly. But this is just what is valuable according to our modified subjective theory of value. So once a subjective theory of value and an objective theory of value are defensibly formulated in the manner I propose, they will lead us to value the same things.

Now it is important to note here that with respect to some of the things we value intrinsically, such as animals and plants, our valuing them depends simply on our ability to discover the value that they actually have based on their qualities, whereas for other things that we value intrinsically, such as our aesthetic experiences and the objects that provided us with those experiences, the value that these things have depends significantly on the way we are constituted. So that if we were constituted differently, what we value aesthetically would be different as well. Of course, the same holds true for some of the things that we value morally. For example, we morally value not killing human beings because of the way we are constituted. Constituted as we are, killing is usually bad for any human that we would kill. But suppose that we were constituted differently such that killing human beings was immensely pleasurable for those humans that we killed, following which they immediately sprang back to life asking us to kill them again. If human beings were constituted in this way, we would no longer morally value not killing. In fact, constituted in this new way, I think we would come to morally value *killing* and the rel-

evant rule for us might be "Kill human beings as often as you can." But while such aesthetic and moral values are clearly dependent on the way we are constituted, they still are not anthropocentric in the sense that they imply human superiority. Such values can be recognized from both an anthropocentric and a non-anthropocentric perspective.

It might be objected, however, that while the intrinsic values of an environmental ethics need not be anthropocentric in the sense that they imply human superiority, these values must be anthropocentric in the sense that humans would reasonably come to hold them. This seems correct. However, appealing to this sense of anthropocentric, Eugene Hargrove has argued that not all living things would turn out to be intrinsically valuable as a non-anthropocentric environmental ethics maintains.[10] Hargrove cites as hypothetical examples of living things that would not turn out to be intrinsically valuable the creatures in the films *Alien* and *Aliens*. What is distinctive about these creatures in *Alien* and *Aliens* is that they require the deaths of many other living creatures, whomever they happen upon, to reproduce and survive as a species. Newly hatched, these creatures emerge from their eggs and immediately enter host organisms, which they keep alive and feed upon while they develop. When the creatures are fully developed, they explode out of the chest of their host organisms, killing their hosts with some fanfare. Hargrove suggests that if such creatures existed, we would not intrinsically value them because it would not be reasonable for us to do so.

Following Paul Taylor, Hargrove assumes that to intrinsically value a creature is to recognize a negative duty not to destroy or harm that creature and a positive duty to protect it from being destroyed or harmed by others. Since Hargrove thinks that we would be loath to recognize any such duties with respect to such alien creatures, we would not consider them to be intrinsically valuable.

Surely it seems clear that we would seek to kill such alien creatures by whatever means are available to us. But why should that preclude our recognizing them as having intrinsic value any more than our seeking to kill any person who is engaged in lethal aggression against us would preclude our recognizing that person as having intrinsic value? To recognize something as having intrinsic value does not preclude destroying it to preserve other things that also have intrinsic value when there is good reason to do so. Furthermore, recognizing a prima facie negative duty not to destroy or harm something and a prima facie positive duty to protect it from being destroyed or harmed by others is perfectly consistent with recognizing an all-things-considered duty to destroy that thing when it is engaged in lethal aggression against us. Actually, all we are doing here is simply applying our Principle of Human Defense, and, as I have argued earlier, there is no reason to think that the application of this principle would preclude our recognizing the intrinsic value of every living being.

Still another objection that might be raised to my reconciliationist argument is that my view is too individualistic, as evidenced by the fact that my principles of environmental justice refer to individual humans, plants, and animals but not specifically to species or ecosystems. Now, I would certainly agree with Paul Taylor that all individual living beings as well as species populations can be benefited or harmed and have a good of their own, and, hence, qualify as moral subjects.[11] But Taylor goes on to deny that species themselves are moral subjects with a good of their own, because he regards "species" as a class name, and classes, he contends, have no good of their own.[12] yet here I would disagree with Taylor because species are unlike abstract classes in that they evolve, split, bud off new species, become endangered, become extinct and have interests distinct from the interests of their members. For example, a particular species of deer but not individual members of that species can have an interest in being preyed upon. Hence, species can be benefited and harmed and have a good of their own, and so should qualify on Taylor's view, as well as my own, as moral subjects. So, too, ecosystems should qualify as moral subjects since they can be benefited and harmed and have a good of their own, having features and interests not shared by their components. Following Lawrence Johnson, we can go on to characterize moral subjects as living systems in a persistent state

of low entropy sustained by metabolic processes for accumulating energy whose organic unity and self-identity is maintained in equilibrium by homeostatic feedback processes.[13] Thus, modifying my view in order to take into account species and ecosystems requires the following changes in my first three principles of environmental justice:

> *A Principle of Human Defense*: actions that defend oneself and other human beings against harmful aggression are permissible even when they necessitate killing or harming individual animals or plants or even destroying whole species or ecosystems.

> *A Principle of Human Preservation*: actions that are necessary for meeting one's basic needs or the basic needs of other human beings are permissible even when they require aggressing against the basic needs of individual animals and plants or even of whole species or ecosystem.

> *A Principle of Disproportionality*: actions that meet non-basic or luxury needs of humans are prohibited when they aggress against the basic needs of individual animals and plants, or of whole species or ecosystems.

But while this modification is of theoretical interest since it allows that species and ecosystems as well as individuals count morally, it actually has little or no practical effect on the application of these principles. This is because, for the most part, the positive or negative impact the application of these principles would have on species and ecosystems is correspondingly reflected in the positive or negative impact the application of these principles would have on the individual members of those species or ecosystems. As a consequence, actions that are permitted or prohibited with respect to species and ecosystems according to the modified principles are already permitted or prohibited respectively through their correspondence with actions that are permitted or prohibited according to the unmodified principles.

However, this is not always the case. In fact, considerations about what benefits non-human species or subspecies as opposed to individuals of those species or subspecies have already figured in my previous argument. For example, I have argued for culling elk herds in wolf-free ranges, but this is primarily for the good of herds or species of elk and certainly not for the good of the particular elk who are being culled from those herds. I also have argued that it would be for the good of farm animals generally that they be maintained under healthy conditions, and then killed relatively painlessly and eaten, rather than that they not be maintained at all. But clearly this is an argument about what would be good for existing flocks or herds, or species or subspecies of farm animals. It is not an argument about what would be good for the existing individual farm animals who would be killed relatively painlessly and eaten. Nevertheless, for the most part, because of the coincidence between the welfare of species and ecosystems and the welfare of individual members of those species and ecosystems, the two formulations of the first three principles turn out be practically equivalent.

In sum, I have argued that whether we endorse an anthropocentric or a non-anthropocentric environmental ethics, we should favor a Principle of Human Defense, a Principle of Human Preservation, and a Principle of Disproportionality as I have interpreted them. In the past, failure to recognize the importance of a Principle of Human Defense and a Principle of Human Preservation has led philosophers to overestimate the amount of sacrificed required of humans. By contrast, failure to recognize the importance of a Principle of Disproportionality has led philosophers to underestimate the amount of sacrifice required of humans. I claim that taken together these three principles strike the right balance between concerns of human welfare and the welfare of non-human nature.

NOTES

1. Aldo Leopold's view is usually interpreted as holistic in this sense. Leopold wrote, "A thing is right when it tends to preserve the integrity, stability and beauty of the biotic community. It is wrong when it tends otherwise." See his *A Sand County Almanac* (Oxford, 1949).

2. Where it is most likely to be morally required is where our negligent actions have caused the environmental problem in the first place.

3. Baird Callicott, "Animal Liberation: A Triangular Affair," *Environmental Ethics* (1980), 311–28.

4. Mark Sagoff, "Animal Liberation and Environmental Ethics: Bad Marriage, Quick Divorce," *Osgood Hall Law Journal* (1984), 297–307.

5. Mary Ann Warren, "The Rigths of the Nonhuman World," in *Environmental Philosophy*, edited by Robert Elliot and Arran Gare (London, 1983), 109–34 and Baird Callicott, *In Defense of the Land Ethic* (Albany, 1989), ch. 3.

6. *Realities for the 90's* (Santa Cruz, 1991), 4.

7. Ibid., 5.

8. Mark Sagoff, "Animal Liberation," 301–5.

9. Holmes Rolston, *Environmental Ethics* (Philadelphia, 1988), 66–8; Murray Bookchim, *The Ecology of Freedom* (Montreal, 1991), xxxvi.

10. Eugene Hargrove, "Weak Anthropocentric Intrinsic Value," in *After Earth Day*, edited by Max Oelschlaeger (Denton, 1992), 147ff.

11. Paul Taylor, *Respect for Nature* [Princeton, NJ: Princeton University Press, 1987], 68–71 and 17.

12. Ibid., 68–71.

13. See Lawrence Johnson, "Toward the Moral Consideration of Species and Ecosystems," *Environmental Ethics*, 14 (1992).

American Terrorism, Environment-Style

DOUG BANDOW

Terrorists are loose in America—eco-terrorists. In August, radical environmentalists apparently burned down an apartment complex under construction in San Diego.

A couple of weeks later, eco-terrorists attacked four SUV dealerships in West Covina, a Los Angeles suburb. Federal agents have arrested for the crime a 25-year-old member of an organization supposedly dedicated to peace and environmentalism.

These attacks were likely perpetrated by the Environmental Liberation Front (ELF), which has boasted of committing arson and bombings. Early last year ELF issued "an open call for direct action." It later took responsibility for torching a Forest Service lab in Pennsylvania.

The Animal Liberation Front (ALF) is similar. The two groups are blamed for $45 million worth of damage in a campaign involving at least 600 arsons and others incidents going back to 1996. ALF's spokesman explained: "It's a war. A long, hard, bloody, war."

Eco-terrorism first gained attention in the early 1970s when "the Fox" engaged in a campaign of eco-sabotage against Chicago-area firms. The group Environmental Action published the self-help guide *Ecotage!* in 1972. Edward Abbey later romanticized eco-terrorism in his novel *The Monkey Wrench Gang.*

Dave Foreman, a former lobbyist for the Wilderness Society, founded Earth First! in 1981. Foreman, later convicted for conspiring to sabotage nuclear power plants in three states, argued that monkey-wrenching "is morally required" as "self-defense on the part of the Earth." After a millworker was seriously injured when a hidden spike shattered a saw blade, Foreman responded: "the old-growth forest in North Idaho is a hell of a lot more important than Joe Six-pack."

Ecoteurs spiked trees and National Forest trails to puncture tires and strung wire to disrupt races. Eco-saboteurs destroyed and electrical substation in Canada, vandalized a ski lift in Arizona, wrecked a utility bridge in Montana, cut power lines in Arizona, Colorado and Utah, and damaged construction equipment at various sites. Ranches were another target.

Aspiring eco-saboteurs imagined even more. The publication *Earth First!* ran an anonymous letter declaring:

"The only way to stop all the destruction of our home is to decrease the birth rate or increase the death rate of people. . . . What we need is a wholesale operation. . . . The simple expedient: biological warfare!"

If only Osama bin Laden had thought to use environmental rhetoric.

Luckily, Earth First! never initiated biological war. Now ELF and ALF have moved to the fore. Arson is their tool of choice, one that is likely to eventually kill people as well as destroy property.

Mainstream environmental groups have done little to discourage eco-saboteurs.

Years ago David Brower, one-time Sierra Club executive director and later chairman of Friends of the Earth, gave office space to Earth First! He explained: "I'm certainly not going to be against civil disobedience."

In fact, he added, "Earth First! makes Friends of the Earth look reasonable. What we need now is an outfit to make Earth First! look reasonable."

ALF and ELF do that.

The vegan campaign coordinator for People for the Ethical Treatment of Animals (PETA), Bruce Friedrich, told the Animal Rights 2001 conference: "If we really believe that animals have the same right to be free from pain and suffering at our hands, then, of course we're going to be blowing things up and smashing windows."

Rick Berman of the Center for Consumer Freedom points to financial ties between PETA and ALF/ELF. The former made a direct contribution to

Doug Bandow, "American Terrorism, Environment-Style," *Human Events* 27 (29 September 2003): 981 (edited). Reprinted with permissions of *Human Events.*

ELF in 2000, and has underwritten the activities of ALF/ELF activists since 1995, including aiding the defense of Rodney Coronado, convicted of arson in 1992.

Existing law covers traditional crimes, but has not targeted organizations fomenting eco-terrorism. Observes the American Legislative Exchange Council, which works with state legislators: "making no legal distinction between the common thug who vandalized a public park and an organized ecoterrorist . . . allows for a significant circular turnover rate, where criminals return to their organizations to commit further crimes in other locations or jurisdictions."

Thus, ALEC has proposed model legislation to prohibit acts of or support for environmental terror-

ism, set penalties for violators, allow victims to sue for treble damages, target organizations that promote ecoterrorism, and allow forfeiture of property used in such offenses. They are not designed for broader use against ever more expansive targets, unlike the old RICO legislation and recent Patriot acts I and II, which have posed potent threats to civil liberties.

Although a higher standard of living makes it easier to protect the environment, some trade-off between ecological and economic values is inevitable. In a democratic society, such disagreements are fought with words, not guns.

But an extremist few have decided to use violence to get their way. They, like al-Qaeda's adherents, threaten American lives and property.

The Land Ethic

ALDO LEOPOLD

When god-like Odysseus returned from the wars in Troy, he hanged all on one rope a dozen slave-girls of his household whom he suspected of misbehavior during his absence.

This hanging involved no question of propriety. The girls were property. The disposal of property was then, as now, a matter of expediency, not of right and wrong.

Concepts of right and wrong were not lacking from Odysseus' Greece: witness the fidelity of his wife through the long years before at last his black-prowed galleys clove the wine-dark seas for home. The ethical structure of that day covered wives, but had not yet been extended to human chattels. During the three thousand years which have since elapsed, ethical criteria have been extended to many fields of conduct, with corresponding shrinkages in those judged by expediency only.

Aldo Leopold, "The Land Ethic," in *A Sand County Almanac* (New York, NY: Ballantine Books, 1966), 237–41, 246–49, 251–54, 261–64 (edited). Reprinted with permission of Random House, Inc.

This extension of ethics, so far studied only by philosophers, is actually a process in ecological evolution. Its sequences may be described in ecological as well as in philosophical terms. An ethic, ecologically, is a limitation on freedom of action in the struggle for existence. An ethic, philosophically, is a differentiation of social from anti-social conduct. These are two definitions of one thing. The thing has its origin in the tendency of interdependent individuals or groups to evolve modes of co-operation. The ecologist calls these symbioses. Politics and economics are advanced symbioses in which the original free-for-all competition has been replaced, in part, by co-operative mechanisms with an ethical content.

The complexity of co-operative mechanisms has increased with population density, and with the efficiency of tools. It was simpler, for example, to define the anti-social uses of sticks and stones in the days of the mastodons than of bullets and billboards in the age of motors.

The first ethics dealt with the relation between individuals; the Mosaic Decalogue is an example. Later accretions dealt with the relation between the individual and society. The Golden Rule tries to integrate the individual to society; democracy to integrate social organization to the individual.

There is as yet no ethic dealing with man's relation to land and to the animals and plants which grow upon it. Land, like Odysseus' slave-girls, is still property. The land-relation is still strictly economic, entailing privileges but not obligations.

The extension of ethics to this third element in human environment is, if I read the evidence correctly, an evolutionary possibility and an ecological necessity. It is the third step in a sequence. The first two have already been taken. Individual thinkers since the days of Ezekiel and Isaiah have asserted that the despoliation of land is not only inexpedient but wrong. Society, however, has not yet affirmed their belief. I regard the present conservation movement as the embryo of such an affirmation.

An ethic may be regarded as a mode of guidance for meeting ecological situations so new or intricate, or involving such deferred reactions, that the path of social expediency is not discernible to the average individual. Animal instincts are modes of guidance for the individual in meeting such situations. Ethics are possibly a kind of community instinct in-the-making.

THE COMMUNITY CONCEPT

All ethics so far evolved rest upon a single premise: that the individual is a member of a community of interdependent parts. His instincts prompt him to compete for his place in the community, but his ethics prompt him also to co-operate (perhaps in order that there may be a place to compete for).

The land ethic simply enlarges the boundaries of the community to include soils, waters, plants, and animals, or collectively: the land.

This sounds simple: do we not already sing our love for and obligation to the land of the free an the home of the brave? Yes, but just what and whom do we love? Certainly not the soil, which we are sending helter-skelter downriver. Certainly not the waters, which we assume have no function except to turn turbines, float barges, and carry off sewage. Certainly not the plants, of which we exterminate whole com-

munities without batting an eye. Certainly not the animals, of which we have already extirpated many of the largest and most beautiful species. A land ethic of course cannot prevent the alteration, management, and use of these 'resources,' but it does affirm the right to continued existence, and, at least in spots, their continued existence in a natural state.

In short, a land ethic changes the role of *Homo sapiens* from conquerer of the land-community to plain member and citizen of it. It implies respect for his fellow-members, and also respect for the community as such.

In human history, we have learned (I hope) that the conquerer role is eventually self-defeating. Why? Because it is implicit in such a role that the conqueror knows, *ex cathedra*, just what makes the community clock tick, and just what and who is valuable, and what and who is worthless, in community life. It always turns out that he knows neither, and this is why his conquests eventually defeat themselves.

In the biotic community, a parallel situation exists. Abraham knew exactly what the land was for: it was to drop milk and honey into Abraham's mouth. At the present moment, the assurance with which we regard this assumption is inverse to the degree of our education.

The ordinary citizen today assumes that science knows what makes the community clock tick; the scientist is equally sure that he does not. He knows that the biotic mechanism is so complex that its workings may never be fully understood.

* * *

SUBSTITUTES FOR A LAND ETHIC

When the logic of history hungers for bread and we hand out a stone, we are at pains to explain how much the stone resembles bread. I now describe some of the stones which serve in lieu of a land ethic.

One basic weakness in a conservation system based wholly on economic motives is that most members of the land community have no economic value. Wildflowers and songbirds are examples. Of the 22,000 higher plants and animals native to Wisconsin, it is doubtful whether more than 5 per cent can be sold, fed, eaten, or otherwise put to economic use. Yet these creatures are members of the biotic community, and if (as I believe) its stability depends on its integrity, they are entitled to continuance.

When one of these non-economic categories is threatened, and if we happen to love it, we invent subterfuges to give it economic importance. At the beginning of the century songbirds were supposed to be disappearing. Ornithologists jumped to the rescue with some distinctly shaky evidence to the effect that insects would eat us up if birds failed to control them. The evidence had to be economic in order to be valid.

It is painful to read these circumlocutions today. We have no land ethic yet, but we have at least drawn nearer the point of admitting that birds should continue as a matter of biotic right, regardless of the presence or absence of economic advantage to us.

A parallel situation exists in respect of predatory mammals, raptorial birds, and fish-eating birds. Time was when biologists somewhat overworked the evidence that these creatures preserve the health of game by killing weaklings, or that they control rodents for the farmer, or that they prey only on 'worthless' species. Here again, the evidence had to be economic in order to be valid. It is only in recent years that we hear the more honest argument that predators are members of the community, and that no special interest has the right to exterminate them for the sake of a benefit, real or fancied, to itself. Unfortunately this enlightened view is still in the talk stage. In the field the determination of predators goes merrily on: witness the impending erasure of the timber wolf by fiat of Congress, the Conservation Bureaus, and many state legislatures.

Some species of trees have been 'read out of the party' by economics-minded foresters because they grow too slowly, or have too low a sale value to pay as timber crops: white cedar, tamarack, cypress, beech, and hemlock are examples. In Europe, where forestry is ecologically more advanced, the non-commercial tree species are recognized as members of the native forest community, to be preserved as such, within reason. Moreover some (like beech) have been found to have a valuable function in building up soil fertility. The interdependence of the forest and its constituent tree species, ground flora, and fauna is taken for granted.

Lack of economic value is sometimes a character not only of species or groups, but of entire biotic communities: marshes, bogs, dunes, and 'deserts' are examples. Our formula in such cases is to relegate their conservation to government as refuges, monuments, or parks. The difficulty is that these communities are usually interspersed with more valuable private lands; the government cannot possibly own or control such scattered parcels. The net effect is that we have relegated some of them to ultimate extinction over large areas. If the private owner were ecologically minded, he would be proud to be the custodian of a reasonable proportion of such areas, which add diversity and beauty to his farm and to his community.

* * *

To sum up: a system of conservation based solely on economic self-interest is hopelessly lopsided. It tends to ignore, and thus eventually to eliminate, many elements in the land community that lack commercial value, but that are (as far as we know) essential to its healthy functioning. It assumes, falsely, I think, that the economic parts of the biotic clock will function without the uneconomic parts. It tends to relegate to government many functions eventually too large, too complex, or too widely dispersed to be performed by government.

* * *

THE LAND PYRAMID

An ethic to supplement and guide the economic relation to land presupposes the existence of some mental image of land as a biotic mechanism. We can be ethical only in relation in something we can see, feel, understand, love, or otherwise have faith in.

The image commonly employed in conservation education is 'the balance of nature.' For reasons too lengthy to detail here, this figure of speech fails to describe accurately what little we know about the land mechanism. A much truer image is the one employed in ecology: the biotic pyramid.

* * *

Plants absorb energy from the sun. This energy flows through a circuit called the biota, which may be represented by a pyramid consisting of layers. The bottom layer is the soil. A plant layer rests on the soil, an insect layer on the plants, a bird and rodent layer on the insects, and so on up through various animal groups to the apex layer, which consists of the larger carnivores.

The species of a layer are alike not in where they came from, or in what they look like, but rather in what they eat. Each successive layer depends on those below it for food and often for other services, and each in turn furnishes food and services to those above. Proceeding upward, each successive layer decreases in numerical abundance. Thus, for every carnivore there are hundreds of his prey, thousands of their prey, millions of insects, uncountable plants. The pyramidal form of the system reflects this numerical progression from apex to base. Man shares an intermediate layer with the bears, raccoons, and squirrels which eat both meat and vegetables.

The lines of dependency for food and other services are called food chains. Thus soil-oak-deer-Indian is a chain that has now been largely converted to soil-corn-cow-farmer. Each species, including ourselves, is a link in many chains. The deer eats a hundred plants other than oak, and the cow a hundred plants other than corn. Both, then, are links in a hundred chains. The pyramid is a tangle of chains so complex as to seem disorderly, yet the stability of the system proves it to be a highly organized structure. Its functioning depends on the co-operation and competition of its diverse parts.

In the beginning, the pyramid of life was low and squat; the food chains short and simple. Evolution has added layer after layer, link after link. Man is one of thousands of accretions to the height and complexity of the pyramid. Science has given us many doubts, but it has given us at least one certainty: the trend of evolution is to elaborate and diversify the biota.

Land, then, is not merely soil; it is a fountain of energy flowing through a circuit of soils, plants, and animals. Food chains are the living channels which conduct energy upward; death and decay return it to the soil. The circuit is not closed; some energy is dissipated in decay, some is added by absorption from the air, some is stored in soils, peats, and long-lived forests; but it is a sustained circuit, like a slowly augmented revolving fund of life. There is always a net loss by downhill wash, but this is normally small and offset by the decay of rocks. It is deposited in the ocean and, in the course of geological time, raised to form new lands and new pyramids.

The velocity and character of the upward flow of energy depend on the complex structure of the plant and animal community, much as the upward flow of sap in a tree depends on its complex cellular organization. Without this complexity, normal circulation would presumably not occur. Structure means the characteristic numbers, as well as the characteristic kinds and functions, of the component species. This interdependence between the complex structure of the land and its smooth functioning as an energy unit is one of its basic attributes.

When a change occurs in one part of the circuit, many other parts must adjust themselves to it. Change does not necessarily obstruct or divert the flow of energy; evolution is a long series of self-induced changes, the net result of which has been to elaborate the flow mechanism and to length the circuit. Evolutionary changes, however, are usually slow and local. Men's invention of tools has enabled him to make changes of unprecedented violence, rapidity, and scope.

* * *

THE OUTLOOK

It is inconceivable to me that an ethical relation to land can exist without love, respect, and admiration for land, and a high regard for its value. By value, I of course mean something far broader than mere economic value; I mean value in the philosophical sense.

* * *

The 'key-log' which must be moved to release the evolutionary process for an ethic is simply this: quit thinking about decent land-use as solely an economic problem. Examine each question in terms of what is ethically and esthetically right, as well as what is economically expedient. A thing is right when it tends to preserve the integrity, stability, and beauty of the biotic community. It is wrong when it tends otherwise.

It of course goes without saying that economic feasibility limits the tether of what can or cannot be done for land. It always has and it always will. The fallacy the economic determinists have tied around our collective neck, and which we now need to cast off, is the belief that economics determines *all* land-use. This is simply not true. An innumerable host of actions and attitudes, comprising perhaps the bulk of all land relations, is determined by the land-users' tastes and predilections, rather than by his purse. The bulk of all land relations hinges on investments of time, forethought, skill, and faith rather than on investments of cash. As a land-user thinketh, so is he.

I have purposely presented the land ethic as a product of social evolution because nothing so important as an ethic is ever 'written.' Only the most superficial student of history supposes that Moses 'wrote' the Decalogue; it evolved in the minds of a thinking community, and Moses wrote a tentative summary of it for a 'seminar.' I say tentative because evolution never stops.

The evolution of a land ethic is an intellectual as well as emotional process. Conservation is paved with good intentions which prove to be futile, or even dangerous, because they are devoid of critical understanding either of the land, or of economic land-use. I think it is a truism that as the ethical frontier advances from the individual to the community, its intellectual content increases.

The mechanism of operation is the same for any ethic: social approbation for right actions: social disapproval for wrong actions.

By and large, our present problem is one of attitudes and implements. We are remodeling the Alhambra with a steam-shovel, and we are proud of our yardage. We shall hardly relinquish the shovel, which after all has many good points, but we are in need of gentler and more objective criteria for its successful use.

CASES FOR ANALYSIS

1. Tigers and Humans

PALAMAU TIGER RESERVE, India—As many as 100,000 tigers are thought to have roamed India 100 years ago. Based on a 2001 census, officials estimate there are just 3,600 tigers left, but conservation activists believe there are far fewer.

The high profile villains are gangs of poachers that kill cats for their pelts and bones, which are used mostly in traditional Chinese medicine. A single tiger carcass can fetch up to $50,000.

The discovery last year that poachers had wiped out every tiger in Sariska, one of India's premier tiger reserves, caused an outcry and demands for a beefing up of security in the parks.

But the threats to the tiger are as varied and complex as the lands they roam: disappearing natural habitat shared with millions of people, a tiger tourism industry that has alienated villagers, a communist rebellion in a core swath of tiger lands and a conservation effort mired in bureaucracy. . . .

Many tiger sanctuaries have people—often India's poorest—living inside them.

Palamau is a stark illustration. It is home to nearly 200 villages inhabited by 100,000 Adivasis, indigenous tribesmen at the bottom of the complex Indian social ladder.

While India's cities are burgeoning into global technology hubs, these communities bear only faint traces of modernity.

In Betla, goats and donkeys wander in and out of low, windowless mud huts with drooping shingled roofs. Huts have no electricity or running water, and the only contact with the outside world comes from three public telephones in the dusty village center.

Residents of Betla and the other villages eke out an existence through subsistence farming—supplemented by what they gather from the forest.

Some 30 tons of firewood and 60 tons of animal fodder are collected each day in the reserve, says P. K. Gupta, a senior forest officer at Palamau. Chunks of forest have been leveled for grazing, and mines encroach—sometimes legally, sometimes not—onto the sanctuary's mineral-rich land, he adds.

"The human pressure on the park is very high," Gupta says. . . .

Despite evidence of increased tiger numbers in the remote park, the animals are elusive. For most visitors, the closest thing is an old stuffed head of a tiger killed 20 years ago by irate villagers and mounted on the wall of the information center.

But that will be gone soon, Gupta says. "It doesn't give the right conservation message."*

Give reasons for your answers to the following questions: To save the tigers, should native residents be forced to give up their lifestyle, which threatens tiger habitats? Should native peoples be forced to give up elements of their folk or religious healing practices that require tiger pelts and bones? If tigers and people cannot possibly coexist in the same area (so that either of them must be forcibly moved to another habitat), which should be forced to move? Is it morally permissible to kill a few tigers to save the entire species—or do the rights of each individual count more than the species?

*Gavin Rabinowitz, "India Hunts for Ways to Save Its Tigers," *MSNBC.com,* 17 February 2006, www.msnbc. msn.com/id/11347534 (accessed 3 December 2006). Reprinted with permission of The Associated Press.

---

2. Saving the Glaciers

HELENA, Mont.—Glacier National Park in Montana and adjacent Waterton National Park in Canada should be declared endangered, because climate change is eliminating glaciers and harming the park environment, a dozen organizations said in a petition presented Thursday.

The Rocky Mountain parks, together known as Waterton-Glacier International Peace Park, are covered by a 1995 international treaty under which they became a UNESCO World Heritage Site. Now they should become a World Heritage Site in Danger, said the groups, which include the Center for Biological Diversity.

"The effects of climate change are well-documented and clearly visible in Glacier National Park, and yet the United States refuses to fulfill its obligations under the World

Heritage Convention to reduce greenhouse gas emissions," said Erica Thorson, an Oregon law professor who wrote the petition submitted to the World Heritage Committee. . . .

Glacier has 27 glaciers, down from about 150 in 1850, said ecologist Dan Fagre, who coordinates global change research for the U.S. Geological Survey at West Glacier.

Endangered status would require the World Heritage Committee to find ways to mitigate how climate change affects the park, Thorson said. Better fuel efficiency for automobiles and stronger energy efficiency standards for buildings and appliances are among the ways to reduce greenhouse pollution that contributes to warming, the petition says.

The proposed designation is "a ridiculous idea" that cannot be supported by sound science, said S. Fred Singer, a retired University of Virginia environmental sciences professor. Singer disputes that greenhouse gases are warming the environment and that governments can curb glacial erosion by stiffening pollution controls.

Of 20 major world glaciers that began shrinking around 1850, about half had stopped shrinking by the end of the 20th century and some were growing, Singer said.

But in a forecast that some scientists have advanced, Kassie Siegel of the Center for Biological Diversity said the glaciers at Glacier park will vanish entirely by 2030 if current trends in climate change continue.

"The United States and Canada must immediately reduce their greenhouse gas emissions to slow the damage," Siegel said.[†]

Justify your answers: Suppose the glaciers' melting would have no appreciable effect on the environment except that they would no longer exist. Would conservationists still be justified in trying to save the glaciers? If so, how could they justify their efforts? If not, why not? Suppose the glaciers could be saved only if the government spends $10 billion on pollution controls—money that would have to be taken away from social programs. Would this cost be worth it? Why or why not?

[†]"Endangered Status for Glacier National Park?" *MSNBC.com*, 16 February 2006, www.msnbc.msn.com/id/11389665/ (3 December 2006). Reprinted with permission of The Associated Press.

3. Ivory-Billed Woodpecker v. Irrigation

As scientists debate whether the ivory-billed woodpecker, once widely assumed to have been extinct for decades, still haunts the Big Woods of Arkansas, environmentalists have enlisted the bird as a key soldier in their fight against a massive irrigation project.

A lawsuit to be heard Monday in federal court in Little Rock asks that work be halted on the U.S. Army Corps of Engineers' Grand Prairie Area Demonstration Project until further environmental studies evaluate its potential effects on the woodpecker.

The $319 million project, which the corps says will save tapped-out groundwater aquifers in a 242,000-acre agricultural region, is "a recipe for disaster" for the bird, says Lisa Swann of the National Wildlife Federation, a plaintiff in the suit.

Not so, says corps biologist Ed Lambert, who maintains that a "biological assessment" done last spring determined Grand Prairie is unlikely to harm the woodpecker.

The irrigation project has been on the table since the mid-1980s, when studies showed that groundwater aquifers in the area, which lies in east-central Arkansas, were being depleted by rice growers. To solve that, the corps is working with farmers to build reservoirs on their land and elsewhere that will be filled via a canal and pipeline network with water pumped from the White River.

The corps says that in addition to helping replenish groundwater supplies, the project will create new waterfowl and shorebird habitat and food supply, reintroduce thousands of acres of native grasses and slow the depletion of hardwood forests.

But Swann's group and others have long fought the Grand Prairie project as a federal boondoggle that poses serious environmental threats and squanders tax dollars to deliver huge subsidies to farmers. This "mammoth sucking machine" would hurt wetlands, degrade water quality and threaten species in the region from ducks to mussels, the National Wildlife Federation says in one publication about Grand Prairie. . . .

Enter the ivory-billed woodpecker, always rare, but presumed extinct for half a century by most ornithologists. Reported sightings of the 20-inch-long black-and-white birds since the 1940s had drawn derision from many experts since ivory-bills bear a strong resemblance to the smaller and rather common pileated woodpecker.

But the possibility that some ivory-bills were still digging beetles and grubs from the bottomland hardwood forests of Arkansas had long fascinated some birders.

Chief among them was Tim Gallagher, editor of Living Bird magazine, published by the Cornell Lab of Ornithology. Gallagher had become fascinated with the ivory-bill story in the 1970s and began working on a book about them in 2001. His research led him to dozens of people who claimed to have seen an ivory-bill, including Gene Sparling, who said he spotted a red-crested male of the species while one on a kayak outing in an eastern Arkansas bayou.

In February 2004, Gallagher and another birder joined Sparling on an expedition to the swamp and saw an ivory-bill for himself. The ensuing hoopla was unprecedented in ornithological circles. Additional expeditions and sightings followed. They culminated in an April 28, 2005, article in the journal Science by Cornell researchers and an official announcement by U.S. Interior Secretary Gail Norton on the same day that the ivory-bill was not extinct.‡

Assume that the woodpecker does exist and that the water project would wipe it out. Should the project proceed or be cancelled? Why? How might a species egalitarian (biocentrist) answer this? A species nonegalitarian? An ecological holist?

‡ Mike Stuckey, "New Star of the Bird World Stars in Lawsuit, Too," *MSNBC.com*, 25 January 2006, www.msnbc.msn.com/id/10929337/ (accessed 3 December 2006). Reprinted with permission.

CHAPTER 15

Animal Rights

One of philosophy's most important functions is to help us critically examine beliefs that we often simply assume without question. Philosophy seems to have played this role especially well in the issue of animal rights, for it was a philosopher who helped engender the current animal rights movement by arguing that something was very wrong with the traditional attitude toward animals (that is, nonhuman animals) and their treatment. The traditional notion is that an animal is merely a resource that humans may dispose of as they see fit: an animal is food, fuel, or fun—something with instrumental value only. Peter Singer was the philosopher who challenged the received wisdom, declaring in his 1975 book *Animal Liberation* that its subject was the "tyranny of human over non-human animals. This tyranny has caused and today is still causing an amount of pain and suffering that can only be compared with that which resulted from the centuries of tyranny by white humans over black humans."[1]

The traditional attitude toward animals has been influential in the West for centuries. It sprang from several sources, including Judeo-Christian thought and the arguments of several distinguished philosophers. The book of *Genesis* declares that God created humans in his own image, "saying to them, 'Be fruitful, multiply, fill the earth and conquer it. Be masters of the fish of the sea, the birds of heaven and all living animals on the earth' " (Genesis 1.28). Aristotle claims that all of nature exists "specifically for the sake of man," that animals are merely instruments for humankind. Thomas Aquinas is remarkably explicit about humans' proper attitude toward animals:

Hereby is refuted the error of those who said it is sinful for a man to kill dumb animals: for by divine providence they are intended for man's use in the natural order. Hence it is no wrong for man to make use of them, either by killing them or in any other way whatever.[2]

Aquinas also says that we should avoid being cruel to animals—but only because cruelty to animals might lead to cruelty to humans. Animal cruelty in itself, he explains, is no wrong. Likewise, René Descartes thinks animals are ours to use any way we want. After all, he asserts, animals are not sentient—they are machines, like mechanical clocks, devoid of feelings and incapable of experiencing pleasure or pain. Immanuel Kant, who thinks that people are not means to an end but ends in themselves, contends that animals are means to the end known as man. Today few would agree with Descartes that animals cannot experience pain, but the traditional idea that animals have no (or low) moral standing is widespread.

Those who reject the traditional attitude remind us that beliefs about the moral status of ani-

[1]Peter Singer, *Animal Liberation*, 2nd ed. (New York: New York Review of Books, 1990), i.

[2]Thomas Aquinas, *Summa Theologica,* from *Basic Writings of Saint Thomas Aquinas,* ed. and annotated Anton C. Pegis (New York: Random House, 1945), Second Part of the Second Part, Question 64, Article 1.

mals influence how animals are treated in the real world—and that treatment, they say, is horrendous on a vast scale. In 2005 in the United Stated alone, more than 10 billion animals were slaughtered for food, including almost 140 million cows, calves, pigs, sheep, and lambs.[3] Critics have charged that the animals are subjected to appalling suffering, including lifelong confinement in spaces so small the animals can hardly move, isolation of veal calves in small crates (and, some say, in almost total darkness), routine mutilation or surgery such as branding and cutting off pigs' tails and chicken's beaks, and the slaughter of chickens and livestock without first stunning them or using any other methods to minimize pain and suffering.[4]

In addition, each year millions of animals—from mice to dogs to primates—are used in laboratory experiments all over the world. Some of this research—no one knows how much—causes significant animal suffering. According to a U.S. government report, in 2004 about 8 percent of larger animals used in experiments (excluding mice and rats) endured "pain or distress" that could not be relieved with medication.

These concerns push us toward the key moral questions that we try to sort out in this chapter: Do animals have instrumental value only? Do they have rights? Do we owe them any moral respect or concern at all? Is it morally permissible to experiment on animals, to raise and kill them for food, to cause them unnecessary pain and suffering? Do animals have the same moral worth as an infant, a mentally incompetent man, a woman with severe senile dementia, or a man in a persistent vegetative state?

ISSUE FILE: BACKGROUND

Fortunately, on these issues there is at least a parcel of common ground. First, almost no one believes, as Descartes did, that animals are equivalent to windup clocks, mechanisms without feelings. Science and common sense suggest that many animals (mostly vertebrates) are *sentient*— that is, they can have experiences. They can experience bodily sensations such as pain and pleasure as well as emotions such as fear and frustration. Sentient beings are thought to have the capacity to suffer. Second, virtually everyone thinks that being cruel to animals—unnecessarily causing them pain or misery—is wrong. Even when we consider this judgment carefully and critically, it seems inescapable. Third, there is general agreement, among philosophers at least, that sentient animals are worthy of some degree of moral respect or concern. Most disputes turn on interpretations of this last point: Exactly how much moral concern do we owe animals? Do they deserve the same level of moral consideration that we give to humans? Do they deserve less? How should we treat them?

Such questions are essentially about the moral status, or moral considerability, of animals. As noted in the previous chapter, something has moral status if it is a suitable candidate for moral concern or respect in its own right, regardless of its relationships to humans. Ethically, we cannot treat a being that has moral status just any way we want, as if it were a mere thing. Whatever we do to such a being, we must take its moral status into account. Another way of expressing the notion of moral status is to say that any being with

[3]U.S. Department of Agriculture, National Agricultural Statistical Services, *Livestock Slaughter: 2005 Summary*, March 2006; USDA, NASS, *Poultry Slaughter: 2005 Summary*, February 2006.

[4]Geoffrey Becker, "Humane Treatment of Farm Animals: Overview and Issues," Congressional Research Service Report RS21978, 18 November 2005 (updated 14 August 2006), www.nationalaglawcenter.org/assets/crs/RS21978.pdf (3 December 2006); People for the Ethical Treatment of Animals, "Petition for Agency Action to Fully Comply with the Mandates of the Humane Methods of Livestock Slaughter Act," 11 December 2001, www.peta.org/feat/usda/petition.html (3 December 2006).

moral status is an object of **direct moral consideration** or concern. That is, such a being is worthy of moral concern for its own sake, not because of its relationship to others. A being that is the object of **indirect moral consideration** is granted respect or concern because of its relationship to other individuals. Human beings are objects of direct moral consideration; some say that animals such as dogs, pigs, and rabbits are too. A screwdriver is not the kind of thing that can be the object of direct moral concern, but it may be of indirect moral concern because of its value to a human being. Some people insist that all nonhuman animals are of indirect moral concern, deriving whatever value they have from their usefulness to humans. Many others reject this view, asserting that sentient animals have independent moral status.

Moral status is typically understood to be something that comes in degrees and that can be overridden or discounted in some circumstances. Philosophers speak of varying levels or weights of moral considerability. Some contend that animals have the same moral status as normal adult humans—that, for example, the interests of animals are as morally important as the comparable interests of humans. Some argue that humans deserve more moral respect or concern than animals, that the interests of humans always take precedence over those of animals. Many maintain that moral considerability varies depending on the species (human or nonhuman), with humans enjoying the greatest degree of moral considerability and other species being assigned lower degrees on a sliding scale. But philosophers disagree on the basis for assigning the different rankings. Whatever a being's moral status, it is usually not viewed as absolute; sometimes it may be overridden or canceled by factors thought to be more important. Some people think, for example, that a dog's moral status prohibits humans from beating it just for fun but may allow beatings under some circumstances—

say, to prevent it from straying into traffic and causing an accident.

Frequently people use the term **animal rights** as a synonym for *moral status*. When they say that animals have rights, they mean only that animals deserve some degree of direct moral considerability. But often the term is used in a more restricted way to refer to a particularly strong type of moral status. In this stronger sense, for an animal to have rights is for it to be entitled to a kind of moral respect that cannot be overridden (or cannot be overridden easily) by other considerations. Those who accept this notion of animal rights may argue that animals should *never* be condemned to factory farms or used in medical experimentation, even if such treatment would make millions of humans happy. Such rights are analogous to rights that people are supposed to have. People are thought to have a right, for instance, not to be unjustly imprisoned—even if their imprisonment would increase the overall happiness of society as a whole. (We take a closer look at strong animal rights in the next section.)

Before examining arguments that animals have moral status or rights, we should cite a few arguments to the contrary. Some people claim that only human beings have moral status and that animals, if they matter at all, have only indirect value as resources or tools for people. If cruelty to animals is wrong, it is wrong only because it makes humans callous or upsets people or damages personal property. The usual tack of those who reject moral status for animals is to argue that only beings that possess a particular property have moral status—a property that animals do not possess while humans do. The proposed status-granting properties are numerous and include having a soul, nurturing strong family bonds, using language, being a member of the human species, and being a person or a moral agent.

The notion that animals lack souls and therefore have no moral status is, of course, a traditional religious view defended on traditional

CRITICAL THOUGHT: Should We Abolish Dog Racing?

Consider this verbal snapshot of the greyhound-racing issue:

> Many greyhounds live in miserable conditions, and many of them are put to death after their racing careers are over. For those who object to animal suffering, the preferred step would be to ensure that greyhounds are allowed decent lives—and to hope that the racing industry is compatible with the goal. But if it is simply impractical for law to ensure that greyhounds live minimally decent lives, some people would argue that greyhound racing should be abolished.*

What position would you take on the moral permissibility of this practice? What argument would you make to support your position? (After reading this chapter, return to this box and reconsider your judgment.)

*Cass R. Sunstein, "Introduction: What Are Animal Rights?" in *Animal Rights: Current Debates and New Directions,* ed. Sunstein and Martha C. Nussbaum (Oxford: Oxford University Press, 2004), 9.

---

religious grounds. Generally philosophers do not take this path, because their focus is on reason and arguments rather than on faith and because philosophical analysis has rendered the concept of a soul problematic or controversial.

The claim that animals have no moral standing because they do not have the kind of strong family relationships exhibited by humans has been undermined not by philosophy but by science. The same goes for the parallel claim regarding animals' language skills. One philosopher sums up the relevant empirical findings:

[M]any species of non-humans develop long-lasting kinship ties—orangutan mothers stay with their young for eight to ten years and while they eventually part company, they continue to maintain their relationships. Less solitary animals, such as chimpanzees, baboons, wolves, and elephants maintain extended family units built upon complex individual relationships, for long periods of time. Meerkats in the Kalahari desert are known to sacrifice their own safety by staying with sick or injured family members so that the fatally ill will not die alone. . . . While the lives of many, perhaps most, non-humans in the wild are consumed with struggle for survival, aggression and battle, there are some non-humans whose

lives are characterized by expressions of joy, playfulness, and a great deal of sex. Recent studies in cognitive ethology have suggested that some nonhumans engage in manipulative and deceptive activity, can construct "cognitive maps" for navigation, and some non-humans appear to understand symbolic representation and are able to use language.[5]

A more common claim is that just *being human*—having the DNA of the human species, in other words—is the property that gives a being moral considerability. If so, then nonhumans do not and cannot have moral status. This view has seemed initially plausible to some, but critics have wondered why simply having human DNA would bestow moral status on a creature.

Perhaps the most telling objection against the human species argument is based on a simple thought experiment. Suppose we humans encounter extraterrestrial creatures who have all the same attributes and capabilities that we have—self-consciousness, intelligence, language skills,

[5]Lori Gruen, "The Moral Status of Animals," *The Stanford Encyclopedia of Philosophy* (Fall 2003 ed.), ed. Edward N. Zalta, http://plato.stanford.edu/archives/fall2003/entries/moral-animal/ (3 December 2006).

reasoning ability, emotions, and more. We would presumably have to admit that these beings have full moral status, just as we do. Yet they are not human. They may not even be carbon-based life forms. Physically they may be nothing like any member of the human species. This strange (but possible) state of affairs suggests that being human is not a necessary condition for having moral status.

Taking a cue from Kant, some philosophers contend that only persons or moral agents can be candidates for moral considerability—and animals do not make the cut. Persons are typically regarded as rational beings who are free to choose their own ends and determine their own actions and values. Moral agents are beings who can make moral judgments and act according to moral reasons or principles. So the basic claim is that since all or most animals are not persons or moral agents, they can have no moral standing. They simply lack the necessary property.

As many critics have pointed out, using personhood and moral agency as criteria for determining moral status has a troublesome drawback: it excludes not only animals from moral considerability but some humans as well. This difficulty is common to all lack-of-some-necessary-property arguments, which we will examine more closely in the next section.

In any case, many think that all these standards for moral status are in a sense beside the point. To them it is obvious that regardless of whether an animal possesses these "higher" capacities and characteristics, it can suffer. They reason that if it can suffer, then it can be wronged by deliberately causing it to suffer. If deliberately hurting it is wrong, it must have some level of moral considerability.

MORAL THEORIES

How might a utilitarian assess the treatment of nonhuman animals? What would he or she say about their moral status? The most famous answers to these questions come from the utilitarian philosopher Peter Singer, credited with kindling through his writings what is popularly known as the animal rights movement. His most celebrated book, *Animal Liberation,* helped spark serious debates about the treatment of animals, the meat industry, and vegetarianism—debates that continue to this day. Classic utilitarianism says that the right action is the one that produces the best balance of happiness over unhappiness (or pain over pleasure), *everyone considered.* Singer's approach is to include *both* animals and humans in this "everyone." The pain and pleasure of *all* sentient beings must be considered when we are deciding which action maximizes the good.

This inclusion of *all* animals (human and nonhuman) in utilitarian calculations is not new, however—it was, in fact, advocated by utilitarianism's founder, Jeremy Bentham (1748–1832):

The day *may* come when the rest of the animal creation may acquire those rights which never could have been withholden from them but by the hand of tyranny. The French have already discovered that the blackness of the skin is no reason why a human being should be abandoned without redress to the caprice of a tormentor. It may one day come to be recognized that the number of the legs, the villosity of the skin, or the termination of the *os sacrum,* are reasons equally insufficient for abandoning a sensitive being to the same fate. What else is it that should trace the insuperable line? Is it the faculty of reason, or perhaps the faculty of discourse? But a full grown horse or dog is beyond comparison a more rational, as well as a more conversable animal, than an infant of a day, or a week, or even a month, old. But suppose they were otherwise, what would it avail? The question is not, Can they reason? nor Can they *talk?* but, Can they suffer?[6]

[6]Jeremy Bentham, *An Introduction to Principles of Morals and Legislation* (1789; reprint, New York: Hafner, 1948), 311.

For both Bentham and Singer, what makes a being worthy of moral concern, what requires us to include it in the moral community, is its ability to experience pain and pleasure—its ability to suffer. Why do humans have moral status? Not, says the utilitarian, because of their capacity for reason, social relationships, and personhood—but because of their capacity for suffering. Likewise, because sentient animals can suffer, they too have moral status. Furthermore, Bentham and Singer argue that because both humans and animals can suffer, they both deserve *equal moral consideration*. As Singer says,

[T]he interests of every being affected by an action are to be taken into account and given the same weight as the like interests of any other being. . . . If a being suffers, there can be no moral justification for refusing to take that suffering into consideration. No matter what the nature of the being, the principle of equality requires that its suffering be counted equally with the like suffering—in so far as rough comparisons can be made—of any other being. If a being is not capable of suffering, or of experiencing enjoyment or happiness, there is nothing to be taken into account.[7]

According to Singer, those who do not give equal moral consideration to both human and nonhuman animals are guilty of **speciesism**—discrimination against nonhuman animals just because of their species. Speciesism, he says, is wrong for the same reason that racism and sexism are wrong: it violates the principle of equal consideration—that is, equal consideration of comparable interests.

Equal consideration of comparable interests, however, does not mean equal treatment. Humans and animals have some interests in common (such as avoiding pain), and they differ dramatically in the possession of other interests (humans are capable of enjoying art and studying philosophy, but animals are not). Singer's utilitarianism demands that when comparable interests are involved, those of humans and those of animals must be given equal weight. A pig's suffering is just as important as a man's or a woman's. If a pig and a man were both experiencing intense pain, we must not assume that the man's pain should be taken more seriously. We should regard the agony of both beings with equal concern. But when interests are not comparable, we need not pretend that they are. We may, for example, give weight to a woman's interest in enjoying a good book, but we would give no weight to this interest in a dog, because a dog has no such interest.

What are the implications of Singer's view for the treatment of animals? For one thing, it implies that our system of meat production is wrong and should be abolished. There is general agreement that currently the meat industry causes immense suffering to millions of sentient creatures. In standard utilitarian calculations if we weigh this extreme suffering against the moderate pleasures it produces (the gustatory enjoyment of humans), we see that the meat industry generates a net balance of evil over good. The alternative to having a meat industry—vegetarianism—would result in far more good than evil. As Singer puts it,

Since, as I have said, none of these [meat industry] practices cater for anything more than our pleasures of taste, our practice of rearing and killing other animals in order to eat them is a clear instance of the sacrifice of the most important interests of other beings in order to satisfy trivial interests of our own. To avoid speciesism we must stop this practice, and each of us has a moral obligation to cease supporting this practice.[8]

Some see a problem in Singer's stance, however, because his call for eliminating meat pro-

[7]Peter Singer, "All Animals Are Equal," *Philosophical Exchange* 1 (1974): 106, 107–8.

[8]Singer, "All Animals Are Equal," 109.

CRITICAL THOUGHT: Should We Experiment on Orphaned Babies?

Consider this controversial argument against speciesism by Peter Singer:

> In the past, argument about vivisection has often missed the point, because it has been put in absolutist terms: Would the abolitionist be prepared to let thousands die if they could be saved by experimenting on a single animal? The way to reply to this purely hypothetical question is to pose another: would the experimenter be prepared to perform his experiment on an orphaned human infant, if that were the only way to save many lives? (I say "orphan" to avoid the complication of parental feelings, although in doing so I am being overfair to the experimenter, since the nonhuman subjects of experiments are not orphans.) If the experimenter is not prepared to use an orphaned human infant, then his readiness to use nonhumans is simple discrimination, since adult apes, cats, mice, and other mammals are more aware of what is happening to them, more self-directing and, so far as we can tell, at least as sensitive to pain, as any human infant.*

What is Singer's point here? Is he advocating the practice of experimenting on orphaned human infants? Suppose you disagree with Singer. What argument would you make against his position?

*Peter Singer, "All Animals Are Equal," *Philosophical Exchange* 1 (1974): 110.

---

duction and embracing vegetarianism does not seem to be fully warranted by his arguments. By Singer's own lights, a humane form of meat production may be morally permissible. If animals could be raised and killed without suffering—if their lives could be pleasant and their deaths painless—then there might be a net balance of good over evil in the process. Then both meat production and meat eating might be acceptable. It seems that Singer's arguments could be used to support reform of the meat production industry just as easily as its total elimination.

As for scientific experimentation on animals, Singer thinks that it might be permissible if the benefits gained from the research outweigh any suffering involved. "[I]f a single experiment could cure a major disease, that experiment would be justifiable," he says.[9] However, he believes that in practice, animal experimentation usually results in more evil than good because often the benefits to humans are negligible.

[9]Singer, *Animal Liberation,* 77–78.

How would a nonconsequentialist view the treatment of animals? Probably the most influential example of the nonconsequentialist approach is that of Tom Regan, another philosopher who has helped define and inspire the animal rights movement. He argues for *animal rights* proper—that is, animal rights in the restricted sense of having moral considerability that cannot be easily overridden, not in the weaker, generic sense of simply possessing moral status. According to Regan,

The genius and the retarded child, the prince and the pauper, the brain surgeon and the fruit vendor, Mother Theresa and the most unscrupulous used car salesman—all have inherent value, all possess it *equally*, and *all have an equal right to be treated with respect,* to be treated in ways that do not reduce them to the status of things, as if they exist as resources for others.[10]

[10]Tom Regan, "The Case for Animal Rights," in *In Defense of Animals,* ed. Peter Singer (Oxford: Blackwell, 1985), 21.

QUICK REVIEW

direct moral consideration—Moral consideration for a being's own sake, rather than because of its relationship to others.

indirect moral consideration—Moral consideration on account of a being's relationship to others.

animal rights—Possession by animals of (1) moral status; (2) strong moral consideration that cannot be easily overridden.

speciesism—Discrimination against nonhuman animals just because of their species.

Regan maintains that such equal inherent value and equal rights apply to animals just as much as they do to humans. More specifically, he says, they apply to all mature mammals, human and nonhuman. Creatures with inherent value must be treated, in Kant's famous phrase, as ends in themselves, not merely as means to an end. Their value or their treatment does not depend on some utilitarian calculation of pain and pleasure. According to Regan, humans and animals have equal value and equal rights because they share particular mental capacities; they are sensitive, experiencing beings—or as Regan says, "experiencing subjects of a life":

[W]e are each of us the experiencing subject of a life, a conscious creature having an individual welfare that has importance to us whatever our usefulness to others. We want and prefer things, believe and feel things, recall and expect things. And all these dimensions of our life, including our pleasure and pain, our enjoyment and suffering, our satisfaction and frustration, our continued existence or our untimely death—all make a difference to the quality of our life as lived, as experienced, by us as individuals. As the same is true of those animals who concern us (those

who are eaten and trapped, for example), they too must be viewed as the experiencing subjects of a life, with inherent value of their own.[11]

How should we treat animals, then, if they have such rights and if these rights are equal to our own? Regan's theory (what he calls the rights view) implies that if it would be wrong to dissect, hurt, torture, eat, cage, hunt, or trap a human, then it would also be wrong to do the same to an animal—and the amount of good that might be produced by such acts is irrelevant. Therefore, Regan concludes, all forms of animal experimentation should be abolished. "Because these animals are treated routinely, systematically as if their value were reducible to their usefulness to others," Regan says, "they are routinely, systematically treated with a lack of respect, and thus are their rights routinely, systematically violated."[12] On the same grounds, he thinks that commercial animal agriculture and commercial and sport hunting and trapping should also be abolished.

MORAL ARGUMENTS

Do animals really have equal rights in the strict sense just mentioned? That is, do nonhuman animals have the same right to respect and moral concern that humans have? Using Tom Regan's rights view as inspiration without sticking strictly to his line of reasoning, let us examine some simple (and simplified) arguments for and against this proposition.

For our purposes, we can state the argument for the rights view like this:

1. Nonhuman animals (normal, fully developed mammals) are experiencing subjects of a life (or "experiencing subjects," for short), just as humans are.

---

[11]Regan, "The Case for Animal Rights," 22.
[12]Regan, "The Case for Animal Rights," 24.

2. All experiencing subjects have equal inherent value.

3. All those with equal inherent value are entitled to equal moral rights (the equal right to be treated with respect).

4. Therefore, nonhuman animals have equal moral rights.

This is a valid argument; the conclusion does follow from the three premises. So we have good reason to accept the conclusion if the premises are true. Are they? Premise 1 is an empirical claim about the mental capacities of animals (again, normal, fully developed mammals). There is scientific evidence suggesting that animals do have at least most of the capacities in question. For simplicity's sake, then, let us assume that Premise 1 is true.

Premises 2 and 3 are much more difficult to sort out. We should not accept them unless there are good reasons for doing so. Good reasons would involve separate arguments that support each of them. Regan has provided such arguments, and several critics have responded to them. Some have said, for example, that the notion of inherent value is obscure and that the link between inherent value and moral rights is unclear. Many others have sidestepped these issues and attacked the conclusion directly, arguing that regardless of whether animals have some moral rights, they surely do not have the *same* moral rights that humans do—that is, the equal right to be treated with respect.

Those who take this latter approach begin with an advantage. Our moral common sense suggests that there must be some sort of difference between the moral status of most humans and that of most animals. We tend to think that accidentally running over a man with our car is morally worse than doing the same to a rabbit. Most of us believe that there is an important moral difference between imprisoning women in cages for later slaughter and doing the same to chickens or hogs—even if we also deem the latter cruel and immoral.

Our intuition about such things can be wrong, of course. So those who reject equal moral rights for animals have offered other considerations. The philosopher Mary Anne Warren, for example, argues that animals do indeed have some moral rights but that there are reasons for thinking that these rights are weaker or less demanding than the rights of humans. For one thing, she notes, the human right to freedom is stronger or more extensive than the animal right to freedom. This right prohibits the unlawful imprisonment of humans, even if the prison is comfortable and spacious. Human dignity and the satisfaction of human aspirations and desires demand a higher degree of freedom of movement than would be required for the satisfaction of the needs or interests of many nonhuman animals. Imprisonment of animals in areas that allow them to satisfy their needs and pursue their natural inclinations, Warren says, "need not frustrate the needs or interests of animals in any significant way, and thus do not clearly violate their rights." In a similar vein, Warren argues that both humans and animals have a prima facie right to life, but this right is generally weaker for animals than for humans. As she puts it, "Human lives, one might say, have greater intrinsic value, because they are worth more *to their possessors*."[13] Humans have hopes, plans, and purposes that make them value continued existence; animals, apparently, lack this forward-looking perspective. Warren adds that nonhuman animals nevertheless have a right to life because, among other things, their premature demise robs them of any future pleasures they might have had.

Regan has responded to such arguments for unequal rights for animals by offering a common counterargument. In general, the arguments contend that animals have less inherent value (and

[13]Mary Anne Warren, "The Rights of the Nonhuman World," in *Environmental Philosophy: A Collection of Readings,* ed. Robert Elliot and Arran Gare (University Park: Pennsylvania State University Press, 1983), 116.

therefore weaker moral rights) because animals lack something that adult humans have—perhaps the ability to reason, intelligence, autonomy, intellect, or some other valuable property. But, Regan says, if this contention is true, then we must say that some humans who lack these characteristics (retarded children or people with serious mental illness, for example) also have less inherent value than normal adult humans and therefore less robust moral rights. In other words, if these critics of equal rights are correct, we are fully justified in treating these "deficient humans" as we would nonhuman animals. "But it is not true," he says, "that such humans . . . have less inherent value than you or I. Neither, then, can we rationally sustain the view that animals like them in being experiencing subjects of a life have less inherent value. *All* who have inherent value have it *equally,* whether they be human animals or not."[14]

SUMMARY

The traditional attitude toward animals is that they are merely resources that humans can dispose of as they see fit; animals have instrumental value only. Buy many reject the traditional view and put forward reasons for supposing that animals have moral status. Something has moral status if it is a suitable candidate for moral concern or respect in its own right.

Some people claim that only humans have moral status and that animals have just indirect value to humans. The usual approach of those who reject moral status for animals is to argue that a being is entitled to moral status only if it possesses particular properties—and that animals do not possess them. These status-granting properties include having a soul, having strong family bonds, using language, being a member of the human species, and being a person or a moral agent.

One of the more common claims is that one must be human to have moral status. Critics, however, have asked what it is about being human that gives one moral status. A thought experiment used against this claim asks us to imagine meeting extraterrestrial creatures who are self-conscious, intelligent, rational, and like ourselves in many other ways. We would presumably have to admit that the aliens have moral status just as we do, even though they are not human. Being human, then, seems not to be necessary for having moral status.

The most famous utilitarian approach to the treatment of animals is that of the philosopher Peter Singer. He argues that the pain and pleasure of animals as well as that of humans must be included in utilitarian calculations. What makes a being worthy of moral concern, he says, is its capacity for suffering, and since both humans and animals can suffer, they both deserve equal moral consideration. Consequently, Singer maintains that our system of meat production is wrong and should be abolished.

The most notable nonconsequentialist approach to the treatment of animals is that of Tom Regan. He argues for strong animal rights on the grounds that all "experiencing subjects of a life" have equal inherent value and therefore an equal right to be treated with respect. Experiencing subjects of a life include healthy, mature mammals (humans and nonhumans). Regan maintains that because such animals have equal rights, all commercial animal agriculture and sport hunting and trapping should be abolished.

[14]Regan, "The Case for Animal Rights," 23.

READINGS

All Animals Are Equal

PETER SINGER

In recent years a number of oppressed groups have campaigned vigorously for equality. The classic instance is the Black Liberation movement, which demands an end to the prejudice and discrimination that has made blacks second-class citizens. The immediate appeal of the black liberation movement and its initial, if limited success made it a model for other oppressed groups to follow. We became familiar with liberation movements for Spanish-Americans, gay people, and a variety of other minorities. When a majority group—women—began their campaign, some thought we had come to the end of the road. Discrimination on the basis of sex, it has been said, is the last universally accepted form of discrimination, practiced without secrecy or pretense even in those liberal circles that have long prided themselves on their freedom from prejudice against racial minorities.

One should always be wary of talking of "the last remaining form of discrimination." If we have learnt anything from the liberation movements, we should have learnt how difficult it is to be aware of latent prejudice in our attitudes to particular groups until this prejudice is forcefully pointed out.

A liberation movement demands an expansion of our moral horizons and an extension or reinterpretation of the basic moral principle of equality. Practices that were previously regarded as natural and inevitable come to be seen as the result of an unjustifiable prejudice. Who can say with confidence that all his or her attitudes and practices are beyond criticism? If we wish to avoid being numbered amongst the oppressors, we must be prepared to re-think even our most fundamental attitudes. We need to consider them from the point of view of those most disad-

Peter Singer, "All Animals Are Equal," *Philosophical Exchange* 1 (1974): 103–16 (edited). Copyright © Peter Singer, 1974, reprinted by permission of the author.

vantaged by our attitudes, and the practices that follow from these attitudes. If we can make this unaccustomed mental switch we may discover a pattern in our attitudes and practices that consistently operates so as to benefit one group—usually the one to which we ourselves belong—at the expense of another. In this way we may come to see that there is a case for a new liberation movement. My aim is to advocate that we make this mental switch in respect of our attitudes and practices towards a very large group of beings: members of species other than our own—or, as we popularly though misleadingly call them, animals. In other words, I am urging that we extend to other species the basic principle of equality that most of us recognise should be extended to all members of our own species.

All this may sound a little far-fetched, more like a parody of other liberation movements than a serious objective. In fact, in the past the idea of "The Rights of Animals" really has been used to parody the case for women's rights. When Mary Wollstonecroft, a forerunner of later feminists, published her *Vindication of the Rights of Women* in 1792, her ideas were widely regarded as absurd, and they were satirized in an anonymous publication entitled *A Vindication of the Rights of Brutes*. The author of this satire (actually Thomas Taylor, a distinguished Cambridge philosopher) tried to refute Wollstonecraft's reasonings by showing that they could be carried one stage further. If sound when applied to women, why should the arguments not be applied to dogs, cats and horses? They seemed to hold equally well for these "brutes": yet to hold that brutes had rights was manifestly absurd; therefore the reasoning by which this conclusion had been reached must be unsound, and if unsound when applied to brutes, it must also be unsound when applied to women, since the very same arguments had been used in each case.

One way in which we might reply to this argument is by saying that the case for equality between men and women cannot validly be extended to non-human animals. Women have a right to vote, for instance, because they are just as capable of making rational decisions as men are; dogs, on the other hand, are incapable of understanding the significance of voting, so they cannot have the right to vote. There are many other obvious ways in which men and women resemble each other closely, while humans and other animals differ greatly. So, it might be said, men and women are similar beings, and should have equal rights, while humans and non-humans are different and should not have equal rights.

The thought behind this reply to Taylor's analogy is correct up to a point, but it does not go far enough. There *are* important differences between humans and other animals, and these differences must give rise to *some* differences in the rights that each have. Recognizing this obvious fact, however, is no barrier to the case for extending the basic principle of equality to non-human animals. The differences that exist between men and women are equally undeniable, and the supporters of Women's Liberation are aware that these differences may give rise to different rights. Many feminists hold that women have the right to an abortion on request. It does not follow that since these same people are campaigning for equality between men and women they must support the right of men to have abortions too. Since a man cannot have an abortion, it is meaningless to talk of his right to have one. Since a pig can't vote, it is meaningless to talk of its right to vote. There is no reason why either Women's Liberation or Animal Liberation should get involved in such nonsense. The extension of the basic principle of equality from one group to another does not imply that we must treat both groups in exactly the same way, or grant exactly the same rights to both groups. Whether we should do so will depend on the nature of the members of the two groups. The basic principle of equality, I shall argue, is equality of consideration; and equal consideration for different beings may lead to different treatment and different rights.

So there is a different way of replying to Taylor's attempt to parody Wollstonecraft's arguments, a way which does not deny the differences between humans and non-humans, but goes more deeply into the question of equality, and concludes by finding nothing absurd in the idea that the basic principle of equality applies to so-called "brutes." I believe that we reach this conclusion if we examine the basis on which our opposition to discrimination on grounds of race or sex ultimately rests. We will then see that we would be on shaky ground if we were to demand equality for blacks, women, and other groups of oppressed humans while denying equal consideration to non-humans.

When we say that all human beings, whatever their race, creed or sex, are equal, what is it that we are asserting? Those who wish to defend a hierarchical, inegalitarian society have often pointed out that by whatever test we choose, it simply is not true that all humans are equal. Like it or not, we must face the fact that humans comes in different shapes and sizes; they come with differing moral capacities, differing intellectual abilities, differing amounts of benevolent feeling and sensitivity to the needs of others, differing abilities to communicate effectively, and differing capacities to experience pleasure and pain. In short, if the demand for equality were based on the actual equality of all human beings, we would have to stop demanding equality. It would be an unjustifiable demand.

Still, one might cling to the view that the demand for equality among human beings is based on the actual equality of the different races and sexes. Although humans differ as individuals in various ways, there are no differences between the races and sexes *as such*. From the mere fact that a person is black, or a woman, we cannot infer anything else about that person. This, it may be said, is what is wrong with racism and sexism. The white racist claims that whites are superior to blacks, but this is false—although there are differences between individuals, some blacks are superior to some whites in all of the capacities and abilities that could conceivably be relevant. The opponent of sexism would say the same: a person's sex is no guide to his or her abilities, and this is why it is unjustifiable to discriminate on the basis of sex.

This is a possible line of objection to racial and sexual discrimination. It is not, however, the way that someone really concerned about equality would choose, because taking this line could, in some circumstances, force one to accept a most inegalitarian society. The fact that humans differ as individuals, rather than as races or sexes, is a valid reply to someone who defends a hierarchical society like, say, South Africa, in which all whites are superior in status to all blacks. The existence of individual variations that cut across the lines of race or sex, however, provides us with no defence at all against a more sophisticated opponent of equality, one who proposes that, say, the interests of those with ratings above 100. Would a hierarchical society of this sort really be so much better than one based on race or sex? I think not. But if we tie the moral principle of equality to the factual equality of the different races or sexes, taken as a whole, our opposition to racism and sexism does not provide us with any basis for objecting to this kind of inegalitarianism.

There is a second important reason why we ought not to base our opposition to racism and sexism on any kind of factual equality, even the limited kind asserts that variations in capacities and abilities are spread evenly between the different races and sexes: we can have no absolute guarantee that these abilities and capacities really are distributed evenly, without regard to race or sex, among human beings. So far as actual abilities are concerned, there do seem to be certain measurable differences between both races and sexes. These differences do not, of course, appear in each case, but only when averages are taken. More important still, we do not yet know how much of these differences is really due to the different genetic endowments of the various races and sexes, and how much is due to environmental differences that are the result of past and continuing discrimination. Perhaps all of the important differences will eventually prove to be environmental rather than genetic. Anyone opposed to racism and sexism will certainly hope that this will be so, for it will make the task of ending discrimination a lot easier; nevertheless it would

be dangerous to rest the case against racism and sexism on the belief that all significant differences are environmental in origin. The opponent of, say, racism who takes this line will be unable to avoid conceding that if differences in ability did after all prove to have some genetic connection with race, racism would in some way be defensible.

It would be folly for the opponent of racism to stake his whole case on a dogmatic commitment to one particular outcome of a difficult scientific issue which is still a long way from being settled. While attempts to prove that differences in certain selected abilities between races and sexes are primarily genetic in origin have certainly not been conclusive, the same must be said of attempts to prove that these differences are largely the result of environment. At this stage of the investigation we cannot be certain which view is correct, however much we may hope it is the latter.

Fortunately, there is no need to pin the case for equality to one particular outcome of this scientific investigation. The appropriate response to those who claim to have found evidence of genetically-based differences in ability between the races or sexes is not to stick to the belief that the genetic explanation must be wrong, whatever evidence to the contrary may turn up: instead we should make it quite clear that the claim to equality does not depend on intelligence, moral capacity, physical strength, or similar matters of fact. Equality is a moral ideal, not a simple assertion of fact. There is no logically compelling reason for assuming that a factual difference in ability between two people justifies any difference in the amount of consideration we give to satisfying their needs and interests. The principle of the equality of human beings is not a description of an alleged actual equality among humans: it is a prescription of how we should treat humans.

Jeremy Bentham incorporated the essential basis of moral equality into his utilitarian system of ethics in the formula: "Each to count for one and none for more than one." In other words, the interests of every being affected by an action are to be taken into account and given the same weight as the like interests of any other being. A later utilitarian, Henry Sidgwick, put the point in this way: "The good of any one individual is of no more importance, from the point of view (if I may say so) of the Universe, than the good of any other."[1] More recently, the leading figures in contemporary moral philosophy have shown a great deal of agreement in specifying as a fundamental presupposition of their moral theories some similar requirement which operates so as to give everyone's interests equal consideration—although they cannot agree on how this requirement is best formulated.

It is an implication of this principle of equality that our concern for others ought not to depend on what they are like, or what abilities they possess—although precisely what this concern requires us to do may vary according to the characteristics of those affected by what we do. It is on this basis that the case against racism and the case against sexism must both ultimately rest; and it is in accordance with this principle that speciesism is also to be condemned. If possessing a higher degree of intelligence does not entitle one human to use another for his own ends, how can it entitle humans to exploit non-humans?

Many philosophers have proposed the principle of equal consideration of interests, in some form or other, as a basic moral principle; but, as we shall see in more detail shortly, not many of them have recognised that this principle applies to members of other species as well as to our own. Bentham was one of the few who did realize this. In a forward-looking passage, written at a time when black slaves in the British dominions were still being treated much as we now treat non-human animals, Bentham wrote:

The day *may* come when the rest of the animal creation may acquire those rights which never could have been witholden from them but by the hand of tyranny. The French have already discovered that the blackness of the skin is no reason why a human being should be abandoned without redress to the caprice of a tormentor. It may one day come to be recognised that the number of the legs, the villosity of the skin, or the termination of the *os sacrum,* are reasons equally insufficient for abandoning a sensitive being to the same fate. What else is it that should trace the insuperable line? Is it the faculty of reason, or perhaps the faculty of dis-

course? But a full-grown horse or dog is beyond comparison a more rational, as well as a more conversable animal, than an infant of a day, or a week, or even a month, old. But suppose they were otherwise, what would it avail? The question is not, Can they reason? nor Can they *talk*? but, *Can they suffer*?[2]

In this passage Bentham points to the capacity for suffering as the vital characteristic that gives a being the right to equal consideration. The capacity for suffering—or more strictly, for suffering and/or enjoyment or happiness—is not just another characteristic like the capacity for language, or for higher mathematics. Bentham is not saying that those who try to mark "the insuperable line" that determines whether the interests of a being should be considered happen to have selected the wrong characteristic. The capacity for suffering and enjoying things is a prerequisite for having interests at all, a condition that must be satisfied before we can speak of interests in any meaningful way. It would be nonsense to say that it was not in the interests of a stone to be kicked along the road by a schoolboy. A stone does not have interests because it cannot suffer. Nothing that we can do to it could possibly make any difference to its welfare. A mouse, on the other hand, does have an interest in not being tormented, because it will suffer if it is.

If a being suffers, there can be no moral justification for refusing to take that suffering into consideration. No matter what the nature of the being, the principle of equality requires that its suffering be counted equally with the like suffering—in so far as rough comparisons can be made—of any other being. If a being is not capable of suffering, or of experiencing enjoyment or happiness, there is nothing to be taken into account. This is why the limit of sentience (using the term as a convenient, if not strictly accurate, shorthand for the capacity to suffer or experience enjoyment or happiness) is the only defensible boundary of concern for the interests of others. To mark this boundary by some characteristic like intelligence or rationality would be to mark it in an arbitrary way. Why not choose some other characteristic, like skin color?

The racist violates the principle of equality by giving greater weight to the interests of members of his own race, when there is a clash between their interests and the interests of those of another race. Similarly the speciesist allows the interests of his own species to override the greater interests of members of other species. The pattern is the same in each case. Most human beings are speciesists. I shall now very briefly describe some of the practices that show this.

For the great majority of human beings, especially in urban, industrialized societies, the most direct form of contact with members of other species is at meal-times: we eat them. In doing so we treat them purely as means to our ends. We regard their life and well-being as subordinate to our taste for a particular kind of dish. I say "taste" deliberately—this is purely a matter of pleasing our palate. There can be no defence of eating flesh in terms of satisfying nutritional needs, since it has been established beyond doubt that we could satisfy our need for protein and other essential nutrients far more efficiently with a die that replaced animal flesh by soy beans, or products derived from soy beans, and other high-protein vegetable products.[3]

It is not merely the act of killing that indicates what we are ready to do to other species in order to gratify our tastes. The suffering we inflict on the animals while they are alive is perhaps an even clearer indication of our speciesism than the fact that we are prepared to kill them.[4] In order to have meat on the table at a price that people can afford, our society tolerates methods of meat production that confine sentient animals in cramped, unsuitable conditions for the entire durations of their lives. Animals are treated like machines that convert fodder into flesh, and any innovation that results in a higher "conversion ratio" is liable to be adopted. As one authority on the subject has said, "cruelty is acknowledged only when profitability ceases."[5] So hens are crowded four or five to a cage with a floor area of twenty inches by eighteen inches, or around the size of a single page of the *New York Times*. The cages have wire floors, since this reduces cleaning costs, though wire is unsuitable for the hens' feet; the floors slope, since this makes the eggs roll down for easy collection, although this makes it difficult for the hense to rest comfortably. In these conditions all the birds' natural instincts are thwarted: they cannot stretch their wings fully, walk freely, dust-bathe, scratch the ground, or build a nest. Although they have never known other conditions, observers have noticed that the birds vainly try to perform these actions. Frustrated at their inability to do so, they often develop what farmers call "vices," and peck each other to death. To prevent this, the beaks of young birds are often cut off.

This kind of treatment is not limited to poultry. Pigs are now also being reared in cages inside sheds. These animals are comparable to dogs in intelligence, and need a varied, stimulating environment if they are not to suffer from stress and boredom. Anyone who kept a dog in the way in which pigs are frequently kept would be liable to prosecution, in England at least, but because our interest in exploiting pigs is greater than our interest in exploiting dogs, we object to cruelty to dogs while consuming the produce of cruelty to pigs. Of the other animals, the condition of veal calves is perhaps worst of all, since these animals are so closely confined that they cannot even turn around or get up and lie down freely. In this way they do not develop unpalatable muscle. They are also made anaemic and kept short of roughage, to keep their flesh pale, since white veal fetches a higher price; as a result they develop a craving for iron and roughage, and have been observed to gnaw wood off the sides of their stalls, and lick greedily at any rusty hinge that is within reach.

Since, as I have said, one of these practices cater for anything more than our pleasures of taste, our practice of rearing and killing other animals in order to eat them is a clear instance of the sacrifice of the most important interests of other beings in order to satisfy trivial interests of our own. To avoid speciesism we must stop this practice, and each of us has a moral obligation to cease supporting the practice. Our custom is all the support that the meat-industry needs. The decision to cease giving it that support may be difficult, but it is no more difficult than it would have been for a white Southerner to go against the traditions of his society and free his slaves; if we do not change our dietary habits, how can we censure those slaveholders who would not change their own way of living?

The same form of discrimination may be observed in the widespread practice of experimenting on other species in order to see if certain substances are safe for human beings, or to test some psychological theory about the effect of severe punishment on learning, or to try out various new compounds just in case something turns up. People sometimes think that all this experimentation is for vital medical purposes, and so will reduce suffering overall. This comfortable belief is very wide of the mark. Drug companies test new shampoos and cosmetics that they are intending to put on the market by dropping them into the eyes of rabbits, held open by metal clips, in order to observe what damage results. Food additives, like artificial colorings and preservatives, are tested by what is known as the "LD$_{50}$"—a test designed to find the level of consumption at which 50% of a group of animals will die. In the process, nearly all of the animals are made very sick before some finally die, and others pull through. If the substance is relatively harmless, as it often is, huge doses have to be force-fed to the animals, until in some cases sheer volume or concentration of the substance causes death.

Much of this pointless cruelty goes on in the universities. In many areas of science, non-human animals are regarded as an item of laboratory equipment, to be used and expended as desired. In psychology laboratories experimenters devise endless variations and repetitions of experiments that were of little value in the first place. To quote just one example, from the experimenter's own account in a psychology journal: at the University of Pennsylvania, Perrin S. Cohen hung six dogs in hammocks with electrodes taped to their hind feet. Electric shock of varying intensity was then administered through the electrodes. If the dog learnt to press its head against a panel on the left, the shock was turned off, but otherwise it remained on indefinitely. Three of the dogs, however, were required to wait periods varying from 2 to 7 seconds while being shocked before making the response that turned off the current. If they failed to wait, they received further shocks. Each dog was given from 26 to 46 "sessions" in the hammock, each

session consisting of 80 "trials" or shocks, administered at intervals of one minute. The experimenter reported that the dogs, who were unable to move in the hammock, barked or bobbed their heads when the current was applied. The reported findings of the experiment were that there was a delay in the dogs' responses that increased proportionately to the time the dogs were required to endure the shock, but a gradual increase in the intensity of the shock had no systematic effect in the timing of the response. The experiment was funded by the National Institutes of Health, and the United States Public Health Service.

In this example, and countless cases like it, the possible benefits to mankind are either non-existent or fantastically remote; while the certain losses to members of other species are very real. This is, again, a clear indication of speciesism.

In the past, argument about vivesection has often missed this point, because it has been put in absolutist terms: would the abolitionist be prepared to let thousands die if they could be saved by experimenting on a single animal? The way to reply to this purely hypothetical question is to pose another: would the experimenter be prepared to perform his experiment on an orphaned human infant, if that were the only way to save many lives? (I say "orphan" to avoid the complication of parental feelings, although in doing so I am being overfair to the experimenter, since the nonhuman subjects of experiments are not orphans.) If the experimenter is not prepared to use an orphaned human infant, then his readiness to use nonhumans is simple discrimination, since adult apes, cats, mice and other mammals are more aware of what is happening to them, more self-directing and, so far as we can tell, at least as sensitive to pain, as any human infant. There seems to be no relevant characteristic that human infants possess that adult mammals do not have to the same or a higher degree. (Someone might try to argue that what makes it wrong to experiment on a human infant is that the infant will, in time and if left alone, develop into more than the nonhuman, but one would then, to be consistent, have to oppose abortion, since the fetus has the same potential as the infant—indeed, even contraception and abstinence might be wrong on this ground, since the egg and sperm, considered jointly, also have the same potential. In any case, this argument still gives us no reason for selecting a nonhuman, rather than a human with severe and irreversible brain damage, as the subject for our experiments.)

The experimenter, then, shows a bias in favor of his own species whenever he carries out an experiment on a nonhuman for a purpose that he would not think justified him in using a human being at an equal or lower level of sentience, awareness, ability to be self-directing, etc. No one familiar with the kind of results yielded by most experiments on animals can have the slightest doubt that if this bias were eliminated the number of experiments performed would be a minute fraction of the number performed today.

Experimenting on animals, and eating their flesh, are perhaps the two major forms of speciesism in our society. By comparison, the third and last form of speciesism is so minor as to be insignificant, but it is perhaps of some special interest to those for whom this paper was written. I am referring to speciesism in contemporary philosophy.

Philosophy ought to question the basic assumptions of the age. Thinking through, critically and carefully, what most people take for granted is, I believe, the chief task of philosophy, and it is this task that makes philosophy a worthwhile activity. Regrettably, philosophy does not always live up to its historic role. Philosophers are human beings and they are subject to all the preconceptions of the society to which they belong. Sometimes they succeed in breaking free of the prevailing ideology: more often they become its most sophisticated defenders. So, in this case, philosophy as practiced in the universities today does not challenge anyone's preconceptions about our relations with other species. By their writings, those philosophers who tackle problems that touch upon the issue reveal that they make the same unquestioned assumptions as most other humans, and what they say tends to confirm the reader in his or her comfortable speciesist habits.

I could illustrate this claim by referring to the writings of philosophers in various fields—for instance, the attempts that have been made by those interested in rights to draw the boundary of the sphere of rights so that it runs parallel to the biological boundaries of the species *homo sapiens,* including infants and even mental defectives, but excluding those other beings of equal or greater capacity who are so useful to us at mealtimes and in our laboratories. I think it would be a more appropriate conclusion to this paper, however, if I concentrated on the problem with which we have been centrally concerned, the problem of equality.

It is significant that the problem of equality, in moral and political philosophy, is invariably formulated in terms of human equality. The effect of this is that the question of the equality of other animals does not confront the philosopher, or student, as an issue in itself—and this is already an indication of the failure of philosophy to challenge accepted beliefs. Still, philosophers have found it difficult to discuss the issue of human equality without raising, in a paragraph or two, the question of the status of other animals. The reason for this, which should be apparent from what I have said already, is that if humans are to be regarded as equal to one another, we need some sense of "equal" that does not require any actual, descriptive equality of capacities, talents or other qualities. If equality is to be related to any actual characteristics of humans, these characteristics must be some lowest common denominator, pitched so low that no human lacks them—but then the philosopher comes up against the catch that any such set of characteristics which covers *all* humans will not be possessed *only by humans.* In other words, it turns out that in the only sense in which we can truly say, as an assertion of fact, that all humans are equal, at least some members of other species are also equal—equal, that is, to each other and to humans. If, on the other hand, we regard the statement "All humans are equal" in some non-factual way, perhaps as a prescription, then, as I have already argued, it is even more difficult to exclude non-humans from the sphere of equality.

This result is not what the egalitarian philosopher originally intended to assert. Instead of accepting the radical outcome to which their own reasonings naturally point, however, most philosophers try to reconcile their beliefs in human equality and animal inequality by arguments that can only be described as devious.

As a first example, I take William Frankena's well-known article "The Concept of Social Justice." Frankena opposes the idea of basing justice on merit, because he sees that this could lead to highly inegalitarian results. Instead he proposes the principle that:

. . . all men are to be treated as equals, not because they are equal, in any respect but simply because they are human. They are human because they have emotions and desires, and are able to think, and hence are capable of enjoying a good life in a sense in which other animals are not.[6]

But what is this capacity to enjoy the good life which all humans have, but no other animals? Other animals have emotions and desires, and appear to be capable of enjoying a good life. We may doubt that they can think—although the behavior of some apes, dolphins and even dogs suggests that some of them can—but what is the relevance of thinking? Frankena goes on to admit that by "the good life" he means "not so much the morally good life as the happy or satisfactory life", so thought would appear to be unnecessary for enjoying the good life; in fact to emphasise the need for thought would make difficulties for the egalitarian since only some people are capable of leading intellectually satisfying lives—or morally good lives. This makes it difficult to see what Frankena's principle of equality has to do with simply being *human*. Surely every sentient being is capable of leading a life that is happier or less miserable than some alternative life, and hence has a claim to be taken into account. In this respect the distinction between humans and non-humans is not a sharp division, but rather a continuum along which we move gradually, and with overlaps between the species, from simple capacities for enjoyment and satisfaction, or pain and suffering, to more complex ones.

Faced with a situation in which they see a need for some basis for the moral gulf that is commonly thought to separate humans and animals, but can find no concrete difference that will do the job with-

out undermining the equality of humans, philosophers tend to waffle. They resort to high-sounding phrases like "the intrinsic dignity of the human individual";[7] They talk of the "intrinsic worth of all men" as if men (humans?) had some worth that other beings did not,[8] or they say that humans, and only humans, are "ends in themselves", while "everything other than a person can only have value for a person."[9]

This idea of a distinctive human dignity and worth has a long history; it can be traced back directly to the Renaissance humanists, for instance to Pico della Mirandola's *Oration on the Dignity of Man*. Pico and other humanists based their estimate of human dignity on the idea that man possessed the central, pivotal position in the "Great Chain of Being" that led from the lowliest forms of matter to God himself; this view of the universe, in turn, goes back to both classical and Judeo-Christian doctrines. Contemporary philosophers have cast off these metaphysical and religious shackles and freely invoke the dignity of mankind without needing to justify the idea at all. Why should we not attribute "intrinsic dignity" or "intrinsic worth" to ourselves? Fellow-humans are unlikely to reject the accolades we so generously bestow on them, and those to whom we deny the honor are unable to object. Indeed, when one thinks only of humans, it can be very liberal, very progressive, to talk of the dignity of all human beings. In so doing, we implicitly condemn slavery, racism, and other violations of human rights. We admit that we ourselves are in some fundamental sense on a par with the poorest, most ignorant members of our own species. It is only when we think of humans as no more than a small sub-group of all the beings that inhabit our planet that we may realize that in elevating our own species we are at the same time lowering the relative status of all other species.

The truth is that the appeal to the intrinsic dignity of human beings appears to solve the egalitarian's problems only as long as it goes unchallenged. Once we ask *why* it should be that all humans—including infants, mental defectives, psychopaths, Hitler, Stalin and the rest—have some kind of dignity or worth that no elephant, pig or chimpanzee can ever achieve, we see that this question is as difficult to answer as our original request for some relevant fact that justifies the inequality of humans and other animals. In fact, these two questions are really one: talk of intrinsic dignity or moral worth only takes the problem back one step, because any satisfactory defence of the claim that all and only humans have intrinsic dignity would need to refer to some relevant capacities or characteristics that all and only humans possess. Philosophers frequently introduce ideas of dignity, respect and worth at the point at which other reasons appear to be lacking, but this is hardly good enough. Fine phrases are the last resource of those who have run out of arguments.

In case there are those who still think it may be possible to find some relevant characteristic that distinguishes all humans from all members of other species, I shall refer again, before I conclude, to the existence of some humans who quite clearly are below the level of awareness, self-consciousness, intelligence, and sentience, of many non-humans. I am thinking of humans with severe and irreparable brain damage, and also of infant humans. To avoid the complication of the relevance of a being's potential, however, I shall henceforth concentrate on permanently retarded humans.

Philosophers who set out to find a characteristic that will distinguish humans from other animals rarely take the course of abandoning these groups of humans by lumping them in with the other animals. It is easy to see why they do not. To take this line without re-thinking our attitudes to other animals would entail that we have the right to perform painful experiments on retarded humans for trivial reasons; similarly it would follow that we had the right to rear and kill these humans for food. To most philosophers these consequences are as unacceptable as the view that we should stop treating non-humans in this way.

Of course, when discussing the problem of equality it is possible to ignore the problem of mental defectives, or brush it aside as if somehow insignificant. This is the easiest way out. What else remains? My final example of speciesism in contemporary philosophy has been selected to show what happens when a writer is prepared to face the question of human equality and animal inequality without ignoring the existence of mental defectives, and without resorting to obscurantist mumbo-jumbo. Stanley Benn's clear and honest article "Egalitarianism and Equal Consideration of Interests"[10] fits this description.

Benn after noting the usual "evident human inequalities" argues, correctly I think, for equality of consideration as the only possible basis for egalitarianism. Yet Benn, like other writers, is thinking only of "equal consideration of human interests." Benn is quite open in his defence of this restriction of equal consideration:

. . . not to possess human shape *is* a disqualifying condition. However faithful or intelligent a dog may be, it would be a monstrous sentimentality to attribute to him interests that could be weighed in an equal balance with those of human beings . . . if, for instance, one had to decide between feeding a hungry baby or a hungry dog, anyone who chose the dog would generally be reckoned morally defective, unable to recognize a fundamental inequality of claims.

This is what distinguishes our attitude to animals from our attitude to imbeciles. It would be odd to say that we ought to respect equally the dignity or personality of the imbecile and of the rational man . . . but there is nothing odd about saying that we should respect their interests equally, that is, that we should give to the interests of each the same serious consideration as claims to considerations necessary for some standard of well-being that we can recognize and endorse.

Benn's statement of the basis of the consideration we should have for imbeciles seems to me correct, but why should there be any fundamental inequality of claims between a dog and a human imbecile? Benn sees that if equal consideration depended on rationality, no reason could be given against using imbeciles for research purposes, as we now use dogs and guinea pigs. This will not do: "But of course we do distinguish imbeciles from animals in this regard," he says. That the common distinction is justifiable is something Benn does not question; his problem is how it is to be justified. The answer he gives is this:

. . . we respect the interests of men and give them priority over dogs not *insofar* as they are rational, but because rationality is the human norm. We say it is *unfair* to exploit the deficiencies of the imbecile who falls short of the norm, just as it would be unfair, and not just ordinarily dishonest, to steal from a blind man. If we do not think in this way about dogs, it is because we do not see the irrationality of the dog as a deficiency or a handicap, but as normal for the species. The characteristics, therefore, that distinguish the normal man from the normal dog make it intelligible for us to talk of other men having interests and capacities, and therefore claims, of precisely the same kind as we make on our own behalf. But although these characteristics may provide the point of the distinction between men and other species, they are not in fact the qualifying conditions for membership, or the distinguishing criteria of the class of morally considerable persons; and this is precisely because a man does not become a member of a different species, with its own standards of normality, by reason of not possessing these characteristics.

The final sentence of this passage gives the argument away. An imbecile, Benn concedes, may have no characteristics superior to those of a dog; nevertheless this does not make the imbecile a member of "a different species" as the dog is. *Therefore* it would be "unfair" to use the imbecile for medical research as we use the dog. But why? That the imbecile is not rational is just the way things have worked out, and the same is true of the dog—neither is any more responsible for their mental level. If it is unfair to take advantage of an isolated defect, why is it fair to take advantage of a more general limitation? I find it hard to see anything in this argument except a defence of preferring the interests of members of our own species because they are members of our own species. To those who think there might be more to it, I suggest the following mental exercise. Assume that it has been proven that there is a difference in the average, or normal, intelligence quotient for two different races, say whites and blacks. Then substitute the term "white" for every occurrence of "men" and "black" for every occurrence of "dog" in the passage quoted; and substitute "high I.Q." for "rationality" and when Benn talks of "imbeciles" replace this term by "dumb whites"—that is, whites who fall well below the normal white I.Q. score. Finally, change "species" to "race." Now re-read the passage. It has become a defence of a rigid, no-exceptions division between whites and blacks, based on I.Q. scores, *not withstanding an admitted overlap* between whites and blacks in this respect. The revised passage is, of course, outrageous, and this not only because we have made fictitious assumptions in our substitutions. The point is that in the original passage Benn was defending a rigid division in the amount of consideration due to members of different species, despite admitted cases of overlap. If the original did not, at first reading strike us as being as outrageous as the revised version does, this is largely because although we are not racists ourselves, most of us are speciesists. Like the other articles, Benn's stands as a warning of the case with which the best minds can fall victim to a prevailing ideology.

NOTES

1. *The Methods of Ethics* (7th Ed.) p. 382.

2. *Introduction to the Principles of Morals and Legislation,* ch. XVII.

3. In order to produce 1 lb. of protein in the form of beef or veal, we must feed 21 lbs. of protein to the animal. Other forms of livestock are slightly less inefficient, but the average ratio in the U. S. is still 1:8. It has been estimated that the amount of protein lost to humans in this way is equivalent to 90% of the annual world protein deficit.

4. Although one might think that killing a being is obviously the ultimate wrong one can do to it, I think that the infliction of suffering is a clearer indication of speciesism because it might be argued that at least part of what is wrong with killing a human is that most humans are conscious of their existence over time, and have desires and purposes that extend into the future. Of course, if one took this view one would have to hold that killing a human infant or mental defective is not in itself wrong, and is less serious than killing certain higher mammals that probably do have a sense of their own existence over time.

5. Ruth Harrison, *Animal Machines* (Stuart, London, 1964).

6. In R. Brandt (ed.) *Social Justice* (Prentice Hall, Englewood Cliffs, 1962): the passage quoted appears on p. 19.

7. Frankena, *op. cit.,* p. 23.

8. H. A. Bedau, "Egalitarianism and the Idea of Equality" in *Nomos IX: Equality,* ed. J. R. Pennock and J. W Chapman, New York 1967.

9. G. Vlastos, "Justice and Equality" in Brandt. *Social Justice,* p. 48.

10. *Nomos IX: Equality:* the passages quoted are on pp. 62ff.

The Case for Animal Rights

TOM REGAN

I regard myself as an advocate of animal rights—as a part of the animal rights movement. That movement, as I conceive it, is committed to a number of goals, including:

- the total abolition of the use of animals in science;
- the total dissolution of commercial animal agriculture;
- the total elimination of commercial and sport hunting and trapping.

There are, I know, people who profess to believe in animal rights but do not avow these goals. Factory farming, they say, is wrong—it violates animals' rights—but traditional animal agriculture is all right. Toxicity tests of cosmetics on animals violates their rights, but important medical research—cancer research, for example—does not. The clubbing of baby seals is abhorrent, but not the harvesting of adult seals. I used to think I understood this reasoning. Not any more. You don't change unjust institutions by tidying them up.

What's wrong—fundamentally wrong—with the way animals are treated isn't the details that vary from case to case. It's the whole system. The forlornness of the veal calf is pathetic, heart wrenching; the pulsing pain of the chimp with electrodes planted deep in her brain is repulsive; the slow, tortuous death of the raccoon caught in the leg-hold trap is agonizing. But what

is wrong isn't the pain, isn't the suffering, isn't the deprivation. These compound what's wrong. Sometimes—often—they make it much, much worse. But they are not the fundamental wrong.

The fundamental wrong is the system that allows us to view animals as *our resources,* here for *us*—to be eaten, or surgically manipulated, or exploited for sport or money. Once we accept this view of animals—as our resources—the rest is as predictable as it is regrettable. Why worry about their loneliness, their pain, their death? Since animals exist for us, to benefit us in one way or another, what harms them really doesn't matter—or matters only if it starts to bother us, makes us feel a trifle uneasy when we eat our veal escalope, for example. So, yes, let us get veal calves out of solitary confinement, give them more space, a little straw, a few companions. But let us keep our veal escalope.

But a little straw, more space and a few companions won't eliminate—won't even touch—the basic wrong that attaches to our viewing and treating these animals as our resources. A veal calf killed to be eaten after living in close confinement is viewed and treated in this way: but so, too, is another who is raised (as they say) 'more humanely'. To right the wrong of our treatment of farm animals requires more than making rearing methods 'more humane'; it requires the total dissolution of commercial animal agriculture.

How we do this, whether we do it or, as in the case of animals in science, whether and how we abolish their use—these are to a large extent political questions. People must change their beliefs before they change their habits. Enough people, especially those elected to public office, must believe in change—must want it—before we will have laws that protect the rights of animals. This process of change is very complicated, very demanding, very exhausting, calling for the efforts of many hands in education, publicity, political organization and activity, down to the licking of envelopes and stamps. As a trained and practising philosopher, the sort of contribution I can make is limited but, I like to think, important. The currency of philosophy is ideas—their meaning and rational foundation—not the nuts and bolts of the legislative process, say, or the mechanics of community organization. That's what I have been exploring over the past ten years or so in my essays and talks and, most recently, in my book, *The Case for Animal Rights*. I believe the major conclusions I reach in the book are true because they are supported by the weight of the best arguments. I believe the idea of animal rights has reason, not just emotion, on its side.

In the space I have at my disposal here I can only sketch, in the barest outline, some of the main features of the book. It's main themes—and we should not be surprised by this—involve asking and answering deep, foundational moral questions about what morality is, how it should be understood and what is the best moral theory, all considered. I hope I can convey something of the shape I think this theory takes. The attempt to do this will be (to use a word a friendly critic once used to describe my work) cerebral, perhaps too cerebral. But this is misleading. My feelings about how animals are sometimes treated run just as deep and just as strong as those of my more volatile compatriots. Philosophers do—to use the jargon of the day—have a right side to their brains. If it's the left side we contribute (or mainly should), that's because what talents we have reside there.

How to proceed? We begin by asking how the moral status of animals has been understood by thinkers who deny that animals have rights. Then we test the mettle of their ideas by seeing how well they stand up under the heat of fair criticism. If we start our thinking in this way, we soon find that some people believe that we have no duties directly to animals, that we owe nothing to them, that we can do noth-

ing that wrongs them. Rather, we can do wrong acts that involve animals, and so we have duties regarding them, though none to them. Such views may be called indirect duty views. By way of illustration: suppose your neighbour kicks your dog. Then your neighbour has done something wrong. But not to your dog. The wrong that has been done is a wrong to you. After all, it is wrong to upset people, and your neighbour's kicking your dog upsets you. So you are the one who is wronged, not your dog. Or again: by kicking your dog your neighbour damages your property. And since it is wrong to damage another person's property, your neighbour has done something wrong—to you, of course, not to your dog. Your neighbour no more wrongs your dog than your car would be wronged if the windshield were smashed. Your neighbour's duties involving your dog are indirect duties to you. More generally, all of our duties regarding animals are indirect duties to one another—to humanity.

How could someone try to justify such a view? Someone might say that your dog doesn't feel anything and so isn't hurt by your neighbour's kick, doesn't care about the pain since none is felt, is as unaware of anything as is your windshield. Someone might say this, but no rational person will, since, among other considerations, such a view will commit anyone who holds it to the position that no human being feels pain either—that human beings also don't care about what happens to them. A second possibility is that though both humans and your dog are hurt when kicked, it is only human pain that matters. But, again, no rational person can believe this. Pain is pain wherever it occurs. If your neighbour's causing you pain is wrong because of the pain that is caused, we cannot rationally ignore or dismiss the moral relevance of the pain that your dog feels.

Philosophers who hold indirect duty views—and many still do—have come to understand that they must avoid the two defects just noted: that is, both the view that animals don't feel anything as well as the idea that only human pain can be morally relevant. Among such thinkers the sort of view now favoured is one or other form of what is called *contractarianism*.

Here, very crudely, is the root idea: morality consists of a set of rules that individuals voluntarily agree to abide by, as we do when we sign a contract (hence the name contractrarianism). Those who understand and accept the terms of the contract are covered directly; they have rights created and recognized by, and protected in, the contract. And these contractors can also have protection spelled out for others who, though they lack the ability to understand morality and so cannot sign the contract themselves, are loved or cherished by those who can. Thus young children, for example, are unable to sign contracts and lack rights. But they are protected by the contract none the less because of the sentimental interests of others, most notably their parents. So we have, then, duties involving these children, duties regarding them, but no duties to them. Our duties in their case are indirect duties to other human beings, usually their parents.

As for animals, since they cannot understand contracts, they obviously cannot sign; and since they cannot sign, they have no rights. Like children, however, some animals are the objects of the sentimental interest of others. You, for example, love your dog or cat. So those animals that enough people care about (companion animals, whales, baby seals, the American bald eagle), though they lack rights themselves, will be protected because of the sentimental interests of people. I have, then, according to contractarianism, no duty directly to your dog or any other animal, not even the duty not to cause them pain or suffering; my duty not to hurt them is a duty I have to those people who care about what happens to them. As for other animals, where no or little sentimental interest is present—in the case of farm animals, for example, or laboratory rats—what duties we have grow weaker and weaker, perhaps to vanishing point. The pain and death they endure, though real, are not wrong if no one cares about them.

When it comes to the moral status of animals' contractarianism could be a hard view to refute if it were an adequate theoretical approach to the moral status of human beings. It is not adequate in this latter respect, however, which makes the question of its adequacy in the former case, regarding animals,

utterly moot. For consider: morality, according to the (crude) contractarian position before us, consists of rules that people agree to abide by. What people? Well, enough to make a difference—enough, that is, *collectively* to have the power to enforce the rules that are drawn up in the contract. That is very well and good for the signatories but not so good for anyone who is not asked to sign. And there is nothing in contractarianism of the sort we are discussing that guarantees or requires that everyone will have a chance to participate equally in framing the rules of morality. The result is that this approach to ethics could sanction the most blatant forms of social, economic, moral and political injustice, ranging from a repressive caste system to systematic racial or sexual discrimination. Might, according to this theory, does make right. Let those who are the victims of injustice suffer as they will. It matters not so long as no one else—no contractor, or too few of them—cares about it. Such a theory takes one's moral breath away . . . as if, for example, there would be nothing wrong with apartheid in South Africa if few white South Africans were upset by it. A theory with so little to recommend it at the level of the ethics of our treatment of our fellow humans cannot have anything more to recommend it when it comes to the ethics of how we treat our fellow animals.

The version of contractarianism just examined is, as I have noted, a crude variety, and in fairness to those of a contractarian persuasion it must be noted that much more refined, subtle and ingenious varieties are possible. For example, John Rawls, in his *A Theory of Justice,* sets forth a version of contractarianism that forces contractors to ignore the accidental features of being a human being—for example, whether one is whiter or black, male or female, a genius or of modest intellect. Only by ignoring such features, Rawls believes, can we ensure that the principles of justice that contractors would agree upon are not based on bias or prejudice. Despite the improvement a view such as Rawls's represents over the cruder forms of contractarianism, it remains deficient: it systematically denies that we have direct duties to those human beings who do not have a sense of justice—young children, for instance, and many mentally retarded humans. And yet it seems reasonably certain that, were we to torture a young child or a retarded elder, we would be doing something that wronged him or her, not something that would be wrong if (and only if) other humans with a sense of justice were upset. And since this is true in the case of these humans, we cannot rationally deny the same in the case of animals.

Indirect duty views, then, including the best among them, fail to command our rational assent. Whatever ethical theory we should accept rationally, therefore, it must at least recognize that we have some duties directly to animals, just as we have some duties directly to each other. The next two theories I'll sketch attempt to meet this requirement.

The first I call the cruelty-kindness view. Simply stated, this says that we have a direct duty to be kind to animals and a direct duty not to be cruel to them. Despite the familiar, reassuring ring of these ideas, I do not believe that this view offers an adequate theory. To make this clearer, consider kindness. A kind person acts from a certain kind of motive—compassion or concern, for example. And that is a virtue. But there is no guarantee that a kind act is a right act. If I am a generous racist, for example, I will be inclined to act kindly towards members of my own race, favouring their interests above those of others. My kindness would be real and, so far as it goes, good. But I trust it is too obvious to require argument that my kind acts may not be above moral reproach—may, in fact, be positively wrong because rooted in injustice. So kindness, notwithstanding its status as a virtue to be encouraged, simply will not carry the weight of a theory of right action.

Cruelty fares no better. People or their acts are cruel if they display either a lack of sympathy for or, worse, the presence of enjoyment in another's suffering. Cruelty in all its guises is a bad thing, a tragic human failing. But just as a person's being motivated by kindness does not guarantee that he or she does what is right, so the absence of cruelty does not ensure that he or she avoids doing what is wrong. Many people who perform abortions, for example, are not cruel, sadistic people. But that fact alone does not settle the terribly difficult question of the moral-

ity of abortion. The case is no different when we examine the ethics of our treatment of animals. So, yes, let us be for kindness and against cruelty. But let us not suppose that being for the one and against the other answers questions about moral right and wrong.

Some people think that the theory we are looking for is utilitarianism. A utilitarian accepts two moral principles. The first is that of equality: everyone's interests count, and similar interests must be counted as having similar weight or importance. White or black, American or Iranian, human or animal—everyone's pain or frustration matter, and matter just as much as the equivalent accepts is that of utility: do the act that will bring about the best balance between satisfaction and frustration for everyone affected by the outcome.

As a utilitarian, then, here is how I am to approach the task of deciding what I morally ought to do: I must ask who will be affected if I choose to do one thing rather than another, how much each individual will be affected, and where the best results are most likely to lie—which option, in other words, is most likely to bring about the best results, the best balance between satisfaction and frustration. That option, whatever it may be, is the one I ought to choose. That is where my moral duty lies.

The great appeal of utilitarianism rests with its uncompromising *egalitarianism*: everyone's interests count and count as much as the like interests of everyone else. The kind of odious discrimination that some forms of contractarianism can justify—discrimination based on race or sex, for example—seems disallowed in principle by utilitarianism, as is speciesism, systematic discrimination based on species membership.

The equality we find in utilitarianism, however, is not the sort an advocate of animal or human rights should have in mind. Utilitarianism has no room for the equal moral rights of different individuals because it has no room for their equal inherent value or worth. What has value for the utilitarian is the satisfaction of an individual's interests, not the individual whose interests they are. A universe in which you satisfy your desire for water, food and warmth is, other things being equal, better than a universe in which these desires are frustrated. And the same is true in the case of an animal with similar desires. But neither you nor the animal have any value in your own right. Only your feelings do.

Here is an analogy to help make the philosophical point clearer: a cup contains different liquids, sometimes sweet, sometimes bitter, sometimes a mix of the two. What has value are the liquids: the sweeter the better, the bitterer the worse. The cup, the container, has no value. It is what goes into it, not what they go into, that has value. For the utilitarian you and I are like the cup; we have no value as individuals and thus no equal value. What has value is what goes into us, what we serve as receptacles for; our feelings of satisfaction have positive value, our feelings of frustration negative value.

Serious problems arise for utilitarianism when we remind ourselves that it enjoins us to bring about the best consequences. What does this mean? It doesn't mean the best consequences for me alone, or for my family or friends, or any other person taken individually. No, what we must do is, roughly, as follows: we must add up (somehow!) the separate satisfactions and frustrations of everyone likely to be affected by our choice, the satisfactions in one column, the frustrations in the other. We must total each column for each of the options before us. That is what it means to say the theory is aggregative. And then we must choose that option which is most likely to bring about the best balance of totalled satisfactions over totalled frustrations. Whatever act would lead to this outcome is the one we ought morally to perform—it is where our moral duty lies. And that act quite clearly might not be the same one that would bring about the best results for me personally, or for my family or friends, or for a lab animal. The best aggregated consequences for everyone concerned are not necessarily the best for each individual.

That utilitarianism is an aggregative theory—different individuals' satisfactions or frustrations are added, or summed, or totalled—is the key objection to their theory. My Aunt Bea is old, inactive, a cranky, sour person, though not physically ill. She prefers to go on living. She is also rather rich. I could make a

fortune if I could get my hands on her money, money she intends to give me in any event, after she dies, but which she refuses to give me now. In order to avoid a huge tax bite, I plan to donate a handsome sum of my profits to a local children's hospital. Many, many children will benefit from my generosity, and much joy will be brought to their parents, relatives and friends. If I don't get the money rather soon, all these ambitions will come to naught. The once-in-a-lifetime opportunity to make a real killing will be gone. Why, then, not kill my Aunt Bea? Oh, of course I *might* get caught. But I'm no fool and besides, her doctor can be counted on to co-operate (he has an eye for the same investment and I happen to know a good deal about his shady past). The deed can be done . . . professionally, shall we say. There is *very* little chance of getting caught. And as for my conscience being guilt-ridden, I am a resourceful sort of fellow and will take more than sufficient comfort—as I lie on the beach at Acapulco—in contemplating the joy and health I have brought to so many others.

Suppose Aunt Bea is killed and the rest of the story comes out as told. Would I have done anything wrong? Anything immoral? One would have thought that I had. Not according to utilitarianism. Since what I have done has brought about the best balance between totalled satisfaction and frustration for all those affected by the outcome, my action is not wrong. Indeed, in killing Aunt Bea the physician and I did what duty required.

This same kind of argument can be repeated in all sorts of cases, illustrating, time after time, how the utilitarian's position leads to results that impartial people find morally callous. It *is* wrong to kill my Aunt Bea in the name of bringing about the best results for others. A good end does not justify an evil means. Any adequate moral theory will have to explain why this is so. Utilitarianism fails in this respect and so cannot be the theory we seek.

What to do? Where to begin anew? The place to begin, I think, is with the utilitarian's view of the value of the individual—or, rather, lack of value. In its place, suppose we consider that you and I, for example, do have value as individuals—what we'll call *inherent value*. To say we have such value is to say that we are something more than, something different from, mere receptacles. Moreover, to ensure that we do not pave the way for such injustices as slavery or sexual discrimination, we must believe that all who have inherent value have it equally, regardless of their sex, race, religion, birthplace and so on. Similarly to be discarded as irrelevant are one's talents or skills, intelligence and wealth, personality or pathology, whether one is loved and admired or despised and loathed. The genius and the retarded child, the prince and the pauper, the brain surgeon and the fruit vendor, Mother Teresa and the most unscrupulous used-car salesman—all have inherent value, all possess it equally, and all have an equal right to be treated with respect, to be treated in ways that do not reduce them to the status of things, as if they existed as resources for others. My value as an individual is independent of my usefulness to you. Yours is not dependent on your usefulness to me. For either of us to treat the other in ways that fail to show respect for the other's independent value is to act immorally, to violate the individual's rights.

Some of the rational virtues of this view—what I call the rights view—should be evident. Unlike (crude) contractarianism, for example, the rights view *in principle* denies the moral tolerability of any and all forms of racial, sexual or social discrimination; and unlike utilitarianism, this view *in principle* denies that we can justify good results by using evil means that violate an individual's rights—denies, for example, that it could be moral to kill my Aunt Bea to harvest beneficial consequences for others. That would be to sanction the disrespectful treatment of the individual in the name of the social good, something the rights view will not—categorically will not—ever allow.

The rights view, I believe, is rationally the most satisfactory moral theory. It surpasses all other theories in the degree to which it illuminates and explains the foundation of our duties to one another—the domain of human morality. On this score it has the best reasons, the best arguments, on its side. Of course, if it were possible to show that only human beings are included within its scope, then a person like myself, who believes in animal rights, would be obliged to look elsewhere.

But attempts to limit its scope to humans only can be shown to be rationally defective. Animals, it is true, lack many of the abilities humans possess. They can't read, do higher mathematics, build a bookcase or make *baba ghanoush*. Neither can many human beings, however, and yet we don't (and shouldn't) say that they (these humans) therefore have less inherent value, less of a right to be treated with respect, than do others. It is the *similarities* between those human beings who most clearly, most non-controversially have such value (the people reading this, for example), not our differences, that matter most. And the really crucial, the basic similarity is simply this: we are each of us the experiencing subject of a life, a conscious creature having an individual welfare that has importance to us whatever our usefulness to others. We want and prefer things, believe and feel things, recall and expect things. And all these dimensions of our life, including our pleasure and pain, our enjoyment and suffering, our satisfaction and frustration, our continued existence or our untimely death—all make a difference to the quality of our life as lived, as experienced, by us as individuals. As the same is true of those animals that concern us (the ones that are eaten and trapped, for example), they too must be viewed as the experiencing subjects of a life, with inherent value of their own.

Some there are who resist the idea that animals have inherent value. 'Only humans have such value,' they profess. How might this narrow view be defended? Shall we say that only humans have the requisite intelligence, or autonomy, or reason? But there are many, many humans who fail to meet these standards and yet are reasonably viewed as having value above and beyond their usefulness to others. Shall we claim that only humans belong to the right species, the species *Homo sapiens*? But this is blatant speciesism. Will it be said, then, that all—and only—humans have immortal souls? Then our opponents have their work cut out for them. I am myself not ill-disposed to the proposition that there are immortal souls. Personally, I profoundly hope I have one. But I would not want to rest my position on a controversial ethical issue on the even more controversial question about who or what has an immortal soul. That is to dig one's hole deeper, not to climb out. Rationally, it is better to resolve moral issues without making more controversial assumptions than are needed. The question of who has inherent value is such a question, one that is resolved more rationally without the introduction of the idea of immortal souls than by its use.

Well, perhaps some will say that animals have some inherent value, only less than we have. Once again, however, attempts to defend this view can be shown to lack rational justification. What could be the basis of our having more inherent value than animals? Their lack of reason, or autonomy, or intellect? Only if we are willing to make the same judgement in the case of humans who are similarly deficient. But it is not true that such humans—the retarded child, for example, or the mentally deranged—have less inherent value than you or I. Neither, then, can we rationally sustain the view that animals like them in being the experiencing subjects of a life have less inherent value. *All* who have inherent value have it *equally*, whether they be human animals or not.

Inherent value, then, belongs equally to those who are the experiencing subjects of a life. Whether it belongs to others—to rocks and rivers, trees and glaciers, for example—we do not know and may never know. But neither do we need to know, if we are to make the case for animal rights. We do not need to know, for example, how many people are legible to vote in the next presidential election before we can know whether I am. Similarly, we do not need to know how many individuals have inherent value before we can know that some do. When it comes to the case for animal rights, then, what we need to know is whether the animals that, in our culture, are routinely eaten, hunted and used in our laboratories, for example, are like us in being subjects of a life. And we do know this. We do know that many—literally, billions and billions—of these animals are the subjects of a life in the sense explained and so have inherent value if we do. And since, in order to arrive at the best theory of our duties to one another, we must recognize our equal inherent value as individuals, rea-

son—not sentiment, not emotion—reason compels us to recognize the equal inherent value of these animals and, with this, their equal right to be treated with respect.

That, *very* roughly, is the shape and feel of the case for animal rights. Most of the details of the supporting argument are missing. They are to be found in the book to which I alluded earlier. Here, the details go begging, and I must, in closing, limit myself to four final points.

The first is how the theory that underlies the case for animal rights shows that the animal rights movement is a part of, not antagonistic to, the human rights movement. The theory that rationally grounds the rights of animals also grounds the rights of humans. Thus those involved in the animal rights movement are partners in the struggle to secure respect for human rights—the rights of women, for example, or minorities, or workers. The animal rights movement is cut from the same moral cloth as these.

Second, having set out the broad outlines of the rights view, I can now say why its implications for farming and science, among other fields, are both clear and uncompromising. In the case of the use of animals in science, the rights view is categorically abolitionist. Lab animals are not our tasters; we are not their kings. Because these animals are treated routinely, systematically as if their value were reducible to their usefulness to others, they are routinely, systematically treated with a lack of respect, and thus are their rights routinely, systematically violated. This is just as true when they are used in trivial, duplicative, unnecessary or unwise research as it is when they are used in studies that hold out real promise of human benefits. We can't justify harming or killing a human being (my Aunt Bea, for example) just for these sorts of reason. Neither can we do so even in the case of so lowly a creature as a laboratory rat. It is not just refinement or reduction that is called for, not just larger, cleaner cages, not just more generous use of anaesthetic or the elimination of multiple surgery, not just tidying up the system. It is complete replacement. The best we can do it comes to using animals in science is—not to use them. That is where our duty lies, according to the rights view.

As for commercial animal agriculture, the rights view takes a similar abolitionist position. The fundamental moral wrong here is not that animals are kept in stressful close confinement or in isolation, or that their pain and suffering, their needs and preferences are ignored or discounted. All these *are* wrong, of course, but they are not fundamentally wrong. They are symptoms and effects of the deeper, systematic wrong that allows these animals to be viewed and treated as lacking independent value, as resources for us—as, indeed, a renewable resource. Giving farm animals more space, more natural environments, more companions does not right the fundamental wrong, any more than giving lab animals more anaesthesia or bigger, cleaner cages would right the fundamental wrong in their case. Nothing less than the total dissolution of commercial animal agriculture will do this, just as, for similar reasons I won't develop at length here, morality requires nothing less than the total elimination of hunting and trapping for commercial and sporting ends. The rights view's implications, then, as I have said, are clear and uncompromising.

My last two points are about philosophy, my profession. It is, most obviously, no substitute for political action. The words I have written here and in other places by themselves don't change a thing. It is what we do with the thoughts that the words express—our acts, our deeds—that changes things. All that philosophy can do, and all I have attempted, is to offer a vision of what our deeds should aim at. And the why. But not the how.

Finally, I am reminded of my thoughtful critic, the one I mentioned earlier, who chastised me for being too cerebral. Well, cerebral I have been: indirect duty views, utilitarianism, contractarianism—hardly the stuff deep passions are made of. I am also reminded, however, of the image another friend once set before me—the image of the ballerina as expressive of disciplined passion. Long hours of sweat and toil, of loneliness and practice, of doubt and fatigue: those are the discipline of her craft. But the passion is there too, the fierce drive to excel, to speak through her body, to do it right, to pierce our minds. That is the image of philosophy I would leave with you, not 'too cerebral' but *disciplined passion.* Of the discipline enough has been seen. As for the passion: there are times, and these not infrequent, when tears come to my eyes when I see, or read, or hear of the wretched plight of animals in the hands of humans. Their pain, their suffering, their loneliness, their innocence, their death. Anger. Rage. Pity. Sorrow. Disgust. The whole creation groans under the weight of the evil we humans visit upon these mute, powerless creatures. It *is* our hearts, not just our heads, that call for an end to it all, that demand of us that we overcome, for them, the habits and forces behind their systematic oppression. All great movements, it is written, go through three stages: ridicule, discussion, adoption. It is the realization of this third stage, adoption, that requires both our passion and our discipline, our hearts and our heads. The fate of animals is in our hands. God grant we are equal to the task.

Difficulties with the Strong Rights Position
Mary Anne Warren

Tom Regan has produced what is perhaps the definitive defense of the view that the basic moral rights of at least some non-human animals are in no way

Mary Anne Warren, "A Critique of Regan's Animal Rights Theory," *Between the Species* 2, no.4 (Fall 1987: 433–41 (edited). Reprinted with permission from Between the Species.

inferior to our own. In *The Case for Animal Rights,* he argues that all normal mammals over a year of age have the same basic moral rights.[1] Non-human mammals have essentially the same right not to be harmed or killed as we do. I shall call this "the strong animal rights position," although it is weaker than the claims made by some animal liberationists in that it ascribes rights to only some sentient animals.

I will argue that Regan's case for the strong animal rights position is unpersuasive and that this position entails consequences which a reasonable person cannot accept. I do not deny that some non-human animals have moral rights; indeed, I would extend the scope of the rights claim to include all sentient animals, that is, all those capable of having experiences, including experiences of pleasure or satisfaction and pain, suffering, or frustration.[2] However, I do not think that the moral rights of most non-human animals are identical in strength to those of persons.[3] The rights of most non-human animals may be overridden in circumstances which would not justify overriding the rights of persons. There are, for instance, compelling realities which sometimes require that we kill animals for reasons which could not justify the killing of persons. I will call this view "the weak animal rights" position, even though it ascribes rights to a wider range of animals than does the strong animal rights position.

I will begin by summarizing Regan's case for the strong animal rights position and noting two problems with it. Next, I will explore some consequences of the strong animal rights position which I think are unacceptable. Finally, I will outline the case for the weak animal rights position.

REGAN'S CASE

Regan's argument moves through three stages. First, he argues that normal, mature mammals are not only sentient but have other mental capacities as well. These include the capacities for emotion, memory, belief, desire, the use of general concepts, intentional action, a sense of the future, and some degree of self-awareness. Creatures with such capacities are said to be subjects-of-a-life. They are not only alive in the biological sense but have a psychological identity over time and an existence which can go better or worse for them. Thus, they can be harmed or benefited. These are plausible claims, and well defended. One of the strongest parts of the book is the rebuttal of philosophers, such as R. G. Frey, who object

to the application of such mentalistic terms to creatures that do not use a human-style language. The second and third stages of the argument are more problematic.

In the second stage, Regan argues that subjects-of-a-life have inherent value. His concept of inherent value grows out of his opposition to utilitarianism. Utilitarian moral theory, he says, treats individuals as "mere receptacles" for morally significant value, in that harm to one individual may be justified by the production of a greater net benefit to other individuals. In opposition to this, he holds that subjects-of-a-life have a value independent of both the value they may place upon their lives or experiences and the value others may place upon them.

Inherent value, Regan argues, does not come in degrees. To hold that some individuals have more inherent value than others is to adopt a "perfectionist" theory, i.e., one which assigns different moral worth to individuals according to how well they are thought to exemplify some virtue(s), such as intelligence or moral autonomy. Perfectionist theories have been used, at least since the time of Aristotle, to rationalize such injustices as slavery and male domination, as well as the unrestrained exploitation of animals. Regan argues that if we reject these injustices, then we must also reject perfectionism and conclude that all subjects-of-a-life have equal inherent value. Moral agents have no more inherent value than moral patients, i.e., subjects-of-a-life who are not morally responsible for their actions.

In the third phase of the argument, Regan uses the thesis of equal inherent value to derive strong moral rights for all subjects-of-a-life. This thesis underlies the Respect Principle, which forbids us to treat beings who have inherent value as mere receptacles, i.e., mere means to the production of the greatest overall good. This principle, in turn, underlies the Harm Principle, which says that we have a direct *prima facie* duty not to harm beings who have inherent value. Together, these principles give rise to moral rights. Rights are defined as valid claims, claims to certain goods and against certain beings, i.e., moral agents. Moral rights generate duties not only to refrain from inflicting harm upon beings with inherent value but also to come to their aid when they are threatened by other moral agents. Rights are not absolute but may be overridden in certain circumstances. Just what these circumstances are we will consider later. But first, let's look at some difficulties in the theory as thus far presented.

THE MYSTERY OF INHERENT VALUE

Inherent value is a key concept in Regan's theory. It is the bridge between the plausible claim that all normal, mature mammals—human or otherwise—are subjects-of-a-life and the more debatable claim that they all have basic moral rights of the same strength. But it is a highly obscure concept, and its obscurity makes it ill-suited to play this crucial role.

Inherent value is defined almost entirely in negative terms. It is not dependent upon the value which either the inherently valuable individual or anyone else may place upon that individual's life or experiences. It is not (necessarily) a function of sentience or any other mental capacity, because, Regan says, some entities which are not sentient (e.g., trees, rivers, or rocks) may, nevertheless, have inherent value (p. 246). It cannot attach to anything other than an individual; species, eco-systems, and the like cannot have inherent value.

These are some of the things which inherent value is not. But what is it? Unfortunately, we are not told. Inherent value appears as a mysterious nonnatural property which we must take on faith. Regan says that it is a *postulate* that subjects-of-a-life have inherent value, a postulate justified by the fact that it avoids certain absurdities which he thinks follow from a purely utilitarian theory (p. 247). But why is the postulate that *subjects-of-a-life* have inherent value? If the inherent value of a being is completely independent of the value that it or anyone else places upon its experiences, then why does the fact that it has certain sorts of experiences constitute evidence that it has inherent value? If the reason is that subjects-of-a-life have an existence which can go better or worse for them, then why isn't the appropriate conclusion that all sentient beings have inherent

value, since they would all seem to meet that condition? Sentient but mentally unsophisticated beings may have a less extensive range of possible satisfactions and frustrations, but why should it follow that they have—or may have—no inherent value at all?

In the absence of a positive account of inherent value, it is also difficult to grasp the connection between being inherently valuable and having moral rights. Intuitively, it seems that value is one thing, and rights are another. It does not seem incoherent to say that some things (e.g., mountains, rivers, redwood trees) are inherently valuable and yet are not the sorts of things which can have moral rights. Nor does it seem incoherent to ascribe inherent value to some things which are not individuals, e.g., plant or animal species, though it may well be incoherent to ascribe moral rights to such things.

In short, the concept of inherent value seems to create at least as many problems as it solves. If inherent value is based on some natural property, then why not try to identify that property and explain its moral significance, without appealing to inherent value? And if it is not based on any natural property, then why should we believe in it? That it may enable us to avoid some of the problems faced by the utilitarian is not a sufficient reason, if it creates other problems which are just as serious.

IS THERE A SHARP LINE?

Perhaps the most serious problems are those that arise when we try to apply the strong animal rights position to animals other than normal, mature mammals. Regan's theory requires us to divide all living things into two categories: those which have the same inherent value and the same basic moral rights that we do, and those which have no inherent value and presumably no moral rights. But wherever we try to draw the line, such a sharp division is implausible.

It would surely be arbitrary to draw such a sharp line between normal, mature mammals and all other living things. Some birds (e.g., crows, magpies, parrots, mynahs) appear to be just as mentally sophisticated as most mammals and thus are equally strong candidates for inclusion under the subject-of-a-life criterion. Regan is not in fact advocating that we draw the line here. His claim is only that normal mature mammals are clear cases, while other cases are less clear. Yet, on his theory, there must be such a sharp line *somewhere*, since there are no degrees of inherent value. But why should we believe that there is a sharp line between creatures that are subjects-of-a-life and creatures that are not? Isn't it more likely that "subjecthood" comes in degrees, that some creatures have only a little self-awareness, and only a little capacity to anticipate the future, while some have a little more, and some a good deal more?

Should we, for instance, regard fish, amphibians, and reptiles as subjects-of-a-life? A simple yes-or-no answer seems inadequate. On the one hand, some of their behavior is difficult to explain without the assumption that they have sensations, beliefs, desires, emotions, and memories; on the other hand, they do not seem to exhibit very much self-awareness or very much conscious anticipation of future events. Do they have enough mental sophistication to count as subjects-of-a-life? Exactly how much is enough?

It is still more unclear what we should say about insects, spiders, octopi, and other invertebrate animals which have brains and sensory organs but whose minds (if they have minds) are even more alien to us than those of fish or reptiles. Such creatures are probably sentient. Some people doubt that they can feel pain, since they lack certain neurological structures which are crucial to the processing of pain impulses in vertebrate animals. But this argument is inconclusive, since their nervous systems might process pain in ways different from ours. When injured, they sometimes act as if they are in pain. On evolutionary grounds, it seems unlikely that highly mobile creatures with complex sensory systems would not have developed a capacity for pain (and pleasure), since such a capacity has obvious survival value. It must, however, be admitted that we do not *know* whether spiders can feel pain (or something very like it), let alone whether they have emotions, memories, beliefs, desires, self-awareness, or a sense of the future.

Even more mysterious are the mental capacities (if any) of mobile microfauna. The brisk and efficient way that paramecia move about in their incessant search for food *might* indicate some kind of sentience, in spite of their lack of eyes, ears, brains, and other organs associated with sentience in more complex organisms. It is conceivable—though not very probable—that they, too, are subjects-of-a-life.

The existence of a few unclear cases need not pose a serious problem for a moral theory, but in this case, the unclear cases constitute most of those with which an adequate theory of animal rights would need to deal. The subject-of-a-life criterion can provide us with little or no moral guidance in our interactions with the vast majority of animals. That might be acceptable if it could be supplemented with additional principles which would provide such guidance. However, the radical dualism of the theory precludes supplementing it in this way. We are forced to say that either a spider has the same right to life as you and I do, or it has no right to life whatever—and that only the gods know which of these alternatives is true.

Regan's suggestion for dealing with such unclear cases is to apply the "benefit of the doubt" principle. That is, when dealing with beings that may or may not be subjects-of-a-life, we should act as if they are. But if we try to apply this principle to the entire range of doubtful cases, we will find ourselves with moral obligations which we cannot possibly fulfill. In many climates, it is virtually impossible to live without swatting mosquitoes and exterminating cockroaches, and not all of us can afford to hire someone to sweep the path before we walk, in order to make sure that we do not step on ants. Thus, we are still faced with the daunting task of drawing a sharp line somewhere on the continuum of life forms—this time, a line demarcating the limits of the benefit of the doubt principle.

The weak animal rights theory provides a more plausible way of dealing with this range of cases, in that it allows the rights of animals of different kinds to vary in strength. . . .

WHY ARE ANIMAL RIGHTS WEAKER THAN HUMAN RIGHTS?

How can we justify regarding the rights of persons as generally stronger than those of sentient beings which are not persons? There are a plethora of bad justifications, based on religious premises or false or unprovable claims about the differences between human and non-human nature. But there is one difference which has a clear moral relevance: people are at least sometimes capable of being moved to action or inaction by the force of reasoned argument. Rationality rests upon other mental capacities, notably those which Regan cites as criteria for being a subject-of-a-life. We share these capacities with many other animals. But it is not just because we are subjects-of-a-life that we are both able and morally compelled to recognize one another as beings with equal basic moral rights. It is also because we are able to "listen to reason" in order to settle our conflicts and cooperate in shared projects. This capacity, unlike the others, may require something like a human language.

Why is rationality morally relevant? It does not make us "better" than other animals or more "perfect." It does not even automatically make us more intelligent. (Bad reasoning reduces our effective intelligence rather than increasing it.) But it is morally relevant insofar as it provides greater possibilities for cooperation and for the nonviolent resolution of problems. It also makes us more dangerous than non-rational beings can ever be. Because we are potentially more dangerous and less predictable than wolves, we need an articulated system of morality to regulate our conduct. Any human morality, to be workable in the long run, must recognize the equal moral status of all persons, whether through the postulate of equal basic moral rights or in some other way. The recognition of the moral equality of other persons is the price we must each pay for their recognition of our moral equality. Without this mutual recognition of moral equality, human society can exist only in a state of chronic and bitter conflict. The war between the sexes will persist so long as there is sexism and male domination; racial conflict will never be eliminated so long as there are racist laws and practices. But to the extent that we achieve a mutual recognition of equality, we can hope to live together, perhaps as peacefully as wolves, achieving (in part) through explicit moral principles what they do not seem to need explicit moral principles to achieve.

Why not extend this recognition of moral equality to other creatures, even though they cannot do the same for us? The answer is that we cannot. Because we cannot reason with most non-human animals, we cannot always solve the problems which they may cause without harming them—although we are always obligated to try. We cannot negotiate a treaty with the feral cats and foxes, requiring them to stop preying on endangered native species in return for suitable concessions on our part.

if rats invade our houses . . . we cannot reason with them, hoping to persuade them of the injustice they do us. We can only attempt to get rid of them.[4]

Aristotle was not wrong in claiming that the capacity to alter one's behavior on the basis of reasoned argument is relevant to the full moral status which he accorded to free men. Of course, he was wrong in his other premise, that women and slaves by their nature cannot reason well enough to function as autonomous moral agents. Had that premise been true, so would his conclusion that women and slaves are not quite the moral equals of free men. In the case of most non-human animals, the corresponding premise is true. If, on the other hand, there are animals with whom we can (learn to) reason, then we are obligated to do this and to regard them as our moral equals.

Thus, to distinguish between the rights of persons and those of most other animals on the grounds that only people can alter their behavior on the basis of reasoned argument does not commit us to a perfectionist theory of the sort Aristotle endorsed. There is no excuse for refusing to recognize the moral equality of some people on the grounds that we don't regard them as quite as rational as we are, since it is perfectly clear that most people can reason well enough to determine how to act so as to respect the basic rights of others (if they choose to), and that is enough for moral equality.

But what about people who are clearly not rational? It is often argued that sophisticated mental capacities such as rationality cannot be essential for the possession of equal basic moral rights, since nearly everyone agrees that human infants and mentally incompetent persons have such rights, even though they may lack those sophisticated mental capacities. But this argument is inconclusive, because there are powerful practical and emotional reasons for protecting non-rational human beings, reasons which are absent in the case of most non-human animals. Infancy and mental incompetence are human conditions which all of us either have experienced or are likely to experience at some time. We also protect babies and mentally incompetent people because we care for them. We don't normally care for animals in the same way, and when we do—e.g., in the case of much-loved pets—we may regard them as having special rights by virtue of their relationship to us. We protect them not only for their sake but also for our own, lest we be hurt by harm done to them. Regan holds that such "side-effects" are irrelevant to moral rights, and perhaps they are. But in ordinary usage, there is no sharp line between moral rights and those moral protections which are not rights. The extension of strong moral protections to infants and the mentally impaired in no way proves that non-human animals have the same basic moral rights as people.

WHY SPEAK OF "ANIMAL RIGHTS" AT ALL?

If, as I have argued, reality precludes our treating all animals as our moral equals, then why should we still ascribe rights to them? Everyone agrees that animals are entitled to some protection against human abuse, but why speak of animal *rights* if we are not prepared to accept most animals as our moral equals? The weak animal rights position may seem an unstable compromise between the bold claim that animals have the same basic moral rights that we do and the more common view that animals have no rights at all.

It is probably impossible to either prove or disprove the thesis that animals have moral rights by producing an analysis of the concept of a moral right and checking to see if some or all animals satisfy the conditions for having rights. The concept of a moral right is complex, and it is not clear which of its strands are essential. Paradigm rights holders ,i.e., mature and mentally competent persons, are *both* rational and morally autonomous beings and sentient subjects-of-a-life. Opponents of animal rights claim that rationality and moral autonomy are essential for the possession of rights, while defenders of animal rights claim that they are not. The ordinary concept of a moral right is probably not precise enough to enable us to determine who is right on purely definitional grounds.

If logical analysis will not answer the question of whether animals have moral rights, practical considerations may, nevertheless, incline us to say that they do. The most plausible alternative to the view that animals have moral rights is that, while they do not have *rights,* we are, nevertheless, obligated not to be cruel to them. Regan argues persuasively that the injunction to avoid being cruel to animals is inadequate to express our obligations towards animals, because it focuses on the mental states of those who cause animal suffering, rather than on the harm done to the animals themselves (p. 158). Cruelty is inflicting pain or suffering and either taking pleasure in that pain or suffering or being more or less indifferent to it. Thus, to express the demand for the decent treatment of animals in terms of the rejection of cruelty is to invite the too easy response that those who subject animals to suffering are not being cruel because they regret the suffering they cause but sincerely believe that what they do is justified. The injunction to avoid cruelty is also inadequate in that it does not preclude the killing of animals—for any reason, however trivial—so long as it is done relatively painlessly.

The inadequacy of the anti-cruelty view provides one practical reason for speaking of animal rights. Another practical reason is that this is an age in which nearly all significant moral claims tend to be expressed in terms of rights. Thus, the denial that animals have rights, however carefully qualified, is likely to be taken to mean that we may do whatever we like to them, provided that we do not violate any human rights. In such a context, speaking of the rights of animals may be the only way to persuade many people to take seriously protests against the abuse of animals.

Why not extend this line of argument and speak of the rights of trees, mountains, oceans, or anything else which we may wish to see protected from destruction? Some environmentalists have not hesitated to speak in this way, and, given the importance of protecting such elements of the natural world, they cannot be blamed for using this rhetorical device. But, I would argue that moral rights can meaningfully be ascribed only to entities which have some capacity for sentience. This is because moral rights are protections designed to protect rights holders from harms or to provide them with benefits which matter *to them*. Only beings capable of sentience can be harmed or benefited in ways which matter to them, for only such beings can like or dislike what happened to them or prefer some conditions to others. Thus, sentient animals, unlike mountains, rivers, or species, are at least logically possible candidates for moral rights. This fact, together with the need to end current abuses of animals—e.g., in scientific research . . . —provides a plausible case for speaking of animal rights.

CONCLUSION

I have argued that Regan's case for ascribing strong moral rights to all normal, mature mammals is unpersuasive because (1) it rests upon the obscure concept of inherent value, which is defined only in negative terms, and (2) it seems to preclude any plausible

answer to questions about the moral status of the vast majority of sentient animals. . . .

The weak animal rights theory asserts that (1) any creature whose natural mode of life includes the pursuit of certain satisfactions has the right not to be forced to exist without the opportunity to pursue those satisfactions; (2) that any creature which is capable of pain, suffering, or frustration has the right that such experiences not be deliberately inflicted upon it without some compelling reason; and (3) that no sentient being should be killed without good reason. However, moral rights are not an all-or-nothing affair. The strength of the reasons required to override the rights of a non-human organism varies, depending upon—among other things—the probability that it is sentient and (if it is clearly sentient) its probable degree of mental sophistication.

NOTES

1. Tom Regan, *The Case for Animal Rights* (Berkeley: University of California Press, 1983). All page references are to this edition.

2. The capacity for sentience, like all of the mental capacities mentioned in what follows, is a disposition. Dispositions do not disappear whenever they are not currently manifested. Thus, sleeping or temporarily unconscious persons or nonhuman animals are still sentient in the relevant sense (i.e., still capable of sentience), so long as they still have the neurological mechanisms necessary for the occurrence of experiences.

3. It is possible, perhaps probable, that some non-human animals—such as cetaceans and anthropoid apes—should be regarded as persons. If so, then the weak animal rights position holds that these animals have the same basic moral rights as human persons.

4. Bonnie Steinbock, "Speciesism and the Idea of Equality," *Philosophy* 53 (1978): 253.

Drawing Lines

JAMES RACHELS

When people are skeptical of the idea that we have moral responsibilities with respect to animals or that we should have laws protecting them, they will ask. "But where do we draw the line?" They may have two things in mind: (1) Where do we draw the line with respect to the *kinds of animals* to whom we have duties, or on whom we should confer legal protection? Do we have duties to fish? Snails? Insects? Viruses? (2) Where do we draw the line with respect to the *kinds of duties* we should acknowledge? Do we have a duty not to harm them? To protect them from harm? To feed them? I will begin by discussing the first question. But as we shall see, the two are related. If we understand the right way to answer one, we will know how to answer the other.

Here is an example of line drawing in the law. The U.S. Animal Welfare Act, enacted in 1966 and amended several times since then, instructs the secretary of agriculture to take steps to protect animals used in various ways, including research. Originally, the act defined *animal* as follows:

The term "animal" means any live or dead dog, cat, monkey (nonhuman primate mammal), guinea pig, hamster, rabbit, or such other warm-blooded animal, as the Secretary may determine is being used, or is intended for use, for research, testing, experimentation, or exhibition purposes or as a pet; but such term excludes horses not used for research purposes and other farm animals, such as, but not limited to livestock or poultry, used or intended for use as food or fiber, or livestock or poultry used or intended for improving animal nutrition, breeding, management or production efficiency, or for improving the quality of food or fiber. With respect to a dog the term means all dogs including those used for hunting, security, or breeding purposes. (Animal Welfare Act as Amended [7 U.S.C. 2132(g)])

James Rachels, "Drawing Lines," in *Animal Rights* (New York: Oxford University Press, 2004), 162–74 (edited). Copyright © 2004 Oxford University Press. Reprinted with permission.

Of course this is not intended as a proper definition of *animal,* but only a specification of which animals are included within the scope of the act.

Mice, rats, and birds are not specifically mentioned, but they seem to be included because they are "warm-blooded animals." However, soon after the act was passed, the secretary of agriculture issued a regulation that excluded them from its scope. There the matter stood until the 1990s, when the Humane Society of the United States and some other pro-animal groups challenged the regulation in court, arguing that there is no legal basis for exempting these species. The court agreed, and the Department of Agriculture began to draft new regulations which would have brought the mice, rats, and birds back under the act's somewhat feeble protections. At this point, Senator Jesse Helms of North Carolina stepped in and proposed an amendment to the act that would make the new regulations unnecessary. He proposed to change the definition of *animal* so that "birds, rats of the genus Rattus, and mice of the genus Mus" would be specifically excluded.[1] The Helms amendment was adopted without debate and was signed into law by President George W. Bush in May 2002.

Why shouldn't mice, rats, and birds have the same status as guinea pigs, hamsters, and rabbits? On what grounds could such distinctions be made? For the American Association of Universities, and others who supported Senator Helms's proposal, the issue appears to have been entirely practical. More than 90 percent of laboratory animals are mice, rats, or birds, so if they don't count, there will be enormously less paperwork needed to comply with federal regulations. On the Senate floor, Mr. Helms also mentioned the "paperwork burden." Of course there is nothing wrong with modifying a policy for the sake of efficiency, especially if the administrative burden would be great and there is no important matter of principle involved.

The problem is that, for those on the other side, there are important matters of principle involved.

The principles are ethical. Central among them is the idea that the interests of animals are important for their own sakes, and that it is indecent of humans not to respect those interests. It is problematic whether ethical principles should be enforced by law, especially when they are not shared by everyone, and I will say nothing about that. But I will assume that at least part of the motivation behind the Animal Welfare Act is a concern for the animals' own interests. This is consistent with the language of the act, which lists as its first purpose "to insure that animals intended for use in research facilities or for exhibition purposes or for use as pets are provided humane care and treatment" (7 U.S.C. 2131[1]).

The fact that the Animal Welfare Act does not treat all animals as equals will not offend most people. Most people—and by this I mean people who are at least moderately thoughtful about such matters—think of some animals as more worthy of protection than others. They seem to think in terms of a hierarchy in which the animal's rank depends, more or less, on its perceived degree of similarity to humans. Thus the mistreatment of primates is seen as a serious matter, and dogs and cats also rate high, but snakes and fish count for little. The act's original definition of *animal* reflects this: "Cold-blooded" animals were never included.

THEORIES OF MORAL STANDING

Theories of moral standing try to answer the question: To whom do we have *direct* duties? A *direct duty* is a duty to an individual as contrasted with a duty that merely involves the individual. If I promise you that I will feed your cat while you are away, the duty created by the promise is not a duty to your cat, even though it involves the cat; it is a duty to you. No one doubts that there can be duties involving animals. The question is whether we have duties *to* them, and if so, why.

The concept of moral standing was introduced by philosophers in the 1970s to deal with a number of issues that had arisen, such as the treatment of animals, but also abortion, euthanasia, and the environment. Philosophers thought they could make progress in these areas by establishing the moral standing of animals, fetuses, comatose persons, trees, and so on. The notion of "standing" was, of course, borrowed from the law. Just as legal standing means that you have the right to bring your claims before a court, moral standing means that, from a moral point of view, you have claims that must be heard—that your interests constitute morally good reasons why you may or may not, be treated in this or that way. So a key question became: What qualifies one for moral standing? Here is a quick summary of four main kinds of theories that have been proposed:

1. The first thought that occurred to many philosophers was that simply being human confers moral standing. This had the advantage of being non-discriminatory, at least as far as humans were concerned. It echoed the rhetoric of the civil rights movement, which proclaimed that people of all races have equal rights "simply in virtue of being human," with no other qualification necessary. But only a little reflection was needed to see that this can't be taken literally. Even if it were true that all and only humans have full moral standing, we should be able to say *what it is* about being human that gives us this special status. Simply being human cannot be what does the job.

2. A more substantial type of theory connects moral standing with such qualities as self-consciousness, autonomy, and rationality. Humans, it was said, have full moral standing because they have such characteristics. These theories have a long history from Aristotle, who believed that human rationality gives us a supremely important place in the scheme of things, to Kant, who held that only self-conscious beings can be direct beneficiaries of obligations. Recently Kantians such as Christine Korsgaard have argued that exercising one's capacity for rational choice necessarily involves acknowledging the special moral status of human beings.

3. Still another idea is that *having moral standing* and *being a moral agent* go together—the same char-

acteristics that make for one make for the other. Thus, you have moral standing if you have the capacity for moral judgment and action. This type of theory is especially attractive to contractarians, who see moral obligations as arising from agreements between people, who are then expected to keep their bargains. John Rawls asks to whom the duties of justice are owed, and he replies: "The natural answer seems to be that it is precisely the moral persons who are entitled to equal justice. . . . they are capable of having (and are assumed to acquire) a sense of justice, a normally effective desire to apply and to act upon the principles of justice, at least to a certain minimum degree. . . . Those who can give justice are owed justice."[2]

However, there is a problem with theories that emphasize qualities like self-consciousness, autonomy, and moral agency: They set the bar too high. Although the proponents of these theories emphasize that moral standing is not limited by definition to normal adult humans—it is at least possible for some nonhuman animals (as well as hypothetical extraterrestrials) to be self-conscious, autonomous persons, or to be moral agents—it turns out that in fact only normal adult humans uncontroversially satisfy such demand criteria. This means, for one thing, that these theories make unwelcome discriminations among human beings. They leave us with a problem about what to say about babies and mentally handicapped people, who may not be self-conscious, autonomous moral agents. Moreover, animals, as is frequently noted, can feel pain, even if they do not possess the fancier qualities. So it seems wrong to torture them, and it seems wrong because of what is being done to them.

4. For this reason, many philosophers, especially utilitarians, were attracted to a more modest theory which says that, to have moral standing, it is only necessary that one be able to feel pain. Thus Mark Bernstein writes: "The realm of the morally considerable is constituted by those individuals with the capacity for modifiable, hedonic conscious experience. If we use 'phenomenology' or 'sentience' as abbreviations for this capacity, we can say that experientialism dictates that all and only those with moral standing are phenomenological or sentient individuals."[3]

Finally, we may note that, in working their way toward a conception of moral standing, many writers take a detour through the concept of personhood. They take "What qualifies one for moral standing?" and "What is a person?" to be essentially the same question. I believe that Joseph Fletcher was the first to produce a list of "conditions for personhood" with an eye to addressing ethical issues,[4] but others soon followed. Mary Anne Warren's list of person-making qualities in her much-anthologized 1973 paper on abortion is perhaps the most famous.[5] Warren produced an account of what it means to be a person—where *person* is not just a biological category but denotes individuals with the psychological and "personal" dimensions of human beings—in order to argue that, because fetuses lack the characteristics of persons, they do not have the full moral rights of persons. This became a familiar strategy. In 1988 some of the literature that had been generated was gathered into an anthology called *What Is a Person?* and the editor wrote:

The problems of personhood . . . are central to issues in ethics ranging from the treatment or termination of infants with birth defects to the question whether there can be rational suicide. But before questions on such issues as the morality of abortion, genetic engineering, infanticide, and so on, can be settled, the problems of personhood must be clarified and analyzed. . . . When qualities/attributes must a being have to be considered a person? Why are those qualities, and not others, significant?[6]

Connecting moral standing with personhood provides an intuitively plausible way of identifying the characteristics that are important for moral standing. We are confident that persons have moral standing, and so, if certain qualities are central to personhood, it is reasonable to conjecture that those qualities are also central to moral standing. If those qualities happen to be the grand, impressive features of human nature that have always led humans to regard themselves as special, so much the better. In this way the appeal to such qualities as rationality, autonomy, self-consciousness, and moral agency were made to seem less arbitrary.

CHARACTERISTICS AND TYPES OF TREATMENT

The theories I have mentioned will be familiar to anyone who is acquainted with the literature produced by moral philosophers since the 1970s. I have summarized these theories, without going in any detail about them, because I want to make a general point about their structure. Despite differences in detail, the theories have this in common: They all assume that the answer to the question of how an individual may be treated depends on whether the individual qualifies for a general sort of status, which in turn depends on whether the individual possesses a few general characteristics. But no answers of this form can be correct. In what follows, I will explain why this is so and why it is important.

Each of the theories offers an account of the relation between (i) how individuals may be treated and (ii) facts about them—facts about their capacities, abilities, and other characteristics, such as whether they are rational, self-conscious, or sentient. But what, exactly, is the relation between the facts about an individual and how the individual may be treated? Let us consider how this works, first for normal adult humans, where our intuitions are firmest.

Facts about people often figure into the reasons why they may or may not be treated in this or that way. Adam may be ejected from the choir because he can't sing. Berry may be given Prozac because she is depressed. Charles may be congratulated because he has just gotten engaged. Doris may be promoted because she is a hard worker. Notice, however that a fact that justifies one type of treatment may not justify a different type of treatment: Unless something unusual is going on, we could not justify giving Betty Prozac on the grounds that she can't sing or throwing Adam out of the choir because he has become engaged.

The same is true of the more impressive characteristics that are mentioned in the theories of moral standing. Autonomy and self-consciousness are not ethical superqualities that entitle the bearer to every possible kind of favorable treatment. Like musical ability and betrothal, they are relevant to some types of treatment but not to others.

Autonomy

Humans are rational, autonomous agents who can guide their own conduct according to their desires and their conceptions of how they ought to live. Does this fact make a difference in how they may be treated? Of course it does. Suppose someone wants to live her life in a way that involves risks we think are foolish. We may try to change her mind; we may point out the risks and argue that they are not worth it. But may we compel her to follow our advice? We may not, for she is, after all, a rational, autonomous agent.

It is different for someone who is not fully rational—a small child, for example. Then we may prevent her from harming herself. The fact that the child is not yet a fully rational agent justifies us in treating her differently than we would treat someone who is a fully rational agent.

Once we understand why autonomy makes a difference in how someone may be treated, in the cases in which it does make a difference, it becomes clear that possession of this quality is not relevant in other sorts of cases. Suppose the treatment at issue is not paternalistic interference, but torture: Why would it be wrong to poke you with a stick? The answer is not that you are autonomous; the answer is that it would cause you pain.

Self-Consciousness

To be self-conscious is to be able to make oneself the object of one's thoughts, to have beliefs about oneself, and to be able to reflect on one's own character and conduct. As the term is used by most philosophers, self-consciousness also includes the capacity for conceiving of oneself as extended through time—for understanding that one has a past and a future.

There are, therefore, a number of goods that self-consciousness makes possible: self-confidence, hope for the future, satisfaction with one's life, the belief that you are someone of value, and the knowledge that you are loved and appreciated by other people. Without self-consciousness, there could be no sense of pride or self-worth. Considered in this light, it is no wonder that some philosophers have singled out self-consciousness as a supremely important human quality.

At the same time, a person who has this capacity is thereby vulnerable to a special range of harms. Because you are capable of reflecting on your own conduct and your own place in the world, you may feel embarrassed, humiliated, guilty, and worthless. Because you can think about your own future, you may despair and lose hope. Your capacity for self-referential beliefs and attitudes makes it possible for you to feel that your life and activities have no meaning, and you can believe, rightly or wrongly, that other people have no regard for you.

This being so, there are ways of treating people that are objectionable on grounds that involve their capacity for self-consciousness. I should not do things that would embarrass or humiliate you. I should not unjustly curse you or hold you in contempt. I should not question or criticize you in ways that would cause you debilitating self-doubt or self-loathing. I should not belittle you in ways that would injure your self-respect. I should not treat you in such a way as to take away your hope for the future.

Moral Agency

Humans have the capacity for moral judgment and action, and this, it is often said, gives them an especially noble nature that sets them apart from other animals. But, self-congratulation aside, how is the possession of this capacity relevant to how an individual may be treated? There are three ways of treating people that are appropriate if they are moral agents.

First, and most obviously, moral agents may merit praise or blame for what they do. Beings who lack a sense of right and wrong are not eligible for such responses.

Second, the fact that someone has moral capacities may be important when we need to influence their conduct. When we are dealing with moral agents, we can reason with them—we can influence their behavior by appealing to their sense of right. This may be better than bribes, threats, or other cajolery not only in that it respects their autonomy, but because such influence might be more stable and longer lasting. Demands for social justice, for example, are more effective in the long run if they address people's consciences than if they are merely exercises of power.

Third, moral agency includes the capacity for cooperating with others, and so moral agents are individuals with whom we can make agreements. This is the critical capacity for rational-choice contractarians, who believe that moral obligations exist only as a result of such agreements. But general views aside, it is important in everyday life to discern whom one can trust and with whom one can profitably cooperate. So this is another respect in which someone's being a moral agent makes a difference in our dealings with them.

The Ability to Feel Pain

The ability to feel pain is perhaps the most obviously relevant characteristic anyone possesses. The fact that it would cause you pain is a complete and sufficient reason why I should not jab you with a stick. This reason does not need to be supplemented or reinforced by considerations having to do with your dignity as a rational being, your autonomy, or anything like that. It is enough that being jabbed hurts.

Of course, your interests as an autonomous agent may be affected by debilitating pain. Chronic pain may prevent you from leading the kind of life you want to lead, and even a short experience of intense pain may have lasting psychological effects. But this only means that, in the case of autonomous beings, there is an additional reason why torture is wrong. The additional reason does not replace the original one, nor is one a mere shorthand for the other.

But regardless of how important the ability to feel pain may be, when other types of treatment are involved it may be irrelevant: What entitles you to remain in the choir is not the same as to what makes it objectionable to poke you with the stick.

We may draw the following conclusions from all this: There is no characteristic, or reasonably small set of characteristics, that sets some creatures apart from others as meriting respectful treatment. That is the wrong way to think about the relation between an individual's characteristics and how he or she may be treated. Instead we have an array of characteristics and an array of treatments, with each characteristic relevant to justifying some types of treatment but not others. If an individual possesses a particular characteristic (such as the ability to feel pain), then we may have a duty to treat it in a certain way (not to torture it), even if that same individual does not possess other characteristics (such as autonomy) that would mandate other sorts of treatment (refraining from coercion).

We could spin these observations into a theory of moral standing that would compete with the other theories. Our theory would start like this: There is no such thing as moral standing *simpliciter*. Rather, moral standing is always moral standing with respect to some particular mode of treatment. A sentient being has moral standing with respect to not being tortured. A self-conscious being has moral standing with respect to not being humiliated. An autonomous being has moral standing with respect to not being coerced. And so on. If asked, toward whom is it appropriate to direct fundamental moral consideration? we could reply: It is appropriate to direct moral consideration toward any individual who has any of the indefinitely long list of characteristics that constitute morally good reasons why he or she should or should not be treated in any of the various ways in which individuals may be treated.

You may think this isn't a very appealing theory. It is tedious: it lacks the crispness of the other theories; it doesn't yield quick and easy answers to practical questions; and worse, it isn't exciting. But it is the truth about moral standing. (I believe it was Bertrand Russell who once said it wasn't his fault if the truth wasn't exciting.)

It would do no harm, however, and it might be helpful for clarity's sake, to drop the notion of "standing" altogether and replace it with a simpler conception. We could just say that the fact that doing so-and-so would cause pain to someone (to any individual) is a reason not to do it. The fact that doing so-and-so would humiliate someone (any individual) is a reason not to do it. And so on. Sentience and self-consciousness fit into the picture like this: someone's sentience and someone's self-consciousness are facts about them that explain why they are susceptible to the evils of pain and humiliation.

We would then see our subject as part of the theory of reasons for action. We would distinguish three elements: what is done to the individual; the reason for doing it or not doing it, which connects the action to some benefit or harm to the individual; and the pertinent facts about the individual that help to explain why he or she is susceptible to that particular benefit or harm:

Action: Poking you with a sharp stick
Reason for not doing that: It would cause you pain.
Facts about you that explain why you are capable of feeling pain: You have conscious experiences and a nervous system of a certain kind: You are sentient.

Action: Telling your husband's friends that he is impotent.
Reason for not doing that: It would humiliate him.
Facts about him that explain why he is capable of being humiliated: He has attitudes and beliefs about himself and about how others regard him: He is self-conscious.

So, part of our theory of reasons for action would go like this: We always have reason not to do harm. If treating an individual in a certain way harms him or her, that is a reason not to do it. The fact that he or she is autonomous or self-conscious, or sentient simply helps to explain why he or she is susceptible to particular kinds of harms.

KINDS OF ANIMALS AND THE ANIMAL WELFARE ACT

How will a morally decent human treat nonhuman animals? The answer will depend, in part, on what we think nonhumans are like, and most of us are willing to attribute a fairly broad range of morally important characteristics to them. Ever since Darwin taught us to see ourselves as kin to the other animals, we have increasingly come to think of them as like us in morally significant ways. We believe that monkeys have cognitive and social abilities similar to our own, that all sorts of animals are self-conscious, and that dogs have qualities such as courage and loyalty. And even if the "lower animals" do not have these impressive qualities, we think it is undeniable that they can at least feel pain.

There are, of course, those who are skeptical about this consensus. Daniel Dennett chides animal rights advocates for assuming too much and for trusting their intuitions too easily. Even the consciousness of animals, he says, can be doubted:

Cog, a delightfully humanoid robot being built at MIT, has eyes, hands, and arms that move the way yours do—swiftly, relaxedly, compliantly. Even those of us working on the project, knowing full well that we haven't even begun to program the high level processes that might arguably endow Cog with consciousness, get an almost overwhelming sense of being in the presence of another conscious observer when Cog's eyes still quite blindly and stupidly follow one's hand gestures. Once again, I plead for symmetry: when you acknowledge the power of such elegant, lifelike motions to charm you into an illusion, note that it ought to be an open question, still, whether you are also being charmed by your beloved dog or cat, or the noble elephant. Feelings are too easy to provoke for them to count for much here.[7]

It is a stretch to doubt the consciousness of "your beloved dog or cat," and there is no evidence that would compel such a major change in how we think of those animals. Indeed, Dennett does not say there is any such evidence: He only pleads for us not to preclude the possibility. The plea for open-mindedness is hard to fault. Nonetheless, I believe the most reasonable approach, when formulating ethical and social policies, is to assume that the prevailing consensus is correct except where we have good evidence to the contrary.

On the fundamental question of whether animals can feel pain, scientific investigations tend to confirm the commonly held belief that most animals, especially the "higher" animals, do feel pain. The mechanisms that enable us to feel pain are not fully understood, but we do know a good bit about them. In humans, nocioceptors—neurons specialized for sensing noxious stimuli—are connected to a central nervous system, and the resulting signals are processed in the brain. Until recently it was believed that the brain's work was divided into two distinct parts: a sensory system operating in the somatosensory cortex, resulting in our conscious experiences of pain, and an affective-motivational system associated with the frontal lobes, responsible for our behavioral reactions. Now, however, this picture has been called into question, and it may be that the best we can say is that the brain's system for processing the information from the nocioceptors seems to be spread over multiple regions. At any rate, the human nociceptive system also includes endogenous opioids, or endorphins, which provide the brain with its natural "pain-killing" ability.

The question of which other animals feel pain is a real and important issue, not to be settled by appeals to "common sense," as Dennett insists. Only a complete scientific understanding of pain, which we do not yet have, could tell us all that we need to know. In the meantime, however, we do have a rough idea of what to look for. If we want to know whether it is reasonable to believe that a particular kind of animal is capable of feeling pain, we may ask: Are there nocioceptors present? Are they connected to a central nervous system? What happens in that nervous system to the signals from the nocioceptors? And are there endogenous opiods? In our present state of understanding, this sort of information, together with the obvious behavioral signs of distress, is the best evidence we can have that an animal is capable of feeling pain.

It is harder to devise experimental tests for the presence of other, more sophisticated capacities. Yet there is some evidence even for such capacities as self-consciousness. One idea is to see whether animals can recognize themselves in mirrors (after it has been established that they know how mirrors work and can recognize other objects in mirrors). In 1970, the psychologist Gordon Gallup devised a clever experiment to test this: While chimpanzees were unconscious, he placed a red mark on one of their eyebrows and ears. Then, he showed each chimp a full-length mirror. The chimps would immediately rub the marked spots and examine their fingers. We are apt to agree with Gallup that this provides strong evidence that the chimps are self-aware. However, Gallup's experiment was subsequently tried on other species, with very different results. Surprisingly, gorillas and monkeys failed the test. But more recently, using a modified form of the Gallup test, Marc Hauser has shown that cotton-top tamarins do show mirror self-recognition.[8]

It is clear, then, that we should proceed cautiously. But bearing all this in mind, let us return to our question: How will a morally decent human treat nonhuman animals? No general answer is possible, because animals are different from one another—a chimpanzee has little in common with a mockingbird. So how, for example, may a chimpanzee be treated? Once again, it depends on what sort of treatment we have in mind. There are lots of ways of treating chimps, just as there are lots of ways of treating people. This means that, if we seriously want to know how chimps may be treated, we will have to consider a long list of treatments and relevant characteristics.

Is there anything about a chimp that makes it objectionable to poke it with a stick? Yes, the chimp can feel pain. Is there anything about a chimp that makes it objectionable to confine it to a barren cage? Yes, chimps are active, intelligent creatures that cannot thrive without a stimulating environment. Is there anything about a female chimp that makes it objectionable to separate her from her babies? Yes, chimpanzee mothers and babies are emotionally bonded in much the same way as are human mothers and babies.

Is there anything about a chimp that makes it objectionable to exclude them from college classrooms? No, they lack the intellectual capacities necessary to participate in college classes. Is there anything about a chimp that makes it objectionable to exclude them from the choir? No, they can't sing.

Is there anything about a chimp that makes it impermissible to forcibly vaccinate it against a disease? No, the chimp lacks the cognitive capacities that would enable it to choose for itself in the relevant sense.

Obviously, we could continue in this way indefinitely. The point, though, is that there is no general answer to the question of how chimps may be treated. There are only the various ways of treating them and the various considerations that count for and against those treatments. Among other things, this means that the question "Where do we draw the line?" is misguided. As we noted at the outset, the question may be taken in two ways: (1) Where do we draw the line with respect to the kinds of animals to whom we have duties? and (2) Where do we draw the line with respect to which duties we have? But in neither instance is there one place to draw the line. There is only an indefinitely long series of lines: Where causing pain is concerned, we draw the line between individuals who can feel pain and individuals who cannot; where separating mothers and babies is concerned, we draw the line between mothers who are bonded with their babies (and babies who need their mothers), and those who are not; and so on.

For purposes of public policy, however, we may need to draw rough lines, and we can do this by attending to the characteristics that are typical of the members of various species and the kinds of treatment that they are likely to receive in relevant contexts. For example, if the relevant context is laboratory research, in which the animals are liable to be separated from their own kind, kept for long periods in sterile cages, and caused a lot of pain, and we are seeking to ensure "humane care and treatment," then it is reasonable to draw the line between species whose members are social, intelligent, and can feel pain, and species whose members lack those qualities.

The Animal Welfare Act's list of included and excluded species is a jerry-rigged affair which looks like the result of compromise and political bargaining. But in some respects it isn't bad. When the context is "research, testing, [and] experimentation," the secretary of agriculture is authorized to ensure "humane care and treatment" for "dog[s], cat[s], monkey[s] (nonhuman primate mammal[s]), guinea pig[s], hamster[s], rabbit[s], or such other warm-blooded animal[s]." The six kinds of animals mentioned by name appear to be no more than examples of the kinds intended; the language of the act includes all warm-blooded animals, *such as* guinea pigs, hamsters, or rabbits. This category seems to capture the social, intelligent, and sensitive animals about whom we should be concerned when they are taken into the laboratory. At the same time, the act's protections do not extend to snakes, snails, or fish, where the presence of the relevant qualities seems less certain. And what of the Helms amendment? In this context, if a mouse or a rat isn't relevantly similar to a guinea pig or a hamster, what is? The Helms amendment is contrary not only to good sense but to the intent of the original legislation. Its adoption was a lamentable step backward.

NOTES

1. The amendment replaced the words "excludes horses not used for research purposes" with "excludes birds, rats of the genus Rattus, and mice of the genus Mus bred for use in research, horses not used for research purposes."

2. John Rawls, *A Theory of Justice* (Cambridge, MA: Harvard University Press, 1971), 505, 510.

3. Mark Bernstein, *On Moral Considerability: An Essay on Who Morally Matters* (New York: Oxford University Press, 1998), 24.

4. Joseph Fletcher, "Indicators of Humanhood: A Tentative Profile of Man," *Hastings Center Report* 2 (November 1972): 1–4.

5. Mary Anne Warren, "On the Moral and Legal Status of Abortion," *Monist* 57 (1973): 43–61. Warren's more recent views are presented in her book *Moral Status: Obligations to Persons and Other Living Things* (Oxford: Clarendon, 1997).

6. Michael F. Goodman, ed., *What Is a Person?* (Clifton, NJ: Humana, 1988), vii.

7. Daniel Dennett, *Brainchildren* (Cambridge, MA: Bradford, 1998), 340.

8. Marc Hauser, *Wild Minds: What Animals Really Think* (New York: Henry Holt, 2000), 100–109.

Our Duties to Animals

Immanuel Kant

Baumgarten speaks of duties towards beings which are beneath us and beings which are above us. But so far as animals are concerned, we have no direct duties. Animals are not self-conscious and are there merely as a means to an end. That end is man. We can ask, 'Why do animals exist?' But to ask, 'Why does man exist?' is a meaningless question. Our duties towards animals are merely indirect duties towards humanity. Animal nature has analogies to human nature, and by doing our duties to animals in respect

Immanuel Kant, "Our Duties to Animals," in *Lectures on Ethics,* trans. Louis Infield (New York: Century Company, Inc. 1930), 239–41 (edited). Reprinted with permission by Century Company.

of manifestations which correspond to manifestations of human nature, we indirectly do our duty towards humanity. Thus, if a dog has served his master long and faithfully, his service, on the analogy of human service, deserves reward, and when the dog has grown too old to serve, his master ought to keep him until he dies. Such action helps to support us in our duties towards human beings, where they are bounden duties. If then any acts of animals are analogous to human acts and spring from the same principles, we have duties towards the animals because thus we cultivate the corresponding duties towards human beings. If a man shoots his dog because the animal is no longer capable of service, he does not fail in his duty to the dog, for the dog cannot judge, but his act is inhuman and damages in himself that humanity which it is his duty to show towards mankind. If he is not to stifle his human feelings, he must practise kindness towards animals, for he who is cruel to animals become hard also in his dealings with men. We can judge the heart of a man by his treatment of animals. Hogarth depicts this in his engravings. He shows how cruelty grows and develops. He shows the child's cruelty to animals, pinching the tail of a dog or a cat; he then depicts the grown man in his cart running over a child; and lastly, the culmination of cruelty in murder. He thus brings home to us in a terrible fashion the rewards of cruelty, and this should be an impressive lesson to children. The more we come in contact with animals and observe their behaviour, the more we love them, for we see how great is their care for their young. It is then difficult for us to be cruel in thought even to a wolf. Leibniz used a tiny worm for purposes of observation, and then carefully replaced it with its leaf on the tree so that it should not come to harm through any act of his. He would have been sorry— a natural feeling for a humane man—to destroy such a creature for no reason. Tender feelings towards dumb animals develop humane feelings towards mankind. In England butchers and doctors do not sit on a jury because they are accustomed to the sight of death and hardened. Vivisectionists, who use living animals for their experiments, certainly act cru-

elly, although their aim is praiseworthy, and they can justify their cruelty, since animals must be regarded a man's instruments; but any such cruelty for sport cannot be justified. A master who turns out his ass or his dog because the animal can no longer earn its keep manifests a small mind. The Greeks' ideas in this respect were high-minded, as can be seen from the fable of the ass and the bell of ingratitude. Our duties towards animals, then, are indirect duties towards mankind.

Our duties towards immaterial beings are purely negative. Any course of conduct which involves dealings with spirits is wrong. Conduct of this kind makes men visionaries and fanatics, renders them superstitious, and is not in keeping with the dignity of mankind; for human dignity cannot subsist without a healthy use of reason, which is impossible for those who have commerce with spirits. Spirits may exist or they may not; all that is said of them may be true; but we know them not and can have no intercourse with them. This applies to good and to evil spirits alike. Our Ideas of good and evil are co-ordinate, and as we refer all evil to hell so we refer all good to heaven. If we personify the perfection of evil, we have the Idea of the devil. If we believe that evil spirits can have an influence upon us, can appear and haunt us at night, we become a prey to phantoms and incapable of using our powers in a reasonable way. Our duties towards such beings must, therefore, be negative.

Speciesism and the Idea of Equality

Bonnie Steinbock

Most of us believe that we are entitled to treat members of other species in ways which would be considered wrong if inflicted on members of our own species. We kill them for food, keep them confined,

Bonnie Steinbock, "Speciesism and the Idea of Equality," *Philosophy* 53, no. 204 (April 1978): 247–56 (edited). Reprinted with permission of Cambridge University Press.

use them in painful experiments. The moral philosopher has to ask what relevant difference justifies this difference in treatment. A look at this question will lead us to re-examine the distinctions which we have assumed make a moral difference.

It has been suggested by Peter Singer[1] that our current attitudes are 'speciesist', a word intended to make one think of 'racist' or 'sexist'. The idea is that membership in a species is in itself not relevant to moral treatment, and that much of our behaviour and attitudes towards non-human animals is based simply on this irrelevant fact.

There is, however, an important difference between racism or sexism and 'speciesism'. We do not subject animals to different moral treatment simply because they have fur and feathers, but because they are in fact different from human beings in ways that could be morally relevant. It is false that women are incapable of being benefited by education, and therefore that claim cannot serve to justify preventing them from attending school. But this is not false of cows and dogs, even chimpanzees. Intelligence is thought to be a morally relevant capacity because of its relation to the capacity for moral responsibility.

What is Singer's response? He agrees that non-human animals lack certain capacities that human animals possess, and that this may justify different *treatment*. But it does not justify giving less consideration to their needs and interests. According to Singer, the moral mistake which the racist or sexist makes is not essentially the factual error of thinking that blacks or women are inferior to white men. For even if there were no factual error, even if it were true that blacks and women are less intelligent and responsible than whites and men, this would not justify giving less consideration to their needs and interests. It is important to note that the term 'speciesism' is in one way like, and in another way unlike, the terms 'racism' and 'sexism'. What the term 'speciesism' has in common with these terms is the reference to focusing on a characteristic which is, in itself, irrelevant to moral treatment. And it is worth reminding us of this. But Singer's real aim is to bring us to a new understanding of the idea of equality. The question is, on what do claims to equality rest? The demand for *human* equality is a demand that the interests of all human beings be considered equally, unless there is a moral justification for not doing so. But why should the interests of all human beings be considered equally? In order to answer this question, we have to give some sense to the phrase, 'All men (human beings) are created equal'. Human beings are manifestly *not* equal, differing greatly in intelligence,

virtue and capacities. In virtue of what can the claim to equality be made?

It is Singer's contention that claims to equality do not rest on factual equality. Not only do human beings differ in their capacities, but it might even turn out that intelligence, the capacity for virtue, etc., are not distributed evenly among the races and sexes:

The appropriate response to those who claim to have found evidence of genetically based differences in ability between the races or sexes is not to stick to the belief that the genetic explanation must be wrong, whatever evidence to the contrary may turn up; instead we should make it quite clear that the claim to equality does not depend on intelligence, moral capacity, physical strength, or similar matters of fact. Equality is a moral ideal, not a simple assertion of fact. There is no logically compelling reason for assuming that a factual difference in ability between two people justifies any difference in the amount of consideration we give to satisfying their needs and interests. The principle of equality of human beings is not a description of an alleged actual equality among humans: it is a prescription of how we should treat humans.[2]

In so far as the subject is human equality, Singer's view is supported by other philosophers. Bernard Williams, for example, is concerned to show that demands for equality cannot rest on factual equality among people, for no such equality exists.[3] The only respect in which all men are equal, according to Williams, is that they are all equally men. This seems to be a platitude, but Williams denies that it is trivial. Membership in the species *homo sapiens* in itself has no special moral significance, but rather the fact that all men are human serves as a *reminder* that being human involves the possession of characteristics that are morally relevant. But on what characteristics does Williams focus? Aside from the desire for self-respect (which I will discuss later), Williams is not concerned with uniquely human capacities. Rather, he focuses on the capacity to feel pain and the capacity to feel affection. It is in virtue of these capacities, it seems, that the idea of equality is to be justified.

Apparently Richard Wasserstrom has the same idea as he sets out the racist's 'logical and moral mistakes' in 'Rights, Human Rights and Racial Discrimination'.[4] The racist fails to acknowledge that the black person is as capable of suffering as the white person. According to Wasserstrom, the reason why a person is said to have a right not to be made to suffer acute physical pain is that we all do in fact value freedom from such pain. Therefore, if anyone has a right to be free from suffering acute physical pain, *everyone* has this right, for there is no possible basis of discrimination. Wasserstrom says, 'For, if all persons do have equal capacities of these sorts and if the existence of these capacities is the reason for ascribing these rights to anyone, then all persons ought to have the right to claim equality of treatment in respect to the possession and exercise of these rights'.[5] The basis of equality, for Wasserstrom as for Williams, lies not in some uniquely human capacity, but rather in the fact that all human beings are alike in their capacity to suffer. Writers on equality have focused on this capacity, I think, because it functions as some sort of lowest common denominator, so that whatever the other capacities of a human being, he is entitled to equal consideration because, like everyone else, he is capable of suffering.

If the capacity to suffer is the reason for ascribing a right to freedom from acute pain, or a right to well being, then it certainly looks as though these rights must be extended to animals as well. This is the conclusion Singer arrives at. The demand for human equality rests on the equal capacity of all human beings to suffer and to enjoy well being. But if this is the basis of the demand for equality, then this demand must include all beings which have an equal capacity to suffer and enjoy well being. That is why Singer places at the basis of the demand for equality, not intelligence or reason, but sentience. And equality will mean, not equality of treatment, but 'equal consideration of interests'. The equal consideration of interests will often mean quite different treatment, depending on the nature of the entity being considered. (It would be as absurd to talk of a dog's right to vote, Singer says, as to talk of a man's right to have an abortion.)

It might be thought that the issue of equality depends on a discussion of rights. According to this line of thought, animals do not merit equal consideration of interests because, unlike human beings, they do not, or cannot, have rights. But I not going to discuss rights, important as the issue is. The fact that an entity does not have rights does not necessarily imply that its interests are going to count for less than the interests of entities which are right-bearers. According to the view of rights held by H. L. A. Hart and S. I. Benn, infants do not have rights, nor do the mentally defective, nor do the insane, in so far as they all lack certain minimal conceptual capabilities for having rights.[6] Yet it certainly does not seem that either Hart or Benn would agree that *therefore* their interests are to be counted for less, or that it is morally permissible to treat them in ways in which it would not be permissible to treat right-bearers. It seems to mean only that we must give different sort of reasons for our obligations to take into consideration the interests of those who do not have rights.

We have reasons concerning the treatment of other people which are clearly independent of the notion of rights. We would say that it is wrong to punch someone because doing that infringes his rights. But we could also say that it is wrong because doing that hurts him, and that is, ordinarily, enough of a reason not to do it. Now this particular reason extends not only to human beings, but to all sentient creatures. One has a *prima facie* reason not to pull the cat's tail (whether or not the cat has rights) because it hurts the cat. And this is the only thing, normally, which is relevant in this case. The fact that the cat is not a 'rational being', that it is not capable of moral responsibility, that it cannot make free choices or shape its life—all of these differences from us having nothing to do with the justifiability of pulling its tail. Does this show that rationality and the rest of it are irrelevant to moral treatment?

I hope to show that this is not the case. But first I want to point out that the issue is not one of cruelty to animals. We all agree that cruelty is wrong, whether perpetrated on a moral or non-moral, rational or non-rational agent. Cruelty is defined as the infliction of unnecessary pain or suffering. What is to count as necessary or unnecessary is determined, in part, by the nature of the end pursued. Torturing an animal is cruel, because although the pain is log-ically necessary for the action to be torture, the end (deriving enjoyment from seeing the animal suffer) is monstrous. Allowing animals to suffer from neg-lect or for the sake of large profits may also be thought to be unnecessary and therefore cruel. But there may be some ends, which are very good (such as the advancement of medical knowledge), which can be accomplished by subjecting animals to pain in exper-iments. Although most people would agree that the pain inflicted on animals used in medical research ought to be kept to a minimum, they would consider pain that cannot be eliminated 'necessary' and there-fore not cruel. It would probably not be so regarded if the subjects were non-voluntary human beings. Necessity, then, is defined in terms of human bene-fit, but this is just what is being called into question. The topic of cruelty to animals, while important from a practical viewpoint, because much of our present treatment of animals involves the infliction of suf-fering for no good reason, is not very interesting philosophically. What is philosophically interesting is whether we are justified in having different stan-dards of necessity for human suffering and for ani-mal suffering.

Singer says, quite rightly I think, 'If a being suf-fers, there can be no moral justification for refusing to take that suffering into consideration'.[7] But he thinks that the principle of equality requires that, no matter what the nature of the being, its suffering be counted equally with the like suffering of any other being. In other words sentience does not simply pro-vide us with reasons for acting; it is the *only* relevant consideration for equal consideration of interests. It is this view that I wish to challenge.

I want to challenge it partly because it has such counter-intuitive results. It means, for example, that feeding starving children before feeding starving dogs is just like a Catholic charity's feeding hungry Catholics before feeding hungry non-Catholics. It is simply a matter of taking care of one's own, some-thing which is usually morally permissible. But whereas we would admire the Catholic agency which did not discriminate, but fed all children, first come, first served, we would feel quite differently about

someone who had this policy for dogs and children. Nor is this, it seems to me, simply a matter of a sen-timental preference for our own species. I might feel much more love for my dog than for a strange child—and yet I might feel morally obliged to feed the child before I fed my dog. If I gave in to the feelings of love and fed my dog and let the child go hungry, I would probably feel guilty. This is not to say that we can simply rely on such feelings. Huck Finn felt guilty at helping Jim escape, which he viewed as stealing from a woman who had never done any harm. But while the existence of such feelings does not settle the morality of an issue, it is not clear to me that they can be explained away. In any event, their existence can serve as a motivation for trying to find a rational justification for considering human interests above non-human ones.

However, it does seem to me that this *requires* a justification. Until now, common sense (and aca-demic philosophy) have seen no such need. Benn says, 'No one claims equal consideration for all mammals—human beings count, mice do not, though it would not be easy to say *why* not. . . . Although we hesitate to inflict unnecessary pain on sentient creatures, such as mice or dogs, we are quite sure that we do not need to show good reasons for putting human inter-ests before theirs.'[8]

I think we do have to justify counting our inter-ests more heavily than those of animals. But how? Singer is right, I think, to point out that it will not do to refer vaguely to the greater value of human life, to human worth and dignity:

Faced with a situation in which they see a need for some basis for the moral gulf that is commonly thought to sepa-rate humans and animals, but can find no concrete differ-ence that will do this without undermining the equality of humans, philosophers tend to waffle. They resort to high-sounding phrases like 'the intrinsic dignity of the human individual'. They talk of 'the intrinsic worth of all men' as if men had some worth that other beings do not have or they say that human beings, and only human beings, are 'ends in themselves', while 'everything other than a person can only have value for a person'. . . . Why should we not attribute 'intrinsic dignity' or 'intrinsic worth' to ourselves?

Why should we not say that we are the only things in the universe that have intrinsic value? Our fellow human beings are unlikely to reject the accolades we so generously bestow upon them, and those to whom we deny the honour are unable to object.[9]

Singer is right to be sceptical of terms like 'intrinsic dignity' and 'intrinsic worth'. These phrases are no substitute for a moral argument. But they may point to one. In trying to understand what is meant by these phrases, we may find a difference or differences between human beings and non-human animals that will justify different treatment while not undermining claims for human equality. While we are not compelled to discriminate among people because of different capacities, if we can find a significant difference in capacities between human and non-human animals, this could serve to justify regarding human interests as primary. It is not arbitrary or smug, I think, to maintain that human beings have a different moral status from members of other species because of certain capacities which are characteristic of being human. We may not all be equal in these capacities, but all human beings possess them to some measure, and non-human animals do not. For example, human beings are normally held to be responsible for what they do. In recognizing that someone is responsible for his or her actions, you accord that person a respect which is reserved for those possessed of moral autonomy, or capable of achieving such autonomy. Secondly, human beings can be expected to reciprocate in a way that non-human animals cannot. Non-human animals cannot be motivated by altruistic or moral reasons; they cannot treat you fairly or unfairly. This does not rule out the possibility of an animal being motivated by sympathy or pity. It does rule out altruistic motivation in the sense of motivation due to the recognition that the needs and interests of others provide one with certain reasons for acting'.[10] Human beings are capable of altruistic motivation in this sense. We are sometimes motivated simply by the recognition that someone else is in pain, and that pain is a bad thing, no matter who suffers it. It is this sort of reason that I claim cannot motivate an animal or an entity not

possessed of fairly abstract concepts. (If some non-human animals do possess the requisite concepts—perhaps chimpanzees who have learned a language—they might well be capable of altruistic motivation.) This means that our moral dealings with animals are necessarily much more limited than our dealings with other human beings. If rats invade our houses, carrying disease and biting our children, we cannot reason with them, hoping to persuade them of the injustice they do us. We can only attempt to get rid of them. And it is this that makes it reasonable for us to accord them a separate and not equal moral status, even though their capacity to suffer provides us with some reason to kill them painlessly, if this can be done without too much sacrifice of human interests. Thirdly, as Williams points out, there is the 'desire for self-respect': 'a certain human desire to be identified with what one is doing, to be able to realize purposes of one's own, and not to be the instrument of another's will unless one has willingly accepted such a role.[11] Some animals may have some form of this desire, and to the extent that they do, we ought to consider their interest in freedom and self-determination. (Such considerations might affect our attitudes toward zoos and circuses.) But the desire for self-respect *per se* requires the intellectual capacities of human beings, and this desire provides us with special reasons not to treat human beings in certain ways. It is an affront to the dignity of a human being to be a slave (even if a well-treated one); this cannot be true for a horse or a cow. To point this out is of course only to say that the justification for the treatment of an entity will depend on the sort of entity in question. In our treatment of other entities, we must consider the desire for autonomy, dignity and respect, but only where such a desire exists. Recognition of different desires and interests will often require different treatment, a point Singer himself makes.

But is the issue simply one of different desires and interests justifying and requiring different treatment? I would like to make a stronger claim, namely, that certain capacities, which seem to be unique to human beings, entitle their possessors to a privileged position in the moral community. Both rats and human beings dislike pain, and so we have a *prima facie* reason not to inflict pain on either. But if we can free human beings from crippling diseases, pain and death through experimentation which involves making animals suffer, and if this is the only way to achieve such results, then I think that such experimentation is justified because human lives are more valuable than animal lives. And this is because of certain capacities and abilities that normal human beings have which animals apparently do not, and which human beings cannot exercise if they are devastated by pain or disease.

My point is not that the lack of the sorts of capacities I have been discussing gives us a justification for treating animals just as we like, but rather that it is these differences between human beings and non-human animals which provide a rational basis for different moral treatment and consideration. Singer focuses on sentience alone as the basis of equality, but we can justify the belief that human beings have a moral worth that non-human animals do not, in virtue of specific capacities, and without resorting to 'high-sounding phrases'.

Singer thinks that intelligence, the capacity for moral responsibility, for virtue, etc., are irrelevant to equality, because we would not accept a hierarchy based on intelligence any more than one based on race. We do not think that those with greater capacities ought to have their interests weighed more heavily than those with lesser capacities, and this, he thinks, shows that differences in such capacities are irrelevant to equality. But it does not show this at all. Kevin Donaghy argues (rightly, I think) that what entitles us human beings to a privileged position in the moral community is a certain minimal level of intelligence, which is a prerequisite for morally relevant capacities.[12] The fact that we would reject a hierarchical society based on degree of intelligence does not show that a minimal level of intelligence cannot be used as a cut-off point, justifying giving greater consideration to the interests of those entities which meet this standard.

Interestingly enough, Singer concedes the rationality of valuing the lives of normal human beings over the lives of non-human animals.[13] We are not required to value equally the life of a normal human being and the life of an animal, he thinks, but only their suffering. But I doubt that the value of an entity's life can be separated from the value of its suffering in this way. If we value the lives of human beings more than the lives of animals, this is because we value certain capacities that human beings have and animals do not. But freedom from suffering is, in general, a minimal condition for exercising these capacities, for living a fully human life. So, valuing human life more involves regarding human interests as counting for more. That is why we regard human suffering as more deplorable than comparable animal suffering.

But there is one point of Singer's which I have not yet met. Some human beings (if only a very few) are less intelligent than some non-human animals. Some have less capacity for moral choice and responsibility. What status in the moral community are these members of our species to occupy? Are their interests to be considered equally with ours? Is experimenting on them permissible where such experiments are painful or injurious, but somehow necessary for human well being? If it is certain of our capacities which entitle us to a privileged position, it looks as if those lacking those capacities are not entitled to a privileged position. To think it is justifiable to experiment on an adult chimpanzee but not on a severely mentally incapacitated human being seems to be focusing on membership in a species where that has no moral relevance. (It is being 'speciesist' in a perfectly reasonable use of the word.) How are we to meet this challenge?

Donaghy is untroubled by this objection. He says that it is fully in accord with his intuitions, that he regards the killing of a normally intelligent human being as far more serious than the killing of a person so severely limited that he lacked the intellectual capacities of an adult pig. But this parry really misses the point. The question is whether Donaghy thinks that the killing of a human being so severely limited that he lacked the intellectual capacities of an adult pig would be less serious than the killing of that pig. If superior intelligence is what justifies privileged status in the moral community, then the pig who is smarter than a human being ought to have superior moral status. And I doubt that this is fully in accord with Donaghy's intuitions.

I doubt that anyone will be able to come up with a concrete and morally relevant difference that would justify, say, using a chimpanzee in an experiment rather than a human being with less capacity of reasoning, moral responsibility, etc. Should we then experiment on the severely retarded? Utilitarian considerations aside (the difficulty of comparing intelligence between species, for example), we feel a special obligation to care for the handicapped members of our own species, who cannot survive in this world without such care. Non-human animals manage very well, despite their 'lower intelligence' and lesser capacities; most of them do not require special care from us. This does not, of course, justify experimenting on them. However, to subject to experimentation those people who depend on us seems even worse than subjecting members of other species to it. In addition, when we consider the severely retarded, we think, 'That could be me'. It makes sense to think that one might have been born retarded, but not to think that one might have been born a monkey. And so, although one can imagine oneself in the monkey's place, one feels a closer identification with the severely retarded human being. Here we are getting away from such things as 'morally relevant differences' and are talking about something much more difficult to articulate, namely, the role of feeling and sentiment in moral thinking. We would be *horrified* by the use of the retarded in medical research. But what are we to make of this horror? Has it moral significance or is it 'mere' sentiment, of no more import than the sentiment of whites against blacks? It is terribly difficult to know how to evaluate such feelings. I am not going to say more about this, because I think that the treatment of severely incapacitated human beings does not pose an insurmountable objection to the privileged status principle. I am willing to admit that my horror at the thought of experiments being performed on severely mentally incapacitated human beings in cases in which I would find it justifiable and preferable to perform the same experiments on non-human animals (capable of similar suffering) may not be a moral emotion. But it is certainly not wrong of us to extend special care to members of our own species, motivated by feelings of sympathy, protectiveness, etc. If this is speciesism, it is stripped of its tone of moral condemnation. It is not racist to provide special care to members of your own race; it is racist to fall below your moral obligation to a person because of his or her race. I have been arguing that we are morally obliged to consider the interests of all sentient creatures, but not to consider those interests equally with human interests. Nevertheless, even this recognition will mean some radial changes in our attitude toward and treatment of other species.

NOTES

1. Peter Singer, *Animal Liberation* (A New York Review Book, 1975).

2. Singer, 5.

3. Bernard Williams, 'The Idea of Equality', *Philosophy, Politics and Society* (Second Series), Laslett and Runciman (eds.) (Blackwell, 1962), 110–131, reprinted in *Moral Concepts*, Feinberg (ed.) (Oxford, 1970), 153–171.

4. Richard Wasserstrom, 'Rights, Human Rights, and Racial Discrimination', *Journal of Philosophy* 61, No. 20 (1964), reprinted in *Human Rights*, A. I. Melden (ed.) (Wadsworth, 1970), 96–110.

5. Ibid., 106.

6. H. L. A. Hart, 'Are There Any Natural Rights?', *Philosophical Review* 64 (1955), and S. I. Benn, 'Abortion, Infanticide, and Respect for Persons', *The Problem of Abortion*, Feinberg (ed.) (Wadsworth, 1973), 92–104.

7. Singer, 9.

8. Benn, 'Equality, Moral and Social', *The Encyclopedia of Philosophy* 3, 40.

9. Singer, 266–267.

10. This conception of altruistic motivation comes from Thomas Nagel's *The Possibility of Altruism* (Oxford, 1970).

11. Williams, op. cit., 157.

12. Kevin Donaghy, 'Singer on Speciesism', *Philosophic Exchange* (Summer 1974).

13. Singer, 22.

CASES FOR ANALYSIS

1. Animal Testing

Protesters for and against animal testing have predicted an escalating conflict after the two sides clashed during weekend demonstrations in Oxford. Both groups pledged to step up campaigns which have already resulted in death threats aimed at advocates of animal testing and panic buttons installed at the home of a leading provivisection protester.

Pro-Test, the group which organised the Oxford rally of scientists, students and patients, plans a march in London which it hopes will draw 5,000 supporters. A spokesman for Speak, the animal rights group campaigning against a new animal research laboratory in Oxford, said the Pro-Test demonstration had left it "fired up" to take tougher action.

Spokesman Mel Broughton said: "They should be worried, not because they are in any danger of violence, but because they have fired us up even more against them and the university." . . .

Many researchers stayed away from the march, fearing reprisals against them and their families. Professor Tipu Aziz, a leading neurosurgeon, said: "This country has thousands of researchers paralysed by fear. That's a travesty of democracy." . . .

A spokesman for the Animal Liberation Front, Robin Webb, yesterday described the Pro-Test marchers as "irrelevant."

"The ALF supporters will completely ignore this protest group and will continue targeting institutions and companies which are directly involved in building the proposed facility," he said.

The Medical Research Council's chief executive, Colin Blakemore, described the Pro-Test demonstration as "immensely gratifying. For a long time, we have needed this kind of collective response. The people want this thuggery and nastiness off the streets of Oxford."*

Which side in this conflict do you sympathize with more? Why? Suppose you are a member of Pro-Test. How would you argue in favor of scientific animal testing? Say you are an ALF supporter.

What arguments could you make for the banning of most (or all) animal testing? Is either side justified in using violence or the threat of violence to further its cause? Why or why not?

*Robert Booth, "Opposing Sides in Animal Testing Row Pledge to Step Up Action," *Guardian Unlimited,* 27 February 2006, education.guardian.co.uk/businessofresearch/story/0,,1718867,00.html (accessed 27 February 2006). Copyright © Guardian News & Media Limited 2006. Reprinted with permission of Guardian News Service.

2. Seal Hunting and the Fate of the Inuit

In the 1980s, postcards were distributed to 12 million United States and United Kingdom households depicting the infamous Canadian Atlantic fisher swinging a bat at a baby seal and eliciting an overwhelming emotional response. Major legislative bodies relented to public pressure with a staggering impact on wildlife management. The collapse of the sealskin market marked a victory for protesters who had waged the most effective, international mass media campaign ever undertaken.

The moral victory for animal rights activists not only hurt Newfoundlanders, it adversely affected thousands of Canadian Inuit living in tiny, remote, Arctic hamlets. Antifur protesters lump all seal-hunting methods together. It is tragic but not surprising that there has been virtually no media coverage of the devastating economic, social, and cultural impact of the collapse of the seal skin market on Inuit. If outsiders had known more about Inuit life, perhaps they would not have so easily dismissed all seal-hunting as unethical and cruel.

Canadian Inuit, who number about 46,000, are part of a circumpolar Inuit community numbering about 150,000 in Greenland, Alaska, and Russia. For Canadian Inuit, the seal is not just a source of cash through fur sales, but the keystone of their culture. Although Inuit harvest and hunt many species that inhabit the desert tundra and ice platforms, the seal is their mainstay. . . .

Inuit no longer use seal oil lamps or kudlik for heating, as did their grandparents. But seal meat, which is extremely high in protein, minerals, and vitamins and very low in fat, is still the most valued meat in many parts of the Arctic. Seal skin mittens and boots continue to provide the greatest protection against the harsh Arctic climate.

Like most people, Inuit respond to structural changes by adapting and innovating. They were already dependent on costly hunting supplies by the 1980s. When fur prices plummeted after the sealskin boycott, their credit and cash flow from furs dried up while the cost of supplies rose. Many families could no longer afford hunting equipment. Their fragile economy was imperiled and their vulnerability increased. Their social order was ruptured as they were deprived of the complex social aspect of sharing seal meat.

Their historical, legal, social, and economic situation already placed them at alarmingly higher risks of poverty and violence than other Canadians even when they live outside the North, as 10,000 Inuit have chosen to do. Life expectancy among the Inuit is 10 years lower than other Canadians. Rates of infant mortality, unemployment, illnesses such as diabetes, violence against women, and overcrowded housing are chillingly high.

One of the most brutal aspects of the lack of cultural continuity is the epidemic of youth suicide striking small communities in clusters where one death rapidly engenders another. But the Inuit, having endured myths and misinformation about their culture for decades, have carried on. . . .

The Inuit are resourceful people who deserve more respectful attention from outsiders.[†]

Provide reasons for your answers: Would a utilitarian like Peter Singer be likely to support a ban on all seal hunting even though it would devastate the Inuit? Would he be likely to approve of the Inuit's hunting if they could always kill the seals painlessly? Would a nonconsequentialist like Tom Regan disapprove of the hunting of the seals under all circumstances? If the fate of the Inuit and the seals was to be decided by either Singer or Regan, which philosopher do you think the Inuit would prefer?

[†]Kirt Ejesiak and Maureen Flynn-Burhoe, "Animal Rights vs. Inuit Rights," *The Boston Globe*, 8 May 2005, www.boston.com/news/globe/editorial_opinion/oped/articles/2005/05/08/animal_rights_vs_inuit_rights/ (accessed 27 February 2006). Reprinted with permission of the authors.

3. Snakes and Snake Charmers

Mumbai, India (Daily News & Analysis)—Every year around Nagpanchami, animal welfare activists play an interesting game of snakes and ladders with snake charmers in the city. The good news, say activists, is that the snakes finally seem to be winning. On Sunday, the Bombay Society for Prevention of Cruelty to Animals (BSPCA) rescued four snakes from Kurla and CST, said snake handler Sunil Ranade who works with the BSPCA.

Snake charmers use the reptiles to make money during the Hindu snake festival. "They earn up to Rs3,000 on Nagpanchami because people pay to watch cobras drink milk," Ranade said.

Thanks to the raids conducted by NGOs like the BSPCA and the Plant and Animal Welfare Society (PAWS), the cruel practice of feeding milk to the snakes has considerably reduced, activists say. "In 1996–97, 670 snakes were seized in the raids. But last year (2005), we rescued just 30. The number of snake charmers coming into the city is gradually going down," said Ranade.

Nilesh Bhanage, general secretary, PAWS-Thane said, "We have been conducting raids since 1998. Then, we seized around 40 snakes on Nagpanchami." But last year, Bhanage's team rescued one cobra. "On Sunday, we found no snakes in Bhandup, Mulund, Kanjur Marg and Vikhroli," said Sunish Subramaniam of PAWS-Mumbai. "This is a good sign as it means snake charmers are afraid of the law," explained Bhanage. The Black cobra, a species highly in demand on Nagpanchami, is usually caught from Rajasthan, Punjab and Haryana.

"The snake charmers keep the snakes hungry for a month so that they can drink the milk offered by the devotees; but, in fact, snakes can't digest milk. They also break their venomous fangs which make the snakes unable to protect themselves. These snakes can't be released back into the wild as they cannot hunt," explained Bhanage.

Wildlife activists say the snakes are bought for Rs400. "In the city they fetch between Rs1,000 and Rs3,000," said Ranade.

"After the festival, the snakes are killed and their skin sold. A skin in good condition can fetch as much as Rs3,000."[‡]

Give reasons for your answers: Do you think the activists were justified in rescuing the snakes from the charmers? Is snake charming itself animal abuse? Do snakes have moral rights? Should snake charming be banned—even if it is the only way some people can make a living? What do you think a utilitarian would say about this practice?

[‡]Deepa Suryanardyan, "Snake Goes Up the Ladder," *Daily News & Analysis,* 30 July 2006, www.dndindia-com/dnaPrint.asp?NewsID=10446314CatID=1 (accessed 7 September 2006). Reprinted courtesy of Daily News & Analysis (Mumbai).

CHAPTER 16

Warfare

Moral questions about warfare are often extremely troubling because the stakes in war are monstrously high and because such queries provoke clashes between widely held moral beliefs—especially these two: that killing people is wrong and that killing in self-defense may sometimes be right. Some veteran soldiers say that the cauldron of war tests the physical and moral mettle of the warrior more severely than any other experience in life. Likewise, weighing the morality of war making can try our moral sensibilities as few other issues can. Part of the role of morality is to help us make sense of, and contend with, the bad parts of life, the evil in the world. And few things can be a greater source of evil—massive, horrific moral evil—than war.

Those who have thought carefully about the moral dimensions of war know that the questions roused can be more than just troubling—they can also be complex. Is resorting to war ever morally permissible? Is it permissible even if it involves the killing of thousands or millions? even if it involves—as it almost always does—the annihilation of innocents? Should we have a policy of *never* resorting to war? If so, should we stick to this policy even if our nation is attacked by another? even if the aggressor is bent on genocide? even if the aggressor intends to kill our neighbors, and only our going to war can stop the slaughter? If self-defense is a valid reason for going to war, when is such action justified—only after we are attacked? When we merely fear that we *may* be attacked? Assuming we are justified in waging war, how exactly should we wage it? Does anything go—the

bombing of civilian targets, the torture of prisoners of war, the use of weapons of mass destruction, the mass killing or ethnic cleansing of whole populations? Or are we obligated to follow certain "rules of war" to contain the carnage? Should we dispense with morality altogether? That is, should we—as some political scientists suggest—forget about trying to apply morality to war and focus on wielding political and military power to advance our own national interests?

Fortunately, as moral philosophers have shown, these complexities are not completely intractable. Let us see then if we can make some headway on this rough terrain.

ISSUE FILE: BACKGROUND

War has reliably ravaged humanity in every era and in virtually every society. Some say it will always be with us, for the propensity for violence is an indelible human trait, as if mass killing was somehow etched into human genes. Others are more optimistic, convinced that someday humans will overcome their aggressive urges and eradicate war from the planet. Whatever the case, perhaps we can draw some encouragement from the fact that the ethics of war—the philosophical study of the morality of warfare—continues to shed light on the subject, yielding more understanding than most people would think possible.

Like war, the study of the right and wrong of war has ancient roots, dating back to great thinkers such as Aristotle (384–322 B.C.E.), Cicero (106–43 B.C.E.), Augustine (354–430 C.E.), Averroës (1126–

1198), Thomas Aquinas (1225–1274), and Hugo Grotius (1583–1645). In fact, their insights on the subject still constitute the core of the best thinking today.

From the beginning, the main ethical questions regarding war have been (1) How—if at all—can war be justified? and (2) Assuming it can be justified, how should it be conducted? Most serious responses to these questions have fallen into three major categories, traditionally labeled *realism, pacifism,* and *just war theory.* **Realism (as applied to warfare)** is the view that moral standards are not applicable to war, which must be judged only on prudence, on how well war serves state interests. War cannot be immoral, only more or less advantageous for the state. Eminent realists of the past include the philosophers Niccolò Machiavelli (1469–1527) and Thomas Hobbes (1588–1679); perhaps the most famous contemporary realist is Henry Kissinger, former U.S. secretary of state for the Nixon administration.

Realists may argue that morality has no part to play in warfare because all moral statements are meaningless or unknowable or because moral norms do not apply to states, just to persons. The former claim denies that there can be appeals to any moral standards at all and is therefore vulnerable to the usual arguments that philosophers make against such moral skepticism (see Chapter 2). To the latter view, some nonrealists may reply that there is no good reason to think that states are exempt from moral judgments. Nonrealists may also insist that despite the seemingly unrestrained brutality of war, common sense suggests that sometimes moral norms do apply to warfare. According to this position, even when people favor a war of extreme, indeed savage, measures, they tend to believe that there are at least some moral limits to what can be done. Most would probably balk at the use of nuclear weapons, or the deliberate killing of children, or the mass rape of all noncombatant women.

Pacifism is the view that war is never morally permissible. (The term is also often used to refer to the broader idea that all violence is wrong or that all killing is wrong.) Pacifists in this sense are opposed to all wars regardless of the reasons behind them. They may or may not, however, be against all uses of personal violence, or violence between individuals. They may believe, for example, that personal violence in self-defense or in law enforcement may be justified.

To make their case, pacifists may argue in a consequentialist vein that war is never justified, because it always produces more bad than good. The catastrophic loss of life and the widespread destruction of war can never offset whatever political or material gains are achieved; riches, land, oil, or power cannot outweigh the carnage. Pacifists may also rely on a nonconsequentialist argument like the following: War is always wrong because in the deliberate killing of human beings it violates a fundamental right—the right to life. This right—which may have either a religious or secular basis—is absolute, admitting no exceptions.

The usual objection to the consequentialist approach is that though war is horrific and often (perhaps usually) produces more bad than good, at least sometimes the results may be good overall. It is possible, this argument goes, that waging a war could save the lives of many more people than are killed in the conflict or that fighting one small war could prevent a much larger one. A common objection to the pacifist's nonconsequentialist line is that even though a person has a right to life, we may be morally justified in killing him or her in self-defense if there is no other way to save our own lives. Thus sometimes killing in war is regrettable but necessary—and therefore morally permissible.

Just war theory is the doctrine that war may be morally permissible under stipulated conditions. It is a centuries-old attempt to understand how war—an enduring form of systematic killing—can be reconciled with our moral presumptions *against* killing. It specifies when resorting to war may be morally justified and how armed conflict should be conducted to meet the minimal demands of morality. Thomas Aquinas produced the most influential discourse on the doctrine, and it has been evolving ever since as both religious and secular thinkers have tried to improve it. Just war theory has become the most widely used lens through which the ethics of war is viewed these days. As one theorist points out,

To be sure, this tradition has often found expression in church law and theological reflection; yet it also appears in codifications and theories of international law, in military manuals on how rightly to conduct war, and—as Michael Walzer has shown in *Just and Unjust Wars*—in the judgments and reactions of common people.[1]

Just war theory is concerned with two main issues: (1) the justification for resorting to war (traditionally labeled **jus ad bellum,** or "the justice of war") and (2) the moral permissibility of acts in war (**jus in bello,** or "justice in war"). Theorists have addressed *jus ad bellum* by specifying that going to war can be morally permissible only if certain requirements are met. In the following list, Aquinas urged the first three requirements, and later thinkers embraced them and added several more. According to the theory, only if all the requirements are met can a war be considered just.

1. *The cause must be just.* War is such a horrifying business that only a just cause—a morally legitimate reason—can justify going to war. The most commonly cited just cause is, as noted previously, self-defense against attack. The usual thinking is that precisely as individuals are entitled to use violence to defend themselves against violent personal attacks, so states have the right to defend against unjust attacks from another

state. The implication here is that states have no right to *instigate* a war.

Many theorists define a just cause broadly: a just cause is resistance to substantial aggression, which has been defined as "the type of aggression that violates people's most fundamental rights."[2] This resistance includes self-defense against external threat, of course. But it also may encompass defending the innocent from deadly attack (as in genocide or "ethnic cleansing," for example), defending people whose basic human rights are being violated by a brutal regime, or defending other states from unjust external attack. Some early theorists thought that wars could be justifiably fought to convert or punish those of a different religion—a view now rejected by philosophers and theologians but still strongly supported in some parts of the world.

Some people argue that war in self-defense is justified only in response to an actual attack; others maintain that an attack need not be actual but only feared—that is, a "preventive war" may be justified. But many contend that to start a war on such grounds is to act on a mere fear of the unknown and to invite other states to launch attacks for no good reason (or for ulterior motives). In response to this worry, a number of theorists maintain that a war is justified only if the threat of attack from another state is "immediate and imminent," which means something like "clearly about to happen." Such a war is properly called preemptive. Much of the debate about the United States' launching a preemptive strike against Iraq in 2003 has been about whether this "immediate and imminent" standard was met as well as about whether the standard is relevant when there might be a danger from weapons of mass destruction.

2. *The war must be sanctioned by proper authority.* The resort to war must be approved by a state's

---

[1]James Turner Johnson, "Threats, Values, and Defense: Does the Defense of Values by Force Remain a Moral Possibility?" *Parameters* 15, no. 1 (Spring 1985).

[2]James P. Sterba, "Reconciling Pacifists and Just War Theorists," *Social Theory and Practice* 18, no. 1 (Spring 1992): 21.

rightful government. As Aquinas says, a just war requires "the authority of the sovereign by whose command the war is to be waged. For it is not the business of a private individual to declare war."[3]

3. *The war should be fought with the right intentions.* Wars must be waged for the sake of the just cause, not moved by some illegitimate motives such as bloodlust, greed, empire expansion, and ethnic hatred. Aquinas continues,

[I]t is necessary that the belligerents should have a rightful intention, so that they intend the advancement of good, or the avoidance of evil. . . . For it may happen that the war is declared by the legitimate authority, and for a just cause, and yet be rendered unlawful through a wicked intention.

4. *Armed conflict should be a last resort.* For a war to be just, all peaceful means of sorting out differences between adversaries should be tried first. Diplomacy, economic pressure, world opinion—all these avenues and others should be exhausted before employing guns and bombs.

5. *The good resulting from war must be proportional to the bad.* The good expected to come from fighting for a just cause must be weighed against the tremendous evils that will inevitably accompany war—death, destruction, pain, and loss on a mass scale.

6. *There must be a reasonable chance of success.* Futile wars should not be waged. Mass killing with no likelihood of achieving anything is unjust. So only if success is reasonably probable should a state resort to war.

Just war theorists believe that it is possible for a resort to war to be morally permissible while the conduct of that war is morally abhorrent. They therefore are concerned not only with *jus ad bellum* but also with *jus in bello,* right action during

the meting out of the violence. They explicitly reject the popular notion that once war commences, there are no moral restraints whatsoever on what can be done to anyone or anything during the conflict. Michael Walzer, the leading contemporary advocate for just war theory, asserts that the popular view is "profoundly wrong":

War is indeed ugly, but there are degrees of ugliness and humane men must, as always, be concerned with degrees. . . . Surely there is a point at which the means employed for the sake of this or that political goal come into conflict with a more general human purpose: the maintenance of moral standards and the survival of some sort of international society. At that point, political arguments against the use of such means are overshadowed, or ought to be, by moral arguments. At that point, war is not merely ugly but criminal.[4]

Traditionally, requirements for *jus in bello*—the so-called rules of war—have included:

1. *Discrimination.* Those fighting a war must distinguish between combatants and noncombatants, never deliberately targeting the latter. People who should not be intentionally attacked are said to have **noncombatant immunity,** a status traditionally reserved for women, children, the elderly, and the sick and injured. Though some noncombatants are almost certain to be killed or harmed in any war, such tragedies are supposed to be unavoidable or unintended and therefore pardonable.

The distinction between combatant and noncombatant is often not very clear, especially when a conflict involves fighters wearing civilian clothes and operating among peaceful inhabitants. Michael Walzer offers a helpful distinction by saying that noncombatants are those who are not "engaged in harm." But some thinkers have tended to blur the line between people usually thought to have noncombatant immunity and those who do not.

[3]Thomas Aquinas, *Summa Theologica,* in *Basic Writings of Saint Thomas Aquinas,* ed. and annotated Anton C. Pegis (New York: Random House, 1945), Second Part of the Second Part, Question 40, Article 1.

[4]Michael Walzer, "Moral Judgment in Time of War," *Dissent* 14, no. 3 (May–June 1967): 284.

They ask, Should people be given immunity if they cheer on their combatants, give them food, and shelter them? Are they really to be regarded as "innocent civilians"?

In any case, the prohibition against intentionally attacking noncombatants is enshrined in international law and widely regarded as the most fundamental "rule of war."

2. *Proportionality.* The use of force should be proportional to the rightful aims of the war—"overkill" is disallowed. Even in bitter conflict, combatants should not kill or destroy more than necessary to achieve the just ends for which the war is waged.

3. *No evil means.* Many just war theorists maintain that certain tactics and weapons in war are "evil in themselves" and thus should never be used regardless of a war's aims. Such evil means are said to include genocide, biological or chemical warfare (use of anthrax and nerve gas, for example), nuclear attack, and mass rape.

4. *Benevolent quarantine.* Soldiers who surrender to their enemies have rights and should be treated accordingly. They must be given "benevolent quarantine" as prisoners of war (POWs)—humane captivity in safe confines removed from the battlefield. In that environment they must not be subjected to execution, torture, starvation, or other forms of serious abuse.

MORAL THEORIES

Both consequentialist and nonconsequentialist perspectives have been given major roles in the ethics of war and peace. On the consequentialist side, utilitarianism has been used both to support and to undermine pacifism. Some have argued, for example, that by utilitarian lights, antiwar pacifism must be true. The philosopher Thomas Nagel provides some examples of such pacifist arguments:

It may even be argued that war involves violence on such a scale that it is never justified on utilitarian grounds—the consequences of refusing to go to war will never be as bad as the war itself would be, even if atrocities were not committed. Or in a more sophisticated vein it might be claimed that a uniform policy of never resorting to military force would do less harm in the long run, if followed consistently, than a policy of deciding each case on utilitarian grounds (even though on occasion particular applications of the pacifist policy might have worse results than a specific utilitarian decision).[5]

Whether good consequences produced by a pacifist stance would always in fact outweigh the bad of war making is, of course, a question of nonmoral fact—and some utilitarians assert that the facts do not help the pacifist's case. These critics say there is no evidence to support the notion that a policy of pacifism always results in less death and suffering. As one philosopher says,

[I]t is worthwhile to point out that the general history of the human race certainly offers no support for the supposition that turning the other cheek always produces good effects on the aggressor. Some aggressors, such as the Nazis, were apparently "egged on" by the "pacifist" attitude of their victims.[6]

Utilitarians can push this kind of argument even further and say that resorting to war is sometimes justified because it results in a better balance of good over bad, everyone considered, than not going to war. (Obviously, they too would need to back up such an empirical claim.) To be consistent, they would also want to base the moral rightness of military actions in war (*jus in bello*) on utilitarian considerations.

As we saw earlier, utilitarian elements are built into just war theory, which is a coherent system of both consequentialist and nonconsequentialist

[5]Thomas Nagel, "War and Massacre," *Philosophy & Public Affairs* 1, no. 2 (Winter 1972): 123–43.
[6]Jan Narveson, "Pacifism: A Philosophical Analysis," *Ethics* 75, no. 4 (1965): 623–24.

CRITICAL THOUGHT: Preemptive War on Iraq

According to most forms of just war theory, a preemptive attack against a state is justified only if that state presents a substantial danger that is "immediate and imminent." As some commentators on just war theory explain, "To establish this condition [of immediate and imminent threat], evidence of planning that is virtually completed needs to be shown."* Now consider the following description of the run-up to the U.S. preemptive strike on Iraq in 2003:

> [President George W. Bush] claimed that he was justified [in going to war with Iraq] so as to prevent (really to preempt) Iraq from attacking the United States. But such talk of prevention is imprecise, for it may refer either to a necessary preemption of an impending attack or merely to an unjustified fear as a pretext for war based on other motivations. In his 2003 State of the Union speech, Bush said that "The British government has learned that Saddam Hussein recently sought significant quantities of uranium from Africa." Such a claim was meant to show that Iraq posed an imminent, not merely a speculative threat to the United States. In addition, Bush said that he was not required to wait for the United States to be attacked, or even to wait for all of the evidence needed to show that Iraq might attack.†

Assume that this passage is an accurate depiction of the prewar situation and is the only relevant information available to you. Would you judge the threat from Iraq to be "immediate and imminent"? Why or why not? Judging from what you have learned about just war theory in this chapter, do you think a fair-minded just war theorist would say the attack on Iraq was justified, or unjustified? Why? Do *you* believe that starting the war was just? What are your reasons?

*Larry May, Eric Rovie, and Steven Viner, introduction to *The Morality of War: Classical and Contemporary Readings,* ed. May, Rovie, and Viner (Upper Saddle River, NJ: Pearson/Prentice Hall, 2006), xi.
†Ibid.

requirements. In our previous list of *jus ad bellum* conditions, the last three requirements are usually taken as consequentialist: (4) last resort, (5) good proportional to the bad, and (6) reasonable chance of success. And the *jus in bello* conditions of discrimination and proportionality are often viewed as rules for maximizing the good for both combatants and noncombatants.

When justifying views on the resort to war, both pacifists and nonpacifists may take a nonconsequentialist approach, appealing to fundamental moral principles rather than to the results of actions. As we have seen, pacifists typically rest their case on the right to life; nonpacifists, on the right of self-defense or the defense of basic human rights generally. The former regard their moral principle as absolute—it allows no exceptions—but the latter may not.

As you would expect, there can be stark differences on many critical matters between the consequentialist and nonconsequentialist. One such issue is the treatment of noncombatants. Absolutist nonconsequentialists maintain that the intentional killing of noncombatants is always morally wrong regardless of the circumstances, but consequentialists insist that sometimes there are exceptions:

Regarding the absolute prohibition on intentional killing of noncombatants, absolutists have been termed "immunity theorists." Immunity theorists hold that it is always morally impermissible to intentionally kill noncombatants in war. Noncombatants are "innocent" and thus immune from attack. . . .

. . . Consequentialists believe that actions in war can be morally justified depending on the end or aim of the action. If it is morally sufficient, the end can justify the means. . . . From this perspective, consequentialists, unlike absolutists, can morally justify the intentional killing of noncombatants or "innocents" in war. A controversial example addressed in this debate is the bombing of Hiroshima and Nagasaki in World War II. Consequentialists can morally justify these bombings. Absolutists, however, contend that these bombings were immoral because these bombings targeted noncombatants.[7]

MORAL ARGUMENTS

Let us examine some arguments involving an issue that in recent years has provoked an enormous amount of intense debate—**humanitarian intervention**. As we saw in the previous pages, the conventional model of a justified resort to war is: one sovereign state defending itself against another's aggression. A state's self-defense is thought to be just cause for unleashing the dogs of war. But humanitarian intervention is a different sort of scenario, for it involves a state (or states) going to war to defend people of another state against the murderous aggression of their own regime. The aggression may appear in the form of genocide, ethnic cleansing, forced starvation, and mass imprisonment or slavery—the kinds of atrocities that occurred thirty years ago in Cambodia and Uganda, and more recently in Somalia, East Timor, Kosovo, and Rwanda. The situations that are said to cry out for humanitarian intervention are both compelling and alien to early just war theory:

The standard cases have a standard form: a government, an army, a police force, tyrannically controlled, attacks its own people or some subset of its own people, a vulnerable minority, say, territorially based or dispersed throughout the country. . . . The attack takes place within the country's borders; it doesn't require any boundary crossings; it is an exercise of sovereign power. There is no aggression, no invading army to resist and beat back. Instead, the rescuing forces are the invaders; they are the ones who, in the strict sense of international law, begin the war. But they come into a situation where the moral stakes are clear: the oppressors or, better, the state agents of oppression are readily identifiable; their victims are plain to see.[8]

To get to the heart of these matters, we want to ask, Is humanitarian intervention ever morally permissible? Those who say yes—the interventionists—might offer an argument like this:

1. An individual has a duty to try to stop an unjust and potentially fatal attack against someone (to intervene), even if defending the victim requires using violence against the attacker (assuming that the defender is capable of acting without too much personal risk, and there is no other way to stop the attack).

2. Humanitarian intervention by a state (or states) is exactly analogous to this type of personal intervention on behalf of seriously threatened victims.

3. Therefore, states have a duty of humanitarian intervention (under the right circumstances).

This argument is, of course, inductive—an argument by analogy. Probably few people would balk at Premise 1: it is a simple moral principle drawn from commonsense morality. Some might insist that a principle declaring that we have a *duty*

[7]Larry May, Eric Rovie, and Steve Viner, in *The Morality of War: Classical and Contemporary Readings,* ed. May, Rovie, and Viner (Upper Saddle River, NJ: Pearson/Prentice Hall, 2006), 200.

[8]Michael Walzer, "The Argument about Humanitarian Intervention," *Dissent* 49, no. 1 (Winter 2002), http://dissentmagazine.org/article/?article=629.

is the well-established doctrine of international conduct that one sovereign state may not meddle in the internal affairs of another. This noninterference principle, says the noninterventionist, seems much stronger than any analogous rule on the personal level. Even interfering in a family conflict in which one family member is being brutally assaulted by the others may seem morally permissible sometimes, while analogous interference in a state's internal conflicts seems less morally clear-cut.

There is much more that can be said both for and against Premise 2, but let us turn to another interventionist argument:

1. All persons have certain supremely important, basic rights—for example, rights to life, to self-determination, and to freedom from harm—rights that must not be violated by either people or states.

2. People who have these basic rights violated are entitled to use force to defend them, and it is morally permissible for other people or states to use force to help in that defense (humanitarian intervention).

3. People or states that violate others' basic rights forfeit their own right not to have force used against them.

4. Therefore, humanitarian intervention is morally permissible in defense of basic rights.

Interventionists are likely to get very little disagreement about either Premise 1 or Premise 3. For a majority of moral philosophers, the concepts of moral rights and their forfeiture are plausible elements in most of the major moral traditions. But Premise 2 is controversial. The idea of people using force in self-defense (to protect their lives or property, for example) is part of commonsense morality, but noninterventionists have questioned the defense of others' rights that involves crossing borders and violating state sovereignty. A critical

to intervene is too strong—better to say that in the right circumstances, intervening is *morally permissible,* not obligatory. Though this complaint may have merit, let us stay with the original wording for simplicity's sake.

Premise 2 is the weak link here. For an argument by analogy to be strong, the two things being compared must be sufficiently similar in relevant ways. In this case, the intervention of an individual to halt an attack on another person must be relevantly similar to an intervention by sovereign states to stop aggression by another state against people within the state's borders. But noninterventionists might claim that the argument is weak because the personal and national circumstances are different in important respects. One difference problem, they would argue, is that the principle embodied in Premise 2 would have us ignore the rights of sovereign states to defend human rights— yet state sovereignty is itself a well-established principle of international relations. So we have a conflict of moral principles. In a utilitarian vein, noninterventionists may also argue that a policy of humanitarian intervention that ignores state sovereignty and attends to the countless violations of rights by a state could lead to perpetual wars everywhere. Some noninterventionists allow that intervention may indeed be necessary in certain extraordinary cases involving genocide, massacres, and other extreme horrors. But they think that intervention should be reserved for these horrors, otherwise, perpetual war will in fact be the norm.

SUMMARY

The main ethical questions regarding war and peace are (1) how—if at all—can the resort to war be justified? and (2) assuming it can be justified, how should it be conducted? Most serious answers to such questions come from three distinct perspectives. Realism, as the term applies to warfare, is the view that moral standards are not applicable to war, though considerations of prudence are. Pacifism is the view that war is never morally permissible. Just war theory is the doctrine that war may be morally permissible under stipulated conditions.

Just war theory is concerned with two fundamental issues: (1) how the resort to war can be justified (called *jus ad bellum*) and (2) what kind of conduct in war can be morally permissible (*jus in bello*). In traditional just war theory, a war can be deemed just if (1) its cause is just, (2) the war is sanctioned by proper authority, (3) the war is fought with rightful intentions, (4) the war is a last resort, (5) the good arising from the war is proportional to the bad, and (6) there is a reasonable chance of success. According to the traditional rules of *jus in bello*, rightful conduct in war requires distinguishing between combatants and noncombatants; using no more force than necessary; using no weapons or tactics that are evil in themselves, such as weapons of mass destruction; and guaranteeing POWs benevolent quarantine.

Depending on how they judge the empirical evidence, utilitarians may with logical consistency take either a pacifist or nonpacifist stand on war. Nonconsequentialists may also consistently support or reject pacifism. Pacifists typically rest their case on the nonconsequentialist principle of the right to life. Nonpacifists may back their case with the nonconsequentialist principles of the right to self-defense or of human rights generally.

One important subject of sharp debate is humanitarian intervention. Interventionists may argue that the intervention of one state in another's internal affairs for humanitarian reasons is analogous to an individual's intervening in a mugging to rescue someone from injury or death—both kinds of actions can be equally justified. Critics complain, however, that the analogy is flawed. Alternatively, interventionists may argue for humanitarian intervention to protect basic human rights. Some say that this approach is problematic because it does not take into account the competing claims of the rights of sovereign states.

READINGS

Pacifism
Douglas P. Lackey

1. VARIETIES OF PACIFISM

Everyone has a vague idea of what a pacifist is, but few realize that there are many kinds of pacifists. (Sometimes the different kinds quarrel with each other!) One task for the student of international ethics is to distinguish the different types of pacifism and to identify which types represent genuine moral theories.

Most of us at some time or other have run into the "live and let live" pacifist, the person who says, "I am absolutely opposed to killing and violence—but I don't seek to impose my own code on anyone else. If other people want to use violence, so be it. They have their values and I have mine." For such a person, pacifism is one life style among others, a life style committed to gentleness and care, and opposed to belligerence and militarism. Doubtless, many people who express such commitments are sincere and are prepared to live by their beliefs. At the same time, it is important to see why "live and let live" pacifism does not constitute a moral point of view.

When someone judges that a certain action, A, is morally wrong, that judgment entails that no one should do A. Thus, there is no way to have moral values without believing that these values apply to other people. If a person says that A is morally wrong but that it doesn't matter if other people do A, then that person either is being inconsistent or doesn't know what the word "moral" means. If a person believes that killing, in certain circumstances, is morally wrong, that belief implies that no one should kill, at least in those circumstances. If a pacifist claims that killing is wrong in *all* circumstances, but that it is permissible for other people to kill on occasion, then

he has not understood the universal character of genuine moral principles. If pacifism is to be a moral theory, it must be prescribed for all or prescribed for none.

Once one recognizes this "universalizing" character of genuine moral beliefs, one will take moral commitments more seriously than those who treat a moral code as a personal life-style. Since moral principles apply to everyone, we must take care that our moral principles are correct, checking that they are not inconsistent with each other, developing and adjusting them so that they are detailed and subtle enough to deal with a variety of circumstances, and making sure that they are defensible against the objections of those who do not accept them. Of course many pacifists do take the business of morality seriously and advance pacifism as a genuine moral position, not as a mere life-style. All such serious pacifists believe that *everyone* ought to be a pacifist, and that those who reject pacifism are deluded or wicked. Moreover, they do not simply endorse pacifism; they offer arguments in its defense.

We will consider four types of pacifist moral theory. First, there are pacifists who maintain that the central idea of pacifism is the immorality of killing. Second, there are pacifists who maintain that the essence of pacifism is the immorality of violence, whether this be violence in personal relations or violence in relations between nation-states. Third, there are pacifists who argue that personal violence is always morally wrong but that political violence is sometimes morally right: for example, that it is sometimes morally permissible for a nation to go to war. Fourth and finally, there are pacifists who believe that personal violence is sometimes morally permissible but that war is always morally wrong.

Albert Schweitzer, who opposed all killing on the grounds that life is sacred, was the first sort of pacifist. Mohandas Gandhi and Leo Tolstoy, who opposed not only killing but every kind of coercion and violence, were pacifists of the second sort: I will call such pacifists "universal pacifists." St. Augustine, who condemned self-defense but endorsed wars against heretics, was a pacifist of the third sort. Let us call him a "private pacifist," since he condemned only violence in the private sphere. Pacifists of the fourth sort, increasingly common in the modern era of nuclear and total war, I will call "antiwar pacifists."

2. THE PROHIBITION AGAINST KILLING

(a) The Biblical Prohibition

One simple and common argument for pacifism is the argument that the Bible, God's revealed word, says to all people "Thou shalt not kill" (Exod. 20:13). Some pacifists interpret this sentence as implying that no one should kill under any circumstances, unless God indicates that this command is suspended, as He did when He commanded Abraham to slay Isaac. The justification for this interpretation is the words themselves, "Thou shalt not kill," which are presented in the Bible bluntly and without qualification, not only in Exodus but also in Deuteronomy (5:17).

This argument, however, is subject to a great many criticisms. The original language of Exodus and Deuteronomy is Hebrew, and the consensus of scholarship says that the Hebrew sentence at Exodus 20:13, "Lo Tirzach," is best translated as "Thou shalt do no murder," not as "Thou shalt not kill." If this translation is correct, then Exodus 20:13 does not forbid all killing but only those killings that happen to be murders. Furthermore, there are many places in the Bible where God commands human beings to kill in specified circumstances. God announces 613 commandments in all, and these include "Thou shalt not suffer a witch to live" (Exod. 22:18); "He that blasphemeth the name of the Lord . . . shall surely be put to death, and all the congregation shall stone him" (Lev. 24:16); "He that killeth any man shall surely be put to death" (Lev. 24:17); and so forth. It is difficult to argue that these instructions are like God's specific instructions to Abraham to slay Isaac: these are general commandments to be applied by many people, to many people, day in and day out. They are at least as general and as divinely sanctioned as the commandment translated "Thou shalt not kill."

There are other difficulties for pacifists who pin their hopes on prohibitions in the Hebrew Bible. Even if the commandment "Thou shalt not kill," properly interpreted, did prohibit all types of killing, the skeptic can ask whether this, by itself, proves that all killing is immoral. First, how do we know that the statements in the Hebrew Bible really are God's word, and not just the guesses of ancient scribes? Second, even if the commandments in the Bible do express God's views, why are we morally bound to obey divine commands? (To say that we will be punished if we do not obey is to appeal to fear and self-interest, not to moral sentiments.) Third, are the commandments in the Old Testament laws for all people, or just laws for the children of Israel? If they are laws for all people, then all people who do not eat unleavened bread for Passover are either deluded or wicked. If they are laws only for the children of Israel, they are religious laws and not moral laws, since they lack the universality that al moral laws must have.

Finally, the argument assumes the existence of God, and philosophers report that the existence of God is not easy to demonstrate. Even many religious believers are more confident of the truth of basic moral judgments, such as "Small children should not be tortured to death for purposes of amusement," than they are confident of the existence of God. For such people, it would seem odd to try to justify moral principles by appeals to religious principles, since the evidence for those religious principles is weaker than the evidence for the moral principles they are supposed to justify.

(b) The Sacredness of Life

There are, however, people who oppose all killing but do not seek justification in divine revelation. Many of these defend pacifism by appeal to the sacredness of life. Almost everyone is struck with wonder when watching the movements and reactions of a newborn baby, and almost everyone can be provoked to awe by the study of living things, great or small. The complexity of the mechanisms found in living bodies, combined with the efficiency with which they fulfill their functions, is not matched by any of the processes in nonliving matter. People who are particularly awestruck by the beauty of living things infer from these feelings that life is sacred, that all killing is morally wrong.

Different versions of pacifism have been derived from beliefs about the sacredness of life. The most extreme version forbids the killing of any living thing. This view was allegedly held by Pythagoras, and is presently held by members of the Jain religion in India. (Those who think that such pacifists must soon starve to death should note that a life-sustaining diet can easily be constructed from milk, honey, fallen fruit and vegetables, and other items that are consumable without prior killing.) A less extreme view sanctions the killing of plants but forbids the killing of animals. The most moderate view prohibits only the killing of fellow human beings.

There is deep appeal in an argument that connects the sacredness of life with the wrongfulness of taking life. Even people who are not pacifists are often revolted by the spectacle of killing, and most Americans would be unable to eat meat if they had to watch how the animals whose flesh they consume had been slaughtered, or if they had to do the slaughtering themselves. Most people sense that they do not own the world they inhabit and recognize that they are not free to do with the world as they will, that the things in it, most especially living things, are worthy of respect and care. Seemingly nothing could violate the respect living things deserve more than killing, especially since much of the taking of human and nonhuman life is so obviously unnecessary.

But with the introduction of the word "unnecessary" a paradox arises. Sometimes—less often than we think, but sometimes—the taking of some lives will save other lives. Does the principle that life is sacred and ought to be preserved imply that nothing should ever be killed, or does it imply that as much life should be preserved as possible? Obviously pacifists take the former view; nonpacifists, the latter.

The view that killing is wrong because it destroys what is sacred seems to imply that killing is wrong because killing diminishes the amount of good in the world. It seems to follow that if a person can save more lives by killing than by refusing to kill, arguments about the sacredness of life could not show that killing in these circumstances is wrong. (It might be wrong for other reasons.) The more lives saved, the greater the quantity of good in the world.

The difficulty that some killing might, on balance, save lives, is not the only problem for pacifism based on the sacredness of life. If preserving life is the highest value, a value not comparable with other, non-life-preserving goods, it follows that any acts which place life at risk are immoral. But many admirable actions have been undertaken in the face of death, and many less heroic but morally impeccable actions—driving on a road at moderate speed, authorizing a commercial flight to take off, and so forth—place life at risk. In cases of martyrdom in which people choose death over religious conversion, life is just as much destroyed as it is in a common murder. Yet, on the whole, automobile drivers, air traffic controllers, and religious martyrs are not thought to be wicked. Likewise, people on life-sustaining machinery sometimes request that the machines be turned off, on the grounds that quality of life matters more than quantity of life. We may consider such people mistaken, but we hardly think that they are morally depraved.

In answering this objection, the pacifist may wish to distinguish between *killing other people* and *getting oneself killed,* arguing that only the former is immoral. But although there is a genuine distinction between killing and getting killed, the distinction does not entail that killing other people destroys life but getting oneself killed does not. If life is sacred, life, including one's own life, must be preserved at all cost. In many cases, people consider the price of preserving their own lives simply to be too high.

(c) The Right to Life

Some pacifists may try to avoid the difficulties of the "sacredness of life" view by arguing that the essential immorality of killing is that it violates the *right to life* that every human being possesses. If people have a right to life, then it is never morally permissible to kill some people in order to save others, since according to the usual interpretation of rights, it is never permissible to violate a right in order to secure some good.

A discussion of the logic of rights in general and the right to life in particular is beyond the scope of this book. But a number of students of this subject are prepared to argue that the possession of any right implies the permissibility of defending that right against aggression: if this were not so, what would be the point of asserting the existence of rights? But if the possession of a right to life implies the permissibility of defending that right against aggression—a defense that may require killing the aggressor—then the existence of a right to life cannot by itself imply the impermissibility of killing. On this view, the right to life implies the right to self-defense, including violent self-defense. It does not imply pacifism.

3. UNIVERSAL PACIFISM

(a) Christian Pacifism

Universal pacifists are morally opposed to all violence, not just to killing. Many universal pacifists derive their views from the Christian Gospels. In the Sermon on the Mount, Christ taught:

> Ye have heard that it hath been said, An eye for an eye, a tooth for a tooth:
>
> But I say unto you, that ye resist not evil: but whosoever shall smite these on the right cheek, turn to him the other also. . . .
>
> Ye have heard it said, thou shalt love thy neighbor, and hate thine enemy. But I say unto you, Love your enemies, bless them that curse you, do good to them that hate you. . . . that ye may be the children of your father which is in heaven: for he maketh the sun to rise on the evil and on the good, and sendeth the rain on the just and the unjust. (Matt. 5:38–45)

In the early centuries of the Christian era, it was widely assumed that to follow Christ and to obey His teaching meant that one should reject violence and refuse service in the Roman army. But by the fifth century, after the Roman Empire had become Christian and after barbarian Goths in 410 sacked Rome itself, Church Fathers debated whether Christ really intended that the Empire and its Church should remain undefended. The Church Fathers noticed passages in the Gospels that seem to contradict pacifism:

> Think not that I am come to send peace on earth: I came not to send peace, but a sword.
>
> For I am come to set a man at variance against his father, and the daughter against her mother, and the daughter-in-law against her mother-in-law. (Matt. 10:34–35)

And there are several instances in the Gospels (for instance, Matt. 8:5–10) in which Jesus encounters soldiers and does not rebuke them for engaging in an occupation that is essentially committed to violence. Rather, he argues, "Render unto Caesar the things which are Caesar's; and unto God the things that are God's" (Matt. 22:21). This would seem to include military service, or at least taxes to pay for the army.

A thorough analysis of whether the Gospels command pacifism is beyond the scope of this book. The passages in the Sermon on the Mount seem to be clearly pacifist; yet many eminent scholars have denied the pacifist message. A more interesting question, for philosophy, if not for biblical scholarship, is this: If Jesus did preach pacifism in the Sermon on the Mount, did He preach it as a *moral* doctrine?

Jesus did not view his teaching as replacing the moral law as he knew it:

> Think not that I am come to destroy the law, or the prophets: I am come not to destroy, but to fulfill. . . .
>
> Till heaven and earth pass, one jot or title shall in no wise pass from the law, till all be fulfilled. (Matt. 5:17–18)

Perhaps, then, the prescriptions of the Sermon on the Mount should be interpreted as rules that one must obey in order to follow Christ, or rules that one must follow in order to obtain salvation. But it does not follow from this alone that everyone has an obligation to follow Christ, and it does not follow from this alone that everyone has an obligation to seek salvation. Even Christians will admit that some people have refused to become Christians and have led morally admirable lives nonetheless, and if salvation is a good, one can nevertheless choose to reject it, just as a citizen can neglect to hand in a winning lottery ticket without breaking the law. If so, the prescriptions of the Sermon on the Mount apply only to Christians seeking a Christian salvation. They are not universally binding rules and do not qualify as moral principles.

(b) The Moral Exemplar Argument

Many people and at least one illustrious philosopher, Immanuel Kant, believe that morally proper action consists in choosing to act in such a way that your conduct could serve as an example for all mankind. (It was Kant's genius to recognize that moral conduct is *essentially* exemplary.) Some universal pacifists appeal to this idea, arguing that if everyone were a pacifist, the world would be a much better place than it is now. This is the argument that Leo Tolstoy (1828–1910) used to support the Gospel prescription not to resist evil.

[Christ] put the proposition of non-resistance to evil in such a way that, according to his teaching, it was to be the foundation of the joint life of men and was to free humanity from the evil that it inflicted on itself. (*My Religion,* Ch. 4) Instead of having the whole life based on violence and every joy obtained and guarded through violence; instead of seeing each one of us punished or inflicting punishment from childhood to old age, I imagined that we were all impressed in word and deed by the idea that vengeance is a very low, animal feeling; that violence is not only a disgraceful act, but also one that deprives man of true happiness. . . .

I imagined that instead of those national hatreds which are impressed on us under the form of patriotism, instead of those glorifications of murder, called wars . . . that we were impressed with the idea that the recognition of any countries, special laws, borders, lands, is a sign of grossest ignorance. . . .

Through the fulfillment of these commandments, the life of men will be what every human heart seeks and desires. All men will be brothers and everybody will always be at peace with others, enjoying all the benefits of the world. (*My Religion,* Ch. 6)

Few would deny that if everyone were a pacifist, the world would be a better place, perhaps even a paradise. Furthermore, since the argument is essentially hypothetical, it cannot be refuted (as many nonpacificists believe) by pointing out that not everyone will become a pacifist. The problem is whether this argument can establish pacifism as a moral imperative.

One difficulty with the argument is that it seems to rely on a premise the truth of which is purely verbal. In what way would the world be a better place if people gave up fighting? The most obvious way is that the world would be better because there would be no war. But the statement "If everyone gave up fighting, there would be no war" is true by definition, since "war" implies "fighting." It is difficult to see how a statement that simply relates the meanings of words could tell us something about our moral obligations.

A deeper problem with Tolstoy's argument is that "resist not evil" is not the only rule that would yield paradise if everyone obeyed it. Suppose that everyone in the world subscribed to the principle "Use violence, but only in self-defense." If everyone used violence only in self-defense, the same consequences would follow as would arise from universal acceptance of the rule "Never use violence." Consequently, pacifism cannot be shown to be superior to nonpacifism by noting the good consequences that would undeniably ensue if everyone were a pacifist.

(c) Gandhian Pacifism

Certainly the most interesting and effective pacifist of the twentieth century was Mohandas Gandhi (1869–1948). Though a devout Hindu, Gandhi developed his doctrine of nonviolence from elementary metaphysical concepts that are by no means special to Hinduism:

Man as an animal is violent but as spirit is nonviolent. The moment he awakes to the spirit he cannot remain violent. Either he progresses towards *ahimsa* [nonviolence] or rushes to his doom. (*Nonviolence in Peace and War,* I, p. 311)

The requirement not to be violent seems wholly negative; sleeping people achieve it with ease. But for

Gandhi the essential moral task is not merely to be nonviolent but to use the force of the soul (*satyagraha*, "truth grasping") in a continual struggle for justice. The methods of applied *satyagraha* developed by Gandhi—the weaponless marches, the sit-downs and sit-ins, strikes and boycotts, fasts and prayers—captured the admiration of the world and have been widely copied, most notably by Martin Luther King, Jr., in his campaigns against racial discrimination. According to Gandhi, each person, by engaging in *satyagraha* and experiencing suffering on behalf of justice, purifies the soul from pollution emanating from man's animal nature:

A *satyagrahi* is dead to his body even before his enemy attempts to kill him, i.e. he is free from the attachments of his body and lives only in the victory of his soul. (*Nonviolence in Peace and War,* I, p. 318) Nonviolence implies as complete self-purification as is humanly possible. (*Nonviolence in Peace and War,* I, p. 111)

By acting nonviolently, pacifists not only purify their own souls but also transform the souls of their opponents: "A nonviolent revolution is not a program of seizure of power. It is a program of transformation of relationships, ending in peaceful transfer of power" (*Nonviolence in Peace and War,* II, p. 8)

Though in most places Gandhi emphasizes the personal redemption that is possible only through nonviolent resistance to evil, the spiritually positive effect of nonviolence on evil opponents is perhaps equally important, since "The sword of the *satyagrahi* is love" (*Nonviolence in Peace and War,* II, p. 59).

Gandhi, then, is far from preaching the sacredness of biological life. What matters is not biological life but the condition of the soul, the natural and proper state of which is *ahimsa*. The evil of violence is that it distorts and disrupts this natural condition of the soul. The basic moral law (*dharma*) for all people is to seek the restoration of their souls to the harmony of *ahimsa*. This spiritual restoration cannot be achieved by violence, but only by the application of *satyagraha*. Disharmony cannot produce harmony; violence cannot, produce spiritual peace.

The "sacredness of life" defense of pacifism ran into difficulties analyzing situations in which taking one life could save many lives. For Gandhi, this is no problem at all: taking one life may save many biological lives, but it will not save souls. On the contrary, the soul of the killer will be perverted by the act, and that perversion—not loss of life—is what matters morally.

The system of values professed by Gandhi—that the highest human good is a harmonious condition of soul—must be kept in mind when considering the frequent accusation that Gandhi's method of nonviolent resistance "does not work," that nonviolence alone did not and could not force the British to leave India, and that nonviolent resistance to murderous tyrants like Hitler will only provoke the mass murder of the innocent. Perhaps the practice of nonviolence could not "defeat" the British or "defeat" Hitler, but by Gandhi's standards the use of military force would only produce a greater defeat, perverting the souls of thousands engage in war and intensifying the will to violence on the opposing side. On the other hand, the soul of the *satyagrahi* will be strengthened and purified by nonviolent struggle against British imperialism or German Nazism, and in this purification the Gandhian pacifist can obtain spiritual victory even in the face of political defeat.

India did not adopt the creed of nonviolence after the British left in 1948, and it is hardly likely that any modern nation-state will organize its international affairs along Gandhian lines. But none of this affects the validity of Gandhi's arguments, which indicate how things ought to be, not how they are. We have seen that Gandhi's principles do not falter in the face of situations in which taking one life can save lives on balance. But what of situations in which the sacrifice of spiritual purity by one will prevent the corruption of many souls? Suppose, for example, that a Gandhian believes (on good evidence) that a well-timed commando raid will prevent a nation from embarking on an aggressive war, a war that would inflame whole populations with hatred for the enemy. Wouldn't a concern with one's own spiritual purity in such a situation show an immoral lack of concern for the souls of one's fellow men?

Another problem for Gandhi concerns the relationship between violence and coercion. To coerce people is to make them act against their will, for fear of the consequences they will suffer if they do not obey. Coercion, then, is a kind of spiritual violence, directed against the imagination and will of the victim. The "violence" most conspicuously rejected by Gandhi—pushing, shoving, striking with hands, the use of weapons, the placing of bombs, and explosives—is essentially physical violence, directed against the bodies of opponents. But if physical violence against bodies is spiritually corrupting, psychological violence directed at the will of opponents must be even more corrupting.

In his writings Gandhi condemned coercion. Yet in practice he can hardly be said to have renounced *psychological* coercion. Obviously he would have preferred to have the British depart from India of their own free will, deciding that it was in their own best interest, or at least morally necessary, to leave. But if the British had decided, in the absence of coercion, to stay, Gandhi was prepared to exert every kind of nonviolent pressure to make them go. And when Gandhi on occasion attempted to achieve political objectives by a "fast unto death," his threat of self-starvation brought enormous psychological pressure on the authorities, who, among other things, feared the riots that would ensue should Gandhi die.

The Gandhian pacifist, then, must explain why psychological pressure is permissible if physical pressure is forbidden. One possible answer is that physical pressure cannot transform the soul of the opponents, but psychological pressure, since it operates on the mind, can effect a spiritual transformation. Indeed, Gandhi characterized his terrifying fasts as acts of education, not coercion. But the claim that these fasts were not coercive confuses the noncoercive intention behind the act with its predictable coercive effects; and if education is the name of the game, the nonpacifist will remark that violence has been known to teach a few good lessons in its day. In many spiritual traditions, what matters essentially is not the kind of pressure but that the right pressure be applied at the right time and in the right way. Zen masters have brought students to enlightenment by clouting them on the ears, and God helped St. Paul to see the light by knocking him off his horse.

In addition to these technical problems, many people will be inclined to reject the system of values from which Gandhi's deductions flow. Many will concede that good character is important and that helping others to develop moral virtues is an important task. But few agree with Gandhi that the development of moral purity is the supreme human good, and that other goods, like the preservation of human life, or progress in the arts and sciences, have little or no value in comparison. If even a little value is conceded to these other things, then on occasion it will be necessary to put aside the project of developing spiritual purity in order to preserve other values. These acts of preservation may require physical violence, and those who use violence to defend life or beauty or liberty may indeed be corrupting their souls. But it is hard to believe that an occasional and necessary act of violence on behalf of these values will totally and permanently corrupt the soul, and those who use violence judiciously may be right in thinking that the saving of life or beauty or liberty may be worth a small or temporary spiritual loss.

4. PRIVATE PACIFISM

Perhaps the rarest form of pacifist is the pacifist who renounces violence in personal relations but condones the use of force in the political sphere. Such a pacifist will not use violence for self-defense but believes that it is permissible for the state to use judicial force against criminals and military force against foreign enemies. A private pacifist renounces self-defense but supports national defense.

(a) Augustine's Limited Pacifism

Historically, private pacifism developed as an attempt to reconcile the demands of the Sermon on the Mount with the Christian duty of charity. The Sermon on the Mount requires Christians to "resist not evil"; the duty of charity requires pity for the weak who suffer the injustice of the strong. For St. Augustine (354–430), one essential message of the Gospels is the good news that this present life is as nothing compared with the life to come. The person who tries to hold on to earthly possessions is deluded as to what is truly valuable: "If any man will sue thee at the law, and take away thy coat, let him have thy cloak also" (Matt. 5:40). What goes for earthly coats should go for earthly life as well, so if any man seeks to take a Christian life, the Christian should let him have it. On this view, the doctrine "resist not evil" is just an expression of contempt for earthly possessions.

But according to Augustine there are some things in this world that do have value: justice, for example, the relief of suffering, and the preservation of the Church, which Augustine equated with civilization itself. To defend these things with necessary force is not to fall prey to delusions about the good. For Augustine, then, service in the armed forces is not inconsistent with Christian values.

One difficulty for theories like Augustine's is that they seem to justify military service only when military force is used in a just cause. Unfortunately, once in the service, the man in the ranks is not in a position to evaluate the justice of his nation's cause; indeed, in many modern nations, the principle of military subordination to civilian rule prevents even generals from evaluating the purposes of war declared by political leaders. But Augustine argues that the cause of justice cannot be served without armies, and armies cannot function unless subordinates follow orders without questioning the purposes of the conflict. The necessary conditions for justice and charity require that some men put themselves in positions in which they might be required to fight for injustice.

(b) The Problem of Self-Defense

Many will agree with Augustine that most violence at the personal level—the violence of crime, vendetta, and domestic brutality, for example—goes contrary to moral principles. But most are prepared to draw the line at personal and collective self-defense. Can the obligation to be charitable justify participation in military service but stop short of justifying the use of force by private citizens, if that force is exercised to protect the weak from the oppression of the strong? Furthermore, the obligation to be charitable does not

exclude acts of charity toward oneself. For Augustine, violence was a dangerous tool, best kept out of the hands of the citizens and best left strictly at the disposal of the state. Beset with fears of crime in the streets, the contemporary American is less inclined to worry about the anarchic effects of private users of defensive force and more inclined to worry about the protection the police seem unable to provide.

For these worried people, the existence of a right to self-defense is self-evident. But the existence of this right is not self-evident to universal or private pacifists, and it was not self-evident to St. Augustine. In the Christian tradition, no right to self-defense was recognized until its existence was certified by Thomas Aquinas in the thirteenth century. Aquinas derived the right to self-defense from the universal tendency to self-preservation, assuming (contrary to Augustine) that a natural tendency must be morally right. As for the Christian duty to love one's enemy, Aquinas argued that acts of self-defense have two effects—the saving of life and the taking of life—and that self-defensive uses of force intend primarily the saving of life. This makes the use of force in self-defense a morally permissible act of charity. The right to self-defense is now generally recognized in Catholic moral theology and in Western legal systems. But it can hardly be said that Aquinas's arguments, which rely heavily on assumptions from Greek philosophy, succeed in reconciling the claims of self-defense with the prescriptions of the Sermon on the Mount.

5. ANTIWAR PACIFISM

Most people who believe in the right to personal self-defense also believe that some wars are morally justified. In fact, the notion of self-defense and the notion of just war are commonly linked: just wars are said to be defensive wars, and the justice of defensive war is inferred from the right of personal self-defense, projected from the individual to the national level. But some people reject this projection: they endorse the validity of personal self-defense, but they deny that war can be justified by appeal to self-defense or any other right. On the contrary, they argue that war always involves an inexcusable viola-

tion of rights. For such antiwar pacifists, all participation in war is morally wrong.

(a) The Killing of Soldiers

One universal and necessary feature of wars is that
soldiers get killed in them. Most people accept such
killings as a necessary evil, and judge the killing of
soldiers in war to be morally acceptable. If the war
is fought for a just cause, the killing of enemy soldiers is justified as necessary to the triumph of right.
If the war is fought for an unjust cause, the killing
of enemy soldiers is acceptable because it is considered an honorable thing to fight for one's country, right or wrong, provided that one fights well
and cleanly. But the antiwar pacifist does not take
the killing of soldiers for granted. Everyone has a
right to life, and the killing of soldiers in war is
intentional killing, a deliberate violation of the
right to life. According to the standard interpretation of basic rights, it is never morally justifiable to
violate a basic right in order to produce some good;
the end, in such cases, does not justify the means.
How, then, can the killing of soldiers in war be
morally justified—or even excused?

Perhaps the commonest reply to the challenge of
antiwar pacifism is that killing in war is a matter of
self-defense, *personal* self-defense, the right to which
is freely acknowledged by the antiwar pacifist. In war,
the argument goes, it is either kill or be killed—and
that type of killing is killing in self-defense. But
though the appeal to self-defense is natural, antiwar
pacifists believe that it is not successful. First of all,
on the usual understanding of "self-defense," those
who kill can claim the justification of self-defense
only if (a) they had no other way to save their lives
or preserve themselves from physical harm except by
killing, and (b) they did nothing to provoke the attack
to which they are subjected. Antiwar pacifists point
out that soldiers on the battlefield do have a way of
saving themselves from death or harm without killing
anyone: they can surrender. Furthermore, for soldiers
fighting for an unjust cause—for example, German
soldiers fighting in the invasion of Russia in 1941—
it is difficult to argue that they "did nothing to provoke" the deadly force directed at them. But if the

German army provoked the Russians to stand and
fight on Russian soil, German soldiers cannot legitimately claim self-defense as a moral justification for
killing Russian soldiers.

To the nonpacifist, these points might seem like
legalistic quibbles. But the antiwar pacifist has an
even stronger argument against killing soldiers in
war. The vast majority of soldiers who die in war do
not die in "kill or be killed" situations. They are killed
by bullets, shells, or bombs directed from safe launching points—"safe" in the sense that those who shoot
the bullets or fire the shells or drop the bombs are in
no immediate danger of death. Since those who kill
are not in immediate danger of death, they cannot
invoke "self-defense" to justify the deaths they cause.

Some other argument besides self-defense, then,
must explain why the killing of soldiers in war should
not be classified as murder. Frequently, nonpacifists
argue that the explanation is found in the doctrine
of "assumption of risk," the idea, common in civil
law, that persons who freely assume a risk have only
themselves to blame if the risk is realized. When a
soldier goes to war, he is well aware that one risk of
his trade is getting killed on the battlefield. If he dies
on the field, the responsibility for his death lies with
himself, not with the man who shot him. By assuming the risk—so the argument goes—he waived his
right to life, at least on the battlefield.

One does not have to be a pacifist to see difficulties in this argument. First of all, in all substantial
modern wars, most of the men on the line are not
volunteers, but draftees. Only a wealthy nation like
the United States can afford an all-volunteer army,
and most experts believe that the American volunteer ranks will have to be supplemented by draftees
should the United States become involved in another
conflict on the scale of Korea or Vietnam. Second, in
many cases in which a risk is realized, responsibility
for the bad outcome lies not with the person who
assumed the risk but with the person who created it.
If an arsonist sets fire to a house and a parent rushes
in to save the children, dying in the rescue attempt,
responsibility for the parent's death lies not with the
parent who assumed the risk but with the arsonist
who created it. So if German armies invade Russia,

posing the risk of death in battle, and if Russian soldiers assume this risk and fight back, the deaths of Russians are the fault of German invaders, not the fault of the defenders who assumed the risk.

These criticisms of German foot soldiers will irritate many who served in the armed forces and who know how little political and military decision making is left to the men on the front lines, who seem to be the special target of these pacifist arguments. But antiwar pacifists will deny that their aim is to condemn the men on the battlefield. Most antiwar pacifists feel that soldiers in war act under considerable compulsion and are excused for that reason from responsibility for the killing they do. But to say that battlefield killings are *excusable* is not to say that they are morally *justified*. On the contrary, if such killings are excusable, it must be that there is some immorality to be excused.

(b) The Killing of Civilians

In the chronicles of ancient wars, conflict was total and loss in battle was frequently followed by general slaughter of men, women, and children on the losing side. It has always been considered part of the trend toward civilization to confine the destruction of war to the personnel and instruments of war, sparing civilians and their property as much as possible. This civilizing trend was conspicuously reversed in World War II, in which the ratio of civilian deaths to total war deaths was perhaps the highest it had been since the wars of religion in the seventeenth century. A very high ratio of civilian deaths to total deaths was also characteristic of the war in Vietnam. Given the immense firepower of modern weapons and the great distances between the discharges of weapons and the explosions of bullets of shells near the targets, substantial civilian casualties are an inevitable part of modern land war. But it is immoral to kill civilians, the antiwar pacifist argues, and from this it follows that modern land warfare is necessarily immoral.

Few nonpacifists will argue that killing enemy civilians is justifiable when such killings are avoidable. Few will argue that killing enemy civilians is justifiable when such killings are the *primary* objective of a military operation. But what about the deaths of civilians that are the unavoidable results of military operations directed to some *other* result? The pacifist classifies such killings as immoral, whereas most nonpacifists call them regrettable but unavoidable deaths, not murders. But why are they not murder, if the civilians are innocent, and if it is known in advance that some civilians will be killed? Isn't this an intentional killing of the innocent, which is the traditional definition of murder?

The sophisticated nonpacifist may try to parry this thrust with analogies to policies outside the arena of war. There are, after all, many morally acceptable policies that, when adopted, have the effect of killing innocent persons. If the Congress decides to set a speed limit of 55 miles per hour on federal highways, more people will die than if Congress sets the speed limit at 45 miles per hour. Since many people who die on the highway are innocent, the Congress has chosen a policy that knowingly brings death to the innocent, but no one calls it murder. Or suppose, for example, that a public health officer is considering a national vaccination program to forestall a flu epidemic. He knows that if he does not implement the vaccination program, many people will die from the flu. On the other hand, if the program is implemented, a certain number of people will die from allergic reactions to the vaccine. Most of the people who die from allergic reactions will be people who would not have died of the flu if the vaccination program had not been implemented. So the vaccination program will kill innocent people who would otherwise be saved if the program were abandoned. If the public health officer implements such a program, we do *not* think that he is a murderer.

Nonpacifists argue that what makes the action of Congress and the action of the public health officer morally permissible in these cases is that the deaths of the innocent, although foreseen, are not the intended goal of these policies. Congress does not want people to die on the highways; every highway death is a regrettable death. The purpose of setting the speed limit at 55 miles per hour is not to kill people but to provide a reasonable balance between safety and convenience. Likewise, it is not the purpose of the public health officer to kill people by giving them vaccine. His goal is to save lives on balance, and every death from the vaccine is a regrettable death. Likewise, in war, when civilians are killed as a result of necessary military operations, the deaths of the civilians are not the intended goal of the military operation. They are foreseen, but they are always regretted. If we do not accuse the Congress of murder and the Public Health Service of murder in these cases, consistency requires that we not accuse military forces of murder when they cause civilian deaths in war, especially if every attempt is made to keep civilian deaths to a minimum.

Antiwar pacifists do not condemn the Congress and the Public Health Service in cases like these. But they assert that the case of war is different in a morally relevant way. To demonstrate the difference, antiwar pacifists provide an entirely different analysis of the moral justification for speed limits and vaccination programs. In their opinion, the facts that highway deaths and vaccination deaths are "unintended" and "regretted" is morally irrelevant. The real justification lies in the factor of consent. In the case of federal highway regulations, the rules are decided by Congress, which is elected by the people, the same people who use the highways. If Congress decides on a 55-mile-an-hour speed limit, this is a regulation that, in some sense, highway drivers have imposed upon themselves. Those people who die on the highway because of a higher speed limit have, in a double sense, assumed the risks generated by that speed limit: they have, through the Congress, created the risk, and by venturing onto the highway, have freely exposed themselves to the risk. The responsibility for these highway deaths, then, lies either on the drivers themselves or on the people who crashed into them—not on the Congress.

Likewise, in the case of the vaccination program, if people are warned in advance of the risks of vaccination, and if they nevertheless choose to be vaccinated, they are responsible for their own deaths should the risks be realized. According to the antiwar pacifist, it is this consent given by drivers and vaccination volunteers that justifies these policies, and it is precisely this element of consent that is absent in the case of the risks inflicted on enemy civilians in time of war.

Consider the standard textbook example of allegedly justifiable killing of civilians in time of war. Suppose that the destruction of a certain bridge is an important military objective, but if the bridge is bombed, it is very likely that civilians living close by will be killed. (The civilians cannot be warned without alerting the enemy to reinforce the bridge.) If the bridge is bombed and some civilians are killed, the bombing victims are not in the same moral category as highway victims or victims of vaccination. The bombing victims did not order the bombing of themselves through some set of elected representatives. Nor did the bombing victims freely consent to the bombing of their bridge. Nor was the bombing in any way undertaken as a calculated risk in the interest of the victims. For all these reasons, the moral conclusions regarding highway legislation and vaccination programs do not carry over to bombing of the bridge.

Nonpacifists who recognize that it will be very difficult to fight wars without bombing bridges may argue that the victims of this bombing in some sense assumed the risks of bombardment by choosing to live close to a potential military target. Indeed, it is occasionally claimed that all the civilians in a nation at war have assumed the risks of war, since they could avoid the risks of war simply by moving to a neutral country. But such arguments are strained and uncharitable, even for those rare warring nations that permit freedom of emigration. Most people consider it a major sacrifice to give up their homes, and an option that requires such a sacrifice cannot be considered an option open for free choice. The analogy between the unintended victims of vaccination and the unintended civilian victims of war seems to have broken down.

(c) The Balance of Good and Evil in War

It is left to the nonpacifist to argue that the killing of soldiers and civilians in war is in the end justifiable in order to obtain great moral goods that can be obtained only by fighting for them. Civilians have rights to life, but those rights can be outweighed by the national objectives, provided those objectives are morally acceptable and overwhelmingly important. Admittedly, this argument for killing civilians is available only to the just side in a war, but if the argument is valid, it proves that there can *be* a just side, contrary to the arguments of antiwar pacifism.

Antiwar pacifists have two lines of defense. First, they can continue to maintain that the end does not justify the means, if the means be murderous. Second, they can, and will, go on to argue that it is a tragic mistake to believe that there are great moral goods that can be obtained only by war. According to antiwar pacifists, the amount of moral good produced by war is greatly exaggerated. The Mexican War, for example, resulted in half of Mexico being transferred to American rule. This was a great good for the United States, but not a great moral good, since the United States had little claim to the ceded territory, and no great injustice would have persisted if the war had not been fought at all.

The Revolutionary War in America is widely viewed as a war that produced a great moral good; but if the war had not been fought, the history of the United States would be similar to the history of Canada (which remained loyal)—and no one feels that the Canadians have suffered or are suffering great injustices that the American colonies avoided by war. Likewise, it is difficult to establish the goods produced by World War I or the moral losses that would have ensued if the winning side, "our side," had lost. Bertrand Russell imagined the results of a British loss in World War I as follows:

The greatest sum that foreigners could possibly exact would be the total economic rent of the land and natural resources of England. [But] the working classes, the shopkeepers, manufacturers, and merchants, the literary men and men of science—all the people that make England of any account in the world—have at most an infinitesimal and accidental share in the rental of England. The men who have a share use their rents in luxury, political corruption, taking the lives of birds, and depopulating and enslaving the rural districts. It is this life of the idle rich that would be curtailed if the Germans exacted tribute from England. (*Justice in War Time*, pp. 48–49)

But multiplying examples of wars that did little moral good will not establish the pacifist case. The pacifist must show that *no* war has done enough good to justify the killing of soldiers and the killing of civilians that occurred in the war. A single war that produces moral goods sufficient to justify its killings will refute the pacifist claim that *all* wars are morally unjustifiable. Obviously this brings the antiwar pacifist head to head with World War II.

It is commonly estimated that 35 million people died as a result of World War II. It is difficult to imagine that any cause could justify so much death, but fortunately the Allies need only justify their share of these killings. Between 1939 and 1945 Allied forces killed about 5.5 million Axis soldiers and about 1 million civilians in Axis countries. Suppose that Britain and the United States had chosen to stay out of World War II and suppose that Stalin had, like Lenin, surrendered to Germany shortly after the invasion. Does avoiding the world that would have resulted from these decisions justify killing 6.5 million people?

If Hitler and Tojo had won the war, doubtless they would have killed a great many people both before and after victory, but it is quite likely that the total of *additional* victims, beyond those they killed in the war that *was* fought, would have been less than 6.5 million and, at any rate, the responsibility for those deaths would fall on Hitler and Tojo, not on Allied nations. If Hitler and Tojo had won the war, large portions of the world would have fallen under foreign domination, perhaps for a very long time. But the antiwar pacifist will point out that the main areas of Axis foreign domination—China and Russia—were not places in which the citizens enjoyed a high level of freedom *before the war began*. Perhaps the majority of people in the conquered areas would have worked out a *modus vivendi* with their new rulers, as did the majority of French citizens during the German occupation. Nor can it be argued that World War II was necessary to save six million Jews from annihilation in the Holocaust, since in fact the war did *not* save them.

The ultimate aims of Axis leaders are a matter for historical debate. Clearly the Japanese had no intention of conquering the United States, and some historians suggest that Hitler hoped to avoid war with England and America, declaring war with England reluctantly, and only after the English declared it against him. Nevertheless, popular opinion holds that Hitler intended to conquer the world, and if preventing the conquest of Russia and China could not justify six and one-half million killings, most Americans are quite confident that preventing the conquest of England and the United States does justify killing on this scale.

The antiwar pacifist disagrees. Certainly German rule of England and the United States would have been a very bad thing. At the same time, hatred of such German rule would be partially fueled by hatred of foreigners, and hatred of foreigners, as such, is an irrational and morally unjustifiable passion. After all, if rule by foreigners were, by itself, a great moral wrong, the British, with their great colonial empire, could hardly consider themselves the morally superior side in World War II.

No one denies that a Nazi victory in World War II would have had morally frightful results. But, according to antiwar pacifism, killing six and one half million people is also morally frightful, and preventing one moral wrong does not obviously outweigh committing the other. Very few people today share the pacifists' condemnation of World War II, but perhaps that is because the dead killed by the Allies cannot speak up and make sure that their losses are properly counted on the moral scales. Antiwar pacifists speak on behalf of the enemy dead, and on behalf of all those millions who would have lived if the war had not been fought. On this silent constituency they rest their moral case.

Reconciling Pacifists and Just War Theorists

James P. Sterba

Traditionally pacifism and just war theory have represented radically opposed responses to aggression. Pacifism has been interpreted to rule out any use of violence in response to aggression. Just war theory has been interpreted to permit a measured use of violence in response to aggression. It has been thought that the two views might sometimes agree in particular cases—for example, that pacifists and just war theorists might unconditionally oppose nuclear war, but beyond that it has been generally held that the two views lead to radically opposed recommendations. In this paper, I hope to show that this is not the case. I will argue that pacifism and just war theory, in their most morally defensible interpretations, can be substantially reconciled both in theory and practice.

James P. Sterba, "Reconciling Pacifists and Just War Theorists," *Social Theory and Practice* 18, no. 1 (Spring 1992): 21–38 (edited). Reprinted with permission of Social Theory and Practice.

In traditional just war theory there are two basic elements: an account of just cause and an account of just means. Just cause is usually specified as follows:

1) There must be substantial aggression;
2) Nonbelligerent correctives must be either hopeless or too costly; and
3) Belligerent correctives must be neither hopeless nor too costly.

Needless to say, the notion of substantial aggression is a bit fuzzy, but it is generally understood to be the type of aggression that violates people's most fundamental rights. To suggest some specific examples of what is and is not substantial aggression, usually the taking of hostages is regarded as substantial aggression while the nationalization of particular firms owned by foreigners is not so regarded. But even when substantial aggression occurs, frequently nonbelligerent correctives are neither hopeless nor too costly. And even when nonbelligerent correctives are either hopeless or too costly, in order for there to be a just cause, belligerent correctives must be neither hopeless nor too costly.

Traditional just war theory assumes, however, that there are just causes and goes on to specify just means as imposing two requirements:

1) Harm to innocents should not be directly intended as an end or a means.
2) The harm resulting from the belligerent means should not be disproportionate to the particular defensive objective to be attained.

While the just means conditions apply to each defensive action, the just cause conditions must be met by the conflict as a whole.

It is important to note that these requirements of just cause and just means are not essentially about war at all. Essentially, they constitute a theory of just defense that can apply to war but can also apply to a wide range of defensive actions short of war. Of course, what needs to be determined is whether these requirements can be justified. Since just war theory is usually opposed to pacifism, to secure a non-question-begging justification for the theory and its requirements we need to proceed as much as possible from premises that are common to pacifists and just war theorists alike. The difficult here is that there is not just one form of pacifism but many. So we need to determine which form of pacifism is most morally defensible.

Now when most people think of pacifism they tend to identify it with a theory of nonviolence. We can call this view "nonviolent pacifism." It maintains that:

Any use of violence against other human beings is morally prohibited.

It has been plausibly argued, however, that this form of pacifism is incoherent. In a well-known article, Jan Narveson rejects nonviolent pacifism as incoherent because it recognizes a right to life yet rules out any

use of force in defense of that right.[1] The view is incoherent, Narveson claims, because having a right entails the legitimacy of using force in defense of that right at least on some occasions.

Given the cogency of objections of this sort, some have opted for a form of pacifism that does not rule out all violence but only lethal violence. We can call this view "nonlethal pacifism." It maintains that

Any lethal use of force against other human beings is morally prohibited.

In defense of nonlethal pacifism, Cheyney Ryan has argued that there is a substantial issue between the pacifist and the nonpacifist concerning whether we can or should create the necessary distance between ourselves and other human beings in order to make the act of killing possible.[2] To illustrate, Ryan cites George Orwell's reluctance to shoot at an enemy soldier who jumped out of a trench and ran along the top of a parapet half-dressed and holding up his trousers with both hands. Ryan contends that what kept Orwell from shooting was that he couldn't think of the soldier as a thing rather than a fellow human being.

However, it is not clear that Orwell's encounter supports nonlethal pacifism. For it may be that what kept Orwell from shooting the enemy soldier was not his inability to think of the soldier as a thing rather than a fellow human being but rather his inability to think of the soldier who was holding up his trousers with both hands as a threat or a combatant. Under this interpretation, Orwell's decision not to shoot would accord well with the requirements of just war theory.

Let us suppose, however, that someone is attempting to take your life. Why does that permit you, the defender of nonlethal pacifism might ask, to kill the person making the attempt? The most cogent response, it seems to me, is that killing in such a case is not evil, or at least not morally evil, because anyone who is wrongfully engaged in an attempt upon your life has already forfeited his or her right to life by engaging in such aggression.[3] So, provided that you are reasonably certain that the aggressor is wrongfully engaged in an attempt upon your life, you would be morally justified in killing, assuming that it is the only way of saving your own life.

There is, however, a form of pacifism that remains untouched by the criticisms I have raised against both nonviolent pacifism and nonlethal pacifism. This form of pacifism neither prohibits all violence nor even all uses of lethal force. We can call the view "anti-war pacifism" because it holds that

Any participation in the massive use of lethal force in warfare is morally prohibited.

In defense of anti-war pacifism, it is undeniable that wars have brought enormous amounts of death and destruction in their wake and that many of those who have perished in them are noncombatants or innocents. In fact, the tendency of modern wars has been to produce higher and higher proportions of noncombatant casualties, making it more and more difficult to justify participation in such wars. At the same time, strategies for nonbelligerent conflict resolution are rarely intensively developed and explored before nations choose to go to war, making it all but impossible to justify participation in such wars.

To determine whether the requirements of just war theory can be reconciled with those of anti-war pacifism, however, we need to consider whether we should distinguish between harm intentionally inflicted upon innocents and harm whose infliction of innocents is merely foreseen? On the one hand, we could favor a uniform restriction against the infliction of harm upon innocents that ignores the intended/foreseen distinction. On the other hand, we could favor a differential restriction which is more severe against the intentional infliction of harm upon innocents but is less severe against the infliction of harm that is merely foreseen. What needs to be determined, therefore, is whether there is any rationale for favoring this differential restriction on harm over a uniform restriction. But this presupposes that we can, in practice, distinguish between what is foreseen and what is intended, and some have challenged whether this can be done. So first we need to address this challenge.

Now the practical test that is frequently appealed to in order to distinguish between foreseen and intended elements of an action is the Counterfactual Test. According to this test, two questions are relevant:

1) Would you have performed the action if only the good consequences would have resulted and not the evil consequences?
2) Would you have performed the action if only the evil consequences resulted and not the good consequences?

If an agent answers "Yes" to the first question and "No" to the second, some would conclude that (1) the action is an intended means to the good consequences; (2) the good consequences are an intended end; and (3) the evil consequences are merely foreseen.

But how well does this Counterfactual Test work? Douglas Lackey has argued that the test gives the wrong result in any case where the "act that produces an evil effect produces a larger good effect."[4] Lackey cites the bombing of Hiroshima as an example. That bombing is generally thought to have had two effects: the killing of Japanese civilians and the shortening of the war. Now suppose we were to ask:

1) Would Truman have dropped the bomb if only the shortening of the war would have resulted but not the killing of the Japanese civilians?
2) Would Truman have dropped the bomb if only the Japanese civilians would have been killed and the war not shortened?

And suppose that the answer to the first question is that Truman would have dropped the bomb if only the shortening of the war would have resulted but not the killing of the Japanese civilians, and the answer to the second question is that Truman would not have dropped the bomb if only the Japanese-civilians would have been killed and the war not shortened. Lackey concludes from this that the killing of civilians at Hiroshima, self-evidently a means for shortening the war, is by the Counterfactual Test classified not as a means but as a mere foreseen consequence. On these grounds, Lackey rejects the Counterfactual Test as an effective device for distinguishing between the foreseen and the intended consequences of an action.

Unfortunately, this is to reject the Counterfactual Test only because one expects too much from it. It is to expect the test to determine all of the following:

1) Whether the action is an intended means to the good consequences;
2) Whether the good consequences are an intended end of the action; and
3) Whether the evil consequences are simply foreseen consequences.

In fact, this test is only capable of meeting the first two of these expectations. And the test clearly succeeds in doing this for Lackey's own example, where the test shows the bombing of Hiroshima to be an intended means to shortening the war, and shortening the war an intended consequence of the action.

To determine whether the evil consequences are simply foreseen consequences, however, an additional test is needed, which I shall call the Nonexplanation Test. According to this test, the relevant question is:

Does the bringing about of the evil consequences help explain why the agent undertook the action as a means to the good consequences?

If the answer is "No," that is, if the bringing about of the evil consequences does not help explain why the agent undertook the action as a means to the good consequences, the evil consequences are merely foreseen. But if the answer is "Yes," the evil consequences are an intended means to the good consequences.

Of course, there is no guaranteed procedure for arriving at an answer to the Nonexplanation Test. Nevertheless, when we are in doubt concerning whether the evil consequences of an act are simply foreseen, seeking an answer to the Nonexplanation Test will tend to be the best way of reasonably resolving that doubt. For example, applied to Lackey's

example, the Nonexplanation Test comes up with a "Yes," since the evil consequences in this example do help explain why the bombing was undertaken to shorten the war. For according to the usual account, Truman ordered the bombing to bring about the civilian deaths which by their impact upon Japanese morale were expected to shorten the war. So, by the Nonexplanation Test, the civilian deaths were an intended means to the good consequences of shortening the war.

Assuming then that we can distinguish in practice between harm intentionally inflicted upon innocents and harm whose infliction on innocents is merely foreseen, we need to determine whether there is any rationale for favoring a differential restriction that is more severe against the intentional infliction of harm upon innocents but is less severe against the infliction of harm that is merely foreseen over a uniform restriction against the infliction of harm upon innocents that ignores the intended/foreseen distinction.

Let us first examine the question from the perspective of those suffering the harm. Initially, it might appear to matter little whether the harm would be intended or just foreseen by those who cause it. From the perspective of those suffering harm, it might appear that what matters is simply that the overall amount of harm be restricted irrespective of whether it is foreseen or intended. But consider—don't those who suffer harm have more reason to protest when the harm is done to them by agents who are directly engaged in causing harm to them than when the harm is done incidentally by agents whose ends and means are good? Don't we have more reason to protest when we are being used by others than when we are affected by them only incidentally?

Moreover, if we examine the question from the perspective of those causing harm, additional support for this line of reasoning can be found. For it would seem that we have more reason to protest a restriction against foreseen harm than we have reason to protest a comparable restriction against intended harm. This is because a restriction against foreseen harm limits our actions when our ends and means are good whereas a restriction against intended harm only limits our actions when our ends or means are evil or harmful, and it would seem that we have greater grounds for acting when both our ends and means are good than when they are not. Consequently, because we have more reason to protest when we are being used by others than when we are being affected by them only incidentally, and because we have more reason to act when both our ends and means are good than when they are not, we should favor the foreseen/intended distinction that is incorporated into just means.

It might be objected, however, that at least sometimes we could produce greater good overall by violating the foreseen/intended distinction of just means and acting with the evil means of intentionally harming innocents. On this account, it might be argued that it should be permissible at least sometimes to intentionally harm innocents in order to achieve greater good overall.

Now it seems to me that this objection is welltaken in so far as it is directed against an absolute restriction upon intentional harm to innocents. It seems clear that there are expectations to such a restriction when intentional harm to innocents is:

1) trivial (for example, as in the case of stepping on someone's foot to get out of a crowded subway);
2) easily repairable (for example, as in the case of lying to a temporarily depressed friend to keep him from committing suicide); or
3) greatly outweighed by the consequences of the action, especially to innocent people (for example, as in the case of shooting one of two hundred civilian hostages to prevent in the only way possible the execution of all two hundred).

Yet while we need to recognize these executions to an absolute restriction upon intentional harm to innocents, there is good reason not to permit simply maximizing good consequences overall because that would place unacceptable burdens upon particular individuals. More specifically, it would be an unacceptable burden on innocents to allow them to be intentionally harmed in cases other than the exceptions we have just enumerated. And, allowing for these exceptions, we would still have reason to favor

a differential restriction against harming innocents that is more severe against the intentional infliction of harm upon innocents but is less severe against the infliction of harm upon innocents that is merely foreseen. Again, the main grounds for this preference is that we would have more reason to protest when we are being used by others than when we are being affected by them only incidentally, and more reason to act when both our ends and means are good than when they are not.

So far, I have argued that there are grounds for favoring a differential restriction on harm to innocents that is more severe against intended harm and less severe against foreseen harm. I have further argued that this restriction is not absolute so that when the evil intended is trivial, easily repairable or greatly outweighed by the consequences, intentional harm to innocents can be justified. Moreover, there is no reason to think that anti-war pacifists would reject either of these conclusions. Anti-war pacifists are opposed to any participation in the massive use of lethal force in warfare, yet this need not conflict with the commitment of just war theorists to a differential but nonabsolute restriction on harm to innocents as a requirement of just means.[5] Where just war theory goes wrong, according to anti-war pacifists, is not in its restriction on harming innocents but rather in its failure to adequately determine when belligerent correctives are too costly to constitute a just cause or lacking in the proportionality required by just means. According to anti-war pacifists, just war theory provides insufficient restraint in both of these areas. Now to evaluate this criticism, we need to consider a wide range of cases where killing or inflicting serious harm on others in defense of oneself or others might be thought to be justified, beginning with the easiest cases to assess from the perspectives of anti-war pacifism and the just war theory and then moving on to cases that are more difficult to assess from those perspectives.

Case 1 where only the intentional or foreseen killing of an unjust aggressor would prevent one's own death.[6] This case clearly presents no problems. In the first place, anti-war pacifists adopted their view because they were convinced that there were instances of justified killing. And, in this case, the only person killed is an unjust aggressor. So surely anti-war pacifists would have to agree with just war theorists that one justifiably kill an unjust aggressor if it is the only way to save one's life.

Case 2 where only the intentional or foreseen killing of an unjust aggressor and the foreseen killing of one innocent bystander would prevent one's own death and that of five other innocent people.[7] In this case, we have the foreseen killing of an innocent person as well as the killing of the unjust aggressor, but since it is the only way to save one's own life and the lives of five other innocent people, anti-war pacifists and just war theorists alike would have reason to judge it morally permissible. In this case, the intended life-saving benefits to six innocent people is judged to outweigh the foreseen death of one innocent person and the intended or foreseen death of the unjust aggressor.

Case 3 where only the intentional or foreseen killing of an unjust aggressor and the foreseen killing of one innocent bystander would prevent the death of five other innocent people. In this case, despite the fact that we lack the justification of self-defense, saving the lives of five innocent people in the only way possible should still provide anti-war pacifists and just war theorists with sufficient grounds for granting the moral permissibility of killing an unjust aggressor, even when the killing of an innocent bystander is a foreseen consequence. In this case, the intended life-saving benefits to five innocent people would still outweigh the foreseen death of one innocent person and the intended or foreseen death of the unjust aggressor.

Case 4 where only the intentional or foreseen killing of an unjust aggressor and the foreseen killing of five innocent people would prevent the death of two innocent people. In this case, neither anti-war pacifists nor just war theorists would find the cost and proportionality requirements of just war theory to be met. Too many innocent people would have to be killed to save too few. Here the fact that the deaths of the innocents would be merely foreseen does not outweigh the fact that we would have to accept the deaths of five innocents and the death of the unjust aggressor in order to be able to save two innocents.

Notice that up to this point in interpreting these cases, we have simply been counting the number of innocent deaths involved in each case and opting for whichever solution minimized the loss of innocent lives that would result. Suppose, however, that an unjust aggressor is not threatening the lives of innocents but only their welfare or property. Would the taking of the unjust aggressor's life in defense of the welfare and property of innocents be judged proportionate? Consider the following case.

Case 5 where only the intentional or foreseen killing of an unjust aggressor would prevent serious injury to oneself and five other innocent people. Since in this case the intentional or foreseen killing of the unjust aggressor is the only way of preventing serious injury to oneself and five other innocent people, then, by analogy with Cases 1–3, both anti-war pacifists and just war theorists alike would have reason to affirm its moral permissibility. Of course, if there were any other way of stopping unjust aggressors in such cases short of killing them, that course of action would clearly be required. Yet if there is no alternative, the intentional or foreseen killing of the unjust aggressor to prevent serious injury to oneself and/or five other innocent people would be justified.

In such cases, the serious injury could be bodily injury, as when an aggressor threatens to break one's limbs, or it could be serious psychological injury, as when an aggressor threatens to inject mind-altering drugs, or it could be a serious threat to property. Of course, in most cases where serious injury is threatened, there will be ways of stopping aggressors short of killing them. Unfortunately, this is not always possible.

In still other kinds of cases, stopping an unjust aggressor would require indirectly inflicting serious harm, but not death, upon innocent bystanders. Consider the following cases.

Case 6 where only the intentional or foreseen infliction of serious harm upon an unjust aggressor and the foreseen infliction of serious harm upon one innocent bystander would prevent serious harm to oneself and five other innocent people.

Case 7 where only the intentional or foreseen infliction of serious harm upon an unjust aggressor and the foreseen infliction of serious harm upon one innocent bystander would prevent serious harm to five other innocent people.

In both of these cases, serious harm is indirectly inflicted upon one innocent bystander in order to prevent greater harm from being inflicted by an unjust aggressor upon other innocent people. In Case 6, we also have the justification of self-defense, which is lacking in Case 7. Nevertheless, with regard to both cases, anti-war pacifists and just war theorists should agree that preventing serious injury to five or six innocent people in the only way possible renders it morally permissible to inflict serious injury upon an unjust aggressor, even when the serious injury of one innocent person is a foreseen consequence. In these cases, by analogy with Cases 2 and 3, the foreseen serious injury of one innocent person and the intended or foreseen injury of the unjust aggressor should be judged proportionate given the intended injury-preventing benefits to five or six innocent people.

Up to this point there has been the basis for general agreement among anti-war pacifists and just war theorists as to how to interpret the proportionality requirement of just means, but in the following case this no longer obtains.

Case 8 where only the intentional or foreseen killing of an unjust aggressor and the foreseen killing of one innocent bystander would prevent serious injuries to the members of a much larger group of people.

The interpretation of this case is crucial. In this case, we are asked to sanction the loss of an innocent life in order to prevent serious injuries to the members of a much larger group of people. Unfortunately, neither anti-war pacifists nor just war theorists have explicitly considered this case. Both anti-war pacifists and just war theorists agree that we can inflict serious injury upon an unjust aggressor and an innocent bystander to prevent greater injury to other innocent people, as in Cases 6 and 7, and that one can even intentionally or indirectly kill an unjust aggressor to prevent serious injury to oneself or other innocent people as in Case 5. Yet neither anti-war pacifists nor just war theorists have explicitly addressed the question of whether we can indirectly kill an innocent bystander in order to prevent serious injuries to the members of a much larger group of innocent people. Rather they have tended to confuse Case 8 with Case 5 where it is agreed that one can justifiably kill an unjust aggressor in order to prevent serious injury to oneself or five other innocent people. In Case 8, however, one is doing something quite different: one is killing an innocent bystander in order to prevent serious injury to oneself and five other innocent people.

Now this kind of trade-off is not accepted in standard police practice. Police officers are regularly instructed not to risk innocent lives simply to prevent serious injury to other innocents. Nor is there any reason to think that a trade-off that is unacceptable in standard police practice would be acceptable in larger scale conflicts. Thus, for example, even if the Baltic republics could have effectively freed themselves from the Soviet Union by infiltrating into Moscow several bands of saboteurs who would then attack several military and government installations in Moscow, causing an enormous loss of innocent lives, such trade-offs would not have been justified. Accordingly, it follows that if the proportionality requirement of just war theory is to be met, we must save more innocent lives than we cause to be lost, we must prevent more injuries than we bring about, and we must not kill innocents, even indirectly, simply to prevent serious injuries to ourselves and others.

Of course, sometimes our lives and well-being are threatened together. Or better, if we are unwilling to sacrifice our well-being then our lives are threatened as well. Nevertheless, if we are justified in our use of lethal force to defend ourselves in cases where we will indirectly kill innocents, it is because our lives are also threatened, not simply our well-being. And the same holds for when we are defending others.

What this shows is that the constraints imposed by just war theory on the use of belligerent correctives are actually much more severe than anti-war pacifists have tended to recognize. In determining when belligerent correctives are too costly to constitute a just cause or lacking in the proportionality required by just means, just war theory under its most morally defensible interpretation:

1) allows the use of belligerent means against unjust aggressors only when such means minimize the loss and injury to innocent lives overall;

2) allows the use of belligerent means against unjust aggressors to indirectly threaten innocent lives only to prevent the loss of innocent lives, not simply to prevent injury to innocents; and

3) allows the use of belligerent means to directly or indirectly threaten or even take the lives of unjust aggressors when it is the only way to prevent serious injury to innocents.

Now it might be objected that all that I have shown through the analysis of the above eight cases is that killing in defense of oneself or others is morally permissible, not that it is morally required or morally obligatory. That is true. I have not established any obligation to respond to aggression with lethal force in these cases, but only that it is morally permissible to do so. For one thing, it is difficult to ground an obligation to use lethal force on self-defense alone, as would be required in Case 1 or in one version of Case 5. Obligations to oneself appear to have an optional quality that is absent from obligations to others. In Cases 2–3 and 5–7, however, the use of force would prevent serious harm or death to innocents, and here I contend it would be morally obligatory if either the proposed use of force required only a relatively small personal sacrifice from us or if we were fairly bound by convention or a mutual defense agreement to come to the aid of others. In such cases, I think we can justifiably speak of a moral obligation to kill or seriously harm in defense of others.

Another aspect of Cases 1–3 and 5–7 to which someone might object is that it is the wrongful actions of others that put us into situations where I am claiming that we are morally justified in seriously harming or killing others. But for the actions of unjust aggressors, we would not be in situations where I am claiming that we are morally permitted or required to seriously harm or kill.

Yet doesn't something like this happen in a wide range of cases when wrongful actions are performed? Suppose I am on the way to the bank to deposit money from a fund-raiser, and someone accosts me and threatens to shoot me if I don't hand over the money. If I do hand over the money, I would be forced to do something I don't want to do, something that involves a loss to myself and others. But surely it is morally permissible for me to hand over the money in this case. And it may even be morally required for me to do so if resistance would lead to the shooting of others in addition to myself. So it does seem that bad people, by altering the consequences of our actions, can alter our obligations as well. What our obligations are under nonideal conditions are different from what they would be under ideal conditions. If a group of thugs comes into this room and make it very clear that they intend to shoot me if each of you doesn't give them one dollar, I think, and I would hope that you would also think, that each of you now has an obligation to give the thugs one dollar when before you had no such obligation. Likewise, I think that the actions of unjust aggressors can put us into situations where it is morally permissible or even morally required for us to seriously harm or kill when before it was not.

Now it might be contended that anti-war pacifists would concede the moral permissibility of Cases 1–3 and 5–7 but still maintain that any participation in the massive use of lethal force in warfare is morally prohibited. The scale of the conflict, anti-war pacifists might contend, makes all the difference. Of course, if this simply means that many large-scale conflicts will have effects that bear no resemblance to Cases 1–3 or 5–7, this can hardly be denied. Still, it is possible for some large-scale conflicts to bear a proportionate resemblance to the above cases. For example, it can be argued plausibly that India's military action against Pakistan in Bangladesh and the Tanzanian incursion into Uganda during the rule of Idi Amin resemble Cases 3, 5, or 7 in their effects upon innocents.[8] What this shows is that anti-war pacifists are not justified in regarding every participation in the massive use of lethal force in warfare as morally prohibited. Instead, anti-war pacifists must allow that at least in some real-life cases, wars and other large-scale military operations both have been and will be morally permissible.

This concession from anti-war pacifists, however, needs to be matched by a comparable concession from just war theorists themselves, because too frequently they have interpreted their theory in morally indefensible ways. When just war theory is given a morally defensible interpretation, I have argued that the theory favors a strong just means prohibition against intentionally harming innocents. I have also argued that the theory favors the use of belligerent means only when such means 1) minimize the loss and injury to innocent lives overall; 2) threaten innocent lives only to prevent the loss of innocent lives, not simply to prevent injury to innocents; and 3) threaten or even take the lives of unjust aggressors when it is the only way to prevent serious injury to innocents.

Obviously, just war theory, so understood, is going to place severe restrictions on the use of belligerent means in warfare. In fact, most of the actual uses of belligerent means in warfare that have occurred turn out to be unjustified. For example, the U.S. involvement in Nicaragua, El Salvador, and Panama, Soviet involvement in Afghanistan, Israeli involvement in the West Bank and the Gaza Strip all violate the just cause and just means provisions of just war theory as I have defended them. Even the recent U.S.-led war against Iraq violated both the just cause and just means provisions of just war theory.[9] In fact, one strains to find examples of justified applications of just war theory in recent history. Two examples I have already referred to are India's military action against Pakistan in Bangladesh and the Tanzanian incursion into Uganda during the rule of Idi Amin. But after mentioning these two examples it is difficult to go on. What this shows is that when just war theory and anti-war pacifism are given their most morally defensible interpretations, both views can be reconciled. In this reconciliation, the few wars and large-scale conflicts that meet the stringent requirements of just war theory are the only wars and large-scale conflicts to which anti-war pacifists cannot justifiably object.[10] We can call the view that emerges from this reconciliation "just war pacifism." It is the view which claims that due to the stringent requirements of just war theory, only very rarely will

participation in a massive use of lethal force in warfare be morally justified. It is the view on which I rest my case for the reconciliation of pacifism and just war theory.[11]

NOTES

1. Jan Narveson, "Pacifism: A Philosophical Analysis," *Ethics* 75 (1965): 259–71.

2. Cheyney Ryan, "Self-Defense, Pacifism and the Possibility of Killing," *Ethics* 93 (1983): 514–24.

3. Alternatively, one might concede that even in this case killing is morally evil, but still contend that it is morally justified because it is the lesser of two evils.

4. Douglas P. Lackey, "The Moral Irrelevance of the Counterforce/Countervalue Distinction," *The Monist* 70 (1987): 255–76.

5. This is because the just means restrictions protect innocents quite well against the infliction of intentional harm.

6. By an "unjust aggressor" I mean someone who the defender is reasonably certain is wrongfully engaged in an attempt upon her life or the lives of other innocent people.

7. What is relevant in this case is that the foreseen deaths are a relatively small number (one in this case) compared to the number of innocents whose lives are saved (six in this case). The primary reason for using particular numbers in this case and those that follow is to make it clear that at this stage of the argument no attempt is being made to justify the large-scale killing that occurs in warfare.

8. Although there is a strong case for India's military action against Pakistan in Bangladesh and the Tanzanian incursion into Uganda during the rule of Idi Amin, there are questions that can be raised about the behavior of Indian troops in Bangladesh following the defeat of the Pakistanian forces and about the regime Tanzania put in power in Uganda.

9. The just cause provision was violated because the extremely effective economic sanctions were not given enough time to work. It was estimated that when compared to past economic blockades, the blockade against Iraq had a near 100% chance of success if given about a year to work. (See *The New York Times,* January 14, 1991.) The just means provision was violated because the number of combatant and noncombatant deaths was disproportionate. As many as 120,000 Iraqi soldiers were killed, according to U.S. intelligence sources.

10. Of course, anti-war pacifists are right to point out that virtually all wars that have been fought have led to unfore-

seen harms and have been fought with less and less discrimination as the wars progressed. Obviously, these are considerations that in just war theory must weigh heavily against going to war.

11. Of course, more needs to be done to specify the requirements of just war pacifism. One fruitful way to further specify these requirements is to appeal to a hypothetical social contract decision procedure as has been done with respect to other practical problems. Here I have simply tried to establish the defensibility of just war pacifism without appealing to any such procedure. Yet once the defensibility of just war pacifism has been established, such a decision procedure will prove quite useful in working out its particular requirements.

Against "Realism"

MICHAEL WALZER

For as long as men and women have talked about war, they have talked about it in terms of right and wrong. And for almost as long, some among them have derided such talk, called it a charade, insisted that war lies beyond (or beneath) moral judgment. War is a world apart, where life itself is at stake, where human nature is reduced to its elemental forms, where self-interest and necessity prevail. Here men and women do what they must to save themselves and their communities, and morality and law have no place. *Inter arma dilent leges*: in time of war the law is silent.

Sometimes this silence is extended to other forms of competitive activity, as in the popular proverb, "All's fair in love and war." That means that anything goes—any kind of deceit in love, any kind of violence in war. We can neither praise nor blame; there is nothing to say. And yet we are rarely silent. The language we use to talk about love and war is so rich with moral meaning that it could hardly have been developed except through centuries of argument. Faithfulness, devotion, chastity, shame, adultery, seduction, betrayal; aggressive, self-defense, appeasement, cruelty, ruthlessness, atrocity, massacre—all these words are judgments, and judging is as common a human activity as loving or fighting.

Michael Walzer, "Against 'Realism,'" in *Just and Unjust Wars* (New York: Basic Books, 2000), 3–20 (edited). Copyright © Basic Books. Reprinted with permission.

It is true, however, that we often lack the courage of our judgments, and especially so in the case of military conflict. The moral posture of mankind is not well represented by that popular proverb about love and war. We would do better to mark a contrast rather than a similarity: before Venus, censorious; before Mars, timid. Not that we don't justify or condemn particular attacks, but we do so hesitantly and uncertainly (or loudly and recklessly), as if we were not sure that our judgments reach to the reality of war.

THE REALIST ARGUMENT

Realism is the issue. The defenders of *silent leges* claim to have discovered an awful truth: what we conventionally call inhumanity is simply humanity under pressure. War strips away our civilized adornments and reveals our nakedness. They describe that nakedness for us, not without a certain relish: fearful, self-concerned, driven, murderous. They aren't wrong in any simple sense. The words are sometimes descriptive. Paradoxically, the description is often a kind of apology: yes, our soldiers committed atrocities in the course of the battle, but that's what war does to people, that's what war is like. The proverb, all's fair, is invoked in defense of conduct that appears to be unfair. And one urges silence on the law when one is engaged in activities that would otherwise be called unlawful. So there are arguments here that will enter into my own argument: justifications and excuses, references to necessity and duress, that we can recognize as forms of moral discourse and that have or don't have force in particular cases. But there is also a general account of war as a realm of necessity and duress, the purpose of which is to make discourse about particular cases appear to be ideal chatter, a mask of noise with which we conceal, even from ourselves, the awful truth. It is that general account that I have to challenge before I can begin my own work, and I want to challenge it at its source and in its most compelling form, as it is put forward by the historian Thucydides and the philosopher Thomas Hobbes. These two men, separated by 2,000 years, are collaborators of a kind, for Hobbes translated Thucydides' *History of the Peloponnesian Wars* and then generalized its argument in his own *Leviathan*. It is not my purpose here to write a full philosophical response to Thucydides and Hobbes. I wish only to suggest, first by argument and then by example, that the judgment of war and of wartime conduct is a serious enterprise.

The Melian Dialogue

The dialogue between the Athenian generals Cleomedes and Tisias and the magistrates of the island state of Melos is one of the high points of Thucydides' *History* and the climax of his realism. Melos was a Spartan colony, and its people had "therefore refused to be subject, as the rest of the islands were, unto the Athenians; but rested at first neutral; and afterwards, when the Athenians put them to it by wasting of their lands, they entered into open war."[1] This is a classic account of aggression, for to commit aggression is simply to "put people to it" as Thucydides describes. But such a description, he seems to say, is merely external; he wants to show us the inner meaning of war. His spokesmen are the two Athenian generals, who demand a parley and then speak as generals have rarely done in military history. Let us have no fine words about justice, they say. We for our part will not pretend that, having defeated the Persians, our empire is deserved; you must not claim that having done no injury to the Athenian people, you have a right to be let alone. We will talk instead of what is feasible and what is necessary. For this is

what war is really like: "they that have odds of power exact as much as they can, and the weak yield to such conditions as they can get."

It is not only the Melians here who bear the burdens of necessity. The Athenians are driven, too; they must expand their empire, Cleomedes and Tisias believe, or lose what they already have. The neutrality of Melos "will be an argument of our weakness, and your hatred of our power, among those we have rule over." It will inspire rebellion throughout the islands, wherever men and women are "offended with the necessity of subjection"—and what subject is not offended, eager for freedom, resentful of his conquerors? When the Athenian generals say that men "will everywhere reign over such as they be too strong for," they are not only describing the desire for glory and command, but also the more narrow necessity of inter-state politics: reign or be subject. If they do not conquer when they can, they only reveal weakness and invite attack; and so, "by a necessity of nature" (a phrase Hobbes later made his own), they conquer when they can.

The Melians, on the other hand, are too weak to conquer. They face a harsher necessity: yield or be destroyed. "For you have not in hand a match of valor upon equal terms . . . but rather a consultation upon your safety . . ." The rulers of Melos, however, value freedom above safety: "If you then to retain your command, and your vassals to get loose from you, will undergo the utmost danger: would it not in us, that be already free, be great baseness and cowardice, if we should not encounter anything whatsoever rather than suffer ourselves to be brought into bondage?" Though they know that it will be a "hard matter" to stand against the power and fortune of Athens, "nevertheless we believe that, for fortune, we shall be nothing inferior, as having the gods on our side, because we stand innocent against men unjust." And as for power, they hope for assistance from the Spartans, "who are of necessity obliged, if for no other cause, yet for consanguinity's sake and for their own honor to defend us." But the gods, too, reign where they can, reply the Athenian generals, and consanguinity and honor have nothing to do with necessity. The Spartans will (necessarily) think only of themselves: "most apparently of all men, they hold for honorable that which pleaseth and for just that which profiteth."

So the argument ended. The magistrates refused to surrender; the Athenians laid seige to their city; the Spartans sent no help. Finally, after some months of fighting, in the winter of 416 B.C., Melos was betrayed by several of its citizens. When further resistance seemed impossible, the Melians "yielded themselves to the discretion of the Athenians: who slew all the men of military age, made slaves of the women and children; and inhabited the place with a colony sent thither afterwards of 500 men of their own."

The dialogue between the generals and the magistrates is a literary and philosophical construction of Thucydides. The magistrates speak as they well might have done, but their conventional piety and heroism is only a foil to what the classical critic Dionysius calls the "depraved shrewdness" of the Athenian generals.[2] It is the generals who have often seemed unbelievable. Their words, writes Dionysius, were appropriate to oriental monarchs . . . but unfit to be spoken by Athenians . . ."[3] Perhaps Thucydides means us to notice the unfitness, not so much of the words but of the policies they were used to defend, and thinks we might have missed it had he permitted the generals to speak as they probably in fact spoke, weaving "fair pretenses" over their vile actions. We are to understand that Athens is no longer itself. Cleomedes and Tisias do not represent that noble people who fought the Persians in the name of freedom and whose politics and culture, as Dionysius says, "exercised such a humanizing influence on everyday life." They represent instead the imperial decadence of the city state. It is not that they are war criminals in the modern sense; that idea is alien to Thucydides. But they embody a certain loss of ethical balance, of restraint and moderation. Their statesmanship is flawed, and their "realistic" speeches provide an ironic contrast to the blindness and arrogance with which the Athenians only a few months later launched the disastrous expedition to Sicily. The *History*, on this view, is a tragedy and Athens itself the tragic hero.[4] Thucydides has given us a morality play in the Greek style. We can glimpse his meaning in

Euripides' *The Trojan Women,* written in the immediate aftermath of the conquest of Melos and undoubtedly intended to suggest the human significance of slaughter and slavery—and to predict a divine retribution:[5]

> How ye are blind
> Ye treaders down of cities, ye that cast
> Temples to desolation, and lay waste
> Tombs, the untrodden sanctuaries where lie
> The ancient dead; yourselves so soon to die!

But Thucydides seems in fact to be making a rather different, and a more secular, statement than this quotation suggests, and not about Athens so much as about war itself. He probably did not mean the harshness of the Athenian generals to be taken as a sign of depravity, but rather as a sign of impatience, toughmindedness, honesty—qualities of mind not inappropriate in military commanders. He is arguing, as Werner Jaeger has said, that "the principle of force forms a realm of its own, with laws of its own," distinct and separate from the laws of moral life.[6] This is certainly the way Hobbes read Thucydides, and it is the reading with which we must come to grips. For if the realm of force is indeed distinct and if this is an accurate account of its laws, then one could no more criticize the Athenians for their wartime policies than one could criticize a stone for falling downwards. The slaughter of the Melians is explained by reference to the circumstances of war and the necessities of nature; and again, there is nothing to say. Or rather, one can *say* anything, call necessity cruel and war hellish; but while these statements may be true in their own terms, they do not touch the political realities of the case or help us understand the Athenian decision.

It is important to stress, however, that Thucydides has told us nothing at all about the Athenian decision. And if we place ourselves, not in the council room at Melos where a cruel policy was being expounded, but in the assembly at Athens where that policy was first adopted, the argument of the generals has a very different ring. In the Greek as in the English language, the word *necessity* "doubles the parts of indispensable and inevitable."[7] At Melos, Cleomedes and Tisias mixed the two of these, stressing the last. In the assembly they could have argued only about the first, claiming, I suppose, that the destruction of Melos was necessary (indispensable) for the preservation of the empire. But this claim is rhetorical in two senses. First, it evades the moral question of whether the preservation of the empire was itself necessary. There were some Athenians, at least, who had doubts about that, and more who doubted that the empire had to be a uniform system of domination and subjection (as the policy adopted for Melos suggested). Secondly, it exaggerates the knowledge and foresight of the generals. They are not saying with certainty that Athens will fall unless Melos is destroyed; their argument has to do with probabilities and risks. And such arguments are always arguable. Would the destruction of Melos really reduce Athenian risks? Are there alternative policies? What are the likely costs of this one? Would it be right? What would other people think of Athens if it were carried out?

Once the debate begins, all sorts of moral and strategic questions are likely to come up. And for the participants in the debate, the outcome is not going to be determined "by a necessity of nature," but by the opinions they hold or some to hold as a result of the arguments they hear and then by the decisions they freely make, individually and collectively. Afterwards, the generals claim that a certain decision was inevitable; and that, presumably, is what Thucydides wants us to believe. But the claim can only be made afterwards, for inevitability here is mediated by a process of political deliberation, and Thucydides could not know what was inevitable until that process had been completed. Judgments of necessity in this sense are always retrospective in character—the work of historians, not historical actors.

Now, the moral point of view derives its legitimacy from the perspective of the actor. When we make moral judgments, we try to recapture that perspective. We reiterate the decision-making process, or we rehearse our own future decisions, asking what we would have done (or what we would do) in similar circumstances. The Athenian generals recognize the importance of such questions, for they defend their policy certain "that you likewise, and others that should have the same power which we have, would do the same." But that is a dubious knowledge, especially so once we realize that the "Melian decree" was sharply opposed in the Athenian assembly. Our standpoint is that of citizens debating the decree. What *should* we do?

We have no account of the Athenian decision to attack Melos or of the decision (which may have been taken at the same time) to kill and enslave its people. Plutarch claims that it was Alcibiades, chief architect of the Sicilian expedition, who was "the principal cause of the slaughter . . . having spoken in favor of the decree."[8] He played the part of Cleon in the debate that Thucydides does record, that occurred some years earlier, over the fate of Mytilene. It is worth glancing back at that earlier argument. Mytilene had been an ally of Athens from the time of the Persian War; it was never a subject city in any formal way, but bound by treaty to the Athenian cause. In 428, it rebelled and formed an alliance with the Spartans. After considerable fighting, the city was captured by Athenian forces, and the assembly determined "to put to death . . . all the men of Mytilene that were of age, and to make slaves of the women and children: laying to their charge the revolt itself in that they revolted not being in subjection as others were . . ."[9] But the following day the citizens "felt a kind of repentance . . . and began to consider what a great and cruel decree it was, that not the authors only, but that the whole city should be destroyed." It is this second debate that Thucydides has recorded, or some part of it, giving us two speeche, that of Cleon upholding the original decree and that of Diodotus urging its revocation. Cleon argues largely in terms of collective guilt and retributive justice; Diodotus offers a critique of the deterrent effects of capital punishment. The assembly accepts Diodotus' position, convinced apparently that the destruction of Mytilene would not uphold the force of treaties or ensure the stability of the empire. It is the appeal to interest that triumphs—as has often been pointed out—though, it should be remembered that the occasion for the appeal was the repentance of the citizens. Moral anxiety, not political calculation, leads them to worry about the effectiveness of their decree.

In the debate over Melos, the positions must have been reversed. Now there was no retributivist argument to make, for the Melians had done Athens no injury. Alcibiades probably talked like Thucydides' generals, though with the all-important difference I have already noted. When he told his fellow citizens that the decree was necessary, he didn't mean that it was ordained by the laws that govern the realm of force; he meant merely that it was needed (in his view) to reduce the risks of rebellion among the subject cities of the Athenian empire. And his opponents probably argued, like the Melians, that the decree was dishonorable and unjust and would more likely excite resentment than fear throughout the islands, that Melos did not threaten Athens in any way, and that other policies would serve Athenian interests and Athenian self-esteem. Perhaps they also reminded the citizens of their repentance in the case of Mytilene and urged them once again to avoid the cruelty of massacre and enslavement. How Alcibiades won out, and how close the vote was, we don't know. But there is no reason to think that the decision was predetermined and debate of no avail: no more with Melos than with Mytilene. Stand in imagination in the Athenian assembly, and one can still feel a sense of freedom.

But the realism of the Athenian generals has a further thrust. It is not only a denial of the freedom that makes moral decision possible; it is a denial also of the meaningfulness of moral argument. The second claim is closely related to the first. If we must act in accordance with our interests, driven by our fears of one another, then talk about justice cannot possibly be anything more than talk. It refers to no purposes that we can make our own and to no goals that we can share with others. That is why the Athenian generals could have woven "fair pretenses" as easily as the Melian magistrates; in discourse of this sort anything can be said. The words have no clear references, no certain definitions, no logical entailments. They are, as Hobbes writes in *Leviathan*, "ever used with relation to the person that useth them," and

they express that person's appetites and fears and nothing else. It is only "most apparent" in the Spartans, but true for everyone, that "they hold for honorable that which pleaseth them and for just that which profiteth." Or, as Hobbes later explained, the names of the virtues and vices are of "uncertain signification."[10]

For one calleth wisdom, what another calleth fear; and one cruelty what another justice; one prodigality, what another magnanimity . . . etc. And therefore such names can never be true grounds of any ratiocination.

"*Never*"—until the sovereign, who is also the supreme linguistic authority, fixes the meaning of the moral vocabulary; but in the state of war, "*never*" without qualification, because in that state, by definition, no sovereign rules. In fact, even in civil society, the sovereign does not entirely succeed in bringing certainty into the world of virtue and vice. Hence moral discourse is always suspect, and war is only an extreme case of the anarchy of moral meanings. It is generally true, but especially so in time of violent conflict that we can understand what other people are saying only if we see through their "fair pretenses" and translate moral talk into the harder currency of interest talk. When the Melians insist that their cause is just, they are saying only that they don't want to be subject; and had the generals claimed that Athens deserved its empire, they would simply have been expressing the lust for conquest or the fear of overthrow.

This is a powerful argument because it plays upon the common experience of moral disagreement—painful, sustained, exasperating, and endless. For all its realism, however, it fails to get at the realities of that experience or to explain its character. We can see this clearly, I think, if we look again at the argument over the Mytilene decree. Hobbes may well have had this debate in mind when he wrote, "and one [calleth] cruelty what another justice . . ." The Athenians repented of their cruelty, writes Thucydides, while Cleon told them that they had not been cruel at all but justly severe. Yet this was in no sense a disagreement over the meaning of words. Had there been no common meanings, there could have been no debate at all. The cruelty of the Athenians consisted in seeking to punish not only the authors of the rebellion but others as well, and Cleon agreed that that would indeed be cruel. He then went on to argue, as he had to do given his position, that in Mytilene there were no "others." "Let not the fault be laid upon a few, and the people absolved. For they have all alike taken arms against us . . ."

I cannot pursue the argument further, since Thucydides doesn't, but there is an obvious rejoinder to Cleon, having to do with the status of the women and children of Mytilene. This might involve the deployment of additional moral terms (innocence, for example); but it would not hang—any more than the argument about cruelty and justice hangs—on idiosyncratic definitions. In fact, definitions are not at issue here, but descriptions and interpretations. The Athenians shared a moral vocabulary, shared it with the people of Mytilene and Melos; and allowing for cultural differences, they share it with us too. They had no difficulty, and we have none, in understanding the claim of the Melian magistrates that the invasion of their island was unjust. It is in applying the agreed-upon words to actual cases that we come to disagree. These disagreements are in part generated and always compounded by antagonistic interests and mutual fears. But they have other causes, too, which help to explain the complex and disparate ways in which men and women (even when they have similar interests and no reason to fear one another) position themselves in the moral world. There are, first of all, serious difficulties of perception and information (in war and politics generally), and so controversies arise over "the facts of the case." There are sharp disparities in the weight we attach even to values we share, as there are in the actions we are ready to condone when these values are threatened. There are conflicting commitments and obligations that force us into violent antagonism even when we see the point of one another's positions. All this is real enough, and common enough: it makes morality into a world of good-faith quarrels as well as a world of ideology and verbal manipulation.

In any case, the possibilities for manipulation are limited. Whether or not people speak in good faith, they cannot say just anything they please. Moral talk is coercive; one thing leads to another. Perhaps that's why the Athenian generals did not want to begin. A war called unjust is not, to paraphrase Hobbes, a war misliked; it is a war misliked for particular reasons, and anyone making the charge is required to provide particular sorts of evidence. Similarly, if I claim that I am fighting justly, I must also claim that I was attacked ("put to it," as the Melians were), or threatened with attack, or that I am coming to the aid of a victim of someone else's attack. And each of these claims has its own entailments, leading me deeper and deeper into a world of discourse where, though I can go on talking indefinitely, I am severely constrained in what I can say. I must say this or that, and at many points in a long argument this or that will be true or false. We don't have to translate moral talk into interest talk in order to understand it; morality refers in its own way to the real world.

Let us consider a Hobbist example. In Chapter XXI of *Leviathan*, Hobbes urges that we make allowance for the "natural timorousness" of mankind. "When armies fight, there is on one side, or both a running away; yet when they do it not out of treachery, but fear, they are not esteemed to do it unjustly, but dishonorably." Now, judgments are called for here: we are to distinguish cowards from traitors. If these are words of "inconstant signification," the task is impossible and absurd. Every traitor would please natural timorousness, and we would accept the plea or not depending on whether the soldier was a friend or an enemy, an obstacle to our advancement or an ally and supporter. I suppose we sometimes do behave that way, but it is not the case (nor does Hobbes, when it comes to cases, suppose that it is) that the judgments we make can only be understood in these terms. When we charge a man with treason, we have to tell a very special kind of story about him, and we have to provide concrete evidence that the story is true. If we call him a traitor when we cannot tell that story, we are not using words inconstantly, we are simply lying.

STRATEGY AND MORALITY

Morality and justice are talked about in much the same way as military strategy. Strategy is the other language of war, and while it is commonly said to be free from the difficulties of moral discourse, its use is equally problematic. Though generals agree on the meaning of strategic terms—entrapment, retreat, flanking maneuver, concentration of forces, and so on—they nevertheless disagree about strategically appropriate courses of action. They argue about what ought to be done. After the battle, they disagree about what happened, and if they were defeated, they argue about who was to blame. Strategy, like morality, is a language of justification.[11] Every confused and cowardly commander describes his hesitations and panics as part of an elaborate plan; the strategic vocabulary is as available to him as it is to a competent commander. But that is not to say that its terms are meaningless. It would be a great triumph for the incompetent if they were, for we would then have no way to talk about incompetence. No doubt, "one calleth retreat what another calleth strategic redeployment . . ." But we do know the difference between these two, and though the facts of the case may be difficult to collect and interpret, we are nevertheless able to make critical judgments.

Similarly, we can make moral judgments: moral concepts and strategic concepts reflect the real world in the same way. They are not merely normative terms, telling soldiers (who often don't listen) what to do. They are descriptive terms, and without them we would have no coherent way of talking about war. Here are soldiers moving away from the scene of a battle, marching over the same ground they marched over yesterday, but fewer now, less eager, many without weapons, many wounded: we call this a retreat. Here are soldiers lining up the inhabitants of a pleasant village, men, women, and children, and shooting them down: we call this a massacre.

It is only when their substantive content is fairly clear that moral and strategic terms can be used imperatively, and the wisdom they embody expressed in the form of rules. Never refuse quarter to a soldier trying to surrender. Never advance with your flanks unprotected. One might construct out of such commands a moral or a strategic war plan, and then it would be important to notice whether or not the actual conduct of the war conformed to the plan. We can assume that it would not. War is recalcitrant to this sort of theoretical control—a quality it shares with every other human activity, but which it seems to possess to an especially intense degree. In *The Charterhouse of Parma*, Stendhal provides a description of the battle of Waterloo that is intended to mock the very idea of a strategic plan. It is an account of combat as chaos, therefore not an account at all but a denial, so to speak, that combat is accountable. It should be read alongside some strategic analysis of Waterloo like that of Major General Fuller, who views the battle as an organized series of maneuvers and counter-maneuvers.[12] The strategist is not unaware of confusion and disorder in the field; nor is he entirely unwilling to see these as aspects of war itself, the natural effects of the stress of battle. But he sees them also as matters of command responsibility, failures of discipline or control. He suggests that strategic imperatives have been ignored; he looks for lessons to be learned.

The moral theorist is in the same position. He too must come to grips with the fact that his rules are often violated or ignored—and with the deeper realization that, to men at war, the rules often don't seem relevant to the extremity of their situation. But however he does this, he does not surrender his sense of war as a human action, purposive and premeditated, for whose effects someone is responsible. Confronted with the many crimes committed in the course of a war, or with the crime of aggressive war itself, he searches for human agents. Nor is he alone in this search. It is one of the most important features of war, distinguishing it from the other scourges of mankind, that the men and women caught up in it are not only victims, they are also participants. All of us are inclined to hold them responsible for what they do (though we may recognize the plea of duress in particular cases). Reiterated over time, our arguments and judgments shape what I want to call *the moral reality of war*—that is, all those experiences of which moral language is descriptive or within which it is necessarily employed.

It is important to stress that the moral reality of war is not fixed by the actual activities of soldiers but by the opinions of mankind. That means, in part, that it is fixed by the activity of philosophers, lawyers, publicists of all sorts. But these people don't work in isolation from the experience of combat, and their views have value only insofar as they give shape and structure to that experience in ways that are plausible to the rest of us. We often say, for example, that in time of war soldiers and statesmen must make agonizing decisions. The pain is real enough, but it is not one of the natural effects of combat. Agony is not like Hobbist fear: it is entirely the product of our moral views, and it is common in war only insofar as those views are common. It was not some unusual Athenian who "repented" of the decision to kill the men of Mytilene, but the citizens generally. They repented, and they were able to understand one another's repentance, because they shared a sense of what cruelty meant. It is by the assignment of such meanings that we make war what it is—which is to say that it could be (and it probably has been) something different.

What of a soldier or statesman who does not feel the agony? We say of him that he is morally ignorant or morally insensitive, much as we might say of a general who experienced no difficulty making a (really) difficult decision that he did not understand the strategic realities of his own position or that he was reckless and insensible of danger. And we might go on to argue, in the case of the general, that such a man has no business fighting or leading others in battle, that he ought to know that his army's right flank, say, is vulnerable, and ought to worry about the danger and take steps to avoid it. Once again, the case is the same with moral decisions: soldiers and statesmen ought to know the dangers of cruelty and injustice and worry about them and take steps to avoid them.

HISTORICAL RELATIVISM

Against this view, however, Hobbist relativism is often given a social or historical form: moral and strategic knowledge, it is said, changes over time or varies among political communities, and so what appears to me as ignorance may look like understanding to someone else. Now, change and variation are certainly real enough, and they make for a tale that is complex in the telling. But the importance of that tale for ordinary moral life and, above all, for the judgment of moral conduct is easily exaggerated. Between radically separate and dissimilar cultures, one can expect to find radical dichotomies in perception and understanding. No doubt the moral reality of war is not the same for us as it was for Genghis Khan; nor is the strategic reality. But even fundamental social and political transformations within a particular culture may well leave the moral world intact or at least sufficiently whole so that we can still be said to share it with our ancestors. It is rare indeed that we do not share it with our contemporaries, and by and large we learn how to act among our contemporaries by studying the actions of those who have preceded us. The assumption of that study is that they saw the world much as we do. That is not always true, but it is true enough of the time to give stability and coherence to our moral lives (and to our military lives). Even when world views and high ideals have been abandoned—as the glorification of aristocratic chivalry was abandoned in early modern times—notions about right conduct are remarkably persistent: the military code survives the death of warrior idealism. I shall say more about this survival later on, but I can demonstrate it now in a general way by looking at an example from feudal Europe, an age in some ways more distant from us than Greece of the city states, but with which we nevertheless share moral and strategic perceptions.

Three Accounts of Agincourt

Actually, the sharing of strategic perceptions is in this case the more dubious of the two. Those French knights so many of whom died at Agincourt had notions about combat very different from our own. Modern critics have still felt able to criticize their "fanatical adherence to the old method of fighting" (King Henry, after all, fought differently) and even to offer practical suggestions: the French attack, writes Oman, "should have been accompanied by a turning movement around the woods . . ."[13] Had he not been "overconfident," the French commander would have seen the advantages of the move. We can talk in a similar way about the crucial moral decision that Henry made toward the end of the battle, when the English thought their victory secure. They had taken many prisoners, who were loosely assembled behind the lines. Suddenly, a French attack aimed at the supply tents far in the rear seemed to threaten a renewal of the fighting. Here is Holinshed's sixteenth century account of the incident (virtually copied from an earlier chronical):[14]

. . . certain Frenchmen on horseback . . . to the number of six hundred horsemen, which were the first that fled, hearing that the English tents and pavilions were a good way distant from the army, without any sufficient guard to defend the same . . . entered upon the king's camp and there . . . robbed the tents, broke up chests, and carried away caskets and slew such servants as they found to make any resistance. . . . But when the outcry of the lackeys and boys which ran away for fear of the Frenchmen . . . came to the king's ears, he doubting lest his enemies should gather together again, and begin a new field; and mistrusting further that the prisoners would be an aid to his enemies . . . contrary to his accustomed gentleness, commanded by sound of trumpet that every man . . . should incontinently slay his prisoner.

The moral character of the command is suggested by the words "accustomed gentleness" and "incontinently." It involved a shattering of personal and conventional restraints (the latter well-established by 1415), and Holinshed goes to some lengths to explain and excuse it, stressing the king's fear that the prisoners his forces held were about to rejoin the fighting. Shakespeare, whose *Henry V* closely follows Holinshed, goes further, emphasizing the slaying of the English servants by the French and omitting the chronicler's assertion that only those who resisted were killed:[15]

Fluellen. Kill the [b]oys and the baggage! 'Tis expressly against the law of arms. 'Tis as arrant a piece of knavery, mark you now, as can be offert.

At the same time, however, he cannot resist an ironical comment:

Gower. . . . they have burned and carried away all that was in the king's tent, wherefore the king most worthily hath caused every soldier to cut his prisoner's throat. O, 'tis a gallant king!

A century and a half later, David Hume gives a similar account, without the irony, stressing instead the king's eventual cancellation of his order:[16]

. . . some gentlemen of Picardy . . . had fallen upon the English baggage, and were doing execution on the unarmed followers of the camp, who fled before them. Henry, seeing the enemy on all sides of him, began to entertain apprehensions from his prisoners; and he thought it necessary to issue a general order for putting them to death; but on discovering the truth, he stopped the slaughter, and was still able to save a great number.

Here the moral meaning is caught in the tension between "necessary" and "slaughter." Since slaughter is the killing of men as if they were animals—it "makes a massacre," wrote the poet Dryden, "what was a war"—it cannot often be called necessary. If the prisoners were so easy to kill, they were probably not dangerous enough to warrant the killing. When he grasped the actual situation, Henry, who was (so Hume wants us to believe) a moral man, called off the executions.

French chroniclers and historians write of the event in much the same way. It is from them that we learn that many of the English knights refused to kill their prisoners—not, chiefly, out of humanity, rather for the sake of the ransom they expected; but also "thinking of the dishonor that the horrible executions would reflect on themselves."[17] English writers have focused more, and more worriedly, on the command of the king; he was, after all, their king. In the later nineteenth century, at about the same time as the rules of war with respect to prisoners were being codified, their criticism grew increasingly sharp: "a brutal butchery," "cold-blooded wholesale murder."[18] Hume would not have said that, but the difference between that and what he did say is marginal, not a matter of moral or linguistic transformation.

To judge Henry ourselves we would need a more circumstantial account of the battle than I can provide here.[19] Even given that account, our opinions might differ, depending on the allowance we were willing to make for the stress and excitement of battle. But that is a clear example of a situation common in both strategy and morality, where our sharpest disagreements are structured and organized by our underlying agreements, by the meanings we share. For Holinshed, Shakespeare, and Hume—traditional chronicler, Renaissance playwright, and Enlightenment historian—and for us too, Henry's command belongs to a category of military acts that requires scrutiny and judgment. It is *as a matter of fact* morally problematic, because it accepts the risks of cruelty and injustice. In exactly the same way, we might regard the battle plan of the French commander as strategically problematic, because it accepted the risks of a frontal assault on a prepared position. And, again, a general who did not recognize these risks is properly said to be ignorant of morality or strategy.

In moral life, ignorance isn't all that common; dishonesty is far more so. Even those soldiers and statesmen who don't feel the agony of a problematic decision generally know that they should feel it. Harry Truman's flat statement that he never lost a night's sleep over his decision to drop the atomic bomb on Hiroshima is not the sort of thing political leaders often say. They usually find it preferable to stress the painfulness of decision-making; it is one of the burdens of office, and it is best if the burdens appear to be borne. I suspect that many officeholders even experience pain simply because they are expected to. If they don't, they lie about it. The clearest evidence for the stability of our values over time is the unchanging character of the lies soldiers and statesmen tell. They lie in order to justify themselves, and so they describe for us the lineaments of justice. Wherever we find hypocrisy, we also find moral knowledge. The hypocrite is like that Russian general in Solzhenitsyn's *August 1914,* whose elaborate battle reports barely concealed his total inability to control or direct the battle. He knew at least that there was a story to tell, a set of names to attach to things and happenings, so he tried to tell the story and attach the names. His effort was not mere mimicry; it was, so to speak, the tribute that incompetence pays to understanding. The case is the same in moral life: there really is a story to tell, a way of talking about wars and battles that the rest of us recognize as morally appropriate. I don't mean that particular decisions are necessarily right or wrong, or simply right or wrong, only that there is a way of seeing the world so that moral decision-making makes sense. The hypocrite knows that this is true, though he may actually see the world differently.

Hypocrisy is rife in wartime discourse, because it is especially important at such a time to appear to be in the right. It is not only that the moral stakes are high; the hypocrite may not understand that; more crucially, his actions will be judged by other people, who are not hypocrites, and whose judgments will affect their policies toward him. There would be no point to hypocrisy if this were not so, just as there would be no point to lying in a world where no one told the truth. The hypocrite presumes on the moral understanding of the rest of us, and we have no choice, I think, except to take his assertions seriously and put them to the test of moral realism. He pretends to think and act as the rest of us expect him to do. He tells us that he is fighting according to the moral war plan: he does not aim at civilians, he grants quarter to soldiers trying to surrender, he never tortures prisoners, and so on. These claims are true or false, and though it is not easy to judge them (nor is the war plan really so simple), it is important to make the effort. Indeed, if we call ourselves moral men and women, we must make the effort, and the evidence is that we regularly do so. If we had all become realists like the Athenian generals or like Hobbists in a state of war, there would be an end alike to both morality and hypocrisy. We would simply tell one another, brutally and directly, what we wanted to do or have done. But the truth is that one of the things most of us want, even in war, is to act or to seem to act morally. And we want that, most simply, because we know what morality means (at least, we know what it is generally thought to mean).

* * *

NOTES

1. This and subsequent quotations are from *Hobbes' Thucydides*, ed. Richard Schlatter (New Brunswick, N.J., 1975), pp. 377–85 (*The History of The Peloponesian War*, 5:84–116).

2. Dionysius of Halicarnassus, *On Thucydides*, trans. W. Kendrick Pritchett (Berkeley, 1975), pp. 31–33.

3. Even oriental monarchs are not quite so toughminded as the Athenian generals. According to Herodotus, when Xerxes first disclosed his plans for an invasion of Greece, he spoke in more conventional terms: "I will bridge the Hellespont and march an army through Europe into Greece, and punish the Athenians for the outrage they committed upon my father and upon us." (*The Histories*, Book 7, trans. Aubrey de Selincourt) The reference is to the burning of Sardis, which we may take as the pretext for the Persian invasion. The example bears out Francis Bacon's assertion that "there is that justice imprinted in the nature of men that they enter not upon wars (whereof so many calamities do ensue) but upon some, at least specious, grounds and quarrels." (Essay 29, "Of the True Greatness of Kingdoms and Estates")

4. See F. M. Cornford, *Thucydides Mythistoricus* (London, 1907), esp. ch. XIII.

5. *The Trojan Women*, trans. Gilbert Murray (London, 1905), p. 16.

6. Werner Jaeger, *Paideia: the Ideals of Greek Culture*, trans. Gilbert Highet (New York, 1939), I, 402.

7. H. W. Fowler, *A Dictionary of Modern English Usage*, second ed., rev. Sir Ernest Gowers (New York, 1965), p. 168; cf. Jaeger, I, 397.

8. *Plutarch's Lives*, trans. John Dryden, rev. Arthur Hugh Clough (London, 1910), I, 303. Alcibiades also "selected for himself one of the captive Melian women . . ."

9. *Hobbes' Thucydides*, pp. 194–204 (*The History of the Peloponnesian War*, 3:36–49).

10. Thomas Hobbes, *Leviathan*, ch. IV.

11. Hence we can "unmask" strategic discourse just as Thucydides did with moral discourse. Imagine that the two Athenian generals, after their dialogue with the Melians, return to their camp to plan the coming battle. The senior in command speaks first: "Don't give me any fine talk about the need to concentrate our forces or the importance of strategic surprise. We'll simply call for a frontal assault; the men will organize themselves as best they can; things are going to be confused anyway. I need a quick victory here, so that I can return to Athens covered with glory before the debate on the Sicilian campaign begins. We'll have to accept some risks; but that doesn't matter since the risks will be yours, not mine. If we are beaten, I'll contrive to blame you. That's what war is like." Why is strategy the language of hard-headed men? One sees through it so easily . . .

12. *The Charterhouse of Parma*, I, chs. 3 and 4; J. F. C. Fuller, *A Military History of the Western World* (n.p., 1955), II, ch. 15.

13. C. W. C. Oman, *The Art of War in the Middle Ages* (Ithaca, N.Y., 1968), p. 137.

14. Raphael Holinshed, *Chronicles of England, Scotland, and Ireland*, excerpted in William Shakespeare, *The Life of Henry V* (Signet Classics, New York, 1965), p. 197.

15. *Henry V*, 4:7, ll. 1–11.

16. David Hume, *The History of England* (Boston, 1854), II, 358.

17. René de Belleval, *Azincourt* (Paris, 1865), pp. 105–6.

18. See the summary of opinions in J. H. Wylie, *The Reign of Henry the Fifth* (Cambridge, England, 1919), II, 171ff.

19. For an excellent and detailed account, which suggests that Henry's action cannot be defended, see John Keegan, *The Face of Battle* (New York, 1976), pp. 107–12.

Kant and Mill in Baghdad

JOHN B. JUDIS

In justifying their war against Iraq, the Bush administration and its supporters based their case primarily on the threat to the United States posed by Iraq's weapons of mass destruction and ties with al-Qaeda. But to date, American and British troops have found no signs of a chemical-, biological- or, more importantly, a nuclear-weapons program and have uncovered only low-level ties to al-Qaeda. And even if they subsequently find a few canisters of mustard gas, or railway tickets from Kandahar to Baghdad, it would hardly confirm America's claims that Saddam Hussein's regime posed a threat to the United States. On the contrary, the absence of weapons of mass destruction (WMD), in particular nuclear weapons, combined with the ease with which the United States rolled over the Iraqi army, strengthens the claims of administration critics that Hussein's regime could have been contained without going to war.

It also looks increasingly implausible that the Bush administration simply made an error of judgment in pressing its case against Iraq. Prior to the war, the United States failed to produce compelling evidence of Iraqi WMD or ties to al-Qaeda. According to United Nations weapons inspector Hans Blix, the evidence that the United States gave him of Iraq's WMD was "pretty pathetic." The Pentagon was also prepared for a short and easy war. That suggests that by the time of the invasion, the Bush administration was primarily concerned with advancing a geopolitical strategy in the region rather than defending Americans against future attack. In all likelihood, George W. Bush lied to the public about the dangers posed by Iraq.

Indeed, since the war's end, the administration and its supporters have changed their argument for the invasion. They now contend that even if the United States has not eliminated a looming WMD threat, it has eliminated a heinous regime. Wrote

New York Times columnist Thomas Friedman, "Bush doesn't owe the world any explanation for missing chemical weapons (even if it turns out that the White House hyped this issue). It is clear that in ending Saddam's tyranny, a huge human engine for mass destruction has been broken." But Friedman and other supporters gloss over the thorny moral issues raised by the invasion. Can the morality of our actions—whether as individuals or nations—be judged simply by the eventual results? Isn't this an instance of the ends justifying the means?

The question of whether the war was justified can best be understood as a conflict between the moral philosophies of Immanuel Kant and those of Jeremy Bentham, John Stuart Mill and the utilitarians. Kant argued that in order to be morally justifiable, actions had to be universalizable—susceptible to becoming universal laws applicable to any individuals. If it is right for A to steal from B, then it will have to be right for B to steal from A, or C from D. Kant's categorical imperative assumes a moral universe of equal beings, all of whom would be subject to the same rights and prohibitions. In making moral choices, Kant contended, human beings treat one another as "ends in themselves." By contrast, the utilitarians, in their most basic form, argued that moral decisions must be judged according to whether they maximize happiness.

Kant and the utilitarians were not trying to say what should be moral but to describe the underlying logic by which we justify our actions. In this respect, each philosophy had its limitations. For instance, a utilitarian could conceivably justify enslaving another human being if it turned out to contribute to the overall sum of human happiness. A Kantian might justify pacifism as universalizable even when his country was threatened with extinction. Ultimately the two principles of moral decision making act as limits on each other: Both must be present in some form for an action to be morally justified. Decisions must respect rights, and they must not make things intolerably worse.

Kant's and the utilitarians' principles were designed to explain how individuals, not nations, justify their actions. But they also helped to explain, and to influence, how nations legitimated international actions. In the 19th century, advanced capitalist countries justified their imperial conquests on utilitarian grounds, claiming to be bringing civilization and prosperity to the backward countries of Asia and Africa. (Karl Marx would credit bourgeois imperialism with drawing "even the most barbarous nations into civilization.") But the rise of modern imperialism, and of rivalries between the imperial powers, led to violent nationalist rebellions and two world wars in which millions perished. These sad events prompted a fundamental reappraisal of international morality.

After World War II—in the Nuremberg trials and the formation of the United Nations—the world's countries embraced a Kantian approach to international relations based upon the recognition of nations as equal sovereign persons (regardless of their size or stage of economic development) with inalienable rights. The UN Charter forbade the "threat or use of force against the territorial integrity or political independence of any state" except if "an armed attack occurs."

Similarly, the Nuremberg tribunal stated that "to initiate a war of aggression . . . is the supreme international crime." Utilitarianism was present, too, but in a supporting role: the UN charter assumed that by granting them inalienable rights, the world's nations would help remove a major cause of war.

In the decades after World War II, the United States and the Soviet Union appeared to violate these principles in Eastern Europe, the Caribbean and Southeast Asia—but in the name of defending themselves against one another. After the Berlin Wall fell in 1989, however, the world seemed ripe for the application of Kantian principles to international relations. UN support for the Gulf War was a textbook case: The world's nations were coming to the defense of a small nation invaded and taken over by a larger, more powerful neighbor. NATO intervention in the Balkans, and particularly in Kosovo, was open to debate but could be justified as the defense of a nation and a people against Serbian aggression without aiming to overthrow and replace the Serbian regime itself. The U.S. and British protection of the Kurds was justifiable along similar lines. And the U.S. invasion of Afghanistan after September 11 was an act of national self-defense.

But the Bush administration, perhaps emboldened by its success in Afghanistan, proceeded to defy the post–World War II principles of international law. Last June, Bush announced a new doctrine of preemptive (really preventive) war against merely potential adversaries. That was meant to justify an invasion of Iraq. Even if this doctrine is seen as a legitimate nuclear-age extension of self-defense, however, the invasion does not seem justified. The United States would have had to demonstrate that the Iraqis had not merely a few chemical weapons (which had failed to deter Iran in the 1980s war) but a burgeoning nuclear program. But no such programs came to light during the inspections or the war. By Kantian standards, the war was aggression without justifiable cause.

Administration officials have tried to justify the war ex post facto entirely on utilitarian grounds—that is, that the war will lead to the democratization or modernization of the Arab region. These arguments echo those of 19th- and early 20th-century imperialists, and indeed some neoconservatives, including Max Boot and Stanley Kurtz, have argued candidly for a return to imperialism. They have replaced the older promise of civilization with that of democracy or of modernization. The Bush administration, fearful of criticism from abroad, has steered clear of explicitly advocating imperialism, but it uses the same utilitarian logic in advancing its aims that European and American proponents of empire used a century ago.

The defenders of a new American imperialism insist that today's America will avoid the pitfalls of the older model. They argue that the United States is an inherently moral nation that will not commit the injustices perpetrated by past imperial aspirants. True, American history, like French and English, is filled with moments of greatness—but also of ignominy, from the Indian wars to the slave trade to the brutal suppression of the Filipino rebels to the Christmas bombing of Hanoi. To put ourselves above the law of nations is to encourage our own tendencies, as well as those of other countries, toward lawlessness.

Defenders of the administration also argue that the United States, unlike imperial Britain or Wilhelm II's Germany, has no serious military rivals and can therefore do what it wants without encouraging a future world war. That may be true—for now. But an arrogant America, strutting across the world stage and invading countries it deems to be merely future adversaries, can incite reprisals and can, over the decades, provoke genuine rivalry. And these rivals will hardly be bound to honor the very rules of international behavior that the United States has already spurned. In its victory over Iraq, the United States can imagine it is instilling democratic principles in the Arab world, but it is also undermining principles designed to protect the world's nations from an even worse fate than autocracy: the ravages of war and the humiliation of conquest.

The Case for Iraq War II

BURTON M. LEISER

As I write these words some forty days after the end of major hostilities in Iraq, Congress, the press, academics, and the public are reassessing the war, and most especially the intelligence upon which the United States and its allies based their decision to pursue war rather than to continue the UN inspection program, as some members of the United Nations Security Council and the United States Congress had urged.

It is perhaps too soon to determine whether the war was a "just war" in the sense that used to be called *jus ad bellum*—a war that was fought for a just cause. But it is certainly a just war insofar as it was *jus in bello*—fought in accordance with the laws of war. The coalition forces did not employ outlawed weapons. Nor did they deliberately target civilians or noncombatants. On the contrary, they appear to have done everything humanly possible to avoid civilian casualties, and indeed, made every effort even to keep the enemy's military casualties to a minimum.

Objections to the war during the months prior to the opening of hostilities consisted essentially of three types: (1) those that were based upon utilitarian considerations, (2) those that presumed that it was possible to resolve the conflict between Saddam Hussein and those who were concerned about his weapons of mass destruction (WMDs) without war, and (3) those that were grounded on interpretations of international law and morality.

The *utilitarian arguments* alleged that dire consequences of one sort or another were likely to result from a military attack on Iraq. Those harmed would be the armed forces of the United States and its allies, innocent Iraqi civilians, the armed forces of Iraq, or other people not directly involved in the combat zone but likely to be affected by it. Other serious consequences of military intervention were thought to involve some injury to the United Nations or to world order as a whole. Here is an incomplete but useful list of some of the predictions of undesirable consequences that were made during the months leading up to the war.

Burton M. Leiser, "The Case for Iraq War II," in *Morality in Practice*, ed. James P. Sterba, 7th ed. (Belmont, CA: Wadsworth/Thomson, 2004), 619–26 (edited). Reprinted with permission by Wadsworth.

- Saddam Hussein was likely to use his weapons of mass destruction on the armed forces assaulting his nation, with potentially devastating effects.

- Saddam was likely to turn his weapons against other states in the region, such as Saudi Arabia, Kuwait, Iran, and most especially Israel, widening the conflict and engulfing the entire region in the flames of war.

- The United States and its allies—but most especially the United States—would suffer the effects of a growing hatred throughout the Arab and Islamic world because of what the Arab "street" would see as American aggression against Islam.

- War would destroy the infrastructure of Iraq and lead to a massive humanitarian crisis. Since Saddam's government was the only one in place, war would leave no effective food distribution system and would lead to widespread starvation and disease.

- The United States would leave Iraq "with its tail between its legs, defeated."

- The rest of the world would see the United States as an arrogant, presumptuous, unilateralist bully, reinforcing attitudes engendered by other recent actions, such as the American administration's refusal to adopt the Kyoto Protocol or to join the International Criminal Court, among others, thus further reducing the esteem in which the rest of the world holds it and consequently reducing American moral influence in the rest of the world.

- If the United States acted against Iraq on its own, without the sanction of the Security Council of the United Nations, it would have dealt a severe blow to the UN's authority throughout the world and to the rule of law internationally.

The *Pollyanaish arguments* boiled down to the following:

- Since Saddam had never used weapons of mass destruction against an adversary who could retal-

iate in kind, it is reasonable to assume that he would not use them against the United States, and therefore containment rather than war should be sufficient.

- The United Nations could compel Iraq to reveal what weapons of mass destruction it possessed, and UN inspections, together with American spy planes and satellites, should be sufficient to monitor such weapons and their destruction.

Finally, as to arguments based on *international law and morality:*

- War is always evil, and it is unthinkable that the United States would launch a preemptive war of aggression against Iraq with all the risks to civilian life, not to mention those of combatants, certain to result from such a war.

- The United Nations Charter, to which the United States is a signatory and for which the United States is largely responsible, forbids preemptive war.

- "You cannot subdue a large and hostile city except by destroying it completely." It will take a "holocaust," a "massacre" of Iraqi civilians to conquer Baghdad.

- In view of the fact that there was no convincing evidence either that Iraq possessed weapons of mass destruction or that it had any hand in terrorist attacks against the United States, there was no justification, under international law, for the United States of launch a war against Iraq.

- No nation is ever entitled to engage in warfare against any other nation except in self-defense, and then only as a last resort. In the absence of clear and convincing evidence that Iraq posed an imminent threat to the United States, there was no legal justification, either under traditional principles of international law or under the charter of the United Nations, for invoking the right of self-defense against Iraq in order to launch a war against it.

- The hidden agenda behind the war was the desire for oil—a materialistic and dishonorable reason for going to war.

UTILITARIAN ARGUMENTS

Utilitarian arguments must of necessity be based upon predictions of the consequences of the actions they purport to judge. If the predictions are ultimately shown to be false—most especially in hindsight, after the events in question have played themselves out—then the judgments themselves must be regarded as incorrect. Despite the fact that I am writing these words just a few weeks following the end of major hostilities, it is nevertheless possible to evaluate the utilitarian arguments. A few remarks should suffice.

Saddam Hussein's forces did not resort to weapons of mass destruction, so their potentially devastating effects did not come to pass. It is noteworthy, however, that critics of the war who employed this argument are now suggesting that Iraq never had such weapons, or at least that the American government[1] and British Prime Minister Tony Blair engaged in lies, evasions, and misdirection in order to persuade the public and other governments to go along with its intention to make war against Iraq. Nor did Saddam attack other nations in the region—largely because of careful strategic planning by the coalition, which early in the conflict disabled rocket launchers that might have targeted Israel, Saudi Arabia, and Kuwait in particular.

The war against Iraq did not spread to other parts of the Middle East. On the contrary, other Arab countries seem to have become less belligerent than they were before the war, and even Syria, responding to thinly veiled threats, has assured the United States that it will cooperate and that it will not offer refuge to Saddam or to other leaders of the Iraqi regime. Some evidence indicates that Syria has expelled some leading Iraqi Baathists and blocked others from entering its territory.

The infrastructure of Iraq was already badly damaged by years of neglect under Saddam Hussein.

Although some infrastructure suffered as a result of bombing during the war, coalition forces have devoted enormous resources to repairing the damage. One of the principal obstacles has been deliberate acts of sabotage against the infrastructure (e.g., power lines, transformers, and oil field equipment) by Saddam loyalists.

Far from leaving Iraq with its tail between its legs, the United States and its coalition partners won a dramatic and swift victory while suffering minimal casualties and inflicting relatively few casualties on the civilian population of Iraq. The crucial test lies in the future, when pressure will be brought to bear by critics in and out of Congress, and most especially in the Arab world, for the coalition to pull its forces out of Iraq prematurely, allowing the vacuum to be filled by extremists who may turn out to be as bad as the regime that has been displaced.

As for the widely held opinion that the United States is arrogant and unilateralist—that opinion was widespread before the war and the war has no doubt done little to ameliorate it. But neither the United States nor any other nation is or should be engaged in a world popularity contest. No American likes to hear his nation described in deprecatory terms; but American foreign policy must be based upon what is in the long-run interests of the United States, and not on the attitudes of other people toward us. As for arrogance, it is difficult to conceive of a government that acts in a more high-handed way than that of France, which seems to presume that its judgments must govern the actions of all other nations, whose ministers threaten other nations with exclusion from the European Union if they fail to go along with French dictates, and whose ambassador to London arrogates to himself the right to refer to another nation as a "shitty little country."[2]

The U.S.-led war against the regime of Saddam Hussein inflicted no damage at all on the United Nations, for the UN had already brought contempt upon itself for its racist policies, its utter incompetence, and its paralysis in the face of major world crises. It is useful to recall here that the UN did not bring much honor on itself when it voted to make

Libya, one of the worst offenders against human rights and a strong supporter of international terrorism, chair of the UN's Human Rights Commission.[3] Iraq, in the meantime, to the great consternation of the United States, had inherited the chairmanship of the UN's Disarmament Commission.[4]

Were the world in general or the Iraqi people in particular worse off at the end of the war than they were before it began? Any fair assessment of the facts would have to conclude that a vast improvement had taken place and that the sum total of human happiness had increased dramatically. One of the world's most monstrous despots had been removed from power, together with is extraordinarily cruel and brutish agents. It came as no surprise to anyone familiar with Saddam's thuggish policies that mass graves containing the remains of thousands of prisoners who had been tortured and executed were found throughout the country. Because of the war and Saddam's decisive defeat, those practices have come to an end. The torture chambers have been shut down, the prisoners have been freed, both those within the prisons and those without. The luxurious palaces that Saddam had built for himself, his sons, and his close associates were revealed to the world. At the same time, photos of the squalor and the suffering people of Iraq were widely disseminated.

Needless to say, the suffering of the Iraqi people was well known before the war. Even the harshest critics of the United States were aware of the deprivations that were inflicted upon the Iraqi population. Ramsey Clark,[5] who is well known as one of the most vigorous defenders of Arab terrorists, has traipsed from campus to campus throughout North America, denouncing the United States for its "genocidal" behavior toward Iraq as he described the starving and sick children who were deprived of adequate food and medicine whom he had encountered in Baghdad and elsewhere in Iraq. He attributed all of this suffering to the American-led boycott of Iraq rather than to the brutal regime that converted oil revenues earmarked for food and medicine to the provision of palaces and luxuries for top members of the regime, but he certainly confirmed the suffering that was taking place in that unfortunate land. The Iraqi government itself invoked the suffering of its people, claiming that the sanctions were at fault. In fact, the sanctions were set up in such a way as to allow food, medicine, and other vital supplies to be imported and paid for by oil that Iraq was permitted to sell. Instead, the funds were diverted by the Iraqi dictator-ship to Saddam's own priorities and those of his cronies.

Kurds and other minorities were forcibly expelled from their homes during Saddam's long reign, and their property was sold and resold to others. Now that the original owners are returning and demanding that the squatters return their property to them, disputes are breaking out; but despite the unhappiness of the squatters (some of whom seem not to have known that title resided in others who had been displaced under duress), there is a sense that justice is being done and that a massive injustice is being remedied.

In short, Iraq is emerging from decades of torture, death, poverty, and gross injustice into a new era that holds promise of peace, freedom, democracy, and the prosperity that should redound to a people who live in a land that possesses one of the most extensive proven reserves of oil in the world. Now that the tyrant has been eliminated, that great wealth can be distributed to the people instead of being plundered for the private enjoyment of a small group of overlords.

POLLYANAISH REASONS FOR NOT GOING TO WAR

The argument that Saddam Hussein would not use weapons of mass destruction against the United States because, after all, he had never used them before against an adversary that was capable of retaliating in kind is a rather intriguing kind of inference. Although it is sometimes reasonable to infer that a given event that will not happen because such an event has never happened before (e.g., that a ewe will not give birth to an egret), such an inference is more likely to be persuasive if something more than the mere fact that such events have not happened in the past can be deduced in support of it. Saddam Hussein's failure to use weapons of mass destruction on adversaries who had the capacity to strike back in kind is not supported by such universal experience as the fact that mammals do not give birth to birds and the wide genetic disparity and modes of reproduction of mammals and birds. In fact, Saddam's willingness to employ WMDs on such powerful forces as those of the United States had not been tested prior to the first Gulf War, and that one experience was scarcely enough to justify such a broad inductive generalization. But more seriously, suppose Iraq had WMDs. Based upon Saddam Hussein's well-established historical record, it would have been utterly foolhardy and irresponsible for any nation to proceed under the assumption that he would not use them. Why, after all, would he have acquired them in the first place, if he did not intend to use them to save himself and his regime in time of peril?

Moreover, nothing that had happened in the previous twenty years was consistent with the proposition that Saddam could have been compelled by the United Nations or any other authority to reveal his WMDs. On the contrary, all of the evidence pointed to further obstructionism by the Iraqi government. As Secretary of State Colin Powell showed the world in his presentations[6] to the Security Council, the Iraqis were quite capable of hiding their WMDs underground or moving them about in mobile units to escape detection. Even the most sophisticated satellite and U-2 surveillance equipment and other forms of intelligence gathering were unable to gather definitive evidence of materials that were so easily concealed. The UN inspection teams, most recently headed by Hans Blix, failed in their mission to uncover the weapons because of obstructions placed in their path by the Iraqis. Absolute certainty was impossible to establish, although there was ample evidence to establish the high likelihood that they did exist. Blix's reports to the UN repeatedly indicated that such weapons did exist, even though his inspectors had been unable to put their hands on them. Even now, after the war, extensive efforts to find such weapons have not been successful. Does it follow that

they do not or did not exist? Not at all. Saddam once admitted to having 8,500 liters of anthrax. The entire stockpile would fill half a tractor-trailer. The ingredients for some biological and chemical weapons could have been combined in a small portable laboratory similar to those that Secretary of State Powell illustrated during his Security Council speeches. It would have even extraordinarily imprudent to act as if Saddam had no such weapons under these circumstances—particularly when the Iraq government had itself admitted that it possessed them, had engaged in numerous subterfuges and diversions in the face of UN-authorized inspections, and had failed to account for those weapons that it had admitted possessing.

Mahdi Shukur Ubaydi, one of Iraq's leading scientists and former head of its uranium enrichment program, has turned over to coalition forces centrifuge components that had been concealed in a barrel buried beneath rose bushes in his garden. He has admitted to investigators that he lied about Iraq's nuclear program before the war. Now, evidently feeling secure against retaliation by the Iraq government because he is out of the country, he says that this equipment was hidden under his rose bushes and was to be brought out and used to enrich uranium for nuclear weapons once the embargo against Iraq was lifted.[7]

The notion that Iraq could be persuaded to disarm peacefully is a completely unrealistic figment of the imagination. There was nothing in the history of the Saddam regime to suggest that such a program had the slightest chance of succeeding, and there was certainly no evidence prior to the war that Saddam intended to cooperate with inspectors, much less anyone planning to dismantle his weapons of mass destruction—assuming that he had any.

In view of the brutal history of Iraqi aggression, not to mention the repression and genocidal actions Saddam had taken against people and groups he considered to be enemies of his regime, and the legitimate fears and concerns engendered by terrorist attacks against the United States on September 11, 2001, as well as those committed both prior to and after that date, it would have been the height of folly to fail to do whatever was necessary to remove what was reasonably perceived to be a potentially lethal threat to the American people and to world peace.[8]

LEGAL AND MORAL ISSUES

As I shall show below, the war against Iraq was not about oil, though the fact that Iraq floats on immense reserves of oil is not irrelevant to the world's interest in it. Nor is it inconsequential insofar as Saddam Hussein's power derived very largely from the fact that he was able to tap the enormous income from Iraq's oil production for his own purposes. Anyone who heats her home in winter, cools it in summer, uses electricity to watch television, heat dinner, and keep a refrigerator and freezer running, and loads her children into her motor vehicle to drive them to school, to Little League, and to piano lessons cannot be indifferent to the energy that fuels all of those activities and more. Without a constant flow of oil, commerce, commodious buildings, education, travel, manufacture, and possibly life as we know it would become impossible. Whether she drives her own motor vehicle or takes public transportation, she cannot, without hypocrisy, sneer at fighting an adversary who would cut off a substantial portion of the world's energy if he could. But as we shall see, there are justifications for the war against Saddam Hussein other than his control over an important oil spigot.

Because of superb strategic and tactical planning, the war against Iraq proceeded very rapidly and by the time it was concluded, the damage done to noncombatants was fairly minimal, coming nowhere near the predicted "holocaust" or "massacre." It now appears that even the Iraqi military did not suffer exceedingly large numbers of deaths because so many of them heeded the warnings and instructions that had been dropped on their positions before the war began, laid down their weapons, and either surrendered or went home. Coalition forces were even careful to avoid bombing important cultural centers and monuments, such as museums and archaeological sites, which suffered far more damage as a result of massive looting and pilfering by local residents during and after the war than from the effects of the war

itself. Neither Baghdad nor any other city was destroyed, though many buildings were reduced to rubble. In order to keep the infrastructure as intact as possible, coalition forces spared bridges, roads, power stations, oil fields, and the like. Iraqi supporters of Saddam Hussein and opponents of the occupation have done far more damage to such facilities than the invading or occupying forces themselves. In short, the war was carried out in such a way that there was minimal loss of life and property. In retrospect, therefore, it is clear that the devastation predicted by opponents of the war failed to materialize.

But that is not a sufficient response to those who argue that war is inherently evil and that no nation ever has a right to subject another to the hazards of war, regardless of the provocation and regardless of the good intentions of those who initiate the action.

It is difficult to know quite how to respond to such an absolutist position. Those who adhere to it are not likely to be persuaded, however rational the response might be. Nevertheless, it is worthwhile to discuss the alternative briefly.

The nations of the world, after all, have never adopted an absolute ban on war, though one might think that the French and Germans had done so when they expressed their intention in the Security Council to vote against authorizing a U.S.-led coalition to go to war with Iraq. (I leave aside for now the question whether the use of armed force had not already been authorized in earlier resolutions dealing with Iraqi disarmament.) When the Charter of the United Nations was adopted, a proposal to define aggression in Article 39 and elsewhere was defeated on the ground that it introduced an undue element of rigidity in the interpretation of the Charter, making it exceedingly difficult to determine, under Article 51, what might properly be regarded as an "armed attack" justifying a response in self-defense. During discussions on the international control of nuclear energy, it was observed that serious violations of the convention might properly be regarded as "armed attack," that is, aggression that under Article 51, a state might respond to as an act of self-defense.[9]

In international law, the right of self-defense has always been regarded as an inherent right, one that was not within the competence of any state other than the one invoking it to judge. Indeed, when the League of Nations Charter was ratified, the signatories reserved to themselves the right to go to war in self-defense and to judge for themselves whether a situation had arisen that justified doing so. France, for example, declared that "Nothing in the new treaty restrains or compromises in any manner whatsoever the right of self-defence. Each nation in this respect will always remain free to defend its territory against attack or invasion; it alone is competent to decide whether circumstances require recourse to war in self-defence." The United Sates and other signatory nations made identical or similar declarations.[10]

Nevertheless, there are those who believe that the justification of self-defense cannot be invoked in support of preemptive war. They base their argument on the following premises: That (1) territorial integrity and political sovereignty are basic rights of states; that (2) any use of force or imminent threat of force by one state against the political sovereignty or territorial integrity of another constitutes aggression and is a criminal act; that (3) the victim is entitled to act in self-defense in case of aggression against it by another state; and that (4) "nothing but aggression can justify war."[11]

In applying this analysis to the 2003 war against Iraq, the obvious weak point is in (2). Just what constitutes aggression? What is an "imminent" threat of force? In domestic law, a person may invoke self-defense against a criminal charge of homicide by proving that he reasonably apprehended that he was in imminent danger of serious bodily harm or death from the person he attacked. He need not wait until he sees the person he identifies as the aggressor pulling the trigger of his gun. By then, it may well be too late. Such rigid adherence to the niceties of law is both irrational and suicidal. The government of a nation may be reasonably apprehensive that its territory is imminently threatened with invasion, or that its citizens are imminently threatened with great bodily harm or death without waiting for the missiles to be fired or the homicide bombers to blow themselves up together with scores of innocent victims, in a passenger plane, a pizza parlor, or a school

bus, before taking action to ward off the perceived threat.

In the case of an international threat, the word "imminent" must be far more elastic than it is in personal confrontations. When a burglar enters my house at night and points a gun at my head, there is no doubt that I am in imminent—i.e., immediate, instant—danger. But imminent dangers to nations may range from weeks to months. When President Kennedy prepared for war and threatened preemptive strikes against the Soviet Union during the Cuban missile crisis, the imminent danger consisted of the unloading and positioning of long-range missiles in Cuba. Those missiles might have been weeks or months from being armed and ready for launch, but they were perceived to be sufficiently threatening to justify risking World War III and the launching of nuclear weapons.

After the terrorist attacks against the territory of the United States on September 11, 2001, American authorities became highly sensitive to the risk of further attacks on the United States, American interests, and its allies. The threat was rightly perceived to be centered most especially in the Middle East and among persons from that part of the world. Once intelligence agencies had developed credible evidence that established a high likelihood that the Iraqi regime possessed nuclear, chemical, or biological weapons and was unwilling, over a period of many years, to permit UN inspectors to look for them unmolested, much less with the cooperation of Iraqi scientists and government officials, it was reasonable to assume that Iraq constituted an imminent threat to the United States as well as to others.

Add to that the fact that Saddam Hussein openly and notoriously aided the Palestinian Arab homicide bombing campaign against Israel by presenting checks for $25,000 each to the families of such bombers, the well-known brutality of the Iraqi regime against Kurdish and Christian minorities within Iraq, dissidents of all kinds, and members of Saddam Hussein's own immediate family; Iraq's use of nerve gases against Iranians and Kurds; and Iraq's war of aggression against Kuwait and its launching of missiles against Israel and Saudi Arabia during that war—and there was ample reason to be apprehensive about the safety of American citizens and the integrity of their homeland against possible attacks launched by Saddam Hussein or his surrogates.

Much has been made of the fact that until now, no clear and convincing evidence has been found of the weapons of mass destruction that were invoked as one of the principal justifications for removing Saddam Hussein's dictatorship from its position of power in Iraq. No doubt nuclear, chemical, and biological weapons are properly called weapons of mass destruction. But such weapons by themselves are unlikely to produce serious damage to anyone. On the other hand, such common weapons as plastic explosives and box cutters can cause immense damage, as the people of Israel, the families of passengers on Pan Am 103, the people of Lockerbie, Scotland, and the 3,000 victims of the 9/11 terrorists found out to their everlasting sorrow.

Those inanimate physical objects are not in themselves weapons of mass destruction. Those who would use them are. Osama bin Laden and Saddam Hussein are the ultimate weapons of mass destruction. Once they and those like them are eliminated, the objects they would use to harm their adversaries become relatively harmless.

When it became clear that Saddam Hussein would use such weapons as were available to him in wars of aggression—as he had already demonstrated by doing so, and as he continued to do by his support of Middle Eastern terrorists—it became clear that neither his neighbors nor those living at greater distances from Iraq, including Americans and Europeans, would be safe if he should decide that they were a danger to him or his interests. A preemptive war in self-defense became fully justified, for he was properly perceived to be an imminent threat to innocent human lives and to world peace.

NOTES

1. I refer throughout to the American government and not to the Bush administration, as some of that administration's opponents and critics prefer to do. Despite the wish in some quarters that George W. Bush were not the President of the United States, the fact is that he was elected and inaugu-rated as President of the United States. His actions and those of the government he heads are actions of the United States of America, and not those of the Bush administration alone. As Hobbes once said, "to whatsoever man or assembly of men shall be given . . . the right to present the person of them all—that is to say, to be their representative—every one, as well he that voted for it as he that voted against it, shall authorize all the actions and judgments of that manor assembly of men in the same manner as if they were his own." Every theory of democracy must make the same assumption, for without it, elections will come to mean nothing. A recent news report referring to "the Bush administration's occupation of Iraq" reflects a shocking failure to appreciate how democracy works.

2. M. Daniel Bernard, quoted in the *Times of London*, Dec. 19, 2001. French spokespersons did not deny that the ambassador made the statement attributed to him, and have not retracted or apologized for it.

3. January 20, 2003, statement by the United States Ambassador to the European Union. The United States, in a departure from tradition, called for a vote on the election of Libya to the chair of the Commission "so that we could leave no doubt about our objection to Libya." He said Muammar Qadhafi's regime detains political opponents, tortures and mistreats prisoners, and restricts freedom of speech, press, assembly, association and religion. "A country with this record does not merit a leadership role in the U.N. System." When asked whether the outcome of the vote, which was favorable to Libya, represented a defeat for the United States, the ambassador responded, "No, this was not a defeat for the United States. It was a defeat for the Human Rights Commission, a defeat for the system which allows countries with egregious abusive records on human rights to become members of the Commission."

4. Condoleeza Rice, the U.S. National Security Advisor, said on February 9, 2003, "Clearly, to have Libya as chairman of the U.N. Human Rights Commission is laughable; to have Iraq in line to become head of the disarmament commission . . . it's laughable. Yes, the United Nations needs to worry about its credibility, but most importantly, the Security Council now needs to worry about its credibility." Radio Netherlands Newsletter, Feb. 10, 2003.

5. I happened to attend former U.S. Attorney-General Clark's lecture at the Pace University School of Law. When a member of the audience asked him whether he had been able to travel to universities in Iraq to talk about Iraqi aggression against Kuwait or Iraq's use of chemical weapons against Iran and against its own Kurdish minority, his complete

response, verbatim, was, "The moment I saw the suit you were wearing, I knew that that was the question you were going to ask." See also accusations he has brought against the United States of genocide against the people of Iraq in a letter to the United Nations Security Council dated February 28, 2001; and his accusations against the United States, the U.N., president Bill Clinton, the members of the U.N. Security Council, and many others of genocide, crimes against humanity, use of a weapon of mass destruction, and other crimes. Clark brought those accusations to the International Criminal Court in November 1996. Many other similar documents are available on the web site of Clark's International Action Center (iacenter.org).

6. February 5, 2003, and March 7, 2003. These statements, together with the documents and recordings to which they refer, are available on the web site of the U.S. Department of State at usinfo.state.gov.

7. Reuters, *New York Times*, June 26, 2003.

8. See Robert J. Lieber, "The Folly of Containment," *Commentary*, April 2003, 15 ff.

9. See Oppenheim-Lauterpacht, *International Law*, 7th ed. (Longmans, Green, 1952), II, 190.

10. Ibid., 187, n. 1.

11. See Michael Walzner, *Just and Unjust Wars* (New York: Basic Books, 1977), 61 f.

Iraqi War II: A Blatantly Unjust War

James P. Sterba

On 19 March 2003, George W. Bush ordered American forces "to disarm Iraq and depose Saddam Hussein."[1] In the course of this second war against Iraq, 172 coalition soldiers lost their lives, and an estimated 3,500 Iraqi civilians and tens of thousand of Iraq soldiers who did not welcome the Americans as liberators also lost their lives before an end to major hostilities was declared on May 1.[2] The justification for Iraqi War II was given by President Bush and by members of his administration starting in early September 2002.[3]

- On 12 September 2002, Bush declared before the United Nations General Assembly that Saddam Hussein "continues to develop weapons of mass destruction." "The first time we may be completely certain he has a nuclear weapon is when, God forbid, he uses one."

- That same month, Bush cited an International Atomic Energy Agency Report that he said showed that Saddam was only months away from

having nuclear weapons, adding "I don't know what more evidence we need."

- In a 7 October 2002 speech, Bush declared: "In 1995, after several years of deceit by the Iraqi regime, the head of Iraq's military industries defected. It was then that the regime was forced to admit that it had produced more than 30,000 litres of anthrax and other deadly biological agents . . . This is a massive stockpile of biological weapons that has never been accounted for, and capable of killing millions."

- On 29 January in his State of the Union message, Bush noted that the British government had learned that Saddam Hussein recently sought significant quantities of uranium from Africa.

- In his presentation to the UN Security Council on 5 February, Secretary of State Colin Powell claimed: "It took years for Iraq to finally admit that it had produced four tons of the deadly nerve agent VX. A single drop of VX on the skin will kill in minutes. Four tons. The admission only came out after inspectors collected documentation as a result of the defection of Hussein Kamel, Saddam Hussein's late son-in-law."

James P. Sterba, "Iraqi War II: A Blatantly Unjust War," in *Morality in Practice*, ed. James P. Sterba, 7th ed. (Belmont, CA: Wadsworth/Thomson, 2004), 626–35 (edited). Reprinted with permission by Wadsworth.

• In that same presentation, Powell claimed that Iraq was linked to Al Qaeda through Abu Musaab al-Zarqawi, who maintained a poison and explosive training camp for Al Qaeda in Northeastern Iraq.

So the main reasons offered by Bush and members of his administration to justify going to war against Iraq were Iraq's possession of weapons of mass destruction, its continuing development of those weapons, and its connection to the Al Qaeda terrorist network.

In addition, Iraq was in a unique predicament with respect to weapons of mass destruction. Following the first war against Iraq, the United Nations Security Council had passed a number of resolutions (seventeen in all), some of which demanded that Iraq destroys all its weapons of mass destruction. So, unlike other nations, for Iraq to continue to possess and develop weapons of mass destruction placed it in violation of UN Security Council resolutions as well.[4] Could all these reasons taken together be thought to suffice to justify Iraq War II?

JUST WAR THEORY

In traditional just war theory, two requirements must be met in order to justify going to war. First, there must be a just cause. Second, just means must be used to fight the war.

In order for there to be a just cause:

1. There must be substantial aggression.

2. Nonbelligerent correctives must be either hopeless or too costly.

3. Belligerent correctives must be neither hopeless nor too costly.

Needless to say, the notion of substantial aggression is a bit fuzzy, but it is generally understood to be the type of aggression that violates people's most fundamental right. To suggest some specific examples of what is and is not substantial aggression, usually the taking of hostages is regarded as substantial aggression while the nationalization of particular firms

owned by foreigners is not so regarded. But even when substantial aggression occurs, frequently nonbelligerent correctives are neither hopeless nor too costly to pursue. And even when nonbelligerent correctives are either hopeless or too costly, in order for there to be a just cause, belligerent correctives must be neither hopeless nor too costly.[5]

Traditional just war theory assumes, however, that there are just causes and goes on to specify just means as imposing two requirements:

1. Harm to innocents should not be directly intended as an end or a means.

2. The harm resulting from the belligerent means should not be disproportionate to the particular defensive objective to be attained.

While the just means conditions apply to each defensive action, the just cause conditions must be met by the conflict as a whole.

THE APPLICATION OF JUST WAR THEORY TO IRAQI WAR II

To meet the requirements of just war theory, there must have been a just cause for Iraqi War II. This means there must have been substantial aggression and the use of nonbelligerent correctives to respond to that aggression must have been hopeless or too costly and the use of belligerent correctives to respond to that aggression must have been neither hopeless nor too costly. But what was the substantial aggression to which the U.S.-led forces were responding? Unlike Iraqi War I, Iraqi War II was not waged to oust Iraqi forces from another country. Rather, it was waged to remove weapons of mass destruction from Iraq itself. The Bush administration claimed that Iraq's possession and development of weapons of mass destruction in violation of UN Security Council Resolutions, together with its ties to Al Qaeda, constituted a threat that we were justified in going to war to eliminate.

Let us assume, for the sake of argument, that a threat can be so serious that it alone can constitute an act of aggression sufficient to justify a military response.[6] For example, some have thought that the Soviet Union's deployment of missiles that could be armed with nuclear warheads in Cuba in 1962 posed such a threat to the United States.[7] So the question is whether Iraq posed such a threat to the United States.

To answer this question, we first need to get clearer about what are weapons of mass destruction. There are three kinds of weapons of mass destruction: nuclear, biological, and chemical.[8] About all these weapons have in common is that they are illegal for at least some countries to use or even possess. For example, while nuclear weapons are legal for some countries such as the United States, Russia, France, and the United Kingdom to possess, they are illegal for other countries to possess who have signed the Nuclear Nonproliferation Treaty. These three kinds of weapons are certainly not equally destructive, and in the case of chemical weapons, they are not really weapons of mass destruction at all. Chemical weapons are basically battlefield artillery weapons. That is how they were used when they were first deployed in France during World War I. After the war, the Geneva Convention of 1925 outlawed their use. That neither side used them in World War II, even though they had built up enormous stocks just in case, was largely due to the fact that neither side could figure out any permanent military advantage from using them. In fact, except for a small-scale use by Soviet and Egyptian troops in the Yemeni civil war in the 1960s, the convention was never violated until the Iran-Iraq War in the 1980s. But that is not so surprising once you consider that poison gas is really not a useful battlefield weapon, except in World War I–style circumstances, where you face an enemy with large numbers of infantry in densely populated trenches. It also helps if you face an enemy who does not have chemical weapons.

Actually, that was the situation that Saddam Hussein found himself in at the beginning of the Iran-Iraq War. Add to that the fact that Hussein's own initial offensive into Iran had failed and that Iranian troops had advanced within a few miles

of Basra, Iraq's second largest city. It was then that Iraq began using mustard gas to stop Iran's "human wave" attacks.[9] They did this with the full knowledge and substantial support of the United States. The Carter administration had in fact encouraged Iraq to go [to] war against Iran. The Reagan administration further increased U.S. support for Iraq as the war progressed.[10]

Declassified U.S. government documents now reveal that Secretary of State George Schultz was given intelligence reports on 1 November 1983 reporting the "almost daily use of CW against Iran."[11] That same month, President Ronald Reagan signed a secret order instructing his administration to do "whatever was necessary and legal" to prevent Iraq from losing the war with Iran. On 20 December 1983, Donald Rumsfeld, then special envoy to the Middle East, now Bush's secretary of defense, traveled to Baghdad to tell Saddam personally that the U.S. government would regard "any major reversal of Iraq's fortunes as a strategic defeat for the West," and that the United States was ready for a resumption of full diplomatic relations immediately. Hussein was reportedly "extremely pleased" with Rumsfeld's visit but wanted to delay resumption of diplomatic relations until the following year.

According to a sworn affidavit prepared for Howard Teicher, a former National Security Council official, the United States, "actively supported the Iraqi war effort by supplying the Iraqis with billions of dollars in credits, by providing military intelligence and advice to the Iraqis, and by closely monitoring third country arms sales to Iraq to make sure Iraq had the military weaponry required."[12] The American government allowed vital ingredients for chemical weapons and missile components to be exported in Iraq, together with samples of all the strains of germs used by the United States to make biological weapons. The United States was also the sole country to vote against a 1986 Security Council statement condemning Iraq's use of mustard gas against Iranian troops.

As many as a hundred thousand of Iran's war deaths in the Iran-Iraq War were due to Iraq's use of poison gas (which the Iranians eventually recipro-cated), but delivering it on a battlefield requires thou-sands of poison gas shells per square mile of battlefield in an artillery barrage.[13] To kill those hun-dred thousand Iranians, Iraq probably used at least that many poison gas shells. Thus, while gas can be a useful battlefield weapon under certain conditions, it is hardly a weapon of choice for terrorists. More damage with a far higher level of confidence that your weapon will work would probably result from using a nail bomb instead of a poison gas dispenser of the same size and weight. That was the lesson that could have been learned from the Japanese cult Aum Shinrikyo's release of sarin gas into the Tokyo sub-way system (eleven packages on five subway lines), which only managed to kill twelve people.

So fifteen years after the Iran-Iraq War, did Sad-dam Hussein's regime still have poison gas weapons, even if they really aren't weapons of mass destruc-tion and even if they are not very useful for terror-ists? It is possible that he did, although the UN arms inspectors who spent seven years in Iraq after Iraqi War I certainly found and destroyed the vast major-ity of Iraqi stocks. Rolf Ekeus, the chief UN inspec-tors from 1991 to 1997, reported to the Security Council that 93 percent of Iraq's major weapons capacity had been destroyed.[14] Since chemical weapons degrade in five years or less, anything not destroyed by the UN inspectors would be useless by now. And the new, large-scale production facilities required to make chemical weapons in sufficient quantities are fairly easy to detect.[15]

But what about biological weapons? Aren't they genuinely weapons of mass destruction? According to Gwynne Dyer, the answer is that nobody really knows how dangerous they are because they have never been used in war, apart from Japanese attacks on eleven Chinese cities before and during World War II, and there does not exist any reliable medical data on the effects of those attacks.[16] Aum Shinrikyo tried to attack the Japanese parliament with botulism toxin in 1990 and in 1993 sprayed anthrax spores from the roof of a building in Tokyo, but moved on to nerve gas because these biological agents produced no discernible effect at all.[17] The only other example

we have of the actual use of bioweapons is the post-9/11 anthrax attacks in the United States, in which a still unidentified terrorist—probably a disgruntled former employee from a U.S. government lab—man-aged to disrupt the mail, inspire a number of hoaxes, but in the end kill only four or five people, clearly not a mass killing by anyone's measure.

In order for biological weapons to qualify as gen-uine weapons of mass destruction, they must have the ability to be dispersed secretly and effectively so as to quickly kill a large number of people. As Dyer points out, in developed countries, this is harder to do than it seems, since the usual human immunities mean that most diseases spread relatively slowly, and that normal medical reporting procedures ensure that outbreaks will quickly be detected and contained by vaccination and quarantine measures.[18] Consider, for example, how the city of Toronto has managed to fairly effectively contain the SARS epidemic that struck the city by quarantining almost 20,000 people.

The one disease that clearly does cause a lot of worry is smallpox, given that most people now have no immunity against it because vaccinations ceased once it was eradicated over thirty years ago. The only surviving samples of the virus, as far as we know, are in government laboratories in the United States and Russia. Of course, it is possible that other countries might have found some way to acquire the virus, but, as Dyer points out, the most realistic measure of the level of threat felt in this regard is the fact that the entire population of Western countries could be protected from smallpox infection by a program of vaccination, but because the vaccine kills about one in a million of the people who take it, that risk is regarded as too high in impose on the general population.[19]

If you really want to determine what military experts think about the comparative value of the dif-ferent weapons that are normally grouped together as weapons of mass destruction, consider the fact that of all the money that has been spent on these weapons since the end of World War II, very little has been spent on chemical and biological weapons. As much as 98 percent of it has been spent on nuclear weapons. Over that period of time, the United States and Russia together have built around fifty thousand nuclear weapons—at the cost of hundreds of billions of dollars, although about half of these weapons have now been destroyed. Five [*sic*] other countries have followed suit—Britain, France, Israel, China, India, and Pakistan have acquired between five hundred and fifty nuclear warheads each. And still other nations are hoping to join this exclusive club. So unless the nuclear powers take credible steps toward nuclear disarmament, their number is likely to grow.[20]

There is also the fear that one or more of these true weapons of mass destruction might fall into the hands of terrorists. At the same time, there is a general consensus that it is unlikely that mere terrorists, lacking the resources of a state, could build such weapons themselves.[21] To make even the simplest of nuclear weapons requires an investment of hundreds of millions of dollars, a lot of electrical power, and access to strictly controlled raw materials and precision machinery. Terrorists are just not going to put a nuclear weapon together in a basement somewhere.[22] But might they not steal or be given one?

The fear that a nuclear weapon might fall into the hands of terrorists probably peaked just after the collapse of the Soviet Union in 1991.[23] At the time, there were large numbers of warheads outside of Russia in other former Soviet republics, and even the security and accounting procedures for nuclear weapons within Russia were somewhat lax. By 1993–1994, however, with American assistance to the Russian authorities, all the weapons were back on Russian soil and security measures had dramatically improved. Of course, we can't be certain that during the period of transition, one or two nuclear warheads did not end up in terrorist hands. But if they did, why would the terrorists wait ten years to use or threaten to use them?

There is, of course, the worry that some "outlaw" state might just give a nuclear weapon to a terrorist group. Members of the Bush administration suggested that that is what Saddam Hussein would have done had he succeeded in acquiring nuclear weapons. Of course, Hussein did spend many billions of dollars over a period of more than a decade (1979–1991)

in an attempt to build nuclear weapons. But if we are to understand what Hussein might have done with them if he had acquired them, we need to understand why he wanted them in the first place. During the time that Hussein was seeking nuclear weapons, he was our friend receiving considerable military and diplomatic support from us. So his goal in acquiring nuclear weapons was not to threaten us but rather to deter Israel, who unlike Iraq, had never signed the Nuclear Nonproliferation Treaty and who, with the help of the French, had secretly assembled about two hundred nuclear weapons.[24] Of course, Saddam would never have been able to match Israel's nuclear arsenal and means of delivery, but having just a few nuclear weapons could have constituted a sufficient deterrent; Israel most likely would never have sought to obliterate Iraq with nuclear weapons, or even threaten to do so, knowing that it might lose one or two of its own cities to a nuclear attack. In addition, Hussein may have been able to extend this deterrence to other Muslim countries as well, thereby securing considerable honor and prestige for himself and his country in the Muslim world. In any case, this was hardly the strategy of a madman. Nor was it morally appropriate for the United Sates to simply press Iraq to disarm, leaving Israel as the undisputed nuclear power in the Middle East. Rather, the United States should have demanded that *all* countries in the Middle East renounce nuclear weapons.

Following Iraqi War I, however, the UN inspectors were able to completely destroy Iraq's potential to make nuclear weapons, and, at the same time, the sanctions made it impossible for Iraq to import the raw materials and specialized equipment needed to restart its nuclear program. So in the run-up to Iraqi War II, Iraq presented no nuclear threat of mass destruction to anyone, and this would have continued to be the case as long as Iraq was kept from importing certain raw materials and specialized equipment and building a large nuclear processing facility. At the same time, to remove the incentive for Muslim countries to acquire nuclear weapons, Israel should have been (and still should be) required to give up its nuclear weapons and sign the Nuclear Nonproliferation Treaty.

Given then that the evidence available before Iraqi War II indicated that Iraq lacked any nuclear weapons, or the wherewithal to develop them, and given that the evidence showed that Iraq could only have had degrading remnants of its past stockpiles of chemical and biological weapons, which in any case were not truly weapons of mass destruction, there clearly was no justification for going to war with Iraq, certainly not one based on a threat of weapons of mass destruction.

Nor was there any justification for going to war based on evidence that Iraq might pass off the small amounts of the chemical or biological weapons it might have to bin Laden and his Al Qaeda network. There was no reputable evidence at all linking bin Laden and Al Qaeda with Iraq. In his presentation to the UN Security Council, Secretary of State Powell claimed that Iraq was linked to Al Qaeda through Abu Musaab al-Zarqawi, who maintained a poison and explosive training camp for Al Qaeda in northeastern Iraq. But this supposed link was undercut by the fact that the camp was maintained in an area of Iraq that is controlled, not by Saddam Hussein, but by the Kurds. Moreover, previous attempts to find a link between Saddam Hussein and Al Qaeda have similarly failed.[25] In fact, it has just now been revealed that independent interrogations of both Abu Zubaydah, an Al Qaeda planner and recruiter, and Khalid Sheikh Mohamed, the Al Qaeda chief of operations, indicated no connections between Al Qaeda and Iraq. But this evidence was never made public by the Bush administration as they pressed for war with Iraq.[26] In fact, the only countries for which there is strong evidence of material support for bin Laden and his Al Qaeda network are Saudi Arabia and Pakistan, and these countries claim to be our allies. Given then that Iraq did not present us with a threat of weapons of mass destruction either directly, or indirectly through Al Qaeda, not even the first requirement of a just cause for Iraq War II was met. There was simply no substantial aggression to respond to here, even when we allow that a threat of an appropriate magnitude could itself constitute substantial aggression. There just was no evidence of such a threat.

Yet maybe the evidence that the United States had before Iraqi War II was inadequate, and maybe now that the U.S.-led forces are in control of Iraq, they will be able to show that Saddam Hussein really did have stockpiles of usable chemical and biological weapons and that he really was attempting to develop nuclear weapons. Of course, the justification for going to war must be based on the evidence that is available before the war. It can't be based on evidence that turns up after the war is over. Even so, now that the war is over, it is interesting to note that no evidence of the relevant sort has turned up. The U.S.-led forces have been in Iraq several months now, and as of this writing, all that has been discovered are two mobile labs that may or may not have been used to produce biological weapons (weapons that in any case I have argued do not really qualify as weapons of mass destruction). However, no chemical or biological weapons themselves, nor any precursors of such weapons, have been found. Before the war, Bush administration officials ridiculed the inability of UN weapons inspectors to turn up evidence of chemical or biological or nuclear weapons, and now without anyone impeding the United States' own search for such weapons, the United States has not been able to uncover anything beyond the two mobile labs. The labs themselves show no trace of such weapons, and Iraqi scientists in custody claim that they were used legitimately to produce hydrogen weather balloons.[27] Yet even if we had had this ambiguous evidence about these two mobile labs, it would not have provided us with sufficient evidence to justify our going to war against Iraq.

THE DELIBERATE DECEPTION OF THE AMERICAN PEOPLE

Unfortunately, the situation with respect to the justification for Iraqi War II is even worse. Not only was there sufficient evidence available showing that Iraq did not threaten us with weapons of mass destruction either directly or indirectly through Al Qaeda, there is also considerable evidence now available that Bush and members of his administration either deliberately lied to us concerning whether Iraq presented such a threat or were grossly incompetent in using intelligence agencies to inform themselves in this regard. It is also unlikely that they were just incompetent. More likely, they deliberately lied to the American people concerning Iraq.

Consider the evidence. In September 2002, Bush cited an International Atomic Energy Report that he said showed that Saddam Hussein was only months away from having nuclear weapons. In fact, the report said no such thing. As Paul Krugman of *The New York Times* recently noted, this "discrepancy" was initially reported for a few hours as the lead story on MSNBC's web site, which bore the headline "White House: Bush Misstated Report on Iraq." Then the story disappeared—not just from the top of the page, but from the site.[28]

In his State of the Union message, Bush claimed that the British government had learned that Saddam Hussein recently sought significant quantities of uranium from Africa. This was reported in a fifty-page document issued by the British government in September 2002. It was based on documents showing that Iraq had tried to buy uranium from Niger so it could build nuclear weapons. As it turns out, earlier Vice President Cheney's office had asked for an investigation of the uranium deal. So a former U.S. ambassador to Africa was dispatched to Niger.[29] In February 2002, according to someone present at the meetings, that envoy reported to the CIA and State Department that the information was unequivocally wrong and that the documents had been forged. One official document was signed with the name of Allele Habibou, a Niger Minister of Foreign Affairs and Cooperation, who had been out of office for over ten years. In addition, the Niger mining program was structured so that a large diversion (500 tons of uranium oxide) was impossible. The envoy's debunking of the forgery was passed around the administration and seemed to be accepted—except that President Bush and members of his administration kept citing it.

In February 2003 the British government issued another report presented as up-to-the-minute British intelligence on Iraq, which Secretary of State Powell praised in his presentation before the UN Security Council.[30] This report was quickly exposed as having been extensively plagiarized (11 out of 19 pages) from three nonsecret published articles.[31] The main article was written by an American postgraduate student and was based on material that was over ten years old. Even typographical errors and anomalous uses of grammar from the original article were included. The only substantial difference in the report is that the estimate of the size of the Fedayeen Saddam given in one of the articles as between 18,000 and 40,000 was inflated to between 30,000 and 40,000. To win support for going to war, the British government needed an up-to-date report, and this unconscionable deception is what the government provided and what the U.S. government endorsed.

As we noted earlier, both Bush and Powell, as well as Cheney and other members of the U.S. government, had cited testimony provided by General Hussein Kamel, Suddam Hussein's son-in-law, who defected in 1995. Kamel testified that Iraq had produced large amounts of chemical and biological weapons, and this part of Kamel's testimony is unfailingly reported by Bush and members of his administration. But Kamel also testified in the same debriefing that Iraq had destroyed all of these weapons. How do you explain this omission except as an attempt to deceive the American people?

A few years ago, President Bill Clinton was almost impeached by the U.S. Senate and driven from office for lying about an affair he had had with White House intern Monica Lewinsky, which was the only charge that a $40 million dollar investigation by Independent Counsel Kenneth Starr was able to bring. At the time, conservative pundit William Bennett, author the *Book of the Virtues* and the *Children's Book of Virtues*, claimed that Clinton by his indiscretions had damaged the American presidency and thereby deserved impeachment.[32] For several months, the investigation into whether Clinton had lied about his relationship with Monica Lewinsky and, if he had, whether this was an impeachable offense, virtually put a halt to any new legislative initiatives by the federal government. Yet in any fair comparison, the lying of President Bush and members of his administration is far more significant than Clinton's actions. President Bush and the members of his administration deprived the United States of the wherewithal to function as a democracy. For a democracy to function, its citizens and especially their representatives must not be deprived of the information they need to make the major decisions affecting the country. Information pertaining to whether a country should go to war or not clearly relates to a major decision for any country. Information pertaining to the private sex life of one of its members, even the president of the republic, is clearly not of that sort. It was only made a topic of public concern in the United States as part of a concerted effort to keep Clinton from implementing his political agenda. By contrast, the lying of President Bush and members of his administration strikes at the heart of the republic. It is nothing less than a criminal attempt that has undermined the functioning of the American democracy, and it should be treated as such. By grossly deceiving the American people about Iraq, President Bush and the members of his administration have also undercut their own legal and moral authority for representing the American people and waging war on our behalf. For this, they should be impeached and/or driven from office.

OTHER POSSIBLE JUSTIFICATIONS FOR THE WAR

In the aftermath of Iraqi War II and the failure to find a nuclear weapons program or the large arsenals of chemical and biological weapons that it was claimed could be deployed within 45 minutes, some have begun to suggest that we really didn't need the threat of weapons of mass destruction to justify our going to war.[33] As Thomas Friedman, the chief foreign affairs columnist for *The New York Times*, put it recently in his Op-Ed piece:

As far as I'm concerned, we do not need to find any weapons of mass destruction to justify this war. Mr. Bush doesn't owe the world any explanation for missing chemical weapons. It is clear that ending Saddam's tyranny [is enough].[34]

In a later Op-Ed piece, Friedman expanded upon his view, distinguishing between the stated reason, the right reason, and the moral reason for going to war against Iraq.[35] The stated reason is, of course, that Saddam had weapons of mass destruction that posed a threat to us. The right reason was that we needed to turn back the hatred for America by doing something good for the Iraqi people—liberating them from Saddam Hussein. And the moral reason was that Saddam Hussein deserved to be overthrown because of his past atrocities. Friedman allows that Bush appealed to the "stated reason" only to get U.S. and world support. But he thinks that the "right reason" and the "moral reason" could have sufficed to justify Iraqi War II. But they could not have sufficed.

In order for reasons to justify a course of action, they must be fittingly related to the course of action; they must be the ends for which the course of action is the most appropriate and effective means. But Iraqi War II is not the most appropriate and effective means for realizing the ends that Friedman endorses. If we had wanted to use $70 billion (the first installment for the war in Iraq) to turn back the hate for America, we could have offered to handsomely resettle all Palestinian refugees and also made a significant dent in world hunger. That would have been a far more appropriate and effective way of pursuing Friedman's "right reason." Friedman's "moral reason" could be exposing and driving from power those in the United States, both inside and outside the Bush administration, who aided and supported Saddam Hussein's past atrocities. That would have done more to show where we really stand on the moral issues at stake. So absent the threat of weapons of mass destruction (which really means the threat of nuclear weapons), there was no justification for Iraqi War II.

It is also important to note that the United States applied considerable pressure and offered large financial incentives in its failed attempt to gain approval from the UN Security Council for Iraqi War II. After the negative vote, the United States took whatever steps it could to punish those countries that voted against it.[36] The United States promised Turkey as much as $26 billion in economic aid to permit U.S. troops to open a northern front against Iraq, but

Turkey's elected parliament voted the offer down.[37] Recently, on a visit to Turkey, U.S. Deputy Secretary of Defense Paul Wolfowitz openly questioned why the Turkish military did not play a stronger role in forcing its elected government to vote in favor of Iraqi War II.[38] So much for the United States' claim to be a strong supporter of democracy in the Middle East.

CONCLUSION

When Americans reflect upon world affairs, most of them regard the two world wars as paradigms of their country's military involvement in other countries. World War I was the "War to End All Wars" and World War II was the "War for Four Freedoms." Both wars are viewed as good wars, although, in fact, only parts of each war were good or just.[39] Most Americans do not like to think too much about other earlier wars that pitted Americans against other nations: the conquest and extermination of American Indian nations, which only ended in 1890, the Mexican-American War of 1846–1848, and the Spanish-American War of 1898. Of course, today Americans might recognize these past wars as unjust, but they usually tend to identify them with a youthful, immature nation, not the American with which they identify that fought in the two world wars. However, if you reflect upon many of the more recent U.S. military interventions into other countries—for example, U.S. interventions into Chile, Nicaragua, Panama, Grenada, Lebanon, Sudan, Afghanistan, and the ten-year-long intervention into Vietnam, which left three million Vietnamese dead—these interventions do tend to resemble more those earlier wars with which [we] do not identify than the two world wars with which we do identify. At least, this is how most people in other countries have come to think about us in recent years as "the greatest threat to peace."[40] And now we have our military occupation of Iraq, the result of a blatantly unjust war that our leaders deceived us into waging. The portents are not good. Under the Bush administration, the United States has definitely begun to strongly reidentify itself with its colonial past. So unless we begin to take meaningful steps to undo the injustice of Iraqi War II and begin to take other steps to show ourselves to be good citizens of the world, we will soon be clearly forced to see ourselves and our country differently, the way many people of other countries already regard us, and I don't think many of us will like what we will see.

NOTES

1. It is worth noting that at the time the U.S. launched its war against Iraq, no public in the world but the Israeli one supported the war under the conditions in which it was launched—that is, without UN support. Jonathan Shell, "The World's Other Superpower," *Nation*, Apr. 14, 2003.

2. http.www.cdi.org/iraq/casualties.cfm, and http://www.wsws.org/articles/2003/may2003/iraq-m05.shtml.

3. As for why the campaign for Iraqi War II began in early September 2002, Andrew H. Card, the White House Chief of Staff explained, "From a marketing point of view, you don't introduce new products in August . . . " Quoted in Chalmers Johnson, "The Sorrows of Empire," http://www.antiwar.com/orig/johnson1.html.

4. It is worth noting here that the U.S. has not been equally concerned with enforcing other Security Council resolutions. There are about 31 UN Security Council resolutions against Israel, mostly in connection with the West Bank and the Gaza strip, land that Israel occupied after the 1967 Arab-Israel War, and 23 resolutions against Turkey in connection with its occupation of Cyprus. Yet both of these countries receive vast amounts of U.S. aid and weaponry, even though they are in blatant violation of UN Security Council resolutions. Given that the U.S. supports the violation of some UN Security Council resolutions while opposing the violation of others, it is clear that its opposition to Iraq has little do to with the mere fact that Iraq is in violation of Security Council resolutions.

5. Built into the "too costly" requirement is the traditional proportionality requirement of just war theory. Clearly, various nonbelligerent and belligerent measures can be too costly either to ourselves, to the other side, or to both sides together. When belligerent measures are too costly either to ourselves or to the other side or to both side together, they are rightly judged disproportionate.

6. This way of thinking about the issue cuts across the distinction between preemptive and preventive war suggesting that the key question to be assessed is not whether the war is preemptive or preventive but how serious is the threat.

7. See Graham Allison, *Essence of Decision* (Boston: Little, Brown, 1971),and Robert F. Kennedy, *Thirteen Days: A Memoir of the Cuban Missile Crisis* (New York: Norton, 1969).

8. In what follows, I rely on Gwynne Dyer's account of the differences between these weapons. See his *Ignorant Armies* (Toronto: The Canadian Publishers, 2003), p. 22 ff.

9. Michael Dobbs, "U.S. Had a Key Role in Iraq Buildup." *Washington Post*, December 30, 2002; Christopher Dickey and Evan Thomas, "How Saddam Happened," in Said Aburish et alia, *Inside Iraq* (New York: Marlow, 2002), pp. 211–224.

10. See William Rivers Pitt with Scott Ritter, *War on Iraq: What Team Bush Doesn't Want You to Know* (New York: Context Books, 2002) p. 20 ff.

11. Dobbs, op. cit.; Research Unit for Political Economy, "Behind the War on Iraq," *Monthly Review*, vol. 55 (2003).

12. *Ibid.*

13. Dyer, op. cit.; Bruce Hoffman, "Terrorism and Weapons of Mass Destruction" (Washington, DC: *Rand*, 1999).

14. Research Unit for Political Economy, op. cit.

15. Pitt and Ritter, op. cit.

16. Dyer, pp. 27–28.

17. Richard Falkenrath et alia, *America's Achilles' Heel* (Cambridge: MIT, 1998), pp. 19–26.

18. Dyer, p. 22 ff.

19. *Ibid.*

20. Unfortunately, recent actions by the U.S. government are only likely to increase the danger from nuclear weapons. After a self-imposed decade-long ban on the research and development of low-yield nuclear weapons, the U.S. Senate Armed Services Committee voted to lift the ban and push ahead with the production of nuclear weapons that would be more usable. Surely other nuclear powers will feel impelled to follow our example. See http://www.wsws.org/articles/2003/may2003/nuci-m14.shtml.

21. Dyer, p. 22 ff.

22. Of course, there is the possibility that terrorists might use radiological weapons; that is, they might combine nuclear waste, say from a hospital, with conventional explosives.

23. Dyer, p. 22 ff.

24. Franc had violated the Nuclear Nonproliferation Treaty in helping the Israelis develop nuclear weapons, and Mordechai Vanunu, who exposed Israel's secret acquisition of nuclear weapons in 1986, was kidnapped by Israeli agents in Rome that same year and has been imprisoned in Israel ever since.

25. David Cortright et al. *Contested Case,* A Report of the Fourth Freedom Foundation and the Joan B. Kroc Institute for International Pace Studies, Policy Brief F8, February 6, 2003.

26. James Risen, "Captives Deny Qaeda Worked with Baghdad." *New York Times*, June 9, 2003.

27. *New York Times*, May 29, 2003; Some of the members of a group of U.S. experts who have more recently seen the labs dispute the claim that these labs were used to make biological weapons. See *New York Times*, June 7, 2003.

28. Paul Krugman, "Matters of Emphasis." *New York Times*, Apr. 29, 2003.

29. See Nicholas Kristoff, "Missing in Action," *New York Times*, May 6, 2003; Seymour Hersh, "Who Lied to Whom? Why Did the Administration Endorse a Forgery about Iraq's Nuclear Program?" *New Yorker*, Mar. 31, 2003, p. 41.

30. See "Iraq-Its Infrastructure of Concealment, Deception and Intimidation," http://www.pm.gov.uk.

31. Glen Rangwala, "Intelligence? The British Dossier on Iraq's Security Infrastructure," 5 February, 2003, http:casi.org.uk/discuss/2003/msg00457.html; Toby Helm, "Fiasco Over the Saddam Dossier," 8 February 2003, http://www.telegraph.co.uk.

32. See Sidney Blumenthal, *The Clinton Wars* (New York: Farrar, Straus and Giroux, 2003), p. 491. More recently Bennett has become known for his multimillion-dollar gambling losses. See Jonathan Alter and Joshua Green, "Gambling: Bennett: Virtue is as Virtue Does?" *Newsweek*, May 12, 2003.

33. In addition to Thomas Friedman, see Michael Schrage, "No Weapons, No Matter," *Washington Post*, May 11, 2003.

34. Thomas Friedman, "The Meaning of a Skull," *New York Times*, Apr. 27, 2003.

35. Thomas Friedman, "Because We Could," *New York Times*, June 4, 2003.

36. In 1990, when Yemen voted against a U.S. Security Council resolution to militarily oust Iraq from Kuwait, a senior American diplomat told the Yemeni ambassador: "That was the most expensive No vote you ever cast." Three days later, a U.S. aid program of $70 million to one of the world's poorest countries was stopped. Yemen began to have problems with the IMF and World Bank, and Saudi Arabia expelled 800,000 Yemeni workers. Later, when the U.S. sought another resolution to blockade Iraq, two other rotating members of the Security Council were duly coerced. Ecuador

was warned about the "devastating economic consequences of a No vote", and Zimbabwe was threatened with new IMF conditions for its debt. Norman Solomon and Reese Erlich, *Target Iraq: What the New Media Didn't Tell You* (New York: Context Books, 2003), pp. 69–70.

37. Dexter Filkins with Eric Schmitt, "Turkey Demands $32 Billion U.S. Aid package if It Is to Take Part in a War on Iraq," *New York Times*, Feb. 19, 2003.

38. http://www.wsws.org/articles/2003/turk-m24.shtml.

39. The firebombing of Dresden and Hamburg and dropping atomic bombs on Hiroshima and Nagasaki were neither good nor just. For an argument to this effect, see my article "Terrorism and International Justice," in my collection *Terrorism and International Justice* (New York: Oxford University Press, 2003), pp. 212–213.

40. According to a *Time* (Europe) poll, 87% of respondents regarded the U.S. as the greatest threat to peace in 2003 (http://www.time.com/time/europe/gdml/peace2003.html).

Humanitarian Intervention: Some Doubts

BURLEIGH WILKINS

If Locke was correct, and I think he was, revolution is justified when there is systematic violation of the rights of life, liberty, and property with no peaceful redress in sight. I believe that secession and even terrorism are also justified when these conditions obtain. But what about humanitarian intervention? Is it also justified in such a situation. Many of us hesitate when confronted by this question, but why? Is it because humanitarian intervention involves military action by some state or states against another state? Is it because it may raise questions about the legitimacy of a state's sovereignty, questions which even the most secure liberal democracy may feel uncomfortable in addressing? Are even more egregious violations of human rights required in the case of humanitarian intervention than in the cases of revolution, secession, and terrorism? Of course, attempted justifications of humanitarian intervention may focus upon issues other than human rights violations, such as the need to establish or reestablish a democracy or to put an end to a vicious civil war, but these issues, although separate from the issue of human rights violations, may nevertheless be related to it. For purposes of this chapter, I shall be

concerned only with human rights violations as a possible ground for humanitarian intervention.

Although it involves the violation of a state's independence and territorial integrity, humanitarian intervention is usually distinguished from war on the ground that the loss of independence and territorial integrity is limited in time and scope. Also it is regarded as a means and not an end, with the end being not conquest or the acquisition of land but the restoration or establishment of protection for basic human rights. But how long before a temporary incursion becomes an occupation? And does not the protection of human rights necessitate at times a change of government, as part of what is sometimes called "a comprehensive settlement"? And what, if anything, can the intervening power(s) do about the culture or way of life which may underlie a government's violation of human rights?

International law seems committed to respect for the sovereignty of states, to the protection of human rights, and to the maintenance of peaceful relations among states. In an ideal world where, say, all states are liberal democracies, all three of these commitments would presumably be honored. There is Michael Doyle's "law" that no democracies ever fight one another, but is this a law or just a trend? In any event, in the real world it may be impossible to provide equal protection for sovereignty, human rights,

Burleigh Wilkins, "Humanitarian Intervention: Some Doubts," in Aleksandar Jokic, *Humanitarian Intervention: Moral and Philosophical Issues* (Peterborough, Ont.: Broadview Press, 2003), 35–44 (edited). Reprinted with permission of Broadview Press.

and peaceful co-existence among states. Here we can note the temptation to treat human rights violations in one state as a threat to the peace and security of all states, or at least of neighboring states, and to use this as a justification for the violation of a nation's sovereignty, although this may in some cases seem farfetched and even disingenuous.

Perhaps humanitarian intervention isn't war, but is it enough like war that the doctrine of just war—with its requirements that a war be fought for a just cause and in a just manner, with an expectation of success, and with a respect for proportionately between the means being employed and the end being sought—can be applied? Would a little fine-tuning help? Justice can be cashed in terms of human rights with the stipulation that the intervention will not become an all-out war and that it will not last too long. *Jus ad interventionem.* It has a fine ring to it! And the numbers are simply appalling: four times as many deaths in the twentieth century at the hands of the victims' own government or as a result of civil strife than from all the wars between states.[1]

Is the model of Good Samaritan intervention by an individual person(s) to assist an individual under attack by another at all helpful here? But these interventions, in those jurisdictions where they are legally mandated, are called for only in cases where the convenience and not the lives of third-party interveners is at risk. Here the law seems to follow common morality: if an individual chooses to risk his or her life to come to the aid of another, this is not considered a duty but a supererogatory act. Does this help explain the cautious manner in which political philosophers speak only of a right of intervention and the silence of philosophers such as Walzer and Rawls on whether humanitarian intervention may be a duty?[2] Make no mistake: humanitarian intervention involves a high probability that the intervening party will take casualties. Sometimes the mere presence of troops may lead to casualties, as "mission creep" is a fact of geopolitical life. This is what happened in Somalia where American troops who were initially dispatched to protect humanitarian aid supplies for a starving populace got caught in a struggle between rival warlords.

However, consider the case where an intervening party takes no casualties, as for example the US-NATO intervention in Kosovo which relied entirely upon high altitude bombings to achieve its objectives. This kind of attack, which critics have likened to shooting fish in a barrel, raises fundamental questions of fairness in how an intervention is conducted.

Might not humanitarian intervention sometimes yield just the opposite effect where the protection of human rights is concerned? There are two real possibilities. An oppressive government may be prompted to become even more oppressive in response to an intervention, with confidence that its supporters and even some of its previous critics will "rally round the flag." Or, once intervention occurs, the leadership of an opposition group may become more militant and disrespectful of the right of others, or the leadership may pass into the hands of a more militant faction with even less respect for human rights than the oppressive regime with which we started out.

Almost everyone agrees that humanitarian intervention might be justified in some cases, but real world examples may prove troublesome. Take the example of the persecution of Jews in Nazi Germany. When would humanitarian intervention have been justified? Before or after *Kristallnacht?* Or only after the Holocaust had begun? By then the West was already at war with Germany for other reasons. What this example shows is the difficulty in pointing to the time when intervention would have become justified, and the certainty that early intervention would have become justified, and the certainty that early intervention would have inevitably escalated into an all-out war that the West was not prepared, militarily or psychologically, to fight. The same is true today when we raise the question of what to do about Tibet or Chechnya. The answer is that we can do very little with powers that have nuclear weapons at their disposal. And, of course, we would not pressure allies such as Turkey over its mistreatment of the Kurds as much as we would pressure non-allies over less severe mistreatment of some of their citizens.

Michael J. Smith in a defense of humanitarian intervention candidly admits that there "simply won't be consistency" in our reactions to human rights violations, but he asks, "Is it more ethical to say that, since I cannot do everything everywhere consistently, I should do nothing?"[3] Smith proposes that we adopt a scale of evil where human rights abuses are concerned; on this scale Virginia's frequent use of the death penalty would rank far below the massacres in Rwanda and Cambodia since "few disinterested observers would urge or welcome the forcible landing of an international military force to prevent Virginia's next execution." Smith seems to believe that there is nothing problematic about how rankings on a scale of evil would be determined. This might be true if the executions in Virginia and the massacres in Rwanda and Cambodia were placed at opposite ends of the scale, but other cases might prove more difficult to rank.

There are, as Smith points out, a few success stories for humanitarian intervention, such as India's intervention in East Pakistan and Tanzania's intervention in Uganda. But India's role in the liberation of Bangladesh, according to some observers, only made matters worse, and, given the history of India-Pakistan relations, it may be that India's intervention was not driven mainly by humanitarian concerns. This leaves us with Tanzania's overthrown of the monstrous Idi Amin in Uganda. Such a small success can hardly lend much support to the principle of humanitarian intervention, and large successes are not to be expected. Undoubtedly, as Smith reminds us, there are moral evils far greater than inconsistency, and to do nothing in the face of evil may well be one of them. It is not, however, the problem of consistency per se that concerns me but the problem of how targets for humanitarian intervention get selected.

Scholars agree that there are no instances of purely humanitarian intervention, and, given what we know about the complexity of human motivation and of the relations among states, this is scarcely surprising. Of course, some cases of allegedly humanitarian intervention are clearly bogus, e.g., Hitler's invasion of Czechoslovakia on the ground of protecting the human rights of the German minority. We all know that for Hitler human rights stopped

with German rights, but other cases are more subtle. Sometimes humanitarian intervention may be used in part to settle old grudges, as was alleged against Boutros Boutros-Ghali where Somalia was concerned, or humanitarian intervention may be used against states which have previously fallen upon disfavor in our eyes. Serbia needs to be taught a lesson, as the American Secretary of State put it during the US-NATO intervention in Kosovo. Intervention may also be used in restoring a state's moral standing in the eyes of others. For example, American intervention in Bosnia was undoubtedly influenced by the desire to overcome anti-American sentiments in the Muslim world arising from the Gulf War and to restore the American "reputation" for fairness and even-handedness. One thing we can be sure of is that humanitarian intervention will not occur if there is a risk of a major conflict in which the intervening power(s) can be expected to take significant casualties. It may be possible to devise a scale of evil, as Smith believes, but there already is a scale of power, and no one seriously believes that evils of great magnitude will trump considerations of relative power.

Because of my doubts about humanitarian intervention I shall not explore in any detail the crucial question of who might best decide whether humanitarian intervention is warranted and who should carry out the intervention. Unilateral intervention by a single state has the advantage of swiftness but runs the risk of partiality and of appearing to be a species of "gunboat diplomacy." Regional organizations should be better at filtering out biases, but they may be dominated by a single great power. The UN may take too long in its decision-making, but it is less likely to be biased and has enjoyed, at least until recently, great moral stature. The UN seems to be the best organization for making a decision about intervention, but the problem of consensus is troubling. Kofi Annan in his report on the tragedy of Srebrenica took responsibility for the UN and the part it played. But politicians and bureaucrats are adroit at taking responsibility in such a way as to shift responsibility. In the "lessons" to be learned from the tragedy, Annan ranked the lack of a common "political will" high on his list of causes which will need to be addressed to avoid future Srebrenicas.[4] However, the lack of a common political will has not been present in all of the activities of the UN as, for example, in the Gulf War which turned on the conquest of one state by another. In cases where there is no common political will, is doing nothing not preferable to the kind of bungling which contributes to disasters like Srebrenica?

The lack of a common political will is, of course, not necessarily confined to the international arena. Domestic support in a state for humanitarian intervention may ebb and flow, depending on the strength of opposed political parties and upon their commitment to a particular humanitarian intervention. One concern I have is the following: once it has been decided that humanitarian intervention is warranted in a particular situation, crucial steps that a more patient diplomacy might pursue may be skipped. An example of this is the haste with which the US and NATO decided to attack Serbia before negotiations were given a real chance—negotiations which were, in fact, a form of ultimatum. There is also the danger of self-righteousness which may lead the UN or other state to make demands which no self-respecting state could possibly accept, such as permitting foreign troops to travel at will throughout its territory or the holding of a plebiscite concerning independence for a contested region.

The current international situation can be characterized as follows. Friends and foes alike are nervous over the US-NATO intervention in Kosovo. How long will troops continue to be deployed there? What will count as a successful termination of the mission? Does it set a precedent for future interventions elsewhere in the name of human rights? Whatever happened to the duty of non-intervention, and what kind of duty is it anyway?

One possible reading of the duty of non-intervention is that it is an absolute duty, and various UN agreements including the Charter appear to support this interpretation. However, many moral philosophers would deny that a duty—or a right—can be absolute, that is, obtaining under all circumstances. Perhaps we should try to move in one of two other directions. We could say that the duty of non-

intervention is *prima facie*, that is, that there is a strong presumption against intervention but one that can be overridden when there are compelling reasons to do so. Or we could try to write out a list of exceptions and make this list an explicit part of the formulation of the duty of non-intervention. What are some of these exceptions? Cases where we are invited to intervene by the legitimate government of a state? Cases where we can prevent or suppress systematic violations of human rights? Cases where we can assist in struggles for "national liberation"? But, except for the case where the intervention is invited, all other cases will be controversial and will call for further elaboration or refinement. The question still remains of whether these elaborations and refinements would be stated as explicit parts of the duty of non-intervention. For various reasons the project of a definitive list of exceptions to any duty—including that of non-intervention—seems doomed to failure. Seeing the duty of non-intervention as *prima facie* becomes a more attractive alternative if only by default. However, it might still be argued that the duty of non-intervention is absolute and that we only need add "except in the case of an emergency." All deontological rules, it is sometimes argued, are properly construed in this way, and the emergency exception would be difficult to satisfy. This may be part of the problem: although some non-emergency but justifiable reasons for intervention may be compelling, one person's emergency may be another person's difficulty which can be resolved short of intervention.

A final possibility is an openly purposive or teleological reading of the duty of non-intervention: it is to be respected except when intervention serves an end or purpose deemed morally justifiable, in accordance with, for example, utilitarianism or Marxism. However, where international law is concerned this purposive or teleological reading of the duty of non-intervention would strain the associative model of the UN and other forms of cooperation among states, as described by Terry Nardin.[5] What is to prevent the protection and especially the promotion of human rights from becoming as divisive as any other teleological reading of the duty of non-intervention? The protection and promotion of human rights might be divisive not only between states that champion human rights and those that do not, but also among states that support human rights but fail to agree on the appropriateness of particular interventions. Consider, for example, the controversies surrounding the Reagan administration's policies in Nicaragua and especially that administration's refusal to acknowledge that the American bombing of Nicaragua's harbors fell under the jurisdiction of the International Court of Justice.

I admit to having grown weary, or at least wary, of disjunctions between doing something and doing nothing. In the present case there are many things which can be done to advance the case of human rights which fall short of humanitarian intervention. One way to ameliorate conflict between liberal and decent societies on the one hand and outlaw states on the other is, simply put, trade. There is Thomas Friedman's "law" that no two countries with Mac-Donalds [sic] have ever gone to war with one another. Where human rights issues are concerned the strategy, which sounds simple in the abstract, is to link trading privileges with the acceptance of human rights covenants, as, for example, was the case with the European Council when it granted trading privileges to Russia. In the eighteenth century, the Chinese Emperor wrote to the emissary of King George III that he did not wish to trade with the British since the Chinese had no interest in Britain's clever gadgets. Fortunately for us, and the prospects of a stable world order, all the world seems made to have the US's clever gadgets. The question of how to take this market for American goods and use it to promote the cause of human rights is, however, a question of statecraft to which, as a philosopher, I have nothing to contribute beyond counsels of prudence. However, in the remainder of this paper I shall explore some conceptual matters which may help clarify the connections between morality and international law.

One possible way to approach this problem is to underscore the moral content of international law and to see it as being in itself an ethical tradition. Of course, this interpretation of international law runs counter to the "realist" school of thought, which reduces all relations among states to questions of national interest. Treaties are made to be broken, according to the realist, whenever one side sees an advantage in doing so, and states are expected to spy not only upon their enemies but upon their friends as well. Trust no one, and promote national self-interest by whatever means are judged to be necessary. Against this bleak picture of the relations among states, which, of course, is not entirely mistaken, it is possible to think of international law as an ethical tradition in its own right similar to natural law theory, Kantianism, utilitarianism, Marxism, etc. This is Terry Nardin's position: ethical traditions evolve over time, and they involve judgments about the application of principles to particular situations.[6] Certainly Nardin is right, since one would be hard pressed to articulate a sharp distinction between legal and moral principles and the ways in which they are applied to particular cases. In what follows, however, I shall be concerned with international law not as an ethical tradition but with the moral obligations to which it gives rise where the conduct of states is concerned.

I begin this final portion of my paper with a confession about international law. I find it to be a perplexing mixture of treaties among states, customary practices among states, the charters and instruments of the United Nations and several regional organizations, the decisions of various international tribunals, and even the writings of international lawyers. International law is so complex and in such a state of change that it cannot, according to some scholars, readily be codified. Then, of course, there is the problem of sanctions or enforcement, a problem so important some commentators have concluded that, strictly speaking, international law is not law at all. Thus, there is something very tentative in what I say when I speak of international law as a legal system.

A municipal legal system differs from mere orders and commands in that it imposes moral duties and obligations upon all members of a society, and there is a general recognition, not limited to legal philosophers, that there is a moral obligation to obey all the laws of a municipal legal system. You cannot pick and choose which laws you will obey. Transposing this picture to international law results in the following: all states are morally bound to respect the provisions of international law, just as individuals are morally bound to respect the provisions of municipal law. But are states the kinds of things that can have moral duties and obligations? Why not, provided we see them as organized groups of individuals bound together by common rules? At the very least it is coherent to say that organized groups of individuals can undertake or enter into agreements with other organized groups of individuals. In fact, this seems to be what actually happens on a daily basis where, for example, the transactions of business corporations are concerned. Where international law is concerned, the agreements between organized groups can be understood in terms of treaties and even customary practices among states.

It is noteworthy that the principles governing the relations among peoples which we find in John Rawls's *The Law of Peoples* are themselves taken from international law. According to Rawls, these principles are: peoples are to observe a duty of non-intervention, peoples are to honor human rights, peoples are to observe treaties and undertakings, and peoples are equal and are parties to the agreements that bind them. Rawls writes that "These familiar and largely traditional principles I take from the history and usage of international law and practice. The parties are not given a menu of alternative principles and ideals from which to select, as they are in *Political Liberalism* or in *A Theory of Justice*. Rather, the representatives of well-ordered peoples simply reflect on the advantages of these principles of equality among peoples and see no reason to depart from them or to propose alternatives."[7] In Rawls's second Original Position, the representatives of liberal and decent hierarchical peoples select principles that are binding upon all peoples, including outlaw states. (Could there ever be an outlaw people for Rawls? Perhaps not, given, for example, the careful way in which he tries to distinguish the Nazi state from the German people. Here he disagrees with David Goldhagen's position in *Hitler's Willing Executioners*. The possibility that a coercive demonic political leadership could in time produce a demonic people merits careful consideration.)[8] If I am correct, both Rawls's

account of the principles governing the relations of people and international law as *it already is* presuppose the idea of international law conceived of as a legal system.

The duty of non-intervention is on my interpretation a moral duty binding upon all states, and it is one of many such duties. Here we should note once more the importance of our conceiving of international law as a legal system. It would be nonsensical to speak of a moral obligation to obey a single principle or to abide by a single agreement standing in isolation from a system of principles or agreements. (There is an analog here, I think, with science where scientific laws are seen as part of a system.) All states are morally bound not to intervene in the domestic affairs of other states. Of course all states are also bound to respect human rights; this would be especially true of the member states of the UN and even more so of those states which have signed the two UN Human Rights Covenants. However there are no provisions in the UN Charter or in these covenants for humanitarian intervention in the domestic affairs of states that do not respect human rights. In the past any such intervention clearly would have been illegal, but now things seem less certain. Perhaps in some circumstances humanitarian intervention may trump the obligation of states not to interfere in the domestic affairs of other states. In this connection it is regrettable, though understandable, that the International Court of Justice refused to rule on the legality of US-NATO intervention in Kosovo. At the risk of sounding like a democratic populist in international law when I am emphatically not a democratic populist where American domestic law is concerned, I think humanitarian intervention gives rise to such complex issues that it should be referred to the legislature. Let the member states of the UN address directly the equation of whether humanitarian intervention is permissible, and if need be let us amend the Charter. Let us vote humanitarian intervention up or down, but let us not leave it to be decided on a case-by-case basis. Law, ideally, should satisfy the requirements of justice, but at the very least states no less than individuals need to know what the legal consequences of certain courses of conduct may be.[9]

I want to conclude on a cautiously optimistic note, which I think is consistent with the interpretation of international law as a legal system. According to *Political Liberalism*,[10] John Rawls's history of how the West evolved in a liberal and tolerant direction, two variables were highlighted as important. First was luck, and second was a growing appreciation on the part of individuals with different belief systems of the mutual advantages arising from limited *modus vivendi* agreements. From this it was a short step, historically speaking, to the moral quest for fair rules of social cooperation. Where relations among states are concerned, the world today has an additional advantage in international law, conceived of as a legal system that gives rise to moral obligations among states. However the question of humanitarian intervention is resolved, whether or not it is seen as a right or even as a duty, all states—not just liberal or decent states—are under an obligation to abide by international law.

NOTES

1. See Sean O. Murphy, *Humanitarian Intervention* (Philadelphia: University of Pennsylvania Press, 1996).

2. Michael Walzer, *Just and Unjust Wars* (New York: Basic Books, 1997). John Rawls, *The Law of Peoples* (Cambridge, MA: Harvard University Press, 1999) 81, 93–94n. Stanley Hoffmann in *The Ethics and Politics of Intervention* (Notre Dame, IN: University of Notre Dame Press, 1996) 12–39, claims that he is more Kantian than Rawls because he believes there is a duty of intervention, but both are more Kantian than Kant who did not believe in intervention.

3. Michael J. Smith, "Humanitarian Intervention: An Overview of the Ethical Issues," *Ethics and International Affairs* 12 (1998): 78.

4. Report of the Secretary General Pursuant to General Assembly Resolution 53/35 (1998).

5. Terry Nardin, *Law, Morality, and the Relations of States* (Princeton, NJ: Princeton University Press, 1983).

6. Terry Nardin, "Ethical Traditions in International Affairs," *Traditions of International Ethics*, ed. Terry Nardin and David R. Mapels (Cambridge: Cambridge University Press, 1992) 1–23.

7. Rawls 41.

8. Rawls 100–01n.

9. Anthony Ellis thinks the small states in the UN would probably defeat any amendment permitting humanitarian intervention. I am not sure this is so, but, if it is, this would reflect a failure by the UN to respect the moral equality of all member states, a failure which could perhaps be alleviated by other changes in the way the UN operates, for example, by changes in the veto powers of the permanent members of the Security Council.

10. John Rawls, *Political Liberalism* (New York: Columbia University Press, 1993).

CASES FOR ANALYSIS

1. War in Bosnia

Bosnia is one of several small countries that emerged from the break-up of Yugoslavia, a multicultural country created after World War I by the victorious Western Allies. Yugoslavia was composed of ethnic and religious groups that had been historical rivals, even bitter enemies, including the Serbs (Orthodox Christians), Croats (Catholics) and ethnic Albanians (Muslims). . . .

A new leader arose by the late 1980s, a Serbian named Slobodan Milosevic, a former Communist who had turned to nationalism and religious hatred to gain power. . . .

In June 1991, Slovenia and Croatia both declared their independence from Yugoslavia soon resulting in civil war. The national army of Yugoslavia, now made up of Serbs controlled by Milosevic, stormed into Slovenia but failed to subdue the separatists there and withdrew after only ten days of fighting. . . .

Aided by Serbian guerrillas in Croatia, Milosevic's forces invaded in July 1991 to 'protect' the Serbian minority. In the city of Vukovar, they bombarded the outgunned Croats for 86 consecutive days and reduced it to rubble. After Vukovar fell, the Serbs began the first mass executions of the conflict, killing hundreds of Croat men and burying them in mass graves. . . .

In April 1992, the U.S. and European Community chose to recognize the independence of Bosnia, a mostly Muslim country where the Serb minority made up 32 percent of the population. Milosevic responded to Bosnia's declaration of independence by attacking Sarajevo, its capital city, best known for hosting the 1984 Winter Olympics. Sarajevo soon became known as the city where Serb snipers continually shot down helpless civilians in the streets, including eventually over 3,500 children.

Bosnian Muslims were hopelessly outgunned. As the Serbs gained ground, they began to systematically round up local Muslims in scenes eerily similar to those that had occurred under the Nazis during World War II, including mass shootings, forced repopulation of entire towns, and confinement in make-shift concentration camps for men and boys. The Serbs also terrorized Muslim families into fleeing their villages by using rape as a weapon against women and girls.

The actions of the Serbs were labeled as 'ethnic cleansing,' a name which quickly took hold among the international media.

Despite media reports of the secret camps, the mass killings, as well as the destruction of Muslim mosques and historic architecture in Bosnia, the world community remained mostly indifferent. . . .

Throughout 1993, confident that the U.N., United States and the European Community would not take militarily action, Serbs in Bosnia freely committed genocide against Muslims. . . .

On February 6, 1994, the world's attention turned completely to Bosnia as a marketplace in Sarajevo was struck by a Serb mortar shell killing 68 persons and wounding nearly 200. Sights and sounds of the bloody carnage were broadcast globally by the international news media and soon resulted in calls for military intervention against the Serbs.

The U.S. under its new President, Bill Clinton, who had promised during his election campaign in 1992 to stop the ethnic cleansing in Bosnia, now issued an ultimatum through the North Atlantic Treaty Organization (NATO) demanding that the Serbs withdraw their artillery from Sarajevo. The Serbs quickly complied and a NATO-imposed cease-fire in Sarajevo was declared.

The U.S. then launched diplomatic efforts aimed at unifying Bosnian Muslims and the Croats against the Serbs. However, this new Muslim-Croat alliance failed to stop the Serbs from attacking Muslim towns in Bosnia which had been declared Safe Havens by the U.N. A total of six Muslim towns had been established as Safe Havens in May 1993 under the supervision of U.N. peacekeepers.

Bosnian Serbs not only attacked the Safe Havens but also attacked the U.N. peacekeepers as well. NATO forces responded by launching limited air strikes against Serb ground positions. The Serbs retaliated by taking hundreds of U.N. peacekeepers as hostages and turning them into human shields, chained to military targets such as ammo supply dumps.

At this point, some of the worst genocidal activities of the four-year-old conflict occurred. In Srebrenica, a Safe Haven, U.N. peacekeepers stood by helplessly as the Serbs under the command of General Ratko Mladic systematically selected and then slaughtered nearly 8,000 men and boys between the ages of twelve and sixty—the worst mass murder in Europe since World War II. In addition, the Serbs continued to engage in mass rapes of Muslim females.

On August 30, 1995, effective military intervention finally began as the U.S. led a massive NATO bombing campaign in response to the killings at Srebrenica, targeting Serbian artillery positions throughout Bosnia. The bombardment continued into October. Serb forces also lost ground to Bosnian Muslims who had received arms shipments from the Islamic world. As a result, half of Bosnia was eventually retaken by Muslim-Croat troops.

Faced with the heavy NATO bombardment and a string of ground losses to the Muslim-Croat alliance, Serb leader Milosevic was now ready to talk peace. On November 1, 1995, leaders of the warring factions including Milosevic and Tudjman traveled to the U.S. for peace talks at Wright-Patterson Air Force base in Ohio.*

For this exercise, assume that the above account of the conflict in Bosnia is accurate. Were the United States and NATO justified in intervening in Bosnia to stop the killing of noncombatants? Why or why not? How would just war theory apply? How might a utilitarian evaluate the permissibility of NATO's military action? What might a nonconsequentialist say about it?

* Philip Gavin, "Genocide in the 20th Century: Bosnia-Herzegovina 1992–1995, 200,000 Deaths," *The History Place,* 1999, www.historyplace.com/worldhistory/genocide/bosnia.htm (accessed 17 February 2006). Written by Philip Gavin, Publisher and Founder of The History Place web site (www.historyplace.com). Reprinted with permission of Philip Gavin.

2. War in Afghanistan

Consider this time line detailing the run-up to the U.S. invasion of Afghanistan in 2001.

September 11—Hijacked airliners are flown into the twin towers of the World Trade Center in New York and the Pentagon, outside Washington DC. A fourth plane crashes in Pennsylvania. In an address to the nation, President Bush describes the attacks as "deliberate and deadly terrorist acts." He says he has directed the US intelligence and law enforcement communities "to find those responsible and bring them to justice," adding that the US "will make no distinction between the terrorists who committed these acts and those who harbor them."

September 12—President Bush declares that the attacks were "acts of war." The United Nations Security Council passes Resolution 1368, recognizing "the inherent right of individual and collective self-defense" and calling on all states to work together to bring the perpetrators of the attacks to justice. The North Atlantic Council for the first time invokes Article 5 of NATO's founding treaty, stating that an armed attack against any member state shall be considered as an attack against all.

September 18—Congress passes a resolution giving the President authorization for the use of force "against those nations, organizations, or persons he determines planned, authorized, committed, or aided the terrorist attacks that occurred on September 11, 2001, or harbored such organizations or persons."

September 20—In an address to a joint session of Congress, President Bush says all the evidence suggests al-Qaeda was responsible for the attacks, and warns the Taliban regime that they must "hand over the terrorists, or they will share in their fate." The Department of Justice issues an Interim Rule stating that non-citizens can be detained for 48 hours without charge, or in the event of an "emergency of other extraordinary circumstance" for "an additional reasonable period of time." . . .

October 4—The British government issues a statement saying it is confident that Osama bin Laden and the al-Qaeda network "planned and carried out the atrocities of 11 September," and setting out the evidence for their conclusion.

October 7—US military forces launch 'Operation Enduring Freedom' against Taliban and al-Qaeda facilities in Afghanistan. In a televised address, President Bush says US actions "are designed to disrupt the use of Afghanistan as a terrorist base of operations, and to attack the military capability of the Taliban regime."[†]

Was the U.S. response to the September 11 attacks a legitimate act of self-defense? Why or why not? According to just war theory, was the U.S. invasion of Afghanistan justified? If so, how does the resort to warfare regarding each of the just war conditions? If not, why not? How does the decision to go to war fail any just war requirements?

[†] Anthony Dworkin and Ariel Meyerstein, "A Defining Moment—International Law Since September 11: A Timeline," *Crimes of War Project,* www.crimesofwar.org/sept-mag/printer-timeline.html (accessed 18 February 2006). Used by permission of Crimes of War Project.

---

3. Genocide in Rwanda

Ten years ago, on April 6, 1994, Rwanda's extremist Hutu government and military led a campaign to exterminate the nation's minority Tutsis.

An estimated 800,000 people were killed in three months of tribal bloodletting. Men, women and children were slaughtered in an orchestrated, pre-planned campaign of genocide not seen since the Jewish Holocaust.

For 100 days the rampant killing continued throughout the country. The machete became Rwanda's symbol of horror.

One much-practised strategy was to drive Tutsis into centers such as churches and schools and then kill them en masse. Stories abound of Tutsis being disabled by having a leg chopped off and left on the ground to await the return of their killers. Tutsis pleading to be put out of their misery quickly. Children being slaughtered in front of their parents. Women being gang raped, subjected to unspeakable acts before being killed.

The world claimed it was unaware of the magnitude of the slaughter. The United Nations peacekeeping force stationed in the country stood by helplessly and watched the massacre unfold.

On a visit to the Rwandan capital, Kigali, in 1998 Clinton apologized for not acting quickly enough or immediately calling the crimes genocide. He said: "It may seem strange to you here, especially the many of you who lost members of your family, but all over the world there were people like me sitting in offices, day after day after day, who did not fully appreciate the depth and speed with which you were being engulfed by this unimaginable terror."[‡]

Should the United States or other governments or the United Nations have intervened militarily to prevent or stop the slaughter in Rwanda? If so, what are your grounds for intervention? If not, why not? Would application of just war theory to the situation have justified intervention? If not, what just war conditions would the intervention have violated?

[‡] "Rwanda Ten Years Ago: How the World Stood Back and Watched a Genocide," *Democracy Now!*, 1 April 2004, www.democracynow.org/article.pl?sid=04/04/01/1621233 (accessed 19 February 2006). Reprinted courtesy of Democracy Now!, www.democracynow.org.

Terrorism and Torture

Too many times and in too many places throughout the world this is how the story goes: From out of nowhere, terrorists strike, killing and maiming shoppers in a mall, travelers in a train station, or passersby on a peaceful street. In the bloody aftermath of the attack, stunned survivors react in shock, fear, and rage. The government responds with police investigations, security measures, formal inquiries, antiterrorist laws, and perhaps military force. The media dissect the story and rehash the horror. Pundits and politicians debate the nature of the threat and how best to defeat it. And even long after the jolting day of terror is past, serious examination of the ethical questions provoked by terrorism is never begun—and so the nature of the evil is misunderstood and the moral response to it misses the mark.

Thus terrorism evokes a familiar dilemma: like all life-and-death issues, it calls for ethical scrutiny, careful evaluation of the moral dimension—but thinking straight about terrorism can be difficult when it hits close to home. "Terrorism upsets people," says the terrorism expert Charles Townshend.

It does so deliberately. That is its point, and that is why it has engrossed so much of our attention in the early years of the 21st century. Insecurity can take many forms, but nothing else plays quite so sharply on our sense of vulnerability. After September 11 we found ourselves in an apparently open-ended and permanent state of emergency, a 'war against terror', whose ramifications are as inscrutable as terrorism itself. Terrorism is never easy to understand, and least of all in the aftermath of a terrorist attack. When society feels under threat, attempts at rational analysis are often openly resisted as giving aid and comfort to, or even sympathizing with, the enemy. Yet without such analysis, combating terrorism seems a baffling contest against an indefinite threat. Although terrorism can sometimes look rational, more often it seems to go straight off the chart of 'common sense'—to be not only unjustifiable, but atrocious, mad, or 'mindless'.[1]

Nevertheless, moral philosophers and others demonstrate that doing ethics is possible even when the subject is the grisly phenomenon of twenty-first century terrorism. The questions involved, however, are thornier than they might seem at first glance: What is terrorism? Is terrorism ever justified? Who commits terrorist acts? Can states commit terrorist acts? Is the United States or any other country guilty of terrorism? For example, was the Allied bombing of German cities in World War II (in which hundreds of thousands of civilians died) a case of state terrorism? How should we treat terrorists? How should we respond to terrorist violence? How much, if at all, should we curtail civil liberties to protect ourselves against terrorism? Can we evaluate the morality of terrorism in the same way we assess the morality of war (by using, for example, just war theory)?

But the questions don't end there. In the public mind, and in the places where terrorists and antiterrorists do battle, terrorism is blood brother

[1]Charles Townshend, *Terrorism: A Very Short Introduction* (Oxford: Oxford University Press, 2002), 1–2.

to torture. Terrorists regularly torture their captives; and sometimes terrorists are tortured by their captors, often at the behest of governments that loudly disavow the terrible deeds. Torture is an ancient, dark art used throughout Western history by authorities to extract confessions and gather evidence for crimes. But in this age of resurgent terrorism, torture has become a tempting tool of the state for thwarting the next terrorist attack or breaking the hidden terrorist cell. And so the moral question will not leave us alone: Is torture ever morally permissible?

ISSUE FILE: BACKGROUND

Most people probably think they know what terrorism is, yet it is notoriously difficult to define. One of the main challenges is to differentiate terrorism from acts of war and violent crimes. In the definition adopted by the U.S. Department of State, terrorism is "premeditated, politically motivated violence perpetrated against noncombatant targets by subnational groups or clandestine agents, usually intended to influence an audience."[2] According to a 1974 British government definition, terrorism is "the use of violence for political ends, and includes any use of violence for the purpose of putting the public, or any section of the public, in fear."[3] For our discussion we can use a broad definition that comprises key elements in common usage: **terrorism** is violence against noncombatants for political, religious, or ideological ends.

---

[2]U.S. Department of State, *Patterns of Global Terrorism 2003* (Washington, DC: U.S. Department of State 2004), xii.

[3]*International Encyclopedia of Terrorism,* 1997 ed., s.v. "The Official View"; quoted in *A Military Guide to Terrorism in the Twenty-first Century,* U.S. Army Training and Doctrine Command, 15 August 2005, version 3.0, available at www.fas.org/irp/threat/terrorism/index (4 December 2006), 1–3.

Some may think terrorism is a recent phenomenon, but its history is long and bloody. The term *terrorism* sprang from the French Revolution's Reign of Terror, in which the new state sanctioned the use of terror against its enemies, real or imagined, executing thousands of mostly ordinary citizens. In the nineteenth century, anarchists aimed to inspire the masses to revolution with terrifying deeds against established regimes. They achieved worldwide attention and spread public alarm—but no revolution—by assassinating several state leaders, including President William McKinley in the United States and Tsar Alexander II in Russia.

The twentieth century had a shockingly large share of terrorism, in both old and new forms driven by familiar and unfamiliar motives. Terrorism in the first half of the century was mostly nationalist (as were terrorist groups in Ireland, Palestine, Algeria, and the Balkans), state-sponsored (by, for example, the Serbian and Bulgarian governments), and state-administered (as in Nazi Germany, Stalinist Russia, and several South American dictatorships). Its preferred form was assassination and mass killing. The second half witnessed more state-sponsored terrorism and the predominance of terrorism that was ideological or religious. Whatever its label, terrorism in this period was distinguished by its heavy reliance on the horrors of airline hijackings, kidnappings, and suicide bombings. According to the Center for Defense Information,

Through the 1960s and 1970s, the numbers of those groups that might be described as terrorist swelled to include not only nationalists, but those motivated by ethnic and ideological considerations. The former included groups such as the Palestinian Liberation Organization (and its many affiliates), the Basque ETA, and the Provisional Irish Republican Army, while the latter comprised organizations such as the Red Army Action (in what was then West Germany) and the Italian Red Brigades. As with the emergence of modern terrorism almost a century earlier, the

United States was not immune from this latest wave, although there the identity-crisis-driven motivations of the white middle-class Weathermen starkly contrasted with the ghetto-bred malcontent of the Black Panther movement.

Like their anti-colonialist predecessors of the immediate post-war era, many of the terrorist groups of this period readily appreciated and adopted methods that would allow them to publicize their goals and accomplishments internationally. Forerunners in this were the Palestinian groups who pioneered the hijacking of a chief symbol and means of the new age globalization—the jet airliner—as a mode of operation and publicity. One such group, Black September, staged what was (until the attacks on America of Sept. 11, 2001) perhaps the greatest terrorist publicity coup then seen, with the seizure and murder of 11 Israeli athletes at the 1972 Olympic Games.[4]

Since around the mid-1990s, the threat of religiously inspired terrorism has expanded dramatically. In 1998, there were 37 incidents of religious terrorism worldwide resulting in 758 deaths. In 2001, there were 99 incidents and 3,275 deaths, most of which occurred in the September 11 attacks on the United States. In 2005, religious terrorists killed 2,061 people throughout the world in 606 incidents.[5] The Council on Foreign Affairs reports that

Religious terrorists seek to use violence to further what they see as divinely commanded purposes, often targeting broad categories of foes in an attempt to bring about sweeping changes. Religious terrorists

come from many faiths, as well as from small cults. . . . Because religious terrorists are concerned not with rallying a constituency of fellow nationalists or ideologues but with pursuing their own vision of divine will, they lack one of the major constraints that historically has limited the scope of terror attacks, experts say. As [the terrorism expert Bruce] Hoffman puts it, the most extreme religious terrorists can sanction "almost limitless violence against a virtually open-ended category of targets: that is, anyone who is not a member of the terrorists' religion or religious sect."[6]

Among the more notorious terrorist incidents of the past thirty years are the following, as described by the U.S. Department of State:

"Bloody Friday," July 21, 1972: An Irish Republican Army (IRA) bomb attack killed eleven people and [injured] 130 in Belfast, Northern Ireland. Ten days later, three IRA car bomb attacks in the village of Claudy left six dead.

Munich Olympic Massacre, September 5, 1972: Eight Palestinian "Black September" terrorists seized eleven Israeli athletes in the Olympic Village in Munich, West Germany. In a bungled rescue attempt by West German authorities, nine of the hostages and five terrorists were killed.

Iran Hostage Crisis, November 4, 1979: After President Carter agreed to admit the Shah of Iran into the US, Iranian radicals seized the U.S. Embassy in Tehran and took 66 American diplomats hostage. Thirteen hostages were soon released, but the remaining 53 were held until their release on January 20, 1981.

Grand Mosque Seizure, November 20, 1979: 200 Islamic terrorists seized the Grand Mosque in Mecca, Saudi Arabia, taking hundreds of pilgrims hostage. Saudi and French security forces retook the shrine after an intense battle in which some 250 people were killed and 600 wounded.

---

[4]Mark Burgess, "A Brief History of Terrorism," *Center for Defense Information,* 2 July 2003, www.cdi.org/program/index.cfm?programid=39 (27 January 2006).

[5]National Memorial Institute for the Prevention of Terrorism (MIPT), *Terrorism Knowledge Base,* www.tkb.org/Home.jsp (27 January 2006).

[6]Council on Foreign Relations, "Types of Terrorism," *Council on Foreign Affairs,* http://cfrterrorism.org/terrorism/types.html (27 January 2006).

Achille Lauro *Hijacking, October 7, 1985:* Four Palestinian Liberation Front terrorists seized the Italian cruise liner in the eastern Mediterranean Sea, taking more than 700 hostages. One U.S. passenger was murdered before the Egyptian government offered the terrorists safe haven in return for the hostages' freedom.

Pan Am 103 Bombing, December 21, 1988: Pan American Airlines Flight 103 was blown up over Lockerbie, Scotland, by a bomb believed to have been placed on the aircraft by Libyan terrorists in Frankfurt, West Germany. All 259 people on board were killed.

World Trade Center Bombing, February 26, 1993: The World Trade Center in New York City was badly damaged when a car bomb planted by Islamic terrorists exploded in an underground garage. The bomb left 6 people dead and 1,000 injured. The men carrying out the attack were followers of Umar Abd al-Rahman, an Egyptian cleric who preached in the New York City area.

Tokyo Subway Station Attack, March 20, 1995: Twelve persons were killed and 5,700 were injured in a Sarin nerve gas attack on a crowded subway station in the center of Tokyo, Japan. A similar attack occurred nearly simultaneously in the Yokohama subway system. The Aum Shinri-kyo cult was blamed for the attacks.

Bombing of the Federal Building in Oklahoma City, April 19, 1995: Right-wing extremists Timothy McVeigh and Terry Nichols destroyed the Federal Building in Oklahoma City with a massive truck bomb that killed 166 and injured hundreds more in what was up to then the largest terrorist attack on American soil.

Terrorist Attacks on U.S. Homeland, September 11, 2001: Two hijacked airliners crashed into the twin towers of the World Trade Center. Soon thereafter, the Pentagon was struck by a third hijacked plane. A fourth hijacked plane, sus-pected to be bound for a high-profile target in Washington, crashed into a field in southern Pennsylvania. The attacks killed 3,025 U.S. citizens and other nationals. President Bush and Cabinet officials indicated that Usama Bin Laden was the prime suspect and that they considered the United States in a state of war with international terrorism. In the aftermath of the attacks, the United States formed the Global Coalition Against Terrorism.

Car Bomb Explosion in Bali, October 12, 2002: A car bomb exploded outside the Sari Club Discotheque in Denpasar, Bali, Indonesia, killing 202 persons and wounding 300 more. Most of the casualties, including 88 of the dead, were Australian tourists. Seven Americans were among the dead. Al-Qaida claimed responsibility. Two suspects were later arrested and convicted. Iman Samudra, who had trained in Afghanistan with al-Qaeda and was suspected of belonging to Jemaah Islamiya, was sentenced to death on September 10, 2003.[7]

To this list we could add many more incidents, and probably most infamous among them would be the March 11, 2004, attacks in Madrid and the July 7, 2005, bombings in London. In Madrid a coordinated series of bombs exploded on four commuter trains, killing 191 people and injuring more than 1,500. Investigators blamed Islamic militants connected to cells in Europe. In London, almost simultaneously four jihadists set off bombs on a double-decker bus and three subway trains, killing themselves and fifty-two other people and injuring hundreds.

The question that all terrorism provokes is, What should be our moral response to it? Many argue that a violent response is the wrong response, that a "war

---

[7]U.S. Department of State, Office of the Historian, Bureau of Public Affairs, "Significant Terrorist Incidents, 1961–2003: A Brief Chronology," March 2004, www.state.gov/r/pa/ho/pubs/fs/5902.htm (27 January 2006).

on terror" is misguided and morally impermissible. The proper response, they say, is dialogue with aggressors, a criminal justice approach instead of military force, and the eradication of the true causes of terrorism—poverty, oppression, suffering, and injustice. As one observer has said,

In my view, the most effective counterterrorism approach would arise from a foreign policy that took the sufferings of people in other countries seriously. A progressive orientation would stand in contrast to today's official counterterrorism, which views suffering as irrelevant, or even as a reason to inflate the terrorist danger.[8]

In the same vein, Pope John Paul II preached against a military response to terrorism. "Violence begets violence," he declared. "War must always be considered a defeat: a defeat of reason and of humanity." He urged world leaders "to persevere in dialogue" and asserted that everything possible must be done to uproot the causes of terror, "especially misery, desperation and the emptiness in hearts."[9]

The opposing view is that violence may in fact be a morally justified reaction to terrorism—that is, morally justified by the lights of just war theory. As noted in the previous chapter, just war theory is the timeworn doctrine that war may be morally permissible if particular requirements are met. It lays out the conditions under which resorting to war would be morally justified (known as the *jus ad bellum* requirements) and specifies the criteria for judging the morality of how it is fought (the so-called *jus in bello* requirements). According to the theory, resorting to war is justified only if (1) its cause is just (usually meaning that the war must be in self-defense), (2) it is sanctioned by proper authority, (3) it is fought with the right intentions, (4) it is fought only as a last resort, (5) the good that comes from the conflict equals or outweighs the evil that arises from it, and (6) there is a reasonable chance of success. Traditionally, the requirements pertaining to the actual conduct of the war have included *discrimination* (noncombatants must be distinguished from combatants and never deliberately targeted), *proportionality* (the use of force should be proportional to the aims of the combat), and *no evil means* (no weapons or tactics that are "evil in themselves," such as chemical weapons or genocide, should ever be used). Some contend that all these criteria can sometimes be met, justifying a carefully measured military response to terrorist attacks. Thus one observer argues that

according to just war theory, defending against this sort of terrorism is a just cause; that within significant constraints sovereign political authorities can have authority to undertake military actions for the sake of this just cause, notwithstanding the nature of organization of the terrorists; and that a political community can pursue such a cause with right intention, even though in the world as it is military efforts to defend against terrorism may well not meet this condition.[10]

Others maintain that government antiterrorism activities and policies (what has been called the "war on terror") have gone too far by undermining civil liberties in the name of security. A prime concern is that some overreaching antiterrorism laws meant to be temporary can easily become permanent. Critics have also charged that repressive governments have used the war on terror as an excuse to violate the human rights and

---

[8]Richard Falk, "Thinking about Terrorism," *The Nation*, 28 June 1986, note that this view was expressed long before the events of September 11, 2001.

[9]"Pope Opposes Military Response to Terrorism," *Catholic World News*, 8 September 2004, www.CWNews.com/news/viewstory.cfm?recnum=32004 (4 December 2006).

[10]Joseph M. Boyle Jr., "Just War Doctrine and the Military Response to Terrorism," *Journal of Political Philosophy* 11, no. 2 (2003): 153–70.

civil liberties of innocent people deemed undesirable by the state.

A more fundamental—and controversial—moral issue is whether terrorist actions can ever be morally justified. Many argue on various grounds that terrorism is never morally permissible, regardless of the merits of the terrorists' cause. The philosopher Haig Khatchadourian, for example, contends that acts of terrorism are always wrong because (1) they violate basic principles of just war theory and, (2) except in rare cases where other overriding moral principles apply, they violate their victims' right to be treated as moral persons. Regarding reason (1), Khatchadourian claims that terrorism in all forms violates the just war principles of discrimination and proportionality. Concerning reason (2), he says that

Treating people as moral persons means treating them with consideration in two closely related ways. First, it means respecting their autonomy as individuals with their own desires and interests, plans and projects, commitments and goals. That autonomy is clearly violated if they are humiliated, coerced and terrorized, taken hostage or kidnapped, and above all, killed. Second, consideration . . . includes sensitivity to and consideration of their feelings and desires, aspirations, projects, and goals. That in turn is an integral part of treating their life as a whole—including their relationships and memories—as a thing of value. Finally, it includes respecting their "culture or ethnic, religious or racial identity or heritage." These things are the very antithesis of what terrorism does to its victims and the victimized.[11]

Similarly, the just war theorist Michael Walzer asserts that terrorism is wrong because it is an indiscriminate attack on the innocent. He thinks that a terrorist attack is worse than rape or murder because these crimes are at least directed at specific persons for particular reasons, even if

those reasons are perverse. But terrorist violence is aimed at no one in particular for no purpose that could be linked to a specific person. For the terrorist, any innocent person who happens to fit into a broad category is as good a target as any other. "Terrorists are like killers on a rampage," says Walzer, "except that their rampage is not just expressive of rage or madness; the rage is purposeful and programmatic. It aims at a general vulnerability: Kill these people in order to terrify those."[12]

Not everyone agrees, however. A few thinkers, while deploring terrorist violence, argue that in some cases terrorism may be morally permissible. In fact, some maintain that particular instances of terrorism can even meet the requirements of just war theory and therefore be justified in the same way that acts of war are justified. For example, one proponent of this view argues that when a stateless group has its right of self-determination thwarted, it may have a just cause—and an organization representing the group can be "a morally legitimate authority to carry out violence as a last resort to defend the group's rights."[13]

Disputes about the moral permissibility of terrorist actions can quickly bring us back to arguments about a plausible definition of terrorism. Suppose, for instance, that the preferred definition of terrorism is a variation on the one proposed at the beginning of this chapter: deliberate use of violence against noncombatants for political or ideological purposes. Interpreted broadly, this definition would apply to many acts that seem to be unambiguous examples of terrorism—the September 11 attacks, the Munich Olympic massacre, the Bali car bombing of October 2002, and many oth-

---

[11]Haig Khatchadourian, *The Morality of Terrorism* (New York: Peter Lang, 1998), 31–32.

[12]Michael Walzer, "Terrorism: A Critique of Excuses," in *Problems of International Justice,* ed. Steven Luper-Foy (Boulder, CO: Westview Press, 1988), 238.

[13]Andrew Valls, "Can Terrorism Be Justified?" in *Ethics in International Affairs: Theories and Cases,* ed. Valls (Lanham, MD: Rowman and Littlefield, 2000), 65–79.

CRITICAL THOUGHT: Terrorists or Freedom Fighters?

On January 5, 2006, BBC News reported on two of the many suicide bombings that have occurred throughout Iraq. One bomb was detonated in Karbala near an important Shia shrine. It killed 60 people and injured more than 100. The other bomb exploded at a Ramadi police recruiting center, killing another 60. At the time, talks were going on among Shia, Sunni, and Kurdish groups to form a coalition government. Iraqi President Jalal Talabini appeared to think that the bombings were meant to cause tension between religious groups and wreck the political process. "These groups of dark terror," he said, "will not succeed through these cowardly acts in dissuading Iraqis in their bid to form a government of national unity."*

Assume that the attacks were terrorist acts carried out by Iraqis intent on ridding Iraq of its Western occupiers and their influence on the government of Iraq (an assumption that may or may not be correct). In that case, was the terrorism morally justified? Why or why not? Should the attackers be called "freedom fighters" instead of terrorists? Could the terrorist acts meet all the conditions of just war theory?

*"Iraq Suicide Bomb Blasts Kill 120," *BBC News Online,* 5 January 2006, http://news.bbc.co.uk/2/hi/middle_east/4583232.stm (5 February 2006).

---

ers. But what about the following cases in which noncombatants were also deliberately killed for political reasons: the Allied bombings of Dresden and other German cities in World War II and the atomic obliteration of Hiroshima and Nagasaki? According to our revised definition, aren't these also terrorist acts? And if so, could not the United States and Britain be classified as terrorist states?

Some are willing to accept such implications of our definition (or similar ones). They think that deliberately targeting noncombatants for political or ideological purposes is never morally acceptable—no matter who does the targeting. So for them, the World War II city bombings were indeed instances of terrorism, and the states doing the bombing were acting as terrorists. Others avoid these repugnant implications by working from a definition that confines terrorism to **nonstate actors**—that is, to individuals or groups that are not sovereign states. (Recall the definition of terrorism offered by the U.S. Department of State—"premeditated, politically motivated violence

perpetrated against noncombatant targets by subnational groups or clandestine agents[.]") Terrorism then would be the killing of innocents by al Qaeda or the Red Brigades, but not by a sovereign polity like the United States. Walzer, however, takes the line that terrorism is never morally justified but that some of the city bombings in World War II *were* justified (and therefore were not terrorism) because they were done in a "supreme emergency"—circumstances in which civilization itself is threatened with eminent destruction.

Struggling with the issue of terrorism will sooner or later lead us to the matter of torture, for these two evils often travel together. The vexing question is whether torture is ever morally justified—specifically, whether it is permissible to use it to prevent terrorist carnage.

Torture is the intentional inflicting of severe pain or suffering on people to punish or intimidate them or to extract information from them. It has been used by both secular and religious authorities for centuries and continues to this day to be applied to hapless victims throughout the world. This, despite worldwide condemnation of the practice and its absolute prohibition in international law, including by United Nations treaties and the Geneva Conventions.

For generations the United States officially opposed torture and prosecuted both American soldiers and the nation's enemies for using harsh methods against captives. But recently the administration of George W. Bush was accused of authorizing and employing interrogation tactics that had long been regarded as torture. The subjects were suspected terrorists, and the purpose of the severe approach was to wrest from them some information that might help authorities crush terrorist groups or prevent future terrorist attacks. Recent reports show that "waterboarding" (simulated drowning) and other extreme techniques have been used against detainees in U.S.-run facilities overseas.

Three questions dominate the debates over the morality of torture: (1) Does torture work? (2) Is torture ever morally acceptable? (3) What should be the state's policy regarding the use of torture?

As usually understood, question 1 is about whether torture is effective in getting reliable information from suspects. Science has yet to definitively answer the question, and the views of expert interrogators conflict. Many intelligence officers claim that torture rarely, if ever, yields useful information; other experts assert that torture occasionally produces valuable data. Some people in both camps worry about the indirect effect of using harsh methods—the damage to American prestige and influence, the increased likelihood of our enemies using torture against us, and the slide down the slippery slope toward the wider use of more brutal means.

For many nonconsequentialists, the answer to question 2 is an absolutist no—torture is the use of a person merely as a means, a clear instance of a lack of respect for a human being. Torture is therefore always wrong. But most people are probably not absolutists; they think that in rare cases there could be exceptions to a no-torture rule. Such a case has come to be known as a "ticking bomb" scenario. Suppose a bomb will soon detonate in a major American city, killing a hundred thousand innocent people. The only way to prevent this massive loss of life is to torture the terrorist who planted the bomb until he reveals its location. Would it be morally permissible to waterboard or electrocute him until he talks? Many think that the obvious answer is yes. Others believe the scenario is too contrived to be taken seriously; ticking-bomb situations don't happen in the real world.

Question 3 is a separate issue entirely. Whether or not we believe that torture would be morally justified in a particular instance, we might take a very different view about legalizing or institutionalizing it. On this matter, there are three main positions: (1) torture should be illegal and never sanctioned in any circumstances; (2) torture should be illegal and officially condemned but unofficially (and secretly) used when necessary; and (3) torture should be a legal instrument of the state, although administered under strict guidelines and oversight.

Those taking the first approach insist that legalizing torture would have devastating consequences. It would corrupt democratic institutions, diminish our moral authority in the world, cause torture to become routine and widespread in society, and arouse worldwide resentment and anger toward us.

Those who prefer the second approach believe that torture may sometimes be necessary (as in ticking-bomb cases) but that acknowledging its use could cause many of the problems that worry those in the first group. Their critics accuse them of hypocrisy, but they see no good alternative to this clandestine, "under the radar" strategy.

The third approach is preferred by many who deplore the hypocrisy of the second group but are convinced that the use of torture is inevitable (a ticking-bomb scenario could actually happen). They hold that if torture is legalized, its use can be better controlled than in any unofficial arrangement, and its abuses and proliferation can be limited. Alan Dershowitz advocates this third way, recommending a system in which official interrogators may use torture only after they acquire permission—"torture warrants"—from a judge.

MORAL THEORIES

How would traditional moral theories have us view the moral justification of terrorism? It seems that act-utilitarianism, arguably the most widely held consequentialist theory, would have to sanction at least some terrorist attacks. The act-utilitarian must admit that it is possible for a terrorist action to yield the best overall results in a situation—and "best overall results" is the overriding factor here. But a utilitarian could not consistently condone terrorist actions that served only the interests of a particular group, for the theory demands that right actions produce the greatest

overall happiness, *everyone considered*. Many (or perhaps most) acts of terrorism are clearly meant to exclusively favor a specific segment of a population; everyone is deliberately *not* considered.

Some writers contend that even though consequentialist moral theories can justify terrorism, the theories can do so "only under conditions that terrorists in the flesh will find it difficult to satisfy." Consider what consequentialism would demand of the terrorist:

First, consequentialist moral theory will focus upon effectiveness and efficiency, upon whether terrorist acts are an effective, efficient means to achieving desirable goals. The question naturally arises, then, whether there is an alternative means available with equal or better likelihood of success in achieving the goal at a reduced cost. If resort to terrorism is a tactic, is there another tactic just as likely to achieve the goal at a cost more easy for us to bear? It is here, of course, that alternatives such as passive resistance and nonviolent civil disobedience will arise and need to be considered. It is here also that account must be taken of the obvious fact that terrorist acts seem often to harden the resistance of those the terrorists oppose. . . . Second, consequentialist moral theory will focus upon the goal to be achieved: Is the goal that a specific use of terrorism is in aid of desirable enough for us to want to see it realized in society at the terrible costs it exacts? . . . And it is here, of course, that doubts plague us, because we are often unsure where justice with respect to some issue falls. . . . Finally, consequentialist moral theory will stress how unsure we sometimes are about what counts as doing justice. On the one hand, we sometimes are genuinely unsure about what counts as rectifying an injustice. . . . On the other hand, we sometimes are genuinely unsure whether we can rectify or eliminate one injustice without perpetrating another.[14]

---

[14]R. G. Frey and Christopher W. Morris, "Terrorism," in *Violence, Terrorism, and Justice,* ed. Frey and Morris (Cambridge: Cambridge University Press, 1991), 1–11.

CHAPTER 17: TERRORISM AND TORTURE ☀ 689

Terrorists themselves sometimes justify their actions on consequentialist grounds: They assert that only terrorism can help them achieve their objectives. But many observers are skeptical of terrorism's power to attain *any* political ends, especially the goal of liberation from an oppressive regime. Walzer observes, "I doubt that terrorism has ever achieved national liberation—no nation that I know of owes its freedom to a campaign of random murder."[15] Certainly terrorism can frighten the public and increase the terrorists' notoriety, but winning a political struggle is a much rougher road. If terrorism is indeed an ineffective strategy, then this fact could form the backbone of a consequentialist argument *against* terrorist acts.

Nonconsequentialist moral theories (or nonconsequentialist moral principles) often yield condemnations of terrorism in all forms. A traditional natural law theorist would insist that terrorism is always wrong because it violates the prohibition against intentionally killing the innocent. Natural law's doctrine of double effect—which disallows intentional bad actions even if they achieve good results—would lead to this conclusion (assuming the definition of terrorism given earlier). Some people, of course, could try to counter this view by rejecting the doctrine of double effect or by questioning the concept of moral innocence. A Kantian theorist or other nonconsequentialist could argue that terrorism is not morally permissible because it violates innocent persons' human rights, their right to life, or their autonomy or because terrorism uses people merely as a means to an end.

Many philosophers view terrorism from the perspective of just war theory, which contains both consequentialist and nonconsequentialist requirements. Some of them argue that terrorism is wrong because it violates key conditions of just war theory—in particular, discrimination, propor-

tionality (both *jus ad bellum* and *jus in bello*), last resort, and just cause. As we saw earlier, some reject this claim and maintain that just war theory, rightly interpreted, shows that in some instances terrorism may be justified because it meets all the conditions.

MORAL ARGUMENTS

Probably the liveliest—and, to some, the most disturbing—moral disputes about terrorism have to do with the moral permissibility of terrorist acts. Consider the tragic events of September 11, 2001. Many people the world over assume without question that those who caused that horrific loss of life committed acts of terrorism that were morally wrong and monstrously evil. And many careful thinkers have come to the same conclusions, albeit by a more reflective, reasoned route. Plenty of people in both groups believe that terrorism is always morally wrong. But some equally reflective observers who are just as horrified by September 11 argue that terrorism may sometimes be permissible (and that many who disagree are being inconsistent, perhaps even hypocritical). We may even hear arguments for the permissibility of terrorism from people sympathetic to certain terrorist causes. Let us look closer at some of these disputes. First, consider this argument:

1. If the killing of innocents is sometimes morally permissible in war, then it is morally permissible in terrorism (defined here as the intentional killing of innocents for political purposes).
2. The killing of innocents is sometimes morally permissible in war.
3. Therefore, the killing of innocents is sometimes morally permissible in terrorism.

This conclusion asserts that we cannot condemn all acts of terrorism out of hand, for some may be morally justified. The argument is that, as

[15]Walzer, "Terrorism," 240.

most people believe, killing innocents in wartime is sometimes permissible. Noncombatants are usually killed and maimed in war because combat so often happens near or among them. Still, most people are willing to accept this "collateral damage" as the inevitable—but regrettable—consequence of waging war. Some "civilian" deaths are unavoidable but morally permissible. Yet if they are morally acceptable in war, they must be morally acceptable aspects of terrorism. After all, both kinds of violence involve the death of innocents during hostilities directed at political ends.

Many critics of this argument would accept Premise 2 but reject Premise 1, insisting that there is a morally significant difference between the killing of innocents in war and in terrorist attacks. They would say that the killing of noncombatants in war is morally permissible because it is unintended; noncombatant deaths happen inadvertently as combatants are targeted. Terrorist killings, however, are wrong because they are intentional. The deliberate slaughter of innocents is never morally acceptable. Obviously, this response is an appeal to the doctrine of double effect.

But some would not accept this appeal, reasoning along the following lines:

While the principle of double effect is plausible in some cases, it is severely defective. To see this, suppose that the September 11 attackers had only intended to destroy the Pentagon and the World Trade Center and had no desire to kill anyone. Suppose that they knew, however, that thousands would die in the attack on the buildings. And suppose, following the attack, they said "We are not murderers. We did not mean to kill these people."

What would be our reaction? I very much doubt that we would think them less culpable. They could not successfully justify or excuse their actions by saying that although they foresaw the deaths of many people, these deaths were not part of their aim. We

would certainly reject this defense. But if we would reject the appeal to double effect in this case, then we should do so in others.[16]

Not everyone would agree with this reasoning, but let us move on to a related argument:

1. Deliberately killing innocents for political or ideological reasons is morally wrong.

2. Deliberately killing noninnocents for such reasons may be morally permissible (as in war or revolution, for example).

3. Some people commonly thought to be innocents are actually noninnocents (they are pseudo innocents).

4. Therefore, deliberately killing pseudo innocents for political or ideological reasons may in some cases be morally permissible.

This argument states formally what is often alleged more casually: some actions usually condemned as instances of terrorism (involving the deliberate killing of innocents) are *not* terrorist acts at all because the "innocents" are not really innocent. This claim (common in some cultures and often uttered by terrorists themselves) is that some people should be judged noninnocents if they, for example, indirectly aid or sympathize with a hated regime, or happen to belong to the same race or religion as those presumed guilty of committing some acts of injustice or oppression, or are simply part of a system or enterprise that adversely affects a favored group. Such an attitude is held by many, most infamously by Osama bin Laden:

The ruling to kill the Americans and their allies—civilian and military—is an individual duty for every Muslim who can do it in any country in which it is possible to do, in order to liberate the Al Aksa Mosque

---

[16]Stephen Nathanson, "Can Terrorism Be Morally Justified?" in *Morality in Practice,* ed. James P. Sterba, 7th ed. (Belmont, CA: Wadsworth/Thomas, 2004), 607.

and the holy mosque from their grip, and in order for their families to move out of all the lands of Islam, defeated and unable to threaten any Muslim.[17]

The precise distinction between innocents and noninnocents (or combatants and noncombatants) in war is controversial among philosophers. But most of these thinkers do acknowledge a clear difference between the two concepts, and many reject the sort of blurring of the distinctions common among those who wish to justify terrorism. A typical argument against such justifications is that if the distinctions are discarded, then anyone and everyone could be deemed guilty and therefore a legitimate target of terrorism. For example, if ordinary individuals who buy bananas and thereby contribute to an economy run by a bloodthirsty dictatorship somehow share the blame for the regime's crimes, then any man, woman, or child could share the guilt—and deserve the terrorist's justice. Attributing guilt to people because of such remote connections to wrongdoing, critics say, seems to reduce the notions of guilt and innocence to absurdity.

[17]From Jeffrey Goldberg, "Inside Jihad U.; The Education of a Holy Warrior," *New York Times Magazine,* 25 June 2000; quoted in Louis P. Pojman, "The Moral Response to Terrorism and the Cosmopolitan Imperative," in *Terrorism and International Justice,* ed. James P. Sterba (New York: Oxford University Press, 2003).

SUMMARY

Terrorism is difficult to define, but for simplicity's sake we can say that it is violence against noncombatants for political, religious, or ideological ends. Terrorism has been with us for centuries, taking various forms—revolutionary, nationalist, state-sponsored, state-run, and religious.

The key question that terrorism provokes is, What should be our moral response to it? Should it always and everywhere be condemned? Or is terrorism sometimes justified? One way to grapple with terrorism is to try to apply the requirements of just war theory to terrorist acts. Many philosophers argue that by the lights of just war theory, terrorism is never morally permissible. Others contend that it is possible for terrorism to meet just war criteria and thereby prove itself justified. Even without reference to just war theory, some argue that terrorism is always wrong because it violates the victims' right to be treated as moral persons, or because it is an indiscriminate attack on the innocent.

A consequentialist moral theory would likely condone terrorism if it maximized happiness or welfare for all concerned, but in actual cases this requirement may make terrorism very difficult to justify. A traditional natural law theory would insist that terrorism is always wrong because it violates the prohibition against intentionally killing the innocent. A Kantian theorist could argue that terrorism is never permissible because it treats persons as mere means to an end.

READINGS

Terrorism: A Critique of Excuses

Michael Walzer

No one these days advocates terrorism, not even those who regularly practice it. The practice is indefensible now that it has been recognized, like rape and murder, as an attack upon the innocent. In a sense, indeed, terrorism is worse than rape and murder commonly are, for in the latter cases the victim has been chosen for a purpose; he or she is the direct object of attack, and the attack has some reason, however twisted or ugly it may be. The victims of a terrorist attack are third parties, innocent bystanders; there is no special reason for attacking them; anyone else within a large class of (unrelated) people will do as well. The attack is directed indiscriminately against the entire class. Terrorists are like killers on a rampage, except that their rampage is not just expressive of rage or madness; the rage is purposeful and programmatic. It aims at a general vulnerability: Kill these people in order to terrify those. A relatively small number of dead victims makes for a very large number of living and frightened hostages.

This, then, is the peculiar evil of terrorism—not only the killing of innocent people but also the intrusion of fear into everyday life, the violation of private purposes, the insecurity of public spaces, the endless coerciveness of precaution. A crime wave might, I suppose, produce similar effects, but no one plans a crime wave; it is the work of a thousand individual decisionmakers, each one independent of the others, brought together only by the invisible hand. Terrorism is the work of visible hands; it is an organizational project, a strategic choice, a conspiracy to murder and intimidate . . . you and me. No wonder

the conspirators have difficulty defending, in public, the strategy they have chosen.

The moral difficulty is the same, obviously, when the conspiracy is directed not against you and me but against *them*—Protestants, say, not Catholics; Israelis, not Italians or Germans; blacks, not whites. These "limits" rarely hold for long; the logic of terrorism steadily expands the range of vulnerability. The more hostages they hold, the stronger the terrorists are. No one is safe once whole populations have been put at risk. Even if the risk were contained, however, the evil would be no different. So far as individual Protestants or Israelis or blacks are concerned, terrorism is random, degrading, and frightening. That is its hallmark, and that, again, is why it cannot be defended.

But when moral justification is ruled out, the way is opened for ideological excuse and apology. We live today in a political culture of excuses. This is far better than a political culture in which terrorism is openly defended and justified, for the excuse at least acknowledges the evil. But the improvement is precarious, hard won, and difficult to sustain. It is not the case, even in this better world, that terrorist organizations are without supporters. The support is indirect but by no means ineffective. It takes the form of apologetic descriptions and explanations, a litany of excuses that steadily undercuts our knowledge of the evil. Today that knowledge is insufficient unless it is supplemented and reinforced by a systemic critique of excuses. That is my purpose in this chapter. I take the principle for granted: that every act of terrorism is a wrongful act. The wrongfulness of the excuses, however, cannot be taken for granted; it has to be argued. The excuses themselves are familiar enough, the stuff of contemporary political debate. I shall state them in stereotypical form. There is no need to attribute them to this or that writer, publicist, or commentator; my readers can make their own attributions.

Michael Walzer, "Terrorism: A Critique of Excuses," in *Problems of International Justice*, ed. Steven Luper-Foy (Boulder, CO: Westview Press, 1988), 237–47 (edited). Reprinted with permission of Steven Luper.

THE EXCUSES FOR TERRORISM

The most common excuse for terrorism is that it is a last resort, chosen only when all else fails. The image is of people who have literally run out of options. One by one, they have tried every legitimate form of political and military action, exhausted every possibility, failed everywhere, until no alternative remains but the evil of terrorism. They must be terrorists or do nothing at all. The easy response is to insist that, given this description of their case, they should do nothing at all; they have indeed exhausted their possibilities. But this response simply reaffirms the principle, ignores the excuse; this response does not attend to the terrorists' desperation. Whatever the cause to which they are committed, we have to recognize that, given the commitment, the one thing they cannot do is "nothing at all."

But the case is badly described. It is not so easy to reach the "last resort." To get there, one must indeed try everything (which is a lot of things) and not just once, as if a political party might organize a single demonstration, fail to win immediate victory, and claim that it was now justified in moving on to murder. Politics is an art of repetition. Activists and citizens learn from experience, that is, by doing the same thing over and over again. It is by no means clear when they run out of options, but even under conditions of oppression and war, citizens have a good run short of that. The same argument applies to state officials who claim that they have tried "everything" and are now compelled to kill hostages or bomb peasant villages. Imagine such people called before a judicial tribunal and required to answer the question, What exactly did you try? Does anyone believe that they could come up with a plausible list? "Last resort" has only a notional finality; the resort to terror is ideologically last, not last in an actual series of actions, just last for the sake of the excuse. In fact, most state officials and movement militants who recommend a policy of terrorism recommend it as a first resort; they are for it from the beginning, although they may not get their way at the beginning. If they are honest, then, they must make other excuses and give up the pretense of the last resort.

The second excuse is designed for national liberation movements struggling against established and powerful states. Now the claim is that nothing else is possible, that no other strategy is available except terrorism. This is different from the first excuse because it does not require would-be terrorists to run through all the available options. Or, the second excuse requires terrorists to run through all the options in their heads, not in the world; notional finality is enough. Movement strategists consider their options and conclude that they have no alternative to terrorism. They think that they do not have the political strength to try anything else, and thus they do not try anything else. Weakness is their excuse.

But two very different kinds of weakness are commonly confused here: the weakness of the movement vis-à-vis the opposing state and the movement's weakness vis-à-vis its own people. This second kind of weakness, the inability of the movement to mobilize the nation, makes terrorism the "only" option because it effectively rules out all the others: nonviolent resistance, general strikes, mass demonstrations, unconventional warfare, and so on.

These options are only rarely ruled out by the sheer power of the state, by the pervasiveness and intensity of oppression. Totalitarian states may be immune to nonviolent or guerrilla resistance, but all the evidence suggests that they are also immune to terrorism. Or, more exactly, in totalitarian states state terror dominates every other sort. Where terrorism is a possible strategy for the oppositional movement (in liberal and democratic states, most obviously), other strategies are also possible if the movement has some significant degree of popular support. In the absence of popular support, terrorism may indeed be the one available strategy, but it is hard to see how its evils can then be excused. For it is not weakness alone that makes the excuse, but the claim of the terrorists to represent the weak; and the particular form of weakness that makes terrorism the only option calls that claim into question.

One might avoid this difficulty with a stronger insistence on the actual effectiveness of terrorism. The third excuse is simply that terrorism works (and nothing else does); it achieves the ends of the oppressed even without their participation. "When the act accuses, the result excuses."[1] This is a consequentialist argument, and given a strict understanding of consequentialism, this argument amounts to a justification rather than an excuse. In practice, however, the argument is rarely pushed so far. More often, the argument begins with an acknowledgment of the terrorists' wrongdoing. Their hands are dirty, but we must make a kind of peace with them because they have acted effectively for the sake of people who could not act for themselves. But, in fact, have the terrorists' actions been effective? I doubt that terrorism has ever achieved national liberation—no nation that I know of owes its freedom to a campaign of random murder—although terrorism undoubtedly increases the power of the terrorists within the national liberation movement. Perhaps terrorism is also conducive to the survival and notoriety (the two go together) of the movement, which is now dominated by terrorists. But even if we were to grant some means-end relationship between terror and national liberation, the third excuse does not work unless it can meet the further requirements of a consequentialist argument. It must be possible to say that the desired end could not have been achieved through any other, less wrongful, means. The third excuse depends, then, on the success of the first or second, and neither of these look likely to be successful.

The fourth excuse avoids this crippling dependency. This excuse does not require the apologist to defend either of the improbable claims that terrorism is the last resort or that it is the only possible resort. The fourth excuse is simply that terrorism is the universal resort. All politics is (really) terrorism. The appearance of innocence and decency is always a piece of deception, more or less convincing in accordance with the relative power of the deceivers. The terrorist who does not bother with appearances is only doing openly what everyone else does secretly.

This argument has the same form as the maxim "All's fair in love and war." Love is always fraudulent, war is always brutal, and political action is always terrorist in character. Political action works (as Thomas Hobbes long ago argued) only by generating fear in innocent men and women. Terrorism is the politics of state officials and movement militants alike. This argument does not justify either the officials or the militants, but it does excuse them all. We hardly can be harsh with people who act the way everyone else acts. Only saints are likely to act differently, and sainthood in politics is supererogatory, a matter of grace, not obligation.

But this fourth excuse relies too heavily on our cynicism about political life, and cynicism only sometimes answers well to experience. In fact, legitimate states do not need to terrorize their citizens, and strongly based movements do not need to terrorize their opponents. Officials and militants who live, as it were, on the margins of legitimacy and strength sometimes choose terrorism and sometimes do not. Living in terror is not a universal experience. The world the terrorists create has its entrances and exits.

If we want to understand the choice of terror, the choice that forces the rest of us through the door, we have to imagine what in fact always occurs, although we often have no satisfactory record of the occurrence: A group of men and women, officials or militants, sits around a table and argues about whether or not to adopt a terrorist strategy. Later on, the litany of excuses obscures the argument. But at the time, around the table, it would have been no use for defenders of terrorism to say, "Everybody does it," because there they would be face to face with people proposing to do something else. Nor is it historically the case that the members of this last group, the opponents of terrorism, always lose the argument. They can win, however, and still not be able to prevent a terrorist campaign; the would-be terrorists (it does not take very many) can always split the movement and go their own way. Or, they can split the bureaucracy or the police or officer corps and act in the shadow of state power. Indeed, terrorism often has its origin in such splits. The first victims are the terrorists' former comrades or colleagues. What reason can we possibly have, then, for equating the two? If we value the politics of the men and women who oppose terrorism, we must reject the excuses of their murderers. Cynicism at such a time is unfair to the victims.

The fourth excuse can also take, often does take, a more restricted form. Oppression, rather than political rule more generally, is always terroristic in character, and thus, we must always excuse the opponents of oppression. When they choose terrorism, they are only reacting to someone else's previous choice, repaying in kind the treatment they have long received. Of course, their terrorism repeats the evil—innocent people are killed, who were never themselves oppressors—but repetition is not the same as initiation. The oppressors set the terms of the struggle. But if the struggle is fought on the oppressors' terms, then the oppressors are likely to win. Or, at least, oppression is likely to win, even if it takes on a new face. The whole point of a liberation movement or a popular mobilization is to change the terms. We have no reason to excuse the terrorism reactively adopted by opponents of oppression unless we are confident of the sincerity of their opposition, the seriousness of their commitment to a nonoppressive politics. But the choice of terrorism undermines that confidence.

We are often asked to distinguish the terrorism of the oppressed from the terrorism of the oppressors. What is it, however, that makes the difference? The message of the terrorist is the same in both cases: a denial of the peoplehood and humanity of the groups among whom he or she finds victims. Terrorism anticipates, when it does not actually enforce, political domination. Does it matter if one dominated group is replaced by another? Imagine a slave revolt whose protagonists dream only of enslaving in their turn the children of their masters. The dream is understandable, but the fervent desire of the children that the revolt be repressed is equally understandable. In neither case does understanding make for excuse—not, at least, after a politics of universal freedom has become possible. Nor does an understanding of oppression excuse the terrorism of the oppressed, once we have grasped the meaning of "liberation."

These are the four general excuses for terror, and each of them fails. They depend upon statements about the world that are false, historical arguments for which there is no evidence, moral claims that turn out to be hollow or dishonest. This is not to say that

there might not be more particular excuses that have greater plausibility, extenuating circumstances in particular cases that we would feel compelled to recognize. As with murder, we can tell a story (like the story that Richard Wright tells in *Native Son,* for example) that might lead us, not to justify terrorism, but to excuse this or that individual terrorist. We can provide a personal history, a psychological study, of compassion destroyed by fear, moral reason by hatred and rage, social inhibition by unending violence—the product, an individual driven to kill or readily set on a killing course by his or her political leaders. But the force of this story will not depend on any of the four general excuses, all of which grant what the storyteller will have to deny: that terrorism is the deliberate choice of rational men and women. Whether they conceive it to be one option among others or the only one available, they nevertheless argue and choose. Whether they are acting or reacting, they have made a decision. The human instruments they subsequently find to plant the bomb or shoot the gun may act under some psychological compulsion, but the men and women who choose terror as a policy act "freely." They could not act in any other way, or accept any other description of their action, and still pretend to be the leaders of the movement or the state. We ought never to excuse such leaders.

THE RESPONSE TO TERRORISM

What follows from the critique of excuses? There is still a great deal of room for argument about the best way of responding to terrorism. Certainly, terrorists should be resisted, and it is not likely that a purely defensive resistance will ever be sufficient. In this sort of struggle, the offense is always ahead. The technology of terror is simple; the weapons are readily produced and easy to deliver. It is virtually impossible to protect people against random and indiscriminate attack. Thus, resistance will have to be supplemented by some combination of repression and retaliation. This is a dangerous business because repression and retaliation so often take terroristic forms and there are a host of apologists ready with excuses that sound remarkably like those of the terrorists themselves. It should be clear by now, however, that counterterrorism cannot be excused merely because it is reactive. Every new actor, terrorist or counterterrorist, claims to be reacting to someone else, standing in a circle and just passing the evil along. But the circle is ideological in character; in fact, every actor is a moral agent and makes an independent decision.

Therefore, repression and retaliation must not repeat the wrongs of terrorism, which is to say that repression and retaliation must be aimed systematically at the terrorists themselves, never at the people for whom the terrorists claim to be acting. That claim is in any case doubtful, even when it is honestly made. The people do not authorize the terrorists to act in their name. Only a tiny number actually participate in terrorist activities; they are far more likely to suffer than to benefit from the terrorist program. Even if they supported the program and hoped to benefit from it, however, they would still be immune from attack—exactly as civilians in time of war who support the war effort but are not themselves part of it are subject to the same immunity. Civilians may be put at risk by attacks on military targets, as by attacks on terrorist targets, but the risk must be kept to a minimum, even at some cost to the attackers. The refusal to make ordinary people into targets, whatever their nationality or even their politics, is the only way to say no to terrorism. Every act of repression and retaliation has to be measured by this standard.

But what if the "only way" to defeat the terrorists is to intimidate their actual or potential supporters? It is important to deny the premise of this question: that terrorism is a politics dependent on mass support. In fact, it is always the politics of an elite, whose members are dedicated and fanatical and more than ready to endure, or to watch others endure, the devastations of a counterterrorist campaign. Indeed, terrorists will welcome counterterrorism; it makes the terrorists' excuses more plausible and is sure to bring them, however many people are killed or wounded, however many are terrorized, the small number of recruits needed to sustain the terrorist activities.

Repression and retaliation are legitimate responses to terrorism only when they are constrained by the same moral principles that rule out terrorism itself. But there is an alternative response that seeks to avoid the violence that these two entail. The alternative is to address directly, ourselves, the oppression the terrorists claim to oppose. Oppression, they say, is the cause of terrorism. But that is merely one more excuse. The real cause of terrorism is the decision to launch a terrorist campaign, a decision made by that group of people sitting around a table whose deliberations I have already described. However, terrorists do exploit oppression, injustice, and human misery generally and look to these at least for their excuses. There can hardly be any doubt that oppression strengthens their hand. Is that a reason for us to come to the defense of the oppressed? It seems to me that we have our own reasons to do that, and do not need this one, or should not, to prod us into action. We might imitate those movements militants who argue against the adoption of a terrorist strategy—although not, as the terrorists say, because these militants are prepared to tolerate oppression. They already are opposed to oppression and now add to that opposition, perhaps for the same reasons, a refusal of terror. So should we have been opposed before, and we should now make the same addition.

But there is an argument, put with some insistence these days, that we should refuse to acknowledge any link at all between terrorism and oppression—as if any defense of oppressed men and women, once a terrorist campaign has been launched, would concede the effectiveness of the campaign. Or, at least, a defense of oppression would give terrorism the appearance of effectiveness and so increase the likelihood of terrorist campaigns in the future. Here we have the reverse side of the litany of excuses; we have turned over the record. First oppression is made into an excuse for terrorism, and then terrorism is made into an excuse for oppression. The first is the excuse of the far left; the second is the excuse of the neoconservative right. I doubt that genuine conservatives would think it a good reason for defending the status quo that it is under terrorist attack; they would have independent reasons and would be prepared to defend the status quo against any attack. Similarly, those of us who think that the status quo urgently requires change have our own reasons for thinking so and need not be intimidated by terrorists or, for that matter, antiterrorists.

If one criticizes the first excuse, one should not neglect the second. But I need to state the second more precisely. It is not so much an excuse for oppression as an excuse for doing nothing (now) about oppression. The claim is that the campaign against terrorism has priority over every other political activity. If the people who take the lead in this campaign are the old oppressors, then we must make a kind of peace with them—temporarily, of course, until the terrorists have been beaten. This is a strategy that denies the possibility of a two-front war. So long as the men and women who pretend to lead the fight against oppression are terrorists, we can concede nothing to their demands. Nor can we oppose their opponents.

But why not? It is not likely in any case that terrorists would claim victory in the face of a serious effort to deal with the oppression of the people they claim to be defending. The effort would merely expose the hollowness of their claim, and the nearer it came to success, the more they would escalate their terrorism. They would still have to be defeated, for what they are after is not a solution to the problem but rather the power to impose their own solution. No decent end to the conflict in Ireland, say, or in Lebanon, or in the Middle East generally, is going to look like a victory for terrorism—if only because the different groups of terrorists are each committed, by the strategy they have adopted, to an indecent end.[2] By working for our own ends, we expose the indecency.

OPPRESSION AND TERRORISM

It is worth considering at greater length the link between oppression and terror. To pretend that there is no link at all is to ignore the historical record, but the record is more complex than any of the excuses acknowledge. The first thing to be read out of it, however, is simple enough: Oppression is not so much the cause of terrorism as terrorism is one of the primary means of oppression. This was true in ancient

times, as Aristotle recognized, and it is still true today. Tyrants rule by terrorizing their subjects; unjust and illegitimate regimes are upheld through a combination of carefully aimed and random violence.[3] If this method works in the state, there is no reason to think that it will not work, or that it does not work, in the liberation movement. Wherever we see terrorism, we should look for tyranny and oppression. Authoritarian states, especially in the moment of their founding, need a terrorist apparatus—secret police with unlimited power, secret prisons into which citizens disappear, death squads in unmarked cars. Even democracies may use terror, not against their own citizens, but at the margins, in their colonies, for example, where colonizers also are likely to rule tyrannically. Oppression is sometimes maintained by a steady and discriminate pressure, sometimes by intermittent and random violence—what we might think of as terrorist melodrama—designed to render the subject population fearful and passive.

This latter policy, especially if it seems successful, invites imitation by opponents of the state. But terrorism does not spread only when it is imitated. If it can be invented by state officials, it can also be invented by movement militants. Neither one need take lessons from the other; the circle has no single or necessary starting point. Whenever it starts, terrorism in the movement is tyrannical and oppressive in exactly the same way as is terrorism in the state. The terrorists aim to rule, and murder is their method. They have their own internal police, death squads, disappearances. They begin by killing or intimidating those comrades who stand in their way, and they proceed to do the same, if they can, among the people they claim to represent. If terrorists are successful, they rule tyrannically, and their people bear, without consent, the costs of the terrorists' rule. (If the terrorists are only partly successful, the costs to the people may be even greater: What they have to bear now is a war between rival terrorist gangs.) But terrorists cannot win the ultimate victory they seek without challenging the established regime or colonial power and the people it claims to represent, and when terrorists do that, they themselves invite imitation. The regime may then respond with its own campaign of aimed and random violence. Terrorist tracks terrorist, each claiming the other as an excuse.

The same violence can also spread to countries where it has not yet been experienced; now terror is reproduced not through temporal succession but through ideological adaptation. State terrorists wage bloody wars against largely imaginary enemies: army colonels, say, hunting down the representatives of "international communism." Or movement terrorists wage bloody wars against enemies with whom, but for the ideology, they could readily negotiate and compromise: nationalist fanatics committed to a permanent irredentism. These wars, even if they are without precedents, are likely enough to become precedents, to start the circle of terror and counterterror, which is endlessly oppressive for the ordinary men and women whom the state calls its citizens and the movement its "people."

The only way to break out of the circle is to refuse to play the terrorist game. Terrorists in the state and the movement warn us, with equal vehemence, that any such refusal is a sign of softness and naiveté. The self-portrait of the terrorists is always the same. They are tough-minded and realistic; they know their enemies (or privately invent them for ideological purposes); and they are ready to do what must be done for victory. Why then do terrorists turn around and around in the same circle? It is true: Movement terrorists win support because they pretend to deal energetically and effectively with the brutality of the state. It also is true: State terrorists win support because they pretend to deal energetically and effectively with the brutality of the movement. Both feed on the fears of brutalized and oppressed people. But there is no way of overcoming brutality with terror. At most, the burden is shifted from these people to those; more likely, new burdens are added for everyone. Genuine liberation can come only through a politics that mobilizes the victims of brutality and takes careful aim at its agents, or by a politics that surrenders the hope of victory and domination and deliberately seeks a compromise settlement. In either case, once tyranny is repudiated, terrorism is no longer an option. For what lies behind all the excuses, of officials and militants alike, is the predilection for a tyrannical politics.

NOTES

1. Machiavelli, *The Discourses* I:ix.

2. The reason the terrorist strategy, however indecent in itself, cannot be instrumental to some decent political purpose is because any decent purpose must somehow accommodate the people against whom the terrorism is aimed, and what terrorism expresses is precisely the refusal of such an accommodation, the radical devaluing of the Other.

3. Aristotle, *The Politics* 1313–1314a.

From *The Morality of Terrorism*

Haig Khatchadourian

TERRORISM: WHAT'S IN A NAME?

What terrorism is or how the word should be employed is a much vexed question, and many definitions of it have been proposed. Some of the conceptual reasons for the lack of agreement on its meaning will become clearer as I proceed, but the fact

Haig Khatchadourian, "What Terrorism Is and Is Not," in *The Morality of Terrorism* (New York: Peter Lang, 1998), 1–38 (edited). Reprinted by permission of Peter Lang Publishing.

that the term is almost invariably used in an evaluative—indeed, highly polemical and emotionally charged—way makes the framing of a neutral definition a difficult task. It is probably no exaggeration to say that, at present, it is as emotional a word as "war." In fact, some think of terrorism as a kind of war, and the mere mention of the word arouses similar anxieties and fears. This was particularly true at the time the initial draft of this chapter was being written, against the backdrop of the Gulf War and President Saddam Hussein's repeated warnings of terrorism against American and European interests world-wide. Not surprisingly, therefore, terrorism is very widely condemned as a major evil plaguing the last decades of the Twentieth century, a century already drenched with the blood of the innocent and the noninnocent in a long series of wars, revolutions, civil wars, and other forms of violence.

The widespread condemnation of terrorism as an unmitigated evil stems in part from the fact that some of those governments or countries, political systems, or regimes, that are the main targets, particularly of state or state-sponsored political violence, use the word as a political-psychological weapon in their fight against the perpetrators and their avowed causes—for example, national liberation from foreign occupation or the overthrow of an oppressive indigenous system or regime. In fighting terrorism targeted at them, the victim groups or countries tend to indiscriminately label all their enemies as "terrorists," including those who practice the least violent kinds of protest, thus stretching the world's already loose usage and vague meaning beyond reason. Despite its notorious vagueness and looseness, some overlap among the multiplicity of the word's definitions and characterizations exists. Quite a number of definitions in the literature, as well as characterizations in the media and in everyday discourse, include the idea that terrorism is the threat or the actual use of violence—the unlawful use of force—directed against civilians (e.g. noncombatants in wartime) *and they alone,* sometimes with the addition of the words, *"for political* purposes." In that respect the moral philosopher Douglas Lackey's definition is typical. With wartime terrorism in mind, he writes: "What separates the terrorist from the traditional revolutionary is a persistent refusal to direct violence at military objectives. Terrorism, on this account, is the threat or use of violence against noncombatants for political purposes. In ordinary war, the deaths of civilians are side effects of military operations directed against military targets. In terrorist operations, the civilian is the direct and intentional target of attack."[1] The same putative core of meaning occurs in other definitions I shall consider.

Although I shall argue that this and similar definitions of "terrorism" are inadequate, Lackey is right in rejecting the definition of former Vice-President George Bush's Task Force on Combating Terrorism, according to which terrorism is "the unlawful use or threat of violence against persons or property to further political or social objectives."[2] That definition, Lackey notes, is too broad, but his own definition suffers from the opposite defect, although it has the merit of not confining the victims of terrorism to civilians. Another example of a too-broad definition is the Task Force's "the threatened or actual use of force or violence to attain a political goal through fear, coercion, or intimidation."[3]

The preceding and most of the other definitions that have been proposed share a more fundamental defect, one that will be noted as we proceed.

Other proposed definitions I have examined are also either too broad or too narrow, or both—a problem faced by "essentialist" definitions in general— often in addition to other defects. Some definitions are too restrictive, being limited to one form of terrorism, for example, political terrorism in the usual, restricted meaning of the word. Still other definitions or characterizations fail because they are overtly or covertly normative (condemnatory) rather than, as definitions ought to be, neutral or nonevaluative. Former President Ronald Reagan's statement that terrorism is the deliberate maiming or killing of innocent people, and his characterization of terrorists as "base criminals," clearly beg the ethical issues. A fuller definition that suffers from the same flaw among others, is proposed by Burton Leiser. Part of his definition is:

Terrorism is any organized set of acts of violence designed to destroy the structure of authority which normally stands for security, or to reinforce and perpetuate a governmental regime whose popular support is shaky. It is a policy of seemingly senseless, irrational, and arbitrary murder, assassination, sabotage, subversion, robbery and other forms of violence, all committed with dedicated indifference to existing legal and moral codes or with claims to special exemption from conventional social norms.[4]

ELEMENTS OF TERRORISM

The main forms of terrorism in existence in the present-day world share at least five important aspects or elements which an adequate description of terrorism must include. They are:

1. The historical and cultural, including the socioeconomic root causes of its prevalence (e.g., the lack or loss of a homeland).
2. The immediate, intermediate and long-range or ultimate goals. Retaliation is an example of the first, while publicity is an example of the second. "The regaining of a lost homeland, the acquisition or exercise of power [by a state], . . . or enforcement of [its] authority",[5] (which F.J. Hacker calls "terrorism from above"[6]), or "the challenge to . . . [a state's] authority" (which he calls "terrorism from below") are examples of long range terrorist goal.
3. The third aspect or element consists in the forms and methods of coercion and force[7] generally resorted to to terrorize the immediate victims and to coerce those who are seriously affected by the terrorism, the victimized. The latter are the individuals, groups, governments, or countries that are intimately connected with the immediate targets and who are themselves the real albeit indirect targets of the terrorist acts. The forms and methods of coercion and force resorted to to define the different *species* or *forms* of terrorism of any given *type*.
4. The nature or kinds of organizations and institutions, or the political systems, practicing or sponsoring the terrorism. For example, in state terrorism the terrorism is practiced by agents of a state, while in state-sponsored terrorism the terrorism is financially, militarily, or in other ways supported but not directly conducted by the sponsoring state or states.
5. The social, political, economic or military context or circumstances in which the terrorism occurs is also important and must be considered. For example, whether the terrorism occurs in time of peace or in wartime. In the latter case, there is also an important ethical dimension in relation to terror-

ist violence or threats to noncombatants, just as in the case of precision "saturation" bombing of towns and cities in Twentieth century warfare. This would become incalculably more important in the case of possible nuclear terrorism.

The one form of terrorism to which (1) above does not normally apply is predatory terrorism—terrorism motivated by greed. But predatory terrorism is relatively unimportant, especially for a discussion of the morality of terrorism such as the present one, since it is clearly immoral. Although seriously flawed, Leiser's definition noted earlier has the merit of incorporating several of the aspects of terrorism I have mentioned. But it fails to spell out the various sorts of causes of terrorism and makes only a passing mention of what it calls the terrorists' "political ends."[8]

DEFINING "TERRORISM"

A fully adequate characterization or formal definition of "terrorism" must be as neutral as possible and not beg the issue of the morality of terrorism in general, in addition to reflecting the five aspects or dimensions of terrorism distinguished above—notwithstanding the word's almost invariably negative connotations, particularly in the Western world.

I stated earlier that Leiser's and certain other definitions of the word describe terrorism as *always* involving the maiming, killing, or coercion of innocent, and *only* innocent, persons, by which Leiser means "persons who have little or no direct connection with the causes to which the terrorists are dedicated."[9] Although this definition is not quite clear on the point, Leiser appears to equate terrorism with what he calls "the victimization of defenseless, innocent persons" as opposed to "the assassination of political and military leaders [political assassination]."[10]

In the current literature the question of whether noninnocents can be included among the immediate victims of terrorism appears to be a very unsettled question. The absence of clarity and fixity—indeed, the ambivalence and uncertainty in current employments of the word—reflect the different users' stand on the *morality* of terrorism and the morality, especially, of the unlawful use of force in general. These uncertainties are intimately connected with uncertainties concerning the distinction between terrorism and "freedom fighting," such as a rebellion, a civil war, an uprising, or a guerilla war aiming, for example, at national liberation. Those who consider the harming of innocent persons an essential feature of terrorism would tend to consider "freedom fighting" as involving, *inter alia,* the maiming, killing or coercing of *non*innocents. That would allow "political assassination" to be classified as a species of "freedom fighting." Leiser states that guerilla warfare is characterized by small-scale, unconventional, limited actions carried out by irregular forces *against regular military forces, their supply lines, and communications."*[11] That description would be perfectly in order provided we stipulate that the targeted soldiers are in the army of their own free will.

The preceding discussion indicates that in addition to being open textured and vague, the various current evaluative concepts of terrorism, like all other evaluative concepts, are, in W. B. Gallie's phrase, "essentially contested."[12] Yet like most vague and unsettled expressions "terrorism" has a "common core of meaning" in its different usages. This core of meaning includes the notion that terrorist acts are acts of coercion or of actual use of force,[13] aiming at monetary gain (*predatory terrorism*), revenge (*retaliatory terrorism*), a political end (*political terrorism*), or a putative moral/religious end (*moralistic/religious terrorism*).

What is absolutely essential for an adequate concept of terrorism and helps distinguish it from all other uses of force or coercion, but which most definitions I have come across lack, is what I shall call terrorism's "bifocal" character. I mean the crucial distinction between (a) the "immediate victims," the individuals who are the immediate targets of terrorism, and (b) "the victimized," those who are the indirect but real targets of the terrorist acts. Normally the latter are individual governments or countries or certain groups of governments or countries, or specific institutions or groups within a given country. The ultimate targets may also be certain social, economic or political systems or regimens which the terrorists

dislike and hope to change or destroy by their terrorist activities.

* * *

TERRORISM AND JUST WAR THEORY

Although the literature on terrorism is constantly growing, very little has been written about the morality of terrorism; perhaps because the writers take it for granted that terrorism is a scourge, always morally reprehensible and wrong: note for instance the common equation of terrorism with murder. . . .

This is not a very auspicious beginning for a moral evaluation of terrorism. From the fact that terrorist acts, including the killing of immediate victims, are prohibited in many if not all municipal legal systems, it does not follow that some or all such acts are *morally* wrong. Calling terrorist killings "murder" begs the complex ethical issues involved, even if one subscribes to the traditional Natural Law theory of law or to a contemporary form of that theory: that is, if one supposes that a putative law is law proper only if it just or moral. Even then the putative immorality of terrorist acts must first be established for the Natural Law legal philosopher or jurist to accept the municipal laws that outlaw terrorist acts as *bona fide* laws rather than (in Aquinas' graphic description) "violence." . . .

Whether at a minimum some terrorist acts committed in the course of a just war or rebellion are morally justified is an important question and will be discussed . . . in relation to just war theory.

* * *

The traditional conditions of a just war are of two sorts: conditions of justified going to war (*jus ad bellum*) and conditions of the just prosecution of a war in progress (*jus in bello*). One of the fundamental conditions of the latter kind is that

The destruction of life and property, even enemy life and property, is inherently bad. It follows that military forces should cause no more destruction than is strictly necessary to achieve their objectives. (Notice that the principle does not say that whatever is necessary is permissible, but that everything permissible must be necessary). This is the principle of necessity: that *wanton* destruction is forbidden. More precisely, the principle of necessity specifies that a military operation is forbidden if there is some alternative operation that causes less destruction but has the same probability of producing a successful military result.[14]

Another fundamental condition is the principle of discrimination or noncombatant immunity, which prohibits the deliberate harming—above all the killing—of innocent persons. In "Just War Theory" William O'Brien defines that condition as the principle that "prohibits direct intentional attacks on noncombatants and nonmilitary targets",[15] and Douglas Lackey, in *The Ethics of War and Peace,* characterizes it as "the idea that . . . civilian life and property should not be subjected to military force: military force must be directed only at military objectives."[16] A third fundamental condition is the principle of proportion, as "applied to discrete military ends."[17] That condition is defined by O'Brien as "requiring proportionality of means to political and military ends."[18] Or as Lackey states it, it is the idea that "the amount of destruction permitted in pursuit of a military objective must be proportionate to the importance of the objective. This is the *military* principle of proportionality (which must be distinguished from the *political* principle of proportionality in the *jus ad bellum*)."[19]

My contention . . . is that these three principles, duly modified or adapted, are analogically applicable to all the types of terrorism distinguished [earlier], and that they are flagrantly violated by them. Indeed, all but the moralistic/religious type of terrorism violate a further condition of just war theory. I refer to the first and most important condition of *jus ad bellum* and one of the most important conditions of a just war in general: the condition of just cause. This condition is defined by Lackey as the rule " . . . that the use of military force requires a just cause," that is, a "wrong received."[20] . . .

Of the four main types of terrorism, predatory, retaliatory and nonmoralistic/religious terrorism clearly run afoul of the just cause condition, understood—in a nutshell—as the self-defensive use of force. Conceivably only some acts of moralistic and moralistic-political/religious terrorism can satisfy that condition. It is clear that the former three types of terrorism violate that condition.

Let us begin with predatory terrorism, terrorism motivated by greed. Like "ordinary" acts of armed robbery, of which it is the terrorist counterpart, predatory terrorism is a crime and is morally wrong. Both cause terror and indiscriminately hurt whoever happens to be where they strike. Indeed, hostage-taking by armed robbers in hopes of escaping unscathed by forcing the authorities to give them a getaway car or plane is an additional similarity to terrorism. It can even be regarded as predatory terrorism itself, particularly if it is systematic and not a onetime affair, since both political and moralistic terrorism tend to be systematic, as [Paul] Wilkinson notes in relation to political terrorism.[21] Even then, armed robbery involving hostage-taking, must be distinguished from the kind of armed robbery that political or moralistic terrorists may indulge in to raise money for their particular political/moralistic/religious ends.

Nonetheless, bona fide predatory (and even retaliatory) terrorism is often unsystematic; like ordinary armed robbery, it may also be a one-time thing. Some well-known terrorist airplane hijackings in the United States for monetary gain have been one-time incidents, although in all but one instance I know of, that was simply because the hijackers were apprehended!

Like predatory terrorism, retaliatory terrorism may or may not be systematic. International terrorism usually includes a systematic policy of retaliation against a hated, enemy state or its citizens. A notorious example a few years ago was the retaliatory terrorism against the United States and its interests, sponsored by Libya, Syria, and/or Iran.

More important for the present discussion, retaliatory terrorism violates, among other moral rules, the just cause condition and the principles of justice, and is consequently wrong. For what is retaliation but another (more euphemistic?) word for revenge, which is incompatible with self-defense as well as due process. That is no less true in war, if retaliatory terrorism is practiced by a country in its efforts to defend itself against aggression. For example, if an attempt is made on the life of the aggressor country's head of state by agents of the victim state in retaliation for attacks on its territory, the assassination attempt would be (a) an act of *terrorism* if it is *intended* to pressure the aggressor's military to end the aggression. But despite its *goal* and the victim's perception of it as part of its national self-defense, it remains (b) an act of retaliation, not an act of self-defense.

What I have said about predatory and retaliatory terrorism in relation to just cause applies to non-moralistic political terrorism, to terrorism whose political goals are *not* moral. An example is when a revolutionary group commits acts of terrorism against a legitimate, democratically elected government it wants to overthrow out of lust for power.

By definition, moralistic terrorism satisfies just cause if "just cause" is interpreted broadly to mean a morally justifiable cause, for example, political terrorism strictly as part of a national liberation movement against a foreign occupier or indigenous oppressive regime. It *may* also satisfy the condition of right intention. Consequently, I shall turn to the other two conditions of just war I mentioned earlier, to ascertain whether even such terrorism can be morally justifiable.

PRINCIPLE OF NECESSITY AND TERRORISM

The principle of necessity states that "*wanton* destruction [in war] is forbidden. More precisely, the principle . . . specifies that a military operation is forbidden if there is some alternative operation that causes less destruction but has the same probability of producing a successful military result."[22] *Pace* Lackey, who regards it as a more precise form of the condition, it is distinct from, although closely related to, the principle that wanton destruction is forbidden in war. If a war *is* a last resort, it would follow that the destruction of life and property is necessary, not wanton. And if it is necessary, it *is* a last resort.

It is clear that predatory terrorism is always a wanton destruction of life or property, and the same is true of retaliatory terrorism; however, the concept of "last resort" is inapplicable to them. If Iran had chosen to

sue the United States for compensation or reparation at the International Court of Justice at the Hague, for the shooting down an Iranian airbus during the Iraq-Iran war, that would have constituted a peaceful, nonviolent *alternative* to any terrorist retaliation against the United States Iran may have sponsored in its aftermath, such as the destruction of Pan Am Flight 103 over Lockerbie, Scotland, which some believe was instigated and financed by Iran and implemented by a notorious Palestinian terrorist. (The United States has steadfastly held Libya, and possibly Syria, responsible for that atrocity.) Logically, retaliation on the one hand and reparation, compensation, or restitution, or other peaceful ways of undoing or rectifying a wrong, are horses of very different colors.

PRINCIPLE OF DISCRIMINATION AND TERRORISM

In many acts of terrorism some or all of the immediate victims and/or victimized are innocent persons, in no way morally connected with or in any degree responsible for the wrong moralistic terrorism is intended to help rectify, hence for the physical or mental harm that the terrorists inflict on them. In predatory terrorism the immediate victims and the victimized are, almost without exception, innocent persons. That is also often true of retaliatory terrorism, at least as far as the immediate victims are concerned. Two very tragic examples in recent memory are the hijacking of the *Achille Lauro,* and the destruction of the Pan Am plane over Lockerbie. In political and political-moralistic terrorism, whether in wartime or in time of peace, some of the immediate victims or some of the victimized are likely to be innocent persons; but some may be noninnocents, such as members (especially high-ranking members) of the military, who are morally responsible for the real or imagined wrong that triggers the terrorism.

The problem of distinguishing innocent and noninnocent persons in relation to different types and forms of terrorism, except terrorism in war, is on the whole less difficult than the much-vexed corresponding problem in relation to war. My position, *mutatis mutandis* in relation to war, simply stated, is this: (1)

"Innocence" and "ominnocence" refer to *moral* innocence and noninnocence, relative to the particular acts, types, or forms of terrorism *T*. (2) Innocence and noninnocence are a matter of degree. (3) A perfectly innocent person is one who has no moral responsibility, a *fortiori*, no causal responsibility at all, for any wrong that gave rise to *T*. A paradigmatically noninnocent person is someone who has an appreciable degree of moral, hence direct or indirect causal responsibility for the wrong, triggering *T*.[23] Between that extreme and paradigmatic noninnocents there would be, theoretically, cases of decreasing moral responsibility corresponding to decreasing degrees of causal responsibility. Her the targets would be noninnocent in some but lesser degree than in paradigmatic cases of noninnocence. (4) Moral responsibility may be direct or indirect, by virtue of a person's direct or indirect role in *T*'s causation—where *T* is triggered or has its root cause(s) in some real injustice or wrong. The degree of a person's innocence may therefore also vary in that way. Everyone whose actions are a proximate cause of the wrong is noninnocent in a higher degree than those whose responsibility for it is indirect. In particular cases it is always possible in principle to ascertain whether an individual is, causally, directly involved. Generally it is also actually possible, although often quite difficult, to do so in practice. Ascertaining who is indirectly responsible and who is not at all responsible is another matter. Since we are mainly concerned with the theoretical problem of the morality of terrorism, that is not too disquieting. But it is of the essence from the point of view of would-be terrorists and that of the law—unless the terrorists happen to be deranged and target innocent individuals or groups they imagine to be morally responsible for the grievances they are out to avenge or redress. Further, the very life of some individuals may depend on the potential terrorists' ability to distinguish innocent from noninnocent persons or groups. Political, retaliatory, or moralistic terrorists, driven by passion or paranoia, often baselessly enlarge, sometimes to a tragically absurd extent, the circle of alleged noninnocent persons. They sometimes target individuals, groups or whole nations having only a tenuous relation, often of a completely innocent kind, to those who have wronged their compatriots or ancestors, stolen their land, and so on. The example given earlier of terrorists striking at the high-ranking officials of governments whose predecessors committed crimes against their people, illustrates this. Another example is terrorism targeting innocent persons presumed to be guilty by association, simply because they happen to be of the same race, nationality, or religion, or enjoy the same ethnic heritage as those deemed responsible for the hurt.

An extreme, horrifying kind of justification of the targeting of completely innocent persons was brought to my attention by Anthony O'Heare.[24] It involves the justification one sometimes hears of the killing of holidaymakers, travelers, and others, in Israel and other terrorist targets, "on the ground that . . . the very fact that they were contributing to the economy and morale of the targeted country [unwittingly] implicated them." As O'Heare comments, that defense is "a disgusting piece of casuistry." Its implications, I might add, are so far-reaching as to be positively frightening. If the travelers or holidaymakers were guilty of a crime against, say, the Palestinian people, as is claimed, then by parity of reasoning all individuals, institutions, groups of peoples, all countries or nations that have any kind of economic dealings with Israel and so contribute to its economy would likewise be guilty of a crime against the Palestinian people and so may be justifiably targeted! But then why exempt those *Arabs* who live in Israel and even those *Palestinians* residing in the West Bank or in the Gaza Strip who are employed in Israel—indeed, all those who spend any amount of money there—from guilt?

Finally, to be able to protect individuals against terrorism, law enforcement agencies as well as governments in general need to be able to protect individuals against terrorism, need to make reliable predictions about who is a likely target of known terrorist organizations. Yet in few other kinds of coercion or other uses of force is the element of unpredictability and surprise greater or the strikes more impelled by emotion and passion than in terrorism. This problem will be later taken up again in a discussion of responses to terrorism.

PRINCIPLES OF PROPORTION AND TERRORISM

In addition to its violation of the moral principles considered above, terrorism may appear to violate two other principles of just war theory: (1) the *political* principle of proportion of *jus ad bellum* and (2) the *military* principle of proportion of *jus in bello*. The former is stated by William O'Brien as requiring that "the good to be achieved by the realisation of the war aims be proportionate to the evil resulting from the war."[25] And "the calculus of proportionality in just cause [that is, the political purpose, *raison d'etat*, "the high interests of the state"] is to the total good to be expected if the war is successful balanced against the evil the war is likely to cause."[26] Lackey describes the political principle of proportionality as stipulating that "a war cannot be just unless the evil that can reasonably be expected to ensue from the war is less than the evil that can reasonably be expected to ensue if the war is not fought."[27]

The military counterpart of the political principle is described by Lackey as the idea that "the amount of destruction permitted in pursuit of a military objective must be proportionate to the importance of the objective. It follows from the military principle of proportionality that certain objectives should be ruled out of consideration on the ground that too much destruction would be caused in obtaining them."[28]

As in the case of war, the main problem facing any attempt to apply the *political* principle of proportion to terrorism is the difficulty of reaching even the roughest estimate of the total expected good *vis-a-vis* the total evil likely to be caused by a series of connected acts of political or *moralistic/religious* terrorism. The crudest estimates of the expected good of some political-moralistic/religious cause against the suffering or death of even one victim or victimized person are exceedingly difficult to come by.

And if we turn from isolated acts of political-moralistic/religious terrorism to a whole series of such acts extending over a period of years or decades, as with Arab or IRA terrorism, the task becomes utterly hopeless. For how can we possibly measure the expected good resulting from the creation of, for example, an independent Catholic Northern Ireland or a Catholic Northern Ireland united with the Irish Republic, and compare it with the overall evil likely to be the lot of the Ulster Protestants in such an eventuality or on different scenarios of their eventual fate—then add the latter evil to the evils consisting in and consequent upon all the acts of terrorism that are supposed to help realise the desired good end? I see no possible way in which these factors can be quantified, hence added or subtracted.

It seems then that we cannot ascertain whether political or moralistic/religious terrorism sometimes or always violates the political principle of proportion. However, it is a patent fact that no political or moralistic/religious terrorist movement in this century—whether Palestinian, Lebanese, Libyan, Syrian, Iranian, Irish, or Algerian—has succeeded in realizing its ultimate or overall political or moralistic objectives. Moreover, these movements have no more chance of success in the future than they have had so far. Palestinian terrorism is typical. Since, in Israel and the West, terrorism is almost synonymous with murder, it is not surprising that instead of helping the eminently just Palestinian cause, Palestinian acts of terrorism (as distinguished from Palestinian resistance, e.g. the intifada) from the very start have hurt that cause almost beyond repair. Not only has terrorism failed to win the Palestinians their human and other rights or brought them any closer to self-determination: it has created strong public sympathy in the West for Israel and turned public attitudes strongly against the Palestinians, or at least their leadership, and has further increased Israeli security concerns.[29] This does enable us, I think, to conclude after all that the preceding types of terrorism are indeed in serious violation of the political principle of proportion. For the result of tallying the evils of terrorist acts in human pain and suffering, death and destruction, against the nonexistent overall benefits leaves a huge surplus of unmitigated evil on the negative side. I refer not only to the evil inflicted by the terrorists upon their victims and the victimized but also the evil they draw upon themselves and their families by risking loss of life, limb, or liberty in ultimately futile pursuit of their dangerous and violent objectives.

We now turn to the military principle of proportionality—in O'Brien's words, the principle that "a discrete military means . . . when viewed independently on the basis of its intermediate military end (*raison de guerre*), must . . . be proportionate . . . to that military end for which it was used, irrespective of the ultimate end of the war at the level of *raison d'etat.*"[30] This principle, applied to discrete military means, O'Brien observes, is in line with the law of Nuremberg, which judged the "legitimacy of discrete acts of the German forces, . . . inter alia, in terms of their proportionality to intermediate military goals, *raison de guerre*. . . . It was a reasonable way to evaluate the substance of the allegations that war crimes had occurred."[31]

The present form of the principle *can* be applied, *mutatis mutandis,* to discrete acts of terrorism provided that their probable intermediate results can be roughly assessed. For example, in evaluating the morality of the *Achille Lauro* seajacking, the short-term and intermediate "political" gains the terrorists expected to receive must be weighed, if possible, against the killing of an innocent passenger and the terrorism visited on the other passengers on board. It can be safely said that apart from the damage the seajacking did to the PLO and to the Middle East peace process as a whole, whatever benefit the seajackers expected to reap from their acts, such as publicity and the dramatization of the plight of the Palestinians under Israeli military rule in the occupied territories, was vastly outweighed by the evils the seajacking resulted in. More important still, the actual and not (as in O'Brien's formulation of the principle) merely the expected outcome of acts of terrorism, good and bad, must be weighed, if possible, against each other. That is, actual proportionality must obtain if, in retrospect, the acts are to be objec-

tively evaluated. But to do so is precisely to assess the outcomes of the acts in terms of consequentialist criteria, and so will be left for later consideration.

The same general factors need to be weighted for the evaluation of other discrete acts of terrorism in relation to the military principle of proportionality; for example, the assassination of members of the Israeli Olympic team in Munich in 1972, the hijacking of TWA flight 847 in Athens, Greece, in 1985, the downing of Pan Am flight 103 over Lockerbie, Scotland, in 1989, and so on.

TERRORISM AND HUMAN RIGHTS

It can be safely said that the belief that all human beings have a (an equal) human right to life, at least in the minimal sense of a negative right to life—a right not to be unjustly or wrongly killed—is held by anyone who believes in the existence of human rights at all. That idea is also found in the United Nations *Universal Declaration of Human Rights.* Thus, Article 3 states, among other things, that "Everyone has the right to life." The importance of our acknowledging such a universal human right is evident: the protection of human life is the sine qua non of the individual's capacity to realize anything and everything—any and all values—a human being is capable of realizing in relation to himself or herself and others. But even if one does not acknowledge a distinct human right, a right to life as such, I believe that one is forced to acknowledge the existence of some protective norms, such as other human rights and/or principles of fairness and justice, that prohibit, except in very special circumstances, the taking of human life. For instance, justice prohibits the execution of an innocent person for a crime he or she has not committed. Or the moral protection of human life can be placed under the protective umbrella of, for example, a human right to be treated as a moral person rather than be used as an "object."

The special exceptional circumstances I have in mind are those in which the right to life is overridden by stronger moral or other axiological claims. They may include the protection of the equal rights of others, including others' right to life itself (such as in the case of soldiers sent by their country to war, to defend the lives and freedoms of their countrymen against an aggressor nation); or situations where a certain act is (1) the lesser or two evils and (2) violates no one's equal human or other moral rights, or the principles of fairness and justice. For instance, in some instances of passive or active euthanasia, or assisted suicide, such as in the case of terminal patients who are suffering unbearable physical pain [condition (1)] and the euthanasia or assisted suicide fulfils the patient's devout wish and desire to die [condition (2)]. Except in such or similar exceptional cases, the deliberate or the knowing killing of innocent persons is morally wrong.

Elsewhere I have argued that we must acknowledge a fundamental human right of all individuals to be treated as moral persons. Further, that the right includes an equal right of all to be free to satisfy their needs and interests, and to actualize their potentials: that is, to seek to realize themselves and their well-being. In addition, I have argued that all human beings have an equal right to equal opportunity and treatment, to help enable them to realize the aforementioned values, either as part of or as implied by the right to be treated as a moral person.

A universal negative human right to life,[32] hence a right to one's physical and mental security and integrity, can be readily derived from the right to equal treatment and opportunity as a premise, if such a right is acknowledged, as a condition of the very possibility of exercising that right at all or any other moral, legal, or other kind of right or rights, including the right to be treated as a moral person as a whole. The rights to equal treatment and opportunity would be empty or meaningless in practice if not in theory if one's security is not protected. Indeed, given Thomas Hobbes' three principal causes of quarrel in human nature—competition, "diffidence" or desire for safety, and the desire for glory in the absence of the protective norm of the equal human right to life and its reinforcement by law, human existence would tend to exemplify Hobbes' State of Nature. There would be "no arts; no letters; no society; and which is worst of all, continual fear, and danger of violent death; and the life of man, solitary, poor, nasty, brutish, and short."[33]

It is clear that if a negative right to life is assumed, terrorists' killings of their immediate victims—unless they satisfy conditions (1) and (2) above—are always morally wrong. In reality, condition (1) may perhaps be sometimes satisfied, but condition (2) cannot ever be satisfied. In fact all types and forms of terrorism I have distinguished seriously violate the human rights of their immediate victims and the victimized as moral persons.

Treating people as moral persons means treating them with consideration in two closely related ways. First, it means respecting their autonomy as individuals with their own desires and interests, plans and projects, commitments and goals. That autonomy is clearly violated if they are humiliated, coerced and terrorized, taken hostage or kidnapped, and above all, killed. Second, consideration involves "a certain cluster of attitudes, hence certain ways of acting toward, reacting to and thinking and feeling about" people.[34] It includes sensitivity to and consideration of their feelings and desires, aspirations, projects, and goals. That in turn is an integral part of treating their life as a whole—including their relationships and memories—as a thing of value. Finally, it includes respecting their "culture or ethnic, religious or racial identity or heritage."[35] These things are the very antithesis of what terrorism does to its victims and the victimized.

In sum, terrorism in general violates both aspects of its targets' right to be treated as moral persons. In retaliatory and moralistic/religious terrorism, that is no less true of those victims or those victimized who are morally responsible in some degree for the wrong that precipitates the terrorist strike than of those who are completely innocent of it. In predatory terrorism, the terrorist acts violate the human right of everyone directly or indirectly hurt by them. For the terrorists the life of the immediate victims and their human rights matter not in the least. The same goes for the victimized. The terrorists use both groups, against their will, simply as means to their own ends. The matter can also be looked upon in terms of the ordinary concepts of *justice* and *injustice.* Terror directed against innocent persons is a grave injustice against them. In no case is this truer than when terrorists impute to their immediate victims or to the victimized guilt by association. It is equally true when the victims are representatives of a government one or more of whose predecessors committed large-scale atrocities, such as attempted genocide, against the terrorists' compatriots or ancestors. True, the present government would be tainted by the original crimes if, to cite an actual case, it categorically refuses to acknowledge its predecessors' guilt and take any steps to redress the grievous wrongs. Similarly, if it verbally acknowledges its predecessors' guilt but washes its hands of all moral or legal responsibility to make amends to the survivors of the atrocities or their families, on the ground that it is a new government, existing decades later than the perpetrators. Yet only if the targeted representatives of the present government themselves are in some way responsible for their government's stand would they be noninnocent in some degree. Otherwise targeting them from a desire for revenge would be sheer murder or attempted murder.

Whenever the victims or victimized are innocent persons, terrorism directed against them constitutes a very grave injustice, like "punishing" an innocent person for a crime he or she has not committed. For in the present sense, justice consists in one's receiving what one merits or deserves, determined by what one has done or refrained from doing.

It may be argued that some terrorist acts *may* be just punishment for wrongs committed by the immediate victims or the victimized themselves, against the terrorists or persons close to them. But first, punishment cannot be just if founded on a denial of the wrongdoer's human as well as other rights. Second, a vast difference exists between terrorist "punishment" and just legal punishment, which presupposes the establishment of guilt by a preponderance of the evidence. By definition, terrorists do not and cannot respect the legal protections and rights of the victims and the victimized, but erect themselves as judges and jury—and executioners—giving the "accused" no opportunity to defend themselves or be defended by counsel against the terrorists' allegations, let alone the possibility of defending themselves physically

against their assailants. This is a further corollary of the terrorists' denial of the moral and legal rights of the victims and victimized.

These strictures apply equally to terrorism from above and from below. The fact that in the former case the terrorist "organization" is the government itself or some arm of government (e.g., its secret police), and that the terrorism is practiced against those of its own citizens it considers dangerous or subversive, does not morally change the situation. It is terrorism by any other name. Such for instance was the situation in Brazil (in the 1960s), Argentina (in the 1970s), Colombia (in the 1980s), and in other Latin American countries when right-wing, anticommunist death squads killed or executed thousands of people suspected of leftist sympathies. In some countries "church and human rights organizations have been particularly hard-hit."[36]

To sum up. The [earlier] discussion of the nature of terrorism . . . prepared the way for the central question [here]: whether terrorism is ever morally right, morally justifiable. To answer that question two kinds of ethical principles/rules were deployed, (A) applicable human rights, and (B) applicable just war principles/rules. A third principle, (C) the application of consequentialist, specifically act- and rule-utilitarian principles/rules to terrorism has been left to Chapter 4. On both (A) and (B), terrorism in general, in all its various types and forms, was found to be always wrong.

Since predatory and retaliatory terrorism, like predation and retaliation in general, are patently wrong, the inquiry was focused on political and moralistic/religious terrorism, which are held by some—with apparent plausibility—to be, in certain circumstances, morally justifiable. However, it was argued that terrorism of both types is wrong, since both violate certain basic human rights and applicable just war principles or rules.

NOTES

1. Douglas Lackey, *The Ethics of War and Peace* (Englewood Cliffs, NJ, 1989), 85.

2. "Report of Vice-President's Task Force on Combating Terrorism," in Lackey, *Ethics*, 85.

3. Charles A. Russell et al., "Out-Inventing the Terrorist," in *Terrorism, Theory and Practice,* Yonah Alexander et al., eds. (Boulder, CO, 1979), 4.

4. Burton M. Leiser, *Liberty, Justice, and Morals* (New York, 1979), 375. Italics in original.

5. Harold J. Vetter et al., *Perspectives on Terrorism* (Pacific Grove, CA, 1990), 8.

6. Frederick J. Hacker, *Crusaders, Criminals, Crazies* (New York, 1977).

7. I use "force" because it is morally neutral or near-neutral, unlike the more common "violence."

8. Leiser, *Liberty, Justice, and Morals,* 375.

9. Ibid.

10. Ibid., 379.

11. Ibid., 381. Italics in original.

12. W. B. Gallie, "Essentially Contested Concepts," *Proceedings of the Aristotelian Society,* n.s., 56 (March 1956), 180ff.

13. Those who use "terrorism" as a condemnatory term would substitute "violence" for "force."

14. Douglas P. Lackey, *The Ethics of War and Peace* (Englewood Cliffs, NJ, 1989), 59. Italics in original.

15. William O'Brien, "Just-War Theory," in Burton M. Leiser *Liberty, Justice, and Morals,* 2nd ed. (New York, 1979), 39.

16. Lackey, *Ethics,* 59.

17. Ibid., 37.

18. Ibid., 30.

19. Ibid., 59. Italics in original.

20. Ibid., 33.

21. See Paul Wilkinson, *Terrorism and the Liberal State,* 2nd ed. (London, 1986).

22. Lackey, *Ethics,* 59. Italics in original.

23. What constitutes an "appreciable degree" of moral responsibility would of course be a matter of controversy.

24. Private communication to the author.

25. O'Brien, "Just War Theory," 37.

26. Ibid.

27. Lackey, *Ethics,* 40.

28. Ibid., 59.

29. A personal note: My own moral condemnation of terrorism and my conviction that it was bound to hurt rather than help the Palestinian cause led me, soon after the Palestinian skyjacking, to send an open letter to the PLO leadership. In the letter I pointed these things out and pleaded that the PLO put an end to such acts. For rather obvious reasons the Beirut publication to which I sent the letter could not publish it.

30. O'Brien, "Just-War Theory," 37.

31. Ibid., 38.

32. As distinguished from a positive human right to life, which includes—over and above the right not to be physically hurt or killed—a right to a minimum standard of welfare.

33. Thomas Hobbes, "Self-Interest," in *Great Traditions in Ethics,* 5th ed., Ethel M. Albert et al., eds. (Belmont, CA, 1984), 134. Reprinted from *Leviathan.*

34. Haig Khatchadourian, "The Human Right to Be Treated as a Person," *Journal of Value Inquiry* 19 (1985): 192.

35. Ibid.

36. Leonard B. Weinberg and Paul B. Davis, *Introduction to Political Terrorism* (New York, 1989), 72.

Terrorism and International Justice

James P. Sterba

INTRODUCTION

How should we think about terrorism within a context of international justice? To answer this question it is helpful to start with a definition of terrorism. Since 1983, the U.S. State Department has defined terrorism as follows:

Terrorism is premeditated, politically motivated violence perpetrated against noncombatant targets by subnational groups or clandestine agents, usually intended to influence an audience.[1]

In a recent U.S. State Department document in which this definition is endorsed, there is also a section that discusses state-sponsored terrorism.[2] It is clear then that the U.S. State Department does not hold that only subnational groups or individuals can commit terrorist acts; it further recognizes that states can commit terrorist acts as well. So let me offer the following definition of terrorism, which is essentially the same as the U.S. State Department's definition once it is allowed that states too can commit terrorist acts, and once it is recognized that it is through attempting to elicit terror (that is, intense fear, fright or intimidation) that terrorists try to achieve their goals. The definition is:

Terrorism is the use or threat of violence against innocent people to elicit terror in them, or in some other group of people, in order to further a political objective.

Using this definition, there is no problem seeing the attacks on New York City and Washington, DC, particularly the attacks on the World Trade Center, as terrorist acts.[3] Likewise, the bombing of the U.S. embassies in Kenya and Tanzania in 1998 as well as the suicide bombings directed at Israeli civilians are terrorist acts.[4]

James P. Sterba, "Terrorism and International Justice," in *Terrorism and International Justice*, ed. James P. Sterba (New York: Oxford University Press, 2003), 206–28 (edited). Copyright © 2003 Oxford University Press. Reprinted with permission.

But what about the U.S. bombing of a pharmaceutical plant in Sudan with respect to which the United States blocked a UN inquiry and later compensated the owner, but not the thousands of victims who were deprived of drugs;[5] . . . or the United States's $4 billion a year support for Israel's occupation of Palestinian lands, . . . which is illegal, that is, in violation of UN resolutions the same sort of resolutions over which the Bush administration now wants to go to war with Iraq that specifically forbid in the case of Israel "the acquisition of territory by force," and which has resulted in many thousands of deaths? If we want to go back further, what about the U.S. support for the Contras in Nicaragua and the death squads in El Salvador, especially during the Reagan years, and the United States's use of terrorist contra-*city* threats of nuclear retaliation during the Cold War and its actual use of nuclear weapons against Hiroshima and Nagasaki at the end of World War II, resulting in over one hundred thousand deaths? Surely, all of these U.S. actions also turn out to be either terrorist acts or support for terrorist acts, according to our definition. How can we tell then, which, if any, of these terrorist acts, or support for terrorist acts, are morally justified?

THE PERSPECTIVE OF JUST WAR THEORY AND PACIFISM

My preferred approach to addressing this question is provided by pacifism and just war theory. This is because I think that pacifism and just war theory provide a very useful way to think morally about terrorism. Thinking morally about terrorism involves trying to think about it from the perspectives of all those involved, which is something we almost never fully manage to pull off, particularly when we are dealing with perspectives that are alien to our own. But the degree to which we fail to reach out and take into account the perspectives of all those involved is the degree to which we fail to reach a morally correct approach to the practical problems we face. That is why pacifism and just war theory are particularly helpful in this context; they tend to keep us focused on what we need to take into account if we are to achieve a morally correct response to terrorism. So this is the approach that I will adopt here.

Most people identify pacifism with a theory of nonviolence. We can call this view "nonviolent pacifism." It maintains that *any use of violence against other human beings is morally prohibited*. Nonviolent pacifism has been defended on both religious and philosophical grounds. New Testament admonitions to turn the other cheek and to love one's enemies have been taken to support this form of pacifism. The Jains of India endorse this form of pacifism and extend it to include a prohibition of violence against all living beings. Philosophically, nonviolent pacifism has also seemed attractive because it is similar to the basic principle of "Do no evil" that is found in most ethical perspectives.

It has been argued, however, that nonviolent pacifism is incoherent. In a well-known article, Jan Narveson rejects nonviolent pacifism as incoherent because it recognizes a right to life yet rules out any use of force in defense of that right.[6] A strict nonviolence principle is incoherent, Narveson argues, because having a right entails the legitimacy of using force in defense of that right at least on some occasions. But nonviolent pacifism does not prohibit all force or resistance in defense of one's rights but only that which is violent.[7] Thus, Rosa Parks was nonviolently defending her rights when she refused to give up her seat in a bus to a white person in Montgomery, Alabama, in 1955.

Some pacifists have thought that the best way to respond to objections like Narveson's is to endorse a form of pacifism that clearly does not rule out all force but only lethal force. We can call this "nonlethal pacifism." It maintains that *any lethal use of force against other human beings is morally prohibited*. This may have been the form of pacifism endorsed by Christians in the early church before the time of Constantine. Mahatma Gandhi is also often interpreted to be defending just this form of pacifism, as rooted in both Christianity and Hinduism. Cheyney

Ryan, attempting to defend this form of pacifism, has argued that a difference between the pacifist and the nonpacifist is whether we can or should create the necessary distance between ourselves and other human beings in order to make the act of killing possible.[8] To illustrate, Ryan cites George Orwell's reluctance to shoot at an enemy soldier who jumped out of a trench and ran along the top of a parapet half-dressed and holding up his trousers with both hands. Ryan contends that what kept Orwell from shooting was that he couldn't think of the soldier as a thing rather than a fellow human being.

However, I do not believe that Ryan's example is compelling as a support for nonlethal pacifism. It is not clear that Orwell's inability to shoot the enemy soldier was because he could not think of the soldier as a thing rather than a fellow human being. Perhaps it was because he could not think of the soldier who was holding up his trousers with both hands as a threat or a combatant.

It also appears that Gandhi himself did not endorse this form of pacifism. In his essay "The Doctrine of the Sword," Gandhi wrote,

I do believe that where there is only a choice between cowardice and violence, I would advise violence. Thus, when my eldest son asked me what he should have done, had he been present when I was almost fatally assaulted in 1908, whether he should have run away and seen me killed or whether he should have used his physical force which he could and wanted to use, and defended me, I told him that it was his duty to defend me even by using violence.[9]

There is, however, a form of pacifism that remains relatively untouched by the criticisms that have been raised against both nonviolent pacifism and nonlethal pacifism. This form of pacifism neither prohibits all uses of force nor even all uses of lethal force. We can call the view "anti-war pacifism" because it holds that *any massive use of lethal force, as in warfare, is morally prohibited*. Some historians claim that this is the form of pacifism endorsed by the early Christian church because, after 180 C.E., but not before, there is evidence of Christians being permitted to serve in the military, doing basically police work, during times of peace. Anti-war pacifism is also the form of pacifism most widely defended by philosophers today, at least in the English-speaking world. Two excellent defenses are Duane L. Cady, *From Warism to Pacifism,* and Robert L. Holmes, *On War and Morality.* Among the members of the primarily U.S. Canadian Concerned Philosophers for Peace, anti-war pacifism seems to be the most widely endorsed pacifist view.

In defense of anti-war pacifism, it is undeniable that wars have brought much death and destruction in their wake and that many of those who have perished in them are noncombatants or innocents. In fact, the tendency of modern wars has been to produce higher and higher proportions of noncombatant casualties, making it more and more difficult to justify participation in such wars.[10] At the same time, strategies for nonbelligerent conflict resolution are rarely intensively developed and explored before nations choose to go to war, making it all but impossible to justify participation in such wars.

In my previous work, I attempted to further defend this form of pacifism by developing it alongside of just war theory. I argue that when just war theory is given its most morally defensible interpretation then it too can be reconciled with the practical requirements of anti-war pacifism.

* * *

. . . We can call the view that emerges from this reconciliation "just war pacifism." It is the view that claims that because of the stringent requirements of just war theory, only very rarely will participation in a massive use of lethal force in warfare be morally justified.

Now one might think that from the perspective of just war pacifism acts of terrorism could never be morally justified. But this would require an absolute prohibition on intentionally harming innocents, and such a prohibition would not seem to be justified, even from the perspective of just war pacifism.[11] Specifically, it would seem that harm to innocents can be justified for the sake of achieving a greater good when the harm is

1. Trivial (e.g., as in the case of stepping on someone's foot to get out of a crowded subway)

2. Easily reparable (e.g., as in the case of lying to a temporarily depressed friend to keep her from committing suicide)

3. Nonreparable but greatly outweighed by the consequences of the action.

Obviously, it is this third category of harm that is relevant to the possible justification of terrorism. But when is intentional harm to innocents nonreparable yet greatly outweighed by the consequences?

Consider the following example often discussed by moral philosophers. A large person who is leading a party of spelunkers gets himself stuck in the mouth of a cave in which flood waters are rising. The trapped party of spelunkers just happens to have a stick of dynamite with which they can blast the large person out of the mouth of the cave; either they use the dynamite or they all drown, the large person with them. Now it is usually assumed in this case that it is morally permissible to dynamite the large person out of the mouth of the cave. After all, if that is not done, the whole party of spelunkers will die, the large person with them. So the sacrifice imposed on the large person in this case would not be that great.

But what if the large person's head is outside rather than inside the cave, as it must have been in the previous interpretation of the case? Under those circumstances, the large person would not die when the other spelunkers drown. Presumably after slimming down a bit, he would eventually just squeeze his way out of the mouth of the cave. In this case, could the party of spelunkers trapped in the cave still legitimately use the stick of dynamite they have to save themselves rather than the large person?

Suppose there were ten, twenty, one hundred, or whatever number you want of splunkers trapped in the cave. At some point, won't the number be sufficiently great that it would be morally acceptable for those in the cave to use the stick of dynamite to save themselves rather than the large person, even if this meant that the large person would be morally required to sacrifice his life? The answer has to be yes, even if you think it has to be a very unusual case when we can reasonably demand that people thus sacrifice their lives in this way.

Is it possible that some acts of terrorism are morally justified in this way? It is often argued that our dropping of atomic bombs on Hiroshima and Nagasaki was so justified. President Truman, who ordered the bombing, justified it on the grounds that it was used to shorten the war. In 1945, the United States demanded the unconditional surrender of Japan. The Japanese had by that time lost the war, but the leaders of their armed forces were by no means ready to accept unconditional surrender. While the Japanese leaders expected an invasion of their mainland islands, they believed that they could make that invasion so costly that the United States would accept a conditional surrender. Truman's military advisors also believed the costs would be high. The capture of Okinawa had cost almost 80,000 American casualties, while almost the entire Japanese garrison of 120,000 men died in battle. If the mainland islands were defended in a similar manner, hundreds of thousands of Japanese would surely die. During that time, the bombing of Japan would continue, and perhaps intensify, resulting in casualty rates that were no different from those that were expected from the atomic attack. A massive incendiary raid on Tokyo early in March 1945 had set off a firestorm and killed an estimated 100,000 people. Accordingly, Truman's Secretary of State James Byrnes admitted that the two atomic bombs did cause "many casualties, but not nearly so many as there would have been had our air force continued to drop incendiary bombs on Japan's cities."[12] Similarly, Winston Churchill wrote in support of Truman's decision "To avert a vast, indefinite butchery . . . at the cost of a few explosions seemed, after all our toils and perils, a miracle of deliverance."[13]

Yet the "vast, indefinite butchery" that the United States sought to avert by dropping atomic bombs on Hiroshima and Nagasaki was one that the United States itself was threatening and had already started to carry out with its incendiary attack on Tokyo. And the United States itself could have easily avoided this butchery by dropping its demand for unconditional Japanese surrender. Moreover, a demand of unconditional surrender can almost never be morally justified since defeated aggressors almost always have certain rights that they never are required to surrender.[14] Hence, the United States's terrorist acts of dropping of atomic bombs on Hiroshima and Nagasaki cannot be justified on the grounds of shortening the war and avoiding a vast, indefinite butchery because the United States could have secured those results simply by giving up its unreasonable demand for unconditional surrender.

A more promising case for justified terrorism is the counter-city bombing by the British during the early stages of World War II. Early in the war, it became clear that British bombers could fly effectively only at night because too many of them were being shot down during day raids by German anti-aircraft fire. In addition, a study done in 1941 showed that of those planes flying at night recorded as having actually succeeded in attacking their targets, only one-third managed to drop their bombs within five miles of their intended target. This meant that British bombers flying at night could reasonably aim at no target smaller than a fairly large city.

Michael Walzer argues that under these conditions, the British terror bombing was morally justified because at this early stage of the war, it was the only way the British had left to them to try to avert a Nazi victory. Walzer further argues that the time period when such terror bombing was justified was relatively brief. Once the Russians began to inflict enormous casualties on the German army and the United States made available its manpower and resources, other alternatives opened up. Unfortunately, the British continued to rely heavily on terror bombing right up until the end of the war, culminating in the fire-bombing of Dresden in which something like one hundred thousand people were killed. However, for that relatively brief period of time when Britain had no other way to try to avert a Nazi victory, Walzer argues, its reliance on terror bombing was morally justified.

Suppose then we accept this moral justification for British terror bombing during World War II. Doesn't this suggest a comparable moral justification for Palestinian suicide bombings against Israeli civilians? Israel has been illegally occupying Palestinian land for thirty-five years now in violation of UN resolutions following the 1967 Arab-Israeli War. Even a return to those 1967 borders, which the UN resolutions require, still permits a considerable expansion of Israel's original borders as specified in the mandate of 1947. Moreover, since the Oslo Peace Accords in 1993, Israeli settlements have doubled in the Occupied Territories. In the year that Sharon has been prime minister, some thirty-five new settlements have been established in the Occupied Territories. In Gaza, there are 1.2 million Palestinians and four thousand Israelis, but the Israelis control 40 percent of the land and 70 percent of the water. In the West Bank, there are 1.9 million Palestinians and 280,000 Israelis, but the Israelis control 40 percent of the land and 37 percent of the water. In addition, Israel failed to abide by its commitments under the Oslo Peace Accords to release prisoners, to complete a third redeployment of its military forces, and to transfer three Jerusalem villages to Palestinian control. Moreover, at the recent Camp David meeting, Israeli's proposals did not provide for Palestinian control over East Jerusalem, upon which 40 percent of the Palestinian economy depends. Nor did Israeli's proposals provide for a right of return or compensation for the half of the Palestinian population that lives in exile (President Clinton proposed that Chairman Arafat should just forget about them), most of them having been driven off their land by Israeli expansion. So the Palestinian cause is clearly a just one, but just as clearly the Palestinians lack the military resources to effectively resist Israeli occupation and aggression by simply directly attacking Israeli military forces. The Israelis have access to the most advanced U.S. weapons and $4 billion a year from the United States to buy whatever weapons they want. The Palestinians have no comparable support from anyone. It is under these conditions that a moral justification for Palestinian suicide bombers against Israeli civilians emerges.[15] Given that the Palestinians lack any effective means to try to end the Israeli occupation or to stop Israel's further expansion into Palestinian territories other than by using suicide bombers against Israeli civilians, why would this use of suicide bombers not be justified in much the same way that Walzer justifies the British terror bombing in the early

stages of World War II?[16] If the Israelis have the ultimate goal of confining most Palestinians to a number of economically nonviable and disconnected reservations, similar to those on which the United States confines Native American Indian nations, then surely the Palestinians have a right to resist that conquest as best they can.[17]

Beginning with just war pacifism, I have argued that there are morally defensible exceptions to the just means prohibition against directly killing innocents. The cave analogy argument aims to establish that conclusion. British terror bombing at the beginning of World War II, but not the American dropping of atomic bombs on Hiroshima and Nagasaki at the end of that war, is offered as a real-life instantiation of that argument. The Palestinian use of suicide bombers against Israeli civilians is then presented as a contemporary instantiation of that very same argument.

Yet even if there is a moral justification for the Palestinian use of suicide bombers against Israeli civilians under present conditions, clearly most acts of terrorism cannot be justified, and clearly there was no moral justification for the terrorist attacks on New York City and Washington, DC, particularly the attacks on the World Trade Center.[18]

Even so, the question remains as to whether the United States was morally justified in going to war against Afghanistan in response to these unjustified terrorist acts. According to just war pacifism, before using belligerent correctives, we must be sure that nonbelligerent correctives are neither hopeless nor too costly. The three weeks of diplomatic activity that the United States engaged in did not appear to be sufficient to determine whether it was hopeless or too costly to continue to attempt to bring Osama bin Laden before a U.S. court or, better, before an international court of law, without military action. We demanded that the Taliban government immediately hand over bin Laden and "all the leaders of Al Qaeda who hide in your land." But how could we have reasonably expected this of the Taliban, given that months after we have overthrown the Taliban government and installed a friendly one, we still have not been able to turn up bin Laden and most of his key associates? How could we have expected that the Taliban government, with its limited resources and loose control over the country, to do in three weeks what we still have not been able to accomplish in over a year?

It is conceivable that our leaders never really expected that the Taliban government would be able to meet our demands even if they had wanted to do so. After we began our military offensive, the Taliban government expressed a willingness to hand over bin Laden and his associates at least for trial in an international court if we would stop our military offensive. But we never took them up on their offer.[19] Perhaps we knew that the Taliban government really lacked the resources to hand over bin Laden and his key associates, even while we used their failure to do so as the justification for our waging a war against them.[20]

Something similar may now be happening in the Israeli-Palestinian conflict. The Israeli government has demanded that Yasir Arafat put a stop to the suicide bombings, and arrest those who are behind them. But it is far from clear that Arafat has the power to do so. The Israeli government, with many more military resources than Arafat has at his disposal, has been unable to put a stop to the suicide bombings; in fact, the number of such bombings has escalated as Israel has escalated its military responses. The Israeli government repeated its demand that Arafat stop the suicide bombings at the same time that it held Arafat under virtual house arrest in Ramallah and attacked members of his Palestinian Authority throughout the Occupied Territories. Clearly, the Israelis must know that Arafat lacks the power to put an end to the suicide bombings in the absence of a political settlement guaranteeing the Palestinians virtually everything they have a right to under the relevant UN resolutions. Moreover, if Arafat is foolish enough to speak out against the suicide bombings, as he has in the past, in the absence of the political guarantees that he needs, the bombings will just continue, and Arafat will be branded as ineffectual. So, either the failure of Arafat to speak out against the suicide bombings or his ineffectiveness at stopping them when he does speak out is used by the Israeli

government as a justification for reoccupying the Palestinian territories and expanding Israeli settlements in them. But neither the actions taken by the Israeli government with respect to the Palestinians nor the actions undertaken by the U.S. government with respect to the Al Qaeda network are morally justified because neither government exhausted its nonbelligerent correctives before engaging in a military response.[21]

In the United States, public opinion rather than the exhaustion of nonbelligerent options has served to motivate our military response to 9/11. The military response has been well received by at least a majority of American people, who want to see their government "doing something" to get bin Laden and fight terrorism. But satisfying public opinion polls is not the same as satisfying the requirements of just war pacifism. The United States first called its military action Infinite Justice and then later, in view of the religious connotations of that term, began calling it Enduring Freedom, but our military action is neither just nor does it acceptably promote freedom unless nonbelligerent correctives are first exhausted, and they were not exhausted in this case. Nor has our military response yet delivered up for trial bin Laden or any of his top associates or even any of the top Taliban leaders, although some were killed by our military action, and some good detective and police work, not military action, has recently led to the capture in Pakistan of Abu Zubaydah, who is thought to be bin Laden's second or third lieutenant.

So, even if the United States itself had not engaged in any related terrorist acts or supported any related terrorist acts, there would still be a strong objection to its relatively quick resort to military force as a response to the terrorist attacks of 9/11. Given that the United States itself arguably has engaged in terrorist acts in Sudan, and through the UN against Iraqi children, as well as has supported terrorist acts through its political and financial support of Israel's illegal occupation of Palestinian lands, and given that these acts of terrorism, and support for terrorism, have served at least partially to motivate terrorist attacks on the United States itself, the United States surely needs to take steps to radically correct its own wrongdoing if it is to respond justly to the related wrongdoing of bin Laden and his followers. Unfortunately this is also something we have not yet done.[22]

What then should we be doing if we are to respect the requirements of just war pacifism in our response to the terrorist attacks of September 11?

1. We should let Israel know in no uncertain terms that our continuing political and financial support depends upon its reaching an agreement with the Palestinians on the establishment of a Palestinian state in accordance with the relevant UN resolutions relatively quickly within, say, three to six months. So many plans for a Palestinian state have been discussed over the years that it should not be that difficult to settle on one of them that accords with the relevant UN resolutions, once Israel knows that it can no longer draw on the political and financial support of the United States to resist a settlement. The evidence of serious negotiations between Israel and the Palestinians will be welcomed by people around the world.

2. The sanctions against Iraq imposed since 1991 must be radically modified to permit sufficient humanitarian assistance to the Iraqi people, particularly the children. (Obviously, I am opposed to a pre-emptive military strike against Iraq—one that does not exhaust nonbelligerent correctives.) According to a UNICEF study done in 1999, if the substantial reduction in child mortality throughout Iraq during the 1980s had continued through the 1990s, there would have been half a million fewer deaths of children under five in the country as a whole during the eight year the period of 1991 to 1998.[23] Moreover, the current oil-for-food program, which was only introduced in 1997 (six years into the sanctions), does not, by the UN's own estimate, provide sufficient food and medicine to prevent conditions in Iraq from getting even worse. This all has to change. The oil-for-food program must immediately be expanded to arrest and reverse the deteriorating humanitarian conditions in Iraq.

3. There should have been three to six months of serious diplomatic negotiations to bring Osama bin Laden and the leaders of his Al Qaeda network either before a U.S. court or, preferably, before an international court of law. Substantial economic and political incentives should have been offered to the relevant individuals and nations to help bring this about. Now that we have overthrown the Taliban in Afghanistan and helped establish a friendly government, we should end our military campaign immediately and return to nonbelligerent correctives, which can include the same sort of good detective and police work that has made possible the capture of Abu Zubaydah, the highest-ranking Al Qaeda member captured to date. This will even give us the unintended benefit of conveying to our enemies and to others that we are serious about engaging in belligerent correctives should the nonbelligerent ones prove ineffective.

One of the main lessons we should have drawn from the 9/11 terrorist attacks on the World Trade Center and the Pentagon is how vulnerable our costly high-tech military defenses are to smart, determined enemies using even the simplest of weapons imaginable—knives and boxcutters. And as bad as 9/11 was, it could have been far worse. There is little doubt that the terrorists who hijacked the airplanes and flew them into the World Trade Center and the Pentagon would not have hesitated to detonate a nuclear explosive, maybe one they would have hidden in the World Trade Center, if they could have done so.

It would also not be that difficult for terrorists to target chemical plants or, more easily, shipments of industrial chemicals such as chlorine that are transported in tank cars and trucks. Before 9/11, only about 2 percent of all the containers that move through U.S. ports were actually inspected. Currently, that number has been doubled, but that still means that 96 percent of such containers that are shipped from all over the world are not inspected when they enter the United States. Detonating thousands of tons of ammonium nitrate loaded on a ship in a harbor would have the impact of a small nuclear explosion.

Just last year, three hundred tons of ammonium nitrate apparently exploded in France, killing twenty-nine people and injuring more than twenty-five hundred.

Building another layer of high-tech military defense, like the $238 billion George W. Bush proposes to spend on a missile defense system, does little to decrease our vulnerability to such terrorist attacks. In fact, because such high-tech military expenditures divert money from projects that would significantly decrease our vulnerability to terrorist attacks, they actually have an overall negative impact on our national security.

What then should we do to prevent future terrorist attacks from being directed at the United States or U.S. citizens? In addition to the changes of policy I mentioned earlier with respect to Israel, Iraq, and Osama bin Laden's Al Qaeda network, there are many other things that the United States could do to project a more just foreign policy. For starters, there are a number of international treaties and conventions, for example, the Kyoto Climate Change Treaty, the Treaty Banning Land Mines, and the Rome Treaty for the establishment of an International Criminal Court, that the United States has failed to sign for reasons that seem to simply favor U.S. special interests at the expense of international justice or what would be of benefit to the world community as a whole.

Furthermore, looking at things from an international justice perspective can require a considerable modification of our usual ways of thinking about the relationships between nations and peoples. From an international justice perspective or, more generally, from a moral perspective, actions and policies must be such that they are acceptable by all those affected by those actions and policies (that is, the actions and policies must be such that they ought to be accepted not necessarily that they are accepted by all those affected by those actions and policies). Thus, the fact that the United States, which constitutes 4 percent of the world's population while using 25 percent of its energy resources, refuses to sign the Kyoto Climate Change Treaty and make the cuts in its energy consumption that virtually all other nations of the world

judge to be fair makes the United States, in this regard, something like an outlaw nation from the perspective of international justice.[24]

Yet the failure of the United States to accord with international justice cuts even deeper. According to the World Food Program, three-quarters of a billion people are desperately hungry around the world. According to that same program, even Afghanistan, the subject of so much of our recent attention, has received only 5 percent of the $285 million in emergency aid it needs to feed its people for the rest of the year. One of two women ministers in the provisional Afghan government, Sima Samar, who is in charge of women's affairs, has an unheated office and no phone or money to effect policies in Afghanistan that would improve the situation for women. There is no way that we can achieve international justice without a radical redistribution of goods and resources from rich to poor to eliminate hunger and desperation around the world.[25] The United States needs to be a champion of this redistribution if it is to be perceived correctly as measuring up to the standard of international justice, and thus to be a just nation, whose resources and people should be respected. But the United States has not done this. In fact, its contribution to alleviate world hunger is (in proportion to its size) one of the smallest among the industrialized nations of the world—roughly .11 percent, which President Bush proposes to increase to .13 percent; Britain's contribution is about three times as much, and Sweden, the Netherlands, and Norway proportionately give about eight times as much.[26]

Clearly, then, there is much that the United States can do if it wants to respond to the terrorist attacks of 9/11 in a way that accords with international justice. I have argued that the best account of pacifism and the best account of just war theory combined in just war pacifism requires that, as soon as possible, the United States put an end to its military response, that the U.S. make it clear that it is taking radical steps to correct for related terrorist acts of its own or of those countries it supports; and that it give nonbelligerent correctives a reasonable chance to work. I have further argued that the United States has to do more to be a good world citizen. It must stop being a conspicuous holdout with respect to international treaties, and it must do its fair share to redistribute resources from the rich to the poor as international justice requires. Only then would the United States be living up to the moral ideals that could make it what it claims to be. In turn, living up to those ideals may prove to be the best defense the United States has against terrorism directed against its own people.

NOTES

1. *Patterns of Global Terrorism—2000*. Released by the Office of the Coordinator for Counterterrorism, April 2001.

2. *Patterns of Global Terrorism—2000*.

3. If we use the just war distinction between combatants and noncombatants, those killed at the Pentagon might be viewed as combatants in some undeclared war.

4. Since the bombings in Kenya and Tanzania were of U.S. government installations, they are only classified as terrorist acts by virtue of the fact that they were intended to maximize civilian casualties.

5. From an interview with Phyllis Bennis, *Z magazine*, September 12, 2001. While the bombing of the pharmaceutical plant may have involved unintentional harm to innocents, refusing to compensate the thousands of victims who were deprived of the drugs they needed is to intentionally harm innocents.

6. Jan Narveson, "Pacifism: A Philosophical Analysis," *Ethics* 75 (1965): 259–271.

7. We can understand "violence" here and throughout the paper as "the prima facie unjustified use of force."

8. Cheyney Ryan, "Self-Defense, Pacifism and the Possibility of Killing," in *The Ethics of War and Nuclear Deterrence*, ed. James P. Sterba (Belmont, CA: Wadsworth Publishing Co., 1985), pp. 45–49.

9. M. K. Gandhi, "The Doctrine of the Sword," in *Nonviolent Resistance* (New York: Schocken Books, 1961), p. 132.

10. Paradoxically, this has been true even as weapons have become more and more precise because now that weapons are more precise, even more targets are selected, and the increased destruction therefrom leads to more civilian deaths, sometimes after open hostilities have ceased. For example, if you knock out a country's water purification facilities, as in Iraq, and then don't let the people in that country import the purification chemicals (or the materials to produce such chemicals) to restore its water purification facilities (because of the possibility of dual use), you can kill lots of noncombatants without directly targeting them with your precision weapons.

11. This is because the requirements of just war pacifism, as I stated them earlier in this article, do not directly address the question of whether there are exceptions to the prohibition on intentionally harming innocents.

12. James Byrnes, *Speaking Frankly* (New York: Harper Row, 1947), p. 264.

13. Winston Churchill, *Triumph and Tragedy* (New York: Houghton Mifflin, 1962), p. 639.

14. Another way to put this is to claim that a right not to have to unconditionally surrender is one of our basic universal human rights.

15. There is a further requirement that must be met here. It is that the Palestinians must have exhausted nonbelligerent correctives. The evidence that this is the case can, I believe, be found in the numerous Palestinian peace initiatives, especially from the early 1970s on when the Palestinians had acquired political standing in the international community. In 1976 the United States vetoed a UN Security Council Resolution calling for a settlement on the 1967 borders, with "appropriate arrangements . . . to guarantee . . . the sovereignty, territorial integrity and political independence of all states in the area and their right to live in peace within secure and recognized boundaries," including Israel and a new Palestinian state in the occupied territories. The resolution was backed by Egypt, Syria, Jordan, the PLO, and the USSR. Israel has rejected every peace plan put forward by the Arabs and the United States except for the bilateral treaty with Egypt and the Oslo Peace Accords, and these Accords have not been, in effect, abandoned by the current Israeli government.

16. Nor will it do to distinguish British terror bombing from Palestinian suicide bombing on the grounds that the Nazis represented an unprecedented evil in human history because at the early stage of World War II, the British could not have know the full character of the Nazi regime.

17. Some will contest whether this correctly represents Israeli intentions. But even in its best offer at Camp David, Israel proposed dividing Palestine into four separate cantons: the Northern West Bank, the Central West Bank, the Southern West Bank, and Gaza. Going from any one area to another would require crossing Israeli sovereign territory and consequently subject movements of Palestinians within their own country to Israeli control. Restrictions would also apply to the movements of goods, thus subjecting the Palestinian

economy to Israeli control. In addition, the Camp David proposal would have left Israel in control of all Palestinian borders, thereby giving Israel control not only of the internal movement of people and goods but international movement as well. Such a Palestinian state would have had less sovereignty and viability than the Bantustans created by the South African apartheid government, which both Israel and the United States once supported. The Camp David proposal also required Palestinians to give up any claim to the occupied portion of Jerusalem. The proposal would have forced recognition of Israel's annexation of all of Arab East Jerusalem. Talks after Camp David in Egypt suggested that Israel was prepared to allow Palestinian sovereignty over isolated Palestinian neighborhoods in the heart of East Jerusalem. However, these neighborhoods would have remained surrounded by Israeli colonies and separated not only from each other but also from the rest of the Palestinian State. Although Yassir Arafat and the Palestinians were roundly condemned in the U.S. media for rejecting the Camp David offer, to my knowledge no maps of the U.S.-Israeli proposal, which would have undercut the claim that it was a reasonable offer, were published in the United States, although they were widely published elsewhere.

18. Al Qaeda have shown themselves capable of inflicting significant damage on both military (the *U.S.S. Cole*) and diplomatic targets (the U.S. embassies in Kenya and Tanzania). So their opposition to the United States could have continued in just this fashion. Moreover, the attack on the Pentagon differs morally from the attack on the World Trade Center, although the deaths of innocent airline hostages is objectionable in both cases. So Al Qaeda could still have effectively waged its war against the United States without attacking the World Trade Center. With respect to the possibility of effectively attacking military or government targets, Al Qaeda is much better situated vis-à-vis the United States and its allies than the Palestinians are vis-à-vis Israel. This is because Al Qaeda can target the far-flung military and government outposts of the United States all around the world, and through such attacks it has effectively brought the United States and its allies to withdraw their military forces from such places as Somalia, Yemen, and even, in terms of effective use, from Saudi Arabia.

19. Of course, it might be questioned whether Al Qaeda effectively exhausted nonbelligerent corrections before it resorted to belligerent ones. If we take Al Qaeda's grounds for just cause to be U.S. support for the Israeli occupation, the U.S. stance against Iraq, U.S. bases in Saudi Arabia, and U.S. support for repressive governments in the Middle East,

then I think we can say that in each case Al Qaeda gave nonbelligerent correctives some chance to work.

20. It is worth noting that the U.S. State Department had been negotiating with the Taliban for handing over bin Laden before 9/11. One Taliban proposal suggested that bin Laden be turned over to a panel of three Islamic jurists, one chosen by Afghanistan, Saudi Arabia, and the United States. When the United States rejected that proposal, the Taliban countered that it would settle for only one Islamic jurist on such a panel. Although the negotiations went on for some time, the United States rigidly held to the position that bin Laden had to be turned over for trial in the United States, and some say the United States thereby missed a chance before 9/11 to get bin Laden before an international court of law. Possibly the United States never believed that the Taliban could deliver on their promises, but why then did it keep negotiating with them for so long?

21. Of course, in theory, one could know or reasonably believe that nonbelligerent correctives are ineffectual or too costly without actually having exhausted them. But, in the cases under discussion, there is no way that one could do this with respect to the particular nonbelligerent correctives under consideration without actually having exhausted them. In addition, making impossible demands in response to an attack and using military means when those demands are not met is just another way not to exhaust nonbelligerent correctives.

22. The reason why the United States must do all these things if it is to justly respond to the related wrongdoing of bin Laden and his followers is that these actions are part of the nonbelligerent correctives that must be employed before the use of belligerent correctives can be justified.

23. "Life and Death in Iraq," *Seattle-Post-Intelligencer*, May 11, 1999. See also Jeff Indemyer, "Iraqi Sanctions: Myth and Fact," *Swans Commentary*, September 3, 2002.

24. The reason that this conclusion follows from an international justice perspective is that it is impossible to imagine how it could be the case that all other nations of the world ought to regard as morally acceptable the self-serving U.S. stance on the Kyoto climate-change treaty.

25. It is sometimes argued that addressing the unjust distribution of resources and meeting the basic needs of people around the world will do little to eliminate terrorism because those who engage in terror are not usually poor people. But while it is probably true that most terrorists are not themselves poor, many of them appear to be motivated by the plight of the poor or by what they perceive

to be other gross injustices, even when they themselves have the means of escaping the harmful effects of those injustices (e.g., Osama bin Laden). So if we intend to rid the world of terrorism in a morally justifiably way, we definitely need to address these questions of international justice. They are part of a nonbelligerent way of ridding ourselves of the threat of terrorism.

26. It might be objected that while Americans are relatively stingy in the foreign aid provided by their government they make up for it with private and corporate largess. But even when U.S. private and corporate giving is taken into account, the United States still gives privately and publicly only half as much as Sweden, Netherlands, and Norway give publicly. The percentage shrinks to only one-quarter as much if we remove the $18 billion that immigrants in the U.S. send to relatives back home, which probably shouldn't be counted as it is not that similar to giving foreign aid to needy people around the world.

Can Terrorism Be Morally Justified?

Stephen Nathanson

Can terrorism be morally justified?

Even asking this question can seem like an insult—both to victims of terrorist actions and to moral common sense. One wants to say: if the murder of innocent people by terrorists is not clearly wrong, what is?

But the question is more complicated than it looks. We can see this by broadening our focus and considering some of the other beliefs held by people who condemn terrorism. Very few of us accept the pacifist view that all violence is wrong. Most of us believe that some acts of killing and injuring people are morally justified. Indeed, most of us think that war is sometimes justified, even though it involves organized, large-scale killing, injuring, and destruction and even though innocent civilians are usually among the victims of war. So, most of us believe that even the killing of innocent people is sometimes morally justified. It is this fact that makes the condemnation of terrorism morally problematic. We pick out terrorism for special condemnation because its victims are civilian, noncombatants rather than military or governmental officials, but we also believe that such killings are sometimes morally permissible.

Seen in a broader context, moral judgments of terrorism often seen hypocritical. They often presuppose self-serving definitions of "terrorism" that allow people to avoid labeling actions that they approve as instances of terrorism, even though these actions are indistinguishable from other acts that are branded with this negative label. On other occasions, moral judgments of terrorism rest on biased, uneven applications of moral principles to the actions of friends and foes. Principles that are cited to condemn the actions of foes are ignored when similar actions are committed by friends.

We need to ask then: Can people who believe that war is sometimes morally permissible consistently condemn terrorist violence? Or are such condemnations necessarily hypocritical and self-serving?

If we are to avoid hypocrisy, then we need both (a) a definition of terrorism that is neutral with respect to who commits the actions, and (b) moral judgments of terrorism that derive from the consistent, even-handed applications of moral criteria.

This paper aims to achieve both of these things. First, I begin with a definition of terrorism and then discuss why terrorism is always wrong. In addition, I want to show that the condemnation of terrorism does not come without other costs. A consistent approach to terrorism requires us to revise some common judgments about historical events and forces us

Stephen Nathanson, "Can Terrorism Be Morally Justified?" in *Morality in Practice*, ed. James P. Sterba, 7th ed. (Belmont, CA: Wadsworth/Thomson, 2004), 602–10 (edited). Reprinted with permission from Stephen Nathanson.

to reconsider actions in which civilians are killed as "collateral damage" (i.e., side effects) of military attacks.

My aim, then, is to criticize both terrorist actions and a cluster of widespread moral views about violence and war. This cluster includes the following beliefs:

1. Terrorism is always immoral.
2. The allied bombing of cities in World War II was morally justified because of the importance of defeating Nazi Germany and Japan.
3. It is morally permissible to kill civilians in war if these killings are not intended.

The trouble with this cluster is that the first belief expresses an absolute prohibition of acts that kill innocent people while the last two are rather permissive. If we are to avoid inconsistency and hypocrisy, we must revise our views either (a) by accepting that terrorism is sometimes morally permissible, or (b) by judging that city bombings and many collateral damage killings are morally wrong. I will defend the second of these options.

DEFINING TERRORISM

I offer the following definition of terrorism to launch my discussion of the moral issues. Terrorist acts have the following features:

1. They are acts of serious, deliberate violence or destruction.
2. They are generally committed by groups as part of a campaign to promote a political or social agenda.
3. They generally target limited numbers of people but aim to influence a larger group and/or the leaders who make decisions for the group.
4. They either kill or injure innocent people or pose a serious threat of such harms to them.

This definition helps in a number of ways. First, it helps us to distinguish acts of terrorism from other acts of violence. Nonviolent acts are not terrorist acts; nor are violent actions that are unrelated to a political or social agenda. Ironically, some terrible kinds

of actions are not terrorist because they are too destructive. As condition 3 tells us, terrorism generally targets limited numbers of people in order to influence a larger group. Acts of genocide that aim to destroy a whole group are not acts of terrorism, but the reason why makes them only worse, not better.

Second, the definition helps us to identify the moral crux of the problem with terrorism. Condition 1 is not the problem because most of us believe that some acts of violence are morally justified. Condition 2 can't be the problem because anyone who believes in just causes of war must accept that some causes are so important that violence may be a legitimate way to promote them. Condition 3 is frequently met by permissible actions, as when we punish some criminals to deter other people from committing crimes. Condition 4 seems closer to what is essentially wrong with terrorism. If terrorism is always immoral, it is because it kills and injures innocent people.

As I have already noted, however, morally conscientious people sometimes want to justify acts that kill innocent people. If a blanket condemnation of terrorism is to be sustained, then we must either condemn all killings of innocent people, or we must find morally relevant differences between the killing of innocents by terrorists and the killing of innocents by others whose actions we find morally acceptable.

TERRORISM AND CITY BOMBING: THE SAME OR DIFFERENT?

Many people who condemn terrorism believe that city bombing in the war against Nazism was justified, even though the World War II bombing campaigns intentionally targeted cities and their inhabitants. This view is defended by some philosophical theorists, including Michael Walzer, in his book *Just and Unjust Wars,* and G. Wallace in "Terrorism and the Argument from Analogy."[1] By considering these theorists, we can see if there are relevant differences that allow us to say that terrorism is always wrong but that the World War II bombings were morally justified.

One of the central aims of Michael Walzer's *Just and Unjust Wars* is to defend what he calls the "war convention," the principles that prohibit attacks on civilians in wartime. Walzer strongly affirms the principle of noncombatant immunity, calling it a "fundamental principle [that] underlies and shapes the judgments we make of wartime conduct." He writes:

A legitimate act of war is one that does not violate the rights of the people against whom it is directed. . . . [N]o one can be threatened with war or warred against, unless through some act of his own he has surrendered or lost his rights.[2]

Unlike members of the military, civilians have not surrendered their rights in any way, and therefore, Walzer says, they may not be attacked.

Given Walzer's strong support for noncombatant immunity and his definition of terrorism as the "method of random murder of innocent people," it is no surprise that he condemns terrorism. At one point, after describing a terrorist attack on an Algerian milk bar frequented by teenagers, he writes:

Certainly, there are historical moments when armed struggle is necessary for the sake of human freedom. But if dignity and self-respect are to be the outcomes of that struggle, it cannot consist of terrorist attacks against children.[3]

Here and elsewhere, Walzer denounces terrorism because it targets innocent people.

Nonetheless, he claims that the aerial attacks on civilians by the British early in World War II were justified. In order to show why, he develops the concept of a "supreme emergency." Nazi Germany, he tells us, was no ordinary enemy; it was an "ultimate threat to everything decent in our lives."[4] Moreover, in 1940, the Nazi threat to Britain was imminent. German armies dominated Europe and sought to control the seas. Britain feared an imminent invasion by a country that threatened the basic values of civilization.

According to Walzer, the combination of the enormity and the imminence of the threat posed by Nazi Germany produced a supreme emergency, a situation in which the rules prohibiting attacks on civilians no longer held. If killing innocents was the only way to ward off this dreadful threat, then it was permissible. Since air attacks on German cities were the only means Britain had for inflicting harm on Germany, it was morally permissible for them to launch these attacks.

Walzer does not approve all of the city bombing that occurred in World War II. The emergency lasted, he thinks, only through 1942. After that, the threat diminished, and the constraints of the war convention should once again have been honored. In fact, the bombing of cities continued throughout the war, climaxing in massive attacks that killed hundreds of thousands of civilians: the bombing of Dresden, the fire bombings of Japanese cities by the United States, and the atomic bombings of Hiroshima and Nagasaki. According to Walzer, none of these later attacks were justified because the supreme emergency had passed.

While Walzer's discussion begins with the special threat posed by Nazism, he believes that supreme emergencies can exist in more ordinary situations. In the end, he supports the view that if a single nation is faced by "a threat of enslavement or extermination[,]" then its "soldiers and statesmen [may] override the rights of innocent people for the sake of their own political community. . . ."[5] While he expresses this view with "hesitation and worry," he nevertheless broadens the reach of the concept of "supreme emergency" to include circumstances that arise in many wars.

The problem for Walzer is that his acceptance of the broad "supreme emergency" exception threatens to completely undermine the principle of noncombatant immunity that lies at the heart of his own view of the ethics of warfare. How can the principle of noncombatant immunity be fundamental if it can be overridden in some cases? Moreover, his condemnation of terrorism is weakened because it seems to be possible that people might resort to terrorism in cases that qualify as supreme emergencies, as when their own people are threatened by extermination or enslavement. Walzer's defense of the bombing of cities, then, seems to be inconsistent with his sweeping denunciation of terrorism.

WALLACE'S ARGUMENT FROM ANALOGY

While Walzer does not directly address the tension between the two parts of his view, G. Wallace explicitly tries to defend the view that terrorism is wrong and that the bombing of cities was justified. According to Wallace, the bombing campaign was justified because it satisfied all four of the following criteria:

1. It was a measure of last resort.
2. It was an act of collective self-defense.
3. It was a reply in kind against a genocidal, racist aggressor.
4. It had some chances of success.

He then asks whether acts of terrorism might be justified by appeal to these very same criteria.

Wallace's answer is that the [acts of] terrorism cannot meet these criteria. Or, more specifically, he says that while any one of the criteria might be met by a terrorist act, all four of them cannot be satisfied. Why not? The problem is not with criteria 2 and 3; a community might well be oppressed by a brutal regime and might well be acting in its own defense. In these respects, its situation would be like that of Britain in 1940.

But, Wallace claims, conditions 1 and 4 cannot both be satisfied in this case. If the community has a good chance of success through the use of terrorism (thus satisfying condition 4), then other means of opposition might work as well, and terrorism will fail to be a last resort. Hence it will not meet condition 1. At the same time, if terrorist tactics are a last resort because all other means of opposition will fail, then the terrorist tactics are also likely to fail, in which case condition 4 is not met.

What Wallace has tried to show is that there are morally relevant differences between terrorism and the city bombings by Britain. Even if some of the criteria for justified attacks on civilians can be met by would be terrorists, all of them cannot be. He concludes that "[E]ven if we allow that conditions (1) and (4) can be met separately, their joint satisfaction is impossible."[6]

Unfortunately, this comforting conclusion—that the British city bombing was justified but that ter-

rorism cannot be—is extremely implausible. Both terrorism and city bombing involve the intentional killing of innocent human beings in order to promote an important political goal. Wallace acknowledges this but claims that the set of circumstances that justified city bombing could not possibly occur again so as to justify terrorism.

There is no basis for this claim, however. Wallace accepts that the right circumstances occurred in the past, and so he should acknowledge that it is at least possible for them to occur in the future. His conclusion ought to be that if city bombing was justifiable, then terrorism is in principle justifiable as well. For these reasons, I believe that Wallace, like Walzer, is logically committed to acknowledging the possibility of morally justified terrorism.

This is not a problem simply for these two authors. Since the historical memory of city bombing in the United States and Britain sees these as justifiable means of war, the dilemma facing these authors faces our own society. We condemn terrorists for intentionally killing innocent people while we think it was right to use tactics in our own wars that did the same. Either we must accept the view that terrorism can sometimes be justified, or we must come to see our own bombings of cities as violations of the prohibitions on killing civilians in wartime.

TERRORISM, COLLATERAL DAMAGE, AND THE PRINCIPLE OF DOUBLE EFFECT

Many of us believe that wars are sometimes justified, but we also know that even if civilians are not intentionally killed, the deaths of civilians is a common feature of warfare. Indeed, during the twentieth century, civilian deaths became a larger and larger proportion of the total deaths caused by war. A person who believes that wars may be justified but that terrorism cannot be must explain how this can be.

One common approach focuses on the difference between intentionally killing civilians, as terrorists do, and unintentionally killing civilians, as sometimes happens in what we regard as legitimate acts of war. According to this approach, terrorism is wrong because it is intentional while so-called "collateral damage" killings and injuries are morally permissible because they are not intended.

This type of view is developed by Igor Primoratz in "The Morality of Terrorism."[7] Primoratz attempts to show why terrorism is morally wrong and how it differs from other acts of wartime killing that are morally permissible.

First, he makes it clear that, by definition, terrorism always involves the intentional killing of innocent people. He then offers a number of arguments to show why such killings are wrong. The first two have to do with the idea that persons are moral agents who are due a high level of respect and concern. He writes:

[E]very human being is an individual, a person separate from other persons, with a unique, irreproducible thread of life and a value that is not commensurate with anything else.[8]

Given the incommensurable value of individual persons, it is wrong to try to calculate the worth of some hoped-for-goal by comparison with the lives and deaths of individual people. This kind of calculation violates the ideal of giving individual lives our utmost respect and concern. Terrorists ignore this central moral ideal. They treat innocent people as political pawns, ignoring their individual worth and seeing their deaths simply as means toward achieving their goals.

In addition, Primoratz argues, terrorists ignore the moral relevance of guilt and innocence in their treatment of individuals. They attack people who have no responsibility for the alleged evils that the terrorists oppose and thus violate the principle that people should be treated in accord with what they deserve.

Terrorists, Pirmoratz tells us, also forsake the ideal of moral dialogue amongst equals. They not only decide who will live and who will die, but they feel no burden to justify their actions in ways that the victims might understand and accept. People who take moral ideas seriously engage in open discussion in order to justify their actions. They engage others in moral debate. Ideally, according to Primoratz, a moral person who harms others should try to act on reasons that are so compelling that they could be acknowledged by their victims. Terrorist acts cannot be justified to their victims, and terrorists are not even interested in trying to do so.

Though these ideas are sketched out rather than fully developed, Primoratz successfully expresses some important moral values. Drawing on these values, he concludes that terrorism is incompatible with "some of the most basic moral beliefs many of us hold."[9]

Primoratz vs. Trotsky

Having tried to show why terrorism is wrong, Primoratz considers an objection put forward by Leon Trotsky, who defended terrorism as a revolutionary tactic. Trotsky claims that people who approve traditional war but condemn revolutionary violence are in a weak position because the differences between these are morally arbitrary. If wars that kill innocent people can be justified, Trotsky claims, then so can revolutions that kill innocent people.

Primoratz replies by arguing that there is an important moral difference between terrorism and some acts of war that kill innocent people. While he acknowledges that the "suffering of civilians . . . is surely inevitable not only in modern, but in almost all wars," Primoratz stresses that the moral evaluation of acts of killing requires that we "attend not only to the suffering inflicted, but also to the way it is inflicted."[10] By this, he means that we need, among other things, to see what the person who did the act intended.

To illustrate his point, he contrasts two cases of artillery attacks on a village. In the first case, the artillery attack is launched with the explicit goal of killing the civilian inhabitants of the village. The civilians are the target of the attack. This attack is the equivalent of terrorism since both intentionally target innocent people, and just like terrorism, it is immoral.

In a second case, the artillery attack is aimed at "soldiers stationed in the village." While the soldiers know that innocent people will be killed, that is not their aim.

Had it been possible to attack the enemy unit without endangering the civilians in any way, they would certainly have done so. This was not possible, so they attacked although they knew that the attack would cause civilian casualties too; but they did their best to reduce those inevitable, but undesired consequences as much as possible.[11]

In this second case, the civilian deaths and injuries are collateral damage produced by an attack on a legitimate military target. That is the key difference between terrorism and legitimate acts of war. Terrorism is intentionally directed at civilians, while legitimate acts of war do not aim to kill or injure civilians, even when this is their effect.

Primoratz concludes that Trotsky and other defenders of terrorism are wrong when they equate war and terrorism. No doubt, the intentional killing of civilians does occur in war, and when it does Primoratz would condemn it for the same reason he condemns terrorism. But if soldiers avoid the intentional killing of civilians, then their actions can be morally justified, even when civilians die as a result of what they do. As long as soldiers and revolutionaries avoid the intentional killing of innocent people, they will not be guilty of terrorist acts.

Problems with Primoratz's View

Primoratz's view has several attractive features. Nonetheless, it has serious weaknesses.

In stressing the role of intentions, Primoratz appeals to the same ideas expressed by what is called the "principle of double effect." According to this principle, we should evaluate actions by their intended goals rather than their actual consequences. An act that produces collateral damage deaths is an unintentional killing and hence is not wrong in the way that the same act would be if the civilians' deaths were intended.

While the principle of double effects is plausible in some cases, it is actually severely defective. To see this, suppose that the September 11 attackers had only intended to destroy the Pentagon and the World Trade Center and had no desire to kill anyone. Sup-

pose that they knew, however, that thousands would die in the attack on the buildings. And suppose, following the attack, they said "We are not murderers. We did not mean to kill these people."

What would be our reaction? I very much doubt that we would think them less culpable. They could not successfully justify or excuse their actions by saying that although they foresaw the deaths of many people, these deaths were not part of their aim. We would certainly reject this defense. But if we would reject the appeal to double effect in this case, then we should do so in others.

In Primoratz's example, the artillery gunners attack the village with full knowledge of the high probability of civilian deaths. The artillery gunners know they will kill innocent people, perhaps even in large numbers, and they go ahead with the attack anyway. If it would not be enough for my imagined September 11 attackers to say that they did not intend to kill people, then it is not enough for Primoratz's imagined soldiers to say that they did not mean to kill the villagers when they knew full well that this would result from their actions.

If we accept Primoratz's defense of collateral damage killings, his argument against terrorism is in danger of collapsing because terrorists can use Primoratz's language to show that their actions, too, may be justifiable. If Primoratz succeeds in justifying the collateral damage killings and if the distinction between these killings and terrorism cannot rest solely on whether the killings are intentional, then the criteria that he uses may justify at least some terrorist acts. Like the soldiers in his example, the terrorists may believe that the need for a particular attack is "so strong and urgent that it prevailed over the prohibition of killing or maiming a comparatively small number of civilians." Consistency would require Primoratz to agree that the terrorist act was justified in this case.

Recall, too, Primoratz's claim that actions need to be capable of being justified to the victims themselves. Would the victims of the artillery attack accept the claim that the military urgency justified the "killing or maiming a comparatively small number of civilians.?"[12] Why should they accept the sacrifice of their own lives on the basis of this reasoning?

In the end, then, Primoratz does not succeed in showing why terrorism is immoral while collateral damage killing can be morally justified. Like Wallace and Walzer, he has trouble squaring the principles that he uses to condemn terrorism with his own approval of attacks that produce foreseeable collateral damage deaths.

The problem revealed here is not merely a problem for a particular author. The view that collateral damage killings are permissible because they are unintended is a very widespread view. It is the view that United States officials appealed to when our bombings in Afghanistan produced thousands of civilian casualties. Our government asserted that we did not intend these deaths to occur, that we were aiming at legitimate targets, and that the civilian deaths were merely collateral damage. Similar excuses are offered when civilians are killed by cluster bombs and land mines, weapons whose delayed detonations injure and kill people indiscriminately, often long after a particular attack is over.

There are many cases in which people are morally responsible for harms that they do not intend to bring about, but if these harms can be foreseen, their claims that they "did not mean to do it" are not taken seriously. We use labels like "reckless disregard" for human life or "gross negligence" to signify that wrongs have been done, even though they were not deliberate. When such actions lead to serious injury and death, we condemn such actions from a moral point of view, just as we condemn terrorism. The principle of double effect does not show that these condemnations are mistaken. If we want to differentiate collateral damage killings from terrorism so as to be consistent in our moral judgments, we will need something better than the principle of double effect and the distinction between intended and unintended effects.

A SKETCH OF A DEFENSE

I want to conclude by sketching a better rationale for the view that terrorist attacks on civilians are always

wrong but that some attacks that cause civilian deaths and injuries as unintended consequences are morally justified.

I have argued that a central problem with standard defenses of collateral damage killings is that they lean too heavily on the distinction between what is intended and what is foreseen. This distinction, when used with the doctrine of double effect, is too slippery and too permissive. As I noted above, it might provide an excuse for the September 11 attacks if (contrary to fact) the attacks were only targeting the World Trade Center *building* and the Pentagon *building* and did not actually aim to kill innocent civilians.

Michael Walzer makes a similar criticism of the double effect principle. Simply not to intend the death of civilians is too easy," he writes. "What we look for in such cases is some sign of a positive commitment to save civilian lives."[13] Walzer calls his revised version the principle of "double intention." It requires military planners and soldiers to take positive steps to avoid or minimize these evils, even if these precautions increase the danger to military forces.

Walzer's rule is a step in the right direction, but we need to emphasize that the positive steps must be significant. They cannot be *pro forma* or minimal efforts. In order to show a proper respect for the victims of these attacks, serious efforts must be made to avoid death and injury to them. I suggest the following set of requirements for just, discriminate fighting, offering them as a sketch rather than a full account. The specifics might have to be amended, but the key point is that serious efforts must be made to avoid harm to civilians. Not intending harm is not enough. In addition, military planners must really exert themselves. They must, as we say, *bend over backwards* to avoid harm to civilians. For example, they must:

1. Target attacks as narrowly as possible on military resources;
2. Avoid targets where civilian deaths are extremely likely;
3. Avoid the use of inherently indiscriminate weapons (such as land mines and cluster bombs) and

inherently indiscriminate strategies (such as high-altitude bombing of areas containing both civilian enclaves and military targets); and

4. Accept that when there are choices between damage to civilian lives and damage to military personnel, priority should be given to saving civilian lives.

If a group has a just cause for being at war and adheres to principles like these, then it could be said to be acknowledging the humanity and value of those who are harmed by its actions. While its attacks might expose innocent people to danger, its adherence to these principles would show that it was not indifferent to their well-being. In this way, it would show that its actions lack the features that make terrorism morally objectionable.

Why is this? Because the group is combining its legitimate effort to defend itself or others with serious efforts to avoid civilian casualties. The spirit of their effort is captured in the phrase I have already used: "bending over backwards." The "bend over backwards" ideal is superior to the principle of double effect in many ways. First, it goes beyond the weak rule of merely requiring that one not intend to kill civilians. Second, while the double effect rule's distinction between intended and unintended results permits all sorts of fudges and verbal tricks, the "bend over backwards" rule can be applied in a more objective and realistic way. It would be less likely to approve sham compliance than is the doctrine of double effect.

The "bend over backwards" rule might even satisfy Primoratz's requirement that acts of violence be justifiable to their victims. Of course, no actual victim is likely to look favorably on attacks by others that will result in the victim's death or serious injury. But suppose we could present the following situation to people who might be victims of an attack (a condition that most of us inhabit) and have them consider it from something like Rawls's veil of ignorance. We would ask them to consider the following situation:

- Group A is facing an attack by group B; if successful, the attack will lead to death or the severest oppression of group A.

- The only way that group A can defend itself is by using means that will cause death and injury to innocent members of group B.

- You are a member of one of the groups, but you do not know which one.

Would you approve of means of self-defense that will kill and injure innocent members of B in order to defend group A?

In this situation, people would not know whether they would be victims or beneficiaries of whatever policy is adopted. In this circumstance, I believe that they would reject a rule permitting either intentional or indiscriminate attacks on civilians. Thus, they would reject terrorism as a legitimate tactic, just as they would reject indiscriminate attacks that kill and injure civilians.

At the same time, I believe that they would approve a rule that combined a right of countries to defend themselves against aggression with the restrictions on means of fighting contained in the "bend over backwards" rule. This would have the following benefits. If one were a member of a group that had been attacked, one's group would have a right of self-defense. At the same time, if one were an innocent citizen in the aggressor country, the defenders would be required to take serious steps to avoid injury or death to you and other civilians.

If people generally could accept such a rule, then actions that adhere to that rule would be justifiable to potential victims as well as potential attackers. This would include actions that cause civilian casualties but that adhere to the "bend over backwards" principle.

I believe that this sort of approach achieves what nonpacifist critics of terrorism want to achieve. I provide a principled basis for condemning terrorism, no matter who it is carried out by, and a principled justification of warfare that is genuinely defensive. Moreover, the perspective is unified in a desirable way. Terrorist actions cannot be morally justified because the *intentional* targeting of civilians is the most obvious kind of violation of the "bend over backwards" rule.

At the same time that these principles allow for the condemnation of terrorism, they are immune to charges of hypocrisy because they provide a basis for criticizing not only terrorist acts but also the acts of any group that violates the "bend over backwards" rule, either by attacking civilians directly or by failing to take steps to avoid civilian deaths.

CONCLUSION

Can terrorism be morally justified? Of course not. But if condemnations of terrorism are to have moral credibility, they must rest on principles that constrain our own actions and determine our judgments of what we ourselves do and have done. To have moral credibility, opponents of terrorism must stand by the principles underlying their condemnations, apply their principles in an evenhanded way, and bend over backwards to avoid unintended harms to civilians. Only in this way can we begin inching back to a world in which those at war honor the moral rules that prohibit the taking of innocent human lives. As long as condemnations of terrorism are tainted by hypocrisy, moral judgments will only serve to inflame people's hostilities rather than reminding them to limit and avoid serious harms to one another.

NOTES

1. Michael Walzer, *Just and Unjust Wars* (New York: Basic Books, 1977); Gerry Wallace, "Terrorism and the Argument from Analogy," *Journal of Moral and Social Studies,* vol. 6 (1991), 149–160.

2. Walzer, 135.

3. Walzer, 205.

4. Walzer, 253.

5. Walzer, 254.

6. Wallace, 155–156.

7. Igor Primoratz, "The Morality of Terrorism?" *Journal of Applied Philosophy,* vol. 14 (1997), 222.

8. Primoratz, 224.

9. Primoratz, 225.

10. Primoratz, 227.

11. Primoratz, 227.

12. Primoratz, 228.

13. Walzer, 155–156.

The War on Terrorism and the End of Human Rights

DAVID LUBAN

In the immediate aftermath of September 11, President Bush stated that the perpetrators of the deed would be brought to justice. Soon afterwards, the President announced that the United States would engage in a war on terrorism. The first of these statements adopts the familiar language of criminal law and criminal justice. It treats the September 11 attacks as horrific crimes—mass murders—and the government's mission as apprehending and punishing the surviving planners and conspirators for their roles in the crimes. The War on Terrorism is a different proposition, however, and a different model of governmental action—not law but war. Most obviously, it dramatically broadens the scope of action, because now terrorists who knew nothing about September 11 have been earmarked as enemies. But that is only the beginning.

THE HYBRID WAR-LAW APPROACH

The model of war offers much freer rein than that of law, and therein lies its appeal in the wake of 9/11.

David Luban, "The War on Terrorism and the End of Human Rights," in *War after September 11,* ed. Verna V. Gehring (Lanham, MD: Rowman & Littlefield, 2003), 51–62 (edited). Reprinted with permission of Rowman & Littlefield Publishers, Inc.

First, in war but not in law it is permissible to us lethal force on enemy troops regardless of their degree of personal involvement with the adversary. The conscripted cook is as legitimate a target as the enemy general. Second, in war but not in law "collateral damage," that is, foreseen but unintended killing of noncombatants, is permissible. (Police cannot blow up an apartment building full of people because a murderer is inside, but an air force can bomb the building if it contains a military target.) Third, the requirements of evidence and proof are drastically weaker in war than in criminal justice. Soldiers do not need proof beyond a reasonable doubt, or even proof by a preponderance of evidence, that someone is an enemy soldier before firing on him or capturing and imprisoning him. They don't need proof at all, merely plausible intelligence. Thus, the US military remains regretful but unapologetic about its January 2002 attack on the Afghani town of Uruzgan, in which twenty-one innocent civilians were killed, based on faulty intelligence that they were al Qaeda fighters. Fourth, in war one can attack an enemy without concern over whether he has done anything. Legitimate targets are those who in the course of combat *might* harm us, not those who *have* harmed us. No doubt there are other significant differences as well. But the basic point should be clear: given Washington's mandate to eliminate the danger of future 9/11s, so far as humanly possible, the model of war offers important advantages over the model of law.

There are disadvantages as well. Most obviously, in war but not in law, fighting back is a *legitimate* response of the enemy. Second, when nations fight a war, other nations may opt for neutrality. Third, because fighting back is legitimate, in war the enemy soldier deserves special regard once he is rendered harmless through injury or surrender. It is impermissible to punish him for his role in fighting the war. Nor can he be harshly interrogated after he is captured. The Third Geneva Convention provides: "Prisoners of war who refuse to answer [questions] may not be threatened, insulted, or exposed to unpleasant or disadvantageous treatment of any

kind." And, when the war concludes, the enemy soldier must be repatriated.

Here, however, Washington has different ideas, designed to eliminate these tactical disadvantages in the traditional war model. Washington regards international terrorism not only as a military adversary, but also as a criminal activity and criminal conspiracy. In the law model, criminals don't get to shoot back, and their acts of violence subject them to legitimate punishment. That is what we see in Washington's prosecution of the War on Terrorism. Captured terrorists may be tried before military or civilian tribunals, and shooting back at Americans, including American troops, is a federal crime (for a statute under which John Walker Lindh was indicted criminalizes anyone regardless of nationality, who "outside the United States attempts to kill, or engages in a conspiracy to kill, a national of the United States" or "engages in physical violence with intent to cause serious bodily injury to a national of the United States; or with the result that serious bodily injury is caused to a national of the United States"). Furthermore, the US may rightly demand that other countries not be neutral about murder and terrorism. Unlike the war model, a nation may insist that those who are not with us in fighting murder and terror are against us, because by not joining our operations they are providing a safe haven for terrorists or their bank accounts. By selectively combining elements of the war model and elements of the law model, Washington is able to maximize its own ability to mobilize lethal force against terrorists while eliminating most traditional rights of a military adversary, as well as the rights of innocent bystanders caught in the crossfire.

A LIMBO OF RIGHTLESSNESS

The legal status of al Qaeda suspects imprisoned at the Guantanamo Bay Naval Base in Cuba is emblematic of this hybrid war-law approach to the threat of terrorism. In line with the war model, they lack the usual rights of criminal suspects—the presumption of innocence, the right to a hearing to determine guilt, the opportunity to prove that the authorities have grabbed the wrong man. But, in line with the law model, they are considered *unlawful* combatants. Because they are not uniformed forces, they lack the rights of prisoners of war and are liable to criminal punishment. Initially, the American government declared that the Guantanamo Bay prisoners have no rights under the Geneva Conventions. In the face of international protests, Washington quickly backpedaled and announced that the Guantanamo Bay prisoners would indeed be treated as decently as POWs—but it also made clear that the prisoners have no right to such treatment. Neither criminal suspects nor POWs, neither fish nor fowl, they inhabit a limbo of rightlessness. Secretary of Defense Rumsfeld's assertion that the US may continue to detain them even if they are acquitted by a military tribunal dramatizes the point.

To understand how extraordinary their status is, consider an analogy. Suppose that Washington declares a War on Organized Crime. Troops are dispatched to Sicily, and a number of Mafiosi are seized, brought to Guantanamo Bay, and imprisoned without a hearing for the indefinite future, maybe the rest of their lives. They are accused of no crimes, because their capture is based not on what they have done but on what they might do. After all, to become "made" they took oaths of obedience to the bad guys. Seizing them accords with the war model: they are enemy foot soldiers. But they are foot soldiers out of uniform; they lack a "fixed distinctive emblem," in the words of The Hague Convention. That makes them unlawful combatants, so they lack the rights of POWs. They may object that it is only a unilateral declaration by the American President that has turned them into combatants in the first place—he called it a war, they didn't—and that, since they do not regard themselves as literal foot soldiers it never occurred to them to wear a fixed distinctive emblem. They have a point. It seems too easy for the President to divest anyone in the world of rights and liberty simply by announcing that the US is at war with them and then declaring them unlawful combatants if they resist. But, in the hybrid war-law model, they protest in vain.

Consider another example. In January 2002, US forces in Bosnia seized five Algerians and a Yemeni suspected of al Qaeda connections and took them to Guantanamo Bay. The six had been jailed in Bosnia, but a Bosnian court released them for lack of evidence, and the Bosnian Human Rights Chamber issued an injunction that four of them be allowed to remain in the country pending further legal proceedings. The Human Rights Chamber, ironically, was created under US auspices in the Dayton peace accords, and it was designed specifically to protect against treatment like this. Ruth Wedgwood, a well-known international law scholar at Yale and a member of the Council on Foreign Relations, defended the Bosnian seizure in war-model terms. "I think we would simply argue this was a matter of self-defense. One of the fundamental rules of military law is that you have a right ultimately to act in self-defense. And if these folks were actively plotting to blow up the US embassy, they should be considered combatants and captured as combatants in a war." Notice that Professor Wedgwood argues in terms of what the men seized in Bosnia were *planning to do*, not what they *did*; notice as well that the decision of the Bosnian court that there was insufficient evidence does not matter. These are characteristics of the war model.

More recently, two American citizens alleged to be al Qaeda operatives (Jose Padilla, a.k.a. Abdullah al Muhajir, and Yasser Esam Hamdi) have been held in American military prisons, with no crimes charged, no opportunity to consult counsel, and no hearing. The President described Padilla as "a bad man" who aimed to build a nuclear "dirty" bomb and use it against America; and the Justice Department has classified both men as "enemy combatants" who may be held indefinitely. Yet, as military law expert Gary Solis points out, "Until now, as used by the attorney general, the term 'enemy combatant' appeared nowhere in US criminal law, international law or in the law of war." The phrase comes from the 1942 Supreme Court case *Ex parte Quirin*, but all the Court says there is that "an enemy combatant who without uniform comes secretly through the lines for the purpose of waging war by destruction of life or property" would "not . . . be entitled to the status of prisoner of war, but . . . [they would] be offenders against the law of war subject to trial and punishment by military tribunals." For the Court, in other words, the status of a person as a nonuniformed enemy combatant makes him a criminal rather than a warrior, and determines *where* he is tried (in a military, rather than a civilian, tribunal) but not *whether* he is tried. Far from authorizing open-ended confinement, *Ex parte Quirin* presupposes that criminals are entitled to hearings: without a hearing how can suspect prove that the government made a mistake? *Quirin* embeds the concept of "enemy combatant" firmly in the law model. In the war model, by contrast, POWs may be detained without a hearing until hostilities are over. But POWs were captured in uniform, and only their undoubted identity as enemy soldiers justifies such open-ended custody. Apparently, Hamdi and Padilla will get the worst of both models—open-ended custody with no trial, like POWs, but no certainty beyond the US government's say-so that they really are "bad men." This is the hybrid war-law model. It combines the *Quirin* category of "enemy combatant without uniform," used in the law model to justify a military trial, with the war model's practice of indefinite confinement with no trial at all.

THE CASE FOR THE HYBRID APPROACH

Is there any justification for the hybrid war-law model, which so drastically diminishes the rights of the enemy? An argument can be offered along the following lines. In ordinary cases of war among states, enemy soldiers may well be morally and politically innocent. Many of them are conscripts, and those who aren't do not necessarily endorse the state policies they are fighting to defend. But enemy soldiers in the War on Terrorism are, by definition, those who have embarked on a path of terrorism. They are neither morally nor politically innocent. Their sworn aim—"Death to America!"—is to create more 9/11s. In this respect they are much more akin to criminal conspirators than to conscript soldiers. Terrorists will fight as soldiers when they must, and metamorphose into mass murderers when they can.

Furthermore, suicide terrorists pose a special, unique danger. Ordinary criminals do not target innocent bystanders. They may be willing to kill them if necessary, but bystanders enjoy at least some measure of security because they are not primary targets. Not so with terrorists, who aim to kill as many innocent people as possible. Likewise, innocent bystanders are protected from ordinary criminals by whatever deterrent force the threat of punishment and the risk of getting killed in the act of committing a crime offer. For a suicide bomber, neither of these threats is a deterrent at all—after all, for the suicide bomber one of the hallmarks of a *successful* operation is that he winds up dead at day's end. Given the unique and heightened danger that suicide terrorists pose, a stronger response that grants potential terrorists fewer right may be justified. Add to this the danger that terrorists may come to possess weapons of mass destruction, including nuclear devices in suitcases. Under circumstances of such dire menace, it is appropriate to treat terrorists as though they embody the most dangerous aspect of both warriors and criminals. That is the basis of the hybrid war-law model.

THE CASE AGAINST EXPEDIENCY

The argument against the hybrid war-law model is equally clear. The US has simply chosen the bits of the law model and the bits of the war model that are most convenient for American interests, and ignored the rest. The model abolishes the rights of potential enemies (and their innocent shields) by fiat—not for reasons of moral or legal principle, but solely because the US does not want them to have rights. The more rights they have, the more risk they pose. But Americans' urgent desire to minimize our risks doesn't make other people's rights disappear. Calling our policy a War on Terrorism obscures this point.

The theoretical basis of the objection is that the law model and the war model each comes as a package, with a kind of intellectual integrity. The law model grows out of relationships within states, while the war model arises from relationships between states. The law model imputes a ground-level community of values to those subject to the law—paradigmatically, citizens of a state, but also visitors and foreigners who choose to engage in conduct that affects a state. Only because law imputes shared basic values to the community can a state condemn the conduct of criminals and inflict punishment on them. Criminals deserve condemnation and punishment because their conduct violates norms that we are entitled to count on their sharing. But, for the same reason—the imputed community of values—those subject to the law ordinarily enjoy a presumption of innocence and an expectation of safety. The government cannot simply grab them and confine them without making sure they have broken the law, nor can it condemn them without due process for ensuring that it has the right person, nor can it knowingly place bystanders in mortal peril in the course of fighting crime. They are our fellows, and the community should protect them just as it protects us. The same imputed community of values that justifies condemnation and punishment creates rights to due care and due process.

War is different. War is the ultimate acknowledgment that human beings do not live in a single community with shared norms. If their norms conflict enough, communities pose a physical danger to each other, and nothing can safeguard a community against its enemies except force of arms. That makes enemy soldiers legitimate targets; but it makes our soldiers legitimate targets as well, and, once the enemy no longer poses a danger, he should be immune from punishment, because if he has fought cleanly he has violated no norms that we are entitled to presume he honors. Our norms are, after all, *our* norms, not his.

Because the law model and war model come as conceptual packages, it is unprincipled to wrench them apart and recombine them simply because it is in America's interest to do so. To declare that Americans can fight enemies with the latitude of warriors, but if the enemies fight back they are not warriors but criminals, amounts to a kind of heads-I-win-tails-you-lose international morality in which whatever it takes to reduce American risk, no matter what the cost to others, turns out to be justified. This, in brief, is the criticism of the hybrid war-law model.

To be sure, the law model could be made to incorporate the war model merely by rewriting a handful of statutes. Congress could enact laws permitting imprisonment or execution of persons who pose a significant threat of terrorism whether or not they have already done anything wrong. The standard of evidence could be set low and the requirement of a hearing eliminated. Finally, Congress could authorize the use of lethal force against terrorists regardless of the danger to innocent bystanders, and it could immunize officials from lawsuits or prosecution by victims of collateral damage. Such statutes would violate the Constitution, but the Constitution could be amended to incorporate antiterrorist exceptions to the Fourth, Fifth, and Sixth Amendments. In the end, we would have a system of law that includes all the essential features of the war model.

It would, however, be a system that imprisons people for their intentions rather than their actions, and that offers the innocent few protections against mistaken detention or inadvertent death through collateral damage. Gone are the principles that people should never be punished for their thoughts, only for their deeds, and that innocent people must be protected rather than injured by their own government. In that sense, at any rate, repackaging war as law seems merely cosmetic, because it replaces the ideal of law as a protector of rights with the more problematic goal of protecting some innocent people by sacrificing others. The hypothetical legislation incorporates war into law only by making law as partisan and ruthless as war. It no longer resembles law as Americans generally understand it.

THE THREAT TO INTERNATIONAL HUMAN RIGHTS

In the War on Terrorism, what becomes of international human rights? It seems beyond dispute that the war model poses a threat to international human rights, because honoring human rights is neither practically possible nor theoretically required during war. Combatants are legitimate targets; noncombatants maimed by accident or mistake are regarded as collateral damage rather than victims of atrocities; cases of mistaken identity get killed or confined without a hearing because combat conditions preclude due process. To be sure, the laws of war specify minimum human rights, but these are far less robust than rights in peacetime—and the hybrid war-law model reduces this schedule of rights even further by classifying the enemy as unlawful combatants.

One striking example of the erosion of human rights is tolerance of torture. It should be recalled that a 1995 al Qaeda plot to bomb eleven US airliners was thwarted by information tortured out of a Pakistani suspect by the Philippine police—an eerie real-life version of the familiar philosophical thought-experiment. The *Washington Post* reports that since September 11 the US has engaged in the summary transfer of dozens of terrorism suspects to countries where they will be interrogated under torture. But it isn't just the United States that has proven willing to tolerate torture for security reasons. Last December, the Swedish government snatched a suspected Islamic extremist to whom it had previously granted political asylum, and the same day had him transferred to Egypt, where Amnesty International reports that he has been tortured to the point where he walks only with difficulty. Sweden is not, to say the least, a traditionally hard-line nation on human rights issues. None of this international transportation is lawful—indeed, it violates international treaty obligations under the Convention against Torture that in the US have constitutional status as "supreme Law of the Land"—but that may not matter under the war model, in which even constitutional rights may be abrogated.

It is natural to suggest that this suspension of human rights is an exceptional emergency measure to deal with an unprecedented threat. This raises the question of how long human rights will remain suspended. When will the war be over?

Here, the chief problem is that the War on Terrorism is not like any other kind of war. The enemy, Terrorism, is not a territorial state or nation or government. There is no opposite number to negotiate with. There is no one on the other side to call a truce or declare a ceasefire, no one among the enemy authorized to surrender. In traditional wars among states, the war aim is, as Clausewitz argued, to impose one state's political will on another's. The *aim* of the war is not to kill the enemy—killing the enemy is the *means* used to achieve the real end, which is to force capitulation. In the War on Terrorism, no capitulation is possible. That means that the real aim of the war is, quite simply, to kill or capture all of the terrorists—to keep on killing and killing, capturing and capturing, until they are all gone.

Of course, no one expects that terrorism will ever disappear completely. Everyone understands that new anti-American extremists, new terrorists, will always arise and always be available for recruitment and deployment. Everyone understands that even if al Qaeda is destroyed or decapitated, other groups, with other leaders, will arise in its place. It follows, then, that the War on Terrorism will be a war that can only be abandoned, never concluded. The War has no natural resting point, no moment of victory or finality. It requires a mission of killing and capturing, in territories all over the globe, that will go on in perpetuity. It follows as well that the suspension of human rights implicit in the hybrid war-law models is not temporary but permanent.

Perhaps with this fear in mind, Congressional authorization of President Bush's military campaign limits its scope to those responsible for September 11 and their sponsors. But the War on Terrorism has taken on a life of its own that makes the Congressional authorization little more than a technicality. Because of the threat of nuclear terror, the American leadership actively debates a war on Iraq regardless of whether Iraq was implicated in September 11; and the President's yoking of Iraq, Iran, and North Korea into a single axis of evil because they back terror suggests that the War on Terrorism might eventually encompass all these nations. If the US ever unearths tangible evidence that any of these countries is harboring or abetting terrorists with weapons of mass destruction, there can be little doubt that Congress will support military action. So too, Russia invokes the American War on Terrorism to justify its attacks on Chechen rebels, China uses it to deflect criticisms of its campaign against Uighur separatists, and Israeli Prime Minister Sharon explicitly links military actions against Palestinian insurgents to the American War on Terrorism. No doubt there is political opportunism at work in some or all of these efforts to piggyback onto America's campaign, but the opportunity would not exist if "War on Terrorism" were merely the code name of a discrete, neatly-boxed American operation. Instead, the War on Terrorism has become a model of politics, a worldview with its own distinctive premises and consequences. As I have argued, it includes a new model of state action, the hybrid war-law model, which depresses human rights from their peacetime standard to the war-time standard, and indeed even further. So long as it continues, the War on Terrorism means the end of human rights, at least for those near enough to be touched by the fire of battle.

SOURCES

On the January 2002 attack on the Afghani town of Uruzgan, see: John Ward Anderson, "Afghans Falsely Held by U.S. Tried to Explain; Fighters Recount Unanswered Pleas, Beatings—and an Apology on Their Release," *Washington Post* (March 26, 2002); see also Susan B. Glasser, "Afghans Live and Die With U.S. Mistakes; Villagers Tell of Over 100 Casualties," *Washington Post* (Feb. 20, 2002). On the Third Geneva Convention, see: Geneva Convention (III) Relative to the Treatment of Prisoners of War, 6 U.S.T. 3317, signed on August 12, 1949, at Geneva, Article 17. Although the US has not ratified the Geneva Convention, it has become part of customary international law, and certainly belongs to the war model. Count One of the Lindh indictment charges him with violating 18 U.S.C. 2332(b), "Whoever outside the United States attempts to kill, or engages in a conspiracy to kill, a national of the United States" may be sentenced to 20 years (for attempts) or life imprisonment (for conspiracies). Subsection (c) likewise criminalizes "engag[ing] in physical violence with intent to cause serious bodily injury to a national of the United States; or with the result that serious bodily injury is caused to a national of the United States." Lawful combatants are defined in the Hague Convention (IV) Respecting the Laws and Customs of War on Land, Annex to the Convention, 1 Bevans 631, signed on October 18, 1907, at The Hague, Article

1. The definition requires that combatants "have a fixed distinctive emblem recognizable at a distance." Protocol I Additional to the Geneva Conventions of 1949, 1125 U.N.T.S. 3, adopted on June 8, 1977, at Geneva, Article 44 (3) makes an important changes in the Hague Convention, expanding the definition of combatants to include nonuniformed irregulars. However, the United States has not agreed to Protocol I. The source of Ruth Wedgwood's remarks: Interview with Melissa Block, National Public Radio program, "All Things Considered" (January 18, 2002); Gary Solis, "Even a 'Bad Man' Has Rights," *Washington Post* (June 25, 2002); *Ex parte Quirin*, 317 U.S. 1, 31 (1942). On the torture of the Pakistani militant by Philippine police: Doug Struck et al., "Borderless Network Of Terror, Bin Laden Followers Reach Across Globe," *Washington Post* (September 23, 2001): "'For weeks, agents hit him with a chair and a long piece of wood, forced water into his mouth, and crushed lighted cigarettes into his private parts,' wrote journalists Marites Vitug and Glenda Gloria in *Under the Crescent Moon*, an acclaimed book on Abu Sayyaf. 'His ribs were almost totally broken and his captors were surprised he survived.'" On US and Swedish transfers of Islamic militants to countries employing torture: Rajiv Chandrasakaran & Peter Finn, "U.S. Behind Secret Transfer of Terror Suspects," *Washington Post* (March 11, 2002); Peter Finn, "Europeans Tossing Terror Suspects Out the Door," *Washington Post* (January 29, 2002); Anthony Shadid, "Fighting Terror/Atmosphere in Europe, Military Campaign/Asylum Bids; in Shift, Sweden Extradites Militants to Egypt," *Boston Globe* (December 31, 2001). Article 3(1) of the Convention against Torture provides that "No State Party shall expel, return ('*refouler*') or extradite a person to another State where there are substantial grounds for believing that he would be in danger of being subjected to torture." Article 2(2) cautions that "No exceptional circumstances whatsoever, whether a state of war or a threat of war, internal political instability or any other public emergency, may be invoked as a justification of torture." But no parallel caution is incorporated into Article 3(1)'s non-*refoulement* rule, and a lawyer might well argue that its absence implies that the rule may be abrogated during war or similar public emergency. *Convention against Torture and Other Cruel, Inhuman or Degrading Treatment or Punishment*, 1465 U.N.T.S. 85. Ratified by the United States, Oct. 2, 1994. Entered into force for the United States, Nov. 20, 1994. (Article VI of the US Constitution provides that treaties are the "supreme Law of the Land.")

Lesser Evils

MICHAEL IGNATIEFF

I. THE FIRE NEXT TIME

It has taken nearly three years, but the 9/11 commissioner and the Supreme Court hearings on enemy combatants have given us our first serious public discussion about how to balance civil liberties and national security in a war on terror. Even so, we have not begun to ask the really hard questions. The hardest one is, Could we actually lose the war on terror?

Consider the consequence of a second major attack on the mainland United States—the detonation of a radiological or dirty bomb, perhaps, or a low-yield nuclear device or a chemical strike in a subway. Any of these events could cause death, devastation and panic on a scale that would make 9/11 seem like a pale prelude. After such an attack, a pall of mourning, melancholy, anger and fear would hang over our public life for a generation.

An attack of this sort is already in the realm of possibility. The recipes for making ultimate weapons are on the Internet, and the matériel required is available for the right price. Democracies live by free markets, but a free market in everything—enriched uranium, ricin, anthrax—will mean the death of democracy. Armageddon is being privatized, and unless we shut down these markets, doomsday will be for sale. Sept. 11, for all its horror, was a conventional attack. We have the best of reasons to fear the fire next time.

A democracy can allow its leaders one fatal mistake—and that's what 9/11 looks like to many observers—but Americans will not forgive a second one. A succession of large-scale attacks would pull at the already-fragile tissue of trust that binds us to our leadership and destroy the trust we have in one another. Once the zones of devastation were cordoned off and the bodies buried, we might find our-

selves, in short order, living in a national-security state on continuous alert, with sealed borders, constant identity checks and permanent detention camps for dissidents and aliens. Our constitutional rights might disappear from our courts, while torture might reappear in our interrogation cells. The worst of it is that government would not have to impose tyranny on a cowed populace. We would demand it for our own protection. And if the institutions of our democracy were unable to protect us from our enemies, we might go even further, taking the law into our own hands. We have a history of lynching in this country, and by the time fear and paranoia settled deep in our bones, we might repeat the worst episodes from our past, killing our former neighbors, our one-time friends.

That is what defeat in a war on terror looks like. We would survive, but we would no longer recognize ourselves. We would endure, but we would lose our identity as free peoples.

Alarmist? Consider where we stand after two years of a war on terror. We are told that Al Qaeda's top leadership has been decimated by detention and assassination. True enough, but as recently as last month bin Laden was still sending the Europeans quaint invitations to surrender. Even if Al Qaeda no longer has command and control of its terrorist network, that may not hinder its cause. After 9/11, Islamic terrorism may have metastasized into a cancer of independent terrorist cells that, while claiming inspiration from Al Qaeda, no longer require its direction, finance or advice. These cells have given us Madrid. Before that, they gave us Istanbul, and before that, Bali. There is no shortage of safe places in which they can grow. Where terrorists need covert support, there are Muslim communities, in the diasporas of Europe and North America, that will turn a blind eye to their presence. If they need raw recruits, the Arab rage that makes for martyrs is still incandescent. Palestine is in a state of permanent insurrection. Iraq is in a state of barely subdued civil war.

Michael Ignatieff, "Lesser Evils," *New York Times* (2 May 2004), section 6 (edited). Reprinted with permission of The New York Times.

Some of the Bush administration's policies, like telling Ariel Sharon he can keep settlements on the West Bank, may only be fanning the flames.

So anyone who says "Relax, more people are killed in road accidents than are killed in terrorist attacks" is playing games. The conspiracy theories who claim the government is manufacturing the threat in order to foist secret government upon us ought to wise up. Anyone who doesn't take seriously a second major attack on the United States just isn't being serious. In the Spanish elections in March, we may have had a portent of what's ahead: a terrorist gang trying to intimidate voters into altering the result of a democratic election. We can confidently expect that terrorists will attempt to tamper with our election in November. Condoleezza Rice, the national security adviser, said in a recent television interview that the Bush administration is concerned that terrorists will see the approaching presidential election as "too good to pass up."

Thinking the worst is not defeatist. It is the best way to avoid defeat. Nor is it defeatist to concede that terror can never be entirely vanquished. Terrorists will continue to threaten democratic politics wherever oppressed or marginalized groups believe their cause justifies violence. But we can certainly deny them victory. We can continue to live without fear inside free institutions. To do so, however, we need to change the way we think, to step outside the confines of our cozy conservative and liberal boxes.

II. THE NECESSITY OF LESSER EVILS

When democracies fight terrorism, they are defending the proposition that their political life should be free of violence. But defeating terror requires violence. It may also require coercion, secrecy, deception, even violation of rights. How can democracies resort to these means without destroying the values for which they stand? How can they resort to the lesser evil without succumbing to the greater?

Putting the problem this way is not popular. Civil libertarians don't want to think about lesser evils. Security is as much a right as liberty, but civil libertarians haven't wanted to ask which freedoms we

might have to trade in order to keep secure. Some conservative thinkers, like those at the libertarian Cato Institute, come down the same way but for different reasons: for them, the greater evil is big government, and they oppose measures that give the executive branch more power. Other conservatives, like Attorney General John Ashcroft, simply refuse to believe that any step taken to defend the United States can be called an evil at all.

But thinking about lesser evils is unavoidable. Sticking too firmly to the rule of law simply allows terrorists too much leeway to exploit our freedoms. Abandoning the rule of law altogether betrays our most valued institutions. To defeat evil, we may have to traffic in evils: indefinite detention of suspects, coercive interrogations, targeted assassinations, even pre-emptive war. These are evils because each strays from national and international law and because they kill people or deprive them of freedom without due process. They can be justified only because they prevent the greater evil. The question is not whether we should be trafficking in lesser evils but whether we can keep lesser evils under the control of free institutions. If we can't, any victories we gain in the war on terror will be Pyrrhic ones.

III. HOW TO THINK ABOUT CIVIL LIBERTIES

Civil liberties are not a set of pesky side constraints, pettifogging legalisms tying democracy's hands behind its back. Ask what the American way of life is, and soon we are talking about trial by jury, a free press, habeas corpus and democratic institutions. Soon we are talking about that freedom and that confident sense of an entitlement to happiness that the Europeans find so strange in this country. Civil liberties are what America is.

Civil liberties may define us, but we have a bad record of jettisoning them when we get scared. We have the A.C.L.U. today because patriotic liberals after World War I were ashamed that the Russian Revolution of 1917 had terrified us into the Red Scare, the Palmer Raids and the needless roundup, arrest and deportation of mostly Eastern European immigrants, whose worst offense was that they had socialist, anarchist or communist illusions. We learned from the Red Scare that we need a civil liberties lobby because frightened majorities do reprehensible things. Between 1917 and 1920, we did ourselves plenty of harm. A congressman, Victor Berger, was denied his seat in the House after being convicted of espionage for writing an antiwar article, and a presidential candidate, Eugene V. Debs, was sentenced to 10 years in prison for delivering an antiwar speech. Aliens were harassed and deported. Legal strikes were smashed, and trade-union leaders were jailed. Indeed, by comparison with the Red Scare or later shameful episodes like Roosevelt's detention of Japanese during World War II, there have been no mass detention camps in the United States since Sept. 11 and no imprisonment for dissent. Not yet anyway.

Even so, after 9/11 we were frightened, and Congress and the government weren't always thinking straight. After the attack, it may have made sense to detain more than 700 aliens on one immigration pretext or another until we could figure out whether there were other sleeper cells at work. But it made a lot less sense to hold them for months (80 days on average) and to deny them lawyers and public due process before we tossed most of them out of the country. It was shameful, as a Justice Department report found, that many Arab and Muslim detainees were abused and harassed in confinement. Civil libertarians like Prof. David Cole of Georgetown nobly stood up and denounced such detainments as the abuses that they were.

But being absolutely right on this issue doesn't make a civil liberties position right on every other issue. Consider the question of a national ID system. Instead of crying "1984," the civil liberties lobby should be taking an honest look at the leaky sieve of the existing driving license ID system and admit how easy it was for the hijackers to talk their way into the ID's that got them onto the planes. Instead of defending a failed ID system, civil libertarians should be trying to think of a better one. One possibility is for Congress to establish minimum national standards for identification, using the latest biometric identifiers. Any legislation should build in a Freedom of Information requirement demanding that the gov-

ernment divulge the data it holds on citizens and purge data that is unsound.

President Bush has been trying to use civil liberties as a wedge issue, campaigning for the swift renewal of the Patriot Act in an effort to portray his rival as soft on the war on terror. The civil liberties lobby has taken the bait, leading the charge against the Patriot Act and its renewal. But partisan politics and civil liberties ideology are making it hard to take an unbiased look at what Bush has actually done. While some aspects of the Patriot Act were vexatious and ill conceived—for example, giving federal agents the power to force librarians and bookstores to divulge what their customers are reading—other parts of the act (and the antiterrorism measures in general) are right-minded. Giving the F.B.I. the same powers to wiretap terrorist suspects that they already use against the Mafia and drug traffickers seems reasonable, particularly because the taps are controlled by court order. Requiring banks and security brokers to file suspicious-activity reports to prevent money-laundering by terrorists sounds like an overdue reform. Enhancing the ability of the C.I.A. and F.B.I. to pool and share information seems like a good idea. As the staff reports of the 9/11 commission have shown, neither agency regularly shared its list of Al Qaeda suspects before Sept. 11 or passed the list to the airlines.

Our vulnerability to attack on 9/11 was not a result just of bureaucratic bungling, dysfunctional Beltway turf wars and plain inertia. The disaster also was a result in part of the unintended consequences of well-meaning measures taken by civil libertarians in the past. Erecting fire walls between domestic intelligence gathering and law enforcement seemed like a positive development in the wake of the abuses of J. Edgar Hoover's F.B.I. These same good intentions led Congress in 1978 to pass the Foreign Intelligence Surveillance Act. This law created a special federal court that meets in secret to rule on requests by counterintelligence officers to put espionage and terrorist suspects under surveillance. These warrants could be issued on lower standards of evidence than those required under the Fourth Amendment rules that regulate warrants issued in standard criminal cases. In order to guarantee that law enforcement would not exploit these lower standards, a legal "wall" was installed between intelligence gathering and criminal investigations. The court could grant F.B.I. intelligence agents a domestic surveillance warrant only if the primary purpose of their surveillance was foreign intelligence, not criminal prosecution.

Richard Clarke, the former television czar, has wisely proposed lowering the wall between domestic law enforcement and intelligence functions. This would allow us to pull all our domestic antiterrorism capabilities into a version of Britain's M15, an agency charged with domestic intelligence-gathering and counterterrorism but without law enforcement responsibilities.

A second victory for civil liberties—the taming of the C.I.A. after its excesses during the Vietnam War era—may have also weakened human intelligence capacities before 9/11. In the wake of disclosures that the C.I.A. had tried to assassinate foreign leaders as well as thousands of Communist political cadres in South Vietnam, Senator Frank Church's Congressional investigation persuaded the Ford administration to rein in the C.I.A. and ban covert assassination activity. At the time, this seemed like a victory for civilian control of intelligence. But C.I.A. veterans like Robert Baer, a former operative in the Middle East, charge that the post-Church controls on the C.I.A. inadvertently created a culture in which agents preferred to sit behind Washington desks, reading reports, rather than risking their lives running informants and agents in the alleyways and tenements of Arab cities. This aversion to risk led the C.I.A. to cease investing in human intelligence and to rely too heavily on satellite and signals intelligence. The United States appears, for example, to have had almost no one on the ground in Iraq after 1998, hence the catastrophic misjudgment by U.S. intelligence about Saddam Hussein's weapons of mass destruction.

But the problems began much earlier. We know now that the war being waged by Islamic fundamentalists against the United States began in 1983 with the bombing of the U.S. Embassy in Beirut and escalated through the African embassy bombings and the attack on the U.S.S. Cole. As the enemy steadily escalated the fight, the C.I.A. needed to have operatives in the bazaars, teahouses and mosques of the Arab world, bribing, importuning and, if necessary, eliminating our enemies. Who doesn't wish we had killed Osama bin Laden in the late 1990's? But the rules of assassination were drawn to outlaw it in so-called peacetime. They were at war with us, and we convinced ourselves that we were not at war with them. Post-Church, we may have betrayed a fatal preference for clean hands in a dark world of terror in which only dirty hands can get the job done.

But dirty hands need not be lawless. If we need a tough counterintelligence service, we do not want it out of control, bribing, suborning, bugging and assassinating anyone it sees fit. To paraphrase Cofer Black, the former C.I.A. counterterrorism chief, we may want to put terrorist heads in boxes, but we need presidents, not C.I.A. operatives or their for-hire hit-men, to decide whose heads we are targeting. There have to be rules, presidential directives controlling the resort to assassination. Congress should weigh in here and call for new legislation. Three rules for targeted assassination seem relatively obvious: only as a last resort, only when capture is impossible without undue risk to American lives and only where death or damage to innocent civilians can be avoided. We need to make sure that assassinations don't do more harm than good. As the Israelis have discovered through their own assassination policy, killing Sheik Yassin of Hamas and his successor may only strengthen Hamas control of Gaza. A war on terror that succeeds tactically—taking out this potential terrorist, breaking up that potential cell—while failing strategically, further enraging the Arab populace, is not a success. So we need rules in a war on terror, first of all to keep free institutions intact and second so that we don't fail in our strategic objective, which is to make America some friends instead of numberless new enemies.

IV. STRIKING A BALANCE

Civil libertarians may tie our hands unduly, while the gung-ho "anything goes" brigade might bring us tactical victories at the price of strategic disaster. Either extreme won't work, so where is the balance to be found?

Let's not pretend it's going to be easy to agree about this. Abiding disagreement about the trade-off between liberty and security is a permanent characteristic of any free society. The founding fathers designed the Constitution to enable our institutions to adjudicate such fundamental disagreements of principle. The key innovation of American government was the system of checks and balances. The founders required the executive branch to justify coercive measures before Congress, and later Justice Marshall in Marbury v. Madison established the principle of judicial review. This system of "adversarial justification" is what keeps us free. Presidents are just like the rest of us: they can justify anything if they have to justify it to only themselves. Our system of government, like trial by jury, puts all coercive measures to the test of hostile, questioning review. Our system is supposed to challenge the president every step of the way. Show me, prove it to me, give me the facts—this is supposed to be the American way.

A war on terror puts this system under real strain. Checks and balances work slowly—Congress must deliberate; the courts must review—and meanwhile, the crisis calls out for decisive action. This is why terrorism's chief impact on democracy—not just in the United States but also in every other free society and especially in Spain and Britain—has been to strengthen the power of presidents and prime ministers at the expense of legislatures and the courts and to increase the exercise of secret government. Much of the war against terror has to be fought in secret, and the killing, interrogating and bribing are done in the shadows. This is democracy's dark secret—the men and women who defend us with a bodyguard of lies and an armory of deadly weapons—and because it is our dark secret, it can also be democracy's nemesis.

The key question is whether free institutions—Congress, courts and the press—are strong enough to keep this secret army under control. Its budget is offline, and its operations are below the Congressional radar. Despite the 9/11 commission's remark-

able exercise in public education, the government is still trying to make the war on terror ever more secret. The administration has fought attempts by the A.C.L.U. to force the Justice Department to disclose how often it has used its expanded authority under the Patriot Act. It has successfully resisted attempts to require disclosure of the names of those detained in investigations after Sept. 11, and an executive order of the president has clamped down on the release of public information relating to critical infrastructure. Obviously, it's a good idea to keep recipes for ricin off government-financed research Web sites, and it's not a good idea to have target detail on critical infrastructure available for download. But adversarial review, as intended by the founding fathers, can't work if ordinary citizens are denied the information they need.

Keeping the war on terror under control also requires judges who are unafraid to challenge presidential power. For nearly two years, the courts deferred to the president's powers as commander in chief, refusing to deny him authority to designate American citizens as "enemy combatants" and allowing him to imprison foreign combatants at Guantánamo beyond the reach of American courts. The president created military tribunals to try foreign combatants, but kept these tribunals free from review by federal courts and free of the due process safeguards that apply in U.S. military courts-martial. To their credit, a group of military defense lawyers assigned to these tribunals has gone public to question whether their defendants stand a chance of a fair trial.

The courts have watched these developments with growing alarm. The judges of the United States Court of Appeals for the Fourth Circuit, even when refusing to grant habeas corpus review to Yaser Esam Hamdi, one of the American enemy combatants currently held in a Navy brig in Charleston, S.C., sounded troubled by the president's powers. The government, they wrote, seems to be "embracing a sweeping proposition—namely that with no meaningful judicial review, any American citizen alleged to be an enemy combatant could be detained indefinitely without charges or counsel on the government's say-so." Now, at last, the Supreme Court is reviewing these presidential powers, and to judge from questioning at the Guatánamo hearings, many justices are troubled by them. As Justice Stephen Breyer said during oral arguments, "It seems rather contrary to an idea of a Constitution with three branches that the executive would be free to do whatever they want, whatever they want without a check." Just as no justice wants to second-guess a president's decision to commit U.S. forces, so no court can afford to defer to the president on the fundamental civil rights of American citizens. The Supreme Court will have to determine whether it was ever in the intentions of the founders to give the president the power to imprison a citizen at pleasure and to hold him beyond the reach of the law, and if these were not their intentions, whether emergency or wartime situations could ever justify such a departure from constitutional safeguards.

Whatever the court decides, Congress may eventually have to decide how much emergency power the president should wield. Bruce Ackerman, a liberal law professor at Yale, has recently proposed a wholesale revision of the president's current power to declare a national emergency, suggesting that if terrorists strike again, the president should be given the authority to act unilaterally for a week and to arrest anyone he sees fit. After a week, Congress would have to vote to renew his powers for a period of 60 days. Thereafter, an overwhelming majority would be required to extend the term further. Better to formalize and control emergency power, Ackerman argues, than to allow the president to slowly accumulate the power of tyranny.

Yet Congress, with rare exceptions—like the joint Congressional inquiry of 2002 into Sept. 11 and the powerful Senate dissents of Robert Byrd and Edward Kennedy—has become as reluctant as the judiciary to subject the president's powers to proper scrutiny. The first Patriot Act was large, cumbersome and poorly drafted, and it passed both the Senate and the House so quickly that it is doubtful Congress really knew what was in it. As the sunset provisions of the act come up for renewal in 2005, Congress has an opportunity to redeem itself.

Thus far, it has not been Congress but the bipartisan commission on 9/11 whose public hearings have focused national debate on civil liberties. It was not Congress that uncovered evidence that the United States has been handing terrorists suspects over to foreign governments like Morocco, Egypt and Jordan for possible torture but diligent reporters like Barton Gellman and Dana Priest of The Washington Post.

Only if our institutions work properly—if Congress reviews legislation in detail and tosses out measures that jeopardize liberty at no gain to security, if the courts keep executive power under constitutional control and if the press refuses to allow itself to become "embedded" with the government—can the moral and constitutional hazards of lesser evils be managed.

V. THE DETENTION ARCHIPELAGO

Even if our institutions do their jobs, the hazards they must manage are considerable. Consider the issue of preventive detention of terrorist suspects. All the major countries on the front line of the war on terror are currently detaining such suspects, often for indefinite periods of time. It is hard to see how a successful counterterrorism campaign can succeed unless the police can arrest and detain suspects on standards of evidence lower than those required for proof of guilt in a criminal trial. Waiting until police have met the Fourth Amendment's exacting standards for search, seizure and arrest would expose innocent civilians to unnecessary risk of terrorist attack. Who doesn't wish the 9/11 hijacker who was pulled over for speeding in the weeks before the attack had been detained until police could check his ID against C.I.A. and F.B.I. watch lists?

Currently, terrorism suspects in the United States can be detained as enemy combatants, held as material witnesses or detained for immigration violations. WE do not even know how many suspects are being held under these categories. If we were to add up all the suspects, citizens and noncitizens held in U.S. institutions, together with those in Guantánamo, Iraq, Afghanistan, Diego Garcia and U.S. brigs and stockades in between, the number might run into the thousands. No one knows how many detainees there are, and that is the crux of the problem: the United States may be operating a global archipelago of detention beyond the law and ken of its citizens. Clearly, there need to be rules to govern detention, and the key rule—one that defines democracy itself—is that no one, citizen or otherwise, should be held without access to public review of his detention by independent judicial authorities. Where they are held, whether offshore or at home, should be immaterial. If they are detained by Americans, they are America's responsibility, and basic due process standards should apply.

Philip Heymann of Harvard Law School has argued that we have to stop holding American citizens indefinitely without charge. We should try them or let them go. If a suspect cannot be brought to trial without revealing evidence that would endanger key informants, then a federal judge could order further detention, but only for a maximum period of two years. After that, the person would have to be brought to trial or released.

Overseas, in Guantánamo, Iraq and elsewhere, where combatant or terrorist detainees are held, the government should create military tribunals that offer detainees the right to challenge the basis of their detention with the assistance of counsel. Of course, this is costly, and of course, some bad characters may talk their way out of America's clutches. Release upon detention, though, does not preclude surveillance upon release. These are hard choices, but we would be better advised to let a few bad characters go than to continue to run a global network of detention facilities that, right now, are an open invitation to abuse.

VI. TORTURE

The abuse we need to talk about is torture. Torture, our founding fathers said, was the vice of tyrannies and its absolute exclusion the mark of free government. At the same time, keeping torture, or at least what used to be called "the third degree," from creeping back into our police squad rooms at home has

required constant vigilance by D.A.'s and honest cops. Now it may be creeping into our war on terror. There is some evidence that the United States has handed key suspects over to Middle Eastern governments for torture. In the metal containers stacked up behind rings of razor wire on Bagram air base in Afghanistan, beatings are reportedly routine, and at least two suspects have died during secret interrogations. It is possible that similar physical methods have been used against detainees from the Hussein regime at Baghdad airport.

Some observers believe such physical methods are inevitable if we hope to break terrorists who are willing to die in attacking us. Alan Dershowitz of Harvard Law School supports an outright ban on torture, but argues that if the United States is going to rely on it, Congress should regulate it by law. Interrogators would at least be required to apply to a court for a "torture warrant," which would se limits to the practice. The evidence extracted by torture would remain inadmissible in court, but it could be used to prevent impending attacks.

Dershowitz's ideas suggest that it is possible to bring the rule of law into the interrogation room, but as an exercise in the lesser evil, it is likely to lead to the greater. Once you allow warrants for genuine "ticking bomb" cases—situations in which torture can prevent an imminent calamity from occurring— little by little, torture may be used when there is no immediate danger. There has never been any certainty, moreover, that information extracted by torture is more reliable than information coaxed out of a suspect by persuasive means. Why should we suppose that pain produces truth? And how can we forget what everyone who has ever been tortured always tells us: those who are tortured stay tortured forever. If you want to create terrorists, torture is a pretty sure way to do so.

Israel has thought hardest about torture in terrorist cases. After watching how interrogation degenerated into torture when the Landau Commission of 1987 allowed physical force in questioning, the Israeli Supreme Court ruled in 1999 that shaking suspects and confining them in chairs tipped forward in painful positions for long periods were violations of

Israel's national and international commitments against torture.

Yet the Israeli Supreme Court also conceded that physical force against suspects sometimes prizes out information that saves lives in ticking-bomb cases. So it allowed interrogators a justifying excuse. Torture was banned absolutely, but interrogators charged with torture could enter evidence that they were seeking to save lives in order to plead to reduced sentences for breaking the rules. An outright ban on torture, rather than an attempt to regulate it, seems the only way a democracy can keep true to its ideal of respecting the dignity even of its enemies. For that is what the rule of law commits us to: to show respect even to those who show no respect for us.

To keep faith with this commitment, we need a presidential order or Congressional legislation that defines exactly what constitutes acceptable degrees of coercive interrogation. Here we are deep into lesser-evil territory. Permissible duress might include forms of sleep deprivation that do not result in lasting harm to mental or physical health, together with disinformation and disorientation (like keeping prisoners in hoods) that would produce stress. What crosses the line into the impermissible would be any physical coercion or abuse, any involuntary use of drugs or serums, any withholding of necessary medicines or basic food, water and essential rest.

Fine idea, you say, but who is to enforce these safeguards? It ought to be the rule that no detainees of the United States should be permanently deprived of access to counsel and judicial process, whether it be civilian federal court or military tribunal. Torture will thrive wherever detainees are held in secret. Conduct disgracing the United States is inevitable if suspects are detained beyond the reach of the law.

VII. CONTROLLING THE PRESIDENT

So far, the basic rules for regulating a war on terror look relatively simple: first, make sure all measures are subjected to review by Congress and the judiciary; second, make sure the law keeps watch over detainees and suspects. In a word, we need to ensure that we wage a war for the rule of law and not a war

against it and that we wage it by means of democratic consent rather than by presidential decree. We have enough of an imperial presidency as it is.

Keeping the president under democratic control if not going to be easy. The dilemmas here are best illustrated by looking closely at pre-emptive war. It is a lesser evil because, according to our traditional understanding of war, the only justified resort to war is a response to actual aggression. But those standards are outdated. They were conceived for wars against states and their armies, not for wars against terrorists and suicide bombs. Against this kind of enemy, everyone can see that instead of waiting for terrorists to hit us, it makes sense to get our retaliation in first. The problem with pre-emption is keeping the president's war power under democratic control.

The president's power to make war is supposed to be balanced by Congress's power to declare it, but in practice, since Vietnam, Congress has not been able to rein in a president bent on the use of force overseas. A war on terror, declared against a global enemy, with no clear end in sight, raises the prospect of an out-of-control presidency. As we learned in the run-up to the war in Iraq, the case for a pre-emptive war is always bound to be speculative, based on doubtful intelligence that will be hard for either an electorate or its representatives, let alone the bureaucracy, to assess for credibility. In the pre-emptive wars of the future—Iraq will not be our last exercise in this moral hazard—our leaders will try to secure our consent by alternately threatening and reassuring us with the phrase "If you only knew what we know."

But as we have found to our cost, this is not nearly good enough. The facts may not be as clear before the event as they are likely to be afterward, but voters must be told what we need to know, before government commits to war in our name. Over Iraq, our name was taken in vain.

We need national and international rules to control such wars. This may require both Congressional legislation and United Nations resolutions. Pre-emptive war can be justified only when the danger that must be pre-empted is imminent, when peaceful means of averting the danger have been tried and have failed and when democratic institutions ratify the decision to do so. If these are the minimum tests pre-emptive war has to meet, the Iraq war failed to meet all three.

Even those—like me—who supported the Iraq war because it might bring freedom and democracy to people who had been gassed, tortured and killed for 30 years had better admit that if our grounds for war had been squarely put to the American people, they probably would have voted to stay home. Worse still, Congress failed to put the president's case for war to adversarial scrutiny and debate. The news media allowed itself to be managed and browbeaten. The war may or may not bring democracy to Iraq eventually, but it hasn't done democracy any good at home.

VIII. A WARRIOR'S HONOR

Regulating a war on terror with ethical rules and democratic oversight is much harder than regulating traditional wars. In traditional wars, there are rules, codes of warriors' honor that are supposed to limit the barbarity of the conflict, to protect civilians from targeting, to keep the use of force proportional and to keep it confined to military objectives. The difference between us and terrorists is supposed to be that we play by these rules, even if they don't. No, I haven't forgotten Hiroshima and My Lai. The American way of war has often been brutal, but at least our warriors are supposed to fight with honor and can be punished if they don't. There is no warrior's honor among terrorists.

The real moral hazard in a war on terror emerges precisely here, in the fact that no moral contact, no expectation of reciprocity, binds us to our enemy. Indeed, the whole logic of terrorism is to exploit the rules, to turn them to their own advantage. If we hesitate to strike a mosque because the rules of war designate it as a protected place, then the smart thing for a terrorist to do is to store weapons and suicide belts there. If our forces start from the presumption that civilian women should be treated as noncombatants, then terrorists will train women to be suicide bombers. If all existing codes of warriors' honor forbid the desecration of bodies, then it is not just

mindless brutality but actually a sound terrorist tactic to drag contractors from a car in Falluja, set them alight and display their severed and burned limbs from a bridge. Such provocations are intended to drag us down to their level.

This is the deepest reason why it is difficult to maintain self-control, let alone democratic control, in a war on terror. We are constantly being tempted to descend to the logic of terror itself. An eye for an eye. A tooth for a tooth. Vengeance is mine, saith the Lord, but unsaintly men and women, seeing their loved ones maimed and butchered, may begin to believe vengeance is theirs by right.

The siren song in any war on terror is "let slip the dogs of war." Let them hunt. Let them kill. Already, we have dogs salivating at the prospect. A liberal society cannot be defended by herbivores. We need carnivores to save us, but we had better make sure the meat-eaters hunt only on our orders.

Taunting us until we let the dogs slip is any canny terrorist's best hope of success. The Algerian terrorists who fought the French colonial occupation in the 1950's had no hope of defeating the armies of France in pitched battle. Their only chance of victory lay in provoking the French into a downward spiral of reprisals, indiscriminate killings and torture so that the Algerian masses would rise in hatred and the French metropolitan population would throw up its hands in disgust. The tactic worked. Terror won in Algeria because France lost its nerve and lost its control of counterterror.

In Iraq, we had better remember the French lesson: we cannot hope to win a war of occupation with harshness alone. We need a political strategy that undermines the terrorist claim that they are fighting a just war against military occupation. We need to turn the place back to Iraqis quickly or we will just have created another losing front in the war on terror.

On all fronts, keeping a war on terror under democratic scrutiny is critical to its operational success. A lesser-evil approach permits preventive detention, where subject to judicial review; coercive interrogation, where subject to executive control; pre-emptive strikes and assassination, where these serve publicly defensible strategic goals. But everything has to be subject to critical review by a free people: free debate, public discussion, Congressional review, in camera if need be, judicial review as a last resort. The war needs to be less secretive, not more. We need to know more about it, not less, even if what we learn is hard. If it comes to it, we need to know, every time we fly, that in case of a hijacking, the president has authorized our pilots to shoot us down if a crash risks killing still more people. In a war on terror, painful truth is far better than lies and illusions.

Above all, we need to keep faith with freedom. When terrorists strike against constitutional democracies, one of their intentions is to persuade electorates and elites that the strengths of these societies—public debate, mutual trust, open borders and constitutional restraints on executive power—are weaknesses. When strengths are seen as weaknesses, it is easy to abandon them. If this is the logic of terror, then democratic societies must find a way to renew their belief that their apparent vulnerabilities are actually a form of strength. This does not require anything new or special. It simply means that those who have charge of democratic institutions need to do their jobs. We want C.I.A. men and women who understand that the dogs of war are needed, but that they need to be on a leash. We want judges who understand that national security is not a carte blanche for the abrogation of individual rights; a free press that keeps asking, Where are the detainees and what are you doing with them? We want a Congress that will not allow national security to prevent it from subjecting executive power to adversarial review. This, after all, is only what our Constitution intends. Our institutions were designed to regulate evil means and control potentially evil people.

The chief ethical challenge of a war on terror is relatively simple—to discharge duties to those who have violated their duties to us. Even terrorists, unfortunately, have human rights. We have to respect these because we are fighting a war whose essential prize is preserving the identity of democratic society and preventing it from becoming what terrorists believe it to be. Terrorists seek to provoke us into stripping off the mask of law in order to reveal the black heart of coercion that they believe lurks behind our promises of freedom. We have to show ourselves and the populations whose loyalties we seek that the rule of law is not a mask or an illusion. It is our true nature.

The Case for Torturing the Ticking Bomb Terrorist

ALAN M. DERSHOWITZ

The arguments in favor of using torture as a last resort to prevent a ticking bomb from exploding and killing many people are both simple and simple-minded. Bentham constructed a compelling hypothetical case to support his utilitarian argument against an absolute prohibition on torture:

Alan M. Dershowitz, "The Case for Torturing the Ticking Bomb Terrorist," in *Why Terrorism Works: Understanding the Threat, Responding to the Challenge* (New Haven: Yale University Press, 2002), 142–63 (edited). Reprinted with permission of Yale University Press.

Suppose an occasion were to arise, in which a suspicion is entertained, as strong as that which would be received as a sufficient ground for arrest and commitment as for felony—a suspicion that at this very time a considerable number of individuals are actually suffering, by illegal violence inflictions equal in intensity to those which if inflicted by the hand of justice, would universally be spoken of under the name of torture. For the purpose of rescuing from torture these hundred innocents, should any scruple be made of applying equal or superior torture, to extract the requisite information from the mouth of one criminal, who having it in his power to make known the place where at this time the enormity was practising or about to be practised, should refuse to do so? To say nothing of wisdom, could any pretence be made so much as to the praise of blind and vulgar humanity, by the man who to save one criminal, should determine to abandon 100 innocent persons to the same fate?

If the torture of one guilty person would be justified to prevent the torture of a hundred innocent persons, it would seem to follow—certainly to Bentham—that it would also be justified to prevent the murder of thousands of civilians in the ticking bomb case. Consider two hypothetical situations that are not, unfortunately, beyond the realm of possibility. In fact, they are both extrapolations on actual situations we have faced.

Several weeks before September 11, 2001, the Immigration and Naturalization Service detained Zacarias Moussaoui after flight instructors reported suspicious statements he had made while taking flying lessons and paying for them with large amounts of cash. The government decided not to seek a warrant to search his computer. Now imagine that they had, and that they discovered he was part of a plan to destroy large occupied buildings, but without any further details. They interrogated him, gave him immunity from prosecution, and offered him large cash rewards and a new identity. He refused to talk. They then threatened him, tried to trick him, and employed every lawful technique available. He still refused. They even injected him with sodium pentathal and other truth serums, but to no avail. The attack now appeared to be imminent, but the FBI still had no idea what the target was or what means would be used to attack it. We could not simply evacuate all buildings indefinitely. An FBI agent proposes the use of nonlethal torture—say, a sterilized needle inserted under the fingernails to produce unbearable pain without any threat to health or life, or the method used in the film *Marathon Man*, a dental drill through an unanesthetized tooth.

The simple cost-benefit analysis for employing such nonlethal torture seems overwhelming: it is surely better to inflict nonlethal pain on one guilty terrorist who is illegally withholding information needed to prevent an act of terrorism than to permit a large number of innocent victims to die. Pain is a lesser and more remediable harm than death; and the lives of a thousand innocent people should be valued more than the bodily integrity of one guilty person. If the variation on the Moussaoui case is not sufficiently compelling to make this point, we can always raise the stakes. Several weeks after September 11, our government received reports than a ten-kiloton nuclear weapon may have been stolen from Russia and was on its way to New York City, where it would be detonated and kill hundreds of thousands of people. The reliability of the source, code named Dragonfire, was uncertain, but assume for purposes of this hypothetical extension of the actual case that the source was a captured terrorist—like the one tortured by the Philippine authorities—who knew precisely how and where the weapon was being bought into New York and was to be detonated. Again, everything short of torture is tried, but to no avail. It is not absolutely certain torture will work, but it is our last, best hope for preventing a cataclysmic nuclear devastation in a city too large to evacuate in time. Should nonlethal torture be tried? Bentham would certainly have said yes.

The strongest argument against any resort to torture, even in the ticking bomb case, also derives from Bentham's utilitarian calculus. Experience has shown that if torture, which has been deemed illegitimate by the civilized world for more than a century, were now to be legitimated—even for limited use in one extraordinary type of situation—such legitimation would constitute an important symbolic setback in the worldwide campaign against human rights abuses. Inevitably, the legitimation of torture by the world's leading democracy would provide a welcome justification for its more widespread use in other parts of the world. Two Bentham scholars, W. L. Twining and P. E. Twining, have argued that torture is unacceptable even if it is restricted to an extremely limited category of cases:

There is at least one good practical reason for drawing a distinction between justifying an isolated act of torture in an extreme emergency of the kind postulated above and justifying the *institutionalisation* of torture as a regular practice.

The circumstances are so extreme in which most of us would be prepared to justify resort to torture, if at all, the conditions we would impose would be so stringent, the practical problems of devising and enforcing adequate safeguards so difficult and the risks of abuse so great that it would be unwise and dangerous to entrust any government, however enlightened, with such a power. Even an out-and-out utilitarian can support an absolute prohibition against institutionalised torture on the ground that no government in the world can be trusted not to abuse the power and to satisfy in practice the conditions he would impose.

Bentham's own justification was based on *case* or *act* utilitarianism—a demonstration that in a *particular case*, the benefits that would flow from the limited use of torture would outweigh its costs. The argument against any use of torture would derive from *rule* utilitarianism—which considers the implications of establishing a precedent that would inevitably be extended beyond its limited case utilitarian justification to other possible evils of lesser magnitude. Even terrorism itself could be justified by a case utilitarian approach. Surely one could come up with a singular situation in which the targeting of a small number of civilians—blowing up a German kindergarten by the relatives of inmates in a Nazi death camp, for example, and threatening to repeat the targeting of German children unless the death camps were shut down.

The reason this kind of single-case utilitarian justification is simple-minded is that it has no inherent limiting principle. If nonlethal torture of one person is justified to prevent the killing of many important people, then what if it were necessary to use lethal torture—or at least torture that posed a substantial risk of death? What if it were necessary to torture the suspect's mother or children to get him to divulge the information? What if it took threatening to kill his family, his friends, his entire village? Under a simple-minded quantitative case utilitarianism, anything goes as long as the number of people tortured or killed does not exceed the number that would be saved. This is morality by numbers, unless there are other constraints on what we can properly do. These other constraints can come from rule utilitarianisms or other principles of morality, such as the prohibition against deliberately punishing the innocent. Unless we are prepared to impose some limits on the use of torture or other barbaric tactics that might be of some use in preventing terrorism, we risk hurtling down a slippery slope into the abyss of amorality and ultimately tyranny. Dostoevsky captured the complexity of this dilemma in *The Brothers Karamazov* when he had Ivan pose the following question to Alyosha: "Imagine that you are creating a fabric of human destiny with the object of making men happy in the end, giving them peace at last, but that it was essential and inevitable to torture to death only one tiny creature—that baby beating its breast with its fist, for instance—and to found that edifice on its unavenged tears, would you consent to be the architect on those conditions? Tell me the truth."

A willingness to kill an innocent child suggests a willingness to do anything to achieve a necessary result. Hence the slippery slope.

It does not necessarily follow from this understandable fear of the slippery slope that we can never consider the use of nonlethal infliction of pain, if its use were to be limited by acceptable principles of morality. After all, imprisoning a witness who refuses to testify after being given immunity is designed to be punitive—that is painful. Such imprisonment can, on occasion, produce more pain and greater risk of death than nonlethal torture. Yet we continue to threaten and use the pain of imprisonment to loosen the tongues of reluctant witnesses.

It is commonplace for police and prosecutors to threaten recalcitrant suspects with prison rape. As one prosecutor put it: "You're going to be the boyfriend of a very bad man." The slippery slope is an argument of caution, not a debate stopper, since virtually every compromise with an absolutist approach to rights carries the risk of slipping further. An appropriate response to the slippery slope is to build in a principled break. For example, if nonlethal torture were legally limited to convicted terrorists who had knowledge of future massive terrorist acts, were given immunity, and still refused to provide the information, there might still be objections to the use of torture, but they would have to go beyond the slippery slope argument.

The case utilitarian argument for torturing a ticking bomb terrorist is bolstered by an argument from analogy—an *a fortiori* argument. What moral principle could justify the death penalty for past individual murders and at the same time condemn nonlethal torture to prevent future mass murders? Bentham posed this rhetorical question as support for his argument. The death penalty is, of course, reserved for convicted murderers. But again, what if torture was limited to convicted terrorists who refused to divulge information about future terrorism? Consider as well the analogy to the use of deadly force against suspects fleeing from arrest for dangerous felonies of which they have not yet been convicted. Or military retaliations that produce the predictable and inevitable collateral killing of some innocent civilians. The case against torture, if made by a Quaker who opposes the death penalty, war, self-defense, and the use of lethal force against fleeing felons, is understandable. But for anyone who justifies killing on the basis of a cost-benefit analysis, the case against the use of nonlethal torture to save multiple lives is more difficult to make. In the end, absolute opposition to torture—even nonlethal torture in the ticking bomb case—may rest more on historical and aesthetic considerations than on moral or logical ones.

In debating the issue of torture, the first question I am often asked is, "Do you want to take us back to the Middle Ages?" The association between any form of torture and gruesome death is powerful in the minds of most people knowledgeable of the history of its abuses. This understandable association makes it difficult for many people to think about nonlethal torture as a technique for *saving* lives.

The second question I am asked is, "What kind of torture do you have in mind?" When I respond by describing the sterilized needle being shoved under the fingernails, the reaction is visceral and often visible—a shudder coupled with a facial gesture of disgust. Discussions of the death penalty on the other hand can be conducted without these kinds of reactions, especially now that we literally put the condemned prisoner "to sleep" by laying him out on a gurney and injecting a lethal substance into his body. There is no breaking of the neck, burning of the brain, bursting of internal organs, or gasping for breath that used to accompany hanging, electrocution, shooting, and gassing. The executioner has been replaced by a paramedical technician, as the aesthetics of death have become more acceptable. All this tends to cover up the reality that death is forever while nonlethal pain is temporary. In our modern age death is underrated, while pain is overrated.

I observed a similar phenomenon several years ago during the debate over corporal punishment that was generated by the decision of a court in Singapore to sentence a young American to medically supervised lashing with a cane. Americans who support the death penalty and who express little concern about inner-city prison conditions were outraged by the specter of a few welts on the buttocks of an American. It was an utterly irrational display of hypocrisy and double standards. Given a choice between a medically administered whipping and one month in a typical state lockup or prison, any rational and knowledgeable person would choose the lash. No one dies of welts or pain, but many inmates are raped, beaten, knifed, and otherwise mutilated and tortured in American prisons. The difference is that we don't see—and we don't want to see—what goes on behind their high walls. Nor do we want to think about it. Raising the issue of torture makes Americans think about a brutalizing and unaesthetic phenomenon that has been out of our consciousness for many years.

THE THREE—OR FOUR—WAYS

The debate over the use of torture goes back many years, with Bentham supporting it in a limited category of cases, Kant opposing it as part of has categorical imperative against improperly using people as means for achieving noble ends, and Voltaire's views on the matter being "hopelessly confused." The modern resort to terrorism has renewed the debate over how a rights-based society should respond to the prospect of using nonlethal torture in the ticking bomb situation. In the late 1980s the Israeli government appointed a commission headed by a retired Supreme Court justice to look into precisely that situation. The commission concluded that there are "three ways for solving this grave dilemma between the vital need to preserve the very existence of the state and its citizens, and maintain its character as a law-abiding state." The first is to allow the security service to continue to fight terrorism in "a twilight zone which is outside the realm of law." The second is "the way of the hypocrites: they declare that they abide by the rule of law, but turn a blind eye to what goes on beneath the surface." And the third, "the truthful road of the rule of law," is that the "law itself must insure a proper framework for the activity" of the security services in seeking to prevent terrorist acts.

There is of course a fourth road: namely to forgo any use of torture and simply allow the preventable terrorist act to occur. After the Supreme Court of Israel outlawed the use of physical pressure, the Israeli security services claimed that, as a result of the Supreme Court's decision, at least one preventable act of terrorism had been allowed to take place, one that killed several people when a bus was bombed. Whether this claim is true, false, or somewhere in between is difficult to assess. But it is clear that if the preventable act of terrorism was of the magnitude of the attacks of September 11, there would be a great outcry in any democracy that had deliberately refused to take available preventive action, even if it required the use of torture. During numerous public appearances since September 11, 2001, I have asked audiences for a show of hands as to how many would support the use of nonlethal torture in a ticking bomb case. Virtually every hand is raised. The few that remain down go up when I ask how many believe that torture would actually be used in such a case.

Law enforcement personnel give similar responses. This can be seen in reports of physical abuse directed against some suspects that have been detained following September 11, reports that have been taken quite seriously by at least one federal judge. It is confirmed by the willingness of U.S. law enforcement officials to facilitate the torture of terrorist suspects by repressive regimes allied with our intelligence agencies. As one former CIA operative with thirty years of experience reported: "A lot of people are saying we need someone at the agency who can pull fingernails out. Others are saying, 'Let others use interrogation methods that we don't use.' The only question then is, do you want to have CIA people in the room?" The real issue, therefore, is not whether some torture would or would not be used in the ticking bomb case—it would. The question is whether it would be done openly, pursuant to a previously established legal procedure, or whether it would be done secretly, in violation of existing law.

Several important values are pitted against each other in this conflict. The first is the safety and security of a nation's citizens. Under the ticking bomb scenario this value may require the use of torture, if that is the only way to prevent the bomb from exploding and killing large numbers of civilians. The second value is the preservation of civil liberties and human rights. This value requires that we not accept torture as a legitimate part of our legal system. In my debates with two prominent civil libertarians, Floyd Abrams and Harvey Silverglate, both have acknowledged that they would want nonlethal torture to be used if it could prevent thousands of deaths, but they did not want torture to be officially recognized by our legal system. As Abrams put it: "In a democracy sometimes it is necessary to do things off the books and below the radar screen." Former presidential candidate Alan Keyes took the position that although torture might be *necessary* in a given situation it could never be *right*. He suggested that a president *should* authorize the torturing of a ticking bomb terrorist, but that this act should not be legitimated by the courts or incorporated into our legal system. He argued that wrongful and indeed unlawful acts might sometimes be necessary to preserve the nation, but that no aura of legitimacy should be placed on these actions by judicial imprimatur.

This understandable approach is in conflict with the third important value: namely, open accountability and visibility in a democracy. "Off-the-book actions below the radar screen" are antithetical to the theory and practice of democracy. Citizens cannot approve or disapprove of governmental actions of which they are unaware. We have learned the lesson of history that off-the-book actions can produce terrible consequences. Richard Nixon's creation of a group of "plumbers" led to Watergate, and Ronald Reagan's authorization of an off-the-books foreign policy in Central America led to the Iran-Contra scandal. And these are only the ones we know about!

Perhaps the most extreme example of such a hypocritical approach to torture comes—not surprisingly—from the French experience in Algeria. The French army used torture extensively in seeking to prevent terrorism during a brutal colonial war from 1955 to 1957. An officer who supervised this torture, General Paul Aussaresses, wrote a book recounting what he had done and seen, including the torture of dozens of Algerians. "The best way to make a terrorist talk when he refused to say what he knew was to torture him," he boasted. Although the book was published decades after the war was over, the general was prosecuted—but not for what he had done to the Algerians. Instead, he was prosecuted for *revealing* what he had done, and seeking to justify it.

In a democracy governed by the rule of law, we should never want our soldiers or our president to take any action that we deem wrong or illegal. A good test of whether an action should or should not be done is whether we are prepared to have it disclosed—perhaps not immediately, but certainly after sometime has passed. No legal system operating under the rule of law should ever tolerate an "off-the-books" approach to necessity. Even the defense of necessity must be justified lawfully. The road to tyranny has always been paved with claims of necessity made by those responsible for the security of a nation. Our system of checks and balances requires that all presidential actions, like all legislative or military actions, be consistent with governing law. If it is necessary to torture in the ticking bomb case, then our governing laws must accommodate this practice. If we refuse to change our law to accommodate any particular action, then our government should not take that action.

Only in a democracy committed to civil liberties would a triangular conflict of this kind exist. Totalitarian and authoritarian regimes experience no such conflict, because they subscribe to neither the civil libertarian nor the democratic values that come in conflict with the value of security. The hard question is: which value is to be preferred when an inevitable clash occurs? One or more of these values must inevitably be compromised in making the tragic choice presented by the ticking bomb case. If we do not torture, we compromise the security and safety of our citizens. If we tolerate torture, but keep it off the books and below the radar screen, we compromise principles of democratic accountability. If we create a legal structure for limiting and controlling torture, we compromise our principled opposition to torture in all circumstances and create a potentially dangerous and expandable situation.

In 1678, the French writer François de La Rochefoucauld said that "hypocrisy is the homage that vice renders to virtue." In this case we have two vices: terrorism and torture. We also have two virtues: civil liberties and democratic accountability. Most civil libertarians I know prefer hypocrisy, precisely because it appears to avoid the conflict between security and civil liberties, but by choosing the way of the hypocrite these civil libertarians compromise the value of democratic accountability. Such is the nature of tragic choices in a complex world. As Bentham put it more than two centuries ago: "Government throughout is but a choice of evils." In a democracy, such choices must be made, whenever possible, with openness and democratic accountability, and subject to the rule of law.

Consider another terrible choice of evils that could easily have been presented on September 11, 2001—and may well be presented in the future: a hijacked passenger jet is on a collision course with a densely occupied office building; the only way to prevent the destruction of the building and the killing of its occupants is to shoot down the jet, thereby killing its innocent passengers. This choice now seems easy, because the passengers are certain to die anyway and their somewhat earlier deaths will save numerous lives. The passenger jet must be shot down. But what if it were only *probable*, not certain, that the jet would crash into the building? Say, for example, we know from cell phone transmissions that passengers are struggling to regain control of the hijacked jet, but it is unlikely they will succeed in time. Or say we have no communication with the jet and all we know is that it is off course and heading toward Washington, D.C., or some other densely populated city. Under these more questionable circumstances, the question becomes *who* should make this life and death choice between evils—a decision that may turn out tragically wrong?

No reasonable person would allocate this decision to a fighter jet pilot who happened to be in the area or to a local airbase commander—unless of course there was no time for the matter to be passed up the chain of command to the president or the secretary of defense. A decision of this kind should be made at the highest level possible, with visibility and accountability.

Why is this not also true of the decision to torture a ticking bomb terrorist? Why should that choice of evils be relegated to a local policeman, FBI agent, or CIA operative, rather than to a judge, the attorney general, or the president?

There are, of course, important differences between the decision to shoot down the plane and the decision to torture the ticking bomb terrorist. Having to shoot down an airplane, though tragic, is not likely to be a recurring issue. There is no slope down which to slip. Moreover, the jet to be shot down is filled with our fellow citizens—people with whom we can identify. The suspected terrorist we may choose to torture is a "they"—an enemy with whom we do not identify but with whose potential victims we do identify. The risk of making the wrong decision, or of overdoing the torture, is far greater, since we do not care as much what happens to "them" as to "us." Finally, there is something different about torture—even nonlethal torture—that sets it apart from a quick death. In addition to the horrible history associated with torture, there is also the aesthetic of torture. The very idea of deliberately subjecting a captive human being to excruciating pain violates our sense of what is acceptable. On a purely rational basis, it is far worse to shoot a fleeing felon in the back and kill him, yet every civilized society authorizes shooting such a suspect who poses dan-

gers of committing violent crimes against the police or others. In the United States we execute convicted murderers, despite compelling evidence of the unfairness and ineffectiveness of capital punishment. Yet many of us recoil at the prospect of shoving a sterilized needle under the finger of a suspect who is refusing to divulge information that might prevent multiple deaths. Despite the irrationality of these distinctions, they are understandable, especially in light of the sordid history of torture.

We associate torture with the Inquisition, the Gestapo, the Stalinist purges, and the Argentine colonels responsible for the "dirty war." We recall it as a prelude to death, an integral part of a regime of gratuitous pain leading to a painful demise. We find it difficult to imagine a benign use of nonlethal torture to save lives.

Yet there was a time in the history of Anglo-Saxon law when torture was used to save life, rather than to take it, and when the limited administration of nonlethal torture was supervised by judges, including some who are well remembered in history. This fascinating story has been recounted by Professor John Langbein of Yale Law School, and it is worth summarizing here because it helps inform the debate over whether, if torture would in fact be used in a ticking bomb case, it would be worse to make it part of the legal system, or worse to have it done off the books and below the radar screen.

In his book on legalized torture during the sixteenth and seventeenth centuries, *Torture and the Law of Proof*, Langbein demonstrates the trade-off between torture and other important values. Torture was employed for several purposes. First, it was used to secure the evidence necessary to obtain a guilty verdict under the rigorous criteria for conviction required at the time—either the testimony of two eyewitnesses or the confession of the accused himself. Circumstantial evidence, no matter how compelling, would not do. As Langbein concludes, "no society will long tolerate a legal system in which there is no prospect in convicting unrepentant persons who commit clandestine crimes. Something had to be done to extend the system to those cases. The two-eyewitness rule was hard to compromise or evade, but the confession invited 'subterfuge.'" The subterfuge that was adopted permitted the use of torture to obtain confessions from suspects against whom there was compelling circumstantial evidence of guilt. The circumstantial evidence, alone, could not be used to convict, but it was used to obtain a torture warrant. That torture warrant was in turn used to obtain a confession, which then had to be independently corroborated—at least in most cases (witchcraft and other such cases were exempted from the requirement of corroboration).

Torture was also used against persons already convicted of capital crimes, such as high treason, who were thought to have information necessary to prevent attacks on the state.

Langbein studied eighty-one torture warrants, issued between 1540 and 1640, and found that in many of them, especially in "the higher cases of treasons, torture is used for discovery, and not for evidence." Torture was "used to protect the state": and "mostly that meant preventive torture to identify and forestall plots and plotters." It was only when the legal system loosened its requirement of proof (or introduced the "black box" of the jury system) and when perceived threats against the state diminished that torture was no longer deemed necessary to convict guilty defendants against whom there had previously been insufficient evidence, or to secure preventive information.

The ancient Jewish system of jurisprudence came up with yet another solution to the conundrum of convicting the guilty and preventing harms to the community in the face of difficult evidentiary barriers. Jewish law required two witnesses and a specific advance warning before a guilty person could be convicted. Because confessions were disfavored, torture was not an available option. Instead, the defendant who had been seen killing by one reliable witness, or whose guilt was obvious from the circumstantial evidence, was formally acquitted, but he was then taken to a secure location and fed a concoction of barley and water until his stomach burst and he died. Moreover, Jewish law permitted more flexible forms of self-help against those who were believed to endanger the community.

Every society has insisted on the incapacitation of dangerous criminals regardless of strictures in the formal legal rules. Some use torture, others use informal sanctions, while yet others create the black box of a jury, which need not explain its commonsense verdicts. Similarly, every society insists that, if there are steps that can be taken to prevent effective acts of terrorism, these steps should be taken, even if they requires some compromise with other important principles.

In deciding whether the ticking bomb terrorist should be tortured, one important question is whether there would be less torture if it were done as part of the legal system, as it was in sixteenth- and seventeenth-century England, or off the books, as it is in many countries today. The Langbein study does not definitively answer this question, but it does provide some suggestive insights. The English system of torture was more visible and thus more subject to public accountability, and it is likely that torture was employed less frequently in England than in France. "During these years when it appears that torture might have become routinized in English criminal procedure, the Privy Council kept the torture power under careful control and never allowed it to fall into the hands of the regular law enforcement officers," as it had in France. In England "no law enforcement officer . . . acquired the power to use torture without special warrant." Moreover, when torture warrants were abolished, "the English experiment with torture left no traces." Because it was under centralized control, it was easier to abolish than it was in France, where it persisted for many years.

It is always difficult to extrapolate from history, but it seems logical that a formal, visible, accountable, and centralized system is somewhat easier to control than an ad hoc, off-the-books, and under-the-radar-screen nonsystem. I believe, though I certainly cannot prove, that a formal requirement of a judicial warrant as a prerequisite to nonlethal torture would decrease the amount of physical violence directed against suspects. At the most obvious level, a double check is always more protective than a single check. In every instance in which a warrant is requested, a field officer has already decided that torture is justified and, in the absence of a warrant requirement, would simply proceed with the torture. Requiring that decision to be approved by a judicial officer will result in fewer instances of torture even if the judge rarely turns down a request. Moreover, I believe that most judges would require compelling evidence before they would authorize so extraordinary a departure from our constitutional norms, and law enforcement officials would be reluctant to seek a warrant unless they had compelling evidence that the suspect had information needed to prevent an imminent terrorist attack. A record would be kept of every warrant granted, and although it is certainly possible that some individual agents might torture without a warrant, they would have no excuse, since a warrant procedure would be available. They could not claim "necessity," because the decision as to whether the torture is indeed necessary has been taken out of their hands and placed in the hands of a judge. In addition, even if torture were deemed totally illegal without any exception, it would still occur, though the public would be less aware of its existence.

I also believe that the rights of the suspect would be better protected with a warrant requirement. He would be granted immunity, told that he was now compelled to testify, threatened with imprisonment if he refused to do so, and given the option of providing the requested information. Only if he refused to do what he was legally compelled to do—provide necessary information, which could not incriminate him because of the immunity—would he be threatened with torture. Knowing that such a threat was authorized by the law, he might well provide the information. If he still refused to, he would be subjected to judicially monitored physical measures designed to cause excruciating pain without leaving any lasting damage.

Let me cite two examples to demonstrate why I think there would be less torture with a warrant requirement than without one. Recall the case of the alleged national security wiretap placed on the phones of Martin Luther King by the Kennedy administration in the early 1960s. This was in the days when the attorney general could authorize a national security wiretap without a warrant. Today no judge would

issue a warrant in a case as flimsy as that one. When Zacarias Moussaoui was detained after raising suspicions while trying to learn how to fly an airplane, the government did not seek a national security wiretap because its lawyers believed that a judge would not have granted one. If Moussaoui's computer could have been searched without a warrant, it almost certainly would have been.

It should be recalled that in the context of searches, our Supreme Court opted for a judicial check on the discretion of the police, by requiring a search warrant in most cases. The Court has explained the reason for the warrant requirement as follows: "The informed and deliberate determinations of magistrates . . . are to be preferred over the hurried action of officers." Justice Robert Jackson elaborated:

The point of the Fourth Amendment, which often is not grasped by zealous officers, is not that it denies law enforcement the support of the usual inferences which reasonable men draw from evidence. Its protection consists in requiring that those inferences be drawn by a neutral and detached magistrate instead of being judged by the officer engaged in the often competitive enterprise of ferreting out crime. Any assumption that evidence sufficient to support a magistrate's disinterested determination to issue a search warrant will justify the officers in making a search without a warrant would reduce the Amendment to nullity and leave the people's homes secure only in the discretion of police officers.

Although torture is very different from a search, the policies underlying the warrant requirement are relevant to the question whether there is likely to be more torture or less if the decision is left entirely to field officers, or if a judicial officer has to approve a request for a torture warrant. As Abraham Maslow once observed, to a man with a hammer, everything looks like a nail. If the man with the hammer must get judicial approval before he can use it, he will probably use it less often and more carefully.

There are other, somewhat more subtle, considerations that should be factored into any decision regarding torture. There are some who see silence as a virtue when it comes to the choice among such horrible evils as torture and terrorism. It is far better, they argue, not to discuss or write about issues of this sort, lest they become legitimated. And legitimation is an appropriate concern. Justice Jackson, in his opinion in one of the cases concerning the detention of Japanese-Americans during World War II, made the following relevant observation:

Much is said of the danger to liberty from the Army program for deporting and detaining these citizens of Japanese extraction. But a judicial construction of the due process clause that will sustain this order is a far more subtle blow to liberty than the promulgation of the order itself. A military order, however unconstitutional, is not apt to last longer than the military emergency. Even during that period a succeeding commander may revoke it all. But once a judicial opinion rationalizes such an order to show that it conforms to the Constitution, or rather rationalizes the Constitution to show that the Constitution sanctions such an order, the Court for all time has validated the principle of racial discrimination in criminal procedure and of transplanting American citizens. The principle then lies about like a loaded weapon ready for the hand of any authority that can bring forward a plausible claim of an urgent need. Every repetition imbeds that principle more deeply in our law and thinking and expands it to new purposes. All who observe the work of courts are familiar with what Judge Cardozo described as "the tendency of a principle to expand itself to the limit of its logic." A military commander may overstep the bounds of constitutionality, and it is an incident. But if we review and approve, that passing incident becomes the doctrine of the Constitution. There it has a generative power of its own, and all that it creates will be in its own image.

A similar argument can be made regarding torture: if an agent tortures, that is "an incident," but if the courts authorize it, it becomes a precedent. There is, however, an important difference between the detention of Japanese-American citizens and torture. The detentions were done openly and with presidential accountability; torture would be done secretly, with official deniability. Tolerating an off-the-book system of secret torture can also establish a dangerous precedent.

A variation on this "legitimation" argument would postpone consideration of the choice between authorizing torture and forgoing a possible tactic necessary to prevent an imminent act of terrorism until after the choice—presumably the choice to torture—has been made. In that way, the discussion would not, in itself, encourage the use of torture. If it were employed, then we could decide whether it was justified, excusable, condemnable, or something in between. The problem with that argument is that no FBI agent who tortured a suspect into disclosing information that prevented an act of mass terrorism would be prosecuted—as the policemen who tortured the kidnapper into disclosing the whereabouts of his victim were not prosecuted. In the absence of a prosecution, there would be no occasion to judge the appropriateness of the torture.

I disagree with these more passive approaches and believe that in a democracy it is always preferable to decide controversial issues in advance, rather than in the heat of battle. I would apply this rule to other tragic choices as well, including the possible use of a nuclear first strike, or retaliatory strikes—so long as the discussion was sufficiently general to avoid giving our potential enemies a strategic advantage by their knowledge of our policy.

Even if government officials decline to discuss such issues, academics have a duty to raise them and submit them to the marketplace of ideas. There may be danger in open discussion, but there is far greater danger in actions based on secret discussion, or no discussion at all.

Whatever option our nation eventually adopts—no torture even to prevent massive terrorism, no torture except with a warrant authorizing nonlethal torture, or no "officially" approved torture but its selective use beneath the radar screen—the choice is ours to make in a democracy. We do have a choice, and we should make it—before local FBI agents make it for us on the basis of a false assumption that we do not really "have a choice." We have other choices to make as well, in balancing security with liberty. It is to these choices that we now turn.

CASES FOR ANALYSIS

1. Bin Laden Justifies Terrorism

[Interview Question 2]: Many of the Arabic as well as the Western mass media accuse you of terrorism and of supporting terrorism. What do you have to say to that?

[Osama] Bin Laden: There is an Arabic proverb that says "she accused me of having her malady, then snuck away." Besides, terrorism can be commendable and it can be reprehensible. Terrifying an innocent person and terrorizing him is objectionable and unjust, also unjustly terrorizing people is not right. Whereas, terrorizing oppressors and criminals and thieves and robbers is necessary for the safety of people and for the protection of their property. There is no doubt in this. Every state and every civilization and culture has to resort to terrorism under certain circumstances for the purpose of abolishing tyranny and corruption. Every country in the world has its own security system and its own security forces, its own police and its own army. They are all designed to terrorize whoever even contemplates to attack that country or its citizens. The terrorism we practice is of the commendable kind for it is directed at the tyrants and the aggressors and the enemies of Allah, the tyrants, the traitors who commit acts of treason against their own countries and their own faith and their own prophet and their own nation. Terrorizing those and punishing them are necessary measures to straighten things and to make them right. Tyrants and oppressors who subject the Arab nation to aggression ought to be punished. The wrongs and the crimes committed against the Muslim nation are far greater than can be covered by this interview. America heads the list of aggressors against Muslims. The recurrence of aggression against Muslims everywhere is proof enough. For over half a century, Muslims in Palestine have been slaughtered and assaulted and robbed of their honor and of their property. Their houses have been blasted, their crops destroyed. And the strange thing is that any act on their part to avenge themselves or to lift the injustice befalling them causes great agitation in the United Nations which hastens to call for an emergency meeting only to convict the victim and to censure the wronged and the tyrannized whose children have been killed and whose crops have been destroyed and whose farms have been pulverized. In today's wars, there are no morals, and it is clear that mankind has descended to the lowest degrees of decadence and oppression. They rip us of our wealth and of our resources and of our oil. Our religion is under attack. They kill and murder our brothers. They compromise our honour and our dignity and dare we utter a single word of protest against the injustice, we are called terrorists. This is compounded injustice. And the United Nations insistence to convict the victims and support the aggressors constitutes a serious precedence which shows the extent of injustice that has been allowed to take root in this land.*

What reasons does Bin Laden give to justify terrorism? He says that terrorism against the noninnocent is permissible—but, by his lights, who are the noninnocent? He lists examples of injustice committed against Muslims. Suppose for the sake of argument that his list is accurate. Would these injustices justify terrorist acts against ordinary citizens or noncombatants? Why or why not?

*John Miller et al., "When Terrorist Response Is Justified: An Interview with Osama Bin Laden," *JUST Response*, 26 November 2003, www.justresponse.net/Bin_Laden3.html (accessed 27 February 2006). From WGBH Educational Foundation. Copyright © 2007 WGBH/Boston.

2. Terrorism and Torture

WASHINGTON—Most Americans and a majority of people in Britain, France and South Korea say torturing terrorism suspects is justified at least in rare instances, according to AP-Ipsos polling.

The United States has drawn criticism from human rights groups and many governments, especially in Europe, for its treatment of terror suspects. President Bush and other top officials have said the U.S. does not torture, but some suspects in American custody have alleged they were victims of severe mistreatment.

The polling, in the United States and eight of its closest allies, found that in Canada, Mexico and Germany people are divided on whether torture is ever justified. Most people opposed torture under any circumstances in Spain and Italy.

"I don't think we should go out and string everybody up by their thumbs until somebody talks. But if there is definitely a good reason to get an answer, we should do whatever it takes," said Billy Adams, a retiree from Tomball, Texas.

In America, 61 percent of those surveyed agreed torture is justified at least on rare occasions. Almost nine in 10 in South Korea and just over half in France and Britain felt that way.[†]

Do you agree with most Americans that the use of torture is sometimes morally permissible in fighting terrorism? If so, what circumstances do you think would justify torture? If not, why not? How might a utilitarian justify (or oppose) torture? How might a Kantian theorist argue against torturing suspected terrorists?

[†]"Poll Finds Broad Approval of Terrorist Torture," *MSNBC.com,* 9 December 2005, www.msnbc.msn.com/id/10345320 (accessed 27 February 2006). Reprinted with permission of The Associated Press.

3. Terrorist Kidnapping and Murder

Kidnapping of Daniel Pearl, January 23, 2002: Armed militants kidnapped *Wall Street Journal* reporter Daniel Pearl in Karachi, Pakistan. Pakistani authorities received a videotape on February 20 depicting Pearl's murder. His grave was found near Karachi on May 16. Pakistani authorities arrested four suspects. Ringleader Ahmad Omar Saeed Sheikh claimed to have organized Pearl's kidnapping to protest Pakistan's subservience to the United States, and had belonged to Jaish-e-Muhammad, an Islamic separatist group in Kashmir. All four suspects were convicted on July 15. Saeed Sheikh was sentenced to death, the others to life imprisonment.[‡]

How did the terrorists try to justify Pearl's murder? Perhaps the terrorists imagined that Pearl was not an innocent victim but was somehow guilty of wrongdoing, if only by association with the West. Is this a plausible justification for the murder? Is it plausible that Pearl was anything but an innocent noncombatant? Why or why not?

‡U.S. Department of State, Office of the Historian, Bureau of Public Affairs, "Significant Terrorist Incidents, 1961–2003: A Brief Chronology," March 2004, www.state.gov/r/pa/ho/pubs/fs/5902.htm (27 February 2006).

CHAPTER 18

Global Economic Justice

A plain fact of the moral life is that in ethical matters small and large, personal and abstract, we wrestle with issues of justice. Whatever our moral outlook, we must sometimes ask, What is just? **Justice** is about persons getting what is fair or what is their due. In the name of justice, we condemn racial discrimination, unequal pay for equal work, and judicial punishment based on a judge's prejudice. For justice's sake, we strive to treat people the same unless there is a morally relevant reason for treating them differently—that is, we try to treat equals equally. For reasons of justice, we act—or feel obliged to act—to change the way things are, to try to make the world or ourselves more just.

Among the more vexing questions of justice are those that emerge when we become aware of people in dire need of something we have, something we could easily supply. Then the questions are, Do we have a duty to give to the needy in order to somehow ease their misery? Do they have a right to some of what we have? If so, how much should we relinquish to them? Would we be justified in refusing to give? Such queries trouble us on two levels—*locally* (pertaining to needy people nearby: in our neighborhood, community, or country) and *globally* (regarding the poor and hungry in other countries). The former has always been a concern. The latter presses us harder than ever because, thanks to our technology and wealth, we now know a great deal about the suffering of people in distant lands and we have the wherewithal to do something about it. In this chapter, we explore the global question What are

our obligations to the impoverished, hungry, dying strangers who are half a world away and who we will never meet?

ISSUE FILE: BACKGROUND

For many people, this moral issue is compelling because the wretchedness of the world's poor is profound and the economic gap between rich and poor is wide. Of the planet's 6 billion people, 1.4 billion of them survive on less than $1.25 a day— that is, in extreme poverty. In 2005, 1 billion of the world's 2.2 billion children were impoverished, with 640 million without adequate shelter and 400 million without safe water. In developing countries, 26,000 children under the age of five die daily from preventable causes.[1]

Economic inequality across the globe has always been with us, but its scale now seems unprecedented. The richest 10 percent of people in the world amass 54 percent of the global income, while the poorest 40 percent get 5 percent. The 40 percent comprise 2.5 billion people who try to live on less than $2 a day. A World Bank study published in 2002 found that the income of less than 50 million of the world's richest people was equal to that of 2.7 billion of the

---

[1]Statistics from UNICEF, "The State of the World's Children 2008," ChildInfo.org, 2008, http://www.childinfo.org/files/The_State_of_the_Worlds_Children_2008.pdf (4 May 2009); The World Bank, "Poverty: At a Glance," April 2009, http://www.worldbank.org/ (4 May 2009); "The State of the World's Children, 2005," UNICEF, 2005, http:www.unicef.org/sowc05/english/sowc05.pdf (11 April 2009).

world's poorest. Perhaps unsurprisingly, the income of 25 million of the richest Americans was equal to that of nearly 2 billion poor people. In 2005, the wealthiest 20 percent of the world consumed over 75 percent of its goods, while the poorest 20 percent consumed only 1.5 percent.[2]

Most careful thinkers agree on such facts and react with dismay and sympathy, but they disagree on the proper moral response to the massive suffering. The disagreements hinge on which moral theory is accepted and on how certain elements of morality are interpreted.

One factor is our distance from those who need help. Suppose you come upon a child drowning in a stream. With very little inconvenience to yourself you could easily save her, and you are the only person in a position to do so. If you walk away, no one will be the wiser. Would you save her? Most people probably would, and many would think they had a *duty* to save her. That is, not to save her would be wrong.

But imagine that the child is not 20 feet away from you but 1 mile or 100 miles or 5,000 miles away. If you somehow had the power to rescue her despite the distance involved, would you be obligated to do so? Most of us assume that we have duties to help those close to us—our family, friends, neighbors, or fellow citizens. After all, we have relationships with these people, and we are often in a good position to aid them. But many believe we have no duty at all to help distant peoples, strangers with whom we have no social or emotional connection. Distance changes our moral obligations; charity begins at home. Others

argue that distance is irrelevant. As one philosopher says, "It makes no moral difference whether the person I can help is a neighbor's child ten yards from me or a Bengali whose name I shall never know, ten thousand miles away."[3]

Another important element in debates over aid to the needy is the notion of rights. A **right** is a person's claim or entitlement to something, a moral demand that obligates others to act accordingly. Someone's **negative right** obligates others *not to interfere* with that person's obtaining something. Someone's **positive right** obligates others *to help that person* obtain something.

Many insist that people possess only negative rights—that is, persons are entitled to be free of coercion or harm or improper restraint. Those who take this line maintain that they have no duty to help the needy, whether near or far. Their obligation is to refrain from interfering in others' lives. They may, out of a sense of charity, give to the destitute, but they are not *morally required* to give anything. Others argue that people have both negative and positive rights and that we thus are obligated to aid the less fortunate, including the poor and hungry of the world. They may contend that everyone has a right to the necessities of life and that the affluent are, therefore, duty-bound to provide them. The have-nots possess a right to the resources of the haves. Exactly how much the have-nots are entitled to, however, is a matter of debate.

Some argue that we must aid the needy of other lands because we have a **duty of beneficence**, a moral obligation to benefit others. The impoverished may not have a right to our resources, but we nevertheless should give what we can to them. If we can help the poor without sacrificing too much of what we have, the argument goes, we should do so.

---

[2]Statistics from United Nations Development Program, "2006 Annual Report: Global Partnership for Development," 2006, http://www.undp.org/publications/annualreport2006/index.shtml (4 May 2009); Branko Milanovic, "The World Income Distribution, 1988 and 1993: First Calculation Based on Household Surveys Alone," *Economic Journal* 112 (January 2002): 51–92; United Nations Development Programme (UNDP), "Human Development Report 1998: Consumption for Human Development" (New York, 1998).

[3]Peter Singer, "Famine, Affluence, and Morality," *Philosophy and Public Affairs* 1, no. 1 (Spring 1972), 23–32.

For a few conscientious people, beneficence seems to require extraordinary sacrifice—they feel obliged to give until their own standard of living is jeopardized. Others accept a duty of beneficence toward the distant needy but try to balance it against other duties, including those to their families and to themselves.

People in this latter group often appeal to a common distinction in morality—that between obligatory and supererogatory actions. Obligatory actions are what duty requires; **supererogatory actions** are "above and beyond" the demands of duty. Supererogatory conduct is not required, but it is praiseworthy. Some think their duty of beneficence is limited and that giving more than required is supererogatory—commendable but optional. Others (many utilitarians, for example) do not recognize supererogatory actions. To them, duty demands that we benefit others as much as possible all the time. If maximum moral effort is required of all our actions, then no actions are supererogatory. On this view, we should give until it hurts, perhaps to the point of greatly reducing our own wealth.

MORAL THEORIES

Concerns about justice emerge in different regions of the moral life. As we saw in earlier chapters, they appear in deliberations about fair punishment for wrongdoing, an issue known as **retributive justice**. Questions regarding the fair distribution of society's goods (income, rights, welfare aid, etc.) are topics of **distributive justice**. The latter applies not only to justice within a society but also to justice between societies—for example, to the global distribution of wealth and resources among rich and poor countries and among rich and poor individuals.

Theories of distributive justice try to explain what makes a particular allocation of economic goods fair or just. They may be part of a broader moral theory such as Kantian ethics or utilitari-

> **VITAL STATS:**
> **The Planet's Poor and Hungry**
>
> - 1.4 billion people live in extreme poverty.
> - Every day, 1 in 7 people goes to bed hungry.
> - 26,000 children under age five die every day from preventable causes.
> - In 2005, the richest 20 percent of the world consumed 75 percent of its goods.
> - 1.1 billion people do not have access to clean drinking water.
> - Each year, 1.8 million children die from diarrhea and other health problems caused by unclean water and inadequate sanitation.
>
> Data from United Nations Development Program, "2006 Annual Report: Global Partnership for Development," 2006, http://www.undp.org/publications/annualreport 2006/index.shtml (4 May 2009); International Food Policy Research Institute, *The Challenge of Hunger 2007*, October 2007, http://www.ifpri.org/media/20071012ghi/ghi07.pdf (5 May 2009).

anism, or they may stand alone as distinctive conceptions of justice. Either way, they often have something interesting to say about the morality of helping or not helping impoverished people of distant lands.

Libertarian theories emphasize individual liberties and negative rights. Exemplified in the writings of Robert Nozick, John Hospers, and others, these perspectives reject positive rights as a violation of personal freedom because such rights force people to contribute to the welfare of others. The central point is that people have a right not to be interfered with and to do whatever they want with their own property as long as they do not violate the liberty rights of others. John Hospers expresses the view like this:

The political philosophy that is called libertarianism . . . is the doctrine that every person is the owner of his own life, and that no one is the owner of anyone else's life; and that consequently every human being has the right to act in accordance with his own choices, unless those actions infringe on the equal liberty of other human beings to act in accordance with *their* choices.[4]

The libertarian asserts that we have no duty to help the poor and hungry of the world; we are not obligated to share our resources with those less fortunate. If we aid the needy, we do so as an act of charity, not because duty commands.

Critics of the libertarian doctrine say that it conflicts with commonsense morality. In strictly libertarian terms, we have no duty to save a drowning child even though we could do so with minimal trouble. But surely when saving her life costs us so little, the critics say, we have a strong duty of beneficence to pull her from the water. The notion that saving her is not morally obligatory but merely optional seems implausible.

Consequentialist or utilitarian theories have been marshaled both to commend the aiding of distant peoples and to deplore it. Taking a utilitarian tack, Peter Singer argues that we can increase the overall good, or utility, in the world if the affluent give large portions of their wealth to the needy in other countries. He thinks his approach would dramatically lower the standard of living for the rich and drastically reduce the suffering of the poor, resulting in a general decrease in misery, starvation, and death. He tries to show that transferring our surplus of goods to those who have little or nothing is not a supererogatory gesture but an inescapable moral obligation.

Others who argue in a consequentialist vein have ended up opposing aid to the world's starving millions. In their view, uncontrolled population growth is the cause of global poverty and starvation. They contend that in developing coun-

tries, population growth is usually unrestrained, so population increases over time, inevitably outstripping available food supplies. Famine soon follows, and many die; but then the balance between population and available food is restored. Giving the starving people food to avert famine would temporarily prevent mass starvation and allow the population to increase again—but that would only postpone the inevitable famine. When this catastrophe does come, many more people will suffer and die than if food were never donated. Thus, on consequentialist grounds, these critics of food aid argue that feeding the hungry in countries where population is unchecked will just lead to greater tragedy. Our moral duty, they say, is not to feed the hungry.

Critics question nearly every assumption behind this argument. They dispute the notions that population growth is the primary cause of famine, that giving food aid is the only option for preventing starvation, and that rich nations bear no responsibility for the plight of the poor in developing countries.

Egalitarian theories hold that justice requires equal distributions of goods among all persons. Some egalitarians insist that everyone be allotted a certain minimum amount of vital goods such as food and medical care. Others claim that only a truly equal share of everything is just. Since all persons have equal value and deserve equal respect, they have equal rights to the world's resources. The world's food, for example, should be shared equally by everyone on the planet. This global equality is the supreme value, even though it requires taking goods from the better-off to give to the needy, thus curtailing the personal liberties of some for the betterment of others.

This latter point provokes considerable criticism from those who believe that individual liberties should take precedence over economic equality—libertarians, for example. They think ensuring that people can use their own legitimately acquired resources as they see fit is more

[4]John Hospers, "What Libertarianism Is," in *The Libertarian Alternative*, ed. Tibor R. Machan (Chicago: Nelson-Hall, 1974), 3.

important than guaranteeing that everyone's needs are met.

MORAL ARGUMENTS

Among the more influential arguments on obligations to the world's needy is Peter Singer's utilitarian case for making major personal sacrifices to aid impoverished, starving people. His argument is straightforward:

1. "[S]uffering and death from lack of food, shelter, and medical care are bad."[5]

2. "[I]f it is in our power to prevent something bad from happening, without thereby sacrificing anything of comparable moral importance, we ought, morally, to do it."[6]

3. Therefore, we are morally obligated to prevent suffering caused by the lack of these necessities.

Singer asserts that our moral duty applies to needy people regardless of their distance from us. "If we accept any principle of impartiality, universalizability, equality, or whatever," he says, "we cannot discriminate against someone merely because he is far away from us (or we are far away from him)."[7]

The argument shows, Singer says, that giving money to famine relief is not an act of charity, a supererogatory gesture—but a moral duty:

Because giving money is regarded as an act of charity, it is not thought that there is anything wrong with not giving. . . . On the contrary, we ought to give the money away, and it is wrong not to do so.[8]

But how much should we give? The second premise requires a drastic change in conventional moral attitudes toward the extent of our obligations:

[W]e ought to give until we reach the level of marginal utility—that is, the level at which, by giving more, I would cause as much suffering to myself or my dependents as I would relieve by my gift. This would mean, of course, that one would reduce oneself to very near the material circumstances of a Bengali refugee.[9]

Singer offers a weaker version of the second premise, even though he thinks the stronger one is closer to the truth: we are duty-bound to prevent something bad from happening as long as we can prevent it without "sacrificing anything morally significant."[10] This principle would require us to contribute to famine relief when doing so would not cost us anything of real importance. If by aiding the poor we would have to forgo buying new clothes or a fancier car, so be it.

Even if we all adopted only the weaker principle, Singer says, society would likely be transformed:

Even if we accepted the principle only in its moderate form, however, it should be clear that we would have to give away enough to ensure that the consumer society, dependent as it is on people spending on trivia rather than giving to famine relief, would slow down and perhaps disappear entirely.[11]

Critics of Singer's strong premise charge that it disregards essential features of the moral life. We may have a duty to help those in need, but we also have obligations involving rights. John Arthur contends, for example, that each person has rights that should not be relinquished even to help others in dire need. Each of us could help others by giving away a kidney or an eye—we could save a life or restore sight to a blind person, and our loss would not be comparable to the terrible loss experienced by someone who will die or be blind for

---

[5]Singer, 231.
[6]Singer, 231.
[7]Singer, 232.
[8]Singer, 235.

[9]Singer, 241.
[10]Singer, 231.
[11]Singer, 241.

lack of our help. But this much sacrifice is not obligatory:

If anything is clear, however, it is that our [moral] code does not *require* such heroism; you are entitled to keep your second eye and kidney. . . . The reason for this is often expressed in terms of rights; it's your body, you have a right to it, and that weighs against whatever duty you have to help. To sacrifice a kidney to a stranger is to do more than is required, it's heroic.[12]

Singer's detractors hold that desert is another factor we must weigh when deciding whether to give food to the hungry. As Arthur says,

Suppose, for example, an industrious farmer manages through hard work to produce a surplus of food for the winter while a lazy neighbor spends his summer fishing. Must our industrious farmer ignore his hard work and give the surplus away because his neighbor or his family will suffer? What again seems clear is that we have more than one factor to weigh. Not only should we compare the consequences of his keeping it with his giving it away; we also should weigh the fact that one farmer deserves the food, he earned it through his hard work.[13]

Others who question Singer's view concede that we have an obligation to aid distant people but maintain that we also have a duty to help those with whom we have a special relationship. As one philosopher explains,

I may have a duty to give of my surplus to help save drowning children in a distant land, but I have a stronger duty to help those with whom I have intimate or contractual ties.[14]

Like Singer, Garrett Hardin also takes a consequentialist approach to the morality of aiding the needy, but he arrives at a very different conclusion. He argues that the rich should *not* aid the poor and hungry because doing so will only invite catastrophe for rich and poor alike.

His argument proceeds by way of metaphors, the most well known being the lifeboat. Rich countries are lifeboats carrying the affluent people of the world in an ocean swarming with the drowning poor, who are desperately trying to scramble into the boats or grasp some of the food on board. Like a country, each lifeboat is limited in the number of people it can sustain, and to maintain a margin of safety it should carry fewer passengers than its maximum capacity. If a boat takes on any more passengers or throws vital supplies to the unfortunates swimming nearby, everyone—rich and poor—will perish. Either the boat will capsize, or those on board will slowly starve. Thus, the only reasonable option is to refuse to help the drowning people. Sadly, millions will be lost, but those already on board will be saved. The conclusion to be drawn, Hardin says, is that the moral duty of affluent countries is not to give aid to the starving, overpopulated ones.

Many take issue with Hardin's argument (and metaphors). A chief complaint is that the lifeboat argument is simplistic, that it ignores some hard facts about rich and poor nations. For instance, Hardin implies that the lifeboats of the rich have no interaction with the poor. But many deny this, asserting that for years rich countries have been taking advantage of poor ones and, therefore, bear some responsibility for the wretched plight of the impoverished:

Haven't colonization and commercial arrangements worked to increase the disparity between the rich and the poor nations of the earth? We extract cheap raw materials from poor nations and sell those nations expensive manufactured goods (for example, radios, cars, computers, and weapons) instead of appropri-

[12]John Arthur, "Equality, Entitlements, and the Distribution of Income," *Philosophy for the 21st Century*, ed. Steven M. Cohn (New York: Oxford University Press, 2003), 677.
[13]Arthur, 678.
[14]Louis P. Pojman, ed., *Life and Death: A Reader in Moral Problems*, 2nd ed. (Belmont, CA: Wadsworth, 2000), 180.

QUICK REVIEW

justice—The morality of persons getting what is fair or what is their due.

right—A claim or entitlement to something; a moral demand that obligates others to honor it.

negative right—A person's right that obligates others not to interfere with that person's obtaining something.

positive right—A person's right that obligates others to help that person obtain something.

duty of beneficence—A moral obligation to benefit others.

supererogatory actions—Conduct that is "above and beyond" duty; not required, but praiseworthy.

retributive justice—Justice concerning fair punishment for wrongdoing.

distributive justice—Justice concerning the fair distribution of society's goods.

libertarian theory of justice—A doctrine emphasizing individual liberties and negative rights, and rejecting positive rights as a violation of personal freedom.

egalitarian theory of justice—A doctrine holding that justice requires equal distributions of goods and social benefits among all persons.

---

ate agricultural goods and training. The structure of tariffs and internal subsidies discriminates selectively against underdeveloped nations. Multinational corporations place strong inducements on poor countries to produce cash crops such as coffee and cocoa instead of food crops needed to feed their own people. . . . Hardin's lifeboat metaphor grimly obscures the fact that we have profited and are profiting from the economic conditions in the third world.[15]

[15]Pojman, 175.

The lifeboat metaphor suggests that supplies are fixed, but critics protest that the reality is far different:

In the real world, the quantity has strict limits, but these are far from having been reached. . . . Nor are we forced to devote fixed proportions of our efforts and energy to automobile travel, pet food, packaging, advertising, corn-fed beef, "defense," and other diversions, many of which cost far more than foreign aid does. The fact is that enough food is now produced to feed the world's population adequately. That people are malnourished is due to distribution and to economics, not to agricultural limits.[16]

The gist of these counterarguments is that the survival of rich countries is not really at stake and that feeding the hungry will not necessarily capsize any boats. The critics conclude that Hardin offers no good reason for our not aiding the needy.

SUMMARY

Justice is about persons getting what is fair or what is their due. Distributive justice pertains to the fair distribution of society's goods and applies to both national and international issues. A central justice issue in global economics is, What is the moral duty of the affluent to the needy of the world?

In answering this question, libertarian theories—which emphasize negative rights—say that we have no duties to the poor. The poor have only negative rights of noninterference; they have no positive rights to be aided by others. Consequentialist theories have been used both to advocate helping the poor and to refrain from helping them, their proponents arguing that the overall benefits and harms of aid are the deciding factor. Egalitarian theories maintain that justice requires equal distributions of goods among all persons.

[16]William W. Murdoch and Allan Oaten, "Population and Food: Metaphors and the Reality," *BioScience* 25, no. 9 (September 1975): 561.

Peter Singer argues that we should make huge sacrifices to aid the impoverished of the world: if it is in our power to prevent something bad from happening without sacrificing anything of comparable moral importance, we should do it. Garrett Hardin contends that we have an opposite duty—not to help the needy. Both Singer and Hardin argue that their preferred course of action results in the overall best consequences.

READINGS

On Justice

JOHN RAWLS

THE ROLE OF JUSTICE

Justice is the first virtue of social institutions, as truth is of systems of thought. A theory however elegant and economical must be rejected or revised if it is untrue; likewise laws and institutions no matter how efficient and well-arranged must be reformed or abolished if they are unjust. Each person possesses an inviolability founded on justice that even the welfare of society as a whole cannot override. For this reason justice denies that the loss of freedom for some is made right by a greater good shared by others. It does not allow that the sacrifices imposed on a few are outweighed by the larger sum of advantages enjoyed by many. Therefore in a just society the liberties of equal citizenship are taken as settled; the rights secured by justice are not subject to political bargaining or to the calculus of social interests. The only thing that permits us to acquiesce in an erroneous theory is the lack of a better one; analogously, an injustice is tolerable only when it is necessary to avoid an even greater injustice. Being first virtues of human activities, truth and justice are uncompromising.

These propositions seem to express our intuitive conviction of the primacy of justice. No doubt they are expressed too strongly. In any event I wish to

inquire whether these contentions or others similar to them are sound, and if so how they can be accounted for. To this end it is necessary to work out a theory of justice in the light of which these assertions can be interpreted and assessed. I shall begin by considering the role of the principles of justice. Let us assume, to fix ideas, that a society is a more or less self-sufficient association of persons who in their relations to one another recognize certain rules of conduct as binding and who for the most part act in accordance with them. Suppose further that these rules specify a system of cooperation designed to advance the good of those taking part in it. Then, although a society is a cooperative venture for mutual advantage, it is typically marked by a conflict as well as by an identity of interests. There is an identity of interests since social cooperation makes possible a better life for all than any would have if each were to live solely by his own efforts. There is a conflict of interests since persons are not indifferent as to how the greater benefits produced by their collaboration are distributed, for in order to pursue their ends they each prefer a larger to a lesser share. A set of principles is required for choosing among the various social arrangements which determine this division of advantages and for underwriting an agreement on the proper distributive shares. These principles are the principles of social justice: they provide a way of assigning rights and duties in the basic institutions of society and they define the appropriate distribution of the benefits and burdens of social cooperation.

John Rawls, "On Justice," in *A Theory of Justice*, rev. ed. (Cambridge, MA: Belknap Press of Harvard University Press, 1999), 3–5, 10–19, 52–54 (edited). Reprinted with permission of Harvard University Press.

Now let us say that a society is well-ordered when it is not only designed to advance the good of its members but when it is also effectively regulated by a public conception of justice. That is, it is a society in which (1) everyone accepts and knows that the others accept the same principles of justice, and (2) the basic social institutions generally satisfy and are generally known to satisfy these principles. In this case while men may put forth excessive demands on one another, they nevertheless acknowledge a common point of view from which their claims may be adjudicated. If men's inclination to self-interest makes their vigilance against one another necessary, their public sense of justice makes their secure association together possible. Among individuals with disparate aims and purposes a shared conception of justice establishes the bonds of civic friendship; the general desire for justice limits the pursuit of other ends. One may think of a public conception of justice as constituting the fundamental charter or a well-ordered human association.

* * *

THE MAIN IDEA OF THE THEORY OF JUSTICE

My aim is to present a conception of justice which generalizes and carries to a higher level of abstraction the familiar theory of the social contract as found, say, in Locke, Rousseau, and Kant. In order to do this we are not to think of the original contract as one to enter a particular society or to set up a particular form of government. Rather, the guiding idea is that the principles of justice for the basic structure of society are the object of the original agreement. They are the principles that free and rational persons concerned to further their own interests would accept in an initial position of equality as defining the fundamental terms of their association. These principles are to regulate all further agreements; they specify the kinds of social cooperation that can be entered into and the forms of government that can be established. This way of regarding the principles of justice I shall call justice as fairness.

Thus we are to imagine that those who engage in social cooperation choose together, in one joint act, the principles which are to assign basic rights and duties and to determine the division of social benefits. Men are to decide in advance how they are to regulate their claims against one another and what is to be the foundation charger of their society. Just as each person must decide by rational reflection what constitutes his good, that is, the system of ends which it is rational for him to pursue, so a group of persons must decide once and for all what is to count among them as just and unjust. The choice which rational men would make in this hypothetical situation of equal liberty, assuming for the present that this choice problem has a solution, determines the principles of justice.

In justice as fairness the original position of equality corresponds to the state of nature in the traditional theory of the social contract. This original position is not, of course, thought of as an actual historical state of affairs, much less as a primitive condition of culture. It is understood as a purely hypothetical situation characterized so as to lead to a certain conception of justice. Among the essential features of this situation is that no one knows his place in society, his class position or social status, nor does any one know his fortune in the distribution of natural assets and abilities, his intelligence, strength, and the like. I shall even assume that the parties do not know their conceptions of the good or their special psychological propensities. The principles of justice are chosen behind a veil of ignorance. This ensures that no one is advantaged or disadvantaged in the choice of principles by the outcome of natural chance or the contingency of social circumstances. Since all are similarly situated and no one is able to design principles to favor his particular condition, the principles of justice are the result of a fair agreement or bargain. For given the circumstances of the original position, the symmetry of everyone's relations to each other, this initial situation is fair between individuals as moral persons, that is, as rational beings with their own ends and capable, I shall assume, of a sense of justice. The original position is, one might say, the appropriate initial status quo, and thus the fundamental agreements reached in it are fair. This explains the propriety of the name "justice as fairness": it conveys the idea that the principles of justice are agreed to in an initial situation that is fair. The name does not mean that the concepts of justice and fairness are the same, any more than the phrase "poetry as metaphor" means that the concepts of poetry and metaphor are the same.

Justice as fairness begins, as I have said, with one of the most general of all choices which persons might make together, namely, with the choice of the first principles of a conception of justice which is to regulate all subsequent criticism and reform of institutions. Then, having chosen a conception of justice, we can suppose that they are to choose a constitution and a legislature to enact laws, and so on, all in accordance with the principles of justice initially agreed upon. Our social situation is just if it is such that by this sequence of hypothetical agreements we would have contracted into the general system of rules which defines it. Moreover, assuming that the original position does determine a set of principles (that is, that a particular conception of justice would be chosen), it will then be true that whenever social institutions satisfy these principles those engaged in them can say to one another that they are cooperating on terms to which they would agree if they were free and equal persons whose relations with respect to one another were fair. They could all view their arrangements as meeting the stipulations which they would acknowledge in an initial situation that embodies widely accepted and reasonable constraints on the choice of principles. The general recognition of this fact would provide the basis for a public acceptance of the corresponding principles of justice. No society can, of course, be a scheme of cooperation which men enter voluntarily in a literal sense; each person finds himself placed at birth in some particular position in some particular society, and the nature of this position materially affects his life prospects. Yet a society satisfying the principles of justice as fairness comes as close as a society can to being a voluntary scheme, for it meets the principles which free and equal persons would assent to under circumstances that are fair. In this sense its members are autonomous and the obligations they recognize self-imposed.

One feature of justice as fairness is to think of the parties in the initial situation as rational and mutually disinterested. This does not mean that the parties are egoists, that is, individuals with only certain kinds of interests, say in wealth, prestige, and domination. But they are conceived as not taking an interest in one another's interests. They are to presume that even their spiritual aims may be opposed, in the way that the aims of those of different religions may be opposed. Moreover, the concept of rationality must be interpreted as far as possible in the narrow sense, standard in economic theory, of taking the most effective means to given ends.

* * *

In working out the conception of justice as fairness one main task clearly is to determine which principles of justice would be chosen in the original position. To do this we must describe this situation in some detail and formulate with care the problem of choice which it presents. These matters I shall take up in the immediately succeeding chapters. It may be observed, however, that once the principles of justice are thought of as arising from an original agreement in a situation of equality, it is an open question whether the principle of utility would be acknowledged. Offhand it hardly seems likely that persons who view themselves as equals, entitled to press their claims upon one another, would agree to a principle which may require lesser life prospects for some simply for the sake of a greater sum of advantages enjoyed by others. Since each desires to protect his interests, his capacity to advance his conception of the good, no one has a reason to acquiesce in an enduring loss for himself in order to bring about a greater net balance of satisfaction. In the absence of strong and lasting benevolent impulses, a rational man would not accept a basic structure merely because it maximized the algebraic sum of advantages irrespective of its permanent effects on his own basic rights and interests. Thus it seems that the principle of utility is incompatible with the conception of social cooperation among equals for mutual advantage. It appears to be inconsistent with the idea of reciprocity implicit in the notion of a well-ordered society. Or, at any rate, so I shall argue.

I shall maintain instead that the persons in the initial situation would choose two rather different principles: the first requires equality in the assignment of basic rights and duties, while the second holds that social and economic inequalities, for example inequalities of wealth and authority, are just only if they result in compensating benefits for everyone, and in particular for the least advantaged members of society. These principles rule out justifying institutions on the grounds that the hardships of some are offset by a greater good in the aggregate. It may be expedient but it is not just that some should have less in order that others may prosper. But there is no injustice in the greater benefits earned by a few provided that the situation of persons not so fortunate is thereby improved. The intuitive idea is that since everyone's well-being depends upon a scheme of cooperation without which no one could have a satisfactory life, the division of advantages should be such as to draw forth the willing cooperation of everyone taking part in it, including those less well situated. The two principles mentioned seem to be a fair basis on which those better endowed, or more fortunate in their social position, neither of which we can be said to deserve, could expect the willing cooperation of others when some workable scheme is a necessary condition of the welfare of all. Once we decide to look for a conception of justice that prevents the use of the accidents of natural endowment and the contingencies of social circumstance as counters in a quest for political and economic advantage, we are led to these principles. They express the result of leaving aside those aspects of the social world that seem arbitrary from a moral point of view.

* * *

THE ORIGINAL POSITION AND JUSTIFICATION

I have said that the original position is the appropriate initial status quo which insures that the fundamental agreements reached in it are fair. This fact yields the name "justice as fairness." It is clear, then, that I want to say that one conception of justice is more reasonable than another, or justifiable with

respect to it, if rational persons in the initial situation would choose its principles over those of the other for the role of justice. Conceptions of justice are to be ranked by their acceptability to persons so circumstanced. Understood in this way the question of justification is settled by working out a problem of deliberation: we have to ascertain which principles it would be rational to adopt given the contractual situation. This connects the theory of justice with the theory of rational choice.

If this view of the problem of justification is to succeed, we must, of course, describe in some detail the nature of this choice problem. A problem of rational decision has a definite answer only if we know the beliefs and interests of the parties, their relations with respect to one another, the alternatives between which they are to choose, the procedure whereby they make up their minds, and so on. As the circumstances are presented in different ways, correspondingly different principles are accepted. The concept of the original position, as I shall refer to it, is that of the most philosophically favored interpretation of this initial choice situation for the purposes of a theory of justice.

But how are we to decide what is the most favored interpretation? I assume, for one thing, that there is a broad measure of agreement that principles of justice should be chosen under certain conditions. To justify a particular description of the initial situation one shows that it incorporates these commonly shared presumptions. One argues from widely accepted but weak premises to more specific conclusions. Each of the presumptions should by itself be natural and plausible; some of them may seem innocuous or even trivial. The aim of the contract approach is to establish that taken together they impose significant bounds on acceptable principles of justice. The ideal outcome would be that these conditions determine a unique set of principles; but I shall be satisfied if they suffice to rank the main traditional conceptions of social justice.

One should not be misled, then, by the somewhat unusual conditions which characterize the original position. The idea here is simply to make vivid to ourselves the restrictions that it seems reasonable to impose on arguments for principles of justice, and therefore on these principles themselves. Thus it seems reasonable and generally acceptable that no one should be advantaged or disadvantaged by natural fortune or social circumstances in the choice of principles. It also seems widely agreed that it should be impossible to tailor principles to the circumstances of one's own case. We should insure further that particular inclinations and aspirations, and persons' conceptions of their good do not affect the principles adopted. The aim is to rule out those principles that it would be rational to propose for acceptance, however little the chance of success, only if one knew certain things that are irrelevant from the standpoint of justice. For example, if a man knew that he was wealthy, he might find it rational to advance the principle that various taxes for welfare measures be counted unjust; if he knew that he was poor, he would most likely propose the contrary principle. To represent the desired restrictions one imagines a situation in which everyone is deprived of this sort of information. One excludes the knowledge of those contingencies which sets men at odds and allows them to be guided by their prejudices. In this manner the veil of ignorance is arrived at in a natural way. This concept should cause no difficulty if we keep in mind the constraints on arguments that it is meant to express. At any time we can enter the original position, so to speak, simply by following a certain procedure, namely, by arguing for principles of justice in accordance with these restrictions.

It seems reasonable to suppose that the parties in the original position are equal. That is, all have the same rights in the procedure for choosing principles; each can make proposals, submit reasons for their acceptance, and so on. Obviously the purpose of these conditions is to represent equality between human beings as moral persons, as creatures having a conception of their good and capable of a sense of justice. The basis of equality is taken to be similarity in these two respects. Systems of ends are not ranked in value; and each man is presumed to have the requisite ability to understand and to act upon whatever principles are adopted. Together with the veil of ignorance, these conditions define the principles of justice as those which rational persons concerned to advance their interests would consent to as equals when none are known to be advantaged or disadvantaged by social and natural contingencies.

There is, however, another side to justifying a particular description of the original position. This is to see if the principles which would be chosen match our considered convictions of justice or extend them in an acceptable way. We can note whether applying these principles would lead us to make the same judgments about the basic structure of society which we now make intuitively and in which we have the greatest confidence; or whether, in cases where our present judgments are in doubt and given with hesitation, these principles offer a resolution which we can affirm on reflection. There are questions which we feel sure must be answered in a certain way. For example, we are confident that religious intolerance and racial discrimination are unjust. We think that we have examined these things with care and have reached what we believe is an impartial judgment not likely to be distorted by an excessive attention to our own interests. These convictions are provisional fixed points which we presume any conception of justice must fit. But we have much less assurance as to what is the correct distribution of wealth and authority. Here we may be looking for a way to remove our doubts. We can check an interpretation of the initial situation, then, by the capacity of its principles to accommodate our firmest convictions and to provide guidance where guidance is needed.

In searching for the most favored description of this situation we work from both ends. We begin by describing it so that it represents generally shared and preferably weak conditions. We then see if these conditions are strong enough to yield a significant set of principles. If not, we look for further premises equally reasonable. But if so, and these principles match our considered convictions of justice, then so far well and good. But presumably there will be discrepancies. In this case we have a choice. We can either modify the account of the initial situation or we can revise our existing judgments, for even the judgments we take provisionally as fixed points are liable to revision. By going back and forth, sometimes altering the conditions of the contractual circumstances, at others withdrawing our judgments and conforming them to principle, I assume that eventually we shall find a description of the initial situation that both expresses reasonable conditions and yields principles which match our considered judgments duly pruned and adjusted. This state of affairs I refer to as reflective equilibrium. It is an equilibrium because at last our principles and judgments coincide; and it is reflective since we know to what principles our judgments conform and the premises of their derivation. At the moment everything is in order. But this equilibrium is not necessarily stable. It is liable to be upset by further examination of the conditions which should be imposed on the contractual situation and by particular cases which may lead us to revise our judgments. Yet for the time being we have done what we can to render coherent and to justify our convictions of social justice. We have reached a conception of the original position.

I shall not, of course, actually work through this process. Still, we may think of the interpretation of the original position that I shall present as the result of such a hypothetical course of reflection. It represents the attempt to accommodate within one scheme both reasonable philosophical conditions on principles as well as our considered judgments of justice. In arriving at the favored interpretation of the initial situation there is no point at which an appeal is made to self-evidence in the traditional sense either of general conceptions or particular convictions. I do not claim for the principles of justice proposed that they are necessary truths or derivable from such truths. A conception of justice cannot be deduced from self-evident premises or conditions on principles; instead, its justification is a matter of the mutual support of many considerations, of everything fitting together into one coherent view.

A final comment. We shall want to say that certain principles of justice are justified because they would be agreed to in an initial situation of equality. I have emphasized that this original position is purely hypothetical. It is natural to ask why, if this agreement is never actually entered into, we should take

any interest in these principles, moral or otherwise. The answer is that the conditions embodied in the description of the original position are ones that we do not in fact accept. Or if we do not, then perhaps we can be persuaded to do so by philosophical reflection. Each aspect of the contractual situation can be given supporting grounds. Thus what we shall do is to collect together into one conception a number of conditions on principles that we are ready upon due consideration to recognize as reasonable. These constraints express what we are prepared to regard as limits on fair terms of social cooperation. One way to look at the idea of the original position, therefore, is to see it as an expository device which sums up the meaning of these conditions and helps us to extract their consequences. On the other hand, this conception is also an intuitive notion that suggests its own elaboration, so that led on by it we are drawn to define more clearly the standpoint from which we can best interpret moral relationships. We need a conception that enables us to envision our objective from afar: the intuitive notion of the original position is to do this for us.

* * *

TWO PRINCIPLES OF JUSTICE

I shall now state in a provisional form the two principles of justice that I believe would be agreed to in the original position. The first formulation of these principles is tentative. As we go on I shall consider several formulations and approximate step by step the final statement to be given much later. I believe that doing this allows the exposition to proceed in a natural way.

The first statement of the two principles reads as follows.

First: each person is to have an equal right to the most extensive scheme of equal basic liberties compatible with a similar scheme of liberties for others.

Second: social and economic inequalities are to be arranged so that they are both (a) reasonably expected to be to everyone's advantage, and (b) attached to positions and offices open to all.

* * *

These principles primarily apply as I have said, to the basic structure of society and govern the assignment of rights and duties and regulate the distribution of social and economic advantages. Their formulation presupposes that, for the purposes of a theory of justice, the social structure may be viewed as having two more or less distinct parts, the first principle applying to the one, the second principle to the other. Thus we distinguish between the aspects of the social system that define and secure the equal basic liberties and the aspects that specify and establish social and economic inequalities. Now it is essential to observe that the basic liberties are given by a list of such liberties. Important among these are political liberty (the right to vote and to hold public office) and freedom of speech and assembly: liberty of conscience and freedom of thought: freedom of the person, which includes freedom from psychological oppression and physical assault and dismemberment (integrity of the person); the right to hold personal property and freedom from arbitrary arrest and seizure as defined by the concept of the rule of law. These liberties are to be equal by the first principle.

The second principle applies, in the first approximation, to the distribution of income and wealth and to the design of organizations that make use of differences in authority and responsibility. While the distribution of wealth and income need not be equal, it must be to everyone's advantage, and at the same time, positions of authority and responsibility must be accessible to all. One applies the second principle by holding positions open, and then, subject to this constraint, arranges social and economic inequalities so that everyone benefits.

These principles are to be arranged in a serial order with the first principle prior to the second. This ordering means that infringements of the basic equal liberties protected by the first principle cannot be jus-tified, or compensated for, by greater social and economic advantages. These liberties have a central range of application within which they can be limited and compromised only when they conflict with other basic liberties. Since they may be limited when they clash with one another, none of these liberties is absolute; but however they are adjusted to form one system, this system is to be the same for all. It is difficult, and perhaps impossible, to give a complete specification of these liberties independently from the particular circumstances—social, economic, and technological—of a given society. The hypothesis is that the general form of such a list could be devised with sufficient exactness to sustain this conception of justice. Of course, liberties not on the list, for example, the right to own certain kinds of property (e.g., means of production) and freedom of contract as understood by the doctrine of laissez-faire are not basic; and so they are not protected by the priority of the first principle. Finally, in regard to the second principle, the distribution of wealth and income, and positions of authority and responsibility, are to be consistent with both the basic liberties and equality of opportunity.

The two principles are rather specific in their content, and their acceptance rests on certain assumptions that I must eventually try to explain and justify. For the present, it should be observed that these principles are a special case of a more general conception of justice that can be expressed as follows.

All social values—liberty and opportunity, income and wealth, and the social bases of self-respect—are to be distributed equally unless an unequal distribution of any, or all, of these values is to everyone's advantage.

Injustice, then, is simply inequalities that are not to the benefit of all.

* * *

The Entitlement Theory of Justice

Robert Nozick

* * *

The term "distributive justice" is not a neutral one. Hearing the term "distribution," most people presume that some thing or mechanism uses some principle or criterion to give out a supply of things. Into this process of distributing shares some error may have crept. So it is an open question, at least, whether redistribution should take place; whether we should do again what has already been done once, though poorly. However, we are not in the position of children who have been given portions of pie by someone who now makes last minute adjustments to rectify careless cutting. There is no *central* distribution, no person or group entitled to control all the resources, jointly deciding how they are to be doled out. What each person gets, he gets from others who give to him in exchange for something, or as a gift. In a free society, diverse persons control different resources, and new holdings arise out of the voluntary exchanges and actions of persons. There is no more a distributing or distribution of shares than there is a distributing of mates in a society in which persons choose whom they shall marry. The total result is the product of many individual decisions which the different individuals involved are entitled to make. Some uses of the term "distribution," it is true, do not imply a previous distributing appropriately judged by some criterion (for example, "probability distribution"); nevertheless, * * * it would be best to use a terminology that clearly is neutral. We shall speak of people's holdings; a principle of justice in holdings describes (part of) what justice tells us (requires) about holdings. I shall state first what I take to be the correct view about justice in holdings, and then turn to the discussion of alternate views.

Robert Nozick, "Distributive Justice," in *Anarchy, State, and Utopia* (New York: Basic Books, 1974), 149–57, 160–63, 167–74 (edited). Reprinted with permission by the Perseus Group.

THE ENTITLEMENT THEORY

The subject of justice in holdings consists of three major topics. The first is the *original acquisition of holdings*, the appropriation of unheld things. This includes the issues of how unheld things may come to be held, the process, or processes, by which unheld things may come to be held, the things that may come to be held by these processes, the extent of what comes to be held by a particular process, and so on. We shall refer to the complicated truth about this topic, which we shall not formulate here, as the principle of justice in acquisition. The second topic concerns the *transfer of holdings* from one person to another. By what processes may a person transfer holdings to another? How may a person acquire a holding from another who holds it? Under this topic come general descriptions of voluntary exchange, and gift and (on the other hand) fraud, as well as reference to particular conventional details fixed upon in a given society. The complicated truth about this subject (with placeholders for conventional details) we shall call the principle of justice in transfer. (And we shall suppose it also includes principles governing how a person may divest himself of a holding, passing it into an unheld state.)

If the world were wholly just, the following inductive definition would exhaustively cover the subject of justice in holdings.

1. A person who acquires a holding in accordance with the principle of justice in acquisition is entitled to that holding.
2. A person who acquires a holding in accordance with the principle of justice in transfer, from someone else entitled to the holding, is entitled to the holding.
3. No one is entitled to a holding except by (repeated) applications of 1 and 2.

The complete principle of distributive justice would say simply that a distribution is just if everyone is entitled to the holdings they possess under the distribution.

A distribution is just if it arises from another just distribution by legitimate means. The legitimate means of moving from one distribution to another are specified by the principle of justice in transfer. The legitimate first "moves" are specified by the principle of justice in acquisition.[1] Whatever arises from a just situation by just steps is itself just. The means of change specified by the principle of justice in transfer preserve justice.

* * *

Not all actual situations are generated in accordance with the two principles of justice in holdings: the principle of justice in acquisition and the principle of justice in transfer. Some people steal from others, or defraud them, or enslave them, seizing their product and preventing them from living as they choose, or forcibly exclude others from competing in exchanges. None of these are permissible modes of transition from one situation to another. And some persons acquire holdings by means not sanctioned by the principle of justice in acquisition. The existence of past injustice (previous violations of the first two principles of justice in holdings) raises the third major topic under justice in holdings: the rectification of injustice in holdings. If past injustice has shaped present holdings in various ways, some identifiable and some not, what now, if anything, ought to be done to rectify these injustices? What obligations do the performers of injustice have toward those whose position is worse than it would have been had the injustice not been done? Or, than it would have been had compensation been paid promptly? How, if at all, do things change if the beneficiaries and those made worse off are not the direct parties in the act of injustice, but, for example, their descendants? Is an injustice done to someone whose holding was itself based upon an unrectified injustice? How far back must one go in wiping clean the historical slate of injustices? What may victims of injustice permissibly do in order to rectify the injustices being done to them, including the many injustices done by persons acting through their government? I do not know of a thorough or theoretically sophisticated treatment of such issues. Idealizing greatly, let us suppose theoretical investigation will produce a principle of rectification. This principle uses historical information about previous situations and injustices done in them (as defined by the first two principles of justice and rights against interference), and information about the actual course of events that flowed from these injustices, until the present, and it yields a description (or descriptions) of holdings in the society. The principle of rectification presumably will make use of its best estimate of subjunctive information about what would have occurred (or a probability distribution over what might have occurred, using the expected value) if the injustice had not taken place. If the actual description of holdings turns out not to be one of the descriptions yielded by the principle, then one of the descriptions yielded must be realized.[2]

The general outlines of the theory of justice in holdings are that the holdings of a person are just if he is entitled to them by the principles of justice in acquisition and transfer, or by the principle of rectification of injustice (as specified by the first two principles). If each person's holdings are just, then the total set (distribution) of holdings is just.

* * *

HISTORICAL PRINCIPLES AND END-RESULT PRINCIPLES

The general outlines of the entitlement theory illuminate the nature and defects of other conceptions of distributive justice. The entitlement theory of justice in distribution is *historical*; whether a distribution is just depends upon how it came about. In contrast, *current time-slice principles* of justice hold that the justice of a distribution is determined by how things are distributed (who has what) as judged by some *structural* principle(s) of just distribution. A utilitarian who judges between any two distributions by seeing which has the greater sum of utility and, if the sums tie, applies some fixed equality criterion to choose the more equal distribution, would hold a current time-slice principle of justice. As would someone who had a fixed schedule of trade-offs between the sum of happiness and equality. According to a current time-slice principle, all that needs to be looked at, in judging the justice of a distribution, is who ends up with what; in comparing any two distributions one need look only at the matrix presenting the distributions. No further information need be fed into a principle of justice. It is a consequence of such principles of justice that any two structurally identical distributions are equally just. (Two distributions are structurally identical if they present the same profile, but perhaps have different persons occupying the particular slots. My having ten and your having five, and my having five and your having ten are structurally identical distributions.) Welfare economics is the theory of current time-slice principles of justice. The subject is conceived as operating on matrices representing only current information about distribution. This, as well as some of the usual conditions (for example, the choice of distribution is invariant under relabeling of columns), guarantees that welfare economics will be a current time-slice theory, with all of its inadequacies.

Most persons do not accept current time-slice principles as constituting the whole story about distributive shares. They think it relevant in assessing the justice of a situation to consider not only the distribution it embodies, but also how that distribution came about. If some persons are in prison for murder or war crimes, we do not say that to assess the justice of the distribution in the society we must look only at what this person has, and that person has, and that person has, . . . at the current time. We think it relevant to ask whether someone did something so that he *deserved* to be punished, deserved to have a lower share. Most will agree to the relevance of further information with regard to punishments and penalties. Consider also desired things. One traditional socialist view is that workers are entitled to the product and full fruits of their labor; they have earned it; a distribution is unjust if it does not give the workers what they are entitled to. Such entitlements are based upon some past history. No socialist holding this view would find it comforting to be told that because the actual distribution *A* happens to coincide structurally with the one he desires *D, A* therefore is

no less just than *D*; it differs only in that the "parasitic" owners of capital receive under *A* what the workers are entitled to under *D*, and the workers receive under *A* what the owners are entitled to under *D*, namely very little. This socialist rightly, in my view, holds onto the notions of earning, producing, entitlement, desert, and so forth, and he rejects current time-slice principles that look only to the structure of the resulting set of holdings. (The set of holdings resulting from what? Isn't it implausible that how holdings are produced and come to exist has no effect at all on who should hold what?) His mistake lies in his view of what entitlements arise out of what sorts of productive processes.

We construe the position we discuss too narrowly by speaking of *current* time-slice principles. Nothing is changed if structural principles operate upon a time sequence of current time-slice profiles and, for example, give someone more now to counterbalance the less he has had earlier. A utilitarian or an egalitarian or any mixture of the two over time will inherit the difficulties of his more myopic comrades. He is not helped by the fact that *some* of the information others consider relevant in assessing a distribution is reflected, unrecoverably, in past matrices. Henceforth, we shall refer to such unhistorical principles of distributive justice, including the current time-slice principles, as *end-result principles* or *end-state principles*.

In contrast to end-result principles of justice, *historical principles* of justice hold that past circumstances or actions of people can create differential entitlements or differential deserts to things. An injustice can be worked by moving from one distribution to another structurally identical one, for the second, in profile the same, may violate people's entitlements or deserts; it may not fit the actual history.

PATTERNING

The entitlement principles of justice in holdings that we have sketched are historical principles of justice. To better understand their precise character, we shall distinguish them from another subclass of the historical principles. Consider, as an example, the principle of distribution according to moral merit. This principle requires that total distributive shares vary directly with moral merit; no person should have a greater share than anyone whose moral merit is greater. (If moral merit could be not merely ordered but measured on an interval or ratio scale, stronger principles could be formulated.) Or consider the principle that results by substituting "usefulness to society" for "moral merit" in the previous principle. Or instead of "distribute according to moral merit," or "distribute according to usefulness to society," we might consider "distribute according to the weighted sum of moral merit, usefulness to society, and need," with the weights of the different dimensions equal. Let us call a principle of distribution *patterned* if it specifies that a distribution is to vary along with some natural dimension, weighted sum of natural dimensions, or lexicographic ordering of natural dimensions. And let us say a distribution is patterned if it accords with some patterned principle. (I speak of natural dimensions, admittedly without a general criterion for them, because for any set of holdings some artificial dimensions can be gimmicked up to vary along with the distribution of the set.) The principle of distribution in accordance with moral merit is a patterned historical principle, which specifies a patterned distribution. "Distribute according to I.Q." is a patterned principle that looks to information not contained in distributional matrices. It is not historical, however, in that it does not look to any past actions creating differential entitlements to evaluate a distribution; it requires only distributional matrices whose columns are labeled by I.Q. scores. The distribution in a society, however, may be composed of such simple patterned distributions, without itself being simply patterned. Different sectors may operate different patterns, or some combination of patterns may operate in different proportions across a society. A distribution composed in this manner, from a small number of patterned distributions, we also shall term "patterned." And we extend the use of "pattern" to include the overall designs put forth by combinations of end-state principles.

Almost every suggested principle of distributive justice is patterned: to each according to his moral merit, or needs, or marginal product, or how hard he tries, or the weighted sum of the foregoing, and so on. The principle of entitlement we have sketched is *not* patterned.[3] There is no one natural dimension or weighted sum or combination of a small number of natural dimensions that yields the distributions generated in accordance with the principle of entitlement. The set of holdings that results when some persons receive their marginal products, others win at gambling, others receive a share of their mate's income, others receive gifts from foundations, others receive interest on loans, others receive gifts from admirers, others receive returns on investment, others make for themselves much of what they have, others find things, and so on, will not be patterned.

* * *

HOW LIBERTY UPSETS PATTERNS

It is not clear how those holding alternative conceptions of distributive justice can reject the entitlement conception of justice in holdings. For suppose a distribution favored by one of these nonentitlement conceptions is realized. Let us suppose it is your favorite one and let us call this distribution D_1; perhaps everyone has an equal share, perhaps shares vary in accordance with some dimension you treasure. Now suppose that Wilt Chamberlain is greatly in demand by basketball teams, being a great gate attraction. (Also suppose contracts run only for a year, with players being free agents.) He signs the following sort of contract with a team: In each home game, twenty-five cents from the price of each ticket of admission goes to him. (We ignore the question of whether he is "gouging" the owners, letting them look out for themselves.) The season starts, and people cheerfully attend his team's games; they buy their tickets, each time dropping a separate twenty-five cents of their admission price into a special box with Chamberlain's name on it. They are excited about seeing him play; it is worth the total admission price to them. Let us suppose that in one season one million persons attend his home games, and Wilt Chamberlain winds up with $250,000, a much larger sum than the average income and larger even than anyone else has. Is he entitled to this income? Is this new distribution

D_2, unjust? If so, why? There is *no* question about whether each of the people was entitled to the control over the resources they held in D_1; because that was the distribution (your favorite) that (for the purposes of argument) we assumed was acceptable. Each of these persons *chose* to give twenty-five cents of their money to Chamberlain. They could have spent it on going to the movies, or on candy bars, or on copies of *Dissent* magazine, or of *Monthly Review*. But they all, at least one million of them, converged on giving it to Wilt Chamberlain in exchange for watching him play basketball. If D_1 was a just distribution, and people voluntarily moved from it to D_2, transferring parts of their shares they were given under D_1 (what was it for if not to do something with?), isn't D_2 also just? If the people were entitled to dispose of the resources to which they were entitled (under D_1), didn't this include their being entitled to give it to, or exchange it with, Wilt Chamberlain? Can anyone else complain on grounds of justice? Each other person already has his legitimate share under D_1. Under D_1, there is nothing that anyone has that anyone else has a claim of justice against. After someone transfers something to Wilt Chamberlain, third parties *still* have their legitimate shares; *their* shares are not changed. By what process could such a transfer among two persons give rise to a legitimate claim of distributive justice on a portion of what was transferred, by a third party who had no claim of justice on any holding of the others *before* the transfer?[4] To cut off objections irrelevant here, we might imagine the exchanges occurring in a socialist society, after hours. After playing whatever basketball he does in his daily work, or doing whatever other daily work he does, Wilt Chamberlain decides to put in *overtime* to earn additional money. (First his work quota is set; he works time over that.) Or imagine it is a skilled juggler people like to see, who puts on shows after hours.

Why might someone work overtime in a society in which it is assumed their needs are satisfied? Perhaps because they care about things other than needs. I like to write in books that I read, and to have easy access to books for browsing at odd hours. It would be very pleasant and convenient to have the resources of Widener Library in my back yard. No society, I assume, will provide such resources close to each person who would like them as part of his regular allotment (under D_1). Thus, persons either must do without some extra things that they want, or be allowed to do something extra to get some of these things. On what basis could the inequalities that would eventuate be forbidden? Notice also that small factories would spring up in a socialist society, unless forbidden. I melt down some of my personal possessions (under D_1) and build a machine out of the material. I offer you, and others, a philosophy lecture once a week in exchange for your cranking the handle on my machine, whose products I exchange for yet other things, and so on. (The raw materials used by the machine are given to me by others who possess them under D_1, in exchange for hearing lectures.) Each person might participate to gain things over and above their allotment under D_1. Some persons even might want to leave their job in socialist industry and work full time in this private sector. I shall say something more about these issues in the next chapter. Here I wish merely to note how private property even in means of production would occur in a socialist society that did not forbid people to use as they wished some of the resources they are given under the socialist distribution D_1. The socialist society would have to forbid capitalist acts between consenting adults.

The general point illustrated by the Wilt Chamberlain example and the example of the entrepreneur in a socialist society is that no end-state principle or distributional patterned principle of justice can be continuously realized without continuous interference with people's lives. Any favored pattern would be transformed into one unfavored by the principle, by people choosing to act in various ways; for example, by people exchanging goods and services with other people, or giving things to other people, things the transferrers are entitled to under the favored distributional pattern. To maintain a pattern one must either continually interfere to stop people from transferring resources as they wish to, or continually (or periodically) interfere to take from some persons resources that others for some reason chose to transfer to them.

* * *

REDISTRIBUTION AND PROPERTY RIGHTS

Apparently, patterned principles allow people to choose to expend upon themselves, but not upon others, those resources they are entitled to (or rather, receive) under some favored distributional pattern D_1. For if each of several persons chooses to expend some of his D_1 resources upon one other person, then that other person will receive more than is D_1 share, disturbing the favored distributional pattern. Maintaining a distributional pattern is individualism with a vengeance! Patterned distributional principles do not give people what entitlement principles do, only better distributed. For they do not give the right to choose what to do with what one has; they do not give the right to choose to pursue an end involving (intrinsically, or as a means) the enhancement of another's position. To such views, families are disturbing; for within a family occur transfers that upset the favored distributional pattern. Either families themselves become units to which distribution takes place, the column occupiers (on what rationale?), or loving behavior is forbidden. We should note in passing the ambivalent position of radicals toward the family. Its loving relationships are seen as a model to be emulated and extended across the whole society, at the same time that it is denounced as a suffocating institution to be broken and condemned as a focus of parochial concerns that interfere with achieving radical goals. Need we say that it is not appropriate to enforce across the wider society the relationships of love and care appropriate within a family, relationships which are voluntarily undertaken?[5] Incidentally, love is an interesting instance of another relationship that is historical, in that (like justice) it depends upon what actually occurred. An adult may come to love another because of the other's characteristics; but it is the other person, and not the characteristics, that is loved. The love is not transferrable to someone else with the same characteristics, even to one who "scores" higher for these characteristics. And the love endures through changes of the characteristics that gave rise to it. One loves the particular person one actually encountered. Why love is historical, attaching to persons in this way and not to characteristics, is an interesting and puzzling question.

Proponents of patterned principles of distributive justice focus upon criteria for determining who is to receive holdings; they consider the reasons for which someone should have something, and also the total picture of holdings. Whether or not it is better to give than to receive, proponents of patterned principles ignore giving altogether. In considering the distribution of goods, income, and so forth, their theories are theories of recipient justice; they completely ignore any right a person might have to give something to someone. Even in exchanges where each party is simultaneously giver and recipient, patterned principles of justice focus only upon the recipient role and its supposed rights. Thus discussions tend to focus on whether people (should) have a right to inherit, rather than on whether people (should) have a right to bequeath or on whether persons who have a right to hold also have a right to choose that others hold in their place. I lack a good explanation of why the usual theories of distributive justice are so recipient oriented; ignoring givers and transferrers and their rights is of a piece with ignoring producers and their entitlements. But why is it *all* ignored?

Patterned principles of distributive justice necessitate *re*distributive activities. The likelihood is small that any actual freely-arrived-at set of holdings fits a given pattern; and the likelihood is nil that it will continue to fit the pattern as people exchange and give. From the point of view of an entitlement theory, redistribution is a serious matter indeed, involving, as it does, the violation of people's rights. (An exception is those takings that fall under the principle of the rectification of injustices.) From other points of view, also, it is serious.

Taxation of earnings from labor is on a par with forced labor.[6] Some persons find this claim obviously true: taking the earnings of n hours labor is like taking n hours from the person; it is like forcing the person to work n hours for another's purpose. Others find the claim absurd. But even these, *if* they object to forced labor, would oppose forcing unemployed hippies to work for the benefit of the needy.[7] And they would also object to forcing each person to work five extra hours each week for the benefit of the needy. But a system that takes five hours' wages in taxes does not seem to them like one that forces someone to work five hour, since it offers the person forced a wider range of choice in activities than does taxation in kind with the particular labor specified. (But we can imagine a gradation of systems of forced labor, from one that specifies a particular activity, to one that gives a choice among two activities, to . . . ; and so on up.) Furthermore, people envisage a system with something like a proportional tax on everything above the amount necessary for basic needs. Some think this does not force someone to work extra hours, since there is no fixed number of extra hours he is forced to work, and since he can avoid the tax entirely by earning only enough to cover his basic needs. This is a very uncharacteristic view of forcing for those who *also* think people are forced to do something *whenever* the alternatives they face are considerably worse. However, *neither* view is correct. The fact that others intentionally intervene, in violation of a side constraint against aggression, to threaten force to limit the alternatives, in this case to paying taxes or (presumably the worse alternative) bare subsistence, makes the taxation system one of forced labor and distinguishes it from other cases of limited choices which are not forcings.

The man who chooses to work longer to gain an income more than sufficient for his basic needs prefers some extra goods or services to the leisure and activities he could perform during the possible non-working hours; whereas the man who chooses not to work the extra time prefers the leisure activities to the extra goods or services he could acquire by working more. Given this, if it would be illegitimate for a tax system to seize some of a man's leisure (forced labor) for the purpose of serving the needy, how can it be legitimate for a tax system to seize some of a man's goods for that purpose? Why should we treat the man whose happiness requires certain material goods or services differently from the man whose preferences and desires make such goods unnecessary for his happiness? Why should the man who prefers seeing a movie (and who has to earn money for a ticket) be open to the required call to aid the needy,

while the person who prefers looking at a sunset (and hence need earn no extra money) is not? Indeed, isn't it surprising that redistributionists choose to ignore the man whose pleasures are so easily attainable without extra labor, while adding yet another burden to the poor unfortunate who must work for his pleasures? If anything, one would have expected the reverse. Why is the person with the nonmaterial or nonconsumption desire allowed to proceed unimpeded to his most favored feasible alternative, whereas the man whose pleasures or desires involve material things and who must work for extra money (thereby serving whomever considers his activities valuable enough to pay him) is constrained in what he can realize? Perhaps there is no difference in principle. And perhaps some think the answer concerns merely administrative convenience. (These questions and issues will not disturb those who think that forced labor to serve the needy or to realize some favored end-state pattern is acceptable.) In a fuller discussion we would have (and want) to extend our argument to include interest, entrepreneurial profits, and so on. Those who doubt that this extension can be carried through, and who draw the line here at taxation of income from labor, will have to state rather complicated patterned *historical* principles of distributive justice, since end-state principles would not distinguish *sources* of income in any way. It is enough for now to get away from end-state principles and to make clear how various patterned principles are dependent upon particular views about the sources or the illegitimacy or the lesser legitimacy of profits, interest, and so on; which particular views may well be mistaken.

What sort of right over others does a legally institutionalized end-state pattern give one? The central core of the notion of a property right in *X*, relative to which other parts of the notion are to be explained, is the right to determine what shall be done with *X*; the right to choose which of the constrained set of options concerning *X* shall be realized or attempted. The constraints are set by other principles or laws operating in the society; in our theory, by the Lockean rights people possess (under the minimal state). My property rights in my knife allow me to leave it where I will, but not in your chest. I may choose which of the acceptable options involving the knife is to be realized. This notion of property helps us to understand why earlier theorists spoke of people as having property in themselves and their labor. They viewed each person as having a right to decide what would become of himself and what he would do, and as having a right to reap the benefits of what he did.

* * *

When end-result principles of distributive justice are built into the legal structure of a society, they (as do most patterned principles) give each citizen an enforceable claim to some portion of the total social product; that is, to some portion of the sum total of the individually and jointly made products. This total product is produced by individuals laboring, using means of production others have saved to bring into existence, by people organizing production or creating means to produce new things or things in a new way. It is on this batch of individual activities that patterned distributional principles give each individual an enforceable claim. Each person has a claim to the activities and the products of other persons, independently of whether the other persons enter into particular relationships that give rise to these claims, and independently of whether they voluntarily take these claims upon themselves, in charity or in exchange for something.

Whether it is done through taxation on wages or on wages over a certain amount, or through seizure of profits, or through there being a big *social pot* so that it's not clear what's coming from where and what's going where, patterned principles of distributive justice involve appropriating the actions of other persons. Seizing the results of someone's labor is equivalent to seizing hours from him and directing him to carry on various activities. If people force you to do certain work, or unrewarded work, for a certain period of time, they decide what you are to do and what purposes your work is to serve apart from your decisions. This process whereby they take this decision from you makes them a *part-owner* of you; it gives them a property right in you. Just as having such partial control and power of decision, by right, over an animal or inanimate object would be to have a property right in it.

End-state and most patterned principles of distributive justice institute (partial) ownership by others of people and their actions and labor. These principles involve a shift from the classical liberals' notion of self-ownership to a notion of (partial) property rights in *other* people.

* * *

May a person emigrate from a nation that has institutionalized some end-state or patterned distributional principle? For some principles (for example, Hayek's) emigration presents no theoretical problem. But for others it is a tricky matter. Consider a nation having a compulsory schemes of minimal social provision to aid the neediest (or one organized so as to maximize the position of the worst-off group); no one may opt out of participating in it. (None may say, "Don't compel me to contribute to others and don't provide for me via this compulsory mechanism if I am in need.") Everyone above a certain level is forced to contribute to aid the needy. But if emigration from the country were allowed, anyone could choose to move to another country that did not have compulsory social provision but otherwise was (as much as possible) identical. In such a case, the person's *only* motive for leaving would be to avoid participating in the compulsory scheme of social provision. And if he does leave, the needy in his initial country will receive no (compelled) help from him. What rationale yields the result that the person be permitted to emigrate, yet forbidden to stay and opt out of the compulsory scheme of social provision? If providing for the needy is of overriding importance, this does militate against allowing internal opting out; but it also speaks against allowing external emigration. (Would it also support, to some extent, the kidnapping of persons living in a place without compulsory social provision, who could be forced to make a contribution to the needy in your community?) Perhaps the crucial component of the position that allows emigration solely to avoid certain arrangements, while not allowing anyone internally to opt out of them, is a concern for fraternal feelings within the country. "We don't want anyone here who doesn't contribute, who doesn't care enough about the others to contribute." That concern, in this case, would have to be tied to the view that forced aiding tends to produce fraternal feelings between the aided and the aider (or perhaps merely to the view that the knowledge that someone or other voluntarily is not aiding produces unfraternal feelings).

NOTES

[1]Applications of the principle of justice in acquisition may also occur as part of the move from one distribution to another. You may find an unheld thing now and appropriate it. Acquisitions also are to be understood as included when, to simplify, I speak only of transitions by transfers.

[2]If the principle of rectification of violations of the first two principles yields more than one description of holdings, then some choice must be made as to which of these is to be realized. Perhaps the sort of considerations about distributive justice and equality that I argue against play a legitimate role in *this* subsidiary choice. Similarly, there may be room for such considerations in deciding which otherwise arbitrary features a statute will embody, when such features are unavoidable because other considerations do not specify a precise line; yet a line must be drawn.

[3]One might try to squeeze a patterned conception of distributive justice into the framework of the entitlement conception, by formulating a gimmicky obligatory "principle of transfer" that would lead to the pattern. For example, the principle that if one has more than the mean income one must transfer everything one holds above the mean to persons below the mean so as to bring them up to (but not over) the mean. We can formulate a criterion for a "principle of transfer" to rule out such obligatory transfers, or we can say that no correct principle of transfer, no principle of transfer in a free society will be like this. The former is probably the better course, though the latter also is true.

Alternatively, one might think to make the entitlement conception instantiate a pattern, by using matrix entries that express the relative strength of a person's entitlements as measured by some real-valued function. But even if the limitation to natural dimensions failed to exclude this function, the resulting edifice would *not* capture our system of entitlements to *particular* things.

[4]Might not a transfer have instrumental effects on a third party, changing his feasible options? (But what if the two parties to the transfer independently had used their holdings in this fashion?) I discuss this question below, but note here that this question concedes the point for distributions of ultimate intrinsic noninstrumental goods (pure utility experiences, so to speak) that are transferable. It also might be objected that the transfer might make a third party more envious because it worsens his position relative to someone else. I find it incomprehensible how this can be thought to involve a claim of justice. * * *

Here and elsewhere in this chapter, a theory which incorporates elements of pure procedural justice might find what I say acceptable, *if* kept in its proper place; that is, if background institutions exist to ensure the satisfaction of certain conditions on distributive shares. But if these institutions are not themselves the sum or invisible-hand result of people's voluntary (nonaggressive) actions, the constraints they impose require justification. At no point does *our* argument assume any background institutions more extensive than those of the minimal night-watchman state, a state limited to protecting persons against murder, assault, theft, fraud, and so forth.

[5]One indication of the stringency of Rawls' difference principle, which we attend to in the second part of this chapter, is its inappropriateness as a governing principle even within a family of individuals who love one another. Should a family devote its resources to maximizing the position of its least well off and least talented child, holding back the other children or using resources for their education and development only if they will follow a policy through their lifetimes of maximizing the position of their least fortunate sibling? Surely not. How then can this even be considered as the appropriate policy for enforcement in the wider society? (I discuss below what I think would be Rawls' reply: that some principles apply at the macro level which do not apply to micro-situations.)

[6]I am unsure as to whether the arguments I present below show that such taxation merely *is* forced labor; so that "is on a par with" means "is one kind of." Or alternatively, whether the arguments emphasize the great similarities between such taxation and forced labor, to show it is plausible and illuminating to view such taxation in the light of forced labor. This latter approach would remind one of how John Wisdom conceives of the claims of metaphysicians.

[7]Nothing hangs on the fact that here and elsewhere I speak loosely of *needs*, since I go on, each time, to reject the criterion of justice which includes it. If, however, something did depend upon the notion, one would want to examine it more carefully. For a skeptical view, see Kenneth Minogue, *The Liberal Mind* (New York: Random House, 1963), pp. 103–112.

What Libertarianism Is

JOHN HOSPERS

The political philosophy that is called libertarianism (from the Latin *libertas*, liberty) is the doctrine that every person is the owner of his own life, and that no one is the owner of anyone else's life; and that consequently every human being has the right to act in accordance with his own choices, unless those actions infringe on the equal liberty of other human beings to act in accordance with *their* choices.

There are several other ways of stating the same libertarian thesis:

1. *No one is anyone else's master, and no one is anyone else's slave.* Since I am the one to decide how my life is to be conducted, just as you decide about yours, I have no right (even if I had the power) to make you my slave and be your master, nor have you the right to become the master by enslaving me. Slavery is *forced* servitude, and since no one owns the life of anyone else, no one has the right to enslave another. Political theories past and present have traditionally been concerned with who should be the master (usually the king, the dictator, or government bureaucracy) and who should be the slaves, and what the extent of the slavery should be. Libertarianism holds that no one has the right to use force to enslave the life of another, or any portion or aspect of that life.

2. *Other men's lives are not yours to dispose of.* I enjoy seeing operas; but operas are expensive to produce. Opera-lovers often say, "The state (or the city, etc.) should subsidize opera, so that we can all see it. Also it would be for people's betterment, cultural benefit, etc." But what they are advocating is nothing more or less than legalized plunder. They can't pay for the productions themselves, and yet they want to see opera, which involves a large number of people and their labor; so what they are saying in effect is, "Get the money through legalized force. Take a little

bit more out of every worker's paycheck every week to pay for the operas we want to see." But I have no right to take by force from the workers' pockets to pay for what I want.

Perhaps it would be better if he *did* go to see opera—then I should try to convince him to go voluntarily. But to take the money from him forcibly, because in my opinion it would be good for *him*, is still seizure of his earnings, which is plunder.

Besides, if I have the right to force him to help pay for my pet projects, hasn't he equally the right to force me to help pay for his? Perhaps he in turn wants the government to subsidize rock-and-roll, or his new car, or a house in the country? If I have the right to milk him, why hasn't he the right to milk me? If I can be a moral cannibal, why can't he too?

We should beware of the inventors of utopias. They would remake the world according to their vision—with the lives and fruits of the labor of *other* human beings. Is it someone's utopian vision that others should build pyramids to beautify the landscape? Very well, then other men should provide the labor; and if he is in a position of political power, and he can't get men to do it voluntarily, then he must *compel* them to "cooperate"—i.e. he must enslave them.

A hundred men might gain great pleasure from beating up or killing just one insignificant human being: but other men's lives are not theirs to dispose of. "In order to achieve the worthy goals of the next five-year-plan, we must forcibly collectivize the peasants . . ."; but other men's lives are not theirs to dispose of. Do you want to occupy, rent-free, the mansion that another man has worked for twenty years to buy? But other men's lives are not yours to dispose of. Do you want operas so badly that everyone is forced to work harder to pay for their subsidization through taxes? But other men's lives are not yours to dispose of. Do you want to have free medical care at the expense of other people, whether they wish to provide it or not? But this would require them

John Hospers, "What Libertarianism Is," in *The Libertarian Alternative: Essays in Social and Political Philosophy*, ed. Tibor R. Machan (Chicago: Nelson-Hall Company, 1974), 3–20 (edited). Reprinted with permission by Nelson-Hall Company.

to work longer for you whether they want to or not, and other men's lives are not yours to dispose of.

The freedom to engage in any type of enterprise, to produce, to own and control property, to buy and sell on the free market, is derived from the rights to life, liberty, and property . . . which are stated in the Declaration of Independence. . . . [but] when a government guarantees a "right" to an education or parity on farm products or a guaranteed annual income, it is staking a claim on the property of one group of citizens for the sake of another group. In short, it is violating one of the fundamental rights it was instituted to protect.[1]

3. *No human being should be a nonvoluntary mortgage on the life of another.* I cannot claim your life, your work, or the products of your effort as mine. The fruit of one man's labor should not be fair game for every freeloader who comes along and demands it as his own. The orchard that has been carefully grown, nurtured, and harvested by its owner should not be ripe for the plucking for any bypasser who has a yen for the ripe fruit. The wealth that some men have produced should not be fair game for looting by government, to be used for whatever purposes its representatives determine, no matter what their motives in so doing may be. The theft of your money by a robber is not justified by the fact that he used it to help his injured mother.

It will already be evident that libertarian doctrine is embedded in a view of the rights of man. Each human being has the right to live his life as he chooses, compatibly with the equal right of all other human beings to live their lives as they choose.

All man's rights are implicit in the above statement. Each man has the right to life: any attempt by others to take it away from him, or even to injure him, violates this right, through the use of coercion against him. Each man has the right to liberty; to conduct his life in accordance with the alternatives open to him without coercive action by others. And every man has the right to property: to work to sustain his life (and the lives of whichever others he chooses to sustain, such as his family) and to retain the fruits of his labor.

People often defend the rights of life and liberty but denigrate property rights, and yet the right to property is as basic as the other two; indeed, without property rights no other rights are possible. Depriving you of property is depriving you of the means by which you live.

. . . All that which an individual possesses by right (including his life and property) are morally his to use, dispose of and even destroy, as he sees fit. If I own my life, then it follows that I am free to associate with whom I please and not to associate with whom I please. If I own my knowledge and services it follows that I may ask any compensation I wish for providing them for another, or I may abstain from providing them at all, if I so choose. If I own my house, if follows that I may decorate it as I please and live in it with whom I please. If I control my own business, it follows that I may charge what I please for my products or services, hire whom I please and not hire whom I please. All that which I own in fact, I may dispose of as I choose to in reality. For anyone to attempt to limit my freedom to do so is to violate my rights.

Where do my rights end? Where yours begin. I may do anything I wish with my own life, liberty and property without your consent; but I may do nothing with your life, liberty and property without your consent. If we recognize the principle of man's rights, it follows that the individual is sovereign of the domain of his own life and property, and is sovereign of no other domain. To attempt to interfere forcibly with another's use, disposal or destruction of his own property is to initiate force against him and to violate his rights.

I have no right to decide how *you* should spend your time or your money. I can make that decision for myself, but not for you, my neighbor. I may deplore your choice of life-style, and I may talk with you about it provided you are willing to listen to me. But I have no right to use force to change it. Nor have I the right to decide how you should spend the money you have earned. I may appeal to you to give it to the Red Cross, and you may prefer to go to prize-fights. But that is your decision, and however much I may chafe about it I do not have the right to interfere forcibly with it, for example by robbing you in order to use the money in accordance with *my* choices. (If I have the right to rob you, have you also the right to rob me?)

When I claim a right, I carve out a niche, as it were, in my life, saying in effect, "This activity I must be able to perform without interference from others. For you and everyone else, this is off limits." And so I put up a "no trespassing" sign, which marks off the area of my right. Each individual's right is his "no trespassing" sign in relation to me and others. I may not encroach upon his domain any more than he upon mine, without my consent. Every night entails a duty, true—but the duty is only that of *forbearance*—that is, of *refraining* from violating the other person's right. If you have a right to life, I have no right to take your life; if you have a right to the products of your labor (property), I have no right to take it from you without your consent. The non-violation of these rights will not guarantee you protection against natural catastrophes such as floods and earthquakes, but it will protect you against the aggressive activities *of other men*. And rights, after all, have to do with one's relations to other human beings, not with one's relations to physical nature.

Nor were these rights created by government; governments—some governments, obviously not all—*recognize* and *protect* the rights that individuals already have. Governments regularly forbid homicide and theft; and, at a more advanced state, protect individuals against such things as libel and breach of contract.

It cannot be by chance that they thus agree. They agree because the alleged creating of rights [by government] was nothing else than giving formal sanction and better definition to those assertions of claims and recognitions of claims which naturally originate from the individual desires of men who have to live in presence of one another.

. . . Those who hold that life is valuable, hold, by implication, that men ought not to be prevented from carrying on life-sustaining activities. . . . Clearly the conception of "natural rights" originates in recognition of the truth that if life is justifiable, there must be a justification for the performance of acts essential to its preservation; and, therefore, a justification of those liberties and claims which makes such acts possible.

. . . To recognize and enforce the rights of individuals, is at the same time to recognize and enforce the conditions to a normal social life.[2]

The *right to property* is the most misunderstood and unappreciated of human rights, and it is one most constantly violated by governments. "Property" of course does not mean only real estate; it includes anything you can call your own—your clothing, your car, your jewelry, your books and papers.

The right of property is not the right to just *take* it from others, for this would interfere with *their* property rights. It is rather the right to work for it, to obtain non-coercively, the money or services which you can present in voluntary exchange.

The right to property is consistently underplayed by intellectuals today, sometimes even frowned upon, as if we should feel guilty for upholding such a right in view of all the poverty in the world. But the right to property is absolutely basic. It is your hedge against the future. It is your assurance that what you have worked to earn will still be there, and be yours, when you wish or need to use it, especially when you are too old to work any longer.

Government has always been the chief enemy of the right to property. The officials of government, wishing to increase their power, and finding an increase of wealth an effective way to bring this about, seize some or all of what a person has earned—and since government has a monopoly of physical force within the geographical area of the nation, it has the power (but not the right) to do this. When this happens, of course, every citizen of that country is insecure: he knows that no matter how hard he works the government can swoop down on him at any time and confiscate his earnings and possessions. A person sees his life savings wiped out in a moment when the tax collectors descend to deprive him of the fruits of his work; or, an industry which has been fifty years in the making and cost millions of dollars and millions of hours of time and planning, is nationalized overnight. Or the government, via inflation, cheapens the currency, so that hard-won dollars aren't worth anything any more. The effect of such actions, of course, is that people lose hope and incentive: if no matter how hard they work the government agents can take it all away, why bother to work at all, for more than today's needs? Depriving people of property is *depriving them of the means by which they live*—the freedom of the individual citizen to do what he wishes with his own life and to plan for the future. Indeed, only if property rights are respected is there any point to planning for the future and working to achieve one's goals. *Property rights are what makes long-range planning possible*—the kind of planning which is a distinctively human endeavor, as opposed to the day-by-day activity of the lion who hunts, who depends on the supply of game tomorrow but has not real insurance against starvation in a day or a week. Without the right to property, the right to life itself amounts to little: how can you sustain your life if you cannot plan ahead? and how can you plan ahead if the fruits of your labor can at any moment be confiscated by government?

Without property rights, no other rights are possible. If one is not free to use that which one has produced, one does not possess the right of liberty. If one is not free to make the products of one's work serve one's chosen goals, one does not possess the right to the pursuit of happiness. And—since man is not a ghost who exists in some non-material manner—if one is not free to keep and to consume the products of one's work, one does not possess the right of life. In a society where men are not free privately to own the material means of production, their position is that of slaves whose lives are at the absolute mercy of their rulers. It is relevant here to remember the statement of Trotsky: "Who does not obey shall not eat."[3]

Indeed, the right to property may well be considered second only to the right to life. Even the freedom of speech is limited by considerations of property. If a person visiting in your home behaves in a way undesired by you, you have every right to evict him: he can scream or agitate elsewhere if he wishes, but not in your home without your consent. Does a person have a right to shout obscenities in a cathedral? No, for the owners of the cathedral (presumably the Church) have not allowed others on their property for that purpose: one may go there to worship or to visit, but not just for any purpose one wishes. Their property right is prior to your or my wish to scream or expectorate or write graffiti on their building. Or, to take the stock example, does a person have a right to shout "Fire!" falsely in a crowded theater? No, for the theater owner has permitted others to enter and use his property only for a specific purpose, that of seeing a film or watching a stage show. If a person heckles or otherwise disturbs other members of the audience, he can be thrown out. (In fact, he can be removed for any reason the owner chooses, provided his admission money is returned.) And if he shouts "Fire!" when there is no fire, he may be endangering other lives by causing a panic or a stampede. The right to free speech doesn't give one the right to say anything anywhere; it is circumscribed by property rights.

Again, some people seem to assume that the right to free speech (including written speech) means that they can go to a newspaper publisher and demand that he print in his newspaper some propaganda or policy statement for their political party (or other group). But of course they have no right to the use of his newspaper. Ownership of the newspaper is the product of his labor, and he has a right to put into his newspaper whatever he wants, for whatever reason. If he excludes material which many readers would like to have in, perhaps they can find it in another newspaper or persuade him to print it himself (if there are enough of them, they will usually do just that). Perhaps they can even cause his newspaper to fail. But as long as he owns it, he has the right to put in it what he wishes; what would a property right be if he could not do this? They have no right to place their material in his newspaper without his consent—not for free, nor even for a fee. Perhaps other newspapers will include it, or perhaps they can start their own newspaper (in which case they have a right to put in it what they like). If not, an option open to them would be to mimeograph and distribute some handbills.

In exactly the same way, no one has a right to "free television time" unless the owner of the television station consents to give it; it is his station, he has the property rights over it, and it is for him to decide how to dispose of his time. He may not decide wisely, but it is his right to decide as he wishes. If he makes enough unwise decisions, and courts enough unpopularity with the viewing public or the sponsors, he may have to go out of business; but as he is free to make his own decisions, so is he free to face their consequences. (If the government owns the television station, then government officials will make the decisions, and there is no guarantee of *their* superior wisdom. The difference is that when "the government" owns the station, you are forced to help pay for its upkeep through your taxes, whether the bureaucrat in charge decides to give you television time or not.)

"But why have *individual* property rights? Why not have lands and houses owned by everybody together?" Yes, this involves no violation of individual rights, as long as everybody consents to this arrangement and no one is forced to join it. The parties to it may enjoy the communal living enough (at least for a time) to overcome certain inevitable problems: that some will work and some not, that some will achieve more in an hour than others can do in a day, and still they will all get the same income. The few who do the most will in the end consider themselves "workhorses" who do the work of two or three or twelve, while the others will be "freeloaders" on the efforts of these few. But as long as they can get out of the arrangement if they no longer like it, no violation of rights is involved. They got in voluntarily, and they can get out voluntarily; no one has used force.

"But why not say that everybody owns everything? That we *all* own everything there is?"

To some this may have a pleasant ring—but let us try to analyze what it means. If everybody owns everything, then everyone has an equal right to go everywhere, do what he pleases, take what he likes, destroy if he wishes, grow crops or burn them, trample them under, and so on. Consider what it would be like in practice. Suppose you have saved money to buy a house for yourself and your family. Now suppose that the principle, "everybody owns everything," becomes adopted. Well then, why shouldn't every itinerant hippie just come in and take over, sleeping in your beds and eating in your kitchen and not bothering to replace the food supply or clean up the mess? After all, it belongs to all of us, doesn't it? So we have just as much right to it as you, the buyer, have. What happens if we *all* want to sleep in the bedroom and there's not room for all of us? Is it the strongest who wins?

What would be the result? Since no one would be responsible for anything, the property would soon be destroyed, the food used up, the facilities nonfunctional. Beginning as a house that *one* family could use, it would end up as a house that *no one* could use. And if the principle continued to be adopted, no one would build houses any more—or anything else. What for? They would only be occupied and used by others, without remuneration.

Suppose two men are cast ashore on an island, and they agree that each will cultivate half of it. The first man is industrious and grows crops and builds a shelter, making the most of the situation with which he is confronted. The second man, perhaps thinking that the warm days will last forever, lies in the sun, picks coconuts while they last, and does a minimum of work to sustain himself. At the time of harvest, the second man has nothing to harvest, nor does he assist the first man in his labors. But later when there is a dearth of food on the island, the second man comes to the first man and demands half of the harvest as his right. But of course he has no right to the product of the first man's labors. The first man may freely choose to give part of his harvest to the second out of charity rather than see him starve; but that is just what it is—charity, not the second man's right.

How can any of man's rights be violated? Ultimately, only by the use of force. I can make suggestions to you, I can reason with you, entreat you (if you are willing to listen), but I cannot *force* you without violating your rights; only by forcing you do I cut the cord between your free decisions and your actions. Voluntary relations between individuals involve no deprivation of rights, but murder, assault, and rape do, because in doing these things I make you the unwilling victim of my actions. A man beating his wife involves no violation of rights if she *wanted* to be beaten. *Force is behavior that requires the unwilling involvement of other persons.*

Thus the use of force need not involve the use of physical violence. If I trespass on your property or dump garbage on it, I am violating your property rights, as indeed I am when I steal your watch; although this is not force in the sense of violence, it *is* a case of your being an unwilling victim of my action. Similarly, if you shout at me so that I cannot be heard when I try to speak, or blow a siren in my ear, or start a factory next door which pollutes my land, you are again violating my rights (to free speech, to property); I am, again, an unwilling victim of your actions. Similarly, if you steal a manuscript of mine and publish it as your own, your are confiscating a piece of my property and thus violating my right to keep what is the product of my labor. Of course, if I give you the manuscript with permission to sign your name to it and keep the proceeds, no violation of rights is involved—any more than if I give you permission to dump garbage on my yard.

According to libertarianism, the role of government should be limited to the retaliatory use of force against those who have initiated its use. It should not enter into any other areas, such as religion, social organization, and economics.

GOVERNMENT

Government is the most dangerous institution known to man. Throughout history it has violated the rights of men more than any individual or group of individuals could do: it has killed people, enslaved them, sent them to forced labor and concentration camps, and regularly robbed and pillaged them of the fruits of their expended labor. Unlike individual criminals, government has the power to arrest and try; unlike individual criminals, it can surround and encompass a person totally, dominating every aspect of one's life, so that one has no recourse from it but to leave the country (and in totalitarian nations even that is prohibited). Government throughout history has a much sorrier record than any individual, even that of a ruthless mass murderer. The signs we see on bumper stickers are chillingly accurate: "Beware: the Government is Armed and Dangerous."

The only proper role of government, according to libertarians, is that of the protector of the citizen against aggression by other individuals. The government, of course, should never initiate aggression; its proper role is as the embodiment of the *retaliatory* use of force against anyone who initiates its use.

If each individual had constantly to defend himself against possible aggressors, he would have to spend a considerable portion of his life in target practice, karate exercises, and other means of self-defenses, and even so he would probably be helpless against groups of individuals who might try to kill, maim, or rob him. He would have little time for cultivating those qualities which are essential to civilized life, nor would improvements in science, medicine, and the arts be likely to occur. The function of government is to take this responsibility off his shoulders: the government undertakes to defend him against aggressors and to punish them if they attack him. When the government is effective in doing this, it enables the citizen to go about his business unmolested and without constant fear for his life. To do this, or course, government must have physical power—the police, to protect the citizen from aggression within its borders, and the armed forces, to protect him from aggressors outside. Beyond that, the government should not intrude upon his life, either to run his business, or adjust his daily activities, or prescribe his personal moral code.

Government, then, undertakes to be the individual's protector; but historically governments have gone far beyond this function. Since they already have the physical power, they have not hesitated to use it for purposes far beyond that which was entrusted to them in the first place. Undertaking initially to protect its citizens against aggression, it has often itself become an aggressor—a far greater aggressor, indeed, than the criminals against whom it was supposed to protect its citizens. Governments have done what no private citizens can do: arrest and imprison individuals without a trial and send them to slave labor camps. Government must have power in order to be effective—and yet the very means by which alone it can be effective make it vulnerable to the abuse of power, leading to managing the lives of individuals and even inflicting terror upon them.

What then should be the function of government? In a word, *the protection of human rights.*

1. *The right to life:* libertarians support all such legislation as will protect human beings against the use of force by others, for example, laws against killing, attempted killing, maiming, beating, and all kinds of physical violence.

2. *The right to liberty:* there should be no laws compromising in any way freedom of speech, of the press, and of peaceable assembly. There should be no censorship of ideas, books, films, or of anything else by government.

3. *The right to property:* libertarians support legislation that protects the property rights of individuals against confiscation, nationalization, eminent domain, robbery, trespass, fraud and misrepresentation, patent and copyright, libel and slander.

Someone has violently assaulted you. Should he be legally liable? Of course. He has violated one of your rights. He has knowingly injured you, and since he has initiated aggression against you he should be made to expiate.

Someone has negligently left his bicycle on the sidewalk where you trip over it in the dark and injure yourself. He didn't do it intentionally; he didn't mean you any harm. Should he be legally liable? Of course; he has, however unwittingly, injured you, and since the injury is caused by him and you are the victim, he should pay.

Someone across the street is unemployed. should you be taxed extra to pay for his expenses? Not at all. You have not injured him, you are not responsible for the fact that he is unemployed (unless you are a senator or bureaucrat who agitated for further curtailing of business, which legislation passed, with the result that your neighbor was laid off by the curtailed business). You may voluntarily wish to help him out, or better still, try to get him a job to put him on his feet again; but since you have initiated no aggressive act against him and neither purposely nor accidentally injured him in any way, you should not be legally penalized for the fact of his unemployment, (Actually, it is just such penalties that increase unemployment.)

One man, A, works hard for years and finally earns a high salary as a professional man. A second man, B, prefers not to work at all, and to spend wastefully what money he has (through inheritance), so that after a year or two he has nothing left. At the end of this time he has a long siege of illness and lots of medical bills to pay. He demands that the bills be paid by the government—that is, by the taxpayers of the land, including Mr. A.

But of course B has no such right. He chose to lead his life in a certain way—that was his voluntary decision. One consequence of that choice is that he must depend on charity in case of later need. Mr. A chose not to live that way. (And if everyone lived like Mr. B, on whom would he depend in case of later need?) Each has a right to live in the way he pleases, but each must live with the consequences of his own decision (which, as always, fall primarily on himself). He cannot, in time of need, claim A's beneficence as his right.

If a house-guest of yours starts to carve his initials in your walls and break up your furniture, you have a right to evict him, and call the police if he makes trouble. If someone starts to destroy the machinery in a factory, the factory-owner is also entitled to evict him and call the police. In both cases, persons other than the owner are permitted on the property only under certain conditions, at the pleasure of the owner. If those conditions are violated, the owner is entitled to use force to set things straight. The case is exactly the same on a college or university campus: if a campus demonstrator starts breaking windows, occupying the president's office, and setting fire to a dean, the college authorities are certainly within their rights to evict him forcibly; one is permitted on the college grounds only under specific conditions, set by the administration: study, peaceful student activity, even political activity if those in charge choose to permit it. If they do not choose to permit peaceful political activity on campus, they may be unwise, since a campus is after all a place where all sides of every issue should get discussed, and the college that doesn't permit this may soon lose its reputation and its students. All the same, the college official who does not permit it is quite within his rights; the students do not own the campus, nor do the hired trouble-makers imported from elsewhere. In the case of a privately owned college, the owners, or whoever they have delegated to administer it, have the right to make the decision as to who shall be permitted on the campus and under what conditions. In the case of a state university or college, the ownership problem is more complex: one could say that the government owns the campus or that "the people" do since they are the taxpayers who support it; but in either case, the university administration has the delegated task of keeping order, and until they are removed by the state administration or the taxpayers, it is theirs to decide who shall be permitted on campus, and what nonacademic activities will be permitted to their students on the premises.

Property rights can be violated by physical trespass, of course, or by anyone entering on your property for any reason without your consent. (If you *do* consent to having your neighbor dump garbage on your yard, there is no violation of your rights.) But the physical trespass of a person is only a special case of violation of property rights. Property rights can be violated by sound-waves, in the form of a loud noise, or the sounds of your neighbor's hi-fi set while you are trying to sleep. Such violations of property rights are of course the subject of action in the courts.

But there is another violation of property rights that has not thus far been honored by the courts; this has to do with the effects of *pollution* of the atmosphere.

From the beginning of modern air pollution, the courts made a conscious decision not to protect, for example, the orchards of farmers from the smoke of nearby factories or locomotives. They said, in effect, to the farmers: yes, your private property is being invaded by this smoke, but we hold that "public policy" is more important than private property, and public policy holds factories and locomotives to be good things. These goods were allowed to override the

defense of property rights with our consequent headlong rush into pollution disaster. The remedy is both "radical" and crystal clear, and if has nothing to do with multibillion dollar palliative programs at the expense of the taxpayers which do not even meet the real issue. The remedy is simply to enjoin anyone from injecting pollutants into the air, and thereby invading the rights of persons and property. Period. The argument that such an injunction prohibition would add to the costs of industrial production is as reprehensible as the pre Civil War argument that the abolition of slavery would add to the costs of growing cotton, and therefore should not take place. For this means that the polluters are able to impose the high costs of pollution upon those whose property rights they are allowed to invade with impunity.[4]

What about automobiles, the chief polluters of the air? One can hardly sue every automobile owner. But one can sue the manufacturers of automobiles who do not install anti-smog devices on the cars which they distribute—and later (though this is more difficult), owners of individual automobiles if they discard the equipment or do not keep it functional.

The violation of rights does not apply only to air pollution. If someone with a factory upstream on a river pollutes the river, anyone living downstream from him, finding his water polluted, should be able to sue the owner of the factory. In this way the price of adding the antipollutant devices will be the owner's responsibility, and will probably be added to the cost of the products which the factory produces and thus spread around among all consumers, rather than the entire cost being borne by the users of the river in the form of polluted water, with the consequent impossibility of fishing, swimming, and so on. In each case, pollution would be stopped at the source rather than having its ill effects spread around to numerous members of the population.

What about property which you do not work to earn, but which you *inherit* from someone else? Do you have a right to that? You have no right to it until someone decides to give it to you. Consider the man who willed it to you: it was his, he had the right to use and dispose of it as he saw fit: and if he deiced to give it to you, this is a windfall for you, but it was only the exercise of his right. Had the property been seized by the government at the man's death, or distributed among numerous other people designated by the government, it *would* have been a violation of his rights: for he, who worked to earn and sustain it, would not have been able to dispose of it according to his own judgment. If he doesn't have the right to determine who shall have it, who does?

What about the property status of your intellectual activity, such as inventions you may devise and books you write? These, of course, are your property also; they are the products of your mind; you worked at them, you created them. Prior to that, they did not exist. If you worked five years to write a book, and someone stole it and published it as his own, receiving royalties from its sales, he would have stolen your property just as surely as if he had robbed your home. The same is true if someone used and sold without your permission an invention which was the product of your labor and ingenuity.

The role of government with respect to this issue, as least most governments of the Western world, is a proper one: government protects the products of your labor from the moment they materialize. Copyright law protects your writing from piracy. In the United States, one's writings are protected for a period of twenty-seven years, and another twenty-seven if one applies for renewal of the copyright. In most other countries, they are protected for a period of fifty years after the author's death, permitting both himself and his surviving heirs to reap the fruits of his labor. After that they enter the "public domain"—that is, anyone may reprint them without your or your heirs' permission. Patent law protects your inventions for a limited period which varies according to the type of invention. In no case are you forced to avail yourself of this protection; you need not apply for patent or copyright coverage if you do not wish to do so. But the protection of your intellectual property is there, in case you wish to use it.

What about the property status of the airwaves? Here the government's position is far more questionable. The government now claims ownership of the airwaves, leasing them to individuals and corporations. The government renews leases or refuses them depending on whether the programs satisfy authorities in the Federal Communications Commission. The official position is that "we all own the airwaves"; but since only one party can broadcast on a certain frequency at a certain time without causing chaos, it is simply a fact of reality that "everyone" cannot use it. In fact the government decides who shall use the airwaves, and one courts its displeasure only at the price of a revoked license. One can write without government approval but one cannot use the airwaves without the approval of government.

What policy should have been observed with regard to the airwaves? Much the same as the policy that was followed in the case of the Homestead Act, when the lands of the American West were opening up for settlement. There was a policy of "first come, first served," with the government parceling out a certain acreage for each individual who wanted to claim the land as his own. There was no charge for the land, but if a man had not used it and built a dwelling during the first two-year period, it was assumed that he was not homesteading and the land was given to the next man in line. The airwaves too could have been given out on a "first come, first served" basis. The first man who used a given frequency would be its owner, and the government would protect him in the use of it against trespassers. If others wanted to use the same frequency, they would have to buy it from the first man, if he was willing to sell, or try to buy another, just as one now does with land.

Laws may be classified into three types: (1) laws protecting individuals against themselves, such as laws against fornication and other sexual behavior, alcohol, and drugs; (2) laws protecting individuals against aggressions by other individuals, such as laws against murder, robbery, and fraud; (3) laws requiring people to help one another; for example, all laws which rob Peter to pay Paul, such as welfare.

Libertarians reject the first class of laws totally. Behavior which harms no one else is strictly the individual's own affair. Thus, there should be no laws against becoming intoxicated, since whether or not to become intoxicated is the individual's own decision; but there should be laws against driving while intoxicated since the drunken driver is a threat to every other motorist on the highway (drunken driving falls into type 2). Similarly, there should be no laws against drugs (except the prohibition of sale of drugs to minors) as long as the taking of these drugs poses no threat to anyone else. Drug addiction is a psychological problem to which no present solution exists. Most of the social harm caused by addicts, other than to themselves, is the result of thefts which they perform in order to continue their habit—and then the *legal* crime is the theft, not the addiction. The actual cost of heroin is about ten cents a shot; if it were legalized, the enormous traffic in illegal sale and purchase of it would stop, as well as the accompanying proselytization to get new addicts (to make more money for the pusher) and the thefts performed by addicts who often require eighty dollars a day just to keep up the habit. Addiction would not stop, but the crimes would. It is estimated that 75 percent of the burglaries in New York City today are performed by addicts, and all these crimes could be wiped out at one stroke through the legalization of drugs. (Only when the taking of drugs could be shown to constitute a threat to *others,* should it be prohibited by law. It is only laws protecting people against *themselves* that libertarians oppose.)

Laws should be limited to the second class only; aggression by individuals against other individuals. These are laws whose function is to protect human beings against encroachment by others, and this, as we have seen, is (according to libertarianism) the sole function of government.

Libertarians also reject the third class of laws totally: no one should be forced by law to help others, not even to tell them the time of day if requested, and certainly not to given them a portion of one's weekly paycheck. Governments, in the guise of humanitarianism, have given to some by taking from others (charging a "handling fee" in the process, which, because of the government's waste and inefficiency, sometimes is several hundred percent). And in so doing they have decreased incentive, violated the rights of individuals, and lowered the standard of living of almost everyone.

All such laws constitute what libertarians call *moral cannibalism.* A cannibal in the physical sense is a person who lives off the flesh of other human beings. A *moral* cannibal is one who believes he has a right to live off the "spirit" of other human beings— who believes that he has a moral claim on the productive capacity, time, and effort expended by others.

It has become fashionable to claim virtually everything that one needs or desires as one's right. Thus many people claim that they have a right to a job, the right to free medical care, to free food and clothing, to a decent home, and so on. Now if one asks, apart from any specific context, whether it would be desirable if everyone had these things, one might well say yes. But there is a gimmick attached to each of them: *At whose expense?* Jobs, medical care, education, and so on, don't grow on trees. These are goods and services *produced only by men.* Who, then is to provide them, and under what conditions?

If you have a right to a job, who is to supply it? Must an employer supply it even if he doesn't want to hire you? What if you are unemployable, or incurably lazy? (If you say "the government must supply it," does that mean that a job must be created for you which no employer needs done, and that you must be kept in it regardless of how much or little you work?) If the employer is forced to supply it at his expense even if he doesn't need you, then isn't he being enslaved to that extent? What ever happened to *his* right to conduct his life and his affairs in accordance with his choices?

If you have a right to free medical care, then, since medical care doesn't exist in nature as wild apples do, some people will have to supply it to you for free; that is, they will have to spend their time and money and energy taking care of you whether they want to or not. What ever happened to *their* right to conduct their lives as they see fit? Or do you have a right to violate theirs? Can there be a right to violate rights?

All those who demand this or that as a "free service" are consciously or unconsciously evading the fact that there is in reality no such things as free services. All man-made goods and services are the result of human expenditure of time and effort. There is no such thing as "something for nothing" in this world.

If you demand something free, you are demanding that other men give their time and effort to you without compensation. If they voluntarily choose to do this, there is no problem, but if you demand that they be *forced* to do it, you are interfering with their right not to do it if they so choose. "Swimming in this pool ought to be free!" says the indignant passerby. What he means is that others should build a pool, others should provide the materials, and still others should run it and keep it in functioning order, so that *he* can use it without fee. But what right has he to the expenditure of *their* time and effort? To expect something "for free" is to expect it *to be paid for by others* whether they choose to or not.

Many questions, particularly about economic matters, will be generated by the libertarian account of human rights and the role of government. Should government have no role in assisting the needy, in providing social security, in legislating minimum wages, in fixing prices, and putting a ceiling on rents, in curbing monopolies, in erecting tariffs, in guaranteeing jobs, in managing the money supply? To these and all similar questions the libertarian answers with an unequivocal no.

"But then you'd let people go hungry!" comes the rejoinder. This, the libertarian insists, is precisely what would not happen; with the restrictions removed, the economy would flourish as never before. With the controls taken off business, existing enterprises would expand and new ones would spring into existence satisfying more and more consumer needs; millions more people would be gainfully employed instead of subsisting on welfare, and all kinds of research and production released from the stranglehold of government, would proliferate, fulfilling man's needs and desires as never before. It has always been so whenever government has permitted men to be free traders on a free market. But why this is so, and how the free market is the best solution to all problems relating to the material aspect of man's life, is another and far longer story. It is told in detail in chapters 3 to 9 of my book, *Libertarianism*.

NOTES

1. William W. Bayes, "What Is Property?" *The Freeman,* July 1970, p. 348.

2. Herbert Spencer, *The Man vs. the State* (1884; reprint ed., Caldwell, Id.: Caxton Printers, 1940), p. 191.

3. Nathaniel Branden, *Who Is Ayn Rand?* (New York: Random House, 1962), p. 47.

4. Murray Rothbard, "The Great Ecology Issue," *The Individualist,* 2, no. 2 (Feb. 1970), p. 5.

Equality and Liberty

KAI NIELSEN

I.

In North America socialism gets a bad press. It is under criticism for its alleged economic inefficiency and for its moral and human inadequacy. I want here to address the latter issue.[1] Looking at capitalism and

Kai Nielsen, "A Moral Case for Socialism," *Critical Review* 3, nos. 3/4 (Summer/Fall 1989): 542–53 (edited). Reprinted with permission of *Critical Review*.

socialism, I want to consider, against the grain of our culture, what kind of moral case can be made for socialism.

The first thing to do, given the extensive, and, I would add, inexcusably extensive, confusions about this, is to say what socialism and capitalism are. That done I will then, appealing to a cluster of values which are basic in our culture, concerning which there is a considerable and indeed a reflective consensus, examine how capitalism and socialism fare with respect to these values.[2] Given that people generally, at least in Western societies, would want it to be the case that these values have a stable exemplification in our social lives, it is appropriate to ask the question: which of these social systems is more likely stably to exemplify them? I shall argue, facing the gamut of a careful comparison in the light of these values, that, everything considered, socialism comes out better than capitalism. And this, if right, would give us good reason for believing that socialism is preferable—indeed morally preferable—to capitalism if it also turns out to be a feasible socio-economic system.

What, then, are socialism and capitalism? Put most succinctly, capitalism requires the existence of private *productive* property (private ownership of the means of production) while socialism works toward its abolition. What is essential for socialism is public ownership and control of the means of production and public ownership means just what it says: *ownership by the public*. Under capitalism there is a domain of private property rights in the means of production which are not subject to political determination. That is, even where the political domain is a democratic one, they are not subject to determination by the public; only an individual or a set of individuals who own that property can make the final determination of what is to be done with that property.[3] These individuals make that determination and not citizens at large, as under socialism. In fully developed socialism, by contrast, there is, with respect to productive property, no domain which is not subject to political determination by the public, namely by the citizenry at large. Thus, where this public ownership and control is genuine, and not a mask for control by an elite of state bureaucrats, it will mean genuine popular and democratic control over productive property. What socialism is *not* is *state* ownership in the absence of, at the very least, popular sovereignty, i.e., genuine popular control over the state apparatus including any economic functions it might have.

The property that is owned in common under socialism is the means of existence—the productive property in the society. Socialism does not proscribe the ownership of private personal property, such as houses, cars, television sets and the like. It only proscribes the private ownership of the means of production.

The above characterizations catch the minimal core of socialism and capitalism, what used to be called the essence of those concepts.[4] But beyond these core features, it is well, in helping us to make our comparison, to see some other important features which characteristically go with capitalism and socialism. Minimally, capitalism is private ownership of the means of production but it is also, at least characteristically, a social system in which a class of capitalists owns and controls the means of production and hires workers who, owning little or no means of production, sell their labor-power to some capitalist or other for a wage. This means that a capitalist society will be a class society in which there will be two principal classes: capitalists and workers. Socialism by contrast is a social system in which every able-bodied person is, was or will be a worker. These workers commonly own and control the means of production (this is the characteristic form of public ownership).[5] Thus in socialism we have, in a perfectly literal sense, a classless society for there is no division between human beings along class lines.[6]

There are both pure and impure forms of capitalism and socialism.[7] The pure form of capitalism is competitive capitalism, the capitalism that Milton Friedman would tell us is the real capitalism while, he would add, the impure form is monopoly or corporate capitalism. Similarly the pure form of socialism is democratic socialism, with firm workers' control of the means of production and an industrial as well as a political democracy, while the impure form is state bureaucratic socialism.

Now it is a noteworthy fact that, to understate it, actually existing capitalisms and actually exiting socialisms tend to be the impure forms. Many partisans of capitalism lament the fact that the actually existing capitalisms overwhelmingly tend to be forms of corporate capitalism where the state massively intervenes in the running of the economy. It is unclear whether anything like a fully competitive capitalism actually exists—perhaps Hong Kong approximates it—and it is also unclear whether many of the actual players in the major capitalist societies (the existing capitalists and their managers) want or even expect that it is possible to have laissez-faire capitalism again (if indeed we ever had it). Some capitalist societies are further down the corporate road than other societies, but they are all forms of corporate, perhaps in some instances even monopoly, capitalism. Competitive capitalism seems to be more of a libertarian dream than a sociological reality or even something desired by many informed and tough-minded members of the capitalist class. Socialism has had a similar fate. Its historical exemplifications tend to be of the impure forms, namely the bureaucratic state socialisms.[8] Yugoslavia is perhaps to socialism what Hong Kong is to capitalism. It is a candidate for what might count as an exemplification, or at least a near approximation, of the pure form.

This paucity of exemplifications of pure forms of either capitalism or socialism raises the question of whether the pure forms are at best unstable social systems and at worse merely utopian ideals. I shall not try directly to settle that issue here. What I shall do instead is to compare *models* with *models*. In asking about the moral case for socialism, I shall compare forms that a not inconsiderable number of the theoretical protagonists of each take to be pure forms but which are still, they believe, historically feasible. But I will also be concerned to ask whether these models—these pure forms—can reasonably be expected to come to have a home. If they are not historically feasible models, then, even if we make a good theoretical moral case for them, we will have hardly provided a good moral case for socialism or capitalism. To avoid bad utopianism we must be talking about forms which could be on the historical agenda. (I plainly here do not take "bad utopianism" to be pleonastic.)

II.

Setting aside for the time being the feasibility question, let us compare the pure forms of capitalism and socialism—that is to say, competitive capitalism and democratic socialism—as to how they stand with respect to sustaining and furthering the values of freedom and autonomy, equality, justice, rights and democracy. My argument shall be that socialism comes out better with respect to those values.

Let us first look at freedom and autonomy. An autonomous person is a person who is able to set her ends for herself and in optimal circumstances is able to pursue those ends. But freedom does not only mean being autonomous; it also means the absence of unjustified political and social interference in the pursuit of one's ends. Some might even say that it is just the absence of interference with one's ends. Still it is self-direction—autonomy—not non-interference which is *intrinsically* desirable. Non-interference is only valuable where it is an aid to our being able to do what we want and where we are sufficiently autonomous to have some control over our wants.

How do capitalism and socialism fare in providing the social conditions which will help or impede the flourishing of autonomy? Which model society would make for the greater flourishing of autonomy? My argument is (a) that democratic socialism makes it possible for more people to be more fully autonomous than would be autonomous under capitalism; and (b) that democratic socialism also interferes less in people's exercise of their autonomy than any form of capitalism. All societies limit liberty by interfering with people doing what they want to do in some ways, but the restrictions are more extensive, deeper and more undermining of autonomy in capitalism than in democratic socialism. Where there is private ownership of productive property, which, remember, is private ownership of the means of life, it cannot help but be the case that a few (the owning and controlling capitalist class) will have, along with the managers beholden to them, except in periods of revolutionary turmoil, a firm control, indeed a domination, over the vast majority of people in the society. The capitalist class with the help of their managers determines whether workers (taken now as individuals) can work, how they work, on what they work, the conditions under which they work and what is done with what they produce (where they are producers) and what use is made of their skills and the like.[9] As we move to welfare state capitalism—a compromise still favoring capital which emerged out of long and bitter class struggles—the state places some restrictions on some of these powers of capital. Hours, working conditions and the like are controlled in certain ways. Yet whether workers work and continue to work, how they work and on what, what is done with what they produce, and the rationale for their work are not determined by the workers themselves but by the owners of capital and their managers; this means a very considerable limitation on the autonomy and freedom of workers. Since workers are the great majority, such socio-economic relations place a very considerable limitation on human freedom and indeed on the very most important freedom that people have, namely their being able to live in a self-directed manner, when compared with the industrial democracy of democratic socialism. Under capitalist arrangements it simply cannot fail to be the case that a very large number of people will lose control over a very central set of facets of their lives, namely central aspects of their work and indeed in many instances, over their very chance to be able to work.

Socialism would indeed prohibit capitalist acts between consenting adults; the capitalist class would lose its freedom to buy and sell and to control the labor market. There should be no blinking at the fact that socialist social relations would impose some limitations on freedom, for there is, and indeed can be, no society without norms and some sanctions. In any society you like there will be some things you are at liberty to do and some things that you may not do.[10] However, democratic socialism must bring with it an industrial democracy where workers by various democratic procedures would determine how they are to work, on what they are to work, the hours of their work, under what conditions they are to work (insofar as this is alterable by human effort at all), what they will produce and how much, and what is to be done with what they produce. Since, instead of there being "private ownership of the means of production," there is in a genuinely socialist society "public ownership of the means of production," the means of life are owned by everyone and thus each person has a *right* to work: she has, that is, a right to the means of life. It is no longer the private preserve of an individual owner of capital but it is owned in common by us all. This means that each of us has an equal right to the means of life. Members of the capitalist class would have a few of their liberties restricted, but these are linked with owning and controlling capital and are not the important civil and political liberties that we all rightly cherish. Moreover, the limitation of the capitalist liberties to buy and sell and the like would make for a more extensive liberty for many, many more people.

One cannot respond to the above by saying that workers are free to leave the working class and become capitalists or at least petty bourgeoisie. They may indeed all in theory, taken *individually*, be free to leave the working class, but if many in fact try to leave the exits will very quickly become blocked.[11] Individuals are only free on the condition that the great mass of people, taken collectively, are not. We could not have capitalism without a working class and the working class is not free within the capitalist system to cease being wage laborers. We cannot all be capitalists. A people's capitalism is nonsense. Though a petty commodity production system (the family farm writ large) is a logical possibility, it is hardly a stable empirical possibility and, what is most important for the present discussion, such a system would not be a capitalist system. Under capitalism, most of us, if we are to find any work at all, will just have to sell (or *perhaps* "rent" is the better word) our labor-power as a commodity. Whether you sell or rent your labor power or, where it is provided, you go on welfare, you will not have much control over areas very crucial to your life. If these are the only feasible alternatives facing the working class, working class autonomy is very limited indeed. But these are the only alternatives under capitalism.

Capitalist acts between consenting adults, if they become sufficiently widespread, lead to severe imbalances in power. These imbalances in power tend to undermine autonomy by creating differentials in wealth and control between workers and capitalists. Such imbalances are the name of the game for capitalism. Even if we (perversely I believe) call a system of petty commodity production capitalism, we still must say that such a socio-economic system is inherently unstable. Certain individuals would win out in this exchanging of commodities and in fairly quick order it would lead to a class system and the imbalances of power—the domination of the many by the few—that I take to be definitive of capitalism. By abolishing capitalist acts between consenting adults, then (but leaving personal property and civil and political liberties untouched), socialism protects more extensive freedoms for more people and in far more important areas of their lives.

III.

So democratic socialism does better regarding the value that epitomizes capitalist pride (*hubris*, would, I think, be a better term), namely autonomy. It also does better, I shall now argue, than capitalism with respect to another of our basic values, namely democracy. Since this is almost a corollary of what I have said about autonomy I can afford to be briefer. In capitalist societies, democracy must simply be *political* democracy. There can in the nature of the case be no genuine or thorough workplace democracy. When we enter the sphere of production, capitalists and not workers own, and therefore at least ultimately control, the means of production. While capitalism, as in some workplaces in West Germany and Sweden, sometimes can be pressured into allowing an ameliorative measure of worker control, once ownership rights are given up, we no longer have private productive property but public productive property (and in that way social ownership): capitalism is given up and we have socialism. However, where worker control is restricted to a few firms, we do not yet have socialism. What makes a system socialist or capitalist depends on what happens across the whole society, not just in isolated firms.[12] Moreover, managers can become very important within capitalist firms, but as long as ownership, including the ability to close the place down and liquidate the business, rests in the hands of capitalists we can have no genuine workplace democracy. Socialism, in its pure form, carries with it, in a way capitalism in any form cannot, workplace democracy. (That some of the existing socialisms are anything but pure does not belie this.)[13]

Similarly, whatever may be said of existing socialisms or at least of some existing socialisms, it is not the case that there is anything in the very idea of socialism that militates against political as well as industrial democracy. Socialists are indeed justly suspicious of some of the tricks played by parliamentary democracy in bourgeois countries, aware of its not infrequent hypocrisy and the limitations of its stress on purely legal and formal political rights and liberties. Socialists are also, without at all wishing to throw the baby out with the bath water, rightly suspicious of any simple reliance on majority rule, unsupplemented by other democratic procedures and safeguards.[14] But there is nothing in socialist theory that would set it against political democracy and the protection of political and civil rights; indeed there is much in socialism that favors them, namely in stress on both autonomy and equality.

The fact that political democracy came into being and achieved stability within capitalist societies may prove something about conditions necessary for its coming into being, but it says nothing about capitalism being necessary for sustaining it. In Chile, South Africa and Nazi Germany, indeed, capitalism has flourished without the protection of civil and political rights or anything like a respect for the democratic tradition. There is nothing structural in socialism that would prevent it from continuing those democratic traditions or cherishing those political and civil rights. That something came about under certain conditions does not establish that these conditions are necessary for its continued existence. That men initially took an interest in chess does not establish that women cannot quite naturally take an interest in it as well. When capitalist societies with long-flourishing democratic traditions move to socialism there is no reason at all to believe that they will not continue to be democratic. (Where societies previously had no democratic tradition or only a very weak one, matters are more problematic.)

IV.

I now want to turn to a third basic value, equality. In societies across the political spectrum, *moral* equality (the belief that everyone's life matters equally) is an accepted value.[15] Or, to be somewhat cynical about the matter, at least lip service is paid to it. But even this lip service is the compliment that vice pays to virtue. That is to say, such a belief is a deeply held considered conviction in modernized societies, though it has not been at all times and is not today a value held in all societies. This is most evident concerning moral equality.

While this value is genuinely held by the vast majority of people in capitalist societies, it can hardly be an effective or functional working norm where there is such a diminishment of autonomy as we have seen obtains unavoidably in such societies. Self-respect is deeply threatened where so many people lack effective control over their own lives, where there are structures of domination, where there is alienated labor, where great power differentials and differences in wealth make for very different (and often very bleak) life chances. For not inconsiderable numbers, in fact, it is difficult to maintain self-respect under such conditions unless they are actively struggling against the system. And, given present conditions, fighting the system, particularly in societies such as the United States, may well be felt to be a hopeless task. Under such conditions any real equality of opportunity is out of the question. And the circumstances are such, in spite of what is often said about these states, that equality of condition is an even more remote possibility. But without at least some of these things moral equality cannot even be approximated. Indeed, even to speak of it sounds like an obscene joke given the social realities of our lives.

Although under welfare-state capitalism some of the worst inequalities of capitalism are ameliorated, workers still lack effective control over their work, with repercussions in political and public life as well. Differentials of wealth cannot but give rise to differentials in power and control in politics, in the media, in education, in the direction of social life and in what options get seriously debated. The life chances of workers and those not even lucky enough to be workers (whose ranks are growing and will continue to grow under capitalism) are impoverished compared to the life chances of members of the capitalist class and its docile professional support stratum.

None of these equality-undermining features would obtain under democratic socialism. Such societies would, for starters, be classless, eliminating the power and control differentials that go with the class system of capitalism. In addition to political democracy, industrial democracy and all the egalitarian and participatory control that goes with that would, in turn, reinforce moral equality. Indeed it would make it possible where before it was impossible. There would be a commitment under democratic socialism to attaining or at least approximating, as far as it is feasible, equality of condition; and this, where approximated, would help make for real equality of opportunity, making equal life chances something less utopian than it must be under capitalism.

In fine, the very things, as we have seen, that make for greater autonomy under socialism than under capitalism, would, in being more equally distributed, make for greater equality of condition, greater equality of opportunity and greater moral equality in a democratic socialist society than in a capitalist one. These values are values commonly shared by both capitalistically inclined people and those who are socialistically inclined. What the former do not see is that in modern industrial societies, democratic socialism can better deliver these goods than even progressive capitalism.

There is, without doubt, legitimate worry about bureaucratic control under socialism.[16] But that is a worry under any historically feasible capitalism as well, and it is anything but clear that state bureaucracies are worse than great corporate bureaucracies. Indeed, if socialist bureaucrats were, as the socialist system requires, really committed to production for needs and to achieving equality of condition, they might, bad as they are, be the lesser of two evils. But in any event democratic socialism is not bureaucratic state socialism, and there is no structural reason to believe that it must—if it arises in a society with skilled workers committed to democracy—give rise to bureaucratic state socialism. There will, inescapably, be some bureaucracy, but in a democratic socialist society it must and indeed will be controlled. This is not merely a matter of optimism about the will of socialists, for there are more mechanisms for democratic control of bureaucracy within a democratic socialism that is both a political and an industrial democracy, than there can be under even the most benign capitalist democracies—democracies which for structural reasons can never be industrial democracies. If, all that notwithstanding, bureaucratic creepage is inescapable in modern societies, then that is just as much a problem for capitalism as for socialism.

The underlying rationale for production under capitalism is profit and capital accumulation. Capitalism is indeed a marvelous engine for building up the productive forces (though clearly at the expense of considerations of equality and autonomy). We might look on it, going back to earlier historical times, as something like a forced march to develop the productive forces. But now that the productive forces in advanced capitalist societies are wondrously developed, we are in a position to direct them to far more humane and more equitable uses under a socio-economic system whose rationale for production is to meet human needs (the needs of everyone as far as this is possible). This egalitarian thrust, together with the socialists' commitment to attaining, as far as that is possible, equality of condition, makes it clear that socialism will produce more equality than capitalism.

V.

In talking about autonomy, democracy and equality, we have, in effect, already been talking about justice. A society or set of institutions that does better in these respects than another society will be a more just society than the other society.[17]

Fairness is a less fancy name for justice. If we compare two societies and the first is more democratic than the second; there is more autonomy in the first society than in the second; there are more nearly equal life chances in the first society than in the second and thus greater equality of opportunity; if, without sacrifice of autonomy, there is more equality of

condition in the first society than in the second; and if there is more moral equality in the first society than in the second, then we cannot but conclude that the first society is a society with more fairness than the second and, thus, that it is the more just society. But this is exactly how socialism comes out vis-à-vis even the best form of capitalism.[18]

A society which undermines autonomy, heels in democracy (where democracy is not violating rights), makes equality impossible to achieve and violates rights cannot be a just society. If, as I contend, that is what capitalism does, and cannot help doing, then a capitalist society cannot be a just society. Democratic socialism, by contrast, does not need to do any of those things, and we can predict that it would not, for there are no structural imperatives in democratic socialism to do so and there are deep sentiments in that tradition urging us not to do so. I do not for a moment deny that there are similar sentiments for autonomy and democracy in capitalist societies, but the logic of capitalism, the underlying structures of capitalist societies—even the best of capitalist societies—frustrate the realization of the states of affairs at which those sympathies aim.[19] A radical democrat with a commitment to human rights, to human autonomy and moral equality and fair equality of opportunity ought to be a democratic socialist and a firm opponent of capitalism—even a capitalism with a human face.

NOTES

1. For arguments about efficiency see David Schweickart, *Capitalism or Worker Control?* (New York: Praeger, 1980) and Samuel Bowles, David M. Gordon and Thomas E. Weisskopf, *Beyond the Wasteland: A Democratic Alternative to Economic Decline* (New York: Anchor Doubleday, 1983).

2. Andrew Levine's work is very important here and my own account has been extensively influenced by his. See Andrew Levine, *Arguing for Socialism* (London: Routledge & Kegan Paul, 1984); Andrew Levine, "On Arguing for Socialism—Theoretical Considerations," *Socialism and Democracy* (Spring/Summer 1968): 19–28; and Andrew Levine, *The Withering Away of the State* (London: Verso, 1987).

3. That this is a system which is distinctive of capitalism and to which there are many working alternatives is shown by

A.M. Honoré, "Property, Title and Redistribution" in Virginia Held, ed., *Property, Profits and Economic Justice* (Belmont, Calif.: Wadsworth Publishing, 1980), 84–92.

4. This is carefully argued for by Andrew Levine. See the references in my second note.

5. Kai Nielsen, "Capitalism, Socialism and Justice" in Tom Regan and Donald Van De Veere, eds., *And Justice for All* (Totowa, N.J.: Rowman and Littlefield, 1982), 264–96.

6. G.A. Cohen, "The Structure of Proletarian Unfreedom," *Philosophy and Public Affairs* 12, no. 1 (Winter 1982): 2–33 and John Exdell, "Liberty, Equality and Capitalism," *Canadian Journal of Philosophy* 11, no. 3 (September 1981): 457–72.

7. Nielsen, "Capitalism, Socialism and Justice," 264–69.

8. Ferenc Fehér, Agnes Heller, György Markus, *Dictatorship over Needs: An Analysis of Soviet Societies* (Oxford: Basil Blackwell, 1983).

9. Cohen, "The Structure of Proletarian Unfreedom."

10. G.A. Cohen, "Freedom, Justice and Capitalism," *New Left Review* no. 26 (March/April 1981) and his "Illusions About Private Property and Freedom," *Issues in Marxist Philosophy*, vol. IV. ed. John Mepham and David-Hillel Ruben (Sussex: Harvester Press, 1981), 223–39.

11. G.A. Cohen, *Karl Marx's Theory of History* (Oxford: Clarendon Press, 1978) 73–7.

12. Levine, *Arguing for Socialism*, 1–11.

13. How far they are from that is shown by Fehér, Heller and Markus, *Dictatorship over Needs*.

14. Claus Offe, *Disorganized Capitalism* (Cambridge, Mass.: MIT Press, 1985), 259–99.

15. Thomas Nagel, *Mortal Questions* (Cambridge: Cambridge University Press, 1979), 106–27.

16. Fehér, Heller and Markus, *Dictatorship over Needs*.

17. John Rawls, *A Theory of Justice* (Cambridge, Mass.: Harvard University Press, 1971); Kai Nielsen, *Equality and Liberty: A Defense of Radical Egalitarianism* (Totowa, N.J.: Rowman and Allanheld, 1985); and Samuel Bowles and Herbert Gintis, *Democracy and Capitalism* (New York: Basic Books, 1986).

18. Levine citations in n 2 above and Nielsen, *Equality and Liberty*.

19. See Richard C. Edwards, Michael Reich and Thomas E. Weisekopf, eds., *The Capitalist System*, 3rd ed. (Englewood Cliffs, N.J.: Prentice-Hall, 1986), and Samuel Bowles and Richard Edwards, *Understanding Capitalism* (New York: Harper and Row, 1985).

Famine, Affluence, and Morality

Peter Singer

As I write this, in November 1971, people are dying in East Bengal from lack of food, shelter, and medical care. The suffering and death that are occurring there now are not inevitable, not unavoidable in any fatalistic sense of the term. Constant poverty, a cyclone, and a civil war have turned at least nine million people into destitute refugees; nevertheless, it is not beyond the capacity of the richer nations to give enough assistance to reduce any further suffering to very small proportions. The decisions and actions of human beings can prevent this kind of suffering.

Peter Singer, "Famine, Affluence, and Morality," *Philosophy & Public Affairs* 1, no. 3 (Spring 1972): 229–36, 240–43 (edited). Reprinted with permission of Wiley-Blackwell Publishers.

Unfortunately, human beings have not made the necessary decisions. At the individual level, people have, with very few exceptions, not responded to the situation in any significant way. Generally speaking, people have not given large sums to relief funds; they have not written to their parliamentary representatives demanding increased government assistance; they have not demonstrated in the streets, held symbolic fasts, or done anything else directed toward providing the refugees with the means to satisfy their essential needs. At the government level, no government has given the sort of massive aid that would enable the refugees to survive for more than a few days. Britain, for instance, has given rather more than most countries. It has, to date, given £14,750,000. For comparative purposes, Britain's share of the nonre-coverable development costs of the Anglo-French Concorde project is already in excess of £275,000,000, and on present estimates will reach £440,000,000. The implication is that the British government values a supersonic transport more than thirty times as highly as it values the lives of the nine million refugees. Australia is another country which, on a per capita basis, is well up in the "aid to Bengal" table. Australia's aid, however, amounts to less than one-twelfth of the cost of Sydney's new opera house. The total amount given, from all sources, now stands are about £65,000,000. The estimated cost of keeping the refugees alive for one year is £464,000,000. Most of the refugees have now been in the camps for more than six months. The World Bank has said that India needs a minimum of £300,000,000 in assistance from other countries before the end of the year. It seems obvious that assistance on this scale will not be forthcoming. India will be forced to choose between letting the refugees starve or diverting funds from her own development program, which will mean that more of her own people will starve in the future.[1]

These are the essential facts about the present situation in Bengal. So far as it concerns us here, there is nothing unique about this situation except its magnitude. The Bengal emergency is just the latest and most acute of a series of major emergencies in various parts of the world, arising both from natural and from man-made causes. There are also many parts of the world in which people die from malnutrition and lack of food independent of any special emergency. I take Bengal as my example only because it is the present concern, and because the size of the problem has ensured that with as been given adequate publicity. Neither individuals nor governments can claim to be unaware of what is happening there.

What are the moral implications of a situation like this? In what follows, I shall argue that the way people in relatively affluent countries react to a situation like that in Bengal cannot be justified; indeed, the whole way we look at moral issues—our moral conceptual scheme—needs to be altered, and with it, the way of life that has come to be taken for granted in our society.

In arguing for this conclusion I will not, of course, claim to be morally neutral. I shall, however, try to argue for the moral position that I take, so that anyone who accepts certain assumptions, to be made explicit, will, I hope, accept my conclusion.

I begin with the assumption that suffering and death from lack of food, shelter, and medical care are bad. I think most people will agree about this, although one may reach the same view by different routes. I shall not argue for this view. People can hold all sorts of eccentric positions, and perhaps from some of them it would not follow that death by starvation is in itself bad. It is difficult, perhaps impossible, to refute such positions, and so for brevity I will henceforth take this assumption as accepted. Those who disagree need read no further.

My next point is this: if it is in our power to prevent something bad from happening, without thereby sacrificing anything of comparable moral importance, we ought, morally, to do it. By "without sacrificing anything of comparable moral importance" I mean without causing anything else comparably bad to happen, or doing something that is wrong in itself, or failing to promote some moral good, comparable in significance to the bad thing that we can prevent. This principle seems almost as uncontroversial as the last one. It requires us only to prevent what is bad, and not to promote what is good, and it requires this of us only when we can do it without sacrificing anything that is, from the moral point of view, comparably important. I could even, as far as the application of my argument to the Bengal emergency is concerned, qualify the point so as to make it: if it is in our power to prevent something very bad from happening, without thereby sacrificing anything morally significant, we ought, morally, to do it. An application of this principle would be as follows: if I am walking past a shallow pond and see a child drowning in it, I ought to wade in and pull the child out. This will mean getting my clothes muddy, but this is insignificant, while the death of the child would presumably be a very bad thing.

The uncontroversial appearance of the principle just stated is deceptive. If it were acted upon, even in its qualified form, our lives, our society, and our world would be fundamentally changed. For the principle takes, firstly, no account of proximity or distance. It makes no moral difference whether the person I can help is a neighbor's child ten yards from me or a Bengali whose name I shall never know, ten thousand miles away. Secondly, the principle makes no distinction between cases in which I am the only person who could possibly do anything and cases in which I am just one among millions in the same position.

I do not think I need to say much in defense of the refusal to take proximity and distance into account. The fact that a person is physically near to us, so that we have personal contact with him, may make it more likely that we *shall* assist him, but this does not show that we *ought* to help him rather than another who happens to be further away. If we accept any principle of impartiality, universalizability, equality, or whatever, we cannot discriminate against someone merely because he is far away from us (or we are far away from him). Admittedly, it is possible that we are in a better position to judge what needs to be done to help a person near to us than one far away, and perhaps also to provide the assistance we judge to be necessary. If this were the case, it would be a reason for helping those near to us first. This may once have been a justification for being more concerned with the poor in one's own town than with famine victims in India. Unfortunately for those who like to keep their moral responsibilities limited, instant communication and swift transportation have changed the situation. From the moral point of view, the development of the world into a "global village" has made an important, though still unrecognized, difference to our moral situation. Expert observers and supervisors, sent out by famine relief organizations or permanently stationed in famine-prone areas, can direct our aid to a refugee in Bengal almost as effectively as we could get it to someone in our own block. There would seem, therefore, to be no possible justification for discriminating on geographical grounds.

There may be a greater need to defend the second implication of my principle—that the fact that there are millions of other people in the same position, in respect to the Bengali refugees, as I am, does not make the situation significantly different from a situation in which I am the only person who can prevent something very bad from occurring. Again, of course, I admit that there is a psychological difference between the cases; one feels less guilty about doing nothing if one can point to others, similarly placed, who have also done nothing. Yet this can make no real difference to our moral obligations.[2] Should I consider that I am less obliged to pull the drowning child out of the pond if on looking around I see other people, no further away than I am, who have also noticed the child but are doing nothing? One has only to ask this question to see the absurdity of the view that numbers lessen obligation. It is a view that is an ideal excuse for inactivity; unfortunately most of the major evils—poverty, overpopulation, pollution—are problems in which everyone is almost equally involved.

The view that numbers do make a difference can be made plausible if stated in this way: if everyone in circumstances like mine gave £5 to the Bengal Relief Fund, there would be enough to provide food, shelter, and medical care for the refugees; there is no reason why I should give more than anyone else in the same circumstances as I am; therefore I have no obligation to give more than £5. Each premise in this argument is true, and the argument looks sound. It may convince us, unless we notice that it is based on a hypothetical premise, although the conclusion is not stated hypothetically. The argument would be sound if the conclusion were: if everyone in circumstances like mine were to give £5, I would have no obligation to give more than £5. If the conclusion were so stated, however, it would be obvious that the argument has no bearing on a situation in which it is not the case that everyone else gives £5. This, of course, is the actual situation. It is more or less certain that not everyone in circumstances like mine will give £5. So there will not be enough to provide the needed food, shelter, and medial care. Therefore by giving more than £5 I will prevent more suffering than I would if I gave just £5.

It might be thought that this argument has an absurd consequence. Since the situation appears to be that very few people are likely to give substantial amounts, it follows that I and everyone else in similar circumstances ought to give as much as possible, that is, at least up to the point at which by giving more one would begin to cause serious suffering for oneself and one's dependents—perhaps even beyond this point to the point of marginal utility, at which by giving more one would cause oneself and one's dependents as much suffering as one would prevent in Bengal. If everyone does this, however, there will be more than can be used for the benefit of the refugees, and some of the sacrifice will have been unnecessary. Thus, if everyone does what he ought to do, the result will not be as good as it would be if everyone did a little less than he ought to do, or if only some do all that they ought to do.

The paradox here arises only if we assume that the actions in question—sending money to the relief funds—are performed more or less simultaneously, and are also unexpected. For if it is to be expected that everyone is going to contribute something, then clearly each is not obliged to give as much as he would have been obliged to had others not been giving too. And if everyone is not acting more or less simultaneously, then those giving later will know how much more is needed, and will have no obligation to give more than is necessary to reach this amount. To say this is not to deny the principle that people in the same circumstances have the same obligations, but to point out that the fact that others have given, or may be expected to give, is a relevant circumstance: those giving after it has become known that many others are giving and those giving before are not in the same circumstances. So the seemingly absurd consequence of the principle I have put forward can occur only if people are in error about the actual circumstances—that is, if they think they are

giving when others are not, but in fact they are giving when others are. The result of everyone doing what he really ought to do cannot be worse than the result of everyone doing less than he ought to do, although the result of everyone doing what he reasonably believes he ought to do could be.

If my argument so far has been sound, neither our distance from a preventable evil nor the number of other people who, in respect to that evil, are in the same situation as we are, lessens our obligation to mitigate or prevent that evil. I shall therefore take as established the principle I asserted earlier. As I have already said, I need to assert it only in its qualified form: if it is in our power to prevent something very bad from happening, without thereby sacrificing anything else morally significant, we ought, morally, to do it.

The outcome of this argument is that our traditional moral categories are upset. The traditional distinction between duty and charity cannot be drawn, or at least, not in the place we normally draw it. Giving money to the Bengal Relief Fund is regarded as an act of charity in our society. The bodies which collect money are known as "charities." These organizations see themselves in this way—if you send them a check, you will be thanked for your "generosity." Because giving money is regarded as an act of charity, it is not thought that there is anything wrong with not giving. The charitable man may be praised, but the man who is not charitable is not condemned. People do not feel in any way ashamed or guilty about spending money on new clothes or a new car instead of giving it to famine relief. (Indeed, the alternative does not occur to them.) This way of looking at the matter cannot be justified. When we buy new clothes not to keep ourselves warm but to look "well-dressed" we are not providing for any important need. We would not be sacrificing anything significant if we were to continue to wear our old clothes, and give the money to famine relief. By doing so, we would be preventing another person from starving. It follows from what I have said earlier that we ought to give money away, rather than spend it on clothes which we do not need to keep us warm. To do so is not charitable, or generous. Nor is it the kind of act which philosophers and theologians have called "supererogatory"—an act which it would be good to do, but not wrong not to do. On the contrary, we ought to give the money away, and it is wrong not to do so.

I am not maintaining that there are no acts which are charitable, or that there are no acts which it would be good to do but not wrong not to do. It may be possible to redraw the distinction between duty and charity in some other place. All I am arguing here is that the present way of drawing the distinction, which makes it an act of charity for a man living at the level of affluence which most people in the "developed nations" enjoy to give money to save someone else from starvation, cannot be supported. It is beyond the scope of my argument to consider whether the distinction should be redrawn or abolished altogether. There would be many other possible ways of drawing the distinction—for instance, one might decide that it is good to make other people as happy as possible, but not wrong not to do so.

Despite the limited nature of the revision in our moral conceptual scheme which I am proposing, the revision would, given the extent of both affluence and famine in the world today, have radical implications. These implications may lead to further objections, distinct from those I have already considered. I shall discuss two of these.

One objection to the position I have taken might be simply that it is too drastic a revision of our moral scheme. People do not ordinarily judge in the way I have suggested they should. Most people reserve their moral condemnation for those who violate some moral norm, such as the norm against taking another person's property. They do no condemn those who indulge in luxury instead of giving to famine relief. But given that I did not set out to present a morally neutral description of the way people make moral judgments, the way people do in fact judge has nothing to do with the validity of my conclusion. My conclusion follows from the principle which I advanced earlier, and unless that principle is rejected, or the arguments shown to be unsound, I think the conclusion must stand, however strange it appears.

* * *

The second objection to my attack on the present distinction between duty and charity is one which has from time to time been made against utilitarianism. It follows from some forms of utilitarian theory that we all ought, morally, to be working full time to increase the balance of happiness over misery. The position I have taken here would not lead to this conclusion in all circumstances, for if there were no bad occurrences that we could prevent without sacrificing something of comparable moral importance, my argument would have no application. Given the present conditions in many parts of the world, however, it does follow from my argument that we ought, morally, to be working full time to relieve great suffering of the sort that occurs as a result of famine or other disasters. Of course, mitigating circumstances can be adduced—for instance, that if we wear ourselves out through overwork, we shall be less effective than we would otherwise have been. Nevertheless, when all considerations of this sort have been taken into account, the conclusion remains: we ought to be preventing as much suffering as we can without sacrificing something else of comparable moral importance. This conclusion is one which we may be reluctant to face. I cannot see, though, why it should be regarded as a criticism of the position for which I have argued, rather than a criticism of our ordinary standards of behavior. Since most people are self-interested to some degree, very few of us are likely to do everything that we ought to do. It would, however, hardly be honest to take this as evidence that it is not the case that we ought to do it.

* * *

[Another] point raised by the conclusion reached earlier relates to the question of just how much we all ought to be giving away. One possibility, which has already been mentioned, is that we ought to give until we reach the level of marginal utility—that is, the level at which, by giving more, I would cause as much suffering to myself or my dependents as I would relieve by my gift. This would mean, of course, that one would reduce oneself to very near the material circumstances of a Bengali refugee. It will be recalled that earlier I put forward both a strong and a moderate version of the principle of preventing bad occurrences. The strong version, which required us to prevent bad things from happening unless in doing so we would be sacrificing something of comparable moral significance, does seem to require reducing ourselves to the level of marginal utility. I should also say that the strong version seems to me to be the correct one. I proposed the more moderate version—that we should prevent bad occurrences unless, to do so, we had to sacrifice something morally significant—only in order to show that even on this surely undeniable principle a great change in our way of life is required. On the more moderate principle, it may not follow that we ought to reduce ourselves to the level of marginal utility, for one might hold that to reduce oneself and one's family to this level is to cause something significantly bad to happen. Whether this is so I shall not discuss, since, as I have said, I can see no good reason for holding the moderate version of the principle rather than the strong version. Even if we accepted the principle only in its moderate form, however, it should be clear that we would have to give away enough to ensure that the consumer society, dependent as it is on people spending on trivia rather than giving to famine relief, would slow down and perhaps disappear entirely. There are several reasons why this would be desirable in itself. The value and necessity of economic growth are now being questioned not only by conservationists, but by economists as well. There is no doubt, too, that the consumer society has had a distorting effect on the goals and purposes of its members. Yet looking at the matter purely from the point of view of overseas aid, there must be a limit to the extent to which we should deliberately slow down our economy; for it might be the case that if we gave away, say, forty percent of our Gross National Product, we would slow down the economy so much that in absolute terms we would be giving less than if we gave twenty-five percent of the much larger GNP that we would have if we limited our contribution to this smaller percentage.

I mention this only as an indication of the sort of factor that one would have to take into account in working out an ideal. Since Western societies gen-

erally consider one percent of the GNP an acceptable level for overseas aid, the matter is entirely academic. Nor does it effect the question of how much an individual should give in a society in which very few are giving substantial amounts.

It is sometimes said, though less often now than it used to be, that philosophers have no special role to play in public affairs, since most public issues depend primarily on an assessment of facts. On questions of fact, it is said, philosophers as such have no special expertise, and so it has been possible to engage in philosophy without committing oneself to any position on major public issues. No doubt there are some issues of social policy and foreign policy about which it can truly be said that a really expert assessment of the facts is required before taking sides or acting, but the issue of famine is surely not one of these. The facts about the existence of suffering are beyond dispute. Nor, I think, is it disputed that we can do something about it, either through orthodox methods of famine relief or through population control or both. This is therefore an issue on which philosophers are competent to take a position. The issue is one which faces everyone who has more money than he needs to support himself and his dependents, or who is in a position to take some sort of political action. These categories must include practically every teacher and student of philosophy in the universities of the Western world. If philosophy is to deal with matters that are relevant to both teachers and students, this is an issue that philosophers should discuss.

Discussion, though, is not enough. What is the point of relating philosophy to public (and personal) affairs if we do not take our conclusions seriously? In this instance, taking our conclusion seriously means acting upon it. The philosopher will not find it any easier than anyone else to alter his attitudes and way of life to the extent that, if I am right, is involved in doing everything that we ought to be doing. At the very least, though, one can make a start. The philosopher who does so will have to sacrifice some of the benefits of the consumer society, but he can find compensation in the satisfaction of a way of life in which theory and practice, if not yet in harmony, are at least coming together.

NOTES

1. There was also a third possibility: that India would go to war to enable the refugees to return to their lands. Since I wrote this paper, India has taken this way out. The situation is no longer that described above, but this does not affect my argument, as the next paragraph indicates.

2. In view of the special sense philosophers often give to the term, I should say that I use "obligation" simply as the abstract noun derived from "ought," so that "I have an obligation to" means no more, and no less, than "I ought to." This usage is in accordance with the definition of "ought" given up by the *Shorter Oxford English Dictionary*: "the general verb to express duty or obligation." I do not think any issue of substance hangs on the way the term is used; sentences in which I use "obligation" could all be rewritten, although somewhat clumsily, as sentences in which a clause containing "ought" replaces the term "obligation."

Lifeboat Ethics

GARRETT HARDIN

* * *

Before taking up certain substantive issues let us look at an alternative metaphor, that of a lifeboat. In developing some relevant examples the following numerical values are assumed. Approximately two-thirds of the world is desperately poor, and only one-third is comparatively rich. The people in poor countries have an average per capita GNP (Gross National Product) of about $200 per year; the rich, of about $3,000. (For the United States it is nearly $5,000 per year.) Metaphorically, each rich nation amounts to a lifeboat full of comparatively rich people. The poor of the world are in other, much more crowded lifeboats. Continuously, so to speak, the poor fall out of their lifeboats and swim for a while in the water outside, hoping to be admitted to a rich lifeboat, or in some other way to benefit from the "goodies" on board. What should the passengers on a rich lifeboat do? This is the central problem of "the ethics of a lifeboat."

First we must acknowledge that each lifeboat is effectively limited in capacity. The land of every nation has a limited carrying capacity. The exact limit is a matter for argument, but the energy crunch is convincing more people every day that we have already exceeded the carrying capacity of the land. We have been living on "capital"—stored petroleum and coal—and soon we must live on income alone.

Let us look at only one lifeboat—ours. The ethical problem is the same for all, and is as follows. Here we sit, say 50 people in a lifeboat. To be generous, let us assume our boat has a capacity of 10 more, making 60. (This, however, is to violate the engineering principle of the "safety factor." A new plant disease or a bad change in the weather may decimate our population if we don't preserve some excess capacity as a safety factor.)

The 50 of us in the lifeboat see 100 others swimming in the water outside, asking for admission to the boat, or for handouts. How shall we respond to their calls? There are several possibilities.

One. We may be tempted to try to live by the Christian ideal of being "our brother's keeper," or by the Marxian ideal (Marx 1875) of "from each according to his abilities, to each according to his needs." Since the needs of all are the same, we take all the needy into our boat, making a total of 150 in a boat with a capacity of 60. The boat is swamped, and everyone drowns. Complete justice, complete catastrophe.

Two. Since the boat has an unused excess capacity of 10, we admit just 10 more to it. This has the disadvantage of getting rid of the safety factor, for which action we will sooner or later pay dearly. More-

Garrett Hardin, "Living on a Lifeboat," *BioScience* 24, no. 10 (October 1974): 561–65, 568 (edited). Reprinted with permission of the American Institute of Biological Sciences.

over, *which* 10 do we let in? "First come, first served?" The best 10? The neediest 10? How do we *discriminate*? And what do we say to the 90 who are excluded?

Three. Admit no more to the boat and preserve the small safety factor. Survival of the people in the lifeboat is then possible (though we shall have to be on our guard against boarding parties).

The last solution is abhorrent to many people. It is unjust, they say. Let us grant that it is.

"I feel guilty about my good luck," say some. The reply to this is simple: *Get out and yield your place to others.* Such a selfless action might satisfy the conscience of those who are addicted to guilt but it would not change the ethics of the lifeboat. The needy person to whom a guilt-addict yields his place will not himself feel guilty about his sudden good luck. (If he did he would not climb aboard.) The net result of conscience-stricken people relinquishing their unjustly held positions is the elimination of their kind of conscience from the lifeboat. The lifeboat, as it were, purifies itself of guilt. The ethics of the lifeboat persist, unchanged by such momentary aberrations.

This then is the basic metaphor within which we must work out our solutions. Let us enrich the image step by step with substantive additions from the real world.

REPRODUCTION

The harsh characteristics of lifeboat ethics are heightened by reproduction, particularly by reproductive differences. The people inside the lifeboats of the wealthy nations are doubling in numbers every 87 years; those outside are doubling every 35 years, on the average. And the relative difference in prosperity is becoming greater.

Let us, for a while, think primarily of the U.S. lifeboat. As of 1973 the United States had a population of 210 million people, who were increasing by 0.8% per year, that is, doubling in number every 87 years.

Although the citizens of rich nations are outnumbered two to one by the poor, let us imagine an equal number of poor people outside our lifeboat—a mere 210 million poor people reproducing at a quite different rate. If we imagine these to be the combined populations of Colombia, Venezuela, Ecuador, Morocco, Thailand, Pakistan, and the Philippines, the average rate of increase of the people "outside" is 3.3% per year. The doubling time of this population is 21 years.

Suppose that all these countries, and the United States, agreed to live by the Marxian ideal, "to each according to his needs," the ideal of most Christians as well. Needs, of course, are determined by population size, which is affected by reproduction. Every nation regards its rate of reproduction as a sovereign right. If our lifeboat were big enough in the beginning it might be possible to live *for a while* by Christian-Marxian ideals. *Might.*

Initially, in the model given, the ratio of non-Americans to Americans would be one to one. But consider what the ratio would be 87 years later. By this time Americans would have doubled to a population of 420 million. The other group (doubling every 21 years) would now have swollen to 3,540 million. Each American would have more than eight people to share with. How could the lifeboat possibly keep afloat?

All this involves extrapolation of current trends into the future, and is consequently suspect. Trends may change. Granted: but the change will not necessarily be favorable. If—as seems likely—the rate of population increase falls faster in the ethnic group presently inside the lifeboat than it does among those now outside, the future will turn out to be even worse than mathematics predicts, and sharing will be even more suicidal.

RUIN IN THE COMMONS

The fundamental error of the sharing ethics is that it leads to the tragedy of the commons. Under a system of private property the man (or group of men) who own property recognize their responsibility to care for it, for if they don't they will eventually suffer. A farmer, for instance, if he is intelligent, will allow no more cattle in a pasture than its carrying capacity justifies. If he overloads the pasture, weeds take over, erosion sets in, and the owner loses in the long run.

But if a pasture is run as a commons open to all, the right of each to use it is not matched by an operational responsibility to take care of it. It is no use asking independent herdsmen in a commons to act responsibly, for they dare not. The considerate herdsman who refrains from overloading the commons suffers more than a selfish one who says his needs are greater. (As Leo Durocher says, "Nice guys finish last.") Christian-Marxian idealism is counterproductive. That it *sounds* nice is no excuse. With distribution systems, as with individual morality, good intentions are no substitute for good performance.

A social system is stable only if it is insensitive to errors. To the Christian-Marxian idealist a selfish person is a sort of "error." Prosperity in the system of the commons cannot survive errors. If *everyone* would only restrain himself, all would be well; but it takes *only one less than everyone* to ruin a system of voluntary restraint. In a crowded world of less than perfect human beings—and we will never know any other—mutual ruin is inevitable in the commons. This is the core of the tragedy of the commons.

One of the major tasks of education today is to create such an awareness of the dangers of the commons that people will be able to recognize its many varieties, however disguised. There is pollution of the air and water because these media are treated as commons. Further growth of population and growth in the per capita conversion of natural resources into pollutants require that the system of the commons be modified or abandoned in the disposal of "externalities."

The fish populations of the oceans are exploited as commons, and ruin lies ahead. No technological invention can prevent this fate: in fact, all improvements in the art of fishing merely hasten the day of complete ruin. Only the replacement of the system of the commons with a responsible system can save oceanic fisheries.

The management of western range lands, though nominally rational, is in fact (under the steady pressure of cattle ranchers) often merely a government-sanctioned system of the commons, drifting toward ultimate ruin for both the rangelands and the residual enterprisers.

WORLD FOOD BANKS

In the international arena we have recently heard a proposal to create a new commons, namely an international depository of food reserves to which nations will contribute according to their abilities, and from which nations may draw according to their needs. Nobel laureate Norman Borlaug has lent the prestige of his name to this proposal.

A world food bank appeals powerfully to our humanitarian impulses. We remember John Donne's celebrated line, "Any man's death diminishes me." But before we rush out to see for whom the bell tolls let us recognize where the greatest political push for international granaries comes from, lest we be disillusioned later. Our experience with Public Law 480 clearly reveals the answer. This was the law that moved billions of dollars worth of U.S. grain to food-short, population-long countries during the past two decades. When P.L. 480 first came into being, a headline in the business magazine *Forbes* (Paddock and Paddock 1970) revealed the power behind it: "Feeding the World's Hungry Millions: How it will mean billions for U.S. business."

And indeed it did. In the years 1960 to 1970 a total of $7.9 billion was spent on the "Food for Peace" program, as P.L. 480 was called. During the years 1948 to 1970 an additional $49.9 billion were extracted from American taxpayers to pay for other economic aid programs, some of which went for food and food-producing machinery. (This figure does *not* include military aid.) That P.L. 480 was a give-away program was concealed. Recipient countries went through the motions of paying for P.L. 480 foods—with IOU's. In December 1973 the charade was brought to an end as far as India was concerned when the United States "forgave" India's $3.2 billion debt (Anonymous 1974). Public announcement of the cancellation of the debt was delayed for two months: one wonders why.

"Famine—1974!" (Paddock and Paddock 1970) is one of the few publications that points out the commercial roots of this humanitarian attempt. Though all U.S. taxpayers lost by P.L. 480, special interest groups gained handsomely. Farmers benefited because they were not asked to contribute the grain—it was bought from them by the taxpayers. Besides the direct benefit there was the indirect effect of increasing demand and thus raising prices of farm products generally. The manufacturers of farm machinery, fertilizers, and pesticides benefited by the farmers' extra efforts to grow more food. Grain elevators profited from storing the grain for varying lengths of time. Railroads made money hauling it to port, and shipping lines by carrying it overseas. Moreover, once the machinery for P.L. 480 was established an immense bureaucracy had a vested interest in its continuance regardless of its merits.

Very little was ever heard of these selfish interests when P.L. 480 was defended in public. The emphasis was always on its humanitarian effects. The combination of multiple and relatively silent selfish interests with highly vocal humanitarian apologists constitutes a powerful lobby for extracting money from taxpayers. Foreign aid has become a habit that can apparently survive in the absence of any known justification. A news commentator in a weekly magazine (Lansner 1974), after exhaustively going over all the conventional arguments for foreign aid—self-interest, social justice, political advantage, and charity—and concluding that none of the known arguments really held water, concluded: "So the search continues for some logically compelling reasons for giving aid . . . " In other words. *Act now, Justify later*—if ever. (Apparently a quarter of a century is too short a time to find the justification for expending several billion dollars yearly.)

The search for a rational justification can be short-circuited by interjecting the word "emergency." Borlaug uses this word. We need to look sharply at it. What is an "emergency?" It is surely something like an accident, which is correctly defined as *an event that is certain to happen, though with a low frequency* (Hardin 1972a). A well-run organization prepares for everything that is certain, including accidents and emergencies. It budgets for them. It saves for them. It expects them—and mature decision-makers do not waste time complaining about accidents when they occur.

What happens if some organizations budget for emergencies and others do not? If each organization is solely responsible for its own well-being, poorly managed ones will suffer. But they should be able to learn from experience. They have a chance to mend their ways and learn to budget for infrequent but certain emergencies. The weather, for instance, always varies and periodic crop failures are certain. A wise and competent government saves out of the production of the good years in anticipation of bad years that are sure to come. This is not a new idea. The Bible tells us that Joseph taught this policy to Pharaoh in Egypt more than 2,000 years ago. Yet it is literally true that the vast majority of the governments of the world today have no such policy. They lack either the wisdom or the competence, or both. Far more difficult than the transfer of wealth from one country to another is the transfer of wisdom between sovereign powers or between generations.

"But it isn't their fault! How can we blame the poor people who are caught in an emergency? Why must be punish them?" The concepts of blame and punishment are irrelevant. The question is, what are the operational consequences of establishing a world food bank? If it is open to every country every time a need develops, slovenly rule will not be motivated to take Joseph's advice. Why should they? Others will bail them out whenever they are in trouble.

Some countries will make deposits in the world food bank and others will withdraw from it: there will be almost no overlap. Calling such a depository-transfer unit a "bank" is stretching the metaphor of *bank* beyond its elastic limits. The proposers, of course, never call attention to the metaphorical nature of the word they use.

THE RATCHET EFFECT

An "international food bank" is really, then, not a true bank but a disguised one-way transfer device for moving wealth from rich countries to poor. In the absence of such a bank, in a world inhabited by individually responsible sovereign nations, the population of each nation would repeatedly go through a cycle of the sort shown in Figure 1. P_2 is greater than P_1, either in absolute numbers or because a deterioration of the food supply has removed the safety factor and produced a dangerously low ratio of resources to population. P_2 may be said to represent a state of overpopulation, which becomes obvious upon the appearance of an "accident," e.g., a crop failure. If the "emergency" is not met by outside help, the population drops back to the "normal" level—the "carrying capacity" of the environment—or even below. In the absence of population control by a sovereign, sooner or later the population grows to P_2 again and the cycle repeats. The long-term population curve (Hardin 1966) is an irregularly fluctuating one, equilibrating more or less about the carrying capacity.

A demographic cycle of this sort obviously involves great suffering in the restrictive phase, but such a cycle is normal to any independent country with inadequate population control. The third century theologian Tertullian (Hardin 1969a) expressed what must have been the recognition of many wise men when he wrote: "The scourges of pestilence, famine, wars, and earthquakes have come to be regarded as a blessing to overcrowded nations, since they serve to prune away the luxuriant growth of the human race."

Only under a strong and farsighted sovereign—which theoretically could be the people themselves, democratically organized—can a population equilibrate at some set point below the carrying capacity, thus avoiding the pains normally caused by periodic

and unavoidable disasters. For this happy state to be achieved it is necessary that those in power be able to contemplate with equanimity the "waste" of surplus food in times of bountiful harvests. It is essential that those power resist the temptation to convert extra food into extra babies. On the public relations level it is necessary that the phrase "surplus food" be replaced by "safety factor."

But wise sovereigns seem not to exist in the poor world today. The most anguishing problems are created by poor countries that are governed by rulers insufficiently wise and powerful. If such countries can draw on a world food bank in times of "emergency," the population *cycle* of Figure 1 will be replaced by the population *escalator* of Figure 2. The input of food from a food bank acts as the pawl of a ratchet, preventing the population from retracing it steps to a lower level. Reproduction pushes the population upward, inputs from the world bank prevent its moving downward. Population size escalates, as does the absolute magnitude of "accidents" and "emergencies." The process is brought to an end only by the total collapse of the whole system, producing a catastrophe of scarcely imaginable proportions.

Such are the implications of the well-meant sharing of food in a world of irresponsible reproduction.

I think we need a new word for systems like this. The adjective "melioristic" is applied to systems that produce continual improvement; the English word is derived from the Latin *meliorare*, to become or make better. Parallel with this it would be useful to bring in the word *pejoristic* (from the Latin *pejorare*, to

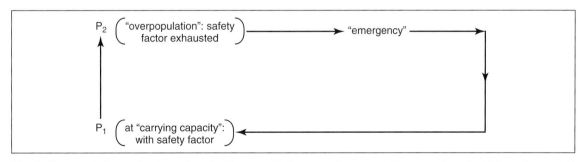

Fig. 1. The population cycle of a nation that has no effective, conscious population control, and which receives no aid from the outside. P_2 is greater than P_1.

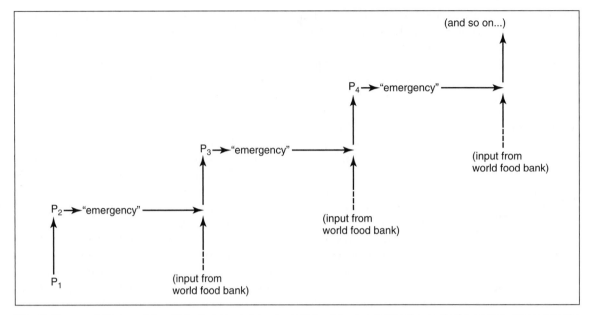

Fig. 2. The population escalator. Note that input from a world food bank acts like the pawl of a ratchet, preventing the normal population cycle shown in Figure 1 from being completed. $P_{II} + I$ is greater than P_{II}, and the absolute magnitude of the "emergencies" escalates. Ultimately the entire system crashes. The crash is not shown, and few can imagine it.

become or make worse). This word can be applied to those systems which, by their very nature, can be relied upon to make matters worse. A world food bank coupled with sovereign state irresponsibility in reproduction is an example of a pejoristic system.

This pejoristic system creates an unacknowledged commons. People have more motivation to draw from than to add to the common store. The license to make such withdrawals diminishes whatever motivation poor countries might otherwise have to control their populations. Under the guidance of this ratchet, wealth can be steadily moved in one direction only, from the slowly-breeding rich to the rapidly-breeding poor, the process finally coming to a halt only when all countries are equally and miserably poor.

All this is terribly obvious once we are acutely aware of the pervasiveness and danger of the commons. But many people still lack this awareness and the euphoria of the "benign demographic transition" (Hardin 1973) interferes with the realistic appraisal

of pejoristic mechanisms. As concerns public policy, the deductions drawn from the benign demographic transition are these:

1) If the per capita GNP rises the birth rate will fall; hence, the rate of population increase will fall, ultimately producing ZPG (Zero Population Growth).

2) The long-term trend all over the world (including the poor countries) is of a rising per capita GNP (for which no limit is seen).

3) Therefore, all political interference in population matters is unnecessary; all we need to do is foster economic "development"—*note the metaphor*—and population problems will solve themselves.

Those who believe in the benign demographic transition dismiss the pejoristic mechanism of Figure 2 in the belief that each input of food from the world outside fosters development within a poor country thus resulting in a drop in the rate of population increase. Foreign aid has proceeded on this assumption for more than two decades. Unfortunately it has produced no indubitable instance of the asserted effect. It has, however, produced a library of excuses. The air is filled with plaintive calls for more massive foreign aid appropriations so that the hypothetical melioristic process can get started.

* * *

REFERENCES

Anonymous. 1974. *Wall Street Journal* 19 Feb.

Borlaug, N. 1973. Civilization's future: a call for international granaries. *Bull. At. Sci.* 29: 7–15.

Boulding, K. 1966. The economics of the coming Spaceship earth. *In* H. Jarrett, ed. Environmental Quality in a Growing Economy. Johns Hopkins Press, Baltimore.

Buchanan, W. 1973. Immigration statistics. *Equilibrium* 1(3): 16–19.

Davis, K. 1963. Population. *Sci. Amer.* 209(3): 62–71.

Farvar, M. T., and J. P. Milton. 1972. The Careless Technology. Natural History Press, Garden City, N.Y.

Gregg, A. 1955. A medical aspect of the population problem. *Science* 121: 681–682.

Hardin, G. 1966. Chap. 9 *in* Biology: Its Principles and Implications, 2nd ed. Freeman, San Francisco.

———. 1968. The tragedy of the commons. *Science* 162: 1243–1248.

———. 1969a. Page 18 *in* Population, Evolution, and Birth Control, 2nd ed. Freeman, San Francisco.

———. 1969b. The economics of wilderness. *Nat. Hist.* 78(6): 20–27.

———. 1972a. Pages 81–82 *in* Exploring New Ethics for Survival: The Voyage of the Spaceship *Beagle*. Viking, N.Y.

———. 1972b. Preserving quality on Spaceship Earth. *In* J. B. Trefethen, ed. Transactions of the Thirty-Seventh North American Wildlife and Natural Resources Conference. Wildlife Management Institute, Washington, D.C.

———. 1973. Chap. 23 *in* Stalking the Wild Taboo. Kaufmann, Los Altos, Cal.

Harris, M. 1972. How green the revolution. *Nat. Hist.* 81(3): 28–30.

Langer, S. K. 1942. Philosophy in a New Key. Harvard University Press, Cambridge.

Lansner, K. 1974. Should foreign aid begin at home? *Newsweek*, 11 Feb. p. 32.

Marx, K. 1875. Critique of the Gotha program. Page 388 *in* R. C. Tucker, ed. The Marx-Engels Reader. Norton, N.Y., 1972.

Ophuls, W. 1974. The scarcity society. *Harpers* 248(1487): 47–52.

Paddock, W. C. 1970. How green is the green revolution? *BioScience* 20: 897–902.

Paddock, W., and E. Paddock. 1973. We Don't Know How. Iowa State University Press, Ames, Iowa.

Paddock, W., and P. Paddock. 1967. Famine—1975! Little, Brown, Boston.

Wilkes, H. G. 1972. The green revolution. *Environment* 14(8): 32–39.

Obligations to Future Generations

M. P. GOLDING

The purpose of this note[1] is to examine the notion of obligations to future generations, a notion that finds increasing use in discussions of social policies and programs, particularly as concerns population distribution and control and environment control. Thus, it may be claimed, the solution of problems in

M. P. Golding, "Obligations to Future Generations," *The Monist* 56, no. 1 (January 1972): 85–99. Reprinted with permission of *The Monist*.

these areas is not merely a matter of enhancing our own good, improving our own conditions of life, but is also a matter of discharging an obligation to future generations.

Before I turn to the question of the basis of such obligations—the necessity of the plural is actually doubtful—there are three general points to be considered: (1) Who are the individuals in whose regard it is maintained that we have such obligations, to whom do we owe such obligations? (2) What, essentially, do obligations to future generations oblige us to do, what are they aimed at? and (3), To what class of obligation do such obligations belong, what kind of obligation are they? Needless to say, in examining a notion of this sort, which is used in everyday discussion and polemic, one must be mindful of the danger of taking it—or making it out—to be more precise than it is in reality.

This cautionary remark seems especially appropriate in connection with the first of the above points. But the determination of the purview of obligations to future generations is both ethically and practically significant. It seems clear, at least, who does not come within their purview. Obligations to future generations are distinct from the obligations we have to our presently living fellows, who are therefore excluded from the purview of the former, although it might well be the case that *what* we owe to future generations is identical with (or overlaps) what we owe to the present generation. However, I think we may go further than this and also exclude our most immediate descendants, our children, grandchildren and greatgrandchildren, perhaps. What is distinctive about the notion of obligations to future generations is, I think, that it refers to generations with which the possessors of the obligations cannot expect in a literal sense to share a common life. (Of course, if we have obligations to future generations, understood in this way, we *a fortiori* have obligations to immediate posterity.) This, at any rate, is how I shall construe the reference of such obligations; neither our present fellows nor our immediate posterity come within their purview. What can be the basis of our obligations toward individuals with whom we cannot expect to share a common life is a question I shall consider shortly.

But if their inner boundary be drawn in this way, what can we say about their outer limits? Is there a cutoff point for the individuals in whose regard we have such obligations? Here, it seems, there are two alternatives. First, we can flatly say that there are no outer limits to their purview: all future generations come within their province. A second and more modest answer would be that we do not have such obli-

gations towards any assignable future generation. In either case the reference is a broad and unspecified community of the future, and I think it can be shown that we run into difficulties unless certain qualifications are taken into account.

Our second point concerns the question of what it is that obligations to future generations oblige us to do. The short answer is that they oblige us to do many things. But an intervening step is required here, for obligations to future generations are distinct from general duties to perform acts which are in themselves intrinsically right, although such obligations give rise to duties to perform specific acts. Obligations to future generations are essentially an obligation to produce—or to attempt to produce—a desirable state of affairs *for* the community of the future, to promote conditions of good living for future generations. The many things that we are obliged to do are founded upon this obligation (which is why I earlier questioned the necessity of the plural). If we think we have an obligation to transmit our cultural heritage to future generations it is because we think that our cultural heritage promotes, or perhaps even embodies, good living. In so doing we would hardly wish to falsify the records of our civilization, for future generations must also have, as a condition of good living, the opportunity to learn from the mistakes of the past. If, in addition, we believe lying to be intrinsically wrong we would also refrain from falsifying the records; but this would not be because we think we have any special duty to tell the truth to future generations.

To come closer to contemporary discussion, consider, for example, population control, which is often grounded upon an obligation to future generations. It is not maintained that population control is intrinsically right—although the rhetoric frequently seems to approach such a claim—but rather that it will contribute towards a better life for future generations, and perhaps immediate posterity as well. (If population control were intrinsically anything, I would incline to thinking it intrinsically wrong.) On the other hand, consider the elimination of water and air pollution. Here it might be maintained that we have a definite duty to cease polluting the environment on the grounds that such pollution is intrinsically bad[2] or that it violates a Divine command. Given the current mood of neopaganism, even secularists speak of the despoilment of the environment as a sacrilege of sorts. When the building of a new dam upsets the ecological balance and puts the wildlife under a threat, we react negatively and feel that something bad has resulted. And this is not because we necessarily believe that our own interests or those of future generations have been undermined. Both views, but especially the latter (Divine command), represent men as holding sovereignty over nature only as trustees to whom not everything is permitted. Nevertheless, these ways of grounding the duty to care for the environment are distinguishable from a grounding of the duty upon an obligation to future generations, although one who acknowledges such an obligation will also properly regard himself as a trustee to whom not everything is permitted. Caring for the environment is presumably among the many things that the obligation to future generations obliges us to do because we thereby presumably promote conditions of good living for the community of the future.

The obligation—dropping the plural again for a moment—to future generations, then, is not an immediate catalogue of specific duties. It is in this respect rather like the responsibility that a parent has to see to the welfare of his child. Discharging one's parental responsibility requires concern, seeking, and active effort to promote the good *of* the child, which is the central obligation of the parent and out of which grow the specific parental obligations and duties. The use of the term "responsibility" to characterize the parent's obligation connotes, in part, the element of discretion and flexibility which is requisite to the discharging of the obligation in a variety of antecedently unforeseeable situations. Determination of the specific duty is often quite problematic even—and sometimes especially—for the conscientious parent who is anxious to do what is good for his child. And, anticipating my later discussion, this also holds for obligations to future generations. There

are, of course, differences, too. Parental responsibility is enriched and reinforced by love, which can hardly obtain between us and future generations.[3] (Still, the very fact that the responsibility to promote the child's good is an obligation means that it is expected to operate even in the absence of love.) Secondly, the parental obligation is always towards assignable individuals, which is not the case with obligations to future generations. There is, however, an additional feature of likeness between the two obligations which I shall mention shortly.

The third point about obligations to future generations—to what class of obligation do they belong?—is that they are *owed*, albeit owed to an unspecified, and perhaps unspecifiable, community of the future. Obligations to future generations, therefore, are distinct from a general duty, when presented with alternatives for action, to choose the act which produces the greatest good. Such a duty is not owed to anyone, and the beneficiaries of my fulfilling a duty to promote the greatest good are not necessarily individuals to whom I stand in the moral relation not having an obligation that is owed. But when I owe it to someone to promote his good, he is never, to this extent, merely an incidental beneficiary of my effort to fulfill the obligation. He has a presumptive *right* to it and can assert a claim against me for it. Obligations to future generations are of this kind. There is something which is due to the community of the future from us. The moral relation between us and future generations is one in which they have a claim against us to promote their good. Future generations are, thus, possessors of presumptive rights.

This conclusion is surely odd. How can future generations—the not-yet-born—*now* have claims against us? This question serves to turn us finally to consider the basis of our obligations to future generations. I think it useful to begin by discussing and removing one source of the oddity.

It should first be noticed that there is no oddity in investing present effort in order to promote a future state of affairs or in having an owed obligation to do so. The oddity arises only on a theory of obligations and claims (and, hence, of rights) that virtually identifies them with acts of willing, with the exercise of sovereignty of one over another, with the pressing of demands—in a word, with *making* claims. But, clearly, future generations are not now engaged in acts of willing, and not now exercising sovereignty over us, and are not now pressing their demands. Future generations are not now making claims against us, nor will it be *possible* for them to do so. (Our immediate posterity are in this last respect in a different case.) However, the identification of claims with making claims, demanding, is plausible within the field of rights and obligations because the content of a system of rights is historically conditioned by the making of claims. Individuals and groups put forward their claims to the goods of life, demand them as their right; and in this way the content is increasingly expanded towards the inclusion of more of these goods.

Nevertheless, as suggestive a clue as this fact is for the development of a theory of rights, there is a distinction to be drawn between *having* claims and *making* claims. The mere fact that someone claims something from me is not sufficient to establish it as his right, or that he has a claim relative to me. On the other hand, someone may have a claim relative to me whether or not he makes the claim, demands, or is even able to make a claim. (This is not to deny that claiming plays a role in the theory of rights.) Two points require attention here. First, some claims are frivolous. What is demanded cannot really be claimed as a matter of right. The crucial factor in determining this is the *social ideal*, which we may provisionally define as a conception of the good life for man. It serves as the yardstick by which demands, current and potential, are measured.[4] Secondly, whether someone's claim confers an entitlement upon him to receive what is claimed *from me* depends upon my moral relation to him, on whether he is a member of my *moral community*. It is these factors, rather than any actual demanding, which establish whether someone has a claim relative to me. (I should like to emphasize that I am not necessarily maintaining that the concepts of a social ideal and a moral community are involved in a theory of every kind of

obligation, but, rather, that they are required by the kind of obligation being considered here.)

The concepts of a social ideal and a moral community are clearly in need of further explanation, yet as they stand the above considerations should serve to relieve a good deal of the oddity that is felt in the assertion that future generations now have claims against us and that they are possessors of presumptive rights. There is, however, a residual sense of peculiarity in the assertion because it still remains to be shown whether future generations are members of our moral community. A discussion of the question of membership in a moral community will, I think, shed light on these subjects.

Who are the members of my moral community? (Who is my neighbor?) The fact is that I am a member of more than one moral community, for I belong to a variety of groups whose members owe obligations to one another. And many of the particular obligations that are owed vary from group to group. As a result my obligations are often in conflict and I experience a fragmentation of energy and responsibility in attempting to meet my obligations. What I ought to desire for the members of one of these groups is frequently in opposition to what I ought to desire for the members of another of these groups. Moral communities are constituted, or generated, in a number of ways, one of which is especially relevant to our problem. Yet these ways are not mutually exclusive, and they can be mutually reinforcing. This is a large topic and I cannot go into its details here. It is sufficient for our purpose to take brief notice of two possible ways of generating a moral community so as to set in relief the particular kind of moral community that is requisite for obligations to future generations.

A moral community may be constituted by an explicit contract between its members. In this case the particular obligations which the members have towards each other are fixed by the terms of their bargain. Secondly, a moral community may be generated out of a social arrangement in which each member derives benefits from the efforts of other members. As a result a member acquires an obligation to share the burden of sustaining the social arrangement. Both of these are communities in which entrance and participation are fundamentally a matter of self-interest, and only rarely will there be an obligation of the sort that was discussed earlier, that is, a responsibility to secure the good of the members. In general the obligations will be of more specialized kinds. It is also apparent that obligations acquired in these ways can easily come into conflict with other obligations that one may have. Clearly, a moral community comprised of present and future generations cannot arise from either of these sources. We cannot enter into an explicit contract with the community of the future. And although future generations might derive benefits from us, these benefits cannot be reciprocated. (It is possible that the [biologically] dead do derive *some* benefits from the living, but I do not think that this possibility is crucial. Incidentally, just as the living could have obligations to the distant unborn, the living also have obligations to the dead. If obligation to the past is a superstition, then so is obligation to the future.)[5] Our immediate posterity, who will share a common life with us, are in a better position in this respect; so that obligations towards our children, born and unborn, conceivably *could* be generated from participation in a mutually beneficial social arrangement. This, however, would be misleading.

It seems, then, that communities in which entrance and participation are fundamentally matters of self-interest, do not fit our specifications. As an alternative let us consider communities based upon altruistic impulses and fellow-feeling. This, too, is in itself a large topic, and I refer to it only in order to develop a single point.

The question I began with was: Who are the members of my moral community? Now it is true that there are at least a few people towards whom I have the sentiments that are identified with altruism and sympathetic concern. But are these sentiments enough to establish for me the moral relationship of owing them an obligation? Are these enough to generate a moral community? The answer, I think, must be in the negative so long as these affections towards others remain at the level of animal feeling. The ancient distinction between mere affection, mere liking, and conscious desire is fundamental here. Genuine concern and interest in the well-being of another must be conscious concern. My desire for another's good must in this event be more than impulsive, and presupposes, rather, that I have a *conception* of his good. This conception, which cannot be a bare concept of what is incidentally a good but which is rather a conception of the good *for* him, further involves that he not be a mere blank to me but that he is characterized or described in some way in my consciousness. It is perhaps unnecessary to add that there is never any absolute guarantee that such a conceived good is not, in some sense, false or fragmentary. Nevertheless, an altruism that is literally mindless—if it can be called "altruism" at all—cannot be the basis of moral community.

But even if it be granted that I have a conception of another's good, I have not yet reached the stage of obligation towards him. We are all familiar with the kind of "taking an interest in the welfare of another" that is gracious and gift-like, a matter of *noblesse oblige*. It is not so much that this type of interest-taking tends to be casual, fleeting and fragmentary—"*cette charité froide qui on nomme altruisme*"—and stands in contrast to interest-taking that is constant, penetrating and concerned with the other's total good. It is, rather, a form of interest-taking, however "conceptual," that is a manifestation of an unreadiness or even an unwillingness to recognize the other's claim (as distinct, of course, from his claiming), the other's entitlement, to receive his good from me. An additional step is, there-fore, required, and I think it consists in this: that I acknowledge this good as a good, that his good is good-to-me. Once I have made this step, I cannot in conscience deny the pertinence of his demand, if he makes one, although whether I should now act so as to promote his good is of course dependent on a host of factors. (Among these factors are moral considerations that determine the permissibility of various courses of action and priorities of duty.) The basis of the obligation is nevertheless secured.

This conclusion, it should be clear, does not entail that I am required to concede the status of an entitlement to every demand that is made by someone in whose well-being I have an interest. Some claims (claimings), as remarked above, are frivolous. The test of this, in the case we have been considering, is my conception of the other's good. This conception is a model in miniature of what I earlier called a *social ideal*. However, the provisional definition of it—a conception of the good life for man—was unnecessarily broad. In using this term, I mean, first of all, to contrast the ideal with a personal ideal of the good life. A personal ideal of the good life is an ideal that is not necessarily maintained as desirable for others to seek to achieve. It is what an individual, given his unique interests and idiosyncrasies, sees as the private end of his striving; while it does not necessarily exclude elements of sociality, it is not social in its purview. By the term "social ideal," however, I mean primarily a conception of the good life for individuals under some general characterization and which can be maintained by them as good for them in virtue of this characterization. The term covers the possibility of a social ideal that is a conception of the good life for individuals characterized in the broadest terms, namely, as human. But a social ideal may be narrower in its scope. For example, one may have a conception of the good life for the city-dweller or for the outdoors type. Since it is possible for me to maintain as good-to-me a variety of ideals bearing upon groups of individuals characterized in different ways, it is possible for me to be a member of more than one moral community. It is in such circumstances, as mentioned earlier, that I will experience the conflicting pulls of obligation and competing claims upon my energy and effort.

(There is admittedly much more to be said in explanation of the nature of social ideals, for they need not be static. The implications of our ideals are not always immediately available, and they are enriched and clarified through experience. They are adaptable to new life-circumstances. And they can also become impoverished. Just as ideals are not static, neither are the characterizations of the individuals to whom the ideals are meant to apply.

Another topic that requires further study is the "logic" of the ideal-claim relationship, a study of the ways in which ideals confer entitlements upon claims. Questions also arise concerning justice and reciprocity. This list could be extended; it is only meant to be suggestive. I make no pretence that I am able to solve these problems at this time.)

So far, in the above account of the generation of my moral community, the question of membership has been discussed solely in reference to those towards whom I initially have the sentiments that are identified with fellow-feeling. But we can go beyond this. Again we take our clue from the history of the development of rights. For just as the content of a system of rights that are possessed by the members of a moral community is enlarged over time by the pressing of claims, demanding, so also is the moral community enlarged by the pressing of claims by individuals who have been hitherto excluded. The claiming is not only a claim for something, but may also be an assertion: "Here I am, I count too." The struggle for rights has also been a counterstruggle. The widening of moral communities has been accompanied by attempts at exclusion. It is important for us to take note of one feature of this situation.

The structure of the situation is highlighted when a stranger puts forward his demand. The question immediately arises, shall his claim be recognized as a matter of right?[6] Initially I have no affection for him. But is this crucial in determining whether he ought to count as a member of my moral community? The determination depends, rather, on what he is like and what are the conditions of his life. One's obligations to a stranger are never immediately clear. If a visitor from Mars or Venus were to appear, I would not know what to desire for him. I would not know whether my conception of the good life is relevant to him and to his conditions of life. The good that I acknowledge might not be good for him. I would not know whether my conception of the good life is relevant to him and to his conditions of life. The good that I acknowledge might not be good for him. Humans, of course, are in a better case than Martians or Venusians. Still, since the stranger appears as strange, different, what I maintain in my attempt to exclude him is that my conception of the good is not relevant to him, that "his kind" do not count. He, on the other hand, is in effect saying to me: Given your social ideal, you must acknowledge my claim, for it *is* relevant to me given what I am; your good is my good, also.[7] If I should finally come to concede this, the full force of my obligation to him will be manifest to me quite independently of any fellow-feeling that might or might not be aroused. The *involuntary* character of the obligation will be clear to me, as it probably never is in the case of individuals who command one's sympathy. And once I admit him as a member of my moral community, I will also acknowledge my responsibility to secure this good for him even in the absence of any future claiming on his part.

With this we have completed the account of the constitution of the type of moral community that is required for obligations to future generations. I shall not recapitulate its elements. The step that incorporates future generations into our moral community is small and obvious. Future generations are members of our moral community because, and insofar as, our social ideal is relevant to them, given what they are and their conditions of life. I believe that this account applies also to obligations towards our immediate posterity. However, the responsibility that one has to see to the welfare of his children is in addition buttressed and qualified by social understandings concerning the division of moral labor and by natural affection. The basis of the obligations is nevertheless the same in both instances.[8] Underlying this account is the important fact that such obligations fall into the area of the moral life which is independent of considerations of explicit contract and personal advantage. Moral duty and virtue also falls into this area. But I should like to emphasize again that I do not wish to be understood as putting this account forward as an analysis of moral virtue and duty in general.

As we turn at long last specifically to our obligations to future generations, it is worth noticing that the term "contract" has been used to cover the kind of moral community that I have been discussing. It

occurs in a famous passage in Burke's *Reflections on the Revolution in France*:

Society is indeed a contract. Subordinate contracts for objects of mere occasional interest maybe dissolved at pleasure—but the state ought not to be considered as nothing better than a partnership agreement in a trade of pepper and coffee, calico or tobacco, or some other such low concern, to be taken up for a little temporary interest, and to be dissolved by the fancy of the parties. It is to be looked upon with other reverence; because it is not a partnership in things subservient only to the gross animal existence of a temporary and perishable nature.

It is a partnership in all science; a partnership in all art; a partnership in every virtue, and in all perfection. As the ends of such a partnership cannot be obtained in many generations, it becomes a partnership not only between those who are living, but between those who are living, those who are dead and those who are to be born.

Each contract of each particular state is but a clause in the great primaeval contract of eternal society, linking the lower with the higher natures, connecting the visible and invisible world, according to a fixed compact sanctioned by the inviolable oath which holds all physical and all moral natures, each in their appointed place.[9]

The contract Burke has in mind is hardly an explicit contract, for it is "between those who are living, those who are dead and those are to be born." He implicitly affirms, I think, obligations to future generations. In speaking of the "ends of such a partnership," Burke intends a conception of the good life for man—a social ideal. And, if I do not misinterpret him, I think it also plain that Burke assumes that it is relatively the same conception of the good life whose realization is the object of the efforts of the living, the dead, and the unborn. They all revere the same social ideal. Moreover, he seems to assume that the conditions of life of the three groups are more or less the same. And, finally, he seems to assume that the same general characterization is true of these groups ("all physical and [all] moral natures, each in their appointed place").

Now I think that Burke is correct in making assumptions of these sorts if we are to have obligations to future generations. However, it is precisely with such assumptions that the notion of obligation to future generations begins to run into difficulties. My discussion, until this point, has proceeded on the view that we *have* obligations to future generations. But do we? I am not sure that the question can be answered in the affirmative with any certainty. I shall conclude this note with a very brief discussion of some of the difficulties. They may be summed up in the question: Is our conception—"conceptions" might be a more accurate word—of the good life for man relevant[10] to future generations?

It will be recalled that I began by stressing the importance of fixing the purview of obligations to future generations. They comprise the community of the future, a community with which we can-not expect to share a common life. It appears to me that the more *remote* the members of this community are, the more problematic our obligations to them become. That they are members of our moral community is highly doubtful, for we probably do not know what to desire for them.

Let us consider a concrete example, namely, that of the maintenance of genetic quality. Sir Julian Huxley has stated:

[I]f we don't do something about controlling our genetic inheritance, we are going to degenerate. Without selection, bad mutations inevitably tend to accumulate; *in the long run, perhaps 5,000 to 10,000 years from now,* we [*sic*] shall certainly have to do some-thing about it . . . Most mutations are deleterious, but we now keep many of them going that would otherwise have died out. If this continues indefinitely . . . then the whole genetic capacity of man will be much weakened.[11]

This statement, and others like it, raise many issues. As I have elsewhere (see footnote 1) discussed the problems connected with eugenic programs, positive and negative, I shall not go into details here. The point I would make is this: given that we do not know the conditions of life of the very distant future generations, we do not know what we ought to desire for them even on such matters as gene constitution. The chromosome is "deleterious" or "advantageous" only relative to given circumstances. And the same argument applies against those who promote certain

social traits by means of genetic engineering (assuming that social traits are heritable). Even such a trait as Intelligence does not escape immune. (There are also problems in eugenic programs having nothing to do with remoteness.) One might go as far as to say that if we have an obligation to distant future generations it is an obligation not to plan for them. Not only do we not know their conditions of life, we also do not know whether they will maintain the same (or a similar) conception of the good life for man as we do. Can we even be fairly sure that the same general characterization is true both of them and us?

The moral to be drawn from this rather extreme example is that the more distant the generation we focus upon, the less likely it is that we have an obligation to promote its good. We would be both ethically and practically well-advised to set our sights on more immediate generations and, perhaps, solely upon our immediate posterity. After all, even if we do have obligations to future generations, our obligations to immediate posterity are undoubtedly much clearer. The nearer the generations are to us, the more likely it is that our conception of the good life is relevant to them. There is certainly enough work for us to do in discharging our responsibility to promote a good life for them. But it would be unwise, both from an ethical and a practical perspective, to seek to promote the good of the very distant.

And it could also be *wrong*, if it be granted—as I think it must—that our obligations towards (and hence the rights relative to us of) near future generations and especially our immediate posterity are clearer than those of more distant generations. By "more distant" I do not necessarily mean "very distant." We shall have to be highly scrupulous in regard to anything we do for any future generation that also could adversely affect the rights of an intervening generation. Anything else would be "gambling in futures." We should, therefore, be hesitant to act on the dire predictions of certain extreme "crisis ecologists" and on the proposals of those who would have us plan for mere survival. In the main, we would be ethically well-advised to confine ourselves to removing the obstacles that stand in the way of immediate posterity's realizing the social ideal. This involves not only the active task of cleaning up the environment and making our cities more habitable, but also implies restraints upon us. Obviously, the specific obligations that we have cannot be determined in the abstract. This article is not the place for an evaluation of concrete proposals that have been made. I would only add that population limitation schemes seem rather dubious to me. I find it inherently paradoxical that we should have an obligation to future generations (near and distant) to determine in effect the very membership of those generations.[12]

A final point. If certain trends now apparent in our biological technology continue, it is doubtful that we should regard ourselves as being under an obligation to future generations. It seems likely that the man—humanoid(?)—of the future will be Programmed Man, fabricated to order, with his finger constantly on the Delgado button that stimulates the pleasure centers of the brain. I, for one, cannot see myself as regarding the good for Programmed Man as a good-to-me. That we should do so, however, if a necessary condition of his membership in our moral community, as I have argued above. The course of these trends may very well be determined by whether we believe that we are, in the words of Burke, "but a clause in the great primaeval contract of eternal society, linking the lower with the higher natures, connecting the visible and invisible world, according to a fixed compact sanctioned by the inviolable oath which holds all physical and all moral natures, each in their appointed place." We cannot yet pretend to know the outcome of these trends. It appears that whether we have obligations to future generations in part depends on what we do for the present.

NOTES

1. This paper is highly speculative, and it is put forward with hesitation. It is an attempt to extend a position developed in my article "Towards a Theory of Human Rights," *The Monist*, 52, No. 4 (1968), 521–549, wherein I also discuss some of the classical and contemporary literature on Rights. See also my paper, "Ethical Issues in Biological Engineering," *U.C.L.A. Law Review*, 15 (1968), 443–479, esp. 451–463, wherein I discuss obligations to future generations and some of the problems they provoke. I know of no other explicit discussion of the topic. The author wishes to thank the Institute of Society, Ethics, and the Life Sciences (Hastings-on-Hudson, New York) for its support.

2. See the remarks of Russell E. Train (Chairman of the Council on Environmental Quality), quoted in *National Geographic*, 138 (1970), 780: "If we're to be responsible we must accept the fact that we owe a massive debt too our environment. It won't be settled in a matter of months, and it won't be forgiven us."

3. Cf. the discussion of *Fernstenliebe* (Love of the Remotest) in Nicolai Hartmann, *Ethics*, trans, by Coit, II (New York: The Macmillan Co., 1932), 317 ff.

4. There is also another factor relevant to determining whether what is demanded can be claimed as a matter of right, namely, the availability of resources of goods. But I am suppressing this for purposes of this discussion.

5. Paraphrasing C. S. Lewis, *The Abolition of Man* (New York: The Macmillan Co., paperback ed. 1969), p.56: "If my duty to my parents is a superstition, then so is my duty to posterity."

6. When Sarah died, Abraham "approached the children of Heth, saying: I am a stranger and a sojourner with you; give me a possession of a burying-place with you, that I may bury my dead out of my sight" (Gen. 23:3, 4). A classical commentary remarks that Abraham is saying: If I am a stranger, I will purchase it, but if I am a sojourner it is mine as a matter of right.

7. Cf. T. H. Green, *Lectures on the Principles of Political Obligation* (New York and London: Longman's, 1959; Ann Arbor: University of Michigan Press, 1967), Sec. 140. I here acknowledge my debt to Green, in which acknowledgment I was remiss in my article on Human Rights.

8. I think it an interesting commentary on our times that the rhetoric of obligation to future generations is so much used just when the family bond has become progressively tenuous.

9. *Reflections on the Revolution in France* (London: Dent, 1910), pp. 93–94.

10. The author at last begs pardon for having to use such an abused word.

11. In *Evolution after Darwin*, ed. by S. Tax, III (Chicago: University of Chicago Press, 1960), p. 61. Emphasis added.

12. On this and other arguments relating to the problem, see Martin P. Golding and Naomi H. Golding, "Ethical and Value Issues in Population Limitation and Distribution in the United States," *Vanderbilt Law Review*, 24 (1971), 495–523.

CASES FOR ANALYSIS

1. Averting Famine

LILONGWE, Malawi—Malawi hovered for years at the brink of famine. After a disastrous corn harvest in 2005, almost five million of its 13 million people needed emergency food aid.

But this year, a nation that has perennially extended a begging bowl to the world is instead feeding its hungry neighbors. It is selling more corn to the World Food Program of the United Nations than any other country in southern Africa and is exporting hundreds of thousands of tons of corn to Zimbabwe.

In Malawi itself, the prevalence of acute child hunger has fallen sharply. In October, the United Nations Children's Fund sent three tons of powdered milk, stockpiled here to treat severely malnourished children, to Uganda instead. "We will not be able to use it!" Juan Ortiz-Iruri, Unicef's deputy representative in Malawi, said jubilantly.

Farmers explain Malawi's extraordinary turnaround—one with broad implications for hunger-fighting methods across Africa—with one word: fertilizer.

Over the past 20 years, the World Bank and some rich nations Malawi depends on for aid have periodically pressed this small, landlocked country to adhere to free market policies and cut back or eliminate fertilizer subsidies, even as the United States and Europe extensively subsidized their own farmers. But after the 2005 harvest, the worst in a decade, Bingu wa Mutharika, Malawi's newly elected president, decided to follow what the West practiced, not what it preached.

Stung by the humiliation of pleading for charity, he led the way to reinstating and deepening fertilizer subsidies despite a skeptical reception from the United States and Britain. Malawi's soil, like that across sub-Saharan Africa, is gravely depleted, and many, if not most, of its farmers are too poor to afford fertilizer at market prices.

"As long as I'm president, I don't want to be going to other capitals begging for food," Mr. Mutharika declared. Patrick Kabambe, the senior civil servant in the Agriculture Ministry, said the president told his advisers, "Our people are poor because they lack the resources to use the soil and the water we have."

The country's successful use of subsidies is contributing to a broader reappraisal of the crucial role of agriculture in alleviating poverty in Africa and the pivotal importance of public investments in the basics of a farm economy: fertilizer, improved seed, farmer education, credit and agricultural research.

Malawi, an overwhelmingly rural nation about the size of Pennsylvania, is an extreme example of what happens when those things are missing. As its population has grown and inherited landholdings have shrunk, impoverished farmers have planted every inch of ground. Desperate to feed their families, they could not afford to let their land lie fallow or to fertilize it. Over time, their depleted plots yielded less food and the farmers fell deeper into poverty.

Malawi's leaders have long favored fertilizer subsidies, but they reluctantly acceded to donor prescriptions, often shaped by foreign-aid fashions in Washington, that featured a faith in private markets and an antipathy to government intervention.*

If, as this story suggests, the World Bank and rich nations offered bad advice to Malawi, do they bear some responsibility for the subsequent food short-ages? Does this story seem to support or under-mine Garrett Hardin's views on helping the needy?

*Celia W. Dugger, "Ending Famine, Simply by Ignoring the Experts," *New York Times*, 2 December 2007, www.nytimes.com/2007/12/02/world/africa/02malawi.html (12 May 2009).

---

2. Developed Countries Failing the Poor

UNITED NATIONS—In criticism aimed primarily at the United States, Japan and the Euro-pean Union, a U.N. report said rich donor nations have failed to deliver on promises to help the world's poorest countries and must increase aid by $18 billion a year.

The report released Thursday also criticized the failure of rich and poor nations to reach a trade pact in seven years of negotiations that would expand global trade opportunities for developing countries to reduce poverty. It called for redoubled efforts to conclude negotiations.

The report was issued ahead of a Sept. 25 meeting of world leaders at U.N. headquarters to step up efforts to achieve the Millennium Development Goals, adopted by world lead-ers at a summit in 2000. The goals include cutting extreme poverty by half, ensuring universal primary school education and starting to reverse the HIV/AIDS pandemic, all by 2015. . . .

U.N. Secretary-General Ban Ki-moon told a press conference that the report "sounds a strong alarm."

"The main message is that while there has been progress on several counts, delivery on commitments made by member states has been deficient, and has fallen behind sched-ule," he said. "We are already in the second half of our contest against poverty. We are running out of time." . . .

Ban noted that total aid from the world's major donor nations amounts to only 0.25% of their combined national income, far below the U.N. target of 0.7%. The only countries to reach or exceed that target were Denmark, Luxembourg, the Netherlands, Norway and Sweden.[†]

Is the failure of rich nations to aid the world's poorest countries morally wrong? Is the giving of aid a moral obligation for rich nations—or just a supererogatory act? What conclusion do you draw from the United States' failure to contribute its promised share of aid?

[†]*USA Today*, "U.N. Report: Developed Countries Failing Poor," 4 September 2008, www.usatoday.com/news/world/2008-09-04-poverty_N.htm (12 May 2009).

3. Singer or Hardin?

CBC News—The Church World Service aid agency is warning that "immediate, massive intervention and assistance" are needed to prevent mass starvation in Kenya.

A team from the humanitarian agency reported recently that many fields are barren and cracked, dried out by the drought that is threatening a third of the east African country's population, or about 10 million people.

What was once among the most fertile land in African can now only support a few struggling plants suitable only for grazing cattle.

"We don't have any food," farmer Lizy Bimba, a Kwale resident, said in Swahili.

In one area, a local official reported that 85 per cent of 5,600 people are facing starvation, the Church World Service team said.

Other farmers have left the land to find what work they can.

"We have been forced to do this so that we get money to buy food," Musa Charo said in Swahili as he broke rocks to earn money to feed his 10 children.

The government declared the food shortage a national disaster on Jan. 16, the UN is appealing for international help and aid agencies warn that the problem will only get worse.[‡]

What would be the proper moral response of rich nations to this impending tragedy? Do you favor Garrett Hardin's approach in which rich countries would not send food aid? Or Peter Singer's path in which affluent individuals would be obligated to give much of their wealth to feed the hungry? Or a middle way in which the rich would have a duty to give some aid but would also have obligations to themselves and to their family and friends? Explain.

[‡]CBC News, "Kenya Facing Mass Starvation: Aid Group," 31 January 2009, www.cbc.ca/world/story/2009/01/31/kenya-famine.html (12 May 2009).

GLOSSARY

abolitionists—Those who wish to abolish capital punishment.

abortion—The deliberate termination of a pregnancy by surgical or medical (with drugs) means.

act-egoism—The theory that to determine right action, you must apply the egoistic principle to individual acts.

active euthanasia—Euthanasia performed by taking a direct action to cause someone's death; "mercy killing."

act-utilitarianism—The theory that right actions are those that directly produce the greatest overall good, everyone considered.

advance directive—A legal document allowing physicians to withhold or withdraw treatments if a patient becomes terminally ill and unable to express his or her wishes.

affirmative action—A way of making amends for, or eradicating, discrimination based on race, ethnicity, and gender.

animal rights—Possesson by animals of (1) moral status; (2) strong moral consideration that cannot be easily overridden.

anthropocentrism—The notion that only humans have moral status.

appeal to authority—The fallacy of relying on the opinion of someone thought to be an expert who is not.

appeal to ignorance—The fallacy of arguing that the absence of evidence entitles us to believe a claim.

appeal to the person—The fallacy (also known as *ad hominem*) of arguing that a claim should be rejected solely because of the characteristics of the person who makes it.

applied ethics—The application of moral norms to specific moral issues or cases, particularly those in a profession such as medicine or law.

argument—A group of statements, one of which is supposed to be supported by the rest.

begging the question—The fallacy of arguing in a circle—that is, trying to use a statement as both a premise in an argument and the conclusion of that argument. Such an argument says, in effect, *p* is true because *p* is true.

biocentrism—The view that all living entities have moral status, whether sentient or not.

capital punishment—Punishment by execution of someone officially judged to have committed a serious, or capital, crime.

categorical imperative—An imperative that we should follow regardless of our particular wants and needs; also, the principle that defines Kant's ethical system.

cogent argument—A strong argument with true premises.

conception—The merging of a sperm cell and an ovum into a single cell; also called *fertilization*.

conclusion—The statement supported in an argument.

consequentialist theory—A theory asserting that what makes an action right is its consequences.

conventional view (of sexuality)—The idea that sex is morally acceptable only between a man and woman who are legally married to each other.

cultural relativism—The view that an action is morally right if one's culture approves of it.

deductive argument—An argument that is supposed to give logically conclusive support to its conclusion.

descriptive ethics—The scientific study of moral beliefs and practices.

direct moral consideration—Moral consideration for a being's own sake, rather than because of its relationship to others.

discrimination—Unfavorable treatment of people on irrelevant grounds.

distributive justice—Justice concerning the fair distribution of society's goods.

divine command theory—A theory asserting that the morally right action is the one that God commands.

doctrine of double effect—The principle that performing a good action may be permissible even if it has bad effects, but performing a bad action for the purpose of achieving good effects is never permissible; any bad effects must be unintended.

duty of beneficence—A moral obligation to benefit others.

ecological holist—One who believes that the fundamental unit of moral consideration in environmental ethics is the biosphere and its ecosystems.

ecological individualist—One who believes that the fundamental unit of moral consideration in environmental ethics is the individual.

egalitarian theory of justice—A doctrine holding that justice requires equal distributions of goods and social benefits among all persons.

emotivism—The view that moral utterances are neither true nor false but are expressions of emotions or attitudes.

equivocation—The fallacy of assigning two different meanings to the same term in an argument.

erotica—Sexually explicit material that does not degrade or subordinate women; also, sexually explicit material that emphasizes mutually satisfying sexual relationships between equals.

ethical egoism—The theory that the right action is the one that advances one's own best interests.

ethics (moral philosophy)—The philosophical study of morality.

ethics of care—A perspective on moral issues that emphasizes close personal relationships and moral virtues such as compassion, love, and sympathy.

eudaimonia—Happiness, or flourishing.

euthanasia—Directly or indirectly bringing about the death of another person for that person's sake.

faulty analogy—The use of a flawed analogy to argue for a conclusion.

Golden Mean—Aristotle's notion of a virtue as a balance between two behavioral extremes.

greatest happiness principle—According to Mill, the principle that "holds that actions are right in proportion as they tend to promote happiness, wrong as they tend to produce the reverse of happiness."

hasty generalization—The fallacy of drawing a conclusion about an entire group of people or things based on an undersized sample of the group.

homosexuality—Sexual relations between people of the same sex.

humanitarian intervention—The act of a state (or states) going to war to defend people of another state against the aggression of their own regime.

hypothetical imperative—An imperative that tells us what we should do if we have certain desires.

imperfect duty—A duty that has exceptions.

indicator words—Terms that often appear in arguments to signal the presence of a premise or conclusion, or to indicate that an argument is deductive or inductive.

indirect moral consideration—Moral consideration on account of a being's relationship to others.

inductive argument—An argument that is supposed to offer probable support to its conclusion.

instrumentally (or extrinsically) valuable—Valuable as a means to something else.

intrinsically valuable—Valuable in itself, for its own sake.

invalid argument—A deductive argument that does not offer logically conclusive support for the conclusion.

involuntary euthanasia—Euthanasia performed on a person against his or her wishes.

jus ad bellum—The justification for resorting to war; the justice of war.

jus in bello—The moral permissibility of acts in war; justice in war.

justice—The morality of persons getting what is fair or what is their their due.

just war theory—The doctrine that war may be morally permissible under stipulated conditions.

Kant's theory—A theory asserting that the morally right action is the one done in accordance with the categorical imperative.

legal moralism—The view that a community's important moral beliefs should have the force of law.

legal paternalism—The view that the government may legitimately restrict citizens' freedom for their own good.

liberal view (of sexuality)—The idea that as long as basic moral standards are respected, any sexual activity engaged in by informed, consenting adults is permissible.

libertarian theory of justice—A doctrine emphasizing individual liberties and negative rights, and rejecting positive rights as a violation of personal freedom.

means-ends principle—The rule that we must always treat people (including ourselves) as ends in themselves, never merely as a means.

metaethics—The study of the meaning and logical structure of moral beliefs.

Miller test—Criteria for judging whether a work is legally obscene, as articulated in *Miller v. California* (1973).

moderate view (of sexuality)—The idea that sex is permissible, whether in marriage or not, if the consenting partners have a serious emotional connection.

morality—Beliefs concerning right and wrong, good and bad; they can include judgments, rules, principles, and theories.

moral statement—A statement affirming that an action is right or wrong or that a person (or one's motive or character) is good or bad.

moral status (or moral considerability)—The property of being a suitable candidate for direct moral concern or respect.

moral theory—An explanation of what makes an action right or what makes a person or thing good.

natural law theory—A theory asserting that the morally right action is the one that follows the dictates of nature.

negative right—A person's right that obligates others not to interfere with that person's obtaining something.

noncombatant immunity—The status of a person who should not be intentionally attacked in war.

nonconsequentialist theory—A theory asserting that the rightness of an action does not depend on its consequences.

nonmoral statement—A statement that does not affirm that an action is right or wrong or that a person (or one's motive or character) is good or bad.

nonstate actors—Individuals or groups that are not sovereign states.

nonvoluntary euthanasia—Euthanasia performed on a person who is not competent to decide the issue and has left no instructions regarding end-of-life preferences. In such cases, family or physicians usually make the decision.

normative ethics—The study of the principles, rules, or theories that guide our actions and judgments.

objectivism—The view that some moral principles are valid for everyone.

obscenity—A characteristic or property believed to render sexually frank material morally or legally unacceptable; also, a legal term used to describe sexually graphic words or images that are not protected by the First Amendment's guarantee of free speech.

pacifism—The view that war is never morally permissible.

passive euthanasia—Euthanasia performed by withholding or withdrawing measures necessary for sustaining life.

perfect duty—A duty that has no exceptions.

person—A being thought to have full moral rights.

physician-assisted suicide—The killing of a person by the person's own hand with the help of a physician.

pornography—Sexually frank images or text meant to cause sexual excitement or arousal.

positive right—A person's right that obligates others to help that person obtain something.

premise—A supporting statement in an argument.

principle of utility—Bentham's "principle which approves or disapproves of every action whatsoever, according to the tendency which it appears to have to augment or diminish the happiness of the party whose interest is in question."

psychological egoism—The view that the motive for all our actions is self-interest.

punishment—The deliberate and authorized causing of pain or harm to someone thought to have broken a law.

quickening—The point in fetal development when the mother can feel the fetus moving (it occurs at about sixteen to twenty weeks).

realism (as applied to warfare)—The view that moral standards are not applicable to war, and that it instead must be judged on how well it serves state interests.

retentionists—Those who wish to retain the death penalty.

retributive justice—Justice concerning fair punishment for wrongdoing.

retributivism—The view that offenders deserve to be punished, or "paid back," for their crimes and to be punished in proportion to the severity of their offenses.

right—A claim or entitlement to something; a moral demand that obligates others to honor it.

rule-egoism—The theory that to determine right action, you must see if an act falls under a rule that if consistently followed would maximize your self-interest.

rule-utilitarianism—The theory that the morally right action is the one covered by a rule that if generally followed would produce the most favorable balance of good over evil, everyone considered.

slippery slope—The fallacy of using dubious premises to argue that doing a particular action will inevitably lead to other actions that will result in disaster, so you should not do that first action.

sound argument—A valid argument with true premises.

species egalitarian—One who believes that all living things have equal moral status.

speciesism—Discrimination against nonhuman animals just because of their species.

species nonegalitarian—One who believes that some living things have greater moral status than others.

statement—An assertion that something is or is not the case.

straw man—The fallacy of misrepresenting someone's claim or argument so it can be more easily refuted.

strong affirmative action—The use of policies and procedures to favor particular individuals because of their race, gender, or ethnic background.

strong argument—An inductive argument that does in fact provide probable support for its conclusion.

subjective relativism—The view that an action is morally right if one approves of it.

supererogatory actions—Conduct that is "above and beyond" duty; not required, but praiseworthy.

terrorism—Violence against noncombatants for political, religious, or ideological ends.

therapeutic abortion—An abortion performed to protect the life or health of the mother.

torture—The intentional inflicting of severe pain or suffering on people to punish or intimidate them or extract information from them.

utilitarianism—A theory asserting that the morally right action is the one that produces the most favorable balance of good over evil, everyone considered.

valid argument—A deductive argument that does in fact provide logically conclusive support for its conclusion.

viability—The stage of fetal development at which the fetus is able to survive outside the uterus.

virtue—A stable disposition to act and feel according to some ideal or model of excellence.

virtue ethics—A theory of morality that makes virtue the central concern.

voluntary euthanasia—Euthanasia performed on a person with his or her permission.

weak affirmative action—The use of policies and procedures to end discriminatory practices and ensure equal opportunity.

weak argument—An inductive argument that does not give probable support to the conclusion.

zoocentrism—The notion that both human and nonhuman animals have moral status.

FURTHER READING

Chapter 1. Ethics and the Examined Life

Anita L. Allen, *New Ethics: A Guided Tour of the Twenty-First-Century Moral Landscape* (New York: Miramax, 2004).

Aristotle, *Nicomachean Ethics,* Book 2, Parts 1 and 4.

Simon Blackburn, *Being Good: A Short Introduction to Ethics* (Oxford: Oxford University Press, 2002).

Donald M. Borchert and David Stewart, *Exploring Ethics* (New York: Macmillan, 1986).

Steven M. Cahn and Joram G. Haber, eds., *Twentieth Century Ethical Theory* (Englewood Cliffs, NJ: Prentice Hall, 1995).

William K. Frankena, *Ethics,* 2nd ed. (Englewood Cliffs, NJ: Prentice-Hall, 1973).

Bernard Gert, *Morality: Its Nature and Justification* (New York: Oxford University Press, 1998).

Brooke Noel Moore and Robert Michael Stewart, *Moral Philosophy: A Comprehensive Introduction* (Belmont, CA: Mayfield, 1994).

Dave Robinson and Chris Garrett, *Introducing Ethics,* ed. Richard Appignanesi (New York: Totem Books, 2005).

Peter Singer, ed., *A Companion to Ethics,* corr. ed. (Oxford: Blackwell, 1993).

Paul Taylor, *Principles of Ethics: An Introduction* (Encino, CA: Dickenson, 1975).

Jacques P. Thiroux, *Ethics: Theory and Practice,* 3rd ed. (New York: Macmillan, 1986).

Thomas F. Wall, *Thinking Critically about Moral Problems* (Belmont, CA: Wadsworth, 2003).

G. J. Warnock, *The Object of Morality* (London: Methuen, 1971).

Chapter 2. Subjectivism, Relativism, and Emotivism

A. J. Ayer, *Language, Truth and Logic* (1936; reprint, New York: Dover, 1952).

Brand Blanshard, "Emotivism," in *Reason and Goodness* (1961; reprint, New York: G. Allen and Unwin, 1978).

Donald M. Borchert and David Stewart, "Ethical Emotivism," in *Exploring Ethics* (New York: Macmillan, 1986).

Richard B. Brandt, chapter 11 of *Ethical Theory: The Problems of Normative and Critical Ethics* (Englewood Cliffs, NJ: Prentice-Hall, 1959).

Jean Bethke Elshtain, "Judge Not?" *First Things,* no. 46 (October 1994): 36–40.

Fred Feldman, chapter 11 of *Introductory Ethics* (Englewood Cliffs, NJ: Prentice-Hall, 1978).

Chris Gowans, "Moral Relativism," *The Stanford Encyclopedia of Philosophy* (Spring 2004 ed.), ed. Edward N. Zalta, http://plato.stanford.edu/archives/spr2004/entries/moral-relativism (2 December 2006).

Melville Herskovits, *Cultural Relativism: Perspectives in Cultural Pluralism,* ed. Frances Herskovits (New York: Random House, 1972).

J. L. Mackie, *Ethics: Inventing Right and Wrong* (Harmondsworth: Penguin, 1977).

Theodore Schick Jr. and Lewis Vaughn, chapter 5 of *Doing Philosophy: An Introduction through Thought Experiments,* 2nd ed. (Boston: McGraw-Hill, 2003).

Peter Singer, ed., chapters 38 and 39 of *A Companion to Ethics,* corr. ed. (Oxford: Blackwell, 1993).

Walter T. Stace, "Ethical Relativism," in *The Concept of Morals* (1937; reprint, New York: Macmillan, 1965).

Paul Taylor, chapter 2 of *Principles of Ethics: An Introduction* (Encino, CA: Dickenson, 1975).

Chapter 3. Evaluating Moral Arguments

Richard Feldman, *Reason and Argument,* 2nd ed. (Upper Saddle River, NJ: Prentice Hall, 1999).

Richard M. Fox and Joseph P. DeMarco, *Moral Reasoning: A Philosophic Approach to Applied Ethics,* 2nd ed. (Fort Worth: Harcourt College Publishers, 2001).

Brooke Noel Moore and Richard Parker, *Critical Thinking,* 7th ed. (Boston: McGraw-Hill, 2004).

Lewis Vaughn, *The Power of Critical Thinking: Effective Reasoning about Ordinary and Extraordinary Claims* (New York: Oxford University Press, 2005).

Chapter 4. The Power of Moral Theories

John D. Arras and Nancy K. Rhoden, "The Need for Ethical Theory," in *Ethical Issues in Modern Medicine,* 3rd ed. (Mountain View, CA: Mayfield, 1989).

Richard B. Brandt, *Ethical Theory: The Problems of Normative and Critical Ethics* (Englewood Cliffs, NJ: Prentice-Hall, 1959).

C. D. Broad, *Five Types of Ethical Theory* (1930; reprint, London: Routledge and Kegan Paul, 1956).

John Hospers, *Human Conduct: Problems of Ethics,* shorter ed. (New York: Harcourt Brace Jovanovich, 1972).

John Rawls, "Some Remarks about Moral Theory," in *A Theory of Justice,* rev. ed. (Cambridge, MA: Harvard University Press, Belknap Press, 1999).

Chapter 5. Consequentialist Theories: Maximize the Good

Jeremy Bentham, "Of the Principle of Utility," in *An Introduction to the Principles of Morals and Legislation* (1789).

C. D. Broad, "Egoism as a Theory of Human Motives," in *Twentieth Century Ethical Theory,* ed. Steven M. Cahn and Joram G. Haber (Englewood Cliffs, NJ: Prentice Hall, 1995).

Steven M. Cahn and Joram G. Haber, eds., *Twentieth Century Ethical Theory* (Englewood Cliffs, NJ: Prentice Hall, 1995).

Fred Feldman, "Act Utilitarianism: Pro and Con," in *Introductory Ethics* (Englewood Cliffs, NJ: Prentice-Hall, 1978).

William Frankena, "Utilitarianism, Justice, and Love," in *Ethics,* 2nd ed. (Englewood Cliffs, NJ: Prentice-Hall, 1973).

C. E. Harris, "The Ethics of Utilitarianism," in *Applying Moral Theories,* 3rd ed. (Belmont, CA: Wadsworth, 1997).

Kai Nielsen, "A Defense of Utilitarianism," *Ethics* 82 (1972): 113–24.

Robert Nozick, "The Experience Machine," in *Anarchy, State and Utopia* (New York: Basic Books, 1974).

Louis P. Pojman, ed., *The Moral Life: An Introductory Reader in Ethics and Literature,* 2nd ed. (New York: Oxford University Press, 2004).

J. J. C. Smart, "Extreme and Restricted Utilitarianism," in *Essays Metaphysical and Moral: Selected Philosophical Papers* (Oxford: Blackwell, 1987).

Paul W. Taylor, "Ethical Egoism," in *Principles of Ethics: An Introduction* (Encino, CA: Dickenson, 1975).

Bernard Williams, "A Critique of Utilitarianism," in *Utilitarianism: For and Against,* ed. J. J. C. Smart and Williams (Cambridge: Cambridge University Press, 1973).

Chapter 6. Nonconsequentialist Theories: Do Your Duty

Stephen Buckle, "Natural Law," in *A Companion to Ethics,* ed. Peter Singer, corr. ed. (Oxford: Blackwell, 1993).

John Finnis, *Natural Law and Natural Rights* (Oxford: Clarendon Press; New York: Oxford University Press, 1980).

C. E. Harris, chapters 6 and 8 of *Applying Moral Theories,* 3rd ed. (Belmont, CA: Wadsworth, 1997).

Mark Murphy, "The Natural Law Tradition in Ethics," The Stanford Encyclopedia of Philosophy (Winter 2002 ed.), ed. Edward N. Zalta, http://plato.stanford.edu/archives/win2002/entries/natural-law-ethics (2 December 2006).

Kai Nielsen, *Ethics without God* (London: Pemberton; Buffalo, NY: Prometheus, 1973).

Robert Nozick, *Anarchy, State and Utopia* (New York: Basic Books, 1974).

Onora O'Neill, "Kantian Ethics," in *A Companion to Ethics,* ed. Peter Singer, corr. ed. (Oxford: Blackwell, 1993).

Louis P. Pojman, "Natural Law," in *Ethics: Discovering Right and Wrong,* 4th ed. (Belmont, CA: Wadsworth, 2002).

James Rachels, chapter 9 of *The Elements of Moral Philosophy,* 4th ed. (Boston: McGraw-Hill, 2003).

Paul Taylor, chapter 5 of *Principles of Ethics: An Introduction* (Encino, CA: Dickenson, 1975).

Thomas Aquinas, *Summa Theologica,* in *Basic Writings of Saint Thomas Aquinas,* ed. and annotated Anton C. Pegis (New York: Random House, 1945).

Robert N. Van Wyk, chapters 4 and 6 of *Introduction to Ethics* (New York: St. Martin's, 1990).

Chapter 7. Virtue Ethics: Be a Good Person

G. E. M. Anscombe, "Modern Moral Philosophy," *Philosophy* 33, no. 124 (January 1958): 1–19.

Philippa Foot, "Virtues and Vices," in *Virtues and Vices and Other Essays in Moral Philosophy* (Berkeley: University of California Press, 1978).

William K. Frankena, "Ethics of Virtue," in *Ethics,* 2nd ed. (Englewood Cliffs, NJ: Prentice-Hall, 1973).

Rosalind Hursthouse, "Virtue Ethics," *The Stanford Encyclopedia of Philosophy* (Fall 2003 ed.), ed. Edward N. Zalta, http:plato.stanford/archives/fall2003/entries/ethics-virtue (2 December 2006).

Alasdair MacIntyre, "The Nature of the Virtues," in *After Virtue: A Study in Moral Theory* (Notre Dame, IN: University of Notre Dame Press, 1984).

Greg Pence, "Virtue Theory," in *A Companion to Ethics,* ed. Peter Singer, corr. ed. (Oxford: Blackwell, 1993).

Chapter 8. Abortion

Daniel Callahan, "Abortion Decisions: Personal Morality," in *Abortion: Law, Choice and Morality* (New York: Macmillan, 1970).

Sidney Callahan, "A Case for Pro-Life Feminism," *Commonweal* 25 (April 1986): 232–38.

Jane English, "Abortion and the Concept of a Person," *Canadian Journal of Philosophy* 5, no. 2 (October 1975): 233–43.

Joel Feinberg, "Abortion," in *Matters of Life and Death,* ed. Tom Regan, 3rd ed. (New York: McGraw-Hill, 1993).

Ronald Munson, "Abortion," in *Intervention and Reflection: Basic Issues in Medical Ethics,* ed. Munson, 7th ed. (Belmont, CA: Wadsworth, 2004).

John T. Noonan Jr., "An Almost Absolute Value in History," in *The Morality of Abortion: Legal and Historical Perspectives,* ed. Noonan (Cambridge, MA: Harvard University Press, 1970).

Louis P. Pojman and Francis J. Beckwith, eds., *The Abortion Controversy: 25 Years After Roe v. Wade: A Reader,* 2nd ed. (Belmont, CA: Wadsworth, 1998).

Roe v. Wade, 410 U.S. 113, 113–67 (1973). Justice Harry Blackman, Majority Opinion of the Court.

Michael Tooley, *Abortion and Infanticide* (Oxford: Clarendon Press; New York: Oxford University Press, 1983).

Chapter 9. Euthanasia and Physician-Assisted Suicide

Tom L. Beauchamp, ed., *Intending Death: The Ethics of Assisted Suicide and Euthanasia* (Englewood Cliffs, NJ: Prentice Hall, 1995).

R. B. Brandt, "The Morality and Rationality of Suicide," in *A Handbook for the Study of Suicide,* ed. Seymour Perlin (New York: Oxford University Press, 1975).

Lonnie R. Bristow, President of the American Medical Association, statement on physician-assisted suicide to the U.S. House of Representatives Committee on the Judiciary, Subcommittee on the Constitution, 104th Cong., 2nd sess., *Congressional Record* 142 (29 April 1996).

Dan W. Brock, "Medical Decisions at the End of Life," in *A Companion to Bioethics,* ed. Helga Kuhse and Peter Singer (1998; reprint, Malden, MA: Blackwell, 2001).

Daniel Callahan, "When Self-Determination Runs Amok," *Hastings Center Report* 22, no. 2 (March/April 1992): 52–55.

Philippa Foot, "Euthanasia," *Philosophy & Public Affairs* 6, no. 2 (1977): 85–112.

Walter Glannon, "Medical Decisions at the End of Life," in *Biomedical Ethics* (New York: Oxford University Press, 2005).

John Lachs, "When Abstract Moralizing Runs Amok," *Journal of Clinical Ethics* 5, no. 1 (1994): 10–13.

Ronald Munson, "Euthanasia and Physician-Assisted Suicide," in *Intervention and Reflection: Basic Issues in Medical Ethics,* ed. Munson, 7th ed. (Belmont, CA: Wadsworth, 2004).

Jeffrey Olen and Vincent Barry, "Euthanasia," in *Applying Ethics: A Text with Readings,* 6th ed. (Belmont, CA: Wadsworth, 1999).

The President's Commission for the Study of Ethical Problems in Medicine and Biomedical and Behavioral Research (Washington, DC: Government Printing Office, 1983).

Bonnie Steinbock and Alastair Norcross, eds., *Killing and Letting Die,* 2nd ed. (New York: Fordham University Press, 1994).

Thomas D. Sullivan, "Active and Passive Euthanasia: An Impertinent Distinction?" *Human Life Review* 3, no. 3 (1977): 40–46.

Robert Young, "Voluntary Euthanasia," *The Stanford Encyclopedia of Philosophy* (Summer 2005 ed.), ed. Edward N. Zalta, http://plato.stanford.edu/archives/sum2005/entries/euthanasia-voluntary/ (2 December 2006).

Chapter 10. Capital Punishment

Hugo Adam Bedau, "Capital Punishment and Social Defense," in *Matters of Life and Death: New Introductory Essays in Moral Philosophy,* ed. Tom Regan, 2nd ed. (New York: Random House, 1986).

Hugo Adam Bedau and Paul Cassell, eds., *Debating the Death Penalty: Should America Have Capital Punishment? The Experts on Both Sides Make Their Best Case* (Oxford: Oxford University Press, 2004).

Gregg v. Georgia, 428 U.S. 153, 153–207 (1976). Justice Potter Stewart et al., Opinion of the Court.

Gregg v. Georgia, 428 U.S. 153, 231–41 (1976). Justice Thurgood Marshall, Dissenting Opinion.

Sidney Hook, "The Death Sentence," *New Leader,* 3 April 1961.

Alex Kozinski, "Tinkering with Death," *New Yorker,* 10 February 1997, 48–52.

Burton Leiser, "The Death Penalty Is Permissible," in *Liberty, Justice and Morals: Contemporary Value Conflicts,* 3rd ed. (New York: Macmillan, 1986).

John Stuart Mill, "Speech in Favor of Capital Punishment," 1868, http://ethics.sandiego.edu/Mill-html (3 January 2007).

Stephen Nathanson, "An Eye for an Eye?" in *An Eye for an Eye? The Morality of Punishing by Death* (Totowa, NJ: Rowman and Littlefield, 1987).

Louis P. Pojman, "Why the Death Penalty Is Morally Permissible," in *Debating the Death Penalty: Should America Have Capital Punishment? The Experts on Both Sides Make Their Best Case,* eds. Hugo Bedau and Paul Cassell (Oxford: Oxford University Press, 2004).

William H. Shaw, "Punishment and the Criminal Justice System," in *Contemporary Ethics: Taking Account of Utilitarianism* (Malden, MA: Blackwell, 1999).

Ernest van den Haag, "On Deterrence and the Death Penalty," *Journal of Criminal Law, Criminology, and Police Science* 60, no. 2 (1969): 141–47.

Chapter 11. Pornography and Censorship

American Booksellers v. Hudnutt, 771 F.2d 323 (7th Cir. 1985).

Ann Garry, "Sex, Lies, and Pornography," *Ethics in Practice,* ed. Hugh LaFollette, 2nd ed. (Malden, MA: Blackwell, 2002).

Helen E. Longino, "Pornography, Oppression, and Freedom," in *Take Back the Night: Women on Pornography,* ed. Laura Lederer (New York: William Morrow, 1980).

Wendy McElroy, "A Feminist Defense of Pornography," in *Sexual Correctness: The Gender-Feminist Attack on Women* (Jefferson, NC: McFarland, 1996).

John Stuart Mill, chapter 1 of *On Liberty* (1859).

Caroline West, "Pornography and Censorship," *The Stanford Encyclopedia of Philosophy* (Fall 2005 ed.), ed. Edward N. Zalta, http://plato.stanford.edu/entries/pornography-censorship/ (8 February 2006).

Mark R. Wicclair, "Feminism, Pornography, and Censorship," in *Social Ethics: Morality and Social Policy,* ed. Thomas A. Mappes and Jane S. Zembaty, 6th ed. (Dubuque, IA: McGraw-Hill, 2002).

Ellen Willis, "Feminism, Moralism, and Pornography," in *Beginning to See the Light: Sex, Hope, and Rock-and-Roll* (Hanover, NH: Wesleyan University Press, 1992).

Chapter 12. Sexual Morality and Marriage

Bruce Bawer, ed., *Beyond Queer: Challenging Gay Left Orthodoxy* (New York: Free Press, 1996).

Raymond A. Belliotti, "Sex," in *A Companion to Ethics,* ed. Peter Singer (Cambridge, MA: Blackwell, 1993).

John Corvino, ed., *Same Sex: Debating the Ethics, Science, and Culture of Homosexuality* (Lanham, MD: Rowman & Littlefield, 1997).

Michael Levin, "Why Homosexuality Is Abnormal," *The Monist* 67 (April 1984): 251–83.

Richard D. Mohr, *The Little Book of Gay Rights* (Boston: Beacon Press, 1994).

Timothy F. Murphy, "Homosexuality and Nature: Happiness and the Law at Stake," *Journal of Applied Philosophy* 4, no. 2 (1987): 195–204.

Vincent C. Punzo, *Reflective Naturalism: An Introduction to Moral Philosophy* (New York: Macmillan, 1969).

Michael Ruse, *Homosexuality: A Philosophical Inquiry* (New York: Blackwell, 1988).

Sam Schulman, "Gay Marriage—and Marriage," *Commentary* (November 2003).

Roger Scruton, *Sexual Desire: A Moral Philosophy of the Erotic* (New York: Free Press, 1986).

Alan Soble, "Philosophy of Sexuality," in *The Internet Encyclopedia of Philosophy* (2006), www.iep.utm.edu/s/sexualit.htm (30 March 2009).

Nancy Tuana and Laurie Shrage, "Sexuality," in *The Oxford Handbook of Practical Ethics,* ed. Hugh LaFollette (New York: Oxford University Press, 2003), 15–41.

Chapter 13. Equality and Affirmative Action

Bernard R. Boxill, "Equality, Discrimination and Preferential Treatment," in *A Companion to Ethics,* ed. Peter Singer, corr. ed. (Oxford: Blackwell, 1993).

Steven M. Cahn, "Two Concepts of Affirmative Action," *Academe* 83, no. 1 (1997): 14–19.

Stephen Carter, *Reflections of an Affirmative Action Baby* (New York: Basic Books, 1991).

Carl Cohen and James P. Sterba, *Affirmative Action and Racial Preference: A Debate* (New York: Oxford University Press, 2003).

Ronald Dworkin, "Bakke's Case: Are Quotas Unfair?" in *A Matter of Principle* (Cambridge, MA: Harvard University Press, 1985).

Walter Feinberg, "Affirmative Action," in *The Oxford Handbook of Practical Ethics,* ed. Hugh LaFollette (Oxford: Oxford University Press, 2003).

Robert Fullinwider, "Affirmative Action," *The Stanford Encyclopedia of Philosophy* (Spring 2005 ed.), ed. Edward N. Zalta, http://plato.stanford.edu/archives/spr2005/entries/affirmative-action/ (4 December 2006).

Ira Katznelson, *When Affirmative Action Was White: An Untold History of Racial History of Twentieth-Century America* (New York: W. W. Norton, 2005).

Albert Mosley, "The Case for Affirmative Action," in *Affirmative Action: Social Justice or Unfair Preference?,* by Mosley and Nicholas Capaldi (Lanham, MD: Rowman and Littlefield, 1996).

Regents of the University of California v. Bakke, 438 U.S. 265, 269–324 (1978). Justice Lewis Powell, Judgment of the Court.

Antonin Scalia, "The Disease as a Cure," *Washington University Law Quarterly,* no. 1 (1979): 147–57.

Richard Wasserstrom, "A Defense of Programs of Preferential Treatment," *Phi Kappa Phi Journal* 58, no. 1 (Winter 1978): 15–18.

Chapter 14. Environmental Ethics

Andrew Brennan and Yeuk-Sze Lo, "Environmental Ethics," *The Stanford Encyclopedia of Philosophy* (Summer 2002 ed.), ed. Edward N. Zalta, http://plato.stanford.edu/archives/sum2002/entries/ethics-environmental/ (4 December 2006).

J. Baird Callicott, "The Search for an Environmental Ethic," in *Matters of Life and Death: New Introductory Essays in Moral Philosophy,* ed. Tom Regan, 2nd ed. (New York: Random House, 1986).

Robert Elliot, "Environmental Ethics," in *A Companion to Ethics,* ed. Peter Singer, corr. ed. (Oxford: Blackwell, 1993).

Garrett Hardin, "The Tragedy of the Commons," *Science* 162 (13 December 1968): 1243–48.

Robert Heilbroner, "What Has Posterity Ever Done for Me?" *New York Times Magazine,* 19 January 1975, 14–15.

Aldo Leopold, "The Land Ethic," in *A Sand County Almanac: And Sketches Here and There* (1949; reprint, New York: Oxford University Press, 1981).

Arne Naess, "The Shallow and the Deep, Long-Range Ecological Movement," *Inquiry* 16 (Spring 1973): 95–100.

Holmes Rolston III, "Values in and Duties to the Natural World," in *Ecology, Economics, Ethics: The Broken Circle,* ed. F. Herbert Bormann and Stephen R. Kellert (New Haven: Yale University Press, 1991).

Albert Schweitzer, "Reverence for Life," in *Civilization and Ethics,* trans. John Naish (London: Black, 1923).

Christopher D. Stone, "Should Trees Have Standing? Toward Legal Rights for Natural Objects" in *Should Trees Have Standing? Toward Legal Rights for Natural Objects* (Los Altos, CA: William Kaufman, 1974).

Lynn White Jr., "The Historical Roots of Our Ecological Crisis," *Science* 155 (March 1967): 1203–7.

Chapter 15. Animal Rights

Carl Cohen, "The Case for the Use of Animals in Biomedical Research," *New England Journal of Medicine* 315 (October 1986): 865–70.

David DeGrazia, *Animal Rights: A Very Short Introduction* (Oxford: Oxford University Press, 2002).

R. G. Frey, "Animals," in *The Oxford Handbook of Practical Ethics,* ed. Hugh LaFollette (New York: Oxford University Press, 2003).

———, *Interests and Rights: The Case against Animals* (Oxford: Clarendon; New York: Oxford University Press, 1980).

Lori Gruen, "Animals," in *A Companion to Ethics,* ed. Peter Singer, corr. ed. (Oxford: Blackwell, 1993).

Mary Midgley, *Animals and Why They Matter* (Harmondsworth: Penguin, 1983).

James Rachels, *Created from Animals: The Moral Implications of Darwinism* (Oxford: Oxford University Press, 1990).

Tom Regan, *The Case for Animal Rights* (Berkeley: University of California Press, 1983).

Tom Regan and Peter Singer, eds. *Animal Rights and Human Obligations,* 2nd ed. (Englewood Cliffs, NJ: Prentice Hall, 1989).

Peter Singer, *Animal Liberation,* 2nd ed. (New York: New York Review of Books, 1990).

———, "Ethics beyond Species and beyond Instincts," in *Animal Rights: Current Debates and New Directions,* ed. Cass R. Sunstein and Martha C. Nussbaum (Oxford: Oxford University Press, 2004).

Bonnie Steinbock, "Speciesism and the Idea of Equality," *Philosophy* 53, no. 204 (April 1978): 247–56.

Cass R. Sunstein and Martha C. Nussbaum, eds., *Animal Rights: Current Debates in New Directions* (Oxford: Oxford University Press, 2004).

Mary Anne Warren, "The Rights of the Nonhuman World," in *Environmental Philosophy: A Collection of Readings* ed. Robert Elliot and Arran Gare (University Park: Pennsylvania State University Press, 1983).

Chapter 16. Warfare

G. E. M. Anscombe, "War and Murder," in *Nuclear Weapons: A Catholic Response,* ed. Walter Stein (New York: Sheed and Ward, 1961).

Cicero, *On Duties,* Book 1.10–14.

Carl von Clausewitz, chapter 1 of *On War* (1832), trans. J. J. Graham, ed. and abridged by Anatol Rapaport (London: Penguin, 1968).

Hugo Grotius, *On the Law of War and Peace* (*De Jure Belli ac Pacis,* 1631), 1, 2, and 3.

James Turner Johnson, "Threats, Values, and Defense: Does the Defense of Values by Force Remain a Moral Possibility?" *Parameters* 15, no. 1 (Spring 1985): 13–25.

Burton M. Leiser, "The Case for Iraq War II," in *Morality in Practice,* ed. James P. Sterba, 7th ed. (Belmont, CA: Wadsworth/Thomson, 2004).

David Luban, "Just War and Human Rights," *Philosophy & Public Affairs* 9, no. 2 (Winter 1980): 160–81.

Larry May, Eric Rovie, and Steve Viner, eds., *The Morality of War: Classical and Contemporary Readings* (Upper Saddle River, NJ: Pearson/Prentice Hall, 2006).

Jeff McMahan, "War and Peace," in *A Companion to Ethics,* ed. Peter Singer, corr. ed. (Oxford: Basil Blackwell, 1993).

Thomas Nagel, "War and Massacre," *Philosophy & Public Affairs* 1, no. 2 (Winter 1972): 123–43.

Jan Narveson, "Pacifism: A Philosophical Analysis," *Ethics* 75, no. 4 (1965): 259–71.

Brian Orend, "War," *The Stanford Encyclopedia of Philosophy* (Winter 2005 ed.), ed. Edward N. Zalta, plato.stanford.edu/archives/win2005/entries/war (20 December 2005).

Henry Shue, "War," in *The Oxford Handbook of Practical Ethics,* ed. Hugh LaFollette (Oxford: Oxford University Press, 2003).

James P. Sterba, "Iraqi War II: A Blatantly Unjust War," in *Morality in Practice,* ed. Sterba, 7th ed. (Belmont, CA: Wadsworth/Thomson, 2004).

Thomas Aquinas, *Summa Theologica,* Second Part of the Second Part, Questions 40, 64, and 69.

Michael Walzer, "The Argument about Humanitarian Intervention," *Dissent* 49, no. 1 (Winter 2002): 29–37.

——, "Moral Judgment in Time of War," *Dissent* 14, no. 3 (May–June 1967): 284–92.

Richard A. Wasserstrom, "On the Morality of War," *Stanford Law Review* 21, no. 6 (June 1969): 1627–56.

John Howard Yoder, "The Tradition and the Real World," in *When War Is Unjust: Being Honest in Just-War Thinking,* 2nd ed. (Maryknoll, NY: Orbis Books, 1996).

Chapter 17. Terrorism and Torture

Joseph M. Boyle Jr., "Just War Doctrine and the Military Response to Terrorism," *Journal of Political Philosophy* 11, no. 2 (2003): 153–70.

Martin L. Cook, "Ethical Issues in Counterterrorism Warfare," in *Contemporary Moral Issues: Diversity and Consensus* Lawrence M. Hinman, 3rd ed. (Upper Saddle River, NJ: Pearson/Prentice Hall, 2005).

R. G. Frey and Christopher W. Morris, "Terrorism," in *Violence, Terrorism, and Justice,* ed. Frey and Morris (Cambridge: Cambridge University Press, 1991).

Robert Fullinwider, "Terrorism, Innocence, and War," in *War After September 11,* ed. Verna V. Gehring (Lanham, MD: Rowman and Littlefield, 2003).

——, "Understanding Terrorism," in *Problems of International Justice,* ed. Steven Luper-Foy (Boulder, CO: Westview Press, 1988).

David Luban, "The War on Terrorism and the End of Human Rights," *Philosophy & Public Policy Quarterly* 22, no. 3 (Summer 2002): 9–14.

Gabriel Palmer-Fernandez, "Terrorism, Innocence, and Justice," *Philosophy & Public Policy Quarterly* 25, no. 3 (Summer 2005): 22–27.

Louis P. Pojman, "The Moral Response to Terrorism and the Cosmopolitan Imperative," in *Terrorism and International Justice,* ed. James P. Sterba (New York: Oxford University Press, 2003).

David Rodin, "Terrorism without Intention," *Ethics* 114 (July 2004): 752–71.

Charles Townshend, *Terrorism: A Very Short Introduction* (Oxford: Oxford University Press, 2002).

Andrew Valls, "Can Terrorism Be Justified?" in *Ethics in International Affairs,* ed. Valls (Lanham, MD: Rowman and Littlefield, 2000).

Michael Walzer, *Just and Unjust Wars: A Moral Argument with Historical Illustrations,* 2nd ed. (New York: Basic Books, 1992).

Chapter 18. Global Economic Justice

William Aiken and Hugh LaFollette, eds. *World Hunger and Morality,* 2nd ed. (Englewood Cliffs, NJ: Prentice Hall, 1996).

Lester R. Brown, *Tough Choices: Facing the Challenge of Food Scarcity* (New York: Norton, 1996).

Joel E. Cohen, *How Many People Can the Earth Support?* (New York: Norton, 1995).

Nigel Dower, "World Poverty," in *A Companion to Ethics,* Peter Singer (Cambridge, MA: Blackwell, 1993).

Steven Luper-Foy, ed., *Problems of International Justice* (Boulder, CO: Westview Press, 1988).

William W. Murdoch and Allan Oaten, "Population and Food: Metaphors and the Reality," *BioScience* 25 (1975): 561–67.

Onora O'Neill, *Faces of Hunger: An Essay on Poverty, Justice, and Development* (London: Allen & Unwin, 1986).

Thomas Pogge, *World Poverty and Human Rights: Cosmopolitan Responsibilities and Reforms,* 2nd ed. (Cambridge: Polity Press, 2008).

Louis P. Pojman, "World Hunger and Population," in *Life and Death: Grappling with the Moral Dilemmas of Our Time,* rev. 2nd ed. (Belmont, CA: Wadsworth, 2000).

Michael J. Sandel, ed., *Justice: A Reader* (New York: Oxford University Press, 2007).

Robert N. Van Wyk, "Perspectives on World Hunger and the Extent of Our Positive Duties," *Public Affairs Quarterly* 2, no. 2 (April 1988): 75–90.

INDEX